Handbook of Research on P2P and Grid Systems for Service-Oriented Computing:
Models, Methodologies, and Applications

Nick Antonopoulos
University of Surrey, UK

George Exarchakos
University of Surrey, UK

Maozhen Li
Brunel University, UK

Antonio Liotta
University of Essex, UK

Volume II

INFORMATION SCIENCE REFERENCE

Hershey · New York

Director of Editorial Content:	Kristin Klinger
Director of Book Publications:	Julia Mosemann
Development Editor:	Christine Bufton
Publishing Assistant:	Kurt Smith
Typesetter:	Carole Coulson
Quality control:	Jamie Snavely
Cover Design:	Lisa Tosheff
Printed at:	Yurchak Printing Inc.

Published in the United States of America by
Information Science Reference (an imprint of IGI Global)
701 E. Chocolate Avenue
Hershey PA 17033
Tel: 717-533-8845
Fax: 717-533-8661
E-mail: cust@igi-global.com
Web site: http://www.igi-global.com/reference

Library of Congress Cataloging-in-Publication Data

Handbook of research on P2P and grid systems for service-oriented computing : models, methodologies and applications / Nick Antonopoulos ... [et al.].
      p. cm.
  Includes bibliographical references and index.
  Summary: "This book addresses the need for peer-to-peer computing and grid paradigms in delivering efficient service-oriented computing"--Provided by publisher.
  ISBN 978-1-61520-686-5 (hardcover) -- ISBN 978-1-61520-687-2 (ebook) 1.
Peer-to-peer architecture (Computer networks)--Handbooks, manuals, etc. 2.
Computational grids (Computer systems)--Handbooks, manuals, etc. 3. Web
services--Handbooks, manuals, etc. 4. Service oriented architecture--
Handbooks, manuals, etc. I. Antonopoulos, Nick.
  TK5105.525.H36 2009
  004.6'52--dc22
                              2009046560

British Cataloguing in Publication Data
A Cataloguing in Publication record for this book is available from the British Library.

All work contributed to this book is new, previously-unpublished material. The views expressed in this book are those of the authors, but not necessarily of the publisher.

Amitava Biswas
Carlos Kamienski
Constandinos Mavromoustakis
Juan Pedro Munoz-Gea
Lu Liu
Marc Frincu
Simon Miles
Dana Petcu
Ryota Egashira
Gino Carrozzo
Rossana Motta
Valeria Bolzonaro
Adetola Oredope
Haris Zisimopoulos
Marco Ballette
Achilleas Achilleos
Ernest Sithole
Antonis Hadjiantonis
Hafiz Munsub Ali
Aldo Campi
Joan Serrat
Marco Aiello
Daniel Ranc
Haitham Cruickshank
Carmelo Ragusa
Rebecca Montanari
Andreas Mauthe
Bart Dhoet
Lisandro Zambenedetti Granville
Nick Papadoglou
Kun Yang
Mohammad Zafiri Eslami
Antonio Cuadra Sánchez
Chigo Okonkwo
Ioannis Christou
Lloyd Wood
Martin Fleury
Luca Caviglione
Paolo Bellavista
Vlado Menkovski
Wei Jie
Heba Kurdi
Man Qi
Simone Ludwig

Anwitaman Datta

Carlos Abalde

Guido Marchetto

Han Liangxiu

Mohammed Hawa

Vassilios Dimakopoulos

Xiao Qin

Eddy Caron

Jochen Furthmueller

Daniel M. Batista

Matthias Quasthoff

List of Contributors

Table of Contents

Volume I

Section 1
Fundamentals of Service-Oriented Computing, P2P and Grids

Section 2
Efficiency

Section 3
Scalability and Robustness

Detailed Table of Contents

Volume I

Section 1
Fundamentals of Service-Oriented Computing, P2P and Grids

Danny Hughes, Katholieke Universiteit Leuven, Belgium
Geof Coulson, University of Lancaster, UK
James Walkerdine, University of Lancaster, UK

This chapter examines each class of contemporary P2P architecture in turn and discusses the suitability of each architecture class for supporting service oriented computing (SOC). Future trends in peer-to-peer architectures are then discussed and multi-layer P2P architectures are highlighted as a promising platform for supporting SOC. This chapter then concludes with a discussion of outstanding issues that must be addressed before peer-to-peer architectures can support SOC.

Heba Kurdi, Brunel University, UK
Maozhen Li, Brunel University, UK
H. S. Al-Raweshidy, Brunel University, UK

This chapter presents a comprehensive taxonomy of Grid systems with an aim to establish a solid foundation in such a rapidly developing field. The taxonomy is based on six design features: type of solution, size of VO, accessibility, interactivity, user-centricity and manageability. Representative emerging Grid projects are reviewed to identify the key implementation approaches and issues related to each emerging Grid that is yet to be explored as a topic of future research.

Numerous studies have been devoted to the problem of resource discovery in P2P networks. Recent research on structured and unstructured P2P systems provides a series of useful solutions to improve the scalability and performance of service discovery in large-scale service-based systems. This chapter systematically reviews recent research studies on P2P search techniques and explores the potential roles and influence of P2P networking in dependable service-based military systems.

This chapter addresses the problem of resource discovery on DHTs. It highlights the close relationship and future opportunities for collaboration between the Grid and P2P communities.

P2P networking paradigm has the potential to integrate independent search engines under a single unified Internet wide search service. Therefore the P2P system will need technologies to capture the meaning of what the users intend to search for and then identify relevant objects. This matching between user's search intention and objects will go beyond simple keyword based comparison. In this chapter the authors present the required techniques to enable Web architecture that satisfy these needs.

Chapter 6

Supporting global scientific collaborations is becoming more and more important due to the increasing complexity of modern scientific problems. Grid computing and the Web-based portal architecture are usually combined to provide scientists with both access to high-end computational resources and means for end-to-end collaborations. This chapter introduces a different architecture, in which a P2P collaborative environment is integrated with Grid-computing services based on a service oriented architecture.

The authors of this chapter offer an extensive review of the state of the art in pervasive computing focusing on service-oriented architecture as a means of implementing several aspects of such systems. It sketches an insightful approach on how SOA combined with P2P and Grids can address solutions to service discovery and composition in pervasive computing environments.

Chapter 8

This chapter identifies the inability of P2P networks to cope with multi-service environments and, thus, proposes a service-oriented architecture to enable service diversification within the same network. Any service offered by a P2P node is published and invoked with the help of a set of other services making the SOA the predominant implementation model of P2P functionality.

Chapter 9

This chapter proposes a management framework that ties together P2P and SOC technologies to reach new work scenarios for the future Internet. Its authors argue that a policy based management middleware offers a good alternative for addressing the dynamic behaviour of P2P nodes: a special intermediary component for the development of emerging SOC/SOA platforms. Although not all the issues have been dealt with here in this work, it can certainly be seen as a step in the right direction.

Chapter 10

This chapter introduces the issues relating to P2P network management. Upon introducing techniques such as traffic shaping and caching, the authors review the most significant developments in the context of ISP and PSP collaboration approaches, including P4P, Biased Neighbor Selection of BitTorrent, Oracle, and Ono. A new approach named 'federation based solution' is finally illustrated.

This chapter discusses the role of business Grids in the coming service market, analysing relevant scenarios and providing a roadmap towards full development and adoption of this technology within the commercial arena.

This chapter focuses on service discovery solutions based on peer-to-peer (P2P) technologies. It presents the distributed lexicographic placement table (DLPT) architecture which provides particular mechanisms for load balancing and fault-tolerance.

With an increasing number of mobile devices for communication and computation the vision of a mobile Grid is becoming more and more attractive. This chapter proposes a scheme for classifying approaches for mobile Grids with respect to the mobile Grid architecture, the kind of shared resources and the way the participants use resources and contribute resources to the Grid. Furthermore, it provides a survey of such efforts, and identifies remaining challenges and future trends.

Section 2
Efficiency

Chapter 14

Stringent requirements on scalability are driving P2P systems to evolve from unstructured to structured architectures. This chapter illustrates the benefits of a service-oriented information plane, built as part of the network control plane, aiming at a reduction of signalling in the overlay network. Through an analytical study, the authors compare this approach with a flooding-based one.

This chapter describes an autonomic network virtualization middleware architecture designed for large-scale distributed applications. The proposed architecture, built upon a new network abstraction (i.e., distributed indexing networks [DIN]), uses end-hosts and proxies at the edge of the network for distributing content to multiple receivers. The authors describe group communication network services analyzing the performance gains in large-scale group communication applications.

In this chapter, an adaptive controller is proposed that dynamically adjusts resource shares to multiple data query requests in order to meet a specified level of service differentiation. The controller parameters are automatically tuned at runtime based on a predefined cost function and an online learning method. Simulation results show that this controller can meet given QoS differentiation targets and adapt to dynamic system resources among multiple data query processing requests.

The authors of this chapter outline existing P2P search mechanisms to improve service discovery in a service-oriented computing environment. They also propose a novel mechanism that utilizes end users' preferences. They deploy a feedback scheme on the preference to the discovered services which is utilized to decide where to forward subsequent queries. Extensive simulations demonstrate that the proposed mechanism meets key requirements such as the selectivity, efficiency and adaptability.

This chapter introduces the concept of cooperation incentives and discusses their design goals and capabilities and how can they improve the characteristics of P2P systems.

This chapter respectively presents the resource discovery in Grid and peer-to-peer (P2P) through an overview of related systems, both historical and emerging. The chapter then discusses the exploitation of both technologies for facilitating the resource discovery within large scale computing systems in a flexible, scalable, fault-tolerant, interoperable and security fashion.

This chapter describes the challenges on resource co-allocation, presents the recent developments over the last decade, and classifies them according to their similar characteristics. In addition, it addresses open research issues and trends such as negotiation, advance reservations, and rescheduling of multi-site applications.

This chapter presents the main characteristics which are necessary for Grid systems to provide quality of service. Twelve Grid systems are described, highlighting their differences and presenting their strong and weak points for the construction of service-oriented Grids.

This chapter focuses on designing energy-efficient Grid system to make it economically attractive and environmentally friendly for parallel applications. It proposes a general architecture for building energy-efficient computational Grids and discusses the potential possibilities of incorporating energy-aware techniques to different layers of the proposed Grid architecture

Section 3
Scalability and Robustness

This chapter discusses the use of peer-to-peer overlay networks to route around failures and congestion points in the Internet. The authors elaborate on the overall architecture of such a system and discuss the implementation of prototype components. Subsequently it is described how the overlay topology can be managed dynamically to achieve the same performance as a full mesh topology with a number of overlay edges that scales linearly with the number of nodes in the network.

This chapter presents a fault-tolerant framework for applications scheduling in large-scale distributed systems (LSDS), with emphasis on Grids. Optimization methods and near-optimal algorithms are presented along with examples solution for dynamic scheduling optimization. The author discusses the important issues relating to multi-criteria optimization, dealing with complex dependencies among tasks, real-time performance and resilience.

Volume II

This chapter presents replication methods applicable to P2P systems. It introduces strategies that can keep replicas up to date so as to achieve a desired level of consistency.

Chapter 26

Anwitaman Datta, Nanyang Technological University, Singapore
Di Wu, Polytechnic Institute of NYU, USA
Liu Xin, Nanyang Technological University, Singapore
Adam Wierzbicki, Polish-Japanese Institute of Information Technology Warsaw, Poland

This chapter focuses redundancy in P2P storage systems, including algorithms of maintenance mechanisms, analytical models to understand system's dynamics, empirical results from simulation experiments as well as experiences from prototype deployments.

Chapter 27

Dimka Karastoyanova, University of Stuttgart, Germany
Frank Leymann, University of Stuttgart, Germany

The robustness of Grid application and infrastructures is the property that is still insufficiently addressed. The major assumption in this work is that Grid services are Web services and Grid applications can be represented in terms of service compositions. The authors argue that the robustness of Grid applications can be improved by using already available mechanisms for enabling flexibility of service compositions and illustrate different approaches.

Chapter 28

Ciprian Dobre, University "Politehnica" of Bucharest, Romania

This chapter contributes to the study of large-scale systems giving emphasis on simulation techniques of Grids and P2P networks. The author, after an extensive review of existing simulation methods and their taxonomies, proposes the principles and a taxonomic system of a general framework for simulating the functionality of distributed systems.

Chapter 29

Bin Li, University of Surrey, UK
Lee Gillam, University of Surrey, UK

In an effort to commoditize Grid systems, the authors of this chapter use risk analysis techniques of Grid resources to predict and assess their availability, reliability and financial risk derived from their failure. This analysis provides essential tools for the automated construction of service level agreements between resource providers and requestors with the aim of reducing investment risks.

After identifying the shortcomings of unstructured and structured P2P networks, the author of this chapter proposes a hybrid solution (VIRGO) exploiting the benefits of both network classes. The unstructured layer supports complex-queries and offers robustness attributes to the network while the structured one ensures discovery in bounded number of messages. VIRGO uses a semantic layer to organise the nodes based on their contents allowing semantic-based content retrieval.

In this chapter, the authors describe a conceptual framework and architecture specification in which normative business contracts can be electronically represented, verified, established, renewed, and so on. In particular, this chapter aims to allow systems containing multiple contracts to be checked for conflicts and violations of business objectives. It illustrates the framework and architecture with an aerospace aftermarket example.

Section 4
Security

Chapter 32

Peer-to-peer (P2P) and Grid systems have become interleaved with human societies. For that reason, they must take into account the behavior and motivations of their human users, like the need for trust and fairness. This chapter describes how P2P and Grid systems encompass and use knowledge about trust and fairness.

This chapter discusses issues regarding trust calculation and management in P2P and Grid systems. The authors provide a theoretical background introducing trust concepts and basic principles behind trust graphs. Then they present an analysis of popular classification schemes in order to present the different types of existing trust functions. Well-known trust mechanisms are analyzed with emphasis on P2P and Grid systems, identifying future directions on this topic.

Chapter 34

This chapter presents a reputation based incentive approach for interactions in P2P systems. A generic architecture for context-aware reputation systems, which can interact with identity-related services like identity providers and policy decision or enforcement points, is presented. More specialized architectures for different environments—business- or consumer-oriented are derived from the generic architecture.

Chapter 35

In the context of Grid security, identity-based cryptography is emerging as a serious contender to the more conventional certificate-based approach. This chapter, starts by examining key limitations of the latter approach and illustrates how identity-based cryptography helps addressing some of them.

This chapter explores a family of mechanisms to enforce fairness in asynchronous collaborative environments, where simple tit-for-tat policies cannot be used. The authors propose solutions relying on enforced neighborhood relations, where each node is restricted in the choice of other nodes to collaborate with. This creates long-term collaboration relationships, where each node must behave well with its neighbors if it wants to be able to use their resources.

Section 5
Service-Oriented Applications of P2P and Grids

This chapter focuses on the indexing of service nodes in these P2P systems, presenting the state-of-the-art solutions concerning P2P-based indexing architectures and a taxonomy of possible services that can be built upon different overlay structures. Finally, emphasis is given to mechanisms implementing service selection based on some cost parameters (e.g., topological proximity) in order to introduce some mechanism based on optimality in case multiple service providers exist.

This chapter advocates migrating sufficient functionality into the network as to allow direct support to Grid computing services. This approach is realized by making use of session initiation protocol (SIP) as the medium to support the signaling among Grid applications and network. The authors elaborate on the advantages of this approach, which benefits directly from the session management capabilities of SIP and enables application-oriented functions.

In service-oriented computing, the assumption is that services can be put together in order to obtain new, composite services. This chapter discusses how peer-to-peer architectures based on multi-agent systems can be used to build reconfigurable infrastructures for dynamic composition of Grid services. The authors introduce the fundamental concepts behind service composition, advocating the adoption of multi-agent systems. A case study helps highlighting emerging trends and issues in this area.

The authors of this chapter, motivated by the competition that network operators face from Web 2.0 service providers, propose the P2P service platform. This platform enables the distributed and efficient management of computation resources and allows flexibility in deploying different service provision strategies while reducing the cost of service deployment infrastructure.

Chapter 41

In this chapter, the authors present the benefits of Fednets for their users deploying a number of usage scenarios and analysing their architecture and lifecycle. They also contribute with the description of a secure access and management (ACM) framework for Fednets that enables self-federation of nodes into groups and P2P-based service provision. ACM allows the nodes to authenticate and authorise each other before they access the resources of their Fednet into which they get organised.

Chapter 42

In an effort to tackle the heterogeneity and adaptability weaknesses of existing Grid middleware in case of pervasive Grid applications, the authors of this chapter propose the Gridkit. The Gridkit addresses the way two complementary component frameworks support an extensible set of interaction paradigms and an extensible set of overlay networks. The chapter finishes with a use-case scenario of Gridkit in a flood detection sensor network.

Chapter 43

Current research and development in ICT has opened new opportunities and threats for both large corporations and small-medium enterprises (SMEs) alike. This chapter examines the role of the large corporations in the digital ecosystem and addresses two major problems which can be major entry barriers for SMEs. The proposed distributed coordination and high connectivity between SMEs can provide a more appropriate business environment for fair competition and collaboration.

In order to provide community networks with proper video services an appropriate middleware support is required to glue together the services and the infrastructures. In this respect, peer-to-peer technology is a very good candidate to achieve this objective and address resource sharing difficulties posed by the power line communication medium. In this chapter, different proposals to provide VoD services using P2P technology are reviewed.

Chapter 45

This chapter discusses the main issues and problems encountered in the transition from the classical symbolic computations based on stand-alone computer algebra systems towards service-oriented symbolic computations, such as building services from legacy codes, discover, compose and orchestrate services as well as standardize the exchange data formats. New approaches to solve at least partially these transition problems have been recently implemented, tested and are revealed in this chapter.

Chapter 46

Today, researchers deploy networks of sensors to collect as much data as possible from different locations for monitoring purposes. The hardware of the sensor nodes must be robust, provide sufficient storage and communication capabilities, and get along with limited power resources. In this chapter the key elements of sensor networks are analysed in order to give an overview of possible applications in the field of monitoring.

Foreword

Peer-to-Peer (P2P) and Grid computing share many common technological challenges: (i) both involve accessing and interacting with distributed resources, such as computational servers, data storage facilities, scientific instruments (such as wireless sensor networks involved in telemetry, to large scale instruments such as telescopes or radio interferometers); (ii) both involve aspects of resource discovery – whereas Grid systems have generally utilized known registry services, the discovery mechanisms in P2P systems are more diverse in nature, ranging from the use of hash tables, to the use of gossiping and flooding protocols. It is also useful to note that both Grid computing and P2P also suffer from similar concerns – such as the absence of suitable business models in deployment, aspects of efficiency and security. Efficiency issues can be of multiple (and in some instances of conflicting) types: energy, cost, and utilization being the more representative examples. Economic models that attempt to compare the impact of these considerations have also been significantly explored in both the P2P and Grid computing communities, although translation of some of this work to wide scale use is still lacking. It is also useful to note that whereas Grid computing has seen a recent decline in interest, P2P systems have continued to demonstrate an enduring interest and a growing user community. Although not a definitive measure, Google Trends provides one graphical representation of this phenomenon, indicating a surge in interest in mid 2007 in P2P systems, which coincided with an increase in video and audio use of P2P tools (such as emergence of Skype and YouTube), along with the growth in social networking (based on data from a study by Cisco systems (Barnett & Sumits, 2008)). Another survey conducted by Sandvine Networks (P2P On, 2008)over the July-September 2008 period, involving 16 million individuals in 18 countries with broadband access, indicates a similar trend, with applications such as video streaming, gaming, VoIP and social networking increasing traffic by almost 50% per subscriber.

Trend 1. Search Volume Index for the term "Grid Computing"

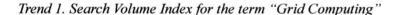
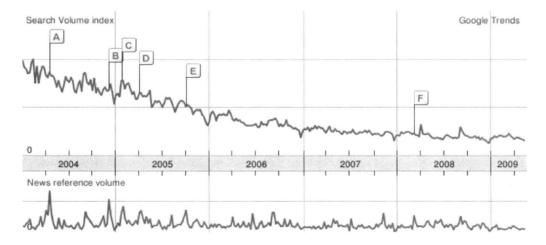

Trend 2. Search Volume Index for the term "P2P" – the scale on the y-axis in this graph is different from that in the Trend 1 graph – and should not be directly compared. It is primarily intended to demonstrate the overall trend over time for a particular search term use (in Google).

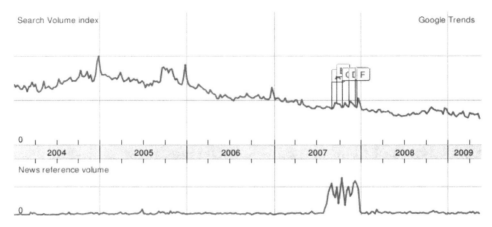

Perhaps, the most interesting trend is seen when we compare the terms P2P, Grid Computing and Cloud Computing – as demonstrated in the graph in Trend 3. Here, it is useful to note that interest in P2P surpasses that in Cloud and Grid computing, and that interest in Cloud computing is only begging to emerge since mid 2008.

Secure access and data privacy remain important challenges for practical deployment of both Grid and P2P systems. The lawsuit against the P2P site "Pirate Bay" (similar to Napster many years ago, but based on Torrent technology) demonstrates that legal sharing of content, and subsequent adoption of these practices by the P2P community remain important challenges. The shutting down of Napster did however lead to positive outcomes, for instance the emergence of legal sharing systems such as KaZaA. Such issues have also limited the adoption of Grid computing in industry, primarily due to data confidentiality and privacy concerns (which remain valid in many Cloud computing deployments available today). Investigating aspects of trust within external providers, and ensuring that these providers will not violate their advertised Service Level Agreements remain barriers that limit use of outsourced ("third party") computational resources in Grid systems.

Given this context, this handbook is timely, as it brings together a collection of articles that address many of the significant challenges that remain in better use of P2P and Grid computing systems. The five sections: (i) fundamental themes; (ii) efficiency; (iii) scalability and robustness; (iv) security and (v) applications, all provide useful surveys and a discussion of possible future directions. Articles in each of the above sections also cover description of particular research projects that are attempting to overcome current technological or usage challenges. The "fundamentals" section covers the use of P2P and Grid technologies in mobile and pervasive devices, mechanisms to support service discovery and network management issues. Some of the articles in this section provide useful introductory material for those new to P2P and Grid technologies – especially the overlap in their features and possible integration. Section 2 on "efficiency" contains articles addressing optimisation strategies related to various aspects of systems management, such as adaptive discovery of data, incentive mechanisms, indexing and resource co-allocation. It is useful to see open research issues and trends being discussed by the authors, in areas such as advanced reservation and the deployment of multi-site applications, driven by a survey of developments over the last decade. Section 3 covers issues related to scalability and service level management, through the use of redundancy or replication (for instance). One particular article, for instance, focuses on the financial risk associated with resource unavailability or failure, with a further

Trend 3. Comparison between term search on "P2P", "Grid Computing" and "Cloud Computing" via the Google search engine

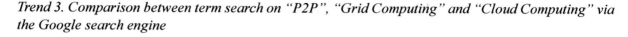

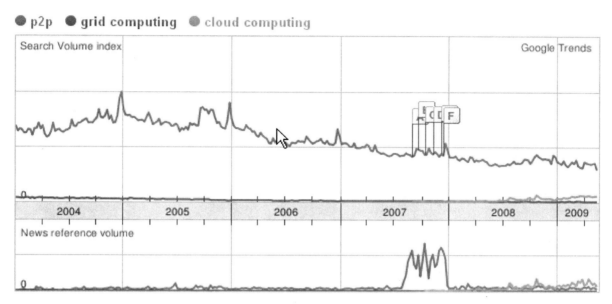

discussion about how Service Level Agreements (and contracts) can be developed to reduce investment risk in this context. When a single resource provider must participate in multiple applications, often it is necessary to support more than one electronic contract – thereby leading to potential conflicts between them. Mechanisms to allow automated verification and conflict detection are therefore essential to enable more efficient use of P2P and Grid computing infrastructure. This aspect is also explored in this section. Section 4 considers various aspects of security in P2P and Grid systems, considering both issues of trust management and identity-based cryptography. Section 5 concludes the book with examples of a number of applications, ranging from Video on Demand (with large multimedia data transfer requirements) to wireless sensor networks (consisting of devices with limited power/energy capability using radio communication with low data transfer requirements, which must operate in a more unstable environment). Hence, a range of different applications have been presented

With the emergence of recent interest in Cloud computing (which, interestingly, encompasses both P2P and Grid technologies), the extensive coverage provided in this handbook will provide useful background material.

Omer F. Rana
Cardiff University, UK
May 2009

Omer F. Rana *is Professor of Performance Engineering at the School of Computer Science, Cardiff University. He has also been the deputy director of the Welsh eScience Centre. He holds a PhD in Computing from Imperial College, London. His research interests include high performance distributed computing, data mining and multi-agent systems.*

REFERENCES

Barnett, T., & Sumits, A. (2008). *Cisco Visual Networking Index Forecast, 2007-2012*. Cisco Systems, Inc. Retrieved from http://www.cisco.com/web/about/ac78/docs/IPTrafficStudy_current_speakerseries_APAC.pdf

P2P On. (2008). *P2P Traffic Reaches Huge Levels, Global Internet Traffic Trends Study Reveals*. Retrieved from http://www.p2pon.com/2008/10/23/p2p-traffic-reaches-huge-levels-global-internet-traffic-trends-study-reveals/

Preface

1. INTRODUCTION & JUSTIFICATION

Service-oriented computing is a popular design methodology for large scale business computing systems. Its underpinning principle is that of modelling a business process as a re-usable service entity that can be connected to a series of other physically distributed services in order to realise a set of predetermined specifications. Interest in further researching and applying the service oriented approach has exponentially increased in the past few years with the development of the Service Oriented Architecture (SOA) and other competing frameworks. A significant number of companies aim to reap the benefit of cost reduction by realising B2B and B2C processes on large-scale SOA-compliant software system platforms. This interest has also been compounded and further strengthened by the massive increase of e-commerce through the online selling of e-content from MP3 music and videos to services and access to specialised content and applications. This phenomenon is bound to continue in the future as big content providers such as music and film production companies forge partnerships with ISPs for on-demand, cost-efficient global content distribution over home broadband connections.

Traditionally, service-oriented computing research has focused on: a) the accurate mapping of real business logic onto software service objects, b) service inter-linking and workflow/transaction management and c) the interfaces and orchestration of the whole scheme by the underlying operating systems and physical hardware. However, this emphasis is quickly shifting towards researching into computing platforms that are capable of supporting this kind of processing. Due to the competitive nature of the aforementioned services, such a platform should be capable of providing a guaranteed quality of service to the customers of the participating businesses. This quality has four dimensions:

- **Efficiency:** The execution and coordination of the realised processes is optimised in terms of data traffic and latency. Data traffic stemming from user queries and downloads is the main cost factor of online content providers and thus its optimisation is a standard long term goal of such businesses. Latency is arguably one of the most important factors affecting customer satisfaction and therefore it should also be within specified acceptable limits.
- **Scalability:** These platforms should be able to scale well as they are intended to be used by massive customer bases. They should also manage to withstand demand during peak times and the "flash crowds" phenomenon.
- **Robustness:** The provisioning of the services needs to have continuously high availability by design and redundancy.
- **Security:** Appropriate levels of security need to be provided to protect both the providers and consumers from malicious or fraudulent activities. In fact, without adequate security provisioning it is highly unlikely that any platform will be considered seriously for such scale of business computing.

Peer-to-Peer (P2P) and Grid computing are two very pertinent fields that have received a significant and sustained research interest in terms of designing and deploying large scale and high performance computational resource sharing systems. Computational resources include anything from files and applications to processing cycles and storage space. Effectively these two fields collectively form the de facto basis for the methodologies and techniques that need to be used to develop performance-driven service-oriented software platforms capable of satisfying the aforementioned four key aspects of quality of service.

P2P and Grids started as two different distributed computing philosophies: Grid computing represented a more business-oriented orchestration of relatively homogeneous and powerful distributed computing resources to optimise the execution of time consuming tasks whereas P2P networks had an emphasis on the discovery and sharing of resources on the edges of a heterogeneous network (i.e. user desktops, etc.) especially in terms of file sharing. However, nowadays these two domains have a very substantial overlap as P2P systems have been borrowing on more traditional Grid techniques for task scheduling and execution and the Grid systems have been deploying P2P oriented techniques for more scalable and versatile resource discovery. In fact with the development of very sophisticated information discovery subsystems within Grids, of P2P overlays dedicated to coordinated parallel and distributed processing and of mobile Grids and P2P networks for ad-hoc sharing of mobile telecoms operator services, it has now become more difficult than ever to differentiate these two approaches.

2. AIM & OBJECTIVES

This handbook aims to address the need for more literature onto the applicability and use of P2P and Grid computing techniques for delivering efficient service-oriented computing. Specifically the book has two key objectives: Firstly to explore how the P2P and Grid paradigms can be used to deliver quality of service in key operations such as the discovery, secure utilisation and coordination of distributed services. Secondly, to use the service-oriented computing as the context of a technical comparison between these two fields. The first objective is closely linked to commercial demand for distributed computing techniques that can form the basis for feasible and efficient solutions for service discovery, secure access and orchestration. The second objective is firmly rooted within the distributed computing academic and research community and its desire to better understand the link between P2P networks and Grids and thus research into potential hybrid solutions.

3. AUDIENCE & CONTRIBUTION

The above objectives make this book appropriate and useful to the following audience:
* researchers and doctoral students working specifically in P2P computing, Grids or SOA implementations and deployments, primarily as a reference publication. Similarly, this book will be useful to researchers in related or more general fields such as distributed computing, software engineering, Web Services, modelling of business processes, etc.
* academics delivering research-oriented modules in the above fields. This handbook can serve as a good collection of related articles to facilitate a broad understanding of this subject and as such it can become one of the recommended texts in such courses.
* professional system architects and developers who could decide to adapt and apply in practice a number of the techniques and processes presented in the book.

- technical managers and IT consultants as a book that demonstrates the potential applicability of certain methods to delivering efficient and secure commercial electronic services to customers globally.

The above categories of readers will find this publication especially appealing as it combines three distinct scholarly contributions:

Firstly it identifies and highlights state-of-the-art techniques and methods from P2P and Grid computing that can be used to build performance-driven service-oriented software platforms. Secondly it uses service-oriented computing as a context to draw a comparison between the P2P and Grid computing paradigms in terms of their ability to provide the necessary quality of service.

Finally, it achieves all of the above through the balanced coverage of both P2P and Grid related research and therefore provides a single reference point for both these technologies. This is academically desirable as the two fields have a significant conceptual overlap and therefore distributed systems researchers are typically interested in knowing about the applicability and usefulness of both P2P and Grids in their research domain. The strong overlapping between them is emphasized by the fact that every major conference, workshop and peer-reviewed journal dedicated on Grid computing typically accepts paper submissions on P2P and vice versa.

4. HANDBOOK CONTENTS

This handbook includes 45 high quality fully refereed chapters organised into five sections.

The first section introduces fundamental concepts, techniques and terminology in the fields of service-oriented computing, P2P and Grid computing through a set of literature review articles. This material effectively sets the scene for the remainder of the book.

The following three sections present state-of-the-art research work that contributes towards one of the four quality of service parameters mentioned in the introduction (namely: efficiency, scalability & robustness and security).

The final section concludes the handbook by presenting real applications and lessons learned from using P2P or Grid approaches to realise various aspects of service-oriented computing.

We are certain that you will find each chapter interesting and potentially useful to your work.

The Editors

Nick Antonopoulos
Georgios Exarchakos
Maozhen Li
Antonio Liotta

Chapter 25
Data Replication in P2P Systems

Vassilios V. Dimakopoulos
University of Ioannina, Greece

Spiridoula Margariti
University of Ioannina, Greece

Mirto Ntetsika
University of Ioannina, Greece

Evaggelia Pitoura
University of Ioannina, Greece

ABSTRACT

Maintaining multiple copies of data items is a commonly used mechanism for improving the performance and fault-tolerance of any distributed system. By placing copies of data items closer to their requesters, the response time of queries can be improved. An additional reason for replication is load balancing. For instance, by allocating many copies to popular data items, the query load can be evenly distributed among the servers that hold these copies. Similarly, by eliminating hotspots, replication can lead to a better distribution of the communication load over the network links. Besides performance-related reasons, replication improves system availability, since the larger the number of copies of an item, the more site failures can be tolerated. In this chapter we survey replication methods applicable to p2p systems. Although there exist some general techniques, methodologies are distinguished according to the overlay organization (structured and unstructured) they are aimed at. After replicas are created and distributed, a major issue is their maintenance. We present strategies that have been proposed for keeping replicas up to date so as to achieve a desired level of consistency.

INTRODUCTION

In a peer-to-peer (p2p) system, a large number of nodes share data with each other. The participation

DOI: 10.4018/978-1-61520-686-5.ch025

of nodes is highly dynamic; nodes may enter and leave the system at will. Since, it is not possible to maintain links with all nodes, for performance as well as for privacy and anonymity reasons, each node maintains links with a selected subset of other nodes, thus forming an *overlay network*. A message between any two nodes in the p2p system is routed through this overlay network which is built on top of the physical one. Thus, two nodes that are neighbors in the overlay network may be many links apart in the physical network.

The overlay network is built to facilitate the operation of a p2p system. In data sharing p2p systems, a basic functionality is discovering the data of interest. A look-up query for data items may be posed at any node in the overlay. The query is then routed through the overlay to efficiently discover the nodes that hold the requested data items. Such query routing must be achieved by contacting as "small" a number of nodes in the overlay as possible and by maintaining as "little" state information at each overlay node as possible.

There are two basic types of overlays: structured and unstructured ones. To assist lookup, *structured overlays* map (keys of) data items to nodes. In structured overlays, the mapping is usually done by hashing the key space of the data items to the id space of nodes. Thus, each node in the overlay maintains a partition of the data space. In structured overlays, lookup reduces to locating the node in the overlay that is responsible for the corresponding data partition. In *unstructured overlays* on the other hand, there is no correlation between nodes and data items.

There are a number of issues regarding the design of a structured p2p system. One design dimension refers to the geometry of the overlay, that is, its structural characteristics. Structured overlays usually follow a regulated topology, such as a ring, tree or grid. Then, upon entering the p2p system, each node takes a specific position in the overlay network. Another design choice is how data are mapped to nodes. The mapping must be fair so that nodes receive similar loads even when the data sets or the operations are skewed. All designs aim at supporting efficiently the basic operations of the overlay, that is, its construction, its incremental maintenance when nodes enter or leave the system, and its search. Efficiency must

be achieved even in the case of high churn, where maintaining the overlay structure incurs a high cost. Most structured overlays guarantee lookup operations that are logarithmic in the number of nodes. Finally, overlays differ with respect to the range of different types of queries that they support.

In unstructured overlays, the topology is not a rigid one. Unstructured overlays are formed by the nodes as they join the system by either selecting randomly a node from a known list of participating peers or by following some loose rules regarding this selection. The resulting topology may have certain properties, however there is no assumption regarding the way the data space is mapped to the address space of the nodes in the overlay. To locate data of interest, a node queries its neighbors in the overlay, which in turn query their neighbors, and so on, until the query hits on a node holding the item. However, this procedure provides no guarantees on the complexity of search.

The topology of an unstructured overlay is built up over time in a decentralized manner as peers join and leave the system. In many existing systems, upon joining the network, a peer selects to connect to another peer essentially at random. In these systems, topologies often tend towards a power-law degree distribution, where some long-lived peers have many connections, while most other peers have a few connections.

To improve performance of lookup, caching or replication[1] of either data or search paths (or both) is possible. Besides improving search, replication may also assist in providing load balancing. Further, replication improves fault tolerance and the durability of data items.

Replication increases the number of copies for each shared piece of data in the system. By doing so, the probability that some or all the data is temporarily or permanently lost significantly decreases, thus the *dependability* of the system in terms of *reliability* and *availability* is increased. Additionally, by having more copies for popular data items, the load for routing and answering queries can be evenly distributed among the servers that hold the copies. This way, the *performance* of query processing is increased in terms of *throughput* and *response time*, since congestions in "hot" servers are avoided. Placing data closer to their requesters, as done by replication, also improves the performance of query processing.

Replication may also improve *data recall*. In structured overlays data recall is not an issue, contrary to unstructured overlays. While unstructured overlays which adopt flooding-based techniques are effective for locating popular data, they are poorly suited for locating rare data. Thus, by replicating the rare data the probability of locating it during query processing increases, consequently increasing data recall. However, replication may affect *data freshness*. P2p systems consist of autonomous peers that can arbitrarily delete or update their content, thus the replicated data can become stale if not updated properly. Updating replicas and cache entries in a p2p system mainly aims at providing soft-state guarantees. Hence, query processing might encounter out-of-date copies of data, thus failing to achieve result freshness.

The cost associated with replication includes the storage cost as well as the maintenance cost in the case of updates. Updates are either initiated by the owner of the copy that was modified (push-based updates) or by the holder of the copy (pull-based updates). Often entries are associated with a time-out value, whose expiration signals the removal of the entry, thus providing only soft-state consistency.

There are two main choices on *what* to replicate: peers may replicate the data items themselves or their location information (index). There is an obvious difference in the required storage space among the two choices. Also, replicating indices does not improve reliability or availability since it does not lead to more physical copies. However, both the placement and the update mechanisms that have been proposed are applicable to both data and index/location replication. Thus we will treat the two cases as equivalent and shall not differentiate between them in what follows.

The rest of this chapter is organized as follows. Replication in unstructured p2p systems is considered first, followed by replication in structured overlays. The results and techniques differ since unstructured p2p systems are treated in essence as "unknown" complex networks, while in structured p2p systems the topology is more or less known in advance and replication schemes may take advantage of it. Next, the problem of keeping the replicas up-to-date is considered where, again, we distinguish between the techniques used for the two types of overlay topology. A final section summarizes the chapter.

REPLICATION IN UNSTRUCTURED P2P NETWORKS

Unstructured topologies evolve in more or less unpredictable ways, as nodes leave and join the overlay at arbitrary positions. As a consequence, they can be effectively modeled as a random graph, or *Erdős-Rényi random graph*. Such a graph with N nodes can be equivalently described in two ways: it is a graph where each of the possible $N(N-1)/2$ edges is present with some fixed probability p; or it is a graph selected uniformly at random among all possible graphs on N nodes and M edges. This is a simple but powerful model, where it can be shown that the degrees of participating nodes follow a Poisson distribution. However, real-world networks have exhibited a behavior that is closer to power-law degree distributions: there are a few highly connected nodes and a large number of nodes with small degree. Thus power-law random graphs or simply *power-law graphs* have been quite popular as a model for p2p networks. Although many replication schemes do not depend on the particular model used for the p2p topology, the choice of this model has strong implications on the analysis of some replication objectives (e.g. determining an optimal number of replicas).

Since in unstructured p2p systems there is no information on where the desired piece of data is placed, mostly "blind" search procedures are used and look-up queries get propagated through the network so as to locate peers offering the data. The usually employed blind search strategies are flooding and random walks, along with their variations, and proposed methods for replication routinely depend on the particular search strategy used for locating items. In *flooding*, a node that receives a query message propagates it to all its neighbors, unless it knows about the item in question. Flooding usually results in fast responses but can easily overload the network with messages, a large percentage of which are unnecessary duplicates. In variations of flooding the query message is sent only to a selected subset of a peer's neighbors, based on certain rules.

During a *random walk* on the other hand, a contacted peer propagates the query to exactly one of its neighbors, selected uniformly at random. Proposed variations bias the selection of the neighbor according to various criteria. This type of search is particularly efficient, especially in certain topologies, but usually results in slow responses. Things can be significantly improved if multiple random walkers are deployed simultaneously. It is a known fact that using random walks, the probability of visiting a node is proportional to its degree, i.e. random walks go through high-degree nodes more frequently (since they are more easily reached due to their large number of neighbors).

To avoid high delays and an overwhelming number of messages, queries are allowed to propagate for a limited number of steps, which is the so-called *time-to-live* (TTL) parameter. The TTL value is included in every query message and gets decremented by 1 at each visited peer. Peers that observe a zero TTL value stop propagating the search any further. It should be obvious, that TTL-limited query propagation may result in *unsuccessful* searches.

In this section we present replication schemes for unstructured p2p networks. The section consists of two parts. In the first part, we discuss theoretical results regarding the optimum number of replicas of each item in the system and practical ways of achieving this. In the second part, we examine methods for placing the generated replicas onto the p2p system nodes.

Number of Replicas

Assume that there are N peers participating in the network and m different data items to be shared among peers. Each peer on average has a storage capacity for storing ρ replicas of data items and the network has a total budget of R copies overall ($R=N\rho$). The *query rate* or *popularity* of item i, q_i, is the probability that any arbitrary peer issues a request for item i.

The problem of determining what is the optimal replica configuration is discussed by Cohen & Shenker (2002), for overlays that are modeled as Erdos-Renyi random graphs. Specifically, the authors deal with the problem of how many replicas of each data item should exist in the network so that the search overhead for locating the item is minimized, with the constraint of fixed storage capacity in the network. Given the query rates for each data item, the objective is determining which fraction p_i of R should be allotted to each data item i, so that the expected search size (ESS), i.e. the number of peers probed during the search process is minimized.

Two natural ways of replicating data items, namely uniform and proportional replication, are shown to be suboptimal under the above assumptions. In *uniform replication* (UR) the same number of replicas is created for each data item, regardless of its query rate. In *proportional replication* (PR) the number of replicas for each data item is proportional to the popularity of the item, so that $p_i \propto q_i$. Although it seems natural to create more replicas for more popular data items so as to favor most common queries, this is done at the expense of rare ones. In fact, it can be shown that the ESS for a successful query is the same for both uniform and proportional replication strategies. The optimal configuration, proved to minimize the expected search size, is *square-root replication* (SR), where the number of replicas of each data item is proportional to the square root of its query rate, i.e. $p_i \propto \sqrt{q_i}$.

Since global knowledge is unavailable at each peer, the authors also consider ways of realizing square-root replication using simple distributed protocols. In one of the simplest, the number of copies created after a successful search is equal to the size of the search, i.e. the number of peers probed during search. At steady state, and under reasonable assumptions, this simple strategy can be shown to converge to SR. The only critical assumption is that the fixed storage capacity of each node is managed through replacement policies that do not depend on the identity and the query rate of the stored items. As such, at a full node, the item that must be deleted so as to make room for another replica cannot be given by usage-based policies such as LRU or LFU but rather by policies like FIFO or random deletions.

Notice that although the idea is quite simple, the size of the search is normally not known. Lv, Cao, Cohen, Li & Shenker (2002) discuss two practical strategies that try to approximate the search size, namely owner and path replication. In *owner replication*, which is used in Gnutella (2003), when a search for a data item is successful (only) the peer that initiated the search process stores a replica of the data item. In *path replication*, each query keeps track of the path it follows from the peer that issues the request to the peer that offers the data item. When the search succeeds, all peers in this path are forced to keep a replica of the data item. Clearly, path replication comes quite closer to approximating the search size and experimental results show that it comes close to achieving SR. Path replication is used on Freenet (Clarke et al, 2002) where all nodes along the search path are forced to create a replica using an *insert* message. Nodes keep both the item and a pointer to the original data holder of the file. The replacement policy used to manage the finite storage space at each node is LRU. Subsequent incoming requests of evicted files, however, can still be served for much longer since the node also holds a pointer to the original holder. It is worth noting that LRU was shown, through detailed simulations (Zhang, Goel, & Govindan, 2004), to be responsible for deteriorating Freenet performance under heavy loads. By just altering the replacement policy so as to force local data clustering, the authors managed to achieve high percentages of successful queries and with small hop counts, even under heavy traffic.

Path replication works only for search strategies based on random walks. Even in such cases however, it may fail to discover the search size. If multiple walkers are used (Lv, Cao, Cohen, Li & Shenker, 2002), only the successful ones will be used to create replicas while the others will be ignored, creating a number of replicas smaller than the total number of visited nodes. To closely approximate the number of probes, Leontiadis, Dimakopoulos & Pitoura (2006) propose the *Pull-then-Push* (PtP) strategy, where replica creation becomes a responsibility of the inquiring peers. PtP replication consists of two phases: the *pull phase* during which the requesting peer is trying to locate the desired data item and the *push phase* which begins after a successful search whereby the requesting peer transmits the data item and causes other peers to hold replicas of it. In order to achieve SR, the number of peers that are probed during the push phase should be equal to the number of peers that where probed during the pull phase. Therefore, it is essential that the same search strategy is used both for searching for the data item (pull) and the data item transmission (push) and with the same hop limit (TTL). Finally, every peer that is probed during the push phase is forced to hold a replica of the data item. PtP works for both flooding and random-walker based strategies and leads easily to SR.

For Erdos-Renyi random graphs, if flooding-based search is used and if the objective is to minimize the search *time* (as opposed to search size) then proportional replication is the optimal configuration as shown by Tewari & Kleinrock (2005). Search time is the shortest distance from the inquiring node where a replica of the queried item is found. Optimality is achieved under the assumption of an ideal "controlled" flooding strategy where search stops immediately when the data item is located. A practical but slightly suboptimal search mechanism that approximates controlled flooding is the expanding rings method described in Lv, Cao, Cohen, Li & Shenker (2002). PR has additional benefits as well, e.g. the minimization of used network bandwidth (estimated as the average number of links traversed per download). Tewari & Kleinrock (2006) additionally consider practical ways of achieving PR. They basically follow owner replication (an inquiring node keeps a copy for itself), which should naturally lead to a number of replicas proportional to the request rates of data items. Again, a crucial factor is the replacement strategy used in managing each node's fixed storage space. Experimentally, all known strategies have good but not optimal performance, with LRU and LFU the better ones. Almost perfect PR can be achieved with a replacement strategy based on random evictions combined with additional replica creations even if the item is found in the inquiring node's storage space.

Placement of Replicas

The works in the previous section deal mostly with determining the optimum number of replicas and with ways to achieve this number, under certain assumptions and constraints. Another approach is to determine *where/how* to place the replicas (without striving for a particular number of them) so as to optimize some objective. For example, the objective may be the minimization of search size or the maximization of the percentage of successful searches.

Gia (Chawathe, Ratnasamy, Breslau, Lanham & Shenker, 2003) has been proposed as an improvement of Gnutella to exploit peer heterogeneity and includes mechanisms that dynamically adapt the overlay topology and the search algorithms. The topology adaptation mechanism ensures that high-capacity nodes are the ones that have high degree. Gia follows *one-hop replication*: an index of the content of every peer is replicated to its immediate neighbors. The rationale behind this is that since high-degree nodes are visited more frequently and high-degree nodes are the ones with high capacity, having them know the content of their neighbors will make them capable of providing answers to a greater number of queries.

Jia, Pei, Li & You (2005) compare various mechanisms for the problem of replica placement in power-law networks. They consider replication of location information (i.e. not the actual data) so as to maximize the overall performance of search queries. The spread mechanisms considered are flooding, percolation-based (randomized) flooding, random walks and high-degree random walks (HDRW). The later is a variation of random walks where a visited peer selects the next peer randomly among its highest-degree neighbors. By spreading location information along an HDRW, more information reaches high-degree nodes more quickly. As a result, because it is well known that search queries gravitate towards the high-degree nodes in the network, potentially more searches will be resolved successfully and quickly. This was confirmed through simulations which showed that for the same message overhead, spreading replicas by HDRW results in better search performance than the other mechanisms, under both flooding-based and random walk-based search.

Morselli, Bhattacharjee, Marsh & Srinivasan (2005) propose *LMS* (Local Minima Search), a search method and replication protocol. Assuming that both peers and data items obtain ids uniformly at random from a given large set (so as to guarantee uniqueness with high probability), the replication mechanism tries to replicate an item with id *i* to peers with id 'close' to *i*. Such a node is called a local minimum for item *i* in that its id is closest to *i* among the ids of all peers in the node's *h*-hop neighborhood, where *h* is a given parameter. A random walk is used first, followed by a deterministic walk that progresses towards the closest local minimum node by selecting at each step the neighbor with the smallest distance from *i*. When this random local minimum is reached, a replica is created if there is not one there already; otherwise, the process is repeated with a random walker of double length. For locating the item, the same procedure is used. A local minimum that receives the query replies with the replica or with a failure message depending on whether it stores the item or not. To improve success rate and response time, multiple such walkers can be utilized. The protocol can achieve quite high query success probabilities but at the expense of a possibly large number of replicas ($O\left(\sqrt{n / d_h}\right)$, where d_h is the minimum size of an *h*-hop neighborhood), which can be a problem if the storage space in each peer is limited.

Maximization of the probability of success is also the subject of the work by Sozio, Neumann & Weikum (2008). They consider the problem of replica placement in arbitrary networks that are searched by random walks. Given the peer capacities and the query rates q_{ij}, i.e. the fraction of all queries (issued in the whole network) for data item *i* by peer *j*, the problem of finding an assignment of replicas to peers so as to maximize the probability of a successful query is shown to be related to the multi-knapsack problem, where there is a set of bins with given capacities and a set of elements each with size and profit and the aim is to find a feasible packing that maximizes the profit. The problem can be tackled by good approximation algorithms, which however are centralized. The authors present *P2R2*, a distributed algorithm to solve the problem, which is based on each peer *j* keeping a special counter for each data item *i*, r_{ij}. The counter r_{ij} is incremented for each query

about *i* that passes through node *j* and is unsuccessful or is satisfied by a peer with larger id. This requires that certain information is piggybacked on the query messages and that random walks are always unfolded to their maximum length even if the item is located at some step earlier than the expiration of TTL. P2R2 leads to a probability of query success which is within a factor of 2 from the optimal.

Summary of Replication in Unstructured P2P Systems

Replication methods that are applicable to unstructured p2p systems provide answers to the questions of how many replicas are created for each data item, according to which optimization criteria, and where those replicas are placed. Table 1 summarizes how replication methods described above deal with each of these issues.

REPLICATION IN STRUCTURED P2P NETWORKS

In structured peer-to-peer networks, data items are stored at specific nodes of the overlay. The mapping of data items to overlay nodes is in general achieved through appropriate hash functions that support a hash table interface with primitives put(key, value) and get(key), where key is the identity of a data item (for instance, the file name). In addition, the nodes in the overlay are organized in rigid topologies, such as a multidimensional ring, grid or an n-dimensional cube. This way, items can be located efficiently. The routing messages for locating an item follow a deterministic path from the requester to the owner of the item.

Ideally, hashing should be such that peer are responsible for roughly the same number of data items. The common underlying assumption for achieving this is that data keys, and in some cases node identifiers, are randomly chosen. However, due to skeweness in the data population, this is

Table 1. Summary of replication methods for unstructured p2p systems

	How many	Where/How	What	Goal
Sqaure-root Replication (Cohen et al, 2002)	Proportional to the square root of the query rate of each data item	-	Data items	Minimum expected search size
Owner Replication (Lv et al, 2002)	Proportional to the query rate of each data item	Only to the requesting peer	Data items	Minimum expected search size
Path Replication (Lv et al, 2002)	Proportional to the number of probes for locating the item	Along the path from the requesting peer to the provider peer	Data items	Minimum expected search size
Pull-then-Push Replication (Leontiadis et al, 2006)	Proportional to the number of probes for locating the item	-	Data items	Minimum expected search size
Proportional Replication (Tewari et al, 2005)	Proportional to the query rate of each data item	-	Data items	Minimum expected search time
Gia (Chawathe et al, 2003)	Equal to the degree of each node	1-hop neighborhood	Location information	Maximum success rate
HDRW (Jia et al, 2005)	Proportional to the number of probes for locating the item	Along a degree-biased search path	Location information	Good success rate and search size
LMS (Morselli et al, 2005)	-	At peers considered as local minima for a data item	Data items	Good success rate and search size
P2R2 (Sozio et al, 2008)	-	At peers resulting in greatest success rate for a data item	Data items	Maximum success rate

not always the case. Furthermore, even when the data items are evenly distributed among the peers of the overlay, non-uniform query workloads may lead to an uneven workload distribution among the peers, resulting in potentially overloading the peers that maintain popular items. Thus, replication techniques are central in achieving both data and workload balance in structured peer-to-peer systems. Furthermore, as in unstructured p2p systems, replication is used to handle peer failures and departures and increase availability. Scalability and performance are also central goals of replication in this context as well.

Most structured p2p systems provide search time logarithmic to the number of nodes in the overlay. Enhancing the basic structured overlays with replication can lead to achieving constant search time in most cases. Since the search path followed for locating an item is deterministic, this can be achieved by proactively placing replicas of each item on appropriate nodes on its search path.

Another common mechanism for implementing replication in DHT-based p2p systems is based on replicating each data item at the *k* neighbors of

the node holding it. Nodes close to each other on the overlay are not likely to be physically close to each other, since the id of a node is based on a hash of its IP address. This provides the desired independence of failures. Besides availability, these replicas can be used to improve query latency; they allow choosing among the *k* replica holders the one that has the lowest reported latency. Fetching from the lowest-latency replica has also the desired side-effect of spreading the load of serving a lookup over the replicas.

An alternative mechanism for realizing replication in DHTs is by using multiple hash functions. By doing so, a data item is mapped and stored at more than one node. This results in increasing availability as well as in improving load balancing. Furthermore, latency may be improved by selecting at each routing step the neighborhood or route that is closest either to the query or to the current node.

Finally, caching in DHTs is based on placing copies on the lookup path, similar to path replication in unstructured p2p systems or to the requestor of an item similar to owner replication.

Replication in Representative Structured P2P Systems

CHORD

Chord (Stoica, Morris, Karger, Kaashoek & Balakrishnan, 2001) is a popular DHT-based p2p system. The Chord protocol uses a variant of consistent hashing to assign to each node and data key an *m*-bit identifier. The identifier of a node is chosen by hashing its IP address, while the identifier of an item is produced by hashing its key. Identifiers are ordered in an identifier circle modulo 2^m. A data item with key i is assigned to the first node whose identifier is equal to or follows i in the circular space. This node is called the *successor* of i.

Each Chord node maintains two sets of neighbors, its successors and its fingers. The successor nodes immediately follow the node in the identifier space, while the finger nodes are spaced exponentially around the identifier space. Each node has a constant number of successors and at most m fingers. The i-th finger of the node with identifier p is the first node that succeeds p by at least 2^{i-1} on the identifier circle, where $1 \leq i \leq m$. The first finger node is the immediate successor of p, where $i = 1$. For a Chord network with N nodes, the number of routing hops for a lookup is $O(\log N)$, while each node only needs to maintain pointers to $O(\log N)$ neighbors.

The core Chord system does not provide for replication or caching. Instead, the replication mechanisms are left as a responsibility of the higher layer applications that use Chord. A typical method for an application to replicate data items in Chord is by using multiple hash functions to store each data item under distinct Chord keys. Furthermore, an application can store replicas of a data item with key i at the k nodes succeeding the successor of i. This is facilitated by the *successor-list* mechanism supported by Chord. In Chord, each node maintains a successor-list with its r nearest successors on the Chord ring. When a node notices that its successor has failed, it replaces it with the first live entry in its successor list. The fact that a Chord node keeps track of its successors means that it can notify the application when successor nodes fail or recover and thus when the application should propagate new replicas.

CAN

The *Content Addressable Network (CAN)* (Ratnasamy, Francis, Handley, Karp & Shenker, 2001) is another popular DHT-based structured p2p network. It uses a virtual *d*-dimensional Cartesian coordinate space or *d*-torus to store (key, value) pairs. Upon entering the system, each node is assigned a zone of this space. The key of each data item is mapped onto a point in the coordinate space using a uniform hash function. Then, the item is stored at the node that owns the zone within which the point lies. Each CAN node maintains a coordinate routing table that holds the IP address and virtual coordinate zone of each of its immediate neighbors in the coordinate space. In a *d*-dimensional coordinate space, two nodes are neighbors if their coordinates overlap along *d*–1 dimensions. Each node routes a message for an item with key i towards its neighbors whose coordinates are closer to that of i. Intuitively, routing works by following the straight line path through the Cartesian space from source to destination coordinates.

CAN supports a variety of replication mechanisms. A node that is overloaded with requests for a specific data item can replicate the data key at each of its neighboring nodes. The key of a popular data item is thus eventually replicated within a region surrounding the original storage node. A node holding a replica of a requested data key may, with a certain probability, choose to either satisfy the request or forward it. The second mechanism is based on the observation that each node can maintain multiple, independent coordinate spaces and be responsible for a different zone in each coordinate space. Each such coordinate space is a called a *reality*. For a CAN with *r* realities, a single node is assigned *r* coordinate zones and holds *r* independent neighbor sets. This form of replication improves data availability. Multiple realities also improve routing fault tolerance, because if routing fails in on one reality, messages can continue to be routed using the remaining realities. It also provides for neighbor selection. To forward a message, a node can check all its neighbors on each reality and forwards the message to the neighbor whose coordinates are the closest to the destination. Thus, using multiple realities reduces the path length and hence the overall CAN path latency. Yet another replication mechanism for improved data availability is to use *k* different hash functions to map a single key onto *k* points in the coordinate space. In this case, a (key, value) pair becomes unavailable only if all *k* distinct nodes become simultaneously unavailable. In addition, queries for a particular hash table entry could be sent to all *k* nodes in parallel thereby reducing the average query latency. Instead of querying all *k* nodes, a node may choose to retrieve an entry from that node which is closest to it in the coordinate space. Finally, with *zone overloading,* a zone may be assigned to more than one node. Each node maintains a copy of all items mapped to the zone to increase availability.

In addition to replication, CAN also supports caching. A CAN peer maintains a cache of the data keys it has recently accessed. Thus, before forwarding a request for a data key towards its destination, a peer first checks whether the requested data key is in its own cache and if so, it can itself satisfy the request without forwarding it any further.

PAST

Pastry (Rowstron & Druschel, 2001a) is a peer-to-peer routing substrate for supporting a variety of applications. In Pastry, each node is assigned a quasi-random 128-bit node identifier (nodeId). The nodeId is used to indicate the position of the node in a circular identifier space, which ranges from 0 to $2^{128} - 1$. Both nodeIds and data keys are treated as a sequence of digits with base 2^b. Pastry routes messages to the node whose nodeId is numerically closest to the given key.

To support routing, each node maintains a routing table, a neighborhood set and a leaf set. The routing table of each node *p* is organized into $\log_{2^b} N$ rows with 2^{b-1} entries each. The 2^{b-1} entries at row *i* of the routing table refer to those nodes whose nodeId has the same first *i* digits with the nodeID of *p*, but a different $i + 1$ th digit. Each such entry contains the IP address of one of the potentially many such nodes, usually the one physically closest to *p*. If no such node is known, the routing table entry is left empty. The leaf set includes the set of nodes with the *L*/2 numerically closest larger nodeIds to *p*, and the L/2 nodes with numerically closest smaller nodeIds to *p*. Lastly, the neighborhood set contains the nodeIds and IP addresses of the *M* nodes that are physically closest to *p*. This set is not normally used for routing, but it is used for maintaining physical locality properties. Typical values of *L* and *M* are 2^b or 2^{b+1}.

Given a message, each node *p* first checks whether the key falls within the range of nodeIds covered by its leaf set. If so, the message is forwarded directly to this node. Otherwise, the routing table is used to forward the message to a node that shares a common prefix with the key by at least one more digit (or *b* bits) than the current node *p*. If no such node is known, the message is forwarded to a node whose nodeId shares a prefix that is as long as the one shared with *p*, but is numerically closer to the key than the nodeId of *p*, by using the leaf set.

In Pastry, replication is not implemented directly. Instead, Pastry provides to the applications built on top of it the functionalities necessary for implementing replication. In particular, applications can use the information maintained in the routing table and the leaf and neighborhood sets to decide where to place replicas. Further, Pastry provides mechanisms for handling peer failures, such as periodically exchanged keep-alive messages.

In particular, *PAST* (Rowstron & Druschel, 2001b) is a p2p file storage system that relies on Pastry to provide routing file queries, multiple replicas of files, and caching for additional copies of popular files. For improved availability, PAST creates *k* replicas of each file and places them to *k* different peers whose nodeId is numerically closest to the 128 most-significant-bits of the identifier of the file (fileId) among all live nodes, where *k* is the replication factor. Since by the way identifiers are assigned to nodes, there is no correlation between these identifiers and the geographic location, network connectivity, ownership or jurisdiction of the nodes, the *k* nodes selected for storing the replicas are highly likely to be diverse in all these aspects and thus unlikely to conspire or be subject to correlated failures or threats.

For maintaining good system-wide storage utilization, PAST uses replica and file diversion. Replica diversion is achieved by allowing a peer that is not one of the *k* numerically closest peers to the fileId of a file to maintain a replica of it, if it is in the leafset of one of those *k* peers. This improves utilization within the nodes in the leaf set. File diversion is performed when the entire leaf set of a node is reaching capacity. A file is diverted to a different part of the identifier space by choosing a different salt in the generation of its fileId.

Replication in PAST aims mainly at improving fault-tolerance and partly at balancing the query load or reducing latency. Creating additional copies for popular files is achieved through caching. PAST uses a form of path replication: copies of files are cached along the search path for the file. In caching a file, however, PAST also considers the storage available at a node. A file is cached at a node only if its size is less than some fraction *c* of the current cache size of the node.

Kademlia

Kademlia (Maymounkov & Mazieres, 2002) is a distributed DHT-based p2p system that employs 160-bit identifiers for both participating nodes and file keys. Every node maintains information about (key, value) pairs "close" to itself. The distance between two objects (keys or nodes) in the 160-bit key space is measured as the bitwise XOR of their ids interpreted as an integer.

Each Kademlia node maintains a routing table that consists of 160 buckets. The *i*th bucket of a node contains up to *k* entries pointing to nodes in distance between 2^i and 2^{i+1}. The buckets are kept constantly updated, as for every received message the node either enters the sender's id in the tail of the appropriate bucket (possibly discarding another entry) or rearranges the entries in the bucket (by refreshing its contact with the least recently seen node).

Lookup is implemented by contacting nodes that have ids close to the id of the requested item. In particular, the inquiring node selects some of the closest nodes from its routing table and queries them, learning about other nodes even closer to the id in question, and so on. The end result is that within $O(\log N)$ steps (with high probability) the node forms a list of the *k* closest nodes to the requested id.

Replication in Kademlia exploits the lookup procedure. To store a (key, value) pair, a Kademlia node first locates the *k* closet nodes to the key, as described above. Then, it sends them a STORE message, creating *k* replicas of the item. Replicas are additionally created dynamically: after each successful search, a replica is placed in the closest node to the key that did not contain the item. The reason behind this is the unidirectionality property of the XOR distance metric which ensures that all searches for an item converge along the same path, no matter where they originate from; placing replicas on the lookup path leads to faster searches, avoiding at the same time hot spots. To ensure the freshness of replicas, Kademlia requires periodic re-publishing of the (key, value) pairs.

P-Grid

P-Grid (Aberer, Cudré-Mauroux, Datta, Despotovic, Hauswirth, Punceva & Schmidt, 2003; Aberer, Datta, Hauswirth & Schmidt, 2005) is a p2p data management system based on building a virtual distributed trie. Data keys are composed by a number of bits. The data key space is recursively bisected so that the resulting partitions carry approximately the same load. One or more peers are associated with each partition. Each partition is uniquely identified by a bit sequence. The bit sequence of a partition is called the path of the peer associated with the partitions. These bit sequences induce a trie structure which is used to implement prefix routing by resolving a key lookup a bit at a time. Each peer maintains for each bit position of its path one or more randomly selected references to a peer that has a path with the opposite bit at this position.

P-Grid implements two forms of replication for fault-tolerance. First, multiple peers are associated with the same key space. This is called structural replication. Then, multiple references are kept in the routing tables, thus providing alternative access paths.

General Replication Strategies

Selective Placement to Reduce Latency

Beehive (Ramasubramanian & Sirer, 2004) is a general replication framework that operates on top of any DHT that uses prefix-routing, such as Chord. In such systems, routing is performed by successively matching a prefix of the data identifier against node identifiers. In general, at each routing step, the query reaches a node that has one more matching prefix with the query than the previous node on the path. A query traveling k hops reaches a node that has k matching prefixes. The central observation behind Beehive is that the length of the average query path will be reduced by one hop when a data item is proactively replicated

at all nodes logically preceding that node on all query paths. For example, replicating the object at all nodes one hop prior to their successor node decreases the lookup latency by one hop. This can be applied iteratively to disseminate items widely throughout the system. Replicating an item at all nodes k hops or lesser from the successor node will reduce the lookup latency by k hops.

Beehive controls the extent of replication in the system by assigning a replication level to each item. An item at level i is replicated on all peers that have at least i matching prefixes with the item. Queries to data items replicated at level i incur a lookup latency of at most i hops. Data items stored only at their successor peers are at level $\log(N)$, while items replicated at level 0 are cached at all the peers in the system. The goal is to find the minimal replication level for each item such that the average lookup performance for the system is a constant C number of hops. Naturally, the optimal strategy involves replicating more popular items at lower levels (on more peers) and less popular items at higher levels. An analytical model provides Beehive with closed-form optimal solutions indicating the appropriate levels of replication for each item. In addition, a monitoring protocol based on local measurements and limited aggregation estimates the relative item popularity and the global properties of the query distribution. These estimates are used, independently and in a distributed fashion, as inputs to the analytical model which yields the locally desired level of replication for each item. Finally, a replication protocol proactively makes copies of the items around the network.

PopCache (Rao, Chen, Fu & Bu, 2007) is based on the observation that in structured p2p system, each node can be seen as the root of a tree. In particular, each node p can be treated as the root of a k-ary tree with its k direct neighbors of p connected by k links as the first level children, the neighbors of neighbors of p added with k^2 links as the second-level children and so on until level $\log_k(N)$, where N is the number of nodes.

Let us denote with T_p the tree having node p as its root. The search from some node to p is the process of greedily approaching the root p along the bottom-up path of T_p. For each data item i, PopCache utilizes the tree T_p that is rooted at the node p responsible for item *i*. Assume that we want to create a total of *m* copies for *i*. First, *k* replicas of *i* are placed on the first level of T_p, then k^2 copies of *i* are placed on the second level and so on, until all *m* replicas are created. For deriving the optimal number of copies per item, two optimization criteria are considered (a) given a maximum number of copies, how to minimize the average latency per query (MAX PREF), and (b) given a targeted threshold how to minimize the number of replicas (MIN COST). The first criterion is similar to that use in unstructured p2p systems, however, in this case, the optimal number of copies per item follows a different proportional principle.

Range Queries

HotRoD (Pitoura, Ntarmos & Triantafillou, 2006) uses replication over Chord to provide fair load distribution in the case of range queries. The key of this implementation is the use a locality-preserving hash function that preserves the ordering of data by mapping consecutive data values to neighboring peers. A range query is pipelined through those peers that store ranges of entries that overlap with the query range. HotRoD detects overloaded peers and distributes their access load among other, under-loaded ones, through replication. In particular, each peer keeps track of the number of times, it was accessed during a time interval *T*, and the average low and high bounds of the ranges of the queries it has processed during this interval. A peer is characterized as overloaded or *hot*, if this number exceeds a system-defined threshold. When a hot peer is detected, replication is initiated. Instead of replicating the content of a single peer, HotRoD replicates *arcs of peers*, where an arc consists of successive neighbors that

correspond to a certain range. This range is defined by the average low and high bounds of the range of the queries processed by the hot peer during the time interval *T*. Replication is achieved by using a multi-rotational hash function to randomly place the replicated arcs on the ring.

Sahin, Gupta, Agrawal & El Abbadi (2004) propose an extension of CAN for caching the results of range queries. In particular, the authors consider a 2-dimensionsal CAN. Each range query [low, high] is hashed at the point (low, high) in the virtual hash space.

Load Balancing

The *LAR protocol* (Gopalakrishnan, Silaghi, Bhattacharjee & Keleher, 2004) primarily addresses replication for load balancing of both the routing load as well as the load of the server holding the item and serving the request. Instead of creating replicas on all peers on a source-destination path as in path replication, the protocol relies on individual server load measurements to precisely choose replication points. The routing process is augmented with lightweight hints that shortcut the original routing and direct queries towards new replicas. Zhu, Zhang, Li & Huang (2007) propose a load prediction algorithm for estimating the load at each peer as well as multiple load thresholds for appropriately adjusting the number of replicas according to the load status of each node.

Alqaralleh, Wag, Zhou & Zomaya (2007) study three replica placements algorithms that can be implemented on top of any prefix-based DHT overlay. They were tested on top of FreePastry. The first algorithm, called CDN-QueryStat, places replicas on peers where queries frequently come from. In the second proposed algorithm, termed CDN-Rand, a peer randomly selects another peer from the id space. Thus, this algorithm tends to distribute replicas uniformly across the network. The third algorithm, CDN-PR, is a priority based approach that tries to minimize the number of peers that store replicas. The motivation is to reduce the overhead of maintaining load statistics. Peers are initially selected to hold replicas as in CDN-QueryStat. A new peer is chosen to hold replicas only if the previously selected peers get saturated with copies. Load balancing is applied, when the access frequency exceed a threshold. Then, a procedure is activated for replica creation and query forwarding.

Datta. Schmidt & Aberer (2007) propose using the query redundancy, that is, the existence of multiple search paths, to achieve better load balancing of both the routing load and the answering load of the server holding the item. They show through simulation, using the P-Grid topology, that, just replicating items and then routing to any of the replicas results in high statistical variation of the query and answering load. Proportional replication was used. To address this imbalance, they propose exploiting the redundant routing table entries used for fault tolerance. To choose among the available peers at each routing step, a cumulative load measure was used where answering queries weighted more than forwarding ones.

P2P-Based Storage and Caching

Dabek, Kaashoek, Karger, Moris & Stoica (2001) have proposed *CFS*, a storage layer based on a DHT that consists of two layers, namely the DHash (a distributed hash table) and Chord layers. The DHash layer performs block fetches for the client and distributes the blocks of each file among the servers. It uses the Chord distributed lookup system to locate the servers responsible for a block. CFS provides distinct mechanisms for replication and caching. Both caching and replication are performed at the level of a file block. CFS places the replica of a block at the r servers immediately after the successor of the block on the Chord ring. The placement of block replicas makes it easy for a client to select the replica likely to be the fastest to download. CFS also caches blocks to avoid overloading servers that hold popular data items. A block is cached at all peers on the search path

after each successful look-up. Cached blocks are replaced in a least-recently-used order. This has the effect of preserving the cached copies close to the successor. In addition, it expands and contracts the degree of caching for each block according to its popularity.

Squirrel (Iyer, Rowstron & Druschel, 2002) is a decentralized p2p system that exploits resources from many desktop machines to achieve the functionality and performance of a dedicated web cache without requiring any additional hardware. Squirrel is built over the routing substrate of Pastry and uses its functionality for locating an object stored at the distributed client caches. It adopts two approaches to create copies: a home-store and a directory approach. In the home-store approach, Squirrel stores objects both at client caches and at their home peer. In the directory approach, the home peer remembers a small number of peers (up to k) that have recently accessed a certain object and keeps pointers to these peers. Then, each request is redirected to a randomly chosen peer among these (called the delegate), which is expected to have a copy of the object locally cached. Comparing these approaches in practice, the home-store method achieves better load balancing than the directory one, since popular objects are associated with rapidly changing directories.

Multiple Mappings

The *"power of two choices"* (Byers, Considine & Mitzenmacher, 2003) proposes a strategy for replica placement for Chord based on multiple hash functions. Each object is hashed using d ($d \geq 2$) hash functions to multiple ids and placed on the least loaded peer among candidates. To locate an item, instead of applying all d hash functions, the peers responsible for the item are connected with each other through *redirection pointers*. Using the redirection pointers, each request received by other peers (candidates) is redirected to the hosting peer. Although, using two or more choices for placement improves load balancing, it still forces a static placement of the data items, which may lead to poor performance when the popularity of items changes over time. One way of addressing this issue is to use the re-direction pointers among the peers and allow items to choose a different peer for placing its replica by periodically re-inserting the items, if their previous choice has become more heavily loaded. The redirection pointers can also be used to facilitate a wide range of load balancing methods that react more quickly than periodic re-insertion, such as allowing an under-utilized peer to perform load-stealing or an overloaded one to attempt load shedding.

Symmetric Replication (Ghodsi, Alima & Haridi, 2005) can be applied to any structured peer-to-peer system. The basic idea is to associate each identifier in the system with f other identifiers. If identifier i is associated with identifier r, any item with identifier i should be stored at the peers responsible for identifiers i and r. Similarly, any item with identifier r should also be stored at the peers responsible for the identifiers i and r. Thus, effectively an identifier space of size N is partitioned into N/f equivalence classes such that identifiers in an equivalence class are all associated with each other. To replicate items with symmetric replication, the peer responsible for identifier i stores all f items with an identifier associated with i. For example, if the identifier 0 is associated with the identifiers 0, 5, 10, 15, any peer responsible for any of the items 0, 5, 10, or 15 has to store all of the items 0, 5, 10, and 15. Hence, if we are interested in retrieving item 0, we can ask the peer responsible for any of the items 0, 5, 10, 15. To implement symmetric replication, each peer in the system augments its routing table to contain for each routing entry f entries, one for each of the replicas of the routing entry. Symmetric replication can be used to send out multiple concurrent requests for an item and then picking the first response that arrives. The advantage of this is twofold. First, it enhances performance. Second, it provides fault tolerance in an end-to-

end fashion, since the failure of a peer along the search path does not require repeating the request as it is likely that another one of the concurrent requests succeeds. It can also be used to achieve proximity neighbor selection in the following way. To route a message to the peer responsible for identifier i, each message in the routing process is augmented with a parameter r that specifies which of the f replicas of i is currently searched for. A peer that receives the request for a replica of i can calculate its distance to all of the f replicas and choose among the f peers the one that has a shorter distance to each respective replica of i. Then, it updates the parameter r in the outgoing message to reflect the new selection.

Locating Replicas

The *Replica Location Service (P-RLS)* (Cai, Chervenak & Frank, 2004) relies on Chord to build a mechanism for locating replicas. Each mapping from logical names (i.e., keys) to physical locations (i.e., replicas) is stored at the root peer of the mapping. P-RLS uses *successor replication*: the root peer replicates the mappings to its k successor peers in the Chord ring for successor routing reliability, where k is the replication factor. As a peer joins to network, it will take over some of the mappings and replicas from its successor peer. When a peer leaves the system, its predecessor will detect its departure, make another peer the new successor, and replicate mappings on the new successor peer adaptively. To avoid unnecessary replication of mappings, each mapping is associated with an expiration time. Besides fault tolerance, successor replication improves data load balance. In Chord, the number of mappings stored at each node is determined by the distance of the node to its immediate predecessor in the circular space, i.e. the "owned region" of the node. With adaptive replication with replication factor k, besides storing the nodes belonging to its own region, each node also replicates the mappings belonging to its k predecessors. Therefore, the number of mappings stored on each node is determined by the sum of $k+1$ continuous owned regions before the node. If the node identifiers are generated randomly, there is no dependency among these continuous owned regions. Thus, intuitively, when the replication factor k increases, the sum of $k+1$ owned region is distributed more normally. To improve query load balance, P-RLS also proposes *predecessor replication*: replicating mappings at the predecessors of the root node. When a predecessor receives a query to the root node, it resolves it locally using its own replica of the mapping without forwarding the request to the root node, thus alleviating hotspots.

To reduce the number of replicas as well as the delay and bandwidth consumption for update propagation, Chen, Katz & Kubiatowicz, (2002) propose organizing the replicas on an application-level multicast tree, called replica dissemination tree (or d-tree) build on top of the overlay network, in their case, Tapestry. Each peer in the d-tree maintains state information only for its parent and its direct children. Two algorithms are proposed for dynamic replica placement. In the first algorithm, called naive placement, a peer stores a replica on the parent server of the requestor peer or on the overlay path server that is as close to the asked peer as possible. The second scheme, called smart placement, chooses as parent the peer with the lowest load among candidates. If more than one of them meets the requirements, then the replica is placed on the overlay path server that is as far from the requestor as possible.

Caching State

EpiChord (Leong, Liskov & Demaine, 2006) is a DHT similar to Chord. Instead of maintaining a finger table per node, EpiChord keeps a cache per node with a list of k successor and k predecessor node. Nodes populate their caches mainly from observing network look-up traffic, and cache entries are flushed from the cache after a fixed lifetime. In particular, each node updates its cache based on information returned by queries and adds an entry to the cache each time it is queried by a node not already in the cache. To lookup an entry, an EpiChord node initiates a number of parallel lookups to the successors and predecessors nodes in its cache. In addition, nodes communicate with their immediate successor and predecessor periodically, exchanging their entire successor and predecessor lists.

Summary of Replication in Structured P2P Systems

Approaches to replication differ on *what* is replicated. Replication may involve either replicating the item itself or its index (i.e. its location). In few cases, the routing table or information about neighbors is also replicated.

There are various methods for achieving replication in structured p2p systems. A very common approach is to place a number of replicas at the immediate neighbors of a node such as the successor nodes in CHORD, the nodes in the leafset in PAST or the peers at the neighboring zones in CAN. Such replicas are easily locatable. The primary reason for this form of replication is fault tolerance. Another approach is to use multiple hash functions to map an item to more than one node. Besides availability, applying multiple hash functions allows the employment of multiple search paths for an item and thus improves query latency and path fault tolerance. Path or owner replication can also be used to improve search for popular items. Finally, to achieve load balancing various approaches base their decision to create replicas purely on the load of each peer. Other approaches include: making more than one node responsible for the same identifier space (such as with zone overloading in CAN or structural relaxation in P-Grid), building multiple overlays (such as with multiple realities in CAN) or building a replica tree on top of the overlay (such as in d-tree).

The number of replicas created is either fixed for all items as a general replication factor of the system (for instance k successors or nearest peers in the identifier space) or varies for each item or node depending on the current system parameters such

as the item popularity or the load at the servers.

Table 2 summarizes the various replication approaches in structured p2p networks.

Table 2. Summary of replication strategies in structured p2p systems

	How many	**Where/How**	**What**	**Goal**
Applications built on top of Chord (Stoica et al, 2001)	k successors	Multiple hash functions, or At the successors of an item	Data items or keys	Failure recovery Load balance
CAN (Ratnasamy et al, 2001)	varies	Neighbor replication Multiple realities Multiple hash functions Zone overloading Caching (i.e. owner replication)	Data items/index entries	Response time Availability Neighbor selection Load balancing
PAST (Rowstron et al, 2001b)	k nearest identifiers	At the k peers whose identifier is numerically closest to the identifier of the file	Files	Fault tolerance
		Caching (path replication)	Files	Query load balance
Kademlia (Maymounkov & Mazieres, 2002)	k replicas plus 1 new per successful lookup	k closest nodes to the key and 1 to next-to--last node on the lookup path	<key, value> pairs	Handle failures and improve latency
P-Grid (Aberer et al, 2005)	-	Multiple peers per key space Multiple route paths	Data keys Routing	Load balancing Fault tolerance
Beehive (Ramasubramanian et al, 2004)	k per item where k depends on item popularity	At all peers k hops before the successor of the item	Data items	Achieves lookup of a constant number of C hops
PopCache (Rao et al, 2007)	Such that to achieve optimal average search (MAX PERF) or a targeted lookup threshold (MIN COST)	On the k-tree induced by the k neighbors of each node	Data items	Query latency
HotRoD (Pitoura et al, 2006)	Arcs of peers	Multi-rotational locality-preserving hash function	Popular data items on arcs of peers	Load balance for range queries
LAR {Gopalakrishnan et al, 2004)	adaptive	Load measurements by individual peers	Data items/index entries	Data and query balance
CDN (Alqaralleh et al, 2007)	adaptive	Frequently query peers, or at random peers or such that to minimize the number of peers holding replicas	Data items	Performance Load balancing Replica maintenance cost
CFS (Dabek et al, 2001)	varies	Caching Replication at the successor	File Blocks	Load balancing Performance
Squirrel (Iyer et al, 2002)	up to k pointers	Caching	Data items (home-store) or Pointers to their location (directory)	Query latency Fault tolerance
Power of two choices (Byers et al, 2002)	d hash functions	Multiple hash functions	Data items	Load balance
Symmetric Replication (Ghodsi et al, 2005)	f nodes	Equivalence classes of related identifiers	Data items	Response time Neighbor selection Fault tolerance
P-RLS (Cai et al, 2004)	k successors and /or predecessors	At the successors	Mappings	Failure recovery, Data balance
		At the predecessors		Query balance
d_tree (Chen et al, 2002)	varies	On a multicast tree built on top of the p2p overlay	Data items	Reduce storage Query latency Improve update efficiency
EpiChord (Leong et al, 2006)	varies	Caching during lookup	Routing state (predecessor and successors)	Query latency Reduce state per node

UPDATES

Replication introduces the overhead of maintaining the replicas of each data item up-to-date. A replica management protocol decides *where* (i.e. at which copies) updates take place, *when* updates propagate to other replicas and *how* the propagation of updates is achieved.

According to the *where* aspect, replication strategies can be classified broadly as single master or primary copy and multi-master or group. *Single master or primary copy* replication is the simplest approach in which each replicated item is owned by a single peer (or owner). The copy held by the owner is called the primary copy. All copies can be read but any update to an item must be first applied to its primary copy and then propagated to the other copies. The advantage of primary copy replication is its simplicity. However, the owner of an item may be a potential bottleneck as well as a single point of failure. The *multi-master* or *group approach* allows multiple peers to hold primary copies of the same data item. All replicas are regarded as equally authoritative. The multi-master approach avoids bottlenecks and single points of failures, however, it increases communication costs and system complexity, since it requires concurrent updates at different replicas to be coordinated and reconciled to solve any potential replica divergences.

In terms of the *when* aspect, update propagation strategies can be implemented either synchronously or asynchronously. A synchronous propagation mechanism updates all replicas before a transaction commits. With the asynchronous strategy, only a subset of the replicas is updated.

Regarding the *how* aspect, most replication management techniques in p2p networks use a combination of push and pull methods to propagate updates as follows. The initiator of an update *pushes* the new value of its copy to a number of other peers in the system. A peer that holds a copy *pulls* other peers to be informed of any potential updates. Most update propagation mechanisms

in p2p systems are *probabilistic* in the sense that they ensure that an update will eventually reach all copies of an item with a certain probability. The propagation of an update may involve a *notification* that the item has been updated, a *state transfer* where the actual new value of the modified data is transferred or an *operation transfer* where the update operation is propagated. Choosing a propagation method depends on the amount of data, bandwidth availability and various system- and application- related characteristics.

Finally, the consistency of replicas refers to the allowable divergence among the various copies of an item. *Strong* consistency does not allow any such divergence and guarantees that each read returns the most current value of an item. *Weak* consistency allows various levels of divergence among copies as well as reads that may return stale values of an item.

To address scalability and dynamicity, most update replication mechanisms in p2p systems support multi-master schemes, probabilistic update propagation and weak consistency.

Individual Peer Techniques

Before proceeding to describe update mechanisms for unstructured and structured p2p systems, we review some techniques that can be followed by individual peers in order to achieve a desired level of confidence or consistency for the items they are interested in.

Vecchio & Son (2005) adapt the traditional quorum consensus schemes to a dynamic p2p environment by letting each peer choose its own quorum level. In effect, each peer decides on the level of confidence of the item it accesses. This way, there is a tradeoff between the incurred message overhead and the achieved consistency levels; the higher the quorum values the higher the message overhead and the lower the possibility of accessing stale data.

The Controlled Update Propagation (CUP) protocol (Roussopoulos & Baker, 2003) allows individual peers to receive and propagate updates only when they have a payoff to do so. Each peer registers with its neighbors for receiving updates only for the items it is interested in. Correspondingly, it propagates any received updates of an item *i* only to the neighbors that have registered their interest for *i*. A node decides whether it is interested in receiving updates for item *i* based on the "profit" it will have; receiving an update is justified if it will save the node the cost of handling queries, i.e. if the node receives frequently queries for item *i* then keeping an up-to-date replica of *i* will allow it to answer these queries immediately, avoiding the overhead of propagating the queries further. Clearly, these policies favor the popular items since these items generate queries most often.

Susarla & Carter (2005) let each peer express their consistency requirements as a vector of options along five different dimensions, on a per-access basis. They argue that different classes of distributed applications, such as file access, database and directory services, and real-time collaborative groupware, have a broad and diverse set of requirements with regards to replica handling. These requirements are classified along the following five, mostly orthogonal, dimensions: (1) concurrency - the degree to which conflicting accesses can be allowed, (2) replica synchronization - the degree to which replica divergence can be tolerated (termed coherence or timeliness) and the types of inter-dependencies among updates that must be preserved upon replica synchronization (termed consistency), (3) failure handling - how data access is handled when some replicas become unreachable or have poor connectivity (4) update visibility - the time at which modifications to local data are made visible globally, and (5) view isolation - the time at which remote updates are made visible locally. To cater for such diverse requirements with regards to replica updates, the *composable consistency model* is proposed along with an outline of its implementation in *Swarm*, a wide area p2p middleware file service. Swarm

allows applications to specify the level for each of the five requirements at every search. Swarm assumes that there is a master server, termed custodian, per file that coordinates the consistency management protocols for the file. There can be more than one custodian per file for fault tolerance. Consistency is achieved through a combination of push and pull operations.

Updates in Unstructured P2P Networks

As mentioned above, the consistency mechanisms that have been proposed use a push-based and/or a pull-based propagation algorithm. One more possibility can be found in the work of Demers et al (1987), who have applied the theory of epidemics to the problem of update propagation in a distributed environment, proposing a number of generic methods. The first method the authors examine is *direct mail*, where the owner of a data item contacts (`mails`) all the other peers at every update. This approach, although simple, can be overwhelming in a p2p network with a large number of nodes. In the *anti-entropy* method each peer regularly chooses a neighbor and by exchanging their content resolves any differences between them (if a newer version of an item is found, it updates its own replica). A peer can either push its content to the other peer letting it check for inconsistencies, or pull content, or even push and pull content at the same time. Another update spreading algorithm considered is *rumor mongering*: at first all peers are considered 'ignorant' when an update is out and the update becomes a 'hot rumor'. If a peer knows of such a rumor, it periodically chooses another peer and tries to communicate the rumor. If the peer sees that the rumor is no longer hot (i.e. most of the peers it contacts already know it), it stops propagating it any further.

If the direct mail method is to be used, a natural plan would be to know (most of) the peers that hold a replica of the particular data item (statefull replication) so as to only contact those upon an update. A mechanism like this is assumed by Datta, Hauswirth & Aberer (2003). The authors study the performance of a generic hybrid push-pull consistency maintenance protocol for p2p environments where peers join and leave the network at a very high rate. At the push phase, the owner sends the updated item, along with its version number, to the peers that hold replicas. This requires knowledge of who holds replicas of what, but the update is not communicated through direct mail; it is rather propagated with a randomized flooding among the affected peers. The owner performs a selective push of its updates to a subset of the peers that will be affected by it (because they have a replica of the updated data item); each peer that receives the update also propagates it to a subset of affected peers it knows, and so on. To reduce the overhead, each message contains a partial list of the peers that have already been contacted. The method is accompanied by a pull phase that takes place whenever a peer is reconnected to the network after a disconnection or has not received updates for a long time (in the spirit of the anti-entropy method); during this pull phase, it contacts online peers with replicas of the items it stores, for their latest versions.

UPTReC – update propagation thought replica chain (Wang, Das, Kumar & Shen, 2007) – exploits similar pull and push mechanisms to scatter updates in decentralized and unstructured p2p systems. The peers that hold the replicas of an item i form a logical bi-directional chain, where each peer maintains information about the k closest peers in the chain in each direction. Peers may join (when a new replica is created) or leave (when removing a replica) by pushing messages at appropriate directions in the chain. Updates are similarly propagated by pushing messages at both directions, informing up to $2k$ nodes; at each direction the furthest known peer undertakes the responsibility of reaching the next bunch of k nodes in the chain and so on. Nodes that reconnect after a disconnection pull in order to synchronize. Maintaining such a chain for every

item reduces the message overhead on updates while also providing better consistency levels than Datta, Hauswirth & Aberer (2003), as shown experimentally.

Wang, Kumar, Das & Shen (2006) consider multi-master replication where all replica holders (termed "replica peers" – RPs) are allowed to update the item. In particular, a subset of RPs become "virtual servers" (VRPs) for the data item. The set of VRPs changes dynamically over time, based on node availability. Any replica peer updating the item contacts a VRP to undertake the update coordination. This "master" VRP first enters an agreement phase with the other VRPs in order to commit the update. When agreement is achieved, the master VRP obtains the updated item from the replica peer and pushes it to the remaining VRPs and to a partial list of the other RPs. Among the other RPs, the update propagation is implemented using a combination of push and pull, where some RPs are only pushing while the others are only pulling. The protocol achieves one-copy serializability, i.e. the concurrent execution of updates on a replicated item has the same effect as a serial execution on a non-replicated item.

Update propagation in the last three methods occurs strictly among the interested peers; although this seems efficient in terms of overheads and consistency levels, it nevertheless incurs the extra state overhead of keeping track of all peers holding a replica of the data item, which could be prohibitive in an unstructured and dynamic p2p network. Three update propagation policies (two based on push and pull techniques and a hybrid one that combines the push and pull policies) are proposed by Lan, Liu, Shenoy & Ramamritham (2003) for practical networks. The authors assume a master-copy schema where the owner of the data item always has the most up to date version and all peers that hold a replica need to be kept consistent; the overlay network is unstructured and the owners do not know who/where replica holders are. To achieve consistency, each data item is associated with a version number which is incremented by the owner every time an update occurs. In the push-based policy, the owner of a data item broadcasts an invalidation message when a data item is modified. The invalidation message is propagated through the network using a flooding algorithm, limited to a predefined number of hops (TTL). When a peer receives an invalidation message, it checks its cache. If it holds a replica of the data item and the stored version is smaller than the received version number, it invalidates the replica in its cache. In the proposed pull-based policy, a peer polls the owner of an item it holds in its cache to determine if the replica is stale or not. An *adaptive polling policy* is used to determine how frequently the peer should poll. It is based on a time-to-refresh (TTR) value associated with each item in the cache, which indicates when the next pull for the item should occur. The TTR is increased by an additive amount C (TTR = TTR+C) if the peer finds out that a data item has not been modified between two successive polls, otherwise TTR is reduced by a multiplicative factor D (TTR = TTR/D). A hybrid push and pull approach can also be used to combine both techniques. In this hybrid scheme, the owner propagates invalidation messages using a limited push. In addition, a peer that holds a replica may pull adaptively to make sure that the replica is valid. TTR can be further tuned by a factor that depends on the degree of a peer; the intuition behind this is that highly connected nodes should poll less frequently since they are potentially easier to reach by the owner push.

An alternative hybrid push/pull update propagation policy, *PtPU*, is proposed by Leontiadis, Dimakopoulos & Pitoura (2006). It is assumed that for the creation of replicas in the p2p network the Pull-then-Push algorithm was used where a peer that requests an item, after a successful search (pull phase) enters a push phase where it transmits replicas of the item using the same algorithm as in the pull phase. Given this replica creation approach, each peer that holds a data item is characterized as *owner* if it is allowed to apply updates,

responsible if it has requested the data item and has forced the creation of replicas or *indifferent* if it has been forced to hold a replica without requesting the data item. In the PtPU policy, the owner performs a limited broadcast of the new version of a data item when an update occurs. If a peer that is characterized as responsible for an item receives the broadcast message with a new version of the data item, it undertakes the task of informing the indifferent peers. This is done by propagating the update message (*U-push phase*) exactly as in the push phase when the replicas were created. Apart from pushing the updates they receive from the owner, responsible peers also pull periodically in order to become aware of more updates. To determine the frequency of the pull, the adaptive polling policy is used, where a TTR value is increased or decreased depending on weather the data item has been changed or not between two successive poll periods.

Updates in Structured P2P Networks

Many update propagation mechanisms in p2p systems use a form of periodic pushing to inform of any updates other holders of data copies. This is particularly useful in terms of updates related to state or routing information. This is often referred to as *soft-state* updates. In P-RLS (Cai, et al, 2004) update propagation is implemented in two phases. In the first phase, the Replica Location Service (LRC) periodically sends soft state updates summarizing its state into the peer-to-peer network. Then, the root peer of each mapping updates its successors immediately to maintain the consistency of the replicated mappings. Soft-state updates are also applied in LAR (Gopalakrishnan et al, 2004) and CAN (Ratnasamy et al, 2001). In CAN, each peer sends periodic update messages to each of its neighbors giving information about its zone coordinates and a list of its neighbors with their zone coordinates. The same policy of periodic update messages is applied to CDN (Alqralleh et al, 2001).

Beehive (Ramasubramanian et al, 2004) exploits the structure of the underlying DHT to provide strong consistency. It ensures that any object modification is propagated to all replicas. In CFS (Dabek et al, 2001) cryptographic verification of updates and server id authentication are used and only owners of data can implement updates. For update dissemination in symmetric replication (Chen et al, 2002), replicas and caches self-organize into a *d*-tree and use application-level multicast to propagate updates. Replicas and caches are always kept up-to-date. P-Grid (Aberer et al, 2003) proposes an update mechanism based on a generic push/pull gossiping scheme that provides probabilistic guarantees for consistency.

Akbarinia, Pacitti & Valduriez (2007) proposed an interesting replica update mechanism for DHT-based p2p networks. Their objective is to provide a mechanism which returns efficiently a current replica of a data item given its key. The proposed update management mechanism relies on timestamps. Data items are replicated using multiple hash functions as in many structured p2p systems. The main difference is that, when a data item is mapped to a peer, each item is associated with a logical timestamp which is stored along with the item. Timestamps are generated through a distributed service that guarantees the monotonicity property for timestamps, i.e. two timestamps generated for the same key are monotonically increasing. This property allows ordering the timestamps generated for the same key according to the time at which they have been generated.

The distributed timestamp generation service uses the underlying DHT. In particular, a hash function is used to map each key with one peer that is held responsible for returning a new timestamp for that key. Each peer that needs a timestamp for an item with a specific key i uses the hash function to locate the peer responsible for generating timestamps for i and sends a timestamp request to it. Upon receiving the request, the responsible peer initializes some local counter to the value of the last generated timestamp for i.

Upon storing an item with timestamp t_s, in case the peer already has a replica of the item with timestamp t_p, the two timestamps are compared so that only the latest version (the one with the largest timestamp) is finally kept. In order to retrieve a data item, a peer first gets a timestamp from the responsible peer and compares it with the results it receives, so that it ensures its currency.

SUMMARY

In this chapter, we have presented replication techniques and mechanisms that have been proposed for p2p networks. Replication is a central mechanism for improving performance and availability in a distributed system. P2p systems introduce new challenges mainly because of their unprecedented scalability and dynamicity. In this chapter, we have focused on replication mainly for improving the response time of search and achieving load balancing.

Note that replication is just one method for achieving redundancy. Alternatively, erasure coding or a combination of replication and erasure coding can be used towards this end. An *erasure code* provides redundancy without the overhead of strict replication. Erasure codes divide an object into m fragments and recode them into n fragments, where $n > m$. The ratio m/n is called the *rate* of encoding. A rate r code increases the storage cost by a factor of $1/r$. The key property of erasure codes is that the original object can be reconstructed from any m fragments. Weatherspoon & Kubiatowicz (2002) have quantified the availability gained using erasure codes. Then, they show that erasure-resilient codes use an order of magnitude less bandwidth and storage than replication for systems with similar mean time to failure (MTTF). They also show that employing erasure-resilient codes increase the MTTF of the system by many orders of magnitude over simple replication with the same storage overhead and repair times. Recent research takes other issues into consideration such as user download behavior (Chen, Qiu & Wu, 2008) and the characteristics of the overlay nodes (Rodrigues & Liskow, 2005) under which replication may outperform erasure codes. Erasure codes and related protocols are beyond the scope of this chapter, since our main focus is on search quality and load balance.

In unstructured p2p systems, most research has focused on determining the appropriate number of replicas as well as on developing practical mechanisms for placing the replicas. Most of the theoretical work on the subject is based on the results of Cohen & Shenker (2002) and assumes a network topology and a search strategy that allow uniform node sampling. Similar results are lacking for other search strategies and more realistic network models (e.g. power-law random graphs). A very limited number of practical algorithms have been presented for the placement of replicas so as to optimize some aspects of search performance. Replication in unstructured p2p systems is currently an area where further theoretical as well as experimental analysis is needed.

As with unstructured p2p, the main reasons for replication in structured p2p systems are availability and performance. In particular with structured p2p, replication is central in improving load balancing caused by skew in the mapping of items to nodes. Replica placement decisions in structured p2p systems often exploit the structure of the underlying overlay. Common choices for placing replicas include the immediate neighboring nodes as well as the nodes on the search path of an item. DHTs also offer alternative mechanisms for realizing replication that are based on the mapping of the data-key space to nodes. One way is by using multiple hash functions to map (store) the same item on multiple nodes. Another way is by assigning the same key space to more than one node (such as with zone overloading in CAN or structural relaxation in P-Grid). Finally, one may build multiple overlays (such as with multiple realities in CAN) or replica trees on top of the overlay (such as in d-tree).

Once replicas are created, a central point is maintaining the replicas up-to-date. Strategies that are based on global knowledge of the replica holders may have the potential to achieve good consistency levels and low message loads, but seem rather inappropriate for dynamic networks that evolve quickly. A logical thing to do in such a case is exploit the p2p network structure for an efficient update scheme, an approach that by nature fits some structured network topologies well. For all other networks most approaches aim at achieving some form of probabilistic consistency, relying on a combination of pushing the updates to neighbors and pulling copies from them.

Since no single optimal solution exists for replica placement or for replica updates, this is expected to be an active area of research for many years. Promising issues include (a) theoretical results regarding the optimal replica placement in various types of unstructured p2p systems, (b) gossiping protocols for update maintenance, (c) replication for fault tolerance, (d) replication to meet the requirements of specific storage-related applications and (e) replication techniques for highly dynamic and unpredictable environments. New research challenges also arise in the area of social networking and in mobile peer-to-peer environments.

REFERENCES

Aberer, K., Cudré-Mauroux, P., Datta, A., Despotovic, Z., Hauswirth, M., Punceva, M., & Schmidt, R. (2003). P-Grid: A Self-organizing Structured p2p System. *SIGMOD Record, 32*(3).

Aberer, K., Datta, A., & Hauswirth, M. (2003). *The quest for balancing peer load in structured peer-to-peer systems* (Tech. Rep. EPFL No. IC/2003/32). Lausanne, Switzerland: Ecole Polytechnique Fédérale de Lausanne.

Akbarinia, R., Pacitti, E., & Valduriez, P. (2007). Data currency in replicated DHTs. In *Proc. SIGMOD 2007 ACM Int'l Conference on Management of Data*, Beijing, China (pp. 211-222).

Alqaralleh, B. A., Wang, C., Zhou, B. B., & Zomaya, A. Y. (2007). Effects of replica placement algorithms on performance of structured overlay networks. In *Proc. IPDPS 2007, IEEE Int'l Parallel & Distributed Processing Symposium*, Long Beach, CA, USA (pp. 1-8).

Byers, J., Considine, J., & Mitzenmacher, M. (2003). Simple load balancing for distributed hash tables. In *Proc. IPTPS 2003, 2nd Int'l Workshop on Peer-to-Peer Systems*, Berkeley, CA, USA.

Cai, M., Chervenak, A., & Frank, M. (2004). A peer-to-peer replica location service based on a distributed hash table. In *Proc. SC2004, ACM/IEEE Conference on Supercomputing*, Pittsburgh, Pennsylvania, USA (pp. 54-54).

Chawathe, Y., Ratnasamy, S., Breslau, L., Lanham, N., & Shenker, S. (2003). Making gnutella-like P2P systems scalable. In *Proc. of SIGCOMM'03*, Karlsruhe, Germany (pp. 407-418).

Chen, G., Qiu, T., & Wu, F. (2008). Insight into redundancy schemes in DHTs. *The Journal of Supercomputing*, *43*, 183–198. doi:10.1007/s11227-007-0126-4

Chen, Y., Katz, R. H., & Kubiatowicz, J. (2002). Dynamic replica placement for scalable content delivery. In *Proc. IPTPS 2002, 1st Int'l Workshop on Peer-to-Peer Systems* (pp. 306-318). Boston, MA, USA.

Clark, I., Miller, S. G., Hong, T. W., Sandberg, O., & Wiley, B. (2002). Protecting free expression online with Freenet. *IEEE Internet Computing*, *6*(1), 40–49. doi:10.1109/4236.978368

Cohen, E., & Shenker, S. (2002). Replication strategies in unstructured peer-to-peer networks. In *Proc. of SIGCOMM'02*, Pittsburgh, Pennsylvania, USA (pp. 177-190).

Dabek, F., Kaashoek, M. F., Karger, D., Morris, R., & Stoica, I. (2001). Wide-area cooperative storage with CFS. In *Proc. of the 18th ACM Symposium on Operating Systems Principles*, Chateau Lake Louise, Banff, Canada (pp. 202-215).

Datta, A., Heuswirth, H., & Aberer, K. (2003, May). Updates in highly unreliable, replicated peer-to-peer systems. In *Proc. of ICDCS 2003, 23rd Int'l Conference on Distributed Computing Systems*, Providence, Rhode Island, (pp. 76-85).

Datta, A., Schmidt, H., & Aberer, K. (2007). Query-load balancing in structured overlays. In *Proc. of CCGrid'07, 7th Int'l Conference on Cluster Computing and the Grid*, Rio de Janeiro, Brazil (pp. 453-460).

Demers, A., Green, D., Hauser, C., Irish, W., Larson, J., Shenker, S., et al. (1987). Epidemic algorithms for replicated database maintenance. In *Proc. PODC 1987, 6th Annual ACM Symposium on Principles of Distributed Computing*, Vancouver, Canada (pp. 1-12).

Ghodsi, A., Alima, L. O., & Haridi, S. (2005). Symmetric replication for structured peer-to-peer systems. In *Proc. DBISp2p'05, 3rd Int'l VLDB Workshop on Databases, Information Systems and Peer-to-Peer Computing* (LNCS 4125, pp. 74-85). Berlin: Springer.

Gnutella. (2003). *Protocol V.0.6 RFC*. Retrieved from http://rfc-gnutella.sourceforge.net

Gopalakrishnan, V., Silaghi, B., Bhattacharjee, B., & Keleher, P. (2004). Adaptive replication in peer-to-peer systems. In *Proc. ICDCS 2004, 24th Int'l Conference on Distributed Computing Systems*, Tokyo, Japan (pp. 360-369).

Iyer, S., Rowstron, A., & Druschel, P. (2002). Squirrel: a decentralized peer-to-peer web cache. In *Proc. PODC 2002, 21st Annual Symposium on Principles of Distributed Computing*, Monterey, California, USA (pp 213-222).

Jia, Z., Pei, B., Li, M., & You, J. (2005). A comparison of spread methods in unstructured P2P networks. In *Proc. of ICCSA 2005, Int'l Conference on Computational Science and its Applications* Singapore (pp. 10-18).

Lan, J., Liu, X., Shenoy, P., & Ramamritham, K. (2003). Consistency Maintenance in Peer-to-peer File Sharing Networks. In *Proc. of WIAPP '03, 3rd IEEE Workshop On Internet Applications*, San Jose, CA, USA (pp. 76-85).

Leong, B., Liskov, B., & Demaine, E. D. (2006). EpiChord: Parallelizing the chord lookup algorithm with reactive routing state management. *Computer Communications, 29*(9), 1243–1259. doi:10.1016/j.comcom.2005.10.002

Leontiadis, E., Dimakopoulos, V. V., & Pitoura, E. (2006). Creating and maintaining replicas in unstructured peer-to-peer systems. In *Proc. of EURO-PAR 2006, 12th Int'l Euro-Par Conference on Parallel Processing* (LNCS 4128, pp. 1015-102). Dresden, Germany: Springer.

Lv, Q., Cao, P., Cohen, E., Li, K., & Shenker, S. (2002). Search and replication in unstructured peer-to-peer networks. In *Proc. of ICS 2002, 16th ACM Int'l Conference on Supercomputing*, New York, New York, USA (pp. 84-95).

Maymounkov, P., & Mazieres, D. (2002), Kademlia: A peer to peer information system based on the XOR metric. In *Proc. of IPTPS 2002, 1st Int'l Workshop on Peer-to-Peer Systems*, Cambridge MA, USA.

Morselli, R., Bhattacharjee, B., Marsh, M. A., & Srinivasan, A. (2005). Efficient lookup on unstructured topologies. In *Proc. PODC 2005, 24th Symposium on Principles of Distributed Computing*, Las Vegas, NV, USA.

Pitoura, T., Ntarmos, N., & Triantafillou, P. (2006). Replication, load balancing and efficient range query processing in DHTs. In *Proc. EDBT 2006*, Munich, Germany (pp. 131-148).

Ramasubramanian, V., & Sirer, E. G. (2004). Beehive: O(1) lookup performance for power-law query distributions in peer-to-peer overlays. In *Proc. NSDI'04, 1st Symposium on Networked Systems Design and Implementation*, San Francisco, CA.

Rao, W., Chen, L., Fu, A., & Bu, Y. Y. (2007). Optimal Proactive Caching in Peer-to-peer Network: Analysis and Application. In *Proc. CIKM 2007, 15th ACM Int'l Conference on Information and Knowledge Management*, Lisbon, Portugal (pp. 663-672).

Ratnasamy, S., Francis, P., Handley, M., Karp, R., & Shenker, S. (2001). A scalable content addressable network. In *Proc. of ACM SIGCOMM*, San Diego, CA, USA (pp. 161-172).

Rodrigues, R., & Liskow, B. (2005). High Availability in DHTs: Erasure Coding vs. Replication. In *Proc. IPTPS 2005*, Ithaca, NY, USA (pp. 226-239).

Roussopoulos, M., & Baker, M. (2003). CUP: Controlled update propagation in peer-to-peer networks. In *Proc. of the Annual USENIX Technical Conference*, San Antonio, Texas, USA (pp. 167-180).

Rowstron, A., & Druschel, P. (2001a). Pastry: Scalable, distributed, object location and routing for large-scale peer-to-peer systems. In *Proc. Middleware 2001, IFIP/ACM Int. Conf. on Distributed System Platforms*, Heidelberg, Germany (pp. 329–350).

Rowstron, A., & Druschel, P. (2001b). Storage management and caching in PAST, a large-scale, persistent peer-to-peer storage utility. In *Proc. of ACM SOSP '01*, Banff, Canada (pp. 188-201).

Sahin, O. D., Gupta, A., Agrawal, D., & El Abbadi, A. (2004). A Peer-to-peer Framework for Caching Range Queries. In *Proc. ICDE 2004, 20th Int'l Conference on Data Engineering*, Boston, USA (pp. 165 -176).

Sozio, M., Neumann, T., & Weikum, G. (2008). Near-Optimal Dynamic Replication in Unstructured Peer-to-Peer Networks. In *Proc. PODS'08, 27th ACM SIGMOD-SIGACT-SIGART Symposium on Principles of Database Systems*, Vancouver, BC, Canada (pp. 281-290).

Stoica, I., Morris, R., Karger, D., Kaashoek, F., & Balakrishnan, H. (2001). Chord: A scalable peer-to-peer lookup service for internet applications. In *Proc. of ACM SIGCOMM*, San Diego, CA, USA (pp.149–160).

Susarla, S., & Carter, J. (2005). Flexible Consistency for Wide Area Peer Replication. In *Proc. ICDCS 2005, 25th IEEE Int'l Conference on Distributed Computing Systems*, Ohio, USA (pp. 199-208).

Tewari, S., & Kleinrock, L. (2005). Analysis of search and replication in unstructured peer-to-peer networks. In *Proc. of SIGMETRICS 2005*, Banff, Canada (pp 404-405).

Tewari, S., & Kleinrock, L. (2006). Proportional replication in peer-to-peer networks. In *Proc. of INFOCOM 2006*, Barcelona, Spain (pp 1-12).

Vecchio, D., & Son, S. H. (2005). Flexible update management in peer-to-peer database systems. In *Proc. IDEAS 2005, Int'l Database Engineering and Applications Symposium*, Montreal, Canada.

Wang, Z., Das, S. K., Kumar, M., & Shen, H. (2007). An efficient update propagation algorithm for p2p systems. *Computer Communications, 30*, 1106–1115. doi:10.1016/j.comcom.2006.11.005

Wang, Z., Kumar, M., Das, S. K., & Shen, H. (2006). File consistency maintenance through virtual servers in P2P systems. In *Proc. ISCC 2006, 11th IEEE Symposium on Computers and Communications*, Sardinia, Italy (pp. 435-441).

Weatherspoon, H., & Kubiatowicz, J. (2002). Erasure Coding vs. Replication: A Quantitative Comparison. In *Proc. of IPTPS 2002*, Cambridge, MA, USA (pp 328-338).

Zhang, H., Goel, A., & Govindan, R. (2004). Using the small-world model to improve Freenet performance. *Computer Networks, 46*, 555–574. doi:10.1016/j.comnet.2004.06.003

Zhu, X., Zhang, D., Li, W., & Huang, K. (2007). Prediction-based fair replication algorithm in structured p2p Systems. In *Proc. ATC 2007, 4th Int'l Conference on Autonomic and Trusted Computing*, Hong Kong, China (pp. 499-508).

KEY TERMS AND DEFINITIONS

Data Replication: Refers to creating and maintaining multiple copies of an item so as to improve performance and reliability.

Overlay Networks: Networks formed between nodes in large scale distributed systems which are built on top of the physical network.

Peer-to-Peer (P2P) Systems: Distributed systems where nodes act as both servers and clients. Characteristics commonly attributed to peer-to-peer systems include node autonomy, large scale and dynamicity.

Replica Placement: Refers to protocols for assigning replicas to nodes in a distributed system.

Replica Updates: Refers to protocols used to maintain consistency among replicas.

Structured Peer-to-Peer Systems: P2P systems where nodes are connected to each other to form specific overlay topologies. The most common structured p2p systems are Distributed Hash Tables (DHTs) where data items are assigned to specific peers based on hashing.

Unstructured Peer-to-Peer Systems: P2P systems where the overlay topology is not rigid and there is no explicit association between the location of data and the location of nodes. Many unstructured p2p systems have power-law degree characteristics.

ENDNOTE

[1] We note here that while both refer to creating copies, caching and replication have some subtle differences. Caching is usually initiated at the clients, in our case, the peers that made the request for an item, while replication is a server-based decision, with possibly system-wide implications. In this chapter, we will not distinguish between replication and caching and we will use the term 'replication' to refer to both of them.

Chapter 26
Maintaining Redundancy in Peer–to–Peer Storage Systems

Anwitaman Datta
Nanyang Technological University, Singapore

Di Wu
Polytechnic Institute of NYU, USA

Liu Xin
NTU Singapore, Singapore

Adam Wierzbicki
Polish-Japanese Institute of Information Technology Warsaw, Poland

ABSTRACT

Peer-to-Peer (P2P) storage systems leverage the combined storage capacity of a network of storage devices (peers) contributed typically by autonomous end-users as a common pool of storage space to store and share content. A major challenge in such a system comprising of autonomous participants is to guarantee quality of service in terms of persistence and availability of the stored content. This chapter focuses on the different possible design choices for maintaining redundancy in P2P storage systems, including algorithm details of maintenance mechanisms, analytical models to understand system's dynamics, empirical results from simulation experiments as well as experiences from prototype deployments.

INTRODUCTION

For diverse reasons including fault-tolerance, load-balance, response time, or geographic distribution of end users, distributed data stores have been around for a long while. Historically this included distributed databases, distributed file systems and Usenet servers among others. Peer-to-peer (P2P) storage is a paradigm which extends those concepts and aims to leverage the combined storage capacity of a network of storage devices (peers) contributed typically by autonomous end-users as a common pool of storage space to store and share content, and is designed to provide persistence and availability of the stored content despite unreliability of the individual autonomous peers in a decentralized environment.

There are many aspects which determine the design space of P2P storage systems. A lot of these

DOI: 10.4018/978-1-61520-686-5.ch026

Figure 1. The design space of P2P storage systems

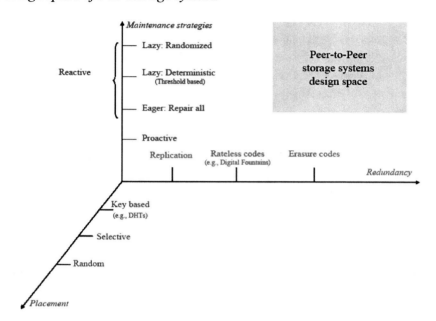

design decisions are pertaining to the fact that to achieve fault-tolerance and load-balancing, redundancy of stored content is necessary. As a consequence – choice of the kind of redundancy to be used (e.g., replication, encoded or mixed), the placement of these redundant objects, and the maintenance of redundancy in presence of churn determine the design axis of p2p storage systems, as shown in Figure 1.

The primary focus of this chapter is along one dimension of this design space - studying different redundancy maintenance strategies, analytical tools to understand the interplay of maintenance and churn, and empirical comparative study of various maintenance strategies.

We first provide background information, including historical context of P2P storage systems and their applications, as well as motivate the problem studied in this chapter - that of maintaining redundancy in P2P storage systems under churn. This will include characterization of churn itself.

We elaborate the various redundancy maintenance strategies (including high level algorithmic

details) of existing maintenance mechanisms. The effectiveness of the maintenance mechanisms, and the dynamics of maintenance under churn have been studied both by constructing analytical models, as well as by simulation experiments.

We outline two analytical models to study storage systems under churn. Markov models are used to study the dynamic equilibrium in P2P storage systems under the hypothetical assumption of how the system would behave if the level of churn is constant. Stochastic differential equations are used to study the system's evolution as the churn level keeps varying.

We then summarize results from simulation based experiments as well as experiences from prototype deployments to study (in)effectiveness and (in)efficiency of the different maintenance mechanisms and garbage collection mechanisms.

Materials presented in this chapter include both our own works and a survey of works done by other researchers, to provide a well-rounded overview of current literature.

Among other implications of the design choices are issues like – "*How are the distributed objects found?" "How is the consistency of mutable content stored redundantly dealt with?"* Such topics are beyond the scope of this chapter. For the first issue – search of objects, readers should refer to structured overlays and DHTs which is one possible mechanism to locate objects in a decentralized manner.

BACKGROUND

Early major attempts of building distributed storage systems were started in the middle of 80s. Most traditional distributed storage systems (e.g., NFS, AFS, CODA, etc) are built on top of reliable dedicated workstations with good network connections, and are implemented in a client-server manner to perform replication, caching and maintenance. It is expensive to build such a system for small companies. The client-server architecture also makes those systems less scalable.

In recent years, Internet growth has inspired a new class of storage systems that adopt the peer-to-peer paradigm. By harnessing the storage space at the edge of the Internet, P2P storage systems can provide inexpensive, scalable, fault-tolerant, and highly-available storage without centralized servers. Some of recent P2P storage systems include Ocean-Store (Kubiatowicz et al., 2000), DHash (Dabek et al., 2004), Total Recall (Bhagwan et al., 2004), etc. In spite of its superior scalability and trivial storage cost compared to traditional systems, P2P storage systems pose many new challenges due to the intrinsic characteristics of autonomous peers.

Unlike traditional distributed systems where failures may be considered rare or abnormal, most P2P systems constantly remain in a state of churn. Churn is incurred due to various reasons, e.g., link outage, user behavior, disk failure, etc. In some cases, churn is temporary as the departed peers may rejoin the system; churn can also be permanent as peers may depart the system forever. It is not easy to distinguish temporary churn from permanent churn.

Maintaining data availability under churn is a challenging issue in P2P storage systems. A basic approach to maintain availability is to provide more redundancy. Redundancy can be achieved either by replication or by using erasure codes. Replication simply stores the same object on multiple nodes without coding, while erasure codes transform a M-fragment object into N ($N > M$) encoded fragments, such that the original object can be reconstructed from any M out of the N encoded fragments. With erasure codes, the same level of availability can be achieved with less storage overhead (Blake & Rodrigues, 2003), however at a higher system design complexity as well as higher communication overhead.

It is also necessary to consider how to choose a set of nodes in the system to store the object replicas (or fragments). One approach is to choose the nodes without considering their characteristics – based on either a deterministic scheme like hashing (as in distributed hash tables) or by making a randomized and arbitrary choice; the other approach is to choose nodes based on certain criteria, such as node lifetime, bandwidth capacity, geographic location, etc. In existing systems, characteristic agnostic schemes such as random placement are widely used due to its simplicity.

Just providing some redundancy cannot guarantee long-term availability due to the effects of permanent churn. Proper maintenance should be performed to restore the lost redundancy. Based on whether maintenance is invoked in reaction to failures or not, existing maintenance strategies can be generalized into two categories: proactive maintenance and reactive maintenance. Proactive maintenance proactively creates new fragments (or replicas) irrespective of whether failures occur or not, while reactive maintenance performs maintenance only in response to failures. Both strategies have its merits, and we will discuss them in more details subsequently.

Existing P2P storage systems differ mainly in the employed strategies on data redundancy, data placement and data maintenance. DHash (Dabek et al., 2004) is a replication-based P2P storage system, which adopts the eager repair and selective placement strategy. Different from DHash, Pond (Rhea et al., 2003), which is a prototype of OceanStore (Kubiatowicz et al., 2000), uses erasure codes to reduce storage overhead, and provides random placement by using a directory. TotalRecall (Bhagwan et al., 2004) is also based on erasure codes and random placement. However, the maintenance strategy is slightly changed. To reduce the maintenance bandwidth, TotalRecall proposes a lazy maintenance scheme and partially allows the temporarily unavailable fragments to be reintegrated at a later time. Carbonite (Chun et al., 2006) extends partial reintegration to full reintegration, and designs a specific multicast mechanism to monitor the fragment availability. Glacier (Haeberlen et al., 2005) focuses on providing high availability to critical data storage by using massive redundancy in an organization environment using mostly available workstations and only a few unstable hosts. Contrary to the above systems based on reactive maintenance, Tempo (Sit et al., 2006) adopts a proactive maintenance strategy to actively produce additional fragments under a given amount of bandwidth.

Besides P2P storage systems, other P2P systems also have requirements of maintaining data availability under churn. In Table 1, we provide a summary of different redundancy, placement and maintenance strategies adopted in typical P2P applications (e.g., web cache, file sharing, content distribution network (CDN), media streaming) besides distributed storage.

MAKING P2P STORAGE SYSTEMS RELIABLE

Redundancy is essential for resilience. However, over time, redundancy is lost because of permanent departure of peers from the system. This necessitates some mechanisms to restore redundancy to make the P2P storage system reliable. Trade-off considerations of redundancy maintenance and achieving resilience have led to the design of several maintenance mechanisms. In this section, we will describe these proposed maintenance strategies as well as some garbage collection mechanisms.

Redundancy Maintenance Mechanisms

Several maintenance mechanisms have been proposed. Based on whether the repair operation

Table 1. Comparison among distributed applications

Distributed Application	Prototype Name	Redundancy Strategy	Placement Strategy	Maintenance Strategy
Storage	Dhash (Dabek et al., 2004)	Replication	Selective	Reactive
	Pond (Rhea et al., 2003)	Erasure Codes	Random	Reactive
	TotalRecall (Bhagwan et al., 2004)	Erasure Codes	Random	Reactive
	Tempo (Sit et al., 2006)	Replication	Selective	Proactive
Web Cache	Squirrel (Iyer, Rowstron, & Druschel, 2002)	Replication	Random or Selective	Reactive
CDN	BitTorrent	Replication	Selective	Proactive
	Avalance (Gkantsidis & Rodriguez, 2005)	Network Coding	Selective	Proactive
File Sharing	eMule	Replication	Selective	Reactive
Streaming	PRM (Banerjee et al., 2003)	Erasure Codes	Selective	Proactive/Reactive

is triggered in response to failures of peers or not they are classified as: (1) *reactive maintenance* and (2) *proactive maintenance*. For the rest of the section we will assume that encoding based redundancy is being used in a storage system, such that originally N encoded distinct fragments for an object is stored, of which, retrieving any M (but no less) fragments ensures that the original object can be reconstructed, though slight variation of the maintenance schemes are also applicable to replicated data.

Eager

The simplest maintenance mechanism is to probe periodically all the peers which are supposed to store encoded fragments of an object, and whenever a probe for some fragments fails, reactively replenish the redundancy by reintegrating new suitable redundant fragments at some live peers. This strategy is referred to as an eager maintenance strategy. Such an eager reactive maintenance mechanism means that the system always operates in a state where redundancy level remains constant (apart from temporary reduction between repair periods).

Lazy

It has been argued and observed that an eager maintenance strategy wastes bandwidth unnecessarily by failing to exploit the fact that often peers come back online along with the stored content. In the design of the TotalRecall storage system (Bhagwan et al. 2004), the authors advocated a lazy maintenance strategy which we call here a "deterministic lazy repair" strategy, distinguishing it from a randomized strategy proposed subsequently by Datta & Aberer (2006) to achieve a more continuous and smoother bandwidth utilization, ensuring that the storage system does not get vulnerable to future (unforeseen) failures.

Deterministic Lazy Repair

In deterministic lazy repair, all peers are probed periodically. When an object has less than T_{dl} encoded fragments available in the system, a repair operation is initiated for that object. $M < T_{dl} < N$ is a design parameter in the maintenance algorithm. Lazy maintenance saves the overhead caused by transient failures. If a few fragments are missing, no action is undertaken, thus no bandwidth is typically wasted in case the peers come back online. However, this approach may suffer from some undesirable effects: (1) Once the threshold is breached, this approach tries to replenish all the missing fragments at once, thus causing spikes in bandwidth usage. (2) By waiting for the redundancy to fall below T_{dl}, the system is allowed to degenerate and become more vulnerable to future (correlated) failures. (3) Before maintenance, the available fragments are accessed more frequently, thus causing access load imbalance.

Randomized Lazy Repair

The randomized lazy repair mechanism (Datta & Aberer, 2006) was proposed to alleviate the shortcomings of the deterministic lazy repair mentioned above, while trying to preserve its benefits. In this approach, fragments of an object are probed in a random order, until T_{rl} live fragments are detected. Thus a random number $T_{rl} + X$ of probes will be required to locate T_{rl} live fragments. Then the X (a random variable) fragments which were detected to be unavailable are replaced by the system. Note that more than X fragments may actually be offline at that moment. The randomized strategy thus tries to find a trade-off between eager (always repair all) and deterministic lazy (repair nothing until a threshold is breached) strategies. Adaptivity is inherent in this randomized strategy, because if most of the fragments are online, then X will be low, and thus there will be fewer replacements, while if a lot of fragments are missing, then X will be higher, and thus more replenishing operations will be carried out.

If $P_i(X=j)$ is the probability that $T_{rl}+j$ fragments are randomly (and sequentially) accessed in order to find T_{rl} live fragments (after which the probing is stopped), when i out of the possible N fragments are actually available, then:

$$P_i(X=j) = \binom{j+T_{rl}}{j} \frac{i!}{N!} \frac{(N-T_{rl})!}{(i-T_{rl})!} \frac{(N-i)!}{(N-i-j)!} \frac{(N-T_{rl}-j)!}{(N-T_{rl})!}$$

Such an inherently adaptive response ensures that bandwidth usage is smooth, and at the same time the storage system does not become vulnerable by waiting too long and doing no repairs at all.

The eager strategy can be considered as a special case of the lazy maintenance strategies (with $T_{dl}=N$ or $T_{rl}=N$ respectively).

Proactive

In a radically different approach, Sit et al. (2006) argued that if the network is not used at all that is wastage, and the critical issue is not how much, but how smoothly bandwidth is used. They proposed to continuously generate and integrate new fragments for each object, subject to local bandwidth budget at peers, irrespective of the number of fragments of an object in the system. Subsequently Duminuco et al. (2007) proposed an adaptive variation. In such a scenario, it is possible that more than N distinct fragments are introduced in the system. While this strategy guarantees that bandwidth usage is smooth (subject to the bandwidth budget), it risks using unlimited amount of storage, which is impractical, even if storage is cheap. Thus, an upper limit N_{max} on the number of fragments to store for each object was introduced. Once the maximum storage limit N_{max} is reached, the proactive strategy is also essentially reduced to act just like eager reactive maintenance.

Garbage Collection Mechanisms

Maintenance strategy regenerates lost redundancy to make system reliable. However, as mentioned before, a peer may leave the system temporarily or permanently. If an offline peer goes online, it brings back the fragments stored locally. This may lead to two kinds of excessive redundancy. If the maintenance operation generates a fragment which is distinct from the fragments that (will) come back, for example, this is the case if rateless codes (Shokrollahi 2006) are used, then the system may eventually have more than N distinct fragments for an object. Otherwise the same fragment will have duplicate copies in the system. Thus the system requires garbage collection to get rid of such excessive redundancy. Here we consider two types of garbage collection mechanisms. One is that we set the upper limit N_{max} on the number of unique fragments maintained for each object. Once this limit is reached, the excessive fragments are garbage collected. This is to ensure that the system's storage space is not exhausted. The other aspect of garbage collection is that when an offline peer goes online, the data fragments stored locally will be garbage collected if a copy (in a more general case, a given number of copies) of the same fragment already exists in the system, which is possible because of the redundancy maintenance mechanisms. This is to ensure that in the system, all the fragments for each object are distinct.

Please note that extra redundancy can be desirable. Allowing more diversity (a larger number, say up to N_{max} of distinct fragments) can make the system more robust against churn, and reduce the need of future maintenance operations. Likewise, even if duplicate copies of encoded fragments do not directly help in increasing availability of an object (because a threshold number of *distinct* fragments are required for object reconstruction), duplicate fragments increase the availability of individual fragments, which in turn helps maintaining diversity at a lower future maintenance cost.

Understanding the Interplay of Churn and Maintenance: Analytical Models

Early works mostly focused on systems design, in which different redundancy strategies, placement strategies and maintenance strategies are employed. However, they lacked theoretical analysis to study the effectiveness and practicality of their approaches under different degrees and types of churn. Some analytical models of storage systems conducted static resilience analysis (Bhagwan et al. 2004) about object availability. Given a target level of availability and the average host availability, their model tried to calculate the number of required redundancy using probability theory. Such analysis was based on the average peer availability and did not capture the time evolution of the storage system and the interplay between object maintenance and churn.

Subsequently analytical models were developed (Datta & Aberer, 2006), (Wu, Tian, Ng, & Datta, 2008) to analyze the dynamics of P2P storage systems providing a deeper understanding of

Table 2. Summary of notation used in representing the P2P storage system's state and analyzing it as a Markov process

Nota-tion	
$S_i(t)$	The probability that i out of the N possible fragments of any object are online at time t just after the maintenance operations.
$\tilde{S}_i(t)$	The probability that i fragments of any object are online at time t just before the maintenance operations (and after churn since time t -1).
$\delta_\downarrow$	The probability that an online peer goes off-line.
$\mu_\uparrow$	The probability that an offline peer returns online.
$\sum S_i(t) = 1$ $\sum \tilde{S}_i(t) = 1$	Normalization for the probability distribution functions.

the effects of various churn, and the interplay of churn and maintenance.

Markov Model for Studying the Dynamic Equilibrium

System Model

The Markov model (Datta & Aberer, 2006) investigates how the system behaves and a maintenance mechanism responds to a particular level of churn. Assume a scenario where traditional erasure code based redundancy is used. An object is said to be in state i at any given time if i out of the N erasure encoded fragments of the object are available in the system at that given time.

In the Markov model for P2P storage system, it does not matter how the system reaches its current state at any time t, and the system's time evolution from that point is analyzed based on its current state and future events induced by churn and maintenance operations. The notations used in the following are summarized in Table 2. A recursive relationship exists between the probability of i fragments being online before or after churn. We illustrate how the analysis technique can be used with the case of deterministic lazy repair (Bhagwan et al. 2004).

Because of churn, we obtain the following:

$$\tilde{S}_i(t+1) = S_i(t)$$

$$- S_i(t) \sum_{l=0}^{i} \binom{i}{l} \delta_\downarrow^l (1-\delta_\downarrow)^{i-l} *$$

$$\left(\sum_{g=0;g\neq1}^{N-i} \binom{N-i}{g} \mu_\uparrow^g (1-\mu_\uparrow)^{N-i-g} \right)$$

$$+ \sum_{j=0}^{i} \sum_{l=0}^{j} S_j \binom{j}{l} \binom{N-j}{g} *$$

$$(1-\delta_\downarrow)^{j-1} \mu_\uparrow^g (1-\mu_\uparrow)^{N-j-g} \quad \text{for} \quad \mathbf{g = i - j + 1}$$

$$\sum_{j=i+1}^{N} \sum_{g=0}^{Min[N-j,i]} S_j \binom{j}{l} \binom{N-j}{g} *$$

$$\delta_\downarrow^l (1-\delta_\downarrow)^{j-1} \mu_\uparrow^g (1-\mu_\uparrow)^{N-j-g} \quad \text{for} \quad \mathbf{1 = j - i + g}$$

[The above equation represents how the system state changes because of churn. The first term represents the outflow from state i because of churn. This happens for any object in state i when any l of its i online fragments go off-line, and any $g \neq l$ of its $N - i$ off-line fragments come online. The second term is the inflow into state i from states $j \leq i$, where the number of fragments for the corresponding state j that go offline l and the number of fragments that come back online g are mutually related such that $g = i - j + l$. The corresponding object ends up into state i from states $j \leq i$. When $i < j$, similar combinatorial arguments hold leading to the third term in the above equation. In addition, $i - g = j - l \geq 0 \rightarrow g \leq i$ and $g \leq N - j$ determine the possible values of the number of fragments coming online g from states $j > i$ which can still cause inflow into state i because of sufficient simultaneous losses. The corresponding loss l is mutually related to g such that $l = j - i + g$.

If deterministic lazy repair is employed (with T_{dl} as repair threshold) as a maintenance mechanism, we also obtain the following:

$$S_N(t+1) = \tilde{S}_N(t+1) + \sum_{j=M}^{T_{dl}} \tilde{S}_j(t+1)$$

For $T_{dl} \leq i < N$, no repair actions are carried out since the threshold is not breached, thus:

$$S_i(t+1) = \tilde{S}_i(t+1)$$

If there are less than the threshold number of fragments available, i.e., $M \leq i < T_{dl}$, full redundancy is restored, so:

$$S_i(t+1) = 0$$

Since the repair operations can not restore redundancy if $i < M$ we get:

$$S_i(t+1) = \tilde{S}_i(t+1)$$

Solving these recursive equations (numerically) provide the system's dynamic equilibrium state for a given level of churn (determined by the parameters $\delta_\downarrow, \mu_\uparrow$). Figure 2 shows an example system state. The Markov model based dynamic equilibrium analysis was the first analytical model to study the dynamics of churn and maintenance operations, in contrast to the previous static resilience analysis, which did not consider these issues, and only determined system vulnerability under a given level of initial redundancy. The probability distribution function of the available objects was a new measure, which revealed more information about the stability and health of the storage system.

Stochastic Differential Equations

The Markov model based study (Datta & Aberer, 2006) assumed a constant level of churn. In reality, the level of churn itself changes over time. To study the system's behavior under changing rate of churn a new stochastic differential equations based model was developed (Wu, Tian, Ng, & Datta, 2008). Such a model can predict the time evolution of online/offline fragments, study the effects of churn and the interplay between object maintenance and churn. The results shed some important insights into object maintenance under churn, which are useful in the optimization of P2P storage systems, e.g., reducing bandwidth usage, provisioning for bandwidth spike, improving system capacity, etc.

System Model
In general, the participating peers in a P2P storage system have the following three states (as shown in Fig. 3).

- **Online state:** The peer is present in the system and the data fragment deployed on that peer is available for access;
- **Offline state:** The peer is not present in the system due to temporary failures. In the

Figure 2. Simulation based validation of the analytical model using M=8, N=32 and T_{dl}=16, where churn level was $\delta_\downarrow$=0.2, $\mu_\uparrow$=0.1

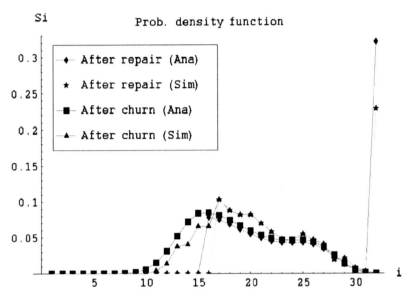

Figure 3. Node transition states

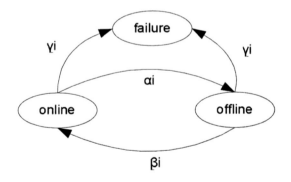

offline state, the fragment still exists in the peer's storage space. The peer will enter the online or failure state at a later time;
- **Failure state:** the peer leaves the system as a result of permanent churn, and the fragment stored on that peer is lost permanently.

Each peer transits between the online and offline states during its lifetime, and finally enters the failure state, which is an absorbing state. Its behavior can be modeled as an alternating ON/OFF

renewal process, with the online/offline session length drawn from certain distributions.

Consider a peer *i* in the system. The events of its temporary failure, recovering and permanent failure are assumed to arrive as Poisson processes, and denoted by N_t^i, N_r^i, N_p^i respectively. The arrival rate of N_t^i, N_r^i, N_p^i are given by $\alpha_i, \beta_i, \gamma_i$. The average values of $\alpha_i, \beta_i, \gamma_i$ over the whole system are denoted by α, β, γ. The sum of α, β, γ is denoted by $\theta = \alpha, \beta, \gamma$.

To model the peer behavior at time t, two random variables $X_i(t)$ and $Y_i(t)$ are defined as follows:

$$X_i(t) = \begin{cases} 1, & \text{peer i is online at time t;} \\ 0, & \text{otherwise.} \end{cases}$$ and

$$Y_i(t) = \begin{cases} 1, & \text{peer i is offline at time t;} \\ 0, & \text{otherwise.} \end{cases}$$

The pair $(X_i(t), Y_i(t))$ provides the necessary information about the peer state: (i) (1, 0) means that the peer is currently online; (ii) (0, 1) means that the peer is now offline; (iii) (0, 0) means that the peer is in the failure state. The evolution of a single peer can be depicted by the following stochastic differential equations:

$$\begin{cases} dX_i = -X_i dN_p^i - X_i dN_t^i + Y_i dN_r^i \\ dY_i = -Y_i dN_p^i - Y_i dN_r^i + X_i dN_t^i \end{cases}$$

Modeling the Effects of Churn

Suppose that a *(N, M)* erasure code is adopted to provide data redundancy, where M is the number of fragments required for object reconstruction, and N is the initial number of generated fragments. Replication can be regarded as a special *(N, 1)* rateless erasure code. Each peer is allowed to hold only one fragment. As to the placement strategy, it is assumed that random placement or selective placement based on the criteria other than lifetime is in use

Definition: For a specific object *o*, the set of peers that hold a fragment of that object is defined as the *Fragment System* of object *o*, which is denoted by *S*. The peers in the fragment system can be either online or offline. The set of online peers is defined as S_{on}, and the set of offline peers is defined as S_{off}.

For the fragment system of a specific object, let $X(t)$ and $Y(t)$ be the number of online fragments and offline fragments at time t. Both $X(t)$ and $Y(t)$ are random variables that follow certain distributions. The evolution of the fragment system caused by churn can be depicted by the following stochastic differential equations:

$$\begin{cases} dX = -\sum_{i=1}^n X_i dN_p^i - \sum_{i=1}^n X_i dN_t^i + \sum_{i=1}^n Y_i dN_r^i \\ dY = -\sum_{i=1}^n Y_i dN_p^i - \sum_{i=1}^n Y_i dN_r^i + \sum_{i=1}^n X_i dN_t^i \end{cases}$$

By taking expectation in the above equations, we have,

$$\begin{cases} dE[X] = -E[X](\gamma + \alpha)dt - E[Y]\beta dt \\ dE[Y] = E[X]\alpha dt - E[Y](\beta + \gamma)dt \end{cases}$$

For convenience, $\overline{X}(t), \overline{Y}(t)$ are used to represent $E[X](t), E[Y](t)$ respectively. By solving the above equations, the evolution of the fragment system under churn can be described by $(\overline{X}(t), \overline{Y}(t))$

$$\begin{cases} \overline{X}(t) = \dfrac{n\beta}{\alpha + \beta} e^{-\gamma t} + \dfrac{n\alpha}{\alpha + \beta} e^{-\theta t} \\ \overline{Y}(t) = \dfrac{n\alpha}{\alpha + \beta} [e^{-\gamma t} - e^{-\theta t}] \end{cases}$$

where

The proof details are presented in the paper (Wu, Tian, Ng, & Datta, 2008).

Real trace-based simulation was conducted to validate the above model. In the experiments, a random set of peers are selected to deploy the fragments of an object. The initial number of encoded fragments is 100. The evolution of the fragment system is shown in Figure 4.

The stochastic differential equation based model well captures the general trend of the system evolution. From the figure, it is observed that the number of online fragments *X(t)* drops quickly in the first few hours, meanwhile, the number of offline fragments *Y(t)* increases rapidly. This phenomenon is due to the effects of temporary churn. In order to guarantee object availability, it is important to use enough redundancy to handle the effects of temporary churn. Later, with the increase of offline fragments, *X(t)* decreases much more slowly as some offline fragments may return to the online state. As to the number of offline fragments *Y (t)*, after the initial increase in the first few hours, *Y(t)* also decreases slowly. The slow drop of both *X(t)* and *Y(t)* is mainly caused by the effects of permanent churn. It indicates that simple redundancy is not enough and maintenance should be performed to replenish the lost redundancy.

Modeling the Interplay Between Object Maintenance and Churn

The above model can be extended to analyze the interplay between object maintenance and churn as well. As reactive maintenance is more popular than proactive maintenance in existing P2P stor-

Figure 4. System evolution under independent churn (N = 100)

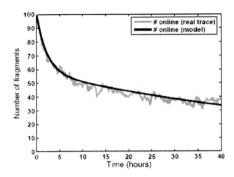

a) Number of online fragments

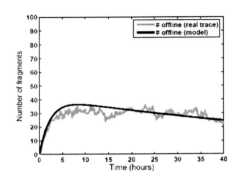

(b) Number of offline fragments

age systems, the following analysis focuses on reactive maintenance.

Denote T as the interval between two consecutive maintenance actions. For Eager repair, $T = T_{probe}$, which is the probing interval; for Lazy Repair, it can be regarded as extending the intervals between two maintenance actions, and a large T is adopted to wait for the return of offline fragments.

Let T_i be the time point that the i-th maintenance happens, T_i^- be the time point just before T_i, and T_i^+ be the time point just after T_i $(i = 0, 1, ...)$. Between the period of $[T_i, T_{i+1})$, the system evolves without any maintenance, and the evolution equations are similar to that in the above section. At the time T_i, the maintenance occurs to restore the lost redundancy.

There are two kinds of reintegration policies: (1) Full reintegration, in which the returned offline fragment is always reintegrated into the fragment system. (2) Partial reintegration, in which only when the downtime of the returned fragment is less than a timeout T_{out} can the fragment be reintegrated. Partial reintegration can reduce the number of fragments that the system should track. In the following, we analyze the above two cases respectively.

1. Full Reintegration

Under full reintegration, every temporarily unavailable fragment will be tracked by the system. In case that the unavailable fragments return online, they can be reintegrated into the system. Note that, full reintegration is not suitable to use together with fixed-rate erasure codes. It is better to employ rateless erasure codes to ensure that every returned fragment is useful.

An indicator function $I_m(x)$ is defined to indicate whether the maintenance can be performed when the number of online fragments equals x. If the maintenance can be performed, $I_m(x) = 1$ otherwise, $I_m(x) = 0$. The impact of the maintenance to the fragment system can be depicted as follows:

$$\begin{cases} X(T_i^+) = X(T_i^-) + I_m(X(T_i^-))(N - X(T_i^-)) \\ Y(T_i^+) = Y(T_i^-) \end{cases}$$

If the maintenance can always be performed, the average number of online/offline fragments just before and after the i-th maintenance can be depicted by:

$$\begin{cases} \overline{X}(T_i^-) = (\psi_3 + \dfrac{1-\psi_1^i}{\psi_1}\psi_2\psi_4)N \\[3mm] \overline{Y}(T_i^-) = \dfrac{1-\psi_1^i}{\psi_1}\psi_2 N \end{cases}$$ and

$$\begin{cases} \overline{X}(T_i^+) = N \\[3mm] \overline{Y}(T_i^+) = \dfrac{1-\psi_1^i}{\psi_1}\psi_2 N \end{cases}$$

where

$$\psi_1 = \frac{\alpha e^{-\gamma T} + \beta e^{-\theta T}}{\alpha + \beta},$$

$$\psi_2 = \frac{\alpha(e^{-\gamma T} - e^{-\theta T})}{\alpha + \beta}, \quad \psi_3 = \frac{\beta e^{-\gamma T} + \alpha e^{-\theta T}}{\alpha + \beta},$$

$$\psi_4 = \frac{\beta(e^{-\gamma T} - e^{-\theta T})}{\alpha + \beta}.$$

Figure 5 illustrates the evolution of the fragment system under reactive maintenance with full reintegration. The initial number of generated fragments is set as **N** = 20. It is found that, due to full reintegration, the number of newly added fragments at maintenance decreases with time elapsing. It is helpful to reduce the maintenance bandwidth. The number of offline fragments $Y(t)$ continues to increase and approaches a steady level.

2. Partial Reintegration

Although it is possible to define a timeout for each offline fragment, let us consider a simple case to facilitate the analysis. In this case, for a fragment that is online at T_i but becomes offline within $[T_i, T_{i+1})$, only when the offline fragment turns online again before T_{i+1} can it be reintegrated.

The evolution of $X(t)$ and $Y(t)$ is a piecewise process at the jump time T_i, which satisfies:

$$\begin{cases} X(T_i^+) = X(T_i^-) + I_m(X(T_i^-))(N - X(T_i^-)) \\[2mm] Y(T_i^+) = 0 \end{cases}$$

For reactive maintenance with partial reintegration, if the maintenance can always be performed,

the number of online/offline fragments just before and after the *i*-th maintenance can be given as below, where ψ_2, ψ_3 are the same as defined previously.

$$\begin{cases} \overline{X}(T_i^-) = \psi_3 N \\ \overline{Y}(T_i^-) = \psi_2\psi_3 N \end{cases} \text{and} \quad \begin{cases} \overline{X}(T_i^+) = N \\ \overline{Y}(T_i^+) = 0 \end{cases}.$$

Figure 6 shows the evolution of the fragment system under reactive maintenance with partial reintegration. Both $X(t)$ and $Y(t)$ exhibit piecewise behavior and the model generally captures the trend of system evolution.

Comparing Different Maintenance Mechanisms: Experimental Studies

In this section, a comparison among different maintenance mechanisms is performed. Firstly, we provide a brief survey about several typical P2P storage systems such as DHash, Pond, Total-Recall, Glacier, Tempo etc, focusing particularly on their maintenance strategies and experimental performance. Then we perform a comparative study of all the main redundancy maintenance mechanisms to find out their pros and cons. The results provide fundamental guidelines for the design of future P2P storage systems.

Existing Systems

In this section, we describe several existing P2P storage systems and put the focus on the redundancy maintenance mechanisms they use. We extract the relevant results from the experiments performed by the authors of these systems to evaluate the performance of the corresponding maintenance mechanisms.

DHash (Dabek et al., 2004)

DHash is DHT-based P2P storage system, which uses Chord lookup service for data location. It uses replication as redundancy scheme because

*Figure 5. System evolution under reactive maintenance with full reintegration (**N** = 20, T = 10 hours)*

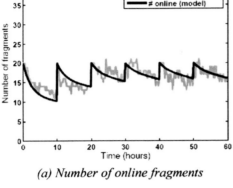
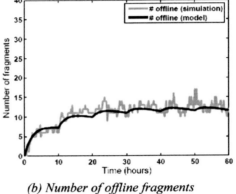

(a) Number of online fragments   *(b) Number of offline fragments*

Figure 6. System evolution under reactive maintenance with partial reintegration (N = 20, T = 10 hours)

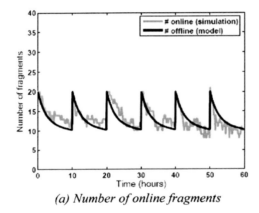
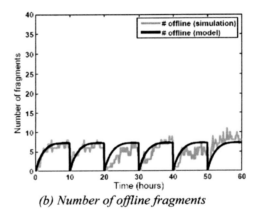

(a) Number of online fragments   *(b) Number of offline fragments*

replication is simple and can avoid high computation overhead and storage space is not expected to be a highly constrained resource. DHash replicates each data block on k servers immediately after the block's successors on the Chord ring to increase availability. After a successor server fails, the block is immediately available at the block's new successor. So DHash uses eager repair strategy to maintain the redundancy. DHash++ is the new version of DHash, the difference between them is that DHash++ uses erasure codes (N= 14 total fragments and M = 7 fragments required to reconstruct the object) instead of replication to provide redundancy.

Experiments show that DHash can work properly when many servers are offline simultaneously. In the experiment in which 1000 objects are inserted into a 1000-server system and each object has 6 replicas, a fraction of servers fail and before Chord starts to rebuild the routing table, 1000 fetches of randomly selected objects are attempted from a single server. Results show that no lookups fail when fewer than 20% of the servers fail and very few when less than 35% fail. Lookup fails only when enough servers fail that some objects lose all six replicas.

Pond (Rhea et al., 2003)

Pond is a prototype implementation of OceanStore (Kubiatowicz et al., 2000). It uses erasure codes for redundancy because erasure codes can achieve much higher tolerance under the same additional storage cost. To reconstruct the original object, Pond uses Tapestry to discover the encoded fragments. Pond also utilizes eager repair to restore redundancy.

The results show that the increase of storage overhead is inversely proportional to the rate of encoding. For instance, encoding an 8KB data block with a rate $r = 1/2$ ($M = 16$ out of $N = 32$ fragments are required to construct the original data block) increases the storage overhead by a factor of 2.7 and when a rate $r = 1/4$ ($M = 16$, $N = 64$) is used, the factor is 4.8.

TotalRecall (Bhagwan et al., 2004)

TotalRecall is a P2P storage system, which automates the task of availability management. It provides user-specified levels of availability while minimizing the overhead needed. TotalRecall utilizes erasure codes. The authors of TotalRecall argued that eager repair makes no distinction between transient departures and permanent departures thus many repair actions are redundant and wasteful. To solve this problem, the authors advocated (deterministic) lazy repair, that is, when the total amount of redundancy falls below a threshold (short-term redundancy factor), the system triggers a repair.

Experiments are performed to compare eager repair and deterministic lazy repair. Different repair strategies require different bandwidth to perform redundancy repair. The results of comparison of bandwidth consumed by eager repair and deterministic lazy repair illustrate the fundamental tradeoffs between redundancy and repair bandwidth. Eager repair can not delay repair repairs and requires more bandwidth. Deterministic lazy repair uses more sophisticated redundancy to delay repair operations and requires less bandwidth. Please note that besides repair strategy, the bandwidth consumption may be also affected by the redundancy schemes used and size of object maintained.

Glacier (Haeberlenm et al., 2005)

Glacier is a distributed storage system that relies on massive redundancy to mask the effect of large-scale correlated failures. Glacier uses erasure codes to spread redundant data uniformly among the storage nodes to generate a certain level of availability. Glacier nodes periodically communicate with each other to detect data loss and regenerate redundancy when necessary. So Glacier uses reactive mechanism to maintain the redundancy.

In the experiments, for each object, Glacier maintains $N = 48$ fragments using erasure codes and any 5 of these fragments are sufficient to reconstruct the object. In this configuration, each object can survive a correlated failure of $f_{max} = 60\%$ of all nodes with guaranteed durability 0.999999 (f_{max} is the probability that any particular node will be affected by the failure). For the traffic statistics, when the network is unstable, maintenance traffic for each host increases but remains at a very low level (below 15 packets per minute).

Tempo (Sit et al., 2006)

Tempo is a distributed hash table that allows users to specify a bandwidth budget to perform proactive replication. Tempo does not aim to reduce overall bandwidth usage but instead tries to ensure not to exceed the maintenance budget. It uses the constant repair rate and is able to smooth the resource consumption for repairs.

Experiments are performed to compare this proactive repair strategy and deterministic lazy repair strategy. For some moments when the number of participating nodes sharply drops and rises, deterministic lazy repair uses orders of magnitude more aggregate bandwidth than Tempo, thus causing spike in bandwidth usage. So Tempo can provide smoother bandwidth utilization. In addition, compared to deterministic lazy repair,

Tempo can also provide more replicas for each object and thus can tolerate future unpredictable correlated failures.

Comparative Study of All Maintenance Mechanisms

Researchers have compared eager repair and deterministic lazy repair, deterministic lazy repair and randomized lazy repair as well as deterministic lazy repair and proactive repair. However, these comparisons are performed in different contexts (different network sizes, different number of objects maintained, different redundancy schemes and different garbage collection strategies). Aiming at fairly comparing different mechanisms, we provide a comprehensive and systematic comparative study of all these maintenance mechanisms under the same context in the following part.

Methodology

We performed trace driven simulation to compare these maintenance mechanisms. Skype superpeer availability data (Godfrey) as well as synthetic data is used in the experiments. Synthetic data is generated based on the behavior of nodes in Skype trace to make the number of available nodes similar to that in Skype trace in the same period (correlated failures are eliminated from the original Skype trace).

To compare the different mechanisms, it is essential to choose parameters for each of the mechanisms that are comparable. Maintaining redundancy is bandwidth intensive, and thus we considered it to be the cost against which to evaluate the benefits of various mechanisms. So we chose the parameter for the deterministic lazy strategy T_{dl} (threshold) in an ad-hoc manner, and measured the aggregate bandwidth usage over the time window. We iterated with various values of T_{rl} (threshold) and B (bandwidth budget) for the randomized lazy and proactive strategies respectively to determine comparable parameter values where aggregate bandwidth usages over the same time

window are the same (Please refer to *Redundancy maintenance mechanisms* section for the meanings of the parameters configured here).

We also considered garbage collection schemes in the experiments. As described in *Garbage collection mechanisms* section, we have two types of garbage collection schemes, one is to garbage collect the replicas that exceed the upper limit (N_{max}) of number of distinct replicas for each object and the other is to garbage collect the replica that the same replica already exists in the system.

Experiment Setting

In the experiments, we assumed that data objects are stored as erasure encoded fragments, such that any $M = 8$ distinct fragments ensure object reconstruction, and originally $N = 32$ distinct fragments are stored in the network. $N_{max} = 32/64$ was the upper limit of number of distinct fragments for each object. The total peer population used in the experiments comprised 2000 homogeneous peers and 4000 objects were encoded and placed on online peers using the random placement strategy at the start of the experiments. The experiments were run for 500 scaled time units (each corresponds to 25 real minutes) and repeated ten times to ascertain that the observed results are consistent. Please note that the bandwidth and parameter values discussed in below results are measured in terms of the number of fragments.

Results

We performed a series of experiments and here we illustrate part of the results to compare the performance of four maintenance mechanisms.

Experiment 1

In this experiment, we used Skype trace, N_{max} was 32 and fragments don't have duplicates. T_{dl} of deterministic lazy repair is 16, T_{rl} of randomized lazy repair is 12 and bandwidth budget of proactive repair is 8. From figure 7(a), we can see that when correlated failures occur, for deterministic lazy repair, 8 objects were lost (the objects that

Figure 7.

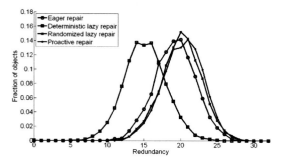

(a). Probability distribution of live fragments at time 243

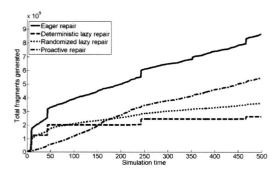

(b). Cumulative number of fragments generated

have less than 8 fragments), while the other three strategies all perform well and similar to each other. Figure 7(b) shows the cumulative number of fragments generated over time. Observe that for eager repair and deterministic lazy repair, there

are several spikes in bandwidth usage (manifested as steps since we show the cumulative number of fragments), which may overwhelm the network traffic. In contrast, bandwidth usage of proactive repair is the smoothest. Randomized lazy repair provides a good compromise because its overall bandwidth usage is modest (less than that of proactive or eager approaches) and its bandwidth usage is much smoother than that of other *reactive* strategies. Note that if the system considers only smoothness of the bandwidth usage then proactive repair wins, while in terms of total bandwidth usage, deterministic lazy repair outperforms all others in this scenario, but by making the system vulnerable.

Experiment 2

In this experiment, we used synthetic data, N_{max} was 64 and each fragment may have multiple duplicates. T_{dl} of deterministic lazy repair is 16, T_{rl} of randomized lazy repair is 11 and bandwidth budget of proactive repair is 7. Since there are no correlated failures in synthetic trace and multiple duplicates for each fragment are allowed, all the maintenance mechanisms can ensure 100% object availability (Figure 8(a)). Even though no object is lost by each maintenance mechanism, all mechanisms perform very differently in terms of bandwidth usage (Figure 8(b)). Notice that in

Figure 8.

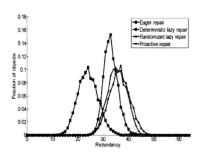

a. Probability distribution of live fragments at time 118

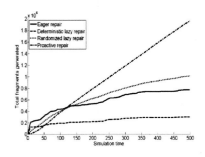

b. Cumulative number of fragments generated

the previous scenario, even if bandwidth is available, proactive strategy would not have used it simply because N_{max} was low. With a higher N_{max} too much bandwidth is wasted by the proactive strategy. In contrast, the randomized strategy provides comparable redundancy at a much lower and relatively smooth bandwidth usage. Even the eager strategy maintains a modest redundancy, and uses even lower amount of bandwidth, but in a spiky manner. The deterministic lazy approach has significantly less bandwidth consumption, though the usage is somewhat spiky. Though the system is relatively more vulnerable to any further failures, it still has adequate redundancy, making it the best choice in this case.

Summary

From the results we can see that there is no clear winner among all the maintenance mechanisms. One mechanism may outperform others in one scenario or measured by a certain metric, but underperform in another scenario or by other metrics. Overall the randomized lazy strategy appears to provide a good tradeoff between total bandwidth consumption and smoothness of bandwidth usage. System designers can use these results as a guide to choose their system design and parameters accordingly.

CONCLUSION

This chapter charts out the various design dimensions of a P2P storage system, delving into the details of redundancy maintenance mechanisms – both in terms of mechanisms to regenerate lost redundancy, as well as garbage collection mechanisms to deal with extra redundancy. Analytical models are showcased to let readers have a better understanding of the interplay between churn and maintenance operations in P2P storage systems. This chapter also discusses major criterions to judge the performance of various maintenance schemes, and reports results from diverse ex-

periments, both to validate analytical models as well as to evaluate the storage systems based on various other metrics (not necessarily studied analytically). Under different circumstances and with different performance priorities, different maintenance schemes perform relatively better than the others, and while there is no outright `best maintenance strategy', the randomized lazy redundancy maintenance strategy provides a good trade-off under diverse environments.

ACKNOWLEDGMENT

This work has been partly supported by Singapore's A*Star SERC Grant No. 072 124 0055 and by the research grant 69/N-SINGAPUR/2007/0 of the Polish Ministry of Science. We used and adapted definitions from Wikipedia when suitable for the key terms accompanying this article.

REFERENCES

Banerjee, S., Lee, S., Bhattacharjee, B., & Srinivasan, A. (2003). Resilient multicast using overlays. *ACM sigmetrics*.

Bhagwan, R., Tati, K., Cheng, Y., Savage, S., & Voelker, G. M. (2004). Totalrecall: System support for automated availability management. In *Proceedings of the 2nd symposium on Networked Systems Design And Implementation (NSDI)*.

Blake, C., & Rodrigues, R. (2003). High availability, scalable storage, dynamic peer network: Pick two. In *Proceedings of the 9th workshop on hot topics in operating systems (hotos-ix)*.

Chun, B.-G., Dabek, F., Haeberlen, A., Sit, E., Weatherspoon, H., Kaashoek, M. F., et al. (2006). Efficient replica maintenance for distributed storage systems. In *Proc. of the 3rd symposium on networked system design and implementation (NSDI)*.

Dabek, F., Li, J., Sit, E., Robertson, J., Kaashoek, M. F., & Morris, R. (2004). Designing a DHT for low latency and high throughput. In *Proceedings of the 2nd symposium on networked systems design and implementation (NSDI)*.

Datta, A., & Aberer, K. (2006). Internet-scale storage systems under churn - a study of the steady state using markov models. In *Proceedings of the sixth IEEE international conference on peer-to-peer computing (P2P)*.

Duminuco, A., Biersack, E., & En-Najjary, T. (2007). Proactive replication in distributed storage systems using machine availability estimation. In *CoNEXT '07: Proceedings of the 2007 ACM CoNEXT conference*.

Gkantsidis, C., & Rodriguez, P. (2005). Network coding for large scale content distribution. In *Proceedings of IEEE infocom*.

Godfrey, B. (2008). *Repository of Availability Traces*. Retrieved May 12, 2008 from http://www.eecs.berkeley.edu/~pbg/availability/

Haeberlen, A., Mislove, A., & Druschel, P. (2005). Glacier: Highly durable, decentralized storage despite massive correlated failures. In *Proceedings of the 2nd symposium on networked systems design and implementation (nsdi)*.

Iyer, S., Rowstron, A., & Druschel, P. (2002). Squirrel: A decentralized peer-to-peer web cache. In *Proceedings of the 21st symposium on principles of distributed computing (podc)*, Monterey, CA.

Kubiatowicz, J., Bindel, D., Chen, Y., Czerwinski, S., Eaton, P., Geels, D., et al. (2000). Oceanstore: An architecture for global-scale persistent storage. In *Proceedings of the ninth international conference on architectural support for programming languages and operating systems*.

Rhea, S., Eaton, P., Geels, D., Weatherspoon, H., Zhao, B., & Kubiatowicz, J. (2003). Pond: The oceanstore prototype. In *Proceedings of usenix file and storage technologies (fast)*.

Saroiu, S. (2004). *Measurement and analysis of internet content delivery systems*. Doctoral Dissertation, University of Washington.

Shokrollahi, A. (2006). Raptor Codes. *IEEE Transactions on Information Theory, 52*(6), 2551–2567. doi:10.1109/TIT.2006.874390

Sit, E., Haeberlen, A., Dabek, F., Chun, B.-G., Weatherspoon, H., Morris, R., et al. (2006). Proactive replication for data durability. In *the 5th international workshop on peer-to-peer systems*.

Wu, D., Tian, Y., Ng, K.-W., & Datta, A. (2008). Stochastic analysis of the interplay between object maintenance and churn. *Elsevier Computer Communications, 31*(2), 220–239.

KEY TERMS AND DEFINITIONS

Churn: In the context of peer-to-peer systems, churn refers to the dynamics of participation of peers in the system by (re-)joining and leaving the system, either temporarily or permanently.

Dynamic Equilibrium: If a steady-state situation in which a reverse process is occurring has a corresponding forward process, at a rate which achieves an exact balance, it is said to be in dynamic equilibrium.

Erasure Codes: Erasure code transforms a message of n blocks into a message with more than n blocks – thus introducing redundancy, such that the original message can be recovered from an arbitrary subset (typically of size n) of those blocks.

Markov Model: A mathematical model assuming that the Markov property holds, that is future states are independent of the past states and are reached through a probabilistic process depending only on the present state.

P2P Storage System: Peer-to-peer (P2P) storage is a paradigm which aims to leverage the combined storage capacity of a network of storage devices (peers) contributed typically by autonomous end-users as a common pool of storage space to store and share content.

Probability Distribution: A probability distribution identifies either the probability of each value of an unidentified random variable (when the variable is discrete), or the probability of the value falling within a particular interval (when the variable is continuous).

Stochastic Differential Equation: A stochastic differential equation is a differential equation in which one or more of the terms is a stochastic process, thus resulting in a solution which is itself a stochastic process.

Chapter 27

Making Scientific Applications on the Grid Reliable Through Flexibility Approaches Borrowed from Service Compositions

Dimka Karastoyanova
University of Stuttgart, Germany

Frank Leymann
University of Stuttgart, Germany

ABSTRACT

The current trend in Service Oriented Computing (SOC) is to enable support for new delivery models of software and applications. These endeavours impose requirements on the resources and services used, on the way applications are created and on the QoS characteristics of the applications and the supporting infrastructure. Scientific applications on the other hand require improved robustness and reliability of the supporting Grid infrastructures where resources appear and disappear constantly. Enabling business model like Software as a Service (SaaS), Infrastructure as a Service (IaaS), and guaranteeing reliability of Grid infrastructures are requirements that both business and scientific application nowadays impose. The convergence of existing approaches from SOC and Grid Computing is therefore an obvious need. In this work we give an overview of the state-of-the-art of the overlapping research done in the area of SOC and Grid computing with respect to meeting the requirements of the applications in these two areas. We show that the requirements of business applications that already exploit service-oriented architectures (SOA) and the scientific application utilizing Grid infrastructures overlap. Due to the limited extent of cooperation between the two research communities the research results are either overlapping or diverging in spite of the similarities in requirements. Notably, some of the techniques developed in each area are needed but still missing in the other area and vice versa. We argue therefore that in order to enable an enterprise-strength service-oriented infrastructure one needs to combine and leverage the existing Grid and Service middleware in terms of architectures and implementations. We call such an infrastructure the Business Grid. Based on the Business Grid vision we focus in this work on presenting

DOI: 10.4018/978-1-61520-686-5.ch027

how reliability and robustness of the Business Grid can be improved by employing approaches for flexibility of service compositions. An overview and assessment of these approaches are presented together with recommendations for use. Based on the assumption that Grid services are Web services, these approaches can be utilized to improve the reliability of the scientific applications thus drawing on the advantages flexible workflows provide. This way we improve the robustness of scientific applications by making them flexible and hence improve the features of business applications that employ Grid resources and Grid service compositions to realize the SaaS, IaaS etc. delivery models.

1. INTRODUCTION

Today, Grid infrastructures are mainly used for scientific computations dealing with considerable amounts of (experimental) data and performing extensive, time-consuming computing tasks. Usually, the hardware and software resources used to run the computations are out of the control of the application owners. The resources used for the computations may be used only for a concrete time period and may appear and disappear in an unpredictable fashion. It has been documented in research publications that the major challenge to be overcome on the Grid is its reliability (Fox & Gannon, 2006).

This book chapter will focus on approaches for making the Grid more reliable. We argue that Grid applications can be made more reliable through making them more flexible. We will present approaches towards flexibility of applications on the Grid. An objective of this work is to show that approaches and infrastructure created by the SOA community can be used for the benefit of the Grid community. Moreover, since approaches from the Grid are needed on the SOA infrastructures, such leverage of concepts and techniques will allow for a mutual amplification of these benefits for both communities. The major assumption in the chapter is that Grid and Web Service technologies can be combined to enable more reliable infrastructure for both business and scientific applications. We argue that only through this combination an infrastructure for supporting both business and

scientific applications can be created, which fosters leverage of existing technologies, mechanisms and techniques, and can provide added value to the users in both domains. We are convinced that the two domains have a lot to leverage and learn from each other and employ the research results to the advantage of both communities.

The chapter will start with an overview of the SOA (Service Oriented Architecture) paradigm, its role model and the operations an SOA infrastructure supports. We also present the Web Service technology as the only available implementation of the SOA paradigm. It is only through service composition that complex business and scientific computations can be enabled, therefore we present an overview of the process-based approach for service composition known from the field of Business Process Management (BPM). In particular, we identify the Business Process Execution Language (BPEL) as the one with the greatest potential to facilitate the creation of complex applications for business and scientific computations. We present the architecture of a (Web) Service Middleware, also known as the Bus or the Enterprise Service Bus (ESB).

Afterwards we shift the focus onto Grid services and existing technologies, whereas we pay the greatest attention to the Web Service Resource Framework (WSRF), which is the latest technology for Gird services and represents the convergence of research efforts of the Grid and SOA communities. WSRF is a framework that allows for representing stateful resources (hardware:

like processors, hard disks, software: applications, processes etc.) as services, whose state, also called properties, can be retrieved, manipulated, and processed in a meaningful way.

We compare the Web Service and Grid technologies, their overlaps and the potential for synergies between them, to facilitate better understanding.

We continue with a discussion about service-based business applications and their most important characteristics, as required by the application domains. We also investigate the characteristics of the existing infrastructures supporting them and identify missing but required functionality. In particular we stress on the need for reliable and scalable applications for enacting business transactions in a dynamic and competitive market. We also present the characteristics of applications currently run on the Grid. Most of the existing applications on the Grid are scientific applications that deal with huge amounts of data and long time to compute or analyse results. Additionally, we emphasise the fact that reliability of the Grid still needs improvements to meet the needs imposed by scientific applications, in particular because of the fact that resources appear and disappear on the Grid constantly. Another drawback of the existing approaches for enabling Grid applications we identify is that the reusability of applications is not fostered to the full and they are not flexible to changes in the environment and fault tolerant. Usually a scientist would create an application from scratch, or just execute the steps needed for a complex computation himself, and wait every time a piece of this computation is run, gather the results, prepare them for the next computation step and start this step. Existing computations implementations, from the areas of e.g. astrophysics, high energy nuclear physics and computational genomics, are not reused across organizations, steps of computations are not pre-defined and cannot be used multiple times with different configurations.

We discuss the vision of Business Grid as the way to follow for enabling reliable, robust and scalable applications. The Business Grid is a composable middleware that combines techniques available on the Bus and in Grid infrastructures. The main characteristics of the Business Grid will be summarized and its architecture is presented. We will show that this architecture addresses the requirements posed on Grid applications from the field of scientific computing and simulation technologies. We argue that instead of creating new concepts, architectures and technologies, the existing once from Grid and SOA can be combined in an advantageous way to support both business and scientific applications. This combination of technologies will enable reliability and scalability for Grid applications and ability to perform long, data intensive computations for business applications. In the same section we will list the requirements on the Business Grid imposed by both business applications and Grid computations. The requirements will be classified according to the characteristics needed and to the supporting infrastructure.

We shall identify the reliability of the Business Grid as the characteristic that needs to be urgently enabled, since both the ESB and the Grid are not yet capable to perform reliably for the needs of application operating on huge data sets for a longer time in a multi-tenant environment. We advocate the support for flexibility of applications on the Business Grid as the instrumental approach towards enabling reliability of such applications.

In order to facilitate the comprehension of the approaches toward flexibility that we present later in this chapter, we start with a classification of approaches to flexibility of applications on the Business Grid. These encompass flexibility on the level of the middleware as well as on the level of the applications. Based on this classification we present approaches towards flexibility of Business Grid applications in detail. These include approaches that enable reaction to failing services like dynamic binding and re-binding, adaptation of process-based applications using new constructs/ extensions to existing process composition languages, using the AOP paradigm, using ontological descriptions of services and processes, and others. Even though most of these approaches have been applied for business applications, we will show that they are applicable and can be leveraged for scientific applications. For each of the approaches we will present the enhancements that need to be made in order to customize them for scientific applications, if necessary. We compare these approaches and identify their advantages and disadvantages. Based on this we produce recommendations about in which cases to apply these approaches and what the effort to employ them would be. The main principle we follow in this comparison is their non-intrusiveness and compliance to standards, as well as reuse of investment in technology and skills.

This chapter will be concluded by an overview of what is missing to enact the Business Grid for it to hold to its promise. At the end we provide a summary and conclusions.

2. SOA, WEB SERVICES AND GRID

2.1 The Service Oriented Architecture (SOA: Overview

SOA is one natural continuation in the evolution of integration technologies (Weerawarana & Curbera & Leymann & Storey & Ferguson, 2005). It aims at enabling interoperability within and across organizations using the *service* abstraction, loose coupling, composability, and fostering technology and investment leverage. An additional goal of SOA is the automation of business processes, which has a great practical importance. Services are self-contained and self-describing units of functionality exposing *stable interfaces* in a unified format independent of implementation specifics and interaction formats and protocols. They render a heterogeneous environment homogeneous. Thus

services allow for standardized access and identification of functionality/applications and thus facilitate application integration. *Loose coupling* is the basic principle of service orientation (Kaye, 2003), (Weerawarana & Curbera & Leymann & Storey & Ferguson, 2005), (Gehlert & Hielscher & Danylevych & Karastoyanova, 2008). In a service-oriented environment the assumptions a service consumer has about a service are reduced; the knowledge about the architectural style, implementation, programming language, native protocols used to realize a service is not needed by the service consumer. Service clients know only the stable interface exposed by the service. The client applications using this service will not break if the implementation of the service is changed as long as the service interface is maintained stable. Loose coupling is also enabled by means of *messaging*, which supports asynchronous mode of communication and enables time and space decoupling of applications.

The SOA architectural style specifies three major *roles* and three *operations* (see Figure 1). Service providers are entities (organizations, persons, departments etc.) that provide services for use by service consumers/clients. The services may be developed by the organization providing them or by any other organization. To enable discoverability of services a discovery component (also called registry or sometimes called broker), is defined as a role in SOA. The provided services are registered with the discovery component and thus made available for discovery by potential service consumers. An entity may play any of the three roles. The *operations* defined by SOA are: find, register and bind. The find operation is used by service consumers to discover services in a service registry. The service providers use the register operation to provide information about their services in the discovery component. Once a client discovers an appropriate service he binds to the service and starts interacting with it. These operations are realized by the service middleware, the so-called service bus (Chappell,

Figure 1. The SOA paradigm and its implementation in terms of the Web Service technology

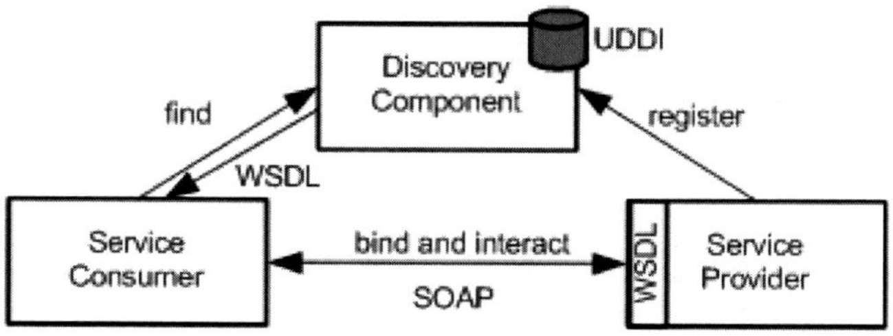

2004), (Leymann, 2005), and are made available to the entities playing any of the SOA roles. The invocation of services is performed by the bus. For this it receives as input from the service consumer the input data for the service invocation and the service description, more precisely a service operation; as a result it returns the output produced by the service. If the service consumer has not provided the location of the service and the access mechanism, it is up to the bus to discover a service on behalf of the client that meets his requirements with respect to functionality and quality characteristics of the service, usually known as quality of service (QoS).

2.2 Web Services

Web services (WSs) are the only existing standardized implementation of SOA. This technology provides a model for use of (existing) applications, not for programming applications. Web services are about virtualisation of applications, which also explains their already huge success in industrial applications and in utility and cloud computing (Mietzner & Leymann, 2008). Services can be implemented in any programming language for any platform, as well as they can be exposed for use via any of the existing interface description languages (IDLs). The novelty in Web services is the notion of binding, which is reflected by the standard language for WS interface description, the Web Service Description Language (WSDL) (W3C, 2001). Unlike any other existing IDL,

WSDL keeps the information about the transport protocol and message encoding separate from the actual interface description (signature). This allows for exposing the same functionality/program/ implementation on different endpoints/ports by combining a service interface description with multiple bindings. This improves modularity and facilitates loose coupling between service providers and consumers.

The WS technology draws on experience in application integration from both academia and industry and meanwhile enjoys a huge support on behalf of industry. The technology has been created for the purposes of application integration and therefore it possesses the features inherent for such a technology (Kaye, 2003), (Weerawarana & Curbera & Leymann & Storey & Ferguson, 2005). WSs enable machine-to-machine interaction across heterogeneous systems/environments by rendering them homogeneous using a unified service interface description format. WSs do not preclude the use of multiple communication modes and transport protocols with different QoS. Of great practical importance is the fact that WSs allow the leverage of existing software and its reuse in new applications in a very flexible manner. WSs can be combined in complex compositions, which can in turn be provided as WS too. The Web Service technology enables composability of technology and specifications. There are many specifications in the WS protocol stack dealing with different concerns of application development and integration. These specifications need not be all used in all WS applications if the features they specify are not needed. Standardization is also one of the major goals of WSs with the purpose of interoperability.

Apart from WSDL, SOAP and UDDI are also considered part of the basic WS protocol stack. SOAP specifies a message format and message processing model independent of the transport protocols used on the message path. UDDI (Universal, Description, Discovery and Integration) defines a data model for storing information about services in service registries and an API for interaction with UDDI registries.

Due to the advantages WSs possess, industry has already invested heavily in creating supporting infrastructures for WSs. There are already even commercial implementations of service buses by all major software vendors.

Recently there have been developments in the area of applying semantic information in the field of WSs, where meta-information about WSs is described in terms of ontologies. This research area targets the improvement of automation of discovery of WSs and their use in business processes across multiple application domains.

The WS technology *virtualizes applications* in a unified manner and thus fosters interoperability and integration. Recently, the need has arisen to *virtualize hardware resources* in particular in the area of scientific computing and simulation, where the computations are lengthy and resource-consuming due to the nature of the computations and the huge amounts of distributed data used and produced. This need was addressed partly by the Grid, and its name stands for a distributed IT infrastructure for advanced science and engineering applications (Foster, 2002), (Foster & Kesselman & Tuecke, 2001).

2.3 Grid and Grid Services

Initially the intent of the *Grid* was to virtualize computing resources and thus supply scientific collaborations with more computing power than

the computing resources each concrete domain provides (i.e. the local IT infrastructures of computing centres). In other words, the Grid is viewed as a solution to the problem of "flexible, secure, coordinated resource sharing among dynamic collections of individuals, institutions and resources" (Foster, 2002). These dynamic collections of individuals, institutions and resources are referred to as "virtual organizations" (Foster, 2002) and can comprise different groups of scientists working on a common goal but can as well be different companies that join forces or are in a supplier-requestor relationship in order to reach a certain (mostly computing intensive) business goal. A fundamental principle virtual organizations follow is the sharing of files or documents, and also of access to programs and even hardware resources.

The organizations that form a virtual organization can only share computing resources if a standardized architecture for the Grid as well as interfaces is at hand to enable the interoperability among Grid resources. The Grid community introduced the Open Grid Services Architecture OGSA (Foster & Kesselman, 2004), which follows the principles of SOA and provides a standardized set of services important in a Grid environment (such as registry, authorization monitoring, data access and others) (Foster & Kesselman & Tuecke, 2001). The technology to realize the OGSA is Web services, thus allowing Grid services to be described and used in a standardized and interoperable manner. The Open Grid Services Infrastructure (OGSI) (Tuecke et al., 2003) and its successor the Web Service Resource Framework (WSRF) (Czajkowski K. et al., 2004), (OASIS WSRF TC, 2008) are specifications that define how to specify stateful Web services that represent stateful resources (such as computers or storage) as they are present in Grid environments. WSRF specifies the so-called *WS-Resource*, which is a WS that allows a unified access to computing resources on the Grid. Apart from possessing a WS interface that exposes the functions a resource

Figure 2. Web service resource

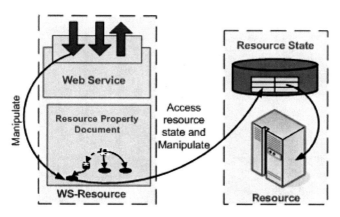

implements in terms of WS operations, the WS-Resource also references a resource property document (see Figure 2**Fehler! Verweisquelle konnte nicht gefunden werden.**). The properties document contains a description of the resource properties and allows for viewing the resource state that may include information like storage capacity, number of discs, processor frequency, resource type, current workload etc.

Additionally, WSRF specifies standardized interfaces for lifecycle control, standardized faults, notifications (WS-Notification) in separate composable specifications, quite in the sense of the WS technology. Compare to the OGSI, where all these orthogonal features were part of one and the same specification, and all OGSI compliant services had to implement all the features, regardless of the requirements.

2.4. Composing WSs and Grid Services

WS and Grid services (i.e. WS-Resources) can be combined in more complex applications using some composition approach. The workflow- or process-based approach (Leymann & Roller, 1999), (van der Aalst & van Hee, 2002) is the most favoured one for creating compositions of services. The process-based approach to service composition, also known as service orchestration, allows composing services in a very flexible manner by means of improved modularity, separation of concerns and configurability. Processes are created in terms of (i) control logic that specifies the sequencing of tasks and the data they exchange, (ii) the functions/services that implement the tasks and (iii) the human participants in an organization that participate in carrying out the tasks. These entities form the so-called workflow/process dimensions. In (Web) service compositions, due to the fact that services do not involve people or hide their participation, the organizational dimension is not present. The definition of a workflow or process used here is based on those presented in BPM (Business Process Management) literature like (Leymann & Roller, 1999) and (van der Aalst & van Hee, 2002). It is important to note that the workflow technology distinguished between a workflow model and workflow instances. A model can be run multiple times, i.e. multiple workflow instances can be executed simultaneously, which brings significant time savings. To the best of our knowledge, based on our participation in multiple projects together with the scientific computing community, the definitions of the notion of workflow first differ from group to group in the scientific world, and second sands for only the sequencing of tasks and the data dependencies.

Figure 3. Interplay among Service compositions, WSs and Grid services

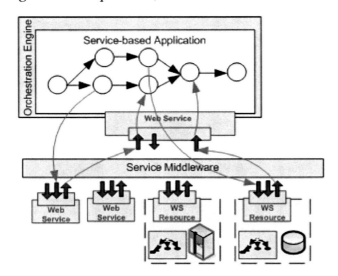

According to these definitions workflows do not include the features from the workflow technology, like: interruptible sequences of tasks, modelling of constraints to transitioning from task to task in a global model of the overall computation, modelling parallel execution of independent tasks, forward and backward recovery, fault handling, staff assignment per task. The available scientific workflow infrastructures do not always distinguish among workflow model and workflow instances; moreover, some of them are tailor-made for a concrete scientific domain, which the workflow engines employed in business applications indeed avoid by implementing a generic workflow meta-model suitable for all application domains. In this work we have as a starting point the workflows or processes as defined by the BPM community.

Usually processes are modelled using some graphical notation, however in order to be executed (on a workflow engine/system) they need to be transformed into some executable format. There are many workflow languages and BPEL (OASIS BPEL TC, 2008) is the standard language for describing service orchestrations. It contains constructs for control flow and data manipulation, as well as the so-called interaction activities which model the interaction with WSs that implement tasks in a workflow, e.g. book hotel, calculate credit risk, generate a mesh in a FEM computation etc. The interaction activities contain references to the service port type and operation and specifies the input and output data. In BPEL the control flow and the functions (WSs) used are predefined during the modelling of the composition and remain unchanged during the process execution. Currently, flexibility of the processes is enabled due to the fact that concrete service implementations (called also ports) can be assigned to tasks during the process deployment onto the execution environment or during run time. For the latter case, it is up to the service bus to discover, select and invoke a concrete service that complies with the specification of the process task and the desired QoS characteristics. The types of services used are however the same during the whole life cycle of the process. Processes are executed by process/orchestration/workflow engines and currently these engines make use of the service middleware to invoke services (see Figure 3). The use of Grid infrastructures for involving WS-Resources into BPEL service orchestrations has great potential and will allow for flexible mixing and interchange of WSs and WS-Resources from the point of view of service orchestrations. This should be addressed by research and engineering efforts in this direction.

BPEL is being extensively used in business applications and all big software vendors have rolled out products with BPEL support. There are preliminary attempts to utilize BPEL for composing scientific computations using existing algorithm and computation implementations (Emmerich & Butchart & Chen & Wassermann & Price, 2005), (Fox & Gannon, 2006), (Leymann, 2006). Admittedly, there are many open issues that still have to be considered in the area of applying the SOA paradigm, Web services and Grid services for scientific applications (SimTech, 2008), (Gannon, 2007). The major critical issues are in particular the robustness, scalability and availability the infrastructure and resources to maintain the long-running scientific application up and running.

A current trend in business applications and supporting infrastructures is to use Grid infrastructures. It is observed that there is a significant lack in support for the use of huge data sets in business applications and in the scenarios where extensive computations are required, like e.g. analysis of customer data, predictions, monitoring of business activities and correlation of such activities, text and multimedia processing and search (Clarin, 2008). While SOA has great success in improving the support for business applications, techniques from Grid can be utilized to enhance this support further. Some of the reasons for the modern SOA infrastructures to not yet support such features can be explained by the requirements business applications up till now had on technologies. Modern business applications however are much more complex and require most of the features mentioned above.

Indeed, both business and scientific applications miss certain features which the other domain has already implemented. Usually, each industry stays in its own confines and keeps developing its own technology and standards. With the advent of service-orientation, which is employed by both communities, now there is a chance to discontinue such practices and unify the efforts in developing composable infrastructures comprising concepts, techniques and implementations from different domains for the mutual benefit. The vision of the service bus (Chappell, 2004) has laid the foundations of the architecture of such a composable infrastructure. It however has considered only application or software services as part of the service landscape. The Grid community has shown that the SOA paradigm can be applied to Grid infrastructures. In the next section we introduce the architecture of the so-called Business Grid, which is meant to combine these two separate developments in a unified infrastructure for business and scientific applications.

3. THE BUSINESS GRID

With the advance of SOA and WSs in particular, the internet has transformed into a ubiquitous integration platform. The Grid resources are also WSs and this provides the opportunity to utilize more, increasingly powerful computing resources across organisations from science and business domains. The enormous potential of the Grid to improve the utilization of idle resources to perform computing intensive tasks or even sell them to any organization becomes evident. The Grid therefore transforms from an infrastructure for scientists into an infrastructure for enterprises, too. It is this unique combination of SOC and Grid paradigms that makes this possible. We argue that the currently divergent infrastructures and research developments can mutually amplify their applicability, features and added-value characteristics if combined in a unified infrastructure. We call such an infrastructure the *Business Grid*. The Business Grid is a vision introduced in our recent research work (Mietzner & Karastoyanova & Leymann, 2008). He we present only an overview of the

Figure 4. Business Grid architecture (Mietzner & Karastoyanova & Leymann, 2008)

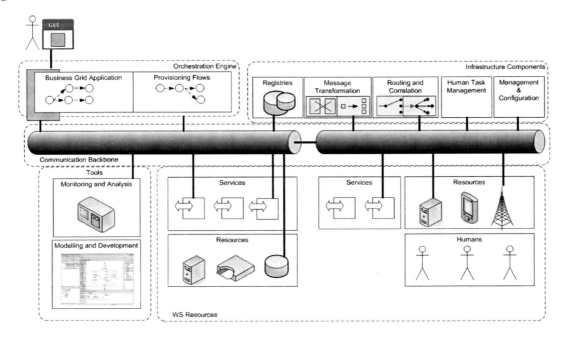

Business Grid to allow for the positioning of the approaches for flexibility discussed in the next sections.

Based on the analysis of requirements imposed on business and scientific applications (Mietzner & Karastoyanova & Leymann, 2008) we can state that business and scientific applications have similar requirements with respect to multiple features like composability of services, modularity, ease of modelling and execution of applications, seamless and transparent support for service discovery, selection and invocation, availability of multiple transport protocols and encoding formats, flexibility, reliability and robustness. These similar requirements have been addressed by the existing infrastructures created in both domains. We also observed that the infrastructures built by these two communities still lack support for features that the opposite community has already enabled. Furthermore, we have also observed that because of the changed application requirements in these two domains the business applications need features available on the Grid

and scientific applications require techniques from service-oriented business infrastructures. The Business Grid has been introduced with the purpose of addressing the collective requirements of these two fields. Our motivation is based on the fact that apart from avoiding the development of overlapping approaches and technologies and duplicate infrastructure implementations, some of the approaches from the Grid may be successfully used to address open issues in the business applications domain, like handling of big data sets, improvements in the long-running execution of applications using provisioning techniques (Keller & Badonnel, 2004), optimization of resource utilization, whereas techniques available in the business applications domain can be utilized to address challenges still prevalent on the Grid, like for instance scalability, flexibility, robustness, composition, and resource/service discovery. The architecture of the Business Grid is presented in Figure 4; for more details consider (Mietzner & Karastoyanova & Leymann, 2008). This architecture is meant to be implemented as a composition of existing implementations of Grid and Service Bus implementations, and the necessary add-ons. It has been meant to provide a framework for integrating existing infrastructures and approaches from the two different domains under the SOA principles of reuse, composability and interoperability.

One example that shows the need to combine techniques from both Grid and SOC is the recognized fact that Grid applications are not yet robust and reliable enough. The service middleware and the workflow engines in an SOA environment provide these features, and since Grid services are Web services it is only natural to reuse the existing techniques for scientific applications that use Grid services. The Business Grid is designed with the idea to reuse as much as possible from the available techniques, one of which is the ability to maintain robustness and reliability of applications using the approaches for flexibility of service compositions.

The ability to react to faults in the environment is flexibility. The faults to which the applications must remain resistant are service faults, failures in the middleware services like discovery and selection, faults in the execution of service compositions either due some unforeseen exceptional situations, or because extensive testing has recommended to exchange services, and others. The assumption is that the applications in a service-oriented environment are service compositions, while the mostly employed approach is the one known from workflow management. Flexibility is needed in order to make business and scientific applications robust even when Grid resources/services are used. We would like to stress once again that only by combining advantageous features from both areas can the Business Grid infrastructure become an enterprise strength one. In the next section we present a classification of approaches for flexibility of service compositions and describe several existing techniques that can be employed on the Business Grid.

4. APPROACHES TO FLEXIBILITY OF BUSINESS GRID APPLICATIONS

Workflows have been used in the last decades for implementing reliable and robust applications. Due to their flexible programming model for separating control logic from the actual functionality to compose, workflows are forward and backward recoverable and can be guaranteed to complete in finite time successfully. Note that a completion of a process, where all the effects of all performed tasks are reversed is also considered successful; success is defined by the business process and the application domain. Parallel execution of tasks, which do not exhibit dependencies, is possible using workflows. Furthermore, workflows are by design capable of performing in heterogeneous environments, especially because the make extensive use of middleware. Note again that multiple instances of the same workflow can be executed, which saves enormous amount of time and human resources. This is identified as a need in scientific computing, where currently only a single run of a computation is performed at a time. Logical units of work can be defined and executed with all-or-nothing semantics – a feature that can be traced back in the history of production workflows (Leymann & Roller, 1999) that evolved from transactional workflows and research in transaction processing.

4.1 Classification of Approaches to Process Flexibility

Even though workflows are a very flexible model for creating applications by predefining a process model optimized for a domain, in some scenarios the process model needs to be adjusted to some unexpected situations, called also changes in the environment. The ability of processes to adapt to the changes in the environment is called flexibility. Adjustments in processes, called also adaptations or changes, can be made for one or more process instances during their execution, or the process model itself may need to be adjusted if the adaptations are relevant for all process instances. Another reason for the necessity of adaptation of processes or instances is the continuous process of business process re-engineering, which targets the continuous improvement and optimization of processes run by enterprises. All process adaptation approaches are applicable for enabling flexibility of service compositions; some additional approaches however are needed because of features inherent for service compositions. These different types of changes are classified in (Karastoyanova, 2006) and the summarized in the following table:

During the design time phase of service compositions, the phase in which the process specifications/definitions are created, any kind of changes in the models can be made. Some of the changes done include the definition of alternative execution paths in the control flow to accommodate different potential situations to which each instance must react as predefined in the control flow; the instance runs along only that alternative path that tackles the situation valid for that instance – this approach is known by the name "flexibility by configuration" (van der Aalst & Jablonski, 2000). Adaptation of service compositions during their execution, or run time, is complex and requires an infrastructure with special features. Whenever a process model is changed the instances that will be created after this change will follow the new model.

For the running process instances first it has to be checked if these instances can at all be modified to reflect the new model depending on their current status/position in the execution of the process. The instances that can be modified according to the new model are said to be migrated to this model. This may require changing the internal workflow engine representation of the instances and the data they use. Additionally, the instanced that cannot be migrated may either be terminated or let complete as specified in the original model. This means that one and the same model would have two versions for a considerable period of time and version management is one

of the implied infrastructure features. Instance migration and the supporting infrastructure are complex areas of current research and are out of the scope of this work. In service compositions only the fixed dimensions of the specification may need to be changed as reaction to environment changes. The control flow specification/model can be adapted by including new tasks or groups of tasks or deleting tasks. Additionally, transition conditions and data can be changed. The functions implementing these tasks may also be changed. All these changes can be performed for both models and one or more instances. Service composition instances may also incorporate a reaction to changes in the environment, e.g. failing WS, the appearance of a new service with better QoS characteristics, adaptation request due to recommendation of a test run (Gehlert & Hielscher & Danylevych & Karastoyanova, 2008), by exchanging a concrete WS implementation that has originally been chosen to perform a task in an instance (Karastoyanova & Houspanossian & Cilia & Leymann & Buchmann, 2005). Approaches enabling all of these types of changes in service compositions already exist and the next section represents an overview of the most advantageous of them.

4.2 Existing Approaches Towards Flexibility of Service Compositions

This section provides an overview of existing approaches towards flexibility of service compositions and assigns them to the concrete group of approaches in the classification presented above.

Consider the following observations (see Figure 5):

- Control logic dimension is fixed in the process models and definitions
- Port types and operations of partner WSs are hard-coded in WS composition models, i.e. the functions dimension is fixed

- A single port type name may identify a simple or a complex functionality
- Concrete participants are typically resolved upon deployment

Since service compositions reference only port types of services, there must be a mechanism to resolve these port types to concrete service endpoints/ports. The mechanism is called *service binding* (see Figure 6A) and there are several strategies defined in literature (Weerawarana & Curbera & Leymann & Storey & Ferguson, 2005) for controlling this mechanism, called *binding strategies*. The static binding strategy

prescribes concrete service ports for each of the tasks in a process during either design time or deployment time; the statically prescribed service ports are used during process execution. Dynamic service binding is a strategy that postulates that the concrete services are to be discovered during process instance execution. It is enabled during both design time and run time. During modelling or deployment time the port types of services that implement a task are specified; these are the functional requirements toward a service. Additionally, the QoS selection criteria, usually provided in terms of WS-Policies, may also be provided. During process execution the process

Figure 5. Service composition specifications reference only port types; the concrete implementations may differ for each of the instances of the same task in a process model

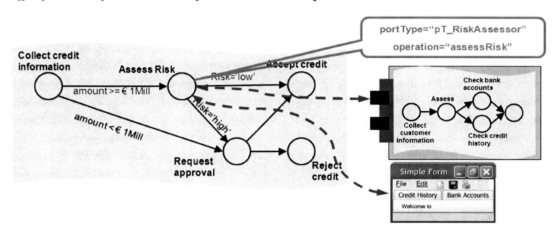

Figure 6. (A) The role of binding strategies in service compositions. (B) Improving flexibility using parameterization

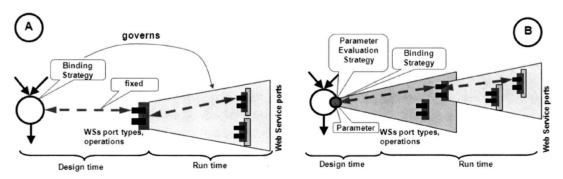

engine delegates the discovery and selection of the concrete services for each of the tasks to the service bus, which uses as input the functional and non-functional properties as provided by the process specification. The dynamic binding is an approach used to enable flexibility for each process instance with respect to the functional dimension of service composition.

4.2.1. Exchanging Concrete Service Implementations During Run Time

The mechanism for discovery, selection and invocation of WS is known by the name *find and bind mechanism* and is utilized during the normal execution of service compositions. It can also be used to exchange services that have been bound for use with a service composition, regardless of the strategy used for the original binding, with another port. This may be necessary in order to handle a fault of a service and the inability of the service middleware to discover a new alternative but compliant service. For the discovery of the new service, the selection criteria must be altered to allow for a discovery at all. Therefore, to enable this, the alternative selection criteria must be provided in the original process model. There are several ways to do this: (a) extend the process definition language to allow for specification of such criteria directly in the interaction activity elements; (b) extend the deployment information by alternative selection policies and use it during execution for the discovery of a substitute for a failed service, which will provide a much more configurable approach.

Approach (a) has already been defined and implemented and detailed report on it can be found in (Karastoyanova & Houspanossian & Cilia & Leymann & Buchmann, 2005). The alternative selection criteria can be provided either via an extension element to the BPEL <invoke> activity automatically, where the alternative policy is available, or manually, where a user provides the alternative selection criteria for the extended

activity in which the attribute modelling the alternative criteria is left empty. To the best of our knowledge, this approach has not been implemented yet.

4.2.2. Parameterized Processes

One approach to make service compositions flexible on the functions dimension in their reaction to changes is enabled by the parameterized processes (Karastoyanova et al., 2006). The approach extends BPEL and provides an extension element in the interaction activities to allow for providing or discovering a port type for the service to be bound using a parameter evaluation strategy (see Figure 6B). Such a strategy is specified during design time but is executed during run time to resolve parameter values. The parameter values may be provided manually by a human participant, or may be provided as a result from a discovery according to service criteria specified in terms of semantic description of services in any of the existing semantic Web services frameworks, or may be copied from a variable. The approach implies particular characteristics of the execution environment since it extends the BPEL core model and hence is not supported by the standard BPEL engines. Additionally, it also requires the integration with an execution environment for semantic Web services (Karastoyanova et al., 2006), (Karastoyanova, 2006), the so-called semantic service bus (Karastoyanova et al., 2007). The use of the approach implies also the use of the dynamic binding strategy, in order to discover the concrete implementation of the discovered port type for each instance of the task, too (see Figure 6B). This approach provides a primitive support for control flow change in service composition since by discovering or specifying a port type and following one of the above observations that a port type may also be implemented by a process, the control flow of the overall service composition is changed.

4.2.3. BPEL^light

BPEL^light (Nitzsche & van Lessen & Karastoyanova & Leymann, 2008) is an extension to BPEL that decouples the process logic from the WSDL descriptions and enable the use of any kind of service interface descriptions. This approach has been implemented prototypically and described in (van Lessen at al., 2007). The BPEL^light specification defines an extension activity which separates completely the process logic from the descriptions of services that allows for associating any kind of service description to the process definitions. During process deployment, the service descriptions are simply supplied together with the process logic. This approach removes the hard-coding to service interfaces into the process models and facilitates the adaptability and reusability of service composition definitions. It is a standard compliant extension of BPEL and can be executed on BPEL compliant engines with the respective extensions. The prototype supports the use of conventional WSs and semantic Web services described in WSMO. For this the BPEL4SWS specification has also been produced and the corresponding engine implementation provided (van Lessen at al., 2007). BPEL4SWS specifies how BPEL^light is used in combination with semantic Web services. Once the service type is discovered based on its semantic description, the discovery of service ports/endpoint is a must. Any other semantic service description framework, like OWL-S and SAWSDL, can also be applied with BPEL4SWS. Through the use of semantics BPEL4SWS improves the discovery of services (port types and ports) through an additional level of abstraction provided by the semantic description of interfaces. This improves further flexibility and reusability of BPEL processes. The approach supports flexibility of the functions dimension of WS compositions and may in some cases enable control flow adaptations similar to the way it is enabled by parameterized processes.

4.2.4. BPEL'n'Aspects

The BPEL'n'Aspects approach for flexibility (Karastoyanova & Leymann, 2009) draws on the ideas of the aspect-oriented programming (AOP) paradigm. The approach enables control flow adaptation of running instances of a process model. It is a non-intrusive approach in the spirit of the AOP paradigm; this means that the original process models are kept unchanged, but using the approach the actual execution of each of the instances of such models may be adapted as needed.

The analogy used to enable the approach follows the AOP paradigm which postulates that upon events of a specified type additional functionality, which has not been part of the original code, can be executed or weaved into the control flow of the original program. We observe a similarity to event notification and reaction to events used in reactive database systems and complex event processing systems.

Following this analogy we treat the BPEL processes the original programs that are executed on BPEL engines; the BPEL engines interpret the BPEL process models and publish navigation events. WSs implement functionalities and can be treated as the functionalities to be weaved in upon a navigation event happening, hence WSs are the advices in AOP terms (see Figure 7). Aspects are specified in terms of WS-Policy (W3C) and aspect references any Web Service (advice) that will represent the additional functionality.

An aspect also specifies upon which event in the process navigation the WS should be executed by means of the so-called pointcut and advice type (before, after and instead). For example a policy, i.e. an aspect, referencing the "Store Debit" operation can be assigned to a process instance of the trip booking process and be executed after the completion of the activity/task "Charge Credit Card" (see Figure 8). Similarly, aspects may be defined to incorporate additional functionality in the process flow before or instead a task, to modify the value of variables or transition conditions on links.

Figure 7. Aspects in the BPEL'n'Aspects approach

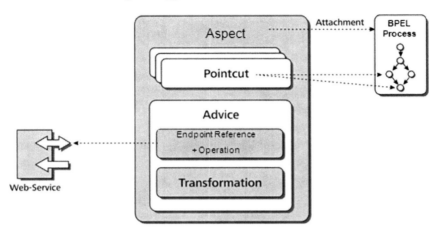

The aspects/WS-Policies are attached to the process models and/or process instances using WS-PolicyAttachment (see Figure 8). This facilitates the better configurability of the approach and allows for combining any aspect definition with any process model.

The implementation of the approach follows the architecture presented in Figure 9. A BPEL engine that is capable of publishing navigation events is needed. The so called custom controller (Khalaf & Karastoyanova & Leymann, 2007) implements the functionality of the weaver.

It is responsible of including the additional functionality for each process instance as defined by the aspects attached to that process instance. The weaver lets only the navigation events for which there is an aspect deployed to be notified. Upon such a notification the WS that constitutes the advice of the corresponding aspect is invoked. This communication (between the process instances and the WSs/advices) is based on the publish/subscribe paradigm and in this particular case uses WS-Notification (WS-N, 2004).

Figure 8. BPEL'n'Aspects approach – example

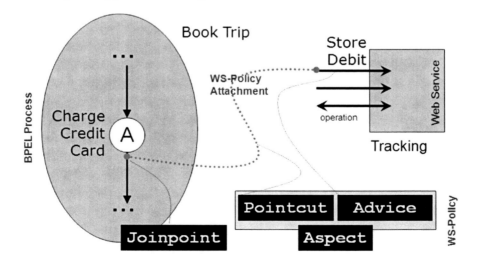

Figure 9. Architecture of the infrastructure implementing the BPEL'n'Aspects approach

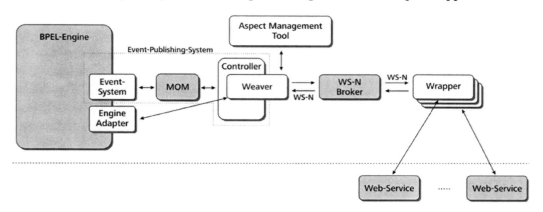

The way to proceed when using the approach is the following:

- Define and deploy the aspect on the supporting infrastructure using the Aspect design and deployment tool (Figure 9)
- Upon subscription the Weaver component subscribes to the navigation event (published by the engine) specified in the point-cut of the aspect, e.g. to the event notifying that the activity "Charge Credit Card" is finished. Additionally, a wrapper is created for the invocation of the WS referenced into the deployed aspect. The wrapper is the component that handles the invocation of the WS/advice.
- Upon this event the Weaver publishes it, and thus the corresponding wrapper is notified (via a predefined topic) and the WS in the aspect is executed, e.g. the WS implementing the operation "Store Debit". The result produced by the WS invocation is returned to the process instance. The effect of the aspect weaving is the inclusion of a new task (i.e. the "Store Debit" task) into the process logic.

The advantages of the BPEL'n'Aspects approach include improvements in modularity and configurability of service compositions, main-

taining the standardization endeavour of the WS technology as a whole, and support for both model evolution and ad-hoc changes in service compositions in a non-intrusive manner. The non-intrusiveness is a very valuable characteristic, since it allows for adapting/extending even existing and running BPEL processes without the necessity to change and redeploy them. Thus the approach tackles a major drawback of other approaches to flexibility presented in this and other works; for further references please consult (Karastoyanova, 2006).

4.3. Assessment of the Flexibility Approaches

The approaches to flexibility of service compositions presented in this chapter enable different types of changes as classified in Table 1. The exchange of concrete services/ports during the execution of service compositions allows for adaptations on the level of functions in processes on per-instance basis. The functions dimension can be modified with respect to the port types used on both models and instances using the approach of process parameterization. This approach can in some cases enable modifications of the control flow of orchestrations. The BPEL'n'Aspects approach has been designed with the purpose to support adaptation of control flows of service com-

Table 1. Classification of adaptation approaches for service orchestrations

Life cycle phase	Modification level	Approach
Design time	Model	Any kind of change possible
	Instance	Flexibility by configuration
Run time	Model	Change in: • functions (port types, operations) • control flow
	Instance	Change in: • functions (port type, operations) • control flow • WS ports or instances

positions and has been demonstrated as a feasible mechanism for adapting BPEL processes. It can also be used to render the functions dimension flexible; the aspects one defines for this must be of the "instead" type, which states that the original task is substituted with another one.

In the scenarios where existing running processes need to be adapted, the best approach to use is BPEL'n'Aspects, since it utilizes existing technology and standard specifications and does not alter the process definition language. It however requires extending the execution environment but all the needed extensions leverage existing very well known technologies and concepts like the WS stack and publish/subscribe.

The rest of the approaches are based on changes in the process definition language and hence imply more changes to the execution engine; on the other hand, tool support and infrastructure for them also exists which facilitates employing them as is.

When choosing an approach for improving the flexibility of service compositions we advise evaluating thoroughly the concrete types of changes needed in the concrete application domain and scenario and use the result of the evaluation during the decision-making process.

5. OPEN ISSUES IN THE FIELD OF THE BUSINESS GRID

The section summarizes some of the open research issues that need to be considered in order to combine the efforts of the SOC and Grid communities and thus supply the foundations of an infrastructure applicable for both business and scientific applications.

Handling huge amounts of data produced and consumed by both scientific and business applications in an SOA is still an open topic. Research done in the field of database management systems, data warehousing and the simulation technology should be leveraged to produce fast results in a standard based manner reusing as much of the existing technology as possible.

Fault handling in business and scientific applications, especially in a domain specific manner, requires not only standardization of the business processes in each of the domains, but also utilizing the advantages of the existing technologies. For example, scientific applications on the Grid are encouraged to take advantage of the workflow technology to enable not only parallel or alternative task execution, but also utilize the inherent backward- and forward-recoverability of workflows supported by workflow management systems. Workflows in combination with SOA enable the creation of fault-tolerant scientific applications in a heterogeneous environment, which directly matches the requirements of scientific computing landscapes.

The available provisioning techniques on the Grid can be utilized to provision enough resources for the execution of business applications in the cases of high workloads and in support of the new application delivery models like Software as a Service (SaaS), Infrastructure as a Service (IaaS), Middleware as a Service (MaaS) etc.

In this relation, it is of utmost importance to design and expose computations as Grid services in a unified manner; note that currently most scientific computations and algorithms are monolithic applications and incorporate features like security, data handling, integration and others, which are orthogonal to the core concern of the applications.

The approached for improving flexibility of applications/compositions and hence their robustness may need to be tuned as to address domain specific requirements. For example, the requirements for robustness in simulation (SimTech), (Taylor et al., 2003) might be different from those in computer linguistics (Clarin, 2008). These requirements still need to be investigated and analysed.

The integration of Grid infrastructures and Bus implementations is not seamlessly possible, since they do not comply with the same general architecture; the introduction of the Business Grid vision provides the necessary framework for this and endeavours to facilitate convergence of the SOC and Grid communities, and the research done by them. Tool support is an obvious must and can be provided once the architecture of a unified architecture is agreed upon. Such support depends on the existence of Domain Specific Languages, and the corresponding extensions to BPEL or other process definition languages. Support for human interaction is still a research issue in SOC and the potential solutions need to take into account the requirements from the scientific domains, too. Reusability of process models and fragments is typically one of the major requirements in both domains and needs to be taken care of. This implies incorporating support for reusability in the modelling tools and the design of process model libraries, including support for debugging and testing. This should all lower the barrier to entry for users.

The appropriate composable execution infrastructure must be put into place. It needs to ensure concurrency, reliability of the middleware and processes running on it, while reusing of existing approaches to ensure leverage of investment in technology and skills.

The performance of this infrastructure must meet the requirements of both domains, and the corresponding performance models, test procedures, evaluation and monitoring infrastructure must be put in place too.

6. SUMMARY AND CONCLUSION

In this work we discussed the potential benefits of combining the SOA and Grid paradigms and the techniques available in these two domains. We are convinced that only the combination of the techniques from the two domains can support enterprise strength applications for business and scientific use. We observe that existing techniques from scientific computing based on Grid infrastructures can be exploited in business applications. Additionally, mechanisms available on the service bus and known from service compositions can be used to address the lack of reliability and robustness in scientific applications on the Grid. This observation is the motivation for introducing a combined infrastructure, called the Business Grid, which exhibits beneficial features applicable in both domains. In this paper we have concentrated on one example of how Grid and SOC techniques can be combined to improve the state-of-the-art. In particular, we have presented approaches for enabling flexibility of service compositions known from business driven research and that they can be applied for scientific Grid applications to tackle reliability and robustness problems under the assumption that Grid services are utilized. We have identified some further synergy opportunities between the business and scientific application domains and argued that the appropriate combination and thorough exploitation of existing approaches can improve the state of the art enormously and grant benefits to the SOC and Grid communities altogether.

REFERENCES

W3C. (2001). *W3C Note: Web services Description Language (WSDL) 1.1.* Retrieved from http://www.w3.org/TR/wsdl

W3C. (n.d.). *W3C member submission: Web services policy framework.* Retrieved from http://www.w3.org/Submission/WS-Policy/

Chappell, D. (2004). *Enterprise service bus.* O'Reilly Media, Inc.

CLARIN Project. (2008). Retrieved from http://www.clarin.eu/

Czajkowski, K., et al. (2004). *From open Grid services infrastructure to WS-resource framework: refactoring & evolution.* Global Grid Forum Draft Recommendation.

Emmerich, W., Butchart, B., Chen, L., Wassermann, B., & Price, S. (2005). Grid service orchestration using the business process execution language (BPEL). *Journal of Grid Computing, 3,* 283–304. doi:10.1007/s10723-005-9015-3

Foster, I. (2002). What is the Grid? - A three point checklist. *GRIDtoday, 1.* Retrieved from http://www.Gridtoday.com/02/0722/100136.html

Foster, I., et al. (2005). *The open Grid services architecture, Version 1.0.* Global Grid Forum, Lemont, Illinois, USA (vol. 30).

Foster, I., & Kesselman, C. (2004). *The Grid 2: Blueprint for a new computing infrastructure.* San Francisco: Morgan Kaufmann Publishers.

Foster, I., Kesselman, C., & Tuecke, S. (2001). The anatomy of the Grid: Enabling scalable virtual organizations. *International Journal of High Performance Computing Applications, 15,* 200–222. doi:10.1177/109434200101500302

Fox, G. C., & Gannon, D. (2006). Workflow in Grid systems. *Concurrency and Computation, 18,* 1009–1019. doi:10.1002/cpe.1019

Gannon, D. (2007). A service architecture for eScience Grid gateways. In *Grid Computing, High-Performance and Distributed Applications (GADA'07).*

Gehlert, A., Hielscher, J., Danylevych, O., & Karastoyanova, D. (2008). Online testing, requirements engineering and service faults as drivers for adapting service compositions. In *Proceedings of MONA+ at ServiceWave2008.*

Karastoyanova, D. (2006). *Enhancing flexibility and reusability of Web service flows through parameterization.* PhD Thesis, TU-Darmstadt, Shaker Verlag.

Karastoyanova, D., et al. (2006). Parameterized BPEL processes: concepts and implementation. In *Proc. of BPM 2006.*

Karastoyanova, D., Houspanossian, A., Cilia, M., Leymann, F., & Buchmann, A. (2005). Extending BPEL for Run Time Adaptability. In *Proceedings of EDOC 2005.*

Karastoyanova, D., & Leymann, F. (2009) BPEL'n'Aspects: Adapting service orchestration logic. In *Proceedings of ICWS 2009.*

Karastoyanova, D., Van Lessen, T., Nitzsche, J., Wetzstein, B., Wutke, D., & Leymann, F. (2007). Semantic service bus: Architecture and implementation of a next generation middleware. In *Proceedings of the 2nd International Workshop on Services Engineering (SEIW) 2007, in conjunction with ICDE 2007.*

Kaye, D. (2003). *Loosely coupled: The missing pieces of Web services.* RDS Press.

Keller, A., & Badonnel, R. (2004). Automating the provisioning of application services with the BPEL4WS workflow language. In *Proceedings of the 15th IFIP/IEEE International Workshop on Distributed Systems: Operations & Management (DSOM 2004)* (LNCS 3278). Berlin, Germany: Springer Verlag.

Khalaf, R., Karastoyanova, D., & Leymann, F. (2007). Pluggable framework for enabling the execution of extended BPEL behavior. In *Proceedings of the 3rd ICSOC International Workshop on Engineering Service-Oriented Application: Analysis, Design and Composition (WESOA 2007)*. New York: Springer.

Leymann, F. (2005). The (Service) Bus: Services penetrate everyday life. In *Proceedings of ICSOC'2005, Amsterdam, LNCS 3826 Springer-Verlag*.

Leymann, F. (2006). Choreography for the Grid: towards fitting BPEL to the resource framework: research articles. *Journal of Concurrency and Computation: Practice & Experience, 18*, 1201–1217. doi:10.1002/cpe.996

Leymann, F., & Roller, D. (1999). *Production workflow: Concepts and techniques*. Upper Saddle River, NJ: Prentice Hall PTR.

Mietzner, R., Karastoyanova, D., & Leymann, F. (2009). Business Grid: Combining Web services and the Grid. *In Special Issue of ToPNoC on Concurrency in Process-Aware Information Systems*. Berlin, Germany: Springer.

Mietzner, R., & Leymann, F. (2008). Towards provisioning the cloud: On the usage of multi-granularity flows and services to realize a unified provisioning infrastructure for SaaS applications. In *Proceedings of the International Congress on Services, SERVICES 2008*.

Nitzsche, J., van Lessen, T., Karastoyanova, D., & Leymann, F. (2008). BPEL^light. In *5th International Conference on Business Process Management (BPM 2007)*.

OASIS BPEL Technical Committee. (2008). Retrieved from http://www.oasis-open.org/committees/tc_home.php?wg_abbrev=wsbpel

OASIS Web services Resource Framework (WSRF) TC. (2008). Retrieved from http://www.oasis-open.org/committees/documents.php?wg_abbrev=wsrf

OASIS WS-BPEL Extension for People. *(BPEL-4People) Technical Committee*. (2008). Retrieved from http://www.oasis-open.org/committees/bpel4people/charter.php

OpenQRM. (2008). Retrieved from http://www.openqrm.org/

Slomiski, A. (2006). On using BPEL extensibility to implement OGSI and WSRF Grid workflows. *Concurrency and Computation, 18*, 1229–1241. doi:10.1002/cpe.1004

Taylor, I. J., et al. (2006). *Workflows for e-Science: Scientific Workflows for Grids*. Berlin, Germany: Springer.

Tuecke, S., et al. (2003). *Open Grid Services Infrastructure (OGSI) Version 1.0*. Global Grid Forum Draft Recommendation. *SimTech: Stuttgart Research Centre for Simulation Technology at the University of Stuttgart*. (n.d.). Retrieved from http://www.simtech.uni-stuttgart.de/

van der Aalst, W., & van Hee, K. (2002). *Workflow Management. Model, Methods and Systems*. Cambridge, MA: MIT Press.

van der Aalst, W. M. P., & Jablonski, S. (2000). Dealing with workflow change: identification of issues and solutions. *International Journal of Computer Systems Science and Engineering, 15*(5).

van Lessen, T., Nitzsche, J., Dimitrov, M., Konstantinov, M., Karastoyanova, D., & Cekov, L. (2007). An Execution Engine for Semantic Business Process. In *2nd International Workshop on Business Oriented Aspects concerning Semantics and Methodologies in Service-oriented Computing (SeMSoC), in conjunction with ICSOC 2007*.

Web services Notification. (2004). Retrieved from http://www-106.ibm.com/developerworks/library/specification/ws-notification/

Weerawarana, S., Curbera, F., Leymann, F., Storey, T., & Ferguson, D. F. (2005). *Web services Platform Architecture*. Upper Saddle River, NJ: Prentice Hall.

Chapter 28
A General Framework for the Modeling and Simulation of Grid and P2P Systems

Ciprian Dobre
University "Politehnica" of Bucharest, Romania

ABSTRACT

The field of modeling and simulation was long seen as a viable alternative to develop new algorithms and technologies and to enable the development of large-scale distributed systems, where analytical validations are prohibited by the nature of the encountered problems. The use of discrete-event simulators in the design and development of large scale distributed systems is appealing due to their efficiency and scalability. In this chapter we focus on the challenge to enable scalable, high-level, online simulation of applications, middleware, resources and networks to support scientific and systematic study of Grid and P2P applications and environments. We describe alternatives to designing and implementing simulators to be used in the validation of distributed systems, particularly Grid and P2Ps.

INTRODUCTION

In the broad area of distributed systems researchers often ask questions such as which scheduling algorithm is best suitable for deploying an application on a given Grid or which caching strategy serves better a community of users that are working in distributed data analysis. The answers to these questions can be obtained in several ways. A solution is to develop purely analytical or mathematical models, but this often leads to NP-complete problems, such as routing, partitioning or scheduling, for which no analytical solution can be found. Another solution consists in conducting live experiments. Unfortunately there are no standard approaches to conduct live experiments on large scale distributed systems. Real-world experiments can be time-intensive, since the execution of applications could last for hours, days, month or even more. In the same time real-world experiments can be labor-intensive, since the entire application needs to be built and functional. The choosing of the right experimental testbed is yet another problem. Real platforms can experience failures that may disrupt the experiments and the

DOI: 10.4018/978-1-61520-686-5.ch028

platform configurations may change drastically while experiments are being conducted. Real-life experiments in most cases are uncontrolled and unrepeatable. And to make things worse, live experiments are limited to testbeds (the particular capabilities of the testbed can affect the outcome) and the obtained results can not be reproduced by others (which is in fact the basis for scientific advances).

Because of such problems *simulation* can prove to be a more elegant solution to conduct experiments. This chapter focuses on the challenge to enable scalable, high-level, online simulation of applications, middleware, resources and networks to support scientific and systematic study of Grid and P2P applications and environments. The field of modeling and simulation was long-time seen as a viable alternative to develop new algorithms and technologies and to enable the development of large-scale distributed systems, where analytical validations are prohibited by the nature of the encountered problems. The use of discrete-event simulators in the design and development of large scale distributed systems is appealing due to their efficiency and scalability. Their core abstractions of process and event map neatly to the components and interactions of modern-day distributed systems and allow the design of realistic scenarios. Compared with the alternative of implementing a new technology directly in real-world to demonstrate its viability, the simulation of distributed systems is a far better alternative because it achieves faster validation results, minimizing the costs involved by the deployment process. Several key advantages make it attractive when compared with conducting live experiments: simulation assume that there is no need to build a real system, the simulated experiments are conducted in a controlled and repeatable fashion, the simulated scenarios have no limitations, and anyone can reproduce the obtained results.

Throughout this we describe new alternatives to designing and implementing simulators to be used in the validation of distributed system tech-

nologies, particularly Grid and P2P related. The chapter is organized as follows. We first present the characteristics of large scale distributed systems such as Grids and P2Ps. We present their specific requirements in terms of modeling and simulation. We then present a comparison study of the most important simulation projects involved in the modeling of distributed systems. The critical analysis is based on the categories proposed for an original taxonomy for comparing simulation instruments for Grid and P2P systems. The proposed taxonomy is particularly focused on the simulation of such systems, hence it introduces categories such as motivation and specific components that are particularly designed to proper categorize the special family of Grid and/or P2P simulation instruments.

BACKGROUND

Distributed systems have become very useful especially for complex scientific applications, involving the processing of very large data volumes, in a very short amount of time, as well as the storage of these data. Taking into account the tremendous popularity of complex distributed systems, favored by the rapid development of computing systems, high speed networks, and the Internet, it is clear that it is imperative, in order to achieve adequate performances in the utilization of these systems, to pick optimal architectures and solutions for designing and deploying distributed systems.

Currently there are many forms of distributed system architectures. Computing in the late 1990s has reached the state of Web-based distributed computing. A basis of this form of computing is distributed computing which is carried out on distributed computing systems. Distributed network systems are now used everywhere. As an example we can recall the well-known network file systems based on the client-server model, the Sun Microsoft's Network File System, known as NFS, that is still in use nowadays. Enterprise development technologies such as CORBA, Enterprise Java Beans, Java 2 Enterprise Edition, and DCOM, are all systems designed to enable the construction of distributed applications.

Several new innovations in networked computing have brought it into the eyes of the public and business, as well as academics. Various levels of hype have surrounded all these ideas at some point, but each of them is still relevant and they form the foundations of Grid computing. Among the first modern distributed architectures were the **cluster systems**. A cluster, a parallel or distributed system that consists of a collection of interconnected computers, is utilized as a single, unified computing resource. **Distributed computing** (or Internet computing) has been given much publicity by the SETI@Home project (Anderson, 2001). The project harnesses idle computing resources to analyze radio signals from space in the hope of finding messages from intelligent extraterrestrial life. The client software, which acts as a screensaver when the computer is not being used, fetches new data over the network, analyses it and sends the results back to the central server.

The **peer-to-peer** (P2P) networking model (Anderson, 2001) forms a completely decentralized system, where every host, or peer, has equal status to any other peer. P2P systems enable direct communication between any two symmetric peers. The most common types of P2P applications are file sharing, distributed computing and storage applications. Projects such as JXTA are developing P2P protocols to enable P2P applications to operate between anything from PCs to mobile devices. Many of the new generation file sharing applications use decentralized indexing servers, making them true P2P applications. Their architectures make it very hard to prosecute copyright violations by users, since no one has overall control of the system. Even though some companies now run legal music downloading services (like Apple's iTunes), other file sharing programs have found new ways around the law enforces,

using completely decentralized network and encrypted communication between nodes, giving anonymity to all users.

Grid computing is considered to be the next phase of distributed computing. It represents an evolving area of computing, where standards and technology are still being developed to enable this new paradigm. All over the world computational Grids are being constructed so that distributed resources can be aggregated and shared among different users and organizations. This development has been driven by the scale of many current and future scientific projects in which the amount of data produced and the computational resources required to analyze it are far greater than previously seen. With such requirements it is not possible to use traditional cluster computing or super-computing at a single location, and scientists are looking to link geographically distributed resources together to form Grids. The hype around Grid computing is not about replacing current technologies but harnessing them all together (cluster computing, web services, P2P, etc.) to work as one unified utility. Grid computing incorporates many of these technologies, together with their characteristics.

In the world of distributed computing Grid computing and P2P systems are currently seen as important new fields, distinguished from conventional distributed computing by their focus on large-scale resource sharing, innovative applications, and, in some cases, high-performance orientation. Today, more than ever, there has been an increased commercial interest and support for such systems. The recent advances in distributed technologies require more than ever the use of simulation for testing and validating solutions designed for such systems more rapidly and with minimal involved costs. Scheduling, data replication, network transfer technologies, are all very hot subjects today and we believe that in the future the interest in a generic simulation framework that can be used to conduct various modeling experiments in the field of distributed systems will be more increased than ever.

The design and optimization of large scale distributed systems require a realistic description and modeling of the data access patterns, the data flow across the local and wide area networks, and the scheduling and workload presented by hundreds of jobs running concurrently and exchanging very large amounts of data. They are semantically different from other distributed systems and therefore performance analysis through simulation requires careful (re)consideration. This thing is particularly difficult, sometimes even impossible, to be considered by anyone without the help of an adequate modeling application. The states of large scale distributed systems are influenced by many internal and external factors, making it impossible to design analytical solutions to predict their behavior. For such reasons the field of modeling and simulation is considered particularly useful for designing distributed systems technologies.

The age of the simulation field that address large scale distributed systems is relatively young. The first simulators were implemented in the late 90[s] (Bricks and MONARC were among the pioneers of the field). This is directly connected with the fact that Grid computing first appeared in 1998. The simulators for such systems are few and many concentrate on specific subjects, such as scheduling or data replication. They were built based on the needs of the scientists working on various Grid or P2P related projects. Most of them represent ad-hoc solutions, built in order to test the validity of a newly proposed technology. The complexity of such systems is one reason why simulators addressing this field are hard to be implemented with generality in mind. There are few simulators for large scale distributed systems that can be used to test a newly proposed scheduling algorithm, and in the same time to validate a new replication strategy and a novel data transfer protocols.

SPECIFIC REQUIREMENTS FOR THE MODELING OF DISTRIBUTED SYSTEMS

We now present the design considerations of simulation models designed for evaluating distributed systems solutions. Such models present special features, as they incorporate specific components and preserve characteristics necessary to design realistic simulation experiments of complex distributed system architectures, consisting of many resources and various technologies, working together to provide a common set of characteristics.

Distributed Systems and their Influence on Simulation Models

Simulation roughly consists of two stages: model development and experiments. In the first stage, a real-world system is formalized into a set of simulation models that not only characterize the relationships inherent in the system, either mathematically, logically, or symbolically, but also are recognizable and executable by computers. These simulation models are executed on computers in the second stage to run experiments and generate results that expose the system characteristics of interest. In order to be useful, a simulation model designed for evaluating large scale distributed systems should incorporate several components and characteristics that are specific to the real-world systems.

The original *distributed system* architecture consists of a collection of autonomous machines connected by communication networks and running software systems designed to produce an integrated and consistent computing environment. Distributed systems represent a solution to enable people to cooperate and coordinate their activities more effectively and efficiently. The key characteristics of a distributed system are: *resource sharing, openness, concurrency, scalability, fault-tolerance* and *transparency* (Coulouris, *et al*, 1994).

In a distributed system, the resources – hardware, software and data – can easily be shared among users. For example, a database server can be shared among a group of users. The *resource sharing* characteristic is ensured by the use of networking components connecting various resources. This characteristic is also important for a simulation model. An adequate model should incorporate a wide set of networking components and protocols to facilitate the modeling of data communication between distributed resources. The simulated entities, included in the model, should also easily share various resources (e.g., a database server could be modeled as being accessible to various tasks running in different locations).

The *openness* characteristic of a distributed system is related to specifying key software interfaces to the system and making them available to software developers so that the system can be extended in many ways. A modeling design preserves this characteristic by following an object-oriented programming approach. The user should also be presented with APIs for interfacing with existing simulated components. He should easily extend the modeling framework with its own modeling components. In addition, the simulated tasks should be able to access various modeling actors such as the networking stack, modeled database servers or processing units by using standard interfaces.

The processing *concurrency* can be achieved by sending requests to multiple machines connected by networks at the same time. For the simulation model this property is equivalent to many simulated processes competing for the same computational resources, as well as concurrent data transfers competing for the same networking resources. A simulation model should therefore incorporate special mechanisms to allow the modeling of concurrent data transfers and processes competing for the same resources. As an example, in MONARC concurrency is achieved using a specialized interrupt mechanism.

The *scalability* characteristic is important because a distributed system composed of a small number of machines should be easily extended to a large number of machines to increase the processing power. In order to preserve this property an adequate simulation model should consider the case of multiple resources connected by simulated networking entities. A modeled distributed system should, therefore, consist of many simulated machines, each composed of both computing and storage elements. A model should furthermore consider the case of a large number of simulated machines, and even allow the dynamical addition of many others. This could be accomplished using an object-oriented design for the simulation model, which could translate in allowing the addition of many instances into a simulation experiment. The number of simulated resources should be limited to only the amount of physical resources available in the system where the simulation is being executed. Conducting simulation experiments is, however, time consuming for several reasons. First, the design of sufficiently detailed models requires in depth modeling skills and usually extensive model development efforts. The availability of sophisticated modeling tools today significantly reduces development time by standardized model libraries and user friendly interfaces. Second, once a simulation model is specified, the simulation run can take exceedingly long to execute. This is due either to the objective of the simulation, or the nature of the simulated model. For statistical reasons it might for example be necessary to perform a whole series of simulation runs to establish the required confidence in the performance meters obtained by the simulation, or in other words make confidence intervals sufficiently small.

Possibilities to resolve these shortcomings can be found in several methods, one of which is the use of statistical knowledge to prune the number of required simulation runs. Statistical methods like variance reduction can be used to avoid the generation of "unnecessary" system evolutions. Statistical significance can be preserved with a smaller number of evolutions given the variance of a single random estimate can be reduced. Importance sampling methods can be effective in reducing computational efforts as well. Naturally, however, faster simulations can be obtained by using more computational resources, particularly multiple processors operating in parallel. It seems obvious, at least for simulation models reflecting real life distributed systems, consisting of components operating in parallel, that this inherent parallelism could be exploited to make better use of all physical computing resources more effectively. One way of copping up with the increasingly power demand coming from the simulation scenarios nowadays is to make use of more processor units, running on different architectures and dispersed around a larger area, in other words one way of keeping up with the simulating scenarios is to distribute the simulation application. Unfortunately, despite over two decades of research, the technology of distributed simulations has not significantly impressed the general simulation community (Fujimoto, 1993). Considerable efforts and expertise are still required to develop efficient simulation programs. There are no "golden rules" that a programmer can follow to guarantee an efficient program.

The *fault-tolerance* characteristic refers to the capability of distributed systems to detect and recover from faults occurring in various layers of the systems. The faults can be of various types, occurring in hardware or software; their occurrences can be transient or permanent. In distributed systems the failure of one machine can be tolerated, for example, if its functionality can be easily replaced by another redundant stand-by machine. So, machines connected by networks can be seen as redundant resources. A software system can be installed on multiple machines so that in the face of hardware faults or software failures, the faults or failures can be detected and tolerated by other machines. In order to validate fault-tolerance solutions for distributed systems a simulation model should at least incorporate the capability

to simulate faults in various levels (applications, processing units, network links), to make use of various fault detection schemes or fault recovery procedures. Considering for example the case of a scheduler allocating jobs to be executed on the underlying distributed resources of a modeled system, a possible fault recovery solution that might be evaluated with a well-designed simulation model consists in allowing the scheduling algorithm to take immediate actions to use the remaining running resources.

Distributed systems can provide many forms of *transparency* such as *location transparency*, which allows local and remote information to be accessed in a unified way, *failure transparency*, which enables the masking of failures automatically, and *replication transparency*, which allows duplicating software/data on multiple machines invisibly. In order to preserve such characteristics into the designed experiment, a simulation model could include several possible mechanisms. For example, in case of network failures, the model could include algorithms that would automatically reroute, if possible, the transiting networking transfers. In case of data handling services failing, replication mechanisms could be used to ensure data consistency. Automation mechanisms could also run in the simulation scenario to ensure data consistency among replicas, as well as to save the data for longer-term usage (write the data in simulated tape deposits for example). A simulated scheduling algorithm could ensure, using various mechanisms, the correct execution of simulated jobs in case of failures occurring in the underlying resources under failure-transparency environments.

A useful simulation model must incorporate many, if not all, of the components and characteristics of Grid and P2P systems. An important aspect of a distributed system is the architecture that defines the system components, specifying the purpose and function of these components, and indicating their interactions. The analysis of the Grid and P2P architectures is a crucial aspect

Table 1. The characteristics of distributed systems and their influence on a simulation model

Characteristic	Possible influence on a simulation model
Resource sharing	Use of networking components and data sharing entities
Openness	Inclusion of easily extendable object-oriented modeling infrastructure and standard interfaces that allow access to the fabric components inside a running simulation experiment
`Concurrency	Inclusion of mechanisms to model concurrent processes and networking transfers (possible based on some interrupt mechanisms)
Scalability	The adoption of an object-oriented simulation model and the use of advanced internal structures to make better use of available physical resources of the underlying stations
Fault-tolerance	Mechanisms to model the occurrence of faults and the possibility to include mechanisms to detect and recover from occurring faults
Transparency	Use of advanced routing algorithms, data replication algorithms, and scheduling algorithms to consider failure-transparency

for developing useful simulation models. The functional requirements of the architecture influence the decision process on what the simulation model should comprise in terms of simulation entities and what properties and characteristics must be preserved.

Characteristics of Large Scale Distributed Systems

Large scale distributed systems, such as Grids, are complex systems that present specific characteristics. According to Bote-Lorenzo (2002), the characteristics of a Grid system can be summarized into 10 main features. First of all, a grid must be able to deal with a number of resources ranging from just a few to millions. The *large scale* characteristic of a Grid brings up the very serious problem of avoiding potential performance degradation as the grid size increases. In order to consider this characteristic, a simulation framework for Grids should allow the modeling of scenarios consisting of a large number of nodes (ranging from few hundreds to thousands). The model should also allow the dynamical addition of others nodes into a running simulation experiment. This could be possible by following an object-oriented approach, allowing the addition of many instances of a simulated resource. In this sense, the simulation model should be scalable,

the number of resources being limited only by the amount of the physical resources of the system where the simulation is being executed. Careful consideration on the modeling engine implementation, the implementation of advanced structures and algorithms at this level, should allow the experimenting with scenarios involving a large number of resources.

Another characteristic of a Grid system is the *geographical distribution* of its resources. The resources pertaining to a grid may be located at distant places. A simulation model should consider that the underlying simulated system is composed of many resources organized into sites, each one being located in geographical distributed locations. The simulated networking stacks should also include special WAN components that connect such distributed farms of resources.

The *heterogeneity*, the vast range of technologies comprising a Grid system, both software and hardware, is one other characteristic. A Grid hosts both software and hardware resources, ranging from data, files, software components or programs to sensors, scientific instruments, display devices, computers, super-computers and networks. In order to allow the simulation of various hardware architectures, a simulation model should allow the grouping of different simulated components altogether. Advanced hardware architectures are, in this case, simulated by envisioning the site as particular hardware

Table 2. The influence of the Grid characteristics on a simulator

Grid characteristic	Influence on the simulation framework
Large scale	Careful design consideration for the simulation model: the use of advanced internal structure could allow the modeling of experiments with many incorporated resources.
Geographical distribution	The inclusion of sites, geographically distributed, in the simulation model. The sites should be connected by special WAN modeled links.
Heterogeneity	Use of various models for hardware components; software architectures captured using probability distributions.
Resource sharing	Represented in the network model.
Multiple administration	Inclusion of a distributed scheduler.
Resource coordination	Resource coordination mechanisms.
Dependable access	Implementation of DAG scheduling algorithms.
Consistent access	Use of standard methods to access the resources.
Pervasive access	The scheduling framework detecting faults and taking appropriate actions.

architecture, having communication channels that are simulated by using networking elements. The software heterogeneity should be modeled through the use of various probability distributions that should be included the simulated model. For example, in case of a data transfer application, the effective quality of the transfer is subject to many influences coming from the software itself or from the underlying networking resources. The actual random fluctuations appearing in the data transfers can be modeled by generating various interrupts in the transmission according to various probability distributions.

Resource sharing is one other characteristic. Resources in a Grid belong to many different organizations that allow other organizations (i.e. users) to access them. Resources, other then the local ones, can be used by applications, promoting efficiency and reducing costs. Yet, this is also one of the main stops in large-scale acceptance of Grid computing, due to problems such as server-hugging or enterprise politics. The simulation model should preserve this characteristic by adopting a mature networking model, with components that simulate the connectivity among the resources being modeled.

The resource sharing characteristic is related to the *multiple administrations* feature. Each organization may establish different security and administrative policies under which their owned resources can be accessed and used. As a result, the already challenging network security problem is complicated even more with the need of taking into account all different policies. This characteristic can translate in the simulation model in the adoption of a distributed scheduler component. Each regional center can contain a local scheduler, and each scheduler can use its own policy to handle the locally available resources.

One other characteristic is *resource coordination*. The resources of a Grid must be coordinated in order to provide aggregated computing capabilities. A Grid aggregates many resources and therefore provides an aggregation of the individual resources into a higher capacity virtual resource. The capability of individual resources is preserved. As a consequence, from a global standpoint the Grid enables running larger applications faster (aggregation capacity), while from a local standpoint the Grid enables running new applications. In a simulation model, if the resource coordination capability is considered, a data replication scenario, for example, can be better simulated by using many geographically disparate sites with multiple simulated database servers, thus making good use of the underlying Grid resources. Such resource coordination mechanisms should be part of an adequate simulation model.

One important aspect provided by any Grid system is the *transparent access*, meaning the user should see the Grid as a single virtual computer. The Grid provides single-sign-on access to any user accessing the system. The possibility to ensure transparency in the simulation model was described in the analysis of the distributed systems presented in the previous section.

A Grid must also assure *dependable access* or the guaranty to deliver services under established Quality of Service (QoS) requirements. The need for dependable service is fundamental since users require assurances that they will receive predictable, sustained and often high levels of performance. In order to preserve this characteristic, a simulation model should also allow the definition of QoS metrics. In order to impose such metrics various politics could be implemented in several components. For example, the scheduler algorithm should consider deadline restrictions, the restrictions that job definitions impose. They should also allow the modeling of DAG scheduling algorithms, where the submitted job could have dependencies specified. In order to preserve QoS requirements, a simulation model should also include a monitoring component that reports when problem appear. This monitoring capability could be implemented, for example, with the help of a resource catalogue.

According to the next characteristic, *consistent access*, a Grid must be constructed with standard services, protocols and interfaces, thus hiding the heterogeneity of the resources while allowing its scalability. Without such standards, application development and pervasive use would not be possible. Every resource being simulated should extend a specific object abstraction in order to preserve this characteristic. The simulation model should also provide standard methods to access the simulated resources.

Finally, *pervasive access* means that a Grid must grant access to available resources by adapting to a dynamic environment in which resources do fail. This does not imply that resources are ev-

erywhere or universally available but that the Grid must tailor its behavior as to extract the maximum performance from the available resources. In the presence of faults in a simulation experiment the scheduling algorithm could take appropriate actions to use the remaining resources. To this date, not many simulators for distributed systems allow the evaluation of fault-tolerance solutions.

The characteristics of the Grid systems must influence the development process of a simulation model specifically designed for Grid technologies. To summarize the specific elements of the simulation model that enables the correct modeling of a Grid environment we can refer to the study conducted in Bagchi (2005). As such, the author presents the features that must be implemented by a simulation model in order to allow the correct modeling of a Grid environment. The identified set of features consists of: *multi-tasking IT resources, job decomposition, task parallelization, heterogeneous resources, resource scheduling,* and *resource provisioning*.

The simulation model must incorporate processing units, database servers, network links, and data storage devices (*multi-tasking IT resources*). The modeled processing unit should consider the case of several tasks being concurrently processed by the resource. An interrupt mechanism could ensure, for example, the modeling of concurrency. In this case, the time needed to complete a task is proportional with the number of other competing tasks. A detailed simulation of the task management within each resource is far too time-consuming when considering Grid environments, with hundreds of resources simulated for the duration of weeks. Instead, when a new task is submitted to a resource, the simulation framework should perform a good approximation of the multi-tasking behavior by re-estimating the completion time of all tasks being processed by that resource.

A workload could be composed of several jobs (*job decomposition*), each one having multiple resource requirements. In this sense, a simulated application could be composed of several jobs, handling various actions with several resource requirements. A job can, for example, be programmed by the user to request data from a database server, to perform some computation using the obtained records and then send the results for further processing to another job. The tasks performed by a job can be correlated with the tasks performed by another one. The dependencies between the jobs can be specified in the form of DAG structures in the simulation model.

A job can be furthermore decomposed into several tasks, each one representing a single resource requirement within the job. Each task in a job may be parallelizable. In the simulation model this can be accomplished if considering a job as being composed of several parallel jobs, each one modeling the action of some task. A simulated job can start new simulated jobs, each one performing specific tasks. This, correlated with the job decomposition characteristic implemented using the DAG structures, can be used to handle the case of *task parallelization*.

Grid resources are *heterogeneous* by their nature. Therefore, the processing time of a task on a resource is subject to performance benchmarks. In the simulation model, the processing entities, as well as other simulated entities, must also be defined in terms of benchmarking units. The computation, data and network models should consider resources with various characteristics and their parameters be generically defined in order to simulate the heterogeneity of resources in the simulation experiments.

Also, a Grid simulator must be able to model *scheduling* policies used by resource brokers to determine on which resource a task will be executed. The simulation scheduler could provide a more advanced scheduling implementation, such as a meta-scheduler, allowing the execution the simulated jobs in a distributed manner, using all sites available. The meta-scheduler could also incorporate a wide-range of user-defined scheduling algorithms. Local scheduling is essential

for a Grid simulation experiments. In the same time, user-defined scheduling algorithms should be easily added in a simulation experiment.

A simulation model should also incorporate the ability to provision resources for processing particular types of tasks. The provisioning policies could be either calendar-based or based on a more dynamic policy. The simulation model should consider the existence of background jobs to handle the execution of specific resource provisioning tasks. Such jobs can be used in dependency with other simulated jobs. In addition, the database server can perform programmed actions, being modeled as a special task in the simulation model. It can simulate special operations such as data archiving on a calendar based designed policy. The automation of resource provision is particularly important to the simulation model because it can be used to experiment with various data replication algorithms and provide flexibility to the simulation scenarios.

Simulation of Complex Computing Models

The simulation of complex realistic computing scenarios presents several research challenges. Such challenges come from the need to simulate complex architectures such as Grids supporting large application requirements, or to realistically model distributed systems consisting of a great number of resources, where many jobs run concurrently, competing for tremendous amounts of processing power and data storage needs.

One objective of a simulation framework is to save valuable time in determining the optimal parameters and configuration of a large scale distributed system, answering important questions without resorting to trial and error with a real testbed. For example, the choice in the scheduling policy can have a dramatic effect on the job processing efficiency in various Grid systems. The choice of using a particular algorithm will affect not just the running of the submitted jobs, but also that of the system as a whole. The simulation model, with its presented characteristics, provides the means to test various resource selection policies, and measure the effect that they have on system performance.

The complexity of a simulation model results from many factors, including both non-technical and technical ones, but the most important one among them is unclear simulation objectives. In many cases, the same simulation objective can be achieved much more efficiently with a simplified model as opposed to a complex one. Hence, given a large, complex real system, it is important to develop the simulation model such that to contain the appropriate level of details to minimize the required computation, but in the same ensure its validity with respect to the simulation objective.

The need to incorporate adequate simplification techniques that preserve the properties of the system being modeled is better illustrated by the study presented in Riley (2002), following the ideas from Paxson & Floyd (1997). In their paper, the authors studied the feasibility of simulating the Internet. They tried to answer the question of how much computation, memory, and disk space is required to simulate a large networking system, consisting of hundreds of million of nodes. The study was conducted using a discrete event simulator and considered a conservative estimation of hosts, routers, links and traffic loads in Internet. The authors estimated that simulating an Internet-scale network for a single second generates $2.9 \cdot 10^{11}$ packet events, and needs 290.000 seconds to finish if a 1 GHz CPU is used. It also requires $2.9 \cdot 10^{14}$ bytes of memory, and $1.4 \cdot 10^{13}$ bytes of disk space for logging the simulation results. In addition, in order to gain more confidence in the results from a simulation, a long simulation run or many independent simulation runs are necessary; this can further prolong the whole execution time. All these lead to the conclusion that packet-oriented simulation of an Internet-scale network is a computationally prohibitive task. The same

conclusion can also be generalized to Grid and P2P systems. A high-granularity complete simulation of a world-wide Grid system is generally not feasible. In practice the simulation models are greatly simplified, using various techniques. The main idea is to try to reduce as much as possible the time needed to conduct the simulation experiment, possible by omitting in the model various uninteresting details of the real-world system or by making gross assumptions on the components being simulated.

The author in Frantz (1995) classified model simplification techniques, based on which components in the model are modified, into three categories: *boundary modification*, *behavior modification*, and *form modification*.

The *boundary modification* approach aims to reduce the input variable space. It is done by either delimiting the range of a particular input parameter or by minimizing the number of input parameters. The latter case conforms to the parsimonious modeling principle, which prefers compact models among those that produce equally accurate results. Model sensitivity analysis can be used to identify input variables that hardly affect the simulation results, and these variables can be eliminated from the simulation model. A simulation model can adopt this technique, for example, by minimizing the number of input parameters. The model could consider only the parameters that affect the simulation results. For example, the input for the processing power of the computation unit is not influenced by the background load of other possible existing processes. Instead the input can be represented by the SI95 performance benchmark unit, an average measure that can be obtained from real systems using different monitoring techniques. Background influences can still be modeled, if the experiment requires such behavior, by using jobs or tasks specifically designed for this purpose. The variations in load can be modeled using various mathematical distributions such that to obtain realistic simulation experiments. The network model also, in order to simplify the simulation conditions, might not consider implicitly background generated noises. Such background noises should be considered inside modeling only if explicitly required by the conditions imposed by the simulation experiment.

In case of *behavior modification* the states of a simulation model are aggregated, in either space or time domain. At some time point in the simulation, the system state can be decomposed into a vector of state variables. Those variables that are closely correlated with each other in certain ways can be aggregated and then replaced by a single one in the simplified model. This is particularly useful when the dynamics of each state variable before aggregation is of little interest to the modeler and the property of the merged variable after aggregation can be easily defined. Aggregation in time domain, sometimes, can also reduce the complexity of simulation models. In case of discrete event simulation the simulation events may be aggregated together when their occurrence times are considerably close and they are thus deemed to happen simultaneously. A simulation model might incorporate this technique, for example, in case of networking. When the dynamics of package flow is of no interest to the simulation experiment, the network model might consider the arrival of a single package to be aggregated into an entire stream. The case of package lost could be treated as if inserting more simulation delay, as experimented by the user in case of various data transferring protocols.

The *form modification* technique considers the simulation model as a "black-box". This means that the model generates results when inputs are fed into it. This approach replaces the original simulation model or submodel with a surrogate one that takes a different, but much simpler, form that does the same or approximate input-output transformation. This technique can take the form of metamodeling. It consists of seeking a simpler mathematical approximation that statistically approaches the original model or submodel. Such a mathematical model can be inferred from the input/

output data observed in real systems or deduced from the rules that govern the dynamics of real systems. A simulation model could incorporate various distributions in order to implement this simplification technique. For example, the job that is being processed can encounter various interferences, therefore its completion time is considered to be generated according to some distribution. The model does not really consider executing background jobs in this case; instead it sees the processing of the job as a black-box, approximating its input-output transformation. The mathematical distributions are frequently used in case of many simulation models designed for large-scale distributed systems simulations.

Even if the model simplification techniques offer the possibility of accelerating simulation of large, complex systems, they come at a price. When details are removed from a simulation model, its validity sometimes becomes doubtful. Therefore, it is always necessary to quantify loss of accuracy when a simplified model is adopted. A simulation framework could present validation in the form of series of testbeds measurements, comparison of resource utilization in real monitoring systems versus the observations drawn from the simulation experiments, or in the form of various queuing theory validation tests.

The simplifications techniques can also lead to less errors being introduced in the design process of the simulation model or in the implementation of the modeling framework. Architects often assume without proof that although their simulator may make inaccurate absolute performance predictions, it will still accurately predict architectural trends. A classic example of simulation errors is presented in Gibson (2000). The FLASH project at Standford was focusing on building large-scale shared-memory multiprocessors. They went from conception, to design, and in the end to actual hardware. Interesting to note is that during this process a total of six years were spent on simulation studies. When the project ended the authors went back and compared the simulation results with the real world results. Surprisingly, the simulations error was up to 30%. In the paper the author categorized the sources of errors into performance bugs, omission of large effects, and lack of sufficient detail. The conclusion of the authors is that a more complex simulator does not ensure better simulation. Surprisingly the simple simulators worked better than sophisticated ones, which were unstable and introduced more errors. What is vital in every simulator implementation in the end is the use of real world observations to tune or calibrate the simulator. The same conclusion is presented by the authors in Vincent (2007).

SIMULATION TOOLS FOR LARGE SCALE DISTRIBUTED SYSTEMS

This section reviews current and previous work in the field of modeling and simulation of large scale distributed systems. We propose a new taxonomy to analyze the most representative modeling instruments for such systems. Previous work has dealt with the more generic case of computing systems simulations, but we state that, based on their specific particularities, the simulators designed for such systems pose special characteristics that can only be highlighted using a specialized methodology. The proposed taxonomy considers both the design characteristics of the large scale distributed systems being simulated, and also the implementation properties of real-world simulation instruments. Based on the proposed taxonomy, we then analyze several simulations tools designed to model large scale distributed systems. We detail their motivations, principles, implementations and applications. We use the categories of the proposed taxonomy to emphasize the pros and cons of each of the surveyed instruments.

Related Work

There are two types of papers that deal with the analysis of various simulation tools for large scale distributed systems. We do not refer to the papers published by various authors in which they compare different existing simulation frameworks just to justify their own simulation tool. We found that, in most cases, these papers tend to be misleading, probably because of the subjectivity of their authors. We refer only to the category of papers that were published in order to objectively analyze and compare existing simulation tools.

Probably the most cited paper is Sulistio (2004). The authors analyzed various parallel and distributed systems simulation tools, proposing a taxonomy to categorize between the various existing modeling frameworks. We state that the taxonomy is appropriate for describing any simulation tool, but is inappropriate to completely describe simulators aiming, for example, at modeling Grid systems. The authors suggest, for example, that based on the purpose of the simulation one of the category according to which we can classify various simulator is the presence of physical time. This property indicates whether the simulation of a system encompasses the physical time factor. We argue that this category is obsolete in case of large scale distributed simulators. Time represents an inherent property in case of large scale distributed systems, and simulators designed for such systems always take this factor into consideration. For example, the networking traffic flow is an inherent time-based process, the job processing also.

Another property according to which the simulation tools can be classified is represented by the modeling framework. According to this taxonomy the simulation tools are categorized into entity-based and event-based. An entity-based modeling framework represents processes to be modeled as entities. Each entity performs its own tasks and communicates with other entities via messaging. In an event-based modeling framework, each task in a modeled process is activated via the arrival of some triggering events. We argue that in reality this category is inconclusive since all simulators that address Grid-related or P2P-related problems use both modeling frameworks. For example, the surveyed simulation tools use entities to simulate various components such as clusters, processing units, network elements, on which external tasks are running, yet they all use events to trigger the evolution of the simulated scenario being run.

In contrast with our proposed taxonomy, the one in Sulistio (2004) is not covering the motivation aspects behind various implementations of simulation tools. Because of the inherent complex structure of the distributed systems many simulators are more focused on some particular areas. Some modeling frameworks were designed specifically for testing various scheduling algorithms, while others target the validation of various data replication strategies. So the motivation behind various simulation tools represents an important aspect that, in our opinion, should be also included in the taxonomy.

In Sulistio (2004) the authors also surveyed various simulation tools and compare them according to their proposed taxonomy. Their survey does not stop to only distributed systems related simulation tools, but rather it is meant as a generic instrument to classify simulators from various computing fields, from communication protocols to Grids. The authors analyzed tools from the networking simulation domain and also from Grid simulation domain. We also include in our surveyed the instruments tested by their taxonomy: Bricks, SimGrid, GridSim. We added several other notorious simulators: OptorSim and MONARC 2. Also, unlike the authors, we consider some aspects such as performance of the execution of various simulation tools, an important aspect to consider, or the validation of the modeling scenarios. The performance consideration represents the effort done by the developers to include state-of-the-art structures in their simulator implementations. It is important if the simulated scenario runs in one

hour or one week. It is not less important for the end-user to have strong confidence in form of validation results of the simulator being used. As presented next, in fact, we found that in practice most of the surveyed simulation tools are not considering any of these two aspects.

Another related paper is Quetier (2005). The authors address some of the problems that we too observed in Sulistio (2004) such as validation and the presenting of the advancements in simulators (they add GangSim and OptorSim to the list of previously surveyed tools). The authors of this paper are not trying to compare the presented simulation tools. Rather, the paper presents only a survey of current trends in Grid simulation. The authors are not sketching any comparisons methods (except for a review of the validation studies carried out in case of the surveyed simulation tools) between the simulation tools. Unlike this paper, we do define means for comparing the various simulation tools, but we also update with the advancements in simulators.

A Taxonomy of Large Scale Distributed Systems Simulation

In this section we define the categories of a taxonomy to describe the most representative modeling instruments for large scale distributed systems. The definition of the taxonomy covers a set of proposed objectives. The taxonomy is as *intuitive* as possible. The taxonomy includes a small and comprehensive set of categories, making it *clear* and *comprising*. In the same time the chosen set of categories allow to differentiate between the most important simulators, thus providing a broad view of the instruments that a researcher can use. The accomplishment of this objective translates into the taxonomy being *usefully* as a methodology for testing the differences between various simulators and in the same time serve as a *guiding* tool for other tools to appear. These properties refer to the capability of the taxonomy to correctly emphasize the characteristics of various simulators, for the purpose of allowing the choosing of an appropriate modeling instrument that serves a specific analysis purpose. We designed the categories of the taxonomy based on an end-user perspective. A scientist confronted with the selection of an appropriate simulation instrument has to choose from several existing tools. He would then start by consulting existing surveys. The survey in Sulistio (2004) poses problems since it does not address issues such the motivation behind a simulation tool, it does not answer the question of which simulation tool would satisfy a proposed performance cost, or it does now reveals any validation considerations. These categories, along with several others, are important in analyzing the simulation tools, so our proposed taxonomy includes them as well.

The design of the taxonomy is based on the survey of the properties of several open-source simulation frameworks. The chosen open-source simulation frameworks best represent the latest research trends in modeling technologies, generally being implemented in various academic environments. We first categorized the simulation tools according to their scope. Many of the existing simulators for large scale distributed systems were implemented to model best only particular classes of problems. Some were implemented to simulate various scheduling algorithms and others were developed to simulate various data movement technologies. The limitations imposed by their considered simulation models originate from the complex structure of such systems.

In categorizing the various simulation tools we then looked at the approaches they adopted to simulate the various constituent components of a large scale distributed system. Of interest to our taxonomy were the adopted designs of the simulated hardware components (networks, processing nodes, cluster organizations, possible database units, etc.), and the simulated software components (schedulers, replication algorithms, data transfer algorithms, etc.). Some tools provide the possibility to integrate components defined by

a user when constructing a simulation scenario; others provide even the ability to integrate in the modeling framework real-life components. A special designed category of our taxonomy considers these aspects too.

Another aspect we considered was the internal design of the applications. We were particularly interested in how the simulator behaves, how it is internally implemented, or what it has to offer. These are details that may not be so obvious at first; some information can be obtained only after looking into more details at the source files, if provided, or by reading the materials published by the architects behind the various tools. The implementation details of a simulation tool constituted an important aspect, not only because only with this information an effective cost estimation can be computed prior to conduct a simulation study, but also because it may mean the difference between running the same simulation test during a period of two weeks or two hours. Various simulation tools are attacking the same problem, for instance simulating various scheduling algorithms, but which one is better to use is one problem that does not an contain an obvious answer. An interesting problem when comparing various simulation tools is validation. Assuming the simulation is executed and results are obtained what guarantees are there that the modeling framework provides correct validation results? This obvious problem is sometimes omitted in reality, with drastic repercussions on the value of the obtained conclusions.

The figure above summarizes our observations. The various properties of any simulator designed to handle technologies related to large scale distributed systems fall in two main categories: the *simulation taxonomy* and the *design taxonomy*. The simulation taxonomy analysis the simulation tools according to the adopted simulation models, while the design taxonomy categorizes the simulation tools according to their design and implementation.

The *simulation taxonomy* comprises five properties. *Motivation* indicates the major target

Figure 1. The categories of the taxonomy

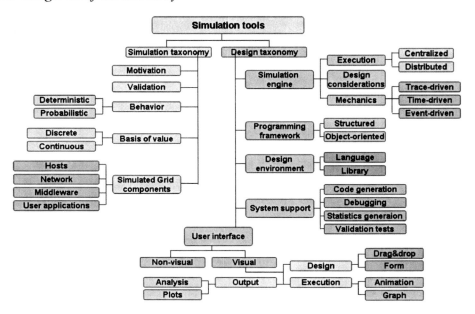

of a simulation tool. According to this taxonomy a modeling instrument can be used to study various data movement optimizations, to investigate scheduling algorithms, to evaluate replication solutions or to study a particular model of a Grid or P2P system. This category considers only the uppermost motivation. If, for example, we consider the case of a simulation tool designed specifically to study various scheduling algorithms, we can observe that in order to study such algorithms the simulator tool must also provide additional support, such as simulated underlying networks or processing nodes. If the underlying Grid components are also simulated then a scientist, with proper mediations, could also test various other scenarios such as different file replication algorithms (assuming the simulator includes the possibility to also simulate data warehouses). But generally such modifications require great amount of work, and, except for the cases when the original developers of a simulation tool redesigned it at some point to comprehend some different classes of Grid related problems, such developments are virtually non-existent. The majority of the Grid simulation projects were developed in the context

of the validation of the Large Hadron Collider (LHC) experiments in CERN and their proposed running conditions. For this reason we often see as possible motivation the categories identified by the authors of the taxonomy described in Venugopal (2006): Data Transport, Data Replication or Scheduling issues.

The *simulated components* taxonomy is important because it classifies simulators according to their capabilities to simulate the layers of the distributed architecture. This taxonomy defines the components of a distributed system, as modeled by the simulation systems. There are four types of components: hosts, network, middleware and user applications. It is very important to have a standardized, complete hierarchy of characteristics that are simulated for all four components of such systems. *Host characteristics* are used to describe the hosts within the distributed environments. Such hosts may contain computing, data storage, and other resources, grouped into single or distributed systems. In a simulation we are interested in the types of host resources capable of being modeled, their organization, as well as the characteristics that are considered for each type of resource. Examples of resource organization in simulation are the "central model" proposed by the Bricks project or the "tier model" proposed by the MONARC project. Of interest for this category are aspects such as how different simulators model the load of the computing nodes, the granularity of jobs being processed, the types of data storage facilities.

The *Network characteristics* category describes the network elements interconnecting hosts within simulated distributed environments. Among network elements there are routers, switches and other devices. This category considers both the types of network devices and the communication protocols that are considered by the various simulation models. The infrastructure communication protocols refers to lower-level protocols such as TCP, UDP, etc. as well as higher-level application protocols such as FTP, NFS, etc.. This category also considers the granularity of the simulation. The simulation of the network can model in detail the flow of each packet through the network, a time consuming operation that leads to better output results, or it can model only the flows of packets going from one end to another in the network. The *middleware characteristics* are used to describe the middleware layer within the simulated environments. Amongst simulated middleware elements this category describes components such as schedulers and various security enforcement components. This category analyses how the middleware system schedules the jobs for execution inside a Grid system, for example. The *user applications* characteristics are used to describe the user applications within the large scale distributed environment.

In classifying different simulation tools based on their capability to model various distributed resources it is important to consider the ability to easily incorporate components dynamically defined at the simulation runtime, for example by the user constructing the scenario experiment. The capability to incorporate new components is crucial in many cases because it's almost impos-

sible to provide the users with a complete set of predefined components to support all possible simulation scenarios. The vast majority of simulation tools provide this capability, but there are also exceptions (Bricks for example).

The *behavior taxonomy* classifies the simulators based on how the simulation proceeds. A deterministic simulation has no random events occurring, so repeating the same simulation will always return the same simulation results. In contrast, a probabilistic simulation has random events occurring, so repeating the same simulation often returns different simulation results.

Basis of value specifies the values that the simulation entities can contain. A discrete simulation has entities only possessing one of many values within a finite range, but a continuous simulation has entities possessing one of many values within a finite range.

The *Validation* category refers to the process of assuring that the conceptual model accurately represents the behavior of a real system. This category analysis the effort put in designing appropriate validation tests in case of each surveyed simulation project. This represents a measure of the reliability offered to the end-user running different modeling scenarios. The validation of the simulation results mainly consists in comparing the results of the simulator with the ones obtained analytically on a mathematically tractable problem or with the results obtained on a real testbed system. Validation is essentially a statistical problem because the number of performable experiments is limited and in general the magnitude of tolerable error depends on the type of obtained results. To this date only a few simulators present validation studies (Bricks, MONARC and SimGrid are such examples).

The *design taxonomy* categorizes simulation tools based on the provided components and features. Each simulation tool exploits a *simulation engine* to implement and execute the simulation model. Here execution refers to the capability of the simulators to make use of the underlying architectures. The authors in Sulistio (2004) see two modes of execution: serial and parallel. We argue that a better taxonomy should classify the simulation tools into centralized and distributed. Shared-memory parallel systems, comprising multiple processors, are becoming more and more accessible as home computing stations. In fact, a pure serial simulation execution, which would make use of only a single processor, can not be a reality when addressing the problem of simulating large scale distributed systems, which are highly complex and in which multiple tasks/jobs are inherently being simultaneous processed. The modern simulation tools make use of at least the threading mechanisms provided by the underlying operating system; they use every processor existing on the underlying computing station. The idea of addressing instead of parallel simulation the term distributed simulation comes back from the early paper of Chandy and Misra (Misra, 1986).

In this taxonomy the simulators designed to use only a single computing unit, no matter if the underlying processing architecture provides multiple processing cores, are called centralized simulators. The second category comprises the simulators designed to make use of multiple processor units, running on different architectures and dispersed around a larger area. There are no pure distributed simulators for modeling large scale distributed systems. The reason for this is that, despite over two decades of research, the technology of distributed simulations has not significantly impressed the general simulation community (Fujimoto, 1993). Considerable efforts and expertise are still required to develop efficient simulation programs.

A simulation tool advances the simulation based on the mechanics defined in the simulation engine. The existing literature divides the types of possible mechanic designs into three categories: the continuous, discrete-event and hybrid categories. In a continuous simulation state changes occur continuously across time. In a discrete-event simulation (DES) state changes

only occur at specific time intervals. Finally, a hybrid simulation comprises both continuous and discrete-event simulations. In case of modeling distributed systems the continuous category identifies the particular case of emulators. An emulator focuses on exact reproduction of external behavior, whilst a simulator concerns an abstract model of the system being simulated. While there are a number of particular good emulator projects for large scale distributed systems (MicroGrid, Grid eXplorer, etc.), we focus our analysis on simulators since their simpler models allow the better observation of the overall behavior of the analyzed system. For this reason we included in the proposed taxonomy only the category of discrete-event simulators.

The taxonomy distinguishes between the different types of discrete-event simulations. A discrete-event simulation adopts a queuing system where queues of events wait to be activated. A trace-driven DES proceeds by reading in a set of events that are collected independently from another environment and are suitable for modeling a system that has executed before in another environment. A time-driven DES advances by fixed time increments and is useful for modeling events that occur at regular time intervals. An event-driven DES advances by irregular time increments and is useful for modeling events that may occur at any time. An event-driven DES is more efficient than a time-driven DES since it does not step through regular time intervals when no event occurs.

The Design Considerations category considers aspects such as the queuing structures adopted in the design of the simulation engine for managing the event lists or the mapping of simulation jobs on physical threads or processes. These aspects, considered by the designers of the simulators, are important because they greatly influence the performance runtime and the capability to model systems consisting of many resources. A system using an $O(1)$ structure for the event list will behave better than another one using an O(log n) queuing structure. The time needed to run a complex simulation experiment can be quite huge when using the second queuing structure solutions, but the implementation of queuing solutions from the first category can take quite long and requires more time researching valuable results. Finding the best suitable queuing structure to be used for the simulation of large scale systems represents an active subject nowadays and this is demonstrated by the great number of papers being published on this subject. There is not a single unanimity accepted queuing structure that performs best when modeling distributed systems, they all tend to behave different depending on various parameters. However, the tree and bucket queuing solutions tend to perform better, according to several studies.

One other aspect to consider is the mapping of the simulation jobs on the underlying threads or processes. Reusing threads, using advanced mapping schemes in which multiple jobs can be simulated running in the same thread context, or any other aspect considered in this direction can yield higher simulation performances. This category considers the optimizations adopted in the design of the simulation engine to either improve the running performances or allow for advanced simulation models to be executed.

The Programming framework determines the programming paradigm that the user needs to be familiar with in order to use the simulation tool. A structured programming framework implements a top-down structured program design, with control passing down the modules in a hierarchy. An object-oriented programming framework expresses the program as a set of objects that communicate with one another to perform simulation tasks. The object-oriented framework is easier to create, maintain and reuse compared with the structured programming framework. SimGrid for example uses structured programming, while GridSim and MONARC 2 use the object-oriented programming.

The Design Environment categorizes the simulators based on the instruments provided to users to design experiments. A good design environment facilitates easy learning and fast usage. A language provides a set of defined constructs for the user to design simulation models. A library provides a set of routines to be used with a supporting programming language. A library-based simulation tool normally gives the user more flexibility in creating and controlling the simulation. An experienced user of the supporting programming language may fine-tune and optimize the simulation by exploiting certain libraries. A language-based simulation tool usually hides low-level implementation details from the user and thus provides less flexibility. Therefore, a language-based tool needs to provide a complete set of well-known constructs to ensure it supports the required level of flexibility. On the other hand, a language-based tool is often easier to learn and use since it is more high-level compared with a library-based tool.

The user interface determines how the user interacts with the simulation tool. A simulator can provide the end-user with an appropriate user interface. A visual user interface is preferred over a non-visual interface because graphical displays enable better interaction and they are easier to use and understand. A visual design interface allows the user to create a simulation model easier and faster compared with a non-visual interface, but the simulator that do provide this facility generally are restricting the types of simulation components that can be inserted in the modeling scene. Using a design interface the user can build the simulation model by dragging and dropping simulation objects and configuring the attributes and values (using forms for example). In contrast, a typical non-visual design interface requires the user to write programming code which requires more time and effort, but also extendibility support for the model. Examples of simulators providing visual design interfaces are GridSim and MONARC 2.

A visual execution interface provides a better

representation of the simulation process. The user can more easily observe and analyze the simulation experiment. Animations provide a good visualization and display the flow of the simulation. Graphs give the graphical version of statistical data captured from the simulation. Without a visual execution interface the user encounters difficulties in analyzing and understanding the simulation results based on huge amounts of statistics and events captured.

The visual output analyzer is probably the most important graphical tool a simulator could have. Generally a simulation generates huge amounts of data. The data is difficult to be analyzed using a pure text format. There are two important categories. The plots are the usual instruments used to represent the output data of the simulation in a graphical format that is more accessible to the end-user. Some tools provide high-level capabilities, being able to not only represent the data but also to analyze it and provide it in a modified and more meaningful way to the end-user. This category includes instruments such as 2D plots (bar graphs, scatter plots, contour maps) and 3D plots (such as surface rendering). The second category includes analysis of the original output results of the simulation, with possible comparison between different sets of results, often from different simulation runs. A simulation instrument that offers more visual capabilities to the end-user to better analyze the results of the simulation scenario is generally preferred by scientists. Interesting to note is that none of the surveyed tools provide a complete visual interface, consisting of all three categories depicted. Most tools have plans to incorporate a visual environment in the future to enable better usability, but implementing a good user interface is not trivial and requires lots of time and effort.

System support provides useful and ready-to-use features that help the user to build an accurate and successful simulation model. The code generation feature produces the resulting simulation code automatically for the user. This allows the user to create the simulation model using a high-level language or simpler visual user interface without worrying about writing complex program code. Debugging facilities enable the user to identify abnormalities and problems in the simulation model more easily and correct them. Statistics related to the simulation allow the user to analyze and justify the simulation model. Without a built-in statistics generation feature, the user needs to write extra separate modules to manually track the simulation execution. The validation test feature is able to help the user identify probable errors or inconsistencies in the simulation model, thus supporting more accurate simulations.

A Critical Analysis of Simulation Tools for Large Scale Systems

Using the categories of the proposed taxonomy, we present an analysis of the properties of seven representative modeling instruments for large scale distributed systems. This study is designed to present the most relevant work in the field of simulation of distributed systems, and to evaluate the capabilities of the presented taxonomy to correctly investigate the capabilities of various simulators designed for such systems.

Bricks, developed by the Tokyo Institute of Technology, in Japan, was the first simulation project developed to investigate different resource scheduling issues using modeling techniques. The Bricks simulation framework allows the simulation of various behaviors: resource scheduling algorithms, programming modules for scheduling, network topology of clients and servers in global computing systems, and processing schemes for networks and servers. In its latest versions Bricks was extended, in order to evaluate the performance of various Data Grid application scenarios, with replica and disk management simulation capabilities. Bricks uses a model which the authors call the "central model". In this simulation model it is assumed that all the jobs are processed at a single site. In contrast with the model, MONARC also proposed another simulation model, called the "tier model", in which jobs are processed according to their hierarchical levels. The tier model was assumed to be necessary due to limitations on the computational and storage resources that could be concentrated at a single site. As opposed to that Bricks is based upon the presumption that it is feasible to construct huge clusters with petascale online storage. This is in conformance with the Grid Datafarm project results that showed that large-scale storage clusters could be constructed feasibly by 2007.

OptorSim is a Data Grid simulator project being developed by the University of Glasgow, in Scotland. It was initially developed by a team of researchers working on the WorkPackage 2 of the European DataGrid project, which was responsible for replica management and optimization, and the emphasis is on this area. The objective of OptorSim is to investigate the stability and transient behavior of replication optimization methods. OptorSim adopts a Grid structure based on a simplification of the architecture proposed by the EU DataGrid project. According to this model the Grid consists of several sites, each of which may provide resources for submitted jobs. Given a Grid topology and resources, a set of jobs to be executed and an optimization strategy as input, OptorSim runs a number of Grid jobs on the simulated Grid. It provides a set of measurements which can be used to quantify the effectiveness of the optimization strategy under the considered conditions.

SimGrid, developed by the Laboratoire de l'Informatique du Parallélisme Ecole Normale Supérieure de Lyon, in France, and by the University of California at San Diego, in U.S.A, is a simulation toolkit that provides core functionalities for the evaluation of scheduling algorithms in distributed applications in a heterogeneous, computational distributed environment. SimGrid aims at providing the right model and level of abstraction for studying scheduling algorithms and generates correct and accurate simulation results. In its current form SimGrid can be used to simulate a single or multiple scheduling entities and timeshared systems operating in a Grid computing environment or to simulate distributed applications in the context of resource scheduling. SimGrid describes scheduling algorithms in terms of agent entities that make scheduling decisions. These agents interact by sending and receiving events via communication channels. SimGrid can be used to simulate compile time and running scheduling algorithms. In the first category, all scheduling decisions are taken before the execution. In the second category some decision are taken during the execution. In accordance with out proposed taxonomy, SimGrid does not provide any of the system support facilities as discussed in the taxonomy. A validation of SimGrid was presented in its very first paper (Casanova, 2001). The validation consisted in comparing the results of the simulator with the ones obtained analytically on a mathematically tractable scheduling problem. SimGrid is considered to be one of the most successfully simulation framework for Grid scheduling and this is demonstrated by the fact that it is used by a vast majority of users (e.g. SimGrid is used for educational purposes at the Ecole Normale Superieure de Lyon).

GridSim, developed by the University of Melbourne, in Australia, is a simulator developed by researchers from the Gridbus project to investigate effective resource allocation techniques based on computational economy. It allows simulation of entities in parallel and distributed computing systems-users, applications, resources, and resource brokers (schedulers) for design and evaluation of scheduling problems. It provides a comprehensive facility for creating different classes of heterogeneous resources that can be aggregated using resource brokers for solving compute and data intensive applications. GridSim supports modeling of heterogeneous computing resources (both time and space shared) from individual PCs to clusters, and various application domains from biomedical science to high energy physics. The focus is very much on scheduling and resource brokering. The GridSim toolkit can be used for modeling and simulation of application scheduling on various classes of parallel and distributed computing systems such as clusters, Grids, and P2P networks. GridSim focuses on Grid economy, where the scheduling involves the notions of producers (resource owners), consumers (end-users) and brokers discovering and allocating resources to users. Its design considers the existence of several brokers, which in SimGrid was introduced only since SimGrid2 (the Agents). GridSim is mainly used to study cost-time optimization algorithms for scheduling task farming applications on heterogeneous Grids, considering economy based distributed resource management, dealing with deadline and budget constraints. In some sense, GridSim is a higher-level simulator compared with SimGrid, which is basically designed to investigate interactions and interferences between scheduling decisions taken by distributed brokers.

The EDGSim simulation project, developed by the University College of London, was developed by Paul Crosby from the University College of London during its PhD as an instrument to model job and data flows around the European DataGrid framework. EDGSim was designed to simulate specifically the performance of the EU DataGrid and concentrates more on the optimization of scheduling algorithms. EDGSim is based on Ptolemy II, a simulator that can be used to simulate systems that comprise heterogeneous components and sub-components. The simulation tool provides a modeling of the flow of computational jobs, physics data and information around a computational grid based on the software being developed by the European Data Grid project. EDGSim uses a multi-tier simulation model.

ChicagoSim, developed by the University of Chicago, is a simulator developed by a team of researchers from the University of Chicago designed to investigate scheduling strategies in conjunction with data location. It is a modular and extensible discrete event Data Grid simulator built on top of the C-based simulation language Parsec. It is designed to investigate scheduling

strategies in conjunction with data location. Its architecture includes a configurable number of schedulers rather than one Resource Broker, for example. It also allows for data replication but with a "push" model in which, when a site contains a popular data file, it will replicate it to remote sites, rather than the "pull" model used in OptorSim. A distributed system in ChicagoSim is modeled as a collection of sites. Each site has a certain number of processors of equal capacity and limited storage.

The final simulation instruments analyzed is MONARC 2. Its simulation model is based on the characteristics of the LHC physics experiments, and is organized in the form of a hierarchy of different sites that are grouped into levels called tiers, mostly based on their resources. MONARC 2 is built based on a process oriented approach for discrete event simulation, which is well suited to describe concurrent running programs, network traffic as well as all the stochastic arrival patterns, specific for such type of simulation. Threaded objects or "Active Objects" (having an execution thread, program counter, stack...) allow a natural way to map the specific behavior of distributed data processing into the simulation program. In order to provide a realistic simulation, all the components of the system and their interactions were abstracted. The chosen model is equivalent to the simulated system in all the important aspects. A first set of components was created for describing the physical resources of the distributed system under simulation. The largest one is the regional center, which contains a farm of processing nodes (CPU units), database servers and mass storage units, as well as one or more local and wide area networks. Another set of components model the behavior of the applications and their interaction with users. Such components are the "Users" or "Activity" objects which are used to generate data processing jobs based on different scenarios. The job is another basic component, simulated with the aid of an active object, and scheduled for execution on a CPU unit by a "Job Scheduler" object.

These simulators include complex sets of wide-area, regional and local-area networks, and heterogeneous sets of compute – and data – servers. The surveyed Grid simulators were analyzed based on their properties and according to the proposed taxonomy. One key characteristic is the motivation driving their implementations. Because of the domain of large scale distributed computing, involving large systems with many jobs running concurrently in heterogeneous mediums, there are not too many simulators that address the general modeling of such systems. The analyzed simulators tend to narrow the range of simulation scenarios to specific subjects, such as scheduling or data replication. There is little room for designing simulations experiments designed to evaluate, for example, a new communication or data-transfer protocol for large scale distributed systems. In particular, this example can only be modeled by simulators such as MONARC 2 and GridSim, tools that incorporate advanced networking modeling stacks. The designs of the surveyed simulators allow only specific classes of problems to be modeled. Most simulators were developed as "ad-hoc" solutions to particular classes of problems. They came into existence as fast solutions to study problems related to particular subjects of interest. The simulation of distributed systems remains a relative young field of research, with only a decade of concrete results, motivated mainly by the needs of the researchers to study possible solutions to their daily problems.

Bricks was among the first simulators to address the field of large scale distributed computing. It was designed and implemented by a team also working on the Ninf project. The people from Ninf wanted an instrument so that they can test various scheduling algorithms and this is why they constructed Bricks. SimGrid was developed in the beginning in the Grid Research and Innovation (GRAIL) Laboratory at San Diego Supercomputing Center, the same team that also developed AppLes, a software environment for adaptively scheduling and deploying application. They needed to test first the algorithms they were going to implement in the AppLes scheduler and this is how they came up with SimGrid. GridSim is part of the larger Gridbus project developed in Australia. Gridbus develops Grid middleware technologies with particular accent on the development of a competitive economy-based Grid scheduler. In order to test their theories on the economy-based Grid scheduling concepts they needed a simulation framework and they constructed GridSim. The next two projects, OptorSim and EDGSim, were both specifically designed on the model of the European DataGrid architecture. In fact, OptorSim was developed as an instrument inside the EU DataGrid project's Data Management Work Package, WP2. The goal of this Work Package was to specify, develop, integrate and test tools and middleware infrastructure to coherently manage and share petabyte-scale information volumes in high-throughput production quality grid environments. OptorSim project was designed specifically for testing various optimization technologies to access data in Grid environments, as this was the objective of the Work Package.

EDGSim was developed by Paul Crosby during his PhD at the University College of London and addresses the problem of analyzing the large volumes of data produced by the HEP experiments and that are using, like OptorSim, the infrastructure provided by the European DataGrid. In USA another PhD student, Kavitha Ranganathan from University of Chicago, working under the supervision of Professor Ian Foster, was researching on data replication and job scheduling. The Chicago-Sim was a byproduct of her PhD research, meant to be a discrete event simulator for modeling large distributed communities.

The development of MONARC started in a period when there were not so many Grid simulation instruments available. In CERN a group of people initiated a project to explore computing models for the LHC projects. As part of this project, a simulator was developed to provide a realistic simulation of distributed computing systems with which different data processing architectures could be evaluated. The MONARC group intended and succeeded to make it as generic as possible, an instrument not limited to scheduling or data replication issues, but instead a tool that would be able to simulate any Grid problem that would arise, as new Grid technologies were constantly being developed and they needed to be able to validate their possible integration into various Grid frameworks.

The internal implementations of the surveyed simulators are closely related to their original motivations. Many simulation instruments were developed to validate scheduling related algorithms; modeling using appropriate simulation instruments was the only feasible solution for doing that (scheduling algorithms are generally NP problems). But the modalities in which various simulators deal with resource scheduling modeling in Grid systems are somewhat different, the various simulators giving a complementary approach solution to each others. Bricks is used in simulating client–server global computing systems that provide remote access to scientific libraries running on high-performance computers and is designed based on a centralized global scheduling methodology. GridSim is able to simulate different classes of heterogeneous resources for a large scale distributed environment that includes both time-based and space-based large-scale resources. It can also be used to simulate application schedulers for single or multiple administrative distributed computing domains such as clusters, P2Ps and Grids. SimGrid supports modeling of resources that are time-shared. The first version of SimGrid, SG, is limited to a single scheduling entity and time-shared system, so it is difficult to simulate multi-user systems in a distributed environment. Therefore, its new version of SimGrid, MSG, was introduced to enhance the low-level SG simulator so that multiple scheduling entities can be simulated.

Like SimGrid, GridSim is a simulator that can

be used to investigate scheduling issues in Grids. GridSim was proposed and designed after SimGrid. Its motivations are quite similar. One main difference concerns its focus on Grid economy, where the scheduling involves the notions of producers (resource owners), consumers (end-users) and brokers discovering and allocating resources to users. Both SimGrid and GridSim consider the existence of distributed brokers (called Agents in SimGrid). GridSim is mainly used to study cost-time optimization algorithms for scheduling task farming applications on heterogeneous Grids, considering economy based distributed resource management, dealing with deadline and budget constraints. In some sense, GridSim is a higher-level simulator compared with SimGrid, which is basically designed to investigate interactions and interferences between scheduling decisions taken by distributed brokers.

The simulation of algorithms for data replication is a subject that is addressed by several of the analyzed simulators. OptorSim and MONARC 2 are the two simulators that include infrastructures for automated replication and replica optimization, both including distributed management components, but with less sophistication in the case of the latter simulation framework.

An important aspect considered in the simulation is the networking layer. Our proposed taxonomy includes this as a special category to compare simulation instruments. All simulators model this underlying network infrastructure, with some having even the ability to simulate realistic experiments by using background traffic. Bricks is able to specify a network topology, bandwidth, throughput and variance of the throughput over time. The background traffic functionality is modeled by using a probabilistic distribution, which is similar to the one found in GridSim. SimGrid has a good network infrastructure that supports TCP transport protocol for a reliable service. It also models background traffic by reading from a trace file generated by NWS. However, SimGrid does not make any distinction between a job computation and a data transfer, since they are modeled as a resource performing a specific task. Therefore, it does not support data packetization. In addition, requesting network status functionalities during runtime in SimGrid are limited to latency and bandwidth of a link. In contrast, GridSim reports more network information than SimGrid, but in a more primitive fashion without the support of an intuitive graphical instrument. OptorSim has a very simple network infrastructure compared to other simulation tools, since it does not support routing, transport protocol or data packetization.

The surveyed simulation tools were analyzed in many papers, particularly in terms of simulations results. OptorSim for example was used

to accurately simulate the behavior of the LCG Data Grid architectures as of 2004 and then of 2008, using the exact conditions described in the computing model documents of the four LHC experiments. The experiments tested various replication strategies and their obtained results prove to be vary important for the experiments that are about to start in CERN. MONARC 2 was used to test various scheduling algorithms, data transport algorithms and infrastructures, data transfer protocols, replication algorithms, all with interesting results that were used in real-world. There are some interesting simulations done using EDGSim. One such simulation showed that data location was important in the scheduling

Table 3. Design comparison of surveyed Grid simulation projects

No.	Simulation tool	Motivation	Basis of value	Simulated Grid components
1	**Bricks**	Resource scheduling in Grid systems	Discrete	Client-Server components organized in a central model; Servers and networking elements modeled as queuing systems; Scheduling Unit as the central simulation component.
2	**OptorSim**	Resource scheduling; Data replication strategies	Discrete	Grid sites composed of Computing Elements and Storage Elements; Computing Elements run one job at a time; Complex network model but lack routing, data transport, packetization; GSs with modeled Resource Broker, Replica Manager and Replica Optimiser.
3	**SimGrid**	Resource scheduling	Discrete	Scheduling tasks; Resource objects: modeled hosts and network links; Grid model can be obtained from traces (ENV and NWS are supported).
4	**GridSim**	Resource scheduling; Simplistic data replication	Discrete	The modeling systems is composed of users, brokers and resources; Both Computational and Data Grids are supported by the simulation model; Networking model takes into consideration QoS, background traffic; Well suited for algorithms designed for Nimrod-G.−
5	**EDGSIM**	Resource Scheduling	Continuous	Jobs submitted using appropriate User Interface; Resource Broker programmed with various Scheduling algorithms; Replica Catalog mapping logical and physical file names; Compute Element models the computation Resource of the Grid; The network model is simple, without considering low-level functionality. −
6	**ChicagoSim**	Resource scheduling; Data replication strategies	Discrete	Three modeled components: the site, the network and the driver; Replica management is carried out at local level; The modeled Grid includes any number of external schedulers, whilst the managing of the files is done locally by a dataset scheduler; Support for modeling various scheduling algorithms and various replica methods. −
7	**MONARC 2**	Generic Grid simulator	Discrete	Processing units, Data Storage, farms, networking, HEP components; Support for the modeling of scheduling algorithms, replica management, networking procedures, etc. Strong support for modeling generic Grid architectures. −

Table 4.

No.	Validation	Execution	User interface	Programming framework	Design environment	System support
1	Performed by replacing the Predictor with NWS	Centralized	Non-visual	Object-oriented	Language	Statistics generation
2	Degenerate tests, fixed values, internal validity	Centralized	Animation	Object-oriented	Library	N/A
3	Fixed values	Centralized	Graphical result analysis	Structured	Library and Language	N/A
4	N/A	Centralized and Distributed	Form	Object-oriented	Library	Code generation Statistics generation
5	N/A	Centralized	Drag-drop, form, graph	Object-oriented	Library and Language	Code generation, debugging, statistics generation
6	N/A	Centralized	Non-visual	Object-oriented	Language	N/A
7	Model Validation Monitored resource utilization vs simulated observations Queuing theory tests	Centralized	Animation Graphical result analysis	Object-oriented	Library	Debugging

decision, but during that particular simulation it is interesting to note that no replication of data was taken into account. A similar simulation was done using MONARC 2, but the data replication was taken into account which led to somewhat different results.

A summary of the capabilities of the surveyed simulation instruments according to the proposed taxonomy is proposed in the following table. The evaluation of the analyzed simulators was mainly based on three criteria: (1) the ability to handle basic Grid functionalities; (2) the ability to schedule compute- and/or data-intensive jobs; and (3) the underlying network infrastructure.

The critical analysis of the surveyed simulators reveals the motivations, principles, implementations and applications of the instruments. The analysis, based on the categories of the taxonomy presented in the previous section, describes the differences between the tools in terms of modeling, implementation and design. The analysis highlighted the specific characteristics of each surveyed instrument, from the design of the simulation model or internal simulation properties

to its implementation. There are advantages and disadvantages with each of the surveyed simulation tools. Interesting enough, even if many of them attack similar problems, being driven by comparable motivations, the analyzed simulators give a complementary approach to each others, allowing exploration of different areas of parameter space. Although the use of a particular simulator depends very much on the scope of the simulation being conducted and the skills of the user, they all cover important aspects of distributed systems, allowing exploration of different areas of parameter space.

FUTURE TRENDS

Large scale distributed systems are today regarded as the solution to developing increasingly large computing applications, designed to answer many of the problems of humanity. Commercially, large scale distributed systems are also becoming more and more appealing and this is reflected in the increasingly interest in the development of such systems coming from major industry players such as IBM, Oracle, Microsoft and many others.

The development of solutions designed for large scale distributed systems, either applications running on top of them or technologies designed to help them, is facilitated by the use of adequate simulation instruments. However, today many of the simulators existing today are too focused on specific technologies, lacking the capability to model generic distributed systems. They do not include all the components and characteristics specific to such systems, leaving the user with the problem of implementing its own solutions on top simulation model. This translates into time and effort and is a reason why many prefer to implement a newly designed technology directly in real-world and evaluate its behavior at runtime.

In the future we believe this lack of generality in simulation model will be increasingly reduced, as designers start to invest more effort into providing more complete modeling solutions. Simulators such MONARC 2 and ChicagoSim already started this trend. Users already see the potential of such simulators. As a consequence, MONARC 2 was already used to evaluate the specific behavior of the LHC experiments (Legrand, 2005), providing valuable information without the need to implement the system in real-world. The experiment tested the behavior of the Tier architecture envisioned by the two largest LHC experiments, CMS and ATLAS. The obtained results indicated the role of using a data replication agent for the intelligent transferring of the produced data. The obtained results also showed that the existing capacity of 2.5 Gbps was not sufficient and, in fact, not far afterwards the link was upgraded to a current 30 Gbps. Other simulators, such as GridSim, SimGrid, OptorSim and many others also are well underway to extend their simulation models to be more generically and address a wider set of possible simulation experiments.

Another problem with existing simulators for large scale distributed systems consists in the lack of evaluation results. A scientist wanting to use a simulator to evaluate a specific technology needs to have increased confidence in the obtained results. He needs evidence that the obtained results also are valid in real-world. Many of the existing simulators designed for large scale distributed systems do not present confidence because they lack proof of their validity. This is due to the nature of the large scale distributed systems, for which analytical models to be compared against the simulation models are hard to design. However, evaluation proof can be obtained in several ways. For example, a well-design simulator must present comparisons between experiments modeling small distributed systems against equivalent real-world testbeds. The comparison between the results obtained in simulation experiments and the monitored parameters of a real-world testbed should be made at least for the networking protocols, for the computing nodes and the storage facilities. If this simplified form of evaluation is conducted for each of the simulated component a general conclusion can be drawn, with higher confidence, for the entire simulation model. Another mechanism designed to facilitate the evaluation of the simulation models consists in the use of queuing theory. The formalism provided by the queuing models is important for the definition and validation of the simulation stochastic models. They provide an analytical model to the problem of testing the randomness introduced by various mathematical distributions. For example, in the simulation of network traffic pattern, queuing models are generally used to describe traffic generation, flows of the transmission and many intrusive problems related with the communication systems.

Another trend relates to the need to model very large distributed systems, consisting of a great number of resources. Many of today's simulators lack the capability to simulate large distributed systems because their simulation engines are limited to the physical resources of the workstations where the experiments are being executed. Today many researchers are interesting in finding solutions to facilitate the simulation of large scale distributed systems. The simulation engine can be optimized, in order to facilitate the evaluation of large scale distributed systems experiments, by using advanced priority queuing structures for the simulation events, by optimizing the way in which simulated entities are being scheduled in simulation for execution, by using various simplifications mechanisms or by using the underlying physical distributed resources of clusters of nodes.

With the advent of large scale distributed systems, today more than ever scientists are looking into simulation as the possible today to answer faster many of the faced problems. However, in order to be useful, a simulator must include solutions to be generic, to present evaluation capabilities (a high confidence) and allow scalability.

CONCLUSION AND OPEN ISSUES

In this chapter we described new alternatives to designing and implementing simulators to be used in the validation of distributed system technologies, particularly Grid and P2P related. We presented the challenges and gave original solutions to the problem of enabling scalable, high-level, online simulation of applications, middleware, resources and networks to support scientific and systematic study of grid applications and environments. We described new alternatives to modeling, designing and implementing simulation instruments for distributed system technologies. Such systems consist of many resources and various technologies, ranging from data transferring to scheduling and data replication, with resources working together to provide a common set of characteristics. Therefore, in order to be useful, a simulation model must preserve several characteristics and include a wide range of possible modeled entities.

We first presented the characteristics of large scale distributed systems such as Grids and P2Ps and their influences in terms of modeling and simulation. We presented several considerations

of simulation models designed for evaluating distributed systems solutions. The identified possible influence can help simulation model designers in building correct generic instruments that can be used to model a wider range of large scale distributed systems. Such generic models must present special features, as, in order to be useful, they incorporate specific components and preserve characteristics necessary to design realistic simulation experiments of complex distributed system architectures, consisting of many resources and various technologies, working together to provide a common set of characteristics.

We then presented a comparison study of the most important simulation projects involved in the modeling of distributed systems. We showed how they relate and differ, their advantages and disadvantages. We demonstrated that, although the use of a particular simulation instrument depends very much on the scope of the simulation being conducted and the skills of the user, they all cover important aspects of distributed systems, allowing exploration of different areas of parameter space.

The critical analysis is based on the categories proposed for an original taxonomy for comparing simulation instruments for Grid and P2P systems. We needed a standardized taxonomic system and, after analyzing the existing work on this subject, we concluded that all existing taxonomies are either too generic or do not consider important characteristics, therefore are not able to sustain a correct comparison. The proposed taxonomy is particularly focused on the simulation of such systems, hence it introduces categories such as motivation and specific components that are particularly designed to proper categorize the special family of Grid and/or P2P simulation instruments.

REFERENCES

Anderson, D. (2001). SETI@Home. *Peer-To-Peer: Harnessing the benefits of a disruptive technology* (pp. 67-77). Sebastopol, CA: O'Reilly.

Bagchi, S. (2005). Simulation of Grid computing infrastructures: Challenges and solutions. *Winter Simulation Conference* (pp. 1773-1780). New York: ACM.

Bote-Lorenzo, M., Dimitriadis, Y., & Gomez-Sanchez, E. (2002). *Grid characteristics and uses: a grid definition*. Technical Report CICYT, Univ. of Valladolid, Spain.

Casanova, H. (2001). Simgrid: a toolkit for the simulation of application scheduling. In *The IEEE International Symposium on Cluster Computing and the Grid (CCGrid'01)* (pp. 430-437). New York: IEEE/ACM.

Coulouris, G., Dollimore, J., & Kindberg, T. (1994). *Distributed systems – Concepts and design*. Reading, MA: Addison-Wesley.

Frantz, F. K. (1995). A taxonomy of model abstraction techniques. In *The 1995 Winter Simulation Conference* (pp. 1413-1420).

Fujimoto, R. M. (1993). Parallel discrete event simulation: Will the field survive? *ORSA Journal on Computing, 5*(3), 213–230.

Gibson, W. (2000). FLASH vs (Simulated) FLASH: Closing the simulation loop. In *ACM Transactions on Modelling and Computer Simulation* (pp. 49-58). New York: ACM.

Legrand, I. C., Dobre, C., Voicu, R., Stratan, C., Cirstoiu, C., & Musat, L. (2005). A simulation study for T0/T1 data replication and production activities. In *The 15th International Conference on Control Systems and Computer Science*.

Misra, J. (1986). Distributed discrete-event simulation. *ACM Computing Surveys, 18*(1), 39–65. doi:10.1145/6462.6485

Paxson, V., & Floyd, S. (1997). Why we don't know how to simulate the Internet. In *The 29th Conference on Winter Simulation* (pp. 1037-1044). Washington, DC: IEEE Computer Society.

Quetier, B., & Capello, F. (2005). *A survey of Grid research tools: Simulators, emulators and real life platforms*. IMACS Survey.

Riley, G. F., & Ammar, M. H. (2002). Simulating large networks – How big is big enough? In *The First International Conference on Grand Challenges for Modelling and Simulation*.

Sulistio, A., Yeo, C. S., & Buyya, R. (2004). A taxonomy of computer-based simulations and its mapping to parallel and distributed systems simulation tools. *Software, Practice & Experience, 34*(7), 653–673. doi:10.1002/spe.585

Venugopal, S., Buyya, R., & Ramamohanaro, K. (2006). A taxonomy of data Grids for distributed data sharing, management and processing. *ACM Computing Surveys, 38*(1), 1–53. doi:10.1145/1132952.1132955

Vincent, J.-M., & Legrand, A. (2007). *Discrete event simulation*. Presentation for Laboratory ID-IMAG, France.

Chapter 29
Grid Service Level Agreements Using Financial Risk Analysis Techniques

Bin Li
University of Surrey, UK

Lee Gillam
University of Surrey, UK

ABSTRACT

Grid computing continues to hold promise for the high-availability of a wide range of computational systems and techniques. It is suggested that Grids will attain greater acceptance by a larger audience of commercial end-users if binding Service Level Agreements (SLAs) are provided. We discuss Grid commoditization, and in particular the use of Grid technologies for certain kinds of financial risk analysis where both data and computation requirements can be substantial. The nature of such analysis, and the need for it to run to completion, suggests the need to guarantee availability and capability in the underlying Grid infrastructure. This further suggests that it is necessary to be able to evaluate the infrastructure in relation both to historic analysis and to the needs of a specific analysis. Our aim, then, becomes one of predicting availability and capability, essentially introducing risk analysis for Grids. Prediction, quantification of risk, and consideration of liability in case of failure, are considered essential for the future provision of Grid Economics – specifically, relating to the provision of SLAs through resource brokers, and comparable to markets in other commodities – but perhaps also more widely applicable to the configuration and management of related architectures such as those of Peer-to-Peer (P2P) and Cloud Computing systems. The authors explore and evaluate some of the factors required for the automatic construction of SLAs, with broad consideration for Financial Risk and the potential formulation of a Grid Economy as a commodity market, which may in future involve the trading and hedging of risk, options, futures and structured products.

DOI: 10.4018/978-1-61520-686-5.ch029

INTRODUCTION

Grid computing has emerged through consideration of secure networked availability of high end computer systems for relatively complex applications, and is reportedly in use in a wide variety of scientific and industrial pursuits. Commercial Grid systems, utility computing, and computing "in the Cloud" are all infrastructural considerations for businesses, and perhaps universities and other academic endeavours, seeking to reduce the costs of their infrastructures. These Grids, Utilities and Clouds can reportedly help organizations to offset environmental impacts and legal requirements relating to the manufacture, delivery, real estate, power and cooling, and subsequent recycling or disposal of the hardware itself. Furthermore, costs relating to ongoing maintenance and software licensing may also be mitigated to some extent. Certain organizations and individuals are variously willing to pay for the use of different forms of commoditized computer systems variously described as kinds of service, for example Software as a Service (SaaS), Platform as a Service (PaaS), Infrastructure as a Service (IaaS) and so on. A number of major IT providers have infrastructural support for SaaS, PaaS and their brethren, and allocate processor hours and storage in managed facilities at fixed prices. The notion, then, is that this enables buyers to focus on the outcomes not the infrastructure, and allows them to rapidly construct applications without entering into procurement and related installation activities from the outset.

To name a few, companies such as HP, Amazon, Google, Sun, Microsoft and IBM already offer or are beginning to promise some form of commoditized servers and pricing models for their Grids, Utilities, and Clouds. These can be used by organizations: (i) directly, for example for running various business services or simulations; (ii) as part of the external-facing business activity, such as supporting a website; (iii) repackaged in some form where a service is sold on to a customer, for example with a relatively simple business model in which some SaaS is built over an infrastructure with a price to the customer that encompasses the cost of the infrastructure. Effective price-performance is going to be a key decision factor in the use of such resources. And yet, commoditization does not necessarily enable the end user to undertake a specific analysis with particular requirements at a given time, to obtain the best price or margin against this analysis, or to manage the risk of the analysis failing and being able to re-run this within limited time. For some applications, the result of analysis may be required at a specific time, beyond which the opportunity to be gained from the analysis is lost. Lacking such assurances of availability, reliability, and, perhaps, liability, is likely to limit numbers of potential end-users. Indeed, a number of Grid Economics researchers have previously suggested that Grids will only be able to attain greater acceptance by a larger audience of commercial end-users if binding Service Level Agreements (SLAs) are provided. This could well be true for Utilities, Clouds, and any other future labelling of computing provision.

The financial sector appears to be one of the principal potential users of substantial commoditized computation, particularly for pricing models and portfolio risk management. However, the limited commercial adoption reported of commoditized infrastructures by the financial sector, preferring instead to maintain bespoke infrastructure with a variety of concomitant costs and related overheads, may suggest that, at minimum, the lack of assurances of availability, reliability and liability may contribute to the apparent lack of adoption of these infrastructures for such use.

Our aim is to support the adoption of such infrastructures by predicting availability and providing for liability through the consideration of risk analysis for Grids. Prediction, quantification of risk, and consideration of liability in case of failure, are considered essential for the future provision of Grid Economics – specifically, relating to the provision of SLAs through resource brokers, and comparable to markets in other commodities – but perhaps also more widely applicable to the configuration and management of related architectures such as those of P2P systems. Much of the literature to date provides a largely theoretical view of Grid Economics, with limited consideration of data analysis. Uncertainty regarding availability of Grid resources, and the ability to monitor resource status so as to predict future availability, provides the major impetus for our current work. From our explorations in financial risk management, and inspired by Kenyon and Cheliotis (2002, 2003), we are now developing an understanding of how to construct risk-balanced portfolios of Grid resources to consider possible formulations of the Grid Economy. Our initial work in financial risk was geared towards greater understanding of risk and its analysis within increasingly complex financial products and markets, to provide for a service-based Financial Grid. In previous work, we have discussed a Financial Grid and sentiment analysis of financial news texts in such an environment (Gillam and Ahmad 2005; Gillam, Ahmad and Dear 2005), combining numeric and textual data to determine whether texts are causal or indicative of market movements. All such analyses place significant demands on available resources, and it is typical to assume availability at any given time; continued use of these applications also provides substantial opportunities for collecting, and simulating, data relating to their execution. Such a Financial Grid must provide accessible algorithms, but it must also make available the requisite computational power at the right time, and execution data may assist here. In a sense, we are focusing on the ability to predict (risks of resource availability for) the ability to predict (risks on financial investments). Risk, here, is the probability of a loss and usually presented in financial applications in monetary terms but may have a different presentation in an SLA.

In this paper, we discuss considerations for the development of the Grid Economy, and how we are working towards an understanding of Grid Economics, in terms of ensuring availability, capability and liability in relation to financial applications. Our considerations may have implications for infrastructures other than Grids, for example incentivized or reward-based Peer-to-Peer (P2P) systems, Cloud Computing environments, and various related kinds of network economics. We are interested in which kinds of financial risk analysis may be applicable for predicting availability and capability, and considering how liability might be formulated. Current research has tended towards focus on SLAs in Grid Economies that involve planning-based systems, which makes an assumption that resources can be reserved with relative predictability. There is little in the literature relating to SLAs for queuing-based systems in which a balance is attempted amongst users for tasks of unknown duration with some, but largely limited, specifications of requirements for the analysis. It is with a Grid Economy involving queue-based systems that we are concerned.

We report initially on the development of Grid-based financial services for calculating portfolio Value at Risk (VaR). In particular, we demonstrate how commonality across three approaches for calculating VaR, characterized by Best (1998), enables us to reuse the Historical analysis and Covariance analysis techniques as parts of a Monte Carlo Simulation technique. We next show typical performance for the Monte Carlo Simulation with different considerations for parallelism. This produces a different set of expectations for analysis in the infrastructure: the computational requirements will vary according to parallelization configured for the number of required simulations, with optimal performance often obtained from some compromise over simulations per node. We discuss implementation for portfolio VaR using the queuing-based system Condor, and monitor resource use during program execution to try to characterize the application and how the infrastructure "reacts" to it. Here, convergence between approaches for computation of risk in portfolios of option-free equities enable us to evaluate our implementation and establish and mitigate performance issues relating to balancing computational speed with calculation accuracy. We next consider how portfolio risk computations may be applied to the construction of various risk-quantified portfolios of computational resources in the UK's National Grid Service (NGS), and how these may be formed into tranches that align availability risk with liability of failure. More complex, structured, investment products such as collateralized debt obligations (CDOs) provide useful points of inspiration for such work. We discuss, finally, how extending specific considerations of financial modelling to Grid Economics may provide for markets for a range computational resources and services, with considerations for a potential formulation of a Grid Economy as a commodity market, and extend this towards trading and hedging of risk, options, futures and structured products.

RELATED WORKS

A number of researchers have addressed a variety of aspects of Grid Economics. Gray (2003) formulates relative costs of networking, computation, database access and database storage, producing dollar-equivalents of network bandwidth, CPU instructions, CPU time, disk space, and database queries. He uses commercial examples in deriving these assessments, which may be helpful in evaluating the costs associated with a particular analysis, but which needs to be rigorously tested with due consideration for reliability and performance factors to work towards cost prediction. Chetty and Buyya (2002) have considered markets in Grid computing by comparison to energy markets: given initial formulations of the Grid as analogous to the electrical grid, this seems to be a natural extension. Computer control of the electri-

cal grid needs to ensure that supply and demand are well-matched, particularly at specific peak demand times. While electrical energy may be storable, the unused capacity of the Grid compute resource is worthless as time elapses, leading to a reduction in value of resource secured but unused. Kenyon and Cheliotis (2003) characterized the Grid commodity/resource as stochastic rather than deterministic; this characterization suggests probabilistic models are possible, in particular through Monte Carlo Simulations. They suggest that the basic building blocks of Grid Economics will not be spot markets but futures contracts, which essentially have the same characteristics as the Grid resources. They also suggest that the selection of Grid resources is often similar to the construction of financial portfolios. Buyya, Abramson and Venugopal (2005) suggest that resource management and scheduling are the most challenging aspects of Grid Economics, and analyze and comment on the differences between current academic and commercial Grid efforts and their own work. Their Economic Grid project emphasizes problems of price setting, market oriented resource management and scheduling. These researchers are aiming to develop a Grid Architecture for Computational Economy (GRACE) and a Grid Resource Broker (GRB) that acts as a meta-scheduler, and have discussed various challenges with building the next generation Grid system which they consider to be an Economic Grid.

In relation to financial grids, many implementations are claimed in the financial sector but relatively few have been reported in the literature. Notable exceptions include the RiskGrid (Donachy 2003) and the Implied Volatility Grid (Macleod 2005), both at the Belfast e-Science Centre, and outputs from the Grid in Finance 2006 Conference. RiskGrid used DataSynapse LiveCluster for job scheduling and Globus toolkit to manage Grid interaction, security and exposure of the VaR service; Implied Volatility Grid used the Sun Grid Engine, JGrid and Globus. Limited information is available regarding these implementations beyond details of technologies used and some performance characteristics. Further work of interest includes Schumacher's (2006) derivatives pricing grid service that uses GEMSS grid infrastructure, tested on architectures ranging from NEC-SX vector computers to PC-Clusters and Germano's work (2006) involving a Monte Carlo pricing application based on the SETI@home project, implemented using C/C++ and FORTRAN code, with significant speed up claimed over the internet. A pricing application in an environment with limited guarantee of the analysis taking place or providing usable results within a specific time period, may be interesting in terms of implementation, but may be some distance from providing the kinds of assurances anticipated.

The closest related work to that detailed in this paper is Kerstin et al (2007) who have reported on the AssessGrid project. AccessGrid relates to the construction of a risk-aware Grid architecture, partly grounded in auction-based planning approaches from almost forty years earlier (Sutherland 1968). AssessGrid attempts to integrate considerations of risk assessment and management through a negotiated SLA among three Grid actors (end-user, broker and resource provider). The authors claim that risk-aware SLAs are only possible in planning-based systems since insufficient estimations are available for queuing-based systems such as Condor and the Sun Grid Engine (SGE). We are aiming to challenge this claim for two reasons: (i) queuing-based systems are in the vanguard; (ii) part of the motivation for our work is to predict the availability of resources for financial risk before the analysis is deployed and; in some senses, we need to create estimations for predicting the ability to predict.

BACKGROUND

Financial Risk Management and Financial Portfolios

Identifying and quantifying risk has become an important aspect of a variety of business and academic pursuits. Risk is an integral part of the real world in general, and the financial world in particular. In financial markets, the word "risk" is often used synonymously with the probability of a known loss, and represented by an amount of money. Various financial crises, including the Asian financial turmoil in 1997 and the 2008 subprime crisis, have emphasized the need for improved understanding of risk analysis to accurately reflect the likelihood of experiencing losses, and the scale of the likely losses involved. Sophisticated mathematical models and measures that carry names such as Black-Scholes, Stress testing, Value at Risk (VaR), etc., are referenced to try to quantify, rather than qualify, expectations for risks. As the quantity of information available for use in calculating risk increases, whether access to information is symmetric – the same data is available to all participants - or asymmetric – different data may be available to different participants though the current price is commonly known - there is an increase to the complexity of models required to estimate the risk and/or the number of simulations and computations required. The choice of the model or the parameters, and the computational tractability of undertaking such analyses, becomes significant.

More complex financial investment strategies tend to involve portfolios. Portfolios can be thought of as collections of named financial assets, or derivatives of these assets, and are variously composed. The return of a portfolio of assets is essentially a weighted average of returns of the individual assets. In selecting the collections, diversification of risk can be a key consideration to ensure that a specific market event, e.g. change in interest rate, has a limited impact on the portfolio as a whole in that all contained assets or derivatives are not equally sensitive to this change. The "Greeks" are often referred to when considering the market sensitivities of financial derivatives: rho (ρ) indicates the change for a small interest rate change; delta (δ) indicates the change in the derivative price in response to small changes in the underlying price; gamma (γ) indicates change in the delta; and so on. A portfolio of derivatives can be hedged to achieve a desired exposure to risk using, for example, delta (δ) hedging. However, there are certain, systemic, risks which cannot be diversified.

Portfolio analysis assumes that investors consider the expected returns and the standard deviation (variance) of returns, a mean-variance framework. Where a new asset contributes to portfolio risk depends on the correlation or covariance of the return and the other assets (β). The preferred portfolio would be one with a high expected return but low standard deviation and low correlation. A high expected return, of course, generally implies higher risk and the lower the correlation, the less the asset will contribute to the overall risk. A negative correlation would offset risk elsewhere in the portfolio, lowering the portfolio standard deviation. Selection is a trade-off between risk and expected returns.

For a single asset investment, the standard deviation of expected returns can be thought of as the market risk, which is not entirely true for the asset in a portfolio where the standard deviation of the asset contributes to the overall portfolio risk. The portfolio risk is made dependent on expected correlations in movements across the assets in the portfolio, the implication being that correlated assets will move together based on the underlying stimulus. To construct a diversified portfolio, the standard deviation of each asset should contribute little to the overall portfolio risk (risk-free asset), and secondly, the correlations among assets would dominate to determine to the portfolio risk (tangent portfolio).

Value at Risk

With increased unpredictability (volatility) of financial markets, large financial institutions began calculating Value at Risk (VaR). VaR can be used to predict market risk, and may also be used to regulate it if sufficient collateral is used

to offset these risks. The "dot com bubble" and so-called credit crunch have demonstrated that use of risk models to produce values in isolation may be insufficient. Furthermore, determining the risk of more complex financial instruments such as asset-backed securities (ABSs) and collateralized debt obligations (CDOs) provides even greater challenge, particularly where improved rationality is needed amongst investors.

VaR is typically related to the computation of values over the distribution of returns (profits and losses). The actual value obtained from this analysis tends to reflect the largest expected loss at a specific confidence level for a specific time. There are three prevalent approaches (Linsmeier and Pearson 1996): (i) Historical Simulation; (ii) Variance-Covariance; (iii) Monte Carlo Simulation. Variation in parameters and assumptions amongst methods results in variation of yields, suggesting that parameter selection depends on factors such as complexity of implementation, ability to deal with options and option-like portfolios, and the reliability of the results. For the three prevalent methods, these factors can be variously assessed, as presented in Table 1.

Selection also depends on data availability (Historical Simulation) and assumptions over the types of distributions considered (Variance-Covariance; Monte Carlo). Commonality in approaches for VaR analysis either for single instrument or a portfolio of financial instruments has been characterized (Best 1998) as:

(A): Mark-to-market the portfolio - evaluate the current price of the portfolio rather than its book value);

(B): Calculate the distribution of portfolio returns;

(C): Compute the VaR of the portfolio.

A distinction is also made between parametric and non-parametric models (Historical: full valuation; Variance-Covariance: analytical valuation; Monte Carlo: stochastic, complete full valuation).

Table 1. VaR methods comparison (Jorion 2002, p230)

Dimensions	VaR methods		
	Historical	Variance-Covariance	Monte Carlo
Implementation difficulty	Easy	Relatively easy	Hard
Explanation difficulty (to manager)	Easy	Easy	Hard
Distribution assumption	Actual	Normal	Normal
Able to deal with options	Yes	No	Yes
Computational time	Short	Short	Long
Accuracy of results	Depends on portfolio	Good	Good
Analysis of sensitivities analysis	No	Possible	Yes
Use Actual Volatilities and Correlations	Yes	Yes	Possible

The parametric model, often referred to as analytical valuation, relies on strong theoretical assumptions and rules that are based on properties of the underlying data. Moreover, the parametric model is only suitable in simple and linear portfolio cases. To balance computational speed and calculation accuracy, the choice of conditional distribution of returns is also important. A normal distribution is usually used since it is easily understood and well described, and higher demands are made of computation if other distributions are used.

It is often assumed in VaR models that returns are normally distributed: most of the returns will be close to the previous price, and the largest profits and losses are rare events. The volatility (standard deviation), holding period (time horizon) and portfolio diversification are the three key drivers of portfolio VaR. The holding period has significant effects on calculating VaR. Generally, a longer holding period results in a bigger value of VaR and holding certain assets reduces the risk in a portfolio. Another important parameter of VaR is confidence level or quantile, which is the interval estimate where the VaR would not be expected to exceed the maximum loss. 99% and 95% confidence levels are most commonly used. The numbers and types of approaches to calculate VaR are growing, and taking account of all of them is beyond the scope of this paper.

Historical Simulation (HS)

Historical Simulation (Linsmeier 1996 and Jorion 2002) comprises the following steps:

HS I. Define the length, period N, of the observation series, and obtain the price change series;

HS II. Obtain a formula that adequately describes a specified portfolio, such as daily returns;

HS III. Specific steps, using daily returns:

a. The price change series is applied to current price to generate hypothetical "historical" profit and loss series of the portfolio;

b. Sort hypothetical profits and losses into quantiles from largest profits to the largest losses;

c. Observe price change from the table equalling or exceeding the confidence level (γ or $1-\gamma$) as the VaR value.

The length of the observed time series, N, significantly affects the VaR value: larger values for N increase the accuracy, but can obscure important changes. Historical VaR for a portfolio is computed as the sum of the hypothetical profits and losses of individual instruments, sorted into quantiles.

Variance-Covariance Method (VC)

For a single instrument, the VC VaR is the product of the standard deviation of changes in instrument price and the quantile of confidence level. The quantile can be calculated using an inverse cumulative probability function of the confidence; therefore the key is obtaining the standard deviation of daily returns. Following Linsmeier (1996) and Jorion (2002), and assuming a normal distribution, the approach involves:

VC I. As HS I.

VC II. As HS II

VC III. Specific steps involving:
   a. Obtaining the mean and standard deviation of the percentage price change series over N periods;
   b. Calculate quantile at the given confidence level, then calculating VaR. Portfolio V-C VaR is associated to a correlation matrix of daily returns for the assets, C, with V as the one row matrix for the position of each individual asset, and V^T is the transpose matrix of V: $\mathrm{VaR} = \sqrt{V * C * V^T}$.

Monte Carlo Simulation (MCS)

The expression "Monte Carlo method" is relatively ambiguous. A "Monte Carlo" experiment uses random numbers in some well-defined sense to examine a problem. In a VaR context, the MCS can be simplified by reusing aspects of both the Historical and Variance-Covariance algorithms, and involves constructing a series of hypothetical "historical" price changes as follows:

MCS I. As HS I / VC I.

MCS II. As HS II / VC II.

MCS III. Specific steps for simulation involving:
   a. As VC III.a

   b. Simulation using random numbers; create correlations, compute eigenvectors and eigenvalues etc
   c. Generating random numbers and correlated simulated price changes. As in HS III.a.
   d. AS HS III.b.
   e. AS HS III.c.

Monte Carlo VaR for portfolios is more complex than for a single instrument. For portfolio VaR, the generated portfolio price changes must be correlated. The correlation matrix of daily returns, the eigenvalues and eigenvectors of the correlation matrix, and the inverse cumulative probability function of the random numbers all need to be produced. Eigenvalues and eigenvectors of the correlation matrix are used to describe how the portfolio price changes are moving in relation to each asset in the portfolio. The eigenvalues indicate the relative importance of each eigenvector, whereas the eigenvectors correspond to the shift in the yield curve. Each eigenvector is structured by elements and each element can be thought to represent an asset. To obtain more accurate results additional computational time is required, especially when dealing with a portfolio which has a large numbers of assets.

Options are characterized as non-linear pay-offs: the relationship between the price at which the option may be exercised and the underlying asset price at exercise time is not linear but functionally associated, so the risk exposure approximation for a portfolio including options is less readily assessable than a portfolio comprising linear pay-off instruments such as bonds and futures. For this reason, Monte Carlo Simulation is preferred since it is possible to construe a mean and standard deviation, and construct a simulated series that can be used to deal with financial options with more accurate risk exposure approximation. The prices generated by Monte Carlo simulation are all theoretically possible with given parameters. The portfolio is then revalued at each of the possible prices.

Collateralized Debt Obligations (CDO)

A CDO is a structured transaction that involves a special purpose vehicle (SPV) in selling credit protection on a range of underlying assets. The underlying assets may be either synthetic or cash. The synthetic CDO involves loans (credit default swaps: CDS), typically including fixed-income assets, bonds and loans; the cash CDO consists of a cash asset portfolio. CDOs were created to provide more liquidity, but at the time of writing may be being variously blamed for inhibiting liquidity in the market. A CDO, and other kinds of structured investments, allows institutions to sell off debt to release capital. A CDO is priced and associated to measurements of riskiness that can be protected (for example, insured against the default on a particular loan). Protection is offered against specific risk-identified chunks of the CDO, called tranches. To obtain protection in each class, a premium is paid depending on the riskiness, reported in basis points, which acts as the insurance policy.

Consider, for example, a typical CDO that comprises four tranches of securities: senior debt, mezzanine debt, subordinate debt and equity. Each tranche is identified as having seniority relative to those below it; lower tranches are expected to take losses first up to specified amounts, protecting those more senior within the portfolio. The most senior tranche is rated as triple-A, then double-A, and so on, with the lowest tranche, equity, unrated. The lowest rated should have the highest returns, but incorporates the highest risk. The senior tranche is protected by the subordinated tranche, and the equity tranche (first-loss tranche or "toxic waste") is most vulnerable, and has to offer higher compensation for the higher risk.

IMPLEMENTING VALUE AT RISK

We have broadly summarized the three main VaR methods above in a way that promotes reusability in implementation, and help to speed not only the time to implementation, but also explorations of distributions and parallelism within the computations. We identified commonality according to Best's characterization (A, B and C, as given previously, for single instrument and portfolio – see Figure 1), and have implemented and evaluated these three VaR methods. Our implementation makes use of the Condor queuing system and, especially, the Java (JDK 1.6.0) Universe, which allows processes to be run on any available Java-supporting system. We have run computations for single instrument VaR and Portfolio VaR on a local cluster that has simultaneously used up to 128 cores provided by 32 IBM HS21 Woodcrest Blades (2 Intel dual core processors, 2.66 GHz, 1333MHz FSB with 4GB RAM per blade). The Condor queuing system manages these 128 cores as a pool, though we currently manually define the level of distribution for the analysis at time of submission.

Running the VaR calculations under Condor requires the creation of a specification of the job, identifying the executable code, I/O details, required libraries, resources and run arguments including number of jobs to be run. This specification is submitted to Condor's queuing system, which undertakes matchmaking operations with available nodes in order to allocate the work according to the specified distribution. It was consideration of removing the manually specified distribution of work that led in part to our motivation for understanding availability, capability and liability.

A portfolio VaR computation using Monte Carlo Simulation involves a correlation of assets and the computation of the corresponding eigenvalues and eigenvectors. As the number of assets in the portfolio increases, the time for the computation increases. Additionally, computation

Figure 1.Portfolio VaR implementation

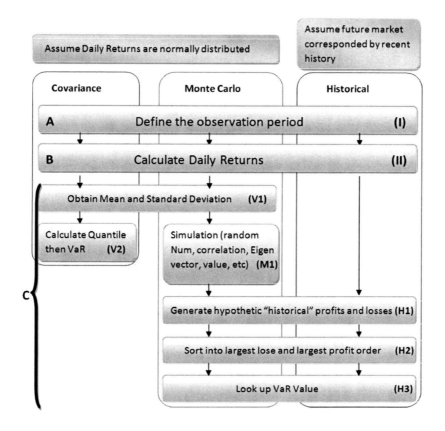

time depends on the time horizon considered, and the longer the horizon, the more sharper the increase in time needed for generating random numbers and price changes. These factors create limits on the complexity and horizon that can be computed on, for example, a single node.

Reusable VaR

Similarities in the three VaR algorithms enable decomposition of the tasks and provide for reuse in implementing an MCS as loosely-coupled parts which can be run separately across machines, including the embarrassingly parallel simulations. The parts comprise: VaR Covariance (obtain Mean and SD); Data Simulation (Generate Hypothetic Prices); and Historical VaR (Daily Return Analysis). We compose the MCS using Condor's sup-

port for directed acyclic graphs (DAGs). Figure 2 shows the nodes of the computations (sub-tasks) with dependencies and flow of data represented by edges. A Condor DAG is specified as the sub-tasks and dependencies between these subtasks required to run and manage the complete job.

In a DAG, the nodes or vertexes represent the computations (sub-tasks), and dependencies are represented by arcs or edges. A DAG file describes the DAG, specifying the order of tasks using PARENT and CHILD relationships, creating the associations to separate task specifications, contained in other files. The specifications, as described earlier, detail the executable code, I/O details, required libraries, resources and run arguments, though to ensure a DAG, each process may only run once. A simple DAG would be composed of four separately speci-fied processes, A, B, C and D. Relationships between

Figure 2. VaR MCS DAG

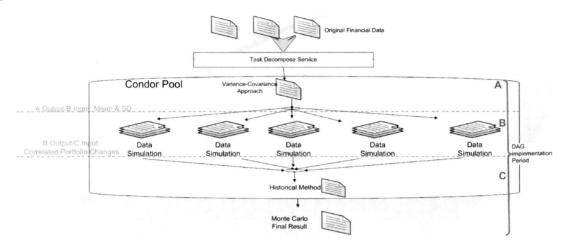

these could be composed as PARENT A CHILD B C; PARENT B C, CHILD D. For this simple DAG, task D would only run following completion of tasks B and C, and neither B nor C would be run unless A had completed. A Condor meta-scheduler called DAG manager (DAGMan) takes care of running the various tasks of the DAG. We have found that it is relatively easy to implement our approach (to be discussed later) using the DAG approach.

Table 2. VaR values comparison

	Expected losses (£)		
Confidence level	HS	VC	MCS
95%	2365.74	2890.82	4064.47
99%	4634.29	4082.18	5736.40

Table 3. Data examination (VaR MCS)

	Mean	SD	95% VaR	99% VaR
Entire input data	0.0001965	0.1752	£2365.74	£4634.29
Second 50% data (Actual market)	-0.0007623	0.1858	£2611.26	£4998.08
Simulated second 50% data	0.0002637	0.2315	£2890.85	£5387.01

TESTING VALUE AT RISK

Single Instrument VaR Evaluation

We tested our implementation of single instrument VaR, with 184,710 closing prices taken every 5 minutes (about 6 years' data between 1997 and 2003), assumed investment of £1 Million, and MCS period of 10,000. This produces the VaR values in Table 2. Monte Carlo results may be larger than those of Variance-Covariance (based on the same mean and standard deviation) and Historical method (based on the same historical data) since the prediction is derived from a wider "possible" range - stochastic and complete full valuation.

Data generated by MCS was compared to market data as a back-test to evaluate fit to the distribution and determine discrepancy in the final value (Table 3). We used the same 184,710 closing prices of every 5 minutes. The first 50% (approximately 3 years) was analysed to obtain the mean and standard deviation, and Monte Carlo Simulations generate a further 50%. The simulated result, compared to actual market data, is about 11% and 8% bigger than actual 95% and 99% confidence levels respectively - sufficient to guide the investment.

Figure 3.VaR MCS time and speedup (single instrument)

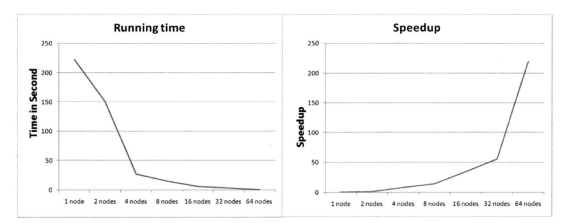

To further test our implementation, 6,400,000 simulations were distributed over 1, 2, 4, 8, 16, 32 and 64 nodes. Figure 3 shows the run-time speed-up: 2 seconds on 64 processors, compared to 220 seconds on one processor.

Linear Option-Free Portfolio VaR Evaluation

For portfolio analysis, results are obtained from VaR calculations for a linear option-free portfolio. We used 20 sets of price data, covering at least 5 years. We used our implementation to calculate VaR for 1 year, 2 year and 5 year holding periods at 95% and 99% confidence levels, using Monte Carlo simulations of 10,000 to 640,000 periods

(quite a heavy workload scenario). Theoretically, longer Monte Carlo simulation periods should improve VaR accuracy. We compare the VC VaR against the Monte Carlo result in each case. The MCS result should be similar to the VC values within the same variable settings, with a 1% standard error normally considered to be sufficiently accurate (Best 1998, pp42-43).

In practice, both results are calculated to cross-validate: an initial consideration was the correctness of the implementation; a subsequent consideration is whether the number of simulations is sufficient. Table 4 presents the results of the analysis. Each scenario runs on a single core, with 20 runs of the MCS calculated over 90000 portfolio price changes. The average MCS result

Table 4. VaR Result (portfolio)

[20 runs, 95%, 90000 simulation, £1m for each asset]						
	10 Assets			**20 Assets**			**40 Assets**
Holding Period	365 days	730 days	1825days	365 days	730 days	1825days	365 days
V-C method:	110188.23	101983.29	162888.99	191759.12	192465.63	265083.82	383518.24
Mean:	110219.06	102009.54	163012.01	191481.70	192354.90	265317.44	383596.19
SD:	516.7701473	442.5305199	521.904809	779.9403801	759.9631925	1110.236801	1566.548775
Tolerance	0.469%	0.434%	0.32%	0.407%	0.395%	0.418%	0.408%
Time (S, mean)	18.7891	20.2455	23.30695	73.6268	68.3625	69.59615	265.7238

Figure 4.VaR MCS Time and Speedup (portfolio)

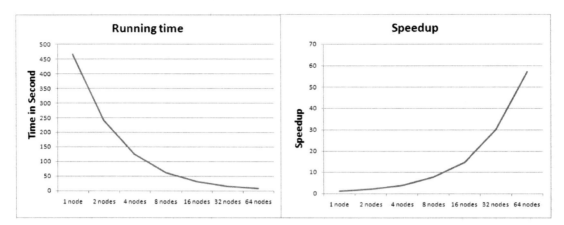

is checked against the VC result, aiming to satisfy the 1% tolerance. The table also shows that the Standard Deviation of the 20 run simulation has converged to approximately 0.5% of the mean value, an acceptable tolerance in practice.

We obtained timings for running our portfolio (MCS DAG), using 640,000 simulations distributed across 1, 2, 4, 8, 16, 32 and 64 nodes. Values are at 95% confidence level, with 20 assets and £20 Million investment portfolio, using 1 year of historical market data. Again, the MCS VaR value is sufficiently close to the VC VaR, and the standard error is within the acceptable tolerance up to distribution across 32 nodes; the implication appears to be that convergence across larger numbers of nodes requires increased numbers of simulations to achieve the equivalent tolerance

(Table 5), and this is being investigated further in relation to the nature of the implementation. The simulation took about 8 minutes on a single core, compared to 8 seconds on 64 cores, with an apparently near-linear speed up of 57.2, although taking speed up at 16 and 64 nodes produces the least compelling values in comparison to speed up at 32 nodes. With 20 assets, 1 year historical data, 95% confidence, 90000 simulation length, we ran the MCS DAG with 5 distributions. With the mean of £191646.78 and 664.09 SD, we obtain 0.346% tolerance. The DAG task finished with 489 seconds (Figure 4), whereas 5 integral MCS tests finished in about 368 seconds (73.62×5).

These different configurations of MCS VaR create different requirements on the infrastructure in terms of distributions and processing

Table 5. VaR speedup (portfolio)

	V-C method	Monte Carlo Simulation for Portfolio						
[95%, 20 assets, 20M GBP investment, 640000 simulation]								
		1 node	2 nodes	4 nodes	8 nodes	16nodes	32 nodes	64nodes
Mean (nodes)	191759.12	191298.14	191776.79	191369	191562.98	191468.41	190995.93	191926.57
SD (nodes)	----	----	749.58976	509.76275	603.59261	1242.3356	2128.3679	2428.5762
Tolerance	----	----	0.391%	0.266%	0.315%	0.649%	1.11%	1.27%
Time Mean	0.61	467.23	241.833	124.229	61.836	32.2905	15.52319	8.168344
Speedup	----	1	1.932036	3.761038	7.555954	14.46958	30.09884	57.20009

time required, and the potential need to increase the number of simulations when increasing the number of nodes in order to achieve the same tolerance. We considered the potential need to produce the results within limited time and to distribute the computation over larger number of nodes as a means to dynamically configure such distributions within shared Grid resources such as the UK's National Grid Service (NGS). At the time of writing, we have been unable to make use of Condor across NGS, and remain to deal with the challenge which is the focus for the remainder of this paper: predicting the availability of resources for computation to ensure job completion within a limited time horizon.

For MCS, selection of the appropriate kind of distribution is a necessary consideration. In portfolios of equities, it is usually assumed that a normal distribution is acceptable since extreme gains and losses are usually rare, while most movements (daily price changes) are close to the previous day's value. In addition to mean-variance, skew and kurtosis can be used to measure the fit to a normal distribution: skew provides a measure of the symmetry, and a normal distribution should have skew close to 0; a positive value is preferred. Kurtosis measures how peaked or flat the data is relative to a normal distribution; kurtosis describes the width of overall distribution and is sometimes referred to as the volatility of volatility. High kurtosis indicates a distinct peak near the mean, with a sharper drop and heavy tails, whereas low kurtosis describes a flatter top. These four moments – mean, variance, skew, kurtosis - are important measures in financial risk management. Efficient portfolio construction can be presented in mean, variance and skewness dimensions: the portfolio return with high mean, low variance and high skewness; kurtosis indicates whether the extreme movement happens.

PROCESSES AT RISK: APPLYING FINANCIAL RISK ANALYSIS TO GRID ECONOMICS

Service Level Agreements (SLAs)

SLAs are often used descriptively in relation to services of particular kinds. Broadly in terms of computer systems, SLAs are documents written for human consumption that relate statically to server management, networking availability, capacity of web servers, and response times of helpdesk and support staff in the event of some kind of failure. Our considerations fit specifically within server management (Paschke, 2006) but we are more interested in how to automatically and dynamically create SLAs that change with the demands on the infrastructure. Binding Service Level Agreements (SLAs) of this kind are considered a key step towards Grid commercialization. A competitive pricing model that makes allowance for failure of computation, would lead towards Grid Economics and brokerage services. The SLA concept and practice brings the notion of risk management to Grid computing: in order to ensure Quality of Service (QoS), the SLA acts as a contract between service providers and particular service customers, possibly negotiated through brokers. The SLA clarifies the nature of the business relationship and the obligations on the parties to the contract. For the user, it should detail the job executions required for a given performance at a given price, involving performance indicators for both customer service, and entailing a price for under-performance or failure (liabilities exercised through some form of penalty). Such SLAs may provide vital assurance for provision of Grid services into the financial sector.

Two frameworks address SLA specification and monitoring: Web Service Agreement (WS-Agreement) developed by Grid Resource Allocation Agreement Protocol (GRAAP) working group of the Open Grid Forum (OGF), and Web Service Level Agreement (WSLA), introduced by

IBM in 2003. As part of Service-Oriented Architecture (SOA), through WS-agreement, an entity could dynamically initiate an SLA representation as a machine-readable and formal contract. The content specified by WS-agreement builds on SOA (driven by agreement), where the service requirement can be achieved dynamically. Based on the XML syntax, these contents can be easily standardized, in terms of agreement templates, machine readable and machine autonomic.

The AssessGrid project (Kerstin, 2007) uses WS-Agreement in the negotiation of contracts between entities. This relies on the consideration of a probability of failure (PoF) which influences price and penalty (liability). Instead of a single risk value, the risk of breaching the terms of the SLA is defined by the PoF and the penalty. The broker acts like a virtual provider in obtaining SLAs from multiple providers and providing a comparison amongst offers. A ranked list is constructed according to price, penalty and PoF depending on the priorities of the end-user. By allowing for trade-offs against price, penalty and PoF, the broker supposedly maximizes the economic benefit to the end user. The end user must still compare SLA offers and somehow make an appropriate selection. The approach appears to focus on comparing amongst separate assured provisions, rather than independently assessing the underlying resource portfolio. In this work, considerations are also limited to planning-based systems.

We consider WS-Agreement (Andreux, 2007) as a structure for our SLAs. WS-Agreement follows general contractual principles, allowing for the specification of the entities involved in the agreement, the work to be undertaken, and the conditions that relate to the performance of the contract. The Service Description Terms are used to identify the work to be done, describing, for example, the platform upon which the work is to be done, the software involved, and the set of expected arguments and input/output resources. Guarantee Terms (GTs) provide assurance between

provider and requester on quality of service (QoS), and should include the price of the service and, ideally, the probably of, and penalty for, failure. For one of our scenarios, an end-user might request a VaR Monte Carlo Simulation, such as those previously, over a portfolio of given names with a specified time horizon, requiring 95% confidence with 20M GBP investment and 640000 simulations run across 32 processors. This will form the SDTs of the SLA, and providers would produce outline agreements by providing the GTs that they can support for such a request.

Grid Resource Monitoring

Collecting information regarding the system status and characteristics is referred to as monitoring. In a Grid environment the Grid resource availability cannot be guaranteed since the nodes might be variously online or offline or unavailable. The value of a monitoring system in a Grid is in providing important information about the system's scope, flexibility, capability and scalability. Apart from Grid information services, monitoring is also crucial in Grid scheduling, performance analysis, prediction, Grid system optimization etc. There are various Grid monitoring systems, including GridRM, NetLogger, Globus MDS, MonALISA and Ganglia (Zanikolas et al, 2005).

The focus of our work is the Ganglia system, since this is currently used across the UK's National Grid Service (NGS), a non-commercial Grid intended for use within the UK's academic research communities that includes 4 major core sites at the Universities of Oxford, Manchester and Leeds, and Rutherford Appleton Labs (RAL). NGS provides access to upwards of 2,000 processors, making the potential scale of available data quite significant. Through Ganglia, it is possible to obtain data for up to 37 system metrics in XML, including use of network bandwidth, temperature and CPU use. Ganglia's monitoring logs are destructively cycled, so to retain a sufficient history of system use we have to automatically capture data for analysis

Figure 5.Samples CPU percentage (sys+user) histogram on the last's year data (per everyday)

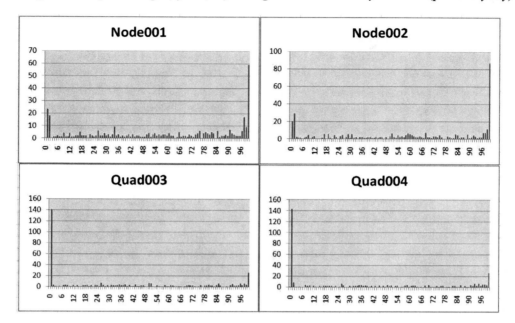

from clusters within NGS using the mechanisms available through Globus. We are collecting Grid resource monitoring data from NGS on an hourly basis to ensure that we retain all time series data points – produced every 15 seconds, but lost in the destructive log cycling. We obtain data from all nodes of major NGS sites that are able to provide this. For the Leeds Cluster, for example, we are obtaining approximately 1.4GB data per day (~ 1/2 TB/year/cluster), prior to removal of overlapping data points.

Our analysis to date has principally concerned CPU use, though time series of other parameters demonstrate similar or related distributions. For the analysis presented here, we selected user and system CPU use for 10 machines from the NGS cluster at Leeds, with data points at 6-minute and daily intervals as available in the dataset. We calculate the mean and standard deviation of series to examine CPU use per day and per year. Many of these distributions have heavy tails - the resource is either close to saturation (nearly 100%) - or unused (see Table 6 and Figure 5). We can still use a normal distribution to produce a benchmarking consideration, but following Malvin (1986) and Fishman (1996) we will move on to consider how to profile the data and identify when different distribution models are required. In particular,

Table 6.

	Samples in Leeds Cluster CPU usage percentage analysis based on a year data (per day)														
	Node001			Node002			Quad003			Quad004			Quad005		
	sys	*user*	*total*	*sys*	*user*	*total*	*sys*	*user*	*total*	*sys*	*user*	*total*	*sys*	*user*	*total*
Mean	1.44	57.3	58.7	2.21	57.9	60.1	1.58	34.4	36.0	1.66	34.3	35.9	1.57	31.9	33.5
SD	2.36	25.3	35.5	6.09	36.8	36.7	7.21	36.8	37.8	6.73	37.1	38.4	7.09	37.3	38.3
Kurtosis	29.7	-1.37	-1.36	51.15	-1.40	-1.32	99.1	-1.23	-1.30	78.8	-1.26	-1.34	71.1	-1.17	-1.26
Sknewness	4.81	-0.32	-0.33	6.82	-0.35	-0.40	9.24	0.58	0.52	8.18	0.57	0.52	7.99	0.68	0.62

we are considering Monte Carlo integration with variance reduction techniques in which the key is choosing sample sets with smaller variance. Here, the sample mean becomes a more accurate estimation while the sample variance decreases; in other words, fewer samples are needed before the sample mean becomes a good approximation.

We next analyze correlations in our sample (Table 7). Within each Group, resource use correlates with some strength, however across these groups the correlations are rather lower – providing an initial indication that these data can be used to manually target analysis. This also encourages us to consider constructing a compute-resource portfolio which we would expect to optimize the overall Grid use. A more substantial future analysis is required to evaluate these assumptions.

Knowing correlations, we next attempt to derive resource portfolios. Following financial analysis, risk-hedging a well constructed low risk portfolio requires assets which are weakly correlated; resources in a risk-reduced Grid portfolio should also be less correlated, so that the risk of a single task failure can be reduced (hedged) – assuming that the queuing system or the task itself are able to retry. The most correlated may indicate the highest combined risk since current use of systems tends to be cluster-oriented. In

other words, submitted jobs may tie up the whole of a specific cluster rather than distributing work across available clusters – which one might expect to be an intended function of a Grid.

For our sample, the lowest correlation occurs between Quad4 and Node1; submitting a task to Quad4 and Node1 may not necessarily improve the speed of execution, but would limit the associated risk of failure. Quad1 and Quad2 seem to move together, indicating an increased combined risk would emerge dependent on behaviour of others. This would suggest at least 2 portfolios could emerge with different characterizations of risk.

Specific portfolio selection steps need to be derived from this pool of Grid instruments. To construct portfolios for CDO-like tranches, we first create the correlation matrix of all the resources from a provider. Next, we select a portfolio size: if 2 resources were needed, for the triple-A tranche we could choose the lowest correlation; the single-B tranche would contain the highest correlation. Submission to AAA is more likely to succeed than to B for two reasons: (i) other workloads assigned only impact part of the portfolio; (ii) the impacted part is supported, through seniority, to enable completion – to the detriment of lower tranches.

Table 7.

Year Total CPU Usage: System + User Correlation Matrix										
	Node1	Node2	Node3	Node4	Node5	Quad1	Quad2	Quad3	Quad4	Quad5
Node1	1									
Node2	0.7746	1								
Node3	0.6384	0.7917	1							
Node4	0.4430	0.5816	0.7695	1						
Node5	0.6313	0.7651	0.7994	0.7964	1					
Quad1	0.1186	0.1615	0.2232	0.1476	0.2166	1				
Quad2	0.1410	0.1959	0.2407	0.1534	0.2239	0.9412	1			
Quad3	0.1623	0.1713	0.2228	0.1938	0.1821	0.8528	0.8807	1		
Quad4	0.1074	0.1530	0.2152	0.1944	0.2164	0.8422	0.8802	0.9284	1	
Quad5	0.0789	0.1125	0.1854	0.1655	0.1664	0.7944	0.8230	0.9050	0.9121	1

Impacts on Resource Portfolios

To evaluate the impact of job submission on Grid resource correlations, we submit various distributions of the Monte Carlo VaR at particular times. Workload was set at 2,048,000 simulations, distributed across up to 64 CPUs with 32,000 simulations each. The correlation matrix was recomputed using 244 records per node (obtained at 20 seconds intervals) following these submissions(Table 8). The following tables use a sample of nodes to demonstrate impacts of running jobs on correlations; these nodes are not always those involved with running differently distributed jobs, and unexpected changes in correlations have been observed that demand further investigation. In pre-submission state, Nodes 125,129 and 111 are strongly positively correlated, implying they are moving together or idling together. Node 102 has strongly negative correlation suggesting an opposite state. With a submission for one unspecified CPUs to run the 2,048,000 simulations, there appears to be no significant impact (Table 9), suggesting that a node

not in this sample is running the job. With a submission for 16 unspecified CPUs to run 128,000 simulations each, there are various changes in correlation coefficients (Table 10), particularly in the shift from strongly negative correlations to slight positive correlations against Node102, and similar behaviour is seen for 64 CPUs (Table 11). Throughout, Node125 and Node129 appear to move together.

Changes in correlations suggest the need to regularly reassess the resource portfolio, and the appropriate time horizon for doing so needs to be established. It may also be possible to interpret and begin to simulate the correlations amongst resources by considering the likely impact λ of executing some job A, where $CorM1 \times \lambda = CorM2$, where CorM1 are correlations before submission, and CorM2 are the correlations after submission. It would be necessary to derive λ experimentally to account for other CPU activity that may be creating unexpected effects mentioned above. Subsequently, we should be able to calculate probability of failure per job, and construct and continuously re-evaluate resource portfolios for SLAs.

Table 8. Correlation Matrix before submissions

	Node102	Node125	Node129	Node111	Node128
Node102	1	-0.957521662	-0.957521662	-0.957521662	0.907078863
Node125	-0.957521662	1	1	1	-0.948241278
Node129	-0.957521662	1	1	1	-0.948241278
Node111	-0.957521662	1	1	1	-0.948241278
Node128	0.907078863	-0.948241278	-0.948241278	-0.948241278	1

Table 9. Correlation Matrix after 2,048,000 simulations submitted to 1 (unspecified) CPU

	Node102	Node125	Node129	Node111	Node128
Node102	1	-0.965889367	-0.965889367	-0.965889367	0.90913573
Node125	-0.965889367	1	1	1	-0.94726895
Node129	-0.965889367	1	1	1	-0.94726895
Node111	-0.965889367	1	1	1	-0.94726895
Node128	0.90913573	-0.94726895	-0.94726895	-0.94726895	1

Table 10. Correlation Matrix after 128,000 simulations submitted to 16 (unspecified) CPUs

	Node102	Node125	Node129	Node111	Node128
Node102	1	-0.691137793	-0.691137793	-0.691137793	0.633760987
Node125	-0.691137793	1	1	1	-0.948206679
Node129	-0.691137793	1	1	1	-0.948206679
Node111	-0.691137793	1	1	1	-0.948206679
Node128	0.633760987	-0.948206679	-0.948206679	-0.948206679	1

Table 11. Correlation Matrix after 32,000 simulations submitted to 64 (unspecified) CPUs

	Node102	Node125	Node129	Node111	Node128
Node102	1	0.032218027	0.032218027	0.032334066	0.181668878
Node125	0.032218027	1	1	0	0.027102074
Node129	0.032218027	1	1	0	0.027102074
Node111	0.032334066	0	0	1	0.610872973
Node128	0.181668878	0.027102074	0.027102074	0.610872973	1

Building SLAs

We construct our Grid SLA, with reference to WS-Agreement, by considering relative pricing of resources of different specifications (Gray 2003), and the associated risk of any item in the portfolio being unable to run or complete its task within a limited timeframe. The liability provides a limit for the expected penalty paid by the service provider for failing to honour the contract. Service providers are likely to want to limit the extent of penalties, for example to 120% of the cost of the contract. Given the nature of need by financial users, setting an example limit might be a difficult proposition since the cost of a missed opportunity may be significantly greater than the expected outlay for the computation. On the other hand, if users demand substantial gearing of liability, one might expect the service providers to increase the cost. There is a risk to be managed on both sides, even before one considers that the computation may be a risk analysis. This integrated consideration, of risk and liability, will likely affect the cost of the offering and place demands on system reliability and performance. The service providers, and the end users, need to be aware of the risk and liability of not satisfying such contracts; the brokers, here, are the portfolio managers, and would need to be able to mitigate risks of failure in the underlying instruments – likely, involving multiple SLAs from providers. Results from our analysis, demonstrated previously, will help to build a ranking system, inspired by CDO models.

This CDO model may help the Grid provider optimize overall system usability as well as maximize the service profit. We will give consideration as follows: firstly, sort resources among the Grid into different classes according to the historical information. The resource with highest availability ranks the top class whereas the bottom class is the lowest availability resource. According to this list, we will make different basis points to guarantee various performances. The top class resource should have highest premium to insure the availability and performance. If under-performance happens with the higher premium, then the higher the penalty will be. We believe that such a framework can bring greater flexibility to the Grid pricing model. The Grid user pays for the use of Grid taking into consideration the budget

Figure 6. Constructing resource portfolio CDO and risk assessment model

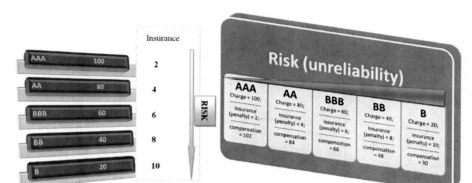

and the task importance. The Grid provider can manage the Grid more efficiently and optimize the overall profit. The SLA for Grid with this framework will distinguish the rights and duties more clearly and reasonably. The risk is quantified on a monetary basis The broker would manage and publish dynamically updated resource CDOs (which may cross different providers) with price and insurance; the end-user worries about the job budget and the published risk. The end-user can select cheaper execution at higher risk (lower seniority); the lower the seniority, the higher the risk that any jobs failing in more senior tranches will force the higher risk jobs to be "kicked out", assuring completion of the more expensive, lower risk jobs.

We consider an initial resource portfolio CDO model here (Figure 6): we classify portfolios into 5 different classes according to correlations of resources with the portfolio. Triple-A indicates the most reliable portfolios, to guarantee most availability (least losses), and jobs are more likely to be finished with these resources. A user would pay the highest price for this level of service, say, 100 units. Single-B represents the most unreliable, hence cheapest, portfolios, where the user suffers highest risk. The increase of proportion of insurance/penalty is in line with the increased risk of failure. The end-user, with a return on the contract, could resubmit with a new budget, but the time

to completion is now increased. The framework should provide flexibility for Grid users to choose services, and improve resource management for the Grid providers.

Compute Node "Defaults"

There are several considerations involved with constructing our SLAs. Consider, for example, Figure 7: a node failing in AAA will have its process passed to a node in AA; since this node may already have a running job, this will equivalently be passed on to A. This continues until the last tranche is reached, where the overall penalty for non-completion of an SLA is at its lowest. This protects the processes in the more senior tranches as well as protecting the resource broker. Since the broker updates SLAs dynamically in terms of price and insurance, while the end-users select service according to its own budget and the given published risk. The more expensive and lower risk submission is always guaranteed the completion, if a job fails within a given tranche, a resource broker may be able to make use of other tranches they have constructed in order to limit the extent of liability through failure. This consideration can be expanded to multiple providers, and future Grids, Utilities and Clouds may benefit from these.

Figure 7. Job failure scenario in Grid resources CDO

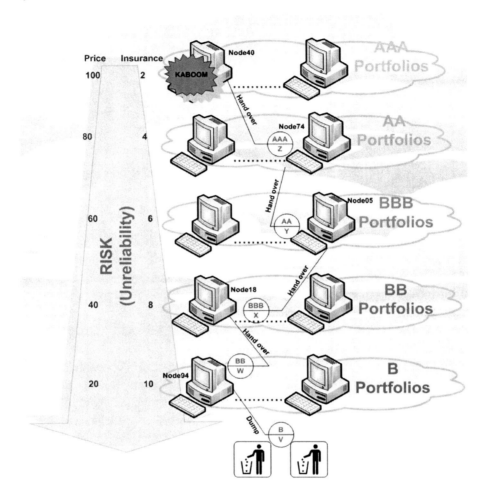

CONCLUSION AND FUTURE WORK

In this paper we have considered the construction of Service Level Agreements (SLAs) by reference to techniques of financial risk analysis. We are working towards using data captured about resources, such as those on the UK's National Grid Service, to be able to construct these SLAs automatically. Such production of SLAs may lead towards markets for Grid computing and for other kinds of compute resources. The aim of our research is to predict availability and capability and introduce risk analysis for portfolios of these resources. Such prediction, quantification of risk, and consideration of liability in case of failure, is

considered essential for Grid Economics – specifically, relating to the provision of SLAs through resource brokers, and comparable to markets in other commodities – but perhaps also more widely applicable to the configuration and management of related architectures such as those of P2P systems and Clouds.

We have explored and evaluated some of the factors required for the automatic construction of SLAs. We reported on the computational challenges for computing portfolio Value at Risk (VaR), demonstrating the commonality in various approaches, and considered providing optimized Grid-based VaR services. As part of our work we have been collecting data regarding computational resource use on the UK's National Grid Service (NGS) and are using these data in combination with the financial techniques to lead towards predicting availability of resources and associated insurance against losses. By obtaining continuous monitoring data from NGS, including CPU user usage percentage, memory usage percentage, network in/out traffic or the overall work load, we can build Grid resource usage time series. Analogous to financial markets, our analysis currently focuses on the distribution, variance, kurtosis and skewness of the time series, as well as the correlations among series. With sufficient historical data, we believe that all these analyses may enable us to predict future resource availability and thereby provide for a Grid Economy. We are looking for similarities in data between financial markets and Grid markets, hoping to adopt a mature financial theory. From earlier discussion in financial derivatives and theory, a well built portfolio can reduce the investment risk. By building a portfolio consisting of Grid resources, the risks of incomplete analysis should decrease substantially, although the overall performance may decrease to ensure lower exposure to risk. This may be good for Grid providers and brokers in reducing the risk of having to pay penalties. The analysis of Grid resource data should also help us to report the usability of a specific application running in the Grid, and through simulation, resource use prediction for different applications with similar characteristics and requirements may be estimatable.

We are still some distance from constructing portfolios automatically so as to quantify and continuously monitor the risk, and beyond that to evaluate the effectiveness of the approach. We will increase our use of the NGS in the near future, which will provide a suitable test bed, and the analysis presented here demonstrates significant potential for our future work, which will involve wider consideration of distributions, and a concrete set of proposals for the pricing of such resources. More substantial analysis is also required to evaluate a wide range of assumptions, including the equivalent to Greeks as a means to characterize the sensitivities of such portfolios, and the expectation that an SLA has duration and may be impacted by a variety of factors not identified in this paper.

REFERENCES

Andrix, A., Czajkowski, K., Dan, A., Keay, K., et al. (2007). *Web Services Agreement Specification (WS-Agreement)*. Grid resource allocation agreement protocol (GRAAP) WG. Retrieved from http://forge.gridforum.org/sf/projects/graap-wg

Best, P. (1998). *Implementing value at risk*, (pp. 1-102), London: Wiley.

Buyya, R., Abramson, D., & Venugopal, S. (2005). *The Grid economy,* In *Special Issue of the Proceedings of the IEEE on Grid Computing*. Los Alamitos: IEEE Press.

Chetty, M., & Buyya, R. (2002). Weaving electrical and computational grids: How analogous are they? *Computing in Science and Engineering*. Retrieved from http://buyya.com/papers/gridanalogy.pdf

Donachy, P., & Stødle, D. (2003). *Risk Grid - Grid based integration of real-time value-at-risk (VaR) services*. EPSRC UK e-Science All Hands Meeting.

Fishman, G. S. (1996). *Monte Carlo. Concepts, Algorithms, and Applications*. New York: Springer-Verlag.

Germano, G., & Engel, M. (2006). City@home: Monte Carlo derivative pricing distributed on networked computers. In *Grid Technology for Financial Modelling and Simulation, 2006*.

Gillam, L., & Ahmad, K. *(2005).* Financial data tombs and nurseries: A grid-based text and ontological analysis. In *Proc. of 1st Intl. Workshop on Grid Technology for Financial Modeling and Simulation (Grid in Finance 2006)*.

Gillam, L., Ahmad, K., & Dear, G. (2005). Grid-enabling Social Scientists: some infrastructure issues. In *Proc. of 1st Intl. e-Social Science Conference*, Manchester, UK. Globus. (n.d.). Retrieved from http://www.globus.org/

Gray, J. (2003). *Distributed computing economics.* Microsoft Research Technical Report: MSRTR-2003-24 (also presented in Microsoft VC Summit 2004, Silicon Valey, April 2004).

Jorion, P. (2002). *Value at risk: The new benchmark for managing financial risk* (2nd Ed.). New York: McGraw-Hill.

Kalos, M. H., & Paula, A. (1986). *Whitlock, Monte Carlo Methods, Vol. 1: Basics.* Hoboken, NJ: John Wiley & Sons.

Kenyon, C., & Cheliotis, G. (2002). Architecture requirements for commercializing grid resources. In *11th IEEE International Symposium on High Performance Distributed Computing (HPDC '02)*.

Kenyon, C., & Cheliotis, G. (2003). *Grid resource commercialization: Economic engineering and delivery scenarios.* In J. Nabrzyski, J. Schopf & J. Weglarz (Eds.), *Grid resource management: state of the art and research issues.* Amsterdam: Kluwer.

Kerstin, V., Karim, D., Iain, G., & James, P. (2007). *AssessGrid, economic issues underlying risk awareness in Grids,* LNCS. Berlin / Heidelberg: Springer.

Linsmeier, T. J., & Pearson, N. D. (1996). *Risk measurement: An introduction to value at risk.* University of Illinois.

Macleod, G., Donachy, P., Harmer, T. J., Perrot, R. H., Conlon, B., Press, J., & Lungu, F. (2005). *Implied volatility Grid: Grid based integration to provide on demand financial risk analysis.* Belfast e-Science Centre, Queen's University of Belfast. NGS ganglia monitoring. (n.d.). Retrieved from http://ganglia.ngs.rl.ac.uk/

NGS. (n.d.). Retrieved from http://www.grid-support.ac.uk/

Paschke, A., & Scappiner-Gerull, E. (2006). A categorization scheme for SLA metrics. In *Multi-Conference Information Systems (MKWI06)*, Passau, Germany.

Schumacher, J., Jaekel, U., & Zimmermann, F. (2006). *Grid services for derivatives pricing,* Grid Technology for Financial Modelling and Simulation.

Sutherland, I. (1968). A futures market in computer time. *Communications of the ACM, 11*(6). The Grid Economy Project. (n.d.). Retrieved from http://www.gridbus.org/ecogrid/index.html

Zanikolas, S., & Sakellariou, R. (2005). A taxonomy of grid monitoring systems. *Future Generation Computer Systems.* Retrieved from http://linkinghub.elsevier.com/retrieve/pii/S0167739X04001190

ADDITIONAL READING

Altmann, J., & Veit, D. (2007). *Grid Economics and Business Models,* In *4th International Workshop, GECON 2007,* Rennes, France, August 28, 2007. Berlin: Springer.

Banks, E. (2006). *Synthetic and structured assets (The Wiley Finance Series).* Hoboken, NJ: Wiley.

Benninga, S. (2006). *Principles of finance with Excel.* New York: Oxford University Press.

Birkenheuer, G., Hovestadt, M., Voss, K., Kao, O., Djemame, K., Gourlay, I., & Padgett, J. (2006). Introducing risk management into the Grid. In *Proc. 2nd IEEE Intl. Conf. on e-Science and Grid Computing*, Amsterdam, The Netherlands.

Buyya, R. (2002). *Economic-based distributed resource management and scheduling for Grid computing*. PhD thesis, Monash University, Australia, April 2002. Retrieved from www.buyya.com/thesis.

Buyya, R., Giddy, J., & Abramson, D. (2001). A case for economy grid architecture for service-oriented Grid computing. In *10th IEEE International Heterogeneous Computing Workshop*, San Francisco, CA.

Chew, L. (1996). *Managing derivative risks: The use and abuse of leverage*. Chichester, UK: Wiley.

Czajkowski, K., Foster, I., Kesselman, C., Sander, V., & Tuecke, S. (2004). Grid service level agreements: Grid resource management with intermediaries. In *Grid resource management: state of the art and future trends* (pp. 119-134). Norwell, MA: Kluwer Academic Publishers. Retrieved from ftp://info.mcs.anl.gov/pub/tech_reports/reports/P1078.pdf

Deacon, J. (2004). *Global securitisation and CDOs (The Wiley Finance Series)*. Hoboken, NJ: John Wiley & Sons.

Dowd, K. (2005). *Measuring market risk*. Chichesterm UK: John Wiley.

Elton, E., Gruber, M., Brown, S., & Goetzmann, W. (2003). *Modern portfolio theory and investment analysis* (6th Ed.). New York: Wiley.

Ferreira, L., et al. (2002). *Introduction to Grid computing with Globus*. IBM Redbook series. Retrieved from http://ibm.com/redbooks

Foster, I., & Kesselman, C. (Eds.). (1999). *The Grid: blueprint for a future computing infrastructure*. San Francisco: Morgan Kaufmann.

Foster, I., Kesselman, C., & Tuecke, S. (2001). The anatomy of the Grid: Enabling scalable virtual organizations. *Int'l J. Supercomputer Applications, 15*(3).

Glasserman, P. (2003). *Monte Carlo methods in financial engineering: v. 53 (Stochastic Modelling and Applied Probability)*. New York: Springer-Verlag.

Grid Economic Services Architecture Working Group. (2003). Global Grid Forum. Retrieved from https://forge.gridforum.org/projects/gesa-wg

Hull, J. (2005). *Fundamentals of futures and options markets* (5th Ed.). Upper Saddle River, NJ: Pearson/Prentice Hall.

Jorion, P., & GARP (Global Association of Risk Professionals). (2007). *Financial Risk Manager Handbook (Wiley Finance)* (4th Ed.). Hoboken, NJ: John Wiley & Sons.

Lalis, Spyros., & Karipidis, A. (2000). An Open Market- Based Framework for Distributed Computing over the Internet. In *First IEEE/ACM International Workshop on Grid Computing (GRID 2000)*, December 2000, Bangalore, India. Berlin: Springer Verlag.

Leff, A., Rayfield, T. J., & Dias, M. D. (2003). Service-Level Agreements and Commercial Grids. *IEEE Internet Computing, 7*(4), 44–50. doi:10.1109/MIC.2003.1215659

Liengme, B. V. (2002). *A guide to Microsoft Excel 2002 for scientists and engineers* (3rd ed.). Oxford: Butterworth-Heinemann.

Loeffler, G., & Posch, P. N. (2007). *Credit Risk Modeling using Excel and VBA (The Wiley Finance Series)*. Hoboken, NJ: Wiley.

Mario, J. M., & Paul, L. F. (2002). *Applied computational economics and finance*. Cambridge, MA: MIT Press.

McCrary, S. A. (2005). *Hedge Fund Course (Wiley Finance)*. Hoboken, NJ: John Wiley & Sons.

Mishkin Frederic, S. (2007). *The economics of money, banking, and financial markets* (8th ed.). Boston: Pearson Addison Wesley.

Nabrzyski, J., Schopf, J., & Weglarz, J. (2004). *Grid Resource Management: State of the Art and Future Trends*. Amsterdam: Kluwer Academic Publishers.

Natenberg, S. (1994). *Option Volatility & Pricing: Advanced Trading Strategies and Techniques* (2nd Ed.). New York: McGraw-Hill.

Rebonato, R. (2004). *Volatility and Correlation: The Perfect Hedger and the Fox (Wiley Finance)* (2nd Ed.). Hoboken, NJ: John Wiley & Sons.

Rouah, F., Rouah, F. D., & Vainberg, G. (2007). *Option Pricing Models and Volatility Using Excel-VBA*. Hoboken, NJ: John Wiley & Sons.

Smithson, C. W. (1998). *Managing financial risk: a guide to derivative products, financial engineer* (3rd Ed.). New York: McGraw-Hill.

Tavakoli, M. J. (2003). *Collateralized Debt Obligations & Structured Finance: New Developments in Cash and Synthetic Securitization* (2nd Ed.). Hoboken, NJ: John Wiley & Sons.

The Options Clearing Corporation. (n.d.). *Characteristics and Risks of Standardized Options and Supplements*, 1997-2007. Retrieved April 2008 from http://www.cboe.com/resources/intro.aspx

The Physiology of the Grid: An Open Grid Services Architecture for Distributed Systems Integration. (n.d.). Retrieved from http://www.gridforum.org/ogsa-wg/

Torben Juul, A. (2006). *Global derivatives: a strategic risk management perspective*. Harlow, UK: Financial Times/Prentice Hall.

Voß, K. (2006). Risk-aware Migrations for Prepossessing SLAs. In *International Conference on Networking and Services (ICNS)*, Silicon Valley, USA.

Wilmott, P. (2006). *Paul Wilmott on quantitative finance* (2nd ed.) (Vol. 1-3). Chichester, UK: Wiley.

KEY TERMS AND DEFINITIONS

Financial Risk Management: An approach to evaluating the likely exposure to losses of particular investments in order to understand and potentially off-set such exposures.

Grid Computing: The use, across administrative domains, of computer resources typically for compute- or data-intensive scientific or industrial problems.

Grid Economy: Treating computational resources like financial instruments, allowing for buying and selling of such resources and the potential for construction and trading of derivates of these.

Monte Carlo Simulation: A range of computational algorithms that generates random samples from distributions with known overall properties that is used, for example, to explore potential future behaviours of financial instruments on the basis of historic properties.

Service Level Agreement (SLA): In Grid computing, a form of contract for the provision of computational services that specifies the requirements of the service and conditions for delivery of that service.

Value at Risk (VaR): A widely used measurement of expected losses at a given confidence, for example the largest potential loss in the worst situation over a specific time horizon.

Volatility: In finance, a measure of price stability or instability of a financial instrument over a particular time horizon, often calculated as the standard deviation over, for example, the difference in the daily close prices (returns) for a specified number of days.

Chapter 30
Virtual Hierarchical Tree Grid Organizations (VIRGO)

Lican Huang
Zhejiang Sci-Tech University, P.R. China

ABSTRACT

The currently two types of main P2P technologies–unstructured and structured approaches do not care about the semantic meaning of the nodes. They do not care about the nodes whose users may take different roles in social groups in the communities. Here, a semantic P2P Network-Virtual Hierarchical Tree Gird Organizations (VIRGO) is described. VIRGO is a hybrid of unstructured P2P and structured P2P technologies by merging a multi-tuple Virtual Hierarchical Overlay Network and random cached network. It has the following properties: Decentralization—VIRGO is fully distributed, robust, and easy-managed; Load balance–Cached nodes in route table help to solve the problem of the load balance in the tree structure; Scalability—Time complexity, space complexity and message-cost of lookup protocol of VIRGO is O (logN), where N is the total number of nodes in the network; Availability–There is at least one path between every two nodes. This chapter gives audience the concepts, framework, protocols and applications about Virtual Hierarchical Tree Gird Organizations (VIRGO). It will point out why VIRGO should exist among lots of P2P technologies.

INTRODUCTION

Although client/server technology has been successful in many IT fields, it has many shortcomings. It is un-scalable, with a single point of failure, and does not fully use resources at the network edge. P2P technology is now considered as the next generation computing model. It is scalable, with efficient use of resources, and processing power at the edge of the network.

There are two types of P2P technologies. Industrial P2P applications such as FreeNet (http://freenet.sourceforge.net/) use an unstructured approach which routes nodes by a "flooding" algorithm. This kind of P2P has the advantages of partial-match querying and robustness, but may cause excess

DOI: 10.4018/978-1-61520-686-5.ch030

network traffic, and lacks guaranteed search. The structured approach is mostly based on Distributed Hash Table (DHT) technologies such as Pastry (Rowstron & Druschel, 2001), CAN (Ratnasamy, Francis, Handley, Karp & Shenker, 2001), and CHORD (Stoica, Morris, Karger, Kaashoek & Balakrishnan, 2001), and is effective in time complexity, but lack partial-match query capability and locality aspects.

The other aspect of the above types of P2P is that they do not care about the semantic meaning of the nodes. They do not care about the nodes whose users may take different roles in social groups in the communities. This leads to lack of powerful solutions for resource discovery by complicated conditions as SQL statement.

Here, a semantic P2P Network—Virtual Hierarchical Tree Gird Organizations (VIRGO) (Huang, 2005) is described. VIRGO is domain related P2P network, which keeps the nodes' semantic meaning and hybrids structured P2P and unstructured P2P. It contains a virtual group tree overlay topology and a random cached netlike topology. It is equally effective in routing messages as structured P2P, but retains the partial-match query and robustness aspects of unstructured P2P. The time complexity, space complexity and message-cost of the VIRGO lookup protocol is O (logN), where N is the total number of nodes in the network. Due to the LRU replacement strategies for caching route nodes, VIRGO is also a load-balanced network.

Grid (Foster, Kesselman & Tuecke, 2001; Foster & Kesselman, 1997) technology is one of the most important one come forth in recent years. In the service-oriented architecture of Grid, how to find Grid services is an important issue. The strategy publishing and discovering services with centralized mode has bad scalability and a single point of failure. P2P (Clark, 2001) has good scalability, but it has some challenges such as security, network bandwidth, and architecture designs, and has difficult to search services which are described by many entities, especially by ontology terms.

Service discovery based on Virtual Hierarchical Tree Gird Organizations (VIRGO) can overcome the above shortages, and can query scope services through SQL-like statements.

DNS becomes a vital component in today's Internet infrastructure. But the existing DNS architecture may encounter problems for the growth of the Internet in the coming IPv6 network. In IPv6 network, there are huge IP address spaces. Therefore, it is reasonable to suppose there are huge numbers of Domain Names. Furthermore, pervasive computing requires more DNS queries. Those above will result in traffic load and latency of DNS lookups. VIRGO_DNS is VIRGO based distributed DNS in IPv6. The DNS servers constructs VIRGO network according to Domain Name Zones (Mockapetris, 1987). The performance of DNS lookups may reach O (1) due to Zipf's law (Huang, 2008b; Jung, Sit, Balakrishnan & Morris, 2001).

In this chapter, we first give backgrounds of related technologies with VIRGO, especially virtual and dynamic hierarchical architecture (VDHA) (Huang, Wu & Pan, 2002; Huang, Wu & Pan, 2003); then presents the framework, protocols and applications of VIRGO in details. Through this chapter the audience should learn the concepts, framework, protocols and applications about VIRGO, and know VIRGO's advantages such as SQL-like scope query compared with lots of other P2P technologies

BACKGROUND

P2P computing is the computing models whose systems share computer resources and services directly. In P2P system, all nodes are both clients and servers. It provides as well as consumes data. It has no centralized data source; and it manages P2P system autonomously. Unlike Client/Server model, any node can initiate a connection with any others. P2P computing can leverage their collective power by taking advantage of existing computing power, computer storage and networking connectivity.

There are two kinds of P2P technologies: un-structural and structural P2P technologies (Kant, Iyer & Tewari, 2002). Un-structural technology such as Gnutella (http://en.wikipedia.org/wiki/Gnutella) uses flooding queries to find the object nodes. The node asks its neighbors for files of interest. Neighbors ask their neighbors, and so on until going through a number of hops that TTL field indicated. It is decentralized and with no single point of failure. However, it cannot ensure correct results. Moreover, search by flooding queries are distributed but still not scalable.

Structured P2P technology such as Chord is the second generation P2P overlay networks Unlike unstructured P2P systems, it is based on a distributed hash table. Each node and each object are hashed into the uniform unique identifiers by distributed hash table. The nodes' identifiers form an overlay topology such as circle, tree. The general interface of this kind of P2P is to store (key, value) pairs (here the key is like a filename, and the value can be file contents), and insert/lookup/delete (key, value) pairs. Structured P2P has advantages of self-organizing, load balanced, fault-tolerant, scalable, and guarantees to query an answer on numbers of hops. But structured P2P based DHT can not query partial keys. There also are systems such as G-ROME system (Exarchakos, G., Salter,J. & Antonopoulos,N.,2006) which interconnects multiple independent DHT-based P2P networks for the purposes of transferring capacity from underutilized to overloaded networks.

The most of all P2P networks are classified as the above two networks. The unstructured P2P network can only flood the messages to neighbors because it has no fixed topologies. Whereas the structured P2P network can only route along some topologies such as tree, ring etc. VIRGO combines structured virtual tree topology and un-structured random cached network. VIRGO routes the message to the next hop by the different way. It selects the node among the nodes in virtual tree topology and random cached nodes with minimum theoretic hops by calculating the

distance of virtual groups between the node and the destination node.

Another difference between the above two types of P2P and VIRGO is that VIRGO keeps the semantic meaning of the nodes, whose users may take different roles in social groups in the communities. By establishing the semantic classified domains, VIRGO can query resources by complicated search conditions as SQL statement.

Virtual and Dynamic Hierarchical Architecture (VDHA)

Virtual and Dynamic Hierarchical Architecture (VDHA) tries to avoid using DHT. In **VDHA** network nodes are grouped virtually (see Figure 1). Nodes can join the group and leave the group dynamically. The groups are virtually hierarchical, with one root-layer, several middle-layers, and many leaf virtual groups (these groups are called VOs). Among these nodes of VOs, one(just one) node (called as gateway node) in each group is chosen to form upper-layer groups, from the nodes of these upper layer groups to form upper-upper-layer groups in the same way, and this way is repeated until to form one root-layer group. In the same group all nodes are capable to be gateway node. Gateway node is the node which is not only in low layer group, but also in up-layer group. Gateway nodes will forward the low-layer group's status information to all the nodes in the up-layer group, and distribute the upper-layer group's status information to all the nodes in the lower-layer group. The numbers of nodes in a VO can be dynamically changed by the way that the node can dynamically join and leave the VO. A VO may join and leave the Grid system as a whole, and this autonomous property makes the large scalable systems possible.

VDHA uses Grid Group Management Protocol (GGMP) (Huang, Wu & Pan, 2003) to construct VDHA network. GGMP has two functions. Firstly, it manages membership of virtual groups and the dynamic virtual group tree. Secondly, when a

Figure 1. Structure of VDHA Note: There are 13 nodes in the grid system. These nodes are grouped as 4 VOs. The number of nodes in each VO is 4,3,3,3 respectively. From each VO we choose one node as gateway node to form two up-layer groups with each having 2 nodes. Then from these two groups, one node each was chosen to form a root group.

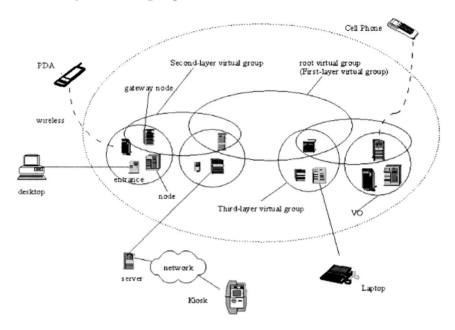

gateway node (Grid node which takes coordinate functions in several different layer virtual groups) fails or leaves, it selects a new one with the maximum weight value from all the on-line nodes in the group the gateway node is involved with. To improve fault-tolerance every member in a virtual group logically contains the group membership list, name and coordinator (a gateway node taking coordinate functions in the virtual group) of the virtual group, and the membership list, name and coordinator of the groups immediately above and below. When there are any changes to the membership of a virtual group, such as a node joining or leaving, these changes are forwarded to the coordinator of the group, which forwards the information to all the members in the group, and to the groups in the neighboring levels. When one coordinator in a virtual group fails, another node in the same virtual group will replace it.

In VDHA, query and discovery protocols are used for querying and discovering some entities such as resources and services, virtual group name, node status, etc. Every node has resources and services which are described by WSDL or ontology languages, etc. Matching the request message is done by the agent of node which has the services. There are two kinds of QDP: Full Search Query and Discovery Protocol (FSQDP) (Huang, Wu & Pan, 2003), which searches all nodes to find nodes that match the request message, and Domain-Specific Query and Discovery Protocol (DSQDP) (Huang, Wu & Pan, 2003), which searches nodes in only specific domains.

FSQDP first finds the root virtual group, and then the coordinator of virtual group of this group forwards the query message to its all members. All of these members execute parallel forwards of the message down to the members of their low-layer groups until leaf virtual groups as Figure 2 shows.

Figure 2. FSQDP searching process

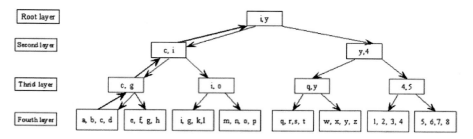

Figure 3. DSQDP searching process

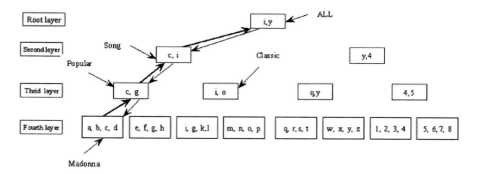

FSQDP is effective, but may cause much traffic. Domain-Specific Query and Discovery Protocol does not have this problem. To use this protocol, the object of virtual group must maintain the catalogue with classifying services from general to detail. It may be done by the nodes' joining the proper virtual group of Grid system. The protocol only searches the nodes whose catalogue matches the request group keywords as Figure 3 shows.

VDHA is suitable for small or medium scale Grid system, which is consisted of many super-computers. It does not belong to P2P system. The disadvantages of **VDHA** are the disruption of the network due to gateway node failure, and bottleneck of computation and communication due to root node's heavy load of computing and heavy traffic of message communications. Because replacing failure gateway node with the new one needs to send message to all members of the related virtual groups, in this time, the VDHA network is broken down. As to query and discovery

protocols, because of all messages pass root node, the queries will be jammed at the root node, and lead to heavy computation at the root node.

VIRTUAL HIERARCHICAL TREE GRID ORGANIZATIONS (VIRGO)

The **VIRGO** overcomes the disadvantages of VDHA and DHT-based structured P2P tech-nologies and inherits the advantages of those technologies by hybridizing unstructured P2P and structured P2P technologies. In a virtual hierarchical overlay network, VIRGO has the following aspects:

- Hybrid of un-structured P2P and structured P2P technology. The structured P2P routes the message to the next hop according to the topology such as tree, ring etc, where as unstructured P2P routes the message to

715

the next hops by flooding to the random neighbours. VIRGO merges an n-tuple replicated virtual tree structured network and a random cached unstructured network. VIRGO routes the message to the next hop by selecting the node with the calculated minimum distance to the destination node among the nodes in virtual tree topology and random cached nodes.

- It is self-organized and decentralized, with an effective lookup protocol for routing messages and a load balanced network.
- It retains the advantage of partial-match querying and the robustness of unstructured P2P networks, and the advantage of effective routing and guarantee search of structured P2P.
- It introduces **scope query** like SQL condition search in database system.

Framework and Protocols of VIRGO

The **VIRGO** is a virtual hierarchical overlay network by hybridizing unstructured P2P and structured P2P technologies. In VIRGO network, there is a core network that consists of stable servers that can access the Internet, and a surrounding circle of thin computers. Machines (called as"clients") in the surrounding circle connect via a node (called as the entrance node) to the core machines by Client/Server technology, whereas the core machines use P2P technology to interact among themselves. This strategy can make the network stable because when nodes join or leave only nodes in the core circle are required to be considered. VIRGO network consists of a prerequisite virtual group tree, which is similar to that described in VDHA (Huang, Wu & Pan, 2003), and random connections cached by least-recently used and minimum distance replacement strategies. The virtual group tree is virtually hierarchical, with one root-layer, several middle-layers, and many leaf virtual groups. Among the nodes of every lower layer virtual groups, N-tuple gateway nodes are

chosen to form upper-layer groups; and from the nodes of these upper-layer groups to form upper-upper-layer groups in the same way; and this way is repeated until one root-layer group is formed (see Figure 4). Random connections cached in a node's routing table are maintained by least-recently used (LRU) and minimum difference (MinD) replacement strategies. The LRU strategy gives a greater chance to frequently requested nodes. The **MinD** strategy gives a greater chance to nodes with differing top prefixes in domain names; this makes VIRGO a distributed network. With randomly cached connections, the netlike VIRGO avoids congestion in the root node of the virtual tree topology, but keeps the advantages of effective message routing in treelike networks. In VIRGO network, every group has a unique group name, such as Science.Biology.Botony, that indicates the group's location in the group tree. The members of a group are nodes with unique Domain Names such as Science.Biology.Botany.BT2 (see Figure 5). The network in Figure 5 is a 2-tuple replicated virtual tree (The nodes with the same character in different layers are actually the same node). For example, BT3, BI1 in the root group come from the same second layer group Science.Biology. The route nodes in the routing table are classified as 'TREE', 'LRU' and 'MinD' types. Every routing node has an ID and its gateway upmost layer, and exists within these groups from bottom layer to gateway upmost layer. BT1(3)means that the node is named as BT1 whose gateway upmost layer is in the third layer.

In order to explain the framework of VIRGO more clearly, we first give some definitions.

- **User** (denoted by user) is the role which accesses the virtual hierarchical overlay networks.
- **Client host** (denoted by cli) is an apparatus (such as desktop computer, PDA, mobile computer, etc), that is used by users to log into the virtual hierarchical overlay network.

Figure 4. Two tuple VIRGO network

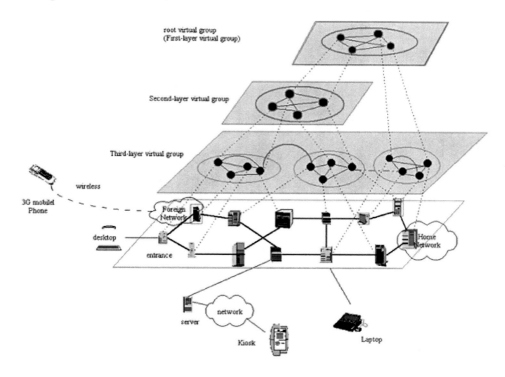

Figure 5. Illustration of lookup and route tables for a two tuple VIRGO network

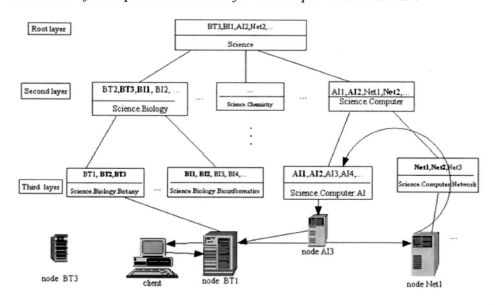

Figure 6. Hop distance

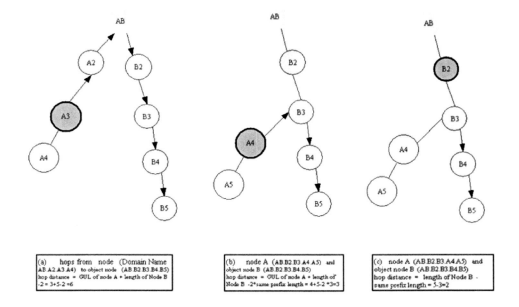

(a) hops from node (Domain Name AB.A2.A3.A4) to object node (AB.B2.B3.B4.B5) hop distance = GUL of node A + length of Node B -2 = 3+5-2 =6

(b) node A (AB.B2.B3.A4.A5) and object node B (AB.B2.B3.B4.B5) hop distance = GUL of node A + length of Node B -2*same prefix length = 4+5-2 *3=3

(c) node A (AB.B2.B3.A4.A5) and object node B (AB.B2.B3.B4.B5) hop distance = length of Node B - same prefix length = 5-3=2

- **Node** (denoted by p) is a basic element in the virtual hierarchical overlay network. Every node has a **Domain Name**, as in DNS, and an Internet IP Address. Gateway (denoted by gn) is a node role which takes part in routing functions in several different layers of virtual groups. A gateway node is a node that is not only in a low-level group, but also is in an upper-level group. Entrance (denoted by ent) is an entrance point of a node for users to log into the virtual hierarchical overlay network.
- **Semantic catalogue** refers to the classification of thins by their semantic meanings.
- **Domain name** (denoted by DN) is a hierarchical domain classification according to the purpose of the network. It is similar to DNS (for example, science.computer.network.Grid). Domain Name Length is the total layers of the Domain Name. In the above example, the length is 4. Every node has a unique Domain Name, and all nodes share a common first prefix (science in the above example). Gateway uppermost layer(denoted

by GUL) is the uppermost virtual group layer that the gateway is in. The layers are ordered from root layer which is labeled as level 1.
- **Virtual group** (denoted by VG) is formed virtually by the gateways nodes. VG^α denotes virtual group with nameα. The group name is part of the node's domain name; that is, in the above example, science, science.computer and science.computer.network are group names.
- **N-tuple virtual group tree** (denoted by NVGT) is a hierarchical tree formed by virtual groups. Among the nodes of the lower layer virtual groups, N-tuple gateway nodes in each group are chosen to form upper-layer groups, and from the nodes of these upper-layer groups to form upper-upper-layer groups in the same way, and this way is repeated until a root-layer group is formed.
- **Node entity** (denoted by NE) is the node's Identification and status. It consists of the **Domain Name**, IP address, GUL of the node, etc.

- **Item of route table** (denoted by IRT) is the record of route table (denoted by routetable). It consists of Node entity (NE), time of last use, and type. Type is classified as TREE, **LRU and MinD**. The node of TREE type is the node in the virtual tree network; a node of LRU type is cached by a least recently-used replacement strategy, and the node with MinD type is cached by minimum difference replacement. The items in the route table are ordered in alphabetical dictionary order by keyword of the node's Domain Name.

Lookup Protocol

The lookup protocol for the VIRGO network is based on the strategy that among nodes in the routing table the node with the minimum distance to the destination node is chosen as the next hop on the route (the theoretical hop distance is calculated as formula in Figure 6). . The strategies of **LRU and MinD** are used for caching route nodes to solve computational and message congestion existing in the tree structure. Figure 5 shows the users using a client via entrance node BT1 (named Science. Biology.Botony.BT1) to request the entities of the destination node named Science.Computer. Network.AI3. The route path of this example is as follows. BT1 –>Net1 (because Net1 has the minimum distance to destination AI3 in BT1's routing table); then Net1–> AI1 (or AI2); then AI1 (or AI2) –>AI3.

The lookup protocol queries the request entities and updates the cached **LRU and MinD** nodes in the route table. The algorithm used by the lookup protocol is as follows:

```
Step 1 cli.send (QUERYMESSAGE,
ent)
Step 2 ent.lookup_ location
(QUERYMESSAGE.DomainName)
Step 3 ent.send(RESULTMESSAGE,
cli);
```

```
Step 4 if ent.macthNodeInRouteT
able(RESULTMESSAGE.ObjectNode.
NE.DomainName)
ent.
RouteTableUpdate(RESULTMESSAGE.
ObjectNode.NE);
else {
if ent.iscachesizeful(LRU)
ent.RouteTableReplacement(RESULT
MESSAGE.ObjectNode.NE, LRU);
else ent.
RouteTableAdd(RESULTMESSAGE.Ob-
jectNode.NE,LRU);
if ent.iscachesizeful(MinD)
ent.RouteTableReplacement(RESULT
MESSAGE.ObjectNode.NE,MinD);
else ent.
RouteTableAdd(RESULTMESSAGE.Ob-
jectNode.NE,MinD);}
```

Here, Function lookup_location locates the destination node by the minimum hops whose algorithm is described as following:

```
Function
p.lookuplocation(QUERYMESSAGE)
routeP = p.selectRouteNodeFromR
outeTable(QUERYMESSAGE.Domain-
Name);
if LengthOfSamePrefix(routeP.
DomainName,QUERYMESSAGE.Domain-
Name)==
LengthOfDomainName(QUERYMESSAGE.
DomainName) {
RESULTMESSAGE= routeP.checkupQue
ryEntities(QUERYMESSAGE);
routeP.send(RESULTMESSAGE,ent);
}
else {
p.send(QUERYMESSAGE,routeP);
if (message sending is suc-
cessful) routeP.lookup_
location(QUERYMESSAGE);
else {
```

```
delete routeP from p.routetable;
p.lookup_
location(QUERYMESSAGE);
  }
}
```

Function selectRouteNodeFromRouteTable chooses the node with the theoretical minimum number of hops to the destination node as the next hop in the route. If there is more than one node with the same minimum number of hops in the route table, a random route node is chosen. The theoretical number of hops to the destination node is calculated as Figure 6 shown.

Maintenance of VIRGO Network

The maintenance of the virtual group tree, initialization of the virtual tree network, the joining of new nodes, the departure of nodes, and the collapse of gateway nodes are all issues that need to be dealt with.

Initialization of VIRGO

When a VIRGO network is planned to establish, we first classify the semantic hierarchical domains, such as music.popular.Brittney.

When a first node creates a new VIRGO network, it sets its own NE(node entity), which includes Domain Name, IP, GUL (value as 1) and type (value as TREE), and creates virtual groups the Domain Name indicated.

Node's Joining VIRGO

When a new node (here denoted as **Pjoin**) joins, it fisrt define its Domain Name, which determines the virtual groups from top to bottom to be joined. Then **Pjoin** finds out the gateway node (denoted as **PgroupToJoin**), which shares the maximum prefix length with the joining node. This step can be done by sending requesting message to any entrance node and then using lookup protocol to find a node which is in the nearest virtual group to the joining virtual group. Because the entrance

node can be one of nodes and is not a fixed node, the joining protocol is decentralized one.

The next steps are as follows:

The joining node sends query message to the gateway node, which forwards the query message to all member nodes of the virtual group. Every node in the virtual group adds the NE of joining node in its route table and responses to the joining node. The joining node adds the NEs of all member nodes of the virtual group. Go to upper layer of virtual group, repeat the process. The pseudo codes are listed as follows:

```
1. Pjoin.send(JOINMESSAGE,
PgroupToJoin)
2. PgroupToJoin.
send(JOINMESSAGE, pi ∈ join-
Group);
3. (pi ∈ joinGroup).send(pi.AP-
PROVEMESSAGE, Pjoin.);
(pi ∈ joinGroup).
RouteTableAdd(Pjoin.NE, TREE);
4. Pjoin..RouteTableAdd(pi ∈
joinGroup.NE,TREE);
5. repeat step 2 to 4 in upper
layer groups until replicated
nodes no less than n-tuple or
root group.
```

Figure 7 shows the establishment of one_tuple **VIRGO** Network for Music Example. The music is classified as two music catalogues: music.popular and music.classic. This VIRGO example network consists of 3 nodes--Node A, B, C. One node can join more than one **virtual group**. After establishing the example VIRGO network, the route tables of all nodes is shown in Table 1.

Node's Leaving VIRGO

When a leaving node (denoted as **Pdpt**) leaves the network, it will notify all the members of the virtual groups from the top layer to the bottom layer which the leaving node within. These members

Figure 7. Establishment of VIRGO network for musical example

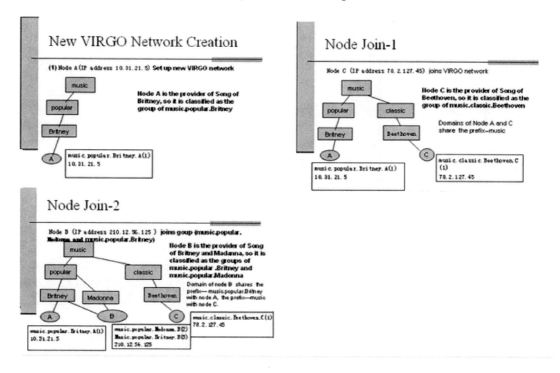

will update their route tables. Each group will select a node to replace this left nodes' gateway role. The main steps in a node's departure from the network are as follows.

1. **Pdpt**.send(LEFTMESSAGE, $p_i \in$ leftgroup);
2. ($p_i \in$ leftgroup).RouteT ableDelete(**Pdpt. NE,TREE**);
3. choose $P_{repalcenode}$ to replace the left node's role;
4. repeat step 1 and 3 in lower layer groups until to the bottom layer group of left node **Pdpt**.

Node's Failure in VIRGO

Nodes may fail or depart without warning. Failure Node (denoted as **Pfail**) is considered to have failed when a node (denoted as **Pnotice**) happens to fail to communicate with node **Pfail** several times. Then node **Pnotice** sends the FAILUREMESSAGE to all the members in the groups from **Pfail**'s top layer to the bottom layer. And every group chooses a node to replace **Pfail**'s gateway role.

1. **Pnotice**, send(FAILUREMESSAGE, $p_i \in$ failgroup);
2. ($p_i \in$ failgroup).RouteTableDelete(**Pfail. NE,TREE**);
3. Choose $P_{repalcenode}$ to replace **Pfail** 's role;
4. repeat step 1 and 3 in lower layer groups until to the bottom layer group of **Pfail**.

Performance Analysis of VIRGO

Availability

Theorem 1. *For an N-tuple virtual group tree, for any two nodes there exists a route path all the time with high probability.*

   Proof: Suppose the time required to replace a failed or departing gateway node is Tr seconds, and the failure or departure frequency of a node within Tr is F(p, Tr). The tree path length of the node to another node is Length, and Pf is the probability that a route path between two nodes fails to exist for all time. Due to the N-tuple replicated gateway nodes, we have:

$$Pf = F(p, Tr)^N * (Length - 1) \qquad (1)$$

If Tr is 60 seconds, and each node fails on average 10 times per day, then $F(p, Tr) = 10*60/(24*60*60) = 1/144$. And if N-tuple is 6 and Length is 10, so Pf is $(1/144)^6 * 9 < 10^{-11}$. This extremely small failure probability only affects performance because nodes can wait Tr time to route again, or the user may make the request once more.

Complexity

If the message is routed along the tree path, then every hop will reduce the distance from the destination node. Because the route table contains TREE portion, every hop reduces the distance from destination node by at least one hop. Therefore,

hops (a,b) and message cost < length(a) + length(b)-1 $\qquad (2)$

Time complexity = O(L) (3),

where L is the tree depth.

Because the gateway existing from root layer to bottom layer groups has the maximum route nodes in the route table, we have:

Items of route table = $L*N_{\_tuple}*nvg + Max\_MinD + Max\_LRU$ $\qquad (4)$

Space complexity = O(L) (5),

where nvg is number of virtual groups, Max_MinD is the maximum number of MinD records in the route table, and Max_LRU is the maximum number of LRU records in the route table. Suppose all leaf virtual groups have the same number of nodes, nvg and all non-leaf virtual groups have the same number of nodes, $nvg * n_{\_tuple}$, then the number of layers L is $\log_{nvg} N$, where N is the total size of the network. So,

Table 1. Route tables of the illustrated example for music providing service

(1) Route table of node A				
ID	IP Address	GUL	Type	Is self?
Music.popular.Britney.A	10.31.21.5	1	TREE	Yes
Music.popular.Britney.B	210.12.56.125	3	TREE	No
Music.popular.Madonna.B	210.12.56.125	2	TREE	No
Music.classic.Beethoven.C	78.2.127.45 1	1	TREE	No
(2) Route table of node B				
ID	IP Address	GUL	Type	Is self?
Music.popular.Britney.A	10.31.21.5	1	TREE	No
Music.popular.Britney.B	210.12.56.125	3	TREE	Yes
Music.popular.Madonna.B	210.12.56.125	2	TREE	Yes
(3) Route table of node C				
ID	IP Address	GUL	Type	Is self?
Music.popular.Britney.A	10.31.21.5	1	TREE	No
Music.classic.Beethoven.C	78.2.127.45 1	1	TREE	Yes

Time complexity and message cost = O(log N) (6)

Space complexity = O(log N) (7)

If the network has total number 108 nodes and 100 nodes per virtual group, then the routing hops to the destination is less than 8 ($2* \log_{100} 108 = 8$). Because VIRGO's lookup strategy is different to other DHT P2P systems, partial-query is possible and has the same time complexity by registering the contents in nodes according to the classification of domain names.

By using a LRU strategy for caching route table, routing to destination node can be partly reduced to just one hop.

Due to the LRU replacement strategy, only recent nodes of interest during a short period need to be cached. Within this short period, N (ent,user,t), which is the number of nodes requested by a user via entrance during the time which covers a whole process from requesting information and getting the result back, is small. We have the following formula:

$$RHR_{ent} = R_{LRU}/(\cup^{Ent}_{user} N(ent,user,t)) \quad (8)$$

Here, RHR(RecordHitRate) is the probability of caching a destination node in the LRU portion of route table of a node. R_{LRU} is the number of LRU cached route table records in the route table. Ent_{user} is the number of users via an entrance node.

Supposing $^{Ent}_{user}$ is 100, N(ent,user,t) is 10, and R_{LRU} 500, then RHR_{ent} = 500/100*10 = 0.5. This means that half of requests just need one hop.

Because formula (8) has no relation with the whole number of nodes in VIRGO network, a large scale system has the same Record Hit Rate. For mobile users, if we cache the nodes of interest in user's owner nodes, and after attaching entrance node, user first sends request to its owner, and then we can obtain the same formula.

Load Balance

For P2P systems load balance is a very important issue. Because the load on the root layer node is the highest message load among all nodes in the network, we here only analyze the root node's message load. We use two strategies to solve the load balance problem. The first is the LRU caching strategy as in the above section. The chance of routing a message through the root node is less than $1-RHR_{ent}$. The second is the minimum difference (MinD) replacement strategy. The message load on root node is as formula 9.

$$Root_{msg}(t) = P_{msg}(user, t)*Nuser * (1-RHR_{ent}) * (1-MinDRHR)^{L-1} /n\_tuple(9),$$

where, N_{User} is the total numer of users in the VIRGO network. MinDRHR (MinDRecordHitRate) is the probability of caching the shorter distance node in a node's MinD portion of the route table than the nodes in its TREE route table. R_{MinD} is the number of MinD cached records in the route table. $P_{msg}(user, t)$ is the probability of the user's sending requested message at time t, which follows a Poisson distribution, is small.

Supposing RHR_{ent} =0.2, MinDRHR=0.99, $NUser_{ent}$ = 10^{10}, the number of nodes is 10^8, N_tuple is 6, nvg is 100, and $P_{msg}(user, t)$= 0.00001, then L = $\log_{100}(108)$ = 4. So, Rootmsg(t) = 0.00001 * 1010 * 0.8 * 0.013/6 = 0.013.

Implementation

The open source project--- VIRGO (http://virgo.sourceforge.net/) consists of core protocol package and application packages such as workflow, distributed file system, distributed DNS, etc. The VIRGO node uses Tomcat as Web Server and Axis as Web service container (see Figure 8). Every node implements Lookup protocol, VIRGO structure maintenance, Web Service matchmaker, and Registry. The VIRGO core program implements all protocols for VIRGO (see Figure 9). The route table is stored by mySQL database. Figure

Figure 8. Software architecture of VIRGO

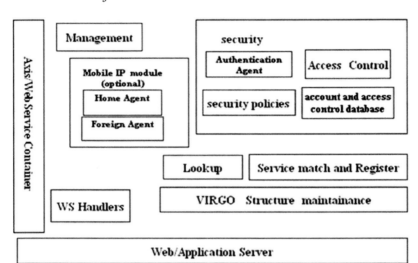

10 shows the processes for client's consuming Web services in VIRGO network.

Applications Built on VIRGO

VIRGO can be used in resource discovery, distributed file system, distributed DNS, etc. Here, we discuss two applications based on VIRGO.

Service Discovery Based on VIRGO

Service Discovery is an important issue in Web Services (http://www.w3.org/TR/ws-arch/) and Grid technologies. The service discovery based on centralized register servers has shortage of crushdown due to single point failure. There are many approaches for distributed service discovery based on P2P technologies (Iamnitchi & Foster, 2001). The un-structural P2P technology such as Freenet using flooding way has shortage of heavy traffic and un-guaranteed search. The structural P2P technology using DHT such as Chord and Pastry loses locality property. Service discovery based on VIRGO (Huang, 2007a; Huang, 2007b; Huang, 2008a) can query scope services like SQL condition search in database system.

As about service matchmaker, semantic Web technologies (Berners-Lee, Hendler & Lassila, 2001) can be used to further enhance semantic service discovery. Service matchmaker by Paolucci, et.al (Paolucci, Kawamura, Payne & Sycara, 2002) use OWL-S to annotate with metadata whose relationships are typically defined with domain ontology. Building on the Rough sets theory, ROSSE (Li, Yu, Omer, R.F. & Wang, 2008) is capable of reducing uncertain properties. In this way, ROSSE Increases the accuracy of service discovery. VIRGO can discover services from huge amount of ones by their semantic meaning. VIRGO use granular computing to solve the vague knowledge of domain classification of Web services. It is reasonable to assume that the knowledge about domain classification for Web Services is granular and there exists boundaries for this knowledge which can be described with several set operations. Supposing that there is a global hierarchical classification of domains, the classification methods for domains are not unique. For a specific domain, someone will use one standard for classification, but others will use other standards for classification. We use roughness function measurement based on P-lower, NP-lower and P-upper, NP-upper approximations

Figure 9. Snapshot of java source codes of VIRGO project

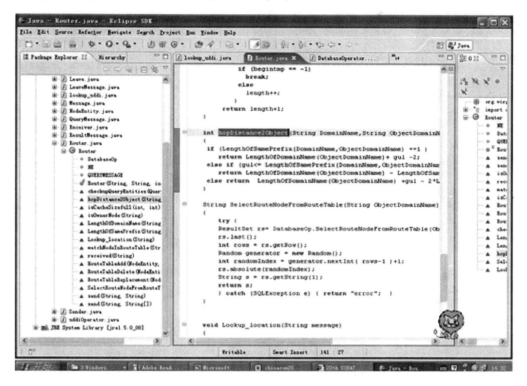

Figure 10. Sequence chart of Web service's consuming in VIRGO network

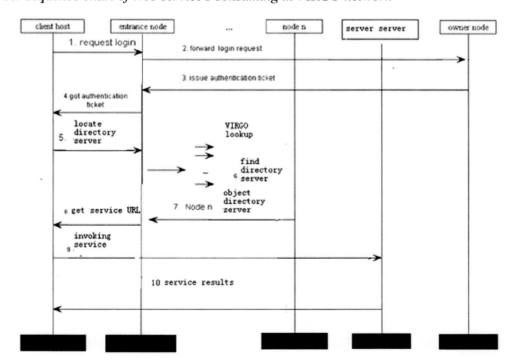

Figure 11. Service catalogue

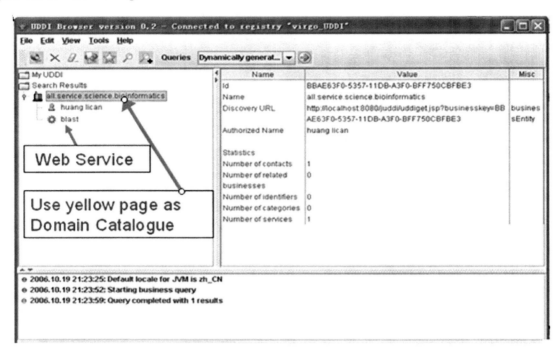

of P set (properties) to find the most suitable web services(Huang & Liu, 2008). We also use the hierarchical algorithm to find the suitable web service effective.

The VIRGO node is taken as service directory. The services are classified into **semantic catalogue**s called as global-hier-part like Domain names. The services are named as "global-hier-part/local-name". The local name part is classified according properties. The services are published into VIRGO nodes. This node then joins with the virtual group whose domain is the same as the service catalogue's domain. For example, if one node provides a song by Madonna, which is classified as music.popular.Madonna, it registers the service into its own repository and joins the virtual group, music.popular.Madonna, in the VIRGO network. Figure 9 shows that the services are classified into all_sicence.science. bioinformatics, and UDDI (http://www.uddi.org/pubs/uddi_v3.htm) yellow page is used as service catalogue(see Figure 11).

We use VIRGO lookup to find URL of web services. Because of services catalogued according to their semantic meaning, we can use sql-like language to find scope services as the following.

```
query::=SELECT{ SUBDOMAIN|ENTITY
|ATTRIBUTE|*|expr[[AS]c_alias]
,expr[[AS]c_alias]...}} FROM
domainref [WHERE search_condi-
tion]; (10)
```

Here, SUBDOMAIN is for querying subdomain for a given super Domain; ENTITY is for querying all entities for a given search condition; ATTRIBUTE is for querying all attributes for a given search condition; expr is for the property queried, which may be a set of properties; [AS] c_alias is the alias name for expr; domainref is for Domain Name, in which we can use * to indicate all sub domains; search_condition is similar to SQL statement in Database.

We use online musical services as example to illustrate the **scope query**.

Operation 1

The form "global-hier-part/?" is to query all services in the global-hier-parts domain. For example, "Britney.popular.music/?" queries all songs by Britney Spears. We can use the following Statement:

```
SELECT * FROM Britney.popular.
music;
```

Operation 2

Suppose that global-hier-part can be expressed as leafDomain.superDomain. The form "?.superDomain/" is to query all leafDomains. This is possible because of the hierarchical structure and the protocols. For example, "?.popular.music" queries all popular singers. We can use the following Statement:

```
SELECT SUBDOMAIN FROM *.popular.
music ;
```

Operation 3

The form "global-hier-part/local-name" is to query specific resource. For example, "Britney.popular.music/Lonely" queries the information of the song-Lonely. We can use the following Statement:

```
SELECT Lonely FROM Britney.popu-
lar.music ;
```

Operation 4

The form "global-hier-part/expression" is to query the resources which satisfy the conditions of the expression indicated. Expression can be scope, maximum, minimum, where condition like SQL statements. For example, "Britney.popular.music/where year between 2006 and 2007" queries all songs by Britney Spears which are produced between 2006 and 2007. We can use the following Statement:

```
SELECT * FROM Britney.popular.
music WHERE Year >=2006 AND Year
<=2007;
```

Distributed DNS Based on VIRGO

Although DNS becomes a vital component in today's Internet infrastructure, the existing DNS architecture may encounter problems for the growth of the Internet in the coming IPv6 network. In IPv6 network, there are huge IP address spaces. Therefore, it is reasonable to suppose there are huge numbers of Domain Names. Furthermore, pervasive computing requires more DNS queries. Those above will result in traffic load and latency of DNS lookups. In today's DNS architecture the servers for TLD zones are bottle neck for lookup of domain names. There are easily to attack by hackers. DNS is unreachable due to the breakdown of root servers. VIRGO based Distributed DNS (Huang, 2008b) may be a choice to solve the above problems.

In this distributed DNS framework based on VIRGO (see Figure 12), DNS servers construct VIRGO network according to domain zones. Every DNS server is the same but some coexist in more than one layer. Every DNS Server maintains a route table and a zone file containing RR records related to its Domain Zone. Route table includes addresses of Foreign Name Servers which are prerequisite for VIRGO Network and cached addresses of Foreign Name Servers which are refreshed by Least Frequently Used Replacement Policy (LFU) based on Zipf's law.

In this framework, all DNS servers maintain route tables. And all route tables have the same top level format shown below, which is also called as Domain Server Node Entity (DSNE) (see Table 2):

The query process is as the following: User program sends QUERY MESSAGE to Local Name Server. If Local Name Server is the authoritative Domain Name Server, then the Local Name

Figure 12. Framework of distributed DNS based on VIRGO

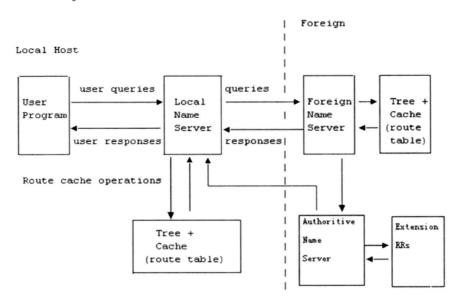

Server will check its RRs to resolve the request Domain name. Otherwise, The Local Name Server will route to the Foreign Name Server which is closer to the authoritative Domain Name Server by calculating theoretical hops. Then the Foreign Name Server routes to the even closer Foreign Domain Name Server. Repeat this process, until the authoritative Domain Name Server has been found. Finally, the authoritative Domain Name Server resolves request Domain Name by check its RR record, and responses to the Local Name Server. The latter will forward the response to the User Program.

The cached addresses of Name Servers are based on Least Frequently Used Replacement Policy (LFU). Because the queries of DNS obeys Zipf's law, with carefully design, the DNS queries may reach O(1) hops.

In Zipf-like query distributions, number of queries (Q_n) to the ith most popular object is:

$$Q_n = C \times i^{-\alpha} \tag{11}$$

Where α is the parameter of the distribution.

The probability distribution function (PDF) is:

$$PDF = C \times i^{-\alpha} / S \tag{12}$$

Table 2. Domain Server Node Entity (DSNE)

Section	Description
DNSI	Domain Name Server Identification of an Domain Server
TYPE	Route TYPE codes (TREE as 0, CHACHE as 1)
GUL	the value of gateway upmost layer of Domain Serve
TTL	the time interval that the route record may be cached before the source of the information should again be consulted.
UTS	Unreachable time stamp. If the route was cached, then refresh it by TTL rule. If the route is gateway node in virtual tree structure, notice to manager to repair it.
IPADDRESSes	IP addresses of the replicated Domain Servers

Here S is the total number of queries.

The cumulative distribution from first most popular object to N most popular object (N is the number of objects) (CumDN) is:

$$CumDN = C / S (N^{1-\alpha}/(1-\alpha) - 1^{1-\alpha}/(1-\alpha)) \qquad (13)$$

This is approximately equal to formula 14.

$$CumDN = C / S (N^{1-\alpha}/(1-\alpha)) \qquad (14)$$

Obviously, the above CumDN value is 1; so

$$C / S = (1-\alpha) / N^{1-\alpha} \qquad (15)$$

The cumulative distribution from first to m-th most popular object (CumDm) is approximately:

$$CumDm = C / S (m^{1-\alpha}/(1-\alpha)) \qquad (16)$$

So, hit rate probability (p) is:

$$p = m^{1-\alpha}/ N^{1-\alpha} \qquad (17)$$

If we cache m DSNEs, then

Average hops (Av) is:

$$Av = \sum((i-1)p^i), i = 1...2L-2 \qquad (18)$$

Here L is the length of domain name.

For example, suppose that total DNS servers N is 1,000,000, and α parameter 0.91 (Jung, Sit, Balakrishnan & Morris, 2001), m is 1000, L is 3, then p is 0.537; and average hops is 1.22.

FUTURE TRENDS

P2P is a next generation computing model. The un-structured and structured P2P technologies at present have some disadvantages. The unstructured P2P technologies route nodes by a "flooding" algorithm, which brings the problems of traffic load and un-guaranteed search. The structured P2P technologies based on DHT breaks the semantic meaning of the nodes. These two kinds of P2P approaches both do not care about the semantic meaning of the nodes. They do not care about the nodes whose users may take different roles in social groups in the communities. The semantic P2P networks are the future trends. VIRGO is a semantic P2P network. Its nodes are identified as semantic classified domain names, and join the network according to their semantic meaning. It may overcome the disadvantages of the current P2P networks by hybridizing un-structured and structured P2P technologies. We are now working at open source project—VIRGO to implement VIRGO protocols and its applications. In the future, we are focusing on two fields about VIRGO. The one is to simulate behaves of VIRGO in Cluster machines and Grid network. The other is to cooperate with companies, universities or research institutes to develop and use VIRGO based applications.

CONCLUSION

Today P2P computing mainly includes two kinds of P2P technologies: un-structural and structural P2P technologies. Un-structural technology uses flooding queries to find the answers. However, it cannot ensure correct results. Moreover, flooding queries search is distributed but still not scalable. Structured P2P technology is mostly based on a distributed hash table. But it can not query resources by complicated search condition. Virtual hierarchical tree grid organizations (VIRGO) is a potential solution to the above problems. VIRGO is a P2P network that merges an n-tuple replicated virtual tree structured network and a random cached unstructured network by least-recently used (LRU) and minimum difference (MinD) replacement strategies. It is self-organizing and decentralized, with an effective lookup protocol for routing messages and a load balanced network. It retains the advantage of partial-match querying and the robustness of unstructured P2P networks, and the advantage of effective routing and guarantee search of structured P2P. The time complexity, space complexity, and message-cost for VIRGO are O(logN) (N being the total number of nodes in the network). The most important advantage of VIRGO is that VIRGO organizes nodes according to semantic catalogues of these nodes' contents; this leads to retrieving information by the mode of scope query like SQL condition searching in database. Through this chapter audience can learn about the concepts, framework, protocols, implementation and applications of VIRGO.

REFERENCES

Berners-Lee, T., Hendler, J., & Lassila, O. (2001). The Semantic Web. *Scientific American, 284*(4), 34–43. doi:10.1038/scientificamerican0501-34

Clark, D. (2001). Face-to-face with peer-to-peer networking. *Computer, 34*(1), 18–21. doi:10.1109/2.970548

Exarchakos, G., Salter, J., & Antonopoulos, N. (2006). *Semantic cooperation and node sharing among P2P networks.* Retrieved from http://personal.cs.surrey.ac.uk/personal/pg/G.Exarchakos/publications/ final_grome.pdf

Foster, I., & Kesselman, C. (1997). Globus: A meta-computing infrastructure toolkit. *The International Journal of Supercomputer Applications, 11*(2), 115–128. doi:10.1177/109434209701100205

Foster, I., Kesselman, C., & Tuecke, S. (2001). The anatomy of the grid: Enabling scalable virtual organizations. *International Journal of High Performance Computing Applications, 15*(3), 200–222. doi:10.1177/109434200101500302

Huang, L. (2005). VIRGO: Virtual hierarchical overlay network for scalable Grid computing. In P.M.A. Sloot, et al. (Eds.), *European Grid Conference (EGC2005), Advances in Grid Computing,* (LNCS Vol. 3470, pp. 911-921). Berlin: Springer-Verlag.

Huang, L. (2007a). A P2P service discovery strategy based on content catalogues. *Data Science Journal, 6,* S492–S499. doi:10.2481/dsj.6.S492

Huang, L. (2007b). Framework for mobile Grid computing by hybridizing structural and un-structural P2P technologies. *International Transactions on Systems Science and Applications, 2*(4), 427–432.

Huang, L. (2008a). Resource discovery based on VIRGO P2P distributed DNS framework In M. Bubak, et al, (Eds.), IC*CS 2008, Computational Science – ICCS 2008,* (LNCS Vol. 5103, pp. 501-509). Berlin: Springer-Verlag.

Huang, L. (2008b). VIRGO P2P based distributed DNS framework for IP V6 Network. In . *Proceedings of, NCM2008,* 698–702.

Huang, L., & Liu, Y. (2008). Domain classification by granular computing used in a P2P approach for Web service discovery. In *Proceedings of Cyberwords2008.*

Huang, L., Wu, Z., & Pan, Y. (2002), Virtual and dynamic hierarchical architecture of E-SCience Grid and relative protocols. In *Proceedings of UK e-Science Programme All Hands Meeting(Poster),* Sheffield, UK. Retrieved from http://www.allhands.org.uk/2002/proceedings/Conference-Digest-AHC-2002.pdf

Huang, L., Wu, Z., & Pan, Y. (2003). Virtual and dynamic hierarchical architecture for e-Science Grid. *International Journal of High Performance Computing Applications, 17*(3), 329–347. doi:10.1177/1094342003173001

Iamnitchi, A., & Foster, I. (2001). On fully decentralized resource discovery in Grid environments. In *Proceedings of International Workshop on Grid Computing.*

Jung, J., Sit, E., Balakrishnan, H., & Morris, R. (2001). DNS performance and effectiveness of caching. In *Proceedings of SIGCOMM Internet Measurement Workshop*, San Francisco.

Kant, K., Iyer, R., & Tewari, V. (2002). A framework for classifying peer-to-peer technologies. In *Proc. of the 2nd IEEE/ACM Int'l Symp. on Cluster Computing and the Grid* (CCGRID02).

Li, M., Yu, B., Omer, R. F., & Wang, Z. (2008). Grid service discovery with rough sets. *IEEE Transactions on Knowledge and Data Engineering, 20*(6), 851–862. doi:10.1109/TKDE.2007.190744

Mockapetris, P. (1987). *Domain names - Implementation and specification.* Specification, RFC1035. Retrieved from http://www.ietf.org/rfc/rfc1035.txt

Paolucci, M., Kawamura, T., Payne, T., & Sycara, K. (2002). Semantic matching of Web service capabilities. In *Proc. First Int'l Semantic Web Conf. (ISWC '02)*, (pp. 333-347).

Ratnasamy, S., Francis, P., Handley, K., Karp, R., & Shenker, S. (2001). A scalable contentaddressable network. In *Proceedings of the 2001 conference on Applications, technologies, architectures, and protocols for computer communications*, (pp.161 – 172). New York: ACM.

Rowstron, A., & Druschel, P. (2001). Pastry: Scalable, distributed object location and routing for large-scale peer-to-pear systems. In *Proceedings of IFIP/ACM International Conference on Distributed Systems Platforms (Middleware).*

Stoica, I., Morris, R., Karger, D., Kaashoek, M. F., & Balakrishnan, H. (2001). Chord: a scalable peer-to-peer lookup service for internet applications. In *Proceedings of the 2001 conference on Applications, technologies, architectures, and protocols for computer communications*, (pp. 149 – 160). New York: ACM.

KEY TERMS AND DEFINITIONS

Availability: Due to n-tuple gateway nodes, every two nodes exits at least one connection path.

Domain Name: The nodes are named as DNS format according to the nodes' interests.

LRU and MinD: Least-recently used (LRU) strategy gives a greater chance to frequently requested nodes. The minimum difference (MinD) strategy gives a greater chance to nodes with differing top prefixes in domain names.

N-Tuple Virtual Hierarchical Tree: The nodes are virtually grouped into hierarchical tree. But, every group has n-tuple gateway nodes.

Scope Query: Because contents are classified into semantic groups and registered into to same semantic nodes of VIRGO network, the query may find scope answers by SQL-like search statements.

Semantic Catalogue: The nodes are semantically classified into catalogues according to their interests.

Virtual and Dynamic Hierarchical Architecture: Abbreviated as **VDHA**. The nodes are virtually grouped into hierarchical tree. Every group has one (just one) gateway node.

Virtual Group: Abbreviated as **VG**. It is formed virtually by the gateways nodes. VG^α denotes virtual group with name α. The group name is part of the node's domain name.

Virtual Hierarchical Tree Grid Organizations: Abbreviated as **VIRGO**. P2P network by Hybridizing un-structured P2P and Structured P2P technologies. The route tables of nodes containing N-tuple Virtual Hierarchical Tree and random cached nodes by the strategy of LRU and MinD.

Chapter 31
Electronic Business Contracts Between Services

Simon Miles
King's College London, UK

Felipe Meneguzzi
King's College London, UK

Nir Oren
King's College London, UK

Nora Faci
University of Lyon, France

Michael Luck
King's College London, UK

Camden Holt
Lost Wax, UK

Sanjay Modgil
King's College London, UK

Gary Vickers
Lost Wax, UK

ABSTRACT

Electronic contracts mirror the paper versions exchanged between businesses today, and offer the possibility of dynamic, automatic creation and enforcement of restrictions and compulsions on service behaviour that are designed to ensure business objectives are met. Where there are many contracts within a particular application, it can be difficult to determine whether the system can reliably fulfil them all, yet computer-parsable electronic contracts may allow such verification to be automated. In this chapter, the authors describe a conceptual framework and architecture specification in which normative business contracts can be electronically represented, verified, established, renewed, and so on. In particular, they aim to allow systems containing multiple contracts to be checked for conflicts and violations of business objectives. They illustrate the framework and architecture with an aerospace aftermarket example.

DOI: 10.4018/978-1-61520-686-5.ch031

INTRODUCTION

It has often been argued that independent entities, such as business services, interacting in a common system, society or environment need to be suitably constrained in order to avoid and solve conflicts, make agreements, reduce complexity, and in general to achieve a desirable social order (Conte & Castelfranchi, 1993; Conte, Falcone & Sartor, 1999). For many, this role is fulfilled by norms, which represent what *ought* to be done by a set of services (when performing functions on behalf of their owning business). Views of norms differ, and include fixed laws that must never be violated as well as more flexible social guides that merely seek to bias behaviour in different ways. Yet the obligations, prohibitions and permissions that may affect service behaviour in a normative system can also be *documented* and communicated between services in the form of *contracts*. Electronic contracts, mirroring the paper versions exchanged between businesses today, offer the possibility of dynamic, automatic creation and enforcement of such restrictions and compulsions on service behaviour. However, where there are many contracts within a particular application, it can be difficult to determine whether the system can reliably fulfil them all; computer-parsable electronic contracts may allow such verification to be automated.

In a peer-to-peer system, organisations, and the services performing functions on their behalf, act as independent peers, with no overall authority, and contracts are necessary to add predictability to behaviour between them. Where there is multiple, independently owned alternatives for a resource or service, contract technology is of particular use. By providing and monitoring contract compliance, applications can make better decisions on which resources or services to take advantage of in the future, a particular problem on Grid systems with a range of reliability issues.

There are two pre-requisites to realistically applying an electronic contracting approach in real-world domains. First, to exploit electronic contracts, a well-defined conceptual framework for contract-based systems, to which the application entities can be mapped, is needed. Second, to support the management of contracts through all stages of the contract life-cycle, we need to specify the functionality required of a contract management architecture that would underlie any such system, leading to ready-made implementations for particular deployments of that architecture. The CONTRACT project (CONTRACT, 2008) aims to do just this. Funded by the European Commission as part of its 6th Framework Program, the project seeks to develop frameworks, components and tools that "make it possible to model, build, verify and monitor distributed electronic business systems on the basis of dynamically generated, cross-organisational contracts which underpin formal descriptions of the expected behaviours of individual services and the system as a whole." In this context, this chapter documents the CONTRACT project's work on both of the pre-requisites identified above. More specifically, the technical contributions described in this chapter are:

- The specification of a model for describing contract-based systems
- The specification of an architecture for managing such systems
- The mapping of an aerospace application to those models

Our approach is distinct in several respects. First, its development is explicitly driven by a range of use cases (Jakob et al., 2008) provided by a diverse set of small and large businesses. One consequence of this diversity is that our approach must account for different practices and possibilities in each stage of the lifecycle of a contract-based system. It is therefore defined in terms of abstract *process types*, to be instantiated in different ways for different circumstances. We provide a non-exhaustive set

Figure 1. The overall structure of the CONTRACT architecture and framework

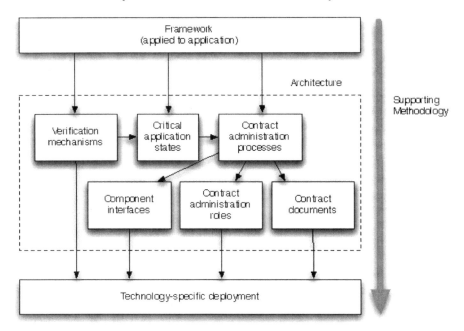

of options for instantiating these process types, and technologies to support these processes. A more specific requirement addressed by our approach is in managing not just fulfilment or violation of contractual obligations, but also other *critical states* of the system with regard to those obligations, such as being in danger of violation, being expected to easily fulfil an obligation, and application-specific states.

In the next section, we provide an overview of the overall structure, introducing the conceptual framework and applying it to a running example. We then discuss how the contractual obligations imply critical states of the system that we may wish to detect and react to in order to effectively manage the system. After that, we describe the architecture: the process types that are required to manage contract-based systems and components that can support such processes. Finally, we discuss related work and conclude with future work.

CONTRACT FRAMEWORK AND ARCHITECTURE

The models and procedures comprising the CONTRACT *framework* and *architecture* are shown in Figure 1. The primary component of this is the framework itself, depicted at the top of the figure, which is the conceptual structure used to describe a contract-based system, including the contracts and the services to which they apply.

From the framework specification of an application, other information is derived. First, understanding the contractual obligations of services allows us to specify the *critical states* that an application may reach. A critical state of a contract-based system with regard to an obligation essentially indicates whether the obligation is fulfilled or fulfillable: achieved, failed, in danger, and so on. This is discussed in the following section. A state-based description, along with the deontic (concerning duties) and epistemic (concerning knowledge) implications of the specified contracts, can then be used to verify a system either off-line or at run-time (Lomuscio & Sergot, 2003) (we do not discuss this further here). The framework specification is used to determine suitable processes for administration of the electronic contracts through their lifetimes, including establishment, update, termination, and renewal. Such processes also include observation of the system, so that contractual obligations can be enforced or otherwise managed, and these processes depend on the critical states identified above. Once suitable administration processes are identified, we can also specify the roles that services play within them, the components that should be part of services to allow them to manage their contracts, and the contract documents themselves. Such process types and roles are described further below.

A Contract-Based System Framework

We first specify a conceptual framework by which contract-based systems can be described. This framework provides a clear indication of how particular applications can exploit contracts and how they must be supported in managing them. By being abstract and generic, such a framework may be used to translate contract data from one concrete format to another.

Contracts document *obligations, permissions* and *prohibitions* (collectively *clauses*) on services and are *agreed* by those services (strictly, it is the

agent enacting the service's logic (W3C, 2008) to which impositions on behaviour apply). Put simply, obligations are statements that services should do something and prohibitions are statement that they should not. Permissions are defined as exceptions to prohibitions: if something was not prohibited, it is not meaningful for a permission to be granted.

The services obliged, permitted and prohibited in a contract are parties to that contract, which specifies *roles* played by services within it. Each clause in a contract applies to roles, to which services are *assigned*, and each service can hold multiple contracts with the same or different parties. The obligation, permission or prohibition defined in a clause is on the service(s) assigned to the role to which the clause applies. A *contract proposal* is a contract that has not yet been agreed by its parties. The concepts are summarised in Table 1.

Aerospace Use Case

To test and illustrate the efficacy of our approach, we adopt an engineering application, based on the aerospace aftercare market, targeted by Lost Wax's agent-based Aerogility platform (Lost Wax, 2008), and used as a running example through the chapter.

The application concerns the continued maintenance of aircraft engines over their lifetime. In this domain, an engine manufacturer is contractually

Table 1. The primary concepts in the CONTRACT framework

Role	A named part that can be played by a service in a system.
Obligation	A statement that a service playing a given role should do something.
Prohibition	A statement that a service playing a given role should not do something.
Permission	An exception to a prohibition for a service playing a given role under given circumstances.
Clause	An obligation, prohibition or permission.
Assignment	A statement that a service should play a given role.
Proposal	A document containing a set of clauses and assignments, where every role referred to which each clause applies has been assigned to a service.
Contract	A proposal to which all assigned services have agreed.

obliged to ensure operators' aircraft have working engines. For an engine to be working, it should not be overdue for regular servicing or left waiting to be fixed after a fault is discovered.

An aircraft's engine can be replaced when it lands at some location if there is a suitable spare engine present at that location. As well as replacing engines to ensure continued operation of the aircraft, an engine manufacturer will service the engines it has removed, so that the serviced engine can be added back into circulation (the "engine pool") and used to replace other engines. In addition to long-term contracts between engine manufacturers and operators, we consider short-term contracts regarding particular instances of servicing engines. These sit in the context of long-term contracts but, by being specified explicitly, allow the parties to use and commit to resources more flexibly. In a long-term contract between an aircraft operator and an engine manufacturer, the manufacturer agrees to service the operator's aircraft to some overall specified standard over the duration of the contract. Such a contract is provided in Table 2, using the framework concepts. Here, the operator specifies a preferred time within which the manufacturer must service an aircraft, and the manufacturer is obliged to meet this in 90% of cases. If the manufacturer does not meet short-term contract requirements (see below), penalties are deducted from the long-term payment

the operator is obliged to make. The operator is obliged to provide adequate engine data so that the manufacturer can fulfil their servicing obligations. Finally, the operator may have demands on the provenance of an engine: operator A may be happy to re-use engines previously used by operators B or C but not those used by D.

In this context, a short-term contract concerns the servicing of a particular aircraft at a particular time (see Table 3). It is again between two parties: the aircraft operator and the engine manufacturer. In this case, the manufacturer has more specific obligations: that they must either service an aircraft in the preferred timescale or pay a penalty, and that they must service it within a maximum period. The limitations on provenance apply in the particular short-term servicing as they do in the long-term aftercare.

Such formal documentation of agreements is important, especially when there are multiple agreements and when these agreements can interact, because they can reveal points of potential or actual conflict. If it is possible to examine such contracts, and determine where these points lie, then one can monitor for violations, or even instigate measures to pre-empt violation. In what follows, these aims inform the elaboration of our architecture. For example, a short-term conflict between two servicing contracts in the aerospace domain occurs when a manufacturer is obliged

Table 2. Long-term aftercare contract

Roles		Manufacturer, Operator
Obligations	O1	Manufacturer agrees to servicing contracts (defined in Table 3) requested by operator during aftercare contract period.
	O2	Manufacturer services engines within the preferred time specified by the servicing contracts in at least 90% of cases.
	O3	Operator pays for servicing of engines, minus any penalties.
	O4	Operator must supply engine health data to the manufacturer in an adequate time to allow problems requiring unscheduled maintenance to be detected.
Prohibitions	P1	Manufacturer is prohibited from supplying engines with parts previously used by other operators not on an approved list (if one is given) or on a disapproved list (if one is given).
Permissions	R1	Manufacturer is allowed to supply engines with parts previously used by other operators on an approved list (if one is given).

Table 3. Short-term servicing contract

Roles		Manufacturer, Operator
Obligations	**O5**	Manufacturer services aircraft in preferred time, or pays penalty (taken out of aftercare contract payment from operator).
	O6	Manufacturer services engine in maximum time.
Prohibitions	**P2**	Manufacturer is prohibited from supplying engines with parts previously used by other operators not on an approved list (if one is given) or on a disapproved list (if one is given).
Permissions	**R2**	Manufacturer is allowed to supply engines with parts previously used by other operators on an approved list (if one is given).
	R3	Operator is allowed to take a penalty from the manufacturer if an aircraft is left on the ground for longer than the preferred time agreed.

Table 4. Basic states (top) and sample pre-achievement sub-states (bottom) of an achievement obligation

State	Properties
Pre-achievement	Not G G achievable Service obliged to achieve G
Succeeded	G
Failed	G unachievable Service obliged to achieve G
Cancelled	No service obliged to achieve G
Sub-State	**Additional Properties**
Initial	
Danger	G in danger of becoming unachievable
Likely Success	Success G' achieved, where G' is a significant subset of G

to service two operators' aircraft at the same time, but can only service one due to a lack of resources. Long-term conflicts are also present, as in a conflict between a servicing contract and an aftercare contract arising when a manufacturer must choose between servicing one operator's aircraft within the maximum time limit and servicing another operator's aircraft within the preferred time, where the manufacturer is in danger of not having serviced the latter operator's aircraft within the preferred time limit for 90% of cases.

CRITICAL STATES OF CONTRACT-BASED SYSTEMS

As mentioned above, a critical state of a contract-based system with regard to an obligation essentially indicates whether the obligation is fulfilled or fulfillable: achieved, failed, in danger, and so on. By identifying the *critical states* of the system with respect to given contractual obligations, it is then easier to determine which of these needs to be checked for and acted upon to ensure that the system performs well. A state-based description can also be used as a basis for verifying whether the system will always result in a desirable state.

Obligation States

Each obligation implies a set of states for the system with regard to that obligation. We classify obligations into three types:

- An obligation to *achieve* some state G, for example to pay an amount
- An obligation to *maintain* some state H, for example to keep aircraft in working order.
- An obligation to *behave* in some way, where that behaviour is to fulfil obligation O(X) whenever event E(X) occurs, for example when aircraft X requires servicing, to service X in an acceptable time.

In part, the critical states of an obligation can be specified independently of the application in which the obligation has force, as we do below for each of the three classes of obligation named.

For an achievement obligation, there are three critical states: *Pre-achievement, Succeeded* and

Table 5. Basic states (top) and sample maintained sub-states (bottom) of a maintenance obligation

State	Properties
Maintained	H Not H achievable Service obliged to maintain H
Succeeded	Not H unachievable
Failed	Not H Service obliged to maintain H
Cancelled	No service obliged to maintain H
Sub-State	**Additional Properties**
Initial	
Danger	Not H in danger of becoming true

Failed. Each has particular properties with regard to the goal state G, as shown in Table 4 (top). In *Pre-achievement*, the goal state is achievable but not yet achieved; in *Succeeded*, the system is in the goal state; and in *Failed*, the goal state is no longer achievable.

Similarly, a maintenance obligation implies three significant states, as shown in Table 5 (top). In the *Maintained* state, the system is in the goal state; in *Succeeded*, the system can no longer leave the goal state; in *Failed*, the system has left the goal state.

As described above, a behaviour obligation triggers the imposition of a further obligation, which we will call the *triggered obligation*, on particular events occurring. The significant states of a behaviour obligation depend on the triggered obligation, but the behaviour obligation has some states of its own, as shown in the top of Table 6. In the *Pre-trigger* state, the triggering event has not yet occurred; in the *Reaction Active* state, an event has occurred but the obligation it has triggered into taking force has not yet reached a *Succeeded* or *Failed* state; in Reaction Failed, that reaction

Table 6. Basic states (top) and sample pre-trigger sub-states (bottom) of a behaviour obligation

State	Properties
Pre-trigger	No new E(X) has occurred Service obliged to achieve G(X), maintain G(X) or behave in way B(X) on every E(X)
Reaction Active	E(a) occurred As Pre-achievement, Maintenance or Pre-trigger state for G(a)/B(a) Service obliged to achieve G(X), maintain G(X) or behave in way B(X) on every E(X)
Reaction Failed	E(a) occurred As respective Failure state for reaction G(a) or B(a) Service obliged to achieve G(X), maintain G(X) or behave in way B(X) on every E(X)
Reaction Succeeded	E(a) occurred As respective Succeeded state for reaction G(a) or B(a) Service obliged to achieve G(X), maintain G(X) or behave in way B(X) on every E(X)
Succeeded	E(X) can never occur again
Cancelled	No service obliged to achieve G(X), maintain G(X) or behave in way B(X) on every E(X)
Sub-State	**Additional Properties**
Initial	
Imminent	E(X) is likely to occur imminently
Likely Complete	E(X) is unlikely to occur again

obligation has reached a *Failed* state, and so the behaviour obligation as a whole has failed; in *Reaction Succeeded* state, the particular reaction obligation has succeeded; and in *Succeeded*, no more applicable events can ever occur and so the behaviour obligation as a whole has succeeded. All obligations also imply a state, *Cancelled*, when the obligation no longer holds.

Significant Sub-States

In addition to the application-independent system states above, applications often refer to significant sub-states part-way between an obligation coming into force and its success or failure. Examples are shown in the bottom portions of Tables 4, 5 and 6. An application may need to detect whether an obligation is in danger of violation and so allocate more resources to ensure that it is fulfilled instead, implying a *Danger* critical state of the system with regard to that obligation as shown in Table 4 (bottom). Or, if an obligation is being fulfilled unexpectedly easily, an application may take advantage by transferring resources being used in support of this obligation to other tasks, for example the *Likely Complete* critical state in Table 6. Interpretation of concepts such as danger or likelihood are application-specific.

Example

As an example, in Table 7 we enumerate critical states for an achievement obligation, O2 in the long-term aftercare contract. It is an achievement

obligation as it describes an eventual state of the system, i.e. 90% of servicing cases were performed in the preferred time period. When the contract first comes into force, i.e. system time is within the contract period, the state *Pre-achievement: Initial* holds. In this state, insufficient cases have been performed to determine whether success is likely. After 5% of cases, the system will be in either *Pre-achievement: Satisfactory* or *Pre-achievement: Danger* states, and may vary between them over the contract period. *Pre-achievement: Satisfactory* holds where 5% of cases were performed within the preferred time, while *Pre-achievement: Danger* holds where between 5% and 10% exceeded that time. The value of taking account of these two states is that transfer of resources between fulfilment of different obligations can be triggered by changes of state. Eventually, the system will reach either *Succeeded* state, where the contract period is exceeded and over 90% of cases were performed on time, or *Failure* state, where over 10% have exceeded the preferred time. The choice of the appropriate sub-states (*Pre-achievement: Satisfactory* and *Pre-achievement: Danger* in this case) is entirely application dependent: considering more states allows finer control as appropriate, but may also add overheads.

ARCHITECTURE OF CONTRACT-BASED SYSTEMS

Aside from modelling contract-based systems using the CONTRACT framework, we also ad-

Table 7. States of aftercare contract obligation O2

Pre-achievement: Initial	Less than (estimated) 5% of servicing cases performed and within contract period
Pre-achievement: Satisfactory	Over 5% of cases performed, less than 5% exceeded preferred time and within contract period
Pre-achievement: Danger	Between 5% and 10% of cases exceeded preferred time and within contract period
Succeeded	Less than 10% of cases exceeded preferred time and beyond contract period
Failed	More than 10% of cases exceeded preferred time

dress the issue of administration: how to manage the processes involved in creating, maintaining, acting on and otherwise processing contracts and contract proposals.

The life-cycle of a contract is viewed as follows. First, a potential contract party discovers services which may provide the functionality they require, and specifies a proposal and negotiates over it with the potential service providers. As part of this process, the parties will agree to how compliance to the obligations will be monitored (see Third-Part Monitoring below). The contract will be agreed to and preserved in independent storage. The contract parties can then perform actions to their obligations in accordance with prohibitions and permissions. This behaviour will be observed and checked by the agreed independent parties. The contract will eventually terminate, possibly leading to renewal if the service required is ongoing.

We identify four key *process types* in the contract life-cycle. *Establishment* brings about the existence of the contract. *Maintenance and Update* ensures a contract's integrity over time. *Fulfilment* brings about the fulfilment of obligations while observing its prohibitions. *Termination or Renewal* end the normative force of the contract, or renew it to apply for a longer period. Each of these process types can be instantiated in different ways, depending on the application and its deployment. The choice dictates the *roles* services must play to fulfil the administration duties implied. Below, we examine each process type in turn.

Establishment

There are many potential ways to establish a contract, varying in complexity. To give an illustration, we present two below.

- **Full proposal establishment process:** Here, one party, the *proposer*, creates a full proposal, excluding some assignments of roles to services, and signs it. It then uses a *registry* to discover services that may fulfil the unassigned contract roles. For each unassigned role in turn, it offers the proposal to a service, a *potential party* it is satisfied can assume that role. If the party is willing, it signs the proposal and returns it. When the last role is filled, a contract is established

- **Template discovery establishment process:** Alternatively, a process may be used in which a service discovers a contract *template* that may be instantiated in a way that fulfils its goals. This implies the use of a *template repository*, where templates can be stored. Such templates may have some assigned roles; that is, they may describe services for which a provider is willing to negotiate terms.

Maintenance and Update

The continued existence and integrity of a contract after establishment is important in reliable systems. As with establishment, there are multiple ways in which this can be achieved, and the functionality that needs to be provided depends on the particular contract and application.

- **Contract store maintenance process:** Here, contract parties use a *contract store* to maintain and control access to contracts. The store is obliged only to allow services to change the contract when all parties send a signed agreement of the change to be made.

- **All party signature maintenance process:** In this process, integrity is preserved by the contract being signed by all parties in a way that prevents editing without detection; for example, digital signatures based on reliable certificates. The signed document includes the contract itself, and an indication of whether it is a revision of a previous version. Each party should check the signatures of the contract before accepting it as binding.

Fulfilment

For every contractual obligation and prohibition, there are certain processes that can be performed to help ensure they are fulfilled. As with the processes above, these imply particular administrative roles that must be played by services. The administrative roles carry with them obligations, prohibitions and permissions, which may be documented in the same contract as the one that is the target of administration, or another contract. The processes below often refer to particular system states with regard to obligations: these are the states specified in the previous section.

- **Observation of fulfilment process:** An *observer* observes state changes to determine whether contractual obligations are being fulfilled. It can notify other services when an obligation is being violated or in danger of violation. An observer X is in an obligation pattern of the following form: "X is obliged to observe for critical state S of contract clause C, and notify registered listeners when it occurs."
- **Management of fulfilment process:** A *manager* is a service that acts when an obligation is not being fulfilled, is in danger of not being fulfilled or a prohibition is breached. It knows about the problem by (conceptually at least) registering to listen to the notifications from an observer.

Manager is a role, and one service may play the role of both manager and observer. The nature of the action taken by a manager may vary considerably. In highly automated and strict applications, an automatic penalty may be applied to a party. In other cases, a management service may be a human who decides how to resolve the problem. Alternatively, a manager may merely provide analysis of problems over the long term, so that a report can be presented detailing which obligations were violated. A manager X is in an obligation pattern of the following form: "X is obliged, whenever the system reaches a critical state S of contract clause C, to perform action A."

An example of an observer's obligation in the aerospace application is shown in Table 8 (top), and of a manager's obligation in Table 8 (bottom). The observer, Checker, is obliged to check that a Danger state has not been reached for the number of suitable engines available at a given location, and the manager, Enforcer, listens to observations on this state and rectifies the situation when it occurs.

Termination and Renewal

Termination of a contract means that the obligations and other clauses contained within it no longer have any force. A contract may be terminated in several ways: (i) it may terminate *naturally* if the system reaches a state in which none of its clauses apply, for example when a contract's period

Table 8. Engine supply checking contract (top) and Engine supply enforcement contract (bottom)

Roles	Checker, Manufacturer, Operator
Obligations	Checker monitors the number of engines available to the manufacturer at a given location that are suitable for a given operator, and notifies registered services if it falls below a minimum quantity.
Roles	Enforcer, Checker
Obligations	Enforcer, on hearing from checker that the number of suitable engines at a location has fallen below a minimum level, transports a suitable engine from another location.

of life expires or all obligations have been met; (ii) it may terminate *by design* if the contract has an explicit statement that the contract is terminated when an event occurs (for example, if one party fails to meet an obligation, the contract is terminated and all others are released from their obligations); or (iii) it may terminate *by agreement*, if parties agree that the contract should no longer hold, and update it accordingly (in line with the process chosen for the Maintenance and Update type above). Renewal of a contract means that a contract that would have imminently terminated naturally is updated so that termination is no longer imminent (again depending on the Maintenance and Update process type above).

Administrative Roles and Components

The processes above all require the fulfilment of particular administrative roles, for example a contract store, registry, observer, or manager. For some of these components, we can provide generic implementations. For example, a contract store, based solely on contract documents and having nothing to do with the application itself, is easy to implement generically. Others, such as managers, need to have application-specific instantiations, as dealing with a contractual obligation not being fulfilled varies greatly between applications. Further details on the specification of these components are available from the CONTRACT website (Contract, 2008).

THIRD-PARTY MONITORING

Detecting and handling obligation violations is essential, in particular as contracts often specify how to react in such circumstances, e.g. the operator taking a penalty for late servicing in clause R3 in Table 3. However, this requires independent contract parties to hold a consistent view of whether a violation has occurred – which is not always trivial to achieve in any distributed system.

As part of our architecture, we attempt to meet this need by two complementary measures. Full details would exceed the scope of this chapter, but we summarise the ideas below and point interested readers to existing publications (Modgil et al. 2009; Meneguzzi et al. 2009).

First, we allow contract parties to name and agree in the contract which observers are jointly *trusted* by all signing parties. The reason for this joint trustworthiness in an observer cannot be application-independent. For example, in a financial situation, a bank may be a trusted third-party observer, whereas in a remote procedure call we may have to rely on the combined reports of the caller and the callee to obtain a trustworthy observation. We, therefore, simply provide the mechanism to declare trusted observers and leave establishing trust to other mechanisms.

Second, we provide a generic, independent monitoring component. This takes as input, a translation of the contract into *augmented transition networks (ATNs)*. Each ATN corresponds to one clause, and consists of a series of nodes connected arcs labelled with observable messages. As messages pass between contract parties, trusted observers report this to the independent monitor, which follows the arcs in the ATNs. This tracking ultimately allows the monitor to declare (to manager services), that a clause is fulfilled or violated. The trace of messages observed also acts as a means to *explain* violations, so providing some supporting evidence for redress.

RELATED WORK

There has been much previous work on various aspects of contract-based system modelling, enactment and administration, and our approach is intended to build on and be compatible with other ideas presented elsewhere. For example, there are many approaches to negotiation which may be used in the establishment of contracts (Lopes Cardoso & Oliveria, 2000), and the administration of contracts can integrate with other useful behaviour, such as observation of fulfilment and violation of obligations potentially feeding into a longer-term assessment of systems (Duran, Torres da Silva, & de Lucena, 2007). Work on multi-party contracts (Xu, 2004) adopt modelling techniques specifically designed to enable detection of parties responsible for contract violation, but do not use normative concepts to regulate behaviour, or model other contract administration processes.

In addition, the wider domains of normative systems and agreement in service-oriented architectures informs our work. Concepts such as norms specifying patterns of behaviour, contract clauses as concrete representations of dynamic norms, management or enforcement of norms itself being a norm, are all already established in the literature (Dellarocas, 2000; Duran, Torres da Silva, & de Lucena, 2007; García-Camino, 2007; Lopez y Lopez, Luck, & d'Inverno, 2005).

However, the approach in this chapter is distinct in that it is concerned with the development of practical system deployments for business scenarios. In particular, business systems operate in the context of wider organisational and inter-organisational processes, so that commitments, providing assurance over the actions of others assumes great importance. While potentially less flexible over the short term, explicit contracts provide just such commitments and are therefore more appropriate for business systems than more flexible, less predictable *ad hoc* approaches (Ghijsen, Jansweijer, & Wielinga, 2007; Muntaner-Perich, de la Rosa, & Esteva, 2007).

We also believe our system to be more widely applicable than some other approaches. By classifying processes into types with different instantiations, the architecture can be incorporated into a wider range of application domains and deployments than fixed protocols would allow. In addition, we describe how administrative functions, such as storing or updating a contract, can be achieved. This contrasts with specifications such as WS-Agreement and Web Services Ser-

vice Level Agreement, where the specifications cover only part of the necessary administration (Andrieux & Czajkowski, 2004; Ludwig, Keller, Dan, King, & Franck, 2003). Abstract architectures for electronic contracting, and associated case studies, have been described elsewhere; most notably in the work of Grefen and Angelov (2002; Angelov & Grefen, 2006). However, accommodation of deontic specifications in order to regulate service behaviour is not modelled in this work. Our approach aims for broad observation and management of obligations and prohibitions, so as to verify whether they are being achieved, prevent failure when in danger of violation and take advantage of success when obligations are being easily met. Some existing work does consider system states with regard to contract clauses (Lopes Cardoso & Oliveira, 2000), but none, to our knowledge, classifies obligations and the critical states they imply as we have done in this chapter, a necessary pre-requisite to observing and managing obligation fulfilment in accordance with a particular application.

Others have raised the issue that observers and managers have, themselves, to be observed and managed (Jones & Sergot, 1993). Here, by modelling observers and managers as services, we allow for the same contract framework to apply to them. However, this clearly has its limits and at some point *trust* between businesses must be explicitly modelled in the system, a topic to be addressed in future work.

CONCLUSION AND FUTURE WORK

In this chapter, we have presented the CONTRACT conceptual framework and architecture, and shown how they apply to aircraft aftercare. By creating a technology-dependent implementation along these lines, an application can take advantage of the reliable coordination provided by electronic contracts. The CONTRACT project aims to allow service-oriented systems to be verified on the basis of their contracts, building on work by Lomuscio et al. on deontic interpreted systems (Lomuscio & Sergot, 2003). While this verification is beyond the scope of this chapter, it places a requirement on our framework that the properties of the target system are identified and isolatable, and a requirement on the architecture that such information can be captured in order to pass to a verification mechanism. Perhaps equally importantly, we also aim for an open source implementation built on Web Services technologies, requiring the architecture to be compatible with such an objective. Finally, taking a very practical standpoint, we have begun to construct a methodology to guide development of applications that use electronic contracts through the process from conceptual framework to deployment. To ensure wide applicability, this will be applied to CONTRACT's other test applications in insurance settlement, software provisioning and certification testing.

ACKNOWLEDGMENT

The CONTRACT project is co-funded by the European Commission under the 6th Framework Programme for RTD with project number FP6-034418. Notwithstanding this fact, this chapter and its content reflects only the authors' views. The European Commission is not responsible for its contents, nor liable for the possible effects of any use of the information contained therein.

REFERENCES

W3C. (n.d.). *Web services architecture*. Retrieved November 11, 2008, from http://www.w3.org/TR/ws-arch/

Andrieux, A., Czajkowski, K., Dan, A., Keahey, K., Ludwig, H., Pruyne, J., et al. (2004). *Web services agreement specification (WS-Agreement)*. Tech. Rep. Global Grid Forum.

Angelov, S., & Grefen, P. (2006). A case study on electronic contracting in on-line advertising - status and prospects. In L. M. Camarinha-Matos, H. Afsarmanesh, & M. Ollus (Ed.), *Network-centric collaboration and supporting frameworks - Proceedings 7th IFIP Working Conference on Virtual Enterprises*, (pp. 419–428). Berlin: Springer.

Conte, R., & Castelfranchi, C. (1993). Norms as mental objects. From normative beliefs to normative goals. In C. Castelfranchi & J.-P. Mueller (Ed.), *5th European Workshop on Modelling Autonomous Agents in a Multi-Agent World, MAAMAW '93*, (pp. 186–196). Berlin: Springer.

Conte, R., Falcone, R., & Sartor, G. (1999). Agents and norms: How to fill the gap? *Artificial Intelligence and Law*, 7, 1–15. doi:10.1023/A:1008397328506

CONTRACT. (n.d.). *Project website*. Retrieved November 12, 2008, from http://www.ist-contract.org/

Dellarocas, C. (2000). Contractual agent societies: Negotiated shared context and social control in open multi-agent systems. In R. Conte & C. Dellarocas (Ed.), *Social order in multiagent systems* (pp. 113-133). Boston: Kluwer Academic Publishers.

Duran, F., Torres da Silva, V., & de Lucena, C. J. P. (2007). Using testimonies to enforce the behaviour of agents. In J. Sichman & S. Ossowski (Ed.), *Coordination, organizations, institutions, and norms in agent systems III* (pp. 25-36). Berlin: Springer.

García-Camino, A. (2007). Ignoring, forcing and expecting concurrent events in electronic institutions. In J. Sichman & S. Ossowski (Ed.), *Coordination, organizations, institutions, and norms in agent systems III* (pp. 15-26). Berlin: Springer.

Ghijsen, M., Jansweijer, W., & Wielinga, R. (2007). Towards a framework for agent coordination and reorganization, AgentCore. In J. Sichman & S. Ossowski (Ed.), *Coordination, organizations, institutions, and norms in agent systems III* (pp. 13-24). Berlin: Springer.

Grefen, P., & Angelov, S. (2002). On τ, μ, π and ε-contracting. In C. Bussler, R. Hull, S. McIlraith, M. E. Orlowska, B. Pernici, & J. Yang (Ed.), *Proceedings of the CAiSE Workshop on Web Services, e-Business, and the Semantic Web,* (pp. 68-77). Berlin: Springer.

Jakob, M., Pechoucek, M., Chábera, J., Miles, S., & Luck, M. Oren, et al. (2008). Case studies for contract-based systems. In M. Berger, B. Burg, & S. Nishiyama (Eds.), *Proceedings of the 7th International Conference on Autonomous Agents and Multiagent Systems (AAMAS 2008)- Industrial and Applications Track,* (pp. 55-62). INESC.

Jones, A. J. I., & Sergot, M. J. (1993). On the Characterisation of Law and Computer Systems: The Normative Systems Perspective. In J.-J.Ch. Meyer & R. J. Wieringa (Ed.), *Deontic logic in computer science: Normative system specification,* (pp. 275–307). New York: John Wiley & Sons.

Lomuscio, A., & Sergot, M. (2003). Deontic interpreted systems. *Studia Logica, 75*(1), 63–92. doi:10.1023/A:1026176900459

Lopes Cardoso, H., & Oliveira, E. (2000). Using and evaluating adaptive agents for electronic commerce negotiation. In M. C. Monard & J. Simão Sichman (Ed.), *Proceedings of the International Joint Conference, 7th Ibero-American Conference on AI: Advances in Artificial Intelligence* (pp. 96-105). Berlin: Springer.

Lopes Cardoso, H., & Oliveira, E. (2007). A contract model for electronic institutions. In J. Sichman & S. Ossowski (Ed.), *Coordination, organizations, institutions, and norms in agent systems III,* (pp. 73–84). Berlin: Springer.

Lopez y Lopez, F., Luck, M., & d'Inverno, M. (2005). A normative framework for agent-based systems. *Computational & Mathematical Organization Theory, 12*(2–3), 227–250. doi:10.1007/s10588-006-9545-7

Ludwig, H., Keller, A., Dan, A., King, R. P., & Franck, R. (2003). *Web service level agreement (WSLA), language specification.* Tech. Rep. Armonk, NY: IBM Corporation.

Meneguzzi, F., Modgil, S., Oren, N., Miles, S., Luck, M., Faci, N., et al. (2009). Monitoring and explanation of contract execution: A case study in the aerospace domain. In *Proceedings of the 8th International Conference on Autonomous Agents and Multiagent Systems (AAMAS 2009) – Industrial and Applications Track.*

Modgil, S., Faci, N., Meneguzzi, F., Oren, N., Miles, S., & Luck, M. (2009). A framework for monitoring agent-based normative systems. In *Proceedings of the 8th International Conference on Autonomous Agents and Multiagent Systems (AAMAS 2009).*

Muntaner-Perich, E., de la Rosa, J. L., & Esteva, R. (2007). Towards a formalisation of dynamic electronic institutions. In J. Sichman & S. Ossowski (Ed.), *Coordination, organizations, institutions, and norms in agent systems III,* (pp. 61–72). Berlin: Springer.

Wax, L. (n.d.). *Aerogility.* Retrieved November 6, 2008, from http://www.aerogility.com/

Xu, L. (2004). A multi-party contract model. *ACM SIGecom Exchanges, 5*(1), 13–23. doi:10.1145/1120694.1120697

KEY TERMS AND DEFINITIONS

Assignment: A statement that an agent should play a given role.

Clause: An obligation, prohibition or permission.

Contract: A proposal to which all assigned agents have agreed.

Obligation: A statement that an agent playing a given role should do something.

Permission: An exception to a prohibition for an agent playing a given role under given circumstances.

Prohibition: A statement that an agent playing a given role should not do something.

Proposal: A document containing a set of clauses and assignments, where every role referred to which each clause applies has been assigned to an agent.

Role: A named part that can be played by a service's agent in a system.

Section 4
Security

Chapter 32
Trust and Fairness Management in P2P and Grid Systems

Adam Wierzbicki[1]
Polish-Japanese Institute of Information Technology Warsaw, Poland

Tomasz Kaszuba[2]
Polish-Japanese Institute of Information Technology Warsaw, Poland

Radosław Nielek[1]
Polish-Japanese Institute of Information Technology Warsaw, Poland

Anwitaman Datta[3]
Nanyang Technological University, Singapore

ABSTRACT

Peer-to-Peer (P2P) and Grid systems serve whole communities of users, and are thus good examples of information systems that should realize social goals. One of the most important social goals is fairness. For that reason, P2P and Grid systems incorporate many mechanisms, algorithms and methods for providing fairness that are referred to as Fairness Management in this chapter. Information systems that serve communities of users can also apply social concepts to support users. Trust is one such concept that is often applied in P2P and Grid systems that apply Trust Management to support users in making decisions under uncertainty that is due to other users' behavior. This chapter describes Trust Management and Fairness Management in P2P and Grid systems, showing that the two subjects are connected. Trust Management can be used to improve fairness without centralized control. The chapter includes a demonstration of fairness emergence due to trust management.

INTRODUCTION

Peer-to-Peer (P2P) and grid systems are instances of Open Distributed Systems that are now widely used in the e-society. For that reason, they must take into account the behavior and motivations of their human

users, like egoism or exploitation of others, and the need for trust and fairness. Information technology aims to support the latter goal by creating systems that encompass and use knowledge about trust and fairness. This chapter is devoted to a description of this trend in P2P and grid systems.

Trust management (TM) uses computational

DOI: 10.4018/978-1-61520-686-5.ch032

models of human trust in order to help users to make decisions under uncertainty that is due to the actions of others. In a P2P or grid system, this decision might concern sharing one's resources with another user when it is uncertain whether she will reciprocate. Other types of decisions must be made by users of P2P applications that have other purposes than resource sharing, like in a P2P game. One of the problems of trust management research is that it is quite generic and can be applied in a variety of areas. In this chapter, we shall introduce a general model of TM developed in the Universal Trust (uTrust) project (http://uTrust.pjwstk.edu. pl) that will be used to organize the discussion of various TM methods described in the literature of P2P and grid systems.

Trust management works by gathering information that can be used to quantify users' trust or reputation. Since this information is usually obtained from untrusted third parties, it is not reliable and TM methods must take into account the credibility of received information and provide incentives for honesty (Fernandes et al., 2004). This problem demonstrates that TM methods in P2P and grid systems must be resistant to adversary behavior that exploits the lack of centralized trusted entities. A list of typical adversaries will be included in the chapter.

Many proposed TM methods in P2P and grid systems use reputation (i.e. information that is based on the history of agents' behavior). However, reputation is always vulnerable to first-time cheating, as well as coalition or discrimination attacks (Dellarocas, 2000a). Other TM approaches (Wierzbicki and Kucharski, 2004; Wierzbicki and Kaszuba, 2007) avoid the use of reputation through the use of cryptography that allows better observation and verification of behavior, even with limited or no use of central control.

P2P and grid systems require fair treatment of users. The problem of freeriders is prevalent in both types of systems, and providing fairness is an important goal, since the lack of fairness is a disincentive to participation in the system. Based

on the theory of equity (Kostreva et al., 2004), this chapter will present methods to evaluate the fairness of various protocols or distributed algorithms in P2P and grid systems.

The two subjects of fairness and trust are inherently connected. For example, it can be shown that the fair behavior establishes expectancy trust. On the other hand, it can also be shown that when efficient trust management is used, then the overall fairness of resource distribution in a system increases. In other words, fairness is an emergent property of trust management (Nielek, 2008). This is relevant information because in distributed systems like P2P systems or the Grid, fairness must often be guaranteed without centralized control; trust management is one of the ways of achieving this goal. The chapter will include a demonstration of fairness emergence due to trust management.

THEORY OF TRUST AND FAIRNESS

Trust Management (TM)

Trust Management TM can be defined as a special method of decision support under uncertainty. The most general and abstract statement of the TM problem is in fact a decision-making problem: an agent considers a situation in which she must make a decision about the choice of action. The outcome of the action is uncertain, as it will depend on the decisions made by other agents. In an open, distributed system (ODS) such as P2P systems or grids, the behavior of agents is autonomous and usually not subject to central control. Moreover, agents often join or leave the system, and the number of agents in the ODS can be very large. Therefore, an agent often interacts with other agents previously unknown to her. This is the reason for the uncertainty of the outcome. The aim of TM is to support the agent in making a decision under uncertainty of establishing trust or distrust towards the other agents on whose actions the decision-maker's welfare depends.

Concepts of Trust and Reputation, Uncertainty and Risk

Trust is a concept derived from the humanities and our own common experience. We apply trust when we purchase goods, use banking services, or employ recommended candidates for a job. It can be defined in the most abstract manner as a relation between a trustor and a trustee in a context. Context is significant because, for example, we would trust a dentist to treat our teeth, but not to perform an operation on an ulcer (here the context depends on the expertise of the trustee). We distinguish two concepts of trust, human trust and computational trust. The term human trust refers to a mental state of humans. Human trust has been studied by psychology, sociology, anthropology, economics and other sciences (such as neuroscience). However, it should be clear that human trust is a very complex concept that can perhaps never be precisely defined and fully understood. Computational trust, on the other hand, is a term that describes representations of trust used in trust management systems. These representations can be based on trust definitions that could also apply to human trust. Moreover, computational trust is usually processed in a way that aims to replicate how humans reason about human trust. Finally, the aim of trust management systems is to establish human trust through computational trust, if the users of the TM system are humans. In some cases, the agents that use the TM system are artificial, and then the TM system only provides information in the form of computational trust that is processed by these agents, (using perhaps some reasoning rules).

Human trust has been defined in various ways in the literature, but two definitions are used most frequently: expectancy trust and dependency trust. Expectancy trust is a subjective, context-dependent expectation that the trustee will choose a specific action in the encounter. This definition is close to definitions proposed in literature, such as (Gambetta, 1988) and (Mui, 2002). Dependency trust can be defined as the subjective, context-dependent extent to which the trustor is willing to depend on the trustee in a situation of uncertainty. This definition is an adaptation of dependency trust definitions proposed by (Jsang et al., 2005) and (Marsh, 1994). The trust theory of (Deutsch, 1973) also supports this definition. A similar definition has been used in sociology (Sztompka, 2007, 1999): trust is defined there as the attitude that allows the trustor to accept a bet on the trustee's behavior. Accepting such bet would imply a willingness to depend on the trustee.

Another concept that can be derived from our common sense and from economics is the concept of reputation. The distinction between trust and reputation is one of the earliest theoretical achievements of Trust Management research. The most abstract definition of reputation is information about the trustee that is available to the trustor and is derived from the history of the trustee's behavior in some contexts. Note that from this definition it can be seen that reputation can establish human trust (and therefore, in some trust management systems, computational trust is not used at all. These TM systems shall be referred to as reputation systems).

For the purposes of this chapter, we shall use a simple definition of risk: risk is the expected variation of the utility of an agent in an encounter. Note that this variation may be calculated precisely only if the agent knows the probabilities of the other agent's behavior (and if the agent's behavior can be modeled probabilistically). Then, the risk is determined by the expected deviation from the expected utility, and is therefore always expressed in the same units as the agent's utility. In many practical cases, there is insufficient information about the encounter and the participating agents to calculate good risk estimates. Instead of the term of risk, we shall use the term of uncertainty to denote the unknown variation of utility. The worst-case estimate of risk could be assumed in such case: if an agent chooses an action in an encounter, then her utility will depend on the actions of other agents. Consequently, the worst case estimate of risk is the difference between the best case utility and the worst case utility for the chosen action.

Trustworthiness and credibility are two concepts that are frequently used in trust management literature. Trust has been defined as a relation; on the other hand, trustworthiness is a property of an agent, not of a relation between two agents. Computational trustworthiness can be calculated from computational trust. Credibility is trust in the context of the truthfulness of received information.

A General Model of TM Systems

In this section we shall introduce a few general concepts used throughout the chapter. These terms can be used to describe various TM methods, ranging from reputation systems to Web services trust management.

Universal Encounter Description

An agent that requests the help of TM service passes the description of the future interaction, called an Encounter. An Encounter (Mui, 2002b) models all possible interactions between agents or applications that use TM services. Relevant information about encounters should include agent identities, context, actions available to agents and their outcomes.

In the case of an Internet auction, encounter data includes the identity of a user (i.e. buyer or seller), and possible actions: sending of purchased goods, or not sending them; paying or not paying the agreed price. For a Web service, encounter data includes an identity and the available actions are the following: returning the correct result of the invocation in reasonable time, returning incorrect results or delaying the reply. Context data for a Web service may include parameters of the Web service that could influence running times. In a P2P file-sharing application, encounter data includes the identities of users who exchange files, and possible actions include the sending or advertising of the available blocks of the file. In a P2P computing application, encounter data again includes the identities of peers, the computing job submitted from one peer to the other, and the response, including observable features such as quality of service and correctness.

Feedback by Universal Proofs

After the encounter, the agent passes feedback information to the TM system. To represent this information, we use the concept of a Proof, a universal representation of an encounter. In the Internet auction, a proof is a history-based report. In the Web service, a proof, called a "security token", delegates trust obtained in previous encounters with trust management authority. We refer to such proof as a recommendation. Proofs can even be prior trust assumptions. Proofs can also be added at any other moment. In the Web service example, proofs could be presented by the agent at the beginning of the scenario, possibly following a trust negotiation procedure. For P2P applications, there have been various types and representations of proofs; however, in our example, the file-sharing application could return a report about the amount and quality of data provided by a peer. Other P2P or grid applications, such as a P2P computation, could use proofs that are base on a comparison of the computation requested from a peer and a second, identical computation done by the requesting peer. Proofs for a P2P grid application can also include information about the computation time.

Fairness Management

After trust management and trust, fairness is the most important concept of this chapter. It is therefore critical to understand it clearly. Although extensively studied (Young, 1994), fairness is a complex concept that depends much on cultural values, precedents, and the context of the problem.

Much of the research on fairness has been done in the area of the social sciences, especially social psychology. The results of this research allow to recognize people's preferences regarding fairness and their understanding of fair behavior. Interestingly, much of the research in that area has been influenced by the seminal work of Deutsch, who is also the author of one of the basic psychological theories of trust (Deutsch, 1975, 1987). To open our discussion on fairness, let us begin with three general kinds of fairness judgments identified by social psychology (Tyler and Smith, 1998): distributive fairness, procedural fairness and retributive fairness. This chapter focuses mostly on distributive fairness. Distributive fairness is usually related to the question of distribution of some goods, resources or costs, be it kidneys for transplantation, parliament mandates, or the costs of water and electricity. The goal of distributive fairness is to find a distribution of goods that is perceived as fair by the concerned agents. Procedural fairness focuses on the perceived fairness of procedures leading to outcomes, while retributive fairness is concerned with rule violation and the severity of sanctions for norm-breaking behavior. It is possible to think of distributive fairness as a special kind of procedural fairness. If a distribution problem can be solved fairly, then a fair procedure would require all agents to take a fair share of the distributed goods or cost. Procedural fairness, however, is also applied in the case when a fair solution cannot be found beforehand or cannot be agreed upon. Both distributional fairness and procedural fairness aim to find fair solutions of distribution problems.

Concepts of Fairness, Reciprocity and Altruism

The most abstract definition of fairness used in this chapter is therefore as follows: fairness means the satisfaction of justified expectations of agents that participate in the system, according to rules that apply in a specific context based on reason and precedent. The reasons and precedents that establish the expectation can differ, depending on the context of the situation. Precedents can, for example, be complex social norms, ranging from ethical norms to tribal customs. Reason can be applied to complex situations not governed by precedent, but even then established procedures or rules can be applied, like for example in a court of law. This general definition applies to distributive, procedural or retributive fairness.

The concepts of reciprocity and altruism can both be considered as special cases of fairness. The rules that govern the behavior of individual agents can be determined by the context of the encounter. In some contexts, fair individual behavior is reciprocal behavior. In other contexts, altruistic behavior is expected of agents (for example in the case of a parent caring for a child). Therefore, most of the reasoning that applies to individual fairness would also apply to agents that behave reciprocally or altruistically, in an appropriate context. On the other hand, sometimes reciprocity and altruism are not individually fair behavior (to make a practical comparison, a salesperson would not behave fairly if she altruistically gave goods away for free). Note that in this chapter, the term altruism will be applied only to the situation when an agent prefers another agent's welfare to her own. An act is said to be altruistic if it is costly to perform but confers a benefit on another agent (Wilson, 1975; Trivers, 1985). Altruism is also widely used (especially in game theory and economics) to mean "un-selfishness" (in constant sum games, the two notions are equivalent). In the terminology used in this chapter, unselfish behavior can be any fair behavior, while altruism has a stronger meaning and is also much more rare.

Theory of Equity

In a fair distribution problem, the objectives of all agents must be taken into consideration. The problem of optimizing the outcomes of all agents can be formulated as a multicriteria problem.

Figure 1. Examples of Lorenz curves

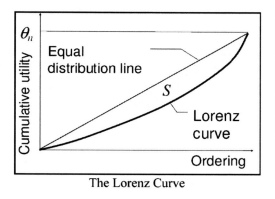

The Lorenz Curve

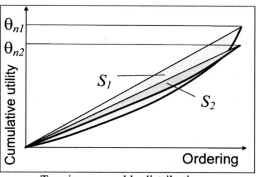

Two incomparable distributions

We shall refer to this as the problem of effective optimization. Effective optimization of agents' outcomes need not have any concern for fairness. The outcomes can be the shares of goods or costs received by agents in an ODS. Let $y=[y_1,...,y_n]$ be an outcome vector of the effective optimization problem (assuming there are n agents that maximize their outcomes). (An optimal solution of this problem is any Pareto-optimal solution: a solution with the property that it is not possible to improve any of its outcome values without worsening others).

The theory of equity can be simply graphically described. The left part of Figure 1 shows one of the key concepts of distributive fairness: the Lorenz curve (to use its name from economics). The Lorenz curve is obtained by first taking the outcomes of all agents that participate in a distribution and putting them in order from worst to best. Then, the ordered outcomes are added one at a time, creating a sequence of cumulative sums, called cumulative ordered sums.

Let us denote this operation by a vector function $\theta(y)=[\theta_1(y),...,\theta_n(y)]$ of the outcome vector. Then, the cumulative ordered sums of agents' outcomes are calculated: starting from the utility of the worst agent (θ_1), then the sum of utilities of the worst and the second worst (θ_2), and so on, until the sum of all agents' utilities, which is denoted on the figure as θ_n. The second line on the figure, the equal distribution line, is simply a straight line connecting the points $(1, \theta_1)$ and (n, θ_n). The area between the two curves, denoted by S, can be seen as a measure of inequality of the agent's utilities. The objective of distributive fairness is to minimize this inequality, making the Lorenz curve as close to the equal distribution line as possible. Note that this objective frequently forms a tradeoff with the objective of maximizing the total sum of agents' utilities (θ_n). The right part of Figure 1 shows two Lorenz curves that correspond to different distributions among the same agents. The first distribution has a higher θ_n, but also a higher inequality, while the second distribution has a lower total of agents' utilities but is more fair. In terms of equitable optimization, the two distributions on the right side of Figure 1 are incomparable - the choice of one of them depends on the preferences of the decision-maker.

By applying cumulative ordered sums, the effective optimization problem is transformed into another multicriteria optimization problem. Therefore, the Lorenz curve actually represents the criteria that need to be optimized in order to achieve equitably efficient (i.e. fair) solutions. These criteria are the cumulative sums of the worst outcomes $\theta_1,...,\theta_n$. The new optimization problem will be called the equitable optimization problem. The Pareto-optimal solutions of equitable optimization problem are a subset of the Pareto-optimal solutions of the effective optimization problem.

Measures of Fairness of Resource Distribution

The area between the Lorenz curve and the equal distribution line can be simply calculated and used as a computable measure of inequality. It can be shown that minimizing this measure leads to fair distributions (Ogryczak et al., 2004). The Gini coefficient (frequently used in economics) is the area S normalized by θ_n: $Gini = \dfrac{S}{2\theta_n}$. Note that minimizing the Gini coefficient to obtain fair distributions can lead to worse total outcomes (i.e. sums of all agent's utilities). Also, the Gini coefficient is not consistent with equitable preference: a distribution that has a smaller Gini coefficient can be dominated in terms of the equitable preference relation by another distribution. This fact is a consequence of the normalization.

Game-Theoretic Approaches to Fairness

Distribution problems in an ODS have a high resemblance to game-theoretic settings. The notion of an encounter itself is similar to a game. However, the conditions of an ODS are usually very complex, and many of the basic assumptions of game theory are too limiting in practice. In fact, much empirical evidence today suggests that the most basic assumptions of game theory: players are selfish; players are strategic; and an equilibrium can be reached, do not apply in practice to the behavior of human agents. Still, concepts of game theory have frequently been applied in ODS, and have also led to practical solutions. A well known example is the application of the Tit-for-Tat strategy for the iterated Prisoner's Dilemma in BitTorrent (cf. below) for the prevention of free-riding. The reason for the usefulness of some game-theoretic concepts is that they have been developed for situations where centralized control is not available. In games, players make autonomous decisions and this similarity to an ODS is sufficient for game-theoretic strategies to be applicable in practical ODS. It is also possible to consider game theory as a pessimistic approximation of human behavior, since it assumes selfish and strategic behavior. In this section, we shall consider non-cooperative game-theoretic concepts that are useful in the theory of fairness.

Non-cooperative games can be used to model a situation when selfish, strategic agents interact in encounters with no incentive to cooperate (there exists no enforcement mechanism of fair behavior). An example of such situation is when peers share files in a P2P overlay network. Every peer is interested to receive files, but is not interested to provide files to others. This situation is usually modeled by the Prisoner's Dilemma (PD) (Axelrod, 1984). This game has two actions for each agent: Cooperate and Defect. The structure of payoffs of the two gains is usually such that the Nash equilibrium in a single game is the choice of the Defect action by all players. The Nash equilibrium is clearly not the utilitarian optimal choice (i.e. a choice that would result in the highest sum of payoffs of all agents). For our example of P2P file sharing, the Nash equilibrium is the choice of never sharing their own files by all peers in the system. As a result, no file would be available in the system for retrieval. The ratio of the highest sum of payoffs of all agents to the sum of payoffs in the worst Nash equilibrium is called the price of anarchy. In our example, the price of anarchy is infinite.

Note here that the concept of a Nash equilibrium in a noncooperative game should only be used if it can be proven that the game players are selfish. If they are not, the Nash equilibrium is not likely to be chosen. Empirical research from behavioral game theory supports the notion that Nash equilibria are rarely chosen by real players.

A more general form of the Prisoner's Dilemma is the n-person PD, also called a Social Dilemma (SD) (Komorita and Parks, 1995, 1994). The SD differs from the PD in several aspects. The negative effects of defection affect not one other agent but many agents involved in the encounter. Also, identifying defectors may be more difficult because the perceived negative results of defection could be caused by any of the other agents. Social dilemmas are further classified into resource dilemmas and public good dilemmas.

TRUST MANAGEMENT IN P2P AND GRID SYSTEMS

In Peer-to-Peer systems, the most common method of trust management is reputation. On the other hand, grid systems can use a TM approach developed for WebServices that allows a more strict access control based on recommendations and delegations. This section summarizes the TM approaches used in P2P and Grid systems.

P2P Reputation Systems

Every designer of a P2P reputation system has to face the following challenges:

- How to establish trust between different peers without trusted third parties or authorities?
- How to gather and evaluate proofs?
- How to deal with adversaries in open P2P systems?

Before we begin discussing how P2P reputation systems may be built, let us consider the last question and present the types of adversaries that can be encountered in a P2P reputation system.

Adversary Models for P2P Trust Management

Several types of adversaries have been proposed for P2P trust management. In their paper, (Kamvar et al., 2003) describe a number of threat models: individual malicious peers that always provide an inauthentic file; malicious collectives that assign maximum trust values to other malicious peers, and malicious spies who provide good files but assign maximum trust values to malicious peers. Malicious peers can provide inauthentic files with a given probability.

(Damiani et al., 2002) review several attacks on P2P networks, such as the self replication attack (i.e. an attack that relies on altering data) and man-in-the-middle attacks. They describe the Mandragore Gnutella worm that responds to all queries and sends a copy of itself instead of the requested data. Man-in-the-middle attacks can be executed by modifying the IP and port of the QueryHit message and sending corrupted data. Moreover, Damiani et al. introduce attacks on reputation systems called pseudospoofing that is a type of whitewashing attack, and the ID stealth attack that uses the Sybil method to multiply peer IDs during query and vote phase. Such attack aims to boost the reputation of the attacker (i.e. shilling attack).

In PeerTrust (Xiong and Liu, 2004) list several adversary models such as modifying information (providing fake resources), man-in-the-middle attacks, or compromising peer settings (e.g. allowing to share specific files like trojans or viruses). In addition to PeerTrust, Srivatsa et al. (Srivatsa et al., 2005) discuss malicious peers referred to as "strategic" who alter their behavior based on their own reputation value. Also, they describe shilling attacks to boost malicious peers' reputation.

Abrams et al. in the cycling partitioning (Abrams et al., 2005) system assume the existence of two types of adversaries: malicious and selfish. Selfish peers wish only to maximize their trust score. Malicious peers aim to minimize the number of authentic downloads in the network and may collaborate to do so.

The dropping of negative proofs has been described in R-CHAIN (Liu et al., 2004). Malicious nodes would like to keep only favorable transaction records and drop unfavorable records. Note that structured P2P systems tend to be more vulnerable to man-in-the-middle attacks and dropping of negative proofs. In structured systems, a strategically placed adversary can control the routing to a chosen peer or group of peers. However, there exist structured systems that use randomized routing and are not vulnerable to routing attacks. On the other hand, unstructured P2P networks are less vulnerable to these attacks as any query is usually sent to multiple neighbors and responses are received via multiple paths.

(Lee et al., 2003) assume that malicious nodes can disseminate arbitrary trust information. All malicious peers in NICE form a cooperating clique. Each malicious peer always reports implicit trust (i.e. maximum value) for every other malicious peer and has a 50% chance of truthful reporting for normal peers.

The described adversary strategies vary from simple to complex ones and can pose varying levels of threats. In general, we can distinguish four main characteristics of adversaries in P2P trust management systems: knowledge, purpose, collaboration degree and complexity.

- **Knowledge:** Adversaries may differ in their knowledge about the system. We distinguish adversaries who base only on their local knowledge; more advanced ones who have knowledge about their neighborhood within the radius k, and adversaries with full system information. To become an adversary with global knowledge, a malicious peer could gather information about the P2P system, for example using a crawler or a gossiping protocol. Using gossiping protocols, the adversary can gather knowledge about the ranking of peers, network interconnections or data distribution, obtaining a global view of at least the distributions of these values.
- **Purpose:** Adversaries may have a variety of objectives. There could be selfish peers (Abrams et al., 2005; Srivatsa et al., 2005; Liu et al., 2004; Xiong and Liu, 2004), whose purpose is simply to boost their

reputation, performance or utility. Such peers can form collectives (Kamvar et al., 2003; Lee et al., 2003; Selcuk et al., 2004) to achieve their goal.

Another type of adversaries are the malicious ones. Their aim is to destroy the P2P system itself (or a part of it) by damaging the query or/and response messages (Abrams et al., 2005), sending corrupted data (Kamvar et al., 2003; Damiani et al., 2002; Selcuk et al., 2004; Xiong and Liu, 2004) or simply by compromising peers (Xiong and Liu, 2004) or making them inoperative (Selcuk et al., 2004; Xiong and Liu, 2004). Adversaries can also attack the Trust Management system itself by executing attacks such as altering feedback information (Lee et al., 2003; Kamvar et al., 2003; Liu et al., 2004), man–in–the–middle attacks (Damiani et al., 2002; Xiong and Liu, 2004) or whitewashing attacks (Damiani et al., 2002; Selcuk et al., 2004).

Some multi-strategy adversaries, described in (Srivatsa et al., 2005), can change their goals depending on their own reputation value.

- **Collaboration degree:** The purpose of an adversary affects her collaboration degree. Some goals cannot be achieved by a single adversary, due to their difficulty or to the possibility of detection. Adversaries can act autonomously (selfish peers), or in collaboration with other adversaries. Collaboration may be occasional, or peers can form a collective (clique) (Kamvar et al., 2003; Lee et al., 2003; Selcuk et al., 2004).
- **Complexity:** Like in the previous aspect, the complexity of an adversary depends on her purpose. Simple attacks may be performed by dropping messages (Liu et al., 2004), tampering with data (Kamvar et al., 2003; Damiani et al., 2002; Selcuk et al., 2004; Xiong and Liu, 2004; Abrams et al., 2005) or altering feedback (Lee et al., 2003; Kamvar et al., 2003; Liu et al., 2004).

Complex attacks can be a combination of simpler attacks. For example, the denial-of-service attack (Selcuk et al., 2004) can be executed by peer collectives. A DoS attack can affect the P2P overlay itself, for example crash some highly connected peers to handicap or even partition the network. This can be exploited by peers who want to modify routing or spoof the identity of other peers.

Adversaries can also perform the Sybil attack (Kamvar et al., 2003; Damiani et al., 2002) to create a number of clones of themselves using different IDs. This attack can be combined with whitewashing to boost the reputation of a peer.

Design of P2P Reputation Systems

Now let us turn to the design of P2P reputation systems. We distinguish four main aspects of every reputation system: types of used proofs, aggregation scope, computed value and resilience to adversaries.

- **Type of used proofs.** Proofs given from peers can be divided into two disjoint groups: reports and observations. Reports are the feedback from peers after their own transactions. Observations are information about the transaction from third party peers (i.e. observers). Systems like NICE (Lee et al., 2003), P2PREP (Cornelli et al., 2002) or proposed by (Selcuk et al., 2004) are based on reports. Proofs can evaluate several criteria like transaction completion, provided transfer, or quality of service. (Wang and Vassileva, 2003) use context-specific ratings which can integrate several criteria (e.g. a peer seeks the provider which has high download speed and good quality of audio files). In PeerTrust (Xiong and Liu, 2004) all types of proofs are used and proofs are weighted by the credibility of the peer. Also, the context factor is taken into consideration. In addition to PeerTrust, Xiong

et al proposed TrustGuard (Srivatsa et al., 2005) in which they claim that only secure proofs can be used. Their TrustGuard credibility filter is based on the similarity of experience between two peers.

- **Aggregation scope.** Full aggregation systems consider proofs from all peers, obtained both from own and third-party interactions. Such aggregation is applied in Eigentrust (Kamvar et al., 2003), Gossiptrust (Zhou and Hwang, 2007a) and PET (Liang and Shi, 2005) systems. This approach has a high accuracy of rating due to the use of full system information, but unfortunately it involves a high computational cost. One of the earliest works on P2P trust management by (Aberer, 2001) has also proposed the use of a structured P2P network (P-Grid), a self-referential, self-contained directory service to store meta-information about peers, including proofs.

Selective aggregation is applied when the performance of the system is more important than accuracy. Systems like (Zhou and Hwang, 2007b; Song et al., 2005; Cornelli et al., 2002; Damiani et al., 2002; Selcuk et al., 2004; Lee et al., 2003; Zhao and Li, 2008; Liu et al., 2004) gather information only from a subset of peers (in most cases from their neighborhood).

- **Computed value.** Global reputation systems (Kamvar et al., 2003; Zhou and Hwang, 2007a,b; Song et al., 2005) are based on the opinions from the whole peer population. Reputation represents an objective evaluation of the trustworthiness of a peer in the system. A system that collects global reputation about objects shared in a P2P networks is Credence, a variant of the popular Limewire client of the Gnutella protocol (Credence, 2006). Credence computes global reputation of shared objects, using an algorithm that weights received votes based on their similarity (the more peers vote similarly, the higher the weight of their vote). Personalized trust measures (Liang and Shi, 2005; Cornelli et al., 2002; Damiani et al., 2002; Selcuk et al., 2004; Lee et al., 2003; Zhao and Li, 2008; Liu et al., 2004) are more often used in open peer-to-peer environments due to problems with obtaining global system information. Such measures are subjective and personalized and can have different values for each peer that is asked evaluation.

- **System resilience.** To prevent peers from unfair behavior, TM systems can use cryptographic methods like Public Key techniques (Xiong and Liu, 2004; Selcuk et al., 2004; Singh and Liu, 2003; Yu et al., 2004). In (Selcuk et al., 2004) every proof provided by peers is signed. Strong authentication of peers is also used in TrustMe (Singh and Liu, 2003) by Singh et al to protect the system from adversaries. (Yu et al., 2004) assumed the use of PKI for naming and authentication in their system in order to detect unreliable or malicious peers.

More sophisticated attacks can be deflected by special algorithms or system designs. (Kamvar et al., 2003) deal with malicious collectives in the basic version of EigenTrust by adding a probability of crawling to a peer that has been recommended a-priori (i.e. is pre-trusted). In the secure version of EigenTrust, authors prevent peers from manipulating their own trust values by assuming that the current trust value of a host should be computed by score managers.

Dropping of negative proofs is a challenge in R-CHAIN (Liu et al., 2004). To prevent the Sybil attack, R-Chain can enforce some proof of work for peers joining the system.

(Selcuk et al., 2004) protect their TM system against denial of service attacks. They add an extra round before the response in which a querying peer receives a puzzle scheme. A querying peer decides in which file versions she is genuinely interested, solves the puzzle and sends the proof-of-work back.

Trust Enforcement Using Cryptography in P2P Systems

In some P2P applications, there exists a possibility and a need for stronger TM techniques than reputation systems. Such techniques rely on cryptographic methods to gather observations about the behavior of other peers. These observations can be used to avoid interactions with unfair peers. Such techniques can be applied for example in P2P games, where a peer can cheat by altering her locally stored game information (i.e. state). Special TM techniques developed in (Wierzbicki and Kaszuba, 2007; Kaszuba et al., 2008) require that a peer should obtain proofs about any modification of her game state. Proofs can only be obtained if the game state was modified in accordance to game rules, that is, fairly. These proofs can then be used to demonstrate the fairness of a game move to the group of peers or, in some more complex cases, to trusted third parties that verify the peer's fairness. After periodic verifications, peers receive certificates that establish their fairness. Other peers can inspect the certificates before every interaction and avoid interactions with peers who do not have a valid verification certificate.

The use of gathered proofs for verification requires cryptographic signatures and a PKI infrastructure. However, the use of distributed PKI can reduce the dependence on centralized certification authorities. The only required centralized elements are trusted third parties. Promising new research has started to investigate the use of secure multiparty computation in P2P systems, an approach that could potentially reduce the reliance on trusted arbiters. Byzantine agreement is another method to reduce the reliance on arbiters, although it cannot always be used. In P2P games, the arbiter is trusted not only to perform the verification correctly but also not to reveal the obtained information to other players.

A similar approach using trusted third parties to supervise transactions has been proposed by (Liu et al., 2004).

Trust Management in Web Services and Grid Systems

Grid systems often use Web services to implement frameworks of grid services. The Web services architecture includes a special Trust Management method that relies entirely on recommendations to establish trust, and does not calculate reputation. The method also relies on trusted third parties: authorities that can issue recommendations to agents who wish to use a Web (or grid) service.

In the Web services TM approach, an agent obtains certain recommendations (called security tokens) after authentication from an authority. When the agent wishes to invoke a Web service, she will present her recommendations. The process of obtaining and presenting recommendations is standardized by the WS-Trust standard.

On the other hand, an agent that provides a service (for example, a member of the grid) can express her preferences concerning recommendations. Various recommendations can be required in order to have access to various services. The requirements of a providing agent can be specified using rules described in the WS-Policy standard. When a requesting agent presents recommendations, the providing agent checks whether her policy is satisfied, and based on this check makes the decision whether to provide the requested service.

The TM method used in Web services and grids can be exploited to support workflows, yet this requires better methods for trust negotiation and retrieval of trust recommendations (Blaze et al., 1996). TM methods can also be used for access control in Grid systems (Colombo et al., 2007).

FAIRNESS MANAGEMENT IN P2P AND GRID SYSTEMS

The problem of fairness management in P2P and grid systems concerns the fairness of access and provision of shared resources. In P2P file sharing, these resources are the access bandwidth of peers. In grids, resources can be CPU time or, more generally, processing time of grid tasks. Unfair behavior in P2P and grid systems is often called free-riding. Peers or grid nodes can sometimes use resources of others without providing resources in return. The goal of fairness management is the increase of fairness in the distribution of used and provided resources. The two distributions are often combined using a distribution of the ratio of used and provided resources. In P2P systems, fairness management works by providing incentives for peers to provide resources to the system. The decentralization of control in P2P systems makes it difficult to manage fairness. Peers can only attempt to control the behavior of others using individual strategies, like in a non-cooperative game. P2P fairness management considers the following measures of fairness of individual peers: sharing ratio and altruistic provision.

Fairness Management in P2P File Sharing

Sharing ratio is defined as the total number of uploaded bytes divided by total bytes downloaded (Mol et al., 2008). A P2P Fairness Management systems' primary objective is to keep the sharing ratio above a certain level for every peer. A sharing ratio of 1 and above is considered fair, since it indicates that a peer uploads the same amount (or more) as she has downloaded. If the sharing ratio drops below a certain level it is possible to exclude the peer from the system.

Altruistic provision is defined as the difference between the expected upload rate and the download rate (Mol et al., 2008; Piatek et al., 2007). Piatek et al. also give an alternative definition of altruistic provision: an upload contribution that can be withdrawn without loss in download performance of the providing peer, given that the other peers use a strategy that is based on the peer's upload contribution.

To assure a fair sharing ratio, BitTorrent uses the choke algorithm described in (Carra et al., 2008; Piatek et al., 2007; Legout et al., 2007). This algorithm has been derived from the game-theoretic Tit-for-Tat strategy and affects the peer selection process. It mostly helps to choose the reciprocating peers, but also prevents the low bandwidth peers from starvation (i.e. optimistic unchoke). The algorithm attempts to prevent malicious peers from free-riding.

An example of a modified BitTorrent client is the BitTyrant project (Piatek et al., 2007), which merges several greedy techniques. The BitTyrant client exploits the original BitTorrent algorithms by altering the reciprocity factor. Authors describe alternative choking algorithms. (Carra et al., 2008) evaluated the Bit-Tyrant modifications. They discovered that BitTyrant's modified algorithms have an unexpected positive impact on system performance.

(Liogkas et al., 2006) proposed other modifications of the BitTorrent algorithm. Their client maximizes client download rate. An extension of their work was made by (Locher et al., 2006). They described different techniques to maximize the peer download rate. Locher et al. designed and implemented a BitTorrent client called BitThief that exploits original choking algorithm. Their client increases its neighborhood set as much as possible to boost the chance of being unchocked by a peer.

Recently, (Meulpolder et al., 2008) proposed the BarterCast reputation algorithm. This algorithm uses an epidemic protocol for peer discovery and downloading statistics exchange. The authors describe how to adapt the BarterCast algorithm to the BitTorrent protocol. Each peer sends only her own statistics (download and upload informa-

tion) to known peers. Peers gather observations and reports received from other known peers. To compute the reputation of third party peers, the MAXFLOW algorithm (Ford-Fulkerson) is used. The authors modify the Bit-Torrent unchoke algorithm by taking a peer' reputation into account. Peers only assign the upload slots to peers that have a reputation above a certain threshold.

The BarterCast algorithm is also used in the TRIBLER system (Pouwelse et al., 2006). TRI-BLER is a modification of the BitTorrent client that allows to use acquaintances (i.e. "helpers") to support a peer's download. These acquaintances are obtained through a social network.

Adversary Strategies Against Fairness Management

(Piatek et al., 2007) and (Liogkas et al., 2006) discuss some adversary strategies against Bittorrent-like P2P Fairness Management systems, such as:

- **Exploiting optimistic unchokes:** This technique uses the whitewashing attack to increase the chance of receiving an optimistic unchoke
- **Downloading only from seeds (Liogkas et al., 2006):** This method is simple because seeds do not need any reciprocation from downloading peers (since they have completed their download). On the other hand, there are usually much fewer seeds and therefore this method reduces the parallelism of downloads.
- **Falsifying block availability:** Another exploit of the unchoke algorithm. A peer has a greater chance of being unchoked if she offers more blocks to others (Liogkas et al., 2006), even if the blocks contain garbage data.

Fairness and Equity in Grid Systems

The problem of fairness management in grids can be approached differently than in P2P systems. Grids can have some measure of central control, or at least a central authority that can suggest an equitably optimal solution, even if it is not capable of enforcing it. Fairness management in grids can be reduced to a scheduling problem. Since all agents use resources provided by various grid members, the problem is how to schedule the tasks of all users on each grid machine. This problem can be made more concrete by assuming a specific model of the grid. Such model needs to specify, for example, whether or not tasks are infinitely divisible, and whether or not certain grid machines are dedicated to certain types of tasks.

The mainstream of the current research on scheduling and resource management (Feitelson et al., 2005) concerns systems in which the performance of all tasks is optimized. Usually, a common metric such as the makespan, or the sum of completion times is optimized and thus all the jobs are treated in a more or less equal manner.

In the context of Grid computing, multi-criteria approaches may be used. Different criteria usually express performance of different jobs (Marchal et al., 2005). A scheduling algorithm is expected to deliver Pareto-optimal solutions. Further restrictions on Pareto-optimal solutions should be imposed in order to achieve equitably optimal solutions.

Grid economic approaches (Buyya et al., 2005) (Wolski et al., 2003) (Kenyon and Cheliotis, 2004) analyze the problem of grid resource management by means of market economy. Each resource has a (monetary) cost for its usage. Each user has a budget to spend for executing her jobs. The problem is that in highly heterogeneous settings the perfect competition assumption, stating that no single participant is able to influence the market price, is hardly fulfilled. Real-world grids, however, are expected to be heterogeneous (Gruber et al., 2006). Solutions that solve the problem of scheduling in heterogeneous systems directly, without relying on free-market assumptions, are therefore desirable.`

There were also some applications of game theory to the problem of grid resource management. (Volper et al., 2004) focus on maintaining good relationships of a node with its neighbors by accepting neighbors' jobs to be executed on the node and therefore increasing the probability that the node's jobs will be accepted by its neighbors in the future. (Kwok et al., 2005) propose a model where individual clusters (e.g. placed in different departments of an university) are visible as one site in the grid. The model assumes that a job has been already accepted for the execution by the site. (Kwok et al., 2005) study which cluster from that site should eventually execute the job. There were also some previous works where the infrastructure was considered a common property and there was selfishness between individual jobs (Angel et al., 2006) (Liu et al., 2005).

An approach that combines game theory and equitable optimization is presented in (Rzadca et al., 2007). The authors introduce an algorithm (called Equitable Walk) that can discover equitably optimal solutions to the global scheduling problem. These solutions can then be proposed by a centralized scheduler to the grid members. Since the solutions are equitably optimal, it can be assumed that fair agents would accept such schedule. However, malicious agents may still exploit the system by locally modifying the equitably optimal schedules to their own advantage. Still, if the number of malicious agents is small, the existence of equitably optimal schedules should provide an incentive for fair agents to participate in the system.

Another strategy of selfish adversaries could be returning incorrect results without running submitted jobs. A similar strategy could be used by malicious adversaries that aim to sabotage the grid computation. Both strategies can be prevented by a random verification of results that requires running the submitted jobs at least twice in the grid system. The behavior of unfair agents could be controlled by a trust management system that receives reports from grid members who have spotted incorrect computation results.

THE EMERGENCE OF FAIRNESS AS A RESULT OF TRUST MANAGEMENT

Fairness management in P2P systems is especially difficult due to the lack of centralized control. The algorithms used to combat freeriders can only try to achieve a local equality of the upload and download throughput. These algorithms are especially unfair to the so-called "altruistic" peers; if these peers have provided a lot of content in the past, they cannot use this content to receive more content in the future. This problem is partially resolved by the BarterCast algorithm that also proposes the use of reputation to solve the problem of fairness management in P2P systems. More generally, let us suppose that it would be possible to use Trust Management methods in order to solve the Fairness Management problem in P2P environments. However, a question arises: do TM methods really have a positive impact on fairness?

When considering the problem of trust management, it seems intuitive to suppose that if all users of the trust management system have similar characteristics, and the system is working well, then all users should have similar utilities. On the other hand, if the trust management system is working poorly because of the presence of adversaries or because of missing proofs, then the utilities of similar users may have significant differences.

From the point of view of the agents who participate in transactions and use a trust management system to cope with uncertainty or risk, the fairness of such system is particularly important. Consider the example of a P2P file sharing application. The users expect that if they behave as fairly as others, they should have a similarly high download rates (when all other factors, such as

access bandwidth variation, can be excluded). In other words, the users of a reputation system expect that the reputation system should treat them as fairly as possible. This expectation of users is a consequence of the general social norm: people expect fair treatment from many social and business institutions, like the stock exchange, banks or supermarkets.

This intuitive reasoning leads to the formulation of a hypothesis: if a trust management system works well, then the utilities of similar users should become more equal. This hypothesis could also be formulated differently: in successful trust management systems, fairness should be an emergent property. We shall refer to this hypothesis as the Fairness Emergence (FE) hypothesis.

Considering Fairness in Trust Management Systems

In a real-world setting, users of trust management systems would be expected to have quite varied levels of utility (perhaps even incomparable ones). How, therefore, do we expect a trust management system to realize the goal of fairness? And how can the Fairness Emergence hypothesis be true?

This concern is based on a frequent misconception that mistakes equality for fairness. If a trader in an Internet auction house has better goods, provides better services and has better marketing than other traders, it is perfectly fair that she should have a larger transaction volume and a larger revenue. In fact, her reputation should increase as well, so the trust management system should in this case support her in getting even more trade. On the other hand, if we have two honest traders that have comparable goods, services, and marketing, yet they have very unequal reputation and transaction volumes, something is certainly wrong in the way the trust management system works.

Therefore, when all other factors can be excluded, equivalent to the ceteris paribus (i.e. all things being equal) assumption from economics, fairness can be identified with distributional fairness. In a laboratory setting, such conditions can be satisfied and we can design trust management systems that realize the goal of fairness, even in the presence of adversaries.

Verifying the Fairness Emergence Hypothesis by Simulation

To verify the Fairness Emergence hypothesis, we have used simulation experiments. The FE hypothesis would hold if we could establish that the reputation system causes an increase in the equity of the distribution of utilities. In particular, we will be interested to study the impact of the quality of the reputation system on the equity of utility distributions.

The simulator is based on the Repast 3.1 platform (REP, 2003) and resembles a P2P file sharing application. In the design of the simulator, we had to make a decision about a sufficiently realistic, yet not too complex, model of the application, user behavior, and the reputation system. We chose to simulate the reputation system and the behavior of users faithfully.

The P2P file sharing application, on the other hand, has been simplified. We simulate the selection of peers using a random choice of a set of potential peers. The choosing peer (i.e. the downloading peer) selects one of the peers that has the highest reputation in the set (and then checks if the selected one has a reputation that is higher than a threshold). After that, the transaction itself is modeled as the Prisoner's Dilemma game. The agents receive payoffs that they add after every transaction.

Agent Behavior

In our simulator, a number of agents interact with one another. There are two types of agents in the system: fair and unfair agents. Unfair agents model adversaries. To test the FE hypothesis, we will focus on the fairness of utility distributions of fair agents. The payoffs of fair and unfair agents will also be compared.

When an agent carries out a transaction, she must make two decisions. The first decision concerns the choice of the transaction partner (peer) and whether or not to engage in the transaction. The agent chooses her partner from a randomly selected set of k other agents (in the simulations of the closed system, k has been equal to 3 or 1). From this set, the agent with the highest reputation is chosen. However, if the highest reputation is lower than a threshold p_{min} choice (in our simulations, fair agents choose partners with reputation at least 0.45, unfair agents - 0.3), then the choosing agent will not engage in any transaction. If the best agent's reputation is sufficiently high, the choosing agent will engage in the transaction with a certain probability p (in the simulations presented here, this probability was 1).

The second decision concerns the agent's behavior in the transaction. This decision can be based on a game strategy that can take into consideration the agent's own reputation as well as the reputation of her partner, the transaction history and other information. We decided to use the famous Tit-for-tat strategy developed by Rapaport but extended by using a reputation threshold: if two agents meet for the first time and one agent's reputation is below p_{min}^{game}, the other agent defects. The strategy used in the simulations presented here has also been based on the threshold p_{min}^{cheat}. In the case when the partner's reputation is higher than p_{min}^{cheat}, the agent would act fairly; otherwise, she would cheat with a certain probability c. In the simulations presented here, fair agents had a cheating probability of 0, while unfair agents had a cheating probability of 0.2 and a reputation threshold of 0 - meaning that unfair agents cheated randomly with a probability of 0.2.

The discovery of proofs by the P2P reputation system has been simulated by making the reports of peers available to the reputation system with a certain probability. In the simulations presented here, the probability of sending a positive report,

p_{rep}^{+} was 1.0, while the probability of sending a negative report p_{rep}^{-} varied from 0 to 1. This choice is based on the assumption about the presence of adversaries who attempt to drop negative proofs. This type of adversary has been discussed frequently in the literature. The assumption is also pessimistic, as our results show that this type of adversary has the highest impact on the performance of the reputation system.

Experiment Setup

In simulations of the closed system, there was a total of 1500 agents, out of which 1050 where fair and 450 were unfair. While the proportion of unfair agents is high, they cheat randomly and at a low probability - so a unfair agent is really a "not totally fair agent".

The simulator can compute reputations using any available feedback. The results of the simulation include: the reputations of individual agents and the total utilities (i.e. payoffs from all transactions) of every agent. In the simulations presented here, an agent's reputation is computed as the proportion of the number of positive reports about the agent to the number of all reports.

All simulations were made using pseudo-random numbers, therefore the Monte Carlo method is used to validate statistical significance. For each setting of the simulation parameters, 50 repeated runs were made, and the presented results are the averages and 95% confidence intervals for every calculated criterion. The confidence intervals were calculated using the t-Student distribution.

We decided to use transaction attempts instead of the number of successful transactions as a stop condition because we believe that an agent would consider each transaction attempt as an expense, and the reputation system would have to work well after as few transaction attempts as possible. In most presented simulations for each turn, 500 transaction attempts have been made.

For each simulation, the first 20 turns were used to warm up the reputation system. It means

that the payoffs are not recorded but an agents' reputation is modified by positive and negative reports. This method has been used to model the behavior of a real reputation system, where the system has a long history of transactions available. Simulating the reputation system without a warm-up stage would therefore be unrealistic.

Simulation Results

To verify the Fairness Emergence hypothesis, we have been interested to investigate the impact of a reputation system on the equity of the agent utility distribution. The equity of utility distributions has been measured using fairness criteria based on the theory of equity; however, other criteria such as the sum of agent utilities are considered as well. The simulations revealed that the Fairness Emergence hypothesis holds in several cases, but not universally; therefore, we have investigated the sensitivity of fairness emergence to various factors that influence the quality of the reputation system.

Fairness Emergence in the Long Term

The first studied effect was the emergence of fairness in the long term. In the simulation experiment, we measured the Gini coefficient and ran the simulation until the Gini coefficient stabilized. This experiment was repeated using three scenarios: in the first one, the agents did not use any reputation system, but selected partners for transactions randomly. In the second experiment, the reputation system was used, but agents submitted negative reports with the probability of 0.2. In the third experiment, negative reports were always submitted.

The results of the three experiments are shown on Figure 2. The Figure plots the average Gini coefficient of fair agents from 50 simulation runs against the number of turns of the simulation. It can be seen that when agents do not use the reputation system, the Gini coefficient stabilizes for

Figure 2. Fairness Emergence in the long term

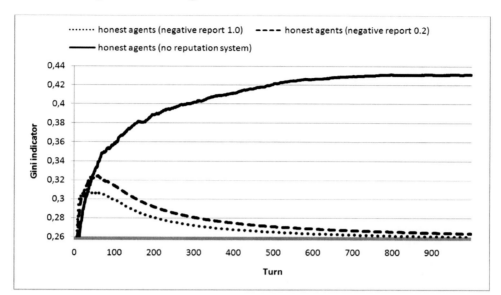

Figure 3. Fairness Emergence in the short term

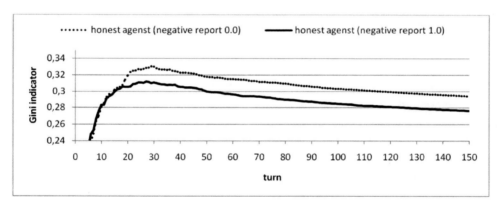

a value that is almost twice as large as the value of Gini that is obtained when reputation is used. Furthermore, there is a clear effect of increasing the frequency of negative feedback: the Gini coefficient decreases faster and stabilizes at a lower value when $p_{rep}^- = 1$. The initial increase of the Gini coefficient from 0 is due to the fact that at the beginning of the simulation the distribution of fair agent utilities is equal (during the warmup stage, utilities of agents are not recorded. All agents start

with a zero utility after warm-up completes).

The result of this experiment seems to be a confirmation of the FE hypothesis. The distributions of fair agents' utilities have a lower Gini coefficient (and a higher total sum of utilities) when the reputation system is used. In our simulation, new agents did not join the system (although the number of agents was large). The average number of successful transactions of an agent was about 270, which is much lower than the number of

Figure 4. Effect of increased choice on Gini coefficient

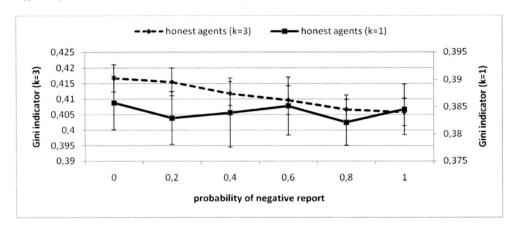

agents; this means that the chance of repeated encounters was low. However, this number is still large. The simulations were continued until a stable state was reached; in practical reputation systems, such situation would not be likely to occur because of the influx of new agents and the inactivity of old ones.

Fairness Emergence in the Short Term

The simulation experiments studied in the rest of this paper were about 8 times shorter than the long-term experiments. For these experiments, the number of successful transactions of an average agent was about 60. Figure 3 shows the Gini coefficient of the distributions of fair agents' utilities. The x axis shows the frequency of sending negative reports by fair agents (unfair agents always sent negative reports). The results show that for low negative report frequencies fairness emerges more slowly. Increasing the quality of a reputation system reduces the time needed for fairness emergence. This effect is apparent very quickly, even after 50 turns of simulation. From now on, fairness emergence in the short term is studied more closely to verify whether the improvement of reputation system quality will cause fairness emergence. In other words, until now we have considered fairness emergence with time, and now we shall consider the effect of the reputation

system's quality on fairness emergence. All further experiments were made in the short term, outside of the stable state of the system.

Effect of Better Usage of Reputation

The usage of reputation by agents had a particularly strong influence on the emergence of fairness. In our simulations, agents chose a transaction partner with the highest reputation. If $k=1$, then the transaction partner was chosen at random and only the threshold p_{min}^{game} was used to consider reputation. If $k=3$, it was less likely that an agent with lower reputation would be chosen as a transaction partner. These two scenarios correspond to the real life situation of peers who are able to select providing peers from a larger set, based on their reputation; on the other hand, it could be possible that the choice is low, because only one peer has the required resources.

We have considered the two scenarios while investigating the impact of the frequency of feedbacks on the reputation system. It turns out that increasing the choice of agents is necessary for the emergence of fairness. Figure 4 shows the effect of increasing the frequency of negative feedback on the Gini coefficient of fair agents. The figure shows two lines that correspond to the scenarios of $k=1$ and $k=3$. It can be seen that if the choice of agents on the basis of reputation is possible, then

Figure 5. Effect of increased choice on sum of utilities

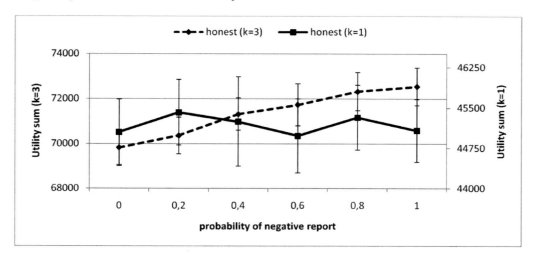

Figure 6. Effect of increased feedback on sum of utilities of all agents

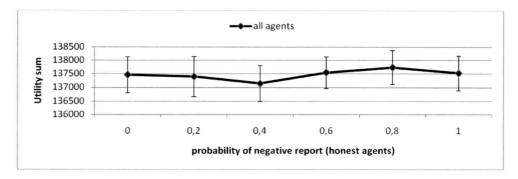

the increase in the number of feedbacks leads to a decrease of the Gini coefficient.

Figure 5 shows the effect of increased choice and varying negative feedback frequency on the sum of fair agents' utilities. It can be seen that once again enabling the choice of partners based on reputation has a positive effect on the welfare of fair agents. For k=3, fair agents had a higher overall sum of utilities than for k=1, and this sum increased when the frequency of negative reports increased. This also explains why the Gini coefficient of fair agents for k=1 was lower than for k=3. Since the sum of utilities was lower for k=1, the Gini coefficient could also be lower, although this does not mean that the distribution of utilities for k=1 was more equitable than for k=3.

Effect of Better Feedback

Better feedback is a prerequisite for increasing the quality of a reputation system. For that reason, we have chosen to investigate the effect of increased feedback on the emergence of fairness. As it has been explained previously, the frequency of negative feedback has been varied from 0 to 1.

Figure 6 shows the effect of increasing negative feedback on the sum of utilities of all agents. It turns out that the total sum was not affected by the increase. This seems to be a paradox, since we are using the iterated Prisoner's Dilemma as a model of our P2P application. In the Prisoner's Dilemma, increased fairness of agents results in an increased sum of all utilities. And increasing

Figure 7. Effect of increased feedback on fair and unfair agents' utilities

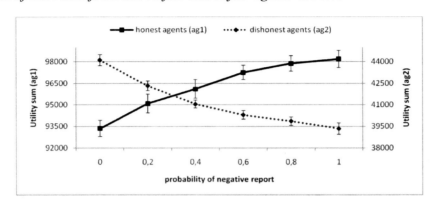

negative feedback from 0 to 1 should result in decreasing the unfair agents' ability to cheat.

This experiment also shows that even assuming the use of a Prisoner's Dilemma as a model of transaction, the use of the sum of all agents' utilities (i.e. the utilitarian paradigm) would lead to a wrong conclusion that the system behavior is not affected. From the utilitarian point of view, the reputation system works equally well when the frequency of negative reports is 0, as when it is equal to 1.

Figure 7 shows that this is not the case. The sum of utilities of fair agents increases, as negative feedback is sent more frequently. On the other hand, the sum of utilities of unfair agents drops.

Figure 8 shows the effect of increased negative feedback frequency on the Gini coefficient. Note that the effect is statistically significant for

the variation of from 0 to 1 (also from 0.4 to 1). Note that these simulations have been made in the short term and that together with the results about the sum of utilities they prove the FE hypothesis: increasing the quality of the reputation system does indeed lead to more equitable distribution of fair agents' utilities, as the hypothesis suggested.

CONCLUSION

This chapter has presented a review of research on trust and fairness management in P2P and grid systems. This research can be viewed as part of a larger trend that could be referred to as social informatics. Social informatics is interested in the solution of social problems (such as providing fairness) using information technology, or in the

Figure 8. Effect of increased feedback on Gini coefficient

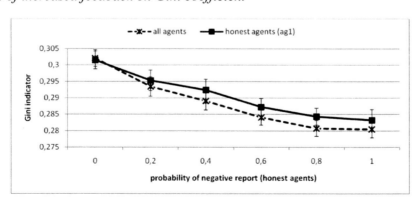

applications of social concepts (such as trust) in virtual social systems. The increase of the number of social applications of open, distributed systems like grids, P2P networks, Web 2.0 services, and many others, is a reason for the increasing importance and interest in social informatics.

The main new finding reported in this chapter is the presentation of the important relationship between trust and fairness management: the emergence of fairness due to trust management. In particular, it has been shown that the use of a reputation system (even with incomplete information, in the presence of adversaries, and outside of stable states) can lead to an emergence of fairness. This fact is important especially in the context of P2P and grid systems, since it allows to conclude that trust management can be used as a distributed tool for fairness management.

Fairness has been evaluated and measured based on the theory of equity. The application of this theory to the problem of fairness management is a new research trend that has been summarized in this chapter. The use of the Gini coefficient together with the sum of all agent utilities is a good alternative to the reliance on the utilitarian approach. Future work on fairness and trust management in open distributed systems will probably involve the study of more sophisticated algorithms that can find equitably optimal solutions. So far, distributed algorithms for finding such solutions are lacking.

REFERENCES

Aberer, K., & Despotovic, Z. (2001). Managing Trust in a Peer-2-Peer Information System. In *Proceedings of the 2001 ACM CIKM International Conference on Information and Knowledge Management, Atlanta, GA,* November 5-10, (pp. 310-317).

Abrams, Z., McGrew, R., & Plotkin, S. A. (2005). A non-manipulable trust system based on eigentrust. *SIGecom Exchanges, 5*(4), 21–30. Retrieved from http://dblp.uni-trier.de/db/journals/sigecom/sigecom5.html#AbramsMP05

Angel, E., Bampis, E., & Pascual, F. (2006). The price of approximate stability for a scheduling game problem. In *Proceedings of Euro-Par*, (LNCS Vol. 4128). Berlin: Springer.

Axelrod, R. (1984). *The Evolution of Cooperation.* New York: Basic Books.

Blaze, M., Feigenbaum, J., & Lacy, J. (1996, May). Decentralized trust management. In *Proc. of 1996 IEEE Symposium of Security and Privacy*, (pp.164–173), Oakland, CA.

Buyya, R., Abramson, D., & Venugopal, S. (2005). The grid economy. *Special Issue on Grid Computing, 93*, 698–714.

Carra, D., Neglia, G., & Michiardi, P. (2008). On the impact of greedy strategies in bittorrent networks: The case of bittyrant. In K. Wehrle, W. Kellerer, S. K. Singhal, & R. Steinmetz, (Eds.), *Peer-to-Peer Computing*, (pp.311–320). Washington, DC: IEEE Computer Society. Available from http://dblp.uni-trier.de/db/conf/p2p/p2p2008.html#CarraNM08

Colombo, M., Martinelli, F., Mori, P., Petrocchi, M., & Vaccarelli, A. (2007). *Fine grained access control with trust and reputation management for globus*, (pp. 1505–1515).

Cornelli, F., Damiani, E., De Capitani di Vimercati, S., Paraboschi, S., & Samarati, P. (2002). Choosing reputable servents in a p2p network. In *WWW*, (pp. 376–386).

Credence. (2006). Sourceforge.net. Retrieved from http://gattaca.cs.cornell.edu/credence/status.html

Damiani, E., De Capitani di Vimercati, S., Paraboschi, S., Samarati, P., & Violante, F. (2002). A reputation-based approach for choosing reliable resources in peer-to-peer networks. In V. Atluri, (Ed.), ACM Conference on Computer and Communications Security, (pp. 207–216). New York: ACM. Retrieved from http://dblp.uni-trier.de/db/conf/ccs/ccs2002.html#DamianiVPSV02

Dellarocas, C. (2000a). Immunizing online reputation reporting systems against unfair ratings and discriminatory behavior. In *Proceedings of the 2nd ACM conference on Electronic commerce*, (pp. 150–157).

Dellarocasm, C. (2000b). Immunizing online reputation reporting systems against unfair ratings and discriminatory behavior. In *Proc. of the 2nd ACM Conference on Electronic Commerce*. Retrieved from http://citeseer.ist.psu.edu/512497.html

Deutsch, M. (1973). *The Resolution of Conflict*. New Haven, CT: Yale University Press.

Deutsch, M. (1975). Equity, equality, and need: What determines which value will be used as the basis of distributive justice? *The Journal of Social Issues, 31*, 137–149.

Deutsch, M. (1987). *Social comparison, social justice, and relative deprivation, chapter Experimental studies of the effects of different systems of distributive justice*, (pp. 151–164). Hillsdale, NJ: Lawrence Erlbaum.

Feitelson, D. G., Rudolph, L., & Schwiegelshohn, U. (2005). Parallel job scheduling a status report. In *Proceedings of JSSPP 2004*, (LNCS Vol. 3277, pp. 1–16). Berlin: Springer.

Fernandes, A., Kotsovinos, E., String, S., & Dragovic, B. (2004). Pinocchio: Incentives for honest participation in distributed trust management. In C. Damsgaard Jensen, S. Poslad, and T. Dimitrakos, (Eds.), *iTrust*, (LNCS Vol. 2995, pp. 63–77). Berlin: Springer. Retrieved from http://dblp.uni-trier.de/db/conf/itrust/itrust2004.html#FernandesKOD04

Gambetta, D. (1998). *Trust: Making and Braking of Cooperative Relations*. Oxford, UK: Basil Blackwell.

Gruber, R., Keller, V., Kuonen, P., Sawley, M.-C., Schaeli, B., Tolou, A., et al. (2006). Towards an intelligent grid scheduling system. In *Proceedings of PPAM 2005*, (LNCA Vol. 3911, pp. 751–757).

Jan-David Mol, J., Pouwelse, J. A., Epema, D. H. J., & Sips, H. J. (2008). Free-riding, fairness, and firewalls in p2p file-sharing. In K. Wehrle, W. Kellerer, S. K. Singhal, & R. Steinmetz, (Eds.), *Peer-to-Peer Computing*, (pp. 301–310). Washington, DC: IEEE Computer Society. Retrieved from http://dblp.uni-trier.de/db/conf/p2p/p2p2008.html#MolPES08

Josang, A., Keser, C., & Dimitrakos, T. (2005). Can we manage trust? In *Trust Management (iTrust 2005)*, (LNCS Vol. 3477). Berlin: Springer. Retrieved from http://www.eu-trustcom.com/ViewDocument.php?tipo=Disem&id=248

Kamvar, S. D., Schlosser, M. T., & Garcia-Molina, H. (2003). The eigentrust algorithm for reputation management in p2p networks. In *Proceedings of the 12th International World Wide Web Conference*.

Kaszuba, T., Rzadca, K., & Wierzbicki, A. (2008). Discovering the most trusted agents without central control. In *proceedings of the Embedded and Ubiquitous Computing (EUC08)*, (Vol. 2, pp. 616-621). Washington, DC: IEEE Computer Society.

Kenyon, C., & Cheliotis, G. (2004). Grid resource commercialization: economic engineering and delivery scenarios. In J. Nabrzyski, J. M. Schopf, & J. Weglarz, (Ed.), *Grid resource management: state of the art and future trends*, (pp. 465–478). Norwell, MA: Kluwer Academic Publishers.

Komorita, S. S., & Parks, C. D. (1994). *Social Dilemmas*. Madison, WI: Brown and Benchmark.

Komorita, S. S., & Parks, C. D. (1995). Interpersonal relations: Mixed-motive interaction. *Annual Review of Psychology, 46*, 183–207. doi:10.1146/annurev.ps.46.020195.001151

Kostreva, M. M., Ogryczak, W., & Wierzbicki, A. (2004). Equitable aggregations and multiple criteria analysis. *European Journal of Operational Research, 158*(2), 362–377. Retrieved from http://dblp.uni-trier.de/db/journals/eor/eor158.html#KostrevaOW04

Kwok, Y.-K., Song, S., & Hwang, K. (2005). Selfish grid computing: Game-theoretic modeling and nas performance results. In *Proceedings of CCGrid*.

Lee, S., Sherwood, R., & Bhattacharjee, B. (2003). Cooperative peer groups in nice. In *Proc. INFOCOM 2003. Twenty-Second Annual Joint Conference of the IEEE Computer and Communications Societies*, (Vol. 2, pp. 1272–1282). Washington, DC: IEEE.

Legout, A., Liogkas, N., Kohler, E., & Zhang, L. (2007). Clustering and sharing incentives in bittorrent systems. *SIGMETRICS Perform. Eval. Rev., 35*(1), 301–312. doi: http://doi.acm. org/10.1145/1269899.1254919.

Liang, Z. & Shi, W. (2005). *Pet: A personalized trust model with reputation and risk evaluation for p2p resource sharing.*

Liogkas, N., Nelson, R., Kohler, E. & Zhang, L. (2006). *Exploiting bittorrent for fun (but not profit).*

Liu, J., Jin, X., & Wang, Y. (2005). Agent-based load balancing on homogeneous minigrids: Macroscopic modeling and characterization. *IEEE Trans. on Parallel and Distributed Systems, 16*(7), 586–598. doi: http://doi.ieeecomputersociety. org/10.1109/TPDS.2005.76

Liu, L., Zhang, S., Dong Ryu, K., & Dasgupta, P. (2004). R-chain: A selfmaintained reputation management system in p2p networks. In D. A. Bader & A. A. Khokhar, (Eds.), *ISCA PDCS*, (pp. 131–136). Retrieved from http://dblp. uni-trier.de/db/conf/ISCApdcs/ISCApdcs2004. html#LiuZRD04

Locher, T., Moor, P., Schmid, S., & Wattenhofer, R. (2006). Free riding in bittorrent is cheap. In *Proc. of HotNets-V*.

Marchal, L., Yang, Y., Casanova, H., & Robert, Y. (2005). A realistic network/application model for scheduling divisible loads on large-scale platforms. In *Proceedings of IPDPS, 01*(48b). doi: http://doi.ieeecomputersociety.org/10.1109/ IPDPS.2005.63

Marsh, S. P. (1994). *Formalising trust as a computational concept.* PhD thesis, University of Stirling, UK.

Meulpolder, M., Pouwelse, J.A., Epema, D. H. J., & Sips, H. J. (2008). *Bartercast: Fully distributed sharing-ratio enforcement in bittorrent.*

Mui, L. (2002). *Computational Models of Trust and Reputation: Agents, Evolutionary Games, and Social Networks.* PhD thesis, Massachusets Institute of Technology, Cambridge, MA.

Ogryczak, W., Kostreva, M. M., & Wierzbicki, A. (2004). Equitable aggregations and multiple criteria analysis. *European Journal of Operational Research, 158*, 362–377. doi:10.1016/j. ejor.2003.06.003

Peyton Young, H. (1994). *Equity: In theory and practice.* NJ: Princeton University Press.

Piatek, M., Isdal, T., Anderson, T., Krishnamurthy, A., & Venkataramani, A. (2007). Do incentives build robustness in bittorrent? In *NSDI, USENIX.* Retrieved from http://dblp.uni-trier.de/db/conf/ nsdi/nsdi2007.html#PiatekIAKV07.

Pouwelse, J. A., Garbacki, P., Wang, J., Bakker, A., Yang, J., Iosup, A., et al. (2006). Tribler: A social-based peer-to-peer system. In *The 5th International Workshop on Peer-to-Peer Systems (IPTPS06)*, (pp. 1–6).

Repastorganization for architecture and development. (2003). Argonne National Laboratory. Retrieved from http://repast.sourceforge.net/docs/ docs_main.html

Rzadca, K., Trystram, D., & Wierzbicki, A. (2007). Fair game-theoretic resource management in dedicated grids. In *CCGRID*, (pp. 343–350). Washington, DC: IEEE Computer Society. Retrieved from http://dblp.uni-trier.de/db/conf/ccgrid/ccgrid2007.html#RzadcaTW07

Selcuk, A. A., Uzun, E., & Pariente, M. R. (2004). A reputation-based trust management system for p2p networks. In *CCGRID '04: Proceedings of the 2004 IEEE International Symposium on Cluster Computing and the Grid*, (pp. 251–258). Washington, DC: IEEE Computer Society.

Singh, A., & Liu, L. (2003). Trustme: Anonymous management of trust relationships in decentralized p2p systems. In N. Shahmehri, R. Lee Graham, & G. Caronni, (Eds.), *Peer-to-Peer Computing*, (pp. 142–149). Washington, DC: IEEE Computer Society. Retrieved from http://dblp.uni-trier.de/db/conf/p2p/p2p2003.html#SinghL03

Song, S., Hwang, K., Zhou, R., & Kwok, Y.-K. (2005). Trusted p2p transactions with fuzzy reputation aggregation. *IEEE Internet Computing, 9*(6), 24–34. Retrieved from http://dblp.uni-trier.de/db/journals/internet/internet9.html#SongHZK05

Srivatsa, M., Xiong, L., & Liu, L. (2005). Trustguard: countering vulnerabilities in reputation management for decentralized overlay networks. In *WWW '05: Proceedings of the 14th international conference on World Wide Web*, (pp. 422–431). New York: ACM. doi:http://doi.acm.org/10.1145/1060745.1060808.

Sztompka, P. (1999). *Trust: A Sociological Theory*. Cambridge, UK: Cambridge University Press.

Sztompka, P. (2007). *Zaufanie. Fundament Spo?eczen'stwa* (Trust. A Foundation of Society). Wydawnictwo Znak.

Trivers, R. (1985). *Social Evolution*. Menlo Park, CA: Benjamin Cummings.

Tyler, T. R., & Smith, H. J. (1998). *The handbook of social psychology*, (Vol. 2, ch. Social justice & social movements, pp. 595–629). Boston: McGraw-Hill.

Volper, D. E., Oh, J. C., & Jung, M. (2004). Game theoretical middleware for cpu sharing in untrusted p2p environment. In *Proceedings of PDCS*.

Wang, Y., & Vassileva, J. (2003). Trust and reputation model in peer-to-peer networks. In *P2P '03: Proceedings of the 3rd International Conference on Peer-to-Peer Computing*, (pp. 150). Washington, DC: IEEE Computer Society.

Wierzbicki, A. (2007). The case for fairness of trust management. *Special issue of Electronic Notes in Theoretical Computer Science*.

Wierzbicki, A., & Kaszuba, T. (2007). Practical trust management without reputation in peer-to-peer games. *Multiagent and Grid Systems, 3*(4), 411–428. Retrieved from http://dblp.uni-trier.de/db/journals/mags/mags3.html#WierzbickiK07

Wierzbicki, A., & Kucharski, T. (2004). *P2p scrabble. can p2p games commence?* Retrieved from http://dblp.uni-trier.de/db/conf/p2p/p2p2004.html#WierzbickiK04

Wierzbicki, A., & Nielek, R. (2008). Fairness emergence through simple reputation. In S. Furnell, S. K. Katsikas, & A. Lioy, (Eds.), *Trust, Privacy and Security in Digital Business* (LNCS, pp. 77–89). Berlin: Springer. Retrieved from http://www.springerlink.com/content/951706w307060326/?p=2d15028d80a94e76b1170c3dc1e3d776&pi=0

Wilson, E. O. (1975). *Sociobiology*. Cambridge, MA: Harvard University Press.

Wolski, R., Brevik, J., Plank, J. S., & Bryan, T. (2003). Grid resource allocation and control using computational economies. In F. Berman, G. Fox, & A. Hey, (Eds.), *Grid Computing: Making The Global Infrastructure a Reality*. Chicester, UK: John Wiley & Sons. Retrieved from http://www.cs.utk.edu/~plank/plank/papers/Grid03.html

Xiong, L., & Liu, L. (2004). Peertrust: Supporting reputation-based trust for peer-to-peer electronic communities. *IEEE Transactions on Knowledge and Data Engineering, 16*(7), 843–857. doi:10.1109/TKDE.2004.1318566

Yu, B., Singh, M. P., & Sycara, K. (2004). Developing trust in large-scale peer-to-peer systems. In *Proceedings of First IEEE Symposium on Multi-Agent Security and Survivability*, (pp. 1–10). Retrieved from http://jmvidal.cse.sc.edu/library/yu04a.pdf

Zhao, H., & Li, X. (2008). H-trust: A robust and lightweight group reputation system for peer-to-peer desktop grid. In *Proc. 28th International Conference on Distributed Computing Systems Workshops ICDCS '08*, (pp. 235–240). doi: 10.1109/ICDCS.Workshops.2008.96.

Zhou, R., & Hwang, K. (2007a). Gossip-based reputation aggregation for unstructured peer-to-peer networks. *ipdps, 0*(95). doi: http://doi.ieeecomputersociety.org/10.1109/IPDPS.2007.370285

Zhou, R., & Hwang, K. (2007b). Powertrust: A robust and scalable reputation system for trusted peer-to-peer computing. *IEEE Trans. Parallel Distrib. Syst., 18*(4), 460–473. Retrieved from http://dblp.uni-trier.de/db/journals/tpds/tpds18.html#ZhouH07

KEY TERMS AND DEFINITIONS

Adversary: Malicious entity whose aim is to weaken or destroy the system. In general adversary can operate independently or form more complex relationship to other adversaries (or normal agents)

Fairness: Measure used to determine whether agents are receiving a fair share of a resources.

Freerider: Type of malicious agent (adversary) who consume more than its fair share of a resource. In peer-to-peer environment freeriders are detected by checking the share ratio value, which is a number determined by dividing the amount of data that agent has uploaded by the amount of data he has downloaded.

Full Aggregation Systems: Systems which uses all gathered proofs (information) as an input to compute requested value. Proofs are gathered from all agents available in the system.

Proof: Feedback passed by the agent to the Trust Management system. Proof can be history-based (report, observation) or delegation-based (recommendation)

Selective Aggregation Systems: Systems, where proofs (information) are gathered from a subset of agents. Such systems performs better than full aggregation systems but have lower accuracy.

Trust: There is a lot of definitions of trust. In our work wee adopt the definition of trust as a tolerance of risk, thus trust and risk values can be expressed on the same scale.

ENDNOTES

[1]   This author has been supported by the research grant 69/N-SINGAPUR/2007/0 of the Polish Ministry of Science
[2]   This author has been supported by the research grant N N516 4307 33 of the Polish Ministry of Science
[3]   This author has been supported by the research grant A*Star SERC GRANT NO: 072 1340055

Chapter 33
Trust Calculation and Management in P2P and Grid Systems

Konstantinos Karaoglanoglou
Aristotle University of Thessaloniki, Greece

Helen Karatza
Aristotle University of Thessaloniki, Greece

ABSTRACT

The significance of efficient security mechanisms in P2P and Grid systems is unquestionable, since security is considered to be a quality of service factor for such systems. Traditional security mechanisms in P2P and Grid systems include encryption, sand-boxing and other access control and authentication mechanisms. Unfortunately these techniques incur additional overhead. By using trust and reputation-based mechanisms, the additional overhead is minimized. The deployment of efficient trust mechanisms results to a safer communication between P2P or Grid nodes, increasing the quality of service and making P2P and Grid technology more appealing. The aim of this book chapter is to lay the theoretical background of concepts such as trust, reputation, trust graphs and trust functions. Furthermore it presents classification schemes for trust functions, discussing the characteristics and differences of each classification. Finally, it analyses popular trust and reputation-based management mechanisms that have been implemented in both P2P and Grid systems.

INTRODUCTION

P2P systems consist of a group of entities called peers that interact with each other without the presence of a central coordinating authority (decentralized P2P systems) (Figure 1). A peer in such a system can

act both as a client and a server (Suryanaranyana & Taylor, 2004). It can request services from other entities as well as provide services to other entities in the system. Each peer has a limited perspective of the system and relies upon information received from other peers to make local autonomous decisions. Decisions made by each decentralized peer may well conflict with those made by other peers.

DOI: 10.4018/978-1-61520-686-5.ch033

A Grid (Figure 2) can be defined as "a large-scale, geographically distributed, hardware and software infrastructure composed of heterogeneous networked resources owned and shared by multiple administrative organizations which are coordinated to provide transparent, dependable, pervasive and consistent computing support to a wide range of applications. These applications can perform distributed computing, high throughput computing, on-demand computing, data-intensive computing, collaborative computing or multimedia computing" (Bote-Lorenzo, Dimitriadis & Gomez-Sanchez, 2004).

P2P and Grid computing are both approaches to distributed computing mainly concerned with the organization of resource sharing in large scale computational environments. Though both types of systems share the common basic concept of resource-sharing, they followed different evolutionary paths. P2P systems focus on dealing with factors such as fault tolerance, transient populations and self-adaptation. On the other hand, research in Grid systems focuses on definitions of common protocols and standardized infrastructures to achieve interoperability.

At first, Grids were comprised by fully dedicated entities. These participating entities communicated with a high trust level, alleviating the requirement of complex reputation and trust models. As time progressed, Grids grew in size and new entities joined the systems. This fact has made the deployment of efficient trust mechanisms in Grid systems a primary concern. P2P applications lack the concept of a pre-defined trust relationship between participating entities. Most P2P applications assume an unsecured

Figure 1. An example figure of a P2P system

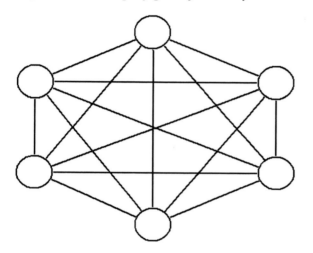

Figure 2. An example figure of a Grid system

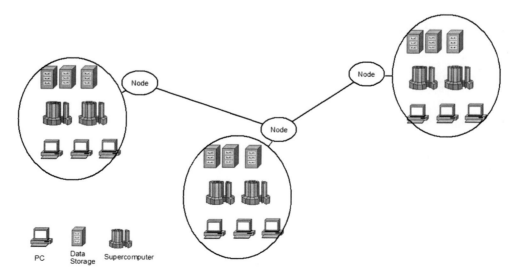

environment at all times. Deployment of trust and reputation mechanisms for P2P systems was always a primary concern. Therefore, both Grid and P2P systems share a common interest in efficient trust-based security mechanisms.

The fact that security in any system is considered a quality of service factor, the significance of efficient security mechanisms is unquestionable. Research work concerning this field suggests the use of security features such as sand-boxing (Chang, Itzkovitz & Karamcheti, 2000), encryption (Schneier, 1996) and other access control and authentication mechanisms. These mechanisms, however, incur additional overhead. Trust and reputation-based mechanisms are aware of the security requirements of the peers or Grid nodes and can perform all the relevant services with a minimized overhead. By using trust and reputation-based mechanisms, P2P and Grid technology becomes more appealing. An efficient trust mechanism results to a safer communication between the entities, increasing the quality of service.

The absence of a single authority that coordinates and monitors the behavior of peers and Grid nodes could lead to negative effects caused by malicious entities. Moreover, the absence of a single authority that coordinates the joining of new entities in these systems could also lead to negative effects since there are no guarantees for the good behavior of the new-joined entities. In decentralized P2P and Grid systems malicious entities may be encouraged to resort to a variety of attacks, such as transmitting false information or posing as other peers or Grid nodes. A trust management mechanism is responsible of defending the system's operation from attacks caused by malicious peers or Grid nodes.

The aim of this book chapter is to lay the theoretical background of concepts used in trust and reputation-based mechanisms. Moreover, well-known and popular approaches of trust management mechanisms in P2P and Grid systems will be presented. These approaches effectively solve practical problems and issues encountered

in P2P and Grid systems while providing complete frameworks for implementing and managing trust relationships between the entities that comprise such systems.

The structure of the book chapter is as follows. In the Background section we present the theoretical trust concepts that have been mentioned in several research works, the basic principles behind trust graphs, the importance of trust functions and metrics, and the different phases that compose the trust life cycle in P2P and Grid systems. The Trust Functions Classification section presents classification schemes for trust functions such as: subjective and objective trust, opinion-based and transaction-based trust, global and local trust, rank-based and threshold-based trust, identity and behavior trust. In the Trust Functions section we present well-known trust functions that are able to manage trust in P2P and Grid systems. Finally, the Future Research Directions section presents future research trends and directions, and the closing section provides our conclusion remarks.

BACKGROUND

Defining Trust and Reputation

The concepts of trust and reputation are closely related. Due to this fact, there is a lack of consensus in bibliography on the definition of both concepts. There are cases where the two concepts are presented to have the same meaning without that being the case. In this section we will present formal definitions of trust and reputation derived from bibliography and we will emphasize in showing that their meanings differ significantly.

Trust is the firm belief in the competence of an entity to act as expected such that this firm belief is not a fixed value associated with the entity but rather it is subject to the entity's behavior and applies only within a specific context at a given time (Azzedin & Mahesswaran, 2002), (Azzedin & Mahesswaran, 2002b). The above definition describes trust as a firm belief in the competence of an entity. Trust is a dynamic value and its value could range from very untrustworthy to very trustworthy. In most trust models the domain of trust is assumed to be in the range of [0, 1], with 0 being very untrustworthy and 1 being very trustworthy. The definition also states that trust depends on the past behavior and past experiences regarding an entity and applies only within a specific context. For instance, an entity X might trust an entity Y to access its local data but not to execute jobs or tasks with its resources. Trust also applies within a given time, meaning that an entity X that trusted an entity Y two years ago does not necessarily trust entity Y now. In most trust models trust decays with time.

The reputation of an entity is an expectation of its behavior based on other entities' observations or information about the entity's past behavior at a given time. The above definition of reputation states that an entity X that wonders on whether to trust an entity Y, can rely on information gathered by other entities in the system. An entity's reputation, therefore, is built on feedback from other entities that had direct interactions with this specific entity. Moreover, reputation of an entity is specified at a given time, meaning that reputation could also change values with the progression of time.

Another notable attempt to define trust and reputation is the one that relates these two concepts with the risks involved in any transaction (Mayer & Davis, 1995), (Josang & Presti, 2004), and (Ruohomaa & Kutvonen, 2005). *Trust is defined as the extent to which an entity is willing to participate in a given action with a given partner, considering the risks and incentives involved.* In this definition trust reflects the risk of dealing with others. Generally, an entity should avoid taking risks that depend on the behavior of entities that it does not trust. At the same time an entity is easily willing to take risks that depend on the behavior of trusted parties. In some sense, how much one trusts others is limited by how much risk one is willing to take.

The definition of the reputation concept according to this approach does not differ significantly from the first definition of reputation we discussed earlier. Reputation is defined as *a perception an entity creates to others through past actions about its intentions and norms.* As the definition implies, the reputation of an entity is derived from its past actions and from the way it behaved to others in the system.

Trust Concepts and Trust Graphs

Trustworthiness is considered to be an indicator of the quality of an entity's services. It is used to predicate the future behavior of an entity. If an entity is considered to be trustworthy, then this entity will possibly provide good services in future transactions (McKnight & Chervany, 1996), (Zhang, Yu, & Irwin, 2004).

In the simplest case *feedback* is defined as information issued by an entity about the quality of services of another entity after a single transaction (Bhattachajee & Goel, 2005), (Zhang, Yu, & Irwin, 2004). Feedback could also be multidimensional, reflecting an entity's evaluation on a variety of aspects of an entity's service such as access to an entity's local data, access to an entity's resources etc.

An *opinion* is an entity's general impression about an entity that provides services. In most cases an opinion is derived from all the feedback on all transactions an entity has conducted with another entity that provides services.

Trust evaluation is a binary action, meaning that an entity evaluates the trustworthiness of another entity and decides whether to trust or not. If an entity A is interested in knowing the trustworthiness of an entity B then we say that A and B are the *source* and *destination* of a trust evaluation respectively.

The framework for creating trust graphs in order to model trust relationships suggests that a trust graph (Figure 3) can be modeled as a directed multi-graph $G\ (V,\ E)$ (Zhang, Yu, & Irwin, 2004). In this graph, V is the set of vertices and E

Figure 3. An example trust graph

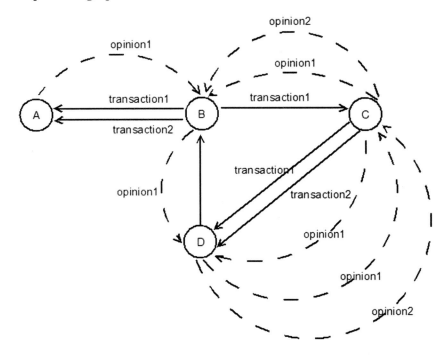

is the set of labeled edges. There are two types of edges: transaction edges and opinion edges. One transaction edge between *A* and *B* represents a relationship where *B* provides a service to *A*. An opinion edge from *A* to *B* represents *A*'s opinion on *B*'s services.

Note that, in a trust graph, there may be multiple transaction edges. *A* and *B* could have conducted more than one transactions between them. Similarly there may be multiple opinion edges, each of which represents *A*'s opinion on a certain type of service provided by *B*.

Managing Trust

Managing trust is crucial for P2P and Grid systems where nodes and users join and leave the system. Therefore, trust mechanisms must understand and manage the trust levels of such dynamic systems. In P2P and Grid systems the trust life cycle is composed of three different phases (Chakrabarti, 2007): trust creation, trust negotiation, and trust management.

- The trust creation phase is generally done before any trusted group is formed or communication between trusted entities is formed. This phase includes mechanisms that develop trust functions and trust policies that are going to be used in order to calculate trust.
- The trust negotiation phase includes the calculation of trust for a new group or node that is now entering the system. As mentioned above, there are no guarantees for the good behavior of new-joined entities in a system. In this phase new-joined entities are evaluated by the trust mechanisms in order to calculate their trust levels.
- The trust management phase is responsible of re-calculating the trust values of users or nodes. The trust management phase differs from mechanism to mechanism. There are some trust mechanisms that re-calculate trust values based on past successful transactions between entities, while others re-calculate trust values based on the

complaints an entity has gathered from past transactions. There are even trust mechanisms that re-calculate trust values based on the progression of time.

TRUST FUNCTIONS CLASSIFICATION

According to (Zhang, Yu, & Irwin, 2004) trust functions can be distinguished into the following four categories depending on the approach used to calculate trust values.

Subjective Trust vs. Objective Trust

If the quality of a service can be objectively measured then an entity's trustworthiness for that service is called objective trust. Otherwise it is called subjective trust. Assume the existence of three entities A, B, and C. A and B are interested in knowing the trustworthiness of entity C. If A and B measure C's trustworthiness objectively they will both conclude to the same level of trustworthiness for entity C. On the other hand, if the measurement of C's trustworthiness happens subjectively, entities A and B may conclude to different results about the trustworthiness of C. An entity's subjective trust may vary greatly when different sources of trust evaluation are considered.

Formally, given a trust function F, if $F(A, C)=F(B, C)$, with A, B, C being entities of the system, then we say F is suitable for objective trust evaluation or F is an objective trust function. Given a trust function F, if $F(A, C) \neq F(B, C)$, with A, B, C being entities of the system, then we say F is suitable for subjective trust evaluation or F is a subjective trust function.

Subjective trust functions and objective trust functions are not comparable. They are suitable for different types of systems, depending on how trust is applied in a system's application.

Transaction-Based vs. Opinion-Based

A transaction-based trust function typically requires information about the transactions between entities in the system. Assume that A is the source of the trust evaluation and B the destination of the trust evaluation. A could conclude to B's trustworthiness based on the information of their past transactions. For instance, A could rely on statistic information about the number of good transactions it has had with B divided by the number of total transactions it has had with B. In another case of trust evaluation based on transactions, A could require information about all the transactions B has had with all the entities of the system. So A could calculate the number of total good interactions B had with all the entities of the system divided by the number of total transactions B had with all the entities of the system. It is obvious that the information about transactions could include only the transactions between A and B or information about the total number of transactions. Depending on how detailed the information about transactions is, the communication cost gets higher.

Opinion-based trust functions give entities the autonomy of forming their own opinions about other entities available in the system without relying on information about transactions. Due to this fact, opinion-based trust functions present a significantly reduced communication cost when compared with transaction-based trust functions. However, an important disadvantage of opinion-based trust functions is that they are easily influenced by malicious users. Assume that entities A and B formed opinions about an entity C. A evaluates C's services as good, but B evaluates C's services as bad (entity B badmouths entity C). By simply looking at these opinions it is difficult for an entity D to form a precise opinion about C.

Global Trust vs. Localized Trust

Trust functions can also be classified according to the way information about transactions or opinions is collected. When complete information about transactions or opinions is required from all the entities of the system, such trust functions are called global trust functions.

There are trust functions that do not require complete information about transactions and opinions in the system, but rely only on localized information. Assume that an entity *A* desires to evaluate the trustworthiness of entity *B*, but has never interacted with *B* in the past. Entity *A* could collect information about the transactions that *B* had with its neighbors. The information *A* collected about *B* includes only the transactions *B* had with neighbors, thus are considered localized.

Typically global trust functions and localized trust functions are considered to be objective-trust functions and subjective-trust functions respectively. It is also important to note that global trust functions have a higher communication cost since they require complete information to reach a result about the trustworthiness of an entity.

Rank-Based vs. Threshold-Based

Even if we reach to the point that we have computed the trustworthiness of an entity of the system, the problem of trust still exists. Should we trust this entity based on its calculated trustworthiness? The classification of rank-based and threshold-based trust functions relies on the nature of the output of a trust function.

Assume that an entity's *A* trustworthiness is 0.7. This means that with a 70% probability entity *A* will provide good services. The question is should we trust entity *A*? Some trust functions have a pre-defined threshold of trustworthiness in order to make trust decisions. If the threshold for trustworthiness is 0.9, then entity *A* is considered to be untrustworthy. These trust functions, where a trust decision is based on a predefined threshold value, are called threshold-based trust functions.

In some other trust functions the level of trustworthiness an entity has, does not show how trustworthy this entity is. In these trust functions the level of trustworthiness makes sense only when it is compared to the level of trustworthiness of other entities. We call such functions rank-based. For instance, assume the existence of entities *A* and *B* with level of trustworthiness 0.9 and 0.95 respectively. Both entities have a high level of trustworthiness, but *B* is considered to be trustworthier. So we decide to use entity *B*, because the other alternative entity *A* has a smaller level of trustworthiness. In other words, entity *B* was preferred when compared with entity *A*.

Another noteworthy approach to classify trust and reputation-based systems is the following. According to (Gutscher, Heesen, & Siemoneit, 2008) three basic trust systems can be distinguished by using different approaches to calculate trust values.

Flat Reputation Systems

This type of trust system is the simplest type available. The reputation values are computed using all available trust opinions from all the entities of the system (Figure 4). All trust opinions have the same weight when trust and reputation values are computed. The problem with this approach lies in the fact that malicious or badmouthing entities have the same influence in the trust calculation as the good and honest ones. Moreover, it is not mandatory for an entity to state trust opinions, thus the collected opinions are not representative for the group of entities comprising a system. This is especially critical for the cases where a single malicious entity poses as other entities using multiple identities. These malicious entities create multiple trust statements in order to influence the way trust is calculated (phenomenon called Sybil-attack) (Douceur, 2002).

Figure 4. Flat reputation

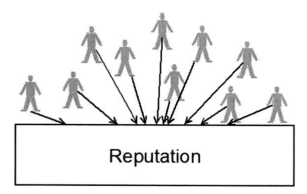

Figure 5. Recursively weighted reputation

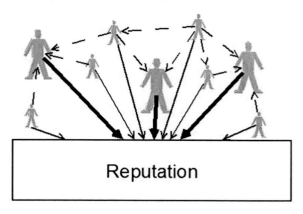

Recursively Weighting Reputation Systems

These types of systems try to improve the quality of the computed reputation value by increasing the weight of higher ranked opinions (Figure 5). It is obvious that the calculation of trust values takes place with an iterative process: the new reputation values are computed from the opinions stated by all other entities in the system weighted by their reputation values computed in the last iteration of the process. The collected opinions in this type of system are still not representative, thus the trust and reputation values are still influenced by the Sybil-attack phenomenon.

Personalized Reputation System with Trust Anchor

These types of systems aim to resist to the Sybil-attack phenomenon (Figure 6). The first step in order to calculate trust and reputation values is to acknowledge a set of a priori trusted entities (trust anchor). This set of entities is responsible of stating trust opinions. The next step is to re-compute trust values using trust opinions from trusted entities only. By this process more and more trustworthy entities are included in the calculation of reputation values. Opinions from untrustworthy entities are ignored as long as the trust anchor entities are trustworthy. This type of reputation systems

Figure 6. Personalized reputation system with trust anchor

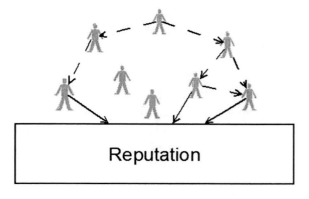

are described as personalized, because different sources of trust evaluation will obtain different reputation values for the same targets depending on the trust anchor they used in the first step of the calculation process.

TRUST FUNCTIONS FOR P2P AND GRID SYSTEMS

This section discusses and analyzes trust functions implemented to manage trust in P2P and Grid systems. These functions are: 'NICE', 'PeerTrust', 'EigenTrust', and 'Trust-aware resource management in Grid computing systems'. The first three

Figure 7. An example trust graph in the NICE framework: Weights present the extent of trust the source has in the sink

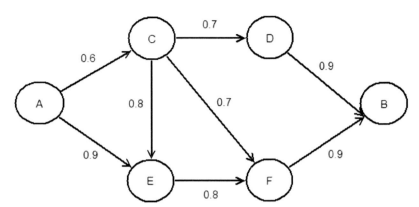

trust functions are applied in P2P systems and the last one in Grid systems.

NICE

NICE framework (Lee, Sherwood & Bhattacharjee, 2003) is a trust and reputation scheme that deals with trust issues in P2P systems. NICE is considered to be a subjective, transaction-based trust function. NICE framework is designed to let the "good" nodes in a system to form robust cooperative groups and also to prevent malicious nodes from entering in these groups. NICE provides three basic services: resource advertisement and location (using a Beaconing-based scheme), secure bartering and trading of resources, and distributed trust valuation.

NICE uses two trust policies in order to protect the integrity of the cooperative groups from malicious users that issue spurious information: trust-based pricing and trust-based trading limits. In trust-based pricing, resources are priced proportional to mutually perceived trust. For instance, consider a transaction between peers *A* and *B* where the trust value from *A* to *B* is 0.5 and the trust value from *B* to *A* is 1. In this case it is obvious that *B* trusts *A* more than *A* trusts *B*. Under trust-based pricing *A* will cooperate with *B* only if *B* offers significantly more to *A* than it gets back

in return. In trust-based trading limits, instead of varying the price of the resource, the amount of the resources bartered is varied. This means that when a peer transacts with a less trusted peer, this specific peer can set a limit to the amount of the resources that will be traded. For instance, using the trust values from the above scenario for peers *A* and *B*, *A* may allow *B* to store 1 MB of data at its host and gradually increase the storage as *B* continues to cooperate well.

For each transaction in the system, each peer involved, creates a signed statement (called cookie) evaluating the quality of the transaction. For example, assume that a successful transaction between *A* and *B* just occurred in which *A* consumed services from *B*. The next step is for peer *A* to evaluate the transaction. After the completion of the transaction, *A* signs a cookie stating that it had a successful transaction with *B*. Now *B* may choose to store this cookie in order to prove its trustworthiness to other peers including *A* for future transactions.

The way trust is calculated in the NICE framework is described using a trust graph. The vertices in the trust graph correspond to the number of different peers available in the system. An edge in the trust graph between two peers *X* and *Y* exists only if *Y* has a signed cookie from *X*. An example trust graph is depicted in Figure 7.

Assume that a peer *A* has acknowledgement of the trust graph in the system and needs to compute peer's *B* trust value, but had no prior transaction with it (note that if *A* had a transaction in the past with *B* there would be an edge between them). In the NICE framework, there are two mechanisms that are used in order to infer trust based on a trust graph: the strongest path, and the weighted sum of strongest disjoint paths.

In the strongest path mechanism, given a set of paths to *A* and in order to compute *B*'s trust value, *A* has to choose the strongest path and use the minimum value edge on the path as a trust value for *B*. In the weighted sum of strongest disjoint paths, instead of choosing only the strongest path, a peer could choose to use contributions from all disjoint paths. Given a set of disjoint paths, *A* can compute a trust value for *B* as a weighted sum of the strength of all of the strongest disjoint paths. To conclude, NICE framework also provides mechanisms that can infer the trust value of a peer based on a given trust graph.

Assume the existence of peers *A* and *B* that had never interacted in the past. In most trust models peer *A* has to prove its trustworthiness to peer *B* in order to use its resources and peer *B* has to verify *A*'s trustworthiness in order to cooperate. In NICE peer *A* has to search for *B*'s cookies and present them to *B* in order to use its resources.

NICE provides an efficient searching mechanism called digest-based search protocol in order to help peers search and store cookies from other peers that hadn't interacted with them in the past. Figure 8 describes an example of the digest-based searching procedure. *A* wants to use *B*'s resources but does not have a signed cookie from *B*. So, *A* starts the search procedure in order to find a cookie path to *B*. In Figure 8 the initial state of cookies and digests in all peers is presented. *A* has a cookie of value 0. 9 from *C* and its digest from *C* shows that *C* has a cookie from *D*. *A* also has a cookie of value 0.8 from *D* and its digest shows that *D* has a cookie from *G*. Finally, *A* has a cookie of value 0.8 from *E* and its digest shows that *E* has a

Figure 8. Initial state of cookies and digests in all peers

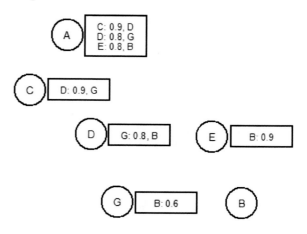

Figure 9. Forwarding queries

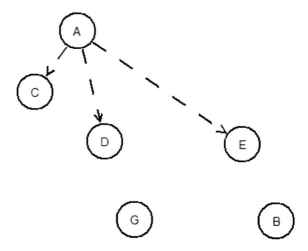

cookie from *B*. In Figure 9 *A* sends its query to all peers, including the ones it didn't have a digest hit (*C* and *D*). *C* won't forward the query since it has no neighbors with a stored cookie from *B*. *D* will forward the query to *G* who has a digest hit for *B*. Now, *G* and *E* return the query to *A* informing it that they have a cookie for *B*. In Figure 11 the two cookie paths *A* searched for are presented, with the strongest path in bold.

Due to the fact that the peers in the system need to prove their trustworthiness in other peers to use their resources, it is clear that peers tend to gather more and more signed cookies from successful transactions and store some of them. What happens when a malicious peer after an unsuccessful transaction is given a signed cookie from another peer that states its bad behavior? Since storing cookies is not mandatory for the peers of the system and malicious peers are able to discard cookies that state their bad behavior, how is the integrity of the system protected?

The integrity of the system is guarded by storing negative cookies. If a peer *A* interacts with a

Figure 10. Results send back to A

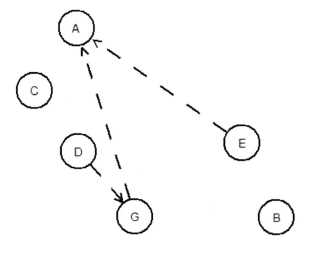

Figure 11. Trust paths (the strongest path shown in bold)

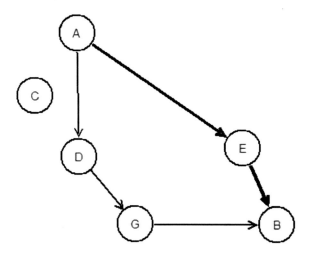

peer *B* and *B*'s behavior was bad, peer *A* should sign a low valued cookie for *B*'s services. Peer *B*, of course, would not want to store a cookie that states that it has low trust value and would normally discard this cookie. In the case of negative cookies, peer *A*, instead of sending the signed cookie to the low trust value peer *B* in order to store it, creates the cookie and stores it itself. In a future request from peer *B*, *A* that now stores the negative cookie, would deny service due to the low trust value of *B*. Negative cookies are also useful not only to the peers that signed them, but to other peers in the system too. Assume that peer *C* wants to interact with peer *B*, but does not have a cookie from it. Peer *C* could initiate a searching procedure for possible negative cookies *B* has. This searching procedure will return to peer *C* a list of peers that it trusts and have had bad interactions with peer *B* in the past. Now peer *C* has all the necessary facts and it can decide whether to transact with *B* or not.

In conclusion, NICE implements techniques that help peers to form robust cooperative groups. It allows peers to identify other good peers and urges them to cooperate, blocking out malicious users that tend to spread spurious information harming the system's integrity. NICE is a totally decentralized trust inference scheme that scales well even with a limited amount of storage at each peer and can be used to implement large distributed applications with no need of central authorities.

PeerTrust

PeerTrust is an objective, transaction-based trust function designed to solve trust issues in decentralized electronic peer to peer communities (Xiong & Liu, 2002), (Xiong & Liu, 2003), and (Aberer, 2001). In such communities peers often have to interact with other unknown peers without the presence of central or other third party authorities. As a result, the risk involved in such interactions is high. PeerTrust is designed in order to decrease the risk involved when interacting with unknown peers.

One solution to the problem of interacting with others would be to use information such as feedbacks about past experiences for the peers of a system in order to make successful trust decisions. The solely use of feedbacks based on past experience for evaluation a peer's trust is inaccurate. Though many trust models decide whether to trust or not based solely on past experiences, PeerTrust suggests that these models are flawed in a number of ways and offer example scenarios to support their point of view.

Assume the existence of peers *A* and *B*. Peer *A* performs 10 interactions with other peers and gets satisfaction for each interaction it has performed. On the other hand, peer *B* performs 100 interactions but only gets satisfaction for 10 of them. Both peers have the same amount of satisfaction (10 successful interactions). It is obvious, though, that peer *A* is considered to be more trustworthy than peer *B*, since peer *B* also has 90 unsuccessful interactions. The unsuccessful interactions of peer *B* are not depicted at all in its past experience.

Another example scenario showing the inaccuracy of using only past experiences is the following. Assume the existence of a trustworthy peer that only interacts with malicious peers and these malicious peers tend to badmouth it to other peers in the system. Though this specific peer in the system is trustworthy, the other peers consider it untrustworthy, since they gather false statements from malicious peers.

To address the above problems PeerTrust evaluates a peer's trust by the degree of satisfaction it receives providing services to other peers in the past. The degree of satisfaction a peer receives reflects to what extent this peer acts in other peers' best interests. The trust evaluation in PeerTrust is based on three important factors: the amount of satisfaction, the number of interactions the peer has with other peers, and a balance factor. By introducing these three important factors for trust evaluation, PeerTrust manages to avoid the flaws encountered in solely feedback-based mechanisms.

The amount of satisfaction a peer receives from others results from the successful interactions it has had with other peers of the system. Thus, a large number of successful interactions for a certain peer mean that this peer is worthy of trust. The solely use of the amount of satisfaction a peer receives is not helpful if not put in a certain context. As a result, an important factor of PeerTrust is the total number of interactions a peer has with other peers in the system. Now the amount of satisfaction a peer had, in the context of the total number of interactions, results to better conclusions for trust evaluation. Finally, the balance factor is used in order to offset false feedback and statements from malicious and badmouth peers. Using the balance factor, the strength of malicious users in a P2P system is effectively reduced.

The basic trust metric that PeerTrust provides in order to evaluate a peer's trust combines the above three factors. Let *P* be the set of *N* peers in an electronic community and *A*, *B* are peers in this community. *I(A, B, t)* is the total number of transactions peer *A* had with peer *B* up to transaction *t*. *I(A, t)* is the total number of transactions peer *A* had with all the other peers in the system, i.e. $\sum_{B \in P, B \neq A} I(A, B, t)$. Let *S(A, B, t)* be the amount of satisfaction peer *A* has with *B* up to transaction *t*. *Cr(B, t)* is the balance factor of trust that offsets the risk of potential false statements from peer *B*. The evaluation of peer's *A* trust up to transaction *t* is defined as a function of *I(A, B, t)*, *S(A, B, t)* and *Cr(B, t)*. With *T(A, t)* being the trust value of peer *A* up to transaction *t*, the trust function is:

$$T\left(A,t\right) = \frac{\sum_{B \in P, B \neq A} S\left(A,B,t\right) \times Cr\left(B,t\right)}{\sum_{B \in P, B \neq A} I\left(A,B,t\right)}$$

So, the trust value of peer *A* is computed as the ratio of the amount of satisfaction that other peers have over *A* balanced by a factor to offset potential malicious behavior from B and the total number of interactions A has with all the other peers in the community P.

The above general trust metric can be easily adapted according to the service-level agreements of any P2P system. Different systems may use different measures and the metric may be adapted in different forms. In PeerTrust the general trust metric was adapted in order to depict a feedback system based on complaints. If a peer receives a complaint from another peer after an interaction, the amount of satisfaction it gets through this in-teraction is 0. Otherwise it gets 1. *C(A, B, t)* is the number of complaints a peer A received from peer B up to transaction t. The balance factor of trust in this adaptation of the complaint feedback system must depict the fact that peers cannot be blindly trusted for their feedbacks. An untrustworthy peer tends to file fake complaints badmouthing other peers. On the contrary, trustworthy peers file true complaints, so there should be a balance factor that offsets the error caused by this behavior of untrustworthy and trustworthy peers. Complaints filed by trustworthy peers should be taken in more consideration in the trust metric than those filed by untrustworthy peers. This is depicted in the trust metric as $C\left(A,B,t\right)\times T\left(B,t\right)$, the credible complaints filed by peer B. The complaint based trust metric that is an adaptation of the general trust metric is the following:

$$T\left(A,t\right)=1-\frac{\sum_{B\in P,B\neq A}C\left(A,B,t\right)\times T\left(B,t\right)}{\sum_{B\in P,B\neq A}I\left(A,B,t\right)}$$

Though the basic implementation of PeerTrust is the complained-based trust metric presented above, PeerTrust could easily be extended in order to cover issues encountered in various P2P electronic communities. The trust metric in PeerTrust does not react to the behavioral change of peers, meaning the change of their behavior as time progresses. For instance, a peer that joined an electronic community could behave well until it

reaches a high reputation and then start behaving completely untrustworthy. If the trust metric needs to be extended in order to take into consideration time as a factor for trust evaluation, PeerTrust suggests building in a sliding time window so that one can give more weight to the latest feedbacks and less weight to old feedbacks. Another exten-sion to PeerTrust is discussed in order to prevent peers with low trust values reentering the system with a new identity. The solution suggested is to assign low trust values to the new joined peers, lower than all the peers comprising the com-munity. This way we create an incentive to peers to keep on improving their trust value instead of exiting the system and reentering with a very low trust value.

PeerTrust is a trust metric implemented for trust management in P2P electronic communities. It uses three basic parameters: amount of satisfac-tion, number of interactions, and balance factor. These parameters are used in order to construct the general trust metric of PeerTrust, which then is adapted in order to depict feedback from a complaint-based system. Moreover, PeerTrust can easily be extended in order to take in consid-eration factors such as the progression of time, and low trust value peers reentering the system with a new identity.

EigenRep

EigenRep is a framework for reputation man-agement in P2P systems (Kamvar, Schlosser & Molina, 2003). The primary goal of EigenRep is to decrease the number of downloads of inau-thentic files from malicious peers. It is a common phenomenon in P2P systems that malicious peers share inauthentic files and respond to any query in the system providing fake files. In EigenRep, each peer is assigned with a global reputation value that reflects the experiences of all peers in the network with this specific peer. Peers use the knowledge of these global reputation values in order to choose from whom peer they will download. This way the system identifies the existent malicious peers and manages to isolate them. The interesting aspect of EigenRep is that it is considered to be a rank-based function. This means that knowing one peer's trustworthiness tells us nothing about the quality of services it provides. The trust values computed in EigenRep show the comparative relations between peers in the system.

The evaluation of a peer to another peer can rely on the transactions between these two peers. One peer may have positive opinions for a peer that provided it with an authentic file, but may have negative opinions for a peer that provided it with an inauthentic file. In this manner EigenRep defines s_{ij} as the difference between the satisfactory transactions peer i had with peer j and the unsatisfactory transactions peer i had with peer j: $s_{ij} = sat(i,j) - unsat(i,j)$.

According to this procedure each peer evaluates other peers based on its experience. However, a peer's experience is considered to be limited, since it only has interactions with a small number of peers in the system. The problem lies for a peer that needs to evaluate another peer with whom it never interacted. This peer should gather evaluations provided by other peers in the system which may be familiar with the unknown peer. In this way, peers share their experiences with each other.

Since there is no central peer that maintains all the local reputation values in the P2P system, it is essential to normalize these local reputation values in some manner before sharing them in the system. EigenRep defines a normalized local reputation value as follows: $c_{ij} = \frac{\max(s_{ij}, 0)}{\sum_j \max(s_{ij}, 0)}$. This definition assigns all the local reputation values to a value between 0 and 1.

When peer i needs to evaluate an unknown peer k, it can ask its friends about their experiences with peer k. Moreover, peer i weighs their opinions by the trust it places in them: $t_{ik} = \sum_j c_{ij} c_{jk}$ and in

matrix notation $\vec{t_i} = C^T \vec{c_i}$, in which $\vec{c_i}$ contains all the normalized local reputation values of peer i to the peers in the system. If peer i needs to broaden its experience even more it can ask its friends about opinions on all the peers in the system.

$$\vec{t_i} = C^T \vec{c_i}, i.e. \begin{pmatrix} t_{i1} \\ \cdots \\ t_{ik} \\ \cdots \\ t_{iN} \end{pmatrix} = \begin{pmatrix} c_{11} & \cdots & c_{k1} & \cdots & c_{N1} \\ \cdots & & & & \cdots \\ c_{1k} & \cdots & c_{kk} & \cdots & c_{Nk} \\ \cdots & & & & \cdots \\ c_{1N} & \cdots & c_{kN} & \cdots & c_{NN} \end{pmatrix} \begin{pmatrix} c_{i1} \\ \cdots \\ c_{ik} \\ \cdots \\ c_{iN} \end{pmatrix}$$

This is a useful way to have each peer gain a view of the system that is wider than its own experience. However, trust values stored in peer i still reflect the experience of peer i and its friends. In order to broaden its view even more, peer i can ask for opinions its friends' friends $\vec{t_i} = (C^T)^2 \vec{c_i}$. If peer i continues this procedure it will have, at some point after n=large iterations, a complete view of the system $\vec{t_i} = (C^T)^n \vec{c_i}$. So, if n is large, the trust vector t will converge to the same vector for every peer i, making t a global reputation vector.

EigenRep also provides solutions for practical issues encountered in P2P systems. There are often peers in the system that are known to be trustworthy. For example, when a P2P system starts to operate, it does so with peers that are trustworthy and want to cooperate. Malicious peers enter such a P2P system later as the system develops. So in every P2P system there could be defined a priori notions of trust and they should be depicted in the trust evaluation process. In EigenRep some distribution p is defined over pre-trusted peers: $p_i = \begin{cases} 1/|P|, i \in P \\ 0, otherwise \end{cases}$. This pre-trusted vector p is used for a number of reasons.

The pre-trusted vector p can be used for inactive peers, i.e. peers that don't download from anybody else or assign a zero score to all other peers. Equation $c_{ij} = \dfrac{\max\left(s_{ij}, 0\right)}{\sum_j \max\left(s_{ij}, 0\right)}$ will not be defined, since for inactive peers the $\sum_j \max\left(s_{ij}, 0\right)$ is equal to zero. For inactive peers the c_{ij} is re-defined as: $c_{ij} = \begin{cases} \dfrac{\max\left(s_{ij}, 0\right)}{\sum_j \max\left(s_{ij}, 0\right)}, & \sum_j \max\left(s_{ij}, 0\right) \neq 0 \\ p_j, & otherwise \end{cases}$

This means that if peer i doesn't know anybody or doesn't trust anybody, it will choose to trust the pre-trusted peers.

The pre-trusted vector p also helps dealing with the formation of malicious collectives. A malicious collective is a group of malicious peers that tend to assign low reputation values to good peers and high reputation values among the malicious peers in the collective in order to subvert the system. EigenRep deals with malicious collectives by defining: $\vec{t}^{(k+1)} = \left(1 - a\right)C^T\vec{t}^{(k)} + a\vec{p}$, where a is a constant less than 1. This way, malicious collectives are broken since peers in the system are obligated to have some trust in the pre-trusted peers in vector p.

By everything we discussed so far, it is obvious that each peer i computes and reports its own trust value with the procedure described above. So malicious peers could easily report false trust values and succeed in subverting the system. This is not true, since EigenRep also offers a secure procedure when computing trust values. The secure version of EigenRep implements mechanisms in order to guarantee the integrity of the computing procedure.

The current trust value of a peer must not be computed by and reside at the peer itself, where it could easily become subject to manipulation. Thus, EigenRep suggests that a different third-party peer in the system should compute the trust value of a peer. This way, malicious peers could tamper the trust evaluation results only when they are supposed to compute a peer's trust value. Since the evaluation of a trust value could still be tampered,

EigenRep suggests that the trust value of a peer in the system should be computed by more than one different peer. When a peer needs to know the trust value of peer i it has to query all the M peers (dubbed 'mother peers' of a peer i) which are used for computing peer i's trust value. In the case that conflicts arise between the mother peers of peer i (malicious mother peers and good mother peers), EigenRep settles them taking a majority vote. This way, opinions from malicious mother peers could be ignored.

EigenRep is a trust framework for decreasing the number of inauthentic files download, which is a common fact in any P2P system. By assigning global reputation values to peers, it helps peers decide from whom to download, achieving to isolate the malicious peers that tend to post inauthentic files in order to subvert the system. EigenRep starts the computing procedure by firstly assigning local reputation values, that are then normalized, and reflect a peer's experience based on its interactions. Then these normalized local reputation values are aggregated in a way that they reflect a much wider view of the P2P system. If the number of iterations of the computing procedure is rather large, the view of the peer about the system will at some point become a whole.

Trust-Aware Resource Management in Grid Systems

Though most research work is focused in dealing with trust issues in P2P systems, there are also attempts to solve trust issues in Grid systems. In (Azzedin & Mahesswaran, 2002), (Azzedin & Mahesswaran, 2002b), a trust-aware resource management is proposed for encouraging domain-to-domain interactions increasing the confidence between the domains for efficient sharing of resources in a distributed Grid environment. Primary goals of this approach are the use of resources in Grid domains without the domains losing their control over their resources and ensuring of confidentiality for others. The trust model presented here deals exclusively with the so-called behavior trust issues. It involves the computation of an entity's trustworthiness based on interactions and the management of such trust evaluations.

The trust model for Grid systems that computes trust and reputation takes into consideration three parameters. Firstly, trust decays with time. If an entity A trusts entity B at a level p, based on an interaction they had five years ago, it is very possible that this entity A does not trust entity B at the same high level p if they haven't transacted since then. A similar suggestion can be noted for the notion of reputation as well. Reputation also decays with time. Secondly, Grid entities tend to form alliances and partnerships with entities they trust more. Finally, the trust model takes into consideration for trust evaluation not only the direct relationship between two entities A and B, but also weighs in the reputation entity B has in the system.

Let A and B denote two domains of entities. The trust relationship based on a specific context c, i.e. printing, storage or computing, at a given time t can be expressed as $\Gamma(A, B, t, c)$ (Equation (1)). Thus, Γ can be computed based on the direct relationship between A and B for c at time t, expressed as $\Theta(A, B, t,)$, and also based on the reputation of B for c at a given time t, expressed as $\Omega(B, t)$. Weights λ and μ are used to weigh in the trust evaluation direct and reputation relationships respectively. Values for λ and μ can be adjusted according to which one of the parameters (direct relationship and reputation relationship) we want to play a bigger role in computing trust. For instance, an entity of the system may have a policy stating that it will compute trust for other entities only by using information from direct relationships and not based on recommendations about reputation. In this case weight μ is 0.

$$\Gamma\left(A, B, t, c\right) = \lambda \times \Theta\left(A, B, t\right) + \mu \times \Omega\left(B, t\right) \quad (1)$$

Direct relationship (Equation (2)) can be computed as a product of the trust level in the direct

trust table (DTT) and the decay function $Y(t_2\text{-}t_1)$, where t_2 is the current time, and t_1 the time of the last interaction between A and B.

$$\Theta\left(A, B, t\right) = DTT\left(A, B\right) \times Y\left(t_2 - t_1\right) \quad (2)$$

Reputation relationship (Equation (3)) is computed as the average of the product of the trust level in the reputation trust table (RTT), the decay function $Y(t_2\text{-}t_1)$, and the recommender trust factor R, which depicts recommendations gathered from all domains F in the system about entity B. The recommender trust factor is used to balance recommendations from malicious Grid entities that could spread false information about an entity.

$$\Omega\left(B, t\right) = \frac{\sum RTT\left(F, B\right) \times R\left(F, B\right) \times Y\left(t_2 - t_1\right)}{\sum F} \quad (3)$$

Each domain in the system maintains direct trust tables (DTTs) that include information about the trust levels of other domains, with which this specific domain had direct interactions. In the same way, each domain maintains reputation trust tables (RTTs) for the reputation trust levels of other domains in the system. It is crucial for the trust model that the information maintained in both direct and reputation tables to be up to date.

Note that the decay function used for computing direct and reputation relationships may differ from domain to domain. This practically means that each domain could use a different trust function depending on the factors that accelerate or de-accelerate trust as time progresses according to its point of view. For instance, a Grid domain could have a policy for decaying trust faster for domains that are not in the same country as it is, though it could decay trust slower for domains that are in the same country.

In order to fully comprehend the proposed trust model in Grid systems, we present an example of two domains A and B that had never interacted in the past. Domain A also is a new-joined domain in the system and domain *B* wishes to use resources that domain *A* offers. The trust evaluation is focused on domain *A* about whether or not to trust domain *B* using its resources. We also assume that domain *A* has recommendations for domain *B* as follows: one third-party domain evaluates the trust level of *B* as value *"D"*, and another third-part domain evaluates the trust level of *B* as value *"C"*. The descriptions of trust levels in a range of *"A"* to *"F"* are presented in Table 1.

In order for domain *A* to permit domain *B* use its resources, it requires a trust level *"F"* for domain *B*. Now domain *A* has to examine if domain *B* abides as an extremely high trust leveled domain. Once the transaction between them begins, domain *A* has to examine if domain *B*'s behavior is good. Let us assume that domain *B* performs poor in this interaction with domain *A* and thus its performance gets a score *"D"* from domain *A*. Domain *A*, now that the transaction is over, has to update its direct trust table (*DTT*) regarding domain *B*, since now these two domains have had an interaction. The trust level of domain *B* in the domain *A*'s *DTT* is set to *"D"*. After updating its *DTT*, domain *A* can update its reputation trust table (*RTT*) in a similar way, setting domain *B*'s trust level to *"D"*. Finally, domain *A* in order to evaluate the recommender trust has to update the recommender trust factor, i.e. *R*. Two third parties gave recommendations to domain *A* about domain *B*. One of them evaluated the trust level of *B* as value *"D"* and another one evaluated the trust level of *B* as value *"C"*. Domain *A* fully agrees with the third-party domain that recommended domain *B*'s trust level as *"D"*. On the other hand, domain *A* disagrees with the third-party domain that recommended domain *B*'s trust level as *"C"*. Taken in consideration these results, it is obvious that domain *A* will weigh more the first third-party's recommendation in future interactions, than recommendations from the second third-party domain.

In conclusion, the presented trust model addresses issues of trust in the distributed Grid envi-

Table 1. Descriptions of trust levels

Trust Level	Description
"A"	Very low
"B"	Low
"C"	Medium
"D"	High
"E"	Very high
"F"	Extremely high

ronment. The trust model can evolve and maintain trust based on direct and reputation relationships. It also takes into consideration the fact that trust and reputation decays with time. The trust-aware resource management in Grid systems is considered to be a formal and efficient model for trust relationships and for the way the trust evaluation occurs, it encourages Grid domains to cooperate based on the trust level of each domain.

FUTURE RESEARCH DIRECTIONS

There are many challenges in the area of trust calculation and management in P2P and Grid systems. We have presented a significant part of research that has been done in this area, but there are also many issues that need to be addressed. This section discusses future research directions regarding issues that arise about the perception of trust when attempting to model it. Moreover, it discusses research directions about more practical problems encountered in P2P and Grid systems.

The majority of the proposed trust models and management frameworks make a number of simplifying assumptions when implementing trust models. The fact that trust is a multidimensional concept makes these assumptions necessary in order to construct a framework to manage trust effectively. But still some may argue that these assumptions may not necessarily hold in real systems. The most challenging direction for the future is dropping these assumptions and enhancing the trust models with more degrees of freedom in order to construct more realistic, richer, complete, and less constrained models and management frameworks.

An important aspect of how trust is perceived is the context of the situation. The main question to consider is whether or not the context of the situation should influence the level of trust a node in the system is willing to accept before any transaction. There are cases of examples in real life that one may trust completely another for a certain situation, but could completely distrust for another situation. Further research is needed in order to successfully include the situational trust evaluation into trust functions and trust management mechanisms. Another point that needs to be considered is to what degree the situational trust should influence one's decision on whether or not to trust another.

Towards the direction of more realistic and complete trust models, a factor called reciprocity should be considered. Reciprocity is defined as the mutual or cooperative interchange of favors or privileges or even revenge between the participant entities in a transaction. For instance, if one entity in the system offers its services to another entity in the system then the second entity would be expected to reciprocate at some point in the future. There is also the negative side of reciprocity. If one entity in the system denies its services to another entity in the system then the second entity could resort to a denial of service at some point in the future. The most challenging aspect of reciprocity is that it is difficult to model. This mutual interchange of favors is completely a human characteristic, therefore it is less predictable.

Apart from the above general issues that need to be considered for more realistic trust functions and models, there are also a number of more practical issues for future consideration. Though many trust models and frameworks have proposed ways of identifying malicious behaviors and solutions to deal with these behaviors, there is still space

for improvement. A future research direction is the discovering of ways to make P2P and Grid systems more robust against malicious behaviors, such as collusions among nodes.

Another issue that needs to be addressed is how to uniquely identify peers or Grid nodes over time and associate their past transaction histories with them. We have discussed cases where malicious peers leave and re-enter the system with new identities. Their new identities offer them a clean start that subsequently will affect the system. These cases of leaving and re-entering the system, thus erasing past histories, is an interesting research direction that needs to be addressed as it is a common phenomenon for P2P and Grid systems.

We have already discussed in previous section that a proper solution to the malicious users, that leave and then re-enter the system, is to assign them with a very low trust value. The problem is that by assigning low trust values in the new joined users, we assign low trust values to innocent new users also. By doing this, innocent new users cannot easily build their reputation in the system. Research work needs to be done in order to discover a way for treating malicious new joined users without affecting the innocent ones.

Finally, there have been proposed ways to create incentive to peers or Grid nodes for constantly trying to improve their reputation. Further research needs to be done for improving these incentive mechanisms in order to efficiently reward good users and properly punish the bad ones. Moreover, efficient incentive mechanisms need to be proposed in order to cover the cases of free-riding users. Free-riding users are an interesting research direction, since these types of users do not behave maliciously. The problem lies to the fact that free-riding users do not contribute to the system. New incentive mechanisms need to be proposed in order to deal efficiently with these cases also.

CONCLUSION

In this book chapter, we discussed issues concerning trust calculation and management in P2P and Grid systems. Firstly, we presented the significance of trust mechanisms in P2P and Grid systems and showed the necessity of these mechanisms in such systems. Then, we presented the theoretical background giving definitions of important trust concepts and providing the basic principles behind trust graphs. Also, we have provided popular classification schemes and analyzed them in order to present the different types and categories of existing trust functions. Furthermore, we presented well-known trust mechanisms and their analysis of how exactly they manage trust issues in P2P and Grid environments. Finally, future research directions about issues yet to be addressed were displayed.

REFERENCES

Aberer, K. (2001). P-Grid: A self organizing access structure for p2p information systems. In *Proceedings of the Cooperative Information Systems, 9th International Conference (CoopIS)*, (LNCS Vol. 2172, pp. 179-194). Berlin: Springer.

Azzedin, F., & Maheswaran, M. (2002a). Evolving and managing trust in Grid computing systems. *Electrical and Computer Engineering, IEEE CCECE, 3*, 1424–1429.

Azzedin, F., & Maheswaran, M. (2002b). Towards trust-aware resource management in Grid computing systems. In *CCGRID 2002, IEEE Computer Society*, (pp. 452-457).

Bhattacharjee, R., & Goel, A. (2005). Avoiding ballot-stuffing in eBay-like reputation systems. In *Proceedings of the 2005 ACM SIGCOMM Workshop on Economics of Peer-to-Peer Systems*, (pp.133-137), Philadelphia, Pensylvania, USA.

Bote-Lorenzo, M., Dimitriadis, Y., & Gomez-Sanchez, E. (2004). Grid characteristics and uses: A Grid definition. In *Postproc. of the First European Across Grids Conference (ACG'03)*, (Springer-Verlag LNCS Vol. 2970, pp. 291-298), Santiago de Compostela, Spain. Berlin: Springer-Verlag.

Chakrabarti, A. (2007). *Grid computing security.* Berlin: Springer.

Chang, F., Itzkovitz, A., & Karamcheti, V. (2000). *User-level resource constrained sandboxing.* Paper presented at the 4th USENIX Windows Systems Symposium, Seattle, Washington.

Douceur, J. (2002). The Sybil attack. In *Proceedings for the 1st International Workshop on Peer-to-Peer Systems, IPTPS 2002*, (Lecture Notes In Computer ScienceLNCS, Vol. 2429, pp. 251-260). Berlin: Springer-Verlag.

Gutscher, A., Heessen, J., & Siemoneit, O. (2008). Possibilities and limitations of modelling trust and reputation. In *Proceedings of the Fifth International Workshop on Philosophy and Informatics (WSPI-2008), Vol. 332, CEUR Workshop Proceedings.*

Josang, A., & Presti, S. L. (2004). Analysing the relationship between risk and trust. In *Trust Management: Second International Conference, iTrust 2004, Proceedings*, (Volume LNCS Vol. 2995/2004, pp. 135–145). Oxford, UK: Springer.

Kamvar, S., Schlosser, M., & Molina, H. G. (2003). The eigentrust algorithm for reputation management in p2p networks. In *Proceedings of World Wide Web Conference 2003*, Budapest, Hungary. New York: ACM, Budapest, Hungary.

Lee, S., Sherwood, R., & Bhattacharjee, B. (2003). Cooperative peer groups in NICE. *INFOCOM 2003, Twenty-second Annual Joint Conference of the IEEE Computer and Communications Societies*, (Vol. 2, IEEE, pp. 1272-1282). Washington, DC: IEEE.

Mayer, C., & Davis, H. (1995). An integrative model of organizational trust. *Academy of Management Review, 20*, 709–734. doi:10.2307/258792

McKnight, D., & Chervany, N. L. (1996). *The meanings of trust.* MISRC Working Paper Series, Technical Report 94-04. Arlson School of Management, University of Minnesota, MN.

Ruohomaa, S., & Kutvonen, L. (2005). Trust management survey. In *iTrust 2005,* (LNCS, pp.77-92)., Berlin: Springer.

Schneier, B. (1996). *Applied cryptography: protocols, algorithms, and source code in C.* New York: John Wiley.

Suryanarayana, G., & Taylor, R. (2004). *A survey of trust management and resource discovery technologies in peer-to-peer applications.* ISR Technical Report UCI-ISR-04-06.

Xiong, L., & Liu, L. (2002). Building trust in decentralized peer-to-peer electronic communities. In *Fifth International Conference on Electronic Commerce Research (ICECR),* Montreal, Canada.

Xiong, L., & Liu, L. (2003). A reputation-based trust model for peer-to-peer ecommerce communities. In *Proceedings of the Fourth ACM Conference on Electronic Commerce,* San Diego.

Zhang, Q., Yu, T., & Irwin, K. (2004). A classification scheme for trust functions in reputation-based trust management. In *ISWC Workshop on Trust, Security, and Reputation on the Semantic Web, Vol. 127, CEUR Workshop Proceedings.*

ADDITIONAL READING

Abdul-Rahman, A., & Hailes, S. (1997). A distributed trust model. *Proceedings of New Security Paradigms Workshop,* (pp. 48-60).

Abdul-Rahman, A., & Hailes, S. (2000). Supporting trust in virtual communities. *In Proceeings of the 33rd Annual Hawaii International Conference on System Sciences (HICSS-33).*

Aberer, K., & Despotovic, Z. (2001). Managing trust in a peer-topeer information system. In *Proceedings of the 10th International Conference on Information and Knowledge Management (CIKM),* pp. 310-317.

Adar, E., & Huberman, B. (2000). Free-riding on Gnutella. *Technical Report,* Xerox PARC.

Atif, Y. (2002). Building trust in e-commerce. *IEEE Internet Computing,* 6(1). doi:10.1109/4236.978365

Blaze, M., Feigenbaum, J., & Lacy, J. (1996). Decentralized trust management. *Proceedings of the 1996 IEEE Symposium on Security and Privacy,* (pp.164-173).

Cornelli, F., Damiani, E., Vimercati, S., Paraboschi, S., & Samarati, S. (2002). Choosing reputable servents in a p2p network. In *Proceedings of the 11th World Wide Web Conference,* Hawaii, USA.

Dimitrakos, T., & Bicarregui, J. (2001). Towards a framework for managing trust in e-services. In *Proceedings of the Fourth International Conference on Electronic Commerce Research (ICECR-4).*

Egger, F. (2000). Towards a model of trust for e-commerce system design. *In CHI2000 Workshop Designing Interactive Systems for 1-to-1 E-Commerce,* 2000.

Foster, I., & Kesselman, C. (1999). *The Grid: Blueprint for a new computing infrastructure.* San Francisco: Morgan Kaufmann.

Golbeck, J., & Hendler, J. (2004). Accuracy of metrics for inferring trust and reputation in Semantic Web-based social networks. In *Proceedings of the International Conference on Knowledge Engineering and Knowledge Management,* Northamptonshire, UK.

Grandison, T., & Sloman, M. (2000). A survey of trust in Internet applications. *IEEE Communications Surveys & Tutorial,* 3(4).

Kautz, H., Selman, B., & Shah, M. (1997). Referral Web: Combining social networks and collaborative filtering. *Communications of the ACM, 20*, 63–66. doi:10.1145/245108.245123

Ketchpel, S., & Garcia-Molina, H. (1996). Making trust explicit in distributed commerce transactions. *In Proceedings of the 16th International Conference on Distributed Computing Systems.*

Khare, R., & Rifkin, A. (1997). Weaving a Web of trust. *World Wide Web (Bussum), 2*(3), 77–112.

Malaga, R. (2001). Web-based reputation management systems: Problems and suggested solutions. *Electronic Commerce Research, 1*(4). doi:10.1023/A:1011557319152

Misztal, B. (1996). *Trust in modern societies.* Cambridge MA: Polity Press.

Mui, L., Mohtashemi, M., & Halberstadt, A. (2002). A computational model of trust and reputation. In *Proceedings of the 35th Hawaii International Conference on System Science.*

Rea, T., & Skevington, P. (1998). Engendering trust in electronic commerce. *British Telecommunications Engineering, 17*(3), 150–157.

Shankar, N., Komareddy, C., & Bhatacharjee, B. (2001, November). Finding close friends over the Internet. *Proceedings of International Conference on Network Protocols.*

Shepherd, M., Dhonde, A., & Watters, C. (2001). Building trust for e-commerce: Collaborating label bureaus. *In Proceedings of the Second International Symposium on Electronic Commerce,* ISEC 2001.

Swarup, V., & Fabrega, J. (1999). Trust: Benefits, models, and mechanisms. In J. Vitek & C. D. Jensen (Eds.), *Secure Internet programming: Security issues for mobile and distributed objects.* (Lecture Notes in Computer Science, 1603, pp. 3). New York: Springer-Verlag.

Yu, B., & Singh, M. (2000). A social mechanism of reputation management in electronic communities. In *Proceedings of the 4th International Workshop on Cooperative Information Agents,* (pp. 154-165).

Zacharia, G., & Maes, P. (2000). Trust management through reputation mechanisms. *Applied Artificial Intelligence, 14*, 881–908. doi:10.1080/08839510050144868

Zacharia, G., Moukas, A., & Maes, P. (1999). Collaborative reputation mechanisms in electronic marketplaces. In *Proceedings of the 32nd Annual Hawaii International Conference on system Sciences (HICSS-32).*

KEY TERMS AND DEFINITIONS

Grid Systems: A large-scale, geographically distributed, hardware and software infrastructure composed of heterogeneous networked resources owned and shared by multiple administrative organizations which are coordinated to provide transparent, dependable, pervasive and consistent computing support to a wide range of applications.

Peer-to-Peer Systems: Consist of a group of entities called peers that interact with each other without the presence of a central coordinating authority (decentralized P2P systems). A peer in such a system can act both as a client and a server. It can request services from other entities as well as provide services to other entities in the system.

Reputation: An expectation of an entity's behavior based on other entities' observations or information about the entity's past behavior at a given time.

Trust: The firm belief in the competence of an entity to act as expected such that this firm belief is not a fixed value associated with the entity but rather it is subject to the entity's behavior and applies only within a specific context at a given time.

Trust Classification: Different categories of trust depending on the approach used to calculate trust values.

Trust Evaluation: A binary action, meaning that an entity evaluates the trustworthiness of another entity and decides whether to trust or not.

Trust Functions: Trust metrics used to calculate trust.

Trust Management: The trust management phase differs from mechanism to mechanism.

There are some trust mechanisms that re-calculate trust values based on past successful transactions between entities, while others re-calculate trust values based on the complaints an entity has gathered from past transactions. There are even trust mechanisms that re-calculate trust values based on the progression of time.

Chapter 34
Taking Trust Management to the Next Level

Rehab Alnemr
Potsdam University, Germany

Matthias Quasthoff
Potsdam University, Germany

Christoph Meinel
Potsdam University, Germany

ABSTRACT

Business often develop proprietary reputation systems for their community, with the side effect of locking users into that service if they wish to maintain their reputation (Bonawitz, Chandrasekhar, & Viana, 2004). Reputation is used in multi-agent models like e-commerce, and distributed computation and reasoning. Currently, virtual communities are using their own reputation values only without exchanging knowledge. Reputation transfer or portability is a controversial subject that is considered either not applicable or of high potentials. Trust is used to carry out decisions in case of uncertainty. In that sense it is used in peer-to-peer (P2P) networks to facilitate its interactions. In P2P networks, peers' willingness to share the content they have and forward the queries plays an important role during the content search process. Using reputation in P2P systems can be an incentive for peers to cooperate. The goal is to have dynamic social networks that work on acquiring, processing, establishing, analyzing, exchanging and evolving of knowledge. In this chapter, the authors are focusing on the use of one of the trust management approaches, namely the reputation-based approach. The connections of trust management to the classic IT security disciplines authorization, trust, and identity management will be laid out. With this background, a generic architecture for context-aware reputation systems, which can interact with identity-related services like identity providers and policy decision or enforcement points, is presented. More specialized architectures for different environments—business- or consumer-oriented—will be derived from the generic architecture.

DOI: 10.4018/978-1-61520-686-5.ch034

INTRODUCTION

Since the rise of the so-called Web 2.0, many social Web sites focusing on people and their relationships have attracted large number of users, and became a marketplace for various business interactions. In these Web communities, reputation related to different contexts needs to be exchanged. The perception, calculation and interpretation of this reputation differ from one community to the other creating the belief that reputation transfer is a matter of fiction. By taking a closer look at the actual difficulties of reputation transfer, we can identify the crucial points of a working reputation transfer system and finally present a means of implementing such framework.

The simplicity of current reputation systems resembles the simplicity of early identity management solutions, which basically consisted of simple databases containing usernames and passwords. Existing work on reputation systems focuses on improving the calculation of reputation values, preventing malicious actions, and deployment into the business world. The achievements in other domains, among them decentralization, standardization, and opening datasets for future enhancements, have not been considered for reputation systems. Reputation models should be capable of including and processing information that cannot be foreseen when developing or implementing the model. This will also make it possible to combine reputation information from independent sources into a more comprehensive view on the reputation of users, services, or agents. Here, a framework is proposed that facilitates the transfer of an agent's reputation from one community to the other by introducing:

- A new representation for the reputation value or profile; Reputation object
- The development of reference models to diminish the distance between multi-perceptions of different communities and platforms.

- The use of reputation centers to facilitate reputation transfer and highlight the importance of their role in analyzing attacks.
- Defining the knowledge domain and the candidate systems that could work with the proposed model.

We are analyzing some of the existing reputation-based communities, categorizing them, and identifying reputation tools that are used. Following that, we are providing guidelines to define the most suitable ontologies to be used in order to build the knowledge base used by the model. The goal is to formalize the proposed model to facilitate integration into real life applications and problems, and to finally develop the standardized reputation reference models.

The chapter is organized as follows; first, the meaning of trust, the use of the reputation-based approach in Web communities, and the role of identity management are being discussed. Afterwards, new concepts and models that add up to form the future vision for reputation based systems and the use of new identity management approaches to ensure the development of these systems are introduced.

TRUST MANAGEMENT

Trust Definition

To trust someone is to have belief on his integrity, to express certain level of dependency and reliability on performance, to expect fulfillment of promises, and to have confidence that this reliability will not be misplaced though of the risks. Trust functions as a way to reduce the complexity of our social life (Luhmann, 1983). In social science, trust can be observed from different point of views: trust meaning, components, types, and sources. The meaning of trust, roughly, can be expressed as:

Trust= dependency + reliability + expectancy + faith + belief + confidence + risk

It can be also categorized as (Uslaner, 2002):

Trust= strategic + particularistic + moralistic

Strategic trust is the trust we gain from daily experience. Particularistic trust is the trust in people like ourselves. It may stem from direct experience or from stereotypes. Moralistic trust or generalized trust is the trust in strangers, especially people who are different from ourselves. It cannot come from interaction with people we know, it cannot come from experience. It is either trusting an organization or a system, or trusting a person:

Trust= organizational trust + Interpersonal trust

From an information source perspective (Kashyap & V, 2004):

Trust source= a priori+ justified belief + facts

where justified belief means reputation that comes from recommendations or direct interaction experience. Sure trust does not compensate lack of knowledge but it gives us some level of certainty to decide on an action.

There are multiple attempts to describe *mistrust*, *distrust* and *un-trust*, yet no definition is standardized for each term. Some believe that mistrust is equal to distrust, and un-trust means *indifference* or *ignorance*. Others define mistrust as a misplaced trust that comes from a direct interaction, distrust as a belief that the other person doesn't have his best interest in his heart, and un-trust as the state of trusting someone but not enough to have a certain interaction.

Defining Digital Identity

A critical point with regards to trust is to recognize interacting participants. In real life this is accomplished, to some degree, by direct or physical interaction. In networked computer systems, it is done through digital identities. Trust values will be assigned to participants and will be used to assess the participant's performance of previous interaction and to estimate the quality of future interactions. It is necessary to guarantee fair judgment, as forged trust values can lead to unfair inclusion or exclusion of participants from future interactions, resulting in potential loss or damage of data, processes, or systems. While the specific connection of trust and identity management will be presented later in this chapter, this section defines some standard identity management concepts for later reference throughout this chapter. To ensure these definitions are in line with recent development in distributed, service-oriented computing, we relate the definitions to the OASIS Reference Model for Service Oriented Architecture (SOA) (MacKenzie, Laskey, McCabe, Brown, & Metz, 2006).

Participants. Trust relationships are relevant between *participants* in an *interaction*, and three different types of participants are relevant to trust management: *Services* are computer programs being accessed by other participants and possibly accessing other services (Cranor, et al., 2006). In that sense services can range from local applications over application plug-ins or applets to whole Web sites. The OASIS SOA Reference Model defines a service more abstract as a "mechanism that brings needs and capabilities together" (MacKenzie, Laskey, McCabe, Brown, & Metz, 2006), but leaves needs and capabilities undefined. The individuals accessing services are called *users*. Both services and users can belong to *organizations*. Digital *identity management* facilitates identifying participants and asserting statements about them. Assessing trust requires knowledge of the relationships and roles of participants and the infrastructure surrounding them.

Interactions. Speaking in terms of the SOA Reference Model, *interaction* happens between participants and services; it is the activity of *using a capability* (MacKenzie, Laskey, McCabe, Brown, & Metz, 2006). Depending on the general system architecture chosen, interaction happens via specialized service interfaces designed for specific interactions or data formats (cf. *information*), or rather via generic, or *uniform interfaces* (Fielding, 2000). Uniform interfaces allow for more flexible and ad-hoc service compositions, and compositions not having been considered at design time. Service interfaces are backed by an *information model* (i.e. syntax and semantics) and a *behavior model* describing actions and processes (MacKenzie, Laskey, McCabe, Brown, & Metz, 2006).

Roles. Both users and services can access, or consume other services, hence act as *service consumers*. On the contrary, users and organizations offering and running, or more general, being responsible for a service are called *service providers* (Cranor, et al., 2006), (MacKenzie, Laskey, McCabe, Brown, & Metz, 2006). As services are related to business functions, the case of one service providing another service is disregarded here as well as the case of an organization accessing a service directly, i.e. without delegating access to a user member of the organization. Besides these roles with regards to specific services, several other relationships can exist between users and organizations: users might *know* each other, be *member* of an organization, and users or organizations might be *contractual partners*.

Infrastructure. Fielding defines three basic concepts describing an infrastructure on an architectural level (Fielding, 2000). Identifying architectural concepts and the participants linked to them in an information system is inevitable when assessing trust relationships on a general level. *Components* generate, process, and store information. Hence, services and computer systems running these services are components. Depending on the level of abstraction, users can be considered accessing services directly, or with the help of mediating computer programs, so called user agents (Cranor, et al., 2006), which are also components. Components communicate over *connectors*, whereas a single component can have multiple connectors, i.e. be accessible over various network interfaces and protocols. *Data* is the information transported over connectors from one component to another. We can differentiate between information inside components and data being serialized information outside components (Fielding, 2000).

Information. The differentiation of data and information is reflected in the separation of abstract Web *resources* and their concrete *representations* (Fielding, 2000). A resource is a piece of information can be abstract in terms of data processing, such as a photograph of the Brandenburg Gate in Berlin. However, the data being transported between components over connectors are representations of the resource, e.g. a fixed-dimensions graphics file in a specific file format. For a single resource there can exist several representations; for a photo there might be a thumbnail graphics, a medium and a high resolution graphic file as well as an HTML page describing the photo and linking to downloadable versions. The distinction of information and data (or resources and representations) conveys among others serious consequences for strong security mechanisms like digital signatures and traditional access control, as those can only be applied to the representations (e.g. the graphics files), not to the resource itself (e.g. the photograph itself). (Quasthoff, Sack, & Meinel, 2007)

Trust Management: Definition and Approaches

In a Service Oriented Architecture (SOA) the need to provide different levels of security between services that handle private information is becoming more critical. These services will need to provide privacy guarantees to prevent delicate information from ending up in the wrong hands. This is not an easy task in a world that has always new participants, laws and policies, requirements, and conditions. In open systems, authentication-based security and privacy schemes are inadequate, due to the fact that principals might be able to provide authentication but are otherwise unknown to the system and thus not authorizable for specific actions. In this case services will adopt the real-world behavior; which is *relying on Trust-relationships*.

Trust-based systems use *Trust* social definition, *a prediction of reliance based on what a party knows about the other party*, to create a framework in which two unrelated parties may establish the trust sufficient to perform sensitive transactions. So in order to establish this trust, organizations or systems, and by consequence services, state policies describing who can do what under what circumstances. This kind of reasoning is needed not only in Web Services but critically in Semantic Web services that exploit the Semantic Web to automate their discovery and interaction. This is because they must autonomously decide what information to exchange and how. The processes that include making assessments and decisions regarding trust relationships are called *trust management*.

As a means to formalize trust negotiation in the web, there are two approaches for managing trust: *policy-based* and *reputation-based*. The two approaches have been developed within the context of different environments and targeting different requirements. On one hand, policy-based trust relies on "strong security" mechanisms such as signed certificates and trusted certification authorities in order to regulate the access of users to services. The result is a binary decision- trusted or not. On the other hand, reputation-based trust relies on a "soft computational" approach. In this case, trust is typically computed from local experiences together with the feedback given by other entities in the network (e.g., users who have used services of that provider)

The two trust management approaches address the same problem - establishing trust among interacting parties in distributed and decentralized systems. However, they assume different settings. While the policy based approach has been developed within the context of structured organizational environments the reputation systems have been proposed to address the unstructured user community. Consequently, they assume different sources for trust (Certificate Authorities and community opinion, respectively) and accordingly employ different mechanisms (Bonatti, Duma, Olmedilla, & Shahmehri, 2005).

In this chapter we are focusing on the reputation-based approach since it is more suitable for e-services because the notions modeled seem more intuitive to the domain.

Several systems nowadays form what we call *Web communities*, which include social networks and unstructured organizations. These communities are formed partially or completely by users on the web like: *eBay, Facebook, isohunt, blogs*, etc. In *User Web* trust is typically computed from local experiences together with the feedback given by other entities in the network (e.g., users who have used services of that provider). The feedback is an expressed opinion of an entity about another entity that forms *recommendation*. *Reputation* is an expectation about an agent behavior based on information about or observations of its past behavior (Rahman & Hailes, 2000). A reputation or rating system attempts to provide concise summaries of a user's history for a given community. In the case of e-markets like *eBay* or *Amazon*, one's reputation is represented by a rating "score" which is calculated based on cumulative rating by its members. Trust management tools are still maturing because they don't contain all phases of trust management (evidence collection, trust specification, establishment, analysis, monitoring, and evolution).

Managing Digital Identity

With the concepts introduced in the previous section, identity management can be described as the combination of the fundamental tasks presented in this section, making up the so-called identity management life cycle. Representations of digital identities can be user profile pages on the WWW, structured data to be used in interaction, such as SAML tokens (OASIS, 2008), or even just one line of text in a password file.

Establishing and describing identities. Digital identities are used to recognize participants that have been dealt with before. It is up to the designer of an information system which of a participant's properties to choose to accomplish this task. These properties can comprise the name, contact data, or passport number, but also less identifying information such as date and time of first interaction, or some other context information like IP addresses used, or just even hash values of these data. Only after a digital identity has been *established*, i.e. has been linked to the participant, we can refer to the identity and further *describe* the participant, i.e. add user profile information and link other attributes to the digital identity. It is important to see that finally destroying a digital identity can be hard. Destroying an identity is virtually impossible if descriptions of the identity in question are controlled by third parties, something which is quite realistic in an open information system like the WWW or an open service infrastructure.

Authentication. Digital identities serve several purposes. On the one hand, they are used to refer to the participant linked to an identity when issuing statements like trust assessments. On the other hand, participants choose a digital identity linked to them or establish a new one when they are about to interact with other participants in an identifiable manner (Cranor, et al., 2006). Using a digital identity in an interaction requires *authentication*, i.e. the confirmation that a digital identity is indeed linked to the participant in the interaction. Depending on the requirements to data protection and other considerations, authentication mechanisms can be designed for varying complexity and security, e.g. by requiring or doing without multi-factor authentication (OASIS, 2008). The specifics of authentication go beyond the scope of this book chapter.

Authorization. Many possible interactions in information systems are actually not desired. Accessing resources or information and triggering specific actions, be it placing orders or placing a call on somebody else's phone, should often be restricted to a subset of potential participants or to specific circumstances. Even in "open" systems where authorization is not required or desired, when excluding spammers and other potential attackers, actually authorization mechanisms are put in place. Authorization decisions can be based on virtually any kind of information, ranging from the digital identity of a participant over other attributes describing the identity, e.g. role or task assignments, to highly dynamic evaluation of context information right before an interaction. Especially in open systems basing authorization on enumeration of authorized digital identities is not feasible and also the definition of pre-defined roles or tasks will be hard (Seigneur & Jensen, 2007). Hence, modern decentralized and open information systems employ more generic attribute-based or context-aware authorization mechanisms, which will also be fed by trust and reputation systems.

Implementing Digital Identity Management

Any identity management architecture can be broken down to an agglomeration of participants and components. While in final implementations some of the components presented in this section could be combined into a single service, especially in open systems this combination can lead to severe interoperability issues, as will be presented later in this chapter. On the contrary, by boiling down each type of service to its core functionality, better flexibility and conceptual soundness can be achieved.

Identity Provider (IdP). Digital identities are managed by special services, so-called *identity providers*. Identity providers are responsible for linking a digital identity to participant with the help of an identifier and authentication mechanisms. In systems where relying parties (i.e. services interacting with identity providers) accept digital identities issued by different identity providers, a participant must either specify its identity provider along with the identifier, or the identity provider must be discoverable from the identifier, e.g. as OpenID does with the help of URI (Recordon & Reed, 2006). As has been mentioned in the previous section, different scenarios can require different security levels. Hence, an identity provider truly designed for serving multiple use cases needs to support flexible combinations of authentication factors. The SAML protocol allows relying parties to request certain authentication mechanisms and identity providers to return the information which authentication mechanisms have actually been used (OASIS, 2008).

Security Token Service (STS). These are specified in the WS-Security specification (OASIS, 2004) and help decoupling participants, services, and the identity provider. Tokens themselves can contain various claims about the identity described, authentication and authorization. They can also contain further information restricting possible uses of the token, e.g. by restricting the validity period or relying parties. Separating STS from the identity provider, results in better cross-domain interoperability and protocol independence.

Policy Decision Point (PDP), Policy Enforcement Point (PEP). As a single identity provider can be used with several services, letting the identity provider decide on authorization for all these potentially unknown services is not feasible. Similarly, due to the potential desire for reuse of authorization and trust policies, the reasoning on authorization and trust decisions takes place at the *policy decision point*, which can be independent of the service or resource being accessed. The service itself only features a *policy enforcement point*, which delegates the authorization decision to the PDP.

Identity Management Architectures

Identity Management Silo. Classic closed-world applications and services—desktop- or Web-based—usually feature a built-in user and password database. Identities are established through invitation, e.g. by administrators or existing users, or self-registration, e.g. in large Web communities. Depending of the potential user base of such a system, legal contracts between the service provider and service users, and the mode of registration (invitation or self-registration) a more or less traceable link will exist between the digital identity and the participant. Disadvantages of such setting are obviously the need of carrying the burden of identity management instead of being able to just use an existing identity management system, and lacking interoperability with other identity-enabled computer systems. However this system architecture is being chosen quite often due to relatively low initial system and policy framework complexity. However, as systems designed around a specific user database usually have severe conceptual limitations with regards to identity management, this approach should is unsuitable for modern open systems except the consequences are well-thought and do not interfere with future development of the system.

Identity Management in the Social Web. The Social Web, also known as Web 2.0, features a specific kind of Web sites allowing users to publish data about themselves, photographs or other text and multimedia content in dedicated Web sites. Especially Social Networking sites like Myspace, Facebook, or LinkedIn can be seen as Identity Providers, because they are centered around their users identity. However, the reuse of the identity described outside the Social Networking site is often limited. Some few Web sites allow further processing of digital identities by publishing some parts of the identities with the help of open, standardized protocols or just by some proprietary interfaces (Winer, 2003). Appropriate open, standardized protocols could involve Semantic Web technologies such as RDF and the Friend of a Friend (FOAF) vocabulary (Brickley & Miller, 2007).. On the other hand, there are emerging Web-scale identity management standards like OpenID (Recordon & Reed, 2006) and CardSpace (Microsoft Developer Network, 2005), which do allow for separation of identity providers and relying parties, and for extensive reuse of digital identities and claims about an identity. Social Web sites offer quite efficient, yet proprietary policy engines based on describing other users from the participant's perspective ("friend" or "family member"). However, all the Social Web sites are still missing to take the next logical step of clearly structuring their services into identity provider functionality ("Who am I?"), policy decision point ("Who can see what parts of my data?"), and the specific business segment—describing events, places and creative work ("Where do I love to go? What did I see there?") etc. This clear structuring along with offering substitution of parts of these services with services from other providers with the help of standardized protocols and data formats would lead to new opportunities to Web users (Quasthoff, 2008).

Identity Management in service-oriented architectures. Identity management in SOA approaches the identity and data portability issues from a different perspective compared to identity management on the Social Web. More precisely, many of the concepts introduced in the previous sections have been fixed in SOA-centric documents and specifications (OASIS, 2004). Where identity management and system architecture on the Social Web can be described as being developed in a bottom-up approach, WS-Security standards have been developed in a rather formal top-down approach. Also, the requirements to business-scale identity management are somewhat

different. The contractual requirements of a company to their employees' identity provider will be more detailed compared to what a Web user expects from some Social Web site. Also, the potentially unlimited number of identity providers a specific service has to cope with will be rather manageable in a enterprise SOA, as likely all employees of a single company, e.g. contractors or customers, will share a common identity management system. Besides the formal approach, which can be a solid basis for concrete implementations, there are three obstacles preventing WS-* standards from becoming the straightforward solution to digital identity management in general: The high level of abstraction and universality of the proposed architecture; the focus on SOAP Web services in implementations along with strong security mechanisms, and the constraint of being able to "federate" legacy enterprise identity management systems, disregarding completely decentralized solutions that will be possible with the help of trust and reputation systems.

Later in this chapter, we outline how the concepts introduced in this section help to combine trust and reputation management with Web-scale identity management to create both a new quality of reputation and digital identity in open, decentralized information systems. In the following sections we introduce our proposed framework, analyze some of the existing tools and define the concepts and terms used in the domain knowledge. Finally, we will present how reputation management and identity management need to be combined in order to finally achieve the proposed model in real-world applications.

CONTEXT-AWARE REPUTATION-BASED FRAMEWORK

Since it is unfeasible for service-oriented entities to keep information on large scale, some flexible degrees of uncertainties, and hence trust, must be established. Until now there is no legitimate authority per jurisdiction to compute trust values. The future vision of these systems is to be able to transfer reputation values from one service or community to the other (from *eBay* to *Amazon*, from *Facebook* to *Flickr*, etc.). These communities should have some common jurisdictions, so the transferred reputation value is meaningful. As human way of thinking, the perception of the degrees of trust differs from one service to another. Transferring reputation values eliminates the need for having to manage different "accounts" in different communities, which can be essential in the e-business world. It can be beneficial also in other situations: when an agent in one platform requests an interaction with another agent in different platform, or when an agent registers in a new platform and does not want to start with zero reputation value.

Mapping identities and transporting identity and reputation information between services requires new, standardized formats and protocols. The information can be expressed with the help of Semantic Web technologies such as RDF, and can then be transported using HTTP. However, the architecture model underlying HTTP (Fielding, 2000) leaves it open how to request and transmit these data, given that this involves authorization and access rights delegation. Existing solutions to access rights delegation such as OAuth (OAuth Workgroup, 2007) are not suitable for large-scale non-interactive service interaction. (Quasthoff, 2008) (Alnemr & Meinel, 2008)

Reputation Objects Instead of Reputation Values

Most of the existing reputation-based systems lack the connection between general reputation and the context of the given reputation. For example: A user, who has ordered a TV set over an online market, received the order later than he expected. When rating the TV factory, most users in this situation give bad rating because of the "late delivery". But that doesn't mean that the

"quality" of the TV is bad for example. *Delivery* and *quality* are two different contexts that should be rated separately.

Usually reputation is viewed as a single value associated with an *entity* or *participant*. Since reputation is a representation of an expected behavior from a service, a person, or an agent, it should be rather viewed as an object that contains the context related to each reputation value and reflects the dynamic nature of trust and its change through time. It is agreed that trust is context-specific even if it holds the same information. For example, a professor in a medical school may simplify treatment information regarding certain disease to his students but will need to use other form of the same information in actual treatment. Therefore the need to link between the *value* and *its meaning* is crucial. Reputation object contains a multidimensional array, a matrix, which represents the reputation linked with its context and the Reputation Reference Trust Model (RRTM) used to calculate this value (discussed in the next section).

```
Object Reputation {
TrustMatrix [context][reputation
value][RRTM];
Time ValidTime;
Credentials PresentedCreden-
tials; //optional
}
```

Associating context with trust sure increase the complexity of the overall system, but it is critical for deriving meaningful trust. (Alnemr & Meinel, 2008)

Developing Reputation Reference Trust Models

There is a big difference between *belief in trustworthiness* and *actions due to trustworthiness*. The distinction is important because if a trustier has past interactions with the trustee that does not mean that all future interactions are guaranteed. Though the trustee is trusted but the action due to this trustworthiness differs every time.

The calculation of reputation values and the perception of the meaning of each value differ from one system to another. If the reputation comes from someone's recommendations, it is important also to take into account the perspective of this recommender. A "very trustworthy person" to him could be a "medium trustworthy person" to you (Rahman & Hailes, 2000). So it is not enough to take "I trust this person" as a recommendation. Even if the recommendation states the context of this trust: "I trust doctor x to treat me". You still need to know several variables like: To what degree the recommender trusts this person? Why and based on what?

Using single values to represent degrees of trust and accordingly user's reputation solved the problem of trust perception. This single value is used to delete the "semantic distance" in trust perception, i.e.: 7 is used instead of saying "this person is very trustworthy", and then the interpretation is left to the one who receives the recommendation. What has not been taking into account is the "semantic reasoning" or the "soft reasoning" behind the 7. One action can be done towards two persons, one will give a rate of 7 to this action and the other will give a score of 5.

We have proposed the use of Reputation Reference Trust Models (RRTM) that explains how particular trust values have been obtained and how they can be interpreted. Publishing the RRTM along with reputation values narrows the difference in perceptions. Reference trust models can be used in this case, to refer to a set of measures that each person based his opinion on. If trust judgment measures of one person are stricter than the others, this person may refuse to take recommendation from others who use softer measures. In this way a participant may make a local evaluation of global information and according to the RRTM which he is using.

The developing of such models involves answering a set of questions such as:

- What is the method used to infer reputation?
- What are the levels of trust? And the distinction between levels? (Golbeck, Parisa, & Hendler, 2003) (Fullam & Barber, 2006)
- What are the semantic and quantitative meanings of each level?
- What is the penalty for first time misplaced trust? What is the threshold that defines the point of total distrust?
- Will distrust be included in the reputation calculations? Is there a distinction between the absence of trust and malicious attack (Victor, Cornelis, & Cock, 2006)?
- Do factors like variance and level of confidence included in the reputation calculations?
- Is there a semantic separation between "belief in trustworthiness" and "actions due to trustworthiness"? Does this fall into *context separation* process?

Forming the models should be followed by forming mapping functions to facilitate reputation transfer from one model to the other. If it is not sufficient to have one trust model that can be used by different platforms, then the solution is to have standard models and mapping functions between them. This decreases the semantic distance of trust definitions, where each entity, platform, service, or agent has different interpretations and measures for trust judgment. (Alnemr & Meinel, 2008)

Developing and Supporting the Use of Trust Reputation Centers

People usually have a tendency to trust recognized organizations. Accordingly, trust sometimes needs to be addressed to an organization. This is because personal experience is not always sufficiently available. We have proposed the development of Trust Reputation Center (TRC) that acts as a trusted third party. But instead of having a set of credentials to supply users with certificates (like a Certificate Authority), the TRC will be a pool of user reputation gathered from different platforms. Each user, agent, or service can have two values that define his reputation: an overall reputation (trusted or non-trusted for malicious users), and a context-based reputation object (RO). When two users from two different platforms (or organizations) establish an interaction, the TRC can be used as a transparent trusted third party. Transparency here means that it will not be enough to get a binary decision (trust or distrust) from the center, but also the RO that details reputation values regarding each context, or a specific context, and the RRTMs used. Interacting users send the center a request to get others reputation objects or values. The request should contain the RRTM used by the platform. The center transfers the stored value to the correspondent value of the requester RRTM using mapping functions.

Another advantage to this approach is that new users, or participants, in any platform or community won't have to start with *zero* reputation but rather with their *transferred reputation*. The center also can act as a negotiator or investigator of agents' reputations in a network. Moreover, using a centered trust party is the possibility of observing ballot stuffing attacks. Ballot stuffing attack is when a group of user may perform unfairly high or low ratings that may affect positively or negatively the user reputation. An observer will identify large variance of a single user's reputation/rating per context. The detection and attenuation of biased ratings will be one of the center tasks. Existing models for analysis can be used (Sherchan, Loke, & Krishnaswamy, 2006). The action that follows the detection may vary from one center to the other. Center components are:

- User Database with the associated reputation objects.
- Reputation Reference Trust Models
- Mapping functions between these models
- Attack Analyzer

The key to success for TRCs is public acceptance among users as well as large communities. The implementation of the TRC can vary from one organization/country to another. Some may choose to use a first time credentials negotiation to construct a record in the center. Others may choose to start with an existing reputation value obtained by users' ratings from one of the web communities. (Alnemr & Meinel, 2008).

In order to adopt this framework (shown in figure 1), the identity of the users should be common in multiple platforms; at least the center should link the identities from one platform to the other. One solution is the deployment of application-independent identity management standards like Cardspace or OpenID.

MODEL'S USE CASE AND DISCUSSION

Stock Market and Real Estate Market: A Use Case

The usability of transferring reputation objects between two communities is best illustrated by an abstract use case. The participants of stock market and real estate market communities are shown in figure2. We are using the use case of one agent, a technical analyst, in the stock market who wants to register in a real-estate community. The reputation object $RO_{StockMarket}$ in a stock market is viewed as the collective value of his reputation in: Real-estate, Forex, Financial, and Commodity.

$$RO_{StockMarket}[ConextS][value]$$

Figure 1. The framework/model

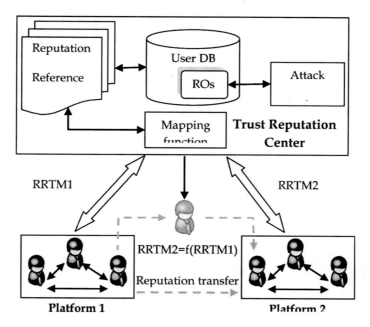

where *ContextS* ∈ {*Credentials, Real-estate, Forex, Financial, Commodity*} and is the domain of all related properties belonging to a stock market agent. In real estate market the properties that describe an agent reputation $RO_{RealestateMarket}$ are: Location, Value Estimation, Quality, Future Value estimation, Marketing skills, and being Friendly.

Figure 2. The stock-real estate markets use case

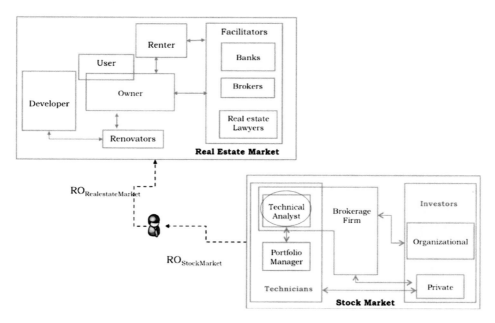

$$RO_{RealestateMarket}[ConextR][value]$$

where *ContextR* $\in$ {*Location, Value Estimation, Quality, Future Value estimation, Marketing skills, Friendliness*} and is the domain of all related properties belonging to a real estate market agent. It is expected from a technical analyst in a stock market, who has high reputation in real-estate stocks, to be experienced in some of the real-estate properties; namely: *value, location,* and part of *future value estimation,* hence the semantic intersection between the two communities' properties. Hence, given the properties values in $RO_{StockMarket}$, the *real-state* property can be transferred and interpreted to create a corresponding $RO_{RealestateMarket}$. However not all the properties can have a value, for example, the value of *Marketing* skills in the transferred reputation object is *zero*.

$$NewAgent\ RO_{RealestateMarket} =$$
$$RO_{StockMarket}[ContextS][value] \cap$$
$$RO_{RealestateMarket}[ContextR][value]$$

The same can be done for communication between existing systems, like:

- eBay and Amazon
- Credit Card rating databases
- Credit Card databases and Western Union
- eBay and PayPal

Framework Strength Points

Benefits of Using Reputation Object

For communities like *eBay, Delicious, Amazon, Allexperts,* etc., the question is since the ratings are written in natural languages, then what are the benefits of the RO attributes? The answer is that there are three proved benefits:

1. Easier to maintain the answers to the eBay and Amazon rating questions. For example: the after buy Questionnaire: *Was the product in the described condition? Was it delivered on time?*
2. Easier to select a seller according to what is most suitable to my requirements. For example: *I need faster delivery service and I don't care about the price*
3. Avoiding Lawsuits by specifying exactly the topic and properties of rating.

That is said, the main reason Reputation object is used is to enforce the connection between general reputation and the context of the given reputation. Without the context, represented as *properties* in that sense, the meaning of the single reputation value is most of the time irrelevant and sometimes even lost.

Reputation Systems and Law

An interesting study about legal challenges that face online reputation systems is being conducted in (Chandler, El-Khatib, Benyoucef, Bochmann, & Adams, 2007). The authors explore legal cases against systems like eBay (California, Grace vs. eBay) and Amazon (cases in UK and USA). The main reason of most of the cases is rating ambiguity. Users misrepresent their rating in a way that both influence negatively the entity being rated and does not correspond to the rating attributes. For example: A used-books seller who was rated badly because the book was not good or too long, although the book was in a very good condition (which is what matters for rating a used-books seller). From the legal point of view, systems like eBay hold no responsibility for users who are expressing their *taste*. What is important from the legal perspective is the distinction between "expressions of fact" and "opinion". Though eBay instituted *limited* assurance coverage; Standard Purchase Protection Program, the problem still exists and growing. What these systems need is specific rating attributes categorized semantically according to the sub contexts of the rated subject. The less vague the rating, the less legal issues arise.

This is achieved if Reputation objects are being used. It can break down the rating into attributes like *delivery* and *quality*. Even quality can be further *sub-categorized* or *detailed out*. By saving this in the object, the user is able to express his opinion and at the same time his rating corresponds directly to these attributes which leads to less lawsuits.

Benefits of Using RRTMs

Going through standardizing reputation trust models is long and needs lots of research. The question is: why standardizing reputation model factors and properties into RRTMs, instead of letting *agents* interact directly and asking directly for the reputation value from the other platform?

The answer is simple, in order to do so, the destination platform has to request for the entire history of the agent from the source platform. This is required to let the destination calculate its own view of trust and reputation, therefore a new value. At the end it is a holistic approach that consumes time and loads the system with too much computation, especially if this is done for every agent or participant who is requesting reputation transfer.

ANALYSIS AND FORMALIZATION OF THE MODEL

In the previous sections, we have laid out the future vision for reputation-based systems and the model that fulfill this vision. To deploy such model, a thorough analysis must take place. This analysis consists of several processes like:

- Defining the domain of reputation systems without being limiting
- Checking the existing systems to avoid current problems and inflexibility
- Defining the categories of the reputation systems

- Defining concepts, terms and relationships that build up a common Ontology to be used by most of reputation systems
- From this ontology, construct a knowledge base that will be used in the model
- Defining the main constructs of the trust relationship
- Determine how identities are handled in the framework
- Give instructions for implementation Reputation Systems Categorized

Reputation systems are fitter for e-services because the notions modeled seem more intuitive to the domain. They can be categorized by characteristics (Chandler, El-Khatib, Benyoucef, Bochmann, & Adams, 2007):

1. The subject of rating
2. The providers of the ratings (open to public or restricted)
3. The business model (revenue derived from an associated online auction, retail channel, advertising, or a public service)
4. Relative Reviews (whether users ratings are relative to the attributes of rating)

The subject of the rating varies from individuals like *Allexperts.com*, *eBay* or *Amazon*, Business like *BizRate.com*, to Articles or posting like in *Kuro5hin.org*, *Slashdot.com* and Products and services like *Epinions.com*.

Reputation systems can also be categorized based on the common features and properties of the online communities:

1. E-market places like *eBay*
2. Opinions and activity sharing sites like *Epinions, Del.icio.us, LastFm*
3. Business/Jobs network sites like *Linkedin. com & Ryze.com*
4. Social/entertainment sites like *Friendster. com & Facebook*

Figure 3. Online reputation systems categorized based on characteristics

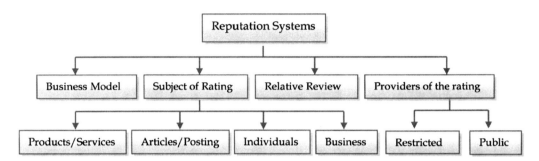

Figure 4. Online reputation systems categorizes based on common features and properties

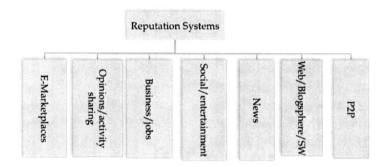

5.   News site like *Kuroshin.org, Slashdot, & Zdnet*
6.   The Web/Semantic Web as for anyone who publish anything – decentralized way
7.   P2P networks where peer clients share opinions about other peers.

In peer-to-peer (P2P) networks, the problem is that the system is open and autonomous by definition. Malicious peers can distribute corrupted files easily or even some peers can download files without letting their files available for download, a technique known as *free riding*. On the other hand, peers can benefit from one active good-peer if they know that he is *good* and *active*. A way to ensure marking both good and bad peers is to let every peer express their opinion to the others. Using reputation concept can be an incentive for peers to cooperate. Interacting peers can provide recommendations, positive or negative, about

other autonomous entities. This encourages more interaction and keeps track of entities behavior.

Reputation systems also can generally be described into two abstract *Reputation Topologies*:

1.   Directly: by users' statements about their experiences (all social networks).
2.   Indirectly: from behavior (*Google*: view the behavior of creating a hyperlink to a Web Page as evidence of the quality, reliability of that web page). Or like the number of cross citations that a given author or journal has accumulated over a period of time. It is a science known as Scientometrics. It is the study of measuring research outputs such as journal impact factors. (Baumgartner & Pieters, 2000)

Figure 5. Terms and concepts used in the model

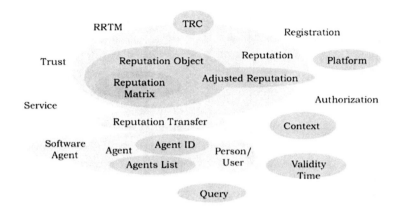

Previous and Existing Reputation Tools and Systems

Most of the existing tools focus on using contextual cues which vary from system to another to evaluate the level of trust that should be placed on a trustee requesting the establishment of a trust relationship. The conceptual function is almost the same in all tools; the change lies in the reputation calculation and dissemination.

For *Poplano 2000*, it uses simple math formulas, specifically designed for solving the problem of searching distributed databases but at the same time constraints cannot be specified. *SECURE* tool reasons about trust, where risk is a significant consideration here. *The Nameless (work of Doyle & Shrobe) 2000* is a probabilistic model that constantly collects security related data about the users from a broad variety of resources including intrusion detection systems, system logs, network traffic analyzers and so forth. Due to this extensive analysis it loads the system with heavy computations and should not be part of a trust agent configuration. In our model, this tool mostly fits into the Attack Analyzer process in the Trust Center. *SULTAN 2003* contains lots of building blocks like specification editor, the analysis engine, the risk service, the trust monitor, and the trust consultant. Having all these processes in one

system, it is expected that it is not lightweight to be installed. (Grandison, Trust Management Tools, 2007)

The problem with these tools and systems that most of them have more than one of the following shortcomings:

- Do not consider interaction between different systems/platforms/services,
- Cannot be fit to avoid legal issues,
- Produce general reputation values regardless of the context,
- Cannot be adjusted to benefit from the ongoing evolution in technology and information science; generally, not adaptive to evolved knowledge,
- Have simple calculations, sometimes even unrealistic,
- Do not consider *distrust,* or
- Do not consider trust monitoring, update and propagation.

Knowledge Base and the Base Constructs of Relationships

To share common understanding of the information structure among agents or services, a common Ontology must be defined. This Ontology should not be used only in one domain but also in multiple domains. This includes defining the system participants, terms used, new and old concepts, and the base constructs of system relationships (Context, measurability and level of trust, cardinality, mathematical properties, and influencing factors like Mistrust, distrust, risk, agreements, experience, diffidence, incentive, and legislation)

This all lead to build up a knowledge base that is needed to help in the decision support process and to enable the reuse of the domain knowledge. Most of the terms and concepts used in the knowledge base are identified in figure 5. (*which suggests some of the terms used in the model, as well as the overall context, viewed as classes and their super classes*)

TRUST MANAGEMENT AND IDENTITY MANAGEMENT

As described earlier in this chapter, moving from identity management silos to Web-scale identity management has required establishing a relatively complex vocabulary and construction kit of components and interactions. The same holds for the integration of Web-scale trust management.

As has been shown, high versatility of identity providers and low dependence of services upon specific identity providers is crucial for achieving an open ecosystem of services and service providers. Similarly the future trust management infrastructure must allow for high flexibility and low interdependence between services, identity providers, and trust reputation centers. Reduced interoperability and intentional hard wiring should be supported in some scenarios, but must not be enforced in the general architecture.

In terms of the basic service vocabulary presented earlier in this chapter, the storage of reputation objects, the mapping function, and the attack analyzer are composable services as shown in Fig. 6. Due to the open nature of reputation—it is not known beforehand what interactions, events, and opinions will finally constitute the reputation of a participant, nor can we know all the contexts in which a participant may gain reputation in future—reputation information should be exchanged in a flexible, but well-defined format. RDF with underlying RDF reputation schemas will be the technology of choice for linking descriptions of interactions ("A purchase has been made"), users ("The user's name is …"), and ratings ("Delivery was quick, technical product quality was good,

Figure 6. Combining trust management and identity management

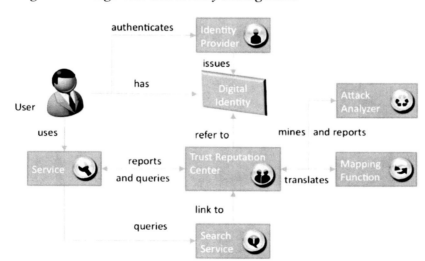

but the product itself is lacking certain features"). It will be the task of the trust reputation center, or a correspondent service, to gather reports by participants, i.e. other users, services, and special services such as the attack analyzer or the mapping function, and to compute meaningful per-context ratings as specified by the requested RRTM.

Due to user privacy concerns, reputation information should not be available for public data retrieval. Rather, the user should have control over which *Trust Reputation Centers* to use, and which services to allow access to his reputation data. From the perspective of services, the user should not be able to hide reputation information. Hence, a reputation search service is required returning a list of TRCs that store reputation information about the user, without automatically revealing this information. When a user first registers with a new Web site, the following actions should be triggered:

1. The Web site queries the reputation search service for the list of TRCs storing reputation information of the user.
2. The Web site asks the user for permission to query the reputation information from the centers returned by the search service.
3. For each of the centers, the user grants or denies access to his reputation data.
4. If access to all reputation centers is granted, the Web site queries and processes the reputation information according to its own RRTM. If access to some TRCs is denied, the Web site can choose one of the following actions.
   a. **Tolerate:** Accept the partial access and proceed, even at risk of deliberately being excluded from processing low reputation information
   b. **Mark***:* Accept the partial access as in a), but add information to the reputation object giving the user low reputation for transparency

   c. **Punish:** Accept the users decision, but refuse to import any data from TRCs, hence considering the user as a new user, starting his reputation information from scratch
   d. **Reject:** Abort user registration

Reject is relevant if the Web site accepts only users with already established reputation, and does not want to *Tolerate* or *Mark* incomplete reputation information.

By the protocol presented, reputation transfer between different Web sites and platforms is possible. At the same time, the user's privacy is respected and the user retains control over his reputation data without giving him the opportunity to hide valuable information.

CONCLUSION

In this book chapter, we have given a definition of trust and trust management. We related trust in information systems to the perception of trust in social science. It can be observed from different point of views: trust meaning, components, types, and sources. Trust management has been defined as the process of making assessments and decisions regarding trust relationships. It has been observed that trust management tools are still maturing and not ready for wide deployment in P2P and other open, distributed systems.

As reputation and trust management requires the notion of digital identity and identity management, the relevant concepts including participants, interactions, roles, infrastructure, and information have been defined. Using these concepts, the identity management lifecycle and prototypical identity management architectures have been laid out.

We introduced our context-aware reputation framework and pointed out the need for complex reputation objects instead of plain reputation values per user. We introduced the notion of standardized reputation reference trust models (RRTM), which explain the point of view on reputation for each Web community. The mediation between these points of view is facilitated by trust reputation centers (TRC). Afterwards we analyzed existing trust management tools. All of them are incapable of adapting to the dynamic requirements in open systems. Last, we presented how the identity management architecture should be combined with the trust management framework presented. In this part, we defined a behavior model for reputation transfer and formalized this into a protocol.

From analyzing reputation systems, tools, and theories, the most important aspect is to provide adjusted reputation that reflects evolving knowledge. Trust management is not only about establishing trust relationships, but also about trust monitoring, update, and propagation. The proposed use of reputation objects along with trust reputation centers and reference models, and the combination with recent identity management technologies forms our contribution.

REFERENCES

Alnemr, R., & Meinel, C. (2008). Getting more from reputation systems: A context–aware reputation framework based on trust centers and agent lists. In *The Third International Multi-Conference on Computing in the Global Information Technology* (pp. 137-142), Greece. Washington, DC: IEEE Computer Society Press.

Baumgartner, H., & Pieters, R. (2000). *The influence of marketing journals: A citation analysis of the discipline and its sub-areas.* The Netherlands: Tilburg University, Center of Economic Research.

Bonatti, P., Duma, C., Olmedilla, D., & Shahmehri, N. (2005). An integration of reputation-based and policy-based trust management. In *Semantic Web Policy Workshop in Conjunction with 4th International Semantic Web Conference,* Galway, Ireland.

Bonawitz, K., Chandrasekhar, C., & Viana, R. (2004). *Portable reputations with EgoSphere.* Cambridge, MA: MIT Internal Report.

Brickley, D., & Miller, L. (2007, November 1). *FOAF Vocabulary Specification 0.91.* Retrieved from http://xmlns.com/foaf/spec/

Chandler, J., El-Khatib, K., Benyoucef, M., Bochmann, G., & Adams, C. (2007). Legal Challenges of Online Reputation Systems. In L. K. R. Song, *Trust in e-services: Technologies, practices and challenges* (pp. 84-111). Hershey, PA: IGI Global.

Cranor, L., Dobbs, B., Egelman, S., Hogben, G., Humphrey, J., Langheinrich, M., et al. (2006, November 1). *The platform for privacy preferences 1.1 (P3P1.1) specification.* Retrieved from http://www.w3.org/TR/P3P11/

Fielding, R. T. (2000). *Architectural styles and the design of network-based software architectures.* Irvine: University of California.

Fullam, K. K., & Barber, K. S. (2006). Learning trust strategies in reputation exchange networks. *Proceedings of the Fifth International Joint Conference On Autonomous Agents And Multiagent Systems* (pp. 1241- 1248). New York: ACM.

Golbeck, J., Parisa, B., & Hendler, J. (2003). Trust networks on the Semantic Web. *In Proceedings of Cooperative Intelligent Agents* (pp. 238-249), Helsinki, Finland. Berlin: Springer.

Grandison, T. (2007). Conceptions of trust: Definition, constructs, and models. In R. Song, L. Korba, & a. G. Yee, (Eds.), *Trust in e-services: Technologies, practices and challenges* (pp. 1-28). Hershey, PA: IGI Global.

Grandison, T. (2007). Trust management tools. In R. Song, L. Korba, & G. Yee, *Trust in e-services: Technologies, practices and challenges,* (pp. 198-216). Hershey, PA: IGI Global.

Kashyap, V., & V, B. (2004). Trust but verify: Emergence, trust, and quality in Intelligent Systems. [Washington, DC: IEEE Xplore.]. *IEEE Intelligent Systems*, 85–88.

Luhmann, N. (1983). *Trust and Power.* Hoboken, NJ: John Wiley & Sons Inc.

MacKenzie, M., Laskey, K., McCabe, F., Brown, P., & Metz, R. (2006, August 1). *Reference Model for Service OrientedArchitecture 1.0.* Retrieved from http://www.oasis-open.org/committees/download.php/19679/soa-rm-cs.pdf

Microsoft Developer Network. (2005, May 1). *Microsoft's Vision for an Identity Metasystem.* Retrieved from http://msdn.microsoft.com/en-us/library/ms996422.aspx

Miranda, H., & Rodrigues, L. (2003). Friend and foes: Preventing selfishness in open mobile ad hoc networks. In *Proc. of 1st International Workshop on Mobile Distributed Computing* (pp. 440- 445), Providence, RI. Washington, DC: IEEE Computer Society Press.

OASIS. (2004, March). *Web Services Security.* Retrieved from http://www-128.ibm.com/developerworks/library/specification/ws-secure/

OASIS. (2008, August 01). *SAML specifications.* Retrieved from http://saml.xml.org/saml-specifications

OAuth Workgroup. O. C. (2007, December 4th). *OAuth Core 1.0.* Retrieved December 4th, 2007, from http://oauth.net/core/1.0/

Quasthoff, M. (2008). Enlightenment 2.0: Facilitating user control in distributed collaborative applications. In *Proc. of the 2008 WI-IAT Doctoral Workshop,* Sydney. Washington, DC: IEEE.

Quasthoff, M., Sack, H., & Meinel, C. (2007). Why HTTPS is not enough – A signature-based architecture for trusted content on the social Web. In *Proc. of the 2007 International Conference on Web Intelligence,* (pp. 820-824), Silicon Valley. Washington, DC: IEEE.

Rahman, A., & Hailes, S. (2000). Supporting trust in virtual communities. In *Proceedings of the 33rd Annual Hawaii International Conference on System Sciences,* (Vol.6, pp.6007), Hawaii.

Recordon, D., & Reed, D. (2006). OpenID 2.0: A platform for user-centric identity management. *Proc. of the 2nd ACM Workshop on Digital Identity Management* (pp. 11-16). Alexandria: ACM.

Seigneur, J.-M., & Jensen, C. D. (2007). User-centric identity, trust and privacy. In R. Song, L. Korba, & G. Yee, *Trust in e-services: technologies, practices and challenges* (pp. 293-322). Hershey, PA: IGI Global.

Sherchan, W., Loke, S. W., & Krishnaswamy, S. (2006). A fuzzy model for reasoning about reputation in web services. *Proceedings of the 2006 ACM symposium on Applied computing* (pp. 1886 - 1892). Dijon, France: ACM.

Uslaner, E. (2002). *The Moral Foundations of Trust.* UK: Cambridge University Press.

Victor, P., Cornelis, C., & Cock, M. (2006). Enhanced recommendations through propagation of trust and distrust. *Proceedings of the 2006 IEEE/WIC/ACM international conference on Web Intelligence and Intelligent Agent Technology,* (pp. 263-266), Hong Kong. Washington, DC: IEEE Computer Society.

Winer, D. (2003, June 1). *XML-RPC Specification.* Retrieved from http://www.xmlrpc.com/spec

KEY TERMS AND DEFINITIONS

Digital Identity: Digital identity is required to describe an entity in the physical world within a digital information system. Besides carrying some identifier, the digital identity will be described with the help of attributes or so-called claims.

Identity Management: Identity Management refers to establishing, describing, and eventually destroying identities. In this chapter, the term mainly refers to managing digital identities, whereas it could generally be used in broader senses as, e.g., for national identity management

Reputation Object: An object that contains a matrix, which represents the reputation linked with its context and the Reputation Reference Trust Model (RRTM) used to calculate this value.

Reputation Reference Trust Models (RRTM): Models that explain how particular trust values have been obtained and how they can be interpreted. They are used to refer to a set of measures that each person based his opinion on.

Reputation-Based Management: Reputation is typically computed from local experiences together with the feedback given by other entities in the network.

Service-Oriented Architecture: Service-oriented architecture (SOA) is an architectural style encapsulating business functionality into separate services, which can be freely composed to realize higher-level business processes. One main argument for SOA is to achieve software components which can easily be reused in other contexts.

Trust Management: A prediction of reliance based on what a party knows about the other party, to create a framework in which two unrelated parties may establish the trust sufficient to perform sensitive transactions. The processes that include making assessments and decisions regarding trust relationships are called trust management.

Trust Reputation Center (TRC): A center that acts as a trusted third party. It is a pool of user reputation gathered from different platforms

Chapter 35
Designing Grid Security Infrastructures Using Identity–Based Cryptography

Hoon Wei Lim
SAP Research, France

ABSTRACT

Public key infrastructure (PKI) is presently deployed in most grid implementations. Existing PKI-based grid systems make extensive use of public key certificates, both long-term and short-term, in order to support various grid security services, such as single sign-on, mutual authentication and delegation. Orthogonally, the emergence of identity-based cryptography (IBC), which is certificate-free, makes possible more lightweight, simpler public key management techniques than that of conventional certificate-based PKI. In this chapter, the authors study how properties of IBC can be used to design alternative grid security infrastructures which support grid security services in a more clean and natural way.

INTRODUCTION

During the emergence of grid projects in the early-2000s, public key infrastructure (PKI) was widely regarded as the technology of choice for supporting security mechanisms making use of public key cryptography. Thus it seems to be a natural choice for the grid community to adopt PKI as the backbone of the Grid Security Infrastructure (GSI) (Foster et al., 1998) for the Globus Toolkit (GT) (Foster & Kesselman, 1997), a leading toolkit used in developing grid applications. Nevertheless, large-scale

DOI: 10.4018/978-1-61520-686-5.ch035

PKIs are known to be difficult to deploy mainly because of issues, such as cost, registration process, trust establishment, key revocation, management of user private keys and support for dynamic security policies (Ellison & Schneier, 2000; Price, 2005). Outside the grid community, many still seem hesitant to adopt PKI.

In order to ease some of the issues related to PKI deployment, a fairly static top-level PKI hierarchy is used in most grid systems. Typically, a government-owned or -supported national-level Certificate Authority (CA) is employed, with participating institutions acting as Registration Authorities (RAs), with responsibility for enrolling their own users. A daily updated simple Certificate Revocation List (CRL) is used to handle public key revocation. To better protect user private keys and to improve accessibility of these keys from anywhere at anytime, online credential repositories, such as MyProxy (Basney et al., 2005), have been developed.

That said, it appears that certificate-based PKI is widely used today in grid applications mainly because it was an available technology. Since the emergence of grid projects, the grid community has been customising and improving the PKI-based GSI to meet the requirements of grid applications. In the GSI, proxy certificates (Tuecke et al., 2004) have been designed and deployed in addition to standard X.509 public key certificates (Housley et al., 2002). Short-lived proxy certificates, typically on the order of hours or days, are used to enable single sign-on and delegation services, and to limit exposure of long-term credentials. However, it is not clear if the extensive use of certificates and its associated key management issues, such as key generation, certification and verification, and the resulting complexity of security services supported by conventional PKI within a large-scale grid environment offers the best possible solution for grid applications. It seems that a more lightweight security architecture is desirable!

This need is amplified by the emergence of wireless grids (Ahuja & Myers, 2006). The availability of wireless devices has been tremendously improving in recent years. These devices can offer additional resources to existing computational grids. For example, wireless devices can supply information on temperature, health, pollution levels, etc. from geographic locations and social settings that are difficult to access through conventional wired networks. Wireless devices are often battery-powered and the energy required for transmission of a single bit of data is over 1000 times greater than that required by a single 32-bit computation (Barr & Asanovic, 2006). Therefore, it is necessary to minimise the communication overheads of any grid security infrastructure if we are to exploit the full potential of wireless grids.

Independent of grid computing, a variant of traditional public key technologies called identity-based cryptography (IBC) (Boneh & Franklin, 2001; Shamir, 1984) has recently received considerable attention. In IBC, a user's public key can be computed based on an identifier which represents the user, for example, the user's email address. The matching private key is produced by a Private Key Generator (PKG) in possession of a system master secret. The concept of IBC avoids the use of public key certificates, hence it seems to offer more lightweight and flexible key usage and management approaches for grid environments than traditional PKI. The emergence and development of IBC presents a sensible opportunity to revisit and redesign, where appropriate, the PKI-based GSI using properties of IBC.

In this chapter, we investigate how properties from IBC can be used to design various security infrastructures for grid applications. We first present a fully identity-based key infrastructure for grid (IKIG) (Lim & Paterson, 2005). We show a customised identity-based authenticated key agreement protocol and a lightweight one-pass delegation protocol that supports short-term identity-based keys. These protocols support single sign-on, authenticated key agreement and credential delegation in IKIG in a natural way.

Although the fully identity-based approach of IKIG is more lightweight than the certificate-based GSI, IKIG inherits key escrow, a property of IBC (since private keys are produced by a PKG). This may not be desirable for some grid applications. We, therefore, also present a dynamic key infrastructure for grid (DKIG) (Lim & Robshaw, 2005), a hybrid certificate/identity-based approach which aims to resolve the key escrow issue. Using this approach, most of the benefits that identity-based techniques offer can be preserved, while eliminating key escrow from the infrastructure.

We then look at yet another security infrastructure based on IBC which focuses on user-friendliness. We present a password-enabled and certificate-free GSI (PECF-GSI) (Crampton et al.,

2007), whereby users are authenticated through the conventional username/password method, yet they are able to perform grid security services using public key cryptographic techniques. In other words, users need to remember only their respective passwords and can avoid managing their cryptographic keys.

BACKGROUND

In this section, we describe some common grid security requirements and give an overview of the Grid Security Infrastructure (GSI) of the Globus Toolkit (GT). We also introduce some basic concepts of identity-based cryptography (IBC).

Example Scenario

We give a simple grid scenario, which captures some common security requirements within a grid environment, such as authentication, access control and delegation.

Let Alice be a member of CryptoGrid. During registration, Alice generates and obtains certification of her public/private key pair, which allows her to perform grid security services. When she wishes to perform a resource demanding task, for example, simulating cryptanalysis on a new cryptographic scheme which may take days to complete, she first generates a job request and signs it with her private key. She then submits her job to the CryptoGrid Gatekeeper through a GT client. The Gatekeeper verifies Alice's signed request and checks if Alice is authorised to access the resources that CryptoGrid provides by consulting its local grid-map file (an access control list mapping users' identities to access permissions). Once the check passes, Alice and the Gatekeeper perform mutual authentication using their respective credentials. Subsequently, Alice delegates her credential to the Gatekeeper through the secure channel that they have established. This enables the Gatekeeper to act on Alice's behalf (without

Alice's manual intervention) every time Alice's job needs to gain access to a new resource.

Based on the job description, the Gatekeeper queries a local replica catalogue to determine suitable resources to run the simulation. Once that has been located, the Gatekeeper passes on the job description to a hosting server. Before the Gatekeeper submits the job to the hosting server, it must perform mutual authentication with the server using the delegated credential from Alice. In some cases, the Gatekeeper may need to further delegate Alice's credential to the hosting server which requires access to other resources to complete Alice's job. For instance, the job may require additional data from a database server. Alice may monitor the progress of the job and possibly change her mind about where or how it is executing. Upon completion of the job, Alice will be notified by the Gatekeeper and the results will be sent back to her. Finally the GT client will clean-up information in the job submission scripts and remove temporary settings that coordinated the job.

Grid Security Infrastructure

The GSI of the GT has been widely deployed to date. The PKI-based GSI focuses on authentication, message protection, and the use of proxy credentials to support single sign-on and credential delegation (Foster et al., 1998; Welch et al., 2004; Welch et al., 2003). In grid applications that employ the GSI, each entity is assigned a unique identity or distinguished name and given a public key certificate signed by a Grid CA. Public key certificates are used to support authentication and key agreement protocols, such as the TLS protocol (Dierks & Allen, 1999). Proxy certificates are used for single sign-on and delegation.

Before a user submits a job request, she must create a proxy certificate which includes generating a new public/private key pair and signing the proxy certificate with her long-term private key. This newly created proxy certificate can then be used for repeated authentication with other grid entities, thus enabling single sign-on. The user's long-term private key does not need to be accessed again until the expiry of the proxy certificate.

For rights delegation from a user A to a target service/resource provider X, three steps are required (Welch et al., 2004):

- X generates a new public/private key pair and sends a request (that is signed with the new private key) to A;
- A verifies the request using the new public key, creates a new proxy certificate, and signs it with her current proxy credential (short-lived private key);
- A forwards the new proxy certificate to X.

MyProxy (Basney et al., 2005), an online credential repository, is now an integral part of the GSI. It implements the virtual smart card concept (Sandhu et al., 2002). As with storing keys in a smart card, a MyProxy server is expected to provide better protection for long-term user private keys than desktop computing environments. Moreover, the MyProxy approach offers credential mobility, in the sense that users can access their respective long-term credentials stored on a My-Proxy server from anywhere.

Identity-Based Cryptography

Identity-based cryptography (IBC) was first introduced by Shamir (1984). Instead of generating and using a random public/private key pair in a public key cryptosystem such as RSA, Shamir conceived the idea of using a user's name or her network address as a public key, with the corresponding private component being generated by a trusted key generation centre. In fact, any type of identifier, for example email address, social security number, telephone number and so forth, can be used, so long it can uniquely identify the user and is readily available to the party that uses it. The main motivation for this approach is to eliminate the need for certificates and the problems that they

bring. Since a user's public key is based on some publicly available information that uniquely represents the user, an identity-based cryptosystem can do away with public key directory maintenance and certificate management. Despite the novel and ambitious conception, Shamir was only able to develop an identity-based signature (IBS) scheme based on the RSA primitive. The construction of an identity-based encryption (IBE) scheme was left as an open problem.

Only in the early 2000's did the emergence of cryptographic schemes based on pairings on elliptic curves result in the construction of a feasible and secure IBE scheme. This area began with the novel work of Sakai et al. (2000) on pairing-based key agreement protocols and signature schemes, and subsequent work on the three-party key agreement protocol by Joux (2000). Boneh & Franklin (2001) then presented the first practical and secure IBE scheme based on the Weil pairings. These three key contributions have stimulated the development of a wide range of pairing-based cryptographic schemes and protocols, for example (Bethencourt et al., 2007; Boldyreva et al., 2008; Chen et al., 2007). More background on cryptography from pairings can be found in (Paterson, 2005).

To give an idea of how IBE works, we now describe a simplified version of the Boneh-Franklin IBE scheme. This is defined by four algorithms, as follows:

- **SETUP:** Given a security parameter, the algorithm generates a set of system parameters (which will be made public) and a master secret (which it keeps private).
- **EXTRACT:** This algorithm is run to extract the private key corresponding to a given public key. It takes the system parameters, the master secret and an arbitrary identifier ID (public key string) as input, and returns a private key.
- **ENCRYPT:** This algorithm uses the system parameters and an identifier ID to encrypt a message, and generates a ciphertext.

- **DECRYPT:** Using the system parameters, a private key and a ciphertext as input, this algorithm returns a plaintext (or possibly an indication that the decryption process has failed).

The SETUP and EXTRACT algorithms are normally executed by a Private Key Generator (PKG), while the ENCRYPT and DECRYPT algorithms are carried out by users. The PKG, in turn, will be managed and controlled by a Trusted Authority (TA), a trusted third party roughly equivalent to a CA in a traditional PKI.

Suppose that Alice wants to send a message secretly to Bob using an IBE scheme. She does not need to first verify the authenticity of Bob's public key by retrieving Bob's public key certificate (which must take place in a conventional PKI). Instead Alice simply encrypts the message with Bob's identifier ID_B, for example his email address <bob@example.com>. Clearly, Alice needs to know Bob's identifier and the system parameters of Bob's TA. If Bob does not already possess the corresponding private key, he has to obtain it from his TA. If the TA is satisfied that Bob is a legitimate receiver, it takes its system parameters, master secret and Bob's identifier ID_B to extract a private key, which will then be used by Bob to decrypt the ciphertext.

In this chapter, we will discuss the use of a variant of IBC called hierarchical identity-based cryptography (HIBC) (Gentry & Silverberg, 2002; Horwitz & Lynn, 2002) for designing grid security infrastructures. HIBC was designed to ease private key distribution in the identity-based setting by having multiple levels of PKGs, analogous to the existing concept of hierarchical PKI (having multiple levels of CAs). It is assumed that these PKGs can be arranged in a rooted tree with users located at the bottom of the tree. More specifically, the root PKG, located at level 0, is trusted to produce private keys for entities at level 1, who in turn act as PKGs for entities in their respective domains at level 2; and users at level t obtain their private keys from their respective PKG at level t-1. Note that all entities in the hierarchy share the same set of system parameters.

Each node in the tree has an identifier. The identifier of an entity is the concatenation of the node identifiers in the path from the root to the node associated with the entity. Hence, the identifier $ID_1, ..., ID_t$ represents an entity at level t whose ancestor at level 1 has identifier ID_1 and whose ancestor at level j has identifier $ID_1, ..., ID_j$.

The first practical, provably secure and fully hierarchical identity-based encryption and signature (HIBE/HIBS) schemes were proposed by Gentry and Silverberg (2002). More recent work on HIBC can be found in (Boneh et al., 2005).

Certificate-Based PKI and Identity-Based PKI

Before describing how properties of IBC/HIBC can be exploited to design grid security infrastructures, it may be useful to first discuss the distinctions between a traditional certificate-based PKI and an identity-based PKI.

The major technical difference between a certificate-based PKI and an identity-based PKI is the binding between the public/private keys and the individual. This can be achieved by using a certificate in the traditional PKI. In the identity-based setting, the public key is bound to the transmitted data while the binding between the private key and the individual is managed by the TA. A public key based on an identifier can be constructed on-the-fly at any time, even before its matching private component is computed.

In terms of key generation, the conventional PKI allows either a user or her CA to create public/private key pairs. However, it is only the TA that can compute private keys in the identity-based setting. This inevitably implies that an identity-based PKI has an escrow facility, which may or may not be desirable. Boneh & Franklin (2001) suggested that key escrow can be circumvented by using multiple TAs and threshold cryptography.

On the other hand, because of this built-in feature, the user always needs to set up an independent secure channel with her TA for retrieving private key material.

For key revocation, Boneh and Franklin proposed the use of date concatenated with the user's identifier to achieve automated key expiry. This may obviate the need for a revocation mechanism. However, it has the disadvantage of increasing the TA's workload, since the TA is required to regularly generate private keys and deliver them to its users.

Table 1 summarises the above comparison between traditional PKIs and identity-based PKIs. More detailed discussions comparing the two architectures can be found in (Burmester & Desmedt, 2004; Paterson & Price, 2003). For discussion of inter-operation between the certificate-based and the identity-based settings and some of the issues that may then arise, see (Price & Mitchell, 2005).

IDENTITY-BASED KEY INFRASTRUCTURE FOR GRID

In this section, we describe a fully developed identity-based infrastructure for grid applications (IKIG) proposed by Lim & Paterson (2005). IKIG makes use of properties from HIBC and it aligns with the security services provided by the GSI adopted in the GT4.

Motivation

Key management that is essential for supporting security mechanisms within a grid environment can be much more complex than in a conventional distributed system. To illustrate this, we refer back to the grid example scenario described earlier. Consider a single secure job submission. Before Alice (A) submits her job request, she must make sure that her proxy credential has been created. When A submits a job through the Gatekeeper (GK), another proxy credential that deals with the job has to be created at the GK. If A delegates her proxy credential to the GK to offload some tasks such as resource allocation and data transfer, the GK would need to create a separate proxy credential signed with A's short-term private key. Should the GK want to further delegate A's proxy credential to resource X, then creation of another proxy certificate is inevitable. The extensive use of standard X.509 certificates and proxy certificates even for a single job submission is evident.

Generation, certification and verification of public keys, distribution of certificates, and other aspects of key management cause non-trivial overheads. For instance, when the GK and resource X perform mutual authentication through the TLS handshake protocol before the job is executed, the GK must transmit the complete certificate chain consisting of: (i) A's long-term and proxy certificates, (ii) the GK's long-term certificate, and (iii) the proxy certificate containing a credential delegated from A to the GK. For

Table 1. Key differences between a certificated-based PKI and an identity-based approach

Feature	Certificate-based PKI	Identity-based PKI
Public key generation	Using random information	Using an explicit identifier
Private key generation	By a user or the CA	By the TA (or PKG)
Key certification	Yes	No
Key distribution	Requiring an integrity protected channel for distributing a new public key from a user to her CA	Requiring an integrity and privacy protected channel for distributing a new private key from the TA to its user
Escrow facility	No (except when key generation is run by the CA)	Yes

X to verify the short-term public key that the GK uses on behalf of *A*, *X* must check the signatures on all the certificates to ensure that *A* has indeed delegated her credential to the GK. It is obvious that when the delegation chain becomes longer, the verification of the short-term public key used at the end of the chain becomes more tedious. Note that this process is repeated every time the GK communicates with a resource provider on *A*'s behalf. Current key and certificate management techniques are likely to cause bottlenecks at the GK and resource *X* when they handle many job requests simultaneously. Hence, we see that although current certificate-based public key management techniques are workable, they seem to be rather heavyweight. On the contrary, it is an essential requirement that key management and the security architecture within a grid environment are lightweight so that a VO that serves as a single virtual supercomputer can be constructed with minimal performance impact.

Generally, IBC has the following attractive properties:

- **Identity-Based:** The use of identity-based public keys in IBC allows any entity's public key to be generated and used on-the-fly without the need for public key certificate verification;
- **Certificate-Free:** IBC does not make use of certificates since public keys can be computed based on some public identifiers;
- **Small key sizes:** Since identity-based cryptographic schemes use pairings which are, in turn, based on elliptic curves, they can have smaller key sizes than more conventional public key cryptosystems such as RSA (Paterson, 2005).

These interesting properties of IBC indicate the possibility of developing an alternative security infrastructure that provides greater flexibility to entities within a grid environment and that offers a more lightweight public key management ap-

proach than traditional PKI. The proposal of IKIG incorporates features that align with the security services provided by the PKI-based GSI, which is an essential requirement of any alternative proposal. The challenge of achieving this lies in the difficulty of creation and management of identity-based proxy credentials, in addition to long-term credentials that are common to most identity-based cryptosystems. By exploiting some properties from HIBC, IKIG facilitates the creation and usage of identity-based proxy credentials in a very natural way. These identity-based proxy credentials, in turn, are needed to support features that match those provided by the GSI.

Design of IKIG

In the IKIG setting, the CA in the current PKI-based GSI is replaced by a TA. The TA's roles including acting as the PKG and supporting other user-related administration and management.

The IKIG approach makes use of both long-term and short-term (proxy) identity-based keys. To match the requirements of the GSI, short-term identity-based keys are used in security services, such as mutual authentication and delegation, during a secure grid job submission. In HIBC, the identifier of an entity can be formed using a meaningful hierarchical (see the section on "Identity-Based Cryptography"). This allows a proxy identity-based public key to be generated naturally, for example, simply by appending an appropriate validity period to the associated identifier before it is transformed into a proxy public key. In other words, a proxy credential for an entity can be generated by simply creating a new entity/node at the next level of the hierarchy.

Figure 1 shows the hierarchical setting of HIBC that matches the hierarchical relationships of various entities within a grid environment, with the TA at level 0, user at level 1 and user proxy at level 2.

The TA distributes long-term private keys to its users (and resource providers) at level 1, who

Figure 1. A hierarchical structure of entities in the IKIG setting

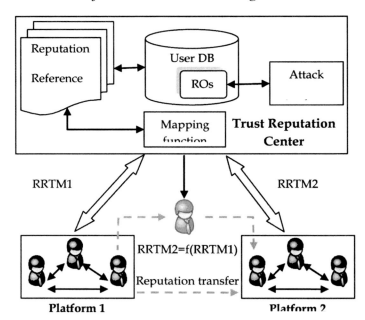

in turn generate short-term private keys for their own proxies (user clients) at level 2. For example, in the IKIG setting, a user A's long-term public key P_A is equivalent to a public key computed using a level-1 identifier ID_A, that is $P_A = f(ID_A)$, assuming f is a key derivation function (part of the system parameters) in a HIBE/HIBS scheme. The corresponding long-term private key S_A is generated by the TA. On the other hand, A can compute a short-term private key SA for her proxy which is at the second level of the hierarchy. In IKIG, the proxy's identifier is defined purely by a lifetime LT_A in some fixed format, and thus A's short-term public key PA is of the form $f(ID_A, LT_A)$. The long-term and short-term credentials of a resource provider can be established in the same manner.

Now that we have described the keys needed by the various entities in the IKIG approach, we can illustrate various security services that IKIG provides in order to secure a job submission. For simplicity in describing the IKIG approach, we assume the user can communicate with the resource provider directly, rather than through a gatekeeper or a resource broker.

Single Sign-On

As with the GSI, the IKIG proposal supports single sign-on through the use of identity-based proxy credentials. With a proxy credential, A does not need to sign on (i.e. access her encrypted long-term private key S_A with her passphrase) again until the expiry of her short-term public/private key pair. Since the users' proxy public keys are based on some identifiers and the matching proxy private keys are stored locally at the user side, user authentication can be performed without any physical intervention from the users and without the need for certificates. Note that users in the IKIG setting do not need to obtain proxy private keys from their respective PKGs (or TAs). This is because through HIBC, the users themselves can act as PKGs for their local proxy clients. Thus proxy private key distribution is not an issue in IKIG.

Authorisation

User A's proxy generates an identity-based signature using a HIBS scheme on her job request using the short-term private key SA. The signed request allows the resource provider or hosting server to first verify the signed job request, and then map A's identifier to its grid-map file before granting access to A. We assume that A's identifier is also forwarded to the resource provider along with her signed request. This allows the resource provider to compute the relevant public key PA to verify the signed request. Clearly, this approach does not require standard or proxy certificates to certify the respective public keys.

Mutual Authentication and Key Agreement

IKIG also supports an identity-based authenticated key agreement protocol based on the TLS handshake. This is needed for A's proxy to perform mutual authentication with the resource provider and subsequently establish a secure channel, which in turn, can be used to protect data confidentiality and integrity, as well as to facilitate delegation of credential, when necessary. In the GSI, this is achieved using the standard TLS protocol (Dierks & Allen, 1999). The identity-based authenticated key agreement protocol is integrated with the widely used TLS protocol so that it can be implemented in existing grid infrastructures without major modification.

In the identity-based TLS handshake approach, HIBE and HIBS schemes are used for message encryption and signing, respectively, in contrast with the typical use of the RSA encryption and signature schemes in the standard TLS protocol. Moreover, the ClientCertificate and ServerCertificate messages of the standard TLS protocol are replaced by ClientIdentifier and ServerIdentifier, respectively. As implied by their names, the ClientIdentifier and ServerIdentifier messages contain information about the identifiers of the involved client and server, respectively. This allows the client's or the server's public key to be computed on-the-fly without the need for obtaining and verifying the validity of the relevant public key certificate.

Delegation

User A may, at her discretion, delegate her credential to a resource provider for later use when necessary.

Currently, the GSI employs a two-pass delegation protocol (Tuecke et al., 2004; Welch et al., 2004) between a delegator and a delegation target. Lim & Paterson (2005) proposed a one-pass delegation protocol which works in the same way as GSI in the sense that the delegator signs a new public key of the delegation target.

As described earlier, the client can easily compute the server's short-term public key based on the server's identifier, and vice versa. By the same reasoning, the delegator can straightforwardly sign the delegation target's new short-term public key which will be used for delegation purposes. This can be done without having the delegation target transmit its chosen short-term public key to the delegator through an authenticated and integrity protected channel. In order to compensate for the removal of certain types of policy enforcement which could have been done through a proxy certificate, the use of a delegation token was proposed in (Lim & Paterson, 2005). The delegation token contains information, such as identifiers of the delegator and the delegation target, the job request, any policy which the delegator wants to enforce on the delegation target, and the validity period of the token.

Key Management

Here, we discuss how cryptographic keys are managed in the IKIG approach.

User Registration

The registration of a new grid user can be done rather similarly to the conventional certificate-based PKI approach. The key difference is that in IKIG, the TA generates a user's long-term private key, whereas in the certificate-based setting, the private key is generated by the user herself.

Key Update

In a grid environment, it is normal practice to renew the user's long-term keys on a yearly basis. In IKIG, this can be done through the TA issuing a new private key directly to the user through a secure channel which can be established via the identity-based TLS protocol described earlier. Assuming that a user's identifier, using the syntax for X.509 certificates (Housley et al., 2002), is of the form "/C=UK/O=eScience/OU=RHUL/CN=Alice/Y=2008" then during the key update, the year field of the identifier can be updated to Y=2009, for example.

This is a more proactive approach as compared to current practice in PKI because the TA can easily compute the user's new long-term public key without requesting a new public key from the user. However, we have to enforce a policy whereby, in the event of compromise of the user's current private key right before the issuance of a new private key, the user must, upon her discovery of the incident, contact her RA in person to obtain a new private key.

Key Revocation

In the IBC setting, a number of revocation mechanisms are possible. We could use a more fine-grained identifier (Boneh & Franklin, 2001). For example, we could extend the user's identifier to include another field which specifies a month, such as: "/C=UK/O=eScience/OU=RHUL/CN=Alice/Y=2008/M=November". This allows automated expiry of public keys after one month (hence the window of exposure is also limited to a month). The granularity of the user identifier must not be so complex that it loses its predictability. However, should this approach prove insufficient, for example in some grid applications requiring high security, then existing PKI revocation mechanisms such as CRLs (Housley et al., 2002) or OCSP (Myers et al., 1999) can be adapted to the IBC setting.

Revocation of short-term keys is a minor concern here. The user creates a new short-term public/private key pair every time she signs on to the system. As with the current GSI setting, we assume the default lifetime for these keys is 12 hours. Upon expiry of the proxy credential, these keys will be deleted from the local file system where they are temporarily stored.

Inter-Operability

For simplicity of exposition, so far we have assumed that users and resource providers have registered with the same TA. If IKIG is to be deployed roughly at the scale of one TA for each country (as with most European grid projects), we expect that the TAs' system parameters would be bootstrapped in the grid system and updated by the users through their GT clients.

As with current grid deployment, trust relationships between TAs can be established through the European Grid PMA without a root TA. System parameters of the TAs are then assumed to be trusted by all users and recognised by the grid system. When a user communicates with a remote resource registered with a foreign TA, the user's grid client will select the foreign TA's system parameters to perform the required cryptographic operations.

Related Work

A number of researchers have recently started exploring the use of IBC in grid security. The first publication on this subject was made by Lim & Robshaw (2004). They described some potential benefits of IBC in a grid security architecture. However, they did not address private key distribution in the IBC setting. More importantly, some of the essential security requirements desired in the GT, such as using proxy credentials for single sign-on and delegation, were also not addressed.

At about the same time, Mao (2004) revisited the GSI proposed for GT2 (Foster et al., 1998) and presented an application of the Sakai et al. (2000) non-interactive identity-based key distribution technique within the GSI authentication framework. It was assumed in (Mao, 2004) that a user, who is from an average or low-end platform, may have to execute many mutual authentication sessions with different resource providers. This would potentially cause a performance bottleneck at the user client. The use of non-interactive session key establishment technique seems to significantly reduce the communication overheads between two key sharing parties. Nevertheless, this may not be the case in practice, particularly in the newer versions of the GT, i.e. GT3 and GT4. A grid user can always delegate her credential to a resource (or resource broker) which can act on the user's behalf. Thus, the performance issues discussed in (Mao, 2004) are only valid for a special scenario whereby a user client is required to contact and perform mutual authentication directly with many resources.

Subsequently, Huang et al. (2005) combined and extended the work of Lim & Robshaw (2004) and Mao (2004), and presented an identity-based security infrastructure which seems to work rather differently to the GSI. Although Huang et al. showed how to perform credential delegation between two parties, each run of their delegation protocol involves additional secure communication with a PKG. This appears to be more costly and tedious than the current delegation techniques for the GSI.

In summary, the potential of IBC has only been partially investigated to date and none of the above proposals so far satisfactorily address the requirements imposed by grid applications (and that are currently met by the GSI). IKIG appears to be the first fully developed identity-based infrastructure for grid applications that does meet these requirements.

DYNAMIC KEY INFRASTRUCTURE FOR GRID

We now describe the concept of a dynamic key infrastructure for grid (DKIG) proposed by Lim & Robshaw (2005). DKIG is a hybrid approach combining identity-based techniques at the user level and traditional PKI to support key management above the user level in the hierarchical structure of a grid environment.

Motivation

We learned earlier that key escrow is inevitable in IBC. Despite that, key escrow seems to be acceptable for most current grid applications since the use of MyProxy in the GSI also involves the same issue. However, we envisage that when computational grids become commercialised and payment is involved, key escrow that prevents strong non-repudiation may become a major issue. Here, strong non-repudiation refers to the inability of any party, including a malicious CA/TA, to impersonate a user by producing a valid signature as if it were generated by the actual user for fraud purposes. Thus in the remaining section, we will look at a means of resolving the key escrow problem while preserving, as much as possible, the advantages that identity-based techniques offer through DKIG.

The term DKIG is intended to capture the notion that a user proxy credential can be created dynamically and on-the-fly based on a static long-term credential. In this hybrid setting, each user publishes a fixed parameter set through a standard X.509 certificate; this parameter set then allows users to act as their own PKGs for the purpose of managing short-term keys which will, in turn, be used for single sign-on and delegation.

Our focus, as in the previous section, will be on simplifying key management aspects of grid applications that rely heavily on both long-term and short-term entity credentials.

Figure 2. The hierarchical structure of entities in the DKIG setting

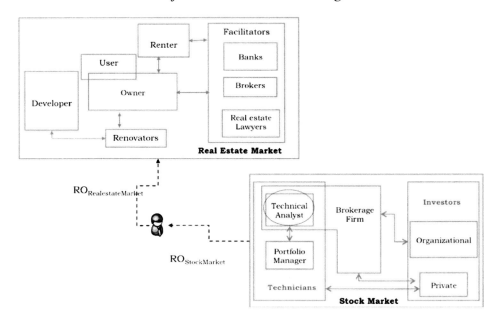

Design of DKIG

As with IKIG, we envisage that the TAs' system parameters in the DKIG setting are boot-strapped into the grid system and can be updated by the users though their GT clients. Also, trust relationships between TAs can be established through a Grid PMA. Note that the TA in the DKIG setting is in fact a traditional CA. For the purpose of consistency in using terminology and to avoid confusion, we stick to the term TA to refer to the key issuance authority in DKIG.

In Figure 2, we show the hierarchy of entities in DKIG. Traditional certificate-based PKI is used by users and resource providers to manage their long-term credentials. The TA issues standard certificates that contain system parameters chosen by users and resources, in a similar way as a typical CA certifies user-chosen public keys. Here, a certificate binds a system parameter set to a user's identity and her master secret, which is used to extract private keys (as a PKG does). These system parameters contain public information required to perform IBE/IBS operations. We

remark that some of these parameters can be fixed to reduce communication costs of the system. Further details of parameter selection are given in (Lim, 2006).

At the user level, the certified system parameters are used by the users (and resources) to extract short-term private keys corresponding to some fixed formatted identifiers. These short-term private keys and identity-based public keys are then taken as input to IBE and IBS schemes for providing security services, such as single sign-on, mutual authentication and delegation. Note that we are not using HIBE and HIBS schemes any longer because in this hybrid approach, identity-based techniques are used starting at the user level. Since the next level is already the user proxy level, non-hierarchical-based IBE and IBS schemes seem to be sufficient. The resulting DKIG approach has the following interesting properties, of which some can be difficult to emulate with conventional PKI:

- The proposal of DKIG not only maintains the hierarchical structure of PKI above the user level, it also provides improved flexibility at the user level (ground level), where peer entities freely create and manage their own proxy credentials without any intervention from a TA/CA.

- The fixed parameter set that each user possesses is different from a proxy certificate. The parameter set can be seen as a long-term "public-key mould" from which other entities can compute short-lived public keys instantly. The corresponding private keys can be generated directly by the entity himself without interacting with the TA, a feature that IKIG also possesses.

- The DKIG framework not only solves the key escrow problem in IBC, it also removes the requirement for short-term private key distribution between the entities and their respective TAs. The latter is an important benefit as distributing short-term private keys using secure channels can be a tedious and expensive operation within a grid environment.

- The replacement of the conventional contents of standard X.509 certificates with identity-based cryptographic system parameters implies minimal changes to the current overall pure PKI-based GSI framework.

- Most of the attractive properties of IBC, such as using identity-based and small-size public keys, can still be preserved in the DKIG setting. Even though each entity needs to publish their system parameters through a certificate, proxy credential management can be done without any use of proxy certificates.

In general, DKIG works in a very similar way to IKIG, but without the key escrow issue. (Hence, details on how DKIG can be used to support various grid security services are omitted from this chapter.) However, each entity in the DKIG setting will possess an authentic and valid certificate that needs to be transmitted to other parties when performing security services such as mutual authentication and delegation. In short, we can regard IKIG as a lightweight solution for grid applications that tolerates key escrow, while we can think of DKIG as a fix to remove the key escrow problem of IKIG at the expense of an acceptable increase in bandwidth requirement and computational cost. Further details on DKIG can be found in (Lim, 2006).

Key Management

We now discuss various key management issues arising in DKIG. In general, management of long-term public keys (in the form of user-selected parameters) in DKIG would be rather similar to the GSI, while short-term credential management may well be more lightweight than the GSI, because of DKIG's avoidance of proxy certificates.

The user registration process in DKIG is almost the same as that of IKIG, except that in DKIG, a user selects her own cryptographic system parameters and submits them to the TA. If approved, the TA generates a certificate and informs the user, through e-mail for example, that the certificate is ready. The user can then download her certificate through an authenticated and integrity protected channel from the TA's server. The user can verify the signature on her certificate by using the TA's public key which is assumed to be bootstrapped in the grid system.

Although DKIG is based on a combination of identity-based and certificate-based approaches, the usual annual key update practice in the GSI can be adopted in our proposal. This is so because certificates are used to carry users' system parameters. Barring any exposure of the user's master secret, the TA can renew the user's current certificate by updating the validity period and serial number of the certificate. Alternatively, the user can pick a new master secret and request a new certificate that would contain fresh system parameters, before the current certificate expires.

In terms of key revocation, since the user's long-term credential is managed in a very similar way as in the GSI, we envisage that a CRL-based method can also be used in DKIG. Clearly, the efficiency of this technique relies on the timeliness of the revocation list update, as well as the willingness of the users to update their local copies of CRLs.

Revocation of proxy credentials is not a major concern here since they will expire automatically within a relatively short period of time.

Related Work

Not long after the publication of Boneh & Franklin's work (2001), Chen et al. (2002) proposed a hybrid certificate-based and identity-based approach related to but different from our work. In Chen et al.'s proposal, they presented a certificate-based approach for TAs above the domain level, e.g. between a domain TA and a root TA, and identity-based techniques for entities below the domain TA. It is assumed that all TAs in this hybrid architecture use non-identity-based public/private keys, while the users have identity-based key pairs. The root TA will verify the public keys or system parameters of the domain TAs and issue certificates accordingly. The domain TAs, in turn, extract identity-based private keys for their respective users using the certified system parameters. Hence, when a user wants to encrypt a message for another user belonging to a different domain, the sender must obtain the system parameters for the domain TA of the receiver and its root TA. Although the proposal of Chen et al. provides a certificate-free approach at the user level, key escrow remains possible since the domain TA possesses a master secret which is used to extract the users' private keys. We note that the security architecture proposed by Smetters & Durfee (2003) for a secure email application (also for secure IP-based communications) using IBC is closely related to Chen et al.'s approach. The architecture proposed by Smetters and Durfee

uses conventional certificate-based PKI above the domain level, while key management within the domain is identity-based. However, private key distribution from a PKG to its users requires the standard TLS protocol which is still certificate-based. In DKIG, this limitation is removed and short-term key management (in the context of a grid application) is fully identity-based.

On the other hand, the key escrow issue of the Boneh-Franklin IBE scheme partly drove the proposals of certificate-based encryption (Gentry, 2003) and certificateless public key cryptography (Al-Riyami & Paterson, 2003). The authors of both proposals split the private key of a user into two components: one computed by the user herself, and another by the TA. Because of this requirement, the user's public key is no longer identity-based. To encrypt a message, the sender must obtain the intended recipient's public key which is an arbitrary string like a conventional public key. Hence, the benefits that identity-based techniques can bring to grid applications may no longer be applicable. Although the certificateless approach of Al-Riyami and Paterson can remove the extensive use of certificates in grid applications, it is not clear if the use of two-component-based private keys will actually simplify current PKI-based public key management in grid applications.

PASSWORD-ENABLED AND CERTIFICATE-FREE GRID SECURITY INFRASTRUCTURE

The third variant of identity-based grid security infrastructure which we will describe is enhancement to IKIG in terms of usability. Crampton et al. (2007) proposed a password-enabled and certificate-free grid security infrastructure (PECF-GSI). The PECF-GSI proposal allows a user to perform single sign-on based only on a password, without requiring a public key infrastructure. This greatly simplifies cryptographic key management from the user's perspective.

Figure 3. A conceptual view of PECF-GSI

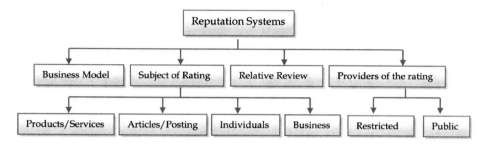

Motivation

Credential acquisition in any security infrastructure which makes use of public key cryptographic techniques is a fairly complicated and time-consuming process. In the UK National Grid Service, for example, obtaining a public key certificate requires the generation of a public/private key pair using a web browser, transmission of the public component to a CA for certification, a face-to-face meeting with an RA to prove user identity and membership in a grid project, and provide justification for her grid usage. The credential acquisition processes that we described for IKIG and DKIG are not less complicated either. Studies have shown that users tend to share credentials within their peer groups because of the cumbersome and time-consuming process of credential acquisition which may take one or up to few weeks (Beckles et al., 2005). This likely introduces security problems, such as increases the risk of private key exposure. Therefore, it is highly desirable to have grid systems with simpler user credential acquisition and management.

Moreover, as described before, key revocation in the identity-based setting can be complicated. Boneh & Franklin (2001) proposed the use of a date concatenated with a user's identifier to achieve automated key expiry. However, this approach has the disadvantage of increasing the workload of the TA (or PKG), since the TA is required to regularly issue private keys to its users.

PECF-GSI was proposed in order to address these issues.

Design of PECF-GSI

As with IKIG, PECF-GSI employs a TA as the root of trust within a grid environment. However in PECF-GSI, a user's long-term credential is simply a password, which she shares with a local domain authentication server. The authentication server is assumed to be accredited by the TA and hosting servers (or resource providers) within the grid environment. Unlike the user, who only has to remember a password, the authentication and hosting servers must obtain the TA's authenticated parameter set through out-of-band mechanisms. This hybrid approach divides the PECF-GSI architecture into two zones: (i) a user-centric zone which employs password-based authentication, and (ii) a server-centric zone which makes use of identity-based PKI (based on HIBC). This is illustrated in Figure 3.

Assuming that the TA in Figure 3 is at level 0 of the hierarchy, it issues private keys using identity-based techniques to the authentication server and the resource provider at level 1. These entities, in turn, issue private keys to their respective children at level 2. Note that the user does not possess any long-term credential issued by the TA; instead she obtains proxy credentials from her authentication server. Hence, the user's proxy (rather than the user) becomes a child of the authentication server in the hierarchy.

Before a user *A* submits a job to a resource provider, for example, she authenticates herself to her local domain authentication server using a secure username/password mechanism. In the

PECF-GSI proposal (Crampton et al., 2007), a password-based TLS protocol was used in line with the widely deployed TLS protocol within grid systems. When the password-based authentication is successful and a secure channel between *A* and her authentication server is established, the server extracts a proxy credential for use by *A*'s proxy. The proxy credential, which comprises a short-term public/private key pair, is transmitted to *A*, along with other required information, such as the TA's system parameters, through the secure channel. We remark that the whole process of single sign-on does not involve any kind of certificate or parameter verification from the user's perspective (we regard verification of parameters as checking the authenticity of the parameters and not validating their number-theoretic structure). Thus, the authentication process is "PKI-free" from the user's perspective.

Subsequently, *A*'s proxy signs her job request (with the new proxy private key), which is then submitted to the resource provider. The rest of the job submission process has been discussed in the previous sections and will not be repeated here.

Key Management

The key issuance process between the TA and domain authentication servers or resource providers are similar to that of IKIG.

On the other hand, it is assumed that users obtain their long-term credentials (passwords) from their respective domain system administrators. One way of doing this is for a system administrator to send an initial password to a new user through email, and requesting the user to change the initial password on her first log-in. Note that user registration in PECF-GSI setting may well be much simpler than applying for an X.509 certificate in the GSI setting or an identity-based credential in the IKIG approach. This is because the user does not have to obtain the necessary credential from a CA/TA.

PECF-GSI deals with revocation of user keys and of hosting server keys in different ways. The

users are never given long-term public keys, instead they are only ever provided with proxy keys, which have a relatively short lifetime. As the window of exposure to compromise is minimised, there is no need for an explicit revocation mechanism for user keys. In this case, the resource providers are trusting authentication servers to only distribute fresh keys to their users if the users' privileges are still valid. The fact that system parameters of the identity-based primitives do not necessarily need to be pre-distributed or bootstrapped, gives rise to easy, flexible and user-friendly deployment of identity-based cryptosystems.

On the other hand, resource providers are issued with long term public keys. In this case, there is a requirement for an explicit revocation mechanism. To allow for the revocation of servers' public keys, the notion of an Identity Revocation List (IRL) was introduced in PECF-GSI, where an IRL is analogous to a CRL in a certificate-based environment. The IRL includes the identity of any server whose key has been revoked. This allows users to verify the validity of a particular resource provider's public key prior to submitting a job to the resource. IRLs are distributed to users by their respective authentication servers via the secure channel established at authentication time. From the user's perspective, this "push" method of distribution simplifies the process of verifying whether a resource provider has had its public key revoked.

Related Work

PECF-GSI is architecturally similar to MyProxy. However, MyProxy relies on a certificate-based PKI. In the MyProxy protocol (Basney et al., 2005), although users are authenticated to their respective MyProxy servers using conventional username/password techniques, server authentication is achieved using the server-authenticated version of the TLS handshake protocol (Dierks & Allen, 1999). This implies the need to protect the root CA's public key certificate on the users' machines and for users to know how to interpret advice concerning certificate checks. It is not an unusual assumption that some machines within the scope of a grid community may lack up-to-date protection in the form of the latest vulnerability patches and virus definitions. There are ways for an attacker to install a bogus root key in the user's browser (Alsaid & Mitchell, 2005). Hence, if MyProxy is used because of the assumption that a desktop is vulnerable to private key exposure, then the desktop may also be at risk from replacement of the associated CA's certificate by the attacker. In short, the user must ensure that the associated certificates bootstrapped in her machine are trustworthy and have not been replaced. On the other hand, in PECF-GSI, a user is required to remember only a password which she shares with her local authentication server.

Recently, Beckles et al. (2005) considered issues related to the usability of the PKI-based GSI, noting that managing certificates can be onerous for general grid users. In an effort to improve the usability of the PKI-based GSI, they adopted Gutmann's plug-and-play PKI (PnP PKI) concept (Gutmann, 2003), which emphasises automated and transparent setup of PKI for the end user. In so doing, Beckles et al. make use of the PKIBoot service of PnP PKI to allow a user to authenticate herself to a PKIBoot server with the standard username/password method. Subsequently, the user can securely retrieve her public key certificate (and optionally her private key) and/or CAs' certificates. This approach can eliminate the difficult tasks involved in correctly establishing trust roots of CAs from the user side. It can also minimise the user's direct involvement in certificate management.

Although the plug-and-play PKI concept seems to make PKI more usable for users, there are still many aspects of PKI that need to be addressed. For example, how can we improve the effectiveness of current key revocation mechanisms, such as CRLs, by exploiting the advantages that the plug-and-play PKI concept could bring? Furthermore, the application of the plug-and-play PKI to the GSI

does not reduce the extensive use of certificates, and certificate chain verification is still required for all grid security services that require certificates. These issues are addressed in PECF-GSI.

CONCLUSION

Security issues in grid applications are numerous due to complex grid properties such as heterogeneity, scalability and adaptability. One of the unique security requirements for grid applications is the use of both standard X.509 and proxy certificates, supported by PKI, to achieve single sign-on, delegation and other security services.

In this chapter, we highlighted some fundamental issues in the PKI-based GSI and discussed the suitability of designing alternative security infrastructures using identity-based cryptography. In conclusion, we believe that an identity-based security infrastructure has more advantages than disadvantages as compared to the PKI-based GSI. Identity-based approaches offer more flexibility in terms of key usage and management than the conventional PKI approach. Although the PKI-based GSI is workable, it is still far from lightweight in terms of the network bandwidth requirement. On the other hand, identity-based approaches consume minimal communication bandwidth since they are certificate-free. The significant saving in message sizes in IKIG augurs well for the on-going transition from transport-level to message-level security based on web services, as well as the emergence of wireless grid applications. In addition, we also showed that identity-based public keys can be used in a very natural way to support various grid security services, such as mutual authentication and delegation.

Moreover, we discussed how the key escrow property that plagues identity-based cryptosystems can be addressed in a grid environment. We also described how an identity-based grid security infrastructure can be made more user-friendly and easier to deploy.

Nevertheless, at the time of writing, no known real world implementation of an identity-based grid security architecture has been carried out either by grid or IBC research communities. This is partly because the study of the application of IBC in grid security at the architectural level is still an ongoing research avenue, and partly because currently available tools and mechanisms used to construct grid systems do not yet have the capability of supporting IBC. Although it is essential to understand and answer various fundamental issues and questions in regards to the suitability of IBC in grid applications, it is also important to examine what are the possible practical or implementation issues related to identity-based solutions. Therefore, in the medium-term, the development of prototypes that implement the described identity-based approaches would seem to be a sensible and natural follow-on.

REFERENCES

Ahuja, S. P., & Myers, J. R. (2006). A survey on wireless grid computing. *The Journal of Supercomputing*, *37*(1), 3–21. doi:10.1007/s11227-006-3845-z

Al-Riyami, S. S., & Paterson, K. G. (2003). Certificateless public key cryptography. In C.S. Laih (Ed.), *Advances in Cryptology - Proceedings of ASIACRYPT 2003*, (LNCS Vol. 2894, pp. 452-473). Berlin: Springer-Verlag.

Alsaid, A., & Mitchell, C. J. (2005). Installing fake root keys in a PC. In D. Chadwick & G. Zhao (Eds.), *Proceedings of the 2ⁿᵈ European Public Key Infrastructure Workshop (EuroPKI 2005)*, (LNCS Vol. 3545, pp. 227-239). Berlin: Springer-Verlag.

Barr, K., & Asanovic, K. (2006). Energy aware lossless data compression. *ACM Transactions on Computer Systems*, *24*(3), 250–291. doi:10.1145/1151690.1151692

Basney, J., Humphrey, M., & Welch, V. (2005). The MyProxy online credential repository. *Journal of Software: Practice and Experience*, *35*(9), 817–826. doi:10.1002/spe.689

Beckles, B., Welch, V., & Basney, J. (2005). Mechanisms for increasing the usability of grid security. *International Journal of Human-Computer Studies*, *63*(1-2), 74–101. doi:10.1016/j.ijhcs.2005.04.017

Bethencourt, J., Sahai, A., & Waters, B. (2007). Ciphertext-policy attribute-based encryption. In *Proceedings of IEEE Symposium on Security and Privacy (SP 2007)*, (pp. 321-334). Washington, DC: IEEE Computer Society Press.

Boldyreva, A., Goyal, V., & Kumar, V. (2008). Identity-based encryption with efficient revocation. In *Proceedings of the 15th ACM Conference on Computer and Communications Security (CCS 2008)*, (pp. 417-426). New York: ACM Press.

Boneh, D., Boyen, X., & Goh, E. (2005). Hierarchical identity based encryption with constant size ciphertext. In R. Cramer (Ed.), *Advances in Cryptology - Proceedings of EUROCRYPT 2005*, (LNCS Vol. 3494, pp. 440-456). Berlin: Springer-Verlag.

Boneh, D., & Franklin, M. (2001). Identity-based encryption from the Weil pairing. In J. Kilian (Ed.), *Advances in Cryptology - Proceedings of CRYPTO 2001*, (LNCS Vol. 2139, pp. 213-229). Berlin: Springer-Verlag.

Burmester, M., & Desmedt, Y. (2004). Identity-based key infrastructures. In *Proceedings of the IFIP TC11 19ᵗʰ International Information Security Conference (SEC 2004)*, (pp. 167-176). Amsterdam: Kluwer.

Chen, L., Cheng, Z., & Smart, N. P. (2007). Identity-based key agreement protocols from pairings. *International Journal of Information Security*, *6*(4), 213–241. doi:10.1007/s10207-006-0011-9

Chen, L., Harrison, K., Moss, A., Soldera, D., & Smart, N. P. (2002). Certification of public keys within an identity based system. In A.H. Chan & V. Gligor (Eds.) *Proceedings of the 5th International Information Security Conference (ISC2002)*, (LNCS Vol. 2433, pp. 322-333). Berlin: Springer-Verlag.

Crampton, J., Lim, H. W., Paterson, K. G., & Price, G. (2007). A certificate-free grid security infrastructure supporting password-based user authentication. In *Proceedings of the 6th Annual PKI R&D Workshop 2007, Interagency Report 7427*, (pp. 103-118). NIST.

Dierks, T. & Allen, C. (1999). The TLS protocol version 1.0. *The Internet Engineering Task Force (IETF)*, RFC 2246.

Ellison, C., & Schneier, B. (2000). Ten risks of PKI: What you're not being told about public key infrastructure. *Computer Security Journal, 16*(1), 1–7.

Foster, I., & Kesselman, C. (1997). Globus: A meta-computing infrastructure toolkit. *The International Journal of Supercomputer Applications, 11*(2), 115–128. doi:10.1177/109434209701100205

Foster, I., Kesselman, C., Tsudik, G., & Tuecke, S. (1998). A security architecture for computational Grids. In *Proceedings of the 5th ACM Computer and Communications Security Conference (CCS '98)*, (pp. 83-92). New York: ACM Press.

Gentry, C. (2003). Certificate-based encryption and the certificate revocation problem. In E. Biham (Ed.), *Advances in Cryptology - Proceedings of EUROCRYPT 2003*, (LNCS Vol. 2656, pp. 272-293). Berlin: Springer-Verlag.

Gentry, C., & Silverberg, A. (2002). Hierarchical ID-based cryptography. In Y. Zheng (Ed.), *Advances in Cryptology - Proceedings of ASIA-CRYPT 2002*, (LNCS Vol. 2501, pp. 548-566). Berlin: Springer-Verlag.

Gutmann, P. (2003). Plug-and-play PKI: A PKI your mother can use. In *Proceedings of 12th USENIX Security Symposium*, (pp. 45-58).

Horwitz, J., & Lynn, B. (2002). Towards hierarchical identity-based encryption. In L.R. Knudsen, (Ed.), *Advances in Cryptology - Proceedings of EUROCRYPT 2002*, (LNCS Vol. 2332, pp. 466-481). Berlin: Springer-Verlag.

Housley, R., Polk, W., Ford, W. & Solo, D. (2002). Internet X.509 public key infrastructure certificate and certificate revocation list (CRL) profile. *The Internet Engineering Task Force (IETF)*, RFC 3280.

Huang, X., Chen, L., Huang, L., & Li, M. (2005). An identity-based grid security infrastructure model. In R.H. Deng, F. Bao, H. Pang & J. Zhou (Eds.), *Proceedings of the 1st International Conference on Information Security Practice and Experience (ISPEC 2005)*, (LNCS Vol. 3439, pp. 314-325). Berlin: Springer-Verlag.

Joux, A. (2000). A one round protocol for tripartite Diffie-Hellman. In W. Bosma (Ed.), *Proceedings of 4th Algorithmic Number Theory Symposium (ANTS-IV)*, (LNCS Vol. 1838, pp. 385-394). Berlin: Springer-Verlag.

Lim, H. W. (2006). *On the Application of Identity-Based Cryptography in Grid Security*. Ph.D thesis, University of London, UK.

Lim, H. W., & Paterson, K. G. (2005). Identity-based cryptography for grid security. In H. Stockinger, R. Buyya & R. Perrott (Eds.), *Proceedings of the 1st IEEE International Conference on e-Science and Grid Computing (e-Science 2005)*, (pp. 395-404). Washington, DC: IEEE Computer Society Press.

Lim, H. W., & Robshaw, M. J. B. (2004). On identity-based cryptography and grid computing. In M. Bubak, G.D.v. Albada, P.M.A. Sloot & J.J. Dongarra (Eds), *Proceedings of the 4th International Conference on Computational Science (ICCS 2004)*, (LNCS Vol. 3036, pp. 474-477). Berlin: Springer-Verlag.

Lim, H. W., & Robshaw, M. J. B. (2005). A dynamic key infrastructure for grid. In P.M.A. Sloot, A.G. Hoekstra, T. Priol, A. Reinefeld & M. Bubak (Eds.), *Proceedings of the European Grid Conference (EGC 2005),* (LNCS Vol. 3470, pp. 255-264). Berlin: Springer-Verlag.

Mao, W. (2004). *An Identity-based Non-interactive Authentication Framework for Computational Grids.* HP Lab, Technical Report HPL-2004-96.

Myers, M., Ankney, R., Malpani, A., Galperin, S. & Adams, C. (1999). Internet X.509 public key infrastructure online certificate status protocol (OCSP). *The Internet Engineering Task Force (IETF),* RFC 2560.

Paterson, K. G. (2005). Cryptography from pairings. In I.F. Blake, G. Seroussi & N.P. Smart (Eds.), *Advances in Elliptic Curve Cryptography. LMS 317,* (pp. 215-251). Cambridge, UK: Cambridge University Press.

Paterson, K. G., & Price, G. (2003). A comparison between traditional public key infrastructures and identity-based cryptography. *Information Security Technical Report, 8*(3), 57–72. doi:10.1016/S1363-4127(03)00308-X

Price, G. (2005). PKI challenges: An industry analysis. In J. Zhou, M-C. Kang, F. Bao & H-H. Pang (Eds.), *Proceedings of the 4th International Workshop for Applied PKI (IWAP 2005), Vol. 128,* (pp. 3-16). Amsterdam: IOS Press.

Price, G., & Mitchell, C. J. (2005). Interoperation between a conventional PKI and an ID-based infrastructure. In D. Chadwick & G. Zhao (Eds.), *Proceedings of the 2nd European Public Key Infrastructure Workshop (EuroPKI 2005),* (LNCS Vol. 3545, pp. 73-85). Berlin: Springer-Verlag.

Sakai, R., Ohgishi, K., & Kasahara, M. (2000). Cryptosystems based on pairing. In *Proceedings of the 2000 Symposium on Cryptography and Information Security (SCIS 2000).*

Sandhu, R. S., Bellare, M., & Ganesan, R. (2002). Password-enabled PKI: Virtual smartcards versus virtual soft tokens. In *Proceedings of the 1st Annual PKI R&D Workshop,* (pp. 89-96). NIST.

Shamir, A. (1984). Identity-based cryptosystems and signature schemes. In G.R. Blakley & D. Chaum (Eds.), *Advances in Cryptology - Proceedings of CRYPTO '84,* (LNCS Vol. 196, pp. 47-53). Berlin: Springer-Verlag.

Smetters, D. K., & Durfee, G. (2003). Domain-based administration of identity-based cryptosystems for secure email and IPSEC. In *Proceedings of 12th USENIX Security Symposium,* (pp. 215-229).

Tuecke, S., Welch, V., Engert, D., Pearlman, L. & Thompson, M.R. (2004). Internet X.509 public key infrastructure proxy certificate profile. *The Internet Engineering Task Force (IETF),* RFC 3820.

Welch, V., Foster, I., Kesselman, C., Mulmo, O., Pearlman, L., Tuecke, S., et al. (2004). X.509 proxy certificates for dynamic delegation. In *Proceedings of the 3rd Annual PKI R&D Workshop,* (pp. 42-58). NIST.

Welch, V., Siebenlist, F., Foster, I., Bresnahan, J., Czajkowski, K., Gawor, J., et al. (2003). Security for grid services. In *Proceedings of the 12th IEEE International Symposium on High Performance Distributed Computing (HPDC-12 2003),* (pp. 48-61). Washington, DC: IEEE Computer Society Press.

KEY TERMS AND DEFINITIONS

Certificate-Free: The use of public keys without requiring binding of the keys with their owners in the form of certificates.

Delegation: The act of a user granting rights to another entity, so that the entity can act on the user's behalf.

Grid Security Infrastructure: An infrastructure used to support security services for grid computing systems.

Identity-Based Cryptography: A variant of public key cryptography in which a public key can be computed based on some identifier information.

Key Agreement: Establishment of a session key between two communication parties.

Public Key Infrastructure: A key management infrastructure required to support the use of public key cryptography.

Single Sign-On: A user is authenticated once only, but is allowed to access different resources or applications within a defined session lifetime.

Chapter 36
Enforcing Fairness in Asynchronous Collaborative Environments

Guillaume Pierre
VU University Amsterdam, The Netherlands

Maarten van Steen
VU University Amsterdam, The Netherlands

ABSTRACT

Many large-scale distributed applications rely on collaboration, where unrelated users or organizations share their resources for everyone's benefit. However, in such environments any node may attempt to maximize its own benefit by exploiting other's resources without contributing back. Collaborative systems must therefore deploy strategies to fight free-riders, and enforce collaborative behavior. This chapter explores a family of mechanisms to enforce fairness in asynchronous collaborative environments, where simple tit-for-tat policies cannot be used. Our solutions rely on enforced neighborhood relations, where each node is restricted in the choice of other nodes to collaborate with. This creates long-term collaboration relationships, where each node must behave well with its neighbors if it wants to be able to use their resources.

INTRODUCTION

Service-Oriented Architectures offer the vision of distributed applications offering functionality to each other, such that complex applications may be realized mostly by composition of existing software components provided by independent parties. An example is the recent popularity of Web mashups, where any programmer can take advantage of service-oriented functionality offered through Web services. However, users of service-oriented applications do expect reasonable performance. This requirement can be translated into: how can a service provide constant performance regardless of the request load addressed to it by independent third parties? Obviously, a single server machine cannot handle arbitrary amounts of load so one must design services such that they can expand their capacity by using additional computing resources when necessary.

One way a service may obtain temporary access to extra resources when it needs them is the use of

DOI: 10.4018/978-1-61520-686-5.ch036

Copyright © 2010, IGI Global. Copying or distributing in print or electronic forms without written permission of IGI Global is prohibited.

collaborative environments. Such environments are characterized by multiple users sharing their resources for everyone's benefit. For example, peer-to-peer file sharing applications can improve everyone's download speed of a file under the condition that those users are willing to donate their resources to upload file contents (Cohen, 2003). Similarly, a service operator may use a collaborative content delivery network, which relies on the willingness of Web server administrators to help each other if one experiences a temporary overload (Pierre and van Steen, 2006); another possible method is to use grid computing, where system administrators are willing to contribute their resources in exchange for future use of global resources (Foster and Kesselman, 1998).

One important issue in such environments is free riding, where some users try to use the shared resources without contributing an equivalent quantity of resources back to the system (Adar and Huberman, 2000). Free riding can be extremely detrimental to the performance of collaborative systems as it decreases the quantity of resources available to users as a whole. Additionally, it produces strain on the remaining good nodes in the system, which reduces the incentive to contribute positively.

An efficient mechanism to enforce collaboration is the tit-for-tat policy, as implemented for example in the BitTorrent file sharing system (Cohen, 2003). This policy dictates that, after a first altruistic interaction, resources are granted to a user under the condition that an equivalent amount of resources is simultaneously contributed back. A few properties of BitTorrent make this scheme effective and easy to apply. First, collaboration is symmetric, meaning that collaboration happens pairwise with no third party involved. Fairness enforcement can thus be realized by the two concerned peers themselves, without requiring the need for external services such as reputation systems. Second, collaboration is local in time in that the balance of respective contributions must be judged as fair by both parties at any instant of

the collaboration. The system therefore does not need to maintain a memory of past interactions.

However, tit-for-tat is not a panacea for solving all fairness issues in collaborative environments. Many such environments rely on asynchronous collaboration, where the services are not provided simultaneously from A to B and from B to A. A good example is a collaborative content distribution network, where Web servers call each other for help only when they experience an overload. For such environments we need more sophisticated mechanisms.

This chapter explores a family of mechanisms to enforce fairness in asynchronous collaborative environments, based on observations from Axelrod (Axelrod, 1984). These observations state that cooperation can emerge only when:

- Nodes retain a unique identity over time
- Interactions are repeated many times between the same pairs of nodes

The intuition between these rules is that, to sustain collaboration between the well-behaving members (and to exclude free-riders), one must rely on some memory of past interactions with other nodes. In a large-scale system this implies that a given node regularly interacts with the same partners over and over again, to have the ability to gain some confidence that they will behave well in the future.

The following sections explore the application of these general principles to two classes of asynchronous collaborative environments. First, we study fairness enforcement in a collaborative content distribution network. In such a system, Web servers may request each other's help when they experience an overload. The interaction is thus necessarily asynchronous because a currently overloaded server cannot be of much help to another overloaded server. It makes more sense that underloaded servers help overloaded servers, thereby creating asynchronous collaboration. We then turn to peer-to-peer grids, where a user can allow jobs from other users to execute on his/her resources in order to gain the rights to later run jobs at other sites. Here, in addition to the fundamental asynchronous nature of the system we need to deal with an extra difficulty: restricting the number of neighbors where a node can execute its jobs has an unacceptable performance impact on the Grid as a whole.. We therefore focus on the way to enforce repeated interaction without limiting the scope of machines where a user may submit jobs.

WHAT IS FAIRNESS?

Defining fairness in collaborative environments is equally difficult as it is in human societies. Ideally, fairness would mean that each party receives resources proportional to their own contribution to the collaborative system. For example, Jain defines fairness in the context of a single resource that must be shared fairly between multiple users (Jain et al., 1984). This metric is meant to evaluate instantaneous fairness, in the sense that one user of the shared resource is not unfairly discriminated compared to the others. However, characterizing fairness in asynchronous collaborative systems is much more complex. On the one hand, a good system must allow resource sharing to be unfair at any point of time: certain nodes only contribute resources while others only receive them. On the other hand, it must distinguish free-riders who intentionally refuse to contribute sufficient resources to the system from nodes that are willing to share their resources but are genuinely unable to do so (e.g., a collaborative Web server may need to refuse to help another one if it already experiences a high load).

In this chapter, we use a definition of fairness similar to that of (Böhm and Buchmann, 2009): the goal of a fairness enforcement system is that the presence of free-riders does not significantly impact the benefits that collaborative nodes get from collaboration. Note that this largely implies that the free-riders do not draw any significant benefit from their actions.

FAIRNESS IN A COLLABORATIVE CONTENT DISTRIBUTION NETWORK

A collaborative content distribution network is an overlay of independent Web servers that organize to offload requests from each other when a server is overloaded (Lal, 2007, Pierre and van Steen, 2006). This guarantee is important because a Web server should expect its request traffic to contain significant bursts of activity (Crovella and Bestavros, 1996). Dimensioning any Web server according to the greatest expected load peak can be extremely expensive, so in practice very few servers are sufficiently provisioned to sustain, for example, the load peak created by having a major news site publish a link to the concerned Web server (Adler). In such situations, it becomes interesting to provision a server for its average load only, and rely on other currently underutilized servers to serve the excess load that the server will occasionally be receiving.

For such a system to work in practice, each server must have the assurance that when an overload will occur, another underloaded server will accept to serve as a backup. A free-riding strategy in such a system could consist of utilizing other server's resources during periods of overload, but deny other servers to use the local resources when the server is underutilized. This system clearly belongs to the category of asynchronous collaborative systems: one server can help another one only if it has spare capacity to donate. On the other hand, although collaboration will at any instant be only unidirectional, no server wants to be systematically exploited by its peers so a fair balance of respective contributions should be maintained in the long run.

Fixed Neighborhoods

The first issue to address is that, like any collaborative environment, collaborative content distribution networks must allow certain levels of altruism to initiate the collaboration. One server must first accept to donate resources to another server with no immediate counterpart, in the hope that the favor will be returned later on. However, although altruism is a necessity to allow collaboration to start, we do not want to allow free-riders to exploit the generosity of every node in the system without ever reciprocating the favor.

We solve this problem by statically assigning a fixed set of helpers to each server. This means in practice that an external entity defines a set of neighbors for each server. These neighboring links are symmetric, so it is easy for a server to decide if a request for help comes from a server that is authorized to do so. This also enforces repeated interaction, since a given server is forced to establish long-term relationships with its neighbors. A free-riding server which would exploit the altruism of its designated neighbors without reciprocating the help would quickly be excluded by these neighbors, and therefore become unable to use the collaborative system any more.

Asynchronous Tit-for-Tat

In an asynchronous collaborative environment such as a collaborative content distribution network, it is impossible to maintain a perfect balance of mutual contributions at all times. Consider a pair of collaborative servers A and B. One of the two (say, A) has to donate resources to B, before B can reciprocate later on. On the other hand, A cannot have hard guarantees that B will effectively reciprocate when requested to do so. The only guarantee that can be provided here is trust, based on previous experience among these two particular servers.

Such trust can be built using two simple mechanisms. First, each server must maintain the balance of mutual contributions it had with each of its neighbors. This allows to limit the amount of generosity toward any neighbor, and to deny resources to a neighbor which would request resources without sufficiently reciprocating in the long term. Second, the maximum tolerated imbalance in respective contributions can be adjusted according to past experience. At the start of a collaboration, this maximum imbalance can be set to a relatively low value, so each server minimizes the risk of being exploited by the other. Later on, if the neighbor behaves well and reciprocates the collaboration, then the maximum imbalance may be increased gradually to expand the scope of the collaboration.

More formally, each server maintains three variables for each of its neighbors: *TotalBytesConsumed*, *TotalBytesServed* and *DeficitThreshold*, representing respectively the resources consumed from and donated to the neighbor, and the maximum tolerated imbalance for this neighbor. A request for resources originating from this peer will be granted under two conditions: (i) the requested server is not itself currently experiencing overload; and (ii) $TotalBytesConsumed - TotalBytesServed < DeficitThreshold$.

While this simple model accurately represents the quantity of resources donated by each server to another, it is not sufficient to account for the quality of service with which one server has helped another. In a content delivery network, it matters a lot at which data transfer rate a server has served its neighbor's data to external clients. Thus, contributions should be expressed not only in terms of the quantity of donated resources, but also with their quality of service. However, the rate at which a neighbor can serve any particular connection does not only depend on the resources it is capable or willing to contribute. The location of the client and the characteristics of the Internet path to that client also contribute to determine the transfer rate of this connection. We should therefore not punish a neighbor server for slow data rates observed on any particular connection.

On the other hand, one can aggregate all requests served by a particular neighbor (for example, using exponential weighted moving average functions) and derive trends to indicate if the global quality of service offered indicates artificial contention created by the neighbor server. By comparing the trend of connection rates delivered by the neighbor to the one it provides to its own clients, a server can decide if the neighbor is playing fair or not, and consequently reward or punish it.

Validating Claims

Enforcing collaboration in a collaborative content distribution network creates one extra difficulty that is not found often in other collaborative systems: to be able to suitably reward or punish a neighbor server according to its behavior, a server must be able to verify the claims that a neighbor server has actually served so many requests at so much data rate. However, the nature of collaborative Web sites makes such verification hard to realize: after a server has redirected a client request to one of its neighbors, it is no longer involved in this request. It therefore cannot verify whether the request was actually served, and at what rate.

One simple solution consists of involving (a fraction of) the clients, such that they report the quality of service they experienced to the origin server. Such systems have actually been built, for example to allow one to detect whether fraudulent content was delivered to the user (Popescu et al., 2003). However, this requires that a significant fraction of end users accept to install extra software to issue such reports.

A possible alternative solution is to exploit the properties of a new mechanism for request redirection, named Versatile Anycast (Szymaniak et al., 2007). With versatile anycast, one server can handoff any of its TCP connections with clients to be served by a neighboring server. The handoff is realized at the IP layer, so that the client-side application does not notice it is being redirected.

After redirection, the connection traffic is routed directly between the client and the neighboring server, with no traffic indirection through the origin server. This form of redirection has the advantage that it allows the origin server to check how much data its neighbors actually deliver to clients, and at which rate. In this scheme, a new client request is always opened with the origin server. If the origin server is overloaded, it can then hand off some of its connections to its neighbors. The neighbor is asked to serve the client requests, then to hand off the connection back to the origin server before closing it. The origin server can then check the data offsets of the TCP socket, and verify how much data has actually been exchanged with the client. The origin server can also measure how much time has elapsed between the connection was handed off from the origin to its neighbor and the time when it was handed off back, and derive the average data rate with which this connection has been served.

Evaluation

We evaluated the proposed approach by studying an implementation of two neighboring servers connected to the Internet by emulated ADSL-like connections, each with 2 Mb/s download bandwidth and 240 kb/s upload bandwidth. We assume that the documents to be served are available at both servers, so no document replication cost is incurred in these experiments. Each server is addressed by a bursty workload, generated using a modified version of S-Client (Banga and Druschel, 1997). This tool allows us to control the burstiness of the traffic addressed to the servers. We express burstiness according to the notation in (Menasce and Almeida, 2001), using two parameters *(a, b)*.

Parameter *a* denotes the ratio between the maximum observed request rate and the average rate during the evaluation period. Parameter *b* denotes the fraction of time during which the instantaneous request rate exceeds the average request rate.

Figure 1. Performance of two Web servers with and without collaboration

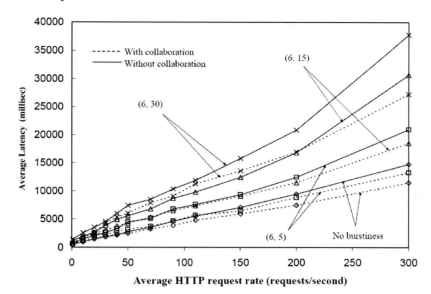

Figure 1 shows the average client-perceived latency of requests addressed to the two servers for several levels of traffic burstiness, with and without collaboration between the two servers. We observe three phenomena: first, obviously, request latency grows when the average request rate grows. Second, for the same average request rate, a bursty traffic is more difficult to serve, as indicated by greater request latency. Finally, we observe that collaboration between the two servers allows to significantly reduce request latencies, especially when the traffic is more bursty. Two servers receiving similarly bursty traffic therefore have a common interest to collaborate.

Figure 2. Performance of a Web server with a free-riding neighbor

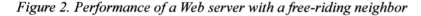
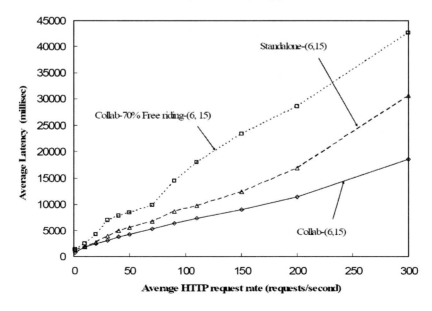

Figure 3. Performance of a Web server with a free-riding neighbor, and enforced collaboration

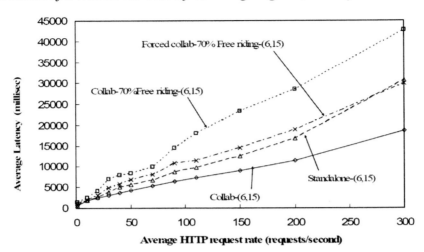

Figure 2 shows the damage that a free-riding neighbor can create. In this example, the free-riding neighbor denies 70% of requests for help from the origin server. In such cases, the origin server must first incur the latency of the denied request for help, then the cost of serving the request itself. We observe that the free-riding neighbor causes an increase of request latency compared to the scenario where the neighbor collaborates, but also compared to the standalone case with no collaboration. We conclude that the best way to behave with a free-riding neighbor is not to collaborate with it any more, since doing so creates an extra burden compared to no collaboration.

Figure 3 shows the performance of the same server when the enforced collaboration mechanisms are activated. The average request latency in the presence of a free-riding neighbor becomes close to the case with no collaboration. This demonstrates that the free-riding neighbor no longer impedes the performance of the origin server.

We conclude this evaluation section with Figure 4, which shows the performance experienced by the free-riding server in these different scenarios. We see that free-riding with no accounting gives this server an extra performance advantage compared to regular collaboration with no free-riding: the free-riding server can exploit the resources

of its collaborative neighbor, without reciprocating. The request latency of the free-riding server therefore improves. However, when we enable the accounting mechanism to enforce collaboration, the free-riding server sees its performance drop to a value close to the case with no collaboration at all. A server therefore has no incentive any more to free ride: using the enforced collaboration, the optimal strategy of any server is to collaborate with its neighbors, for everyone's shared benefit.

FAIRNESS IN A PEER-TO-PEER GRID

A different kind of asynchronous collaborative environment is a peer-to-peer grid (Foster and Kesselman, 1998, Weel, 2008). Here, collaboration happens when a node issues a computational job to be executed by some number of its peers. Similar to the situation of collaborative content delivery networks, each compute node is expected to accept running computations on behalf of other users, in order to gain the rights to later execute jobs on other nodes. Peer-to-peer grids however present two important differences with collaborative content distribution networks. First, in a peer-to-peer grid, a node expecting to run a job at

Figure 4. Performance of a free-riding server

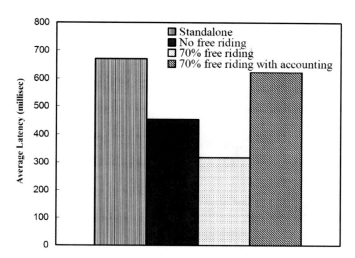

other nodes expects to find several remote peers simultaneously available to run the computation. Second, it is not a necessity that jobs should start executing immediately after they are requested: a reasonable delay before execution starts is acceptable in most cases.

In such a system, restricting collaboration to a fixed number of neighbors severely reduces the performance of the Grid itself: if this set is significantly smaller than the total size of the grid, this greatly restricts the available periods when a sufficient number of neighbor nodes can be simultaneously available. Increasing the number of neighbors per node is not a satisfactory solution either: doing this would increase the possibility for a node to free ride, by exploiting the initial altruism of each of its neighbors.

We therefore see that a node cannot be restricted to running jobs only at its direct neighbors without greatly reducing the efficiency of the system. In the worst case, a computation request would require more nodes than the number of neighbors, and thus could not execute at all. On the other hand, we need to keep a notion of neighbors, since these are the core of the mechanisms to avoid exploitation of the well-behaving nodes.

We address this dilemma by building an economic system between nodes: each node is

assigned a small number of neighbors. A node can of course trade resources with its direct neighbors, similarly to the solution discussed for collaborative content distribution networks. However, it can also trade resources with nodes that are not its direct neighbors: in such case, it must find a path of neighboring nodes that leads to the desired compute node. Intermediate nodes in this path are thus expected to mediate the collaboration between the requester node and the compute node. For example, if node A has a credit with node B, and node B has a credit with node C, then we can use the path A → B → C: B can act as a mediator to allow node A to use resources from node C. The problem thus translates into being able to find a path of nodes having credit with each other from the requesting node to the providing nodes (we assume that each compute node can carry only one computation at a time).

Fairness Enforcement Algorithm

Fairness enforcement in our collaborative grid works in two phases. First, when a job scheduling request is issued by one node requesting resources from its peers, the grid uses a decentralized scheduling algorithm to identify nodes that will be simultaneously available in the near future, and may be used to run this job (Fiscato et al., 2008). This algorithm initially selects a (random) set of nodes capable of executing the job together. It then iteratively improves its choice of nodes to find groups capable of starting the execution as soon as possible. This algorithm identifies groups of nodes based on their scheduled availability only, irrespective of fairness issues.

Each time an improved schedule is found for a given job, the initiator must check if it will be able to acquire rights to use the selected nodes. In other terms, it must find a path in the graph of neighboring relationships that links it to each of the selected nodes, and where each intermediate node is willing to mediate the resource usage. If at least one such path cannot be found, the schedule is declared invalid. The initiator then requests the scheduling algorithm to propose another solution, and so on.

A path of neighboring nodes will successfully mediate access to resources under the condition that each node would normally accept the job if it was initiated by its direct predecessor in the path. For example, a request from node A for a 1-hour long job to be executed by node C will be successful using path A → B → C if A has sufficient credit with B, and B has sufficient credit with C. If the path is found to be valid, then B will spend 1 hour of its credit with C, and gain 1 hour of credit with A. One could imagine a variant where node B would charge an additional contribution to A in payment for its brokering service.

Fairness enforcement within the whole collaborative grid is realized by the conjunction of multiple local neighboring relationships. In the example above, if A is a free-rider, then after exploiting B's initial generosity, A will not be able to use any path A → B → *. After it has exhausted the generosity of all its neighbors, A is effectively excluded from the collaboration, unless it starts reciprocating again.

One important case in this scheme is the case where A and C behave well in the system, but the chosen mediator B is a free-rider. In such

case, C will deny the resources to B so the path is unusable. A must therefore be able to find an alternative path composed of well-behaving nodes that connects it to C.

Finding Paths in the Overlay

In the above described system, it is crucial to design the graph of neighboring relationships carefully. This graph should have the following properties:

1. Nodes should be able to efficiently find paths from each other in the graph.
2. If one path fails, then nodes should be able to find an alternative path to the same destination.
3. Neighboring relationships must be symmetric: if node A considers B as its neighbor, and potentially requests B for resources, then B must also consider A as its neighbor and regularly request A for resources so that A can balance its credit with B.

The first requirement suggests the use of a DHT overlay between the compute nodes. Each node is initially assigned an ID by an external entity. When it joins the DHT, its list of neighbors in the fairness system is defined as the list of its fingers in the DHT. Organizing nodes along a DHT structure allows nodes to find paths of length $O(\log n)$ from each other, where n is the number of nodes in the system.

Most existing DHTs also allow to support the second requirement: if one path is considered as invalid, then one can easily find alternative paths leading to the same destination. Supporting the third requirement is however more difficult: most DHT systems do not impose that the links between their nodes are symmetric. This rules out traditional DHTs like Chord and Pastry.

We decided to base our neighboring overlay on Voronoi Diagrams, as is also done in the VoroNet overlay (Beaumont et al., 2007). In this

Figure 5. A Voronoi diagram (Weisstein)

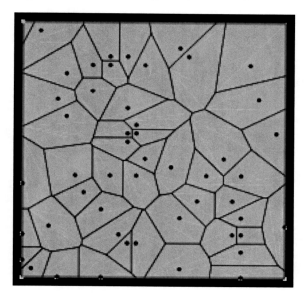

Figure 5. A Voronoi diagram (Weisstein)

overlay, each node is assigned a 2-dimensional coordinate randomly by an external entity. A Voronoi diagram associates each node s with a cell C(s), consisting of all points closer to s than to any other node. An example Voronoi diagram is shown in Figure 5. Each node, represented by a dot, maintains neighborhood relationships with the nodes responsible for contiguous cells. A Voronoi-based overlay has several interesting properties: (i) one can easily route messages by using geographical routing, where a message is always forwarded to one's neighbor that is closest to the destination; (ii) geographical routing also makes it easy to find alternative paths to a destination, for example by routing a message to one's second-closest neighbor; (iii) neighborhood relationships are symmetric by construction; (iv) Voronoi diagrams guarantee short paths between nodes, and maintain a small node degree, in average around 6.

When a node joins the Grid, it is assigned a coordinate by an external entity. It then joins the VoroNet overlay, by routing a message to its new coordinate and establishing neighborhood relationships with the nodes holding a cell contiguous to its own. On average this neighborhood

will contain 6 links; the new node is thus forced to establish good reciprocating relationships with them in order to benefit from the grid after using the initial altruism that the new neighbors will grant. Neighbors can easily check that the new node should indeed be included in their list. Importantly, when new nodes join or old nodes leave the system, the implied changes in neighborhood relationships remain local to the coordinates of the joined or departed node, so most neighborhood relationships remain unchanged.

Evaluation

We evaluate the performance of the fairness enforcement algorithm on a simulated 100-node grid. Every time unit, we submit 20 jobs requesting 5 machines for a duration of 5 time units each. Jobs are created during the first 5 time units, then no more job is submitted until the grid becomes idle again. Jobs are issued at randomly selected nodes. Each experiment lasts 100 time units: a job that has not started executing after this delay is considered as having failed.

Figure 6 shows the impact of the fairness algorithm on the scheduling algorithm, when no free-rider is present. When no fairness algorithm is present, most jobs start executing within 6 time units after they are submitted. No job fails. When using direct reciprocity, nodes exchange resources only with their direct neighbors, without actually building paths to nodes further away in the overlay. The scheduling quality drops considerably: the waiting time before a job starts increases greatly, and 8 jobs fail. When using transitive reciprocity, nodes are authorized to build paths of any length to each other through the overlay, and trade resources along these paths. The quality of scheduling is nearly as good as the first case, with most jobs starting to execute within 10 time units after being submitted. We however note that 6 jobs fail, meaning that a number of paths are considered invalid. Although in this experiment no node is actively free-riding, not every node has the

Figure 6. Impact of the fairness algorithms on scheduling performance

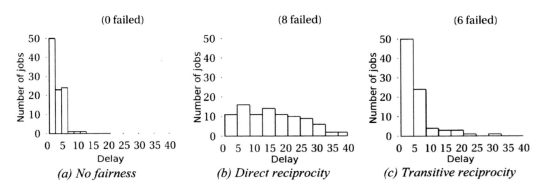

(a) No fairness (b) Direct reciprocity (c) Transitive reciprocity

Figure 7. Performance in the presence of 10% free-riding nodes

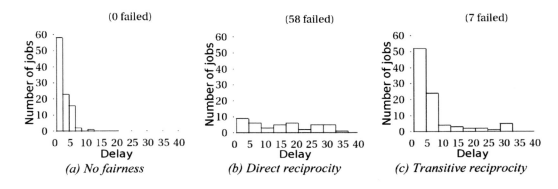

(a) No fairness (b) Direct reciprocity (c) Transitive reciprocity

opportunity to execute enough jobs for its peers before it needs resources from its neighbors.

Figure 7 shows the impact of the presence of 10% free-riding-nodes in the system. When no reciprocity is present, jobs get scheduled similarly to the first case, albeit with slightly greater delays. In other terms, free-riders can exploit the resources of the well-behaving nodes. Direct reciprocity enforces fairness, but at an unacceptably high cost: 58 jobs fail, most of which were issued by well-behaving nodes. When using transitive reciprocity, we enforce fairness at a much more acceptable cost. The delay before jobs can execute is higher than with no reciprocity, due to the higher number of failing paths passing through a free-rider. However, only 7 jobs fail: most of these jobs are the ones issued by free-riders after their neighbor's initial generosity has expired.

CONCLUSION

Many large-scale distributed applications rely on collaboration, where unrelated users or organizations share their resources for everyone's benefit. However, in such environments any node may attempt to maximize its own benefit by exploiting other's resources without contributing back. Collaborative systems must therefore deploy strategies to fight free-riders, and enforce collaborative behavior.

Tit-for-tat mechanisms have been deployed successfully in systems such as BitTorrent. However, tit-for-tat requires that collaboration is local in time. We studied two examples of asynchronous collaborative systems, where collaboration cannot be local in time. In such systems, applying instantaneous tit-for-tat mechanisms is not sufficient because one node must help the other before the second can reciprocate. Nodes therefore need to maintain a memory of past interactions, and determine their collaborative behavior according to this past experience. This requires that each node, including the well-behaving ones, is restricted to a limited number of other nodes to interact with. In the case of collaborative content distribution networks this is relatively easy to achieve, as in principle any node may help any other when the need arises. We can thus build efficient pairwise fairness enforcement mechanisms. In the case of a collaborative grid, the application performance depends on the ability to use any peer in the system to execute jobs. Direct pairwise reciprocity mechanisms severely hamper the performance of the system itself. Instead, we have shown that using simple transitive economic incentives, one can enforce collaboration with reduced impact on the overall system performance.

Incentive mechanisms discussed in this chapter have the property that they rely only on local decisions: each node decides autonomously on what is fair or not, without the need to report selfish behavior to a higher authority. Yet, the ability of free-riders to disrupt the collaboration is restricted to the initial generosity of their direct neighbors. We believe that this property is key to building truly large-scale collaborative systems, where unrelated nodes gracefully collaborate with each other, whether they like it or not.

REFERENCES

Adar, E., & Huberman, B. A. (2000). Free riding on Gnutella. *First Monday, 5*(10). Adler, S. (n.d.). *The slashdot effect: An analysis of three internet publications.* Retrieved from http://ssadler.phy.bnl.gov/adler/SDE/SlashDotEffect.html

Axelrod, R. (1984). *The Evolution of Cooperation.* New York: Basic Books.

Banga, G., & Druschel, P. (1997). Measuring the capacity of a web server. In *Proceedings of the USENIX Symposium on Internet Technologies and Systems.*

Beaumont, O., Kermarrec, A.-M., Marchal, L., & Riviere, E. (2007). VoroNet: A scalable object network based on Voronoi tessellations. In *Proceedings of the Parallel and Distributed Processing Symposium.*

Böhm, K., & Buchman, E. (2009). Free Riding-Aware Forwarding in Content-Addressable Networks. *VLDB Journal.*

Cohen, B. (2003). Incentives build robustness in BitTorrent. In *Proceedings of the Workshop on Economics of Peer-to-Peer Systems.*

Crovella, M., & Bestavros, A. (1996). Explaining world wide web traffic self-similarity. In *Proceedings of the ACM SIGCOMM Conference.*

Fiscato, M., Costa, P., & Pierre, G. (2008). On the feasibility of decentralized grid scheduling. In *Proceedings of the Workshop on Decentralized Self-Management for Grids, P2P, and User Communities,* Venice, Italy.

Foster, I., & Kesselman, C. (1998). *The Grid: Blueprint for a New Computing Infrastructure.* San Francisco: Morgan Kaufmann Publishers.

Jain, R., Chiu, D. M., & Hawe, W. (1984). *A Quantitative Measure of Fairness and Discrimination for Resource Allocation in Shared Systems.* DEC Research Report TR-301.

Lal, N. (2007). *Enforcing collaboration in a collaborative content distribution network.* Master's thesis, Vrije Universiteit, Amsterdam, The Netherlands.

Menasce, D. A., & Almeida, V. A. F. (2001). *Capacity Planning for Web Services.* Upper Saddle River, NJ: Prentice Hall.

Pierre, G., & van Steen, M. (2006). Globule: a collaborative content delivery network. *IEEE Communications Magazine, 44*(8), 127–133. doi:10.1109/MCOM.2006.1678120

Popescu, B. C., Crispo, B., & Tanenbaum, A. S. (2003). Secure data replication over untrusted hosts. In *Proceedings of the 9th Workshop on Hot Topics in Operating Systems.*

Szymaniak, M., Pierre, G., Simons-Nikolova, M., & van Steen, M. (2007). Enabling service adaptability with versatile anycast. *Concurrency and Computation, 19*(13), 1837–1863. doi:10.1002/cpe.1213

Weel, J. (2008). *Gossiptron: Efficient sharing on the grid without central coordination.* Master's thesis, Vrije Universiteit, Amsterdam, The Netherlands.

Weisstein, E. W. (n.d.). *Voronoi diagram.* From MathWorld - A Wolfram Web Resource. Retrieved from http://mathworld.wolfram.com/VoronoiDiagram.html

Section 5
Service–Oriented Applications of P2P and Grids

Chapter 37
Service Providers Indexing Using P2P Systems

G. Marchetto
Politecnico di Torino, Italy

M. Papa Manzillo
Politecnico di Torino, Italy

L. Torrero
Politecnico di Torino, Italy

L. Ciminiera
Politecnico di Torino, Italy

F. Risso
Politecnico di Torino, Italy

ABSTRACT

The idea of sharing resources across the network has become very popular during the last few years, leading to a diversified scenario in which shared resources include not only files and videos but also storage and CPU cycles. A new trend is to extend this paradigm toward a distributed architecture in which multiple network nodes cooperate to provide services in a distributed fashion, thus ensuring robustness and scalability. Peer-to-peer (P2P) overlays are the natural solution to achieve this goal as, thanks to their simplicity and flexibility, they can change their topology in order to fit the needs of the different kinds of services that can be provided on top of them. This chapter focuses on the indexing of nodes (i.e., the service providers) in these P2P systems, presenting the state-of-the-art solutions concerning the P2P-based indexing architectures and a taxonomy of possible services that can be built upon different overlay structures. Finally, emphasis is given to mechanisms implementing service selection based on some cost parameters (e.g., topological proximity) in order to introduce some mechanism based on optimality in case multiple service providers exist.

DOI: 10.4018/978-1-61520-686-5.ch037

INTRODUCTION

Sharing resources across the network became a mainstream technology in the mid-Eighties when Microsoft/IBM LAN Manager and UNIX NFS appeared on the market. At that time, sharing was mainly intended for disks and printing resources and was limited to local area networks. Only some years later, these systems were extended in order to operate also across the Internet; this required also deep changes, e.g., in case of IBM/Microsoft LAN Manager, the original NetBEUI protocol (which was non-routable) had to be replaced with TCP/IP. Before that, sharing was mainly intended as a way to use CPU cycles of a powerful super-computer (and, later, minicomputer) from other remote terminals.

The tremendous growth in terms of processing and storage capabilities in the recent years made the idea of resource sharing extremely interesting, since most of modern PCs have a huge amount of resources (CPU cycles, disk space, and, recently, bandwidth) that are not used for most of the time, and that can be shared without penalizing the local user of the machine. Therefore, the idea of sharing resources across the network has become very popular, leading to diversified scenarios in which shared resources include not just files but also storage (e.g., distributed file systems), bandwidth (e.g., network proxies, anonymizers, or real-time video streaming) and CPU cycles. In general, this same idea has broadened to en-compass not only basic resources available on the different machines, but also application services (i.e. application software providing some sort of service to other users over the network).

The resulting situation is that the same term is used with different meanings, in different contexts and communities. It is important to introduce defi-nitions of the most important terms used in this chapter, without claiming that those definitions are universally accepted. The human users or some automatic routines require *services* – e.g. some mathematical computation on special hardware, the content of one file, a telephone call, some disk space. A service is accessible by contacting one or more *service providers*, which are hosted in one or more network *nodes*, with the access to a specific service provider available on a single node. Each *node* may supply the access to one or more service providers. A service may require the use of other services, in order to be executed, resulting in a composed service. However, from the point of view of the indexing of nodes pro-viding a service, there is no distinction between composed and non-composed services.

The transition from early days *resource shar-ing* to nowadays *distributed systems* has been pos-sible thanks to two important changes: (a) a shift in the technical paradigm that enables resource sharing, and (b) a new user-level perspective. With respect to the first point, resource sharing was previously based mostly on a client-server paradigm (a server shared its resources with a set of clients), while recently each user is a service provider and a client at the same time. The unprecedented number of *service providers* required the development of a new generation of technologies, which are able to organize such systems in a more efficient way than the old centralized topology (which is the paradigm commonly adopted in client-server applications). With respect to the second point, systems are becoming *transparent* to the end-user. While in the early days a user was able to select if a given resource was local or remote, in the most recent systems the user asks for a service, and the systems provides it to him. While the user do not know the physical location of the resource (neither he wants to know), the system has to keep into consideration additional parameters that are typical in a location-aware distributed system. For instance, when a user ask for storage capabilities, such system does not have to locate simply a service provider with enough disk space, but this location must be possibly close enough so that the user does not even recognize that its data is flowing through the network.

Peer-to-Peer (P2P) and *Grid Computing* are the most common categories of applications currently in use that support advanced service sharing. In particular, P2P applications are currently characterized by a large-size distributed systems in which users dynamically exchange specific services, such as files – e.g., *Gnutella* (Klinberg & Manfredi, 2002), *eMule* (Breitkreuz, 2009), *bitTorrent* (Cohen, 2008) – or interact with each other – e.g., *Skype (*Baset & Schulzrinne, 2006). The basic concept of the P2P paradigm is that a *peer* relationship exists among all nodes in the network, which hence act as both client and server. Each peer may offer some services to the others (acting as a server) but can also exploit services offered by other peers (i.e., acting as a client). The system is extremely dynamic and it is able to cope with very high rates of node insertion/deletion within the system itself. On the other hand, Grid mainly refers to distributed systems usually intended to provide support to intensive computation tasks and complex data management. Generally, Grid systems are composed by a smaller number of nodes with respect to the P2P case. P2P and Grid recently met in what is known as *Desktop Grid computing* – *e.g.,* SETI@home (Anderson et al., 2008), *Folding@home* (Pande et al., 2009)–, i.e., a distributed computing paradigm that aims to exploit unused resources (storage, computational power, etc.) available on widely located (home) computers. The ubiquity of these systems is clearly observable from the number of platforms supported by the *Folding@home* project: the most common operating systems with single or multiple CPUs, Sony PlayStation3, ATI and NVIDIA GPU. Desktop Grids are essentially distributed systems where nodes with limited resources (e.g., few free CPU cycles) can submit jobs to other available peers. This paradigm can be generalized to a distributed service-oriented platform where users can ask for specific services to each other. The idea is that services that are currently provided by centralized solutions can migrate to decentralized P2P-based approaches,

thus ensuring performances, scalability, and robustness. An example of such approach is *Cloud Computing*, where resources distributed over the Internet are used to provide network-based services to a large amount of customers. For instance, the cloud computing paradigm can even be used to implement distributed data centers, as well as to provide computational power to thin clients (e.g., mobile devices like smartphones), which can acquire from "the cloud" the resources they need.

This chapter reports on the state-of-the-art solutions for the development of a proper indexing architecture in these P2P-based service-oriented platforms. A taxonomy of possible services that can be build upon an overlay network is provided. Furthermore, existing overlay architectures are analyzed and classified in order to identify which better support the specific types of provided services with respect to service localization. For instance, service localization refers to the task of indexing the available service providers and provides a scalable method to locate them when requested. In particular, the chapter presents the key aspects that are needed to leverage the characteristics of the underlying overlay topology in order to best fit the specific service requirements. The following section briefly reviews the basic principles of the P2P paradigm, with particular attention to the mechanisms that have been devised for information lookup in such systems; this section lays the ground for the following one, showing which mechanisms can be actually used to search for services and service providers. The third section of the chapter indeed introduces some different classes of services and illustrates the most significant solutions discussed in literature concerning the P2P-based service-oriented indexing architectures. The last part of the chapter presents some solutions proposed to ensure proximity-aware selection of service providers in a P2P environment, i.e., the capability to access the closest service provider, when multiple choices are available. Such mechanisms have been recently introduced in P2P systems in order to optimize network traffic (that may become massive, in some cases) and service access times, and therefore represents the future trends of the research effort in this area; in this respect, proximity-aware and indexing mechanisms complement each other in the effort of improving system performances.

BACKGROUND

One of the most important features in new-generation distributed systems such as Grid and Peer-to-peer applications is that they rely on the concept of overlay networks. An *overlay network* is a virtual infrastructure built on top of another, underlying, network. Each participating node has a set of adjacencies with other overlay nodes, independently of the underlying topology. Nodes in the overlay can be thought of as being connected by virtual or logical links, each of which corresponds to a path in the underlying network, possibly through many physical links. As result, the overlay shape is independent of the underlying topology and can change rapidly, even adapting to new requirements (e.g., new services) or new constraints (e.g., a change in the network status). Sundararaj et al. (2004) were aware of this when proposed their Virtuoso middleware. Indeed, Virtuoso has been designed to present to the final users a grid based infrastructure made up of virtual machines as a network made up of real computers. To do this Virtuoso uses two main components: VNET and VTTIF. VNET is the component that creates a virtual network that makes possible to move the virtual machines, without changing their virtual network address. The Virtual Topology and Traffic Inference Framework (VTTIF) is used to monitor the application topology (i.e. the number and the localization of the application processes) and to estimate the performances of the underlying network. Since network performances may change during time, VTTIF makes possible to decide if it is necessary to relocate the virtual machines running the application processes, thus achieving the best performances.

From the topological point of view, overlays can be divided in centralized topologies, also known as "hub and spoke" (a node is placed as the "hub" node, and all the other nodes setup a direct virtual link to it) and decentralized topologies (nodes setup virtual links among each other without relying on a hub node). Decentralized overlays, adopted in today's P2P networks, are usually further classified in *unstructured* (nodes can assume an arbitrary position in the overlay, although some additional rule are often used to organize the overlay as a whole), and *structured* (a node with a given characteristic is always placed in a precise position of the overlay). Unstructured and structured overlays differ in the type of architecture that peers construct, and in the policies they use to find service providers. In particular, in unstructured overlays, the relations among peers are not established according to predefined rules and hence there is no specific structure over which queries can be routed during service lookup procedures. On the contrary, in structured overlays peers are linked together according to well defined policies, so that they build a very precise (and deterministic) structure. Services are assigned to specific peers according to well-defined rules, thus service queries are reduced to the location of the peer responsible for the searched service. This can be performed efficiently by applying routing protocols over the structure.

None of these structures is optimal for every service and expected load: for instance, a *centralized* topology may be a good choice for a limited-size directory service, while it may not be suitable for a service that involve a large number of nodes and generate a huge load, due to the non-negligible overhead on the central node. Therefore, a more detailed description of the above categories is provided in the following.

Centralized P2P Overlays

Grid systems usually adopt this topology due to their generally small size: the hub acts as centralized scheduler and distributes jobs among the participating nodes. The centralized topology was also used in first-generation file-sharing P2P systems, such as Napster (Napster, 2001). Clearly, this solution cannot scale to a global overlay where millions of nodes use the infrastructure. Hence, decentralized topologies (structured and unstructured) have been proposed to overcome these scalability issues[1] and are currently adopted in the most common P2P networks.

Unstructured Overlays

Whenever a peer joins an unstructured overlay, it establishes a fixed number of connections with some of the other peers, which thus become its neighbors. Since the random component of this neighbor selection procedure is in general extremely high, peers result forming a random topology, which is lacking of any regularity in its structure. Hence, there are no relationships between services and their placement over the network, with consequent problems related both the efficiency and the effectiveness of specific service lookups as queries have to be *flooded* throughout the entire network in order to find the required service. Flooding is a routing technique that implies that a request received by a peer should be broadcasted to all its neighbors (except to the original sender). This technique is able to reach the target service, wherever it may be located in the overlay. In case of multiple copies, all of them will be reached by the request, and multiple copies of the same request may reach the same peer, in case of multiple paths within the overlay[2]. Flooding makes the communication highly reliable, because all the peers and all the possible paths are scanned, but it also generates a large amount of traffic over the network, caused by all the copies of the message. Hence, it is clear that such a

solution cannot scale to large networks because of the traffic it produces. Controlled flooding is a possible improvement that associates a lifetime (i.e., a Time-To-Live, TTL) to queries, so that they expire after a predefined number of hops they encompass (if the query does not find the service). This limits the overhead on the network, but clearly it introduces a non-zero probability that queries does not locate services even if they exist in the overlay, because not all the peers are involved in the search (i.e., a lookup procedure could result in a false negative). In both cases, each time a node that holds the queried service is reached by flooding, it generates a reply to the sender so that it can start exploiting the service. If more than one service provider is discovered by flooding, the sender can chose one among them or use all copies (or a subset of them) in order to achieve load balancing and/or better performance.

Search Improvements

Several techniques have been proposed to further reduce the overhead due to broadcast flooding. *Dynamic Query* (Fisk, 2008) consists in probing few neighbors with a small TTL value first with the aim of estimating the popularity of the searched service. This is used as initial input for an iterative process which, neighbor by neighbor, estimates the number of peers that have to be contacted in order to obtain the desired number of service providers (which might be more than one, e.g., in order to achieve load balancing), consequently evaluates a proper TTL for the query, and then sends it to the specific neighbor. This process lasts until the required number of service providers is reached or all neighbors have been visited. Another approach is the *Random Walk* (Lv et al., 2002) search, which is based on randomly selecting k neighbors at each hop to which propagating the query (which usually has a limited TTL). This method produced a very low overhead, but has the serious drawback of being greatly dependent on the network topology concerning the achieved performance. A simple extension to this method (Tsoumakos & Roussopoulos, 2003) consists in forwarding random walks toward the k neighbors that previously were able to satisfy the greatest number of queries. The performance of the network can further increase if nodes disseminate the knowledge they have about service locations (i.e., if service indexes are replicated in more peers). This can be obtained in a scalable way by applying well-known dissemination algorithms (Bailey, 1957). These algorithms have been implemented in many efficient protocols for P2P overlays. These protocols are usually known as *gossiping protocols*.

Topology Alternatives: Flat and Hierarchical Topologies

Concerning the overlay topology, unstructured networks can basically be classified in two major classes: *flat* and *hierarchical* topologies. The former makes every peer having roughly the same number of incoming links, thus the probability of being reached by queries is about the same for each node. The main issue of this topology is that nodes with limited bandwidth capabilities can be saturated by high traffic load due to queries, thus drastically reducing the performance of the entire network as showed by Truelove (2000). Hierarchical topologies overcome this issue by introducing a two-tier hierarchy of peers. Depending on its availability, bandwidth and connectivity (i.e., if it is placed behind NAT/Firewall module), a node is classified as *leaf node* or *supernode*. Basically, stable nodes with public IP address, without strict security constraints, and with large-bandwidth network connection become supernodes, the others are leaves. Leaves can only connect to supernodes, which are connected to both leaves and other supernodes. Furthermore, leaves register services they offer to the community at supernodes they connect to, so that it is sufficient for query messages to flood only among supernodes for finding the required service. In essence, only supernodes

actively participate at the overlay and search consists in exploring the service indexes stored in these nodes. This ensures that nodes with high bandwidth capabilities exclusively handle query messages, thus sensibly increasing the efficiency with respect to the pure flat topology.

Experimental studies (Hong, 2001; Matei et al., 2002; Saroiu et al., 2002) showed how hierarchical overlays usually evolve in scale-free topologies where the in-degree of nodes (i.e, the number of incoming edges) follows a power law distribution. Basically, supernodes continue to increase their degree by accepting new connections, thus the older is the node, the higher is its in-degree. This means that few nodes have very high degree (the oldest supernodes), a number of peers have average in-degree (the middle-aged supernodes), and the greatest part of peers have a very low in-degree (young supernodes and leaves). Adamic et al. (2001) showed how the power law characteristic of these topologies can significantly improve performance of random walk searches and proposed an algorithm that takes advantage of the existence of high degree nodes (usually called *hubs*): whenever a peer needs to locate a service, it starts a random walk, which, at each node, is forwarded to the neighbors with the highest degree. The running principle of this algorithm is that high degree nodes are expected to answer many queries, as they know many peers (i.e., they manage many services).

Clearly the main strength of unstructured overlays is the simplicity. Nodes join the overlay by connecting to some randomly chosen existing peers (which have to be supernodes in hierarchical networks) and during their lifetime they do not have to maintain any particular structure. Topologies described above simply define a hierarchy, but connections among nodes are established using a pseudo-random algorithm and can randomly change during peer lifetime. As highlighted above, this simplicity is paid for by the non-deterministic performance of service lookups. If we exclude the broadcast flooding (which cannot be used for its scalability issues), all search algorithms are based on random movements of query messages throughout the network and thus they cannot guarantee neither the success of the query resolution nor its maximum duration in terms of number of hops required.

Structured Overlays

In structured overlays, services are not randomly distributed among peers, but they are placed at specific locations determined according to some well-defined rules. The organization of stored information enables the deployment of effective routing protocols for their lookups, which are (*i*) deterministic and (*ii*) able to locate the service (or to decide that it is not present) in a bounded number of hops (which logarithmically grows with the network size, in most of the cases).

The idea is to introduce a Distributed Hash Table (DHT) in order to define a distributed indexing system for service location. Basically, a hash function is used to define a key space over which services are mapped. The key space is partitioned, so that each participating peer is responsible for a specific interval. Each service is assigned to the peer responsible for the key value that maps the service on the key space. Hence, lookups simply consist in moving throughout the DHT towards the node responsible for the searched key. Efficient routing can be achieved if nodes are organized in structures (i.e., well-defined rigid topologies) supporting the deployed DHT. For this reason these systems are called structured overlays.

Thanks to their service lookup guarantees, structured overlays are very attractive for applications that require locating rare services: the DHT ensures that a query message reaches the requested service in a small bounded number of hops, even if only one service provider exists. This is a great enhancement with respect to the unstructured overlays, where lookups of rare items might perform very poorly. Clearly, these lookup features are obtained to the detriment of

the system simplicity as nodes have to follow the above mentioned stringent rules concerning the overlay construction. In particular, nodes have to connect to a set of well-defined existing peers when joining the overlay, and maintain the constructed topology when new nodes join or existing nodes leave the overlay.

Some examples of structured overlays are: *Content Addressable Network (CAN)* (Ratnasamy et al., 2001), *Chord* (Stoica et al., 2001), *Kademlia* (Maymounkov & Mazieres, 2002), *Pastry* (Rowstron & Druschel, 2001), Bamboo (Rhea et al., 2004), *Tapestry* (Zhao et al., 2004), *Viceroy* (Malkhi et al., 2002), etc. An extensive and detailed description of these technologies is outside the scope of this chapter. However, Chord and Kademlia are presented in the following because of their heavy impact in this research field (both are cited by thousands of scientific papers).

Chord

Chord was one of the first technologies using a structured paradigm in the P2P context. Despite its relative oldness, several subsequent, even recent, works cite Chord and use it for drawing a comparison. In order to understand the operating principles of Chord, consider enumerating in increasing order a finite set of points on a circle: each point, is connected to a set of other points (similar to drawing some chords on such a circle), whose value is always greater than the considered one. In Chord, the set of points represents the key space and a hash function is adopted to map both nodes (usually their IP address) and services in this space. Each service is assigned to the node whose identifier has the smallest key value that is greater than the evaluated service key. The chords described above are the connections that each node has to maintain to support the DHT operation. In particular, nodes maintain pointers (chords) to other nodes whose identifiers are a power of two far away from them[3]. For example, given a 4-bit key space, a node whose hash value is 10 might

Figure 1. Service location in a 4-bit key space Chord network

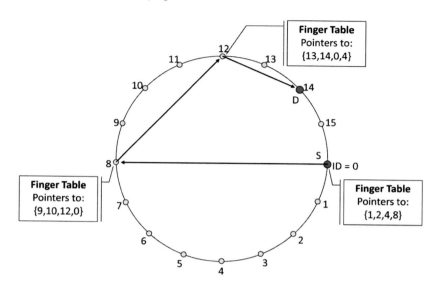

have a chord to nodes whose hash value is 11, 12 and 14 since $11 = 10+2^0$, $12 = 10+2^1$ and $14 = 10+2^2$. These connections are stored in a table, called finger table, and they are used for service location. Lookup messages are forwarded at each node using the entry in the table which points to the peer whose key is the greatest value that is less or equal than the searched service key. This ensures messages encompass no more than $O(\log N)$ hops to reach the required service. The lookup procedure is exemplified in Figure 1 for a Chord network built over a 4-bit key space.

When a node joins, a portion of keys handled by its successor in the circle have to be reassigned to the new peer. Analogously, when a peer leaves, keys it is responsible for have to be assigned to its successor in the circle. In both cases, finger tables of nodes have to be updated in order to guarantee routing operation.

The main issue of this algorithm may be that nodes can disconnect for unpredictable events (e.g. power loss, system crash, etc.), and they can leave the overlay in an inconsistent state (the finger tables may point offline nodes). For limiting this issue, Chord introduces a periodic overlay restructuring that may turn out in a heavy resource expense.

Kademlia

Kademlia tries to solve the Chord restructuring issue using a less rigid routing and, at same time, making nodes learn from their physiological searches through the overlay. In Kademlia, services and nodes are mapped in a 160-bit key space. Services are stored in the k closest peers in the key space. Distances in Kademlia are defined as the bitwise exclusive OR between two points in the key space. Each node maintains a set of 160 lists containing pointers to other peers. In particular, the ith list contains pointers to up to k nodes at distance d from the node, $2^i \le d < 2^{i+1}$. These lists are called k-buckets. To lookup a service, a node sends up to n (usually three) lookup messages in parallel to n peers chosen in the closest non-empty k-bucket. The n nodes reply with a message containing the k nodes closest to the searched key. This procedure is iterated until the sender finds the node responsible for the required service. Nodes have to be considered as leaves in a binary tree. The idea is that at each iteration the sender explores a region of the binary tree which is closer to the destination. Given the construction principles of k-buckets, it follows that lookup procedures last $O(\log N)$ iterations.

Figure 2 exemplifies a service lookup in a simple Kademlia network based on a 3-bit key space. The sender S (node 1) has to contact the destination D (node 5), which is responsible for the searched service. It starts to send a query message to node 6, which is the closest node to the destination that it knows (Figure 2(a)).

For the construction rules of k-buckets, node 6 has a deeper knowledge of the tree region containing node 5, i.e., considering the distance metric of Kademlia, node 5 is only $2^2 - 1$ units far from node 6, which hence can reach it through some node in its second k-bucket. Node 6 inserts the address of node 4 in its answer, which is then contacted by node 1 (Figure 2(b)). Node 4 is 1 unit far from node 5, i.e., its first k-bucket must contain node 5. Hence, node 4 conveys the address of node 5 to node 1, which can complete the lookup (Figure 2(c)). Peers gradually fill their k-buckets with the nodes they learn from the received messages.

In Kademlia, nodes update their *k*-buckets any time they receive a message and, only if they do not receive any message from some network area, they execute a light and localized refresh procedure. The resiliency of the resulting structure allows peers to avoid a graceful procedure when leaving the overlay. A new node that wants to join the overlay has to know at least one participating peer: it inserts this node in the proper *k*-bucket, and searches itself on the network in order to fill its *k*-buckets and to communicate its presence to other nodes.

P2P-BASED INDEXING SOLUTIONS

The main issue concerning the deployment of distributed services over P2P overlays is the selection of the P2P infrastructure that better fits the requirements of the specific service deployed. A number of different services can benefit from this novel distributed paradigm, ranging from the sharing of files (which was the precursor of this idea) or CPU cycles, to video streaming or

Figure 2. Service location in a 3-bit key space Kademlia network

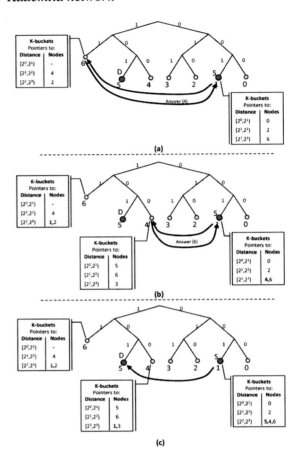

traffic relaying. Clearly, each service has different characteristics, which need to be properly supported by the underlying P2P infrastructure, so that users can efficiently access the offered features. For example, in a file sharing system users have to be able to quickly locate a specific file (rare, in general). On the contrary, if the offered service is the sharing of CPU cycles, the user is generally interested in locating any of the many nodes satisfying certain requirements (e.g., CPU speed not less than 1.5 GHz). However, as typically happens in the Desktop-Grid scenario, CPU cycles could be only one component of a more complex sharing service (including, for example, storage) which allows users to specify several additional parameters (e.g., interest for Linux rather than Windows machines). What these distributed architectures require is a proper indexing system for *services* and *service providers*. We can divide services in the following three classes according to their requirements and the estimate number of servants that are equivalent from the user point of view:

- **Class 1:** A service based on large groups of existing service providers considered equivalent by users (potentially all participating nodes form a single group).
- **Class 2:** A service based on small groups of service providers that users can consider equivalent (potentially every single node forms a group).
- **Class 3:** A highly customizable service (based on either many or few equivalent service providers) where users can specify multiple and complex service parameters.

In the first class of service under examination a large number of peers provide the same functionality, thus the goal is to locate one available service provider, with a possible optimization of the instance that is found with respect to some parameters (e.g., response time, available bandwidth, available CPU power). In this context the number of copies predominates over the number of distinct services available. In the second class of service, even if the number of existing service providers is large, the number of service providers a user can consider equivalent is small. In this context, users have to locate rare specific service providers. The third class of service considered (i.e, a highly customizable service) is characterized by the need to express complex queries in order to describe the service the user expects to receive. This class can be seen as a generalization of the other ones enriching queries with complex multi-dimensional attributes. As it will be shown in the following, this generalization implies a greater complexity and a smaller efficiency. Then

services are included in this class only if complex multi-dimensional attributes queries are strictly necessary. Otherwise the first two classes better fit the services. Attributes can specify exact values or ranges, thus defining four different types of multi-dimensional queries:

- **Exact Queries:** A user is interested in locating one or more service providers whose value for a given attribute is equal to a specified exact amount; "*FIND a node with Storage Capacity = 3 GB, File System = NTFS* " is an example of 2-dimensional exact query in a simple distributed storage system.
- **Sampling Queries:** A user is interested in locating any service provider whose value for a given attribute is within a specified range (i.e., a "sampling" service provider within a range); "*FIND a node with Access Bandwidth ≥ 2 Mb/s* " is an example of 1-dimensional sampling query in a distributed traffic relaying system.
- **Range Queries:** A user is interested in locating all service providers whose value for an attribute is within a specified range, e.g., "*FIND ALL nodes with 3 GB ≤ Storage Capacity ≤ 10 GB*".
- A multi-dimensional combination of these three types.

The following sections analyze these classes of service (also providing some examples) and report on the most important existing indexing solutions that can efficiently support each of them.

Service Based on Large Groups of Equivalent Service Providers

There are several examples of applications relaying on geographically distributed services that, from the point of view of users, are basically interchangeable. Let us think about a simple distributed storage system, where users are interested in locating a node with enough disk space to contain their files. The aim of the lookup is not to find a specific peer, but any of the many that can contain users' file. Another interesting example is SETI@ home, the distributed computing project developed at the University of California, Berkeley to utilize free CPU cycles over the Internet to processing complex data originated by radio telescopes, with the aim of Searching for Extraterrestrial Intelligence (SETI). Also in this case the key point is to find any of the available nodes.

Some indexing solutions were proposed in this context with the aim of fulfilling the service requirements and, in the same time, optimizing the overlay operation with respect to one or more functional aspects, such as the message forwarding overhead and the load balancing among peers. This section includes a detailed overview of some of these indexing architectures. In particular, we present:

- A P2P approach for service location in grid environments defined by Iamnitchi & Foster (2003).
- A P2P-based grid information service, developed by Puppin et al (2005).
- A uniform sampling based approach to locate service providers in a P2P environment (Awan et al, 2006).
- The DIStributed COnnectivity Service (DISCOS), proposed by Ciminiera et al (2008) for traffic relays lookup. In this context all nodes in the overlay are equivalent, as all of them can provide relaying service; hence, this is an example that perfectly fits with the characteristics of this class of services.

A P2P Approach for Service Location in Grids

Imanitchi & Foster (2003) proposed a P2P-based service indexing infrastructure where nodes are divided into virtual organizations (VO). Every participant publishes services it can offer on known peers within its organization. Users that need a specific service, typically send a request to a known node in the P2P overlay. This node processes the request: if it can provide the queried service, it replies to the sender, otherwise, it forwards the request to one or more of the known peers. The proposed solution partitions a general service discovery into four architectural components:

- The *membership protocol*, which specifies how nodes join the overlay and how they discover existing nodes in the overlay.
- The *overlay construction*, a function used to select the set of peers that are effectively part of the overlay. Indeed common networks include extremely heterogeneous peers, with different computing power, bandwidth and storage capabilities. To ensure efficiency, only the peers whose capabilities meet specific requirements should participate actively to the P2P overlay, according to the hierarchical P2P paradigm.
- The *preprocessing*, referring to all the procedures that can be executed before the lookup with the aim of enhance its performances. For example, service prefetching is considered a preprocessing technique.
- The *request processing*, which performs the parsing of an incoming query message at a node. It has a *local component* and a *remote component*. The local component is used to decide if the request can be satisfied at the local node. The remote component implements the request propagation rule, i.e., it defines how the node propagates the request if it cannot be satisfied locally.

Although more sophisticated techniques can be applied, Imanitchi & Foster (2003) assume a simple solution for the first three architectural components and elaborate on the fourth, specifically on its remote component. In particular, (*i*) a joining node is supposed to discover offline at least one existing peer to connect to (membership protocol), (*ii*) all new nodes are supposed to be accepted in the overlay (overlay construction), and (*iii*) no preprocessing is done. Given also the straightforward assumption for the local component of the request processing to be based on perfect matching (i.e., only the requests that exactly match the services provided by the peer are accepted), four forwarding strategies for the remote component have been considered:

- **Random walk:** The next peer is chosen randomly among the known peers
- Learning based: a request is forwarded to the peer that has answered a similar request before. If no knowledge is available, the query is forwarded randomly.
- **Best neighbor:** Each peer records the number of request answered by each one of its neighbors; the query is forwarded to the neighbor that answered the largest number of requests.
- **Learning based + best neighbor:** This strategy is equal to the learning based with the exception of the case where no neighbor knowledge is available; best neighbor strategy is used instead of the random choice in this situation.

Imanitchi & Foster (2003) evaluated these approaches by simulation. They focused on search costs, assuming TTL message set to infinite. The best approach resulted to be the learning based strategy. For a network of thousands of nodes, the average number of hops contacted to get a positive answer was around 20. A key advantage of the learning based strategy is the ability to take advantage from the query response similarity by using a possibly large cache. Indeed, at the system startup the strategy performs poorly, but as soon as nodes build their caches performances rapidly improve.

This work is a preliminary study about applicability of P2P techniques in Grid environment.

In particular the evaluated search methods are typical of unstructured P2P topologies.

A P2P-Based Grid Information Service

The unstructured flavor of P2P technologies is also used by Puppin et al (2005) that propose a distributed Grid environment based on a hierarchical unstructured P2P overlay. In particular, super-peers are used as servers for clusters of leaf-peers that form a virtual organization. The system is made up of two key entities: the *agent* and the *aggregator*. The agent runs on leaf-peers and is used to publish the service information of the node into a super-peer, while the aggregator runs on super-peers and collects service data, replies to queries, and, eventually, forwards them to other peers. In addition, the aggregator maintains an index of the services handled by the neighbor peers. Inside a virtual organization, super-peers may be replicated for load balancing and robustness purposes. In particular, super-peers within the same virtual organization can share the workload and ensure that information about available services is not lost when one of them leaves. When an agent publishes a service, the related information is spread to every aggregator (i.e., every super-peer) of the virtual organization. Agents then periodically send updates concerning the service status. The aggregators build a P2P overlay over which queries are routed during service lookups.

In order to improve routing efficiency and reduce flooding overhead, Puppin et al. (2005) introduced the *hop count routing index*, which is used to route messages according to the number of data elements that can be reached within a given number of hops The hop count routing index of a node is organized as a $M \times N$ matrix, where M is the number of neighbors and N is the horizon of the index, i.e., the maximum number of hops. The nth position in the mth row counts the number of services of a specific type that can be reached through neighbor m in n hops. The example in

Figure 3. Query routing example

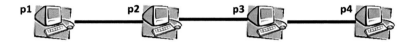

Routing table of peer p2

	Reachable in 1 hop	Reachable in 2 hops
Path	# Storage resources	# Storage resources
p3	2	9
p1	4	0

Figure 3 helps to understand how this routing algorithm works. Node 'p2' must determine which node in its neighborhood will be the next hop for a query concerning "memory"; the routing algorithm chooses node 'p3' as it enables reaching 9 memory services in two hops. When a new super-peer joins the overlay it sends information about the data it is responsible for to its neighbors: these neighbors update their tables and consider the joining peer 1 hop far from them.

The lookup algorithm operates as follows. A generic node performing a service lookup sends the query message to a super-peer. This peer starts evaluating locally the request and, eventually, forwards the message to the next hop using the hop count routing index. If a super-peer has not neighbors, it replies with a negative answer to the requesting node, which chooses another peer from its neighborhood and repeats the procedure. A TTL value, decremented at every hop, is used to define the horizon of messages. The algorithm aims at locating as many services as possible within a given TTL, in order to imitate the behavior of service locators in Grids. It may be seen as an improved version of the already mentioned controlled flooding with lifetime.

A Uniform Sampling Based Approach to Locate Service Providers

Previous architectures, even if based on unstructured P2P technologies, do not focus on load balancing among service providers. This may be an important issue as unstructured topologies do not have regularity by construction, thus possibly distributing service requests and, consequently, the load in a non uniform way among service providers – i.e., some service providers are returned from index system more frequently than others. For instance, this may happen if a service provider is indexed in a very popular and well connected area of the overlay while another one is indexed in an unpopular and not well connected area: in the former case the service provider may result more loaded than in the latter. Awan et al. (2006) proved that this problem can be solved by designing a lookup infrastructure where service providers are selected through a uniform sampling based mechanism. A trivial approach to obtain uniform sampling would be to create a centralized index of the existing service providers and pick up one randomly every time a service request occurs. Clearly, this approach is unfeasible for robustness and scalability reasons: the central server would be a single point of failure and would have to handle the periodical status updates sent by nodes, with consequent prohibitive overhead. To avoid this, the uniform sampling is realized through random walks. According to Awan et al (2006), "*a random walk of a given length samples uniformly at random from a set of nodes of a connected network if and only if the walk terminates at any node 'i' belonging to the network, with probability 1/N, where N is the number of nodes in the network*".

Random walk effectiveness is conditioned by the next hop choice at each node. The simplest approach consists in choosing the next hop uniformly among all neighbors, namely, if a node has four neighbors, the probability to move to any of them is 0.25. It can be proved that after a random walk encompassing $O(\log N)$ hops, the probability distribution of target nodes becomes stationary (Lovász, 1996). However, in most unstructured overlays, the probability distribution of target nodes reached through random walks is stationary but not uniform, as the probability of terminating at a node is directly proportional to the degree of the node. So, in a Gnutella-like overlay, where degrees may vary significantly, the above described approach does not lead to a uniform sampling. To overcome this problem, Awan et al (2006) propose the Random Weight Distribution (RWD) algorithm within their work concerning the sharing of CPU cycles over P2P networks. This algorithm is defined to set up transition probabilities p_{ij} (i.e., the probability that a service provider lookup message at a node i is forwarded to node j) of the overlay nodes in order to enable an efficient uniform sampling to random walks. The algorithm proceeds as follows. During the initialization phase, all the transition probabilities are set to:

$$p_{ij}^{rwd} = \begin{cases} 1/\rho & i \neq j \quad j \in \Gamma(i), \rho \geq d_{\max} \\ 1 - d_i/\rho & i = j \\ 0 & otherwise \end{cases}$$

where ρ is a static system parameter that must be greater than the maximum degree $d_{\max}$, $\Gamma(i)$ represents the neighborhood of node i and d_i is the degree of the node. After this initialization phase, each node starts "distributing" randomly and symmetrically the initial value of its self-transition probability (referred to as the *weight* of the node) among its neighbors. The distribution algorithm terminates at a node when either the node weight or the weight of all its neighbors becomes zero.

The algorithm converges to a global symmetric transition probability matrix. The authors proved that this is a sufficient condition for a random walk to yield a uniform sampling.

Distributed Connectivity Server (DISCOS)

Ciminiera et al (2008) proposed the DIStributed COnnectivity Service (DISCOS) as a distributed solution to ensure connectivity across Network Address Translators (NATs). NATs were developed with a client-server paradigm in mind: an internal client can contact an external server and obtain the required services. For this reason, the deployment of such NATs highly limits the end-to-end connectivity of all the applications that use different paradigms (e.g., VoIP and P2P). In particular, nodes behind NAT cannot be directly contacted (e.g., for establishing a multimedia session with them) by external nodes, unless proper traversal strategies are used. NAT traversal strategies consist of two main mechanisms: the *hole punching* and the *relaying*. The common idea is to make the NAT believe that the initiator is always the internal host: by doing this the NAT will create a temporary binding with the remote host, thus allowing incoming packets delivery. The *hole punching* technique tries to do this by establishing bidirectional channels between hosts. The basic idea is that internal hosts keep a persistent connection with an external rendezvous server, which is used to contact them from the outside. Then, hosts start to exchange probe packets in order to create bindings (or "holes", according to the hole punching terminology) across the NAT. This allows them to switch to direct communication exploiting the created holes. If hole punching fails, for example if hosts are behind NATs that impair end-to-end connectivity, the only solution available is *relaying*: hosts maintain persistent connections with an external node (the relay server) which handles and forwards all packets of the session. DISCOS distributes rendezvous and relaying functionalities (currently provided by central servers, with consequent lack in robustness and scalability) among participating nodes with enough resources (e.g., a public network address, a wideband Internet connection and free CPU cycles), which build a gossip-based unstructured P2P networks. These nodes are called *connectivity peers*. The DISCOS overlay is used by nodes behind NAT to locate a connectivity peer whenever they need rendezvous or relaying service. Lookups are based on iterative queries to connectivity peers: when a queried peer cannot provide the service (for example because it is busy), it provides the querying node with a set of other peers it knows; the querying node then contact these peers. Distributed NAT traversal is clearly an example of Class 1 service, as nodes behind NAT are interested in locating one of the available peers, preferably in a short time.

The paper shows how combining a gossip-based service provider advertisement with a scale-free overlay topology is a key point for ensuring architecture simplicity and fast service provider lookup. In a gossip-based scale-free network, hubs receive a large number of advertisement messages. Thus, they have the opportunity to learn a large number of new service providers that they can provide to users when queried. For this reason, queries are directed to hubs. DISCOS essentially exploits — and generalizes to the case of a single service provided by many nodes — the results achieved by Adamic et al. (2001) about random walk searches in scale-free overlays. Proper advertisement policies are defined to guarantee that peers build and maintain a scale-free topology, according to an approximated Barabasi-Albert model (Albert & Barabasi, 2002).

It is worth noticing that DISCOS has been engineered and validated on a Session Initiation Protocol (SIP) (Camarillo et al., 2002) — i.e., the popular signaling protocol usually deployed to manage Voice over IP (VoIP) sessions — infrastructure, but the solution is more general and it can be seen as a mechanism to efficiently support service provider location in the context of Class 1 services.

Services Based on Small Groups of Equivalent Service Providers

The distributed services belonging to this class differ from the ones discussed before. If previously the purpose of users was to find an available service provider among the many equivalent peers present in the network, here lookups consist in searching very rare services. In this class of services, each peer (or a small set of them) covers a specific role in the service provided by the infrastructure and is not interchangeable with any other. This makes harder the service provider localization procedure as now the infrastructure must be able to locate the particular peer (or the set of peers) that matches the service request.

A use-case of this class of services consists in providing to an application the different types of resources it needed for its execution in a distributed environment. These resources include computational resources, storage, and so on, thereby making fundamental the simultaneous availability of different service providers specialized in different fields. Czajkowski et al. (1999) define this problem as "the co-allocation problem" that consists in the allocation, configuration (i.e. the initializing phase of an application) and monitoring/control functionalities for the resource ensemble required by the application.

In the following, some architectures developed to support this class of services are reported:

- Gnutella (Klinberg & Manfredi, 2002), a file sharing system based on an unstructured topology.
- Kad (Stutzbach & Rejaie, 2006), a file sharing infrastructure based on the Kademlia structured overlay.
- RELOAD (Baset et al., 2008), a service oriented P2P infrastructure used to locate peers and establish channels among them.
- A "loosely consistent" DHT proposed by Traversat et al. (2003) in the context of the JXTA framework.

- SpiderNet (Gu et al., 2004), an architecture supporting the Service Composition paradigm, which is briefly introduced as an example of service belonging to this class; Service Composition consists in fact in combining two or more specific services together to form a complex service.

Gnutella

Indexing in a file sharing environment is a typical example of this class of services: every file can be stored, according to its popularity, by a medium or a small number of nodes. Generally speaking, these nodes are equivalent and the number of available files is large. The solution proposed by Gnutella (Klinberg & Manfredi, 2002) relies on an unstructured overlay. The system, nowadays, is based on an open protocol used by many, mature, applications. Early versions of this protocol used a flat topology but, for scalability issues, the infrastructure switched to a hierarchical paradigm starting from the 0.6 version. The already mentioned *Dynamic Query* (Fisk, 2008) was developed in this context.

Nodes that want to join the network try to connect to one of the several well-known, stable, bootstrap nodes, which are likely to be always available. Starting from 0.6 version, these bootstrap nodes are likely to be supernodes (in this system *ultrapeers*). The list of bootstrap nodes can be obtained from a website or kept in memory from the last time the node joint the network

Exploiting the mechanism of controlled flooding described in the unstructured overlays section, joining nodes send *ping* messages through the chosen ultrapeer. The answers, that flow using the reverse path of requests, are called *pong* and are generated by all nodes that receive the ping message. Using this mechanism, the newly joint nodes can establish new connections with other nodes. Starting from 0.6 version, the pong message caching was introduced for reducing the bandwidth consumption. This technique allows

the first ultrapeer to provide directly the list of its neighbors, avoiding the flooding mechanism.

The search mechanism relies on the flooding of *query* messages and the consequent *query response* messages. Evidently, the difference between these messages and the ping/pong couple consists in the condition that triggers the response: in the ping case every node answers, in the other case just nodes that known the requested file answer.

Once the requesting node has collected a list of results, it can start the download trough *get* and *push* messages. Unlike the query and ping messages, which are routed through the overlay, the effective file transmission happens directly between nodes.

Gnutella furnishes a working system, worldwide adopted since 2000, that uses relatively simple algorithms. Unfortunately, since it relies on controlled flooding technique, it can fail to locate an available service and can require a not bounded research time.

Kad

In 2003, the developers of the popular open source project eMule decided to add a decentralized indexing system to their application. They chose to rely on the newly presented Kademlia overlay and developed Kad. This solution overcomes the false negative results issue of controlled flooding, but at expense of greater complexity. Increasing the complexity makes easier to incur in implementation errors; for example Stutzbach & Rejaie (2006) reported on three bugs that had a deep impact on efficiency of Kad.

The implementation is substantially compliant to the description exposed by Maymounkov & Mazieres (2002) but uses a 128 bit key space instead of the 160 bit space described in the Kademlia specification. This has been done to maintain the compatibility with the eDonkey centralized protocol, which uses the MD4 hash algorithm to univocally identify the files. Other small differences include the expiration time of stored data and slightly modifications in the mechanism for adding data redundancy in the overlay.

Resource Location and Discovery (RELOAD)

REsource LOcation And Discovery (RELOAD), instead, address a completely different requirement: it focus on a P2P signaling protocol that can be used to build a distributed service infrastructure over the Internet. This is obtained through a self organizing overlay network service which supports efficient routing of messages among nodes and provides an efficient procedure for nodes to store data in the overlay. As described in Baset et al. (2008), RELOAD ensures these features by deploying a Chord-based overlay. According to the overlay principles of operation, nodes and services have a unique numeric identifier. RELOAD also considers *client nodes*, which have a unique identifier but are not part of the overlay because of their limited amount of resources (e.g., storage space, computing power, or battery power). The idea is that client nodes rely on an overlay peer to complete their functionalities. The architecture of RELOAD includes several layers:

- A *usage layer*, that defines an application specific usages of the generic services provided in the overlay.
- A *routing layer*, used to route messages through the overlay.
- A *storage component*, which is used to store and retrieve data.
- A *forwarding layer*, which provides packet forwarding services between nodes.
- A *topology plugin*, which implements the specific overlay algorithm. As mentioned before, Baset at al. (2008) define support for a Chord DHT. However, other DHTs can be implemented by manipulating this component.
- The core component of the architecture is the routing layer, which serves different purposes:

- It handles the requests sent through the usages, acting as a backend for every usage defined for RELOAD. The interaction with the usage layer is done via the abstract Message Routing API.
- It interacts directly with the storage to fetch and store data and with the topology plugin to handle overlay management messages.
- Typically, it performs queries on the overlay through the topology plugin in order to determine toward which peer sending an outgoing message..

To route messages among peers, RELOAD uses the recursive mechanism typical of Chord, i.e., each node reached by a query message forwards it to the known peer that is closest to the destination. The related response reaches the requesting node following the reverse path. However, RELOAD also supports a basic *iterative routing mode* where intermediate nodes just reply to the requesting node indicating the next hop to which forwarding the message.

RELOAD can support different applications running on it by means of the usage layer and can be used to create and handle channels among peers, to exchange data, enable media flows, and so on. If a peer wants to establish a channel with another peer, through RELOAD the target peer is locate starting from its unique identifier. Then the calling peer sends what is defined as an Attach Message to the called, in order to establish a channel with him. The infrastructure routes the message through the overlay until the target node is reached. Then, the called node sends an Attach Message on the reverse path, so that a bidirectional channel is established. RELOAD establishes a connection between users, but does not handle sessions: it only provides a logical channel to enable the session establishment.

A Loosely Consistent DHT for the JXTA Framework

Traversat et al. (2003) proposed a loosely consistent DHT (i.e., a particular structured system where peers have not to maintain a consistent view of the distributed hash status) for searching, publishing services, and routing queries in a JXTA (Williams, V., & Petrovic, M., 2008) network. JXTA is an open source project started by Sun Microsystems, Inc. and aims at providing a common P2P overlay infrastructure that can be used to implement a large variety of applications and services. Basically, the protocols included in JXTA standardize the procedures peers use to discover each other, advertise their own services, and discover services. The peers belonging to the JXTA overlay organize themselves into *peergroups*. These groups are sets of peers having common interests and that define common routing policies. By default, all peers also belong to the *world peergroup* that, consequently, includes all the peers in the overlay.

In the JXTA specification, nodes are divided in two hierarchical categories:

• The *rendezvous peers*, which are part of the overlay and maintain a distributed index of the published services inside each group.
• The *edge peers*, which publish their services in the rendezvous peers and use them for service lookups. Services advertisements are propagated among rendezvous peers only within the same peergroup.

Peergroups may offer services provided by all their peers, ensuring service availability even if multiple peers leave the overlay. In addition, peers may offer services that are provided individually. Since the mechanism used to locate resources in JXTA has to deal with service providers offering different services, this means that peers are not equivalent and the presented infrastructure falls under the class discussed in this section.

Traversat et al (2003) pointed out how the high maintenance overhead characterizing DHT-based overlays may drastically affect the effectiveness of a distributed service infrastructure because of the high rate with which nodes can join and leave in this context. Hence, given the importance of the lookup efficiency of DHTs for some applications, they propose an alternative solution to the standard JXTA, where rendezvous peers are organized in a loosely-consistent DHT. The system is "loosely-consistent" because of the procedure used for converging the rendezvous peer views, i.e., the lists of known peers belonging to the same peergroup that are stored locally at each rendezvous peer. Indeed, each rendezvous peer periodically selects a set of the peers in its view and sends a list of know peers to them, thus allowing the update of other rendezvous peer views. If the pinged peers do not respond, they are simply purged from the views. Since this procedure consists only in rendezvous peers exchanging locally peer information with other known peers, no global maintenance is done. This behavior may lead to temporarily or permanently inconsistent rendezvous peer views, thus making the entire overlay loosely consistent. However, in order to ensure service availability even in case of high churn rate, whenever an edge peer sends a service advertisement to a rendezvous peer, the rendezvous publishes the service not only on the rendezvous peer derived by the hashing function, but also on its immediate neighbors. By doing this, if the rendezvous peer storing the key related to the service leaves the overlay, the service key is still available on other rendezvous peers. This mechanism makes the overlay robust to inconsistent rendezvous peers views. Indeed, if a rendezvous peer is queried for a service and the peer responsible for the related key has gone offline, the queried peer detects the failure (i.e., the standard hash-based lookup over the DHTs fails) and immediately recomputes its peer view, thus forwarding the request to one of the immediate neighbors of the node that left. Since such neighbors store the key as well, the request is answered successfully and the node providing the service is located.

Service Composition: SpiderNet

Another interesting area to explore in this context is the Service Composition, which consists in combining two or more services together to form a more complex service. Hence, in this case the "final" service is a composition of several Class 2 services. A Service Composition framework usually receives a complex application that is subdivided in different tasks. These, in turn, are scheduled to nodes of a distributed environment. Innovative algorithms are currently under study, which are capable to schedule tasks on heterogeneous computational environments (i.e. service providers specialized in different services). For instance, Topcuoglu et al. (2002) defined two algorithms that perform task scheduling on heterogeneous environments. These differ from each other for the methodology they use for ranking tasks and, thus, change the assignment to service providers. Even though details of such algorithms are outside the scope of this presentation, it is useful to underline how authors also proved the efficiency of the proposed algorithms by extensive experimentation. Gu et al. (2004) define a different approach where the Service Composition mechanism can be considered as an extension of service discovery techniques and which uses the services offered by overlay nodes to perform tasks. In particular, Gu et al. (2004) propose a service oriented P2P framework called SpiderNet, where peers provide service components. SpiderNet can automatically map user composite service requests into an application service in the P2P overlay. The composite service request is made up of two parts:

• The function graph, defined as the graph where vertices are the required service functions, i.e., the specific functionalities composing the final service. Service functions are connected each other by two types of links:

• Dependency links, used to indicate that the output of a function is used as the input of the successor.

• Commutation links, used to indicate that the composition order of two functions can be inverted.

The function graphs are direct acyclic graphs where each node implements different functionalities.

• Quality of service requirements, indicating quality parameters for the service functions.

The service functions are dynamically mapped to peers of the overlay. This dynamic mapping requires the ability to locate service providers quickly and without the need to repeat searches. Indeed, as observed by Czajkowski et al. (1999), the infrastructure must be able to handle sudden crashes of service providers, thus replacing them quickly. In addition, it may happen that service providers that were supposed to provide computational resources actually cannot do that as they result overloaded by other running processes when the application is initialized. Hence, it is necessary to implement a quick localization mechanism to give the opportunity to the user to find an alternative service provider. To achieve these goals SpiderNet locates the required service providers using a DHT based on Pastry. First of all, when a peer providing a service component wants to join the overlay, it registers its service functionalities by storing related metadata into the DHT. To determine the peer responsible for the metadata, a key is computed by hashing the function name of the service component. When a peer wants to discover other peers providing specific service components, the requester computes the hash of each function name of each service component needed; then the requester looks up the DHT to determine the peers that will handle each service component.

A Highly Customizable Service Based on Attribute Values

Services belonging to this class are defined as highly customizable. This means that a user can add some attributes to the query to customize the requested service. Basically, these attributes are combined in service requests to define multi-dimensional queries, which have to be forwarded by the infrastructure to the peer that best matches the specified requirements. A user can perform essentially four types of multi-dimensional queries: (*i*) exact queries (i.e., queries that specify exact values for the attributes), (*ii*) sampling queries (i.e., queries that search any service provider whose value for one or more attributes is within given ranges), (*iii*) range queries (i.e., queries that search all service providers within a range), or (*iv*) a combination of them. While the first two types of queries can be supported by most of the solutions presented before, range queries are more knotty to handle. This class includes all services that require this kind of queries. This section will discuss in detail solutions designed to support these queries. In particular, next subsections will discuss:

- SWORD, a scalable service discovery service for wide area distributed systems presented by Oppenheimer et al. (2005).
- Mercury, a scalable protocol that supports multi-attribute range queries providing explicit load balancing (Bharambe et al, 2004).

SWORD

SWORD (Oppenheimer et al., 2005) is a scalable service discovery service for wide area distributed systems. Applications making use of SWORD are typically sensitive not only to per-node characteristics but also to inter-node ones; for this reason, SWORD allows queries for one or more *groups* of service providers, characterized by per-node, intra-group, and inter-group attribute values. For example a user may require a set of computing machine placed in North America with certain processing capabilities: these machines form a group. The same user may ask for another group of nodes placed in Italy with different computing capabilities. In addition, the user can specify in the request some intra-group attributes (e.g., the bandwidth availability between each pair of nodes within the group) and inter-group attributes (e.g., the maximum latency between nodes belonging to two different groups). Attributes may specify range values, preferred values within each range, and the sensitivity to the deviation from the preferred values using per-attribute penalty functions.

It is possible to distinguish two main components in SWORD architecture: the *query processor* and the *optimizer*. The query processor retrieves all the nodes matching the specified requirements, while the optimizer selects the ones that minimize the penalty functions defined in the query.

Nodes participating at the SWORD infrastructure are divided in two categories: the *server nodes*, which built a P2P overlay based on a Bamboo DHT (Rhea et al., 2004), and the *reporting nodes*, which publish (and periodically update) offered services into the server nodes through ad-hoc messages (the *measurement reports*), which basically consist in <attribute, value> pairs. Hence, reporting nodes offer the service, while server nodes implement the above mentioned query processor in a distributed way. A key is computed from each measurement report and used to determine which server node will be responsible for storing the reported information. This association is obtained by applying a particular function which maps contiguous values for a given attribute to contiguous values in the key space. Hence, it results that each server node is responsible for a well-known range of values for one or more attributes. Note that this is not a feature of typical DHT-based overlays and is the key point that enables range queries support in such systems. In SWORD, only per-node attributes are stored in the DHT. Inter-node attributes are handled through semi-centralized servers.

Figure 4. Example of the SingleQuery routing approach

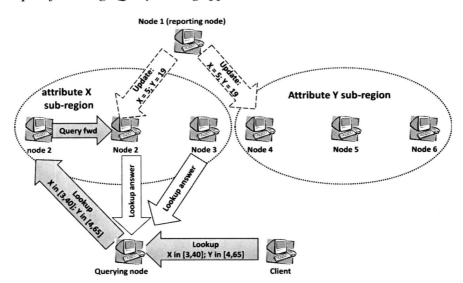

To issue a lookup, a node sends a request to any node of the infrastructure. The node that receives the lookup request is called *query node* and acts as a proxy, i.e., it sends subrequests to one or more server nodes. Lookups performed in SWORD include multi-dimensional range queries based on both per-node attributes and inter-nodes attributes. In particular, besides some straightforward solutions based on the deployment of semi-centralized index servers, two totally distributed approaches are defined to handle multi-dimensional range queries based on per-node attributes:

- **Single Query:** This approach is based on the fact that each measurement report includes all the attribute values representing a reporting node. This means that a multi-dimensional measurement report is sent to all server nodes responsible for the ranges in which the specified values of each attribute lie. These server nodes store <attribute, value> pairs for all the specified attributes. Even though this approach causes a consistent updating overhead, it allows sending a multi attribute query only to the nodes responsible for the target range of

one of the attributes. In more detail, the query is forwarded to a peer responsible for a key contained in the range of one of the specified attributes and then it is forwarded (using the successor pointer of the Bamboo DHT) to all the other nodes responsible for the keys in the queried range of that attribute. The attribute chosen is called *range search attribute* and is selected in order to minimize the number of nodes in the DHT that will be traversed by the query. Consider for example the multi-attribute lookup showed in Figure 4. The reporting node 'node 1' sends the reports update concerning all the attributes to all the involved node servers. A client who wants to perform a multi-attribute query, simply selects one attribute (for example 'X') and sends the query to one of the nodes belonging to the set that is responsible for that attribute. Then the multi-attribute query is completed forwarding the query to the remaining nodes of that set.

- **MultiQuery:** In this solution, reporting nodes send measurement reports related to different attributes to different sets of

Figure 5. Example of the MultiQuery routing approach

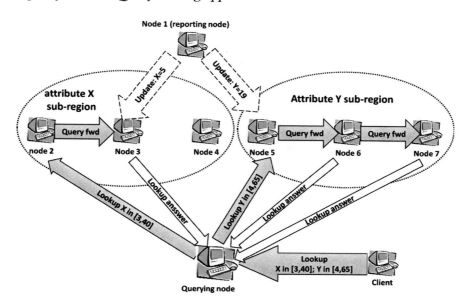

server nodes. This means that, given two attributes 'X' and 'Y', there is a set of server nodes responsible for the values of 'X' that is disjointed from the set of server nodes responsible for the values of 'Y'. This result in less bandwidth usage when sending reports and in less storage space required on peers. However it is no longer possible to forward a multi-dimensional range query only to one node responsible for one of the specified attribute range. Queries must be sent in parallel by the query node to as many server nodes as is the number of specific attributes. Figure 5 provides a MultiQuery example.

Once the multi-attribute range query concerning per-node attributes has been answered, the servers responsible for inter-node attributes are queried. Then, the optimizer selects the nodes that minimize the penalty functions.

Mercury

Range queries are supported by DHTs by introducing a particular mapping function for associating services to the overlay nodes, so that contiguous ranges of attribute values are mapped in contiguous portions of the key space. This may lead to a non uniform distribution of data among nodes, since some ranges of a given attribute may be more popular than others and, thus, nodes responsible for those ranges may result overloaded. Bharambe et al. (2004) proposed Mercury, a structured scalable solution that supports multi-attribute range queries with explicit load balancing among nodes. The authors validate this architecture in the context of a distributed gaming application, where is used to maintain the state of each player.

Mercury introduces the concept of *routing hubs* – i.e. logical collections of nodes responsible for a specific attribute. Each routing hub is organized in a circular overlay, where each node is responsible for a range of contiguous data values. New data values for the attributes are inserted in the infrastructure using data records, i.e. sets of attribute/value pairs. All the data/value pairs of a data record are replicated in all the hubs that are responsible for each attribute in the data record. This behavior leads to a high data replication that makes possible to query a single hub to perform multi-attribute range queries. To understand

Figure 6. Query routing in Mercury

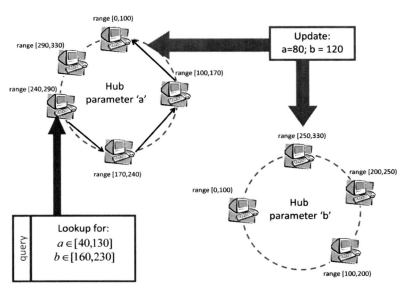

how this mechanism works, let us consider the scenario depicted in Figure 6. The red rectangle labeled "update" is a data record that is used to insert new values for the attributes 'a' and 'b', which, for example, may be considered the co-ordinates of a point in the space. The data record is copied integrally in both the hubs responsible for each one of the present attributes. To do this, the hub responsible for 'a' stores a copy of the data-record in the node responsible for the data range that includes the value of 'a' announced in the data-record. The hub responsible for 'b' performs the same operation: the data record is copied in the node responsible for the range that includes the announced value of 'b'. When the query is performed, only one of the hubs is contacted. According to the figure, let us assume that the hub responsible for 'a' is the queried one. To determine the nodes responsible for the range, the node responsible for the smallest value in the range is contacted first. In the example, this node is the one that handles the [0,100) interval. Then the query is forwarded to the successor of this node in the circular overlay. This forwarding procedure continues until the node responsible for the largest value of the range is reached. In the

example considered, the procedure terminates at the node responsible for the interval [100, 170). These two nodes are able to completely satisfy the multi-attribute range query because they also have a copy of the values of y previously announced in the data-record. From this example it is clear that if the query is routed to the hub whose attribute corresponds to the greatest range present in the query, many nodes in the hub will be contacted (since the interval is large, many contiguous nodes cover it). So in the real Mercury operation, the hub is not chosen randomly: the hub related to the attribute having the smallest range in the query is chosen and the query is forwarded to it (according to the terminology used by the authors, the queried hub is the one that is "most selective" for that query). The presented mechanism resembles the SingleQuery mechanism of SWORD.

Mercury defines an explicit load balancing mechanism to avoid peers to be overloaded when some attribute ranges are more popular than others. The solution consists in increasing the density of nodes in the portions of the value ranges that are heavily loaded, so that heavy loaded value ranges are smaller than the ones that are lightly loaded. Using an ad-hoc random sampling algorithm, nodes can estimate the density of peers in different parts of the hub. This allows them to determine the average load of the whole system and, consequently, their actual load level with respect to the other peers. A node that realizes to be heavily loaded sends probe messages on the network in order to discover lightly loaded peers. Once a probe finds a lightly loaded node, this node is asked to gracefully leave the overlay and to join the heavily loaded portion of the network.

Discussion on Service Classification

The service classification proposed in the previous paragraphs consists in three service classes. The first class includes the services that are provided by large groups of service providers while the second class is made up of different services offered by different groups of service providers. As mentioned, these groups are supposed to be small or even to contain just one service provider. The third class covers the services that may be highly customizable by the user, thus allowing queries including ranges of attributes. The previous paragraphs also presented examples of techniques falling under these categories. A conclusion that could derive from this section is that, although potentially both unstructured and structured overlays may be used for the first two classes, the existing literature tends to associate unstructured overlays to the services of the first class and structured overlays to the services of the second class. The relatively frequent adoption of unstructured overlays for the first class could be justified observing that the ability of structured overlays to quickly locate a specific service (obtained to the detriment of the system simplicity) is not required in a context where the number of equivalent service providers predominates over the number of distinct services available (Chawathe et al., 2003). On the contrary, the features of structured overlays may be significant to achieve good performances in the context of the second class of services, thus justifying the frequent

choice for a DHT. Indeed, in the second class of services the number of service providers that can be considered equivalent is relatively small, thus making the localization of rare specific service providers the main issue concerning the access to a given service.. Hence, the non-deterministic lookup performance of unstructured overlays may lead to a non negligible probability of missing a service provider that is actually available, with the consequent need to repeat the request. Even though the examined cases suggest this association, there are important exceptions that must be considered, and the previous sections provided examples in that sense. For instance, Gnutella, based on an unstructured overlay, is used to locate files, even though the file location service falls under the second class. This can be explained considering that in file sharing the download time predominates over the search time. So the additional time needed to locate files using an unstructured overlay may be acceptable, considering also that unstructured overlays are easier to develop, require a small maintenance overhead and are more robust to high churn when compared to structured overlays. Another interesting example consists in overlays where the same peers provide services belonging to different classes. For example P2PSIP (Bryan & Lowekamp, 2007) is a peer-to-peer overlay originally designed to locate users in a SIP (Camarillo et al., 2002) infrastructure. SIP is an application protocol used to establish media sessions; users are identified by Universal Resource Identifiers (URI) that are bound to temporary network addresses related to node where the user is currently located. To establish a media session with another user, it is necessary to retrieve the temporary address bound to the URI: this is made possible by centralized servers called SIP proxy servers that interact with a location services used to store such bindings. P2PSIP distributes the lookup functionality of the proxy server integrating it directly into peers that join the overlay forming a distributed lookup service. The overlay is typically a DHT. This lookup service falls under the second class, since only a specific node stores lookup information about a user. Subsequently NAT/firewall related issues have been taken into consideration by the developers of P2PSIP, which decided to add the relaying functionality enabling users behind NATs and firewalls to make and receive calls. Since all the service providers offer the same service, the relaying service falls under the first class. However service providers are located by performing a sort of random walk on the DHT: a key is randomly chosen and then the node responsible for that key is located and used as relay.

Considering now the third class of services, it is worth noticing that solutions proposed in the context of this class can also support services belonging to the other two classes, but add more complexity that is not necessary for these services. However, the indexing techniques used for the third class can perform range queries that are not possible when using other methodologies, thus adding flexibility that enables complex searches. The presence of range of attributes makes possible to implement some sort of QoS oriented searches that are not possible otherwise. For example, services consisting in CPU intensive tasks may require strict performances in terms of CPU clock frequency to meet certain levels of quality in terms of computational performances. So it is necessary to locate the service providers having CPU clocks in certain ranges. This can be done using range queries, thus ensuring that the computational tasks will be assigned to nodes that meet the QoS requirements. However, it is worth noticing that it is possible to implement a full QoS oriented queries through range queries only if the parameter of the quality of service can be stored in the index. For example, if there are QoS requirements concerning network bandwidth, it is not possible to use range queries to find a service provider that meets the requirements. This is because network bandwidth is influenced by both the endpoints of the communication; indeed it is not only determined by the service provider,

but also by the other node that asks for service. In general, it is not possible to store in the index such information for all the possible pairs.

PROXIMITY AWARE SELECTION

This section focuses on an issue that has attracted much attention in recent works on P2P systems: the *cost of contacting different service providers*. In the case where multiple service providers satisfy the user requirements, the client wants to locate the one that minimizes a cost function. Often the chosen cost function is the *distance* — i.e., clients should be able to use the topologically closest provider among all the available ones. The lack of this feature can turn in criticality: for example (Aggarwal et al., 2007) have shown that, in the case of Gnutella, at least 34% of file downloads is, actually, performed with a peer in a different AS, even if the same file is present on a peer in the same autonomous system as the client. This may have serious consequences in applications that make heavy use of bandwidth. Besides the serious case of file sharing, an extreme, though real, scenario is depicted by (Abadie et al., 2007). The European Organization for Nuclear Research (CERN) generates about 15PB raw and elaborated data per year; these information have to be spread across about 150 research sites in tens of countries. In this scenario, if the service provider distance is not taken in account, there is a large bandwidth waste. Moreover, this can results in longer transfer times, as data are moved across some network bottleneck that could be avoided with a smarter peer selection. These issues make the proximity aware search a fundamental improvement in the near future and a critic feature for next generation distributed systems.

The issue of determining the best service provider is orthogonal from the mechanism used for organizing the overlay—i.e., structured or unstructured network or, even, centralized server—and from the type of service (class 1, 2, or 3), but it requires that multiple service providers exist in the network.

After the search task, the requester has a subset R of all service providers S — i.e., $R \subseteq C$. The vast majority of current solutions uses a greedy approach for choosing the service providers among R: they select nodes that are available sooner. This approach is sub optimal because there is no guarantee that these nodes are closer to the requester and, thus, a large number of network hops might be required. This can influence negatively both the delay and the bandwidth (the probability to incur in a bottleneck increases) available between the two parties. Moreover, this may have an additional side effect for Internet Service Providers, which may experience an increasing demand in their upstream bandwidth due to necessity to contact remote entities. For instance, the fact that a requester does not select service providers based on their proximity, may further impair the capability of the system of selecting "near" nodes: if service providers become busy for distant requesters they cannot accept future requests from clients closer to them.

In order to select the best service provider, it is necessary to define algorithms that compute the distance between nodes and that force users to ask services preferably from closer nodes. The first step lies on determining the distance between the requester and the nodes in R. At first sight, this task looks easy because tools like the standard traceroute, combined with queries to whois databases for obtaining the AS number of each hop, allows a quite accurate measure of topological distance between the requester and any other node. Unfortunately this is not an efficient approach for, at least, two reasons: from user point of view, executing a traceroute and, for each hop, a whois query is extremely resource and time expensive, thus the start-up time is likely to be not acceptable. Moreover, assuming that start-up is not an issue, there are issues from the operator point of view: traceroute is resource-expensive for routers while whois queries, if done directly to official databases, can produce an excessive load on the servers of Internet Registries.

Lighter approaches rely on the assumption that the distance is directly proportional to round-trip time (RTT). Also in this case the solution looks simple in principle and consists in measuring directly the RTT by using tools like the standard ping. Even if this solution is lighter (and less accurate) than traceroute approach, often is not acceptable because is too time and resource consuming, especially for large cardinalities of the set R.

Distributed Binning

The first approach from a chronological point of view consists in binning users localized in the same topological area and, preferentially, using services offered by nodes belonging to the same bin of requester. This technique is discussed in (Ratnasamy et al., 2002) and requires that each node, independently, executes some initial steps:

1. Measurement of the RTT between the node itself and a pre-determined and common set of nodes, called landmarks.
2. Sorting of the landmarks in ascending order of measured RTT.
3. Classification of landmarks, according a predetermined schema based on RTT value

Let us assume, for example, that the predetermined set is composed by three landmarks, and the schema splits the range in three levels. Assume that the three classes of RTT are defined as follows: level 0 for RTT between [0, 100] ms, level 1 for RTT between [100, 200] ms and level 2 for RTT above 200 ms. If the distance of node n_1 from landmarks l_1, l_2 and l_3 are 192 ms, 65 ms and 85 ms respectively, the n_1 bin is "$l_2 l_3 l_1$: 001".

When a service provider is not available in the same bin of requester, the source is selected between peers belonging to similar bins (e.g., requester in $l_2 l_3 l_1$: 001 and source in $l_2 l_3 l_1$: 011 — i.e., just one different class).

Evaluation has been done through a simulative approach and shows that, as expected, increasing the number of landmarks results in more fine-grained binning and, thus, a better ratio between the average latency among users belonging to different bins and the average latency among users belonging to same bin. It has also been shown that, after three different delay levels, only minor gains can be achieved. Moreover, according to authors' results, this technique enables the selection of optimal mirror in about half of cases, while, in almost all other cases, the chosen mirrors are less than a factor of two away from the optimal one.

Vivaldi

As discussed above, the direct measurement of RTT between each couple of nodes when the set of nodes is extremely large is time and resource consuming. For this reason the Vivaldi algorithm (Dabek et al., 2004) has been developed: this technique allows the estimation of RTT between a large number of nodes with a small number of direct measurements.

This algorithm assigns, to each node, coordinates not necessarily related to a physical characteristic, but such that the distance is directly proportional to RTT. At the beginning, each node is labeled with a default coordinate and the following steps aim to gradually minimize the initial error. The minimization process uses the following squared-error function:

$$E = \sum_i \sum_j (L_{ij} - \|x_i - x_j\|)^2$$

where L_{ij} is the actual RTT between each i and j nodes of the system, and $\|x_i - x_j\|$ is their distance in the coordinate space. The squared error function was chosen for having a parallel to the displacement in a mass-spring system. Minimizing the system error is similar to minimizing the energy in a spring network.

From Hooke's law we can obtain the force F_{ij} applied to the node i from the spring between i

and j:

$$\vec{F}_{ij} = (L_{ij} - \|x_i - x_j\|) \times \vec{u}(x_i - x_j)$$

where $u(x_i\text{-}x_j)$ is the unit vector that gives the force direction. Each node i, regularly, measures the RTT toward another node j asking its coordinate. Then it corrects its position following the spring force. That is to say each node corrects its estimated position according the rule:

$$\vec{x}_i = \vec{x}_i + \delta \times \vec{F}_{ij}$$

where δ determines how deeply a node correct its coordinates. This rule is biased toward more recent measures. This can be an advantage for dynamic networks (like P2P or desktop grids ones) where the old samples, often, are outdated.

The δ parameter is determinant for system behavior: a large δ causes the nodes to move very rapidly while a small one allows the nodes explore low energy areas. The first behavior is desirable for new nodes that still have to determine their position in the coordinate system. While, increasing the accuracy of node localization, low values of δ may be considered good for avoiding that wrong measurements lead to large spurious movements. Since the force depends on both nodes of each pair, this consideration should be applied to the localization accuracy of both nodes. Thus, δ is given by:

$$\delta = c_c \frac{local\_error}{local\_error + remote\_error}$$

where c_c is a normalization coefficient ($c_c<1$). This formula should achieve quick convergence (with high local error, δ approaches 1), low oscillation (with small local error, δ approaches 0) and resilience with high error nodes (with high remote error, δ approaches 0).

Once every node has its coordinates, the RTT is estimated as the distance between the coordinates of nodes.

Figure 7. Locality prediction for oblivious clients architecture

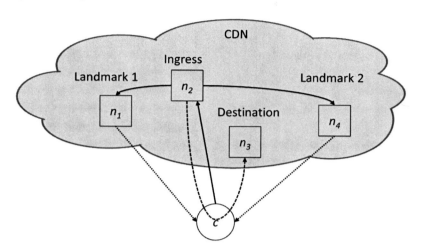

The Vivaldi algorithm, described above, can be used with any coordinate system that supports magnitude, addition and subtraction operations. Euclidean, spherical and height vector coordinate system have been analyzed. Simulative results show that 2D Euclidean system performs better than spherical one, while the height vector achieve better results than 3D Euclidean system, producing better results than the 2D version. The height vector is composed by a 2D Euclidean coordinate system plus a height. The 2D coordinate models the high-speed internet core, while the height reproduces the extra delay due to the access link (e.g., telephone modems or DSL). The difference with the 3D Euclidean system relies on the fact that the height must be always added – i.e., the distance between two nodes is given by the sum of first height plus the Euclidean distance plus the second height.

Authors' estimations showed that the RTT prediction error is one order of magnitude smaller than the real value.

Locality Prediction for Oblivious Clients

There are some contexts in which the requester does not even know that he is interfacing to a P2P network, but uses standard client-server protocols (e.g., HTTP, DNS). A noticeable example of this class of services is content delivery networks (CDN). In this context the service provider is always a web mirror and the locality-awareness is obtained with the support of companies that manage CDNs and that need to keep up-to-date large and costly maps of internet topology. In order to cope with this kind of locality-related issue, Shanahan & Freedman (2005) describe a technique that enables the selection of web mirror characterized by the lowest delay with respect to the requester. This is achieved through a small number of direct measurements, which make use of a set of landmarks.

As depicted by Figure 7, the architecture is fairly simple: the requester queries a randomly chosen mirror (e.g., known through the DNS service). This mirror is called ingress node and it asks other k mirrors, called landmarks, to measure the RTT with the client. The results of these queries are collected by the ingress node. This one can choose the most convenient mirror, called destination, and redirect the client there.

In order for this approach to be implemented, each mirror needs to know the RTT between itself and any other mirror in the network. This would require $O(n^2)$ direct measures or, more efficiently,

O(n) measures exploiting coordinate systems. The authors used the Vivaldi coordinate system described above.

The study analyzed four main issues:

1. Landmarks selection
2. Choice of the destination — i.e., the selected mirror
3. Number of direct measurements for each request — i.e., number of chosen landmarks
4. Number of measurements iterations for each request, as will be explained later

The first analyzed issue is the landmarks selection. Three different options have been analyzed for this issue: the simplest option consists in choosing randomly the landmark among all the available mirrors. The second method tries to have well distributed landmarks, which can be selected through the creation of random subsets and the choice of subset that minimize the following equation:

$$\left| mean(D_n) - mean(D_k) \right|^2 + \mathrm{var}(D_k)$$

where D_n is the set of all pair-wise distances for the subset n, while set n is the whole network and k is the analyzed subset. These distances are computed using Vivaldi. Finally the third method, called sphere, require that the ingress node makes the first RTT measure and then choose k-1 landmarks between the mirrors with a similar RTT. The name is due to the consideration that the landmarks are chosen on the surface of delay sphere with radius equal to the RTT with the client.

The second issue is the choice of selected mirror. There are two alternative options: the first relies on ingress node collect the information from landmark nodes and select as destination the landmark with the smallest value of RTT. Using this approach the destination can only be one of the landmarks. The second technique requires using Vivaldi also for clients. The ingress node use the measured RTT to compute Vivaldi coordinates

for client. Using this method the destination can be any mirror.

The third issue — i.e., the number of required measures — is analyzed using a simulative approach and is described later.

With respect to the fourth issue, these algorithms can be reiterated using the destination as input for the successive iteration. If the landmarks are randomly chosen, there is no benefit, but, with the sphere system, the radius is gradually smaller, while the ingress node should choose landmarks closer to the client at each iteration, with the well-distributed algorithm.

Experiments on the PlanetLab testbed (Peterson & Culler, 2008) show that sphere metric obtain best prediction results than the well-distributed algorithm and the random technique.

As expected, increasing the number of landmark lowers the prediction error but it is more resource expensive. Anyway using just three landmarks the predictive error is about four times better than random selection — i.e., one single landmark.

Surprisingly, the approach that computes Vivaldi coordinates also for clients yields strictly worse performance than the destination selection between landmarks when using a small number of measures. This can be explained with the biased choice of landmarks (e.g., close to the client) that does not permit to obtain accurate coordinates.

As expected, increasing the number of iterations and using the spherical system, the prediction error was lower at the expense of increased resource cost and convergence time.

Finally, the extra delay due to the choice of a suboptimal mirror, using this algorithm, is up to one order of magnitude less than the random selection.

SG-2

Also the SG-2 protocol (Jesi et al., 2007) uses Vivaldi but it is adopted for obtaining a proximity-aware topology, which is organized as a two level overlay. The highest level includes superpeers—i.e., nodes with superior performances that can serve a large number of other nodes, while the lowest lever is constituted by the others, called clients. Superpeers are connected to each other in delay spheres with radius equal to $tol + \delta$ where both tol and δ are system parameters chosen according the delay distribution of every nodes pairs at network layer . Clients try to connect to the most powerful superpeer within a delay radius of tol—i.e., the superpeer that can serve the greatest number of clients in the acceptable radius. The target overlay is composed by as few superpeers as possible. The SG-2 architecture is composed by four layers:

1. Virtual coordinate service
2. Peer sampling service
3. Local multicast service
4. Superpeer management service

The virtual coordinate service is based on the Vivaldi system described in a previous section. This system is fundamental because enables nodes to determine their delay with any other node by just knowing its virtual coordinate.

The peer sampling service is provided by Newscast (Jelasity et al., 2003), a gossip based network. Each node, independently by its computational power, knows c random nodes and it is aware of their Vivaldi coordinates. Periodically, it select one of the known nodes, update the corresponding timestamp that represent the last time that it has been checked, and the two nodes performs an exchange of their view — i.e., they merge the list of nodes with which they are connected to and each of them keeps only the c nodes with the more recent timestamp.

The local multicast service allows users to send messages to all nodes that are in a delay sphere centered on the sender. Nodes have to specify their Vivaldi coordinates s_m and the delay radius parameter r_m. The message is sent to all nodes known through Newscast and that have an estimated

delay with s_m less or equal to r_m. Recipients with a probability equal to $p = 1 - e^{-s/\theta}$ drop the message otherwise they read it and forward the message following the same rule of previous sender. In this way they act also as intermediate nodes. In the drop probability formula, s is the number of times the node has seen this message, while θ is a system parameter that should be chosen as a trade-off between a faster overlay convergence and a lower network consumption. This mechanism is used to avoid flooding.

Finally, the superpeer management service is used for choosing the optimal set of superpeer. Each node has a list of supernodes (spv) and a list of normal peers (clv). The algorithm uses two types of multicast messages:

1. SP-BCASTs, sent by superpeers and including the sender identifier, its capacity (in terms of standard nodes that can serve) and the dispatch timestamp
2. CL-BCASTs, sent by normal nodes when they are seeking a superpeer to register with and including just the sender identifier and the dispatch timestamp

A superpeer that receives a SP-BCAST message executes the following algorithm:

*   It inserts the new superpeer in clv or updates its timestamp
*   If the receiver is more powerful than the sender – i.e., it can serve more clients – it tries to takeover the other superpeer:
    ◦   It compute the number of clients n_f it can still manage
    ◦   It asks the sending superpeer to migrate n_f of its current users to the receiver.
*   If the receiver has no client yet and the latency with the other superpeer is less than or equal to tol, it becomes a normal peer and try to register itself, as user, with the other superpeer

When a client receive a SP-BCAST, it executes the following algorithm:

- It inserts the superpeer in *spv* or updates its timestamp
- If the client is not registered yet with a superpeer, it tries to register itself with the superpeer
- If the client is already registered with a superpeer but the new one is more powerful, it tries to migrate to the new superpeer

When a superpeer receives a CL-BCAST message and it has room enough for serving another client, it contacts the sender notifying its capacity and its availability for acting as superpeer.

When a client receives a CL-BCAST message, the node can switch to superpeer mode with the following probability:

$$p = \frac{s^2}{s^2 + \Theta^2}$$

where s is a coefficient directly proportional to the number of CL-BCAST messages received while Θ is a threshold computed for the node in that time instant. The Θ is directly proportional both to the node computational power and the time spent, in the past, to act as superpeer. The Θ varies with the time according the following formula:

$$\Theta(t) = \Theta(t-1) + (\alpha \cdot (t - t'))$$

where t is the current cycle and t' is the last cycle in which the node became a superpeer while α is a system parameter used for limiting the time influence.

Authors' simulations showed that was possible to construct overlay in which almost all the nodes can communicate within latency constrains similar to the average RTT of nodes at network level, the synergy between these mechanisms is exploited.

Oracle

Recently, a new architecture has been proposed that relies on the ISP support for measuring distances. ISPs are in a privileged position because they have an accurate knowledge of their topology and, they can estimate the approximate distance for every destination, because they are aware of routing (e.g., OSPF, BGP) messages. The first algorithm, in chronological order, is described in Aggarwal et al. (2007) and uses one centralized server, called oracle, for each ISP.

The requester uses the traditional indexing system for collecting a list of service providers. Before starting to send any request, the user asks the oracle (and, hence, the provider) to order the nodes in the previous list. The ISP can take into account different parameters for sorting the list, according to its objectives. Among the possible parameters, for each node in the network the oracle can take into account:

- Topological and geographical distance, e.g., same point of presence (PoP) of requester, same city, same region.
- Performances of routes between requester and supplier: expected delay, bandwidth, etc.
- Link congestion, enabling, thus, traffic engineering of P2P traffic

- While, for each node outside the AS of the ISP it is possible to evaluate:

- The number of AS hops, obtained analyzing the BGP announcements
- The distance to the edge of the AS
- The bandwidth, congestion and peering agreements

Once the list is sorted, the requester queries the service suppliers following the list order. This technique can be exploited for a large number of application, e.g., file sharing, overlay construction for unstructured networks, choice between mirrors or service suppliers. Simulative works on file sharing applications showed that this method definitely increases the locality of the file transfers, where transfers between two users that belong to the same AS increases one order of magnitude.

However, this approach has some issues: from the ISP point of view, it allows an attacker to obtain the network topology making ad-hoc requests to the oracle. From the user point of view, there are some privacy concerns about oracle centrality.

P4P

The oracle approach introduces another structural issue when the requested service is very popular and uniformly spread worldwide. The problem resides in the common limit of the indexing systems — i.e., structured or unstructured networks or centralized servers. If a very large number of replicas are stored in the indexing system, supply the complete list to all requesters would be very resource expensive or, for unstructured network, not feasible. In this case, generally, the subset R of results available for the requester is much smaller than the complete set C. Unfortunately, the subset is often obtained by randomly choosing some elements from the complete set. Thus the oracle can only choose a local minimum within the nodes contained in the subset. In this case, the improvement guaranteed by the oracle might be limited. This negative scenario can be very common: for example in the first type (see section "Service based on a large number of equivalent service providers") of services — i.e., all infrastructure is devoted to a single service — all requests belongs to this scenario.

P4P technology (Xie et al., 2008) is rooted in this issue and the solution lies on placing the locality awareness inside the indexing service keeping, anyway, to obtain locality information by the ISP. On this technology, the oracle is superseded by iTrackers. The latters do not order the lists, instead they offer to the indexing system the information needed for ranking the sources. This information can include:

- Policies of a network, e.g., time-of-day link usage
- Distances between users grouped according to a policy, e.g., distances between ISP points of presence (PoPs)

The distances may take into account of topological distance, bandwidth and/or financial cost of links, traffic engineering objectives.

The information offered by an iTracker can be obtained and used both by centralized indexing services (e.g., BitTorrent Tracker) and nodes constituting DHTs. In this way the indexing service can return optimal subsets of result.

CDNs as Oracles

A technique, in some way, similar to the distributed binning is the oracle-based Content Delivery Network (Choffnes & Bustamante, 2008). This algorithm requires a pre-determined and common landmark. Nevertheless unlike distributed binning, it does not make direct measures of RTT or distance, instead it try to exploit the knowledge of the CDN about the internet topology.

Each node do multiple DNS queries for obtaining the IP address of a website managed by a CDN (e.g., www.akamai.com). The network redirects the user to one of closest mirrors. Collecting these results, each node has the following ratio-map:

$$\mu_{a,w} = \left\langle m_1 \Rightarrow p_1, m_2 \Rightarrow p_2, \ldots, m_n \Rightarrow p_n \right\rangle$$

This means that the node a, querying the address w, has been redirected to the m_1 mirror with probability p_1, to the mirror m_2 with probability p_2 and so on. Every time two nodes a and b have to evaluate their distance they use the method of cosine similarity:

Figure 8. Example of a working system: n represents the requester, p the probability with which n is redirected to the mirror m_1 while μ_n is the resulting ratio-map.

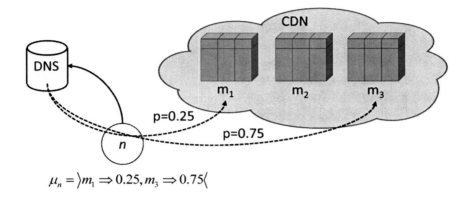

$$\cos\_sim(\mu_{a,w}, \mu_{b,w}) = \frac{\sum_{i \in I_{a,w}}(\mu_{a,w,i} \cdot \mu_{b,w,i})}{\sqrt{\sum_{i \in I_{a,w}} \mu^2_{a,w,i} \cdot \sum_{i \in I_{b,w}} \mu^2_{b,w,i}}}$$

where $I_{n,w}$ is the set of mirror server found for website w by node n and $\mu_{n,w,i}$ is the probability of being redirect to the mirror i by the node n for the website w. The result lies between 0 (no mirror in common) and 1 (all mirrors in common). If the value of cosine similarity is greater than a certain threshold (authors' choice was 0.15), the algorithm suggests to exchange data between these nodes.

The evaluation of this algorithm was done through a prototype: a plugin for the popular BitTorrent client Azureus. Due to the fact that Azureus and current implementation of BitTorrent lack of support to this technology, there are some limitations:

1. The exchange of ratio-maps can be done exclusively between nodes and not through the indexing system. Thus, there is the same issue, described above, that caused the evolution of oracle system to the P4P technique

2. It is hard to discover the localization, and thus the distance, for nodes that do not have the plugin. Since the prototype was installed only by 120,000 end users this scenario could be very common.

3. The only way for biasing the Azureus behavior and favoring close nodes was to allow them to skip the queue and start the download immediately. It would be useful granting them more bandwidth than far nodes, but it was not possible to implement this mechanism, for lack of support in Azureus API.

The statistical data collected by the plugin shows that, using this technology, the median number of IP hops toward a recommended node is less than half the number of hops toward a peer selected by actual implementation of Azureus. Moreover one-third of connections created with this algorithm are inside the same AS.

As expected, the latency decreases: the median value is two orders of magnitude less than the actual median.

Nevertheless, the average transfer speed has not been increased. The problem might rely on ISPs that heavily limit the access bandwidth. Thus, for users belonging to such ISPs could be more convenient, from a bandwidth point of view, to obtain files from outside the autonomous system. To this point, authors cite the case of a specific ISP that offers high performance inside its network (50Mb/s) while limits the bandwidth for connection with external nodes. In this context the CDN based oracle enable a median download rate higher by nearly one order of magnitude because it selects preferably local sources, which do not suffer of strict bandwidth limitations.

CONCLUSION

This chapter describes how distributed services can be efficiently deployed on peer-to-peer overlays, which are becoming the foundation of an increasing number of nowadays applications. In fact, distributed overlay can be considered an improvement over centralized solutions due to their better scalability characteristics and to their robustness, obtained by replicating the same functionalities on multiple peers. However, due to the large variety of services and the different properties associated to different types of overlays, we cannot define a specific underlying peer-to-peer topology that may be universally deployed and that is appropriate for any application. Indeed, the key issue in distributing services over peer-to-peer overlays is the service selection, i.e., the possible techniques to locate and choose service providers that offer a specific service. The effectiveness of these techniques is highly influenced by the type of service requested and by the number and distribution of service providers. Different types of searches for service retrieval require potentially different underlying peer-to-peer overlay topologies, i.e., unstructured peer-to-peer overlay topologies or structured ones. We have investigated three separated service classes, in order to find possible correlations with the service providers indexing mechanisms. The first service class assumes that peers offer a small group of services and that there are many equivalent peers. The analysis of the literature shows how the mechanisms widely adopted rely on unstructured overlays. The second class, on the contrary, requires the ability to locate a precise service provider offering a specific service among a large set of alternatives, with relatively small groups of equivalent providers. In this context, the most popular solution, although relevant exceptions exist, is the adoption of structured overlays. This may be due to unstructured overlays difficulty to precisely locate a service provider. Service composition, i.e., the capability to subdivide a service in sub-services assigned to separate peers, has been considered part of the second class of services. This is because, from the indexing point of view, the sub-services can be considered like independent services that must be bound to specific service providers offering specific functionalities. Finally, the third class requires the ability to improve service requests information by adding range queries on additional attributes in order to better define the needs of the user. DHTs are a valuable solution that permits range queries among *all* service providers enabling the choice of best ones. However it as been observed that multi-attributes range queries require modifications in the DHT algorithms to be handled efficiently.

Under these assumptions, the chapter analyzes relevant solutions that best fit to the characteristics of each class, thus providing a general overview of the current state-of-the-art available solutions to bring service oriented architectures in peer-to-peer environments.

Since the amount of data generated by some services may be huge (even 15PB/year), the choice of topologically close service providers may be a critical task. This may be seen as an additional step for refining searches, i.e., the localization of the best service provider in case multiple service providers exist. In fact, this requires the implementation of a clever mechanism of selection that is based on the concept of service cost, in a way that looks similar to the routing problem, i.e., the problem of path selection in current packet switching networks. Several research groups have investigated this problem, and it appears that one of the most important parameters to take into account is the service distance, i.e., the capability to select the service provider that is closest to the requester. This cost criteria might be able to guarantee fair end-do-end delay and fits into one of the biggest problem in nowadays ISP networks, i.e., the necessity to keep most of the traffic within the autonomous system in order to save costly links toward their upstream providers.

It is worth noticing how most of the solutions reviewed in this chapter have not been widely deployed in real environments and, thus, it is hard to clearly determine which technology will predominate. Moreover, the success or failure of such technologies is also driven by their diffusion that, in turn, strongly depends by the richness and relevance of the services that will be supported.

REFERENCES

Abadie, L., Badino, P., Baud, J., Casey, J., Frohner, A., Grosdidier, G., et al. (2007). Grid-Enabled Standards-based Data Management. In *24th IEEE Conference on Mass Storage Systems and Technologies, 2007. MSST 2007,* (pp. 60-71). doi: 10.1109/MSST.2007.4367964

Adamic, L. A., Lukose, R. M., Puniyani, A. R., & Huberman, B. A. (2001). Search in power-law networks. *Physical Review E: Statistical, Nonlinear, and Soft Matter Physics, 64*(4), 46135. doi:10.1103/PhysRevE.64.046135

Aggarwal, V., Feldmann, A., & Scheideler, C. (2007). Can ISPS and P2P users cooperate for improved performance? *SIGCOMM Comput. Commun. Rev., 37*(3), 29–40. doi:. doi:10.1145/1273445.1273449

Albert, R., & Barabási, A. (2002). Statistical mechanics of complex networks. *Reviews of Modern Physics, 74,* 47–97. doi:10.1103/RevModPhys.74.47

Anderson, D. P., Werthimer, D., Korpela, E., Cobb, J., Lebofsky, M., Bankay, R., et al. (2008). *SETI@home.* Retrieved November 18, 2008, from http://setiathome.berkeley.edu/

Awan, A., Ferreira, R. A., Jagannathan, S., & Grama, A. (2006). Unstructured peer-to-peer networks for sharing processor cycles. *Parallel Computing, 32*(2), 115–135. doi:10.1016/j.parco.2005.09.002

Bailey, N. T. J. (1957). *The Mathematical Theory of Epidemics.* New York: Hafner.

Baset, S., Jennings, C., Lowekamp, B., Rescorla, E., & Schulzrinne, H. (2008). *Resource Location and Discovery (RELOAD), P2P SIP working group.* In internet draft.

Baset, S. A., & Schulzrinne, H. G. (2006). An Analysis of the Skype Peer-to-Peer Internet Telephony Protocol. In *Proceedings INFOCOM 2006. 25th IEEE International Conference on Computer Communications,* (pp. 1-11). doi: 10.1109/INFOCOM.2006.312

Bharambe, A. R., Agrawal, M., & Seshan, S. (2004). Mercury: supporting scalable multi-attribute range queries. In *Proceedings of the 2004 conference on Applications, technologies, architectures, and protocols for computer communications* (pp. 353-366). Portland, OR: ACM. doi: 10.1145/1015467.1015507

Breitkreuz, H. (2009). eMule Project Home Page. *eMule Project.* Retrieved February 15, 2009, from http://www.emule-project.net

Bryan, D. A., & Lowekamp, B. B. (2007). Decentralizing SIP. *Queue, 5*(2), 34–41. doi:. doi:10.1145/1229899.1229910

Camarillo, G., Rosenberg, J., Schulzrinne, H., Johnston, A., Peterson, J., Sparks, R., et al. (2002). SIP Session Initiation Protocol. In *IETF Request for Comment 3261.*

Chawathe, Y., Ratnasamy, S., Breslau, L., Lanham, N., & Shenker, S. (2003). Making gnutella-like P2P systems scalable. In *Proceedings of the 2003 conference on Applications, technologies, architectures, and protocols for computer communications* (pp. 407-418). Karlsruhe, Germany: ACM. doi: 10.1145/863955.864000

Choffnes, D. R., & Bustamante, F. E. (2008). Taming the torrent: a practical approach to reducing cross-isp traffic in peer-to-peer systems. In *Proceedings of the ACM SIGCOMM 2008 conference on Data communication* (pp. 363-374). Seattle, WA: ACM. doi: 10.1145/1402958.1403000

Ciminiera, L., Marchetto, G., Risso, F., & Torrero, L. (2008). Distributed connectivity service for a SIP infrastructure. *Network, IEEE, 22*(5), 33–40. doi:10.1109/MNET.2008.4626230

Cohen, B. (2008, February 28). The BitTorrent Protocol Specification. *BitTorrent.org*. Retrieved February 15, 2009, from http://www.bittorrent.org/beps/bep_0003.html

Czajkowski, K., Foster, I., & Kesselman, C. (1999). Resource co-allocation in computational grids. In . *Proceedings of the The Eighth International Symposium on High Performance Distributed Computing, 1999*, 219–228. doi:10.1109/HPDC.1999.805301

Dabek, F., Cox, R., Kaashoek, F., & Morris, R. (2004). Vivaldi: a decentralized network coordinate system. *SIGCOMM Comput. Commun. Rev., 34*(4), 15–26. doi:10.1145/1030194.1015471

Fisk, A. (2008). Gnutella Dynamic Query Protocol v0.1. *Gnutella Developer's Forum*. Retrieved November 14, 2008, from http://www9.limewire.com/developer/dynamic_query.html

Gu, X., Nahrstedt, K., & Bin, Yu. (2004). SpiderNet: an integrated peer-to-peer service composition framework. In *Proceedings of the 13th IEEE International Symposium on High performance . Distributed Computing, 2004*, 110–119. doi:10.1109/HPDC.2004.1323507

Hong, T. (2001). Performance. In *Peer-to-Peer: Harnessing the Benefits of a Disruptive Technology,* (pp. 203-241). Sebastopol, CA: O'Reilly Media.

Iamnitchi, A., & Foster, I. (2003). A peer-to-peer approach to resource location in Grid environments. In *Grid resource management: state of the art and future trends* (pp. 413-429). Amsterdam: Kluwer Academic Publishers.

Jelasity, M., Kowalczyk, W., & van Steen, M. (2003). *Newscast computing*. Amsterdam: Vrije Universiteit Amsterdam, Department of Computer Science.

Jesi, G., Montresor, A., & Babaoglu, O. (2007). Proximity-Aware Superpeer Overlay Topologies. *Network and Service Management . IEEE Transactions on, 4*(2), 74–83. doi:10.1109/TNSM.2007.070904

Klinberg, T., & Manfredi, R. (2002, June). Gnutella 0.6. *Gnutella Development Forum*. Retrieved from http://groups.yahoo.com/group/the_gdf

Lovász, L. (1996). Random walks on graphs: A survey. *Combinatorics, Paul Erdös is Eighty, 2*, 353-398.

Lv, Q., Cao, P., Cohen, E., Li, K., & Shenker, S. (2002). Search and replication in unstructured peer-to-peer networks. In *Proceedings of the 2002 ACM SIGMETRICS international conference on Measurement and modeling of computer systems* (pp. 258-259). Marina Del Rey, CA: ACM. doi: 10.1145/511334.511369

Malkhi, D., Naor, M., & Ratajczak, D. (2002). Viceroy: a scalable and dynamic emulation of the butterfly. In *Proceedings of the twenty-first annual symposium on Principles of distributed computing* (pp. 183-192). Monterey, CA: ACM. doi: 10.1145/571825.571857

Matei, R., Iamnitchi, A., & Foster, P. (2002). Mapping the Gnutella network. *Internet Computing, IEEE, 6*(1), 50–57. doi:10.1109/4236.978369

Maymounkov, P., & Mazieres, D. (2002). Kademlia: A peer-to-peer information system based on the XOR metric. In *Proceedings of the 1st International Workshop on Peer-to-Peer Systems* (Vol. 258, p. 263). Berlin: Springer.

Napster protocol specification. (2001, March 12). *OpenNap*. Retrieved February 15, 2009, from http://opennap.sourceforge.net/napster.txt

Oppenheimer, D., Albrecht, J., Patterson, D., & Vahdat, A. (2005). Design and implementation tradeoffs for wide-area resource discovery. In *Proceedings of the 14th IEEE International Symposium on High Performance Distributed Computing, 2005, HPDC-14*, (pp. 113-124). doi: 10.1109/HPDC.2005.1520946

Pande, V. S., Bacallado, S., Beberg, A., Bowman, G., Brandman, R., Branson, K., et al. (2009). *Folding@home*. Retrieved February 15, 2009, from http://folding.stanford.edu/

Peterson, L., & Culler, D. (2008). PlanetLab testbed. *PlanetLab Consortium*. Retrieved November 16, 2008, from http://www.planet-lab.org

Puppin, D., Moncelli, S., Baraglia, R., Tonellotto, N., & Silvestri, F. (2005). A Grid Information Service Based on Peer-to-Peer. In *Euro-Par 2005 Parallel Processing* (pp. 454-464). doi: 10.1007/11549468

Ratnasamy, S., Francis, P., Handley, M., Karp, R., & Schenker, S. (2001). A scalable content-addressable network. In *Proceedings of the 2001 conference on Applications, technologies, architectures, and protocols for computer communications* (pp. 161-172). San Diego, CA: ACM. doi: 10.1145/383059.383072

Ratnasamy, S., Handley, M., Karp, R., & Shenker, S. (2002). Topologically-aware overlay construction and server selection. In *Proceedings of IEEE INFOCOM 2002, Twenty-First Annual Joint Conference of the IEEE Computer and Communications Societies*, (Vol. 3, pp. 1190-1199). doi: 10.1109/INFCOM.2002.1019369

Rhea, S., Geels, D., Roscoe, T., & Kubiatowicz, J. (2004). Handling churn in a DHT. In *Proceedings of the annual conference on USENIX Annual Technical Conference* (pp. 10-10). Boston: USENIX Association.

Rowstron, A. I. T., & Druschel, P. (2001). Pastry: Scalable, Decentralized Object Location, and Routing for Large-Scale Peer-to-Peer Systems. In *Proceedings of the IFIP/ACM International Conference on Distributed Systems Platforms Heidelberg* (pp. 329-350). Berlin: Springer-Verlag.

Saroiu, S., Gummadi, K. P., & Gribble, S. D. (2002). *A measurement study of peer-to-peer file sharing systems*, (Tech. Rep. No. UW-CSE-01-06-02). Seattle, WA: University of Washington, Department of Computer Science & Engineering.

Shanahan, K., & Freedman, M. (2005). Locality Prediction for Oblivious Clients. In *Peer-to-Peer Systems IV*, (pp. 252-263). doi: 10.1007/11558989

Stoica, I., Morris, R., Karger, D., Kaashoek, M. F., & Balakrishnan, H. (2001). Chord: A scalable peer-to-peer lookup service for internet applications. In *Proceedings of the 2001 conference on Applications, technologies, architectures, and protocols for computer communications*, (pp. 149-160). San Diego, CA: ACM. doi: 10.1145/383059.383071

Stutzbach, D., & Rejaie, R. (2006). Improving Lookup Performance Over a Widely-Deployed DHT. In *Proceedings INFOCOM 2006, 25th IEEE International Conference on Computer Communications*, (pp. 1-12). doi: 10.1109/INFOCOM.2006.329

Sundararaj, A. I., Gupta, A., & Dinda, P. A. (2004). Dynamic topology adaptation of virtual networks of virtual machines. In *Proceedings of the 7th workshop on Workshop on languages, compilers, and run-time support for scalable systems*, (pp. 1-8). Houston, TX: ACM. doi: 10.1145/1066650.1066665

Topcuoglu, H., Hariri, S., & Min-You Wu. (2002). Performance-effective and low-complexity task scheduling for heterogeneous computing. *Parallel and Distributed Systems, IEEE Transactions on, 13*(3), 260-274. doi: 10.1109/71.993206.

Traversat, B., Abdelaziz, M., & Pouyoul, E. (2003). *Project JXTA: A Loosely-Consistent DHT Rendezvous Walker*. Sun Microsystems, Inc. Retrieved November 16, 2008, from http://research.sun.com/spotlight/misc/jxta-dht.pdf

Truelove, K. (2000). *To the bandwidth barrier and beyond*. Clip 2, Inc.

Tsoumakos, D., & Roussopoulos, N. (2003). Adaptive probabilistic search for peer-to-peer networks. In *Proceedings of the Third International Conference on Peer-to-Peer Computing, 2003, (P2P 2003)*, (pp. 102-109).

Williams, V., & Petrovic, M. (2008). JXTA Framework. *JXTA Community Project*. Retrieved November 16, 2008, from https://jxta.dev.java.net/

Xie, H., Yang, Y. R., Krishnamurthy, A., Liu, Y. G., & Silberschatz, A. (2008). P4P: provider portal for applications. In *Proceedings of the ACM SIGCOMM 2008 conference on Data communication*, (pp. 351-362). Seattle, WA: ACM. doi: 10.1145/1402958.1402999

Zhao, B., Ling Huang, Stribling, J., Rhea, S., Joseph, A., & Kubiatowicz, J. (2004). Tapestry: a resilient global-scale overlay for service deployment. *Selected Areas in Communications, IEEE Journal on, 22*(1), 41-53. doi: 10.1109/JSAC.2003.818784

ENDNOTES

[1]   Another reason that drove the development of decentralized overlays was the vulnerability of centralized solutions to being shut down by police and other authorities in case of copyright violations. For example, Napster was shut down by a U.S. Federal Court in 2001. However, these legal reasons are not related to the focus of this chapter, which assumes the deployment of P2P overlays for the provision of law compliant distributed services.

[2]   Another problem of flooding is that requests may circulate forever, in the likely case the overlay can be modeled as a cyclic graph. A possible solution consists in recording inside each request all the IDs of the peers already visited. When a new request is received, the peer scans this list, looking for its own ID; if this is the case, the request is dropped because it is returning to the same place after traveling on a closed path.

[3]   If the node exactly distant a power of two is missing, a node connects to the peer at the shorter distance that is greater that the considered power of two.

Chapter 38
SIP Protocol for Supporting Grid Computing

Aldo Campi
University of Bologna, Italy

Franco Callegati
University of Bologna, Italy

ABSTRACT

This chapter advocates migrating sufficient functionality into the network as to allow direct support to grid computing services. This approach is realized by making use of session initiation protocol (sip) as the medium to support the signaling among grid applications and network. The authors elaborate on the advantages of this approach, which benefits directly from the session management capabilities of sip and enables application-oriented functions.

INTRODUCTION

Grid computing is migrating from traditional high performance and distributed computing to pervasive and utility computing based on heterogeneous networks and clients. The success of this new range of services is directly linked to the effectiveness of the networking infrastructure used to deliver them.

Grid computing services aim at integrating and manage resources according to application requirements and within distributed, heterogeneous, dynamic environments. On the other hand, networks and, in particular their control planes, regardless of the specific implementation, deal with topology, capacity, connectivity and routing. In general, these two worlds have very different perspectives and talk very different languages. So far the direct link between the application and the network is still missing and the applications usually rely on virtual overlay topologies that provide connectivity according to a pre-defined scheme and are built a-priori in the network.

The present typical scenario is that, as proposed for instance by the Open Grid Forum (Open Grid Forum, n.d.), applications talk end-to-end and resource management is provided by means of

DOI: 10.4018/978-1-61520-686-5.ch038

web-services, an approach that has the merit to provide a standard and flexible communication (Tuecke, Czajkowski, Foster, Graham, Kesselman, Maguire, et al, 2003)(Foster, Berry, Djaoui, Grimshaw, Horn, Kishimoto, et al, 2004). This is a typical overlay approach with associated merits and drawbacks. In particular it may result in inefficiencies in the use of the network resources and in limited functionalities with respect to what achievable with a more integrated approach. Moreover limitations exist for implementations targeting large populations of users in terms of scalability, fault tolerance, performance, quality of service provisioning etc.

An alternative approach may be that of migrating into the network the intelligence needed to support the Grid computing services, making the network node capable of interacting with the network in an application oriented language. The realization of this goal requires the disintegration of numerous barriers that normally separate application services, IT resources (computing systems) and networks. This chapter discusses this scenario and proposes a possible approach to solve the problem, based on an application layer signalling protocol able to work with a broad spectrum of existing and future IP protocols and services.

Up to now the application layer services (e.g. resource discovery, reservation, etc.) have been deployed with some form of centralized mechanisms based on web services, without bothering of exploiting any knowledge of the transport services. The result is that, in most cases, the Grid signaling is segregated on a separate infrastructure while the transport network is used as a best effort transport facility to carry the application data almost independently from the signaling. The reasons for this can be found in the fact that service provisioning is an operator task for the part concerning network connectivity and is a user "private" task for the part concerning IT resources. Currently, operator and user do not communicate and service provisioning is not available "on-the-fly" at the user premises.

Some solutions to provide users with an abstract view of the network resources (resource virtualization) have been proposed already, like the User-Controlled Light-paths (UCLP) by Bill St. Arnaud (St. Arnaud, et al, 2004)(St. Arnaud, et al, 2006). In UCLP users manage the optical network resources they own through a web service-based infrastructure. UCLP is based on the Grid services concept and builds on the Jini and JavaSpaces technologies. Similarly in the framework of the ITU-T there has been effort in the direction and trying to standardize high-level triggering of network services. The most significant example is the ITU-T Next Generation Network (NGN) architecture (Cochennec, 2002)(ITU-T Recommendation Y.2001, 2004) (ITU-T Recommendation Y.2011, 2004)(Recommendation Y.2012, Functional requirements and architecture of the NGN release 1, 2006). Through the logical partitioning of functions into a Service Stratum and Transport Stratum, NGN is capable of abstracting the connectivity services over a IP-based service-oriented network architecture.

Moreover there are three large research projects focus on developing mechanisms for end-to-end coordinated reservations across network domains of geographically distributed high-end computing resources:

- **PHOSPHORUS (EU-IST-** http://www.ist-phosphorus.org)**: Focuses on enabling on-demand end-to-end network services across multiple heterogeneous domains, treating the underlying network as a first class Grid resource, thus developing integration between application middleware and transport networks.
- **Enlightened computing (NSF-** http://www.enlightenedcomputing.org)**: Develops Grid middleware that views the network as a Grid resource at the same level as the compute and storage resources, thus allowing applications to dynamically request computing and storage

resources along with the necessary dedicated bandwidth.

- **G-Lambda (JPN-** http://www.g-lambda. net**)**: Establishes a standard Web service interface (Grid Network Service/Web Service Interface GNS-WSI) between the Grid resource manager and the network service manager.

The first two approaches are user-centric since the user can have knowledge and in some cases control of the network topology and resources, while the G-Lambda has a network centric approach.

All these works provide very valuable contributions and ideas but with the lack of generality to be applicable to a general mass market Grid computing application on a general and public networking infrastructure. They are either limited to specific networking scenarios or to specific application scenarios. Moreover in case of a public network operated by networks operators they do not allow an easy separation between user and operator responsibilities.

The step forward proposed here is based on the idea to implement a signalling architecture that can make the Grid applications and the network evolve into a fully integrated infrastructure while still allowing to keep a clear separation of the roles of users and applications, as well as of different network domains. The idea is that the boundaries between application, network control and information transport disappear thanks to an integration layer provided by the new signalling infrastructure.

The core of the proposal is to provide full application aware networking for Grid networks by means of a single signalling protocol, thus providing the application with the opportunity to request a given resource (i.e. remote storage space, remote computation, media stream, etc.) and the communication facilities required to connect to it with proper grade of service fully relying on the network infrastructure.

To this purpose, the following action points are crucial to this end:

- Make the application capable of exchanging semantically rich messages with the network to issue service requests for the negotiation and reservation of the needed resources;
- Choose a semantically rich language that is general enough to be useable by any sort of application for any possible kind of task;
- Define a "technology independent" methodology to control network resources by mapping the service request into network control plane directives.

Some preliminary studies in this direction appeared recently offer the user-controlled invocation of connectivity service, IT service management as well as general service composition, but all these research efforts were still focus on specific scenarios or on specific sub-problems (Baroncelli, Martini, Martini, & Castodi, 2007)(Baroncelli, Martini, Valcarnghi & Castoldi, 2006)(Simeonidou, Zervas, Nejbati, Callegati, Campi, & Cerroni, 2007)(Ciulli, Carrozzo, Giorgi, Zervas, Escalona, Qin, et al, 2008)(Zervas, Nejabati,Campi, Qin, Simeonidou, Callegati, et al, 2007). This work aims at providing a full view of the possible solution to the problem, considering at once all the various issues to be addressed.

The chapter will propose to use the Session Initiation Protocol (SIP) (Rosenberg, et al, 2002) as the medium to support the signalling underlining the aforementioned action points. By exploiting the session management message flows already provided by SIP, we will show that it is possible to implement application oriented functions such as resource publication, resource discovery and resource reservation, including communication facilities (i.e. QoS). This is done in conjunction with the use of high level application languages that are embedded into the payload of SIP messages at due time. We will show that the session management messages can carry both a Grid application protocol (i.e. Job Submission Description Language (Anjomshoaa, et al, 2005)) and a general resource description payload that contains the application request to the network in a user oriented language.

The core result is that test-bed implementations have shown that the aforementioned objectives can be reached without any major implementation effort, using existing building blocks, suitably arranged and extended.

It is worth mentioning that for communications spanning over multiple network domains the problem of signalling is in general more complex that in a single network domain. The obvious reason is that each administrative entity involved along the path has responsibility on its domain and may not be fully coordinated with the others. In the remainder of this work we do not consider the multi-domain issue, which will be subject of further investigation, and focus on QoS guarantee within a single network domain.

THE BUILDING BLOCKS OF APPLICATION ORIENTED NETWORKING FOR GRID COMPUTING

In this section we outline the general architecture of the proposed solution and related building blocks. The starting point is the consideration that Grid computing is the results of several coordinated actions between application and network. Moreover the quality of service issue is more and more important since, in general, Grid applications have rather stringent QoS requirements and communication without QoS guarantees may be rather meaningless.

Because of these reasons we believe that the migration of application oriented functions into the network must adopt a state-full approach to be able to track and manage the state of the communication and the associated QoS.

The key building block to support Grid services is an application signalling language able to:

- Accept and understand the publication of information about the availability of Grid computing resources and the related access policies;
- Accept and understand the Grid application requests;
- Search if the resources required are available and negotiate the best possible answer to the requests of the specific application;
- Provide access to the network resource in order to transport information of various sizes as effectively and efficiently as possible.

Accomplishing all these tasks at once is not easy, most of all because they span over several logical layers of the network stack. Today's solutions usually focus "horizontally" on a subset of them, while an integrated "vertical" solution is still missing. It can be achieved by exploiting the concept of communication session. A session layer into the network has the capability to maintain an end-to-end state of the communication that is more general than the single (TCP for instance) connection. The session can be spread over several connections and/or data flows, interrupted, retrieved, re-routed etc. and a session oriented protocol like SIP provides all the messages and primitives to perform these actions.

Therefore the session layer match very well with the need to manage a connection oriented communication between remote application entities with several general features. What about the management of all the rest? Who will provide primitives in the network to manage resources, discover them, authorize their use etc.?

It is rather trivial to exploit the SIP protocol together with the implementation of a few ad-hoc modules to make the session layer support these functions, with a rather general approach that proves to be extensible and very flexible. The key

point is the capability of SIP to carry whatever payload we like in the body of the signalling messages (such for instance the session initiation message INVITE) and of the SIP proxy to store "users profiles" i.e. information about rights of access, service policies etc.[1]

Building on these capabilities the technical solution described in this chapter is based on the following general concepts:

- Grid users and Grid resource are seen as SIP terminals (User Agents – UA) that can register to a SIP proxy providing information on their network location and state at the time of registration;
- The SIP proxy keeps the information for later use, in particular for resource discovery and reservation;
- A service request is issued as a session set-up request, including in the payload of the signalling messages higher layer protocols that specify all the requirements of the application (type and amount of resources needed, including network resources);
- The SIP proxy will establish the session if it is possible to satisfy the requirements, possibly re-negotiating them.

How these actions are performed is a matter of implementation, and will be discussed in the remainder of the chapter. Surely it is easy to understand that they can be accomplished if:

- One or more application protocols to exchange application related information between the terminals and the SIP proxy exists, are carried in the payload of the signalling messages and can be interpreted by ad-hoc modules in the proxy;
- Is defined a model of interaction, together with the related protocols, to transfer the application requests to the network, in order to identify and reserve the network resources requested by the communications.

As an example let's consider the reservation. Generally speaking the Grid application can be successfully served if both the application resources to execute the required processing and the network resources required to exchange the related data are available. If we consider the network reservation two models are possible to finalize it:

- The end-to-end model, requiring that the peers have the capability to map the media streams of a session into network resource reservations. For example, IP Multimedia Subsystem (IMS) (Poikselka, et al, 2006) supports several end-to-end QoS models and terminals may use link-layer resource reservation protocols (PDP Context Activation), Resource ReSer-Vation Protocol (RSVP), or Differentiated Services (DiffServ) directly. Anyway, today the option of using RSVP has been removed (it is not used by anyone in practice) and DiffServ is being used as transport QoS mechanism (mapping PDP context QoS information to DSCP parameters) (End-to-end Quality of Service (QoS) Concept and Architecture, n.d.).
- A core oriented approach where the transport network already provides QoS oriented service classes (for instance using DiffServ) and the sessions are mapped directly into this classes by the network itself.

Nonetheless in both models the sequence of actions to be performed in the network are mapped into:

- Check by means of the network Control Plane if enough resources are available
- Reserve the network resources providing the QoS required

Before entering into the details of a possible implementation let us first review the three basic problems to be addressed: session management using the SIP protocol, interacting with the network Control Plane and interacting with applications by means of application level languages.

Session Management and the Session Initiation Protocol (SIP)

The Session Initiation Protocol (SIP) is an IETF application layer protocol used for establishing and managing sessions. The concept of session is well known in networking but also in general real life and is related to a set of activities performed by a user that can be logically correlated. In networks several exchanges of information (either in parallel or series) may be part of a single session. The session may be manipulated by the user or the network according to the needs, for instance a session may be suspended, retrieved etc.

SIP deals with session-oriented mechanisms, regardless the scope(s) of a session. It specifies the message flows required to initiate, terminate and modify sessions. In other words, SIP does not provide services but provides primitives that can be used to implement services on top of sessions. For example, SIP can locate a user and deliver an opaque object to its current location. It is also neutral to the transport protocol and can run on top of almost all existing protocols (TCP, TLS, UDP). Thanks to these characteristics SIP scales well, is extensible, and sits comfortably in different architectures and deployment scenarios. Because of these features SIP has become the core protocol of the IMS architecture that promises to pave the path towards ubiquitous communication over heterogeneous networks.

SIP limits itself to a modular philosophy and focuses on a specific function set, thus maximizing interoperability with existing and future protocols and applications. In the perspective of this work SIP is used at its best to manage the sessions:

- Sessions are used to handle the communication requests and maintain their state by mapping it into session attributes

- Sessions are mapped into a set of networking resources with QoS guarantees
- The SIP protocol is used to manage the sessions, to provide user authentication, session set-up, suspension and retrieval, as well modification of the service by adding or taking away resources or communication facilities according to the needs.

Interaction with the Network Control Plane

Talking about the network control plane (CP) we have already pointed out the importance to address heterogeneous networks with different levels of capacity, flexibility and intelligence. Of course different networks have different control planes with different capabilities. For instance, the GMPLS control plane for optical network is tailored to reliable high bandwidth and connection oriented data transmission, but lacks fast bandwidth provisioning. Wi-Fi is able to provide fast mobile access but with a limited reliable bandwidth segmentation.

How it is possible that SIP supports network related functions such as network resource reservation and QoS management, when the network control plane uses primitives that are not directly accessible by SIP and may depend on the network technology. This is where new modules must be created. SIP has the capability to store attributes for a session and modify them according to the needs.

What is needed is a framework to describe the network resources in an abstract way in the SIP proxy and then implement a module that maps this abstract representation into specific control plane directive to the given networking technology. The framework must be general enough to be able to identify a wide variety of resources as well as resources' state.

To this purpose we have chosen the Resource Description Framework (RDF) (RDF/XML Syntax Specification, 2004) that is a general-purpose language, defined by W3C, for representing information. RDF provides general method of modelling information through a variety of syntax formats, allowing the formalization of a wide variety of resources as well as resources state. The idea to use a language based on RDF to describe networks related concepts is not new. The Network Description Language (NDL) proposed in (Van der Ham, Grosso, Dijkstra & de Laat, 2006) provides ontology for computer networks and can be used to easily describe, for instance, a network topology.

Application Level Protocols

Applications do communicate with their specific languages to implement a service instance. Protocols exist to express the end-user needs, find the resources a user wants and reserve them for use. Of course, the application protocols are related to a particular application.

In this work we deal with two different types of application protocols, focusing on application specific and network specific information. The former is used by the end-users to find the computational resources needed and exchange the description of requirements of jobs. The Job Submission Description Language (JSDL) is the protocol currently existing to this end. The latter is used by the end-users to specify the requirements of the requested service in terms of communications facility. There is no protocol to date dedicated to this task. We have proposed a new one, called Network Resource Description Language, exploiting the Resource Description Framework.

JSDL is a language to describe the requirements of computational jobs in Grid environments. The JSDL language contains a vocabulary and XML Schema that facilitates the expression of requirements as a set of XML elements. The specification focuses on the description of computational tasks to be submitted to traditional high-performance computer systems. JSDL describes the submission aspects of a job as well as job state with the following general categories

- Job identification requirements as Job name, description;
- Resource requirements, such as total RAM available, total swap available, CPU clock speed, number of CPUs, Operating System, etc.;
- Data requirement, such as the maximum amount of CPU time, wallclock time, or memory that can be consumed, etc.

JSDL does not cope with the network resources needed to support the communication related to a given Grid service.

On the other hand, the network requirements are exchanged between end-users and network using the Network Resource Description Language (NRDL). NRDL is based on RDF and extend the Network Description Language (Van der Ham, Grosso, Dijkstra & de Laat, 2006). NDL is an RDF vocabulary defined to describe network elements and network topologies. It does not fit with our needs since we would like to deal with network "resources" rather than with network "objects". In the case of interest here the RDF syntax must be able to describe "communication needs", general enough to provide network information exchange independently from the networking technology.

NRDL formalizes a communication relationship between two network equipments enriching the communication with detailed information about QoS and network requirements (i.e. Bandwidth, jitter, delay, etc...) For the purpose of the work described in this chapter a detailed presentation of NRDL is not necessary. Up to now we have used a simple vocabulary as an instrument for the test-bed implementations. The success of the experiments prove that the approach is viable and we are currently working on the detailed NRDL ontology syntax (including list of classes and proprieties).

Figure 1. Schematic of the Application Aware architecture. The session layer is placed between the application and the transport network. The figure shows nodes, coupling the AO-M with the transport switches.

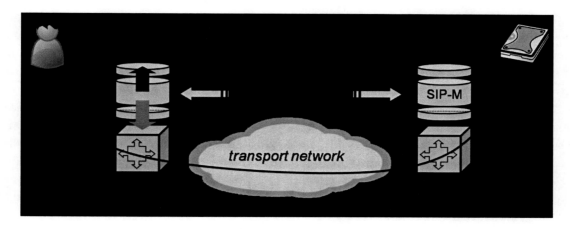

APPLICATION ORIENTED NETWORKING ARCHITECTURE

This section describes the proposed architecture and the relevant building blocks. The logical architecture is presented in Figure 1 where three logical layers are in evidence, an application layer application, a session layer managing the signalling and the network layer which provides the mapping between service and network requests by means of the network control plane.

Application Oriented Modules

The Application Oriented Modules (AO-M) is the block responsible of the application aware networking. The AO-M represents the node where all application and network requests are routed. The logical scheme of the AO-M is that shown in Figure 1. It is logically sub-divided into three modules:

- **SIP module (SIP-M):** Is built around a SIP proxy implementing standard SIP communication facilities, having the task to map the communication needs into sessions. SIP-M is, in same way, the heart of the

AO-M, it is responsible for managing the Session Layer, find the next hop and forward any SIP messages to the destination;

- **Application module (APP-M):** Parses and partially understands the application protocols that may be encapsulated in the SIP messages. APP-M represent the application oriented part of the AO-M. The APP-M is equipped with a relational database where it is possible to store some kind of application or network data;

- **Network module (NET-M):** Network module (NET-M) is able to interact with the network control plane in order to activate the transport striatum with a predefined QoS. The NET-M modules is the only technology dependent module in the AO-M. In fact the NET-M interact to the network control plane according to type of transport network, for instance GMPLS control plane. The functions relegated to this module are mainly oriented to the transport stratum activation and management. NET-M has a direct interface to the network Control plane to check and reserve resources.

The SIP-M is enhanced with interfaces towards the upper and lower module. Combining the communication capabilities of APP-M and SIP the AO-M may assist applications into publishing, searching and reserving resources, thus understanding the related communication needs and mapping them into sessions. Thanks to the "network oriented" module the SIP-M may trigger the networks into creating the connections required to transport the data flow according to the service profile of a given session.

Combining the communication capabilities of APP-M and SIP-M the AO-M may assist applications into publishing, searching and reserving resources, thus understanding the related communication needs and mapping them into sessions. Thanks to the NET-M the SIP-M may send the information about the service profile of a given session to the network CP, that will trigger the networks into creating the connections required to transport the data flow.

Layer Integration

The SIP driven session layer and the network transport layer controlled by the network control pane can co-exist with different levels of integration (Figure 2).

- **Pure overlay (Figure 2.a):** The AO-Ms are placed into the edge routers only and the application resources (e.g. computing and storage) and network resources are managed separately in an overlay manner. The users (i.e. the application) use the SIP protocol to negotiate the IT communication session. When the session is set the SIP-M triggers the NET-M that is responsible to request a data path between the edge routers involved in the session to the network control plane. Then the session data cut through the transport plane.
- **Fully integrated (Figure 2.b):** The network control plane is enriched with SIP functionalities, to realize a pure application

aware network interworking with the session layer. All network nodes are fully functional AO-M nodes.

- **Partial integration (Figure 2.c):** In between the two solutions just presented this solution still segregates most of the intelligence of the SIP layer at the boundaries of the network. The AO-M in the edge nodes are fully functional and logically identical to those mentioned before. On the other hand the AO-M in the core node is equipped with a subset of functionalities, to satisfy the best performance/complexity trade-off. For instance the AO-M could be limited to a SIP-M functioning as a light proxy with forwarding capabilities and to the NET-M with network resource management functions.

RESOURCE MANAGEMENT

The resource management concerns all operations regarding the resources information exchange (i.e. publication and discovery) as well as resources reservation. As already outlined we propose to use the session layer with the SIP signalling to support resource management in an integrated manner within the network. To this end we assume that resources and users are divided into domains. A domain is an organization that is particularly indicated in a Grid network oriented to consumer applications where a large number of resources and users can be present.

With the general term of resources we intend both application and network resources. Since this research is applied to Grid Networks the application resources (i.e. storage space, computational power, etc.) are resources of use for Grid applications. On the other hand, network resources are all the resources concerning the network layer (bandwidth available, etc.).

Thus, referring to a generalized resource, the proposed resource management operations follow in principles three different phases:

Figure 2. Schematics of the various network architectures: a) overlay, b) fully integrated and c) partially integrated

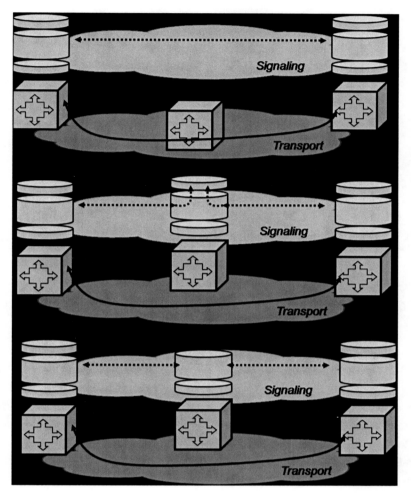

- **Resource publication:** Each available resource must publish its own availability to the AO-M. The publication phase allows the collection of network and application resource into the network nodes equipped with AO-Ms.
- **Resource discovery:** Allows users to find a set of available resources into the network including their network location and terms of availability.
- **Resource reservation:** Allows the reservation of both application resources in the application domain, and network resources in the network domain. Resource reservation can follow different paradigms depending on the network capability to reserve resources with a define QoS and depending on the interaction between application and network reservation. The interaction model between application and network is envisaged in the following.

The resources are managed by processors behaving as SIP User Agents, i.e. are able to perform the typical signalling of a standard SIP terminal. In the following we discuss how the various phases can be implemented using SIP.

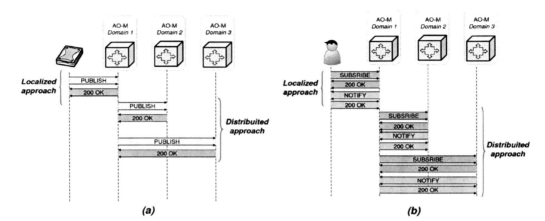

Figure 3. Schematics of the resource management: a) resource publication, b) resource discovery

(a)   (b)

Resource Publication

Resources (application and network) are announced to the AO-M by means of a SIP PUBLISH message, Figure 3.(a), a standard SIP message encapsulates into the body a resource descriptor. The resource descriptor must address the resource (i.e. resource's SIP address), capability, availability and state.

To this purpose a NRDL document can be successfully used as a generic resource descriptor. When the state of a resource changes, the SIP UA responsible of the resource prepares a NRDL document reporting the detailed resource state. The document is encapsulated in a SIP PUBLISH message and sent to the AO-M. Here it is parsed by the SIP-M and the NRDL payload in the body is sent to the APP-M where updated resource capability and availability are stored into the APP-M database. Depending whether the information must be propagated in the network the PUBLISH message may be forwarded to adjacent AO-M or not.

Depending on the domains two approaches are possible:

- **Localized approach:** In order to avoid uncontrolled messages propagation, PUBLISH messages can be forwarded only in the Home domain of the UA. A PUBLISH message can not reach any AO-M in a different domain or subdomain. This approach is particularly indicated in domains with few resources where the probability to find a free resource is acceptable.

- **Distributed approach:** In order to spread the resources state into the network SIP PUBLISH messages can be propagated to any AO-M nodes, even crossing SIP domain borders. To avoid unnecessary messages if a PUBLISH arrives in an AO-M that already know the resource with the same parameters, the AO-M module sends back a SIP error response and the PUBLISH propagation stops in that node. The distribute approach should be used only in a federated inter-domain environment where predefined agreements can restrict uncontrolled messages propagation.

Every time the state of a particular resource changes, the SIP UA responsible of the resource can update the resource status by means of a new PUBLISH message. Obviously to avoid network overload some sort of time windowing can be implemented to limit the number of PUBLISH messages since resources may change their state very rapidly.

Moreover in order to avoid scalability problems an intelligent trade-off between Localized and Distributed approach should be done in real networks.

Resource Discovery

Any SIP UA can request a set of particular resources exploiting the SIP protocol presence notification mechanism (Roach, 2002). A resource is associated with a SIP address (i.e. a UA of the SIP network) and has a set of proprieties with a state. A SIP UA send a request by issuing a SIP SUBSCRIBE message, Figure 3.(b) to the AO-M, the characteristics of the request are included in the SIP message body by means of a descriptor language.

The descriptor language must have the capability to express a set of requirements in both network and application domain.

Again the specific description language used is not a major matter since the APP-M can be extended to understand any new application descriptor. As mentioned before for the time being we assume JSDL and NRDL can be embedded in the SIP SUBSCRIBE message.

NRDL can express the network requirements (i.e. Bandwidth, QoS, etc.) while JSDL is the standardized language for expressing Job submission.

Depending on where the database of the available resources is maintained the SUBSCRIBE arrives to the closest AO-M node where the message is parsed by the SIP-M module. The message body is forwarded to the APP-M where it is processed. The APP-M starts a seeking phase into the resources database where all the published resources are stored.

Whatever the requested resources are found or not, the AO-M node send a NOTIFY message back to the UA, Figure 3.(b).

The NOTIFY message encapsulates the NRDL which describes the position and the availability of a free set of resources or an information massage.

The information massage notifies the UA about the state of the research with a detailed semantic information. For instance, an information massage can report information like: seeking not complete, seeking in progress, resource not available, resource not present, etc... In this work, we will not go through a detailed description of the information massage.

The two approaches allowed in the resource discovery follow in principle the approaches used in resource publication:

- **Localized approach:** SUBSCRIBE message can not be forwarded out of the Home Domain or Sub-domain. Using the Localized approach the probability to find a free resource is reduced, on the other hand since the SUBSCRIBE massage is not effect by the propagation phase, the final NOTIFY response is given in a shorter period. Moreover, the Localized approach guarantee a fully controlled environment with trusted resources.

- **Distributed approach:** In order to have a high probability to find a free resource the SUBSCRIBE message can be propagate by any AO-M nodes to any Domains or Sub-domains. The SUBSCRIBE Distributed approach is effected by the same issues advised in the Resource publication section. Moreover, because every search phase is followed by a notification one, by means of a SIP NOTIFY messages, the waste of bandwidth and consequentially the network congestion can became intolerable if the Distributed approach is applied widely.

Obviously, the NOTIFY message are effected by congestion control issues. In fact, an update NOTIFY message is sent from the AO-M modules to the SIP UA every time the state of the subscribed resources change. Congestion control mechanism should be apply to cope with messages overload.

Resource Reservation

The resource reservation will be performed by means of the SIP request used to established a dialog between two UAs (Rosenberg, et al, 2002). This is the time when the network QoS issue should also be addresses, since the reservation could be subject to the availability of given network resources. To make the presentation more effective addressing one problem at a time, this section does not deal with QoS. The QoS management issue will be dealt within the dedicated section that will follow. Therefore for the case here presented the reservation will be provided by a standard SIP INVITE without the SIP extension for the QoS (Camarillo, 2002).

Encapsulated into the INVITE there is either a JSDL document describing the job requirement or a NRDL document or even both. The INVITE message goes though the network and arrives at the UA destination, that acknowledges the request by sending back a 200 OK positive response. Otherwise a response message error is raised depending of the resource state. A SIP ACK message follows to close the INVITE transaction.

The SIP INVITE message can be used to implement resource discovery and reservation in two different approaches.

- **Single phase**: A single SIP INVITE message perform both resource discovery and reservation at the same time.
- **Two phases**: Two different mechanisms are use sequentially for resource discovery and reservation.

Both Single and two phases approach has been the subject of the study in many published papers. The testing and the detailed results are described in the following works (Campi, Cerroni, Callegati, Zervas, Nejabati & Simeonidou, 2007) (Simeonidou, Zervas, Nejebati, Callegati & Cerroni, 2007) (Zervas, Qin, Nejabati, Simeonidou, Callegati, Campi & Cerroni, 2007)(Zervas, Qin, Nejabati, Simeonidou, Campi, Cerroni, & Callegati, 2008) (Callegati, Campi, Corazza, Simeonidou, Zervas, Qin & Nejabati, 2008).

Single Phase Approach

The single phase approach is presented in Figure 4.(a), where both resource discovery and reservation mechanisms are performed at the same time. In some way, the single phase approach defines an anycast procedure for reservation, in fact, the user with data to be processed remotely sends a request to the closest AO-M in the form of an INVITE SIP message. Encapsulated into the INVITE there is a description language describing the request, for instance in Grid network is the JSDL document which describes the job requirement.

Obviously, the first phase is to publish Grid resources to the AO-M, by means of a SIP PUBLISH message as already explained.

The SIP-M module passes the job requests to its application middleware (APP-M) that performs a resource discovery algorithm to find out whether there are enough computing resources available within its known resources. If the answer is "yes" the AO-M would start establishing the session, if it is "no" it would forward the message to the other AO-M modules in the network to look for the requested resources until the message arrive to an available resource or it is dropped. If a resource is found the INVITE is acknowledged and a session between user and resource is created, thus reserving the resource usage.

Depending of the interaction model between network and application many resource reservation with QoS requirements can be applied (see next paragraph).

Two Phases Approach

The two phases approach is shown in Figure 4.(b). At first a resource discovery with a notifications mechanism is performed then a direct reservation by the client follows to complete the reservation.

Figure 4. Schematics of the resource reservation approaches: (a) single phase, (b) two phases

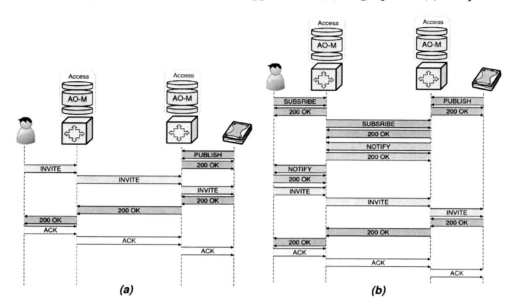

(a) *(b)*

In this approach the Grid resources are published to the attached AO-M with a PUBLISH message. A user requesting resources sends a SUBSCRIBE message to the nearest AO-M. The AO-M checks the status of its own resources and if they can satisfy the request then notifies the client. Otherwise, the SUBSCRIBE message is propagated to the other known AO-M (with a Localized or Distributed approach) either by utilizing sequential or parallel forking in order to discover the requested resources. The AO-M with available resources sends a NOTIFY message back to UA. The NOTIFY is used to communicate to the UA the availability and location of the resources (i.e. address of the end point or AO-M or domain).

After the resource discovery the user knows the location (SIP name or network address) of the resource and can attempt a direct reservation by an INVITE message.

RESOURCE RESERVATION WITH SIP QOS MANAGEMENT

As already outlined, end users may interact with the network control plane but to date this interaction can not be general and technology independent. Nonetheless is possible to imagine interaction models between application and network layer to guarantee the establishment of a session with network QoS guarantee. In the following, given that a session set-up phase is always started with an INVITE message sent by the caller to the callee, some examples of different approaches are given exploiting the SIP messages syntax.

- **Network reservation during session set up (Figure 5.a):** While the INVITE message goes through the network (e.g. with anycast procedures) a network path is reserved before the INVITE message reaches the resource destination. Network reservation is performed step by step and always before application reservation, Fig. 5.a.1. Each network portion is independent

Figure 5. Interaction models between application and network (a) Network reservation during session set up (b) Network reservation before application reservation (c) Network reservation before session set up (d) Network reservation after application reservation (e) Network reservation after session set up

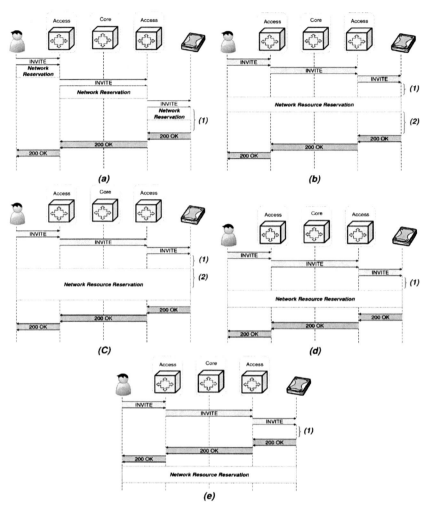

and reserved on the fly during the INVITE path. This method can be used for very fast provisioning purpose.

• **Network reservation before application reservation (Figure 5.b):** As soon as the INVITE message arrives at the destination and application resources are checked, the network reservation starts, Fig. 5.b.1. After the network resources are reserved the application resource is reserved and the session started, Fig. 5.b.2. In this case, the network reservation is performed before

application reservation as a whole network path. Moreover, the application domain must wait the end of the entire network reservation before reserving any resources. This is the case of VoIP calls.

• **Network reservation before session set up (Figure 5.c):** As soon as the INVITE message arrives at the destination, and the application resources are found, the application (Fig. 5.c.1) and network (Fig. 5.c.2) resource reservations are started in parallel. Once both reservations are completed independently and both the application resource and the network path are available the session is started. In this case the whole session can starts only when both application and network resources have been reserved. This can be the case of standard Grid sessions.

- **Network reservation after application reservation (Figure 5.d):** The INVITE message arrives at the destination and application resources are checked and reserved, Fig. 5.d.1. Then, network reservation starts into the network and as soon as the path between Grid user and Grid resource is established, the application session is started. This can be used when few application resources are available and the probability to find a free resource application is low.

- **Network reservation after session set up (Figure 5.e):** The INVITE message arrives at the destination and application resources are checked and reserved, immediately the application session can start without having any network resources reserved, Fig. 5.e.1. Then, network reservation starts and as soon as the path between Grid user and Grid resource is established, the application session already started can take advantage moving the transmission state from best-effort to QoS enable. This can be used when the QoS is not crucial for the application (or at least not in the beginning part of the session).

The management of the QoS issue is not part of the standard SIP protocol but the issue is there and, a Resource Management framework was defined for establishing SIP sessions with QoS. The solution proposed in (Handley & Jacobson, 1998) exploits the concept of pre-condition. The pre-condition is a set of "desiderata" that are negotiated during the session set-up phase between the two SIP UAs involved in the communication. If the pre-conditions can be met by the underlin-

ing networking infrastructure then the session is set up, otherwise the set-up phase fails and the session is not established.

The pre-conditions simply require that participants use end-to-end existing resource reservation mechanisms to reserve what is needed before establishing the session (e.g. RSVP, PDP context activation etc.).

The framework requires the SIP user agents to reserve network resources before establishing the session, so that the user is not alerted of the incoming communication if the network resources required are not available.

This scheme is mandatory because the reservation of network resources frequently requires learning the IP address, port, and session parameters of the callee. Moreover, in a bidirectional communications the QoS parameters must be agreed upon between caller and callee. Therefore the reservation of network resources can not be done before an exchange of information between caller and callee has been finalized. This exchange of information is the result of the initial offer/answer message exchange at the beginning of the session start up. The information exchange sets the pre-conditions to the session. If the pre-conditions can be met the session is then established.

Weakness of the Current Resource Management Framework

The current framework says that the QoS pre-conditions are included into the SDP message, using two state variables: *Current status* and *Desired status*.

Consequently, the SIP UA treats these variables as all other SDP media attributes (Rosenberg & Schulzrinne, 2002).

The current and desired status variables are exchanged between UAs using offers and answers in order to have a shared view of the status of the session.

The framework has been proposed for VoIP applications and the chosen solution is tailored to this specific case. Consequentially, it has some limitations when considering a generalized application aware environment, enumerated in the following.

- Both session and Quality of Service parameters are carried by the same SDP document. Thus, a session established with another session protocol (i.e. Job Submission Description Language (JSDL)) is not possible.
- The pre-condition framework imposes a strict "modus operandi", since pre-conditions must be met before alerting the user. Therefore network reservation must always be completed before service reservation.
- Since the network reservation is performed by the UAs at the edge of the network, only a mechanism based on end-to-end reservation is applicable.
- QoS is performed on each single connection, without the ability of grouping connections resulting from sessions established by others.
- Since SDP is a protocol based on lines description, it has a reduced enquiring capability. Moreover, only one set of pre-conditions can be expressed by SDP. Multiple negotiations of pre-conditions are not possible.
- The SDP semantic is rather limited. It is not possible to specify detailed QoS parameters since the SDP lines are marked with "QoS" parameter without specifying any additional detail (i.e. delay, jitter, etc...).

Given these issues we believe that an extended resource management framework is needed in order to achieve a general framework for QoS for application oriented network supporting advantage applications such as Grid computing. In the next section we propose an extension to the framework to generalize its applicability to the case of the *Network reservation before session set up* scenario that we believe to be the more likely to be used in a Grid network. Extensions to other scenarios is possible and will be presented in future works.

The Extended Resource Management Framework

The extension to the existing framework can be implemented exploiting the following ideas:

- Keep the QoS mechanisms out of SIP protocol. The specific end-user application will manage the interaction model;
- Do not limit the framework to the use of the SDP protocol but allow more general protocols in the SIP payload at session start-up;
- Separate the information about the request and requirement related to the application layer from the information about request and requirements at the network layer, using two different protocols to carry them;
- Allow as many re-negotiation as possible of the pre-conditions both at session start-up and while the session is running.

The extended Resource Management framework for QoS is based on an approach close to a *Network Service Subscription* model. This different approach is motivated by the wiliness of keeping the QoS framework out of the current SIP mechanism for reservation.

Regarding the protocols to declare the pre-conditions we propose to make a distinction between application and network protocol. In the following:

- **Application Description Protocol (ADP):** Is used to describe application requirements, for instance JSDL which is a consolidate language for describing Job submission for Grid networks.
- **Network Resource Description Language (NRDL):** Is used to describe the network

Figure 6. Example of resource reservation Call Flow at session set-up with QoS

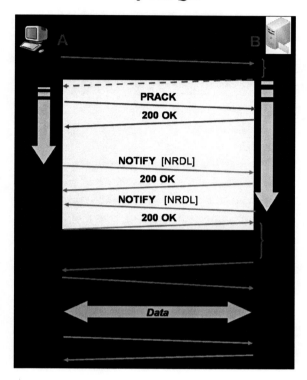

requirements and QoS requests. The use of a complete different document descriptor for QoS allow the use of many ADPs for describing application requirements, and not only the SDP.

The NRDL is a general method of modeling information and has the capability to describe both resources and the resources state. For this reason NRDL can be used instead of SDP as a more general description language for network resources. Furthermore, because NRDL is a structured language, it is possible to enrich its semantic at will with the detailed information about QoS (i.e. Bandwidth, jitter, delay, etc...). The meaning of using NRDL for describing network requirements is motivated by maintaining the QoS approach technology independent.

The main advantage of this approach is that the network does not need the capability to un-

derstand the ADP since the QoS requirements are only described in the NRDL.

The main drawback is that a link between ADP and NRDL is needed; and therefore some sort of "interface" has to be implemented in the UA on top of a standard SIP UA.

The extension to pre-condition negotiation is implemented exploiting two concepts already present is SIP:

- INVITE multi-part message: that is an INVITE that carries more than one protocol in the payload (multi-body), in this case for instance NRDL (express network requirements) and JSDL (express Job requirements);
- NOTIFY message (Roach, 2002): a message that allows the exchange of information related to a "relationship" between two UAs, for instance a session that is starting up or that is already running.

Details about the extension of the SIP management framework can be found in (Callegati & Campi, 2008).

Resource Reservation with QoS

In Figure. 6 is presented an overview of the call flow in an end-to-end scenario where the network and application resource reservation is a pre-condition to the session set up. User A sends an initial INVITE multi-part message including both the network QoS requests and an application protocol for the application requests.

The QoS requests are expressed by means of an NRDL document while the application protocol depends on the type of application (i.e. SDP for VoIP, JSDL for Grid computing, etc...)

A does not want B to start providing the requested service until the network resources are reserved in both directions and end-to-end. B starts checking if the service is available, if so it agrees to reserve network resources for this session before starting the service. B will handle resource reservation in the B → A direction, but needs A to handle the A → B direction.

To indicate so, B returns a 183 (Session Progress) response with an NRDL document describing the quality of service from its point of view.

This first phase goes on with the two peers exchanging their view of the desired QoS of the communication, thus setting the "pre-conditions" to the session in term of communications quality.

Then both A and B start the network resource reservation. When an UA finishes to reserve resources in one direction, it sends a NOTIFY message to the other UA to notify the current reservation status by a NRDL document in the message body. The NOTIFY message is used to specify the notification of an event. Only when the network channel meets the pre-condition B starts the reservation of the desired resources in the application domain, and session establishment may complete as normally.

Once the service is ready to be provided B send back a 200 OK message to A. Data can be exchanged by the two end-point since both application and network resourced have been reserved. BYE message close the dialog.

The main differences with the current approach are:

- Use of a separated NRDL document in an multi-part INVITE message. The INVITE message starts a SIP dialog between parties. The peer NRDL is carried by a 183 response.
- Use of NOTIFY messages instead of UPDATE. Since ADP and NRDL are separated (even if carried by the same INVITE message) the UPDATE message can be sent only by UA A and can be used to update both ADP and NRDL. The NOTIFY can be sent by both UAs and is related to NRDL only and guarantees that the issues of network resource reservation is addressed independently from that of application resource reservation. The NOTIFY

messages have Dialog-ID, From and To tag equal to the INVITE message.
- The INVITE message implies the opening of a logical relationship between the peers (a subscription) that ends with the dialog tear down. Each time that the network reservation state changed a NOTIFY message is used to notify the changes for a specific subscription.

Detailed results of the resource reservation testing with QoS are been reported in the following publications (Callegati & Campi, 2008) (Martini, Campi, Baroncelli, Martini, Torkman, Zangheri et al, 2009).

CONCLUSION

In this chapter we have addressed the issue of managing application and network resource in a consumer Grid scenario. The starting concept is that a more effective approach to the solution of these problems could be achieved by delegating directly to the network some crucial functions such as resource publication, discovery and reservation. This is achievable by means of a general signalling infrastructure embedded in the network with the capability to interact directly with the end user applications, as well as with the network functional sub-blocks.

We have discussed the possibility to implement such a concept by means of a session layer that is part of the network control plane and may be implemented using the SIP signalling protocol.

Research works and experiment already published and ongoing show that SIP provides a high degree of flexibility and can be configured to support application and network oriented functions such as application resource advertisement and discovery, application and network resource reservation, QoS management etc. over a variety of networking technology.

Moreover, these functional schemes can be adapted to support different application languages

(JSDL, NRDL etc.) as well as different level of network intelligence by suitably integrating SIP with the existing network control planes.

We strongly believe this proposal may be a breakthrough in the implementation of this sort of services since it solves a large degree of problems with a very limited implementation effort, since many of the basic building blocks are based on existing and well established technologies.

REFERENCES

Anjomshoaa, A. et al. (2005, November). *Job submission description language (JSDL) specification v. 1.0*. Open Grid Forum document GFD.56.

Baroncelli, F., Martini, B., Martini, V., & Castoldi, P. (2007, May 21-25). A distributed signalling for the provisioning of on-demand VPN services in transport networks. In *10th IFIP/IEEE International Symposium on Integrated Network Management (IM 2007)*, Munich, Germany.

Baroncelli, F., Martini, B., Valcarenghi, L., & Castoldi, P. (2006, July 16-18). Service Composition in Automatically Switched Transport Networks. *IEEE International Conference on Networking and Services (ICNS'06)*, Silicon Valley, CA.

Callegati, F., & Campi, A. (2008). Extension of Resource Management in SIP, GridNets 2008, Beijing

Callegati, F., Campi, A., Corazza, G., Simeonidou, D., Zervas, G., Qin, Y., et al. (2009). SIP-empowered Optical Networks for Future IT Services and Applications. *IEEE Communications Magazine*.

Camarillo, G., et al. (2002, October). *Integration of Resource Management and Session Initiation Protocol (SIP)*. IETF RFC 3312.

Campi, A., Cerroni, W., Callegati, F., Zervas, G., Nejabati, R., & Simeonidou, D. (2007). SIP Based OBS networks for Grid Computing. In *Proceedings of ONDM 2007*, Athens, Greece.

Campi, A., Cerroni, W., Corazza, G., Callegati, F., Martini, B., Baroncelli, F., et al. (2009). *SIP-based Service Architecture for Application-aware Optical Network*. In *ICTA 2009*.

Ciulli, N., Carrozzo, G., Giorgi, G., Zervas, G., Escalona, E., & Qin, Y. (Eds.). (2008). Architectural approaches for the integration of the service plane and control plane in optical networks. *Optical Switching and Networking*, 5, 94–106. doi:10.1016/j.osn.2008.01.002

Cochennec, J.-Y. (2002, July). Activities on next-generation networks under Global Information Infrastructure in ITU-T. *IEEE Comm Mag*.

End-to-end Quality of Service (QoS) Concept and Architecture. (n.d.). 3GPP TS 23.107.

Foster, I., Berry, D., Djaoui, A., Grimshaw, A., Horn, B., Kishimoto, H., et al. (2004, July 12). *Open Grid Service Architecture V1.0*.

Handley, M. & Jacobson, V. (1998, April). *SDP: session description protocol, RFC 2327*. Internet Engineering Task Force.

ITU-T, Recommendation Y.2012. (2006, September). Functional requirements and architecture of the NGN release 1.

ITU-T Recommendation Y.2001. (2004, December). General overview of NGN, December 2004.

ITU-T Recommendation Y.2011. (2004, October). General principles and general reference model for Next Generation Networks.

Martini, B., Campi, A., Baroncelli, F., Martini, V., Torkman, K., Zangheri, F., et al. (2009). *SIP-based Service Platform for On-demand Optical Network Services*. In *OFC 2009. Open Grid Forum*. (n.d.). Retrieved from http://www.ogf.org/

Poikselka, M., et al. (2006). *The IMS: IP Multimedia Concepts and Services* (2nd Ed.). Hoboken, NJ: Wiley.

RDF/XML Syntax Specification. (2004, February 10). W3C Recommendation.

Roach, A. B. (2002, June). *Session Initiation Protocol (SIP)-Specific Event Notification.* IETF RFC 3265.

Rosenberg, J., et al. (2002, June). *SIP: Session Initiation Protocol.* IETF RFC 3261.

Rosenberg, J., & Schulzrinne, H. (2002). *An offer/answer model with session description protocol (SDP).* RFC 3264, Internet Engineering Task Force, June 2002.

Simeonidou, D., Zervas, G., Nejabati, R., Callegati, F., Campi, A., & Cerroni, W. (2007, September 10-14). SIP empowered OBS Network Architecture for Future IT Services and Applications. In *Proceedings of IEEE Broadnets 2007,* Raleigh, NC.

Simeonidou, D., Zervas, G., Nejabati, R., Callegati, F., Campi, A., & Cerroni, W. (2007, September). SIP-enpowered OBS Network Architecture for Future IT Services and Applications. In *Proc. of Broadnets 07,* Raleigh, NC.

St. Arnaud, B., et al. (2004). A Grid Oriented Lightpath Provisioning System. In *Proc. of Globecom 2004,* Dallas, TX.

St. Arnaud, B., et al. (2006, November). Layer 1 Virtual Private Network Management by Users. *IEEE Comm. Mag.*

Tuecke, S., Czajkowski, K., Foster, I., Graham, S., Kesselman, C., Maquire, T., et al. (2003, April 5). *Open Grid Service Infrastructure V1.0.*

Van der Ham, J., Grosso, P., Dijkstra, F., & de Laat, C. T. (2006, November 11 - 17). Semantics for hybrid networks using the network description language. In *Proceedings of the 2006 ACM/IEEE Conference on Supercomputing,* Tampa, FL.

Zervas, G., Nejabati, R., Campi, A., Qin, Y., Simeonidou, D., Callegati, F., et al. (2007, September). Demonstration of a Fully Functional Optical Burst Switched Network with Application Layer Resource Reservation Capability. In *33nd European Conference on Optical Communication (ECOC 2007),* Berlin, Germany.

Zervas, G., Qin, Y., Nejabati, R., Simeonidou, D., Callegati, F., Campi, A., & Cerroni, W. (2008). SIP-enabled Optical Burst Switching architectures and protocols for application-aware optical networks. *Computer Networks.*

Zervas, G., Qin, Y., Nejabati, R., Simeonidou, D., Campi, A., Cerroni, W., & Callegati, F. (2008). Demonstration of Application Layer Service Provisioning Integrated on Full-Duplex Optical Burst Switching Network Test-bed. In *OFC 2008,* California, USA.

ENDNOTE

[1] SIP supports these two features oriented to the VoIP application that is the most typical field where it is used. Basically the SIP proxy must be able to authenticate a user registering to the proxy and the Session Description Protocol (SDP) [15] is used as the application language used to specify session attributes.

Chapter 39

Agent–Based Infrastructure for Dynamic Composition of Grid Services

Matthew Adigun
University of Zululand, South Africa

Johnson Iyilade
University of Zululand, South Africa

Klaas Kabini
University of Zululand, South Africa

ABSTRACT

The service-oriented computing paradigm is based on the assumption that existing services can be put together in order to obtain new composite services. This chapter focuses on how peer-to-peer architectures based on multi-agent systems can be used to build highly dynamic and reconfigurable infrastructure that support dynamic composition of grid services. The chapter starts by providing an overview of key technologies for SOC. It then introduces dynamic service composition and challenges of composing grid services. The authors further motivate for Multi-agent system approach in SOC and why it becomes important in service composition. They then present our research effort, AIDSEC, an agent-based infrastructure for dynamic service composition, describing its architecture, implementation and comparison with some related work in the literature. In addition, the chapter raises some emerging trends in SOC and the particular challenges they pose to service composition. They conclude by suggesting that a solution based on multi-agent system is required for composing services that possess capabilities of autonomy, reliability, flexibility, and robustness.

INTRODUCTION

The Service Oriented Computing (SOC) paradigm is currently a promising methodology for engineer-

ing applications in both scientific and industrial communities (Bhatia, 2005). It promises a world of distributed services that are loosely coupled to flexibly create dynamic business processes and agile applications that may span many organizations and computing platforms.

DOI: 10.4018/978-1-61520-686-5.ch039

A major assumption of the SOC approach is that services can be combined together in order to obtain new, composite services. The implication of this is that future enterprise and scientific applications do not have to be developed from the scratch but assembled on the fly from an ecosystem of services available on a network such as the grid (NGG Report, 2006). This is already having revolutionary impact on the way software applications are designed, architected, delivered and consumed.

Building scientific or business applications that utilize distributed services is one of the challenges facing the SOC research community today. Traditional software engineering methodologies are often inadequate in addressing the complexity and dynamic nature of large-scale distributed systems. Classical techniques for composing services are procedural and only define how different services ought to be invoked e.g. in terms of ordering and parallelism among them. They are geared for low-level invocation of services, and not specially geared for enabling composition (Singh & Huhns, 2005). Moreover, a number of existing techniques are too rigid and are controlled by a centralized composition engine. They are, therefore, inadequate for service composition, especially, when services require capabilities of autonomy, flexibility and robustness.

Interestingly, there has been an explosion of interest in peer-to-peer (P2P) methodology as a promising approach for engineering large scale distributed systems (Bhatia, 2005). P2P systems generally, offer the advantages of scalability, reliability, and robustness over traditional server-based systems (Verma, 2004). Multi-agent Systems (MAS) have thus, emerged as a P2P methodology that address the issues of organizing large-scale software systems and could, therefore, complement existing methodologies for SOC. Agents are autonomous, computational entities that can be viewed as perceiving their environment through sensors and acting upon them through effectors (Bradshaw, 1997). Many existing and potential industrial applications of multi-agent systems in engineering large-scale systems are found in many fields such as e-commerce, telecommunications, transportation, sensor network, scheduling, and manufacturing (Weiss, 1999). Multi-agent systems would, therefore, be invaluable in emerging SOC environments especially in developing and analyzing intricate models and theories of interactivity and collaboration among Collaborative Virtual Enterprises (CVEs) and Virtual Organizations (VOs). Moreover, agents provide greater flexibility and robustness in how services are used and created by operating rationally in a variety of environmental circumstances and context that change in a usually unforeseen manner.

We, therefore, present in this chapter an approach that augment current service-based technologies with multi-agent system for dynamic composition of grid services.

The rest of the chapter is organized as follows:

- In the Background section, we present a general introduction to drivers of a new approach to software development that led to the emergence of the SOC paradigm, followed by a short introduction of web services and grid services as two key technologies for implementing services. We further introduce the semantic web and its importance to advancing the vision of SOC;
- Then, in the Dynamic Service Composition section, we introduce the basic concepts of service composition, and then discuss the challenges of dynamic composition of grid services;
- In the section that follows, we present Multi-agent system in SOC by first introducing agents and multi-agent systems; we then present a motivation for MAS in SOC and thereafter, draw abstractions for composition of services;

- Subsequently, we present our research effort AIDSEC – an agent-based infrastructure for dynamic composition of grid services. We start by presenting a sample usage scenario that informed the design considerations of AIDSEC, then discuss its architecture, operation, implementation, and comparison with related work;
- In the Future trend section, we present emerging trends that drives the future of SOC and the implication for service composition;
- Finally, the last section presents the conclusion.

BACKGROUND

Drivers of a New Approach to Software Development

Business organizations have recently been facing the pressure of cutting down costs of Information Technology (IT) investment and maximizing the utilization of existing technologies. They must at the same time, strive to serve customers, be more competitive, and respond to business strategic priorities. Two major themes behind all these are heterogeneity and change (Endrei et al, 2004).

Heterogeneity is a killer problem for business organizations because most enteprises are comprised of different systems, applications, and architectures of different ages and technologies that need to interoperate within and across the organization (Singh, 2004). Integrating products from many vendors is often a nightmare. Businesses, however, cannot afford to take a single-vendor solution approach because that would make their application suites and IT infrastructure inflexible.

Change is another major theme that describes the challenges business organizations face. Consumers are demanding new product offerings at a rate unimaginable. With the global deployment and broad use of networking technologies like the Internet, globalization and e-business are the order of the day. Globalization has led to a more fierce competition, resulting in shortening of product cycles as companies look to gain advantage over their competitors. It has equally given consumers a wealth of information on competitive product offering available over the Internet. Additionally, the dynamism of today's operating business environment requires ability for businesses to respond to changes in the system in a way not anticipated before.

Businesses must, therefore, rapidly adapt in order to cope in today's dynamic and competitive business environments and the IT infrastructure must allow them to do so. Consequently, business organizations are evolving from operating as isolated business entities towards a new ecosystem business paradigm with more focus on the extended supply chain and partner access to business services. In the new ecosystem paradigm, business services are componentized and distributed on the network.

The IT industry's response to these trends has also been evolving in parallel. As shown in Figure 1, this has led to evolution of various software architectures, ranging from the traditional monolithic to current architecture based on services. A very apparent reality for the IT industry, however, is that business applications could no longer be developed from the scratch as monolithic programs, as they have been done in the past, but composed by reusing, as much as possible, already existing code or other assets in the ecosystem. This has been a very big challenge for the IT industry.

Generally, it was believed that any viable solution to address this challenge must have at least, three key characteristics (Endrei et al, 2004):

i. *It must be loosely coupled* (i.e it must be developed as individual modules and distributed to allow reuse. This is important, especially, to address changing requirements);

Figure 1. Evolution of software architectures (Endrei et al, 2004)

ii. *It must be protocol independent* (i.e. it must allow components developed with different technologies and running in different platforms to interoperate); and

iii. *It must be location transparent* (i.e it must present the entire application components to the end-user as if they are running locally).

Initially, it was thought that such reuse could be achieved by object-oriented programing methodologies. However, the scale of an object is too small, which makes it difficult to develop a new application based on already-existing objects. Later, Component-based software engineering (CBSE) promised to accelerate software development significantly, due to the larger scale of the components when compared to objects. However, designing, developing, and maintaining components and component-based applications for reuse is a very complex process, which places high requirements not only on the component functional and non-functional properties, but also on the development organization. Interoperability of heterogeneous component was a major challenge of CBSE.

Key players within the IT industry, however, believed that we are close to a satisfactory answer to the challenge with the emergence of the Service Oriented Computing (SOC) paradigm. Service Oriented Computing (SOC) enables the development of distributed applications that consist of mutually independent services executing in heterogeneous environments. It is based on the Service Oriented Architecture (SOA), which is an architectural style for building software applications that use services available in a network such

as the web. It promotes loose coupling between the services so that they can be reused and composed. Among the benefits of this software methodology to business organizations includes: faster time to market, reduction in programing complexity and costs, flexible customization of products and lower maintenance costs.

Implementing Service Oriented Computing

A number of efforts have been going on within the industrial and scientific communities to develop core infrastructures and standards for realizing the vision of SOC. The two technologies that have emerged for implementing services out of these efforts are *web services* and *grid services*. The former is an industry-led effort while the latter is driven by the need of the scientific community. However, in recent years, these two types of service implementation approaches have technically converged to a large extent with the only difference being, essentially, that of application focus (Koehler & Alonso, 2007). We, briefly, highlight the key features of the two approaches.

Web Services

According to the World Wide Web consortium (W3C) (W3C, 2002b),

A web service is a software system identified by a uniform resource identifier (URI) whose public interfaces and bindings are defined and described using extensible markup language (XML). Its definition can be discovered by other software systems. These systems may interact with the Web

service in a manner prescribed by its definition using XML-based messages conveyed by Internet protocols.

Web services primarily address the issues of discovery and invocation of services on the Internet.

Today, web service has received wide acceptance as an important distributed computing approach for integrating extremely heterogeneous applications over the Internet because it is based on standards (Andrian et al, 2003). Standards are a collection of specifications, rules, and guidelines formulated and accepted by the leading market participants (Brydon et al, 2004). They, however, do not prescribe implementation details. Standards enable web services developed by different vendors to be interoperable. Unfortunately, there is an abundance of web service standards today, and it is not always easy to recognize how these standards are grouped and how they relate to each other. A more comprehensive categorization of web services standards is provided in (IBM, n.d):

The *de facto* standards established for web services describe (Brydon et al, 2004):

- **Common markup language for communication:** This facilitates communication between service providers and requestors, as each party is able to read the exchanged information based on the embedded markup tags. Web services use eXtensible Markup Language (XML) for the common markup language.

- **Common Message format for exchanging information:** For effective communication, the parties must be able to exchange messages according to an agreed-upon format. By having such format, parties who are unknown to each other can communicate effectively. Representational State Transfer (REST) and Simple Object Access Protocol (SOAP) are currently the widely used message formats for Web services.

- **Common service specification formats:** There must be a common format that all service providers can use to specify the service details, such as the service type, how to access the service, and so forth. This enables service providers to specify their services so that any requestor can understand and use them. Web Services Description Language (WSDL) provides web services with common specification formats.

- **Common means for service lookup:** In the same way that providers need a common way to specify service details, service requestors must have a common way to look up and obtain details of a service. By having these common, well-known locations and a standard way to access them, services can be universally accessed by all providers and requestors. Universal Description, Discovery and Integration (UDDI) specification defines a common means for registering and looking up web services.

Grid Services

The Grid computing idea started within the scientific and academic communities as a way of enabling computing resources, data and services on demand. Foster and Kesselman in 1998 defined computational grid as follows (Foster & Kesselman, 1998):

A computational grid is a hardware and software infrastructure that provides dependable, consistent, pervasive, and inexpensive access to high-end computational capabilities.

The definition was primarily centered on the computational aspects of grids. Later, the definition was broadened with more emphasis on collaboration and resource sharing and thereby, addressing the social and policy issues. Therefore, the most common definition of grid in use today is (Foster et al, 2001):

Coordinated resource sharing and problem solving in dynamic, multi-institutional virtual organizations.

Many early efforts in grid led to *ad hoc* solutions for resource integration. However, since web service standards are already popular and widely deployed, it becomes clear that Grid computing could benefit from capabilities provided by web services. This motivated the Global Grid Forum (GGF) (GGF, 2002) to formulate the Open Grid Services Architecture (OGSA) which is based on web services (Tuecke et al, 2002). The core of OGSA is a *grid service*. A grid service is an interface associated with a grid resource. The grid resource and its state are controlled and managed via grid services. There are two key frameworks for implementing grid services: the Open Grid Service Infrastructure (OGSI) and the Web Service Resource Framework (WSRF). However, the WSRF provides a superior approach to developing grid services and is, therefore, commonly used in most grid service implementations. The two frameworks have reference implementations in Globus Toolkit 3 (GT3) and Globus Toolkit 4 (GT4) respectively (Foster, 2005).

It must, however, be noted that, although, grid services are implemented using web-services technology, there are some fundamental differences between them (Sotomayor & Childers, 2006):

- One, in a grid service, the state of a resource or service is often important and, therefore, may need to persist across transactions. A web service is, however, stateless and does not need to keep the state information. This means, plain web services are stateless (i.e there is no memory between separate transactions invoked on the same service instance. They can not remember information about last invocation).
- Two, a grid service addresses the issue of a virtual resource and its state management and since grid environment is dynamic, a

grid service can be transient rather than persistent. A web service, however, addresses the issue of discovery and invocation of persistent services.

- Three, a grid service can be dynamically created and destroyed, unlike a Web service, which is often presumed available if its corresponding WSDL file is accessible to its client.

But, in spite of these differences, it must be pointed that, even though the Web Services Resource Framework (WSRF) is a specification tailored to Grid computing to enable closer control of stateful resources (eg computations) through Web services, the specification can be used in many business applications because business settings now frequently involve computation-intensive and decision-support components often with dedicated hardware which are the hallmark of scientific applications (Koehler & Alonso, 2007; Singh, 2004). Also, business applications would benefit from the high availability and superior implementation model offered by grid services. Although, currently there is no consensus on how grid computing would support business applications. This is partly due to its traditional focus on addressing the computational challenge of scientific applications. In the literature, two key ideas seem prevalent:

- First, grid computing can provide *IT level* support, where the grid is used to take advantage of underutilized computing capacity to solve business problems and provide IT level infrastructure to support business applications. This aligns with the traditional use of grid.
- Second, grid computing technology can be applied at *business process level.* This is in view of the convergence of the two technologies for implementing services - grid and web services. One such idea is the Business Process Grid (Zhang et al, 2004)

which focuses on business process provisioning through the grid. Research focus, in this case, is at business process-level and not at the low-level resource level. Similar view of applying grid beyond IT level had been echoed in a number of other initiatives such as the Business Grid (Nessi-Grid, 2006) and the Service Oriented Knowledge Utilities, SOKU (NGG report, 2006) of the UK Framework Programme. In this sense, grid provides the infrastructure for assembling next-generation business applications on the fly from an ecosystem of services on the grid and thereby, enhancing performance of systems in critical business areas such as enterprise resource planning (ERP), customer relationship management (CRM), supply chains, partner relationships, and product lifecycles. Some of the key issues to be addressed include business process orchestration and choreography, grid service workflow management, grid service selection and composition. This would provide the needed support for some on-going trends in e-business such as outsourcing (Dibbern et al, 2004), Software-as-a-Service (SaaS) (Vassiliadis et al, 2004; Vassiliadis et al, 2006), Business-to-Business (B2B) and Business-to-Consumer (B2C) integration and collaborative commerce (Andrian et al, 2003).

We, therefore, suggest grid as a unified next-generation SOC infrastructure for both e-business and e-science. Also, an ecosystem of services in a virtual organization would, typical, consist of few persistent (web) services and potentially many transient (grid) services (Sotomayor & Childers, 2006).

Semantic Web

Another very important technology that is paramount to realizing the vision of SOC is the Semantic Web (Berners-Lee, et al, 2001). A large-scale SOC environments typically involves a number of participants (processes, services, resources, organizations), each with different data, information and expertise. We need a way to ensure these participants communicate in understandable terms.

The grid community has appreciated the value of applying Semantic Web technologies to the information and knowledge aspects of Grid applications. This has led to the Semantic Grid. According to De Roure et al (2001):

The Semantic Grid is an extension of the current Grid in which information and services are given well-defined meaning, better enabling computers and people to work in cooperation.

To achieve this, technologies such as ontologies are used to define different data sources that are to be shared on the grid (Brown, 2005; Heflin, 2004; Gomez-Perez et al, 2004). It is concerned with how to represent (in terms of structure), store, manipulate and share knowledge in a formal way so that it may be used to accomplish a given task. This implies the need to arrive at an agreed knowledge representation of the data from heterogeneous data sources (Quix et al, 2002). Ontology can generally be captured using representational languages such as Resource Description Framework (RDF) (Decker et al, 2002a,b), the DARPA Agent Modeling Language (DAML) coupled with the Ontology Interchange Language (OIL) (the combination was also known as DAML+OIL) (DAML, 2001; Hender & McGuiness, 2001), the Web Ontology Language (OWL) and more generally ontologies (Heflin & Hender, 2000).

Beyond understanding the semantics of data, the *Semantic Web Services* have equally emerged to define semantics for services (process-level).

This came out of the realization that WSDL does not contain semantic descriptions, it only specifies the structure of message components using XML schema constructs. Knowing the semantics of the service enable us to better able to use it to fulfil application needs. Therefore, a solution to create semantic for web services is by mapping concepts in a Web service description (WSDL specification) to ontological concepts. Some of the approaches and initiatives towards specifying Web Services using semantics and ontologies include: OWL-S (OWL-S, 2004), RDFS (2004), SWSI (SWSI, 2004), SWWS (SWWS, 2004), WSML (WSML, 2004), WSMO (WSMO, 2004), WSMX (WSMX, 2004), and WSDL-S (Akkiraju, et al, 2006)

DYNAMIC SERVICE COMPOSITION

Having laid some background on trends in distributed computing towards SOC and presenting some key technologies that have emerged for realizing the vision of SOC, our aim in this section is to introduce dynamic composition of services and some challenges to dynamic composition of grid services.

Service Composition Concepts

Central to the Service Oriented Computing idea are *services*. Services generally, provide network-accessible capabilities and can be invoked or consumed and reused (Zhang et al, 2007). As illustrated in Figure 2, a service can be *atomic* (e.g Service A) in that it provides all of the required functionality contained within itself, or *composite* (e.g Service B uses Services X, Y and Z) that is, it may itself be made up from other services combined in some fashion (Nessi-Grid, 2006). Furthermore, services (whether atomic or composite) are provided and consumed. Provided service can exist within a single organization or sourced from different organizations. This can be used to define a number of business relationships and models between organizations that

can range from *static* to *dynamic* (Nessi-Grid, 2006). Our focus in this chapter is not actually on the relationship between service owners but on an efficient way of composing application that utilizes services (application modules) that are available in a grid ecosystem and typically owned by members of the Virtual Organization (VO). We, therefore, define *service composition* as any form of putting services together to achieve some desired functionality (Singh & Huhns, 2005). The service composition process can be *static* or *dynamic*. A *static composition* allows the service requestor to build an abstract model of the tasks that should be carried-out during the execution of the service at design and/or compile time (Alamri et al, 2006). The abstract model is a representation of the set of tasks including the control and the data dependency among them. *Dynamic composition*, on the other hand, is achieved by creating the abstract model of tasks and selecting the atomic services automatically without the interference of the service requestor in the composition process (Alamri et al, 2006). Static composition may work fine in environments where service components do not or only rarely change. In reality, most service environments are highly flexible and dynamic. New services become available on a daily basis and the number of service providers is constantly growing. Therefore, service composition processes should be able to transparently adapt to environment changes, and to adapt to customer requirements with minimal user intervention. Thus, the desirability of a dynamic composition approach.

In view of the fact that services can be composed to realize a desired functionality, both web services and grid communities have formulated process-level standards that allow services to be assembled as part of a workflow. Some of the process-level standards for Web services include:

- *XLANG* (Thatte, 2001), developed by Microsoft and used to describe how a process works as part of a business flow.

Figure 2. Service A is atomic while Service B is composite (Incorporating services X,Y, and Z) (Nessi-Grid, 2006)

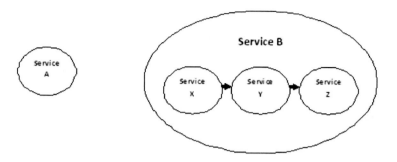

- *Web Services Flow Language (WSFL)* (Snell, 2001), initially developed by IBM, is a graph-based language that defines a specific order of activities and data exchanges for a particular process.
- *Web Services Choreography Interface (WSCI)* (W3C, 2002a), initially developed by Sun, SAP, BEA and Intalio, is a block-structured language that describes the messages exchanged between Web services participating in a collaborative exchange.
- *Business Process Execution Language for Web Services (BPEL4WS)* (Curbera et al, 2002), proposed by IBM, Microsoft and BEA, builds on WSFL and XLANG and combines the features of the block structured XLANG and the graph-based WSFL. BPEL4WS is replacing XLANG and WSFL.
- *Business Process Modelling Language (BPML)* (BPML, 2002), a metalanguage for modelling business processes. The specification was developed by Business Process Management Initiative (BPMI).

There are also standards relating to composition of grid services. Many of them aim to augment traditional workflow technology defined by web services especially to address the requirements of grid applications. Key workflow languages used in Grid include Grid Workflow Execution Languange (GWEL) (Cybok, 2004), Grid Service Flow Language (GSFL) (Krishnan, et al, 2002), GALE (Beiriger et al, 2000), and SWFL (Huang & Walker, 2003).

Two main perspectives on service composition seem to be prevalent (Singh & Huhns, 2005):

- **Orchestration:** This takes the view that composition is a partial order of operations that need to be executed. A central process (which can be another web service) takes control over the involved web services and coordinates the execution of different operations on the web services involved in the operation. This is done as per the requirements of the orchestration. Examples are workflow representations and process languages such as BPEL4WS. Orchestration is usually used in private business processes.
- **Choreography:** This does not rely on a central coordinator but rather takes the view that a composition is a set of message exchanges between participants. It is a collaborative effort focused on exchange of messages in public business processes. The message exchanges are constrained to occur in various sequences and may be required to be grouped into various transactions. Examples are in WSCL and WSCI.

We would later see that composition techniques based on orchestration and choreography only address the ordering of service components and not really geared for composition especially when services have to cooperate with one another throughout the lifecycle of the composition process.

Some Challenges to Dynamic Composition of Grid Services

There are a number of challenges to dynamic composition of grid services. Here are some of them:

1. **High uncertainties:** In grid systems, services are nomadic in nature, implying that they constantly enter and leave the environment anytime. Service unavailability at runtime may jeopardize the entire composition process especially when the composition has time constraints.
2. **Time constraints:** In most cases compositions are constrained by deadlines. The composition deadline is the time in which a particular composition is expected to be available or formed.
3. **Scalability:** Large-scale deployment of grid services would involve large directories with thousands or millions of services. Performing discovery and the selection of services in such grid directories will surely degrade the system performance if effective matchmaking algorithms or mechanisms are not employed.
4. **Changing requirements:** Changing user and system requirements are the norm rather than the exception in dynamic environments. Composition must be flexible so that it can be modified at runtime when user objectives or specifications changes. Furthermore, adaptation to system requirement changes is desirable because it ensures system reliability and robustness.

5. **Semantic disparity:** The grid environment is a shared virtual world where information is exchanged and resources shared. A major challenge is how to resolve the semantic differences of information shared by participants. As we earlier pointed out, the work of the semantic web is already addressing this need.

MULTI-AGENT SYSTEMS IN SERVICE ORIENTED COMPUTING

We now want to introduce agent and multi-agent systems and present a motivation for multi-agent system in dynamic composition of grid services especially in addressing some of the challenges outlined above.

Agent and Multi-Agent Systems

Software Agents

Although, there is no consensus on what exactly an agent is, but according to (Weiss, 1999) an *agent* is a computational entity such as a software or a robot that can be viewed as perceiving and acting upon its environment and that is autonomous in that its behaviour at least partially depends on its own experience. Autonomy is the most essential feature, which differentiates the agent from other simple programs (Jennings & Wooldridge, 1998). Software agents are important paradigm and development technology for software engineering in many areas including, intelligent user interfaces (Lieberman, 1997), electronic commerce (Nwana et al., 1998), business process management (Jennings et al, 2000), and digital libraries (Atkins et al, 1996). According to Wooldridge and Jennings (Wooldridge & Jennings, 1995), if a piece of software has the characteristics of autonomy, social ability, reactivity, and pro-activity, it is an agent in weak notion. On top of these characteristics, if the software has further characteristics of adaptability, mobility, veracity, and rationality, it becomes an agent in strong notion.. However, the weak agency model is the widely accepted (Woolridge and Jennings, 1995). According to the weak agency model, agents enjoy the following properties (Wang, 2007):

- **Autonomy:** Agents operate without the direct intervention of human or others, and have some kind of control over their actions and internal state (Castelfranchi, et al, 1992)
- **Social ability:** Agents interact with each other agents (and possibly humans) via some kind of agent communication language (Genesereth & Ketchpel, 1994)
- **Reactivity:** Agents perceive their environment (e.g the physical world, or the Internet) and respond in a timely fashion to changes that occur in it
- **Pro-activeness:** Agents do not simply act in response to their environment, they are able to exhibit goal-directed behavior

Multi-Agent Systems (MAS)

A *Multi-agent System (MAS)* consists of a society of multiple coexisting agents. Multi-agent systems (MAS) stem from the fields of distributed computing and distributed artificial intelligence (DAI) about four decades ago (Stone & Veloso, 2000). To benefit maximally from agents, we need a means for them to enable them to interact with each other at a high level (Singh & Huhns, 2005). Cao et al, (2001) gave the following reasons why a multi-agent system is suitable for addressing many real life problems than a centralized solution:

- Real life problems are usually physically or functionally distributed (e.g air traffic control, manufacturing system, health care, etc)
- Complex systems are often beyond direct control. They operate through the cooperation of many interacting subsystems, which may have their independent interest and modes of operation
- The complexity of a number of problems dictates a local point of view. When the problems are too expensive to be analyzed as a whole, solutions based on local approaches are more efficient
- Centralized structures are difficult to maintain and reconfigure, inefficient to satisfy real-world needs and costly in the presence of failures. Also, the amount of knowledge to manage is very large
- Real-world problems are heterogeneous. Heterogeneous environments may use different data and models, and operate in different modes

Motivation for MAS in SOC

There are a number of requirements for SOC that must be addressed for it to have large-scale deployment in open systems. Current service technologies are inadequate in addressing these needs and, therefore, other software engineering methodologies must be sought and employed. We discussed some of them as follows:

First, classical grid systems are server-based and, therefore, do suffer some performance problem (Bhatia, 2005). Current grid systems have a small user base typically a few hundreds. For example, if we consider that, from the viewpoint of OGSA, everything on the grid would be a service, these include applications, files, and instruments. Looking at just files, they would be roughly millions on any particular machine. If we then assume one million machines, we can imagine the scale? No doubt, this would increase the complexity of interactions of services beyond what a centralized server can effectively cope with. Also, centralization introduces a single point of failure. Therefore, as the grid gets to the mainstream of becoming the infrastructure for large-scale SOC, it will have to adopt a solution approach that scale well as number of resources increase. Augmenting current server-based grid system with a MAS architecture, therefore, offers the following performance benefits (Weiss, 1999):

- **Speed-up and efficiency:** Agents can operate asynchronously and in parallel, and this can result in an increased overall speed (provided that the overhead of necessary coordination does not outweigh this gain)
- **Robustness and reliability:** The failure of one or several agents does not necessarily make the overall system useless, because other agents already available in the system may take over their part
- **Scalability and flexibility:** The system can scale to an increased problem size by adding new agents, and this does not necessarily affect the operationality of the other agents

Second, Singh & Huhns (2005) discussed some major ways in which MAS technology could, potentially, extend current service implementation technologies (grid and web services) as follows:

- **Increasing their level of awareness:** A service knows only about itself, but not about its users, clients, or customers. Agents are often self-aware at a metalevel, and through learning and model building gain awareness of other agents and their capabilities as interactions among the agents occur.
- **Making them active:** Services are passive until invoked whereas agents are inherently communicative.
- **Autonomy:** For services to apply naturally in open environments, they need to be autonomous. Autonomy is a natural characteristic of agents.
- **Cooperation:** Agents are cooperative, and by forming teams and coalitions can provide higher-level and more comprehensive services.

Abstractions for Composition

From the foregoing, when service composition is treated as a workflow, the execution model of the composition is trivial and is only suitable for a closed environment. Workflows only define the ordering of services and do not capture deeper interactions of services. Singh & Huhns, (2005) provided the following useful abstraction for service composition that is suitable for open and dynamic environments such as grids:

- **Autonomy:** Services are provided by different organizations that might have local policies and interests; we should respect the autonomy of services during the composition process and not require them to be subservient to other services. In essence, services should be designed to be proactive and interact flexibly on their own terms.
- **Heterogeneity:** Because services are heterogeneous, there is the need for expressive, standardizable representations: this should be done for both data and services.
- **Long-lived and evolving:** Services are long-lived and evolving, and operate in environments that produce exceptions. Appropriate mechanisms must be put in place to handle such exceptions and ensure dynamic reconfigurability.
- **Cooperative:** Services can be (and ought to be) cooperative, the abstraction must represent how they behave in the awareness of the behaviour of other services.

These abstractions justify the suitability of the multi-agent systems approach for composition of grid services with capabilities of autonomy, heterogeneity, reliability, flexibility and robustness. It is in view of these abstractions for composition that we now introduce AIDSEC as discussed in the following section.

AIDSEC: AN AGENT-BASED INFRASTRUCTURE FOR DYNAMIC SERVICE COMPOSITION

In this section, we present our research effort, Agent-based Infrastructure for Dynamic Service Composition (AIDSEC) that demonstrates the need for a flexible and adaptive infrastructure for service composition. In other to put the problem addressed by AIDSEC in context, we start with a sample usage scenario and present some design considerations for AIDSEC. Thereafter, we discuss AIDSEC architecture, operation, and comparison with some existing work.

A Sample Usage Scenario

The use case presented here is based on a fictitious business-to-business (B2B) model of a South African-based travel agent company, called Planit (Pty) Ltd (hereafter, referred to as Planit). Planit specializes on planning trips of its clients which include flight booking, hotel booking and car rental. She offers a Business to Consumer (B2C) web portal that allows clients to make travel arrangements and also specify their trip preferences.

Let us consider a South African businessman named Joe, who intends to use Planit travel service to arrange his next business trip from Durban to Johannesburg. Joe will access Planit's web portal to make travel arrangements for his trip. In this case, he may be interested in: (1) booking a cheap flight from Durban to Johannesburg that would not cost him more than R1,500; (2) renting an executive-class car that would drive him from the airport to the place of his business meeting; (3) he may, also, be interested in a hotel that is not far from the location of his business meeting. Using Planit web portal, he is able to specify all the configurations required for reservation processing. These include, the time and day of his trip, the type of room he needs and in what location, payment method and so on.

To process Joe's request, Planit web portal application will access the company's internal services as well as external partner services since Planit is part of a collaborative network of tourism businesses in South Africa who formed a virtual organization for the purpose of sharing their business services. Conventionally, in the underlying service delivery infrastructure, Planit application will make use of a predefined workflow to aggregate the required services that comprise the travel package. In most cases, such workflows are static, which means they are only constrained to the services specified in their descriptions and their structure cannot be dynamically modified when new requirements are available at runtime. For example, if Joe wishes to add another request to check the weather conditions of his destination, it becomes practically impossible to dynamically incorporate a weather service to meet Joe's demands using conventional approach. In this sense, a more flexible approach becomes essential.

In addition to this, the execution of Planit's workflow for the travel service is centralized, making the travel service not to scale with the number of user requests. Although, the travel service offered by Planit deals with a handful of base services, but there are times when the scale of base services becomes so large that the execution of the composite service takes a very long time to complete. In this case, decentralization of control in the service delivery infrastructure is essential to improve scalability, reduce communications costs and avoid single locus of failure.

Moreover, if we imagine a case where a hotel reservation fails while a flight has been booked and the client has already been charged a flight fee, the system need to be able to manage the transaction and ensure necessary compensation in case of any undesired situation. It will be required that failure be communicated to the flight service so that flight reservation is cancelled.

Figure 3. AIDSEC architecture

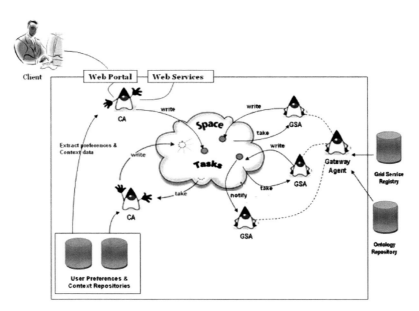

Design Considerations

From the foregoing, we identify the following design considerations for AIDSEC:

- **Flexibility:** Must allow composition to be configured at runtime according to requirements changes;
- **Autonomy:** Must ensure services independent and maintain the interests of their providers while participating in complex interactions.
- **Scalability:** Must be able to scale with increase in number of constituent services including the services to be discovered and selected.
- **Pro-activeness:** It must allow service providers to take the initiative to search consumers in order to improve the performance of matchmaking.
- **Fault-tolerance:** Must ensure composition is able to adapt to any type of fault or exception that occurs at runtime due to service unavailability or other uncertainties.

- **Deadline-driven:** Must ensure composition is synthesized within expected timeframe.

Overview of AIDSEC Architecture

The AIDSEC architecture, illustrated in Figure 3, is based on the concepts of Multi-agent Systems, OGSA-compliant stateful grid services and tuple spaces (Gelernter, 1985). The multi-agent system is implemented as autonomous and decentralized agents that operate on local limited knowledge. Decentralization of multi-agent systems is utilized, in this case, to achieve a fault tolerant and scalable dynamic service composition platform. The tuple space was used to achieve flexible and decoupled communications between agents. Using a tuple space, the agents can flexibly collaborate in a transparent manner while maintaining global coherence. In AIDSEC, there are three types of agents, namely: the *Client Agent* (CA), *Grid Service Agent* (GSA) and the *Gateway Agent* (GA). AIDSEC also include other support components such as *Grid Service Registry (GSR), Ontology*

Figure 4. Client agent components

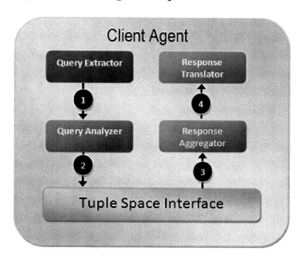

Figure 5. Grid service agent components

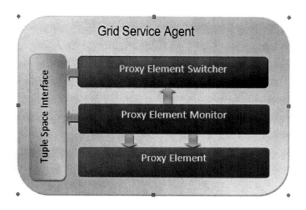

Registry (OR), and *User Preference and Context Repository (UPCR)*.

The CA is responsible for collecting complex user requests, decomposing them and publishing them on the tuple space. Thereafter, it synthesizes composition plans and present composition results to the user. The GSA serves in executing published tasks, while the GA is responsible for creating the GSA based on available services in the GSR. The GSR is a registry such as the Grid MDS or the UDDI that enables providers to register their service offerings. The OR is a repository that stores semantic description of published grid services. Lastly, the UPCR stores information pertinent to user profiles and context that is used by the CA for

further customization. Figure 4 shows the internal components of the CA while Figure 5 shows the components of GSA.

AIDSEC Operation

We describe here the operation of AIDSEC and present discussions on how it addresses the challenges posed by the use-case scenario presented earlier. AIDSEC addresses dynamic service composition as a problem that involves the following phases: *task decomposition and representation, dynamic service matchmaking, dynamic composition synthesis, execution and monitoring*, and *dynamic service configuration or adaptation*.

Task Decomposition and Representation

A *task* is a high level goal or objective that an end user wants to achieve. In most cases, end users specify their tasks as high level or abstract goals that can be simple or complex. Complex tasks can be further decomposed into simpler ones so that they can be assigned to appropriate processing entities or services. Tasks are carried out by services and, for simplicity, we assume each simple task can be mapped to a single atomic service. The distinction between a task and a service is quite simple: a task describes what the user wants to achieve including the constraints that are associated with it, while a service deals with how the goal is realized under the given constraints.

In the *Planit* scenario presented, *Joe* can make a request to book his business trip and specify his request, in natural language, as follows:

I want to go on a business trip to Sandton, Johannesburg, book a flight that is less than R1500, reserve an executive car and also reserve a hotel that is near to the location of my business meeting.

This request is sent to the CA in AIDSEC, which will accept it together with the user preferences. The CA then parse it and partition it into a set of sub-requests represented as a pair of task, and associated constraints. In this case, the above request will be partitioned into tasks like:

```
<book flight | price < 1500>,
<reserve car | class =executive>
and <book hotel | location =
near>.
```

These sub-tasks are then represented as an object of type Task which consists of attributes such as task_id, task_desc, task_status, and plan_id. Thereafter, the CA will dynamically create its own local interaction space and then publishes the sub-tasks along with their associated constraints into the tuple space. The CA, however, maintains the identity of its created interaction space.

Dynamic Service Matchmaking

The next phase of AIDSEC operation is service matchmaking. Service matchmaking in AIDSEC is achieved through a set of "active" grid services implemented as distributed matchmakers who pro-actively search the tuple space for tasks that they can contribute to. Pro-active distributed matchmakers are employed in this case to reduce the discovery and selection time of conventional centralized matchmaker. Pro-activeness gives services the ability to initiate interactions rather than to remain passive until invoked as in conventional passive architectures. The distinction between a pro-active and reactive approach is illustrated in Figure 6. Besides, pro-activeness enables agents to maintain their autonomy while participating flexibly in complex interactions. The distributed matchmakers are implemented as grid services wrapped inside agents (called GSA). Our assumption is that a GSA is given a single task thus, a GSA cannot perform multiple tasks simultaneously. During the startup of AIDSEC platform, the Gateway Agent creates all GSAs based on available services and deploys them to the AIDSEC platform. Each created GSA consists

of the running agent code, a semantic description and the bindings of its associated services. The GA creates the GSA by listening to different grid service registries and upon registration of a new service in the global registries, it creates a new local GSA to represent the service.

Therefore, when the CA publish *Joe*'s request as a simple primitive tasks in the tuple space, the GSAs will start matching their semantic descriptions with the requirements of the published tasks. For example, in the tourism business ecosystem, there might be HotelGSAs that represent different hotel services; FlightGSAs representing different flight services and CarHireGSAs representing different car rental services. Each of these services will search the tuple space in order to find a task that best suits its semantic descriptions. In this context, a FlightGSA will search the tuple space to locate the *<book flight>* task that fit its semantic description. If a GSA find a task that matches its criteria, it will: (i) change the task status in the space from "available" to "assigned"; (ii) query the task_id, plan_id and result_id of the task; (iii) leave its service description on the task in the space; and (iv) wait for the its execution plan to be available in order to start executing the task.

Figure 6. Passive and active approaches to grid service discovery

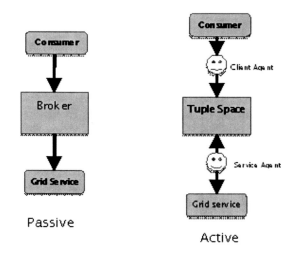

Passive

Active

Note that if the status of the task in the tuple space is "assigned", other GSAs will assume that the task is occupied and not attend to it.

Dynamic Composition Synthesis

After the matchmaking process, the CA will synthesis execution plans for each GSA based on the published semantic service descriptions on tasks. Execution plans are synthesized by creating a graph which maps the inputs and outputs of all services which have left their semantic descriptions on published tasks. Thereafter, the graph is partitioned into partial plans (see sample partial task execution plan in Figure 7), which are then published in the tuple space for consumption by the GSA. In this case, all the GSAs will coordinate the execution flow of composite service using their partial plans. Besides, AIDSEC composition model is unique in that it synthesizes composition plans based on available services at runtime. After plans for tasks are published on the tuple space, the status of each task then changes from "assigned" to "ready".

Execution and Monitoring

On getting the partial execution plan, each GSA will initiate and monitor execution of the service it represents. Therefore, the execution of the service provided by the GSA starts just after the GSA has retrieved the execution plan corresponding to its assigned task from the tuple space. All GSAs will receive their execution plans by periodically checking the tuple space for plan availability using the plan_id. Hence, if the GSA retrieves a valid plan that corresponds to its assigned task, it will first check the plan for dependencies that needs to be satisfied before task execution. This includes the execution policies that define how the task should be adapted during execution. If there are no dependencies defined in its plan description, the GSA will check whether are there is any notification or instruction it is supposed to receive before initiating execution. If there are no messages or instructions, the GSA will change the status of the task on the tuple space from "ready" to "running" and immediately start task execution by invoking the corresponding service. However, if there are task dependencies, the GSA will first check the execution policies to determine whether execution can commence without waiting for task

Figure 7. A sample partial task execution plan for Hotel service

```
<plan>

<task id = "1324676687" name = "Hotel">
  <dependencies>
  <dependency id = "2342543251" name = "Flight" type = "">
    <outputList>
    <output name = "flight_ticket" type = "FlightTicket">
    </outputList>
      </dependency>
  </dependencies>
  <execution-policy>
      <dependency-constraints availability = "all">
          <dependency-constraints availability = "single">
  </execution-policy>
  </task>
  </plan>
```

Figure 8. AIDSEC implementation overview

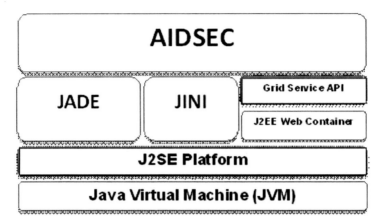

dependencies. If it is possible, the GSA will commence on task execution, otherwise it will wait until the relevant dependencies becomes available. Finally, the GSA will publish the results of a successful service execution into a tuple space as a result entry which is identified by a result_id associated with the completed task.

Dynamic Service Configuration or Adaptation

During the execution stage, a service might fail while executing its assigned task due to exceptions in its internal logic and become temporarily unavailable. In such case, the GSA representing the service will autonomously adapt by modifying the status of its assigned task from "running" to "failed". It will also query the execution state of the service and publish it into the tuple space. The execution state can then be made available to any other waiting GSA in the same service category so as to continue from the point of failure.

In addition, the system also adapts composition to changes in user requirements at runtime. In our scenario, if *Joe* requires the travel service to include weather service, this could be dynamically incorporated to the running composite service since the service composition does not depend on a predefined workflow. In another case, if *Joe*

decided to cancel car booking service because he has already spoke to a friend to pick him up at the airport, the CA may send instruction to terminate the car booking while allowing the rest of the services to continue execution unimpeded.

AIDSEC Implementation

We have implemented all the functionalities of AIDSEC and tested with the use-case scenario described above. All the functionalities were implemented with Java technologies and relevant frameworks. A layered overview of AIDSEC implementation is shown in Figure 8. The Java Agent Development Environment (JADE) (JADE, 2005) framework was used to implement all the agent's roles in the system. Java Interface for Network Infrastructure (JINI) (JINI, 1994) technology provided JavaSpaces service which is a Java based tuple space implementation derived from Linda coordination model. Grid services were implemented using the Globus Toolkit 4 Java Web Service core API (Globus Alliance, 2005) and deployed into the Apache Tomcat Web Container (Apache, 1998). An open source implementation of UDDI 2.0 registry JUDDI (Apache, 2003) was used as the registry to publish grid services and IBM UDDI4J (Tidwell, 2001) was used to programatically interact with the

JUDDI. WSDL4J (2005) was used parse WSDL descriptions during the publication process of WSDL interface description in the JUDDI. The Gateway Agent uses WSDL2Java (2000) to generate proxy stubs used by GSAs to invoke the service implementation. The task execution plan is generated as an XML file which is represented in the tuple space as a Java object. Finally, OWL-S (2004) was used to describe the service profiles for grid services.

Comparison with Related Work

Although, there are various taxonomy that could be used in classifying approaches for dynamic services composition in the literature, for lack of space, we would only compare our approach with workflow techniques and a few multi-agent systems. However, we summarize some key approaches for dynamic service composition (with their strengths and limitations) in Table 1.

Currently, most WSRF-compliant grid systems adopt service composition/orchestration techniques that are procedural and based on workflow. Infact, there are almost over 100 workflow management systems in use today but the most popular ones are seen in projects such as Triana Project (2003), Taverna (2004), and JIGSA (2005). Workflow technology general suffers critical limitations as follows (Singh & Huhns, 2005):

- They are often too rigid because they are constructed prior to use and are enforced by some central authority
- The rigidity also causes productivity losses by making it harder to accommodate the flexible, adhoc reasoning that is the strong suit of human intelligence
- They lack adaptation mechanism to runtime changes in system requirements

In order to eliminate the rigidity of workflow techniques, many other research endeavours have tried to augment workflow approaches with adaptation mechanisms. The Rudder project (Li & Parashar., 2006) has some interesting similarities with our own work since they also employ multi-agent systems and use tuple space for coordination. A major difference of our work from Rudder is that we employed decentralized matchmakers in order to achieve scalable and efficient service discovery while Rudder uses a central matchmaker for service discovery. Moreover, AIDSEC is a pure agent-based system wrapped on grid services for service composition while Rudder employs agents to augment workflow.

Furthermore, in the work reported by Muller et al (2006), a pure agent-based system was proposed for service composition. However, coordination of service agents' activities is achieved through coalition formation. A problem with coordinat-

Table 1. Summary of key approaches for dynamic service composition

Approach	Techniques	Strengths	Limitations
Workflow e.g Triana (2003) Rudder(Li & Parashar., 2006)	BPML, BPEL, WSCI, GWEL WSFL, GWL	Fault Handling and Compensation Mechanism.	-Centralized execution model. -Rigid. -Priori knowledge
AI Planning e.g SHOP2 (2004)	Situation Calculus HTN Planning, Rule Based Planning	Automatic composition.	- Suitable for close and static environments. -Domain knowledge.
Formal e.g CRESS (Turner, 2000)	Petri nets, Process Algebra, Finite State Automata	Verification and Validation.	-Centralized execution model.
Multi-agent System e.g Muller et.al (2006)	Coalition Formation.	Emergent behavior based on alliance formation.	-Assume all agents know about each other's preferences. -Computational Complexity

ing agents' activities using coalition formation (Nwana et al, 1996) is computational complexity. Also, the amount of knowledge required of the agent is much because it assumes that each agent has knowledge of the utility models of other agents. Moreover, communication is high between agents and, therefore, resulting in some overhead. AIDSEC is designed to enable agent operate on limited knowledge and thereby decoupled in time and space.

FUTURE TRENDS

Current SOC environments are still very rudimentary with just a few participants. The emphasis unfortunately, has been on the execution of individual services or ordering of services and not the important problems of how services are selected and how they collaborate to provide higher-levels of functionality. The next stage in the evolution of SOC will drive the move towards pervasive service environment where services would become widely available in everyday home, office and play environments which will then result in higher degree of diversity and heterogeneity of the end-systems (Hunns et al, 2005). Future SOC environments would, therefore, be more populous, distributed and dynamic thereby, requiring greater collaboration and interaction of diverse entities. The maturity and proliferation of online ontologies through the Semantic Web technologies would further allow independently developed services to be dynamically selected, engaged, composed and executed in a context sensitive manner. This would bring new requirements for composing services on the fly especially services whose requirements are not known apriori. Services can equally collaborate to intelligently realize an application need without any human interaction involved. It is then important that services become "alive" and "active" by utilizing other techniques that can facilitate greater interaction in order to meet these challenges. We suggest a multi-agent

system as a promising complement. In the emerging grid service ecosystem, rather than waiting for discovery, services can proactively determine how they can contribute to a particular application without violating their own autonomy.

CONCLUSION

In this chapter, we discussed the business trends that have led to the evolution of SOC for developing business applications. We have introduced key service technologies that are used for realizing the vision of SOC including web and grid services. We have, also, pointed out the vital role of the Semantic Web in SOC. We have then looked at the key concepts of dynamic service composition and enumerated some challenges to dynamic composition of grid services. In view of the challenges of dynamic composition of grid services, we presented multi-agent systems and motivated for MAS approach in SOC. We suggested some abstractions for service composition and opined that such abstractions can only be realized by using an agent-oriented approach for service composition. Subsequently, we have also tried to demonstrate key concepts discussed in this chapter through a case study of our own research endeavour - AIDSEC (Agent-based Infrastructure for Dynamic Service Composition). In the chapter, we have presented its design, implementation and compared it with some related work. The key strengths of AIDSEC as presented in this chapter include its respect for autonomy of service providers, scalability, decentralized matchmaking (thereby speeding up service discovery), decentralized composition execution and also adaptation to runtime changes in user and system requirements. We equally have raised some interesting trends in the future of SOC and how it would impact dynamic composition of services. It could then be concluded that in order to cope with the scale and level of interactivity required for dynamic service composition in emerging SOC environments, current technologies for implementing services would have to be augmented with an agent-based approach especially where services require capabilities such as autonomy, heterogeneity, flexibility and robustness.

ACKNOWLEDGMENT

This research work described in this chapter is supported by Telkom, THRIP, HUAWEI, and the National Research Foundation (NRF) of South Africa. The authors are grateful for their financial support.

REFERENCES

W3C. (2002a). *Web Service Choreography Interface (WSCI) 1.0*. Retrieved November 10th, 2008 from http://www.w3.org/TR/wsci/

W3C. (2002b). Retrieved from http://www.w3.org

Akkiraju, R., Farrell, J., Miller, J., Nagarajan, M., Schmidt, M., Sheth, A., & Verma, K. (2006). *Web service semantics: WSDLS*. Retrieved February 20, 2007 from http://www.w3.org/Submission/WSDL-S

Alamri, A., Eid, M., & El Saddik, A. (2006). Classification of state-of-the-art dynamic web services composition techniques. *International Journal of Web and Grid Services*, 2(2). doi:10.1504/IJWGS.2006.010805

Andrian, C., Peter, H., Aditya, G., Sim, K., & George, D. (2003). *Using Portal Technology for Collaborative e-Commerce*. White Paper. Retrieved January 13th, 2006 from www.dsl.uow.edu.au/publications/techreports/collins04portal.pdf

Apache. (1998). Retrieved from http://tomcat.apache.org/

Apache. (2003). Retrieved from http://ws.apache.org/juddi/

Atkins, D. E., Birmingham, W. P., Durfee, E. H., Glover, E. J., Mullen, T., & Rundensteiner, E. A. (1996). Toward inquiry-based education through interacting software agents. *IEEE Computer*, 29(5), 67–76.

Beiriger, J. I., Johnson, W. R., Bivens, H. P., Humphreys, S. L., & Rhea, R. (2000). Constructing the ASCI Computational Grid. In *Proceedings of the Ninth International Symposium on High Performance Distributed Computing (HPDC 2000)*, Pittsburgh, PA. Washington, DC: CS Press.

Berners-Lee, T., Hendler, J., & Lassila, O. (2001). The Semantic Web. *Scientific American*, 34–43. doi:10.1038/scientificamerican0501-34

Bhatia, K. (2005). *Peer-To-Peer Requirements On The Open Grid Services Architecture Framework*. GGF document by the OGSAP2P Research Group. Retrieved from www.ggf.org

BPML. (2002). Retrieved November 10th, 2008 from www.ebpml.org/bpml.htm

Bradshaw, J. M. (1997). An introduction to software agents. In J. M. Bradshaw (Ed.), *Software agents* (pp. 3-46). Cambridge, MA: AAAI Press/The MIT Press.

Brown, M. C. (2005). *What is the semantic grid*. Retrieved from http://www.ibm.com/developerworks/grid/library/gr-semgrid/

Brydon, S., Murray, G., Ramachandran, V., Singh, I., Stearns, B., & Violleau, T. (2004). *Designing Web Services with the J2EE platform*. Reading, MA: Addison Walley Publishers.

Cao, J. (2001). *Agent-based Resource Management for Grid Computing*. Unpublished doctoral dissertation. University of Warwick, Coventry, UK

Castelfranchi, C., Miceli, M., & Cesta, A. (1992). Dependence relations among autonomous agents. In *Proceedings of the 3rd European Workshop on Modeling Autonomous Agents and Multi-Agent Worlds (pp. 215-231)*. Amsterdam: Elsevier Science Publisher.

Curbera, F., Goland, Y., Klein, J., Leymann, F., Roller, D., Thatte, S., & Weerawarana, S. (2002). Business Process Execution Language for Web Services, Version 1.0. Retrieved November 10th, 2008 from http://download.boulder.ibm.com/ibmdl/pub/software/dw/specs/ws-bpel/ws-bpel1.pdf

Cybok, D. (March 2004). *A Grid Workflow Infrastructure, Presentation in GGF-10*. Berlin, Germany.

DAML. (2001). *The DARPA Agent Markup Language*. Retrieved from http://www.daml.org

De Roure, D., Jennings, N. R., & Shadbolt, N. R. (2001). *The Semantic Grid: A future e-Science infrastructure*. Retrieved 15th May, 2007 from http://www.semanticgrid.org/documents/semgrid-journal/semgrid-journal.pdf

Decker, S., Prasenjit, M., & Sergey, M. (2002b). Framework for the Semantic Web: An RDF tutorial. *IEEE Internet Computing*, *4*(6), 68–73.

Decker, S., Sergey, M., van Harmelen, F., Fensel, D., Klein, M., & Broekstra, J. (2002a). The Semantic Web: The roles of XML and RDF. *IEEE Internet Computing*, *4*(5), 63–74. doi:10.1109/4236.877487

Dibbern, J., Goles, T., Hirschheim, R., & Jayatilaka, B. (2004). Information Systems Outsourcing: A survey and analysis of the literature. *The Data Base for Advances in Information Systems*, *35*(4), 6–102.

Endrei, M., Ang, J., Ansanjani, A., Chua, S., Comte, P., Krogdahi, P., et al. (2004). Patterns: Service-Oriented Architecture and Web Services. *IBM Redbooks*. Retrieved May 17th, 2007 from www.ibm.com/redbooks

Foster, I. (2005). Globus Toolkit 4: Software for Service Oriented Systems. In H. Jin, D. Reed, & W. Jiang, (Eds.), *NPC 2005*, (LNCS 3779, pp. 2 – 13). Retrieved November 10th, 2008 from http://www.globus.org/alliance/publications/papers/IFIP-2005.pdf

Foster, I., & Kesselman, C. (1998). *The Grid: Blueprint for a New Computing Infrastructure*. San Francisco: Morgan Kaufmann Publishers.

Foster, I., Kesselman, C., & Tuecke, S. (2001). The Anatomy of the Grid: Enabling scalable virtual organizations. [Retrieved from www.globus.org/research/papers/anatomy.pdf]. *International Journal of High Performance Computing Applications*, *15*(3), 200–222. doi:10.1177/109434200101500302

Gelenter, D. (1985). Generative Communication in Linda. *ACM Transaction of Prog. Lang. Syst.*, *1*(7), 80–112. doi:10.1145/2363.2433

Genesereth, M. R., & Ketchpel, S. P. (1994). Software agents. *Communications of the ACM*, *37*(7), 48–53. doi:10.1145/176789.176794

GGF. (2002). Retrieved from http://www.gridforum.org

Globus Alliance. (2005). *Globus Toolkit 4 Java WS Core*. Retrieved from http://www.globus.org/toolkit/docs/4.0/common/javawscore/

Gomez-Perez, A., Fernandez-Lopez, M., & Corcho, O. (2004). *Ontological Engineering with examples from the areas of Knowledge Management, e-commece and the Semantic Web*. London: Springer-Verlag.

Heflin, J. (2004). *OWL Web Ontology Language.* Retrieved April 2006 from http://www.w3.org/TR/webont-req/

Helfin, J., & Hendler, J. A. (2000). Dynamic Ontologies on the Web. In *Proceedings of the National Conference on Artificial Intelligence (AAAI)* (pp. 443-449).

Hender, J., & McGuiness, D. L. (2001). DARPA Agent Markup Language. *IEEE Intelligent Systems, 15*(6), 72–73.

Huang, H., & Walker, D. (2003). Extensions to Web Service Techniques for Integrating Jini into a Service-Oriented Architecture for the Grid. In *Proceedings of the International Conference on Computational Science 2003 (ICCS '03),* Melbourne, Australia, (LNCS). Berlin: Springer-Verlag.

Huhns, M.N., Singh, M.P., Burstein, M., Decker, K., Durfee, K.E., Finin, T.et al. (2005) Research Directions for Service-oriented Multiagent Systems. *Internet Computing, IEEE, 9*(6), 65 – 70.

Hwagyoo, P., Woojong, S., & Heeseok, L. (2004). A role-driven component-oriented methodology for developing collaborative commerce systems. *Information and Software Technology,* (46): 819–837.

IBM. (n.d). Retrieved October 17th, 2008, from http://www.ibm.com/developerworks/webservices/standards/

JADE. (2005). Retrieved from http://jade.tilab.com/

Jennings, N. R., Norman, T. J., Faratin, P., & Odgers, B. (2000). Autonomous agents for business process management. *International Journal of Applied Intelligence, 14*(2), 145–189.

Jennings, N. R., & Wooldridge, M. J. (1998). *Agent technology: Foundations, Applications and Markets.* Berlin: Springer-Verlag.

JIGSA. (2005). Retrieved from http://www.grid-workflow.org/snips/gridworkflow/space/JIGSA

JINI. (1994). Retrieved from http://www.sun.com/software/jini/

Koehler, J., & Alonso, G. (2007, July). Service Oriented Computing. *Ercim News, 70,* 15–16.

Krishnan, S., Wagstrom, P., & Laszewski, G. (2002). *GSFL: A Workflow Framework for Grid Services. Preprint ANL/MCS-P980-0802.* Argonne, IL: Argonne National Laboratory.

Li, Z., & Parashar, M. (2006). *An Infrastructure for Dynamic Composition of Grid Services.* Retrieved from www.caip.rutgers.edu/TASSL/Papers/rudder-grid-06.pdf

Lieberman, H. (1997). Autonomous Interface Agents. In *proceedings of CHI conference on Human Factors in Computer Systems* (pp. 67-74).

Muller, I., Kowalczyk, R., & Braun, P. (2006). Towards Agent-based Coalition Formation for Service Composition. In *Proceedings of the IEEE/WIC/ACM International Conference on Intelligent Agent Technology.* Retrieved from ieexplore.ieee.org/iel5/4052878/4052879/04052901.pdf

Nessi-Grid. (2006). Networked European Software and Services Initiative – Grid. *Grid vision and strategic research agenda.* Retrieved from www.nessi-europe.com/

Nwana, H. S., Rosenschein, J., Sandholm, T., Sierra, C., Maes, P., & Guttman, R. (1998). Agent-mediated electronic commerce: Issues, challenges, and some viewpoints. In *Proceedings of 2nd ACM International Conference on Autonomous Agents* (pp. 189-196).

Nwana, S., Lee, L., & Jennings, N. R. (1996). Coordination in Software Agent Systems. *BT Technology Journal, 14*(4).

OWL-S. (2004). *OWL-based Web service ontology*. Retrieved February 20, 2007 from http://www.daml.org/services/owl-s/

Quix, C., Schoop, M., & Jeusfeld, M. (2002). Business Data Management for Business-To-Business Electronic Commerce. *SIGMOD Record, 31*(1). doi:10.1145/507338.507348

RDFS. (2004). *RDF vocabulary description language 1.0: RDF schema, W3C*. Retrieved October 24, 2006, from http://www.w3.org/TR/rdf-schema/

NGG Report. (2006). Future for European Grids: GRIDs and Service Oriented Knowledge Utilities. *Vision and Research Directions 2010 and Beyond*. Retrieved from semanticgrid.org/NGG3

SHOP2. (2004). Retrieved from http://www.cs.umd.edu/projects/shop/

Singh, M. P. (2004). Agent-based Abstractions for Software Development - Accommodating Complexity in Open Systems. In F. Bergenti, M.P. Gleizes, F. Zambonelli, (Eds.), *Methodologies and Software Engineering for Agent Systems - The Agent-Oriented Software Engineering Handbook*. Amsterdam: Kluwer Academic Publishers.

Singh, M. P., & Huhns, M. (2005). *Service-Oriented Computing: Semantics, Processes, Agents*. Hoboken, NJ: John Wiley & Sons.

Snell, J. (2001). *Introducing the Web Services Flow Language*. Retrieved from November 10th, 2008, http://www.ibm.com/developerworks/library/ws-ref4/

Sotomayor, B., & Childers, L. (2006). *Globus Toolkit 4: Programming Java Services*. San Francisco: Morgan Kauffman publishers.

Stone, P., & Veloso, M. (2000). *Multiagent systems: A Survey from a Machine Learning Perspective*. Tech. Rep. CMU-CS-97-193. Pittsburgh, PA: Carnegie Mellon University, School of Computer Science.

SWSI. (2004). *Semantic Web services initiative (SWSI)*. Retrieved February 20, 2007 from http://www.swsi.org/

SWWS. (2004). *Semantic Web enabled Web service*. Digital Enterprise Research Institute (DERI).

Taverna. (2004). Retrieved from http://taverna.sourceforge.net/

Thatte, S. (2001). *XLANG Web Services for Business Process design*. Retrieved from http://www.ebpml.org/xlang.htm

Tidwell. (2001). *UDDI4J: Matchmaking for Web services*. Retrieved from http://www.ibm.com/developerworks/library/ws-uddi4j.html

Triana Project. (2003). Retrieved from http://www.trianacode.org/

Tuecke, S., Czajkowski, K., Foster, I., Frey, J., Graham, S., Kesselman, C., & Jennings, N. R. (2002). *Grid Service Specification*. Presented at GGF4, February, 2002. Retrieved from http://www.globus.org/research/papers.html

Turner, K. (2000). *Communication Representation Employing Systematic Specification*. Retrieved from http://www.cs.stir.ac.uk/~kjt/research/cress.html

Vassiliadis, B., Giotopoulos, K., Votis, K., Sioutas, S., Bogonikolos, N., & Likothanassis, S. (2004). Application Service Provision through the Grid: Business Models and Architectures. In . *Proceedings of International Conference on Information Technology: Coding and Computing, 1*, 367–371. doi:10.1109/ITCC.2004.1286481

Vassiliadis, B., Stefani, A., Tsaknakis, J., & Tsakalidis, A. (2006). From Application Service Provision to Service Oriented Computing: A Study of the IT Outsourcing Evolution. *Telematics and Informatics, 23*, 271–293. doi:10.1016/j.tele.2005.09.001

Verma, D. C. (2004). *Legitimate Applications of Peer-to-Peer Networks*. Hoboken, NJ: John Wiley & Sons.

Wang, L. (2007). Toward Agent-Based Grid Computing. In H. Lin (Ed.), *Architectural design of multi-agent systems: technologies and techniques,* (pp. 173-188). Hershey, PA: IGI Global publishing.

Weiss, G. (1999). *Multiagent Systems: A modern approach to distributed artificial intelligence.* Cambridge, MA: The MIT Press.

Woolridge, M., & Jennings, N. R. (1995). Intelligent Agents: Theory and Practice. *The Knowledge Engineering Review, 10*(2), 115–152. doi:10.1017/S0269888900008122

WSDL2Java. (2000). Retrieved from http://ws.apache.org/axis/java/user-guide.htm

WSDL4J. (2005). Retrieved from http://sourceforge.net/projects/wsdl4j

WSML. (2004). Web Service Modeling Language (WSML). Retrieved February 20, 2007 from http://www.wsmo.org/wsml/

WSMO. (2004). Web Services Modeling Ontology(WSMO). Retrieved February 20, 2007 from http://www.wsmo.org

WSMX. (2004). Web services execution environment (WSMX). Retrieved February 20, 2007 from http://www.wsmx.org

Zhang, L., Li, J., & Lam, H. (2004). Toward a Business Process Grid for Utility Computing. *IT Professional, 6,* 62–64. doi:10.1109/MITP.2004.25

Zhang, L., Zhang, J., & Cai, H. (2007). *Services Computing.* Berlin: Co-published by Tsinghua University Press and Springer- Verlag.

KEY TERMS AND DEFINITIONS

Dynamic Service Composition: Service composition is the process of putting services together to achieve some desired functionality. The process can be static or dynamic. In dynamic service composition, the creation of the abstract task model and participating services is done at runtime.

Grid Services: A grid service is an interface associated with a grid resource. It is implemented using OGSI or WSRF frameworks. It is a special adaptation of web services technology for grid environment. However, we consider grid services as the de-facto service implementation technology for emerging applications in both scientific and business domain.

Multi-Agent System: A software agent is a computational entity that can be viewed as perceiving and acting upon its environment and that is autonomous in that its behaviour at least partially depends on its own experience. A multi-agent system consists of a population of agents.

Service: A service is a coarse-grained, discoverable software entity that exists as a single instance and interacts with applications and other services through a loosely coupled message-based communication model. Service could be implemented using grid service or web service technologies

Virtual Organizations (VO): These are dynamic group of individuals, groups or organizations who define the conditions and rules for sharing resources in a grid environment. In OGSA, resources are accessed through their service interface. Therefore, the term "resources" could be loosely abstracted to cover a wide range of concepts including physical resources individuals and their expertise, capabilities and frameworks. The resources provided by members of the VO for sharing form the components of the grid service ecosystem.

Web Services: A web service is a software system identified by a Uniform Resource Identifier (URI) whose public interfaces and bindings are defined and described using XML–based messages conveyed by Internet protocols.

Workflow: A workflow is an activity that addresses some need by carrying specified control and data flows among sub-activities that involve information resources and possibly humans e.g loan processing workflow involves: filling out a form, clerk reviews its completeness, auditor verifies information, and a supervisor invokes an external credit agency.

Chapter 40
Exploiting P2P Solutions in Telecommunication Service Delivery Platforms

Antonio Manzalini
Telecom Italia, Italy

Roberto Minerva
Telecom Italia, Italy

Corrado Moiso
Telecom Italia, Italy

ABSTRACT

Network Operators provide Telecommunication services according the "Network Intelligence" paradigm based on centralized sets of specialized resources. Their major competitors in offering new services are Web2.0 Service Providers, which adopt the "Web as a platform" approach: services, designed according to client-server paradigm, are deployed on large, but cost effective, data centers able to satisfy an increasing number of service requests. Web2.0 Service Providers seem to have a technological edge on service delivery over Network Operators. To face this threat, Network Operators could adopt P2P technology, as an alternative to "Network Intelligence" and client-server paradigms, to build future proof service platforms, "naturally" open and extensible by users and communities, and leveraging connectivity, their main asset. This chapter describes motivations and characteristics of a novel service platform based on P2P technology for delivering Telecommunication and ICT services. It includes also an analysis of technical advantages, and considerations on business and costs aspects.

INTRODUCTION

The consolidation of distributed processing capabilities (e.g., Cloud Computing), the spread of adaptive computing techniques (e.g., P2P, Grid Computing), opportunistic communication mechanisms (wireless sensor network, mesh networking), the Web2.0 approach and its evolutions (semantic web, dataweb) pose new challenges to the traditional telecommunication world. What can Network Operators (NOs) do in this environment?

DOI: 10.4018/978-1-61520-686-5.ch040

In a traditional approach, named Network Intelligence [Minerva & Moiso, 2004], NOs develop functionally capable systems, able to support supplementary services on top of a major capability: the call control, or the session control in IP Multimedia Subsystem (IMS). This paradigm enables the construction of a limited set of communication services. The large part of the Internet services is instead focusing on data retrieval. The two major computing paradigms of the Internet, the Client-Server (CS), and the Peer-to-Peer (P2P), are good for data services and are not wholly exploited in Telco related solutions.

Web 2.0 service providers (SPs) have extended the common usage of the CS, by setting-up huge Data Centers made out of general purpose computing machines. SPs have a clear technological advantage in the delivery of large scale services over many NOs: the Data Center infrastructure, comprised of hundred of thousand of servers, is becoming so complex to manage and so expensive to build from scratch that many NOs simply cannot close the technological gap in a short time period. This prevents them to be better competitors in the Internet service realm.

Conversely, P2P technology enables new services and in particular the massive file sharing in large communities. The strength of the solution is the cooperative working of several networked nodes that are part of a community. The P2P technology is not only about file sharing, it is a distributed processing technique that fosters the sharing of resources and the cooperation between different nodes in order to reach a common goal.

The CS and the P2P approaches fit better than the Network Intelligence paradigm [Isenberg, 1998] into the Internet service scenario. Currently NOs are refurbishing the network infrastructure moving towards All-IP networks. This yields to the opportunity to rethink to the network control and service infrastructure. NOs adopt an "IMS+SDP approach", which, as described in the following section, consists of deploying a SDP (Service De-livery Platform) on top of an IMS infrastructure. These technologies are implemented according to the traditional attitude of NOs: they are centralized and over-imposed over an IP Network. They are expensive; do not follow the IP approach of having intelligent nodes and simple networks, and do not scale in the same manner as the Web Data Center do. Besides, they are mainly focused on the delivery of NOs' communication services, and are not suitable to promote new business eco-systems for broader classes of services. The NO embracing the "IMS+SDP approach" can lag behind the SPs in programming, governing and build a service layer infrastructure.

Therefore, NOs need to welcome other technologies that allow them to compete with the offering of services of the Web Actors: P2P technologies are a disruptive means to compete with the Web SPs

The rest of this Chapter summarizes the current approaches for delivering telecommunication services, the evolution trends, and some critical issues from the NO's standpoint. Then, it describes how an advanced P2P platform could address the identified critical issues: the proposed solution would replace the server-centric approaches with a highly distributed solution involving both end-users terminals, and computing and communication resources in the domains of NOs and SPs. Finally, the chapter analyzes the advantages and opportunities concerning the adoption of the proposed solution.

BACKGROUND

Telecommunication services are currently provided according to the Network Intelligence approach, where they are created, executed and managed by a "Service Architecture", comprising a set of systems implementing network functions needed for the service delivery. Services are characterized by a "business logic" that uses basic Telco features (e.g., call/session control, end-user presence and

Figure 1. General Structure of an SDP

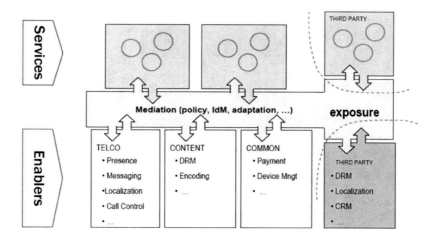

location, messaging, charging). Currently, services interact with Telco features and terminals through a wide set of protocols, each one specialized to deal with specific capabilities. Most of the currently deployed "service layers" are implemented as "vertical" platforms, i.e., "silos", each of them specialized to provide a specific service class on a specific network. This makes it hard to combine functions belonging to different silos without costly integration efforts.

For overcoming this situation, the service layer is evolving towards a "horizontal" approach, named Service Delivery Platform (SDP). According to [Kimbler & Taylor, 2008], it is characterized by:

• The separation of execution environments running the service logic from the Enablers that provide reusable Telco and IT functions implemented through the telecommunication network control and resources
• The possibility to share the Enablers among several service execution environments

An SDP (*Figure 1*) is built around a "service bus" for passing and controlling events and commands between reusable functionalities. It provides "mediation" functions, including Policy Management, Identity Management, and protocol adaptation. Some Services and Enablers can be provided by third parties through an exposure function.

The introduction of SDP is often coupled with the deployment of IMS, for the delivery of voice and multimedia services over a controlled IP networks and different (both fixed and mobile) access networks. IMS architecture (*Figure 2*) is based upon the separation of functions at transport, control and service levels. The Control Layer comprises servers for the control and management of communication/service sessions and the interworking with the traditional telecommunication switched network. The Service Layer encompasses disjointed servers for the management of user data and identity, application servers for implementing IMS Enablers (e.g., Presence or Messaging) and for executing service logic. These Enablers and application servers are integrated in an SDP.

NOs through SDP want to compete with Web2.0 SPs, which adopted a radically different approach for their service infrastructure highly optimized for the delivery of so-called Web2.0 services. For instance, Google has built an infrastructure of general purpose servers (probably, more than 400 thousands). The software architecture is CS based and is specialized for search and

Figure 2. IMS architecture

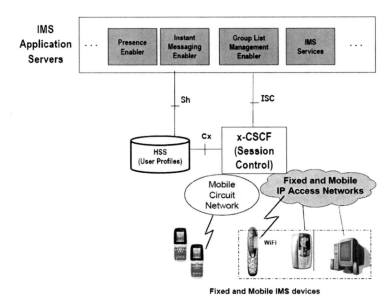

indexing. It provides for distributed replication of data and functions. Google software architecture is highly distributed and it is well-designed to manage large data centers that work like a GRID (Global Resource Information Database) computing network. Google has a lot of storage and processing power that is used for building advanced applications. This architecture offers high-level availability, and scalability, at very low CAPEX (Capital Expenditure), and OPEX (Operational Expenditure) costs.

Both Network Intelligence and CS paradigms aim at logically clustering in a few points (in the network or at the edges in data centers) the resources and the services accessible by many "simple" clients.

An alternative approach to Network Intelligence and CS paradigms is to implement a highly distributed architecture, based on computing nodes interconnected in a P2P way on an overlay network. P2P technologies allow the deployment of systems and applications orchestrating resources and service logic in a decentralized manner, blurring the distinction among clients and servers. P2P sees each node participating to a networked

communication as an entity having full rights to use, share, and offer resources and features to all the other nodes in a network. This uniformity makes the network of peers more homogeneous and resilient with respect to centralized CS and Network Intelligence approaches. In pure P2P networks there is neither the idea of centralized nodes governing the communication between peers, whilst this concept is central to CS and Network Intelligence solutions.

The P2P approach is very flexible, in one hand it can support specialized solutions [Milojicic, 2003], tailored for the execution of specific services; examples are Skype for VoIP (Voice over IP), Gia for content distribution, VidTorrent for video distribution. Besides, P2P can be used as a general purpose platform: e.g., JXTA [Gong, 2001] provides a set of libraries and protocols for the development of P2P applications.

The concept of a P2P service platform used by NOs for creating a generic service provision and delivery ecosystem is not generally pursued. Studies in this area focus on a single service approach, i.e., P2P is used for providing a single class of services by NOs [Schwan, Strauss & Tomsu,

2007], or they focus on the usage of P2P in the field of IT services. The reason for such a lack in literature has, at least, two causes:

- NOs see P2P as a threat more than a practical technology for service delivery
- NOs are concerned with P2P issues related to Quality of Services (QoS) to provide to users

Instead, P2P is a viable solution for telecommunication services especially when autonomics functions are added to the platform.

Even if NOs disregard P2P applications, they have a great impact on the network: a significant amount of IP traffic is generated by P2P applications used for file sharing, real-time communications and live media streaming. Current P2P applications usually have little knowledge of the underlying network topology, and they choose their peers based on measurement and statistics which often lead to suboptimal choices from the underlying network perspective. The IETF initiative named ALTO (Application-Layer Traffic Optimization) aims at investigating standard solutions for optimizing traffic generated by P2P applications through the access to information on link and network layer [Gurbani & Marocco, 2008]. An analogous proposal is P4P: a flexible framework enabling explicit cooperation between P2P overlay and network infrastructure [Xie & Krishnamurthy, 2008]. These approaches lead to a win-win situation in which NOs optimize the usage of the network and P2P overlays optimize the functionalities offered to the peers. ALTO and P4P are two initiatives, together to [Aggarwal, Feldmann & Scheideler, 2007], that come closer to the definition of a P2P infrastructure for NOs. In any case, they do not define a service architecture, but just mechanisms for a better usage of the network by overlays.

P2P can be exploited in a more general way developing a generic (i.e., service independent) telecom oriented distributed platform. It decouples the execution environments from the underlying infrastructure, by creating overlay networks on top of (heterogeneous) computing and communication resources, and it optimizes the usage of underlying networked resources. Some distributed service execution environments based on overlay networks have been proposed but they do not completely fulfill the requirements of NOs. For instance, the Service Oriented P2P System [Gerke, 2003] combines P2P with SOA (Serviced Oriented Architecture), in order to allow the definition of component-based P2P applications. A similar approach is adopted in SESAM project [Conrad, 2005], aimed at the development of a highly flexible, scalable and technology-independent architecture for distributed service delivery. Finally, the SELFMAN project [SELFMAN, 2008] focused on large-scale distributed applications that are "self-managing" by combining component models and structured overlay networks. The distributed service platform proposed in the following section does not limit the distribution of the execution to SOA based processing and to orchestration of Web Services, but it extends its applicability towards distributed services components interacting in a more flexible way, as required by real-time, event-driven and session-based computations of Telco services.

Provide broad definitions and discussions of the topic and incorporate views of others (literature review) into the discussion to support, refute or demonstrate your position on the topic.

TOWARDS A P2P INFRASTRUCTURE FOR NETWORK OPERATORS

Challenges for a P2P Service Platform for Network Operators

The trend for service delivery leads NOs to adopt the "IMS+SDP approach", i.e., the deployment of SDP coupled with IMS infrastructure. Even if this solution is an improvement over silos-based solutions, it has limitations in scalability and dynamic adaptation:

- Service logic is mainly "centralized" with limited distribution of functions: its components (e.g., exposed as Web Services) are mainly used to access Telco features and not to other business logics and features;
- Composition and configuration of service logic are static with limited dynamic adaptation to the service execution context;
- Deployment of services on servers is performed according to some off-line planning with limited dynamic adaptation to performance, and fault conditions;
- Capability of handling data intensive applications, requiring a real-time view of the huge volume of highly dynamic information, is limited.

These solutions focus on the development and deployment of services in the domain of NOs and SPs: such characteristic does not enable new business models. There is the need to enable new ecosystems, where services and service components are created by several actors: NOs, SPs, content providers, and "Prosumers".

Finally, these solutions do not reduce the total costs of ownership, from both CAPEX (servers for executing services are expensive and are not used in an optimal way) and OPEX (costs related to the operation of the infrastructure and the service management are slightly reduced).

NOs could adopt a radically new approach for the delivery of Telco/ICT services: a highly distributed solution that exploits the self-management, reliability and scalability characteristics of P2P architectures. "Traditional" server-centric solutions for service control (based on SDP and IMS) are replaced by a cooperating set of computing nodes supporting the distribution of service executions and service data.

Aiming at the provision of ICT services, the P2P Service Platform (PSP) goals are twofold:

- Provision of many classes of ICT services (not limited to communication or data services), in a multi-domain context;
- Overcoming the QoS issues of current P2P systems enabling an optimization of the usage of the physical layer and the overlay itself.

PSP must be a multi-service platform, able to support both session-based/asynchronous/person-to-person type of services, and client-server/request-response type of services. Examples of enabled services range from multimedia communication services (e.g., multiparty calls, multimedia conferences, interactive messaging), to content-media sharing and access services, (e.g. file/content-sharing, real-time media streaming, etc.) possibly among closed-user groups, from situated services over huge amount of dynamic data, to service environments for virtual communities or social networks. PSP must provide a set of shared capabilities enabling the execution and the possible co-operation of multiple (P2P) applications.

Extending the reach of service provision should be coupled with the ability to optimize the network infrastructure. PSP has to consider how to improve the efficient usage of the underlying infrastructure, through an optimized supervision of the whole platform and of applications running on it.

PSP organizes the computing nodes, interconnected through a potentially heterogeneous communication infrastructure (e.g., made out of different networks), in a set of interworking peers. Each peer provides basic functions for the execution of services (structured in interacting components), and for the creation and the maintenance of the overlay networks. The computing nodes could by either servers or servers clusters deployed indifferently in interacting domains: NO's nodes, end-users' devices (e.g., PDAs, mobile phones, laptops), Customer Premise Equipment (Residential Gateways, Set Top Boxes), sensors networks (or their aggregation proxy), etc. For

Figure 3. Layers in PSP peers

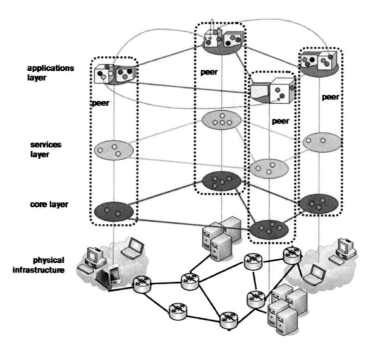

NOs (and, potentially, for SPs), one of the main issues concerns the PSP functions deployment strategies on computing nodes, either in the NO domain or in the end-user domain, by taking into account parameters concerning availability of the functions, security, privacy, trustiness, and avoiding the bottlenecks of a CS infrastructure.

PSP, therefore, aims at addressing the identified challenges and, thus, enabling a "carrier-grade" P2P platform for service delivery alternative to the traditional server-centric one adopted by NOs.

Differently from many P2P solutions that focus on the delivery of ICT services as specific applications, the PSP offers a set of basic capabilities enabling the deployment and execution of "application overlays", and the creation of eco-systems of composable services. PSP is not only a set of libraries for the development of P2P applications, but also a run-time distributed platform enabling the optimized allocation and sharing of computing, communication and Telco resources and an environment for composing

features stemming from a composite services/overlays eco-system.

A layered architecture is adopted in order to foster the reuse, the decoupling, and the sharing of platform capabilities, so to ease the dynamic introduction of new features and provide an optimized allocation of resources to the services and the application overlays.

A P2P Platform for Telco/ICT services

PSP implements functions for handling different overlays. It decouples the service execution functions from the underlying communication and computing infrastructure: each PSP overlay organizes the computing nodes, interconnected through a potentially heterogeneous communication infrastructure, in a set of peers, each providing functions for connectivity and execution of services and service components [Alfano, Manzalini & Moiso, 2007].

Functions implemented by peers can be organized in a functional layered model (*Figure 3*): applications, services and core layers.

There is no a client-server relationship between the three logical layers of the PSP: the layering is intended to introduce only a functional organization of peers composing the platform. At the lowest layer the relation between the physical network and the controlling peers is based on an "event-command" paradigm at the higher layers the relation is P2P.

Applications Layer consists of a set of application specific functions, structured in terms of distributed communicating components. Such components rely on features offered by the Services Layer, and deployed through the capabilities made available by the Core Layer, in charge for managing the overlays and abstracting the computing and communication resources. Therefore, the application logic and data are distributed across all the peers involved in the application execution (and replicated so to achieve suitable levels of fault-tolerance and scalability), in opposite to the client-server model, where they are rigidly assigned to server nodes (i.e., computing nodes of a server farm).

Services Layer provides general services for the execution of applications. Services include functions for the composition, distribution, execution (e.g., scheduling, distribution, interaction of components), and supervision of services and service components:

- The distributed caching/storage/sharing of contents and real-time data (e.g., service session information, logical names-physical addresses mappings), including techniques for data propagation, indexing and search;

- Identity Management for dealing with identities of end-users and service/content providers involved in the service delivery;

- FCAPS (i.e., fault, configuration, accounting, performance and security) supervision areas at the level of service execution.

Additional services should guarantee the interworking with external systems, and networks, such as platforms implementing Telco capabilities (e.g., IMS control, location systems), and Operations and Business Support Systems (OSS/BSS) systems.

Core Layer provides an abstraction of the underlying computing and communication infrastructure and offers basic capabilities to the Services and Applications Layers (aiming at building a sort of Autonomic infrastructure for making the entire overlay more resilient, configurable and robust). Examples are:

- Basic capabilities to build, maintain, and supervise the overlay(s), by discovering peers to be introduced in the overlay(s), and handling dynamic and unpredictable events (e.g., protecting from security attacks, mitigating failures of computing nodes, reacting to and smoothing traffic picks, providing a fair usage of shared resources);

- Basic capabilities for creating and controlling DHTs (Distributed Hash Tables), for building distributed data bases to store information and contents;

- Capabilities for unique logical addressing of peers, for handling computing nodes with dynamically assigned addresses, and Network Address Translation, and for optimized routing of messages between peers (e.g., the capability of P2PSIP, a P2P variant of the SIP protocol [Baumgart, Heep & Krause, 2007]);

- Capabilities for peer communications supporting multiple classes of applications (e.g. conversational, streaming, real-time multimedia, file/content sharing, grid/elastic computing, etc.) with different levels of QoS;

- Capabilities for optimization of the overlay topology (e.g., in case of introduction/deletion of nodes), by exploiting the information of the underlying physical networking infrastructure (P4P approach);

Figure 4. Functional overview of PSP

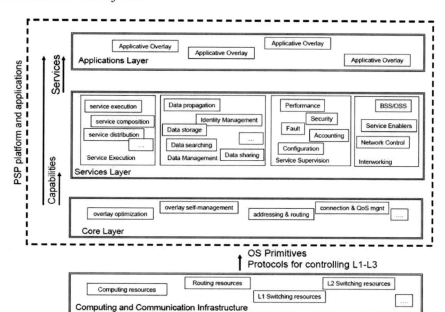

- Capabilities for creation and management of "groups" of peers sharing the same "properties", e.g., the discovery of new peers to be included in the group, the optimized location and routing between peers in a group.

Core and Services Layers offer, respectively, their capabilities and services (structured as aggregation of software components) through a set of APIs; these can be locally accessible by means of programming primitives, or remotely, by means of distributed processing communication mechanisms.

Core Layer capabilities interact with the underlying computing and communication resources through APIs offered by the node operating systems, and protocols offered by the network infrastructure, for the control of L1-L3, such as access to routing and topology information (e.g., P4P), QoS management, and traffic optimization (e.g., through flow management [McKeowen, Parulkar & Peterson, 2008]).

Figure 4 summarizes the architecture of the PSP and its interface with computing and communication resources.

The Core Layer guarantees robustness and scalability for the overlay(s) in a distributed context. These requirements are addressed by designing the core layer functions with autonomic capabilities, e.g., self-management and self-organization.

PSP is defined as P2P + Self-* autonomic algorithms. The introduction of Autonomic and Self-organization capabilities represents a major area of innovation of P2P systems. Self-organization is defined as "a process where the organization (constraint, redundancy) of a system spontaneously increases, i.e., without this increase being controlled by the environment or an encompassing or otherwise external system" [Heylighen, 1997].

In P2P architectures, self-organization is a basic requirement for handling scalability, resilience and highly dynamic connection of resources, and ownership costs. P2P systems can scale unpredictably in number of peers, users, and load. Level of scalability results in an increased probability of failures, which in turn requires self-maintenance and self-repair of the systems. At the same time, adaptation is required to handle connections changes caused by peers connecting and disconnecting from the P2P systems (e.g. high churn rate in wireless networks). Finally, distributions and complexity of P2P architectures require self-management solutions for hiding complications to human operators and ownership costs.

Overlay Topology and Deployment Options

PSP guarantees fairness and optimization in resources allocation and a number of pre-designed components to aggregate in order to implement and deploy overlays according to flexible policies and topologies. Specifically, networking capabilities are orchestrated in a distributed fashion according to the needs of the specific overlay and the available physical resources. The PSP implements fairness algorithms for guarantee an optimized usage of the available resource avoiding the problem of the "tragedy of commons".

For the allocation of computing power, PSP overlays might adopt pure or hybrid P2P solutions. Different deployment options range from instantiation of peers only in the NO environment to the instantiation of peers also on other domains (e.g., the user domain). A viable deployment option is a fully decentralized architecture, where peers are deployed on both end-user and network spaces. The deployment of peers on end-user devices is a fundamental requirement in order to realize an open infrastructure enabling open service eco-systems and active roles of end-users (i.e., prosumption). Moreover, it allows exploiting computation and storage capabilities of nodes external to the NO domains, so reducing the total cost of ownership of the service platform (e.g., by reducing power costs and equipment costs) and improving the efficiency in the usage of communication links among the network and the edge systems. In addition to end-user devices, PSP peers can be deployed on devices at the edge of the network, but still owned and operated by NOs (or SPs); examples are network gateways, residential/home gateways, etc., which could offer a greater level of stability and reliability than end-

user devices: in fact, peers deployed on end-user terminals, in particular on the mobile ones, can have a higher level of churn rate.

This fully decentralized deployment has the advantage of a distributed infrastructure, whose overall functionalities are not compromised by the failure of one or more peers; this does not exclude the degradation on performance/availability of some capabilities that require a "carrier-grade" quality. As a consequence, NOs and SPs could consider adopting a hybrid architecture, where some of the peers are "specialized" to execute some functions critical for the service delivery.

In the proposed hybrid architecture peers can interact directly without the need to involve "specialized" peers; moreover, "specialized" peers are peers themselves, which execute an optimized set of functions: this deployment option for PSP differs, thus, from traditional peer-superpeer architectures, where superpeers are logically centralized for the localization of shared resources or contents.

Providers could deploy the "specialized" peers on computing nodes in their network infrastructure (if any), or in the one of the NO, both characterized by greater levels of availability, due to reliable connectivity, or churn rate limited to faults (*Figure 5*). Similar architectures, confining critical functions on specialized nodes, are adopted in P2P solutions for specific telecommunication services, e.g., Skype.

Several criteria could be adopted for identifying the critical functions executed by specialized peers. Examples are: identity management (including authentication, authorization, and profile information), accounting for used resources, fairness and optimization of shared resource usage (e.g., connectivity, overlay maintenance), security related functions. PSP overlays of specialized peers may spread across multiple administrative domains, to guarantee co-operations in multi-domain service ecosystem.

The structure of the single overlay could be optimized, by exploiting information such as network topology, information on QoS, traffic load,

Figure 5. Deployment of PSP on heterogeneous infrastructure

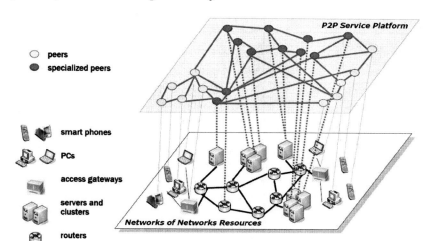

etc, which are available in the operator's network infrastructure (e.g., through P4P).

Both deployment options (pure or hybrid) strongly differ from client-server architecture, based on server farms. In PSP, service logic and functions are distributed on all the nodes, both end-user devices and network servers, while in a CS solution, service logic is deployed on large server farms, and end-user devices execute clients providing a rich interface to access the service. Moreover, scalability of CS solutions requires the introduction of new servers, while PSP solutions directly scale with the number of end-users, with the introduction of peers deployed on end-user devices, or, in addition, on new (low cost) servers.

Optimized Resource Allocation

Two optimization aspects concern the allocation of PSP resources: the optimization of networking protocols used for the communication among peers and the optimization of the allocation and usage of available resources.

For the first problem, the solution proposed is the adoption of a game-theoretic approach. Game-theory is used to determine the optimal value for parameters configuring the different layers in the protocol stack according to varying requirements

and communication resource availability. As a matter of fact, game theory has been widely applied to communications problems [Saraydar & Mandayam, 2002], [Yu & Ginis, 2002]. However, existing formulations tend to focus manly on the physical layer.

According to Internet layered architecture (ISO-OSI) each layer in the protocol stack hides the complexity of the layer below and provides a service to the layer above.

Cross layer solutions fit better in highly dynamic distributed and unpredictable infrastructures (as those supported by PSP). Vertical cross layer optimization implies harmonize various protocol layers into a single coherent theory, aiming at a global optimization of the network. A usual strategy is splitting the optimization problem into two steps: first considering each layer as a solver in isolation (iterating on a set of variables and using local information, thus implicitly assuming that also other layers are designed optimally) and finally studying the cross layer interactions to perform an overall vertical optimization.

PSP adopts an alternative game-theoretic approach to carry out (for application services demand) a global optimization from different goals, i.e., SP(s) (and consequently users of the overlay) and NO(s).

Figure 6. Example of cross-layer design

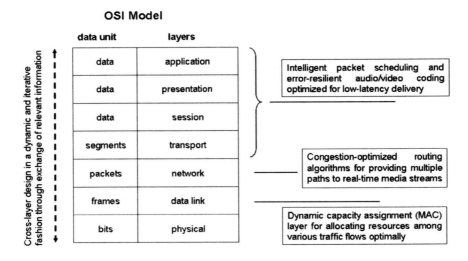

The overall optimization problem is decomposed into two sub-problems for optimizing certain utility functions both for the SP and the NO. As an example, SP's utility functions could be functions (or combinations) of bit-rate, reliability, delay, jitter, or power level; on the other hand, NOs' utility functions can be functions (or combination) of congestion level, energy efficiency, network lifetime, or collective estimation error. Clearly, not every game has a Nash equilibrium, neither is the equilibrium necessarily stable; as such a set of sufficient conditions should be identified for existence, uniqueness, and stability of the Nash equilibria for both games.

Finally, primal-dual algorithms should be used iteratively for executing the two games and updating shadow prices to coordinate the physical layer supply and the application services demand. This should assure that the overall optimization process reaches a good balance between the two optimization sub-problems.

Let's consider the example of cross-layer optimization for design of an ad-hoc wireless network (*Figure 6*) to provide delay-critical applications, such as conversational voice or real-time video [Setton & You, 2005]. Design implies inter-working across all layers of the ISO-OSI protocol stack to leverage the flexibility offered by joint optimization of some parameters.

Capacity of individual wireless links to support delay-constrained traffic (possibly in multiple service classes) should be properly adjusted with adaptive link layer techniques. Dynamic capacity assignment in the Media Access Control (MAC) layer is intended to allocate resources among various traffic flows optimally; a congestion-optimized routing algorithm is expected to provide multiple paths to real-time media streams; finally at the transport and application level, intelligent packet scheduling and error-resilient audio/video coding will be optimized for low-latency delivery over ad-hoc wireless networks. PSP components performing and controlling above techniques will integrate in a dynamic and iterative fashion. Components will exchange relevant information such as link capacities, traffic flows, packet deadlines and rate-distortion preamble of the source data across the entire protocol stack.

The second optimization aspect considered is the allocation of resources (e.g., computational power, communication bandwidth, telecommunication capabilities, such as messaging or positioning systems) for fulfilling the service requests performed by end-users. A common approach is

948

enriching application services with the ability to negotiate the resources to be allocated for execution [Stratford & Mortier, 1999].

Auction is one of the most investigated approaches [Vickrey, 1961]. Most state-of-art solutions feature a common space (playing both the role of resource discovery and allocation) in which multiple negotiations lead to contracts for the allocation of overlay resources to applications services.

Let's consider a simple example: when an application service requires resources, it registers its requirements as an auction. This information is then distributed to the bidders, i.e., entities in charge of allocating a given type of resources according to some allocation policy, by a specific overlay that in turn collects any bids. Different "pricing" policies and bidding criteria could be used to express different allocation strategies, such as optimal/balanced allocation of shared resources in a service infrastructure, or applying some power savings.

As described by Magrath (2005), auction approach has the advantages to be fully distributed, with the possibility to dynamically and autonomously self-organize the overlay between resource requestors and resource managers.

Independently from the chosen overlay structure and policies there are two levels of optimization granted by the PSP: an internal one that guarantees an optimal organization and allocation of resources within the single overlay for its users; an external one that guarantees the fair allocation of resources among several competing overlays.

Platform Capacity

The construction of a new Data Center for providing services according to the CS paradigm is an expensive process both in terms of development and resources to allocate to servers. The "Capacity" (in a qualitative meaning) of the CS platforms com-

prises connectivity (in terms of total bandwidth available to the data center), processing power, and storage. A Data Center has to be well dimensioned in order to support the constant increase in demand for services. A CS model implies that, at the growth of the number of users, the number of servers increases (as well as in other capabilities like bandwidth and storage).

Generalizing, the set of capabilities of CS systems is given by the global Capacity made available by the servers in the data center itself:

Capacity of Centralized System = {Bs, Ss, Ps}

where: Bs = bandwidth of the Server System

Ss = storage of the Server System

Ps = processing in the Server System

There is the need to cope with performance issues and the balancing of server usage, and this is not an easy task for CS systems.

In terms of global capacity, P2P systems show (from a qualitative point of view) very interesting capabilities due to resource sharing and distributed allotment granted by any single participating peer. A description of the global capacity could be represented as:

Capacity of P2P System = $\sum (b_i, s_i, p_i)$

where: b_i = bandwidth of node *i* in the overlay

s_i = storage of node *i* in the overlay

p_i = processing of node *i* in the overlay

Functionalities and capacity of a P2P network grow on the basis of the number of participants to the overlay. However part of these capabilities is used for the management of the overlay itself: the management and control functions are distributed over many different nodes in order to allow the network to perform its functions even in presence of a high dynamic behavior of the peers.

Overlay networks "consume" bandwidth because the peers need to share or replicate data and resources/functions so that services can be dependably provided. In doing this, they tend to consume as much bandwidth is made available. From the NO perspective this feature can be seen as a problem but also as an opportunity: the management of an overlay network does not require a great amount of centralized processing and storage power, many functions are demanded to edge nodes (to peers) that use their own capabilities in order to contribute to the functioning of the entire network. This allows saving in infrastructural investments but at the same time, it facilitates the provision of services to large communities. The "price" for this infrastructural agility is the request for bandwidth, and bandwidth availability is the asset of NOs. For this reason, optimized P2P solutions (optimized in the sense of PSP) could be an important asset for NOs in order to compete in the provision of new services.

FUTURE RESEARCH DIRECTIONS

The unstructured grow of Internet may lead to an infrastructure becoming too large, brittle and not optimized for future services and applications. Given such increasing complexity of the network, very soon even traditional software programs will not be able to get a good grip on Internet [Clark, Wroclawski & Sollins, 2005].

Tomorrow's Internet is expected to overcome current limitations and to address emerging trends including: mobility, the spread of large numbers of heterogeneous nodes and devices, the mass digitization of media, the emergence of software as services, constraints imposed by resources, the emergence of new models of services and interaction, and the need for improved security and privacy features, etc.

Research communities are studying new Internet architectures which should make it more easy and convenient to use, while making possible to abstract from heterogeneity of various techniques and technologies. It is widely recognized that an effective tomorrow's Internet design requires to adapt and flex under unpredicted pressures and dynamics. This implies a modularized (e.g. design by variation) and optimized architecture (e.g. cross-layer optimization) allowing all Parties to interact in an open way. Internet is likely to become an ecosystem seamless integrating heterogeneous nodes and devices for enabling any-layers services (e.g. network, transport services but as real-time communications, contents sharing, sensing, actuation, etc.) for human-to-human, human-to-machine and machine-to-machine interactions.

Future Internet [Manzalini, 2008] will be like an adaptive network of networks (e.g. showing adaptive behavior from simple self-organized networking of local entities) rather than a static and complicated one; openness, self-organization and self-adaptation (defined as a set of rules whereby global patterns emerge from the interaction of lower level components) would allow overcoming some current tussles and limitations of Internet (e.g. static behavior, missing optimization), improving flexibility (e.g. adaptability and situation awareness) and even hiding (management and operation) complexities to human operators.

The PSP architecture presented in this Chapter is likely to meet most of above requirements, so to become an enabler for the provisioning of services on the Future Internet. PSP could be exploited in interesting new applications. One of the possible application fields is cloud computing, i.e., the ability to dynamically create computational clouds for performing specific computing and storage tasks. This distributed application could be executed on the PSP adopting an approach à la Google. Networked applications can be retrieved using hashing mechanisms; specialized peers can be involved into the distributions and control of the application components: computations and related data can be distributed and replicated over different peers. Specialized peers have the task to manage the computational loads and to reconcile the different flows into meaningful results and return those to the originator. Due to the highly dynamic behavior of the P2P network, specialized peers have to replicate several time the same part of the application over different nodes in order to ensure that at least one of them will be able to complete the entire computation. This introduces the need to replicate the instances of computation and data, having an impact on the total capacity of the solution. This issue requires specific studies to tune the best strategy for replicating the components.

Another interesting field of application is the so call dissemination network [D'Ambrosio & Fasano, 2008]: the name refers to a new architecture made available in order to better support the data service needs of Internet users. In the proposed architecture all the information is hashed and indexed and made available though a highly distributed platform. Specialized peers can play a relevant role in here enabling NOs to act as brokers of information, scattered over many peers. Also in this case, policies and mechanisms are to be put in place in order to guarantee the persistence of the data even in a highly dynamic situation.

CONCLUSION

NOs are providing Telecommunication services with a Network Intelligence paradigm, whose architecture is based on a centralized set of resources. Today, a major threat for NOs comes from Web2.0 SPs (e.g. Google, Yahoo! etc), who, on the other hand, are adopting the so-called paradigm "web as a platform": in particular, they built up large data centers able to satisfy rapidly all the service requests coming from a constantly increasing number of users.

Even if P2P is considered by many NOs as a threatening technology, this chapter has shown

that it can be adopted to face competition of Web2.0 SPs.

The P2P Service Platform is able to address critical issues of the platforms for service delivery currently adopted by NOs: the proposed solution replaces the server-centric approaches with a highly distributed solution potentially involving both end-users terminals and computing and communication resources in the domain of NOs and SPs. The implementation of PSP on the physical architecture of communication and computation resources is particularly flexible allowing different deployment strategies: from overlay functionalities heavy relaying and instantiated in controlled environments to overlay spanning unreliable and uncontrolled environments but able to use any resource available. In particular, it considered how to map peers and specialized peers on nodes in the controlled network and at its edge, and how the information in the network could be exploited to optimize the architecture of the overlay. This enables a new approach for the operators: the offering of "Platform As A Service" or "Infrastructure As A Service".

PSP approach guarantees an intrinsic solution for scalability, allowing the seamless introduction of new nodes, and fault management without centralized supervision; moreover, it enables an efficient usage of computing resources, with dynamic adaptation according to the changes of service loads.

From a business perspective, PSP approach would enable a cross-domain platform, which would support a new eco-system of services, offered by several actors. The PSP could be leveraged to produce/consume/combine services and content according to innovative business models: new value chains in the provisioning of Telco/ICT services could be created and this approach would be a factor characterizing the Future Internet.

Finally, from the costs perspective, the PSP would reduce the expenditure in the service infrastructure, because computing nodes could be used with greater efficiency and could be based on component-on-the-shelf (COTS) servers, instead of specialized hardware/software. Moreover, computing and storage could be seamlessly distributed through the platform, by giving an active role also to the systems deployed in other domains; finally, the self-organizing properties of P2P solutions, enriched with autonomic capabilities, would reduce the operation/management costs of the platform as a whole, and would enable the adoption of energy saving policies.

REFERENCES

Aggarwal, V., Feldmann, A., & Scheideler, C. (2007). Can ISPs and P2P Users Cooperate for Improved Performance? *ACM SIGCOMM Computer Communication Review, 37*(3), 29–40. doi:10.1145/1273445.1273449

Alfano, R., Manzalini, A., & Moiso, C. (2007). Distributed Service Framework: an innovative open eco-system for ICT/Telecommunications. In *1st Conference on Autonomic Computing and Communication Systems*. New York: ACM Digital Library.

Baumgart, I., Heep, B., & Krause, S. (2007). A P2PSIP Demonstrator Powered by OverSim. In *7th IEEE Conference on P2P Computing* (pp. 243-244). New York: IEEE Computer Society.

Clark, D., Wroclawski, J., Sollins, K., & Braden, R. (2005). Tussle in cyberspace: defining tomorrow's Internet. *IEEE/ACM Transactions on Networking, 13*(3), 462-475.

Conrad, M., Dinger, J., Hartenstein, H., Schöller, M., & Zitterbart, M. (2005). Combining Service-Orientation and P2P Networks. In *Kommunikation in Verteilten Systemen* (pp. 181-184). Kaiserslautern, Germany: GI-Edition.

D'Ambrosio, M., Fasano, P., Marchisio, M., Vercellone, V., & Ullio, M. (2008). Providing Data Dissemination Services in the Future Internet. In *IEEE Globecom WTC2008* (pp. 1-6). New York: IEEE Computer Society.

Gerke, J., Hausheer, D., Mischke, J., & Stiller, B. (2003). An Architecture for a Service Oriented P2P System. *Praxis der Informationsverarbeitung und Kommunikation, 2*(03), 90–95. doi:10.1515/PIKO.2003.90

Gong, L. (2001). JXTA: A Network Programming Environment. *IEEE Internet Computing, 5*(3), 88–95. doi:10.1109/4236.935182

Gurbani, V., & Marocco, E. (2008). *Application-Layer Traffic Optimization (ALTO) Problem Statement*. IETF Internet-Draft. Retrieved April 14, 2009, from http://tools.ietf.org/html/draft-marocco-alto-problem-statement-02

Heylighen, F. (1997). Self-organization. In *Principia Cybernetica Web'*. Brussels: Principia Cybernetica. Retrieved April 14, 2009, from http://pespmc1.vub.ac.be/SELFORG.html

Isenberg, D. (1998). The dawn of the "stupid network". *ACM NetWorker, 2*(1), 24–31. doi:10.1145/280437.280445

Kimbler, K., & Taylor, M. (2008). *SDP 2.0 – Service Delivery Platforms in the Web2.0 Era*. Egham, UK: The Moriana Group. Retrieved April 14, 2009, from http://www.morianagroup.com

Magrath, S., Chiang, F., Markovits, S., Braun, R., & Cuervo, F. (2005), Autonomics in telecommunications service activation. In *Autonomous Decentralized Systems 2005,* (pp. 731-737). New York: IEEE Computer Society.

Manzalini, A. (2008). Tomorrow's open Internet for Telco and Web federations. In *Conference on Complex, Intelligent and Software Intensive Systems* (pp. 567-572). New York: IEEE Computer Society.

McKeowen, N., Parulkar, G., & Peterson, L. (2008). OpenFlow: enabling innovation in campus networks. *ACM SIGCOMM Computer Communication Review, 38*(2), 69–74. doi:10.1145/1355734.1355746

Milojicic, D. S. (2003). *P2P Computing.* Technical Report No. HPL-2002-57. Palo Alto, CA: HP Laboratories Palo Alto.

Minerva, R., & Moiso, C. (2004). The Death of Network Intelligence? In *15th IEE International Symposium on Services and Local Access* (pp. 157-168). London: IEE.

Saraydar, C., Mandayam, N. B., & Goodman, D. J. (2002). Efficient Power Control via Pricing in Wireless Data Networks. *IEEE Transactions on Communications, 50*(2), 291–303. doi:10.1109/26.983324

Schwan, N., Strauss, T., & Tomsu, M. (2007). P2P VoIP & MMoIP for Public Services – Requirements and Architecture. In *International Conference on Intelligence in Networks 2007.* Sterling, VA: Neustar. Retrieved Feb. 19, 2009, from www.icin.biz

SESAM Project. (2008), *Self Organization and Spontaneity in Liberalized and Harmonized Markets.* Retrieved Feb. 19, 2009, from http://dsn.tm.uni-karlsruhe.de/english/sesam-project.php

Setton, E., Yoo, T., Zhu, X., Goldsmith, A., & Girod, B. (2005). Cross-layer Design of Ad Hoc Networks for Real-Time Video Streaming . *IEEE Wireless Communications Magazine, 12*(4), 59–65. doi:10.1109/MWC.2005.1497859

Stratford, N., & Mortier, R. (1999). An Economic Approach to Adaptive Resource Management. In *7th Workshop on Hot Topics in Operating Systems,* (pp. 142-147). New York: IEEE Computer Society.

Vickrey, W. (1961). Counterspeculation, Auctions, and Competitive Sealed Tenders. *The Journal of Finance, 16*(1), 8–37. doi:10.2307/2977633

Xie, H., Krishnamurthy, A., Silberschatz, A., & Yang, Y. R. (2008). *P4P: Explicit Communications for Cooperative Control Between P2P and Network Providers.* Retrieved April 14, 2009, from http://www.dcia.info/documents/P4P_Overview.pdf

Yu, W., Ginis, G., & Cioffi, J. (2002). Distributed Multiuser Power Control for Digital Subscriber Line. *IEEE Journal on Selected Areas in Communications, 20*(5), 1105–1115. doi:10.1109/JSAC.2002.1007390

ADDITIONAL READING

Anastasopoulos, M. P., Vasilakos, A. V., & Cottis, P. G. (in press). An Autonomic Framework for Reliable Multicast: A Game Theoretical Approach based on Social Psychology. *ACM Transactions on Autonomous and Adaptive Systems . Special Issue on Adaptive Learning in Autonomic Communication.*

Babaoglu, O., Canright, G., Deutsch, A., Caro, G. A., & alii (2006). Design Patterns from Biology to Distributed Computing. *ACM Transaction on Autonomous and Adaptive Systems, 1*(1), 26-66.

CASCADAS Project. (2009). *ACE Toolkit open source.* Retrieved April 14, 2009, from http://sourceforge.net/projects/acetoolkit/.

Deussen, P., Ferrari, L., Manzalini, A., & Moiso, C. (in press). Highly Distributed Supervision for Autonomic Networks and Services. In *Fifth Advanced International Conference on Telecommunications - AICT2009.* New York: IEEE . *Computers & Society.*

Jelasity, M., Montresor, A., & Babaoglu, O. (2005). Gossip-based Aggregation in Large Dynamic Networks. *ACM Transactions on Computer Systems, 23*(3), 219–252. doi:10.1145/1082469.1082470

Kephart, J., & Chess, D. (2003). The Vision of Autonomic Computing. *IEEE Computer, 36*(1), 41–50.

Liu, H., Bhat, V., Parashar, M., & Klasky, S. (2005). An Autonomic Service Architecture for Self-managing Grid Applications. In *6th IEEE/ACM International Workshop on Grid Computing* - GRID2005. New York: IEEE Computer Society.

Maes, S. H. (2007). Service Delivery Platforms as IT Realization of OMA Service Environment: Service Oriented Architectures for Telecommunications. In *Wireless Communications and Networking Conference 2007* - WCNC 2007 (pp. 2883-2888). New York: IEEE Computer Society.

Mamei, M., Menezes, R., Tolksdorf, R., & Zambonelli, F. (2006). Case Studies for Self-organization in Computer Science. *Journal of Systems Architecture, 52*(8), 443–460. doi:10.1016/j.sysarc.2006.02.002

Manzalini, A., Zambonelli, F., Baresi, L., & Di Ferdinando, A. (in press). The CASCADAS Framework for Autonomic Communications. In A. Vasilakos, M. Parashar, S. Karnouskos, & W. Pedrycz (Eds.), *Autonomic Communication*. Heidelberg: Springer.

Michiardi, P., Marrow, P., Tateson, R., & Saffre, F. (2007). Aggregation Dynamics in Service Overlay Networks. In *1st International Conference on Self-Adaptive and Self-Organizing Systems* (pp. 129-140). New York: IEEE Computer Society.

Minerva, R. (2008). On Some Myths about Network Intelligence. In *International Conference on Intelligence in Networks* - ICIN2008. Retrieved April 14, 2009, from www.icin.biz. Sterling: Neustar.

Minerva, R., & Demaria, T. (2007). There is a Broker in the Net… its name is Google. In *International Conference on Intelligence in Networks* - ICIN2007. Retrieved April 14, 2009, from www.icin.biz. Sterling, VA: Neustar.

Minerva, R., Manzalini, A., & Moiso, C. (in press). Bio-inspired Autonomic Structures: a middleware for Telecommunications Ecosystems. In A. Vasilakos, M. Parashar, S. Karnouskos, & W. Pedrycz (Eds.), *Autonomic Communication*. Heidelberg: Springer.

Ohnishi, H., Yamato, Y., & Kaneko, M. Moriya, & alii (2007). Service Delivery Platform for Telecom-Enterprise-Internet Combined Services. In *Global Telecommunications Conference 2007* - GLOBECOM '07 (pp. 108-112). New York: IEEE Computer Society.

Poikselka, M., & Mayer, G. (2009). *The IMS: IP Multimedia Concepts and Services*. London: Wiley.

Samimi, F. A., McKinley, P. K., Sadjadi, S. M., & Tang, C., Shapiro, & J. K., Zhou, Z. (2007). Service Clouds: Distributed Infrastructure for Adaptive Communication Services. *IEEE Transactions on Network and System Management, Special Issue on Self-Managed Networks . Systems and Services, 4*(2), 84–95.

Stephen, E. A. (2005). The Google Legacy - How Google's Internet Search is Transforming Application Software. *Infornortics, 2005*(9). Retrieved April 14, 2009, from www.infonortics.com/ publications/google/google-legacy.html.

Sterritt, R., Parasharb, M., Tianfieldc, H., & Unland, R. (2005). A concise introduction to autonomic computing. *Advanced Engineering Informatics, 19*, 181–187. doi:10.1016/j.aei.2005.05.012

KEY TERMS AND DEFINITIONS

Autonomic Computing: This term was coined by IBM's term to indicate a technology for introducing self-managing capabilities into Information Technology. Goal is to shift the burden of management tasks such as fault, configuration, maintenance, and performance management from people to technology itself (i.e., by enhancing the systems with self-* capabilities). In this context, self-organization is defined as a process where the organization of a system spontaneously increases, i.e., without this increase being controlled by the environment or an encompassing or otherwise external system.

Cross-Layer Design: it is a technical approach that implies optimizing the design parameters of various protocol layers into a single coherent way, thus aiming at a global optimization of the network.

Network Intelligence: Network Intelligence is the architectural approach used by Telecommunication operators to develop telecommunication services. It is based on a centralized set of servers which execute the service logic and are able to control, through specialized protocols, network and service resources deployed in the telecommunication network infrastructures. Intelligent Network and IMS are examples of solutions structured according to the Network Intelligence approach.

Network Operator: A network operator is a traditional telecommunication operator owning both a network infrastructure (i.e., routers, switches, transport nodes) and a service delivery infrastructure (e.g., servers, data centers).

Prosumer: Prosumer is a portmanteau word formed by contracting the word *prod*ucer with the word cons*umer*. This term, adopted in the context of Web2.0, indicates people and/or entities acting at the same time as producer and consumer of contents, data and services.

Quality of Service: It is a generic term referring to the level of quality of a certain service. QoS definition depends on the specific service quality parameters (e.g., jitter, delay, errors).

Resource Negotiation: Resource negotiation includes those mechanism adopted by distributed applications and services for discovering and negotiating the usage of shared resources that required for their execution. An auction protocol, for example, can be used for resource optimal allocation.

Service Oriented Architecture (SOA): It is a distributed software architecture where software systems are structured in a set of reusable and shared software components, offering, to other components, functions over a network through well defined interfaces (e.g., by using Web Services, or CORBA IDL).

Service Provider: Service Provider is an enterprise owning and operating a service delivery infrastructure.

Telco Enablers: They provide reusable capabilities implemented through the telecommunication network control and resources. Examples of Telco Enablers provide capabilities for location, messaging, call control. Usually, they offer interfaces used by service logic to control the provided functions; these interfaces are structured in a set of commands and events.

Chapter 41
Fednets:
P2P Cooperation of Personal Networks Access Control and Management Framework

Malohat Ibrohimovna
Delft University of Technology, The Netherlands

Sonia Heemstra de Groot
Delft University of Technology, The Netherlands

ABSTRACT

A personal network (PN) is a network of a user's personal devices and services, cooperating with each other independently of their geographical location to provide ubiquitous services to the user. PNs can be the producers and consumers of the services, content and resources. They can also export the subsets of their personal resources and services to other PNs. In such cases, PNs may form a group-oriented secure network called a Federation of Personal Networks (Fednet). A Fednet is a temporal, ad-hoc opportunity or purpose driven network of PNs, in which PNs collaborate with each other to share resources and services in a peer-to-peer manner. A Fednet is a pervasive and ubiquitous computing technology that enables the users to enjoy cooperation and promises exciting opportunities for different applications in various fields, such as education, healthcare, entertainment, business and emergency.In this chapter, the authors discuss PN technology expanding on the concept of Fednet. They provide example scenarios for Fednets, showing their potential impact to the quality of life of their users. Furthermore, they present the architecture and lifecycle of a Fednet. They explain the interactions of the main architectural components during its lifecycle and present a framework for the secure access control and management for a Fednet. The framework provides a controlled collaboration of PNs, where each PN controls the access to its resources and services. Finally, the authors provide a brief overview of some of the existing resource sharing group-oriented networks related to Fednets.

DOI: 10.4018/978-1-61520-686-5.ch041

Figure 1. Example of a personal network

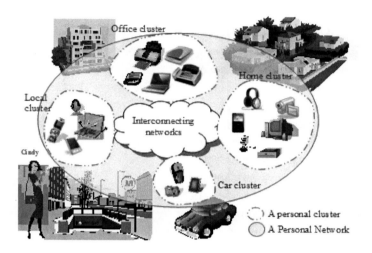

1. INTRODUCTION

Recent developments in device technologies resulted in various personal digital devices equipped with networking capabilities that enable them to communicate with each other, forming a person-centric network. A personal network (PN) (Niemegeers & Heemstra de Groot, 2003) is an example of a person-centric network. It is a network of a user's personal digital devices that cooperate with each other regardless of their geographical location. Some of the devices in the PN can be located at home, others in a user's office or car, and some of the devices the user can carry with her/him. Based on their location, personal devices can be grouped into clusters. A simple PN consists of a local cluster around the user. The local cluster can be extended with remote clusters, such as an office cluster, home cluster and car cluster by means of interconnecting infrastructures. Together they form a distributed personal environment of a user. This is illustrated in Figure 1.

The concept of a personal network and its design challenges have inspired many projects that investigated different aspects of PNs, such as the Dutch projects Freeband PNP2008 (2004-2008) and QoS for PNs at home (2004-2008), and the European IST projects Magnet and Magnet

Beyond (2006-2008). The European project Pac-Woman (2003) has research outcomes useful for the research on personal networking.

Personal devices of the user in the PN, communicating with each other independently of their geographic location, can provide ubiquitous services to the user, such as remote babysitting, remote control and monitoring of one's house, content sharing and conferencing services. In some situations it is beneficial and even crucial to share these personal resources and services with others to achieve a common goal that otherwise, by means of a single PN, would not be possible. Examples are: sharing digital media for business or entertainment, sharing sensor information from different sources for rescue of people in a disaster relief operation or getting real-time information from devices that belong to other people in healthcare applications. To achieve a common goal, different persons' PNs can federate into a group-oriented network. Then a personal network that is tailored to the needs of one person will grow into a network of a group of persons who share a subset of their resources and services with each other.

The idea of group communication of personal networks, the so-called *Federation of Personal Networks* (Fednet) for sharing personal resources to achieve a common goal, was first introduced by Niemegeers & Heemstra de Groot (2005). A Fednet is a temporal, ad-hoc opportunity or purpose driven network of PNs. PNs in a Fednet cooperate and share resources in a peer-to-peer manner, i.e. PNs are 'peers' to each other and have equal responsibilities and capabilities in providing/consuming the services. Therefore we consider Fednets a P2P network of personal networks.

Research in Fednets is still in its infancy. The main challenge in sharing personal resources in Fednets is the control of the access to the shared resources. Up till now, little attention has been paid to the design of the access control mechanisms for Fednets. The major issues in the access control in Fednets are: protecting the privacy sensitive information such as PN's structure and services, and keeping the control over personal resources and services; high dynamism in availability of personal resources and services; and changing access rights of Fednet members depending not only on their behavior but also on the goals of the Fednet and total availability of resources.

Different aspects of PNs and their federations have been studied in the European projects Magnet and Magnet Beyond (2006-2004). Some of the achievements of the projects include new optimized air interfaces for low and high data rates, self-organization in PNs, new routing and mobility protocols for PNs and their federations and business models. Although federations have received some attention, the issues related to the access control in Fednets were considered on a conceptual level. No detailed studies were done to compose a consistent and complete solution. In this chapter, we propose a framework for secure access control and management for a Fednet (ACM framework) as one of the solutions to realize Fednets.

This chapter is organized as follows. In Section 2, we introduce Fednets and give examples. In Section 3, we describe Fednets in terms of their lifecycle and architecture. In Section 4, we present the ACM framework for Fednets and define its objectives and functions. In Section 5,

we explain the operation of the ACM framework from the discovery till the dissolution of the Fednet and briefly discuss early experimental results of prototyping. In order to place Fednets among existing technologies and paradigms, in Section 6, we give a brief overview of existing resource-sharing group-oriented networks. Finally, we conclude and discuss future research opportunities in Section 7.

2. FEDERATION OF PERSONAL NETWORKS

By adding extra functionality to a PN, it is possible to create a P2P network on top of a PN, i.e. a Fednet, to share personal resources and services among different PNs. While the essence of a PN is providing the user with personal ubiquitous services, the essence of a Fednet is sharing these ubiquitous services with others for a common goal. Fednet is a temporal, ad hoc, opportunity or purpose driven, secure group-oriented network where the users may be the producers and consumers of the services, content and resources in the Fednet. The PNs in a Fednet collaborate with each other and share resources and services in a P2P manner. The P2P cooperation of PNs allows us to place Fednets among P2P technologies. However, depending on the situation and context, client-server applications can also be supported by Fednets.

In Fednets PNs export their personal services to each other, the Fednet as such is perceived as a pool of services. This pool of services can also be made accessible to the outside world, i.e. when Fednets export their federated services to third parties. Furthermore, it might be possible to build a hierarchy of Fednets, in which different Fednets export to each other a subset of their federated services. However, this topic is out of the scope of this chapter.

The applications enabled by Fednets span multiple domains, ranging from entertainment to

Figure 2. A Fednet composed of four PNs to share photos and videos

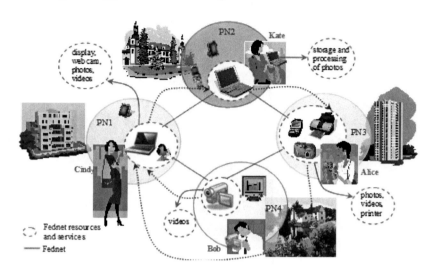

business, from emergency to healthcare. Fednets can be conceived of as an emergency network, an entertainment network, an educational network, a social network, a healthcare network or as another one that might be envisaged by ubiquitous and pervasive communications in the future. In this section, we give some examples of Fednets in different contexts.

2.1 Business: Sharing Digital Media in a Common Workspace

As a first example of a Fednet we consider Figure 2. It represents is a temporal network composed by the PNs of four colleagues that have attended a conference together. In the conference some of them have taken photos and videos. After the conference they want to look to the photos and videos together. For this purpose they form a Fednet that contains a subset of the resources in their PNs. These subsets are composed by a web camera and a laptop (PN1), a computer with photo-editing software (PN2), a digital photo camera and a photo printer (PN3) and a digital video camera (PN4). This is illustrated in Figure 2.

In this Fednet, colleagues can share with each other several types of resources (i.e. photos and videos) and services (i.e. display, photo-editing

and printing services). Note that because the PNs share only a subset of their resources, those PN resources that are not included in the Fednet will not be visible or accessible to other PNs. The Fednet creates a virtual common workspace to its participants to share their personal resources and services in a secure way. Once the colleagues have finished sharing videos and photos, editing and printing photos, they dissolve the Fednet. This illustrates temporal nature of the Fednet.

2.2 Emergency: Sharing Sensor Information and Camera Images for Rescue of People in Disaster Relief

In emergency situations, such as a disaster relief operation, it might become crucial to share information, such as videos, photos, temperature, location or any other data valuable to the efficacy of the operation. In such situations, Fednets can enable professionals involved in the operation to share sensor information, camera view or network access to the infrastructure for the rescue of people in a disaster or for some other common goal in emergency situations.

Figure 3 illustrates an emergency situation, in which a fire explosion in the building puts the lives of people living or working there in dan-

Figure 3. A Fednet composed in emergency situation

ger. Imagine there are several professionals (fire fighters, police officers, medical specialists and environmental analysts) involved in the rescue operation and they all have their PNs. Cindy is a professional in charge of coordinating the rescue operation. Kate is a medical doctor, who coordinates the first medical aid for the rescued people. Alice is an environmental analyst who is a specialist in the construction of the building and the risk assessment in case of the disasters, such as fire, earthquake, storm or flooding. She also has access to the archives and construction databases. Bob is a chief fireman who is in charge of coordinating the fight with the fire and rescue of the people that are trapped in the building and cannot escape without help.

Alice, the environmental specialist, has to work out the quick rescue plan, taking into account the specifics of the building. In order to fulfill her job efficiently, she needs the temperature and location values of the fire points in the building to analyze statistically the collapsing risk of the building. She also needs the view from different sides of the building to evaluate the damage to the building. Bob, the fireman, needs the view of

the building from the other sides to coordinate efficiently the operation of his fire brigade. Cindy, the coordinator, needs to be able to monitor visually all entrances of the building. She also needs to know the approximate number of people that need to be rescued people to call for additional ambulances and to inform the police officers to clear the road for the ambulance machines. Kate, the medical doctor, needs to have the view from the building so that she can organize the first medical aid and dispatch the injured to the hospital. Kate also needs online contact with the hospital rescue team to transfer files to them.

All of them have information that might be valuable to the others for a successful operation. To obtain the necessary information from each other, they form a Fednet consisting of the following: Cindy (PN1): a wireless access point to share the connection to the infrastructure, a video camera and a web camera to share the view of the building; Kate (PN2): a laptop and a webcam to share the view of the building; Alice (PN3): a webcam to share the view of the building, a wireless access point to share the connection to the infrastructure for transferring images and files from Kate to

Figure 4. A Fednet composed for a healthcare application

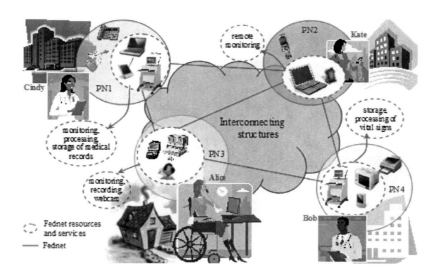

the hospital and a printer to provide the detailed rescue plan with hints for rescuing people, indicating the weak points of the construction; Bob (PN4): temperature and location sensors on his uniform to share sensor information, a webcam mounted on his helmet to share the view from the building. Once the Fednet is formed, all this valuable information is available to all members of the Fednet.

2.3 Healthcare: Sharing Real-Time Information to Detect Dangerous Situations

An example of a Fednet in healthcare environment is illustrated in Figure 4 as the network, formed between family members (Kate and Alice) and medical professionals (Cindy and Bob) to provide ambient assisted living. The Fednet here will allow sharing real-time information, access to medical information of specific vital signs, video images of Alice, who is sick and lives unattended. Alice's personal devices in her PN monitor specific vital signs and regularly report to Kate's PN and the PNs of medical doctors Cindy and Bob. As a result, they are kept informed about the situation and can detect potentially dangerous situations,

such as upcoming seizures, in order to provide with the timely medical aid.

2.4 Other Examples

In addition to these examples, there are other situations in which the concept of Fednets could be applied. For example, e-*entertainment* realized by cooperating personal devices of friends, allows friends who met at a restaurant, to exchange their holiday pictures. Their kids exchange music and play games forming another Fednet (Niemegeers & Heemstra de Groot, 2005). Another example is a virtual classroom created with PNs of students for e-*learning* that enables them to conduct regular seminars, to share study materials, tests, exams and hints on assignments.

3. LIFECYCLE AND ARCHITECTURE OF FEDNETS

A Fednet is a dynamic entity, because it evolves incrementally as more PNs join, and it ceases to exist when all PNs leave it. Therefore a Fednet has a lifecycle that reflects the phases of its existence. In this section, we describe the lifecycle of

Figure 5. The lifecycle of a Fednet

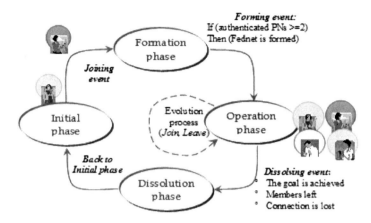

a Fednet. Furthermore, we present the architecture of a Fednet.

3.1 The Lifecycle

Fednets have a temporal nature with a lifecycle comprising the consecutive and interlinked phases of its existence. We have identified four phases: initial, formation, operation, and dissolution. Dividing the lifecycle into phases makes it easier to understand the internal processes of a Fednet and their interrelations with each other. Figure 5 illustrates the lifecycle of a Fednet.

Initial Phase

Before its creation, a Fednet is in its *Initial phase*. The Initial phase includes all processes and actions that come before the actual formation of a Fednet, such as profile creation and discovery. There are two types of profiles: a Fednet profile and a member profile. A *Fednet profile* contains the minimally required information for the PNs who wants to join a Fednet, such as the name and the goal of the Fednet and its contact information. The goal of a Fednet can be specified as "file sharing", "virtual meeting", "online gaming", etc. To join a Fednet, a new member must create a *membership profile*, which contains information about the PN, such as its identity/name, contact information (e.g. IP address), and a list of services offered to the Fednet. For a PN who wants to federate 'Discovery' process is a discovery of an existing Fednet to join, while for a Fednet it is the discovery of a new member to invite.

Formation Phase

Once the discovery is successful, 'Joining' event triggers the *Formation phase*. In the formation phase, the authentication and authorization processes take place. Members first authenticate each other and establish security associations between each other to secure their further communication. Then the accepted members of a Fednet receive a special token, e.g. a *membership credential* that proves that they belong to the Fednet. A Fednet requires at least two members in order to be formed. When there are two authenticated PNs, for example, Cindy's PN and Kate's PN, a Fednet is formed and enters its *Operation phase*.

Operation Phase

The operation phase includes the main processes of the Fednet's lifecycle, such as the mutual interactions between the PNs towards reaching the goals of the Fednet. In this phase, a Fednet is in use, i.e. the resources and services shared between the Fednet members can be utilized. During the operation phase, new members (for example, Alice's PN and Bob's PN) can join the Fednet. Members can also leave the Fednet. This process is called the *evolution* of a Fednet. The evolution makes the Fednet dynamic, because its members and available services change over time. Figures 2-4 illustrate different instances of a Fednet in its operation phase.

Dissolution Phase

Dissolving event triggers the *Dissolution phase*. Dissolution is the phase in which a Fednet is terminated. There are three types of dissolution: graceful, forced, and abrupt. *Graceful dissolution* takes place when the goals of a Fednet have been fulfilled. *Forced dissolution* takes place when the necessary requirements are no longer met, e.g. insufficient number of members for the Fednet to operate, insufficient resources, or impossibility of reaching the goal of the Fednet. *Abrupt dissolution* happens suddenly, without prior warning. It happens when the constituent networks are not available anymore, or when connectivity is lost. In the dissolution phase all security associations are cleared, the members are informed and (optionally) the history of interactions of the members is stored for future use. In Section 5 we explain the lifecycle of the Fednet illustrated in Figure 2.

3.2 Architecture

There are two approaches to the architecture of a Fednet: (1) using network overlays between PNs (MAGNET, 2006-2008) and (2) using service proxies at the gateways of PNs in MAGNET, (2006-2008) and PNP2008, (2004-2008). The difference between the two approaches is in the service access control and service provisioning. In the overlay approach the Fednet is formed as an overlay between all personal devices participating in the Fednet. In this overlay all devices and services are visible and accessible from outside the PN. Therefore, in this approach each personal device in the Fednet carries out the service access control, while providing a service to others. This is the approach adopted in PNP2008.

In a proxy-based approach PNs see each other as a single point of access at the gateways. Personal devices and services are not directly accessible from outside the PN, neither are they visible to other PNs. In the proxy-based approach, the services of a PN are provided at the gateway of a PN by means of service proxies. In addition, the access control to the PN services is at the gateway of a PN, so other personal devices inside the PN do not need to have access-control capabilities. This allows each PN to have a separate security domain in a Fednet and to keep its autonomy. This advantage over the overlay-based approach has been our main motivation for choosing the proxy-based architecture in our work (Ibrohimovna & Heemstra de Groot, 2008, July). The proxy-based architecture of a Fednet is presented in Figure 6.

The architectural components of a proxy-based Fednet are the following:

- The *Fednet manager* (FM) is a centralized entity in a Fednet and is responsible for the management and control of the entire Fednet, which includes creating/dissolving the Fednet and accepting/removing Fednet members.
- The *Fednet agent* (FA) is responsible for federation-related management and control functions for its PN, such as joining/leaving a Fednet and controlling access to personal resources and services.
- The *Gateway Node* (GW) is a device through which a PN communicates with other PNs by making one of its network interfaces publicly available.
- The *Service Proxy* is a functional component that is located at the gateway nodes of the PN. It prevents direct access for

Figure 6. Basic proxy-based architecture of a Fednet composed of two PNs

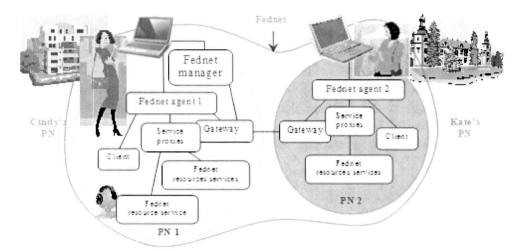

other Fednet members to the personal devices and services of a PN by making the
services available at the gateway of a PN.
The service proxy contains a piece of application code that imitates the behavior of
the service and acts as an intermediary between the client and the service.
- *Fednet services* are the services offered by
a PN to a Fednet.
- A *client* is an application or a personal
device within a PN requesting a Fednet
service.

Location of the Fednet Manager
We distinguish between two modes of functioning of a Fednet: with *internal Fednet manager*
and with *external Fednet manager*. The Fednet
manager is considered to be *external* when it is
located outside the Fednet. This is the case of a
Fednet initiated by a third party, such as a provider, who takes the responsibility of creating and
managing the Fednet. This third party acts only
as a manager of the Fednet and may be located in
the infrastructure. The external Fednet manager
can also be hosted by a PN, which only plays a
role of a manager of this Fednet. The architecture
with external Fednet manager suits the scenarios
when the Fednet membership is expected to be

large and requires a dedicated manager; or when
a specific federating service is being offered by
a third party, for example, in an on-line gaming
environment.

The infrastructure support may not always
be available for PNs to federate; or there may be
no trusted third party available for hosting the
Fednet manager functionality. In such situations
ad-hoc functioning might be an option to federate.
This is the motivation for having a Fednet with
an *internal* Fednet manager. Figure 6 illustrates
a Fednet architecture, in which this functionality
is hosted by one of the participating PNs (Cindy's
PN). This is the case when a Fednet is created in a
spontaneous manner, by one of the PNs and other
PNs join the Fednet. No third party is involved
in the creation and managing of the Fednet. An
interesting part of this approach is that it gives
flexibility, i.e. the location of the Fednet manager
is not fixed - it can be delegated or handed over to
another PN. There are several ways to do that: by
backing up or handing over the Fednet manager
functionality, or by electing a new one. However,
this might introduce overhead due to reestablishing
security associations between the PNs.

The disadvantages of the approach with the
external Fednet manager are: being dependent on
the trusted third party and having a single point

Figure 7. The ACM framework

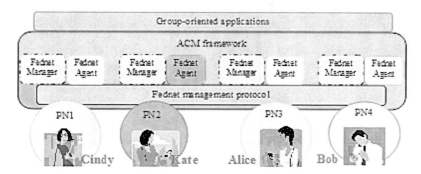

of failure at the Fednet. The disadvantage of the approach with the internal Fednet manager for the PNs hosting the manager functionality, is overhead introduced due to the management activities.

4. ACCESS CONTROL AND MANAGEMENT FRAMEWORK FOR FEDNETS

When people cooperate with each other, the following issues arise related to controlling the access to their personal resources and services: *How to authenticate each other?, Who can be authorized to access the personal services?* and *What is allowed to do for authorized users?* These issues point to the main challenge in Fednets, which is maintaining and managing a secure cooperation between PNs that belong to different persons. Secure cooperation requires proper access control mechanisms to personal resources and services. In this section, we present the access control and management framework for Fednets.

4.1 Objectives

To tackle the challenges of maintaining and managing a secure cooperation in Fednets, we designed a framework for secure Access Control and Management for a Fednet (ACM framework) illustrated in Figure 7. The objectives of the ACM framework are:

- To enable PNs to *federate* into a Fednet in a secure way;
- To provide a *user-centred approach* for forming and managing a Fednet;
- To enable PNs to run group-oriented applications using the formed Fednet through *common interfaces*;
- To facilitate the management of the Fednet, by allowing *a single sign-on* to the Fednet and its services.

4.2 Components

The main building blocks of the ACM framework are the Fednet manager, the Fednet agent and the Fednet management protocol. Since there is one FM per Fednet, it is sufficient that one of the PNs plays the role of manager by hosting the Fednet manager functionality. Therefore the Fednet manager is illustrated with dashed boxes in Figure 7. The Fednet Manager has the following functions:

- **Management function:** To create the Fednet profile and advertisements, to manage the formation, evolution and dissolution of a Fednet;
- **Fednet access control function:** To produce decisions on the access control to the Fednet and to issue membership credentials for the Fednet members.

- **Service directory look up function:** To provide the directory service to Fednet members and to maintain the list of the Fednet members and their contributions during the Fednet operation.

The *Fednet agent* (FA) acts on behalf of a PN within the Fednet and therefore it is the required functionality for every PN in federating with other PNs. The Fednet agent administers and manages the resource of the PN that are made accessible to the Fednet. The Fednet Agent has the following functions:

- **Management function:** To coordinate the PN services to which a PN can grant temporal access within a Fednet, to manage the participation of a PN in the Fednet, to create a membership profile, to join and leave the Fednet;
- **Service Access Control function:** To produce access control decisions to PN services;
- **Service Proxy configuration function:** To configure a requested service proxy to a particular member in a Fednet.

The *Fednet management protocol* is a protocol between PNs to enable them to communicate with each other. Using the Fednet management protocol, PNs can initiate and join a Fednet, exchange authorization messages and manage the formation, the operation and the dissolution of the Fednet.

4.3 Access Control

When people share their personal resources and services, it is crucial to provide proper access control. We took a two-level approach for the access control in Fednets. We chose this approach because it gives a separation of concerns in controlling access. The *first-level* is the control over access to the Fednet. It is carried out by the

Fednet manager when a new member requests to join a Fednet. By the successful first-level access control, a new member joins the Fednet. The first-level access control can be considered as a *'single sign-on'* to the Fednet.

The *second-level* is the control over access to the Fednet services, carried out by the FA of a PN when a Fednet service located in this PN is requested. This allows a PN to keep control over its personal resources and services. This meets the preferences of PN owners, who usually do not prefer delegating the access control rights over their personal resources to a third party. By the successful second-level access control, the requested Fednet service can be utilized.

4.4 Management

This list of members and services in the Fednet, which is maintained at the FM, is created at the Formation phase and updated according to the evolution of the Fednet. The list is updated when members join or leave. Moreover, when a service becomes available or unavailable, the service list is updated accordingly. Table 1 gives an example of the list of members and resources/services that is maintained by the FM of the Fednet illustrated in Figure 2.

A centralized entity for the management facilitates the management, especially with dynamically joining and leaving PNs within the Fednet. However, the FM as a centralized entity might cause a single point of failure. A possible solution to this problem might be assigning backups to the FM in the Fednet, which are sleeping and inactive, but they can be activated when needed. This is a topic for future work.

5. OPERATION OF THE ACM FRAMEWORK

In this section, we describe the operation of Fednets starting from the discovery of PNs till

Table 1.An example list of members and services of the Fednet maintained by an FM

Members	Fednet resources and services	Contact information of a Fednet agent
Cindy's PN	Display, webcam, photos and videos	IP address, port number
Kate's PN	Storage and processing of photos	IP address, port number
Alice's PN	Photos, videos and printing	IP address, port number
Bob's PN	Videos	IP address, port number

the disbanding of the Fednet. We explain the interactions between the main components of the Fednet architecture presented in Section 3.2 by means of the example illustrated in Section 2.1. In this example, Cindy (PN1), Kate (PN2), Alice (PN3) and Bob (PN4) form a Fednet to share digital media.

5.1 Discovery

PNs and Fednets use advertisements in order to discover each other. A Fednet advertisement contains {the goal of the Fednet and the contact information of the Fednet manager}. A PN advertisement contains {the PN name and contact information of the Fednet agent}. The advertisements can be distributed using pull or push methods. In *pull* method the advertisements are published at predefined locations, such as online databases or directories and can be retrieved from there. *Push* method represents a local broadcast of the advertisements in the vicinity. We distinguish the following possible types of discovery in forming a Fednet: discovery of a Fednet to join, discovery of a new PN to invite to the Fednet and discovery of a peer PN to federate into a Fednet.

5.2 Joining the Fednet and the First-Level Access Control

When the discovery process is accomplished, joining event triggers the first-level access control. Figure 8 illustrates how Cindy's PN and Kate's PN form a Fednet as a result of a successful first-level access control.

The first-level access control consists of the following processes: Authentication, Policy evaluation and token granting.

Authentication

Once the Fednet manager and agent have discovered each other, the formation phase of the federation lifecycle begins. This is the phase in which the first-level access control takes place. First, the Fednet manager and agent authenticate each other. One approach for authentication is the SSL/TLS handshake protocol, which also establishes security associations between authenticated parties. TLS, Transport Layer Security (Dierks & Rescorla, 2006), is a widely deployed protocol for securing network traffic. The protocol allows applications to communicate in a way that is designed to prevent eavesdropping, tampering, or message forgery. It is possible to provide security for an application protocol by inserting TLS between the application and network layers. Using TLS has advantages, such as the creation of a secure, transparent channel for the communication between PNs, the use of custom certificates to authenticate each other and the possibility of resuming a previously established secure channel.

Figure 8 illustrates the authentication and establishment of a secure channel between the Fednet manager and Fednet agent 2 using the TLS handshake protocol. To protect the communication by the secure authenticated channel created by the handshake protocol of the TLS, the FM and the FA first obtain certificates to prove

Figure 8. Joining the Fednet and the first-level access control

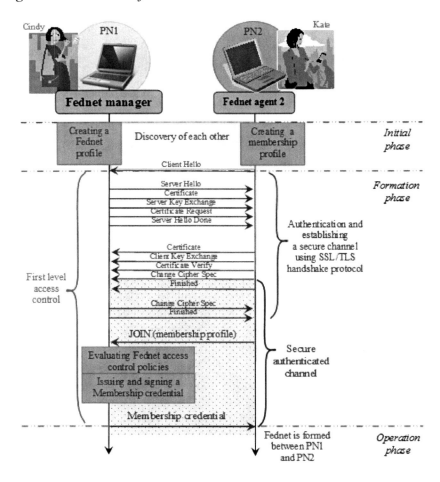

their identities. *Certificates* bind the identity of the owner of the certificate with its public key. These certificates are signed by a common root certification authority. Once the FM and the FA have successfully verified the authenticity of their certificates, the cipher suits to be used further to secure the communication are negotiated. After that, they establish a secure association, i.e. an authenticated encrypted channel that provides confidential communication between the FA and the FM.

Policy Evaluation

When both parties are authenticated, Fednet agent 2 sends a 'JOIN' request message to the Fednet

manager containing its *membership profile* created in the Initial phase. This is depicted in Figure 8. The Fednet manager carries out the authorization process by evaluating the Fednet access control policies. Simple examples of policies are: checking whether the PN is blacklisted, how many and what services it offers to the Fednet.

During the policy evaluation a member type is assigned to the PN. For example, if the member type is assigned based on the contributions PNs made in the Fednet, then the membership type could be *contributor*, *peer* or *free rider*. In this case, a *contributor* can be a member who contributes to the Fednet with a certain number of services (Nservice), for example Nservice > 2. A *peer* can be a member who contributes with little number

Table 2. Assigning a membership class based on the member type

Member type	Membership class	Privileges to use specific services
Contributor	Golden	Multiple access through the lifetime of the Fednet
Peer	Silver	Multiple access for a definite period of time
Free rider	Bronze	Single access for a definite period of time

of services, for example Nservice = 1. A *free rider* can be member who only consumes the services and does not contribute.

Membership Class

Membership class defines the ranking of a member within a particular Fednet. This ranking is important in the second-level access control process, i.e. accessing the Fednet services, because each membership class is associated with different privileges to use the services. Therefore, based on the member type and the membership class, the access to the services is different. The privileges to use the services are defined by the service owner, i.e. by the PN. Table 2 illustrates an example mapping of member type to membership class and examples of privileges.

Token Granting: Membership Credential

Once a member's membership class has been defined, a special token is issued to the member. This token is used in the member's future communications within this Fednet to prove its membership. It can be in the form of a *membership credential*, digitally signed by the Fednet manager and verifiable by other members of the Fednet. This credential stores the information that authenticates the owner of the credential. The membership credential includes {the Fednet name, the PN name, membership class and the validity period for this credential}. The membership credential is signed with the private key of the FM. The membership credential provides the PNs with a '*single sign-on*' to the Fednet, because

PNs can use their membership credentials in their interactions with other PNs of the Fednet to prove their membership.

Figure 8 shows the issuing and providing the membership credential by the FM hosted in Cindy's PN to Kate's PN. After that the Fednet is formed between Cindy's PN and Kate's PN and the Fednet enters its operation phase. Other PNs can also join the Fednet by successfully accomplishing the first-level access control.

5.3 Service Lookup

Fednet services contain subsets of services offered to the Fednet by different PNs to share with others. We classify Fednet services into 'common' and 'specific' services. Whether a service is common or specific is defined by the owner of the service. Access control is different for common services and specific services. *A common service* is accessible to all Fednet members upon presenting their membership credentials, which means that the membership credential also provides a single sign-on to the common services of the Fednet. A set of common services in a Fednet is defined at the initial phase. A common service can be, for example, a forwarding service, a display service, a printing service, internet access, storage facilities, etc.

A service lookup is a common service that is provided by the FM to all members of the Fednet. Assume that PN2 requests a service. To discover the service in the Fednet, Fednet agent 2 contacts the Fednet manager for a service lookup using a secure authenticated channel, as is illustrated in Figure 9.

Figure 9. A service lookup process

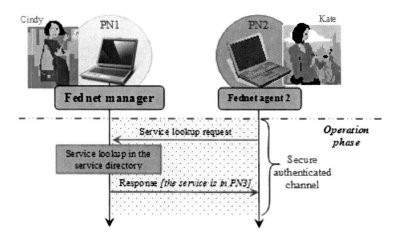

Service lookup request contains the requested service name and PN2's membership credential. The Fednet manager searches the service directory for the service information, i.e. the location of the service and the requirements to access the service (e.g. minimally required membership class to access the service). Then, the Fednet manager returns the lookup result to Fednet agent 2, stating that the requested service is located in PN3.

On demand polling the FM by the PNs for the service lookup, instead of regularly sending the updated service lists to the PNs, saves bandwidth, reduces the number of exchanged messages and prevents the PNs from storing the stalled information about the services in a Fednet.

The remaining services in the Fednet are called *specific services*, which require the second-level access control procedure, i.e. evaluating service access policies by the Fednet agents in each PN. An example of a specific service can be a file-sharing service. The access rights to this service can be different: copying a file, modifying a file, deleting a file or duplicating a file. The service access control policies define which of these actions are allowed to the Fednet members: for example, copying a file is allowed, but not modifying or deleting a file. Distinguishing between the common and specific Fednet services introduces some

flexibility for the PN owners. When contributing to a Fednet, the PN owners can differentiate between specific services and common services and decide themselves what and how much to contribute to a Fednet.

5.4 Service Request and the Second-Level Access Control

The second-level access control is the access control to the Fednet services and it takes place in the operation phase of the Fednet. The second-level access control is triggered by the service request and contains the following processes: Authentication, Policy evaluation and token granting.

Authentication

Figure 10 illustrates PN2's service request to PN3, e.g. Kate is requesting a service from Alice.

First, Fednet agent 2 initiates an authentication process between PN2 and PN3. Again we suggest using the TLS handshake protocol for the authentication. As was explained in Section 5.2, each PN obtains a membership credential, which proves its membership to this Fednet. This membership credential is signed by the FM's private key. During the handshake the PNs present each other their membership credentials, which they can verify with the FM's public key. The advantage of using the membership credential here for authentication is the optimization of the message exchange. By verifying the membership credential the PNs authenticate each other and at the same time they verify the membership of the PN to this Fednet. So, the membership credential is used as a token for a single sign-on in the Fednet and its common services. When the authentication is successful, a secure channel is established and the PNs can communicate over this secure channel, as is shown in Figure 10.

Policy Evaluation

Using a secure channel established by the TLS handshake protocol, Fednet agent 2 sends a service request to Fednet agent 3. This triggers the policy evaluation. Fednet agent 3 evaluates service access control policies to produce an authorization decision for PN2. Examples of the policies are:

```
Check the requested service
type,
If it is a common service,
    Then access is granted at
the preconfigured service proxy,
If the service is marked as spe-
cific,
    Then check the membership
class.
```

Further refinement in the access control decision is done by the policies based on the membership class specified in the membership credential and the PN owner-defined service access privileges. For the example given in Table 2, this refinement will be as follows:

```
If (membership class is Golden)
Then grant multiple access
throughout the lifetime of the
Fednet
```

```
If (membership class is Silver)
Then grant multiple access for a
definite period of time
If (membership class is Bronze)
Then grant single access for a
definite period of time.
```

Token Granting: Service Proxy Configuration

If the access control decision is positive, then the proxy of the required service is configured at the gateway of PN3 to be accessed by PN2. To configure the proxy, first, a *service proxy token* (i.e. a token to inform the service proxy) is issued and sent to the service proxy. The service proxy token includes the following information:

```
{Fednet name, PN2 name, service
name, membership class (service
access privileges), port num-
ber}.
```

Second, a *service access token* (i.e. a token to inform the client) is issued and sent to PN2 (i.e. Fednet agent 2) which includes the followings:

```
{Fednet name, PN2 name, service
name, port, IP address}.
```

In this way, Fednet agent 2 is notified about the contact information of the service proxy through which the service can be accessed. Finally, to access the service, PN2 contacts the IP address at the port indicated in the token. The service proxy compares the Fednet name, the PN name and the service name indicated in the service proxy token. If they match the service proxy provides the service or the access to the service.

Figure 10. Service request and the second-level access control

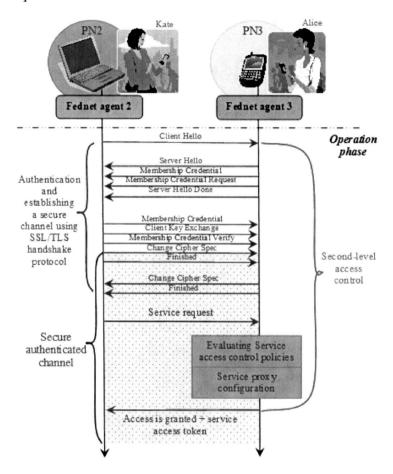

5.5 Leaving the Fednet and Dissolution of the Fednet

The process of leaving the Fednet can be initiated by the FM asking a PN to leave the Fednet, it can be also initiated by the PN who wants to leave the Fednet, or it can happen due to connection faults. Figure 11 illustrates the case in which Kate wants to leave the Fednets and sends the 'LEAVE' request to the FM. The FM carries out administrative tasks, such as removing security association and saving the history and experience with this PN for future use. The same procedure is done at Fednet agent 2. After acknowledging the 'LEAVE' request, Kate's PN is considered to have left the Fednet and the Fednet consist only

of three members, i.e. Cindy, Alice and Bob.

As was discussed in Section 4.4, the FM maintains the lists of members and the services of the Fednet. In a dynamic environment it is possible that a member loses the connection with the Fednet when the connection is down. One way for the FM to have the up-to-date information about the current members and services of the Fednet is by applying periodic "*I am alive*" messages sent by the FA to the FM. When such messages have not been received for a definite period of time, the PN is considered to have left the Fednet.

Figure 12 shows the *graceful dissolution* of a Fednet, which is one of the ways discussed in Section 3.1 to dissolve the Fednet. In this case, the FM sends a 'DISSOLVE' message to all members.

Figure 11. Leaving the Fednet

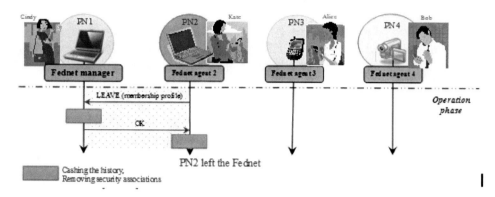

Figure 12. The Fednet dissolution process

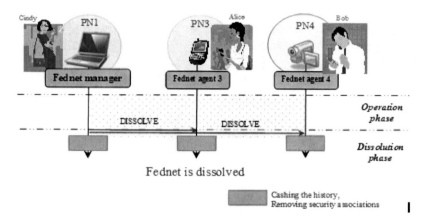

Consequently, security associations are removed, history is saved and the Fednet is dissolved. The *forced dissolution* contains similar message exchange. However the *abrupt dissolution* does not contain these message exchanges, since the dissolution is caused by the connectivity failure. The issues related to the abrupt dissolution are the issues of fault tolerance, availability, reliability and self organization that would call a separate in-depth research.

In this section, we provided the full picture of how the Fednet operates from the discovery of its members till its dissolution. The approach taken in this section is one of the possible solutions to realize the Fednets.

5.6 Early Experimental Results

In this subsection, we briefly describe early experimental results from prototyping the ACM framework, which is being carried out to support the ongoing research. Although the prototyping is still ongoing, it provides with many insights to the problem, helps to reflect on the theoretical design and to refine it. For prototyping we use Java on Window XP. The prototype is meant to run on the gateways of the PNs, assuming that the PNs are formed and functioning. The prototype enables PNs to federate with each other, to manage forming, evolution and dissolution of Fednets. The prototype of the framework includes common services, such as a lookup service, provided by the Fednet manager to all Fednet agents within the Fednet and a conference service between the Fednet members to exchange text messages.

We tested the implemented code on two HP laptops for a local ad hoc scenario to emulate the case with four PNs illustrated in Section 2.1. In the set up, each of the laptops runs two PNs. We tested the code to form Fednets with internal and with external Fednet managers. In the first case, one of the PNs hosts the Fednet manager functionality and also participates in the Fednet. Therefore, this Fednet has the architecture with internal FM functionality. The running of the code was successful. 'PNs' formed a Fednet through 'the first-level access control'. Furthermore, the Fednet services can be requested through 'the second-level access control', in which the 'server PN' provides a service access token to the 'client PN'.

The implemented architecture with internal Fednet manager is suitable for the Fednets of small sizes, i.e. involving a few PNs. The reason is that in this architecture, one of the participants is responsible to manage the Fednet and when there is a large number of participants, it would be unfeasible for a participant-PN to manage the Fednet. In this case, it would be particularly important to have an external dedicated manager for the Fednet. Therefore, the implementation code was tested also for forming a Fednet with external Fednet manager, in which, one of the PNs plays a role of a dedicated Fednet manager. This architecture shows better scalability in comparison with the architecture with the internal Fednet manager.

The user can set his preferences to the first-level access control as automatic or user-assisted modes through the user interface of the prototype. In the automatic setting, PNs automatically form a Fednet when a suitable Fednet (e.g. matching goal) and members (e.g. matching PN name) are discovered. The user preferences on the second-level access control can be set as well. If automatic mode is chosen, the access to the services is controlled by user-defined policies, whereas, in user-assisted mode, the service owner will be prompted to accept or deny the service request. The automatic and user-assisted options give flexibility to the users, since depending on the situation, context and the application nature, the users can set their preferences as automatic or user-assisted modes for joining, forming Fednets and access control to their resources.

Currently we are investigating the ways the service proxy functionality can be implemented for service provisioning in Fednets. Additionally, the ongoing work includes the dynamic access control to the Fednet resources, which should take into account the behavior of the members as well as the availability of the Fednet services.

6. RELATED TECHNOLOGIES

In this section, we discuss the relation between Fednets and other existing paradigms and group-oriented technologies.

6.1 Fednets and Resource Sharing Group-Oriented Systems

This subsection presents a brief overview of some resource sharing group-oriented systems reported in literature.

A *grid* (Foster, Kesselman & Tuecke, 2001) is a hardware and software infrastructure that allows sharing resources across organizational boundaries. Grid computing offers powerful distributed computing resources to optimize the execution of time consuming tasks, whereas Fednets have smaller scope and represent ad hoc on demand sharing of personal resources and services.

Secure Virtual Enclaves (SVE) (Shands, Yee, Jacobs & Sebes, 2001) is a middleware infrastructure that enables multiple organizations to provide each other with restricted access to the organizational information databases. Fednets and SVE differ in administrative domains, in the nature of sharing the resources and the scope of applications.

Wireless community networks (WCN, 2003) and *P2P wireless networks confederation* (P2P-WNC) (Efstathiou, Frangoudis & Polyzos, 2006) are examples of Internet access sharing. *WCN* is a development of interlinked networks using wireless technologies to provide Internet access in areas where the conventional connection services are expensive or not available. *P2PWNC* is a community of administrative domains, built on WCNs, and offers wireless Internet access to each others' registered users based on incentive techniques. While WCN and P2PWNC are tailored to a specific application, i.e. sharing Internet access, sharing Internet access is just one of the possible applications of Fednets. Therefore WCN and P2PWNC can be seen as special cases of Fednets.

The access control mechanisms used in these technologies are different, access control policies (grids, SVE), privileges (grids), grid map file (grids), file encryption-decryption keys (P2P file-sharing networks) and list of registered users (WCN, P2PWNC). The complexity of the access control mechanisms is different from technology to technology. Furthermore, in the literature we encountered distributed and centralized access control to the shared resources. In (Ibrohimovna & Heemstra de Groot, 2008, October.) we provide an overview of the access control mechanisms used in the above mentioned technologies. Since grids have a dedicated infrastructure support, grid approaches for the access control would be suitable for the Fednets which have the infrastructure support and the architecture with an external Fednet manager. The approaches of VOMS (Alfieri, Cecchini, Ciaschini, dell'Agnello, Frohner, Gianoli et al., 2003) and CAS (Pearlman, Welch, Foster, Kesselman & Tuecke, 2002) facilitate the access control and management in the Fednets with a large number of members, since there are dedicated VOMS administrators and CAS servers for this task. The approach taken in PRIMA (Lorch & Kafura, 2004) could be used for dynamic on-demand creation and management of user accounts for small groups of Fednet members.

The major difference between the Fednet concept and the paradigms mentioned above is that a Fednet is built on top of personal networks using a variety of personal resources and services. The resources and services are part of a personal network and not an organization with system managers. Furthermore, the availability of these personal resources and services is very dynamic. In addition, the access rights of Fednet members may change in time, depending on their behavior but also on the goals of the Fednet and total availability of resources. Moreover, Fednets are applicable in different contexts: family, entertainment, education, research, business, healthcare and emergency. They have a potential to cover a variety of P2P application categories, such as communication and collaboration (instant messaging), distributed computation (sharing available processing power), internet service support (sharing internet connection, multicasting services) and content distribution (digital media sharing). Therefore Fednets can evolve into a new generation of P2P networks with service-orientation and personalization features that allow users to share their personal resources in a seamless, secure and flexible way.

6.2 Fednets and the Flavour of a Service-Oriented Architecture

According to the Organization for the Advancement of Structured Information Standards (OASIS), a service-oriented architecture (SOA) can be defined as "a paradigm for organizing and utilizing distributed capabilities that may be under the control of different ownership domains. It provides a uniform means to offer, discover, interact with, and use capabilities to produce desired effects consistent with measurable preconditions and expectations" (MacKenzie, Laskey, McCable, Brown & Metz, 2006). A SOA specifies how to connect applications and data for service consumers on demand. This implies that a SOA is a collection of services that communicate with each other. This communication can include a simple data transfer and even communication of services coordinating some activity. The examples of Fednets given in Section 2 show that based on the context and the situation, every instance of a Fednet is oriented to a particular service or an application, e.g. for sharing digital media for business environments, for sharing sensor information, view and other services in disaster relief and sharing vital sign information for an assisted living environment in healthcare. These scenarios bring us to the world of service-oriented architectures. From this point of view, Fednets can be seen as a form of SOA.

SOA signifies cross-domain integration of disparate services, by using common standards for the description of service interfaces and by integrating heterogeneous applications. This implies that in SOA, interfaces are platform-independent, thus a client from any device using any operating system in any language can use the service. This matches very well with the philosophy behind Fednets. The idea of realizing Fednets using service proxies can make personal services in different PNs available through common interfaces, hiding the details of underlying technologies, the services and the internal structure of PNs.

In the past, service-oriented architectures were associated with the use of technologies such as Decentralized Component Object Model (DCOM) or Object Request Brokers (ORB) for providing a set of distributed services. Nowadays, the SOA has entered grids and the P2P computing world. The concepts of grids, P2P and SOA are more and more intervened with each other. For example, composite concepts such as P2P grids (Uppuluri, Jabisetti, Joshi & Lee, 2005) and service-oriented P2P appeared in academia. Fednets can become part of future tendencies on integration of various paradigms such as grids, P2P and SOA. The Fednet is, in fact, *a grid of personal networks* or a *service-oriented P2P cooperation of personal networks*.

7. CONCLUSION AND FUTURE TRENDS

A Fednet is an example of pervasive and ubiquitous computing technology. It is a group-oriented networking concept that might be very attractive to users due to its potential impact on the quality of life. In this chapter, we presented the concept of a Fednet through various examples. We described its architecture and lifecycle. In addition, we presented a framework for secure access control and management for Fednets (ACM framework), which provides a controlled collaboration of personal networks where each personal network controls the access to its resources and services. The framework contains software components that run on the PNs to federate them into a Fednet, to coordinate them in the Fednet, and to provide authenticated communication and a single sign-on to the Fednet and its common services. Furthermore, the framework enables group-oriented P2P service sharing applications on top of PNs. The added value of the ACM framework is that it enables independent PNs to federate and manage the Fednet in a secure and organized way, i.e. before sharing their personal resources and services, members authenticate each other and give authorizations to access their services. Thus, the ACM framework can be the means for personal services of different owners to be connected with each other in a secure way.

The results presented in this chapter reflect our initial research on Fednets. The implementation and testing of the ACM framework is currently ongoing work. Speaking about further development, it would be interesting to investigate the participation of PNs in multiple Fednets. We anticipate that the management of a Fednet in this case is more complex. Another interesting challenge is hosting multiple Fednets in one PN, where each Fednet represents a separate realm, i.e. a separate security domain. In Fednets PNs export their personal services to each other; it would be also interesting to investigate the challenges of Fednet hierarchies, i.e. when Fednets export their federated services to other Fednets or to third parties. Although the dynamic cooperation of PNs in the Fednet and the impact of the reputation information in this cooperation have not been investigated here, it would be an interesting avenue for future research.

We envisage different application areas of Fednets such as education, healthcare, entertainment, business and emergency. The advantages of personal networks and their federations will become more obvious as the number of personal devices increases. Observe that although nowadays we have just a few devices, in the near future this number is expected to increase tremendously. It is predicted by the Wireless World Research Forum or WWRF (Jefferies, 2007) that 10 years from now, there will be 7 trillion wireless devices serving 7 billion people, that is, on the average 1000 wireless devices per person. The large proliferation of all types of sensors and portable devices with networking facilities will result in new paradigms for service oriented computing. Fednets are an example of this. Personal networks and their federations can be seen as a next generation networking concept that allows organizing a big part of these devices in order to make them cooperate in an effective way.

REFERENCES

Alfieri, R., Cecchini, R., Ciaschini, V., dell'Agnello, L., Frohner, A., Gianoli, A., et al. (2003). Voms: An authorization system for virtual organizations. In *Proceedings of the 1st European Across Grids Conference*, Santiago de Compostela.

Dierks, T., & Rescorla, E. (2006). *The Transport Layer Security (TLS) Protocol Version 1.1, RFC 4346.*

Efstathiou, E. C., Frangoudis, P. A., & Polyzos, G. C. (2006). Stimulating Participation in Wireless Community Networks. In *Proceedings of IEEE INFOCOM'06*, Barcelona, Spain.

Foster, I., Kesselman, C., & Tuecke, S. (2001). The Anatomy of the Grid: Enabling Scalable Virtual Organizations. *The International Journal of Supercomputer Applications, 15*(3).

Ibrohimovna, M., & Heemstra de Groot, S. (2008, July). Proxy-based Fednets for sharing personal services in distributed environments. In [Athens, Greece.]. *Proceedings of, ICWMC2008*, 150–157.

Ibrohimovna, M., & Heemstra de Groot, S. (2008, October). Sharing resources in group-oriented networks: Fednet and related paradigms. In [Valencia, Spain.]. *Proceedings of UBICOMM, 08*, 430–437.

Jefferies, N. (2007). *Global Vision for a Wireless World, Wireless World Research Forum, 18th WWRF meeting*, Helsinki, Finland.

Lorch, M., & Kafura, D. (2004). The prima grid authorization system. *Journal of Grid Computing, 2*(3), 279–298. doi:10.1007/s10723-004-5408-y

MacKenzie, M., Laskey, K., McCable, F., Brown, P. F., & Metz, R. (2006). *OASIS – Reference Model for Service Oriented Architecture 1.0*. Retrieved from http://www.oasis-open.org/

Magnet, I. S. T. *6FP MAGNET*. (2006-2008). Retrieved from http://www.ist-magnet.org, http://magnet.aau.dk/

Niemegeers, I., & Heemstra de Groot, S. (2003). Research issues in ad-hoc distributed personal networking. *Wireless Personal Communications, 26*(2-3), 149–167. doi:10.1023/A:1025522402484

Niemegeers, I., & Heemstra de Groot, S. (2005). FEDNETS: Context-Aware Ad-Hoc Network Federations. *Wireless Personal Communications, 33*(3-4), 305–318. doi:10.1007/s11277-005-0574-1

PacWoman. (2003). Retrieved from http://www.imec.be/pacwoman

Pearlman, L., Welch, V., Foster, I., Kesselman, C., & Tuecke, C. (2002). A community authorization service for group collaboration. In *Proceedings of the IEEE 3rd International Workshop on Policies for Distributed Systems and Networks.*

PNP 2008, The Dutch Freeband Communications Project PNP2008. (2004-2008). Retrieved from http://www.freeband.nl

QoS for PNs at home, The Dutch Freeband Communications Project QoS for PNs at home. (2004-2008). Retrieved from http://qos4pn.irctr.tudelft.nl

Shands, D., Yee, R., Jacobs, J., & Sebes, E. J. (2001). Secure Virtual Enclaves: Supporting Coalition Use of Distributed Application Technologies. [TISSEC]. *ACM Transactions on Information and System Security, 4*(2), 103–133. doi:10.1145/501963.501964

Uppuluri, P., Jabisetti, N., Joshi, U., & Lee, Y. (2005). P2P Grid: Service Oriented Framework for Distributed Resource Management. In *Proceedings of the 2005 IEEE SCC'05*, (Vol.1, pp. 347-350).

WCN. *Wireless Community Networks.* (2003). Retrieved from http://wcn.cnt.org

ADDITIONAL READING

Ait Yaiz, R., den Hartog, F., & Selgert, F. (2006). On the Definition and Relevance of Context-Awareness in Personal Networks. In *Proceedings of the 1st International Workshop on Personalized Networks (PerNets 2006),* pp.1-6. San José, California, USA.

Baken, N., van Boven, E., den Hartog, F., & Hekmat, R. (2004, September). A four-tiered hierarchy in a converged fixed-mobile architecture, enabling Personal Networks. *The Journal of The Communications Network, 3*(3).

Chrevrollier, N., Passchier, I., den Hartog, F., & de Jonge, M. (2008). Towards sustainable mobility by introducing Personal Networks in Intelligent Transportation Systems. *Presented at the 7th European Congress and Exhibition on Intelligent Transport Systems and Services,* June 4-6, 2008.

Den Hartog, F., Blom, M., Lageweg, C., Peeters, M. E., Schmidt, J. R., van der Veer, R., et al. (2007). *First experiences with Personal Networks as an enabling platform for service providers.* In Proceedings of MobiQuitous 2007 (pp. 1-8). Philadelphia, USA.

Den Hartog, F., Schmidt, H., & de Vries, A. (2006). On the Potential of Personal Networks for Hospitals. *International Journal of Medical Informatics, 75*(9), 658–663. doi:10.1016/j.ijmedinf.2006.04.005

Den Hartog, F., Schmidt, J., & de Vries, A. (2005). Personal Networks Enabling Remote Assistance for Medical Emergency Teams. *The Journal on Information Technology in Healthcare., 3*(6), 377–385.

Den Hartog, F. T. H., Joosten, R., & Selgert, F. (2009). Architecture of a Personal Network Service Layer. *In Proceedings of the workshop UbiIslands.* Berlin, 27 April 2009.

Fledderus, E., Rietkerk, O., den Hartog, F., Niemegeers, I., & Heemstra de Groot, S. (2006). Towards Viable Personal Networks and FedNets – a Value-Web Perspective. *Wireless Personal Communications, 38*(1), 103–115. doi:10.1007/s11277-006-9043-8

Gu, Y., Prasad, V., Lu, W., & Niemegeers, I. (2007). Clustering in Ad Hoc Personal Network Formation. International Conference on Computational Science. pp. 312-319. Wireless and Mobile Systems track. *In Springer Lecture Notes in Computer Science* (4490).

Gu, Y., Prasad, V., & Niemegeers, I. (2008). A Mobility Model for Personal Networks. *In the Mediterranean Ad Hoc Networking Workshop (Med-Hoc-Net)*, Palma de Mallorca, Spain, June 23-27, 2008.

Ibrohimovna, M., & Heemstra de Groot, S. (2009). Resource sharing and access control in group-oriented networks: Fednet and related paradigms. To appear in *International online Journal on Advances in Intelligent Systems.* 2(1).

Ibrohimovna, M., & Heemstra de Groot, S. (2009, May). A framework for access control and management in dynamic cooperative and federated environments. To appear *In Proceedings of AICT2009,* Venice/Mestre, Italy.

Ibrohimovna, M., Heemstra de Groot, S., & Zhou, J. (2009, January). Secure and Dynamic Cooperation of Personal Networks in a Fednet. *In Proceedings of CCNC2009,* Las Vegas, USA. 978-1-4244-2309-5/09/$25.00 ©2009 IEEE.

Ineke, N., Prasad, V., Niemegeers, I., & Heemstra de Groot, S. (2007) Ad Hoc Federation of Networks (FedNets) - Mechanisms and Requirements. *WILLOPAN, IEEE COMSWARE,* Bangalore, India. 10.1109/COMSWA.2007.382501.

Jacobsson, M. (2008). Personal Networks – An Architecture for Self-Organized Personal Wireless Communications, *Doctoral dissertation*, TU Delft, June 17, 2008.

Jacobsson, M., Niemegeers, I., & Heemstra de Groot, S. (To be published in 2010). *Personal Networks: Wireless Networking for Personal Devices.* A book. Publisher: John Wiley & Sons.

Jehangir, A., & Heemstra de Groot, S. (2007). Securing inter-cluster communication in Personal Networks. *In Proceedings of the 2nd International Workshop on Personalized Networks.* Philadelphia, USA. 10.1109/MOBIQ.2007.4451053.

Joosten, R. _ Joosten, S.)2007'. Rules for Identity and Access Control. *In Proceedings of the IFIP Summer School on The Future of Identity in the Information Society.* August 2007, Karlstad.

Lo, A., Lu, W., Jacobsson, M., Prasad, V., & I. Niemegeers. (2007). Personal Networks: An Architecture for 4G Mobile Communications Networks. *Telektronikk Journal,* 103 (1).

Lu, W., Gu, Y., Prasad, V., Lo, A., & Niemegeers, I. (2007). A Self-organized Personal Network Architecture. *International Conference on Networking and Services ICNS '07 (*pp. 36-41). Athens, Greece.

Lu, W., Prasad, V., Lo, A., & Niemegeers, I. (2007) A Framework for the Self-organization of Personal Networks. *In Proceedings of the 2nd International Workshop on Personalized Networks* (pp. 1-8). Philadelphia, USA.

Onur, E., Jacobsson, M., Heemstra de Groot, S., & Niemegeers, I. (2008). Manageable Bubbles of the Future Internet: Personal Super Virtual Devices. *Presented in the 21st Wireless World Research Forum Meeting.* Stockholm, Sweden, October 13-15, 2008.

Peeters, M., & den Hartog, F. (2006). A concrete example of a Personal Network architecture. *In Proceedings of the 3rd IEEE Consumer Communications and Networking Conference.* Vol. 1 (pp. 514–518). Las Vegas, NV, USA.

Prasad, V., Jacobsson, M., Heemstra de Groot, S., Lo, A., & Niemegeers, I. (2005). Architectures for Intra-Personal Network Communication. *In Proceedings of the 3rd ACM International Workshop on Wireless Mobile Applications and Services on WLAN Hotspots WMASH'05* (pp. 115 – 118). Cologne, Germany.

Prasad, V., Li, Y., Jacobsson, M., Lo, A., & Niemegeers, I. (2008). FEW-PNets - A Framework for Emulations of Wireless Personal Networks. *In the IEEE International Symposium on a World of Wireless, Mobile and Multimedia Networks (WOWMOM'08).* Newport Beach (CA), USA, June 23-27, 2008.

Vazifehdan, J., Jacobsson, M., & Niemegeers, I. (2009). A Generic Framework for Gateway and Access Network Selection in Personal Networks. *In Proceedings of the Third International Workshop on Personalized Networks (Pernets'09).* Las Vegas, Nevada, USA.

Wu, Y., & Niemegeers, I. (2006). A Cognitive Architecture for Personal Networks. In *Proceedings of the First International IFIP TC6 Conference on Autonomic Networking.* Paris, France.

Zhou, J., Jacobsson, M., & Niemegeers, I. (2007). Cross Layer Design for Enhanced Quality Routing in Personal Wireless Networking. *In Proceedings of the 2nd International Workshop on Personalized Networks.*

Zhou, J., Jacobsson, M., Onur, E., & Niemegeers, I. (2008). Factors that Impact Link Quality Estimation in Personal Networks. *In the 8th International Symposium On Computer Networks (ISCN'08),* Istanbul, Turkey, June 18-20, 2008.

KEY TERMS AND DEFINITIONS

Access Control in Fednets: Control of the access over the personal resources and services in personal networks who are participating in the Fednet.

Federation of Personal Networks: A Federation of Personal Networks is a group-oriented secure network of Personal Networks, in which Personal Networks collaborate with each other to share personal resources and services in a peer-to-peer manner to achieve a common objective.

Fednet (Abbreviation for a Federation of Personal Networks): A Fednet is a group-oriented secure network of Personal Networks, in which Personal Networks collaborate with each other to share personal resources and services in a peer-to-peer manner to achieve a common objective.

Fednet Agent: The entity in a personal network for federation-related management and control functions, such as joining/leaving a Fednet and the access control to the PNs' resources and services.

Fednet Manager: A centralized entity in a Fednet that is responsible for the management and control of the entire Fednet.

Lifecycle of a Fednet: The phases of the Fednet's existence starting from its conception till its termination.

Personal Network: Personal network is a network of a user's personal devices and services, cooperating with each other independently of their geographical location to provide ubiquitous services to the user.

Service Proxy: In the context of Fednets, it is a functional component located at the gateway of a PN. It prevents direct access for other Fednet members to the personal devices and services of the PN by making the services available at the gateway of the PN.

Sharing Personal Resources and Services: Exporting a subset of personal resources and services to others. A cooperation between personal networks, where they can be producers and consumers of personal resources and services.

Chapter 42
Overlay–Based Middleware for the Pervasive Grid

Paul Grace
University of Lancaster, UK

Danny Hughes
University of Lancaster, UK

Geoff Coulson
University of Lancaster, UK

Gordon S. Blair
University of Lancaster, UK

Barry Porter
University of Lancaster, UK

Francois Taiani
University of Lancaster, UK

ABSTRACT

Grid computing is becoming increasingly pervasive; sensor networks and mobile devices are now connected with traditional Grid infrastructure to form geographically diverse complex systems. Applications of this type can be classified as the Pervasive Grid. In this chapter we examine how traditional Grid technologies and middleware are inherently unsuited to address the challenges of extreme heterogeneity and fluctuating environmental conditions in these systems. We present Gridkit, a configurable and reconfigurable reflective middleware that leverages overlay networks and dynamic software in response to the requirements of the Pervasive Grid. We also illustrate how Gridkit has been used to deploy a flood monitoring application at a river in the north west of England; this demonstrates both the flexibility Gridkit provides, and how dynamic adaptation optimises performance and resource consumption.

DOI: 10.4018/978-1-61520-686-5.ch042

INTRODUCTION

The Grid promises computing as a utility, where distributed computational resources are brought together and can be openly accessed by many via a standardized infra-structure—Grid middleware. Originally concerned with the computational power of networked PCs and cluster computers this has been extended to include pervasively deployed resources embedded within environments. The Pervasive Grid (Davies et al., 2004) merges the vision of ubiquitous computing with traditional Grid computing. The following present some of the many examples of this Pervasive Grid in action:

- **Environmental monitoring and control.** In order to predict natural phenomena such as floods, hurricanes, and volcanic eruptions, scientists collect data and feed this into computationally intensive prediction models. These systems involve networked sensor devices deployed "in the field" that monitor the environment, collect data and then distribute this, via communication networks, to models that may be running local to the monitored site, or running off-site (typically a traditional high-performance Grid).
- **Transport.** Next generation transport systems are embracing pervasive computing. Traffic monitoring systems consisting of sensor devices at the roadside, along with embedded devices within cars collect real-time data that is input to complex traffic models to help improve traffic flow. Similarly the ability for cars to communicate with one another using vehicular ad-hoc networks (VANETS) have been used to improve road safety, by warning drivers or autonomously taking evasive action.
- **Healthcare.** Remote patient monitoring devices e.g. those that are embedded in the home, or mobile devices carried by the patient monitor their current state of health and are integrated into large-scale healthcare systems to improve standards of patient care. This can include detecting potential problems and informing a suitable healthcare professional.

From these application types it is clear that there is an increasing trend towards *diversity* in Grid applications. Here, two key characteristics of the Pervasive Grid that must be addressed by future middleware are:

1. **Extreme heterogeneity of Grid technologies.** At the *device* level we envisage a spectrum of devices ranging from large cluster computers through to mobile devices, embedded devices and wireless sensors. At the *network* level, the range of network types in use has grown to include: high-speed local networks; lower-speed wide-area networks; infrastructure-based wireless networks; ad-hoc wireless networks and specialised sensor networks. At the *middleware* level, the range of middleware-level communications services in use is expanding from basic point-to-point interactions (e.g. SOAP messaging and RPC), to "interaction paradigms" such as: reliable and unreliable multicast; workflow; media streaming; publish-subscribe; tuple-space/ generative communication; and peer-to-peer based resource location or file sharing.
2. **Fluctuating environmental conditions.** Wireless sensor networks deployed on site, mobile computing devices, and ad-hoc networking are all subject to fluctuating conditions in the environment e.g. network quality of service (QoS), resource availability (e.g. battery power), changing location, devices in range, etc.

Dealing with these characteristics is a fundamental challenge for future Grid middleware, and one that is demonstrably not addressed by existing platforms. We argue that Grid middleware must be flexible and configurable to meet a wide range of application requirements across heterogeneous systems; and importantly should be able to dynamically adapt its behaviour to ensure that it continues to provide the required level of service in the face of changing operating conditions.

In this chapter, we describe Gridkit (Grace et al., 2008) a component-based, *reflective middleware* for the Pervasive Grid. The use of software components as building blocks allows the middleware to be flexibly deployed on heterogeneous devices. Subsequently, reflection is used as a principled approach to adapt these components at run-time. A novel feature of Gridkit is that it leverages *overlay networks* to tackle the problems of network heterogeneity. Overlay networks are virtual communication structures that are logically "laid over" an underlying physical network such as the Internet or a wireless ad-hoc networking environment. The benefits of the overlay approach are that it can mask the heterogeneity of the underlying networked infrastructure, it can provide needed network services (e.g. application level multicast) in network environments that don't support them, and it is inherently configurable and run-time adaptive so as to be able to address the high degree of dynamicity inherent to pervasive computing environments.

The final part of this chapter examines how Gridkit has been used to deploy a real world application that predicts flooding in a river valley in the North-West of England. In the context of this application, hydrologists deploy sensors (such as depth and flow-rate sensors); and a wireless sensor network is used to: i) feed information into off-site flood prediction models executing upon a traditional computational Grid, and ii) create a "local Grid" of sensors for performing flood prediction computations on site. In this example, we illustrate both the flexibility of middleware deployment across devices, and the use of dynamic adaptation to optimize the performance of the

sensor network and conserve valuable resources such as battery power.

ADAPTIVE SYSTEMS SOFTWARE

The Pervasive Grid is characterised by change, and as such, next generation Grid software must by capable of dynamically adapting its behaviour in response to this change. In this section we introduce techniques from the field of dynamic software adaptation and in particular focus on the Lancaster philosophy for developing adaptive systems software; this combines three fundamental software technologies: *software components, computational reflection* (Maes, 1987), and *component frameworks* (Szyperski, 1998). Here we examine each technology in detail, thus providing the necessary expertise to understand how the Gridkit middleware operates once the three are combined.

Software Components

Architecture-based runtime software adaptation (OReizy et al., 1998) is a well-established approach to change the behaviour of software over time. Here software components act as the building blocks of adaptive software, and as the unit of change. Inspired by this prior work, **OpenCom** (Coulson et al., 2008) was developed as a general component model designed to support the development of dynamically adaptive systems software (and in particular reflective middleware). An outline of this component model is illustrated in Figure 1.

Here, *components* are language-independent encapsulated units of functionality and deployment that interact with other components exclusively through "interfaces" and "receptacles". *Interfaces* describe the behaviour offered by each component and are expressed in terms of sets of operation signatures and associated datatypes. Importantly, components support multiple in-

Figure 1. The OpenCom component model

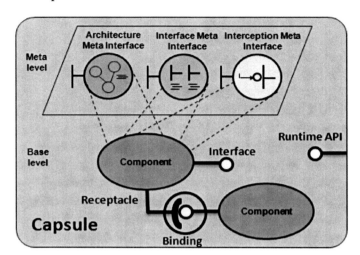

terfaces: this is useful in embodying separations of concern (e.g. between base functionality and component management). *Receptacles* are the corresponding "required" interfaces that are used to explicitly describe the dependencies of one component on other components; *bindings* are then the associations between a single interface and a single receptacle.

Components are deployed and executed within a *Capsule;* these are kernel-like environments that offer a runtime API to manage the contained components. This API provides operations to create component instances, delete component instances, create bindings and destroy bindings. Hence, using this interface components can be deployed and bindings created at any time during run-time (this is called *third-party deployment*). We have developed a wide range of capsules for different devices—e.g. for a Unix or Windows process on a PDA or PC; a RAM chip on a sensor mote; and others; thus allowing software adaptation to take place across heterogeneous pervasive devices.

Reflection

Reflection is the capability of a system to reason about itself and act upon this information. Hence, a reflective system maintains a representation of itself that is causally connected to the underlying system that it describes. This is known as the CCSR or Causally Connected Self Representation (Maes, 1987). The CCSR is often referred to as the meta level, and the system itself the base level. Hence, changes made at the meta-level via this self-representation are reflected in the underlying base-level, and vice versa. Reflection is seen as a principled approach to carry out dynamic adaptation.

Figure 1 also illustrates how OpenCom provides reflective behaviour to the component developers. Each traditional OpenCom component (described as a base component) has access to a set of three meta-space behaviours (each with a separate *meta-interface*):

- The *interface* meta-interface supports the inspection of the component's provided and required interfaces, and the operations available on these interfaces. It also allows third-parties to dynamically invoke methods.
- The *architecture* meta-interface accesses the software architecture of a component (in the following section we will investigate these composite components in further detail). The meta-representation is

a component graph describing the set of connected components, where a connection maps between a required and provided interface in the same address space. Hence, the architecture meta-interface has operations to inspect the current component configuration and also to make changes to this graph structure (which will then be reflected in the base component).

• The two prior meta-interfaces focus on the structure of a system; whereas the *interception* meta-interface allows reflection to manage the behaviour of the system. This interface supports the dynamic insertion of interceptors, these typically describe behaviour to be performed before an operation is executed (a pre interceptor) or after (a post interceptor). Such capabilities provide the ability to add non-functional behaviour implementation into the system at run-time; notable examples would be monitoring or security checks.

Component Frameworks

A Component framework (CF) is a composite component that encapsulates a configuration of components whose role is related to a specific behaviour domain. Hence, this is an abstraction for supporting architectural adaptation as prescribed by (OReizy et al., 1998). In terms of middleware, a component framework could manage a set of network protocol components, service discovery components or buffer management mechanisms. These framework elements also act as the life support environment for the contained components i.e. the framework contains mechanisms to verify valid component configurations (e.g. enforcing a strict stacking architecture for network protocol composition), and it also makes decisions when to perform a dynamic reconfiguration, utilizing appropriate adaptation mechanisms to ensure that these are carried out in a safe and consistent manner. A fundamental requirement of adaptation is

that the system is placed in a safe-state before the adaptation is executed. (Kramer & Magee, 1985) termed this state *Quiescence*; and this involves ensuring that there is no ongoing active computation within the component architecture.

Importantly, component frameworks can either be *node-local* (i.e. the component configuration they manage is within a single address space) or *distributed* (i.e. the component configuration is spread (or replicated) across a number of distinct machines). In the appendix we describe the mechanisms that underpin adaptation for the interested reader. Richer examples of real component frameworks will be presented within the Gridkit middleware.

GRIDKIT: RECONFIGURABLE OVERLAY BASED MIDDLEWARE

The role of middleware is to provide communication services (e.g. resource discovery, remote procedure calls, messaging, and many others) in the face of end-system, operating system and network heterogeneity; and to simplify the task of the application developer by managing the problems of distribution. Established Grid middleware have achieved some success in providing these services; however, in relation to the problems of the Pervasive Grid we believe that they are limited in three respects:

1. Current middleware solutions are *'network-style centric'*. That is, their operation is suited to individual network types, they cannot work in another network type, or across network types. For example, Grid middleware e.g. Globus (Foster et al., 2001) are reliant on the properties of fixed networks such as connectivity. Alternatively, middleware for wireless infra-structure networks or ad-hoc networks typically focus on addressing the problems of network disconnection and mobility.

2. Monolithic implementations of middleware are typically targeted to specific device types (and the majority for high-end desktop PCs or servers). These lack the flexibility to be deployed on the embedded, mobile and sensor devices found in the Pervasive Grid.

3. Middleware technologies typically support individual communication services, e.g. resource discovery, Remote Procedure Call (RPC), publish-subscribe, etc. However, one-size does not fit all network types, and will not optimally work for all types of applications; for example, data sharing is well suited to ad-hoc interaction in ad-hoc and sensor networks, whereas RPC is better suited to infrastructure networks.

One possible solution to these problems is to employ *separate middleware solutions* for different devices, network domains and communication services. This solution is evident in the piece-meal nature of current Grid middleware: e.g. SOAP for messaging, JMS for publish-subscribe, GridFTP for data streaming, and OGSA-DAI for database access. However, this ad-hoc approach has numerous problems:

*   The responsibility for middleware composition and integration adds considerable complexity to the application developer's task.
*   The middleware infrastructure becomes redundant and heavyweight due to potentially common functionality being duplicated across multiple implementations (e.g. network transport, resource management, and security).
*   Individual middleware implementations may only operate in certain environments and/or under certain network conditions (e.g. separate publish-subscribe implementations are typically used for infrastructure-based and for ad-hoc networks)—this again leads to redundant deployment, this time of whole middleware services.

Therefore, Gridkit has been designed to provide a flexible range of middleware services across a range of network domains and device types. This common software framework aims to transparently hide the complexities of heterogeneity and middleware configuration from the application developer and also provide consistent programming APIs for communication services. By achieving these requirements Gridkit is a natural tool to support the development of Pervasive Grid applications. In this section we focus on the overall architecture of Gridkit describing its core component framework and how configurations are generated.

The Gridkit Architecture

An illustration of the high-level software architecture of Gridkit is provided in Figure 2. The framework is built from OpenCom components and executes within the OpenCom kernel represented at the bottom of the diagram. Each of the boxes above describe an individual component framework related to a particular domain of Gridkit's functionality; these illustrate a central philosophy of capturing domain behaviour within individual frameworks in order for them to be developed and optimized individually by domain experts. Briefly, the *overlays framework* is a distributed framework for the deployment of multiple overlay networks. In practice, this amounts to hosting, in a set of distributed overlay framework instances, a set of per-overlay plug-in components. This framework provides a virtualized view of network behaviour (in potentially many different environments) to allow higher level services and frameworks to be easily deployed without being concerned about the underlying network heterogeneity.

Above the overlays framework is a set of further "vertical" frameworks that provide functionality in various orthogonal areas, and can optionally be included or not included on different devices. The frameworks are as follows: the *interaction framework* accepts multiple interaction type plug-ins (e.g. RPC, publish-subscribe, group

Figure 2. The Gridkit architecture

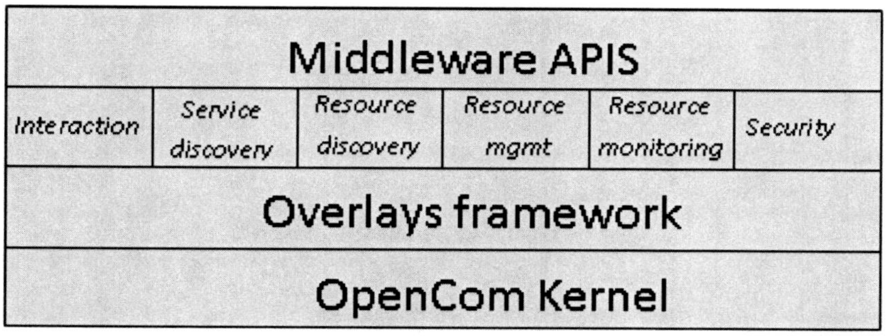

communication); the *service discovery framework* accepts plug-in strategies to discover application services (e.g. SLP, UPnP, Salutation); the *resource discovery* framework accepts plug-in strategies to discover resources such as CPUs and storage (e.g. peer-to-peer search); the *resource management* and *resource monitoring* frameworks are respectively responsible for managing and monitoring resources; and the *security* framework provides general security services for the rest of the frameworks.

The Overlays Framework

The overlays framework (as visualised in Figure 3) is an OpenCom component framework that is deployed on each participating node in the distributed system. The framework accepts 'plug-in' components that offer various types of overlay-related behaviour. More specifically, the types of components that can be plugged into the framework are as follows.

Overlay plug-ins. These are per-node implementations of network overlays. For example, Figure 3 shows four overlay plug-ins: TBCP (Mathy et al., 2001) which is an Internet Scale application level multicast protocol; the Chord Key-Based Routing (KBR) overlay (Stoica et al., 2001) is a lookup protocol to find the nearest host to a given identifier in a ring-structured overlay; Scribe (Castro et al., 2002) is a multicast protocol layered directly upon key-based rout-

ing behaviour; and the Chord Distributed Hash Table (DHT) is a decentralised service similar to a hash table, where data is stored and retrieved from the overlay node closest to the hash of the data's key.

Interface plug-ins. While overlay plug-ins provide different types of behaviour, interface plug-ins capture common API patterns that can be shared by multiple overlays. We have used the key abstractions described in (Dabek et al., 2003) as the basis of these APIS, as these are generally considered the de-facto standard for overlay interfaces. Figure 3 shows interface plug-ins for DHT and multicast overlays. The indirection provided by interface plug-ins isolates higher-layer software from the idiosyncrasies of individual overlay plug-ins, facilitates application-transparent adaptation, and encourages a principled approach to the development of 'families' of overlays plug-ins, each of which shares a common API.

One of the key features of the framework is that multiple overlays can operate simultaneously in the framework either in mutual isolation (cf. TBCP in Figure 3) or in a stacking relationship (e.g. Scribe and Chord DHT are both stacked atop Chord KBR). Hence, multiple types of overlay behaviour can support a wide range of middleware services, and re-using lower-level plug-ins reduces the duplication of networking implementation. The overlay plug-in abstraction is applied uniformly throughout the communication stack. For example, transport protocols like

Figure 3. An example configuration of the open overlays framework

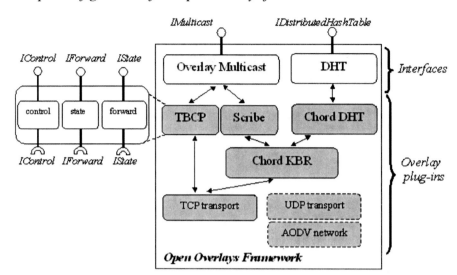

TCP or UDP are represented as overlay plug-ins (as seen at the bottom of Figure 3); these could be replaced by an AODV overlay plug-in at the network layer should the device be operating in a MANET environment.

The overlay plug-ins are themselves coarse-grained modules; hence, we also propose a software pattern for developing these plug-ins that promotes configuration, reconfiguration, and re-use at a finer-grained level within each overlay. Each Overlay plug-in is a 'mini' component framework, each of which, as shown in the left part of Figure 3, is composed of three distinct components that respectively encapsulate the following areas of behaviour:

i.   **Control behaviour,** in which the node co-operates with its peer control element on other nodes to build and maintain an overlay-specific virtual network topology;

ii. **Forwarding behaviour** that determines how the overlay will route messages over the aforementioned virtual topology;

iii. **State** information that is maintained for the overlay; e.g. nearest neighbours.

Each of these three elements exposes a standard interface, IControl, IForward, and IState respectively, which enables the free composition of overlays (subject to the configuration constraints discussed below). We refer to this three-element architecture as the overlay pattern. The motivation for the overlay pattern is to achieve flexibility in terms of both configuration and dynamic reconfiguration by enabling both control and forwarding behaviour to be independently replaced without loss of state information. We see an example of this fine-grained adaptation in the flood monitoring application discussed later.

Benefits of the Overlay Framework

In terms of the effectiveness, the overlays framework provides benefits in three key dimensions (note we leave the demonstration of reconfiguration benefits until later).

Generality. Table 1 lists the network types that have been developed for and deployed within the overlay framework. From this list, it is clear that the framework can provide a general range of network services across a range of heterogeneous environmental conditions. There are different

Table 1. Descriptions of some implemented overlay plug-ins

Overlay Name	Description and configurability options
Chord KBR	A large-scale KBR overlay based on the Chord algorithms (Stoica et al., 2001).
DHT	A storage overlay for a decentralised lookup of large amounts of data (equivalent of hash table behaviour).
Pastry KBR	A KBR overlay based on Pastry (Rowstron et al., 2001).
Failure Monitor	Monitoring overlay based upon the algorithms described in (vanRennesse et al., 1998); this detects node failures and notifies other members of the overlay.
SCAMP	A scalable group membership overlay with gossip-based forwarding as described by (Ganesh et al., 2001).
Scribe	A multicast overlay that can be layered on top of any KBR overlay (e.g. Chord or Pastry) as described by (Castro et al., 2002). This is well suited to large-scale and highly dynamic multicast memberships.
Spanning Trees	A tree structured overlay for fan-in routing i.e. routing data from individual nodes to the root of the tree. These are well suited to static ad-hoc network deployments (e.g. networked sensors). These can be configured to different tree topologies e.g. shortest hop trees or fewest hop trees.
TBCP	A wide area multicast overlay for Internet scale multicast membership with a low degree of membership churn as described by (Mathy et al., 2001).

types of KBR protocols (e.g. Chord and Pastry), a DHT overlay, multicast protocols (e.g. Scribe and TBCP), gossip overlays (Scamp), and more specialised overlays such as a node failure monitoring overlay, and a spanning tree overlay for fan-in routing in network sensors. Further more in terms of providing *virtualisation* of network services to higher-level middleware services Table 1 also illustrates the range of overlays that can be virtualised by common interfaces, e.g. multicast and DHT network resources.

Configurability. To measure the configurability of the framework we calculated the number of possible configurations in each of four profiles (i.e. an 'empty' profile consisting of only the framework itself, a 'WSN' profile for wireless sensor network environments containing only the spanning tree overlays, a 'multicast' profile for all the multicast overlays from Table 2, and a 'full' profile containing all 8 overlays. The numbers, which are summarised in the rightmost column of Table 2, result from an exhaustive enumeration of all the configurations reachable. The results show that the more complex and well-populated profiles support a very large number of possible configurations; e.g. the 'full' profile has 26,999. Furthermore, the overlay pattern contributes significantly to the configurability of the framework by supporting

Table 2. Configurability results and overheads for framework profiles

Profile	Static Memory cost of Overlay plug-ins (KB)	Total configurations
Empty	60	1
WSN	146	4
Multicast	169	89
Full	252	26,999

fine-grained configuration of individual overlays. Consider, for example, a Gnutella implementation with either a random-walk-based, or a flooding-based forwarder; or a tree overlay with a control element that either contains or doesn't contain a self-repair algorithm.

Resource overhead. What is the resource overhead incurred by the overlays framework when providing such configurability and generality? We performed three experiments to determine this.

These employed components executing on a Java 1.5.0.10 virtual machine on a networked workstation with a 3.0 GHz Pentium 4 processor, 1 Gbyte of RAM and running Windows XP. The first experiment (see Table 2) investigated the *static storage footprint* costs; i.e. the disk space required to store the framework, and components. It can be seen that the base framework requires

60K before any plug-ins are added. In the second experiment (see Table 3), we evaluated *dynamic memory overhead* by measuring the RAM footprint of overlay plug-ins while they were in operation (i.e. joined to a running overlay). We can see that the basic framework with no plug-ins is responsible for a high percentage of the overall footprint (65% on average; note, however, that this figure includes 6,392 Kbytes for the JVM and 600 KBytes for the OpenCOM kernel). We can again reduce overhead in a given deployment through the profiling mechanism. More complex configurations, e.g. the layering of Scribe over a Chord KBR obviously increases the footprint size, but by a small margin, e.g. adding Scamp to TBCP results in a 164 Kbytes increase.

Finally, the third experiment (again, see Table 3) investigated *configuration performance* by measuring the time needed to configure new plug-ins based on a sample of configurations from the different profiles (e.g. TBCP in the full profile, etc.). While it is clear that configuration performance is largely tied to the complexity of the configuration in terms of the numbers of configuration rules and plug-ins involved, and the number of inter-component connections etc., the overall cost of configuration is largely negligible compared to time for a node to join an overlay (e.g. Pastry averages 5 to 10 seconds for node joins).

The Interaction Framework

Gridkit's interaction framework provides a common framework for an extensible set of so-called *pluggable interaction paradigms*, or *PIP*s. The overall architecture and context of the interaction framework is illustrated in Figure 4. Here individual PIPs are component frameworks implementing a particular type of communication service. For example, an RPC PIP will typically have components that: marshal and unmarshal RPC messages, forward these to appropriate local objects, and manage object lifetimes; whereas a publish-subscribe PIP will contain components to: parse/construct event messages, maintain subscription information, and match events against subscriptions. These are implemented with the philosophy of separating the interaction framework from the overlay framework to promote the reuse of overlays and thus conserve resources—i.e. different interactions may re-use overlay configurations that are already in place (for example, a topic-based publish-subscribe PIP and a reliable multicast PIP might both share a multicast tree overlay). The design of the interaction framework is guided by the following principles:

1. The selection and use of PIPs by applications should be straightforward;
2. The programming model of each PIP should be independent of how it is implemented

Table 3. Performance times and dynamic memory costs of typical configurations

Configuration	#Components	#Bindings	Profile	Configuration time (ms)	Dynamic memory (KB)
Empty	0	0	Full	N/A	10,448
Empty	0	0	Sensor	N/A	8,352
Spanning tree	5	12	Sensor	191	11,452
TBCP	6	12	Full	211	15,144
SCAMP	5	9	Full	152	13,708
Scribe/KBR	9	27	Full	486	16,652
Scribe + TBCP	13	39	Full	592	16,972
TBCP+SCAMP	10	21	Full	281	15,308

Figure 4. The interaction framework

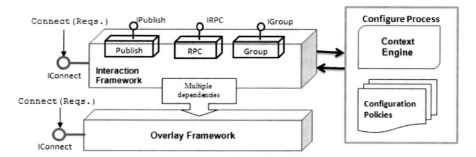

over different (overlay) network types and conditions;

In line with the principles above, we have made every effort to simplify the API of the interaction framework. General experience in the development of reflective middleware has taught us that highly configurable systems are often a two edged sword: configurability is certainly a good thing, but too often the benefits are outweighed by the inconvenience and complexity of having to write many lines of baroque code to achieve a desired configuration. In many cases, this complexity is so great that developers ignore the available flexibility and use only a small number of default configurations. This is especially relevant in the case of the interaction framework as (unlike the overlay framework) it is generally used directly by application developers.

To illustrate the abstractions provided to application developers we give an example of a generic API. In the *IPublish* API for publish-subscribe PIPs (see below), *createChannel()* creates an event dissemination channel or network. This can be an individual channel for all events (e.g. a broker network) or a specific topic channel (implemented by an individual group). *Publish()* disseminates an event on the channel. Apart from the primary content, additional information (an example could be the location of the publisher) can be passed using the *Context* parameter. *Subscribe()* subscribes to a particular channel and takes a

content/context filter (subscriptions are defined in a dedicated filter language, and an *EventListener* as parameters. The event listener will respond to the *matchedEvent* notification. From this interface, the transparency from configuration and overlay heterogeneity is clear.

```
TopicID =
createChannel(UserDefinedID);
joinChannel(ChannelID);
publish(TopicID, Content, Con-
text);
subscribe(TopicID, Filter, Even-
tListener);
Notification -> matchedEvent;
```

Configuring Middleware Behaviour

We now describe how middleware behaviour is configured in Gridkit. Given a request for a particular PIP by the application developer, we show how the interaction framework and overlay framework are configured. Our approach here employs a notion of so-called *binding contracts*. More specifically, PIP interfaces have attached to them sets of *name-value pairs* that embody PIP-specific information such as the name of the PIP, its purpose, constraints on its use, and the QoS it provides. Correspondingly, the receptacles of application components that want to use PIPs have *predicates* attached to them whose terms refer to the name-value pairs attached to potentially matching PIP interface references. The binding contract elements (i.e. name-value pairs and predicates) are attached to receptacles and interface references using native facilities of our component model (i.e. the 'interface' meta-interface). This process repeats throughout the Gridkit architecture i.e. the interaction framework requests behaviour from the overlay framework using the same approach and configuration mechanism.

Based on binding contracts, we provide a simple generic API to the interaction framework of the form *connect(receptacle)* to which the potential user of a PIP submits its receptacle. This is illustrated to the left of Figure 4. Given this, the interaction framework selects, instantiates, and configures a PIP instance based on the following information:

- The set of PIPs currently registered with the interaction framework;
- The predicates attached to the offered receptacle;
- The advice of a *context engine* which follows the design as proposed by (Capra et al., 2003) which supports additional name-value pairs the value of which varies dynamically according to the context of the host machine (e.g. battery life, network connectivity etc.).
- *Declarative configuration rules* are XML-based expressions that specify the

configuration possibilities supported by the profile. As an example, a configuration rule could state that when a 'multicast' service is requested by the application, and the current network context is 'fixed infrastructure with no IP multicast support', then the TBCP overlay plug-in should be instantiated and configured beneath the 'overlay multicast' interface plug-in.

Consider a Gridkit installation that is described by Table 4. This shows the plug-ins that are currently registered with the interaction and overlay frameworks, and the context on each of the two device types, namely a PC or a PDA. It also shows the current set of name-value pairs for the plug-ins and the per-device context. *RelMsg* means reliable messaging; *GrpMem* means group membership; and *Net* means network type (i.e. either fixed infrastructure or ad-hoc networking). Given this installation, consider the processing of a request on the interaction framework of the form *connect(publish_receptacle)* for a Publish PIP where there is a predicate of the form *RelMes=F* attached to *publish_receptacle*. The steps involved in processing this request are as follows:

- **Step 1:** The *connect()* call is issued on the interaction framework as already described.
- **Step 2:** The interaction framework retrieves from the engine, context relevant

Table 4. An example Gridkit installation

Framework	Generic API	Item	Name-value pairs
Interaction	*IPublish*	Publish	RelMes: F
	IGroup	Group1	RelMes: F; GrpMem: T
		Group2	RelMes: F; GrpMem: F
Overlay	*IGroupMessage*	ALM	RelMes: F; Net: fixed
	IGroupMessage	ProbMcast	RelMes: F; Net: adhoc
	IGroupMembers	Gossip	RelMes: F; Net: fixed; Net: adhoc
Context	N/A	PC	Net: fixed
		PDA	Net: adhoc

to the type of PIP being requested (in this case *Net: fixed* for PC, or *Net: adhoc* for PDA).

- **Step 3:** A pattern matching algorithm fires the appropriate configuration policy, instantiates the PIP and then decides on a suitable overlay to underpin the PIP.
- **Step 4:** The script issues a *connect(alm_ receptacle)* call on the overlay framework and the process is repeated.

For a request for a *Group* PIP with a receptacle predicate of *RelMes=F and GrpMem=T*. A similar process to the above will be carried out with the *Group1* PIP being selected (because of the specification of *GrpMem=T*), and underpinned by *ALM* and *Gossip* overlays on the PC, and *ProbMcast* and *Gossip* overlays on the PDA (due, as above, to the contextual differences). The Gossip overlay is used to gossip about group membership (as required by the *GrpMem=T* part of the predicate).

Finally, the interaction framework also supports *dynamic monitoring* of currently instantiated binding contracts. Using this facility, either party to the binding contract (including the context engine) can force a re-evaluation of the contract by altering their respective 'side' of the contract. For example, the user of the framework can drive reconfiguration of a PIP by altering the predicates attached to its receptacle. To detect such changes, the component model's 'interception' meta-interface is used to attach a 'dynamic contract evaluator' to the receptacle-interface binding, which is executed every time a call is made across the binding, and raises an exception if it finds the binding contract to be no longer valid. This exception can either be handled by the user of the framework or by the framework itself, e.g., delete the PIP instance or attempt to reconfigure it. As an example, the context engine might change a name-value pair to reflect the fact that a live Ethernet MAC layer no longer exists, and the framework might on that basis change the underlying overlay from

IP-based multicast routing to an ad-hoc network based multicast approach.

GRIDKIT IN A FLOOD MONITORING APPLICATION

We now describe how Gridkit has been used to develop a real-world Pervasive Grid scenario: namely a wireless sensor network-based real-time flood forecasting in a river valley in the north west of England. In this scenario, a wireless sensor network (WSN) comprising of 20 nodes has been deployed to monitor depth and flow conditions along a 2.5KM stretch of river. We discuss the hardware, software and networking solutions that were chosen and then deployed on site. Subsequently we discuss the dynamic nature of the environment and present how dynamic reconfiguration of the overlay framework is used to improve both the performance and resource consumption of the application.

The GridStix Sensor Devices

Each sensor node (known as 'GridStix') comprises a 400MHz XScale CPU, 64MB of RAM and 16MB of flash memory. They have the capability to communicate via three types of networks: i) 802.11b/g for high performance long range networking, ii) Bluetooth for low power short range networking, and iii) GPRS/UMTS to connect to the Internet. Each GridStix is powered by a 4 watt solar array and a 12V 10Ah battery. They run Linux 2.6, version 1.4 of the JamVM Java virtual machine. Finally, they provide options to connect a number of different sensors:

- Pressure-based depth sensors that connect via ADC Channels.
- Ultrasound-based flow monitoring that connect via RS-232.
- A Digital camera for image-based flow measurement that connect via Ethernet.

The devices themselves are shown in Figure 5; this illustrates the combined package of sensor board, and power supply; and how they are deployed in the river. Here a sensor in the water is connected directly to the GridStix device. Note, that the device is relatively large, as in such a scenario there is no requirement to minimise the size of the sensor.

GridStix Software Configurations

The flood monitoring system monitors water depth (using pressure sensors) and flow-rate (using a combination of image-based flow measurement and ultrasound flow measurement). This data is then fed into flood models which then predict when flooding is likely to occur, before notifying interested stakeholders of these events. In this application the following requirements of Gridkit are important:

1. **To perform flood prediction using spatial flood models.** This must collect data from all sensor nodes, forward this data to the root nodes of the sensor network whose role is to then distribute data off-site (using GPRS/UMTS) where the models execute. Notably, these models are computationally complex and require traditional cluster or Grid computing solutions.

2. **To perform site-local flood prediction using Point-prediction models (Beven et al., 2005).** Here, data is collected from the sensors and then forwarded to root nodes who manage the execution of the models on-site because there is significantly less computational overhead compared to spatial models.

3. **To use image-based flow measurement to help flood prediction.** Digital imaging sensors (e.g. a digital camera) collect data sets that cannot easily be transmitted off-site (without significant expense due to their size). Hence, flow measurement is performed at the site; however, the computational costs prohibits single sensor execution, hence the task must be distributed across the local sensors (c.f. a local mini-grid).

Figure 5 also illustrates the location of the deployed sensor network. The sensors are placed at locations along the river; depending on the distances between sensors, different networks are used to communicate e.g. Bluetooth and 802.11b for shorter distances, GPRS for longer communication. To meet the communication requirements of flood prediction application described above, we deploy the Gridkit wireless sensor network profile. In the interaction framework the publish-subscribe PIP is employed; a node can be just a publisher (e.g. a child node), just a subscriber, or, optionally, it can act as a broker in the event service (e.g. a root node). Underpinning this framework is a set of overlays for the distribution of events towards sinks. This is also customizable from: i) a centralized spanning tree using Dijkstra's shortest path algorithm, or ii) a fewest hop tree. *Fewest hop* (FH) spanning trees are optimised to maintain a minimum number of hops between any given node and the root. FH trees minimise the data loss that occurs due to node failure, but are sub-optimal with respect to power consumption. *Shortest path* (SP) spanning trees are optimised to maintain a minimum distance in edge weights from any given node to the distinguished 'root' node; edge weights are derived from the power consumption of each pair-wise network link. SP trees tend to consume less power than FW trees, but offer poorer performance;

Finally, at the physical network level (i.e. the bottom level of the overlays framework) each node can use either *Bluetooth* or *WiFi* (802.11b). Both technologies have extremely different throughput, energy, and range properties. WiFi provides the highest throughput and longest range, but a cost of energy consumption almost an order of mag-

Figure 5. The GridStix sensors deployed at the river

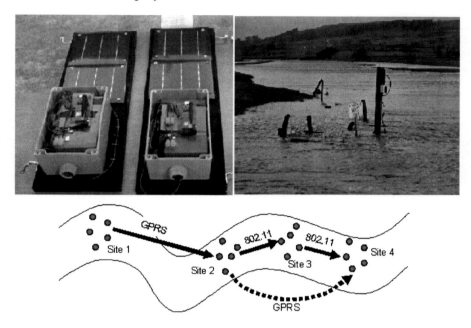

nitude higher than Bluetooth. Typically Bluetooth would be used in quiescent conditions, and WiFi in imminent flooding situations.

Dynamic Reconfiguration

This Pervasive Grid application necessitates rich support for heterogeneous network technologies. On the one hand, networking support must be sufficiently power-efficient that nodes may operate for extended periods of time. On the other hand, applications such as image-based flow prediction also require high performing (and implicitly power hungry) networking support. This need for heterogeneity is further compounded by varying resilience requirements: During quiescent periods, when flooding is unlikely, data may reach the off-site cluster with a high delay. Faults in the network may take a long time to be recovered from, since they might only jeopardise the completeness of measurement logs. In these periods, a low energy consumption is a prime requirement to maximise the life-time of the sensor network. By contrast, when a flood is imminent, we want the network

to react quickly, while providing a high degree of resilience (e.g. a low sensitivity to disruptions), even if this means its energy supplies get depleted much more rapidly. Hence, we examine how dynamic reconfiguration of the overlays framework can meet these demands.

Triggering Reconfiguration

Reconfiguration is supported in our sensor network though the Distributed Component Framework facility included in the Overlays Framework. The reconfiguration 'triggers' that drive the system from one configuration to another are expressed with declarative configuration rules, summarised in Figure 6 in the form of a state transition diagram (to avoid excessive presentational complexity, the diagram represents a drastically simplified view of the implemented system i.e. only two of the possible states of the system). We also show the pseudo-code rule relating to each of the transitions.

The triggers/rules are based upon optimising configurations for three factors: latency, resilience and power consumption in different environmen-

Figure 6. Reconfiguration states and triggers (simplified)

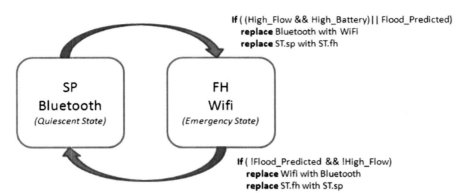

tal contexts. To determine these configurations a number of experiments were performed on the real sensor network deployment. These experiments are described in full detail in (Grace et al., 2008) and describe how the states are chosen. There are three important context types at the base of reconfiguration. First, *High_Flow* is a context that is detected by attaching a video camera to some of the nodes, pointing this at the river surface, and estimating river flow rates by carrying out some simple image processing on the resultant images. Secondly, *Flood_Predicted* is provided by point prediction models which provide localised predictions of water depth based on the collated readings of depth sensors in the immediate locality. Finally, *High_Battery* is measured by collecting the current power readings of individual sensor nodes. For a simplified explanation: we can see in the diagram that when flooding is predicted we switch to the more resilient fewest hop tree that consumes more power, but in a quiescent state we switch to the shortest path tree to conserve resources.

The Benefits of Reconfiguration

We evaluated reconfiguration primarily through simulation of the Gridkit middleware in operation in an example sensor deployment. This is because it provided the control to simulate events that trigger

reconfiguration. For this, we developed the *GridStix simulator* which models the low-level properties of each node (available CPU, available Battery, solar panel power production) and each pairwise network link (round-trip-time, power-consumption, bandwidth, delay, jitter, loss). This low-level data has been measured empirically on the real-world system, which makes the simulator highly accurate for this scenario. The visualisation sub-system of the simulator is shown in Figure 7 illustrating FH (left) and SP (right) overlay configurations.

The simulation was configured as follows: The simulation period is 24 hours (midnight-to-midnight). Each node enters the simulated period with a battery at 50% charge. Flood conditions begin at 12PM and last until 6PM (the approximate mean duration of a flood event at the site). Dawn occurs at 8AM from which time solar power production is set to WINTER_SUN, when flood conditions begins at 12PM, solar power production is set to HEAVY_CLOUD, finally night falls at 8PM (approximately mimicking late winter conditions, when flooding is most prevalent). All nodes were programmed to wake for one minute in every hour. During quiescent conditions nodes transmit sensor readings at a rate of one per minute. During flooding condition, nodes transmit sensor readings at a rate of one per second. This is commensurate with the increased requirements of performing real-time flood modelling.

Figure 7. FH (left) and SP (right) Spanning Trees in the Gridstix simulator

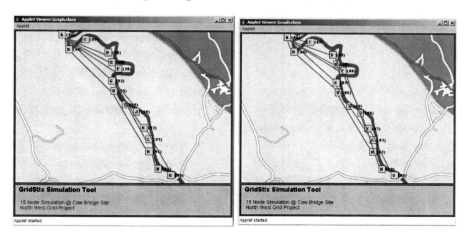

Throughout the simulated period, the system's performance has been evaluated in the context of three key metrics:

1. **Resilience:** The resilience of the network is a function of the extent to which the failure of a given node reduces the overall connectedness of the network. We measure this as the number of viable routes between each node and the root.
2. **Power consumption:** Although the GridStix are equipped with solar panels, power consumption is still an extremely important factor. We infer this from the per-node battery power consumed throughout the test.
3. **Performance:** We measure this in terms of the latency with which messages can be relayed from each sensor node to the root node.

We measured in the simulation for three types of overlays: i) an SP configuration, ii) a FH configuration, and iii) the adaptive configuration defined by Figure 6. In the simulation the flooding is detected (at noon), and the middleware reconfigures from using a low-power SP tree to a high-performance FH tree. We found the following key results:

Resilience

- As FH trees have a typically lower node degree they tend to be more resilient to node failure.
- SP trees have a typically higher degree and are therefore significantly more vulnerable to node failure.
- Where nodes reconfigure between overlays during flooding, system resilience matches SP during quiescent periods and FH during flooding periods (i.e. it is more resilient, but at the expense of power).

Battery Power

- SP trees maintain the highest possible battery life throughout the test.
- FH trees result in the greatest battery power consumption (though at the expense of performance and resilience as shown).
- Where the system reconfigures at flood time from an SP to a FH configuration, battery power is maximised during quiescent conditions (i.e. approximating SP), while increasing during flooding conditions (i.e. approximating FH); though at the same time providing better performance and resilience.
- The power consumed by reconfiguration, both in the transmission of reconfiguration

messages and in CPU-usage is acceptably low.

Performance

- FH configurations demonstrate a mean reporting latency of 11ms, while SP offers a reporting latency of 28ms (though consuming significantly less power).
- When the system reconfigures from an SP configuration during quiescent conditions to an FH configuration during flood conditions, performance is correspondingly low during quiescent conditions, but high during flood conditions (though at the expense of power).

In summary, testing on a real-world system illustrates the benefits of overlay reconfiguration. By configuring to a low-power overlay during normal conditions and a high performing and resilient overlay during flood conditions, battery life is extended, while maintaining system functionality during critical conditions. We also found that the cost of reconfiguration in terms of additional power consumed, and reconfiguration time does not significantly affect the power costs and performance of the sensor network.

FUTURE TRENDS FOR GRID MIDDLEWARE

The implementation approach currently favoured by Grid middleware (e.g. OGSA) is to layer the Grid environment on top of existing web services platforms. Although these platforms are a useful starting point, they have significant limitations as a Grid middleware support infrastructure for the next generation of applications required within the Pervasive Grid. Here we examine how Grid middleware can follow the trends from the wider middleware community, and also the lessons learned from configurable and reconfigurable

middleware (like proposed in this chapter).

Firstly, Grid middleware is extremely limited, in comparison to object-based middleware platforms (e.g. RM-ODP and CORBA, and industry-developed platforms like Java RMI, Enterprise JavaBeans, DCOM, and the .NET remoting architecture) in the following areas:

- **The provision of generic (horizontal, or breadth-oriented) services:** For example, CORBA supports generic reusable services like fault tolerance, persistent state, automated logging, load-balancing, transactional object invocation, event distribution, and many others;
- **Scalability and performance:** For example, EJB and the CORBA Component Model have sophisticated support for the automated activation/ passivation of stateful services, and natively support services that span multiple machines/ networks; in addition performance engineering has been the subject of intensive research in the object-based middleware community over the last 10 years.

In contrast, horizontal services are conspicuously lacking in current Grid environments and there is great potential here for reuse from the wider field. And in terms of performance, the application focus of web services-derived middleware has traditionally been on e-Commerce where dependability and security are far more important than performance.

Secondly, web services-derived platforms have little or no support for QoS specification and realisation. We believe that such facilities will be increasingly demanded by sophisticated pervasive applications. We also believe that a prime cause of this deficiency is an over-reliance by web services platforms on SOAP as a communications engine. Although very flexible and general, SOAP clearly shows its limitations when relied on exclusively:

- It is inappropriate for Grid applications involving large-volume scientific datasets mainly due to its use of XML as an on-the-wire data representation. This is highly demanding in terms of bandwidth, memory and processing cycles (especially compared to earlier standards like CORBA's CDR). Alternatively it also heavyweight when considering the embedded and sensor devices discussed in this chapter.
- Although it offers some flexibility in terms of support for different interaction types (e.g., choice of request-reply or one-way messages), it does not support the comprehensive range of interaction types proposed within this chapter.

The OGSA design recognises the limitations of exclusive reliance on SOAP, and leaves room for non-SOAP bindings (e.g. using CORBA IIOP and, potentially, other bindings that do have some support for QoS). However, OGSA does not currently specify any particular framework whereby such bindings can be integrated into the distributed programming model, and it similarly does not provide any framework for generic QoS specification/ enforcement.

Thirdly and finally, Grid middleware does not make use of advanced middleware research which is investigating highly configurable (and run-time reconfigurable) reflective and component-based middleware technologies. A prime, and highly successful, example of such a platform is the open source JBoss application server (Fleury & Reverbel, 2003). The basic philosophy of advanced middleware (c.f. Gridkit) is to support configurability, extensibility and adaptability as fundamental system properties. In particular, the approach enables alternative policies (e.g. security policies, replication policies, service (de)activation policies, priority-assigned invocation paths, thread scheduling) and components (e.g. protocols, buffer managers, loggers, debuggers, demultiplexers) to be configured in or out at deploy-time,

and reconfigured at run-time (e.g. on the basis of dynamically evolving conditions).

Overall, our view is that next generation Grid middleware can and should leverage the results of the wider middleware field as discussed above. In doing so, it can retain key web services-derived characteristics (loose coupling, XML-based data structuring, reliance only on ubiquitous Internet standards) while additionally folding in some of the key benefits of the wider field—in particular, the availability of generic services, and scalability and performance engineering know-how offered by 'standard' middleware; and the increased flexibility and configurability promised by advanced middleware research.

CONCLUSION

In this chapter we have presented the case for novel Grid middleware solutions to tackle the problems of heterogeneity and dynamic change in Pervasive Grid applications. We have documented how the Gridkit middleware addresses some of the many challenges; in particular how two complementary component frameworks support an extensible set of interaction paradigms and an extensible set of overlay networks. The combination of the two frameworks enables a wide range of pluggable interaction paradigms to be instantiated in a wide range of network environments. Notably, we have also presented a real world flood monitoring application that illustrates the effectiveness of the middleware in both supporting the developer deploy a working solution, and also in optimising the performance of the system in the face of changing conditions. We illustrated how the co-ordinated reconfiguration of middleware components across a sensor network deployment provided performance gains, resilience gains, and improved battery life.

Based upon these results we are particularly interested in supporting challenging scenarios involving 'extreme' network heterogeneity e.g.

involving systems that span a sensor network, a fixed grid environment, and a loosely-connected MANET. This is a fundamentally challenging issue in that it is not yet understood even how to design overlays that can successfully span such environments, let alone an overarching framework. In addressing this challenge, we do not foresee major problems in applying the basic tenets of our framework on individual nodes; it will be the distributed deployment and reconfiguration issues involving distributed adaptation that will present the major challenges (e.g. making appropriate choices in terms of distributed versus centralised configurators, quiescence and validation algorithms, membership protocols, etc.).

REFERENCES

Beven, K., Romanowicz, R., Pappenberger, F., Young, P., & Werner, M. (2005). The Uncertainty Cascade in Flood Forecasting. In *Proceedings of the ACTIF meeting on Flood Risk,* Tromsø.

Capra, L., Emmerich, W., & Mascolo, C. (2003). CARISMA: Context-Aware Reflective Middleware System for Mobile Applications. *IEEE Transactions on Software Engineering, 29*(10), 929–945. doi:10.1109/TSE.2003.1237173

Castro, M., Druschel, P., Kermarrec, A.-M., & Rowstron, A. (2002). SCRIBE: A Large-Scale and Decentralised Application-Level Multicast Infrastructure. *IEEE Journal on Selected Areas in Communications, 20*(8), 1489–1499. doi:10.1109/JSAC.2002.803069

Coulson, G., Blair, G., Grace, P., Joolia, A., Lee, K., Ueyama, J., & Sivaharan, T. (2008). A Generic Component Model for Building Systems Software. *ACM Transactions on Computer Systems, 27*(1), 1–42. doi:10.1145/1328671.1328672

Dabek, F., Zhao, B., Druschel, P., Kubiatowicz, J., & Stoica, I. (2003). Towards a Common API for Structured P2P Overlays. In *Proceedings of the Second International Workshop on Peer-to-Peer Systems (IPTPS).*

Davies, N., Friday, A., & Storz, O. (2004). Exploring the Grid's Potential for Ubiquitous Computing. *IEEE Pervasive Computing / IEEE Computer Society [and] IEEE Communications Society, 3*(2), 74–75. doi:10.1109/MPRV.2004.1316823

Fleury, M., & Reverbel, F. (2003). The JBoss Extensible Server. In *Proceedings of the IFIP/ACM Middleware Conference,* (LNCS, pp. 344-354). Berlin: Springer Verlag.

Foster, I., Kesselman, C., & Tuecke, S. (2001). The Anatomy of the Grid: Enabling Virtual Organizations. *The International Journal of Supercomputer Applications, 15*(3).

Ganesh, A., Kermarrec, A., & Massoulie, L. (2001). SCAMP: Peer-to-peer lightweight membership service for large-scale group communication. In *Proceedings of the 3rd International Workshop on Networked Group Communication.*

Grace, P., Hughes, D., Porter, B., Coulson, G., Blair, G., & Taiani, F. (2008). Experiences with Open Overlays: A Middleware Approach to Network Heterogeneity. In *Proceedings of the 3rd ACM International EuroSys Conference* (123-136). New York: ACM Press.

Kon, F. (2000). *Automatic Configuration of Component-Based Distributed Systems.* PhD Thesis, University of Illinois at Urbana-Champaign, Urbana, IL.

Kramer, J., & Magee, J. (1990). The evolving philosophers problem: Dynamic change management. *IEEE Transactions on Software Engineering, 16*(11). doi:10.1109/32.60317

Maes, P. (1987). Concepts and Experiments in Computational Reflection. In *Proceedings of OOPSLA '87, of ACM SIGPLAN Notices* (Vol. 22, pp. 147-155). New York: ACM Press.

Mathy, L., Canonico, R., & Hutchison, D. (2001) An Overlay Tree Building Control Protocol. In *Proceedings of Networked Group Communication*, (LNCS Vol. 2233, pp. 76-87). Berlin: Springer.

Oreizy, P., Medvidovic, N., & Taylor, R. N. (1998). Architecture-based runtime software evolution. In *Proceedings of the 20th international Conference on Software Engineering.*

Rowstron, A., & Druschel, P. (2001). Pastry: Scalable, Distributed Object Location and Routing for Large-scale Peer-to-Peer Systems. In *Proceedings of the International Middleware Conference Middleware*, (LNCS, pp. 329-350). Berlin: Springer Verlag.

Stoica, I., Morris, R., Karger, D., Kaashoek, M. F., & Balakarishnan, H. (2001). Chord: A Scalable Peer-to-Peer Lookup Service for Internet Applications. In *Proceedings of ACM SIGCOMM*, (pp. 149-160).

Szyperski, C. (1998). *Component Software, Beyond Object-Oriented Programming.* New York: ACM Press/Addison-Wesley.

van Renesse, R., Minsky, Y., & Hayden, M. (1998). A Gossip-Based Failure Detection Service. In *Proceedings of Middleware '98, the IFIP International Conference on Distributed Systems Platforms and Open Distributed Processing*, (pp. 55-70).

KEY TERMS AND DEFINITIONS

Computational Reflection: The capability of a system to introspect its own structure and behaviour via a meta-representation, and make changes to this representation that are reflected in the running system.

Dynamic Adaptation: The addition, removal or replacement of software elements (e.g. components) at runtime i.e. while the system is performing its core operations.

Middleware: System software that typically resides between the application and the operating system that provides a distributed programming paradigm that supports the developer overcome the challenges of distributed computing.

Overlay Network: A logical networking infrastructure (topology and routing management) layered over the existing physical network infrastructure.

Pervasive Grid: A Grid infrastructure that embraces resources embedded in the environment e.g. in the form of networked sensors and mobile devices.

Reflective Middleware: A configurable and reconfigurable middleware platform that uses reflection as a principled mechanism to dynamically adapt middleware behaviour to changing environmental context.

Software Component: A third party deployable software module that has private data and a set of provided and required interfaces that explicitly describe the component's behaviour.

APPENDIX: COMPONENT FRAMEWORKS

We now provide more detailed information about how dynamic adaptation is carried out by software frameworks, and aim to identify the challenges involved for the future development of adaptive Grid software.

Component frameworks manage the adaptation of components contained wholly within themselves. The elements for adapting a component framework can be seen in Figure 8. Here, there are four key elements important to the adaptation process.

- *The architecture meta-interface provides the adaptation operations to the party performing the adaptation. These allow the framework to be inspected and dynamically reconfigured. Hence an adaptation is performed through a transactional sequence of method calls on this interface.*
- *Validation of reconfigurations. Providing open access to a system (through the prior meta-interface) and allowing run-time changes increases the risk of third party attack. To guard against this, each software framework exports a 'health check' mechanism through the plug-in interface named IAccept. A component encapsulating knowledge about valid dynamic reconfigurations for this framework is then plugged into the framework here. When a reconfiguration is performed it is validated against this health check; any invalid reconfigurations are blocked and the framework is rolled back to the previous safe state.*
- *A quiescence mechanism places the framework in a state ready to be adapted. For this purpose, each framework provides a readers/writers lock. Every normal interface operation accesses the lock as a reader. Any call through the architecture meta-interface to change the configuration accesses the lock as a writer (a writer can access the lock when there are no readers). Hence, this ensures that there is no executing thread within the framework for the duration of the adaptation.*
- *Configuration Management. The configurator pattern (Kon, 2000) illustrated to the left offigure 8underpins adaptations. A configurator acts as the unit of autonomy for making decisions about when and how to change the framework (based upon a set of Event-Condition-Action rules stored in a set of policies). When an event is detected (typically a context change notified by the context engine), operations on the architecture meta-interface are called to make the change.*

Figure 8. Component frameworks

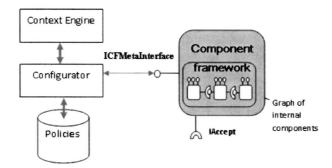

Chapter 43
Digital Ecosystems:
Challenges and Proposed Solutions

A. R. Razavi
University of Surrey, UK

P. Krause
University of Surrey, UK

S. Moschoyiannis
University of Surrey, UK

ABSTRACT

Current research and development in ICT has opened new opportunities and threats for both large corporations and SMEs alike. Many SMEs see the new Digital Ecosystem as a new open frontier where they can enter, innovate and compete with large corporations on an equal footing. This chapter examines the role of the large corporations (the keystones) in the digital ecosystem and presents solutions about the emergence of two major problems that if left unanswered will result in the creation of major entry barriers for SMEs. The authors' proposed distributed coordination and high connectivity between SMEs can provide a more appropriate business environment for fair competition and collaboration.

INTRODUCTION

The aim of this chapter is to introduce the concept of Digital Ecosystems, analyse the challenges, and then discuss some of the proposed solutions and ongoing research in this domain. Our main thesis is that current digital infrastructures for collaborative working introduce serious barriers to adoption of, and innovation within, the digital economy by Small to Medium-sized Enterprises (SMEs) and micro-enterprises. Using the ecosystem metaphor, this implies that currently Digital Ecosystems

favour "keystone species". Yet it is the long tail of less-dominant "species" that typically provides the pool of innovation and response diversity (in cases of external shocks to the system) in healthy ecosystems. To address this bias, we will argue that advanced Peer-to-Peer architectures are critical in order to fully realise the potential of the World Wide Web to collaborative business and knowledge sharing.

We will discuss these risks in more detail in the next section. Since 2002, the EU funded DBE and, subsequently, OPAALS projects have been developing approaches to addressing these risks and empowering SMEs in the digital economy. Follow-

DOI: 10.4018/978-1-61520-686-5.ch043

ing the review section, we will then progress with discussion of the architecture, formal framework, detailed design and implementation of a digital infrastructure that supports collaboration and service innovation amongst enterprises, without violating the "local autonomy" of the participants.

DIGITAL ECOSYSTEM: A SHORT HISTORICAL REVIEW (FROM METAPHOR TO REALITY)

The concept of "business ecosystem" appears to have been first introduced in a well-cited article of James F. Moore in 1993 ("Predators and Prey: The New Ecology of Competition" (Moore, 1993)), where he compared the business environment to an ecological system. The metaphor "business ecosystem" is used to describe the business environment as an economic community, which "is supported by a foundation of interacting organizations and individuals – the organisms of the business world" (Moore, 1993). This comparison of economy to biology has been seen as extremely relevant and useful, not only because it improves our understanding of the roles and interconnectedness of various actors in the business ecosystem, but also because it explicates the increasing connectivity and complexity of these systems.

Of course, one can consider an economy to be a national business ecosystem (Rothschild, 1995) composed of many smaller systems, all of which are directly or indirectly interconnected. What many call an industry can now be considered to be either an ecosystem in itself or part of a larger one. These business ecosystems are populated by (some loosely) interconnected organisms: businesses, consumers, the government and other stakeholders.

As far as the business population of each business ecosystem is concerned, the majority is composed of Small and Medium size Enterprises (SMEs) along with a few large ones, the so-called keystones. Marco Iansiti and Roy Levin compare

the role of these keystone companies to those of keystone species in nature (Iansiti & Levien, 2004). They argue that we live in an interconnected world, the landscape of which is made of a network of networks, with keystones at the hubs and niche players surrounding the hubs.

In nature a Keystone species is defined as "a species whose effect is large and disproportionately large relative to its abundance" (Power et al., 1996). It is also argued that Keystones help in determining or regulating the number and type of other species in their communities. The keystone concept has been adopted in both computer and business literature but recently the correctness of the analogy has been questioned. As an example, Payton et al. (Payton, Fenner, & Lee, 2002) provides some of these arguments on the concept in its original context, namely the definition and role of keystones in ecology.

Technological innovations have always led to the creation of new companies by entrepreneurs who have tried to take advantage of those innovations to create a competitive advantage for themselves in the marketplace; which in turn necessitated the adaptation of those innovations by the older established companies.

The Industrial Age and Business Ecosystems

Until relatively recently, the rate of diffusion and adaption of new technologies was rather slow. Lack of speedy communication was one of the reasons behind this glacial diffusion rate. For example, new machines were invented and used in one part of the world without being introduced and used in other parts. A good example of this is the printing press, which was invented in China a few hundred years prior to its "re-invention" in Germany in 1439.

However, the industrial revolution (1760-1840) (Iansiti & Levien, 2004) reduced the distance between the continents. The improvements in steam engines (steam locomotives, 1804), invention of telegraph in 1830s and later the telephone in the 1860s effectively reduced distances between towns, countries and continents. This reduction in distance also opened new markets, allowing manufacturers and producers to increase production capacity, which in turn led to increasing size of these companies.

Indeed the origins of the modern diversified corporations can be traced back to the creation of large corporations at the beginning of the last century; when mass-production (brought about by innovations in work methods and mechanical automation) allowed many companies to grow rapidly and prosper at a rate that had never been seen before in history. Companies such as Ford, General Motors, Standard Oil Company and others grew from small businesses to large corporations (keystones), whose turnover matched the GNP of many small nations.

In this era competition, by and large, was seen as "dominate or absorb" with one exception: the creation of cartels. "Price competition among large-scale rivals proved mutually destructive to profits and after a brief period of cut-throat competition, business enterprise turned to cartels, trusts and other monopolistic forms of organisation designed to eliminate price competition" (Dillard, 1967). Here the theories of Cournot (Cournot, 1960) (monopoly, duopoly, and oligopoly), first published in 1838, were put to work. This allowed the owners, the so-called "robber barons" (Josephson, 1962), to concentrate on increasing internal efficiency of their organisations.

Part of this internal efficiency was achieved by focusing on economies of scale, i.e. to produce a product faster, better and cheaper than competitors, using mass-production (changes in the supply side). As the competition intensified and marketing and customer demand became more important, these companies began to change their focus to economies of scope (Chandler, 1990); that is producing "different products" faster, better and cheaper. But by entering to the Information age, the rules and playground has changed substantially.

Information Age and Digital Business Ecosystems

A Digital Business Ecosystem or Innovation Ecosystem results from the structurally coupled and co-evolving digital ecosystem and business ecosystem (Nachira, 2002) and (Nachira, Dini, Nicolai, Louarn, & Leon, 2007). A network of digital ecosystems will offer opportunities of participation in the global economy to SMEs and to less developed or remote areas. These new forms of dynamic business interactions and global co-operation among organisations and business communities, enabled by digital ecosystem technologies, are deemed to foster local economic growth.

The role of keystones has dramatically changed from the industrial age to the information age. Technological evolutions usually give birth to new industries where start-ups and existing SMEs, because of their size (agility), typically enter first, becoming the first movers. First movers generally have the advantage of registering patents, establishing brand names and changing the economics of the market; ultimately making it difficult for others to enter and compete and so on. In young industries, first movers have the ability to, in a very short time, become industry leaders or keystones. We have seen this with Microsoft and personal computer operating systems. In the connected digital world, this first mover advantage has been very rewarding for these companies. First movers have managed to become strong hubs with many links, becoming almost impervious to competition from smaller actors.

By considering the Internet as a provided network for digital ecosystems, the network can be described as a network that has no predetermined structure and expands in a random fashion. New nodes (computers) constantly connect and disconnect themselves to the network via links (vertices) to other computers. Studies (Barabási & Albert, 1999), (Barabási, Albert, & Jeong, 2000) have shown that the topology of this network follows a power-law distribution; which means that often a few nodes evolve in such a way to attract a large number of links while many nodes continue to exist with only a few links. This is especially true for the World Wide Web (WWW) where page links act as links to other pages and hence internet sites. This gives those nodes with large number of links, and companies that own them, a disproportionate power in the network; First movers have managed early-on to become large hubs. SMEs in this sector have very little chance of becoming hubs. The entry barriers in this sector are getting higher and higher. If by chance or design an SME manages to acquire a number of links (e.g., Alibaba.com in China), it is bought (Alibaba was acquired by Yahoo) and integrated into the existing hub.

In such an environment, first movers take advantage of their position and try to establish themselves as the industry leaders. As such they constantly try to either set the industry standard or change the proposed standards to their own advantage. So here we see two distinct problems: the first being the structure of the networks where hubs try to dominate[1] and the second being the question of standards being set for the creation of applications that will be running on those networks[2].

The other challenge is the coordination of information systems of different enterprises over the net. The ideal solution, as has been proposed and pursued, is to establish mechanisms that allow different businesses with different practices, equipment and technologies to seamlessly and effectively communicate with each other. One of the solutions that is being widely explored by major players and other organisations has been Service Oriented Architecture (SOA). But note that this is more of a mind-set or a development philosophy than anything else. As such the concept has been around for a number of years and did not become interesting for major software developers and vendors until the emergence of the concept of a Web Service (WS). A WS is defined as "a

software system designed to support interoperable machine-to-machine interaction over a network" (Booth et al., 2004).

The whole concept of SOA revolves around services and loose coupling (Singh & Huhns, 2005). "The goal of SOA is to allow fairly large chunks of functionality to be strung together to form ad hoc applications which are built almost entirely from existing software services. The larger the chunks, the fewer the interface points required to implement any given set of functionality; however, very large chunks of functionality may not be granular enough to be easily reused. Each interface brings with it some amount of processing overhead, so there is a performance consideration in choosing the granularity of services. The great promise of SOA is that the marginal cost of creating the n-th application is zero, as all of the software required already exists to satisfy the requirements of other applications. Only orchestration is required to produce a new application." ("Service-oriented architecture - Wikipedia, the free encyclopedia").

However, currently there is a foundational problem. Both of the currently extant coordination protocols for business transactions, violate loose coupling on one side and offer just one pattern of behaviour (this is important as it relates to clarifying the completion protocol in a transaction and determining the recovery method in respect to that protocol (Razavi, Krause, & Moschoyiannis, 2006)) for participants of transactions, on the other (Vogt, Zambrovski, Gruschko, Furniss, & Green, 2005). This tight coupling results in the participants (e.g. SMEs) losing their local autonomy (their local state of business will be visible to the coordinator). At the same time the pattern of behaviour supported by the coordinator framework (do-compensate (Furnis & Green, 2005)), forces participants to apply specific methods of fault recovery during a transaction failure (Razavi, Moschoyiannis, & Krause, 2007), (Razavi, Moschoyiannis, & Krause, 2007c). This not only enforces a specific problem solving method in the event of a failure (which is known by the companies supporting the protocols) but also imposes the responsibility of sorting the failure out to participants.

The other crucial concerns related to digital ecosystems have been raised by a new generation of applications on the Internet, the so-called Web 2.0 (OREILLY, 2005). Apart from unclear security and safety measures, digital ecosystems are extending their business models behind the boundary of conventional business environments. As a result, the coordination model is freely granted full access to an individual's social network. Despite the currently formative business plans of these large organisations, the potential side effects of such violations of privacy offer considerable benefits to those organisations, with minimal benefit to the individuals (some of the general issues have been discussed in (Barnes, 2006)).

These problems provide significant barriers to the inclusion of SMEs and micro-enterprises in the digital economy. They also act as major barriers to service innovation. We will now explore our proposed solutions to these problems.

DIGITAL ECOSYSTEMS: DISTRIBUTED AGENTS

As discussed in the previous section, current protocols in transaction frameworks targeted at supporting business activities between networked organizations provide a centralized solution, which not only violates the primary concept (loose-coupling) of Service Oriented Computing (SOC) but also does not cover all aspects of their business activities. This creates tight dependencies which are susceptible to the risk that comes with a single point of failure in the framework. In contrast, our proposed model, from the very beginning and early prototypes, advocates a fully distributed solution and relies on the P2P interactions between the platforms (here, participants) (Razavi et al., 2006), (Razavi, Moschoyiannis, & Krause, 2007a).

As the kernel of each platform, we have designed a software agent which is responsible for coordinating the participant's business activities (transactions). This local agent also archives the information related to these activities (corresponding VPTNs) and improves the general connectivity

Figure 1. Local agent for each participant

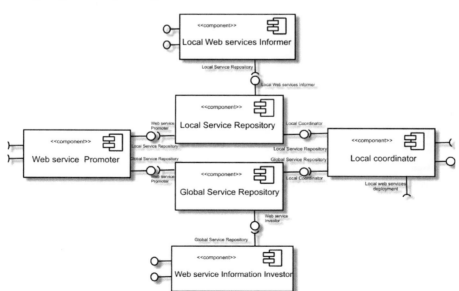

Figure 2. Local agents communication diagram

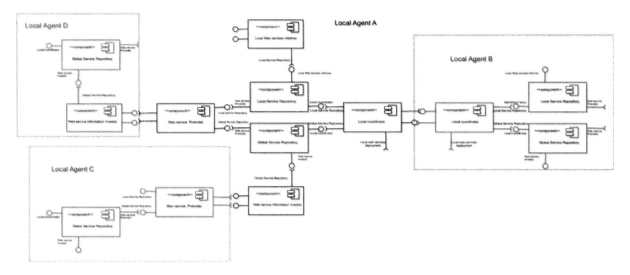

of the network (its digital ecosystem), and in doing so it contributes to the so-called *network growth* (Razavi et al., 2007a). This is an important aspect when it comes to sustainability, especially in a fully distributed solution. This leads up to the main definition of a digital ecosystem (recall section II) which is represented in Figure1, highlighting the fact that there should be no centralized point of command and control in a digital ecosystem.

Figure 1 shows the structure of the local software agent of each participant. The '*local coordinator*' component coordinates the service requests to and from the local platform. In other words, it deploys services of the platform, coordinates the transactions and archives their information in the '*local service repository*'. In this way, all participants of a transaction will keep the archived information of the transaction. The '*local web service informer*' component updates any changes of local services in the '*local service repository*' and relevant participants can be notified of the changes through the '*web service promoter*'. The links to other participants will be kept in the '*global service repository*'. Note that at this stage, participants of different VPTNs are connected to each other [in (Razavi et al., 2007a) this is called the *birth stage* of the underlying

network]. For reducing the possibility of failures and increasing the network stability (Section V), the network connectivity, i.e. the number of links to other participants, may change. These changes will be done by two components; the '*web service information investor*', for updating new links to the global repository and the '*web service promoter*', for promoting new links to other participants [in (Razavi et al., 2007a) this is referred to as the *growth stage*]. Figure2 shows a diagram, where four agents are communicating; Agent A and B are Participating in a Transaction (Section IV) and Agent D and C are involved in the network growth for increasing the connectivity (Section V).

DIGITAL ECOSYSTEMS: LOCAL COORDINATION

Transaction Context

In previous work (Razavi et al., 2007c) we have described the use of a tree structure to represent transactions that involve the execution of services. This allows us to capture nested sub-transactions - the internal actions that need to take place in the course of execution of the transaction. To respect the loose-coupling of the underlying services, which is a basic premise of Service-Oriented Computing (SOC) (Papazoglou, 2003), (Papazoglou & Georgakopoulos, 2003), each participant provides its services and requests services of others through a coordinator component. Its purpose is to manage the communication between the different participants' platforms and the deployment of the corresponding services.

Drawing upon the latest work on the SOC computing paradigm (Papazoglou, Traverso, Dustdar, Leymann, & Kramer, 2006), we have considered different composition types which allow for various modes of service interaction in our model. Figure 3 shows a transaction tree with five basic services - a1, a2 and a3 of a local platform with coordinator component CC1, b1 of CC2, and c1 of CC3 - whose order of execution is determined by the corresponding composition types [transaction context symbols are based on

the notation that first appeared in (Haghjoo & Papazoglou, 1992)].

We note that the example transaction given in Figure 3 is an adaptation of that found in (Moschoyiannis, Razavi, & Krause, 2008) and will be extended in this section to illustrate the key ideas as well as to show how these build on previous work in (Moschoyiannis, Razavi, Yongyan Zheng, & Krause, 2008), (Moschoyiannis et al., 2008).

A transaction tree determines the Participants and the respective services required for performing a business activity. In this sense, it sets the context of the conversation to follow and is issued by the Initiator of the transaction. In (Moschoyiannis et al., 2008) we have provided a schema for describing transaction contexts. The derived XML description of the transaction tree of our example (given in Figure 3) can be found following (Razavi & Moschoyiannis, 2008). The service interactions implied by a transaction tree can be

Figure 3. Transaction context

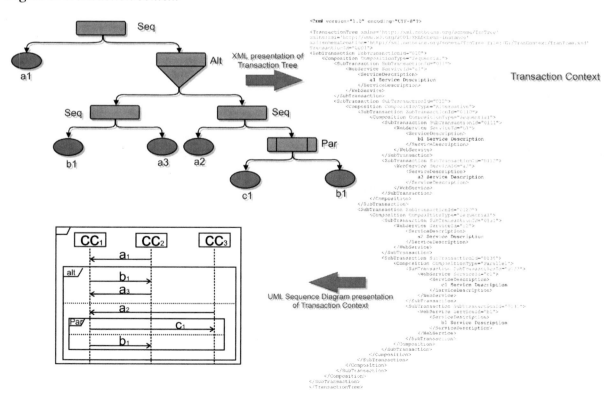

modelled using a UML interaction diagram. The sequence diagram in Figure 3 shows the three coordinator components of the participants in the transaction and the required service invocations between them. It can be seen that the behavioural scenarios, as given by the corresponding sequence diagram, determine the order of execution of the participating components' services.

As mentioned earlier, in a transactional setting we also need to deal with faults that may arise at any stage during execution. These may be due to some service being unavailable (service failure or traffic bottleneck on the local platform) or some participant being temporarily disconnected due to network failure. We have seen that a long-running transaction should either complete successfully or not take place at all. So in the event of a failure, previous parts of the transaction that have already taken place should be 'undone' or be compensated for. We will mention this, after explaining the execution script of the transaction.

Transaction Script

In (Moschoyiannis et al., 2008) we describe a formal language for long-running transactions that allows to determine the patterns of interaction the underlying service invocations should follow in order to guarantee a successful outcome.

A transaction T is associated with a set of coordinator components C and a set of actions M. Our interest is in the observable events on the coordinator components and thus actions can be understood as service invocations between the participating components, as shown for example in the scenario of Figure 4. Hence, each component in C is associated with a set of actions which correspond to deploying (its own) or requesting (others') services. If we denote this set by $\mu(i)$, for each $i \in C$, the previous sentence can be expressed more formally by defining the function μ:
$$C \rightarrow P(M)^3 \text{ and requiring that } \bigcup_{i \in C} \mu(i) \subseteq M.$$
As can be seen in Figure 3, a transaction has a number of activation or access points, namely

the interfaces of the coordinator components participating in the interaction. Thus, instead of modelling the behaviour of a transaction by a sequential process, which would generate a trace of a single access point, we consider a number of such sequences, one for each component, at the same time. This draws upon Shields' vector languages (Shields, 1997) and leads to the definition of the so-called transaction vectors.

Transaction vectors. Let T be a transaction. We define V_T to be the set of all functions $\underline{v}: C \rightarrow M^*$ such that $\underline{v}(i) \in \mu(i)^*$.

By $\mu(i)^*$ we denote the set of finite sequences over $\mu(i)$. Mathematically, the set V_T is the Cartesian product of the sets $\mu(i)^*$, for each i. Effectively, transaction vectors are n-tuples of sequences where each coordinate corresponds to a coordinator component in the transaction (hence, n is the number of leaves) and contains a finite sequence of actions that have occurred on (coordinator of) that component. When an action occurs in the transaction, that is to say when a service is called on a coordinator component, it appears on a new transaction vector and at the appropriate coordinate.

The idea is that the particular subset of transaction vectors, for a given transaction, expresses the ordering constraints necessary in the corresponding orchestration of the underlying services. For instance, in the transaction of Figure 4, following action a1, there is a choice between b1 on the coordinator component CC2 and a2 on CC1. Whenever b1 happens, it is followed by a3 on component CC1 whereas a2 is followed by c1 and b1 which happen concurrently on CC3 and CC2, respectively. Notice that the order structure in case of concurrent actions (as in b1 and c1 here) exhibits the characteristic structure of a finite lattice: A lattice is simply a mathematical way of representing partial orders in some set of entities (actions in our case). This means that after the behaviour described by vector $\underline{u} = (a1a2, \Lambda, \Lambda)$ both independent action vectors $\alpha1 = (\Lambda, b1, \Lambda)$ and $\alpha2 = (\Lambda, \Lambda, c1)$ take place, resulting in

Figure 4. Transaction script

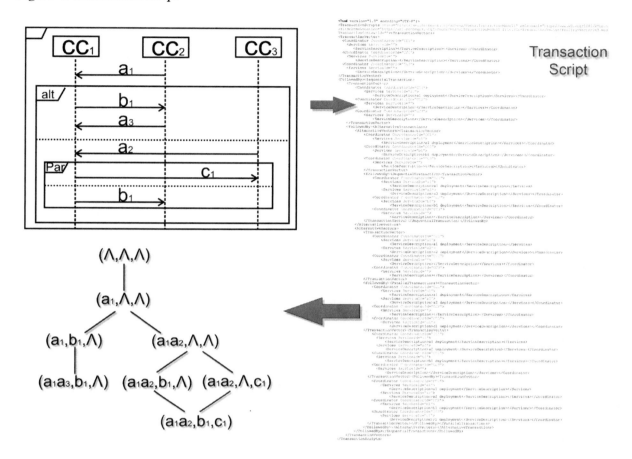

the behaviour described by vector $v = (a1a2, b1, c1)$, which is their least upper bound (i.e. no other action can be "squeezed in" before v).

The additional structure provided by the notion of independence allows to go round the lozenge once and always end up with the behaviour in which both actions happened concurrently (this can be seen in (Moschoyiannis et al., 2008)). As we will see in the next subsection, this also applies to going backwards and allows to compensate concurrently for concurrent forward actions.

The order structure of the transaction language determines the pattern the underlying service interactions between the coordinator components in the transaction should follow. Starting with the empty vector, and following the pattern of Figure 3, each subsequent action (or concurrent

actions) take place in going forward until the transaction as a whole terminates successfully. In (Moschoyiannis et al., 2008), we have provided a schema for deriving the XML description of the order structure of a transaction language. These so-called transaction scripts describe the interactions between different coordinator components (recall Figure 2) and determine the order in which the underlying services need to be deployed. Figure 4 shows the transaction script generated from the vector-based behavioural description of the transaction in our approach

Transaction scripts reflect the corresponding transaction languages and hence describe the dependencies between services of different participants' coordinator components, in terms of the orderings of the underlying service invoca-

Figure 5. Execution history

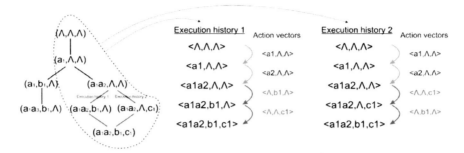

tions. This means that when the scripts are parsed they provide the full transaction history, resulting from the actual deployment of the transaction, but based on the associated formal semantics of the transaction. The XML schemas and further details on transaction scripts can be found (downloaded) following (Razavi & Moschoyiannis, 2008).

Execution History

So far we have described the use of transaction languages in expressing the forward behaviour of a transaction in terms of the orderings of the underlying service executions, and these can be analysed prior to deployment in determining the set of allowed sequences of actions. In our approach, the transaction history is captured in the order structure of the corresponding transaction language which is used to express forward behaviour and is reflected in the derived transaction scripts. As shown in Figure 4 a transaction language which includes alternative actions will have different allowed *execution paths*. These start from the empty vector and lead to (one of) the largest vectors in the language. The largest vectors describe maximal behaviour of the transaction, in the sense that they do not describe an earlier part of behaviour than any other vector does. In the transaction language of Figure 4 there are two maximal vectors, namely $\underline{v1} = (a1a3, b1, \Lambda)$ and $\underline{v2} = (a1a2, b1, c1)$. This means that one allowed sequence of execution is $a1 \rightarrow b1 \rightarrow a3$ and the other is $a1 \rightarrow a2 \rightarrow (b1$ concurrently

with $c1$). Note that both allowed sequences end up in a maximal vector which corresponds to the behaviour exhibited when the transaction executes successfully until it terminates. Thus, in both cases the transaction produces a consistent state. In other words, transaction consistency is attained by reaching a maximal vector in the transaction language. The existence of two maximal transaction vectors in this case means that there are two alternative execution traces that lead to successful completion of the transaction.

When the transaction is actually deployed, then of course only one of the allowed sequences of actions can occur. In our example, this would depend on how the choice between a2 and b1, after a1 has occurred, is resolved. Figure 5 shows the case where a2 occurred after a1, and hence the right branch of the Hasse diagram with the transaction language was actually deployed. It can be seen that each vector in turn is obtained by coordinate-wise concatenation with the appropriate action vector, according to the allowed sequence of actions along the particular execution path.

This distinction between the set of all allowed sequences of actions and the allowed sequence of actions that *actually* takes place when the transaction is deployed is important when considering compensations. Naturally, when a failure makes further progress impossible, we would only want to compensate for actions that actually happened up to that point and not for every possible action in the transaction. We will refer to the actual path of execution during a run of the transaction as the *execution history* of the particular deployment of the transaction. In Figure 5 it appears there are two execution histories but these are the result of concurrency (between b1 and c1) and therefore, they are equivalent. This is because the series of concatenations with action vectors differ only in the order of the *independent* action vectors $\alpha 1 = (\Lambda, b1, \Lambda)$ and $\alpha 2 = (\Lambda, \Lambda, c1)$, and consequently they correspond to the same allowed sequence of actions.

This notion of independence is what allows us to identify equivalent behaviours in the presence of concurrency, something that is not possible when adopting an interleaving model, as done in (Butler, Hoare, & Ferreira). The benefit of being able to identify equivalent execution histories can perhaps be seen most clearly when it comes to compensation in transaction recovery, where as we will see it is only required to compensate once for all equivalent execution histories.

Coordination and Transaction Failure

In this part we extend our approach to coordinating long-running transactions to handle compensations. This is to address occasions where some failure happens mid-way through execution in which case we need to have a way to express compensating sequences of actions that need to take place in going '*backwards*' while effectively undoing all previously successful forward actions. The operation per coordinator is called *right-cancellation,* which it is equivalent to calling a cancelation for a service [a formal definition of this can be found in (Moschoyiannis et al., 2008) and (Razavi, Moschoyiannis, & Krause, 2007b)]. Figure 6 shows the case where a failure occurs after service a2 of component CC2 has been invoked. This means that it is no longer possible for the transaction to produce a consistent state by reaching the maximal vector (a1a2, b1, c1), as dictated by the allowed sequence of actions in its execution history. Consequently, the transaction needs to be recovered and this implies returning

to the (consistent) state the system was in before the transaction started.

We have seen how right-cancellation can be applied to generate compensating sequences of actions for the full recovery of a transaction. Full recovery however, can be costly in terms of resources, delays, business relations and so on. Additionally, in a highly transactional environment dependencies may also exist across transactions so the effect of a recovered transaction may be magnified. For this reason it is desirable to avoid full recovery wherever possible. One way to do this is to design transactions with a number of alternative scenarios of execution; in other words, allow for multiple execution histories in the corresponding transaction script. In such cases, our approach comes with the provision for forward recovery which is a mechanism for avoiding full recovery. The aim is during compensation to explore whether there is any possibility for successfully terminating the transaction following a different execution history to the one originally deployed, instead of compensating for the whole execution history.

This is possible in our approach because all the execution histories are captured in the transaction language. Hence, in recovering a given execution history which failed, after the next forward action(s) is compensated for we check whether the resulting vector is also part of a different execution history. If this is the case, then we attempt to go forward by performing the execution in accordance with the allowed sequence of actions in that alternative execution history. As shown in the green box, Figure 6, in going backwards, and while cancelling out one action (or a set of concurrent actions) at a time, we look each time whether there is an alternative path from the vector we arrived on (after applying the compensating action(s)) leading to a maximal vector (successful outcome). For those familiar with logic programming, this is directly analogous to the use of backtracking when searching for a successful solution to a goal.

Figure 6. Transaction life-cycle

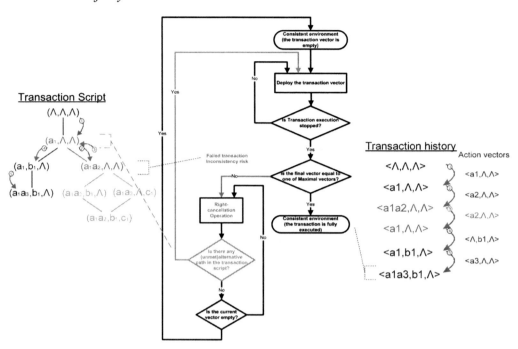

Data Inconsistency in Business Transactions

According to the definition of (Gray & Reuter, 1993), a transaction that is started when a system is in a consistent state may make the state temporarily inconsistent, but it must terminate by producing a new consistent state. In conventional transactions, this has been provided by applying isolation theorems [This maintains the illusion that each transaction runs in *Isolation*. The conventional mechanism for doing so is to use an S/X (Share/eXclusive) Lock, (Bernstein, Hadzilacos, & Goodman, 1987) and (Gray & Reuter, 1993)]. Violation of the isolation property is related to various dependency cycles. As with conventional transactions, cyclic dependencies in long-running transactions are categorized into three generic forms [full details can be found in most transactional or database books such as (Date, 2003) or (Gray & Reuter, 1993)];

- **Lost updates:** The first sub-transaction's *write* (deploying the data) is overwritten by the second sub-transaction which uses *write* based on the initial value of the object.

- **Dirty read:** A sub-transaction *read*s an object which has been *written* before by another uncommitted sub-transaction which also *write*s to it again after the *read* action. This means the first sub-transaction may find inconsistency in the object.

- **Unrepeatable read:** A sub-transaction *read*s an object that is then *read* by another sub-transaction which also *write*s to it after its *read* action and commits. Meanwhile, the first sub-transaction *read*s the object again, and may find an inconsistency in the object.

These show cycles in access to objects, called a *wormhole*, which we explain later in this section. First we should to formalize the long-running transaction's execution according to its accessing of objects. In defining an execution of a long-running transaction we use the standard term *schedule*. A *schedule* of a long-running transaction is any sequence-preserving merge of the actions (i.e. reading, writing, aborting, committing) of a set of sub-transactions into a single sequence for the set of sub-transactions and is denoted by:

$$S = st, a, o_i \, i = 1, \ldots, n$$

Each step of the history $<st,a,o>$ is an action a by sub-transaction st on object o. By analysing a history, we can capture all dependencies (WRITE→WRITE, WRITE→READ and READ→WRITE) into a dependency relation DEP[H], where two sub-transactions are dependent if they engage in actions on a common version of an object.

Wormhole Theorem

This theorem is a well-known theorem in isolation theory. In what follows we outline how it can be adapted to determine wormhole-free transactions of the kind considered in our approach, i.e. long-running transactions. Hence, before using the classic theorem and its proof (Gray & Reuter, 1993) we introduce the equivalent concept and notation in long-running transactions, and then adapt the proof to long-running transactions. The dependencies in the history of a long-running transaction can define a time ordering of the sub-transactions. Conventionally this ordering is signified by the relation $<<<_H$, (or simply by $<<<$ when the history is clear from context), and is the *transitive closure* of the dependency relation, DEP[H]. $<<<_H$ is the smallest relation satisfying:

$$f \; ST, o, ST' \in DEP\big[H\big] \; for \; some \; object \; version \; o, \textbf{or}$$

$$\begin{pmatrix} ST <<<_H ST'' \; and \; ST', o, ST' \in DEP\big[H\big] \\ for \; some \; sub-transactions \; ST'', and \; some \; object \; o \end{pmatrix}$$

In terms of the dependency graph, we can say that $ST<<<ST'$ if there is a path in the dependency graph from sub-transaction ST to sub-transaction ST'.

The $<<<$ ordering defines the set of all sub-transactions that run before or after ST;

$$BEFORE\big(ST\big) = \big\{ ST \big| ST <<< ST \big\}$$

$$AFTER\big(ST\big) = \big\{ ST \big| ST <<< ST \big\}$$

If ST is fully isolated (i.e., it is the only sub-transaction, or it's *read* and *write* objects are not accessed by any other sub-transactions), then it's BEFORE and AFTER sets are empty, and it can be scheduled in any way. When a sub-transaction is both after and before another distinct sub-transaction (ST here), it is called *wormhole transaction* (ST' here):

$$ST \in BEFORE\big(ST\big) \cap AFTER\big(ST\big)$$

It is not hard to see that serial histories do not have wormholes - in a serial history, all the actions of one transaction precede the actions of another, i.e. the first cannot depend on the outputs of the second.

Based on the wormhole theorem, a history is isolated if, and only if, it has no wormhole sub-transactions (Gray & Reuter, 1993). On the other hand, the isolated histories have the *unique* property of having no wormholes. The theorem dictates that a history that is not isolated has at least one wormhole; $ST<<<ST'<<<ST$. (i.e. ST' has critical dependencies on an uncommitted transaction).

In graphical terms we can say that if the dependency graph has a cycle in it, then the history is not equivalent to any serial history because some sub-transaction is both before and after another sub-transaction. A wormhole in a particular history is a sub-transaction pair in which ST ran before ST' which ran before ST. In the next section, we propose a mechanism for avoiding wormholes using our distributed coordinators.

Internal Dependencies

We have shown that by avoiding wormholes we can release results between sub-transactions of a long-running transaction. In doing so, we use the dependency graph to trace released data items (objects) between each participant. This graph is updated regularly and potential cycles (wormholes) can be detected in each step. As this graph captures dependencies between sub-transactions of a transaction we call it the Internal Dependency Graph (IDG).

For clarifying access-rights, inside of each participant we use a simple lock mechanism which is compatible with the conventional S/X Lock. The only difference with an S/X Lock is the UN-Lock mechanism. Since participants are executing a sub-transaction and the result can only be visible in that particular long-running transaction, instead of unlocking the data we introduce an internal lock I-Lock which unlocks the data items in the context of a particular transaction. This means the data item will only be available for other sub-transactions of the transaction, which are executing in other participants. As mentioned in the beginning of the section, the execution of a transaction will be performed by the 'local coordinator' of the participants. Figure 7 shows a simple example.

Figure 7 shows part of a long-running transaction, where a parallel composition between services c1 and b1 has a data-dependency. We have assumed that service c1 is a service offered by participant P1 and service b1 is provided by participant P2. Based on the transaction context described in the beginning of this section, c1 and b1 can be deployed in the context of two sub-transactions (STc1 and STb1). When participant P1, deploys the service c1 the service creates a data-item K as the output (notice that P1 uses X-Lock for writing/creating the object) and sub-

transaction STc1 commits and releases the result for other sub-transactions. To do this P1 uses I-Lock and a pre-request for the object while the IDG is created for the object. Our example illustrates the case where participant P2 needs the output of c1 (STc1). It can use the result, which has been released by I-Lock, and if there is a dependency between the two sub-transactions present in the corresponding IDG ($STc1 <<< STb1$), also shown in the figure, P2 uses S-Lock for reading K and proceeds to use it as the input in service b1. Then P2 can again release it by using I-Lock on the data-item. Any subsequent usage of the data-item will be done by checking and updating the IDG. In this way, local coordinators can avoid any cycle (e.g., $STc1 <<< STb1 <<< ... <<< STc1$).

Partial Results by Using Conditional Commit

As the life-cycle of long-running transactions is long, occasionally releasing results between these transactions before their termination (commit/rollback) can be valuable for a digital ecosystem (Razavi et al., 2006), (Moschoyiannis et al., 2008) in covering a range of B2B scenarios. However, these 'partial results' can be costly - in case of abortion of the first long-running transaction we may face cascading abortion (Razavi et al., 2007b). Earlier in this chapter, we provided a mechanism for *forward recovery* and here we consider a similar approach in term of data-orientation (in case of abortion of the first transaction - this is further discussed in the next section). As the partial results are released before the actual commit of a long-running transaction, the mechanism for releasing them is called *Conditional Commit*. For conditional commit again we use a dependency graph in combination with the wormhole theorem. It is important to note that:

- In the first place two long-running transactions had full invisibility towards each other. therefore the released data-item from

Figure 7. Internal dependency diagram

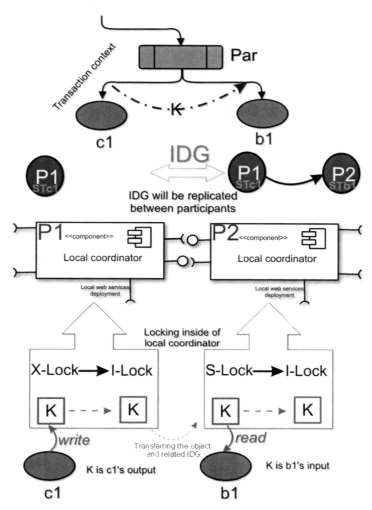

the first long-transaction has to be read by the second transaction

- As all the data-items are in the deployment level they will be created by the transaction in the first place. This means the first operation on a data-item for any long-running transaction will be a *write* (in fact, it can take place in one of its sub-transactions but this is the primary assumption of SOA).

Therefore in any conditional commit between transaction T1 and T2 there is a *write →read* dependency and as the first transaction is not fully committed, any *write* operation can create a wormhole (*T1<<<T2<<<T1* in terms of *write →read →write*). That is why after releasing the partial result the data-item will be read-only and this cannot change until the first transaction commits. Note also that the second transaction cannot commit before the first one does and as a result it will have a commit dependency. For addressing this limitation, we define a C-Lock for the conditional commit of partial results and the dependency graph for releasing these data-items is called *External Dependency Graph* (EDG). In addition to capturing the dependencies on particular data-items released between transactions, this graph also captures the commit dependency.

Figure 8. External dependency graph

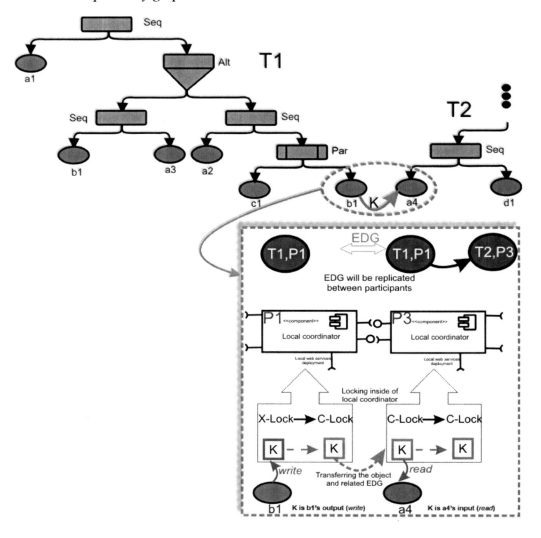

By using the EDG the second transaction can not commit unless it receives a confirmation from the first transaction that it has committed. Figure 8 shows an example of using conditional commit.

In Figure 8 transaction T1 releases the partial result (data-item K) to transaction T2. As a result, the related External Dependency Graph (EDG) will be created by coordination of Participant P1 (one of T1's participants which has done the last action on data-item K), and the graph is shared by P3 (one of T2's participants which is going to do the first *read* operation on data-item K). The

important point is that the C-Lock has been used for data-item K and the lock will be inherited by any participants which are going to use the data-item. In this way, the data-item will remain 'Locked' until the transaction, the one which has created the data-item (*originator transaction*; here, T1), commits. Meanwhile, in terms of abortion in the originator transaction, all dependent transactions should be rolled back. In the next section we describe the recovery procedure that needs to take place.

Recovery

We start with the well-known 'Rollback theorem' and build our recovery procedure around the concepts of degenerating the transactions and, of course, avoiding wormholes. In this respect we use the rollback theorem (A transaction that unlocks an exclusive lock and then does a '*Rollback*' is not well-formed and is a potential wormhole, unless the transaction is degenerate). As the theorem is well known, we refer the interested reader to (Gray & Reuter, 1993) for the actual proof. The important point of the theorem is that we have to degenerate the transaction to affect rollback. For this purpose we can use the logs provided by the dependency graphs and trace them. The only caveat is that the digital ecosystem network is distributed and therefore there is no centralised synchronisation. This entails that there is a risk for wormholes.

Two Phase Recovery

For avoiding wormholes, we have designed the recovery procedure in line with our consistency model (logs/locks) for concurrency control. Overall, Recovery Management in combination with the concurrency control procedure runs in two phases:

- **Preparation phase:** This consists of sending a message (abort/restart) to the participants of all sub-transactions that puts them (and their data) into an isolated mode (preparing for recovery). This helps avoid any propagation of inconsistent data and possibility for creating wormhole during the actual rollback.
- **Atomic Recovery Transaction routine:** The recovery routine will be run as an atomic procedure that can rollback and cancel deployed services of sub-transactions by using correct data-items.

Both phases in recovery management rely strongly on tracing the corresponding dependency graphs. This is where the necessary information for finding the changes on data-items, in different participants, and to undo them and bring back the system to a consistent state. Figure 9 shows a sample scenario that extends that presented earlier in Figure 8.

According to Figure 9, a failure happens for T1 while participant P1 was trying to execute the transaction. The participant P1 has to stop any further progress on T1 and uses its EDG and IDG for informing about the failure on T1. As shown in the figure, participant P3 uses some results from P1 for transaction T2, which means P3 has to start a similar procedure for transaction T2. This is the external dependency. Participant P3 now uses its IDG, which indicates that the participant P2 needs to be informed for stopping the potential execution of transaction T1 (in this case, it will be the sub-transaction STb1 of transaction T1). In fact, it has to inform any dependent transaction or sub-transactions by checking its related graphs to cater for all internal dependencies. Now for stopping the transaction progress (isolation of T1 affection) upon failure, we need an internal structure inside of the local coordinator.

DIGITAL ECOSYSTEMS: NETWORKING AND CONNECTIVITY

Digital Ecosystem as a Network of Business participants

A digital ecosystem can be conceptualized as the result of several business transactions where each transaction creates a private network, the so-called *Virtual Private Transaction Network* (VPTN). Conceptually, we consider D_U as all Digital Ecosystems, where T_U is all of the possible transactions in these Ecosystems and P_U all possible participants of the Ecosystem. Each transaction is the result of compositions of services

Figure 9. Recovery procedure

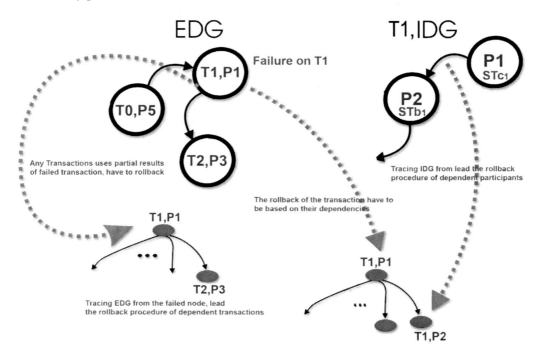

from several participants. This can be described by the pair (t, P_t), where P_t is the set of participants which are involved in a transaction t. The universe of digital ecosystems comprises all of the possible transactions and their participants and can be defined as:

$$D_U = \left\{ (t, P_t) \middle| t \in T_U \wedge P_t \subset P_U \right\}$$

We define a specific Digital Ecosystem *DE*, as a subset of D_U, where all of its participants, by engaging in its transactions, are connected.

Each VPTN can be recognised by the transaction of its participants (t, P_t) where

$$P_t = \left\{ Participant \sin volved\ in\ Transaction\ t \right\}$$

In this paradigm, the maximum number of links which any one participant may have is just the number of participants minus one (they do not link to themselves):

$$|P_t| - 1$$

In our transaction model, coordination of the underlying services is distributed and addresses both the order and the data dependencies, and hence the actual number of links in a single transaction is always less than this:

$$1 \leq No\ of\ links\ for\ a\ node in\ (t, P_t) \leq |P_t| - 1 \tag{1}$$

But based on the definition of a digital ecosystem, individual VPTNs can have overlaps that make a connected network (participants can engage in multiple transactions). Therefore, nodes can be involved in several VPTNs and as a result, they will have additional links through this participation in different transactions. Studies show most business networks follow the power-law distribution degree (Barabási & Albert, 1999), which means that a very small number of nodes are involved in the majority of the transactions,

Figure 10. Digital ecosystem of connected VPTNs

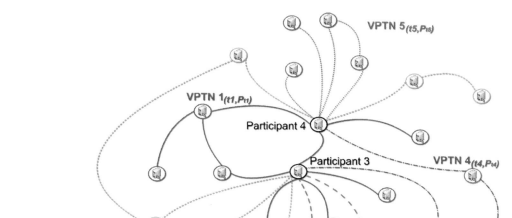

and even in each transaction these "keystones" will have the maximum numbers of links.

Figure 13 shows a simple digital ecosystem, where '*Participant 4*' and '*Participant 3*', are involved in all of the VPTNs, and in each VPTN they get the majority of links.

This has as a drawback that any problem in either '*Participant 4*' or '*Participant 3*' (or both) can cause serious disruptions in all the VPTNs. In addition, a simple failure on '*Participant 4*' or '*Participant 3*' can fragment the network, which means even if the involvement of '*Participant 4*' or '*Participant 3*' was restricted to alternative service composition, still the transactions may not be executed. Moreover, since '*Participant 4*' and '*Participant 3*' have gotten this important role based solely on their business transactions they may not be the best candidate for providing connectivity for the network. In other words, their emergence as a highly connected node has been driven by the volume of transactions they take part in and no other factor. This raises the question of whether it is desirable for a digital business ecosystem to rely on very few nodes in general. Before addressing such aspects, we show how each VPTN will react to a failure and how it can be recovered, how the cost of failure can be reduced, and how full abortion of the transaction can be avoided. After that, we examine how the possibility for failures can be reduced all together.

Link Replication, and Connectivity

Normally the connections (links) to other participants of the digital ecosystem have been established by the '*global service repository*', where the addresses of other service providers (participants) and the description of their services have been kept. For inserting (or modifying) a new participant to the repository and its services, the 'web service information investor' component will be involved. For introducing the participant to another participant the 'web service promoter' will be used.

Figure 11. Link replication

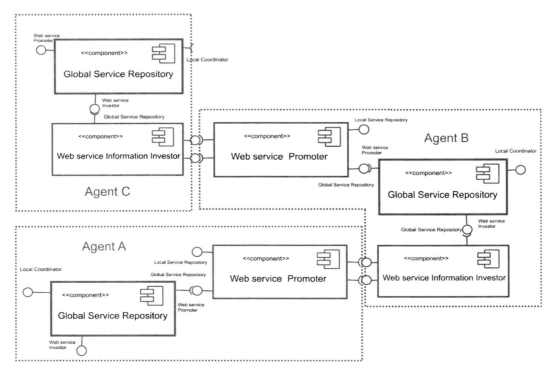

It can be seen that for increasing the connectivity we use three components of the component-based design of each participant. Figure 11 shows the relationships between these components of three participants (their software agents). Participant B ('*Agent B*'), receives all of the connections of Participant A ('*Agent A*') through its '*web service information investor*' when participant A ('*Agent A*') provides them through its '*web service promoter*'. Similarly, participant B ('*Agent B*') provides its connections (links to the other participants) to the '*web service information investor*' of participant C ('*Agent C*'). We call this procedure *Link Replication*. It is important to mention that it is possible to have *partial link replication* where there is no need to replicate or pass to other participants all of the connections of a given participant.

Fully Connected VPTN and Digital Ecosystem

As we mentioned at the beginning of this section, one of the significant risks for the VPTNs of a digital ecosystem (transactions of the network) is disconnection between participants of a transaction which amounts to low connectivity inside the VPTNs. It seems the primary solution for the problem is to use the link replication procedure between the participants. By repeating link replication in each participant, within a limited time, all participants in a VPTN will be connected together. As a result we will have a fully connected VPTN, which if it is built based on transaction t and participant P_t each node will have $|P_t|$- 1 links.

Where this may seem like an ideal solution for each VPTN, the result can in fact be devastating for the digital ecosystem and consequently the majority of transactions could fail. As a digital ecosystem is a connected network through its

Figure 12. Fully disconnected VPTNs

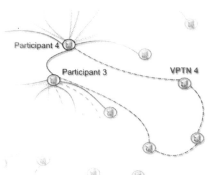

VPTN 4 in our sample DE

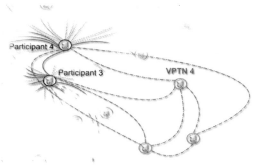

VPTN 4 after increasing interconnections

transactions, the VPTNs have overlaps on some of the their participants (there are some intersections between different VPTNs' participants) and as mentioned, studies show most business networks follow the power-law distribution degree (Barabási & Albert, 1999). This means that he digital ecosystem relies on very few participants (nodes) to stay connected and these small numbers of participants are involved in the majority of the transactions, i.e. these few participants will be in most VPTNs.

Now if we apply *link replication*:

each participant in the VPTN will have

$$|P_t| - 1$$

links. Therefore a participant R which is involved in transactions

$$\{t_m, \cdots, t_n\}$$

will have up to

$$\sum_{i=m}^{n} |P_t| - (m + n)$$

links.

Based on the second point above, very few participants are involved in the majority of transac-

tions. Therefore by applying *link replication* in this way this small number of participants will have a very large increase of links. This increases their traffic dramatically and it is highly probable they may collapse as a result, which means a potentially large number of transactions will be failed. More importantly, based on the first point, as the digital ecosystem relies on them to stay connected, the whole digital ecosystem will be fragmented. Figure 12 shows this situation which his generally rather difficult for a network to recover from.

On the left side of Figure 12 VPTN4 from the sample digital ecosystem presented in Figure 10, is shown, and on the right-side we can see the result of *link replication* on all participants of the VPTN4. As *link replication* in a similar way has been applied for all other VPTNs, participant 3 and participant 4 which are involved in several transactions face the large increases of links which can bring traffic complexity. While the *link replication* itself seems quite useful for increasing connectivity, the way and on which participant it is applied can be crucial for the general performance of the digital ecosystem (and even each VPTN).

Stable Nodes, Link Replication and Permanent Clusters

In general, we can say the best candidates for link replication inside each VPTN and connecting

Figure 13. Permanent clusters and virtual super peers

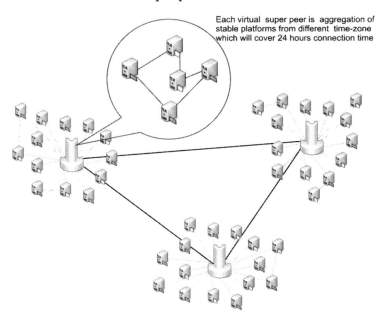

VPTNs together are the most stable participants (nodes) in each VPTN [the stability function, according to the DE sector this can vary, the general function in (Razavi, Moschoyiannis, & Krause, 2008) can be used]. Connecting these participants, the link replication can be done by using the '*Global Service Repository*' of each candidate-participant from each VPTN (as has been shown in Figure 2). However, we cannot warranty full stability of the network and still cannot avoid the occasional fragmentations. Even in the best case, this is still dependent on each candidate-participant's availability and if the total online time of all stable nodes cannot cover the full '*active-time*' of the network, the network will collapse for some period of time, precisely that in which all candidates are not available.

Therefore, in contrast with conventional super peers, we try in our network design to move towards a more dynamic architecture which does not rely on just a few permanent nodes. Central to our approach is finding permanent clusters on the network. More specifically, we are identifying aggregations of stable nodes, where node stability is determined as in the previous section. For do-

ing so, the most stable nodes from different time zones must be chosen, in a way that they cover the digital ecosystem's '*active-time*' (for reasonably large ecosystems, 24 hours). More specifically, we are trying to find permanent clusters through the most stable nodes.

The important part in determining permanent clusters is discovering different aggregations of these time zones which can cover 24 hour availability. Any union of the stable nodes in the aggregations (which provides the full '*active-time*' - 24 hour availability coverage) are actual permanent clusters. Figure 13, shows the simple situation in which the most stable nodes have been selected from two sets of time zones which can cover 24 hour service availability to form permanent clusters.

Virtual Super Peers

By using stable nodes from permanent clusters, as shown in Figure 13, we can create *Virtual Super Peers* (VSPs) which are effectively permanent clusters of nodes in the network. These can provide the desired stability for the digital ecosystem.

The strong connection between the virtual super peers themselves on one hand and the connection between them and their nodes decrease the probability for fragmentation. Depending on the level of reliability required for the network, it is possible to include further redundant stable platforms from each available time zone. For example, in Figure 13 we have included two stable nodes from one time-zone and three stable nodes from the other one (the green and creamy coloured signs show different time zones).

In this manner, the good connectivity can cause more reliable transactions at the VPTNs level. Meanwhile the traffic is spread over the virtual super peers and there is less risk of bottleneck at peak time. Participants (nodes) within a virtual super peer need to keep information only about nodes in their cluster and about neighbouring VSPs so at off-peak time the amount of redundant information processing is reduced dramatically as compared to the classical Super Peers solution.

Since choosing stable participants (nodes) is done based on the stability measurement which is given by a function of their Expected Availability Time (EAT) and the Disconnection Period of a node during EAT, whose value varies over time, is a *dynamic* process and hence the virtual super peers are also formed dynamically. This means the topology can change from time to time and new nodes can be added to the permanent clusters as the structure of the virtual super peers changes. A node can become part of a virtual super peer, when its node stability increases and overcomes some threshold, and nodes that are super peers may not be able to cope with the increased number of connections they get, and possibly increased number of transactions they perform and lose their virtual peer status. Within a digital ecosystem for business, SMEs would be expected to invest at that time (in hardware, processing power, bandwidth etc.) and become again part of a virtual super peer in future. It is in this sense that the topology evolves to reflect the usage and demands of the

participants who benefit from and contribute to the 'sustainability' of the network.

Additionally, network congestion can change the maximum level of node stability which in turn affects the selection of the most stable nodes in forming the permanent clusters. High congestion of packages can increase or decrease network reliability (higher traffic on few virtual super peers can potentially create a bottleneck and even cause fragmentation). In a digital business ecosystem, the major part of the traffic is the result of business activities, which are effectively long-lived transactions. These have been virtualised in VPTNs and therefore, using the effect of VPTNs for making VSPs and their client nodes, can increase stability of each virtual super peer. Furthermore, we expect a reasonable cluster coefficient on account of having VPTNs as the main building blocks, which we have seen are formed from transactions. This means its participants are in relevant domains – by connecting them to several VSPs we actually increase the probability for that. We also expect a fair distribution degree on the account of propagating links to VSPs. This means that instead of being concerned with individual links for each node, aggregate links of VSPs come into play.

Finally, reusing business activity results (or service-on-fly as a result of composite services (Papazoglou, 2005)(Papazoglou et al., 2006)) and explorative service composition (Yang, Papazoglou, & van den Heuvel, 2002) are other factors which can be considered for higher performance within a digital business ecosystem and can provide potential for creating so-called *virtual vendors* (Razavi et al., 2007a).

The Dynamic Mechanism for Choosing VSPs

In the first step, the most stable participant in each VPTN (participants of a transaction) should be selected for keeping vital information about the transaction and its participants. In this sense, the network provides a level of durability with

Figure 14. Dynamic mechanism for increasing stability

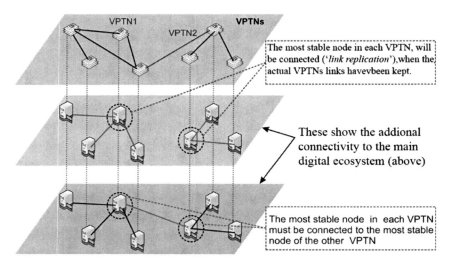

minimum cost from participants and it provides a greater chance for forward recovery even in terms of failure in one of the participants of a transaction. Effectively, this makes our mechanism, fully effective with regard to what is referred to as (in purely transactional literature, the solved problem is called) *omitted results*, which is a problem relating to preserving as much progress-to-date as possible in the event of aborting a transaction (the details about complexity of the problem can be found in our previous work (Razavi et al., 2007)).

In the next step, by connecting the most stable nodes of each VPTN together, the first level of strong connectivity and suitable nodes for VSPs are created. Figure 14 shows the internal structure of each VPTN and the connection between VPTNs. The internal structure of a VPTN contains a lot of information from the transaction level such as log structures, lock schemes for ensuring consistency in recovery mentioned above, local coordinator design, formal analysis of the required interactions and recoverability (Razavi et al, 2007b), along with alternative scenarios for forward recovery. Now by using the most stable node, we let the optimisation in transactions to be performed and any waste of resources as the result of weak connectivity will be avoided.

The direct effect of connecting VPTNs together is a raising of the cluster coefficient for the network. Conversely, connecting the most stable nodes of VPTNs together provides the opportunity of choosing the best candidate locally between these stable nodes for the permanent cluster. Choosing nodes of the permanent cluster in this way results in a virtual super peer that provides fair traffic distribution at the VSN level (each virtual super peer will take care of its local VPTNs). The main concept behind forming permanent clusters stays the same, i.e., selecting the most stable nodes from different time zones which can cover 24 hours online time.

JXTA and DE Model

We have started to work with IPTI in Brazil ('Instituto de Pesquisas em Tecnologia e Inovação' http://ipti.org.br/) for providing an implementation of the model. The aim here is to exploit the characteristics of the transaction model, mostly in terms of interaction-based service composition and the fine-grained lock scheme, in supporting complex interactions within the collaborative platform *guigoh* (http://www.guigoh.com/Home. do) and improve its social network aspects. In the first instance we have been looking at reducing the traffic complexity of the interactions and adding provision for business services.

The first implementation uses JXTA protocols, which are defined as a set of XML messages which allow any device connected to a network to exchange messages and collaborate independently of the underlying network topology (https://jxta.dev.java.net/). The first prototype of this work, together with preliminary documentation, can be found in the opensource project 'flypeer' and can be downloaded from (http://kenai.com/projects/flypeer). Based on our roadmap, by growth of participants, the dynamicity of VSPs comes into play and the consistency model can be fully distributed. At the moment, in collaboration with IPTI we have examined the transaction context, through sample service-oriented scenarios, where the main services are optimised for creating parallel, sequential and alternative compositions of virtual online conferences. This has included the full distributed transactional communication (exchange of messages, initiating a transaction, and terminating the transaction). The P2P relationship between participants and their services has been supported in a purely loosely-coupled manner.

In the next steps, we plan to extend the implementation prototype by considering more complex scenarios and introducing additional traffic complexity through incorporating more heavy services, such as voice and video streams. In addition, we are looking at introducing a larger number of transaction participants and work is in progress in integrating the user interface for monitoring the model.

The Model on an XMPP Implementation

Our work on distributed coordination of long-running transactions involving the deployment of services started in the Digital Business Ecosystem (DBE) project. The support for a distributed transaction model initially targeted the DBE Studio (Razavi et al, 2006) which can

be understood as a service container for search and deployment of services from various service providers, and specifically SMEs. The DBE Studio implemented by TechIdeas (http://techideas.es/) uses the so-called FADA network. Experience with FADA has shown the network to become unstable in certain respects. Subsequent analysis and further experimentation under the real DBE studio implementation revealed certain problems relating to connectivity and fragmentation. Such aspects have also been highlighted by our simulations reported earlier.

Currently, the work led by TechIdeas is steered towards using XMPP (http://xmpp.org/tech/) protocols and a first implementation of this is a new platform called *Sironta* (http://www.sironta.com/). XMPP at its core is a technology for streaming XML over a network. Our transaction framework is concerned with optimising transactions in terms of the XML context, the consistency model for the interactions. In the OPAALS project ("OPAALS Website - Opaals Home Page") there is a roadmap for integrating this work with Techideas' implementation in order to provide a customised infrastructure for the service-oriented platform Sironta.

Figure 15 outlines the general idea behind the integration of the two approaches which involves modelling XMPP servers onto customised SME's servers. In this case, the digital ecosystem infrastructure described in this paper can act as a SMEs transactional cloud, which dynamically optimises itself to respond to the usage that is being made of it based on the transactions taking place between participating organisations.

DIGITAL ECOSYSTEMS: DISCUSSIONS AND FURTHER POTENTIALS FOR RESEARCH

This chapter has provided a snapshot of the development of an infrastructure to support open collaborations within Digital Ecosystems, as it

Figure 15. XMPP implementation for digital ecosystem

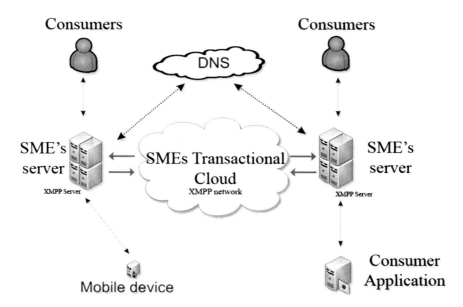

moves towards implementation. The key feature of this work is that it expands the concept of P2P computing to include full sharing of the infrastructure that supports collaboration and orchestration of business activities. We should also mention that, although it is outside the scope of the current chapter, the infrastructure is also supported by a fully distributed identity and trust model.

This can be thought of as a move towards *Community Cloud Computing*, "C3", in which all the computational resources (both hardware and software) needed to support a community/ecosystem are provided from within that community. There are potential environmental benefits to this, since the processing resources are provided through spare capacity within the ecosystem. Our simulations indicate this could significantly reduce the need for dedicated server farms. But most importantly, this frees the community from any dependencies on third parties or specific individuals within the community. *And* it ensures that all the added value that is generated by that community, business services and knowledge resources, can be fairly traded.

As well as the high-level view, there are also some more detailed benefits of this infrastructure. For example, the proposed lock scheme, here considered within the transaction model, allows for simultaneous editing on different parts of a document without conflict. This is being incorporated in the *guigoh* e-learning collaborative platform in collaboration with IPTI as outlined in the previous section.

As mentioned before, a digital ecosystem is a highly dynamic environment for a variety of reasons and failures of various types are to be expected. Therefore, our efforts so far have been targeted at providing a stable network that exhibits increased connectivity and resilience to fragmentation.

In order to get a handle on how the network topology evolves under the events of nodes joining and leaving the network, we have been looking at biological models of growth in living organisms. Of particular interest seems to be the study of molecular networks of lipids and proteins in (Rzhetsky & Gomez, 2001) which exhibit scale-free characteristics and have interesting properties with respect to connectivity. Preliminary investigations show that these aspects are driven by the major evolutionary events in growth in molecular networks, namely *domain duplication* and *innovation*. We are currently examining ways to inform the reaction of the network, possibly in terms of the neighbouring nodes, to the event of a node joining the network or leaving. This can be coupled with the component-based design of the local software agent on each participating node, and this is certainly an aspect of the work that we are keen to investigate further.

REFERENCES

Barabási, A. L., & Albert, R. (1999). Emergence of Scaling in Random Networks. *Science, 286*(5439), 509. doi:10.1126/science.286.5439.509

Barabási, A. L., Albert, R., & Jeong, H. (2000). Scale-free characteristics of random networks: the topology of the world-wide web. *Physica A: Statistical Mechanics and its Applications, 281*(1-4), 69-77.

Barnes, S. B. (2006). A privacy paradox: Social networking in the United States. *First Monday, 11*(9).

Bernstein, P. A., Hadzilacos, V., & Goodman, N. (1987). *Concurrency control and recovery in database systems*. Boston: Addison-Wesley Longman Publishing Co., Inc.

Booth, D., Haas, H., McCabe, F., Newcomer, E., Champion, M., Ferris, C., et al. (2004). *Web Services Architecture, W3C Working Group Note 11 February 2004*. Retrieved from http://www.w3. org/TR/ws-arch

Butler, M., Hoare, T., & Ferreira, C. A trace semantics for long-running transactions. In *Proceedings of* (Vol. 25, pp. 133–150). Berlin: Springer.

Chandler, A. D. (1990). *Scale and Scope: The Dynamics of Industrial Capitalism*. Cambridge, MA: Harvard University Press.

Cournot, A. A. (1960). *Researches into the mathematical principles of the theory of wealth, 1838* (p. 213). New York: A.M. Kelley.

Date, C. (2003). *An Introduction to Data Base Systems* (8th ed., p. 1024). Upper Saddle River, NJ: Pearson Education.

Dillard, D. D. (1967). *Economic Development of the North Atlantic Community: Historical Introduction to Modern Economics/Dudley Dillard*. Upper Saddle River, NJ: Prentice-Hall.

Furnis, P., & Green, A. (2005). *Choreology Ltd. Contribution to the OASIS WS-Tx Technical Committee relating to WS-Coordination, WS-Atomic-Transaction, and WS-BusinessActivity*, (November 2005). Retrieved from http//www. oasis-open. org/committees/download.php/15808

Gray, J., & Reuter, A. (1993). *Transaction Processing: Concepts and Techniques*. San Francisco: Morgan Kaufmann.

Haghjoo, M. S., & Papazoglou, M. P. (1992). TrActorS: a transactional actor system for distributed query processing. In *Distributed Computing Systems 1992, Proc. of the 12th International Conference on*, (pp. 682-689).

Iansiti, M., & Levien, R. (2004). *The Keystone Advantage: What the New Dynamics of Business Ecosystems Mean for Strategy, Innovation, and Sustainability* (pp. 304). Cambridge, MA: Harvard Business School Press.

Josephson, M. (1962). *The Robber Barons: the Great American Capitalists: 1861-1901*. New York: A Harvest Book.

Moore, J. F. (1993). Predators and Prey: A New Ecology of Competition. *Harvard Bus. Rev., 71*, 75–83.

Moschoyiannis, S., & Razavi, A. R. Yongyan Zheng, & Krause, P. (2008). Long-running Transactions: Semantics, schemas, implementation. In *Digital Ecosystems and Technologies, 2008. DEST 2008. 2nd IEEE International Conference on* (pp. 20-27). doi: 10.1109/DEST.2008.4635168.

Moschoyiannis, S., Razavi, A. R., & Krause, P. (2008). Transaction Scripts: Making Implicit Scenarios Explicit. In *ETAPS 2008 - FESCA '08, ENTCS*. New York: Elsevier.

Nachira, F. (2002). *Towards a Network Of Digital Business Ecosystems Fostering the Local Development*.

Nachira, F., Dini, P., Nicolai, A., Louarn, M., & Leon, L. (2007). *Digital Business Ecosystems*. Brussels: European Commission. *OPAALS Website - Opaals Home Page*. (n.d.). Retrieved December 22, 2008, from http://www.opaals.org/

O'Reilly, T. (2005). *What is Web 2.0: Design Patterns and Business Models for the Next Generation of Software*.

Papazoglou, M. P. (2003). Service-Oriented Computing: Concepts, Characteristics and Directions. In *Proceedings of the Fourth International Conference on Web Information Systems Engineering* (Vol. 3). Washington, DC: IEEE Computer Society Press., December.

Papazoglou, M. P. (2005). Extending the Service-Oriented Architecture. *Business Integration Journal*, 7(1), 18–21.

Papazoglou, M. P., & Georgakopoulos, D. (2003). Service-Oriented Computing. *Communications of the ACM*, 46(10), 25–28. doi:10.1145/944217.944233

Papazoglou, M. P., Traverso, P., Dustdar, S., Leymann, F., & Kramer, B. J. (2006). Service-oriented computing: A research roadmap. *Service Oriented Computing (SOC)*.

Payton, I. J., Fenner, M., & Lee, W. G. (2002). *Keystone Species: The Concept and Its Relevance for Conservation Management in New Zealand*. Dept. of Conservation.

Power, M. E., Tilman, D., Estes, J. A., Menge, B. A., Bond, W. J., & Mills, L. S. (1996). Challenges in the quest for keystones. *Bioscience*, 46(8), 609–620. doi:10.2307/1312990

Razavi, A., Krause, P., & Moschoyiannis, S. (2006). Deliverable D24.5: DBE Distributed Transaction Model. *Project Acronym: DBE, European Community, Framework, Contract No: 507953*.

Razavi, A., Moschoyiannis, S., & Krause, P. (2007). Concurrency Control and Recovery Management in Open e-Business Transactions. In *Proc. WoTUG Communicating Process Architectures (CPA 2007)*, (pp. 267–285).

Razavi, A. R., & Moschoyiannis, S. (2008). *FESCA WORKSHOP 2009 xml Sources*. Retrieved December 22, 2008, from http://www.computing.surrey.ac.uk/personal/st/S.Moschoyiannis/trnscripts/

Razavi, A. R., Moschoyiannis, S., & Krause, P. (2007a). *Preliminary Architecture for Autopoietic P2P Network focusing on Hierarchical Super-Peers, Birth and Growth Models*. OPAALS Project (OPAALS project Deliverable D3.1). Retrieved from http://files.opaals.org/OPAALS/Year_1_Deliverables/WP03/OPAALS_D3.1-final_submitted.pdf

Razavi, A. R., Moschoyiannis, S., & Krause, P. (2007b). *Report on formal analysis of autopoietic P2P network, together with predictions of performance*. OPAALS project (Deliverable D3.2). Retrieved from http://files.opaals.org/OPAALS/Year_1_Deliverables/WP03/OPAALS_D3.2_final.pdf

Razavi, A. R., Moschoyiannis, S. K., & Krause, P. J. (2007c). A Coordination Model for Distributed Transactions in Digital Business EcoSystems. *Digital Ecosystems and Technologies (DEST 2007)*. Los Alamitos, CA: IEEE Computer Society Press.

Razavi, A. R., Moschoyiannis, S. K., & Krause, P. J. (2008). A scale-free business network for digital ecosystems. In *Digital Ecosystems and Technologies, 2008. DEST 2008. 2nd IEEE International Conference on*, (pp. 241-246).

Rothschild, M. (1995). *Bionomics: Economy As Ecosystem* (Reissue., pp. 448). New York: Henry Holt & Company.

Rzhetsky, A., & Gomez, S. M. (2001). *Birth of scale-free molecular networks and the number of distinct DNA and protein domains per genome* (Vol. 17, pp. 988-996). Cambridge, UK: Oxford Univ. Press.

Service-oriented architecture. (n.d.). Wikipedia, the free encyclopedia. Retrieved December 21, 2008, from http://en.wikipedia.org/wiki/Service-oriented_architecture

Shields, M. W. (1997). *Semantics of parallelism.* New York: Springer.

Singh, M. P., & Huhns, M. N. (2005). *Service-Oriented Computing: Semantics, Processes, Agents.* Hoboken, NJ: Wiley.

Vogt, F. H., Zambrovski, S., Gruschko, B., Furniss, P., & Green, A. (2005). Implementing Web Service Protocols in SOA: WS-Coordination and WS-BusinessActivity. *CECW, 5,* 21–28.

Yang, J., Papazoglou, M. P., & van den Heuvel, W. J. (2002). Tackling the Challenges of Service Composition in e-Marketplaces. In *Proceedings of the 12th International Workshop on Research Issues on Data Engineering: Engineering E-Commerce/E-Business Systems (RIDE-2EC 2002),* San Jose, CA.

ENDNOTES

[1]   The power of these hubs is so strong that even large companies with sufficient financial resources and know-how such as Microsoft have trouble competing effectively in these segments. Similarly, as Microsoft used its size and financial resources (derived from its operating system) to spread its wings and expand into different segments, these hubs are also trying to establish themselves as Goliaths in other areas.

[2]   Example of this is variety of protocols and standards on security, resource sharing, identity, etc which in several cases are not compatible or are in contrast with each other.

[3]   P(M) denoting the power set, or set of all possible subsets of M.

Chapter 44
Providing VoD Services in Community Networks Using P2P Technology

Juan Pedro Muñoz-Gea
Polytechnic University of Cartagena, Spain

Josemaria Malgosa-Sanahuja
Polytechnic University of Cartagena, Spain

Pedro Jose Piñero-Escuer
Polytechnic University of Cartagena, Spain

Joan García-Haro
Polytechnic University of Cartagena, Spain

ABSTRACT

Thanks to the technological development, the production of multimedia content is no longer restricted to content providers. End-users communities are enabled to efficiently share, distribute, manage, and consume audio-visual contents. In this context, community networks are expected to play a central role. This kind of networks can be understood as the sum of all networks that interconnect devices in the homes, and the homes in a neighbourhood. They can use diversity of technologies, and among all of them, PLC (power line communication) is a very good alternative. In order to provide community networks with proper video services an appropriate middleware support is required to glue together the services and the infrastructures. In this respect, P2P (peer-to-peer) technology is a very good candidate to achieve this objective. On the other hand, there are several aspects of the PLC medium that make it difficult to share resources fairly but they can be solved using P2P technology. In this work, different proposal to provide VoD services using P2P technology are reviewed.

DOI: 10.4018/978-1-61520-686-5.ch044

INTRODUCTION

VoD (Video-on-Demand) services have traditionally consisted of the large scale distribution of AV (audio-visual) content from the content servers (providers) to the end-users (consumers). However, nowadays, digital AV content can be produced at a relatively low cost. Thus, end-users may eventually become both providers and consumers, and they can participate and collaborate actively in a *community network*. In this context, community networks are the sum of all networks that interconnect media devices in the homes and the homes in a neighborhood. This is possible because in the near future, all the media elements will have a network capacity attached to them (like cable, 3G, WiFi, Bluetooth, or power line transmission). This concept is called *networked media* (Networked Media of the Future, 2007).

Networking technologies that interconnect devices in the homes may be categorized as wireless, wired and no-new-wires networks. Among all of them, the no-new-wires networks are the most promising for in-home networking. In this category there are several possibilities: phone line, cable and power line networks. The major drawback of phone line and cable networks is the limited number of available connection points. On the other hand, residential power lines are the most pervasive networks in the home. Recently, the broadband communication over power line networks has attracted much interest in academy and industry. The Open PLC European Research Alliance has developed OPERA specification for the last mile access, and the HomePlug Powerline Alliance has developed the HomePlug AV specification for in-home networking. With this technology, the PLC medium can be considered appropriate to implement *community networks*.

In order to provide community networks with proper video services an appropriate middleware support is required to glue together the services and the infrastructures. In this respect, P2P (peer-to-peer) technology is a very good candidate to achieve this objective. On the other hand, there are several aspects of the PLC medium that make it difficult to share resources fairly but that can be solved using P2P technology. First, line attenuation increases exponentially with distance and it causes the problem of "hidden nodes" to arise frequently. That is, two nodes that are unaware of each other may transmit simultaneously resulting in interference at the receiving node. In addition, all the electronic or electrical equipment connected to the power lines is regarded as noise resources on the power line. Some of them generate broadband noise, while others inject impulse of noise. The previous characteristics make that during certain periods of time some of the devices connected to the PLC network have serious difficulties to communicate among them. Thus, if the applications use the traditional client-server architecture, where there is only a source of information (the server), it is possible that it suffers from several discontinuities in the provision of the information. In this scenario, a P2P network can solve the problems, because in this kind of networks every node acts a source of information, and if one of them is unavailable the application can search an alternative one.

In this work, we review the different proposal to provide VoD services using P2P technology. Recently, there have been a number of successful deployments for *live* P2P streaming. However, the question has remained open whether P2P technologies can be used to provide VoD services. It is more challenging to design a P2P VoD service than a P2P live streaming system because even though a large number of users may be watching the same video, they are asynchronous to one another (different users may watch different portions of the same video at any given moment). We focus on *mesh-based* P2P VoD systems. For these systems, we review several buffer-forwarding and storage-forwarding approaches, studying the mechanisms to find partners with expected data and the mechanism to collaborate among them for content delivery.

IN-HOME/IN-BUILDING NETWORKING

Home networking is defined by the Consumer Electronics Association (CEA) Board of Directors as follows (Consumer Electronics Association, 2008): "*A home network interconnects electronic products and systems, enabling control of them, and remote access to any available content such as music, video or data*". The key points in this definition are connection, access, and control (Rose, 2001).

Nowadays, the most important requirement for a home network is (Hughes & Thorne, 1998) that it is able to support for video and data transmission from a variety of sources in the home, provisioning of intra-home communication as a home LAN. On the other hand, a real increase in bandwidth, coverage and latency reduction is demanded for in-home networks. The reason is that DSL and cable operators are providing Triple Play services (consisting of video, voice and data), and the entry point of the twisted pair (or the cable) into the home is seldom close to the television (Gutierrez et al., 2005). Therefore, home networks are the candidate to provide connectivity between the home entry point and the different media devices at home.

Broadband Home Technologies

Candidate networking technologies to provide convenient and widespread residential networking services may be categorized as wireless, wired and no-new-wires networks. In (Yu-Ju et al., 2003) a discussion of networks in the three categories above is given. Next, this discussion is summarized.

Wireless networks can be constructed by installing multiple interconnected wireless access points. The main benefit of using wireless networks is the freedom to move around while maintaining network connectivity. The most interesting and widely accepted wireless networking technology is the 802.11 family: 802.11b operates in the 2.4 GHz band and provides a maximum data rate of 11 Mbps; 802.11a supports speeds of up to 54 Mbps and operates in the 5 GHz band; 802.11g provides data rates up to 54 Mbps in the 2.4 GHz band; finally, 802.11n, which will be finalized in December 2009, will support data rates up to 300 Mbps in the 5 Ghz and/or 2.4 Ghz bands.

For wired networks, Ethernet technology is the most extensively used. However, it is required to install special cabling in existing home or other buildings, and it may be costly.

For the no-new-wires networks category, there are several possibilities: phone line, cable, and power line networks. The major drawback of phone line and cable networks is the limited number of available connection points. On the other hand, residential power lines are the most pervasive networks in the home. Recently, the broadband communication over power line networks has attracted much interest in academy and industry. Open PLC European Research Alliance (OPERA) (OPERA, 2009) and HomePlug Powerline (HomePlug, 2009) Alliance have developed new generation of specifications separately (i.e. OPERA specifications and HomePlug AV). However, the aims of the two alliances are different: OPERA specification focuses on the last miles access and HomePlug AV focuses on in-home networking. With the available technology, the PLC medium can be considered appropriate to implement *community networks*. Therefore, we are going to concentrate on this technology along this chapter.

PLC for In-Home/In-Building Networking

The world's most widely deployed PLC system is the HomePlug standard developed by the HomePlug Powerline Alliance (HomePlug, 2009). The first standard was the HomePlug 1.0 which appeared in the year 2000. It was designed mainly to distribute broadband Internet access in the home. This standard has been widely deployed in the market and it is used internationally by home networking equipment manufacturers. The Home-Plug 1.0 standard was followed by HomePlug AV which appeared in the year 2005. Its objective is to allow the distribution of audio/video content within the house, as well as data.

HomePlug AV employs advanced physical and medium access control (MAC) technologies that provide a 200 Mbps power line network. The physical layer utilizes this 200 Mbps rate to provide 150 Mbps information rate. The MAC layer is designed to be highly efficient, support-ing both TDMA and CSMA/CA based access. The TDMA access provides quality of service (QoS) guarantees including guaranteed bandwidth reservation, high reliability and tight control of latency and jitter. The CSMA/CA access provides four priority levels.

On the other hand, HomePlug AV also pro-vides advanced capabilities consistent with new networking standards. For example, it offers tight security based on 128-bit AES and makes provision for dynamic (automatic) change of the encryption keys and for several different user experiences in setting up security and admitting stations to the network.

Nowadays, there are about 70 certified Home-Plug products, which can be found in (HomePlug Products, 2009). Within this set there are prod-ucts of important companies like Cisco-Linksys (Cisco-Linksys, 2009) or Netgear (Netgear, 2009). The simplest product is the HomePlug Ethernet adapter. This product connects the Ethernet devices to the HomePlug network. The adapter is con-nected to the wall outlet and the Ethernet device is connected with a network cable to the adapter. Other available HomePlug products are hubs, bridges, switches and routers. The hubs, bridges and switches have several Ethernet connections and one HomePlug connection. Therefore, they can be used to simultaneously connect several Ethernet devices to a HomePlug network. The routers can have several Ethernet, HomePlug

Figure 1. PLC in-home network

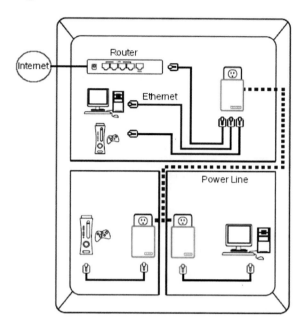

and Wireless interfaces and they can be used to configure different topologies.

Figure 1 represents a HomePlug network installed in a two floor house. On the first floor a personal computer and a video game console with Ethernet interfaces are connected to the power line by means of two HomePlug Ether-net adapters. On the second floor a HomePlug bridge is used to connect a personal computer and a video game console with the HomePlug network. The HomePlug bridge is also used to connect the power line network to the Internet by means of a Ethernet router. As can be seen, the main advantage of this kind of networks is that the only additional equipment needed to configure this network are the HomePlug Ethernet adapters and the bridges. It is not necessary to install new wires in the house.

This technology can be also used to connect several apartments of the same building, and several nearby houses. In order to do that, the only necessary condition is that all the apartment and houses share the same power line. Figure 2 represents an example of this configuration.

Figure 2. PLC network for two houses

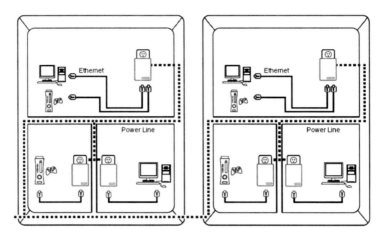

However, the power line medium has a high attenuation, and it makes difficult to communicate different devices in distant places. In order to solve this problem it is possible to use a Home-Plug repeater. In (González-Castaño et al., 2005) the authors developed a repeater at MAC level. Its main distinctive features are transparency (no planning is necessary) and availability (it is built from off-the-shelf hardware).

On the other hand, nowadays some companies are adding HomePlug circuits directly into multimedia home entertainment equipment to provide the high-speed connection for the multimedia content. Among the products attached with HomePlug circuits can be networked HDTV flat panel LCD or Network Area Storage (NAS) equipment (Gigle, 2009). By this way, it will not be necessary any additional equipment (like Ethernet adapters) to connect the electrical appliances to the PLC network.

COMMUNITY NETWORKING

Former community networks were originated as small local Internet companies managed by people that live in the same area with the objective of providing reliable access to the Internet almost all the time (Lasek & Rajaravivarma, 2007). The general structure of this network might consist of several large or small residential buildings as well as single family houses. All buildings are connected to the main server and the Internet access, which are located in one of the buildings (the "main building").

The main advantage of this kind of community networks is their low cost, because they usually use open source software and the cost of the hardware is very low. However, there are other two very important advantages. The first one is the faster access to information of local interest and the second one is the provision of services to the neighborhood, services of importance for (and customized by) the community. In this way, a community network can serve as a content sharing architecture for high-quality multimedia data (Chung et al., 2008). For example, after a community member acquires a live program via a broadcasting channel or a broadband access network, the other members can share the program without having to receive the same program from outside the network.

Existing Community Networks

Community networks have a number of requirements to be successful. First of all they have to be as open as possible to the users and to the developers. Being open enables anyone within the community to actively use the network and participate in the building. Another constraint is that the network should be reliable and low-cost at the same time. The 802.11b standard is frequently used because of the availability of equipment, open source drivers and the cost of the hardware. The standard is defined for home and office use, but with special antennas it is also applicable for crossing longer distances outdoors (up to a maximum of approximately 15 km).

Using these networks people can share resources among each other and they can connect to the Internet. These networks are established by a number of volunteers and they are operated and owned by a community of users. Some of these networks in Europe are the following: Athens Wireless Metropolitan Network, Athens (Greece); Wireless Leiden, Leiden (Netherlands); RedLibre, Guadalajara (Spain); SOWN, Southampton (United Kingdom).

On the other hand, in (Chung et al., 2008) authors adopt the fiber channel arbitrated loop (FC-AL), which is a typical structure to organize storage area networks (SANs), to build a community network. Such several advantages as high bandwidth, long distance support, and a fairness arbitration algorithm, make FC-AL suitable as a fast network connecting a large number of devices. The proposed community network, combined with consumer devices as personal video recorders (PVRs), serves as a content sharing architecture for high-quality TV programs in a residential area. After a community member acquires a live program via a broadcasting channel or a broadband access network, the other members can share the program without having to receive the same program from outside the network. However, the main inconvenient of this technology is that supporting scalable community networks in an economical way without using expensive fiber channel switches is very difficult.

PLC for Community Networking

In order to implement an extensive PLC community network the Homeplug AV standard is not appropriate. Therefore, it is necessary to take advantage of the solutions designed to provide last mile access to the Internet, because these solutions are able to connect the houses in a neighborhood in an efficient way.

One of the most promising specifications for the PLC last mile access has been developed by the Open PLC European Research Alliance (OPERA) project. The first phase of the OPERA Project (OPERA 1) started in January 2004 and it finished in December 2005. The members of the project were PLC operators, power utilities, technology providers, developers and universities. As a result of this project several operators started offering Internet access using the PLC technology. For example, in Spain, Iberdrola (Iberdrola, 2009), a power utility, offered a service of up to 2 Mbps. However, this service was given up in the year 2007 by several technical problems. The previous problems caused the beginning of OPERA 2.

The second phase of the OPERA Project (OPERA 2) started in January 2007 and it has finished in December 2008. This second phase solves the detected technical problems and it is considered as a very promising solution to offer PLC last mile access.

Figure 3 represents the structure of an electrical supply network. As can be seen, the indoor power line grids are linked together by the low voltage (LV) network and fed at the LV transformer. The electricity network which spans from each medium-to-low voltage transformer to the electricity users fed by those transformers is known as a LV cell.

The OPERA PLC network is composed of three types of nodes:

- **Head End Equipment (HE)** which connects the PLC network to the backbone network.

Figure 3. Structure of electrical supply networks

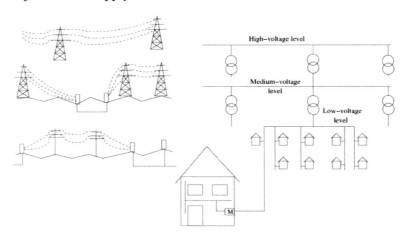

- **Frequency/Time Repeater Equipment (TDR/FDR)** which is used to extend the coverage of the network.
- **Customer Premises Equipment (CPE)** which connects the end user to a PLC access network.

The PLC connectivity within a LV cell is provided in a tree topology, with a HE which connects the LV cell to the medium voltage network. CPE's may be connected directly to the HE or through a series of repeaters. Repeaters increase the range of the PLC signal by retransmitting the signal that they receive either at a different frequency to the signal that they receive (Frequency Division) or in different time slots (Time Division). Figure 4 represents the distribution of a PLC cell.

Most of the features that allow more than 200 Mbps data transmission reside in the physical layer. Combined with the OPERA power mask mechanism, a continuous range of bandwidths from 3 to 33 MHz can be achieved. In its 30 MHz mode, OPERA systems provide a maximum physical throughput of 204.94 Mbps. For more information about OPERA, the reference (OPERA, 2009) can be consulted.

The necessary equipment to implement a community network using PLC technology are the CPEs, in order to connect the home networks

Figure 4. OPERA powerline access technology

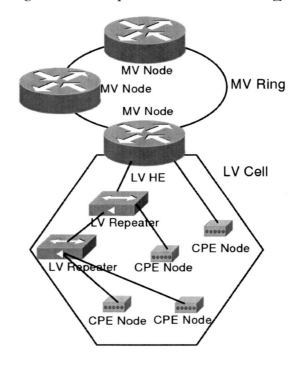

to the access networks, and the TDR repeaters, to extend the coverage of the access network. Nowadays, this equipment is only available by power utilities and PLC operators, but in the near future they would be accessible for the rest of users. It is important to say that both, HomePlug and OPERA networks, are perfectly compatible.

However, at the moment, another solution to connect the in-home HomePlug networks is to use the wireless technology, as it is used to implement wireless community networks. As it was previously presented, the 802.11b standard can achieve a distance of up to 15 km using special antennas.

PLC CHANNEL CHARACTERISTICS

It is necessary to take into account that there are several aspects of the PLC medium that make it difficult to share resources fairly. First, line attenuation increases exponentially with distance- which is in contrast to radio propagation- and it causes the problem of "hidden nodes" to arise more frequently, that is, two nodes that are unaware of each other may transmit simultaneously resulting in interference at the receiving node.

In addition, the PLC networks usually have several line discontinuities with impedance mismatches. Multipath reflections are generated at these discontinuities, which results in the time dispersion in the power line. The time dispersion is characterized by the delay spread (the total time interval during which signal reflections with significant energy arrive at the destination from the origin) and in a PLC network it typically amounts to several microseconds. The time dispersion generates overlapping between consecutive symbols (intersymbol interference (ISI)) (Abad et al., 2003).

On the other hand, all the electronic or electrical equipment connected to the power lines is regarded as noise resources on the power grid. Some of them generate broadband noise (electrical motors), while others (light dimmers and electrical switches) inject impulse of noise. In addition, the environment creates noise in the power lines: the so-called ingress (e.g., radio stations transmitting at medium and shortwave bands). Therefore, the various types of noise can be classified as follows (Abad et al., 2003):

- Background noise (stationary over periods from seconds to hours): produced by a sum of numerous low-power noise sources, by the ingress of radio stations transmissions in the medium, and by working electrical appliances
- Impulsive noise (varies from microseconds to milliseconds): caused mainly by light dimmers

In order to solve the previous problems, at the physical level HomePlug uses Orthogonal Frequency Division Multiplexing (OFDM). OFDM is a spectrum efficient modulation technique, which uses simultaneous transmission of a large number of narrow band carriers. These carriers divide a large frequency channel into a number of subchannels. Subchannels can differ greatly in their quality, defined by their S/N ratios. Adaptive coding modulation for each subchannel solves this problem by giving each subchannels an appropriate capacity, and by switching off those with a poor channel condition. A HomePlug device constantly monitors the powerline medium for sudden changes in the channel transfer function. Rate adaptation for each subchannel occurs in two ways: by changing the modulation between DQPSK (Differential Quadrature Phase Shift Keying) and DBPSK (Differential Binary Phase Shift Keying), and by changing the convolutional FEC (Forward Error Correction) rate between ¾ and ½.

PROVIDING VOD STREAMING USING P2P NETWORKS

In order to provide community networks with proper video services an appropriate middleware support is required to glue together the services and the infrastructures. The middleware organizes end-user applications and service providers in a way that is most suitable for the peculiar requirements of video services. In this respect, P2P (peer-to-peer) overlay networks are a very good candidate to achieve this objective. Overlay networks are virtual communications infrastructures implemented "on top of" an underlying physical network such as the Internet. There are two main reasons to build an overlay: to force some special routing in the network (e.g. multicast routing, or QoS routing) and/or to organize application-level entities in order to efficiently provide some form of service to large scale communities.

In addition, P2P technology can help to solve some problems which can appear in the PLC medium. As it was previously presented, all the electrical equipment connected to the power lines generate noise in the power grid, and the channel response of the PLC medium can change abruptly when electrical appliances are connected and disconnected. Therefore, it is possible that some outlets in the power grid are unavailable for a while, and it cannot be possible to perform a data transmission from those outlets. In these cases, the distributed nature of P2P technology can solve this problem: if the communication with one outlet is impossible, the communication mechanism can try to locate another outlet which provides the same information as the failed outlet.

P2P VoD Systems

P2P systems, initially developed to support IP multicast and file-sharing, have moved beyond that functionality. With the increasing bandwidth capacity provided by the Internet, they are also proving to be key technologies for the delivery of video streaming. The basic solution for streaming video over the Internet is the client-server model. However, the bandwidth provision at video servers must grow proportionally with the client population, and it makes the server based video streaming solutions expensive (Liu et al., 2008).

Recently, there have been a number of successful deployments for "live" P2P streaming. Coolstreaming (Zhang et al., 2005), which was built in March 2004, has been recognized as one

of the earliest large-scale P2P live streaming systems. It was constructed using a new concept called *data-driven* model, which is somewhat similar to the technique used in BitTorrent. Since then, there have been several commercial systems that have attracted a large number of viewers, such as PPLive (PPLive, 2004) and SopCast (Sopcast, 2008). However, it is more challenging to design a P2P VoD service than a P2P live streaming. The reason for this is that, although a large number of users may be watching the same video, they are asynchronous to one another; that is, different users may watch different portions of the same video at any given moment.

A fundamental component of any P2P VoD system is its overlay network structure, related to the organization of participating peers into an overlay structure. Based on this component, P2P VoD streaming systems can be broadly classified into *tree-based* and *mesh-based* categories. The tree-based systems have well organized overlay structures and they typically distribute video by actively pushing data from a peer to its children peers. One major drawback of tree-based streaming systems is their vulnerability to peer departure, which will temporarily disrupt video delivery to all peers in the subtree rooted at the departed peer. On the other hand, in a mesh-based P2P streaming system, peers are not confined to a static topology. Instead, peer relationships are established/terminated based on the content and bandwidth availability on peers. This kind of system tries to achieve fast file downloading by swarming. With this method, a file is divided into small size segments, and the server disperses them to different users. The users download from their neighbors the segments that they currently do not have. Since multiple neighbors are maintained at any given moment, mesh-based video streaming systems are highly robust to peer's failures. This chapter is going to concentrate on mesh-based approaches.

An important component of any mesh-based P2P VoD system is the content forwarding policy, that is, the way the multimedia content is stored and transmitted to each participating peer through the overlay. There are two main categories for this component: the *buffer-forwarding* and the *storage-forwarding* approaches. In the buffer-forwarding approach each client caches a limited number of segments around its current "play offset". In the storage-forwarding approach each peer stores a great number of random video segments at its local storage (such as hard disk).

The design of mechanisms to find partners with expected data is also a key aspect in mesh-based P2P VoD systems. It is very challenging to develop an efficient suppliers search mechanism among a large population of collaborative peers. Due to scalability concerns, the search structure should have a distributed structure with sub-linear search efficiency, for example, a distributed hash table (DHT). In the buffer-forwarding approaches, peers are sorted in the search structures by the play offset. Given the play offset as the sorting key, these methods support random search in a distributed manner. On the other hand, in the storage-forwarding approaches, each peer stores a number of segments randomly chosen from the segments of the video. In this way, there are multiple copies of each segment in the network. When a client wants to play a segment, it first looks for the supplying peers of that segment and then sends requests to those peers for the service.

The collaboration with partners for content delivery (*data scheduling*) is another very important and challenging problem in mesh-based P2P VoD systems. The scheduling scheme in mesh-based P2P VoD systems has two main components: how to evaluate and assign media requests from many peers, and how to construct media requests and send all of them to adequate neighbors. For the buffer-forwarding approaches, many heuristics have been proposed to address this issue, such as round robin or smallest-delay. Some recently proposed schemes use network coding to improve the system throughput. On the other hand, for the storage-forwarding approaches several modifica-

tions of the BitTorrent piece selection algorithm have been proposed. In addition, the use of rate-less coding, such as LT or Raptor codes, is a new alternative to address this issue.

In this work, different proposals to provide VoD services using P2P technology are reviewed. These proposals are classified and analyzed in order to give an overview of the state of the art until now.

Overlay Network Structure for P2P VoD

As it was previously said, a key aspect of any P2P VoD system is the organization of participating peers into an overlay structure. Based on this component P2P VoD streaming systems can be broadly classified into two categories: *tree-based* and *mesh-based*.

Tree-Based Network Structures

Tree-based P2P systems were originally designed to be used as multicast structures at the application layer without network layer support (i.e. IP). However, in this kind of system the users are synchronous, and in a VoD service the users' behavior is strongly asynchronous. Therefore, the use of a tree-based P2P system to provide VoD services is not direct. In the last years, several mechanisms have been proposed to solve this problem. For example, in (Guo et al., 2003) the authors designed a tree-based P2P VoD system inspired by the patching scheme (Hua et al., 1998). Users that arrive within a predefined time interval *T* constitute a session, and together with the server they form a tree-based P2P system. The server starts streaming the entire video over the tree, and when a new client joins the session, it joins the tree and retrieves the stream from it. In addition, the new client must obtain a *patch*, the initial portion of the video that it has missed (from the start of the session to the time it joined the base tree). The patch is available at the server

Figure 5. A snapshot of the patching scheme with T=10 at time 40

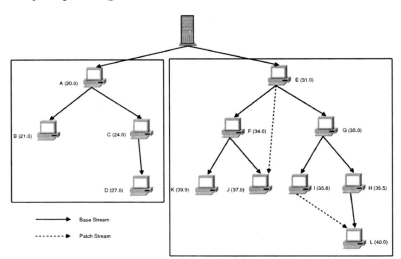

as well as other users who have already cached the patch. Figure 5 illustrates a snapshot of the solution above when a new user arrives at time 40. Each user is marked with its arrival time to the system. It shows two sessions, starting at time 20 and 31, respectively, with time interval *T* equal to 10. User E has to create a new session because its arrival time to the system (31) is out of time interval *T* of user A (20 + 10 = 30). One major drawback of tree-based streaming systems is their vulnerability to peer departure, which will temporarily disrupt video delivery to all peers in the subtree rooted at the departed peer.

Mesh-Based Network Structure

Peers in mesh-based P2P systems are not confined to a static topology, rather they dynamically connect to a subset of random peers in the system. This kind of system tries to achieve fast file downloading by swarming. With this method, a file is divided into small size segments and the server disperses them to different users. Peers periodically exchange information about their data availability, and the users download from their neighboring peers the segments that they currently do not have. These segments have to be received before their playback time.

In theory, the P2P system can support arbitrary number of concurrent users if individual users contribute sufficient uplink bandwidth. However, peers dynamically join and leave the system (peer churn phenomenom). Peer churn introduces dynamics and uncertainty into the P2P network and degrades the users' viewing quality. To fully utilize users upload bandwidth and achieve the highest downloading throughput possible, the segments at different users have to be different from each other so that there is always something to exchange. This is the so-called *diversity requirement* in mesh-based P2P system.

Block diversity improves the systems throughput, but could become a problem during playback time since video blocks have to provide continuity and be played in sequential order. Users need to receive blocks sequentially and not in a random order to watch the movie while downloading. Moreover, due to the asynchronous nature of VoD service, the users are interested in different parts of content at any given moment. The availability of different content blocks is also skewed by users' behavior. Therefore the challenge of designing a mesh-based P2P VoD scheme rests on the right balance between the overall system efficiency and the conformation to the sequential playback requirement for asynchronous users.

On the other hand, since multiple neighbors are maintained at any given moment, mesh-based systems are highly robust to peers' failures. This is the main reason why this chapter is going to concentrate on mesh-based approaches. Within this kind of networks, several suppliers search and data scheduling mechanisms for both storage-forwarding and buffer-forwarding approaches are going to be introduced.

Forwarding Approaches

The content forwarding policy is another important component of any P2P VoD system. By this, the way the multimedia content is stored and transmitted to each participating peer through the overlay is meant. There are two main categories for this component: the *buffer-forwarding* and the *storage-forwarding* approaches.

Buffer-Forwarding

In the buffer-forwarding approach, each client caches a limited number of segments around its current *play offset,* and it exchanges its cached segments with partners who have close play offset and can thus provide the expected data with high probability. The users need to search for such partners when joining or taking a VCR operation. Since the contents buffered in one peer are continuously changing, an additional structure is needed for the partner search. In this structure the participating peers organize themselves based on the playback progress. After locating the partners, the user collaborates with them to schedule the data transmission and exchange the content. This approach has two main drawbacks: First, a peer only redistributes the video, that it is currently watching, to the peers that are watching approximately the same video scene, and it does not redistribute the content that it has stored in its storage. Second, the upload bandwidth of the idle peers cannot be utilized, since they have no buffered content.

Storage-Forwarding

In the storage-forwarding approach each peer stores a great number of random video segments at its local storage (such as hard disk). This approach can be used when peers have a large storage capacity. For example, in Vmesh (Yiu et al., 2007) each peer keeps a list of peers who have the previous and the next video segments. Following the list, it can quickly find the peers with the next requested segments. Furthermore, a peer also keeps a list of peers storing the same segment for load balancing purpose. If a node is loaded, it redirects some of its requests to other peers on its list. The main drawback of this kind of systems is the need to have a big storage capacity in order to achieve a good performance. In addition, the upload bandwidth of the peers has to be high enough to support several connections.

Suppliers Search

A key aspect in mesh-based P2P VoD systems is the design of mechanisms to find partners with expected data. It is very challenging to develop an efficient suppliers search mechanism among a large population of collaborative peers. Due to scalability concerns, the search overlay should have a distributed structure with sub-linear search efficiency. Today, some distributed structures have been proposed with logarithmic search efficiency, for example, the DHT (distributed hash table) structure.

Searching in Buffer-Forwarding

In the buffer-forwarding approaches, peers are sorted in the distributed search structures by the play offset. Given the play offset as the sorting key, these methods support searching mechanisms in a distributed manner. However, the maintenance cost of these search structures is not trivial, since all peers need to be registered in the structure. Some buffer overlapping may occur among the

Figure 6. Neighbor distribution over rings for peer P

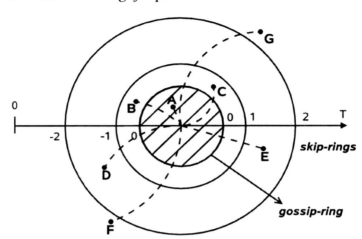

different nodes, and removing the nodes whose buffer range is fully covered by other nodes does not reduce the total buffer coverage. The BAS (buffer-assisted search) structure (Chi et al., 2007) tries to maintain as few peers as possible for better search efficiency. In other words, it wants to minimize the search structure size without sacrificing the search effectiveness. This problem can be formulated as the Minimum Buffer Cover (MBC), which is a variation of the well-known NP-hard problem Minimum Set Cover.

However, there are other systems that use more novel management schemes. For example, in RINDY (Cheng et al., 2007), a video is divided into a series of timeslots which encapsulate the content of one second, and the buffer window can contain at most w timeslots. The distance between any two peers is calculated from their current playing positions. For instance, the distance from peer j to peer i is $d_{ji} = cur_j - cur_i$. If d_{ji} is negative, then the playing position of peer j is behind of that of peer i and peer j is called a *back-neighbor* of peer i; otherwise peer j is called a *front-neighbor* of peer i. The neighbors are organized into a series of concentric, non-overlapping logical rings according to their relative distances (see Figure 6). The radius of the i-th ring is $w \cdot 2^i$ (the i-th ring covers the area between the two circles with radii

$w \cdot 2^{i-1}$ and $w \cdot 2^i$). A peer's innermost ring, whose ring number is zero, is responsible for collecting some neighbors with close playing positions (this ring is called *gossip-ring*). Outer rings are mainly used to improve the speed of lookup operations (these rings are called *skip-rings*). For the gossip-ring, each peer keeps track of at most m neighbors, called *near-neighbors*; for each skip-ring, a peer tries to maintain at most k *front far-neighbors* and k *back far-neighbors*.

Searching in Storage-Forwarding

In the storage-forwarding approach, depending on the capacity of its local storage, each peer stores a number of segments randomly chosen from the N segments of the video. In this way, there are multiple copies of each video segment in the network. When a client wants to play a segment, it first looks for the supplying peers of that segment and then sends requests to those peers for the service. If there is no supplying peer, the requesting peer requests the media server for the target segment as the last resort. In this section the searching mechanisms of two representative storage-forwarding proposals are presented.

In Vmesh (Yiu et al., 2007), each storage peer should register its segments in a DHT network in

Figure 7. In VMesh, peers keep a list of peers who possess the next/previous/current segments for random reeking and load balancing purposes

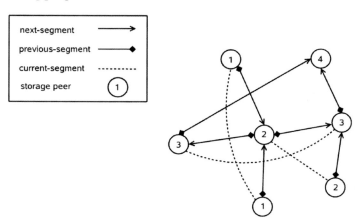

order to allow other peers to locate them. A new client searches for its segment of interest in the DHT network and starts playing the video when the requested data arrives. Then, it continues to request the next segment when the current one is nearly finished. In order to shorten the segment location latency, the peers also form an overlay mesh among themselves. This overlay mesh is represented in Figure 7. In this figure every circle represents a peer and the number inside represents the ID of the segment it holds. Each peer keeps a list of pointers (i.e., the IP addresses) pointing to some peers which store the next video segment and the previous video segment. By using the pointer list, clients could request for the locations of the next required segment. Besides, for the load balancing issue, each peer also keeps a list of pointers to some peers which are storing the same segment. If a node is loaded, it redirects some of its requests to other peers on its list.

BulletMedia (Vratonjic et al., 2007) also uses a DHT to store information about content location within the peers of the mesh overlay. However, the DHT does not store information at a segment granularity, instead, sets of contiguous segments are deterministically grouped into *chunks* (e.g., 100 segments in a chunk), and each one is assigned a unique key (*chunkId*). Each peer monitors

its local content cache and when all associated segments with a particular *chunkId* are present, the peer inserts an entry into the DHT. When a peer performs a seek operation, it determines the *chunkId* of the block and queries the DHT.

Data Scheduling

Data scheduling is an additional important and challenging problem in mesh-based P2P VoD systems. The scheduling scheme in mesh-based P2P VoD systems has two main components: how to evaluate and assign media requests from many peers, and how to construct media requests and send all of them to adequate neighbors.

Scheduling in Buffer-Forwarding

For the buffer-forwarding approaches, many heuristics have been proposed to address this issue, such as round robin or smallest-delay. These schemes suffer from inefficient use of network resources in large and heterogeneous networks. Some recently proposed schemes use network coding (NC) to improve the system throughput.

Wang & Liu (Wang & Liu, 2008) proposed directly applying the linear NC into VoD streaming. The original data segments are denoted as

Figure 8. BiToS structure

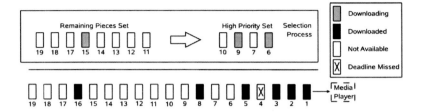

$c_1, c_2, \ldots, c_w$, where w is called *coding window (CW)*. A random linear coding on $\{c_i\}$ is a vector $f = \sum \beta_i \times c_i$, for $i \in (1 \ldots w)$, where the coefficient vector β is randomly generated in a finite field F_4 of size q. f_i also spans a range of w. If all f_i are linearly independent, once a node has a subset of f_i that spans range w, it can recover all the w original segments by solving a set of linear equations.

However, it is difficult to apply network coding to VoD systems because some segments may miss the playback deadline before being decoded, which causes severe performance degradation. In conventional network coding the CW is always the same as the number of expected segments. The deadline-aware network coding (DNC) (Chi et al., 2007) scheme tries to use a CW that is as large as possible for better coding efficiency while controlling the CW size so that no segment misses its play deadline. DNC estimates the CW to be the maximum number of segments that can be retrieved from the partners before the most urgent deadline. Then the problem is to find an assignment for retrieving segment *j* from partner *i*, so that the number of received segments is maximized before the most urgent deadline. The authors transformed the DNC problem into the Max-Flow problem.

Scheduling in Storage-Forwarding

For the storage-forwarding approaches several modifications of the BitTorrent piece selection algorithm have been proposed. On the other hand,

when individual peers are under common control (this is the case of residential home gateways or set-top boxes-STBs-under the control of a content provider), the use of rateless coding such as LT or Raptor codes is a new alternative to address this issue.

BitTorrent regards all data units, called chunks, as equally important, and it employs Tit-for-Tat (TFT) strategy in determining to which neighbors a peer serves content, that is, a peer favors a neighbor who transmits data in return. However, in a VoD system the highest priority is given to the chunks close to their playback time. BiToS (Vlavianos et al., 2006) attempted to support the VoD service by modifying the piece selection algorithm of BitTorrent. A peer in BiToS has three components, as shown in Figure 8: The *received buffer* stores all the data blocks that have been received, the *high priority set* contains the video blocks close to their playback time which have not been downloaded yet, and the *remaining piece set* contains the blocks that have not been downloaded. A block in high priority set is downloaded with probability *p* while one in the remaining pieces set is downloaded with probability *1-p*. By setting the value of *p* greater than 0.5, the blocks in the high priority set are given preference over the ones in the remaining pieces set to be downloaded earlier.

In (Suh et al., 2007) the peers are set-top boxes (STBs), which are under the control of a content provider. Each video is chopped into windows of contiguous data of size *W*, and it is pushed to a population of STBs (supposing that there are *M* STBs). The authors propose two data placement schemes: full-striping and code-based. The full striping scheme stripes each window in M blocks, each of size W/M, and each one is pushed to only one box. A full window is reconstructed at a particular box by concurrently downloading $M-1$ distinct blocks for the window from the other $M-1$ boxes. Code-based placement tries to reduce the maximum number of simultaneous connections that a box can serve to y (for some $y<M-1$). In order to achieve this it applies LT coding (Luby, 2002). It divides each window into k source symbols, and generates Ck coded symbols (C is called the expansion ratio). A viewer can reconstruct a window of a video by concurrently downloading any Cky/M distinct symbols from an arbitrary set of y boxes out of $(M-1)$ boxes.

Scalable Multi-Stream Coding

In P2P VoD systems, the rate at which a peer can receive a video will fluctuate because of peer churn. As peer come and go, the ratio of the offered upload bandwidth to the demanded upload bandwidth for a given video fluctuates. Buffering can be used to mitigate the effects of short term variations in bandwidth availability. However, if the demand for upload bandwidth exceeds the supply for a long period of time, buffering is ineffective. Therefore, to deal with long term variations in available bandwidth, *scalable multi-stream coding* is a natural candidate for P2P VoD system.

In the *single layer* coding with high-rate erasure coding (SLRS, (Li, 2004)) the media stream is broken up into "data units", so that each "data unit" is independently decodable. For example, a data unit can be a group of pictures (GOP). A data unit is then divided into M blocks and Reed-Solomon (RS) coding is employed to generate a total of N blocks for each data unit, with $N>>M$. Each block is assigned a unique block number. The blocks with the same block number from different "data units" are grouped to generate a substream.

These N substreams are distributed to up to N supplying peers. The receiving peer can recover the original video stream from any M substreams. However, a "data unit" is non-decodable if less than M blocks are received for this unit.

Layered Coding (LC) and Multiple Description Coding (MDC) divide the video in *several layers* and they distribute them separately in the network. Peers will reproduce the video with more or less quality in function of the number of layers that they receive. However, both mechanisms have fundamental differences. LC divides the video in different kind of layers: a base layer and one or more extra information layers. The peer needs the base layer in order to reproduce the video with a minimum quality and adding extra information layers the video wins quality. If a packet of the base layer is lost, the video is not reproduced during that time. MPEG-4 Fine Grain Scalable (FGS) (Li, 2001) is a popular scheme for creating layered coding. An FGS encoder encodes the video into a base layer and a scalable enhancement layer. The enhancement layer is then sliced into $M-1$ substreams, creating a total of M substreams.

On the other hand, MDC divides the video in M equal layers. It is only necessary a layer (either of them) in order to reproduce the video with a minimum quality and it wins quality receiving more layers, up to the maximum quality that is achieved receiving the M layers. MD-FEC (Puri & Ramchandran, 1999) is a popular scheme for multiple description coding. Each data unit (e.g., a GOP) is partitioned into M layers. For $k=1, ..., M$, the kth layer is further divided into k equal-length groups. A Reed-Solomon (RS) code is then applied to the k groups of each layer to yield M groups per layer. Description m is formed by packing bits from group m from all layers. At the receiver, if any m of the M descriptions are received for a data unit, the decoder can recover the first m layers of the original bitstream.

FUTURE RESEARCH DIRECTIONS

In the near future, community networks can serve as content sharing architectures for multimedia data among the near neighbors, providing services of importance to the community. These networks interconnect the homes in a neighborhood. In this chapter it has been proved that, among all the available technologies, power line communication (PLC) is a good candidate. The main advantage of this technology is that no new cabling or street digging is required to reach all the homes in the neighborhood. For this reason, it is predicted that in the near future several community networks will be implemented with this technology.

On the other hand, in the last years, P2P technology has been proved to be very appropriate to supply streaming services. Therefore, it can also be applied in a PLC community network environment, trying to exploit all the pros of the emerging P2P approaches, such as autonomicity, self-configuration, resilience, scalability, openness, and so on. In this environment, it is envisaged that storage-forwarding approaches will be more frequently adopted. The reason is that the media devices available in these networks will have a great storage capacity, and the available bandwidth will be great enough to support several connections.

With respect to the suppliers search and data scheduling mechanisms, we have the following comments. For the suppliers search mechanism, the formation of an overlay mesh among all the nodes, similar to that presented in Vmesh, will be a very promising solution. In addition, this mechanism will be combined with a DHT structure, in order to support the joining of new nodes and the VCR operations. This structure is likely to implement some additional mechanism, such as the one presented in BulletMedia, in order to improve the system performance.

The previous searching mechanisms can be complemented with a data scheduling mechanism based on the use of rateless coding. This coding

strategy can help us solve some of the problems of the PLC channel, such as the intersymbol interference (ISI) and the noise. A rateless code generates indefinitely coded symbols from a finite-length message, and its performance is measured by the least number of received symbols to decode the message perfectly. Rateless codes were first designed by Luby. He devised the well-known *LT codes* (Luby, 2002). Maymounkov and Shokrollahi independently designed improved rateless codes, namely *online codes* and *raptor codes* (Maymounkov, 2002), (Shokrollahi, 2006), respectively.

CONCLUSION

Community networks are expected to play a central role in the immediate future. People can make communities for content sharing among home networks as people do on current P2P file sharing communities. PLC is one of the most promising technologies to implement home networks. With multiple outlets in almost every room, residential power lines are the most pervasive networks in the home. In addition, PLC is not restricted to home networks; it also includes the low voltage access networks. With this organization, PLC can be considered an appropriate technology to implement community networks.

On the other hand, an appropriate middleware support is required to glue together the services and the infrastructures. The middleware organizes end-users applications and service providers in a way that is most suitable for the peculiar requirements of video services. In this respect, P2P overlay networks are a very good candidate to achieve this objective. Recently, there have been a number of successful deployments for live P2P streaming. However, it is more challenging to design a P2P VoD service than a P2P live streaming because although a large number of users may be watching the same video, they are asynchronous to one another.

An important component of any P2P VoD system is the content forwarding policy, that is, the way the multimedia content is stored and transmitted to each participating peer through the overlay. There are two main categories for this component: the buffer-forwarding and the storage-forwarding approaches. In addition, in P2P VoD systems suppliers search and data scheduling are identified as two main mechanisms. Several mechanisms for both storage-forwarding and buffer-forwarding approaches have been introduced.

ACKNOWLEDGMENT

This research has been supported by project grant TEC2007-67966-C03-01/TCM (CON-PARTE-1) and it is also developed in the framework of "Programa de Ayudas a Grupos de Excelencia de la Región de Murcia, de la Fundación Séneca, Agencia de Ciencia y Tecnología de la RM (Plan Regional de Ciencia y Tecnología 2007/2010)". Juan Pedro Muñoz-Gea also thanks the Spanish MEC for a FPU (AP2006-01567) pre-doctoral fellowship.

REFERENCES

Abad, J., Badenes, A., Blasco, J., Carreras, J., Dominguez, V., & Gomez, C. (2003). Extending the power line LAN up to the neighborhood transformer. *IEEE Communications Magazine, 41*(4), 64–70. doi:10.1109/MCOM.2003.1193976

Cheng, B., Jin, H., & Liao, X. (2007). Supporting VCR functions in P2P VoD services using ring-assisted overlays. In . *Proceedings of the IEEE International Conference on Communications, 2007*, 1698–1703. doi:10.1109/ICC.2007.284

Chi, H., Zhang, Q., Jia, J., & Shen, X. (2007). Efficient search and scheduling in P2P-based media-on-demand streaming service. *IEEE Journal on Selected Areas in Communications, 25*(1), 119–130. doi:10.1109/JSAC.2007.070112

Chung, S., Kim, E., & Liu, J. C. L. (2008). A scalable PVR-based content sharing architecture for community networks. *IEEE Transactions on Consumer Electronics, 54*(3), 1192–1199. doi:10.1109/TCE.2008.4637606

Cisco-Linksys. (2009). Retrieved from http://www.linksysbycisco.com/

Consumer Electronics Association. (2008). Retrieved from http://www.ce.org/

Gigle Semiconductor. (2009). Retrieved from http://www.gigle.biz/

González-Castaño, F. J., Gil-Castiñerira, F. J., Rodelgo-Lacruz, M., & Asorey-Cacheda, R. (2005). Off-the-shelf transparent HomePlug range extension. In *Proceedings of the 10th IEEE Symposium on Computers and Communications 2005,* (pp. 179-184).

Guo, Y., Suh, K., Kurose, J., & Towsley, D. (2003). P2Cast: peer-to-peer patching scheme for VoD service. In *Proceedings of the 12th International Conference on World Wide Web,* (pp. 301-309).

Gutierrez, D., Torres, L. M., Blasco, F., Carreras, J., & Riveiro, J. C. (2005). In-home plc ready for triple play. In *Proceedings of 2005 International Symposium on Power Line Communications and its Applications,* (pp. 366-370).

HomePlug Certified Products. (2009). Retrieved from http://www.homeplug.org/kshowcase/view

HomePlug Power Alliance. (2009). Retrieved from http://www.homeplug.org/

Hua, K., Cai, Y., & Sheu, S. (1998). A multicast technique for true video-on-demand services. In *Proceedings of the 12th ACM International Conference on Multimedia* (pp. 191-200).

Hughes, S., & Thorne, D. J. (1998). Broadband in-home networks. *BT Technology Journal, 16*(4), 71–19. doi:10.1023/A:1009639628587

Iberdrola. (2009). Retrieved from http://www.iberdrola.es/

Lasek, K., & Rajaravivarma, T. (2007). Design aspects of a hybrid community LAN environment. In . *Proceedings of IEEE SoutheastCon, 2007*, 669–673.

Li, J. (2004). *Peerstreaming: A practical receiver-driven peer-to-peer media streaming system*. Microsoft Research, Tech. Rep. MSR-TR-2004-101.

Li, W. (2001). Overview of fine granularity scalability in mpeg-4 video standard. *IEEE Transactions on Circuits and Systems for Video Technology, 11*, 301–317. doi:10.1109/76.911157

Liu, Y., Guo, Y., & Liang, C. (2008). A survey on peer-to-peer video streaming systems. *Peer-to-Peer Networking and Applications, 1*(1), 18–28. doi:10.1007/s12083-007-0006-y

Luby, M. (2002). LT Codes. In *Proceedings of the 43rd Symposium of Foundations of Computer Science* (p. 271).

Maymounkov, P. (2002). *Online codes*. New York University, Tech. Rep. TR2002-833.

NETGEAR. (2009). Retrieved from http://www.netgear.com/

Networked Media of the Future. (2007). White paper available at: http://cordis.europa.eu/fp7/ict/netmedia/publications_en.html

OPERA. (2009). http://www.ist-opera.org/

PPLive. (2004). http://www.pplive.com/

Puri, R., & Ramchandran, K. (1999). Multiple description source coding through forward error correction codes. In *33rd Asilomar Conf. Signals, Systems and Computers*.

Rose, B. (2001). Home networks: a standards perspective. *IEEE Communications Magazine, 39*(12), 78–85. doi:10.1109/35.968816

Shokrollahi, A. (2006). Raptor codes. *IEEE Transactions on Information Theory, 52*(5), 2033–2051. doi:10.1109/TIT.2006.872855

Sopcast. (2008). Retrieved from http://www.sopcast.org

Suh, K., Diot, C., Kurose, J., Massoulié, L., Neumann, C., Towsley, D. F., & Varvello, M. (2007). Push-to-peer video-on-demand system: Design and evaluation. *IEEE Journal on Selected Areas in Communications, 25*(9), 1706–1716. doi:10.1109/JSAC.2007.071209

Vlavianos, A., Iliofotou, M., & Faloutsos, M. (2006). Bitos: Enhancing bittorent for supporting streaming applications. In . *Proceedings of INFOCOM, 2006*, 1–6.

Vratonjic, N., Gupta, P., Knezevic, N., Kostic, D., & Rowstron, A. (2007). Enabling dvd-like features in P2P video-on-demand systems. In *P2P-TV '07: Proceedings of the 2007 workshop on peer-to-peer streaming and IP-TV*, (pp. 329-334).

Wang, D., & Liu, J. (2008). A dynamic skip list-based overlay for on-demand media streaming with VCR interactions. *IEEE Transactions on Parallel and Distributed Systems, 19*(4), 503–514. doi:10.1109/TPDS.2007.70748

Yiu, W. P. K., Jin, X., & Chan, S. H. G. (2007). Vmesh: Distributed segment storage for peer-to-peer interactive video streaming. *IEEE Journal on Selected Areas in Communications, 25*(9), 1717–1731. doi:10.1109/JSAC.2007.071210

Yu-Ju, L., Latchman, H. A., Newman, R. E., & Katar, S. (2003). A comparative performance study of wireless and power line networks. *IEEE Communications Magazine, 41*(4), 54–63. doi:10.1109/MCOM.2003.1193975

Zhang, X., Liu, J., Li, B., & Yum, T. S. (2005). Coolstreaming/donet: A data-driven overlay network for peer-to-peer live media streaming. In . *Proceedings of IEEE INFOCOM, 2005,* 2102–2111.

ADDITIONAL READING

Afkhamie, K. H., Katar, S., Yonge, L., & Newman, R. (2005). An overview of the upcoming HomePlug AV standard. In Proceedings of *2005 International Symposium on Power Line Communications and its Applications*. (pp. 400-404).

Cheng, B., Liu, X., Zhang, Z., & Jin, H. (2007). A measurement study of a peer-to-peer video-on-demand system. In Proceedings of *The 6th International Workshop on Peer-to-Peer Systems (IPTPS 2007)*.

Dutta-Roy, A. (1999). Networks for homes. *IEEE Spectrum, 36*(12), 26–33. doi:10.1109/6.809120

Gotz, M., Rapp, M., & Dostert, K. (2003). Power line channel characteristics and their effect on communication system design. *IEEE Communications Magazine, 42*(4), 78–86. doi:10.1109/MCOM.2004.1284933

Huang, Y., Fu, T. Z. J., Chiu, D. M., Lui, J. C. S., & Huang, C. (2008). Challenges, design and analysis of a large-scale p2p-vod system. *ACM SIGCOMM Computer Communication Review, 38*(4), 375–388. doi:10.1145/1402946.1403001

Katar, S., Krishnam, M., Mashburn, B., Afkhamie, K., Newman, R., & Latchman, H. (2006). Beacon schedule persistence to mitigate beacon loss in HomePlug AV networks. In Proceedings of *2006 International Symposium on Power Line Communications and its Applications*. (pp. 184-188).

Majumder, A., & Caffery, J. (2004). Power line communications. *IEEE Potentials, 23*(4), 4–8. doi:10.1109/MP.2004.1343222

Meng, H., Guan, Y. L., & Chen, S. (2005). Modeling and analysis of noise effects on broadband power-line communications. *IEEE Transactions on Power Delivery, 20*(2), 630–637. doi:10.1109/TPWRD.2005.844349

Mol, J. J. D., Pouwelse, M., Meulpolder, M., Epema, D., & Sips, H. (2008). Give-to-Get: Free-riding-resilient video-on-demand in p2p systems. In Proceedings of *SPIE, Multimedia Computing and Networking Conference (MMCN)*. (volume 6818, article 681804).

Pavlidou, N., Han Vinck, A. J., Yazdani, J., & Honary, B. (2003). Power line communications: state of the art and future trends. *IEEE Communications Magazine, 41*(4), 34–40. doi:10.1109/MCOM.2003.1193972

Pinho, L. B., & Amorin, C. L. (2006). Assessing the efficiency of stream reuse techniques in P2P video-on-demand systems. *Journal of Network and Computer Applications, 29*(1), 25–45. doi:10.1016/j.jnca.2004.10.009

Rose, B. (2001). Home networks: a standard perspective. *IEEE Communications Magazine, 39*(12), 78–85. doi:10.1109/35.968816

Tager, S., & Waks, D. J. (2002). End-user perspectives on home networking. *IEEE Communications Magazine, 40*(4), 114–119. doi:10.1109/35.995860

Yu-Ju, L., Latchman, H. A., Newman, R. E., & Katar, S. (2003). A comparative performance study of wireless and power line networks. *IEEE Communications Magazine, 41*(4), 54–63. doi:10.1109/MCOM.2003.1193975

KEY TERMS AND DEFINITIONS

Community Network: Community networks are the sum of all networks that interconnect devices in the homes and the homes in a neighborhood.

Home Network: Home network is a residential local area network, and it is used to connect multiple devices within the home.

IPTV (Internet Protocol Television): Television content that, instead of being delivered through traditional broadcast and cable formats, is received by the viewer through the technologies used for computer networks.

P2PTV: It refers to P2P applications designed to distribute video streams in real time on a P2P network.

Power Line Communications: It is the use of existing electrical cables to transport data, and it has been around for a very long time. Power utilities have been using this technology for many years to send or receive data on the power grid using the existing infrastructure.

Streaming Video: It is content send in compressed form over the Internet and displayed by the viewer in real time. With streaming video a Web used does not have to wait to download a file to play it.

Video-on-Demand: Video on Demand systems allow users to select and watch video content on demand. VOD systems either stream content through a set-top box, allowing viewing in real time, or download it to a device such as a computer, digital video recorder, personal video recorder or portable media player for viewing at any time.

Chapter 45
Service–Oriented Symbolic Computations

Dana Petcu
Institute e-Austria Timisoara, Romania

Georgiana Macariu
Institute e-Austria Timisoara, Romania

Alexandru Cârstea
Institute e-Austria Timisoara, Romania

Marc Frîncu
Institute e-Austria Timisoara, Romania

ABSTRACT

Service-oriented computing is an interesting paradigm not only for building business applications but also for scientific applications requiring a loosely-coupled communication system between its components. In particular, scientific applications involving symbolic computations that are both computational and data intensive have proved in the last years to be adequate for implementation in service-oriented architectures, mainly due to the standards promoted for communications or service discovery. This chapter discusses the main issues and problems encountered in the transition from the classical symbolic computations based on stand-alone computer algebra systems towards service-oriented symbolic computations, such as building services from legacy codes, discover, compose and orchestrate services, standardize the exchange data formats. Moreover, several new approaches to solve at least partially these transition problems have been recently implemented, tested and are revealed in this chapter.

1. INTRODUCTION

In the last decade the symbolic approach gained considerable recognition as a viable tool for solving large-scale engineering problems. Symbolic computations are currently applied in a number

DOI: 10.4018/978-1-61520-686-5.ch045

of disciplines where mathematical models and calculations take place. Advanced applications in many areas of computer science, such as computer aided design or software development, VLSI design, geometric modeling and reasoning, robot programming, are currently using symbolic computations. Also, symbolic methods have lately become popular in life sciences, in particular in studying human genome.

Symbolic solution of mathematical problems involves manipulations of symbolic objects, like logical or algebraic formulae, rules or programs. Simple examples for symbolic computations are polynomial operations, large integer arithmetic, or primitives. Unlike the numerical approach, one of the main goals of the symbolic approach is exactness. Developments in symbolic computing are lagging relative to numerical computing, mainly because of the inadequacy of available computational resources, both computer memory and processor power.

Due to the complexity of the symbolic algorithms, sophisticated tools, namely Computer Algebra Systems (CASs), were developed already three decades ago to help the progress in this field. Real problems for which a mathematical model can be extracted are often easily solved with these tools. Classical usage examples are coming from mechanics. Parametric studies are simplified on account of the possibility to extract a solution as an expression of the variable parameters. Maple and Mathematica are world-wide well known to be commercial solutions for general purposes. Other categories of CASs are the ones that are dedicated towards special fields or the ones designed with open sources – such as GAP for group theory or Kant for number theory. Due to either the commercial aim or the complexity of the implementation, CASs may be included in the category of legacy software.

Despite the progress in the hardware capabilities, the applicability of complex symbolic computing algorithms is still a problem since they may require computing and memory resources that are not available on a single machine. A classical example is the solution of polynomial equation systems with more than four variables and high polynomial degree – Groebner base detection is the theoretic solution, but in practice the detection cannot be done in reasonable time. Besides, the specialization of some CAS has the drawback to not be able to solve specific problems and the ability to collaborate with other CASs could prove of great importance in this case.

The solution found already three decades ago to reduce the time response of the complex symbolic algorithms implementations and increase the number of problems that can be solved with CASs was to use supercomputers and, more recently, computer clusters (HPC solution). Symbolic computing algorithms were designed to profit from the parallel computing paradigm.

The rapid development of network technologies within the last decade offered the opportunity to exploit considerable more computational power by combining the resources shared by interconnected supercomputing centers (Grid-based solution) or disparate computational resources (Internet-based solution). A pro argument in favor of Grid and Internet-based solutions besides the efficiency and the scale is the social one. The high cost of supercomputers and clusters, ownership and other administrative issues prevent regular user access. Their resources are reserved for well defined purposes. Given the context, sharing resources in collaborative architectures may represent a viable solution. Anyone participating in such structures can potentially access the resources, at virtually no cost, and has the opportunity to use this infrastructure. Thus, services may be implemented by users who want to share their latest achievement with their collaborators.

While CAS speedup and scalability are improved through parallel and Grid-based systems, the inter-operability and CAS capability enhancements are the basic issues encountered in loosely coupled architectures that offer, as main advantages, reusability of components and robustness of the obtained software solution. Service Oriented Architectures (SOA) tends to represent the main model of the applications built nowadays. Applications built upon Web services offer the advantage of standard mechanisms to describe components' interfaces and standard structure of the messages exchanged between components. In addition, the latest Grid technologies combine these capabilities with standard mechanisms that allow exposing resources of any kind, of hardware or software nature, at high level of abstraction and provide means to create reliable and secure computational infrastructure.

In order to explain the differences between the above described approaches, we consider the simple example of multiplying large integers with the Karatsuba algorithm (presented for example in (Grabmeier et al, 2003)). Being a recursive algorithm it can be easily split between several processors in order to obtain a fast response when two integers with billion of digits are multiplied (HPC solution). When we have a large set of smaller integers, say one million peers of integers with million digits to be multiplied, we can apply a solution based on volunteer computing using the computers of all our friends who are currently connected to the Internet (Internet-based solution). Yet if the set includes larger integers, we need a more professional solution – the cluster of clusters, such that in each cluster runs a parallel version of the Karatsuba algorithm (Grid-based solution). If the large integers are generated from instance in the frame of GAP and supposing the internal functions for multiplications are slow, the user could want to search from inside Maple for a fast service outside GAP to do the multiplication, e.g. in KANT, send the result back to GAP to find the group that is corresponding this result, and retrieve the group elements (SOA solution).

This chapter exposes the technical issues related to the process of creating a broad distributed architecture built upon symbolic computing services. It discusses the main issues related to the transition of the stand-alone tools for symbolic computations towards service-oriented architectures and presents several solutions that were proposed in the frame of an on-going research program SCIEnce, aiming to create a European symbolic computation infrastructure.

The chapter is organized as follows. The next section describes shortly the recent efforts to build service-oriented computing infrastructures based on Web and Grid services. Section 3 presents the approaches taken in the frame of SCIEnce. The final sections concern the future trends and conclusions.

2. OVERVIEW OF THE EFFORTS TO BUILD WEB AND GRID-BASED MATHEMATICAL SERVICES

A comprehensive overview of the achievements in Web and Grid-based symbolic computations at the level of 2004 has been provided in the book chapter (Petcu et al, 2006). We will point here only the principal issues and underline the influence of SOA on the field of symbolic computations reflected by the most significant developments reported in the last years. The classical design issues of distributed system that will be discussed in relation with symbolic computations are as follows: the common data representation format agreed between communicating parties, the technology that allows components of the architecture to interconnect and the reliable mechanism permitting services to be both advertised and discovered by potential clients.

2.1. Data Representation Problems and Solutions

The common understanding between components can only be achieved if the messages carry semantic information. This is mandatory with CASs, as every system has its own internal data representation format. In the context of mathematical formulae, semantic mechanisms must allow different software package to determine the meaning of messages. For example, in the formulae that expresses the area of a circle $A = PI * R^2$ it is significant to determine that R represents a variant while "PI" is a substitute for the well known mathematical constant π.

The OpenMath standard (OpenMath Society, 2004) was introduced in the last decade as a solution to solve the semantic problem. Representing mathematical formulae using the OpenMath standard may be done using either the XML encoding format, more suitable for communication over Internet, or the binary format. An alternative to OpenMath is MathML (also XML based). Its capabilities to describe mathematical formulae makes it more suited for presentation level, such as integration with HTML Web pages rather than for describing semantic reach content.

Most of the solutions that aimed to build an architecture based on CASs having different data representational formats considered using as an intermediate format one of the two formats presented above. Despite the efforts conducted in the last years, a small number of current CASs are able to manage objects using above mentioned formats. Therefore the inter-operability between the CASs is still an unsolved problem.

2.2. Interconnection Problems and Solutions

The experience gained in the last decades in the symbolic computing field emphasizes the need of a distributed architecture that is able to interconnect different CASs and combine their functionality for solving complex problems. Problems arising in particular fields of symbolic computing can be often solved only by using specialized CASs (see the SOA solution described in Section 1) or can require computational resources that may exceed available resources provided by a single machine (see the HPC solution described in Section 1).

CASs lack of support for network interactions represents a major drawback. These systems had been initially conceived as standalone command-line tools. Reengineering, an invasive procedure, could not be regarded as a viable approach owing to the high complexity of these systems. In spite of these obstacles, different approaches to create a symbolic distributed architecture were considered in the last two decades.

Recently, GEMLCA (Delaittre et al, 2005) offered a solution to deploy legacy code applications as Grid services, but it is not versatile enough to allow multiple calls that target the same application instance. A custom wrapper approach that would interact with the CAS using a tailored mechanism, ranging from I/O operations (in case of a CAS that can be used in command-line mode) to TCP/IP sockets (where available), represents a more appropriate solution.

Result of an academic activity, the MathWeb-SB (Zimmer et al, 2006) is a software bus that is able to combine mathematical services using brokers and CORBA technology. Distributed object technologies are not well suited for large scale applications spread over multiple computational domains. Another solution is JavaMath (Solomon 2001) which uses Java RMI technology to interconnect for example GAP and Maple. In its latest version, OpenMath is used to encode messages sent between a Java coordinator and remote GAP and Maple instances. Amongst the issues that arise with these implementations, security and lack of service discovery mechanisms are the most notable ones.

2.3. Advertise, Discover and Compose Services

Newer technologies such as Web and Grid services responded to the above described problems and were generally favored by all newest systems that aim to interconnect different CASs.

A general framework for the description and provision of Web-based mathematical services was designed within the frame of MONET (Smirnova et al, 2004) project whose purpose was to demonstrate the applicability of the semantic Web to the world of mathematical software. Contrary to MathWeb-SB shortly described above, this framework allows dynamic discovery of services based on published descriptions which express both their mathematical and non-mathematical attributes. Furthermore, a symbolic solver wrapper was designed to provide an environment that encapsulates CASs and exposes their functionalities through symbolic services. Maple has been chosen as computational engine in the initial implementation and is loaded from the XML configuration file. Later on, Axiom was used to demonstrate the ability to incorporate different computational engines without changes.

To complete MONET's framework, the Mathematical Services Description Language (MSDL) was introduced to describe mathematical Web services so that these services can be discovered by clients. It implements a service description model that uses a decomposition of descriptors into multiple inter-linked entities: problem, algorithm, implementation, realization. An implementation of the concept, MathBroker (Baraka et al 2005), is based on a Web registry to publish and discover mathematical Web services.

The GENSS project (GENNS Consortium, 2005) followed the ideas formulated by MONET with the aim to combine Grid computing and mathematical Web services using a common open agent-based framework. Its research was focused on matchmaking techniques for advertisement and discovery of mathematical services, as well as design and implementation of an ontology for symbolic computing problems. This concept proved to be well suited for mathematical services, but ontologies are not developed enough to represent the foundation of a reliable system.

Maple and Mathematica providers implemented software solutions tailored for clusters and local area networks. The Grid Computing Toolbox (MapleSoft, 2008) and gridMathematica (Wolfram Research, 2003) have similar goals. They both allow computations that can be executed in parallel to be distributed over a local area network or a cluster. Passing the boundaries of a local network induces communication latencies and security problems, such as open ports, that are not tackled by these products. While they cannot be accounted as wide distributed architectures, MapleNET (MapleConnect, 2006) and Web-Mathematica (Wolfgang Research, 2001) permit

setting up dedicate servers that can be accessed through Web pages. Thus, remote users have access to complicated mathematical solvers using simple interfaces available within Web browsers. Composing services is a challenge for the user.

The recently initiated project SAGE (Stein, 2008) proposes an integrated system in which users interact with the SAGE front-end and the contributing CASs are attached to the system through backend servers. SAGE is a free open-source mathematics software system that combines the power of existing open-source packages into a common Python-based interface. Unfortunately, in order to communicate with the CASs, SAGE uses a custom internal representation.

GridSolve (YarKhan et al, 2007), a component of one of the earliest Grid systems developed, the NetSolve, is a middleware between desktop systems equipped with simple APIs and the existing services supported by the Grid architecture—this API is available for Mathematica. Details about other two academic initiatives that targeted to demonstrate the suitability of Grid architectures for symbolic computing, MathGridLink and Maple2G, may be found in (Petcu et al, 2006). The latest developments in Grid technology fields, WSRF Grid services, tend to represent the dominant solution for securely exposed computational resources.

Recent solutions to the CAS inter-operability problem through service-oriented approach were proposed by an on-going international collaborative project – SCIEnce. The technical goal in the SCIEnce project is to create a framework that will allow services to be both provided and consumed by any CAS. An important distinction from previous designed frameworks is that it uses OpenMath to facilitate third party developers to expose their software using a new OpenMath-based communication protocol. The following sections present the latest achievements of the SCIEnce project relative to a particular middleware component that is based on Web and Grid services, namely SymGrid-Services. Lessons learned during the development process may be applied in other similar application domains.

3. SYMGRID SOLUTIONS

The main aim of the SCIEnce project (Symbolic Computation Infrastructure for Europe, http://www.symbolic-computation.org), funded in the frame of the European Commission Programme FP6 is to improve integration between CAS developers and application experts. The project includes developers from four major CASs: GAP, Maple, MuPAD and KANT.

The SCIEnce project is subscribing to two main research directions. The first one refers to software composability, through the development of standards and implementations for symbolic computation software to use Web services, Grid services and OpenMath technologies, allowing them to be efficiently composed to solve complex problems. The second one is concerned with the symbolic computations on Grids by designing middleware to allow the production of Grid-enabled symbolic computation systems and constructing research prototypes supporting security, scheduling and resource broking appropriate for complex symbolic computing applications on computational Grids.

From the development point of view, the main objectives are: the development of CASs extensions that permit inter-communication via a common standard service interface; the development of middleware to allow production of Web or Grid-enabled symbolic computation systems; promote and ensure uptake of recent developments in programming languages, including automatic memory management into a symbolic computation system.

The five years work-plan concerning the Grid services started in 2006 and includes the followings stages. The first one, already finalized, has produced a portable framework, SymGrid, that allows not only symbolic computations to ac-

cess Grid services but also symbolic components to be exploited as part of complex applications on a computational Grid (these components are described in Section 3.3). The second one, the current on-going stage, is referring to the development of resource brokers that will support the irregular workload and computation structures that are frequently found in symbolic computations (subsection 3.3.4). The last one, planned for the near future, will implement a series of applications that will demonstrate the capabilities and limitations of Grid computing for symbolic computations.

3.1. Issues, Controversies, Problems

The SymGrid framework tempts to tackle a series of problems which were not completely addressed by any of the available solutions for Grid-based symbolic computing services described in the previous section. More precisely, none of them conforms to all three of the following basic requirements (that are addressed by SymGrid):

a. Deploy and discover symbolic computing services
b. Access available services from within the symbolic computing system
c. Couple different symbolic services into a coherent whole

A general problem for distributed systems to be solved also in the frame of SymGrid is related to the user knowledge and burden. Hiding the complexity of the background system from the users of usual tools for symbolic computations is one of the steps to be undertaken by SymGrid. The users may not be aware of the existing tools that solve their problems or they may not be able to make the best choice of tool. Moreover it is not realistic to install all possible computer algebra packages locally on the user's computer, to maintain locally up-to-date working versions or to solve software licensing issues. Likewise different systems have different names for the same operation and wrap data differently. To deal with these issues, SymGrid offers a solution to deploy various symbolic computing tools over the grid and discover the operations performed by symbolic packages based on a standard taxonomy/semantic interface.

One novelty of SymGrid consists also in the fact that it is the only current middleware package that allows generic access to both Web and Grid symbolic and non-symbolic computing services from within a symbolic computing system requiring only minor additions to the system. Subsections 3.3.1 and 3.3.2 give a detailed description of how SymGrid achieves this.

One of the most important issues to deal with in the implementation of SymGrid is related to the integration of multiple symbolic systems in a single framework. This difficulty is a consequence of the heterogeneity characterizing the systems and their native platform, as well as of domain-specific patterns for computations in the new loosely coupled infrastructures oriented towards services. A related problem is the openness of the CAS to communication with external codes. An analysis performed in the frame of SCIEnce's programme in order to estimate the efforts involved in the transition towards service-oriented infrastructures revealed that only several CASs can be remotely accessible, still almost none of them use a standard data model for interactions with other CASs. A first solution to the problem is constructing special wrappers for the CASs (see subsection 3.3.2). Additionally, the SCIEnce's programme intends to promote a standard in the communication between existing tools for symbolic computations. The proposal for this standard is briefly described in subsection 3.2.

The composition of services is another challenge due at least to the following facts. The workflow is expected to be described from within CASs that have currently no such facilities. Interrupting, changing and rerunning a workflow is expected to be required in long running symbolic computations and the current mechanisms for workflow executions are not allowing these management facilities to be implemented in an easy way. Several solutions related to these issues are presented in subsection 3.3.3.

In order to permit efficient scheduling of symbolic computing applications on Grids, it is desirable to have scheduling mechanisms that can anticipate dynamic changes in parallelism for an application and respond to these changes by dynamically tuning the resources allocated to the application. The design of an adaptive prescient scheduler for symbolic computations is a difficult task to overcome. While solutions were proposed for iterative numerical codes, symbolic programs can be worse than numeric ones because of dynamic data dependencies, irregular parallelism (structure and workload), complex symbolic data structures or difficulty to estimate resource requirements. Details about how SymGrid handles this problem are presented in subsection 3.3.4.

A non-trivial issue is also to find the best examples highlighting the benefits of using the loosely coupled heterogeneous infrastructures and test suites to tune the system performance. Such an example that was already identified is the search for groups with orders within a given range of values. This problem requires two nested levels of parallelism, a search across and within families of groups of the same order. Moreover, it is characterized by a high irregularity because of different complexity for different groups and the variation in number of groups of each order. More examples can be found in (Freundt et al, 2008).

3.2. The Standard Proposal: Symbolic Computation Software Composability Protocol

OpenMath 2 (OpenMath Society, 2004) is the current standard for representing mathematical objects with their semantics. Its main idea is to allow object exchange between various programs,

Figure 1 Example of SCSCP procedure call

```
<OMOBJ>
    <OMATTR>
        <OMATP>
            <OMS cd="scscp1" name="call_ID" />
            <OMSTR>ieat_9055</OMSTR>
        </OMATP>
        <OMA>
            <OMS cd="scscp1" name="procedure_call" />
            <OMA>
                <OMS cd="SCSCP_transient_1" name="WS_factorial" />
                <OMI>3</OMI>
            </OMA>
        </OMA>
    </OMATTR>
</OMOBJ>
```

as well as object storing in databases and publishing on Web. Two encodings are allowed – XML and binary format.

In order to allow a simple way for communication between the CASs, a protocol called Symbolic Computation Software Composability Protocol (SCSCP) has been recently developed with the hope to become soon a standard in the field of service-oriented symbolic computing. SCSCP enables different mathematical software packages not only to exchange mathematical objects, but also to request calculations and store and retrieve remote objects, either locally or remotely. The first proposal can be found in (Konovalov & Linton, 2007).

The protocol is XML-based. In particular, the protocol messages are written in OpenMath language and its TCP-sockets-based implementation uses XML processing instructions to delimit these messages or to indicate major failures that may arise during the processing of a request. An example of a SCSCP message representing a call for a procedure called WS_factorial which computes the value of 3! exposed by a SCSCP-enabled CAS is presented in Figure 1.

SCSCP specification defines semantic and technical descriptions and allows sequences of OpenMath-encoded messages to and from CASs through remote procedure calls, returning the result

of a successfully completed procedure and a signal about the procedure termination. The protocol supports calling functions with mathematical objects as arguments, on either a local or remote system, as well as sending back successful results or failure reports. It also supports basic options such as limits on memory or CPU and information like memory or CPU time used.

In SCSCP the protocol messages are represented as OpenMath objects (OM). Both transmission of actual mathematical objects and references to them are supported. The service designer can choose the data to be represented as strings, binaries or in other formats (Om-foreign, like in MathML). Moreover, SCSCP has support for remote objects: the client may indicate a preference for the reply to contain a full mathematical object or a reference to that same object. The last option serves in the case a client prefers to let almost all computations be performed remotely and details of the mathematical objects are not transmitted unless necessary. The transmission of references can be used in subsequent requests too. For example, in the case it is needed to construct and manipulate large mathematical objects on Grids it is possible to send over the Internet only the properties the user is interested in.

Initially a Content Dictionary (OpenMath CD) named *cascal1* was developed to define three main kinds of messages, respectively for procedure call, completeness and termination (Konovalov & Linton, 2007). Options that may be added to the call message are referring to runtime, debug level, minimum and maximum memory, returned object or returned cookie. The information that may be supplied with the result is referring to runtime, memory or cookie.

Currently two Content Dictionaries for SC-SCP, called *scscp1* and *scscp2,* are available (Roozemond, 2008). The objects in the *scscp2* CD are more complex than those in *cascall1.* The symbols in this CD serve two purposes: on the one hand, working with remote objects through store, retrieve and unbind and determining the procedures a system supports through getting allowed heads, signature, service description, or setting the signature or service description.

Using SCSCP, a CAS may offer services for the following clients: Web services using SOAP/HTTP protocols serving some remote clients; Grid middleware; another instance of the same CAS (in a parallel computing context); or a different CAS running on the same computer or remotely.

The specification assumes two possible ways of implementation. The first is a standard socket-based implementation through which a CAS can talk locally or remotely via ports with a SCSCP service (in this case, not a Web service). Communication takes place using port 26133, reserved for SCSCP by the Internet Assigned Numbers Authority (IANA). The other implementation is a Web service using standard SOAP/HTTP wrappings for SCSCP messages.

SCSCP support, both as server and as client, is currently available for development versions of GAP, KANT, and MuPAD. Examples of SCSCP usage within GAP and MuPAD have been recently provided in (Freundt et al, 2008). In particular, the GAP implementation of the SCSCP allows GAP to work as an SCSCP server and client: communication goes via TCP/IP protocol and handles OpenMath encoding, the new symbols from the *scscp1* and *scscp2* CDs are supported,

as well as OM attributes and references. The user-level functionality provided by the GAP package refers to installing procedures available as SCSCP services, running the SCSCP server, sending request to the server and getting result, and store/retrieve procedures allowing to work with remote objects.

Furthermore, a Java implementation of SCSCP was developed as a framework to enable third party developers to expose their software easily (Freundt et al, 2008).

One of the most important advantages of using SCSCP is the fact that a CAS user does not need to know details about the remote CAS that he/she invokes. For instance, he/she uses the GAP syntax to invoke from GAP through SCSCP a computation that is done in KANT without knowing how the object described in GAP will look in KANT. This is possible due to standardized way of transmitting the mathematical objects.

3.3. SymGrid Components

This subsection presents the main components and subcomponents of SymGrid, the service-oriented open framework proposed by SCIEnce. The two main components, shown in Figure 2, are the SymGrid-Par which supports the construction of high-performance applications on computational Grids, and the SymGrid-Services which manages Web and Grid services.

SymGrid-Par is the most prominent and complex service provided by the SymGrid. Its design and implementation are described in details in (Hammond et al, 2007; Al Zain et al 2007b; Al Zain et al 2008). The SymGrid-Par middleware is used to orchestrate computational algebra components into a parallel application and allows parallel symbolic computations to be executed on a computational Grid. SymGrid-Par components communicate using the Symbolic Computation Software Composability Protocol (described in section 3.2), which in turn builds on OpenMath. SymGrid-Par provides an API for parallel hetero-

Figure 2. The SymGrid middleware

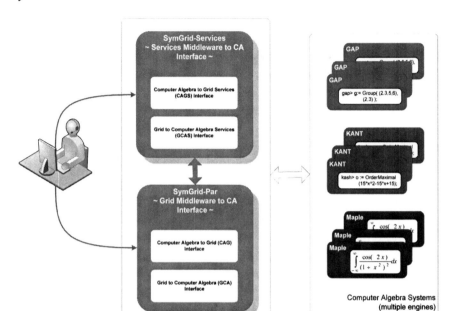

geneous symbolic components, which extends the Grid-GUM (Al Zain et al 2007a), and has two generic interfaces: the CAG and GCA interfaces (acronyms for Computer Algebra to Grid and Grid to Computer Algebra). The former consists of the CAS to Grid middleware, that links CASs to the Grid-GUM and the latter represents the Grid middleware to CAS, which links the Grid-GUM to these systems. The aim of the CAG/GCA interfaces is to enable CASs to execute on computational Grids, e.g. on a loosely-coupled collection of Grid-enabled clusters. SymGrid-Par orchestrates symbolic components into Grid applications by allowing ultra-lightweight thread creation, distributed virtual shared memory, multi-level scheduling, automatic thread placement, automatic datatype-specific marshalling/unmarshal-ling. A GAP library has been built as demonstrator.

The SymGrid-Services middleware is used to access, from a CAS, Grid and Web services and to access and compose the CASs facilities deployed as Grid and Web services. It is based on the WSRF standard that ensures uniform access to Grid and Web services. A GAP library is available also for this SymGrid component. As in the case of the SymGrid-Par, the SymGrid-Services have two interfaces to be detailed in the next sections: the CAGS (Computer Algebra to Grid Service) interface and the GCAS (Grid to Computer Algebra Service) interface. CAGS links CASs to external Grid or Web services, while GCAS uses Web and Grid services for exposing and integrating CASs into a service-oriented architecture and allowing service composition. The following sections are referring the SymGrid-Services.

3.3.1 EXTERNAL ACCESS: CAGS Solution to Access Web and Grids from Within a CAS

CAGS allows CASs to leverage their computing capabilities with the ones offered by external Grid or Web services. An example of application was given in the SOA solution for large integer multiplication presented in Section 1. More us-

Figure 3. UML component diagram of CAGS

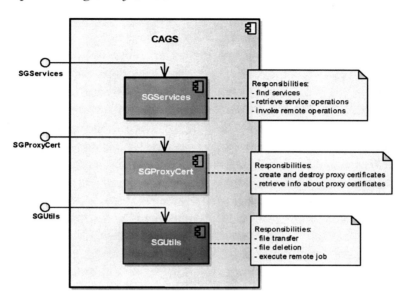

age examples are provided in (Petcu et al, 2008). Details about the implementation are furnished in (Cârstea et al, 2007a). Here we will present shortly the CAGS functionality.

A CAS user must be able to: discover services, connect to remote services, call remote operations, run jobs and transfer files in a seamless fashion. Therefore SymGrid-Services's CAGS provides three interfaces each implemented by a corresponding component as depicted in Figure 3.

The first component, SGServices, provides three kinds of operations: retrieval of a list of services registered with a certain Web or Grid services registry, retrieval of signatures for the operations exposed by a service and call facilities to remote operations. The second component, SGProxyCert handles issues arising from the need to support 'single sign-on' for users of the Grid and delegation of credentials, namely the creation and destruction of proxy certificates, retrieval of information about the owner of a certificate and about the lifetime of a proxy certificate. The last component, SGUtils provides additional functionality for file transfer, file deletion and remote job execution.

All CAGS components are implemented in Java. A CAS can access the functionality provided by these three components by launching a script which creates a child process executing CAGS. This process then communicates with the CAS using standard input/output streams to pass parameters and return values. The same mechanism can be used by any other system which requires the capabilities of CAGS.

One of the initial SymGrid-Services targets is GAP. A demonstrator library of GAP functions was built to allow a GAP user to access the CAGS functionality without the need to know the details of the implementation. Since Java cannot be invoked directly from a GAP program, the solution described above is to invoke instead a shell script that starts a Java program using the *InputOutputLocalProcess* function of the GAP system. For the GAP user this is transparent. He simply calls the GAP functions defined in the additional library just as he would call any other GAP function.

Three categories of services were used for the initial tests: general Web services, domain-specific symbolic Web services such as those provided by MONET and GENSS, and simple test Grid services deployed on a single cluster and wrapping publicly available CASs (CoCoA, Fermat, GAP, Kant, Macaulay, MuPAD, PARI, Singular and Yacas). The test services were arranged in a Globus container (registry). The registry can be interrogated to obtain the list of services registered to that registry (for example, one can obtain the list of service URLs representing all services in the registry whose names include a specific substring). Once the address of a service is known, CAGS can supply the signatures of the operations exposed by the service (for example the list of operations supported by that service that relate to OpenMath). Based on the list of the exposed methods, the user can then discover all details that are needed to call a specific method.

For instance, the GAP code snippet below retrieves the list of Grid services registered with the Globus service container running at the address matrix.info.uvt.ro and afterwards lists the operations provided by the Grid service with the URI https://matrix.info.uvt.ro:8082/wsrf/services/GapService. The last line of code sends a GAP command (a classical symbolic operation on integers, factorization) for remote execution.

SG_GridServiceList("https://matrix.info.uvt.ro:8082/wsrf/services/","");

SG_OperationList("https://matrix.info.uvt.ro:8082/wsrf/services/GapService", "");

SG_CallOperation("http://matrix.info.uvt.ro:8082/wsrf/services/GapService", "execute", "FactInt(5645648)");

3.3.2. WRAP: GCAS Solution for Wrapping CAS as Web and Grid Services

As shown in subsection 3.1 one major issue for Grid-enabled symbolic computing is represented by the deployment of symbolic services. Consider for example the benefit of exposing a service that allows the computation of the exact derivate of an input function to be used at run-time by a code implementing a numerical method that requires a partial derivate of a multi-variables function provided by the user.

SymGrid-Services component GCAS aims to expose CASs functionality as services running on SymGrid infrastructure. The interaction between these services can lead to increased computing efficiency required for solving complex symbolic problems and consequently, it was considered necessary for GCAS to be able to also compose the deployed services.

Figure 4 presents the overall structure of the GCAS component of SymGrid-Services. The CAS Server is one of the main components along with the *Client Manager* and the *Orchestration Engine* that are presented in subsection 3.6. The CAS Server was first presented in the paper (Cârstea et al, 2007c) and its current improvements are presented in (Macariu et al 2008). The main functionality of the CAS Server is to enable any CAS to expose its functions for remote access. Note that several CASs can be exposed through the same CAS Server at the same time. For security reasons, the CAS Server will not allow a client to invoke any CAS function. Further, the client can find what functions are exposed by interrogating the CAS Server.

The integration of legacy software (i.e. CASs) in service oriented architectures must consider three major issues: wrapping the legacy system, exposing technology and data encoding.

The first and most important issue the CAS Server component design must deal with is to find ways to expose CAS functions in order to make them available by means specific for Web service invocation. A significant number of existing CASs is not conceived to be remotely accessible. Most of them allow interaction only through command-line interfaces. Only few of them have special facilities like socket connec-

Figure 4. The GCAS component

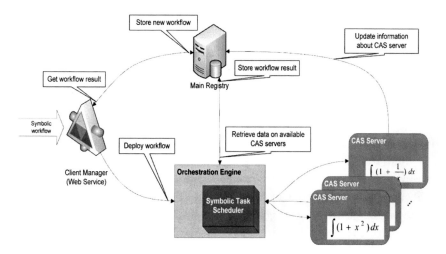

Figure 5. The CAS server

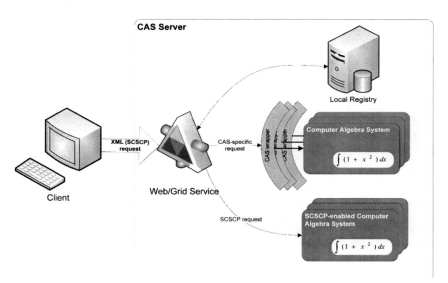

tions or multi-threading. Generally, redesigning these systems to allow modern communication with outside world cannot be achieved easily. Due to these reasons, SymGrid-Services proposes a wrapper approach for integrating CASs into the Grid while simultaneously allowing integration of CASs which implement the SC-SCP protocol described in the next subsection (see Figure 5).

Wrapping legacy software and exposing their functionality using service technologies involve creation of a three level architecture at the server side: the Web/Grid service, the CAS wrapper and the CAS. This architecture is illustrated in Figure 5. The service has the role of receiving function calls from the client as SOAP messages, solving them using one of the underlying CASs and returning the result(s) of the computation to the client. Direct communication with the CAS is handled by the CAS wrapper specially built for that CAS.

The mechanism used by the wrapper to interact with the legacy software component depends on the native technology of the legacy component. The wrapper may use TCP/IP sockets, redirecting of the I/O streams for a process, input and output files or it may have to use JNI encapsulation. On a regular basis, a SymGrid wrapper communicates with a CAS by redirecting I/O streams in a program level encapsulation style. This is the approach that has been used for the GAP and the KANT computer algebra systems. A different mechanism was employed for Maple, since this CAS provides a Java API for interaction with other systems.

As it can be seen in Figure 5, the CAS Server also exposes functionality provided by CASs which implements the SCSCP protocol. At the moment SCSCP versions of GAP, Kant, MuPAD and Maple are under development. For such CASs the communication with the CAS uses TCP/IP sockets. Since the protocol used for communication is the same for all CASs, there is no need for a specific wrapper for each CAS and the service can communicate directly with the CAS.

Exposing full CAS functionality is difficult because of the high number of functions that a CAS implements. As shown in the experiments described by Cârstea et al (2007a), a service with many operations exposed makes impossible the dynamic creation and invocation of the service achieved by the CAGS component. Moreover, the WSDL 2.0 standard explicitly forbids that operations with the same name exist within the same service definition, while in a CAS functions from different libraries can have the same name. Another issue is security since exposure of certain functions allowing changes in the execution environment could represent a security gap.

The approach considered by SymGrid-Services is for the Grid service to provide a generic operation that receives the CAS function name and

parameters as inputs. Nevertheless, this solution has some drawbacks too. Deploying such services into a service container is not efficient as obtaining the list of exposed functions and assuring access to them on a per user basis is not trivial. To overcome this situation, a registry mechanism was created to allow the administrator of the server to register CAS functions into a database. The general execution schema associated with this approach is composed from several steps. Initially, the client invokes the remote operation on the service. Then the server verifies that the CAS is available on the server and that the function encoded in the call object is available. If successful, the server returns a unique job identifier that identifies the job and starts the execution. At a later moment the client will use the job identifier to retrieve information about the status of the job and the results of the computation (the interaction between the client and the server is carried out in an asynchronous manner).

As mentioned above, a simple tool allows the administrator of the machine to register into a CAS registry the CAS functions he wants to expose. Every function exposed by a CAS will have an entry in the registry. A method that does not appear in this registry is consequently considered inaccessible for remote invocations (for example each CAS' system functions). Each local CAS Server registry will send periodically information about exposed functions to the main registry used by Client Manager and Orchestration Engine components of GCAS.

One important aspect of the interactions between the client and the legacy system is the model used for data exchange. The data model used by the client must be mapped to the internal data model of the legacy software. Currently, the available CASs use a variety of encoding standards, from plain text to XML structured documents. Thanks to the benefits involved in representation and manipulation of data in a structured manner, the XML standard was adopted as the natural choice for machine to machine interaction. XML representation of mathematical objects was achieved by OpenMath standards (see the next subsection). The SCSCP-enabled CASs in Figure 5 can process such OpenMath requests received through a socket. This simplifies the mechanism for accessing them as the service can send the function calls directly to them without the need of using an additional CAS wrapper.

The CAS Server is implemented using Java SDK with supporting tools and software from Globus Toolkit, Apache Axis and Tomcat, as well as RIACA's OpenMath Java API. The generic services implemented in the CAS Server architecture invoke CAS functions that are applied to OpenMath objects as described in the following subsection.

3.3.3. COMPOSE: SymGrid-Services' Solution to Compose Web and Grid-Based Symbolic Services Using Workflows

Remember the example provided in Section 1 concerning the SOA solution where within Maple the user wants to call several services that are pipelined in order to provide the final result.

The solution to a complex problem using multiple procedures is often described using workflows which couple different symbolic services. Currently workflow implementation technologies are able to combine the results obtained by invoked black-box components like software services. While most of the classical composition examples are referring to static composition that is achieved at design time by specifying all the details of the composition, in dynamic composition of services, the decision on which services have to be called in order to solve a particular problem is done at runtime. Implementing dynamic composition of services is a clear requirement in the case of symbolic computations services due to the high degree of usage in research that imposes to allow any combination of services.

Specialized languages for describing Web service workflows are usually XML based lan-

guages (e.g. BPEL) because they are well suited for automated machine processing. Graphical interfaces usually used to create workflows and assist in deploying the fresh described workflow are not useful for a CAS user who wants to write the workflow in its known CAS environment.

Dynamic discovery techniques have been recently proposed in the frame of projects like MONET or GENSS that were described in Section 2. The discovery process in MONET uses special ontology language and problem description language to retrieve the right mathematical services by interrogating modified UDDI registries. A similar agent-based approach is also used in GENSS. SymGrid-Services' approach is different: the discovery process uses as selection criterion the functionality implemented by a certain service to handle each OpenMath call object.

The solution implemented by SymGrid-Services dynamic generation of BPEL workflows and several examples proving the benefits of the approach have been recently described in (Cârstea et al 2007b). One important aspect of the proposed approach is that the service composition is achieved using standard workflow patterns without any modification of the underlying CASs.

The main components of SymGrid-Services/GCAS necessary for carrying out the workflow execution and managing related issues are the Client Manager, the Orchestrator Engine that executes the workflow, and several CAS Servers that expose CAS functionality as Grid services.

The construction and deployment of composed Grid services in a dynamic fashion is available through the CAS' usual interface. General workflow patterns are helping the CAS user to describe the sequence of service calls. The resulted description is deployed and executed by SymGrid components implemented using Java SDK relaying on the ActiveBPEL workflow engine and PostgreSQL database servers.

Several patterns that apply to SymGrid services composition were pointed out in (Cârstea et al 2008a). The most common workflow patterns are the following. A sequence pattern represents the sequential execution of two or more tasks. If several tasks may be executed in parallel a parallel split pattern can be used. A group of tasks may have to be executed only if a condition is met – such behavior may be expressed using conditional patterns. The exclusive choice pattern selects, amongst several branches, a branch that should be executed. The multichoice pattern allows several branches to be executed in parallel if the individual condition for each branch is met. There are also situations when the same action must be applied several times to various arguments – this behavior is expressed as the multiple instances with prior knowledge pattern, when the exact number of iterations is known, and as multiple instances without prior knowledge, when an external call is expected to end the loop execution. A common functionality is to enable the user to interrupt the execution of a running process – the cancel pattern.

The communication models used to interact with partner services can be abstracted as several conversational patterns. A common pattern, the request/reply pattern, allows a synchronous invoke of a partner service. The one way invocation pattern covers the situation when the sender only wants to transmit a message to the partner service and does not expect a response message to be issued so the client may continue its execution. Asynchronous communication is useful when the required computation time is relatively long. A compound pattern that is particularly useful is a combination of two request/reply patterns, where the reply message is used only as an acknowledgment (when the service client sends a request and receives the result at a later time as a callback message). In the GCAS component, the Orchestration Engine uses non-blocking asynchronous communication between the workflow and the partner CAS Servers.

The Client Manager component uses BPEL to express workflows built using the above patterns. Several patterns, such as the sequence pattern and parallel/split pattern, have direct correspondence with existing BPEL activities. Yet most of the

patterns, such as conversational patterns, were implemented in SymGrid-Services using complex constructions and the Java API offered by the ActiveBPEL engine. Conversational patterns cannot be implemented straight-forward because they require adding the corresponding invocation task, input and output variables and links with partner WSDL documents to the resulting BPEL document. The lack of prior knowledge about the structure of the new workflow imposes that these details are generated just before deployment. Predefined structure of the Web/Grid services' interfaces and a standard encoding format for the data representation, namely OpenMath, makes composing these services possible. In the context of arbitrary Web services, implementing conversational patterns would be impossible without additional semantic information being available. Besides, patterns like exclusive choice or multiple choices were implemented both with and without synchronization.

The composition of services is specified at the client level in an Abstract Workflow Language (AWL) that is a simple XML language, simpler than BPEL. In this way it is easier for any CAS developer to extend the CAS with support for constructing complex workflows. As an example, a GAP package was developed. This package defines GAP functions which build workflows using the AWL language transparently to the CAS user. Using AWL instead of BPEL also enables future extensions of the Client Manager component which could interact with workflow engines which use a language distinct from BPEL.

Figure 6 presents a workflow where two tasks are executed in parallel. Each of the tasks is defined using SCSCP OpenMath objects that will be sent to CAS Servers exposing a GroupIdentificationService function, respectively a GroupByIdNumber function. The GroupIdentificationService determines the number in the GAP Small Groups Library of the permutation group given by its generators. The second task retrieves the group [24, 12] from GAP Small Groups Library.

Figure 6. A workflow example describing parallel tasks

```
<workflow xmlns="http://ieat.ro">
  <parallel>
    <invoke invokeID="invoke_0">
      <casid>GAP</casid>
      <call>
        <OMOBJ>
          <OMATTR>
            <OMATP>
              <OMS cd="scscp1" name="call_ID" />
              <OMSTR>ieat_9055</OMSTR>
            </OMATP>
            <OMA>
              <OMS cd="scscp_transient_1"
                name="GroupIdentificationService"/>
              <OMA>
                <OMS cd="group1" name="group" />
                <OMA>
                  <OMS cd="permut1" name="permutation" />
                  <OMI>2</OMI><OMI>3</OMI><OMI>1</OMI>
                </OMA>
                <OMA>
                  <OMS cd="permut1" name="permutation" />
                  <OMI>1</OMI><OMI>2</OMI><OMI>4</OMI><OMI>3</OMI>
                </OMA>
              </OMA>
            </OMA>
          </OMATTR>
        </OMOBJ>
      </call>
    </invoke>
    <invoke invokeID="invoke_1">
      <casid>GAP</casid>
      <call>
        <OMOBJ>
          <OMATTR>
            <OMATP>
              <OMS cd="scscp1" name="call_ID" />
              <OMSTR>ieat_9056</OMSTR>
            </OMATP>
            <OMA>
              <OMS cd="scscp1" name="procedure_call" />
              <OMA>
                <OMS cd="scscp_transient_1" name="GroupByIdNumber" />
                <OMI>24</OMI><OMI>12</OMI>
              </OMA>
            </OMA>
          </OMATTR>
        </OMOBJ>
      </call>
    </invoke>
  </parallel>
</workflow>
```

The composition description is further translated by the Client Manager component into a BPEL workflow. The main part of the resulted BPEL document is the corresponding translation of the workflow described at client side. Starting the workflow can be done exclusively by invoking the composed service that results after deploying the workflow. In order to avoid the time expense of deploying the same workflow several times, the user can access already deployed workflows. For each received computation request the CAS Server creates a new symbolic Grid service to handle the request. Once the computation is finished a callback to the BPEL process is made.

The user specifies the workflow to be executed and then submits it to a server. The result can be obtained at a later time without having to maintain the connection with the server. Managing the workflow at the server level may allow the client to obtain the result faster than managing the workflow at the client side. The server may also provide load balancing and failure management by using a specialized workflow engine.

In order to be usable in a workflow constructed by the Client Manager, a Web/Grid service needs to meet some constraints:

a. It must implement callback mechanisms to provide the result to the client of the service (e.g. the workflow engine)

b. It must implement mechanisms that permit delaying the callback call that sends the result

c. It must offer through their exposed interface information relevant for the centralized management system

As mentioned in subsection 3.1, additional to the ability to orchestrate services, the ability to manage workflows after deployment plays an important role. Not all workflow management systems (like ActiveBPEL) provide such management capabilities for the workflows they execute. The node that manages the orchestration of the services may be the best choice to implement management features such as starting/resuming a workflow execution. Unfortunately, it is not yet implemented by any public available execution engine and implementing such functionality within the workflow engine requires modifications of the engine.

One of the essential features introduced by the SymGrid-Services system is the ability to control the execution of the workflow. Pausing a task may prove useful in some contexts as stand-alone functionality. It can be also used to alter the computation result of a task, manually.

Although pausing the CAS Server means that the service is hindered to make the callback invoke, the computation carried out by the corresponding CAS is not actually paused. By preventing the service to send back the result of the computation to the service orchestration engine, none of tasks dependent on the current task is able to be started. Moreover, SymGrid-Services offers the ability to pause the execution of a service and then, to set the value of the result to a value that is independent and is not modified by the actual execution of the task – this approach offers the possibility to experiment different scenarios based on the same workflow.

Not only the entire workflow, but also the execution of a workflow branch may be paused on-demand by delaying the callback that provides the result of an invoke. As a result, by pausing and resuming, it is possible to execute only sections of the original workflow. Doing this, some of the management functionality is pushed out of the node that manages the execution of the workflow. The role of this node remains important because it stores valuable information about the current status of the execution, the services that were invoked and the results that were already obtained.

A possible usage scenario of the management operations described above is presented in Figure 7.

The user can obtain the list of the invoked workflow tasks and the structure of a workflow previously submitted as a list of task identifiers and, respectively, a list of dependencies between tasks. Afterwards he/she can pause a task, change its result, resume it or simply stop it.

Every time a CAS user calls one of these operations on a specified task, the request is sent to the Client Manager component. The Client Manager determines the URL of the CAS Server responsible for the execution of the task and sends the request to this server.

In order to test the features related to work-flow submission and management, the SymGrid-Services workflow facilities are integrated into a portal. The portal allows free testing of several features of SymGrid-Services among them being the ability to submit workflows using the Abstract Workflow Language or GAP-like functions and to control the workflow as described above. The portal is available for testing at http://matrix.info.uvt.ro:8080/portal/.

Figure 7. A workflow management scenario

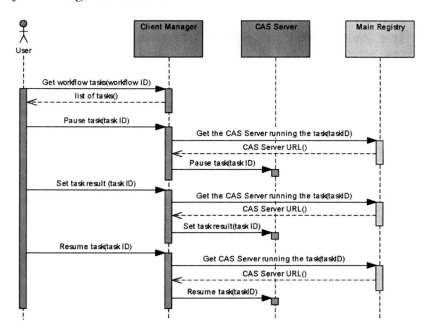

3.3.4. OPTIMIZE: SymGrid' Solution for Adaptive Resource Brokering and Scheduling

One of the innovations that SymGrid wants to promote in the parallel and distributed computing communities is an adaptive and prescient scheduler coupled with a dynamic resource contract negotiator. Consider an example involving large integer (more than 60 digits) factorizations which has strong implications in the field of cryptography. Due to the various existing serial or parallel algorithms with different complexities, this is representative for the scenario in which runtime estimation of the problem on any resource is a hard or almost impossible problem. A scheduling algorithm designed for this kind of problems should be prescient in terms of possessing foresight of system and application needs, and would dynamically interact with running computations in order to obtain foreknowledge of future needs. From the existence of an adaptive prescient scheduler can profit both the Grid application developers through the move of the attention from the low level imple-

mentation issues to high level of abstraction and resource providers through a higher usage of their resources. However in heterogeneous and highly dynamic environments such as Grids it is difficult to foresee the future configuration or behavior of any application or even of the environment itself. This is even more difficult if we add to the scenario problems such as the one presented in the previous example. An alternative in the form of using historical known data from problems belonging to the same complexity class combined with using templates, based on some user provided information for placing the problem in certain runtime intervals could be more appropriate.

The challenging issues are related to the irregularities in symbolic computations that hinder the cost estimation for complex symbolic computations and furthermore, the construction of contract resource negotiators and resource brokers for these complex computations. Taking into account the example provided at the beginning of this section we can identify a series of such problems. By exposing CASs as services it is almost impossible to have a foresight on the algorithm which will be used in the computation and therefore its time complexity. This also implies difficulties in estimating runtimes due to possible data and algorithm parallelism. In addition, the related example shows that it is also difficult to even estimate runtimes based on similar past results as the runtime of the given problem depends only on the currently used input and not on similar ones used in the past.

Janjic et al (2008) have recently presented the design of a dynamic, adaptive prescient scheduler for SymGrid-Par programs that possesses both foresight of future application behavior and foreknowledge of future application needs. It does this by predicting application level parallelism and some knowledge on its current state. The proposed mechanism is dynamic in that decisions about the resources allocated to an application are made during its execution, rather than beforehand. It is also adaptive in that scheduling decisions for an application will take into consideration information that is obtained from previous executions of the same application. The application informs the scheduler of important information about its future execution, such as the number of threads, the amount of communication between those threads, the granularity of threads and the potential parallelism that may be induced by each thread. The scheduler will then use this information to determine the most appropriate resources that should be allocated to the application. The final versions of the scheduler and the resource broker are expected to be available in 2009.

Frincu (2009) presents a dynamic scheduling algorithm based on a multiple queue model. The basic idea behind the algorithm is that rescheduling should be done at certain well chosen intervals and that the efficiency of the rescheduling depends on those intervals. Each time a task is rescheduled it is migrated to another queue where its chances of being executed earlier and even faster are greater. Also, due to the heterogeneity of the execution platforms the algorithm takes into account factors such as transport costs and

different execution times on different machines. The runtime estimates could come from various sources such as a prescient mechanism like the one presented in the previous paragraph or from user given initial estimates which will be then used against a template to match the problem into a certain runtime interval based on its complexity and input data.

The scheduler involved in planning the execution of workflow tasks has been designed as an integrated module inside the Workflow Orchestration Engine (See Figure 4). Its aim is to allow dynamic binding of scheduling algorithms to the SymGrid platform. This approach was considered as it is desirable to separate the scheduling from the actual execution and to allow different scheduling algorithms to be tested in the frame of planning mathematical problems which are to be executed on service exposed CASs.

4. FUTURE TRENDS

A number of major new obstacles need to be overcome by SCIEnce and the symbolic computing community in the near future. Amongst the most important future developments are mechanisms for adapting to dynamic changes in either computations or systems. This is especially important for symbolic computations, which may be highly irregular in terms of data structures and general computational demands and which therefore present an interesting challenge to current and projected technologies for Grids in terms of their requirements for autonomic control.

Another issue to deal with is the fact that communication of data in XML-based formats has the drawback of slowing the communications when the data to be sent are huge. Adaptive schemes that avoid the transmission of large XML-documents are under construction.

Adoption on a larger scale of the SCSCP protocol is essential for the impact of the SCIEnce proposals into the scientific community. While the first step, validation by the scientific community has been already undertaken, future steps intending to reach as much as possible a large community dealing with symbolic computations need to be carefully pursued.

As pointed in the first sections, finding the computational patterns to be used in complex applications and which are matching the characteristics of service-oriented computing infrastructures is a key element in the adoption of the new concepts and their implementations by the user communities.

5. CONCLUSION

Several approaches have been proposed to tackle with the issues raised in the transition of symbolic computing tools towards a service-oriented computing infrastructure:

- Generic access from within classical tools for symbolic computing, computer algebra systems to the outer world currently full of Web-based or Grid-based computational services
- Deployment and discovery of symbolic computing facilities exposed as Web or Grid services
- Standard proposal for communication protocol for mathematical objects
- Computer algebra system's user-friendly service composition facilities based on workflows and patterns
- Design of an adaptive scheduler and resource negotiation

Future developments are expected in what concerns the implementation of the adaptive scheduler and resource negotiator, the identification of computational patterns adequate to the service-oriented infrastructures, as well as the identification of the applications that have the highest benefit from the transition towards the new kind on infrastructures.

ACKNOWLEDGMENT

This research is partially supported by EU FP6 grant RII3-CT-2005-026133 SCIEnce: Symbolic Computing Infrastructure for Europe.

REFERENCES

Al Zain, A., Hammond, K., Trinder, P., Linton, S., Loidl, H. W., & Costantini, M. (2007b). SymGrid-Par: design a framework for executing computational algebra systems on computational Grids. In *Procs. ICCS'07, Intl. Conference on Computer Science Beijing,* (LNCS 4488, pp.617–624). Berlin: Springer.

Al Zain, A., Trinder, P., Michaelson, G., & Loidl, H. (2008). Evaluating a High-Level Parallel Language (GpH) for Computational GRIDs. *IEEE Transactions on Parallel and Distributed Systems*, *19*(2), 219–233. doi:10.1109/TPDS.2007.70728

Al Zain, A., Trinder, P. W., Loidl, H. W., & Michaelson, G. J. (2007a). Supporting high-level Grid parallel programming: the design and implementation of Grid-GUM2. In *Procs. UK e-Science Prog. All Hands Meeting.*

Baraka, R., Caprotti, O., & Schreiner, W. (2005). A Web registry for publishing and discovering mathematical services. In *Procs. EEE-05* (pp.190-193). Washington, DC: IEEE Computer Society Press.

Cârstea, A., Frîncu, M., Konovalov, A., Macariu, G., & Petcu, D. (2007c). On service-oriented symbolic computing. In R. Wyrzykowski, J. Dongarra, K. Karczewski, J. Wasniewski (Eds.), *Parallel Processing and Applied Mathematics,* (LNCS Vol. 4967, pp.843-851). Berlin: Springer.

Cârstea, A., Frîncu, M., Macariu, G., & Petcu, D. (2007b). Composing Web-based mathematical services. In *Procs. SYNASC 2007* (pp.327–334). Washington, DC: IEEE Computer Society Press.

Cârstea, A., Frîncu, M., Macariu, G., Petcu, D., & Hammond, K. (2007a). Generic access to Web and Grid-based symbolic computing services: the SymGrid-services framework. In *Procs. ISPDC 2007* (pp.143–150). Washington, DC: IEEE Computer Society Press.

Cârstea, A., Macariu, G., Petcu, D., & Konovalov, A. (2008a). Pattern based composition of Web services for symbolic computations. In M. Bubak, G.D. van Albada, J. Dongarra, P.M.A. Sloot (Eds.), *Computational Science,* (LNCS Vol. 5101, pp.126–135). Berlin: Springer.

Delaittre, T., Kiss, T., Goyeneche, A., Terstyanszky, G., Winter, S., & Kacsuk, P. (2005). GEMLCA: running legacy code applications as Grid services. *Journal of Grid Computing, 3*(1-2), 75–90. doi:10.1007/s10723-005-9002-8

Freundt, S., Horn, P., Konovalov, A., Linton, S., & Roozemond, D. (2008). Symbolic computation software composability. In S. Autexier et al. (Eds.), *AISC Calculemus MKM,* (LNAI 5144, pp.285-295). Berlin: Springer.

Frîncu, M. (2009). Dynamic Scheduling Algorithm for Heterogeneous Environments with Regular Task Input from Multiple Requests. In N. Abdennadher, D. Petcu (Eds.), *Grid and Pervasive Computing,* (LNCS 5529, pp.205-216). Berlin: Springer.

GENSS Consortium. (2005). *Grid-enabled numerical and symbolic services.* Retrieved November 2008 from http://genss.cs.bath.ac.uk/

Grabmeier, J., Kaltofen, E., & Weispfenning, V. (2003). *Computer Algebra Handbook.* Berlin: Springer.

Hammond, K., Al Zain, A., Cooperman, G., Petcu, D., & Trinder, P. (2007). SymGrid: a framework for symbolic computation on the Grid. In A.M. Kermarrec, L. Bouge, & T. Priol (Eds.), *Parallel Processing,* (LNCS 4641, pp.447–456). Berlin: Springer.

Janjic, V., Hammond, K., & Yang, Y. (2008), Using application information to drive adaptive grid middleware scheduling decisions. In Procs. 2nd workshop on Middleware-application interaction. *ACM International Conference Proceeding Series,* (Vol. 306, pp.7-12). New York: ACM Press.

Konovalov, A., & Linton, S. (2007). *Symbolic Computation Software Composability Protocol Specification.* CIRCA preprint 2007/5, University of St Andrews. Retrieved November 2008 from http://www-circa.mcs.st-and.ac.uk/preprints.html

Macariu, G., Cârstea, A., Frîncu, M., & Petcu, D. (2008). Towards a Grid oriented architecture for symbolic computing. In *Procs. ISPDC'08.* Washington, DC: IEEE Computer Society.

MapleConnect. (2006). *MapleNet.* Retrieved November 2008 from http://www.maplesoft.com/products/ maplenet

MapleSoft. (2008). *Grid Computing Toolbox.* Retrieved November 2008 from http://www.maplesoft.com/products/toolboxes/Grid-Computing/

OpenMath Society. (2004). *OpenMath 2.0.* Retrieved November 2008 from http://www.openmath.org/

Petcu, D., Cârstea, A., Macariu, G., & Frîncu, M. (2008). Service-oriented symbolic computing with SymGrid. *SCPE, 9*(2), 111–125.

Petcu, D., Tepeneu, D., Paprzycki, M., & Ida, T. (2006). Symbolic computations on Grids. In B. Di Martino, J. Dongarra, A. Hoisie, L. T. Yang, H. Zima, (eds.), *Engineering the Grid,* (pp. 91–107). Valencia, CA: American Scientific Publishers.

Roozemond, D. (2008). *OpenMath Content Dictionary: scscp2.* Retrieved November 2008 from http://www.win.tue.nl/SCIEnce/cds/scscp2.html

Smirnova, E., So, C. M., & Watt, S. M. (2004). Providing mathematical Web services using Maple in the MONET architecture. In *Procs. MONET Workshop.* Retrieved November 2008 from http://monet.nag.co.uk/cocoon/monet/proceedings/

Solomon, A., & Struble, C. A. (2007). JavaMath - an API for Internet Accessible Mathematical Services. Asian Symposium on Computer Mathematics, Matsuyama, Japan, September 2001. In Shirayangi, K., Yokoyama, K. (Ed.), *Proceedings of Asian Symposium on Computer Mathematics*, (pp.151-160). Singapore: World Scientific

Stein, W. (2008). *Sage Mathematics Software*. London: The Sage Group. Retrieved November 2008 from http://www.sagemath.org/

Wolfram Research. (2001). *WebMathematica*. Retrieved November 2008 from http://www.wolfram.com/ products/webmathematica/

Wolfram Research. (2003). *gridMathematica*. Retrieved November 2008 from http://www.wolfram.com/ products/gridmathematica/

YarKhan. A., Dongarra, J. & Seymour, K. (2007). GridSolve: The evolution of network enabled solver. In A. Prescott (ed), *Procs. WoCo9, Series IFIP Intern. Federation for Information Processing,* (vol. 239, pp.215–224). Berlin: Springer.

Zimmer, J., Franke, A., & Kohlhase, M. (2006). *MATHWEB-SB: A software bus for MathWeb.* Retrieved November 2008 from http://www.mathweb.org/mathweb/

KEY TERMS AND DEFINITIONS

CAS: Computer Algebra System
SOA: Service-oriented architecture
CD: Content Dictionary
WS: Web Service
GT4: Globus Toolkit version 4
WSDL: Web Services Description Language
GSI: Grid Security Infrastructure
WSRF: Web Service Resource Framework
OM: OpenMath
SCSCP: Symbolic Computation Software Composability Protocol

Chapter 46
Applications of Wireless Sensor Networks

Corinna Schmitt
Technische Universität München, Germany

Georg Carle
Technische Universität München, Germany

ABSTRACT

Today the researchers want to collect as much data as possible from different locations for monitoring reasons. In this context large-scale wireless sensor networks are becoming an active topic of research (Kahn1999). Because of the different locations and environments in which these sensor networks can be used, specific requirements for the hardware apply. The hardware of the sensor nodes must be robust, provide sufficient storage and communication capabilities, and get along with limited power resources. Sensor nodes such as the Berkeley-Mote Family (Polastre2006, Schmitt2006) are capable of meeting these requirements. These sensor nodes are small and light devices with radio communication and the capability for collecting sensor data. In this chapter the authors review the key elements for sensor networks and give an overview on possible applications in the field of monitoring.

INTRODUCTION

The goal of using a wireless sensor network is to collect a variety of data, to store and analyze the data and to provide the information to other devices. Applications can be found in structural health monitoring (e.g. the Golden Gate Bridge Project (Kim2006)) or in habitat monitoring (e.g. monitoring animal behavior). Other applications for wireless sensor networks are traffic monitoring, industrial automation, and battlefield surveillance (Ilyas2004, Karl2005, Tavares2008).

Because of the characteristic of the environment smart technologies are very interesting. Different types of sensors nodes, also called motes, have been developed in order to meet the varying requirements. Berkeley Motes (Levis2003, Levis2004,

DOI: 10.4018/978-1-61520-686-5.ch046

Figure 1. Information flow from WSN up to a user

Figure 2. Components of a sensor node

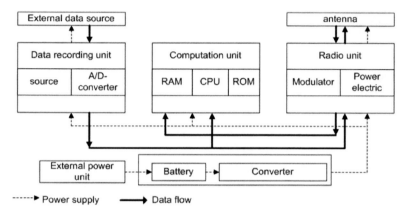

Schmitt2006) have become highly popular because they allow quick development, are of small size and support different sensors.

The remaining part of the chapter is structured as follows. In section 1 a brief overview of the history of sensor networks is given. In section 2 the theoretical background together with the limitation of wireless sensor networks is described and the common Berkeley Motes are characterized. In the third section different approaches corresponding to structural health and habitat monitoring using wireless sensor networks are presented. Finally future trends are mentioned and a summary is given.

BACKGROUND

In this section the corresponding keywords in the field of wireless sensor networks are mentioned which will be characterized in more detail in section two.

Today the industrial production is able to produce very small mobile devices (Warneke2001).

Two sorts can be distinguished: very small, specialized nodes, and larger nodes with commercial off-the-shelf (COTS) components.

An embedded system is a specialized computer which is used for device control (e.g. cars, mobiles, hand-held-units, washing machine). Typically, the end user has no control over it because the device is hidden.

Embedded systems and highly embedded systems can be differentiated. Highly embedded systems would be particularly small, resulting in highly limited resources. This implies the use of sophisticated hardware, in combination with the use of suitable, special operating systems. Data can be collected by a variety of sensors. After collection, this data has to be transmitted to other nodes. Thus, wireless sensor systems have to support highly developed communication.

Wireless sensor nodes have their own energy supply provided by batteries or solar cells. Some sensor nodes have processors that allow to process data before passing it on. Different technologies for wireless transmission are used such as infrared or radio frequency technology. A sensor node consists of several components which are illustrated in figure 2 in section two.

Wireless sensor networks (WSNs) (Röm04, Haenselmann2006) have a decentralized structure in which messages cannot be addressed directly to their destination. Instead messages are sent to neighboring nodes (e.g. using a local broadcast). Nodes that receive messages have to decide whether to further forward the received data. Due to the absence of planned connectivity between specific nodes, these networks are called ad-hoc networks. Another problem of these networks is their limitations concerning security and anonymity.

Like the short description of WSNs above implicit special software (e.g. TinyOS for Berkeley Motes) must be developed to optimize the quality of the established network. Therefore the developers have to look at the requirements of the environment where to use the network and also at the participating components and their limitations. On important aspect is the realization of energy saving procedures and memory saving methods for data acquiring and transmission within the network.

1. HISTORY OF SENSOR NETWORKS

Sensor network research started in the 1980s. At that time it used to be called Distributed Sensor Networks. Typical applications were military (e.g. radar systems, audio sensors to track down submarines). Due to the process of miniaturization of electronic devices, new application areas became of interest, leading to additional research tasks. Nowadays, sensor networks can be found in many different areas, such as observation of the environment, medical applications, and areas of daily live such as surveillance in supermarkets. Fault tolerance, production costs, area of usage, hardware, communication, location, and the energy consump-

tion are essential for developing components of sensor networks.

2. THEORETICAL BACKGROUND OF SENSOR NETWORK TECHNOLOGY AND REQUIREMENTS

In this section the general aspects of a sensor network and the corresponding requirements are described. In the field of monitoring the Berkeley Motes are frequently used. They are also characterized in this section. A good overview of the wireless sensor network technology gives (Raghavendra2004).

2.1. Communication Within a Network

As mentioned above a wireless sensor network has special requirements based on the equipment and different limitations. Those are more specified in the upcoming sections. Because of the limited requirements it is essential to a look on communication possibilities in a network together with possible problems which might occur. A possible setup is shown in figure 1.

WSN networks can have different topologies. Well known ones are the star, ring, bus, tree mesh or fully connected topology. Corresponding to the chosen topology the devices are more or less connected to each other. Medium Access Control protocols for WSNs can use one of the following techniques:

- Frequency Division Multi Access (FDMA)
- Code Division Multiple Access (CDMA)
- Time Division Multiple Access (TDMA)

The decision on which Medium Access Control protocol is influenced by factors such as collision probability, protocol overhead, and resulting possible throughput.

Distributed networks may have many possible paths from the source to the destination. Different routing schemes such as fixed or adaptive schemes can be used. The fixed schemes work with routing tables which consist of information like next available routing node and destination node. These schemes have many disadvantages which increase with the number of nodes in the network.

Communication networks can exhibit problems like deadlocks or livelocks. A deadlock means that buffers of participants communicating with each other are full, resulting in protocol instances waiting for each other. In a livelock affected nodes are able to communicate but the transmitted messages never reach their destination. This can happen in case of a routing loop.

2.2. General Aspects of a Sensor Node

Sensor networks consist of different sensor nodes that communicate with each other via radio frequency communication links. Figure 2 shows the cooperation of the components, as well as the power supply and the data flow between the different components of a sensor node.

Energy consumption is a limited factor in wireless sensor networks. The life time of a battery is determined by several factors: the dimension of the battery that is limited by the device size, the material used, the power consumption (discharge) and the surrounding temperature. Accumulators in combination with solar cells can be used to increase the life time of the battery, so the system is able to recharge itself, thereby providing sufficient energy for all components. Many wireless sensor node systems have realized energy save modes. If a part of the system is not used it is shut down or sleeps and is woken up when needed.

A converter component takes energy from the battery and provides constant voltage for connected components. If the battery voltage decreases and a higher voltage than provided by the battery is needed, the converter can supply the higher voltage, at the cost of larger current discharging the battery, thereby decreasing battery lifetime.

In the following, we present core components of a wireless sensor node and give information of their energy consumption:

• Typically, the computation unit together with the radio unit has the largest energy consumption.
• The data recording and storage unit typically consumes significantly less energy. This unit consists of the following 4 components: the physical signal translator, the converter for electrical signals, the signal adapter and the A/D-converter. The external data source is given by the data that the sensors recorded.

Sensor nodes have limited energy resources. Therefore the energy consumption must be low. Typically, a combination of some of the following approaches is required for achieving needed lifetime:

• Usage of large battery packs;
• Not fully processing all messages by all nodes receiving the messages;
• Distinguishing node types by their maximum possible communication distance (short / long distance);
• Introducing breaks in which processors and functional units are shut down;
• Energy-aware scheduling of processor usage;
• Using data compression to reduce the amount of data that needs to be transmitted
• Sending data with high data rate and short duration;
• Receiving data at predefined times, thereby allowing to sleep in-between.

Another interest task is the communication between the participating sensor nodes. The participating structure of the communicating ar-

Figure 3. Types of communication

Direct transmission

Multihop

Clustering

chitecture should be mentioned here shortly. The communicating architecture of a sensor network can be subdivided into the five layers: application layer, transport layer, network layer, data link layer, and physical layer.

Most important for wireless sensor networks are physical layer, data link layer and network layer, i.e. layers one to three. The network layer provides different communication models for the sensor network, including direct transmission, multi-hop transmission and clustering, as illustrated in figure 3.

Important in the development of an operating system for sensor nodes is support of energy efficient usage of the system, such as the ability to shut down unused components.

Not only energy is a limiting factor for wireless sensor nodes, but also limited computing and memory resources. A suitable communication architecture for wireless sensor to take this into account adequately. The operating system for wireless sensor nodes has to support the following points as well:

- Low memory capacity and energy efficiency
- Concurrency
- Variety in design and application of the sensor node
- Availability

Sensor nodes both send and receive data. As memory of the nodes is low, buffer space available for the routing protocol is also rather limited.

Figure 4. Picture of Berkeley Mote vs. quarter

2.3. Special Aspects Concerning Berkeley Motes

In the field of monitoring Berkeley Motes are very interesting for the researchers. In 2000 Jason Hill and David Culler from the University of California at Berkeley/USA developed an operating system – TinyOS – within the framework of a DARPA project. TinyOS (TinyOS2004) is one of the most prevalent operating systems for sensor nodes.

Berkley Motes (Gupta2004) contain a microprocessor, Static Random Access Memory (SRAM), and Electrically Erasable and Programmable Read-Only Memory (EEPROM). Actor and sensor components, radio interfaces, and serial

Figure 5. Development of the hardware platforms (Levis2004)

Mote	WeC	rene	dot	mica	mica2	mica2 dot	iMote	btNode
Released	1999	2000	2001	2002	2003	2003	2003	2003
Processor	4 MHz				7 MHz	4 MHz	12 MHz	7 MHz
Flash (code, kB)	8	8	16	128	128	128	512	128
RAM (kB)	0,5	0.5	1	4	4	4	64	4
Radio (KBaud)	10	10	10	40	40	40	460	460
Radio Type	RFM				ChipCon	ChipCon	ZeevoBT	Ericsson BT
controller	Atmel						ARM	Atmel
Expandable	no	yes	no	yes	yes	yes	yes	yes

interfaces are attached (Hill2000).

The first prototype contained a master control unit, an Atmel 90LS8535, which is an 8bit architecture with a 16bit address space, an 8kb Flash, and a 512 Bytes SRAM. The following energy saving modes have been realized:

- Idle mode: just the processor is shut down.
- Power-down mode: everything besides the interrupt circuit, which reloads the system, will be shut down
- Power-save mode: equivalent to the power down mode, at which only a timer that reloads the system regularly runs

The radio sender/receiver is a simple transceiver with an antenna, where the sending and receiving unit can be altered. Three control modes are possible: sending, receiving, and shut down. The prototype contains LEDs, a shot resistor, a sensor for temperatures, output devices, and digital input devices. Such a node is shown in the following picture.

Throughout the years newer versions have been developed, which contain a faster master control unit, a bigger flash-memory, and RAM. Further improvements are the sensors that have been moved to a sensor board, which is linked to the main board via a bus. The development of different versions is explained in Figure 5.

As already mentioned, TinyOS (TinyOS2004) is the operating system of the Berkeley Motes. In general it is an operating system which suitable for hardware with significantly limited resources (e.g. Berkeley Motes). TinyOS has an efficient multithreading engine, which is composed of a two-level-scheduler for threads. Figure 6 illustrates the schema of TinyOS with regard to the two-level-scheduler and the communication between different components.

The two-level-scheduler allows to distinguish:

- Tasks which contain current tasks like network routing and data preparation. These tasks have a relatively long lifetime. Their executions can be shortly suspended by hardware events that have to be worked on.
- Events that have to be worked on as fast as possible. Therefore, the operating system prevents long-time blocking of events by applications, thereby preventing data loss.

Based on the two-level-scheduler it is important to take the consumption of electricity of the main board into account, thus guaranteeing an efficient way of processing parallel running data streams.

The parts which merge sensors, processing and communication units are further important components of the operating system. These parts contain a Command Handler dealing with Commands, and an Event Handler which makes an immediate reaction to a state change possible. Higher level components communicate with lower levels components via Commands, which send a return value after execution or dispatch

Figure 6. TinyOS schema (Adapted from Körber2006)

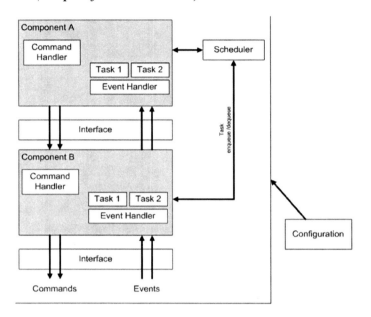

about success or failure. Thus a Command cannot cause Events. The Event Handler deals with Events, which can be caused directly or indirectly by hardware interrupts. Events can cause Events of higher levels. Frames contain the data memory of a component. Within a component Tasks are running, which have been started by Commands, Events, or other Tasks from the same component. Typical features of Tasks are the atomic structure, and the "run-completion" semantic, i.e. a Task cannot be stopped and stops itself when finished.

This knowledge allows a classification of the components into three types (Hill2000):

- Hardware abstraction components: Mapping of physical hardware into a components model. One of the components is the RFM, which operates the pins of the RFM sender/receiver, and informs other components of successful transmission via Events.
- Synthetic hardware components: Mapping of progressive hardware, e.g. the radio-byte-hardware, which sends data to the RFM, and gives a signal when a whole byte has been sent.
- High level software components: They contain the application-logic. They control components, and calculate the routing, and other data information. (e.g. Messaging-Module, which fractionizes messages into packages, and reassembles receives packages back into messages.)

As mentioned above the operating system has a modular structure. The Message Module, for example, calls Commands of a component which is located in the package-layer, and deals with the corresponding Events. As this simple description shows, the assembling of single modules through a simple interface explanation is easy. The communication method is comparable to functional calls, which very common in a variety of computer languages.

2.4. Wireless Sensor Networks (WSNs)

In the previous section technical details of Berkeley Motes were briefly described. This section characterizes a WSN.

In a WSN, the nodes communicate via radio frequency with each other. Nodes may have special sensor boards with different sensors like light sensors, accelerometers, and microphones. A sensor board can be attached to the basic node to collect different environmental data. While a large amount of data can be collected, storage is limited. Therefore, collected data should be processed and transmitted to other nodes. In this setting, an ad-hoc network with multi-hop option is used typically. When data from the wireless sensor network gets propagated to a computer with significant resources for storage, the data can be stored finally for further analysis. If the data is transmitted to all nodes in the network, redundancy may occur, possibly requiring to detect and to filter out the redundancy.

3. APPLICATIONS: MONITORING BY USING BERKELEY MOTES

A typical application of sensor nodes is to gain information about the environment. If constructions are monitored, the technical term of this application area is "structural health monitoring" (SHM). It is used to analyze the changes in the structure of the building, which can affect the performance (e.g. Golden Gate Bridge Project). Another approach is habitat monitoring where animal behavior is observed. These two monitoring approach can also be divided by the network type – static or mobile.

Other important application areas are remote healthcare monitoring, agricultural monitoring as well for automobile applications.

Corresponding projects are described in subsequent sections.

3.1. Structural Health Monitoring

The "Golden Gate Bridge Project" and the "Great Duck Island Project" are structural health monitor-

ing projects that apply stationary nodes. Due to the resulting network structure, appropriate routing algorithms are not very complex. In both projects it is possible to transmit collected data directly to neighboring nodes located at fixed positions. This allows simple processing of captured data. These two projects are described in more detail in the subsection sections.

3.1.1. The "Golden Gate Bridge Project"

The "Golden Gate Bridge Project" is located in San Francisco, USA (Kim2006). This project deals with the structural health monitoring (SHM) problem. The aim is to observe the ambient vibration of the structure. Berkeley-Motes are placed at different points of the bridge.

In this project the first approach was to use Mica2 motes. The nodes use 8MHz Atmega 128L microcontroller with 128KB program memory and 4KB of RAM. The radio chip used is a Chipcon CC1000 with a data rate of 38.4Kbaud. The radio frequency used is 433MHz. The node has an external 512 KB EEPROM for data storage. The sensor board used is an accelerometer board that consists of several accelerometers (e.g. ADXL 202E, Silicon Designs 1221L), one thermometer and four analog to digital converters (ADC).

Due to the construction of the bridge it is essential to measure two directions perpendicular to the bridge span – one up-down and one across the span. For the towers two directions must be measured – along the span and across the span. The accelerometer of the ADXl 2002E type can measure in perpendicular directions to each other. This information is not enough for the structural health monitoring of the bridge thus the accelerometers of the Silicon Designs 1221L type is needed. Those measure the axis. The ADXL 202E has a range from -2G to 2G for big movements, e.g. earthquakes, and the other type has a narrow range of -0.1G to 0.1G to sample ambient vibrations.

The arrangement of the sensors and the antenna

dimension is based on the Golden Gate Bridge construction. The collected information is transmitted from sensor node to sensor node. The longest hop distance is 280 ft. This distance can be increased by using bidirectional antennas. This antenna type is not compatible with the Mica2 mote, but with the micaZ mote that uses standard IEEE 802.15.4 radio running at 2.4GHz. A compromise must be made between the needed power for the transmission and the number of needed hops, because of the limited power resources. The node transfers data one third of its time; otherwise is in an idle state. With these requirements and a usage of three Tadrian 5930 batteries supplying 3.6V a working period of three weeks can be realized.

In this application area, it is important for reliable information to ensure high sample accuracy, high frequency sampling, time synchronization, stable operation of a large-scale multi-hop network, reliable command dissemination and reliable data collection. All these requirements can be realized when the operation of data collection is divided into three phases:

1. **Data acquisition:** Samples the vibration data of the structure, and logs it into EEPROM
2. **Data collection:** Transfers data reliable to an external computing resource
3. **Data processing & feedback:** Runs analysis algorithm, determines health status, and sends feedback to nodes if needed

The data acquisition is realized with regular sampling by uniform intervals. The sampling frequency is 200Hz. The component FTSP is responsible for the time synchronization that provides 67μs error over 59- node 11-hop network.

In the data collection phase the component MintRout is needed for the large-scale multi-hop network. Important for a correct structural analysis is a complete data collection which is archived by retransmission. The data collection is also responsible for the needed sampling cycles. It is important to keep in mind: the less compu-

tational power, the less memory storage and the less energy. The service STRAW – Scalable Thin and Rapid Amassment Without loss – works with multi-hop on good scalability and optimizes the interval between the packets (Kim2006).

In the last step of the data collection the PC collects the whole transmitted data, analysis them, and runs a diagnosis of the structural health. If, for instance, a new calibration is essential, a feedback is send to the nodes.

This sensor network and the strategy are successfully tested on a small footbridge from the City of Berkeley to Berkeley Marina before it was established on the Golden Gate Bridge.

3.1.2. The "Great Duck Island Project"

Another interesting application area is explored in the "Great Duck Island Project" in Maine, USA (Yang2002, Polastre2006, Baer2003), where biologists observe microclimates in and around nesting burrows of Storm Petrels – a kind of sea bird. The researchers observe the occupancy of the burrows and the conditions of the burrows surrounding. The aim is the developing of a habitat monitoring kit. They put sensor devices from the Mica Family of the Berkeley Motes in the underground nest as well as on 4-inch stilts outside their burrows. The devices record data about the birds and their behavior. They are transmitted to a gateway node which transmits the data to a computer or laptop in the research station. After that it is transferred to a satellite dish to transmit it to the base laboratory at Berkeley, USA.

This project uses Mica2dots and Mica2 motes. The Mica2 mote works with two AA batteries. The node has several places for sensors. It consists of an Atmega 128L processor, a 916MHz and 433MHz radio transmitter. The power management shows that the processor needs 12mA, if it is in the "wake-up mode" and otherwise less than 1microA. The Mica2dot's diameter is 25mm, the multi-channel radio has a range up to 300m and it is working with 2.8v SAFT LO34SX batteries rated at 860mAhr. The processor needs 8mA in the "wake-up mode" and otherwise less than 15microA. The sensor board used in this project consists of several sensors (Szewczyk2004):

- Non-contact temperature module: Melexis MLX90601
- Temperature and humidity sensor: Sensirion SHT11
- light sensor: TAOS TSL2550
- Sensor for barometric pressure: Intersema MS5534A

The sensor network consists of 30 sensor nodes, which are divided into two groups – the burrow nodes and the weather nodes. The burrow nodes observe the occupancy of the burrow by using a non-infrared thermopiles and temperature/humidity sensor. The weather node is used for the monitoring of the surface microclimate.

The small size of the nodes and their automatically running allows the biologists to observe the habitat without stepping in the current ecosystem. The nodes should observe the habitat for a period of nine months. The information collected is periodically broadcasted over a single radio hop or a multi-hop corresponding to their distance to the base station.

3.2. Habitat Monitoring

The second group of applications deals with tasks corresponding to habitat monitoring. The main difference to the other projects mentioned is that the nodes and the base station are mobile and not static anymore. The information flow is enormous and every node needs a big storage to store its data and the received data of other nodes.

In this section the "ZebraNet Project" and the "Rat movement tracking Project" are described. The project names implicits that the hardware has to be adapted to the size of the observed animals and their environment.

3.2.1. The "ZebraNet Project"

In general, the aim of animal observation is to collect information about the animal's behavior. The University of Princeton, USA (Juang2002) has developed the "ZebraNet Project" where zebras wear a tracking collar that weighs 1090g and consists of the following part (Zhang2004):

- Global Positioning System (GPS) chip – GPS-MS1E
- CPU
- 640KB flash memory – uBlox chip
- Short-range radio (100m, 19.2Kbps) – Linux Technologies SC-PA series
- Long-range radio and Packet Modem for transfers over 8km with 2.4Kbps
- Lithium-Ion batteries with capacity of five days
- Solar cell array

The characteristic of this sensor system is the long term animal tracking, even supporting long distances. All the nodes are mobile and build a wireless sensor network. This arrangement allows the scientists to find and follow zebras throughout their environment and to be able to collect additional information. The project is located at the Mpala Research Centre in central Kenya. The biologists observe Plains zebra (*E. burchelli*). They build tight-knit uni-male, multi-female breeding groups. The observations did reveal that movements of so-called "harems" are determined by the females, but the direction is caused by the males. Thus, only the male need to wear the collars for collecting sufficient information.

For this application, the designers' goal is to collect as much information as possible for about one year requiring little energy for the nodes only, which is achieved by the following conditions:

- Every three minutes the position in located by GPS
- Every hour detailed activity logs are taken

for three minutes

The communication between the nodes is realized by ad-hoc routing. The most important challenge is that the observers must be mobile in order to represent the base station, which therefore can cause that the "base station" is not available for the nodes. When the researches want to collect the information, they drive through the area and stop near a water hole because the zebras will go there if they are thirsty due to the limited water resources. Because of this situation, the collected data must be transmitted to other nodes to secure the transmission to a base station, which is realized by a hierarchical system, which means a node that is in the surrounding of the base station has a higher number than the others. Every node transmits its data to the node with the highest number in its surrounding; finally the data will raise the base station. A disadvantage of this system is the exorbitant data flow over the whole system.

3.2.2. The "Rat Movement Tracking Project"

In this project (Schmitt2006) the used hardware needs to be smaller and the power resource is smaller, because the nodes are not allowed to be heavy due to the rats' size and cannot be recharged by solar cells as mentioned in the "ZebraNet Project". The only static part of the network is the base station which should be localized at an often frequented place, e.g. at burrow entries; thus it might not have connectivity to the other nodes at all times. Rats normally live in burrow systems and the surrounding earth prevents the communication with the outside; thus, a GPS sensor would not provide useful location information. Data transfer between nodes is important to ensure a transmission of collected data of every node to the base station, which is why a rather large storage capacity at the nodes is needed. The storage capacity must be sufficiently large to store the nodes' data and the transmitted data of

other rats until the storage is emptied when being close enough to the base station. In this project Mica2dots nodes were used because they did meet the requirements of the scenario.

3.3. Remote Healthcare Monitoring

A specific approach for remote healthcare monitoring has been explored by the University of Technology in Sydney. As the human population becomes older, medical surveillance becomes more and more important. Based on the situations in the nursing homes and the financial situation of the government it is better to care for the people at their homes instead in aged-care facilities. The medical care should not suffer from this situation. The healthcare industry aims for developing remote monitoring systems for remotely monitoring people at home (Lubin2005).

In this project the researchers use Berkeley Mica2 motes in a test bed environment with a PDA and a network management application. The PDA is a mobile monitor with access to the internet. The combination of PDA and motes provides a multi-functional aspect, increasing flexibility at low costs, A graphical front-end was created to display the readings from the sensors in real-time.

3.4. Agricultural Monitoring

In the field of agricultural monitoring (Baer2003) first approaches started in 2003. In the Okanagan Valley in British Columbia, USA a network of 65 motes is used to collect temperature data of several acres of vines. The analyzed data determines which grapes to plant and where to irrigate. The same system is also used for defense aspects corresponding to increased heat and humidity. The aim of the project is to develop a high-yield viticulture.

Another project was developed for testing water in Palmdale, California, USA. The aim of the government is to re-use the wastewater on farms. This is only possible if the water quality is appropriate corresponding to the nitrates level. The idea is to bury sensors to track the pollutant and finally to warn the farmers to stop the water usage.

Wireless sensor networks are used also for fire fighting and seismology analysis in California, USA. The UC Berkeley developed the project FireBug (Doolin2004). This project establishes a network which consists of golf ball-sized sensor motes. The sensor nodes can be dropped ahead of an inferno and send the collected data (e.g. temperature) about the current situation back out. Over time, the researchers hope to deploy sensors in the wilderness as a way to anticipate hot spots. The UCLA Department of Earth and Space Sciences, Center for Embedded Networked Sensing developed a network for seismology analysis (Husker2004). The network consists of 50 seismometers located around the San Andreas Fault to analyze the movement of the giant tectonic plates. The devices record faint rumbles and allow the researchers to calculate the depth of the fault and to pinpoint locations. The understanding of those data leads to a better forecasting.

3.5. Automobile Applications

The automobile industry is interested in using wireless sensor networks for intra-vehicle and inter-vehicle aspects. To the first group count applications such as reducing wiring in vehlicles, monitoring of areas difficult to access, and providing simple access to useful information. In the field of inter-vehicle task the main aspect is improving driving safety. Here the automobiles should collect information about dangerous conditions, traffic jams and road signs. This data must then be provided to the other vehicles. Such scenarios are analyzed with the help of Berkeley Motes in scenarios tested at the Instituto de Telecomunicações in Portugal (Tavares2008). Information gathered is acceleration and fuel consumption, identification of incorrect tire pressure, failures

of illumination, and evaluation of the vital signals of the drivers.

FUTURE TRENDS

In the future the development will go on. The equipment may become cheaper and consist of more sensors. The application area will grow. Monitoring might be possible in the human body by using sensor technology. Due to the fast technology's development the variety of communication methods are growing day by day, and the already existing ones gain more and more quality. To make the data collection more effective and efficient the research goes on and the analysis possibilities will grow corresponding to the researchers interests. Perhaps in the future the information might be available by mobile devices so the users can work with the data when they are out of office and will not need a wired connection to the server anymore. The small node technology will be adapted to more monitoring fields such as military areas, industrial production and defense aspects.

CONCLUSION

As a conclusion the wireless sensor nodes are a good possibility to monitor different aspects of the environment. With an effective programming and a look on the requirements the resources of sensor nodes can be used effectively. If many nodes are used an effective network can be realized which provides a fast monitoring with small investment. Sensor nodes have many tasks such as data acquisition and communication to other nodes. This functionality requires sufficient computing, memory, communication and energy resources. At the same time, all these resources are very limited. As a consequence the resources must be used efficiently. Important for mobility is the ability to maintain communication among mobile devices. As existing solutions are not able to meet all challenging requirements, additional research efforts are needed for more effective communication methods and improved data and power management in wireless sensor networks.

REFERENCES

Baer, M. (2003). The Ultimate on-the-fly Network. *On Newsstands Now, 11*(12). Retrieved November 20, 2008, from http://www.wired.com/wired/archive/11.12/network.html

Doolin, D. M., Sitar, D., & Glaser, S. (2004). *Software Architecture for GPS-enabled Wildfire Sensorboard*. Civil and Environmental Engineering, University of California, Berkeley, USA. Retrieved November 20, 2008, from http://firebug.sourceforge.net/interface_poster.pdf

Gupta, A. (2004). *Wireless Sensor Networks Research*. Department of Computer Science, Western Michigan University, USA. Retrieved November 20, 2008, from http://www.cs.wmich.edu/wsn/

Haenselmann, T. (2006). Sensornetworks. *GFDL Wireless Sensor Network textbook*. Retrieved November 20, 2008, from http://www.informatik.uni-mannheim.de/~haensel/sn_book/

Hill, J., Szewczyk, R., Woo, A., Hollar, S., Culler, D., & Pister, K. (2000). System Architecture Directions for Networked Sensors. [New York: ACM.]. *ACM SIGPLAN Notice, 35*(11), 93–10. doi:10.1145/356989.356998

Husker, A., Stubailo, I., Kohler, M., & Davis, P. (2004). *Seismic Network Development Preparations*. Center for Embedded Network Sensing, UCLA, Los Angeles, CA. Retrieved November 20, 2008 from http://www.cens.ucla.edu/Education/RR_Posters/Research%20Review/027_Husker.pdf

Ilyas, M., & Mahgoub, I. (2004). *Handbook of sensor networks: Compact wireless and wired sensing systems*. Boca Raton, FL: CRC Press.

Juang, P., Oki, H., Wong, Y., Martonosi, M., Peh, L. S., & Rubenstein, D. (2002). Energy-Efficient Computing for Wildlife Tracking: Design Tradeoffs and Early Experiences with ZebraNet. *The Proceeding of ASPLOS-X,* (pp. 96-107). New York: ACM.

Kahn, J. M., Katz, R. H., & Pister, K. S. J. (1999). Next century challenge: mobile networking for "Smart Dust." In *Proceedings of the 5th annual ACM/IEEE international conference on Mobile computing and networking,* (pp. 271-278). New York: ACM.

Karl, H., & Willing, A. (2005). *Protocols and Architectures for Wireless Sensor Networks*. New York: Wiley & Son.

Kim, S., Pakzad, S., Culler, D., Demmel, J., Fenves, G., Glaser, S., & Turon, M. (2006). Wireless Sensor Networks for Structural Health Monitoring. In *Conference On Embedded Networked Sensor Systems,* (pp 427-428). ACM: New York.

Körber, H. J. (2006). *Low Power Wireless Sensor Networks*. Lecture Elektrische Messtechnik, Helmut Schmidt Universität, Universität der Bundeswehr Hamburg. Retrieved November 20, 2008, from www.hsu-hh.de/download-1.4.1.php?brick_id=YYgNZmeQf1vZvACt

Levis, P., Lee, N., Welsh, M., & Culler, D. (2003). TOSSIM: Accurate and Scalable Simulation of Entire TinyOS Applications. In *Conference on Embedded Networked Sensor Systems* (pp. 126-137). New York: ACM.

Levis, P., Madden, S., Gay, D., Polastre, J., Szewczyk, R., Woo, A., et al. (2004). The Emergence of Networking Abstractions and Techniques in TinyOS. In *Proceedings of the 1st conference on Symposium on Networked Systems Design and Implementation,* (pp. 1-1). Berkeley, CA: USENIX Association.

Lubin, E., Lawrence, E., & Navarro, K. F. (2005). Wireless Remote Healthcare Monitoring with Motes. In *Proceedings of the International Conference on Mobile Business* (pp. 235-241). Washington, DC: IEEE Computer Society.

Polastre, J. (2003). *Design and Implementation of Wireless Sensor Networks for Habitat Monitoring*. Unpublished master thesis, University of California at Berkeley, Department of Electrical Engineering and Computer Sciences.

Polastre, J., Szewczyk, R., Mainwaring, A., Culler, D., & Anderson, J. (2006). Analysis of wireless sensor networks for habitat monitoring. *Wireless Sensor Network*, (pp. 399-423). New York: Springer Science+Buisness Media, LCC.

Raghavendra, C. S., Sivalingam, K. M., & Znati, T. (2004). *Wireless Sensor Networks*. New York: Springer Science+Buisness Media, LCC.

Römer, K., & Friedemann, M. (2004). The Design Space of Wireless Sensor Networks. *IEEE Communications Society*, *11*(6), 54–61.

Schmitt, C. (2006). *Animal Observation using embedded technologies – Rat movement tracking*. Unpublished diploma thesis, Eberhard-Karls University, Wilhelm-Schickard-Institute for Computer Sciences, Germany, Tuebingen.

Szewczyk, R., Mainwaring, A., Polastre, J., & Culler, D. (2004). An analysis of a large scale habitat monitoring application, *Conference on Embedded Networked Sensor Systems*, (pp. 214-226). New York: ACM.

Tavares, J., Velez, F. J., & Ferro, J. M. (2008). Application of Wireless Sensor Networks to Automobiles. *Measurement Science Review*, *8*(3), 65–70. doi:10.2478/v10048-008-0017-8

Tiny, O. S. *Homepage* (2004). UC, Berkeley, California, USA. Retrieved November 20, 2008, from http://www.tinyos.net

Warneke, B., Last, M., Liebowitz, B., & Pister, K. S. J. (2001). Smart Dust: Communication with a Cubic-Millimeter Computer. *Computer*, *34*(1), 44–51. doi:10.1109/2.895117

Yang, S. (2002). *Wireless sensors from UC Berkeley and Intel researchers help conversation biologists monitor exclusive seabird in Maine*. Berkeley, CA: University of California at Berkeley, Media Relations. Retrieved November 20, 2008, from http://www.universityofcalifornia.edu/news/article/4602

Zhang, P., Sadler, C. M., Lyon, S. A., & Mortonosi, M. (2004). Hardware Design Experience in ZebraNet, (n.d.). *Conference On Embedded Networked Sensor Systems*, (pp. 227-238).New York: ACM.

Zimmermann, H. (1980). Innovations in Internetworking, OSI Reference Model – The ISO Model of Architecture for Open Systems Interconnection. [Norwood, MA: Artech House Inc.]. *IEEE Transactions on Communications*, 425–432. doi:10.1109/TCOM.1980.1094702

ADDITIONAL READING

Akyildiz, I., Su, W., Sankarasubramaniam, Y., & Cayirci, E. (2002). A survey on sensor networks .*Communications Magazine, IEEE*, *40*, 102–114. doi:10.1109/MCOM.2002.1024422

Carman, D., Kruus, P., & Matt, B. (2002). Constraints and approaches for distributed sensor network security, *DARPA Project report, (Cryptographic Technologies Group, Trusted Information System, NAI Labs Perrig, A.; Stankovic, J. & Wagner, D. (2004), Security in wireless sensor networks, *Commun. ACM* . ACM, 47, 53–57.

Pottie, G. (1998), Wireless sensor networks. *Information Theory Workshop*, (pp. 139-140)

Walters, J., Liang, Z., Shi, W., & Chaudhary, V. (2007), Wireless Sensor Network Security: A Survey.*Security in Distributed, Grid, Mobile, and Pervasive Computing,* Auerbach Pub

KEY TERMS AND DEFINITIONS

Ad-Hoc Network: A self-configuring network of routers which are connected by links.

Embedded System: A specialized computer that is used for device control where the user has no control of it because it is hidden from him.

Multihop Communication: Means that the message needs to hop over several subsystems until it reaches the final destination.

Sensor Network: A network which consists of different sensor nodes that can communicate with each other. If the network consists of wireless component it is a so called wireless sensor network (WSN).

Sensor Nodes: Represent the basis for the sensor networks and consist of a great number of single components like the data recording unit, computation unit, radio unit, external data source, actors for mobility and an antenna.

Sensors: Devices that measure data from the environment and which they can pass on.

Structural Health Monitoring (SHM): Deals with the observation of structural health in different research fields like building health or animal observation.

Two-Level Scheduling: Describes a method to more efficiently perform process scheduling.

Compilation of References

Abad, J., Badenes, A., Blasco, J., Carreras, J., Dominguez, V., & Gomez, C. (2003). Extending the power line LAN up to the neighborhood transformer. *IEEE Communications Magazine, 41*(4), 64–70. doi:10.1109/MCOM.2003.1193976

Abadie, L., Badino, P., Baud, J., Casey, J., Frohner, A., Grosdidier, G., et al. (2007). Grid-Enabled Standards-based Data Management. In *24th IEEE Conference on Mass Storage Systems and Technologies, 2007. MSST 2007,* (pp. 60-71). doi: 10.1109/MSST.2007.4367964

Abalde, C., Gulías, V. M., & Castro, L. M. (2008). Efficient discovery of widely distributed and non-volatile resources on DHTs. In A. Mellouk, J. Bi, G. Ortiz, D. K. W. Chiu, & M. Popescu (Ed.), *ICIW'08: Proceedings of the Third International Conference on Internet and Web Applications and Services* (pp. 370-376). Washington, DC, USA: IEEE Computer Society Press.

Abdelzaher, T. F., Shin, K. G., & Bhatti, N. (2002). Performance guarantees for Web server end-systems: A control-theoretical approach. In *IEEE Transactions on Parallel and Distributed Systems*, Vol. 13

Aberer, K. (2001). P-Grid: A self organizing access structure for p2p information systems. In *Proceedings of the Cooperative Information Systems, 9th International Conference (CoopIS),* (LNCS Vol. 2172, pp. 179-194). Berlin: Springer.

Aberer, K., & Despotovic, Z. (2001). Managing Trust in a Peer-2-Peer Information System. In *Proceedings of the 2001 ACM CIKM International Conference on Information and Knowledge Management, Atlanta, GA,* November 5-10, (pp. 310-317).

Aberer, K., & Despotovic, Z. (2001). Managing trust in a peer-to-peer information system. In *10th International ACM Conference on Information and Knowledge Management (CIKM)* (pp. 310–317).

Aberer, K., Cudré-Mauroux, P., Datta, A., Despotovic, Z., Hauswirth, M., Punceva, M., et al. (2003). Advanced peer-to-peer networking: The P-grid system and its applications. *PIK Journal - Praxis der Informationsverarbeitung und Kommunikation, Special Issue on P2P Systems*.

Aberer, K., Cudré-Mauroux, P., Datta, A., Despotovic, Z., Hauswirth, M., Punceva, M., & Schmidt, R. (2003). P-Grid: A Self-organizing Structured p2p System. *SIGMOD Record, 32*(3).

Aberer, K., Datta, A., & Hauswirth, M. (2003). *The quest for balancing peer load in structured peer-to-peer systems* (Tech. Rep. EPFL No. IC/2003/32). Lausanne, Switzerland: Ecole Polytechnique Fédérale de Lausanne.

Aberer, K., Datta, A., & Hauswirth, M. (2005). Multi-faceted Simultaneous Load Balancing in DHT-Based P2P Systems: A New Game with Old Balls and Bins. In *Self-star Properties in Complex Information Systems* (pp. 373-391).

Abrams, Z., McGrew, R., & Plotkin, S. A. (2005). A non-manipulable trust system based on eigentrust. *SIGecom Exchanges, 5*(4), 21–30. Retrieved from http://dblp.uni-trier.de/db/journals/sigecom/sigecom5.html#AbramsMP05

Abramson, D., Buyya, R., & Giddy, J. (2002). A computational economy for grid computing and its implementation in the Nimrod-G resource broker. *Journal of*

Future Generation Computer Systems, 18(8), 1061–1074. doi:10.1016/S0167-739X(02)00085-7

Acosta, W., & Chandra, S. (2007). Improving search using a fault-tolerant overlay in unstructured p2p systems. In *Parallel Processing, 2007. ICPP 2007. International Conference on*, page 5.

Adamic, L. A., Lukose, R. M., Puniyani, A. R., & Huberman, B. A. (2001). Search in power-law networks. *Physical Review E: Statistical, Nonlinear, and Soft Matter Physics, 64*(4), 46135. doi:10.1103/PhysRevE.64.046135

Adar, E., & Huberman, B. A. (2000). Free riding on Gnutella. *First Monday, 5*(10).

Adjie-Winoto, W., Schwartz, E., Balakrishnan, H., & Lilley, J. (1999). The design and implementation of an intentional naming system. In *SOSP '99: Proceedings of the seventeenth ACM symposium on Operating systems principles* (Vol. 33, pp. 186-201). New York: ACM Press.

Adler, M., Halperin, E., Karp, R., Vazirani, V. (2003). A stochastic process on the hypercube with applications to peer-to-peer networks. *STOC 2003.*

Adler, S. (n.d.). *The slashdot effect: An analysis of three internet publications.* Retrieved from http://ssadler.phy.bnl.gov/adler/SDE/SlashDotEffect.html

AFS. (2008). *Andrew File System.* Retrieved December 5, 2008, from http://www.openafs.org/

Agarwal, A., Norman, D. O., & Gupta, A. (2004). *Wireless grids: Approaches, architectures, and technical challenges.* Working Paper 4459-04. MIT Sloan School of Management.

Aggarwal, V., & Feldmann, A. (2008, May). *ISP-Aided Neighbor Selection in P2P Systems.* Retrieved from http://www.funchords.com/p2pi/28%20aggarwal-p2pi.pdf

Aggarwal, V., Feldmann, A., & Scheideler, C. (2007). Can ISPs and P2P Users Cooperate for Improved Performance? *ACM SIGCOMM Computer Communication Review, 37*(3), 29–40. doi:10.1145/1273445.1273449

Aho, A., & Lee, D. (2000). Hierarchical networks and the LSA n-squared problem in OSPF routing. In *IEEE Global Telecommunications Conference* (pp. 379-404).

Ahuja, S. P., & Myers, J. R. (2006). A survey on wireless grid computing. *The Journal of Supercomputing, 37*, 3–21. doi:10.1007/s11227-006-3845-z

Akbarinia, R., Pacitti, E., & Valduriez, P. (2007). Data currency in replicated DHTs. In *Proc. SIGMOD 2007 ACM Int'l Conference on Management of Data,* Beijing, China (pp. 211-222).

Akkiraju, R., Farrell, J., Miller, J., Nagarajan, M., Schmidt, M., Sheth, A., & Verma, K. (2006). *Web service semantics: WSDLS.* Retrieved February 20, 2007 from http://www.w3.org/Submission/WSDL-S

Akogrimo. (n.d.). Retrieved May 1, 2009, from http://www.mobilegrids.org/

Al Zain, A., Hammond, K., Trinder, P., Linton, S., Loidl, H. W., & Costantini, M. (2007). SymGrid-Par: design a framework for executing computational algebra systems on computational Grids. In *Procs. ICCS'07, Intl. Conference on Computer Science Beijing,* (LNCS 4488, pp.617–624). Berlin: Springer.

Al Zain, A., Trinder, P. W., Loidl, H. W., & Michaelson, G. J. (2007). Supporting high-level Grid parallel programming: the design and implementation of Grid-GUM2. In *Procs. UK e-Science Prog. All Hands Meeting.*

Al Zain, A., Trinder, P., Michaelson, G., & Loidl, H. (2008). Evaluating a High-Level Parallel Language (GpH) for Computational GRIDs. *IEEE Transactions on Parallel and Distributed Systems, 19*(2), 219–233. doi:10.1109/TPDS.2007.70728

Al-Ali, R., Hafid, A., Rana, O., & Walker, D. (2003). QoS adaptation in service-oriented Grids. In *Proceedings of the 1st International Workshop on Middleware for Grid Computing (MGC2003).* Retrieved November 12, 2008, from http://www.wesc.ac.uk/resources/publications/pdf/MGC289_final.pdf

Alamri, A., Eid, M., & El Saddik, A. (2006). Classification of the state-of-the-art dynamic web services composition techniques. *International Journal of Web and Grid Services*, *2*(2), 148–166. doi:10.1504/IJWGS.2006.010805

Albert, R., & Barabási, A. (2002). Statistical mechanics of complex networks. *Reviews of Modern Physics*, *74*, 47–97. doi:10.1103/RevModPhys.74.47

Albert, R., & Barabasi, A. L. (2000). Topology of evolving networks: local events and universality. *Physical Review Letters*, *85*, 5234–5237. doi:10.1103/PhysRevLett.85.5234

Alberts, D. S., & Hayes, R. E. (2005). *Power to the Edge.* Command and Control Research Program (CCRP) Publications Series.

Albrecht, K., Arnold, R., Gahwiler, M., & Wattenhofer, R. (2004). Aggregating information in peer-to-peer systems for improved join and leave. In *P2P '04: Proceedings of the Fourth International Conference on Peer-to-Peer Computing* (pp. 227-234). Washington, DC, USA: IEEE Computer Society Press.

Alda, S., & Cremers, A. B. (2005). Towards Composition Management for Component-based Peer-to-Peer Architectures. *Elsevier Electronic Notes in Theoretical Computer Science*, *114*(1), 47–64. doi:10.1016/j.entcs.2004.02.067

Alfano, R., Manzalini, A., & Moiso, C. (2007). Distributed Service Framework: an innovative open eco-system for ICT/Telecommunications. In *1st Conference on Autonomic Computing and Communication Systems*. New York: ACM Digital Library.

Alfieri, R., Cecchini, R., Ciaschini, V., dell'Agnello, L., Frohner, A., Gianoli, A., et al. (2003). Voms: An authorization system for virtual organizations. In *Proceedings of the 1st European Across Grids Conference*, Santiago de Compostela.

Alhusaini, A. H., Prasanna, V. K., & Raghavendra, C. S. (2000). A framework for mapping with resource co-allocation in heterogeneous computing systems. In C. Raghavendra (Ed.), *Heterogeneous Computing Workshop* (pp. 273-286). Los Alamitos, CA: IEEE Computer Society.

Alhusaini, A. H., Raghavendra, C. S., & Prasanna, V. K. (2001). Run-time adaptation for grid environments. In B. Werner (Ed.), *International Parallel and Distributed Processing Symposium* (pp. 864-874). Los Alamitos, CA: IEEE Computer Society.

Ali, H. A., Salem, M. M., & Hamza, A. A. (2007). A framework for scalable autonomous P2P resource discovery for the Grid implementation. *International Journal of Computer Science and Engineering*, *1*(3), 145–154.

Allen, G., Angulo, D., Foster, I., Lanfermann, G., Liu, C., & Radke, T. (2001). The Cactus Worm: Experiments with dynamic resource discovery and allocation in a Grid environment. *International Journal of High Performance Computing Applications*, *15*(4), 345–358. doi:10.1177/109434200101500402

Almeida, D., Baptista, C., Silva, E., Campelo, C., Nunes, C., Costa, B., et al. (2005). Using Service-Oriented Architecture in Context-Aware Applications. In *Brazilian Symposium on GeoInformatics – GEOINFO, INPE* (pp. 15-29).

Almeira, H., Costa, E., Paes, R., & Percusich, A. (2004). Compor: a methodology, a component model, a component based framework and tools to build multiagent systems. *CLEI Electronic Journal, 7*(1).

Almes, G., Kalidindi, S., & Zekauskas, M. (1999, September). *A One-way Delay Metric for IPPM.* RFC 2679 (Proposed Standard).

Alnemr, R., & Meinel, C. (2008). Getting more from reputation systems: A context–aware reputation framework based on trust centers and agent lists. In *The Third International Multi-Conference on Computing in the Global Information Technology* (pp. 137-142), Greece. Washington, DC: IEEE Computer Society Press.

Alonso, G., Casati, F., Kuno, H., & Machiraju, V. (2004). *Web Services - Concepts, Architecture and Applications.* London: Springer.

Al-Oqily, I., & Karmouch, A. (2009). Towards automating overlay network management. *Academic Press Journal of Network and Computer Applications*, *32*(2), 461–473. doi:10.1016/j.jnca.2008.02.013

Alqaralleh, B. A., Wang, C., Zhou, B. B., & Zomaya, A. Y. (2007). Effects of replica placement algorithms on performance of structured overlay networks. In *Proc. IPDPS 2007, IEEE Int'l Parallel & Distributed Processing Symposium,* Long Beach, CA, USA (pp. 1-8).

Al-Riyami, S. S., & Paterson, K. G. (2003). Certificateless public key cryptography. In C.S. Laih (Ed.), *Advances in Cryptology - Proceedings of ASIACRYPT 2003,* (LNCS Vol. 2894, pp. 452-473). Berlin: Springer-Verlag.

Alsaid, A., & Mitchell, C. J. (2005). Installing fake root keys in a PC. In D. Chadwick & G. Zhao (Eds.), *Proceedings of the 2nd European Public Key Infrastructure Workshop (EuroPKI 2005),* (LNCS Vol. 3545, pp. 227-239). Berlin: Springer-Verlag.

Amazon Elastic Compute Cloud. *Developer Guide.* (2008). Retrieved February 15, 2009, from http://awsdocs.s3.amazonaws.com/EC2/latest/ec2-dg.pdf

Amazon. (n.d.). *Amazon Web Services. Amazon elastic compute cloud (amazon EC2).* Retrieved May 11, 2009, from http://aws.amazon.com/ec2/

Amazon-EC2. (2008). *Amazon Elastic Computing Cloud.* Retrieved December 5, 2008, from http://aws.amazon.com/ec2/

American National Standards Institute. (1997). *American National Standard X9.30.2-1997: Public key cryptography for the financial services industry - Part 2: The secure hash algorithm (SHA-1).*

Amin, K., Laszewski, G., & Mikler, A. (2004, October). *Toward an architecture for ad hoc grids.* Argonne, USA: Argonne National Laboratory. Retrieved May 11, 2009, from http://www-unix.mcs.anl.gov/~laszewsk/papers/vonLaszewski-adhoc-adcom2004.pdf

Amoretti, M., Zanichelli, F., & Conte, G. (2005). SP2A: A service-oriented framework for P2Pbased Grids. In *ACM International Conference Proceeding Series: Vol. 117. 3rd international workshop on Middleware for grid computing* (pp. 1-6).

Amoretti, M., Zanichelli, F., & Conte, G. (2008, April). Enabling Peer-To-Peer Web Service Architectures With JXTA-SOAP. In *Proceedings of IADIS International Conference e-Society 2008,* Algarve, Portugal.

Ananthanarayanan, G., Padmanabhan, V. N., Ravindranath, L., & Thekkath, C. A. (2007). COMBINE: Leveraging the power of wireless peers through collaborative downloading. In E. W. Knightly, G. B. Borriello, & R. Cáceres (Eds.), *Proceedings of the 5th International Conference on Mobile Systems, Applications, and Services (MobiSys 2007),* (pp. 286-298). San Juan, Puerto Rico.

Andersen, C. F. (1996). *A Computational Model of Complex Concept Composition.* Unpublished master's thesis, Dept CS, Univ Texas at Austin.

Andersen, D., Balakrishnan, H., Kaashoek, F., & Morris, R. (2001). Resilient Overlay Networks. In *Symposium on Operating Systems Principles* (pp. 131–145)

Anderson, D. (2001). SETI@Home. *Peer-To-Peer: Harnessing the benefits of a disruptive technology* (pp. 67-77). Sebastopol, CA: O'Reilly.

Anderson, D. P. (2004, November). BOINC: A System for Public-Resource Computing and Storage. In *proceedings of the 5th IEEE/ACM workshop on Grid Computing (Grid '04),* Pittsburgh, USA (pp. 4-10).

Anderson, D. P., Cobb, J., Korpela, E., Lebofsky, M., & Werthimer, D. (2002). SETI@home – An experiment in public resource computing. *Communications of the ACM, 45*(11), 56–61. doi:10.1145/581571.581573

Anderson, D. P., Werthimer, D., Korpela, E., Cobb, J., Lebofsky, M., Bankay, R., et al. (2008). *SETI@home.* Retrieved November 18, 2008, from http://setiathome.berkeley.edu/

Anderson, T., Arpacie, R., Culler, D., Dahlin, M., Dusseau, A., & Ghormley, D. (1995). A case for networks of workstations (now). *IEEE Micro, 15*(1), 54–64. doi:10.1109/40.342018

Andradea, N., Brasileiroa, F., Cirnea, W., & Mowbray, M. (2007). Automatic Grid assembly by promoting collaboration in Peer-to-Peer grids. *Journal of Parallel and Distributed Computing, 67,* 957–966. doi:10.1016/j.jpdc.2007.04.011

Andreozzi, S., Sgaravatto, M., & Vistoli, C. (2003). Sharing a Conceptual Model of Grid Resources and Services. In *Proceedings of the Conference on Computing in High Energy and Nuclear Physics (CHEP 2003)*, La Jolla, CA, USA, Mar 2003.

Andrian, C., Peter, H., Aditya, G., Sim, K., & George, D. (2003). *Using Portal Technology for Collaborative e-Commerce*. White Paper. Retrieved January 13th, 2006 from www.dsl.uow.edu.au/publications/techreports/collins04portal.pdf

Andrieux, A., Czajkowski, K., Dan, A., Keahey, K., Ludwig, H., Pruyne, J., et al. (2004). *Web services agreement specification (WS-Agreement)*. Tech. Rep. Global Grid Forum.

Andrzejak, A., & Xu, Z. (2002). Scalable, efficient range queries for grid information services. In R. L. Graham & N. Shahmehri (Eds.), *Proceedings of 2nd International Conference on Peer-to-Peer Computing (P2P 2002)* (pp. 33-40). Washington, DC: IEEE Computer Society

Angel, E., Bampis, E., & Pascual, F. (2006). The price of approximate stability for a scheduling game problem. In *Proceedings of Euro-Par*, (LNCS Vol. 4128). Berlin: Springer.

Angelov, S., & Grefen, P. (2006). A case study on electronic contracting in on-line advertising - status and prospects. In L. M. Camarinha-Matos, H. Afsarmanesh, & M. Ollus (Ed.), *Network-centric collaboration and supporting frameworks - Proceedings 7th IFIP Working Conference on Virtual Enterprises*, (pp. 419–428). Berlin: Springer.

Anjomshoaa, A. et al. (2005, November). *Job submission description language (JSDL) specification v. 1.0*. Open Grid Forum document GFD.56.

Annavaram, M., Grochowski, E., & Shen, J. (2005, June). Mitigating Amdahl's law through EPI throttling. In *Proc. 32nd Annual International Symposium on Computer Architecture (ISCA'05)* (pp. 298-309).

Antonopoulos, N., & Salter, J. (2004). Efficient Resource Discovery in Grids and P2P Networks. *Internet Research, 14*, 339–346. doi:10.1108/10662240410566926

Antonopoulos, N., & Shafarenko, A. (2001). An Active Organisation System for Customised, Secure Agent Discovery. *The Journal of Supercomputing, 20*(1), 5–35. doi:10.1023/A:1011122319458

AOL. (n.d.). Retrieved from http://video.aol.com
Aqualab. (n.d.). Retrieved from http://www.aqualab.cs.northwestern.edu/

Apache. (1998). Retrieved from http://tomcat.apache.org/

Apache. (2003). Retrieved from http://ws.apache.org/juddi/

Apache. (2008). *Apache muse – A Java-based implementation of WSRF 1.2, WSN 1.3, and WSDM 1.1*. Retrieved November 5, 2008 from http://ws.apache.org/muse/index.html.

Apostolopoulos, G., Williams, D., Kamat, S., Guerin, R., Orda, A., & Przygienda, T. (1999). *QoS routing mechanisms and OSPF extensions, RFC 2676*. Internet Engineering Task Force (IETF).

Arasu, A., Babcock, B., Babu, S., Datar, M., Ito, K., Nishizawa, I., Rosenstein, J., & Widom, J. (2003). STREAM: The Stanford Stream Data Manager. *IEEE Data Engineering Bulletin, March*.

Arenas, A. (2006). *State of the art survey on trust and security in Grid computing systems*. FP6 CoreGrid project report.

Arora, M., Das, S., & Biswas, R. (2002). A De-centralized Scheduling and Load Balancing Algorithm for Heterogeneous Grid Environments. In *ICPP.Workshops* (pp. 499-505).

Asokan, N., Schunter, M., & Waidner, M. (1997). Optimistic protocols for fair exchange. In *4th ACM Conference on Computer and Communications Security* (pp. 7–17).

Aspnes, J., & Shah, G. (2007). Skip graphs. *ACM Trans. Algorithms, 3*(4), 37. doi:10.1145/1290672.1290674

Atkins, D. E., Birmingham, W. P., Durfee, E. H., Glover, E. J., Mullen, T., & Rundensteiner, E. A. (1996). Toward inquiry-based education through interacting software agents. *IEEE Computer, 29*(5), 67–76.

Atkinson, S. R., & Moffat, J. (2005). *The Agile Organization.* Command and Control Research Program (CCRP) Publications Series.

Aumage, O., & Mercier, G. (2003). MPICH/MADIII: A cluster of clusters enabled MPI implementation. In F. Titsworth & D. Azada (Eds.), *International Symposium on Cluster Computing and the Grid* (pp. 26). Los Alamitos, California: IEEE Computer Society.

Avaki. (2008). *Sybase Avaki for Data Grid.* Retrieved December 5, 2008, from http://www.sybase.com/products/allproductsaz/avakieii/sybaseavakifordatagrid

Avizienis, A. (1985). The n-version approach to fault-tolerant software. *IEEE Transactions on Software Engineering, 11,* 1985. doi:10.1109/TSE.1985.231893

Avnur, R., & Hellerstein, J. (2000). Eddies: Continuously adaptive query processing. In *Proceedings ACM SIGMOD 2000,* (pp. 261-272).

Awan, A., Ferreira, R. A., Jagannathan, S., & Grama, A. (2006). Unstructured peer-to-peer networks for sharing processor cycles. *Parallel Computing, 32*(2), 115–135. doi:10.1016/j.parco.2005.09.002

Awerbuch, B., Patt-Shamir, B., & Varghese, G. (1996). Self-Stabilizing End-to-End Communication. *Journal of High Speed Networks, 5*(4), 365–381.

Axelrod, R. (1984). *The Evolution of Cooperation.* New York: Basic Books.

Azar, Y., Broder, A., Karlin, A., & Upfal, E. (2000). Balanced Allocations. *SIAM Journal on Computing, 29*(1), 180–200. doi:10.1137/S0097539795288490

Azougagh, D., Yu, J.-L., Kim, J.-S., & Maeng, S. R. (2005). Resource co-allocation: A complementary technique that enhances performance in grid computing environment. In L. Barolli (Ed.), *International Conference on Parallel and Distributed Systems* (Vol. 1, pp. 36-42). Los Alamitos, CA: IEEE Computer Society.

Azzedin, F., & Maheswaran, M. (2002). Evolving and managing trust in Grid computing systems. *Electrical and Computer Engineering, IEEE CCECE, 3,* 1424–1429.

Azzedin, F., & Maheswaran, M. (2002). Towards trust-aware resource management in Grid computing systems. In *CCGRID 2002, IEEE Computer Society,* (pp. 452-457).

Azzedin, F., & Maheswaran, M. (2003). Trust modeling for peer-to-peer based computing systems. In *IPDPS: Year of Publication 2003. International Parallel and Distributed Processing Symposium* (pp. 99.1). Washington, DC: IEEE Computer Society

Azzedin, F., Maheswaran, M., & Arnason, N. (2004). A synchronous co-allocation mechanism for grid computing systems. *Cluster Computing, 7*(1), 39–49. doi:10.1023/B:CLUS.0000003942.73875.29

Azzedin, F., Maheswaran, M., & Mitra, A. (2006). Applying a trust brokering system to resource matchmaking in public-resource grids. *Journal of Grid Computing, 4,* 247–263. doi:10.1007/s10723-006-9041-9

Bader, D. (2007). *Petascale Computing Algorithms and Applications.* New York: Chapman and Hall/CRC.

Baer, M. (2003). The Ultimate on-the-fly Network. *On Newsstands Now, 11*(12). Retrieved November 20, 2008, from http://www.wired.com/wired/archive/11.12/network.html

Bagchi, S. (2005). Simulation of Grid computing infrastructures: Challenges and solutions. *Winter Simulation Conference* (pp. 1773-1780). New York: ACM.

Bai, C., Schlesewsky, B. I., Wang, L., Hung, Y. C., Schlesewsky, M., & Burkhardt, P. (2008). Semantic composition engenders an N400: evidence from Chinese compounds. *Neuroreport, 19*(6), 695. doi:10.1097/WNR.0b013e3282fc1eb7

Bailey, D. (2006). Power efficiency metrics, for the top500. Top500 BoF, Supercomputing 2006.

Bailey, N. T. J. (1957). *The Mathematical Theory of Epidemics.* New York: Hafner.

Baird, I. (2003). *Grids in practice: A platform perspective Middleware Spectra.* Retrieved May 11, 2009, from http://middlewarespectra.com/grid/

Balakrishnan, H. (2003). Looking Up Data in P2P Systems. *Communications of the ACM, 46*(2), 43–48. doi:10.1145/606272.606299

Balazinska, M., Balakrishnan, H., & Karger, D. (2002). INS/Twine: A scalable peer-to-peer architecture for intentional resource discovery. In *Pervasive'02: Proceedings of the First International Conference on Pervasive Computing* (pp. 195-210). Berlin: Springer.

Banavar, G., Chandra, T. D., Mukerjee, B., Nagarajarao, J., Strom, R. E., & Sturman, D. C. (1999). An efficient multicast protocol for content-based publish-subscribe systems. In . *Proceedings of ICDCS, 1999,* 262–272.

Bandwidth management for peer-to-peer applications [F5 white paper]. (2007) Retrieved from http://www.f5.com/pdf/ white-papers/rateshaping-wp.pdf

Banerjee, S., Kommareddy, C., Kar, K., Bhattacharjee, B., & Khuller, S. (2003, April). Construction of an efficient overlay multicast infrastructure for real-time applications. *IEEE Infocom.*

Banerjee, S., Lee, S., Bhattacharjee, B., & Srinivasan, A. (2003). Resilient multicast using overlays. In *SIGMETRICS '03: Proceedings of the 2003 ACM SIGMETRICS international conference on Measurement and modeling of computer systems* (pp. 102–113). New York: ACM.

Banerjee, S., Lee, S., Bhattacharjee, B., & Srinivasan, A. (2003). Resilient multicast using overlays. *ACM sigmetrics.*

Banga, G., & Druschel, P. (1997). Measuring the capacity of a web server. In *Proceedings of the USENIX Symposium on Internet Technologies and Systems.*

Barabási, A. L., & Albert, R. (1999). Emergence of Scaling in Random Networks. *Science, 286*(5439), 509. doi:10.1126/science.286.5439.509

Barabási, A. L., Albert, R., & Jeong, H. (2000). Scale-free characteristics of random networks: the topology of the world-wide web. *Physica A: Statistical Mechanics and its Applications, 281*(1-4), 69-77.

Baraka, R., Caprotti, O., & Schreiner, W. (2005). A Web registry for publishing and discovering mathematical services. In *Procs. EEE-05* (pp.190-193). Washington, DC: IEEE Computer Society Press.

Barham, P. Dragovic, B., Fraser, K., Hand, S., Harris, T. L., Ho, A., Neugebauer, R., Pratt, I., & Warfield, A. (2003). Xen and the art of virtualization. In C. Roisin, E. V. Munson, & C. Vanoirbeek (Eds.), *Proceedings of the 19th ACM Symposium on Operating Systems Principles* (pp. 164–177). New York: ACM.

Barkai, D. (2001). *Peer-to-peer computing: Technologies for sharing and collaborating on the net.* Santa Clara, CA: Intel Press.

Barnes, S. B. (2006). A privacy paradox: Social networking in the United States. *First Monday, 11*(9).

Baroncelli, F., Martini, B., Martini, V., & Castoldi, P. (2007, May 21-25). A distributed signalling for the provisioning of on-demand VPN services in transport networks. In *10th IFIP/IEEE International Symposium on Integrated Network Management (IM 2007),* Munich, Germany.

Baroncelli, F., Martini, B., Valcarenghi, L., & Castoldi, P. (2006, July 16-18). Service Composition in Automatically Switched Transport Networks. *IEEE International Conference on Networking and Services (ICNS'06),* Silicon Valley, CA.

Barr, K., & Asanovic, K. (2006). Energy aware lossless data compression. *ACM Transactions on Computer Systems, 24*(3), 250–291. doi:10.1145/1151690.1151692

Baset, S. A., & Schulzrinne, H. G. (2006). An Analysis of the Skype Peer-to-Peer Internet Telephony Protocol. In *Proceedings INFOCOM 2006. 25th IEEE International Conference on Computer Communications,* (pp. 1-11). doi: 10.1109/INFOCOM.2006.312

Baset, S., & Schulzrinne, H. (2005). An analysis of the Skype Peer-to-Peer Internet Telephony Protocol. Technical Report CUCS-039-04, Department of Computer Science, Columbia University.

Baset, S., Jennings, C., Lowekamp, B., Rescorla, E., & Schulzrinne, H. (2008). *Resource Location and Discovery (RELOAD), P2P SIP working group.* In internet draft.

Basney, J., Humphrey, M., & Welch, V. (2005). The My-Proxy online credential repository. *Journal of Software: Practice and Experience, 35*(9), 817–826. doi:10.1002/spe.689

Bastida, L., Nieto, J. F., & Tola, R. (2008). Context-aware service composition: a methodology and a case study. In *SDSOA '08: Proceedings of the 2nd international workshop on Systems development in SOA environments* (pp. 19-24).

Basu, S., Banerjee, S., Sharma, P., & Lee, S. J. (2005). NodeWiz: Peer-to-peer resource discovery for Grids. In *CCGRid'05 . Proceedings of IEEE International Symposium on Cluster Computing and the Grid, 1*, 213–220. doi:10.1109/CCGRID.2005.1558557

Batista, D. M., & da Fonseca, N. L. S. (2007). A Brief Survey on Resource Allocation in Service Oriented Grids. In *Globecom Workshops - 1st IEEE Workshop on Enabling the Future Service-Oriented Internet* (pp. 1-5). Washington, DC: IEEE.

Batista, D. M., & da Fonseca, N. L. S. (2008). Empowering Grids with flexibility to cope with uncertainties. In *ICC Workshops '08 - (CAMAD 2008)* (pp. 227-231). Washington, DC: IEEE.

Batista, D. M., da Fonseca, N. L. S., Miyazawa, F. K., & Granelli, F. (2008). Self-adjustment of resource allocation for Grid applications. *Computer Networks, 52*(9), 1762–1781. doi:10.1016/j.comnet.2008.03.002

Battelle, J. (2005). *The Search: How Google and Its Rivals Rewrote the Rules of Business and Transformed Our Culture.* Portfolio Hardcover.

Baumgart, I., Heep, B., & Krause, S. (2007). A P2PSIP Demonstrator Powered by OverSim. In *7th IEEE Conference on P2P Computing* (pp. 243-244). New York: IEEE Computer Society.

Baumgartner, H., & Pieters, R. (2000). *The influence of marketing journals: A citation analysis of the discipline and its sub-areas.* The Netherlands: Tilburg University, Center of Economic Research.

Bayardo, R. J., Crainiceanu, A., & Agrawal, R. (2003). Peer-to-Peer sharing of Web applications. In *Proceedings of WWW2003*, Budapest, Hungary.

BBC. (2006). *Chilly chip shatters speed record.* Retrieved December 5, 2008, from http://news.bbc.co.uk/1/hi/technology/5099584.stm

Beaumont, O., Kermarrec, A.-M., Marchal, L., & Riviere, E. (2007). VoroNet: A scalable object network based on Voronoi tessellations. In *Proceedings of the Parallel and Distributed Processing Symposium.*

Beaver, D. d., & Rosen, R. (1978). Studies in scientific collaboration: Part i. The professional origins of scientific co-authorship. *Scientometrics, 1.*

Beckles, B., Welch, V., & Basney, J. (2005). Mechanisms for increasing the usability of grid security. *International Journal of Human-Computer Studies, 63*(1-2), 74–101. doi:10.1016/j.ijhcs.2005.04.017

Beiriger, J. I., Johnson, W. R., Bivens, H. P., Humphreys, S. L., & Rhea, R. (2000). Constructing the ASCI Computational Grid. In *Proceedings of the Ninth International Symposium on High Performance Distributed Computing (HPDC 2000)*, Pittsburgh, PA. Washington, DC: CS Press.

Belqasmi, F., Glitho, R., & Dssouli, R. (2008). Ambient Network Composition. *IEEE Network, 22*(4), 6–12. doi:10.1109/MNET.2008.4579765

Belwood, T., Capell, S., Clement, L., Colgrave, J., Dovey, M. J., Feygin, D., et al. (2004). *UDDI Spec TC.* Retrieved November 2, 2008, from http://www.oasis-open.org/committees/uddi-spec/doc/spec/v3/uddi-v3.0.2-20041019.htm

Benini, L., & Micheli, G. D. (1998). *Dynamic Power Management: Design Techniques and CAD Tools.* Norwell, Massachusetts: Kluwer Academic Publishers.

Bergman, M. K. (2001). White paper: The deep Web: Surfacing hidden value. *Journal of Electronic Publishing, 7*(1). doi:10.3998/3336451.0007.104

Berners-Lee, T., Fielding, R., & Masinter, L. (1998). *Uniform resource identifier (URI), generic syntax.*

Retrieved September 22, 2008, from http://www.ietf. org/rfc/rfc2396.txt

Berners-Lee, T., Hendler, J., & Lassila, O. (2001). The Semantic Web: A new form of Web content that is meaningful to computers will unleash a revolution of new possibilities. *Scientific American, 284*(5), 34–43. doi:10.1038/scientificamerican0501-34

Bernstein, P. A., & Goodman, N. (1981). Concurrency control in distributed database systems. *ACM Computing Surveys, 13*(2), 185–221. doi:10.1145/356842.356846

Bernstein, P. A., Hadzilacos, V., & Goodman, N. (1987). *Concurrency control and recovery in database systems.* Boston: Addison-Wesley Longman Publishing Co., Inc.

Berry, M. W., Dumais, S. T., & O'Brien, G. W. (1995). Using linear algebra for intelligent information retrieval. *SIAM Review, 37*(4), 573–595. doi:10.1137/1037127

Best, P. (1998). *Implementing value at risk*, (pp. 1-102), London: Wiley.

Bethel, W., Siegerist, C., Shalf, J., Shetty, P., Jankun-Kelly, T., Kreylos, O., & Ma, K.-L. (2003). *VisPortal: Deploying Grid-enabled visualization tools through a Web-portal interface.* Tech. Rep. No.LBNL-52940, Lawrence Berkeley National Laboratory.

Bethencourt, J., Sahai, A., & Waters, B. (2007). Ciphertext-policy attribute-based encryption. In *Proceedings of IEEE Symposium on Security and Privacy (SP 2007)*, (pp. 321-334). Washington, DC: IEEE Computer Society Press.

Beven, K., Romanowicz, R., Pappenberger, F., Young, P., & Werner, M. (2005). The Uncertainty Cascade in Flood Forecasting. In *Proceedings of the ACTIF meeting on Flood Risk*, Tromsø.

Bhagwan, R., Tati, K., Cheng, Y., Savage, S., & Voelker, G. M. (2004). Totalrecall: System support for automated availability management. In *Proceedings of the 2nd symposium on Networked Systems Design And Implementation (NSDI)*.

Bhagwan, R., Varghese, G., & Voelker, G. M. (2003). *Cone: Augmenting DHTs to support distributed resource discovery* (Tech. Rep. CS2003-0755). San Diego, CA: University of California, Department of Computer Science and Engineering.

Bhagyavati, & Kurkovsky, S. (2004). Emerging issues in wireless computational grids for mobile devices. In *Proceedings of the 8th World Multiconference on Systemics, Cybernetics and Informatics (SCI-2004)*, Orlando, FL, USA. BUILDER_UK. (2003, August). *OGSI-based system management: Manageability services for linux.* Retrieved May 11, 2009, from http://uk.builder.com/ whitepapers/0,39026692,60109062p-39000780q,00. htm

Bharambe, A. R., Agrawal, M., & Seshan, S. (2004). Mercury: Supporting scalable multi-attribute range queries. In *SIGCOMM '04: Proceedings of the 2004 conference on Applications, technologies, architectures, and protocols for computer communications* (pp. 353-366). New York: ACM Press.

Bharambe, A. R., Herley, C., & Padmanabhan, V. N. (2006). Analyzing and Improving BitTorrent Performance. In *25th IEEE International Conference on Computer Communications (INFOCOM)* (pp. 1-12).

Bhaskar, P., & Ahamed, S. I. (2007). Privacy in Pervasive Computing and Open Issues. In *The Second International Conference on Availability, Reliability and Security (ARES'07)* (pp. 147-154).

Bhatia, K. (2005). *Peer-To-Peer Requirements On The Open Grid Services Architecture Framework.* GGF document by the OGSA P2P Research Group. Retrieved from www.ggf.org

Bhattacharjee, R., & Goel, A. (2005). Avoiding ballot-stuffing in eBay-like reputation systems. In *Proceedings of the 2005 ACM SIGCOMM Workshop on Economics of Peer-to-Peer Systems*, (pp.133-137), Philadelphia, Pensylvania, USA.

Bhoj, P., Ramanathan, S., & Singhal, S. (2000, May). Web2K: Bringing QoS to Web servers. HP Labs Technical Report, HPL-2000-61.

Bianchini, R., & Rajamony, R. (2004). Power and energy management for server systems. *Computer, 37,* 68–74. doi:10.1109/MC.2004.217

Bickerton, D. (1990). *Language & species.* IL: The University of Chicago Press.

Bindal, R., Cao, P., Chan, W., Medval, J., Suwala, G., Bates, T., & Zhang, A. (2006, July). Improving Traffic Locality in BitTorrent via Biased Neighbor Selection. In *Proceedings of the ICDCS,* Lisboa, Portugal. *Bittorrent.* (n.d.). Retrieved from http://www.bittorrent.com

Biswas, A., Mohan, S., & Mahapatra, R. (2008). Optimization of semantic routing table. In *Computer Communications and Networks, 2008. ICCCN '08. Proceedings of 17th International Conference on* (pp. 1-6).

Biswas, A., Mohan, S., & Mahapatra, R. (2009). Search Co-ordination by Semantic Routed Network. In *18th International Conference on Computer Communications and Networks,* US Virgin Islands.

Biswas, A., Mohan, S., Panigrahy, J., Tripathy, A., & Mahapatra, R. (2009). Representation and Comparison of Complex Concepts for Semantic Routed Network. In *10th International Conference on Distributed Computing and Networking (ICDCN),* Hyderabad.

Biswas, A., Mohan, S., Tripathy, A., Panigrahy, J., & Mahapatra, R. (2009). Semantic key for meaning based searching. In *3rd IEEE International Conference on Semantic Computing,* Berkeley, CA.

Bittorrent Inc. (2008). Retrieved October 2008 from http://www.bittorrent.com/

Blake, C., & Rodrigues, R. (2003). High availability, scalable storage, dynamic peer network: Pick two. In *Proceedings of the 9th workshop on hot topics in operating systems (hotos-ix).*

Blaze, M., Feigenbaum, J., & Lacy, J. (1996, May). Decentralized trust management. In *Proc. of 1996 IEEE Symposium of Security and Privacy,* (pp.164–173), Oakland, CA.

Blythe, J., Jain, S., Deelman, E., Gil, Y., Vahi, K., Mandal, A., & Kennedy, K. (2005). Task scheduling strategies for workflow-based applications in Grids. In *IEEE International Symposium on Cluster Computing and Grids (CCGRID'05), volume 2* (pp. 759-767). Washington, DC: IEEE.

Böhm, K., & Buchman, E. (2009). Free Riding-Aware Forwarding in Content-Addressable Networks. *VLDB Journal.*

Boivie, R., Feldman, N., & Metz, C. (2000). On the Wire - Small Group Multicast: A New Solution for Multicasting on the Internet. *IEEE Internet Computing, 4*(3), 75–79. doi:10.1109/4236.845393

Boldyreva, A., Goyal, V., & Kumar, V. (2008). Identity-based encryption with efficient revocation. In *Proceedings of the 15th ACM Conference on Computer and Communications Security (CCS 2008),* (pp. 417-426). New York: ACM Press.

Bolie, J., et al. (2006). *BPEL Cookbook: Best Practices for SOA-based Integration and Composite Applications Development.* UK: Packt Publishing.

Bolze, R. (2006). Grid'5000: A large scale and highly reconfigurable experimental Grid testbed. *International Journal of High Performance Computing Applications, 20*(4), 481–494. doi:10.1177/1094342006070078

Bolze, R., Cappello, F., Caron, E., Daydé, M., Desprez, F., & Jeannot, E. (2006). Grid'5000: a Large Scale and Highly Reconfigurable Experimental Grid Testbed. *International Journal of High Performance Computing Applications, 20*(4), 481–494. doi:10.1177/1094342006070078

Bonatti, P., Duma, C., Olmedilla, D., & Shahmehri, N. (2005). An integration of reputation-based and policy-based trust management. In *Semantic Web Policy Workshop in Conjunction with 4th International Semantic Web Conference,* Galway, Ireland.

Bonawitz, K., Chandrasekhar, C., & Viana, R. (2004). *Portable reputations with EgoSphere.* Cambridge, MA: MIT Internal Report.

Boneh, D., & Franklin, M. (2001). Identity-based encryption from the Weil pairing. In J. Kilian (Ed.), *Advances in Cryptology - Proceedings of CRYPTO 2001,* (LNCS Vol. 2139, pp. 213-229). Berlin: Springer-Verlag.

Boneh, D., Boyen, X., & Goh, E. (2005). Hierarchical identity based encryption with constant size ciphertext. In R. Cramer (Ed.), *Advances in Cryptology - Proceedings of EUROCRYPT 2005,* (LNCS Vol. 3494, pp. 440-456). Berlin: Springer-Verlag.

Boniface, M., Phillips, S. C., & Sanchez-macian, A. (2007). Dynamic Service Provisioning Using GRIA SLAs. In *Non Functional Properties and Service Level Agreements in Service Oriented Computing Workshop, NFPSLA-SOC'07.*

Booth, D., Haas, H., McCabe, F., Newcomer, E., Champion, M., Ferris, C., et al. (2004). *Web Services Architecture, W3C Working Group Note 11 February 2004.* Retrieved from http://www. w3. org/TR/ws-arch

Borch, N. T. (2005). Improving semantic routing efficiency. In *Second International Workshop on Hot Topics in Peer-to-Peer Systems, 2005. HOT-P2P 2005* (pp. 80-86).

Borch, N. T., & Vognild, L. K. (2004). Searching in variably connected P2P networks. In *International MultiConference in Computer Science & Computer Engineering.*

Bote-Lorenzo, M., Dimitriadis, Y., & Gomez-Sanchez, E. (2002). *Grid characteristics and uses: a grid definition.* Technical Report CICYT, Univ. of Valladolid, Spain.

Bote-Lorenzo, M., Dimitriadis, Y., & Gomez-Sanchez, E. (2004). Grid characteristics and uses: A Grid definition. In *Postproc. of the First European Across Grids Conference (ACG'03),* (Springer-Verlag LNCS Vol. 2970, pp. 291-298), Santiago de Compostela, Spain. Berlin: Springer-Verlag.

Boutaba, R., & Aib, I. (2007). Policy-based Management: A Historical Perspective. *Journal of Network and Systems Management, 15*(4), 447–480. doi:10.1007/s10922-007-9083-8

Bowen, N. S., Nikolaou C. N., & Ghafoor A. (1992, March). On the Assignment Problem of Arbitrary Process Systems to Heterogeneous Distributed Computer Systems. *Institute of Electrical and Electronics Engineers Transaction on Computers, 41*(3).

Box, D., Ehnebuske, D., Kakivaya, G., Layman, A., Mendelsohn, N., Nielsen, H. F., et al. (2000, May 8). *Simple Object Access Protocol (SOAP) 1.1.* Retrieved from http://www.w3.org/TR/2000/NOTE-SOAP-20000508/

BPML. (2002). Retrieved November 10th, 2008 from www.ebpml.org/bpml.htm

Bradshaw, J. M. (1997). An introduction to software agents. In J. M. Bradshaw (Ed.), *Software agents* (pp. 3-46). Cambridge, MA: AAAI Press/The MIT Press.

Braumandl, R., Keidl, M., Kemper, A., Kossmann, D., Kreutz, A., Seltzsam, S., & Stocker, K. (2001). Object-Globe: Ubiquitous query processing on the Internet. *The VLDB Journal, 10*(1), 48–71.

Bray, T., Paoli, J., Sperberg-McQueen, C. M., Maler, E., & Yergeau, F. (2006). *Extensible markup language (XML) 1.0* (4th Ed.). Retrieved September 16, 2008 from http://www.w3.org/TR/REC-xml/

Breitkreuz, H. (2009). eMule Project Home Page. *eMule Project.* Retrieved February 15, 2009, from http://www.emule-project.net

Brickley, D., & Miller, L. (2007, November 1). *FOAF Vocabulary Specification 0.91.* Retrieved from http://xmlns.com/foaf/spec/

Broder, A., & Mitzenmacher, M. (2004). Network applications of bloom filters: A survey. *Internet Mathematics, 1*(4), 485–509.

Brodie, M., Rish, I., Ma, S., & Odintsova, N. (2003). Active probing strategies for problem determination. In *the Eighteenth International Joint Conference on Artificial Intelligence.*

Brogi, A., & Popescu, R. (2008), Workflow Semantics of Peer and Service Behaviour. In *2nd IFIP/IEEE International Symposium on Theoretical Aspects of Software Engineering,* Nanjing, China (pp. 143-150).

Brown, M. C. (2005). *What is the semantic grid.* Retrieved from http://www.ibm.com/developerworks/grid/library/gr-semgrid/

Brunkhorst, I., Dhraief, H., Kemper, A., Nejdl, W., & Wiesner, C. (2003). Distributed queries and query optimization in schema-based p2p-systems. In *Proceedings of the International Workshop on Databases, Information Systems and Peer-to-Peer Computing (DBISP2P)* (pp. 184-199).

Bryan,D.A.,&Lowekamp,B.B.(2007).DecentralizingSIP. *Queue, 5*(2), 34–41. doi:. doi:10.1145/1229899.1229910

Bryan, D., Draluk, V., Ehnebuske, D., Glover, T., Hately, A., Husband, Y. L., et al. (2002, July 19). *The UDDI Version 2 API Specification*. Retrieved from http://uddi. org/pubs/ProgrammersAPI-V2.04-Published-20020719. htm

Bryce, R. (2000, December). Power struggle. *Interactive Week*. Retrieved on November 9, 2008 from http://www.zdnet.com.au/news/business/soa/Power-struggle/0,139023166,120107749,00.htm.

Brydon, S., Murray, G., Ramachandran, V., Singh, I., Stearns, B., & Violleau, T. (2004). *Designing Web Services with the J2EE platform*. Reading, MA: Addison Walley Publishers.

BSM. (2008). Wikipedia Business Service Management definition. Retrieved December 5, 2008, from http://en.wikipedia.org/wiki/Business_Service_Management

Bucur, A. I. D., & Epema, D. H. J. (2003). The performance of processor co-allocation in multicluster systems. In F. Titsworth & D. Azada (Eds.), *International Symposium on Cluster Computing and the Grid* (pp. 302-309). Los Alamitos, CA: IEEE Computer Society.

Bucur, A. I. D., & Epema, D. H. J. (2003). Priorities among multiple queues for processor co-allocation in multicluster system. In R. Bilof (Ed.), *Annual Simulation Symposium* (pp. 15-27). Los Alamitos, CA IEEE Computer Society.

Bucur, A. I. D., & Epema, D. H. J. (2007). Scheduling policies for processor coallocation in multicluster systems. *IEEE Transactions on Parallel and Distributed Systems, 18*(7), 958–972. doi:10.1109/TPDS.2007.1036

Burke, S., Campana, S., Lanciotti, E., & Lorenzo, M. P., Miccio, V., Nater, C., Santinelli, R., & Sciaba, A. (2009).

gLite 3.1 user guide manuals series. Retrieved February 10, 2009, from https://edms.cern.ch/file/722398//gLite-3-UserGuide.pdf

Burmester, M., & Desmedt, Y. (2004). Identity-based key infrastructures. In *Proceedings of the IFIP TC11 19th International Information Security Conference (SEC 2004)*, (pp. 167-176). Amsterdam: Kluwer.

Butler, M., Hoare, T., & Ferreira, C. A trace semantics for long-running transactions. In *Proceedings of* (Vol. 25, pp. 133–150). Berlin: Springer.

Butt, A. R., Zhang, R., & Hu, Y. C. (2006). A self-organizing flock of condors. *Journal of Parallel and Distributed Computing, 66*(1), 145–161.

Buyya, R. (2005). Grid computing: Making the global cyberinfrastructure for eScience a reality. *Computer Society of India (CSI) Communications, 29*(1). Retrieved May 11, 2009, from http://www.gridbus.org/~raj/papers/CSICommunicationsJuly2005.pdf

Buyya, R., Abramson, D., & Giddy, J. (2000). Nimrod/G: An Architecture of a Resource Management and Scheduling System in a Global Computational Grid. In *HPC Asia 2000*, May 14-17, 2000, Beijing, China (pp 283 – 289).

Buyya, R., Abramson, D., & Giddy, J. (2001). A case for economy Grid architecture for service oriented Grid computing. In *Proceedings of the 15th International Parallel and Distributed Processing Symposium* (pp. 776-790). Washington, DC: IEEE.

Buyya, R., Abramson, D., & Venugopal, S. (2005). The Grid Economy. *Proceedings of the IEEE, Special Issue on Grid Computing, 93*(3), 698-714.

Buyya, R., Abramson, D., Giddy, J., & Stockinger, H. (2002). Economic models for resource management and scheduling in Grid computing. *Journal of Concurrency: Practice and Experience, Grid computing special issue,* 1507-1542.

Buyya, R., Yeo, C. S., & Venugopal, S. (2008). Market-oriented cloud computing: Vision, hype, and reality for delivering IT Services as computing utilities. In *Proceedings of the 10th IEEE International Conference on High*

Performance Computing and Communications (pp.5-13). Los Alamitos, CA: IEEE Computer Society.

Byers, J., Considine, J., & Mitzenmacher, M. (2003). Simple load balancing for distributed hash tables. In *Proc. IPTPS 2003, 2ⁿᵈ Int'l Workshop on Peer-to-Peer Systems*, Berkeley, CA, USA.

Byers, J.W., Considine, J., Mitzenmacher, M., & Rost, S. (2004). Informed content delivery across adaptive overlay networks. IEEE/ACM Transactions on Networking, 12(5), 767- 780.

Cai, M., Chervenak, A., & Frank, M. (2004). A peer-to-peer replica location service based on a distributed hash table. In *Proc. SC2004, ACM/IEEE Conference on Supercomputing,* Pittsburgh, Pennsylvania, USA (pp. 54-54).

Cai, M., Frank, M., Chen, J., & Szekely, P. (2005). MAAN: A multi-attribute addressable network for Grid information services. *Journal of Grid Computing, 2*(1), 3–14. doi:10.1007/s10723-004-1184-y

Callegati, F., & Campi, A. (2008). Extension of Resource Management in SIP, GridNets 2008, Beijing

Callegati, F., Campi, A., Corazza, G., Simeonidou, D., Zervas, G., Qin, Y., et al. (2009). SIP-empowered Optical Networks for Future IT Services and Applications. *IEEE Communications Magazine*.

Calvert, K., Zegura, E., & Bhattacharjee, S. (1996). How to model an Internetwork. In *Proc. of Infocom*.

Camarillo, G., & García-Martín, M. (2008). *The 3G IP Multimedia Subsystem (IMS): Merging the Internet and the Cellular Worlds*. New York: John Wiley & Sons.

Camarillo, G., et al. (2002, October). *Integration of Resource Management and Session Initiation Protocol (SIP)*. IETF RFC 3312.

Camarillo, G., Rosenberg, J., Schulzrinne, H., Johnston, A., Peterson, J., Sparks, R., et al. (2002). SIP Session Initiation Protocol. In *IETF Request for Comment 3261*.

Campi, A., Cerroni, W., Callegati, F., Zervas, G., Nejabati, R., & Simeonidou, D. (2007). SIP Based OBS networks for Grid Computing. In *Proceedings of ONDM 2007*, Athens, Greece.

Campi, A., Cerroni, W., Corazza, G., Callegati, F., Martini, B., Baroncelli, F., et al. (2009). *SIP-based Service Architecture for Application-aware Optical Network.* In *ICTA 2009*.

Cao, J. (2001). *Agent-based Resource Management for Grid Computing*. Unpublished doctoral dissertation. University of Warwick, Coventry, UK

Capit, N., Costa, G. D., Georgiou, Y., Huard, G., Martin, C., Mounie, G., et al. (2005). A batch scheduler with high level components. In *International Symposium on Cluster Computing and the Grid* (pp. 776-783). Los Alamitos, CA: IEEE Computer Society.

Capit, N., Da Costa, G., Georgiou, Y., Huard, G., Martin, C., & Mounié, G. (2005). A Batch Scheduler with High Level Components. In . *Proceedings of CCGRID, 2005*, 776–783.

Cappello, F., Caron, E., Dayd'e, M. J., & Desprez, F. J'egou, Y., Primet, P. V.-B., et al. (2005). Grid'5000: a large scale and highly reconfigurable grid experimental testbed. In *International conference on grid computing* (p. 99-106). Los Alamitos, CA: IEEE.

Cappello, F., Djilali, S., Fedak, G., Herault, T., Magniette, F., Néri, V., & Lodygensky, O. (2005). Computing on large-scale distributed systems: Xtrem Web architecture, programming models, security, tests and convergence with Grid. *Future Generation Computer Systems, 21*(3), 417–437. doi:10.1016/j.future.2004.04.011

Capra, L., Emmerich, W., & Mascolo, C. (2003). CARISMA: Context-Aware Reflective Middleware System for Mobile Applications. *IEEE Transactions on Software Engineering, 29*(10), 929–945. doi:10.1109/TSE.2003.1237173

Cardellini, V., Casalicchio, E., Colajanni, M., & Yu, P. S. (2002). The state of the art in locally distributed Web-server systems. [CSUR]. *ACM Computing Surveys, 34*(2), 263–311. doi:10.1145/508352.508355

Cardoso, R. S., & Issarny, V. (2007). Architecting Pervasive Computing Systems for Privacy: A Survey. In

Proceedings of the Sixth Working IEEE/IFIP Conference on Software Architecture (pp. 26).

Cardoso, R. S., Mokhtar, B. S., Urbieta, A., & Issarny, V. (2007). EVEY: enhancing privacy of service discovery in pervasive computing. In *Proceedings of the 8th ACM/IFIP/USENIX international conference on Middleware, SESSION: Work in progress* (pp. 27).

Carey, M. J. (2008). SOA What? *IEEE Computer, 41*(3), 92–94.

Caromel, D., di Costanzo, A., Gannon, D., & Slominski, A. (2005), Asynchronous Peer-to-Peer Web Services and Firewalls. In *Proceedings of the 7th International Workshop on Java for Parallel and Distributed Programming* (pp. 183.1).

Caron, E., Datta, A., Petit, F., & Tedeschi, C. (2008). Self-Stabilization in Tree-Structured Peer-to-Peer Service Discovery Systems. In *Proceedings of the twenty seventh International Symposium on Reliable Distributed Systems*.

Caron, E., Desprez, F., & Tedeschi, C. (2006). A Dynamic Prefix Tree for the Service Discovery Within Large Scale Grids. In *Proceedings of the sixth IEEE International Conference on Peer-to-Peer Computing (P2P2006)*.

Caron, E., Desprez, F., & Tedeschi, C. (2008). Efficiency of Tree-Structured Peer-to-Peer Service Discovery Systems. In *Proceedings of Parallel and Distributed Processing (IPDPS 2008, Hot-P2P workshop)*.

Carra, D., Neglia, G., & Michiardi, P. (2008). On the impact of greedy strategies in bittorrent networks: The case of bittyrant. In K. Wehrle, W. Kellerer, S. K. Singhal, & R. Steinmetz, (Eds.), *Peer-to-Peer Computing,* (pp.311–320). Washington, DC: IEEE Computer Society. Available from http://dblp.uni-trier.de/db/conf/p2p/p2p2008.html#CarraNM08

Cârstea, A., Frîncu, M., Konovalov, A., Macariu, G., & Petcu, D. (2007). On service-oriented symbolic computing. In R. Wyrzykowski, J. Dongarra, K. Karczewski, J. Wasniewski (Eds.), *Parallel Processing and Applied Mathematics,* (LNCS Vol. 4967, pp.843-851). Berlin: Springer.

Cârstea, A., Frîncu, M., Macariu, G., & Petcu, D. (2007). Composing Web-based mathematical services. In *Procs. SYNASC 2007* (pp.327–334). Washington, DC: IEEE Computer Society Press.

Cârstea, A., Frîncu, M., Macariu, G., Petcu, D., & Hammond, K. (2007). Generic access to Web and Grid-based symbolic computing services: the SymGrid-services framework. In *Procs. ISPDC 2007* (pp.143–150). Washington, DC: IEEE Computer Society Press.

Cârstea, A., Macariu, G., Petcu, D., & Konovalov, A. (2008). Pattern based composition of Web services for symbolic computations. In M. Bubak, G.D. van Albada, J. Dongarra, P.M.A. Sloot (Eds.), *Computational Science,* (LNCS Vol. 5101, pp.126–135). Berlin: Springer.

Carzaniga, A., Rosenblum, D. S., & Wolf, A. L. (2000). *Content-based addressing and routing: A general model and its application* (Technical report). Department of Computer Science, University of Colorado.

Casanova, H. (2001). Simgrid: a toolkit for the simulation of application scheduling. In *The IEEE International Symposium on Cluster Computing and the Grid (CCGrid'01)* (pp. 430-437). New York: IEEE/ACM.

Casier, K., Verbrugge, S., Colle, D., Pickavet, M., & Demeester, P. (2004). Using Aspect-Oriented Programming for Event-Handling in a Telecom Research Software Library. In *8th International Conference on Software Reuse (ICSR)*, Madrid, Spain.

Castelfranchi, C., Miceli, M., & Cesta, A. (1992). Dependence relations among autonomous agents. In *Proceedings of the 3rd European Workshop on Modeling Autonomous Agents and Multi-Agent Worlds (pp. 215-231)*. Amsterdam: Elsevier Science Publisher.

Castro, M., Costa, M., & Rowstron, A. (2003, November). Should we build Gnutella on a Structured Overlay. In *Proceedings of the 2nd Workshop on Hot Topics in Networks (HotNets-II)*, Cambridge, MA, USA (pp. 131-136).

Castro, M., Druschel, P., Kermarrec, A.-M., & Rowstron, A. (2002). SCRIBE: A Large-Scale and Decentralised Application-Level Multicast Infrastructure. *IEEE Journal on Selected Areas in Communications, 20*(8), 1489–1499. doi:10.1109/JSAC.2002.803069

CERN. (2007). *Worldwide LHC computing Grid*. Retrieved November 12, 2008, from http://lcg.web.cern.ch/LCG/

Chakrabarti, A. (2007). *Grid computing security*. Berlin: Springer.

Chakraporty, D., Joshi, A., Finin, T., & Yesha, Y. (2006). Toward Distributed service discovery in pervasive computing environments. *IEEE Transactions on Mobile Computing, 5*(2), 97–112. doi:10.1109/TMC.2006.26

Chakravarti, A. J., Baumgartner, G., & Lauria, M. (2005). The organic grid: Self-organizing computation on a peer-to-peer network. *IEEE Transactions on Systems, Man, and Cybernetics. Part A, Systems and Humans, 35*(3), 373–384. doi:10.1109/TSMCA.2005.846396

Chakravarti, A. J., Baumgartner, G., & Lauria, M. (2006). Self-organizing scheduling on the organic grid. *International Journal of High Performance Computing Applications, 20*(1), 115–130. doi:10.1177/1094342006061892

Chan, L., & Karunasekera, S. (2007). Designing configurable publish-subscribe scheme for decentralised overlay networks. In *AINA'07: Proceedings of the IEEE 21st Inter- national Conference on Advanced Information Networking and Applications* (pp.102-109). Washington, DC: IEEE Computer Society.

Chan, P., & Abramson, D. (2007). A Scalable and Efficient Prefix-Based Lookup Mechanism for Large-Scale Grids. In *third IEEE International Conference on e-Science and Grid Computing* (e-Science 2007).

Chandler, A. D. (1990). *Scale and Scope: The Dynamics of Industrial Capitalism*. Cambridge, MA: Harvard University Press.

Chandler, J., El-Khatib, K., Benyoucef, M., Bochmann, G., & Adams, C. (2007). Legal Challenges of Online Reputation Systems. In L. K. R. Song, *Trust in e-services: Technologies, practices and challenges* (pp. 84-111). Hershey, PA: IGI Global.

Chandrasekaran, S., Cooper, O., Deshpande, A., Franklin, M. J., Hellerstein, J. M., Hong, W., et al. (2003). TelegraphCQ: continuous dataflow processing. In *Proceedings ACM SIGMOD 2003* (pp. 668).

Chang, F., Itzkovitz, A., & Karamcheti, V. (2000). *User-level resource constrained sandboxing*. Paper presented at the 4th USENIX Windows Systems Symposium, Seattle, Washington.

Chang, T., Fan, J., Ahamad, M., Popescu, G., & Liu, Z. (2005). Preference-aware overlay topologies for group communication. In *Proceedings of Globecom 2005*.

Chang, T., Popescu, G., & Codella, C. (2002). Scalable and Efficient Update Dissemination for Interactive Distributed Applications. In . *Proceedings of ICDCS, 2002*(July), 143–151.

Chapin, S., Karpovich, J., & Grimshaw, A. (1999). The legion resource management system. In *Proceedings of the 5th Workshop on Job Scheduling Strategies for Parallel Processing,*(pp.162-178). Berlin: Springer-Verlag.

Chappell, D. (2004). *Enterprise service bus*. Sebastopol, CA: O'Reilly Media, Inc.

Chase, J. S., Irwin, D. E., Grit, L. E., Moore, J. D., & Sprenkle, S. (2003). Dynamic virtual clusters in a grid site manager. In *International Symposium on High-Performance Distributed Computing* (p. 90-103). Los Alamitos, CA: IEEE Computer Society.

Chawathe, Y., McCanne, S., & Brewer, E. *(2000). RMX: Reliable Multicast for Heterogeneous Networks. In* Proceedings of the IEEE Infocom '00, *Tel-Aviv, Israel, March.*

Chawathe, Y., Ratnasamy, S., Breslau, L., Lanham, N., & Shenker, S. (2003). Making Gnutella-like P2P System scalable. In *Proceedings of the 2003 Conference on Applications, Technologies, Architectures, and Protocols for Computer Communications* (pp.407-418). New York: ACM.

Cheema, A. S., Muhammad, M., & Gupta, I. (2005). Peer-to-peer discovery of computational resources for Grid applications. In *GRID'05: Proceedings of the Sixth IEEE/ACM International Workshop on Grid Computing* (pp. 179-185). Washington, DC: IEEE Computer Society Press.

Chen, G., Qiu, T., & Wu, F. (2008). Insight into redundancy schemes in DHTs. *The Journal of Supercomputing, 43*, 183–198. doi:10.1007/s11227-007-0126-4

Chen, H., Jin, H., Sun, J., Deng, D., & Liao, X. (2004). Analysis of large-scale topological properties for peer-to-peer networks. In *Proceedings of the 4th IEEE International Symposium on Cluster Computing and the Grid* (pp. 27-34).

Chen, J. O. U. R. N. A. L., & DeWitt, D. J., Tian, F., & Wang, Y. (2000). NiagaraCQ: A scalable continuous query system for Internet databases. In *Proceedings ACM SIGMOD 2000* (pp. 379-390).

Chen, L., Cheng, Z., & Smart, N. P. (2007). Identity-based key agreement protocols from pairings. *International Journal of Information Security, 6*(4), 213–241. doi:10.1007/s10207-006-0011-9

Chen, L., Harrison, K., Moss, A., Soldera, D., & Smart, N. P. (2002). Certification of public keys within an identity based system. In A.H. Chan & V. Gligor (Eds.) *Proceedings of the 5th International Information Security Conference (ISC2002),* (LNCS Vol. 2433, pp. 322-333). Berlin: Springer-Verlag.

Chen, Y., Katz, R. H., & Kubiatowicz, J. (2002). Dynamic replica placement for scalable content delivery. In *Proc. IPTPS 2002, 1st Int'l Workshop on Peer-to-Peer Systems* (pp. 306-318). Boston, MA, USA.

Cheng, B., Jin, H., & Liao, X. (2007). Supporting VCR functions in P2P VoD services using ring-assisted overlays. In . *Proceedings of the IEEE International Conference on Communications, 2007*, 1698–1703. doi:10.1109/ICC.2007.284

Cheng, Y., Leon-Garcia, A., & Foster, I. (2008). Toward an Autonomic Service Management Framework: A Holistic Vision of SOA, AON, and Autonomic Computing. *IEEE Communications Magazine, 46*(5), 138–146. doi:10.1109/MCOM.2008.4511662

Chervenak, A., Foster, I., Kesselman, C., Salisbury, C., & Tuecke, S. (2001). The Data Grid: Towards an architecture for the distributed management and analysis of large scientific datasets. *Journal of Network and Computer Applications, 23*, 187–200. doi:10.1006/jnca.2000.0110

Chess, D. M., Segal, A., Whalley, I. N., & White, S. R. (2004). Unity: Experiences with a prototype autonomic computing system. In *the First International Conference on Autonomic Computing* (pp. 140–147). Washington, DC: IEEE Computer Society.

Chetty, M., & Buyya, R. (2002). Weaving electrical and computational grids: How analogous are they? *Computing in Science and Engineering.* Retrieved from http://buyya.com/papers/gridanalogy.pdf

Chi, C. X., Huang, D. W., Lee, D., & Sun, X. R. (2002). Lazy flooding: A new technique for signaling in all optical network. In *IEEE/OSA Optical Fiber Communication Conference and Exhibit* (pp. 551–552).

Chi, H., Zhang, Q., Jia, J., & Shen, X. (2007). Efficient search and scheduling in P2P-based media-on-demand streaming service. *IEEE Journal on Selected Areas in Communications, 25*(1), 119–130. doi:10.1109/JSAC.2007.070112

Choffnes, D. R., & Bustamante, F. E. (2008). Taming the torrent: a practical approach to reducing cross-isp traffic in peer-to-peer systems. In *Proceedings of the ACM SIGCOMM 2008 conference on Data communication* (pp. 363-374). Seattle, WA: ACM. doi:10.1145/1402958.1403000

Christensen, E., Curbera, F., Meredith, G., & Weerawarana, S. (2001, March 15). *Web Services Description Language (WSDL) 1.1.* Retrieved from http://www.w3.org/TR/2001/NOTE-wsdl-20010315

Chu, D. C., & Humphrey, M. (2004, November). Mobile OGSI.NET: Grid computing on mobile devices. In *Proceedings of the Fifth IEEE/ACM International Workshop on Grid Computing* (pp. 182-191).

Chu, J., Labonte, K., & Levine, B. (2002). Availability and locality measurements of peer-to-peer filesystems. In *Proceedings of SPIE ITCom 2002: Scalability and Traffic Control in IP Networks.*

Chu, Y. H., Rao, S., Seshan, S., & Zhang, H. (2002). A case for end system multicast. *Journal of Selected Areas in Communications, IEEE, 20*(8), 1456–1471. doi:10.1109/JSAC.2002.803066

Chun, B.-G., Dabek, F., Haeberlen, A., Sit, E., Weatherspoon, H., Kaashoek, M. F., et al. (2006). Efficient replica maintenance for distributed storage systems. In *Proc. of the 3rd symposium on networked system design and implementation (NSDI).*

Chung, S., Kim, E., & Liu, J. C. L. (2008). A scalable PVR-based content sharing architecture for community networks. *IEEE Transactions on Consumer Electronics, 54*(3), 1192–1199. doi:10.1109/TCE.2008.4637606

Ciminiera, L., Marchetto, G., Risso, F., & Torrero, L. (2008). Distributed connectivity service for a SIP infrastructure. *Network, IEEE, 22*(5), 33–40. doi:. doi:10.1109/MNET.2008.4626230

Cisco. (n.d.). *Service Control Engine.* Retrieved from http://www.cisco.com/en/US/products/ps6151/index.html

Cisco-Linksys. (2009). Retrieved from http://www.linksysbycisco.com/

Ciulli, N., Carrozzo, G., Giorgi, G., Zervas, G., Escalona, E., & Qin, Y. (Eds.). (2008). Architectural approaches for the integration of the service plane and control plane in optical networks. *Optical Switching and Networking, 5,* 94–106. doi:10.1016/j.osn.2008.01.002

CLARIN Project. (2008). Retrieved from http://www.clarin.eu/

Clark, D. (2001). Face-to-face with peer-to-peer networking. *Computer, 34*(1), 18–21. doi:10.1109/2.970548

Clark, D., Wroclawski, J., Sollins, K., & Braden, R. (2005). Tussle in cyberspace: defining tomorrow's Internet. *IEEE/ACM Transactions on Networking, 13*(3), 462-475.

Clark, I., Miller, S. G., Hong, T. W., Sandberg, O., & Wiley, B. (2002). Protecting free expression online with Freenet. *IEEE Internet Computing, 6*(1), 40–49. doi:10.1109/4236.978368

Clarke, I., Sandberg, O., Wiley, B., & Hong, T. W. (2001). Freenet: A distributed anonymous information storage and retrieval system. In *Designing privacy enhancing technologies: International workshop on design issues in anonymity and unobservability* (pp.46-66). Berlin: Springer-Verlag.

Clip2. (2002). *Gnutella Protocol Specification v0.4.* Retrieved October 5, 2008, from www9.limewire.com/developer/gnutella_protocol_0.4.pdf

Cloud-Wiki. (2008). Wikipedia Cloud Computing definition. Retrieved December 5, 2008, from http://en.wikipedia.org/wiki/Cloud_computing

Cluster. (2008). Cluster Resources Moab Cluster suite. Retrieved December 5, 2008, from http://www.cluster-resources.com/pages/products/moab-cluster-suite.php

Cochennec, J.-Y. (2002, July). Activities on next-generation networks under Global Information Infrastructure in ITU-T. *IEEE Comm Mag.*

Coen, M., Phillips, B., Warshawsky, N., Weisman, L., Peters, S., & Finin, P. (1999). Meeting the computational needs of intelligent environments: the Metaglue system. In *Proceedings of the 1st International workshop on managing interactions in smart environments* (pp. 201-212).

Cohen, B. (2003). Incentives build robustness in BitTorrent. In *Proceedings of the Workshop on Economics of Peer-to-Peer Systems.*

Cohen, B. (2008, February 28). The BitTorrent Protocol Specification. *BitTorrent.org.* Retrieved February 15, 2009, from http://www.bittorrent.org/beps/bep_0003.html

Cohen, E., & Shenker, S. (2002). Replication strategies in unstructured peer-to-peer networks. In *Proc. of SIGCOMM'02,* Pittsburgh, Pennsylvania, USA (pp. 177-190).

Colarelli, D., & Grunwald, D. (2002, November). Massive Arrays of Idle Disks for Storage Archives. *Proc. of the 15th High Performance Networking and Computing Conference. Cool'n'Quiet Technology Installation Guide for AMD Athlon 64 Processor Based Systems.* (n.d.). Retrieved on February 22, 2008 from http://www.amd.com/us-en/assets/content_type/DownloadableAssets/Cool_N_Quiet_Installation_Guide3.pdf

Colle, D., Maesschalck, S. D., Pickavet, M. P., Demeester, P., Jaeger, M., & Gladisch, A. (2002). Developing control plane models for optical networks. In *IEEE/OSA Optical Fiber Communication Conference and Exhibit* (pp. 757-759).

Colombo, M., Martinelli, F., Mori, P., Petrocchi, M., & Vaccarelli, A. (2007). *Fine grained access control with trust and reputation management for globus*, (pp. 1505–1515).

Comellas, F., Ozón, J., & Peters, J. G. (2000). Deterministic small-world communication networks. *Information Processing Letters*, 76(1), 83–90. doi:10.1016/S0020-0190(00)00118-6

Common Object Request Broker Architecture. *Core Specification*. (2004). Retrieved September 6, 2008, from http://www.omg.org/docs/formal/04-03-12.pdf

Condor Project. (n.d.). Retrieved October 12, 2008, from http://www.cs.wisc.edu/condor/

Condor-G. (2008). Contor-G website. Retrieved December 5, 2008, from http://www.cs.wisc.edu/condor/condorg/

Conrad, M., Dinger, J., Hartenstein, H., Schöller, M., & Zitterbart, M. (2005). Combining Service-Orientation and P2P Networks. In *Kommunikation in Verteilten Systemen* (pp. 181-184). Kaiserslautern, Germany: GI-Edition.

Conrad, M., Funk, C., Raabe, O., & Waldhorst, O. P. (2008). Legal compliance by design - technical solutions for future distributed electronic markets. *Journal of Intelligent Manufacturing*, 19(6).

Consumer Electronics Association. (2008). Retrieved from http://www.ce.org/

Conte, R., & Castelfranchi, C. (1993). Norms as mental objects. From normative beliefs to normative goals. In C. Castelfranchi & J.-P. Mueller (Ed.), *5th European Workshop on Modelling Autonomous Agents in a Multi-Agent World, MAAMAW '93*, (pp. 186–196). Berlin: Springer.

Conte, R., Falcone, R., & Sartor, G. (1999). Agents and norms: How to fill the gap? *Artificial Intelligence and Law*, 7, 1–15. doi:10.1023/A:1008397328506

CONTEXT. (n.d.). Retrieved February 13, 2009, from http://www.context.upc.es/

CONTRACT. (n.d.). *Project website*. Retrieved November 12, 2008, from http://www.ist-contract.org/

Cooper, B. F. (2004). A content model for evaluating peer-to-peer searching techniques. In *Proceedings of the 5th ACM/IFIP/USENIX International Middleware Conference* (pp. 18 - 37).

Cooper, B. F. (2004). Guiding queries to information sources with InfoBeacons. In *Proceedings of the 5th ACM/IFIP/USENIX International Middleware Conference* (pp. 59 - 78).

Cooper, K., Dasgupata, A., Kennedy, K., Koelbel, C., Mandal, A., Marin, G., et al. YarKhan, A., & Dongarra, J. (2004). New Grid Scheduling and Rescheduling Methods in the GrADS Project. In *NSF Next Generation Software Workshop, International Parallel and Distributed Processing Symposium*, Santa Fe, April 2004.

Cornelli, F., Damiani, E., De Capitani di Vimercati, S., Paraboschi, S., & Samarati, P. (2002). Choosing reputable servents in a p2p network. In *WWW*, (pp. 376–386).

Cornwell, J., Fette, I., Hsieh, G., Prabaker, M., Rao, J., Tang, K., et al. (2007). User-Controllable Security and Privacy for Pervasive Computing. In *Proceedings of the 8th IEEE Workshop on Mobile Computing Systems and Applications (HotMobile 2007)* (pp. 14-19).

Costa, M., Castro, M., Rowstron, A., & Key, P. (2004), PIC: Practical Internet coordinates for distance estimation. In *International Conference on Distributed Systems*.

Coulouris, G., Dollimore, J., & Kindberg, T. (1994). *Distributed systems – Concepts and design*. Reading, MA: Addison-Wesley.

Coulson, G., Blair, G., Grace, P., Joolia, A., Lee, K., & Ueyama, J. (2004). OpenCOM v2: A Component Model for Building Systems Software. In *Proceedings of IASTED Software Engineering and Applications (SEA'04)*.

Coulson, G., Blair, G., Grace, P., Joolia, A., Lee, K., Ueyama, J., & Sivaharan, T. (2008). A Generic Component Model for Building Systems Software. *ACM Transactions on Computer Systems, 27*(1), 1–42. doi:10.1145/1328671.1328672

Cournot, A. A. (1960). *Researches into the mathematical principles of the theory of wealth, 1838* (p. 213). New York: A.M. Kelley.

Couvares, P., Kosar, T., Roy, A., Weber, J., & Wegner, K. (2007). Workflow Management in Condor. In *Workflows for e-Science*. Berlin: Springer-Verlag.

Cowan, N., Nugent, L. D., Elliott, E. M., Ponomarev, I., & Saults, J. S. (1999). The Role of Attention in the Development of Short-Term Memory: Age Differences in the Verbal Span of Apprehension. *Child Development, 70*(5), 1082–1097. doi:10.1111/1467-8624.00080

Crampton, J., Lim, H. W., Paterson, K. G., & Price, G. (2007). A certificate-free grid security infrastructure supporting password-based user authentication. In *Proceedings of the 6th Annual PKI R&D Workshop 2007, Interagency Report 7427,* (pp. 103-118). NIST.

Cranor, L., Dobbs, B., Egelman, S., Hogben, G., Humphrey, J., Langheinrich, M., et al. (2006, November 1). *The platform for privacy preferences 1.1 (P3P1.1) specification.* Retrieved from http://www.w3.org/TR/P3P11/

Credence. (2006). Sourceforge.net. Retrieved from http://gattaca.cs.cornell.edu/credence/status.html

Crespo, A., & García-Molina, H. (2002). Routing indices for peer-to-peer systems. In *ICDCS'02: Proceedings of the 22nd International Conference on Distributed Computing Systems* (pp. 23-32). Washington, DC: IEEE Computer Society Press.

CrossGrid. (n.d.). Retrieved June 28, 2006, from http://www.crossgrid.org/

Crovella, M., & Bestavros, A. (1996). Explaining world wide web traffic self-similarity. In *Proceedings of the ACM SIGCOMM Conference.*

Cuenca, J., Gimenez, D., & Martinez, J.-P. (2006). Heuristics for work distribution of a homogeneous parallel dynamic programming scheme on heterogeneous systems. *Institute of Electrical and Electronics Engineers on Heterogeneous Computing Workshop.*

Cuenca-Acuna, F. M., Peery, C., Martin, R. P., & Nguyen, T. D. (2003). Planetp: Using gossiping to build content addressable peer-to-peer information sharing communities. In *IEEE International Symposium on High Performance Distributed Computing (HPDC).*

Cugini, F., Giorgetti, A., Andriolli, N., Paolucci, I., Valcarenghi, L., & Castoldi, P. (2007). Multiple path computation element (PCE) cooperation for multi-layer traffic engineering. In *IEEE/OSA Optical Fiber Communication Conference and Exhibit* (pp. 1-3).

Culicover, P. W., & Jackendoff, R. (2005). *Simpler syntax* [Oxford linguistics]. Oxford, UK: Oxford University Press.

Culicover, P. W., & Jackendoff, R. (2006). The simpler syntax hypothesis. *Trends in Cognitive Sciences, 10*(9), 413–418. doi:10.1016/j.tics.2006.07.007

Curbera, F., Duftler, M., Khalaf, R., Nagy, W., Mukhi, N., & Weerawarana, S. (2004). Unraveling the Web Services Web: An Introduction to SOAP, WSDL, and UDDI. *IEEE Internet Computing, 6*(2), 86–93. doi:10.1109/4236.991449

Curbera, F., Goland, Y., Klein, J., Leymann, F., Roller, D., Thatte, S., & Weerawarana, S. (2002). Business Process Execution Language for Web Services, Version 1.0. Retrieved November 10th, 2008 from http://download.boulder.ibm.com/ibmdl/pub/software/dw/specs/ws-bpel/ws-bpel1.pdf

Curbera, F., Meredith, G., & Weerawarana, S. (2001). *Web Services Description Language (WSDL) 1.1.* Retrieved October 6, 2008, from http://www.w3.org/TR/wsdl

Cybok, D. (March 2004). *A Grid Workflow Infrastructure, Presentation in GGF-10.* Berlin, Germany.

Czajkowski, K., Ferguson, D., Foster, I., Frey, J., Graham, S., Maguire, T., et al. (2004). *From open grid services infrastructure to ws-resource framework: Refactoring & evolution.* Fujitsu Limited, International Business Machines Corporation, The University of Chicago.

Czajkowski, K., Foster, I. T., Kesselman, C., Sander, V., & Tuecke, S. (2002). SNAP: A protocol for negotiating service level agreements and coordinating resource management in distributed systems. In D. G. Feitelson, L. Rudolph, & U. Schwiegelshohn (Eds.), *8th international workshop job scheduling strategies for parallel processing* (Vol. 2537, p. 153-183). Berlin: Springer.

Czajkowski, K., Foster, I., & Kesselman, C. (1999). Resource co-allocation in computational grids. In *International Symposium on High Performance Distributed Computing* (pp. 219-228). Los Alamitos, CA: IEEE Computer Society.

Czajkowski, K., Foster, I., Karonis, N., Kesselman, C., Martin, S., Smith, W., et al. (1998). A resource management architecture for metacomputing systems. In D. G. Feitelson & L. Rudolph (Eds.), *International Workshop on Job Scheduling Strategies for Parallel Processing* (Vol. 1459, pp. 62-82). Berlin: Springer.

D'Ambrosio, M., Fasano, P., Marchisio, M., Vercellone, V., & Ullio, M. (2008). Providing Data Dissemination Services in the Future Internet. In *IEEE Globecom WTC2008* (pp. 1-6). New York: IEEE Computer Society.

da Costa, C. A., Yamin, A. C., & Geyer, C. F. R. (2008). Toward a general software infrastructure for ubiquitous computing. *IEEE Pervasive Computing / IEEE Computer Society [and] IEEE Communications Society*, 7(1), 64–73. doi:10.1109/MPRV.2008.21

Dabek, F., Cox, R., Kaahoek, F., & Morris, R. (2004, August). Vivaldi: A Decentralized Network Coordinate System. In the *Proceedings of SIGCOMM 2004*, Portland, OR.

Dabek, F., Cox, R., Kaashoek, F., & Morris, R. (2004). Vivaldi: a decentralized network coordinate system. *SIGCOMM Comput. Commun. Rev.*, 34(4), 15–26. doi:. doi:10.1145/1030194.1015471

Dabek, F., Kaashoek, M. F., Karger, D., Morris, R., & Stoica, I. (2001). Wide-area cooperative storage with CFS. In *Proc. of the 18th ACM Symposium on Operating Systems Principles,* Chateau Lake Louise, Banff, Canada (pp. 202-215).

Dabek, F., Li, J., Sit, E., Robertson, J., Kaashoek, M. F., & Morris, R. (2004). Designing a DHT for low latency and high throughput. In *Proceedings of the 2nd symposium on networked systems design and implementation (NSDI)*.

Dabek, F., Zhao, B., Druschel, P., Kubiatowicz, J., & Stoica, I. (2003). Towards a Common API for Structured P2P Overlays. In *Proceedings of the Second International Workshop on Peer-to-Peer Systems (IPTPS)*.

Dally, W., Carvey, P., & Dennison, L. (1998, August). The Avici Terabit Switch/Rounter. In *Proc. Hot Interconnects* (Vol. 6, pp. 41-50).

Damiani, E., De Capitani di Vimercati, S., Paraboschi, S., Samarati, P., & Violante, F. (2002). A reputation-based approach for choosing reliable resources in peer-to-peer networks. In V. Atluri, (Ed.), ACM Conference on Computer and Communications Security, (pp. 207–216). New York: ACM. Retrieved from http://dblp.uni-trier.de/db/conf/ccs/ccs2002.html#DamianiVPSV02

Damiani, E., di Vimercati, S. D. C., Parabosci, S., & Samaranti, P. (2003). Managing and Sharing Servents' Reputations in P2P Systems. *IEEE Transitions on Data Knowledge Engineering*, 15(4), 840–854. doi:10.1109/TKDE.2003.1209003

DAML. (2001). *The DARPA Agent Markup Language*. Retrieved from http://www.daml.org

Dantas, R., Fidalgo, J., Sadok, D., Kamienski, C., & Ohlman, B. (2008), Policies for the Management of Ambient Networks: From Theory to Practice. In *8th IEEE International Workshop on Policies for Distributed Systems and Networks* (pp. 37-45).

DAS-3. (n.d.). Retrieved from http://www.cs.vu.nl/das3/index.shtml

DASM. (2008). *DataSynapse Dynamic Application Service Management*. Retrieved December 5, 2008, from http://www.datasynapse.com/solutions

DataGrid. (2003). *DataGrid Security design*. Deliverable 7.6.

DataSynapse-Grid. (2008). *Data Synapse Grid Server.* Retrieved December 5, 2008, from http://www.datasynapse.com/gridserver

Date, C. (2003). *An Introduction to Data Base Systems* (8th ed., p. 1024). Upper Saddle River, NJ: Pearson Education.

Datta, A., & Aberer, K. (2006). Internet-scale storage systems under churn - a study of the steady state using markov models. In *Proceedings of the sixth IEEE international conference on peer-to-peer computing (P2P).*

Datta, A., Hauswirth, M., John, R., Schmidt, R., & Aberer, K. (2005). Range Queries in Trie-Structured Overlays. In *Fifth IEEE International Conference on Peer-to-Peer Computing.*

Datta, A., Heuswirth, H., & Aberer, K. (2003, May). Updates in highly unreliable, replicated peer-to-peer systems. In *Proc. of ICDCS 2003, 23rd Int'l Conference on Distributed Computing Systems,* Providence, Rhode Island, (pp. 76-85).

Datta, A., Schmidt, H., & Aberer, K. (2007). Query-load balancing in structured overlays. In *Proc. of CCGrid'07, 7th Int'l Conference on Cluster Computing and the Grid,* Rio de Janeiro, Brazil (pp. 453-460).

Davies, N., Friday, A., & Storz, O. (2004). Exploring the Grid's Potential for Ubiquitous Computing. *IEEE Pervasive Computing / IEEE Computer Society [and] IEEE Communications Society, 3*(2), 74–75. doi:10.1109/MPRV.2004.1316823

DCOM. (n.d.). Retrieved from September 6, 2008, from http://en.wikipedia.org/wiki/Distributed_Component_Object_Model.

De Roure, D. (2005). The semantic grid: Past, present and future. The Semantic Web: Research and Applications. In *Proceedings of the Second European Semantic Web Conference(ESWC 2005)* (pp. 726). *edutain@grid project.* (n.d.). Retrieved February 13, 2009, from http://www.edutaingrid.eu/

De Roure, D., Jennings, N. R., & Shadbolt, N. R. (2001). *The Semantic Grid: A future e-Science infrastructure.*

Retrieved 15th May, 2007 from http://www.semanticgrid.org/documents/semgrid-journal/semgrid-journal.pdf

De Vleeschauwer, B., De Turck, F., & Dhoedt, B. Demeester. P., Wijnants, M., & Lamotte, W. (2008). End-to-end QoE Optimization Through Overlay Network Deployment. In *International Conference on Information Networking (ICOIN),* Pusan, Korea.

De Vleeschauwer, B., De Turck, F., Dhoedt, B., & Demeester, P. (2004, September). On the Construction of QoS Enabled Overlay Networks. In *Quality of Future Internet Services (QofIS)* (LNCS 3266, pp. 164–173).

De Vleeschauwer, B., De Turck, F., Dhoedt, B., & Demeester, P. (2006, November). Online management of QoS enabled overlay multicast services. In *Proceedings (on CD-ROM) of IEEE GLOBECOM 2006, the Global Telecommunications Conference,* San Francisco, California, USA.

De Vleeschauwer, B., De Turck, F., Dhoedt, B., & Demeester, P. (2006, September). Dynamic algorithms to provide a robust and scalable overlay routing service. In International Conference on Information Networking, ICOIN 2006, Sendai, Japan (LNCS 3961, pp. 945-954).

De Vleeschauwer, B., De Turck, F., Dhoedt, B., & Demeester, P. (2008). Server Placement and Path Selection for QoS Enabled Overlay Networks. *Wiley Interscience European Transactions on Telecommunications.*

De Vleeschauwer, B., Simoens, P., Van de Meerssche, W., De Turck, F., Dhoedt, B., Demeester, P., et al. (2007). Enabling Autonomic Access Network QoE Management Through TCP Connection Monitoring. In *First IEEE workshop on autonomic communications and network management, ACNM.*

Dean, J., & Ghemawat, S. (2004). MapReduce: Simplified data processing on large clusters. In *Proceedings of the 6th Conference on Symposium on Operating Systems Design & Implementation* (pp.10). Berkeley, CA: USENIX Association.

Dean, M., & Schreiber, G. (2004). *OWL web ontology language reference.* Retrieved December 5, 2008, from http://www.w3.org/TR/owel-ref

Decker, J., & Schneider, J. (2007). Heuristic scheduling of grid workflows supporting co-allocation and advance reservation. In B. Schulze, R. Buyya, P. Navaux, W. Cirne, & V. Rebello (Eds.), *International Symposium on Cluster Computing and the Grid* (pp. 335-342). Los Alamitos, CA: IEEE Computer Society.

Decker, S., Prasenjit, M., & Sergey, M. (2002). Framework for the Semantic Web: An RDF tutorial. *IEEE Internet Computing, 4*(6), 68–73.

Decker, S., Sergey, M., van Harmelen, F., Fensel, D., Klein, M., & Broekstra, J. (2002). The Semantic Web: The roles of XML and RDF. *IEEE Internet Computing, 4*(5), 63–74. doi:10.1109/4236.877487

DeFanti, T., Foster, I., Papka, M., Stevens, R., & Kuhfuss, T. (1996). Overview of the I-WAY: Wide area visual supercomputing. *The International Journal of Supercomputer Applications, 10*(2), 123–130. doi:10.1177/109434209601000201

DEISA. (2008). *DEISA website*. Retrieved December 5, 2008, from http://www.deisa.eu/

Delaittre, T., Kiss, T., Goyeneche, A., Terstyanszky, G., Winter, S., & Kacsuk, P. (2005). GEMLCA: running legacy code applications as Grid services. *Journal of Grid Computing, 3*(1-2), 75–90. doi:10.1007/s10723-005-9002-8

Dellarocas, C. (2000). Contractual agent societies: Negotiated shared context and social control in open multi-agent systems. In R. Conte & C. Dellarocas (Ed.), *Social order in multiagent systems* (pp. 113-133). Boston: Kluwer Academic Publishers.

Dellarocas, C. (2000). Immunizing online reputation reporting systems against unfair ratings and discriminatory behavior. In *Proceedings of the 2nd ACM conference on Electronic commerce*, (pp. 150–157).

Demchenko, Y. (2005). *White Collar Attacks on Web Services and Grids*. Work in Progress, Draft Version 0.3, Advanced Research Group, University of Amsterdam.

Demers, A., Green, D., Hauser, C., Irish, W., Larson, J., Shenker, S., et al. (1987). Epidemic algorithms for replicated database maintenance. In *Proc. PODC 1987, 6th Annual ACM Symposium on Principles of Distributed Computing*, Vancouver, Canada (pp. 1-12).

DePaoli, F., & Mariani, L. (2004). Dependability in Peer-to-Peer Systems. *IEEE Internet Computing, 8*(4), 54–61. doi:10.1109/MIC.2004.9

Deriaz, M. (2005). *A thesis proposition: Service Oriented Computing in a P2P Architecture*. Retrieved July 13, 2008, from http://cui.unige.ch/~deriazm/publications/ThesisPropositionSOC.pdf

Dertouzos, M. L. (1999). The future of computing. *Scientific American, 281*(2), 52–55. doi:10.1038/scientificamerican0899-52

Deshpande, A., Hellerstein, J. M., & Raman, V. (2006). Adaptive Query Processing: Why, How, When, What Next. In *Proceedings ACM SIGMOD 2006* (pp. 806-807).

Deutsch, M. (1973). *The Resolution of Conflict*. New Haven, CT: Yale University Press.

Deutsch, M. (1975). Equity, equality, and need: What determines which value will be used as the basis of distributive justice? *The Journal of Social Issues, 31*, 137–149.

Deutsch, M. (1987). *Social comparison, social justice, and relative deprivation, chapter Experimental studies of the effects of different systems of distributive justice*, (pp. 151–164). Hillsdale, NJ: Lawrence Erlbaum.

Diao, Y., Gandhi, N., & Hellerstein, J. L. Parekh, S., & Tilbury, D.M. (2002). *MIMO Control of an Apache Web server: Modeling and controller design*. American Control Conference.

Diao, Y., Hellerstein, J. L., & Parekh, S. (2002). Using fuzzy control to maximize profits in service level management. *IBM Systems Journal, 41*(3).

Dibbern, J., Goles, T., Hirschheim, R., & Jayatilaka, B. (2004). Information Systems Outsorurcing: A survey and analysis of the literature. *The Data Base for Advances in Information Systems, 35*(4), 6–102.

Dierks, T. & Allen, C. (1999). The TLS protocol version 1.0. *The Internet Engineering Task Force (IETF)*, RFC 2246.

Dierks, T., & Rescorla, E. (2006). *The Transport Layer Security (TLS) Protocol Version 1.1, RFC 4346.*

Dillard, D. D. (1967). *Economic Development of the North Atlantic Community: Historical Introduction to Modern Economics/Dudley Dillard.* Upper Saddle River, NJ: Prentice-Hall.

Dingledine, R., Freedman, M. J., & Molnar, D. (2001). Accountability. In *Peer-to-Peer: Harnessing the Power of Disruptive Technologies* (pp. 217-340). Sebastopol, CA: O'Reilly & Associates.

DMTF. (2008). *Distributed Management Task Force.* Retrieved November 15, 2008, from http://www.dmtf.org

Dolev, S. (2000). *Self-stabilization.* Cambridge, MA: MIT Press.

Donachy, P., & Stødle, D. (2003). *Risk Grid - Grid based integration of real-time value-at-risk (VaR) services.* EPSRC UK e-Science All Hands Meeting.

Dong, S., Karniadakis, G. E., & Karonis, N. T. (2005). Cross-site computations on the TeraGrid. *Computing in Science & Engineering, 7*(5), 14–23. doi:10.1109/MCSE.2005.92

Dongarra, J., Du Croz, J., Hammarling, S., & Duff, I. S. (1990). A Set of Level 3 Basic Linear Algebra Subprograms. *ACM Transactions on Mathematical Software, 16*(1), 1–17. doi:10.1145/77626.79170

Doolin, D. M., Sitar, D., & Glaser, S. (2004). *Software Architecture for GPS-enabled Wildfire Sensorboard.* Civil and Environmental Engineering, University of California, Berkeley, USA. Retrieved November 20, 2008, from http://firebug.sourceforge.net/interface_poster.pdf

Douceur, J. (2002). The Sybil attack. In *Proceedings for the 1st International Workshop on Peer-to-Peer Systems, IPTPS 2002,* (Lecture Notes In Computer Science LNCS, Vol. 2429, pp. 251-260). Berlin: Springer-Verlag.

Douglis, F., Krishnan, P., & Marsh, B. (1994). Thwarting the Power-Hunger Disk. In *Proc. Winter USENIX Conf.,* (pp.292-306).

Downey, A. B. (1999). Using pathchar to estimate Internet link characteristics. In *Proceedings of ACM SIGCOMM '99* (pp. 241–250).

DRMAA. (2008). *Distributed Resource Management Application API.* Retrieved December 5, 2008, from http://www.drmaa.org/

Duan, Z., Zhang, Z., & Hou, Y. T. (2003). Service overlay networks: SLAs, QoS, and bandwidth provisioning. *IEEE/ACM Trans. Netw., 11*(6), 870–883.

Duminuco, A., Biersack, E., & En-Najjary, T. (2007). Proactive replication in distributed storage systems using machine availability estimation. In *CoNEXT '07: Proceedings of the 2007 ACM CoNEXT conference.*

Duran, F., Torres da Silva, V., & de Lucena, C. J. P. (2007). Using testimonies to enforce the behaviour of agents. In J. Sichman & S. Ossowski (Ed.), *Coordination, organizations, institutions, and norms in agent systems III* (pp. 25-36). Berlin: Springer.

Dustdar, S., & Schreiner, W. (2005). A survey on web services composition. *International Journal of Web and Grid Services, 1*(1). doi:10.1504/IJWGS.2005.007545

Eastlake, D. E., & Jones, P. E. (2001, September). *US Secure Hash Algorithm 1 (SHA1), Internet Engineering Task Force, RFC3174.* Retrieved from http://www.faqs.org/rfcs/rfc3174.html

ebXML Business Process Specification Schema Technical Specification v2.0.4. (2006). Retrieved October 28, 2008, from http://docs.oasis-open.org/ebxml-bp/2.0.4/OS/spec/ebxmlbp-v2.0.4-Spec-os-en.pdf

Edge, D. (1979). Quantitative measures of communication in science: A critical review. *History of Science, 17,* 102–134.

Efe, K. (1982, June). Heuristic Models of Task Assignment Scheduling in Distributed Systems. *IEEE Transactions on Computers,* 50–60.

Efstathiou, E. C., Frangoudis, P. A., & Polyzos, G. C. (2006). Stimulating Participation in Wireless Community Networks. In *Proceedings of IEEE INFOCOM'06*, Barcelona, Spain.

Egashira, R., Enomoto, A., & Suda, T. (2003). Distributed discovery using preference for query hits. In *Proceedings of the 18th IEEE Annual Workshop on Computer Communications* (pp. 210 – 216).

Egashira, R., Enomoto, A., & Suda, T. (2004). Distributed and adaptive discovery using preference. In *Proceedings of 2004 Symposium on Applications and the Internet Workshops* (pp. 395 – 401).

Egashira, R., Enomoto, A., & Suda, T. (2005). Distributed service discovery using preference. In *Proceedings of the 1st IEEE/ICST International Conference on Collaborative Computing: Networking, Applications and Worksharing.*

EGEE. (2008). *EGEE Overview*. Retrieved December 5, 2008, from http://eu-egee.org/fileadmin/documents/style-template/template_infosheet_general.doc

EGEE. (n.d.). Retrieved September 25, 2008, from http://www.eu-egee.org/

Eger, K., & Killata, U. (2008). Bandwidth trading in BitTorrent-like P2P networks for content distribution. *Journal of Computer Communications, 31*(2), 201–211. doi:10.1016/j.comcom.2007.08.005

EGGE-2. (2008). *EGEE website*. Retrieved December 5, 2008, from http://www.eu-egee.org/

EGI. (2007). *The Future European Grid Infrastructure - Towards a common sustainable e-infrastructure*. EGI Preparation Team. Vision Paper prepared for the EGI Workshop, Munich.

EGO. (2008). *Platform Enterprise Grid Orchestrator*. Retrieved December 5, 2008, from http://www.platform.com/Products/platform-enterprise-grid-orchestrator

EJB. (n.d.). Retrieved September 6, 2008, from http://java.sun.com/products/ejb/

El-Ansary, S., Alima, L. O., Brand, P., & Hari, S. (2003). Efficient broadcast in structured P2P networks. In *Peer-to-Peer Systems II* (LNCS 2735, pp. 304-314). Berlin, Germany: Springer.

Elenius, D. (2003). *Service discovery in peer-to-peer networks*. Unpublished master's thesis, Inköping Institute of Technology, Sweden.

Elfatatry, A. (2007). Dealing with Change: Components versus Services. *Communications of the ACM, 50*(8), 35–39. doi:10.1145/1278201.1278203

Ellison, C., & Schneier, B. (2000). Ten risks of PKI: What you're not being told about public key infrastructure. *Computer Security Journal, 16*(1), 1–7.

Elmroth, E., & Tordsson, J. (2007). *A standards-based grid resource brokering service supporting advance reservations, coallocation and cross-grid interoperability.* Manuscript submitted for publication.

Elnikety, S., Dropsho, S. G., & Zwaenepoel, W. (2007). Tashkent+: Memory-aware load balancing and update filtering in replicated databases. *ACM SIGOPS Operating Systems Review, 41*(3), 399–412. doi:10.1145/1272998.1273037

Elnozahy, E. N. M., Kistler, M., & Rajamony, R. (2002, February). Energy-Efficient Server Clusters. *International Workshop Power-Aware Computer Systems.*

El-Sayed, A., Roca, V., & Mathy, L. (2003). A survey of proposals for an alternative group communication service. IEEE Network, Jan/Feb.

Emmerich, W., Butchart, B., Chen, L., Wassermann, B., & Price, S. (2005). Grid service orchestration using the business process execution language (BPEL). *Journal of Grid Computing, 3*, 283–304. doi:10.1007/s10723-005-9015-3

eMule Project. (2008). Retrieved October 2008 from http://www.emule-project.net

eMule. (.n.d.). Retrieved from http://www.emule.com

Endrei, M., Ang, J., Ansanjani, A., Chua, S., Comte, P., Krogdahi, P., et al. (2004). Patterns: Service-Oriented Architecture and Web Services. *IBM Redbooks.* Retrieved May 17th, 2007 from www.ibm.com/redbooks

End-to-end Quality of Service (QoS) Concept and Architecture. (n.d.). 3GPP TS 23.107.

Enterprise Grid Alliance. (2005). *Enterprise grid alliance reference model v1.0.* Retrieved May 11, 2009, from http://www.ogf.org/gf/docs/?final&all

EnterTheGrid. (2007, October). 36 national grids initiatives in Europe support the EGI concept. *EnterTheGrid – PrimeurMonthly.* Retrieved May 11, 2009, from http://enterthegrid.com/primeur/07/articles/monthly/AE-PR-10-07-48.html

Environment Protection Agency. (2006). *Power Usage of Data Centers.* Last retrieved on November 9, 2008 from http://www.energystar.gov/ia/partners/prod_development/downloads/EPA_Datacenter_Report_Congress_Final1.pdf

Erikson, H. (1994). Mbone: the multicast backbone. *Communications of the ACM, 37,* 54–60. doi:10.1145/179606.179627

Erl, T. (2005). *Service-oriented architecture: Concepts, technology, and design.* Upper Saddle River, NJ: Prentice Hall PTR.

Erl, T. (2007). *SOA Principles of Service Design.* Upper Saddle River, NJ: Prentice Hall PTR.

Ernemann, C., Hamscher, V., & Yahyapour, R. (2002). *Economic Scheduling in Grid Computing* (LNCS 2537, pp. 128-152). Berlin: Springer-Verlag.

Ernemann, C., Hamscher, V., Schwiegelshohn, U., Yahyapour, R., & Streit, A. (2002). On advantages of grid computing for parallel job scheduling. In *International Symposium on Cluster Computing and the Grid* (pp. 39). Los Alamitos, CA: IEEE Computer Society.

Ernemann, C., Hamscher, V., Streit, A., & Yahyapour, R. (2002). Enhanced algorithms for multi-site scheduling. In M. Parashar (Ed.), *International Workshop on Grid Computing* (Vol. 2536, pp. 219-231). Berlin: Springer.

Erwin, D. (Ed.). (2003). *UNICORE Plus final Report - Uniform Interface to Computing Resources.* Forschungszentrum Jülich.

Erwin, D. W., & Snelling, D. F. (2001). UNICORE: A grid computing environment. In *Euro-Par 2001 Parallel Processing* (pp. 825-834). Berlin/Heidelberg, Germany: Springer.

e-Science (2008). *4th IEEE International Conference on e-Science, 2008.* Retrieved November 12, 2008, from http://escience2008.iu.edu/

ESG. (2008). *Earth System Grid (ESG).* Retrieved November 12, 2008, from http://www.earthsystemgrid.org/

ETSI-TC-Grid. (2008). *European Telecommunications Standards Institute Technical committee GRID.* Retrieved December 5, 2008, from http://www.etsi.org/website/technologies/grid.aspx

European DataGrid. (n.d.). Retrieved September 16, 2008, from http://eu-datagrid.web.cern.ch/eu-datagrid/

Exarchakos, G., Salter, J., & Antonopoulos, N. (2006). *Semantic cooperation and node sharing among P2P networks.* Retrieved from http://personal.cs.surrey.ac.uk/personal/pg/G.Exarchakos/publications/ final_grome.pdf

Eymann, T., Reinicke, M., Ardaiz, O., Artigas, P., de Cerio, L. D., Freitag, F., et al. (2003). Decentralized vs. centralized economic coordination of resource allocation in Grids. In *Proceedings of the 1st European Across Grids Conference.*

Fahmy, S., & Kwon, M. (2007). Characterizing overlay multicast networks and their costs. IEEE/ACM Transactions on Networking (TON), 15, 373-386.

Fahringer, T., Jugravu, A., Pllana, S., Prodan, R., Seragiotto, C., & Truong, H. (2005). ASKALON: a tool set for cluster and Grid computing. *Research Articles, Concurr. Comput. Pract. Exper., 17*(2-4), 143–169. doi:10.1002/cpe.929

Fang, L., Slominski, A., & Gannon, D. (2005). Web Services Security and Load Balancing in a Grid Environment. In *6th IEEE/ACM International Workshop on Grid Computing.*

Fangpeng, A., & Akl, S. (2006, January). *Technical Report No. 2006-504 Scheduling Algorithms for Grid Computing: State of the Art and Open Problems.*

FAROO. (n.d.). Retrieved from www.faroo.com/

Farrel, A., Vasseur, J.-P., & Ash, J. (2006). *A path computation element (PCE)-based architecture.* RFC 4655, Internet Engineering Task Force (IETF).

Faye, D., Nachouki, G., & Valduriez, P. (2007). Semantic Query Routing In Senpeer, A P2P Data Management System. In *Network-Based Information Systems* (pp. 365-374). Berlin, Germany: Springer.

Feamster, N., Andersen, D. G., Balakrishnan, H., & Kaashoek, M. F. (2003). Measuring the effects of internet path faults on reactive routing. In *SIGMETRICS*, 126–137.

Feitelson, D. G., Rudolph, L., & Schwiegelshohn, U. (2005). Parallel job scheduling a status report. In *Proceedings of JSSPP 2004,* (LNCS Vol. 3277, pp. 1–16). Berlin: Springer.

Feldman, M., Lai, K., Stoica, I., & Chuang, J. (2004). Robust Incentive Techniques for Peer-to-Peer Networks. In *5th ACM Conference on Electronic Commerce* (pp. 102–111).

Feng, Q., & Dai, Y. (2007). LIP: A Lifetime and Popularity Based Ranking Approach to Filter out Fake Files in P2P File Sharing Systems. In *International workshop on Peer-To-Peer Systems.*

Fergus, P., Mingkhwan, A., Merabti, M., & Hanneghan, M. (2003). DiSUS: Mobile Ad Hoc Network Unstructured Services. In M. Conti, S. Giordano, E. Gregori, & S. Olariu (Eds.) *Personal wireless communications* (pp. 484-491). Berlin/Heidelberg, Germany: Springer.

Ferguson, D. F., Pilarinos, D., & Shewchuk, J. (2007). The Internet Service Bus. *The Architecture Journal, 13*(1).

Fernandes, A., Kotsovinos, E., String, S., & Dragovic, B. (2004). Pinocchio: Incentives for honest participation in distributed trust management. In C. Damsgaard Jensen, S. Poslad, and T. Dimitrakos, (Eds.), *iTrust,* (LNCS Vol. 2995, pp. 63–77). Berlin: Springer. Retrieved from http://dblp.uni-trier.de/db/conf/itrust/itrust2004. html#FernandesKOD04

Ferrari, D., Gupta, A., & Ventre, G. (1997). Distributed advance reservation of real-time connections. *Multimedia Systems, 5*(3), 187–198. doi:10.1007/s005300050055

Ferscha, A., Hechinger, M., Mayrhofer, R., & Oberhauser, R. (2004). A light-weight component model for peer-to-peer applications. In *Proceedings 24th International Conf. on Distributed Computer Systems Workshops* (pp. 520-527).

Fessant, F. L., Handurukande, S., Kermarrec, A. M., & Massoulie, L. (2004). Clustering in peer-to-peer file sharing workloads. In *Proceedings of 3rd International Workshop on Peer-to-Peer Systems* (pp. 217-226).

Fielding, R. T. (2000). *Architectural styles and the design of network-based software architectures.* Irvine: University of California.

FIPS. *(2008).* Secure hash standard (SHS). federal information processing standards.

Fiscato, M., Costa, P., & Pierre, G. (2008). On the feasibility of decentralized grid scheduling. In *Proceedings of the Workshop on Decentralized Self-Management for Grids, P2P, and User Communities,* Venice, Italy.

Fisherl, K. M., & Lipson, J. I. (2004). Information Processing Interpretation of Errors in College Science Learning. *Instructional Science, 14,* 49-74.

Fishman, G. S. (1996). *Monte Carlo. Concepts, Algorithms, and Applications.* New York: Springer-Verlag.

Fisk, A. (2008). Gnutella Dynamic Query Protocol v0.1. *Gnutella Developer's Forum.* Retrieved November 14, 2008, from http://www9.limewire.com/developer/dynamic_query.html

Fleury, M., & Reverbel, F. (2003). The JBoss Extensible Server. In *Proceedings of the IFIP/ACM Middleware Conference,* (LNCS, pp. 344-354). Berlin: Springer Verlag.

Force.com Web Services API Developer's Guide. (2008). Retrieved October 15, 2008, from http://www.salesforce. com/us/developer/docs/api130/apex_api.pdf

Ford, B., Srisuresh, P., & Kegel, D. (2005). Peer-to-peer communication across network address translators. In *Proceedings of the annual conference on USENIX Annual Technical Conference* (pp. 13).

Forge, S., & Blackman, C. (2006). *Commercial Exploitation of Grid Technologies and Services*. Drivers and Barriers, Business Models and Impacts of Using Free and Open Source Licensing Schemes, SCF Associates for DG Information Society and Media.

Foster, I. (2001). The anatomy of the grid: Enabling scalable virtual organizations. *The International Journal of Supercomputer Applications, 15*(3), 200–222. doi:10.1177/109434200101500302

Foster, I. (2002). The Grid: A new infrastructure for 21st century science. *Physics Today, 55*(2), 42–47. doi:10.1063/1.1461327

Foster, I. (2002). What is the Grid? A three point checklist. *GRIDToday, 1*(6). Retrieved November 12, 2008, from http://www-fp.mcs.anl.gov/~foster/Articles/WhatIsTheGrid.pdf

Foster, I. (2005). Globus Toolkit 4: Software for Service Oriented Systems. In H. Jin, D. Reed, & W. Jiang, (Eds.), *NPC 2005*, (LNCS 3779, pp. 2 – 13). Retrieved November 10th, 2008 from http://www.globus.org/alliance/publications/papers/IFIP-2005.pdf

Foster, I. (2005). Globus toolkit version 4: Software for service-oriented systems. In *IFIP International Conference on Network and Parallel Computing* (LNCS 3779, pp. 2-13).

Foster, I. (2005). Service Oriented Science . *Science Magazine, 308*(1), 814–817.

Foster, I., & Iamnitchi, A. (2003). On death, taxes, and the convergence of peer-to-peer and grid computing. In M.F. Kaashoek & I. Stoica (Eds.), *Lecture Notes in Computer Science, Peer-to-Peer Systems II* (Vol. 2735, pp. 118-128). Heidelberg, Germany: Springer-Berlin.

Foster, I., & Kesselman, C. (1997). Globus: A metacomputing infrastructure toolkit. *The International Journal of Supercomputer Applications and High Performance Computing, 11*(2), 115–128. doi:10.1177/109434209701100205

Foster, I., & Kesselman, C. (1998). *The GRID – Blueprint for a new computing infrastructure.* San Francisco: Morgan Kaufmann.

Foster, I., & Kesselman, C. (1999). Computational grids. In I. Foster & C. Kesselman (Eds.), *The grid: Blueprint for a new computing infrastructure* (pp. 15-51). San Francisco: Morgan-Kaufman.

Foster, I., & Kesselman, C. (1999). Globus: A toolkit-based grid architecture. In I. Foster & C. Kesselman (Eds.), *The Grid: Blueprint for a new computing infrastructure* (pp.259-278). San Francisco: Morgan Kaufmann.

Foster, I., & Kesselman, C. (2003). *The grid 2: Blueprint for a new computing infrastructure.* San Francisco: Morgan Kaufmann.

Foster, I., Berry, D., Djaoui, A., Grimshaw, A., Horn, B., Kishimoto, H., et al. (2004, July 12). *Open Grid Service Architecture V1.0.*

Foster, I., et al. (2005). *The open Grid services architecture, Version 1.0.* Global Grid Forum, Lemont, Illinois, USA (vol. 30).

Foster, I., Kesselman, C., & Tueck, S. E. (2001). The anatomy of the grid: Enabling scalable virtual organizations. *The International Journal of Supercomputer Applications, 15*(3), 200–220. doi:10.1177/109434200101500302

Foster, I., Kesselman, C., & Tuecke, S. (2001). The anatomy of the Grid: Enabling scalable virtual organizations. *International Journal of High Performance Computing Applications, 15*(3), 200–222. doi:10.1177/109434200101500302

Foster, I., Kesselman, C., Lee, C., Lindell, B., Nahrstedt, K., & Roy, A. (1999). A distributed resource management architecture that supports advance reservations and co-allocation. In *International Workshop on Quality of Service* (pp. 27-36). Piscataway, NJ: IEEE Computer Society.

Foster, I., Kesselman, C., Nick, J., & Tuecke, S. (2002). *The physiology of the Grid: An open Grid services ar-*

chitecture for distributed systems integration. Retrieved October 10, 2008, from http://www.globus.org/alliance/publications/papers/ogsa.pdf

Foster, I., Kesselman, C., Tsudik, G., & Tuecke, S. (1998). A security architecture for computational Grids. In *Proceedings of the 5th ACM Computer and Communications Security Conference (CCS '98),* (pp. 83-92). New York: ACM Press.

Foster, I., Kishimoto, H., Savva, A., Berry, D., Djaoui, A., Grimshaw, A., et al. (2005). *The open grid services architecture, version 1.0.* Global Grid Forum (GGF).

Fox, G. C., & Gannon, D. (2006). Workflow in Grid systems. *Concurrency and Computation, 18,* 1009–1019. doi:10.1002/cpe.1019

Fox, G., & Walker, D. (2003). *e-science gap analysis* (UK e-science Technical Report Series COSPA Knowledge Base). Retrieved May 11, 2009, from http://hdl.handle.net/2038/1515

Fraigniaud, P., & Gauron, P. (2006). D2B: A de Bruijn based content-addressable network. *Theoretical Computer Science, 355*(1), 65–79. doi:10.1016/j.tcs.2005.12.006

Frank, K., Suraci, V., & Mitic, J. (2008). Personalizable service discovery in pervasive systems. In *Fourth International Conference on Networking and Services, ICNS 2008* (pp. 182-187).

Frantz, F. K. (1995). A taxonomy of model abstraction techniques. In *The 1995 Winter Simulation Conference* (pp. 1413-1420).

Frei, A. (2005). *Jadabs – An adaptive pervasive middleware architecture.* Unpublished doctoral dissertation, Swiss Federal Institute of Technology, Zurich, Switzerland.

Freundt, S., Horn, P., Konovalov, A., Linton, S., & Roozemond, D. (2008). Symbolic computation software composability. In S. Autexier et al. (Eds.), *AISC Calculemus MKM,* (LNAI 5144, pp.285-295). Berlin: Springer.

Frey, J., Tannenbaum, T., Livny, M., Foster, I., & Tuecke, S. (2002). Condor-G: A computation management agent for multi-institutional Grids. *Cluster Computing, 5*(3), 237–246. doi:10.1023/A:1015617019423

Friese, T., Freisleben, B., Rusitschka, S., & Southall, A. (2003). A framework for resource management in peer-to-peer networks. In *Revised Papers from the International Conference NetObjectDays on Objects, Components, Architectures, Services, and Applications for a Networked World* (LNCS 2591, pp. 4-21). Berlin, Germany: Springer.

Friese, T., Smith, M., & Freisleben, B. (2004, November). Hot service deployment in an ad hoc grid environment. In *Proceedings of the Second International Conference on Service Oriented Computing (ICSOC '04)* (pp. 75-83).

Frîncu, M. (2009). Dynamic Scheduling Algorithm for Heterogeneous Environments with Regular Task Input from Multiple Requests. In N. Abdennadher, D. Petcu (Eds.), *Grid and Pervasive Computing,* (LNCS 5529, pp.205-216). Berlin: Springer.

Frolund, S., & Guerraoui, R. (2002). e-Transactions: end-to-end reliability for three-tier architectures. *IEEE Transactions on Software Engineering, 28*(4), 378–395. doi:10.1109/TSE.2002.995430

Fu, Y., Chase, J., Chun, B., Schwab, S., & Vahdat, A. (2003). Sharp: An Architecture for Secure Resource Peering. In *9th ACM Symposium on Operating Systems Principles* (pp. 133–148).

Fudenberg, D., & Tirole, J. (1991). *Game theory.* Cambridge, MA: MIT Press.

Fujii, K., & Suda, T. (2006). Semantics-based dynamic Web service composition. *International Journal of Cooperative Information Systems, 15*(3), 293–324. doi:10.1142/S0218843006001372

Fujimoto, R. M. (1993). Parallel discrete event simulation: Will the field survive? *ORSA Journal on Computing, 5*(3), 213–230.

Fullam, K. K., & Barber, K. S. (2006). Learning trust strategies in reputation exchange networks. *Proceedings of the Fifth International Joint Conference On Autonomous Agents And Multiagent Systems* (pp. 1241- 1248). New York: ACM.

Funk, C., Schultheis, A., Linnhoff-Popien, C., Mitic, J., & Kuhmunch, C. (2007). Adaptation of composite services in pervasive computing environments. In *IEEE International Conference on Pervasive Services* (pp. 242-249).

Furfaro, F., Grimaldi, A., Nigro, D., Pupo, L., & Cicirelli, F. (2004). *Management architecture for distributed measurement services.* In *Proceedings of the 21st IEEE Instrumentation and Measurement Technology Conference* (Vol. 2, pp. 974-979).

Furnis, P., & Green, A. (2005). *Choreology Ltd. Contribution to the OASIS WS-Tx Technical Committee relating to WS-Coordination, WS-AtomicTransaction, and WS-BusinessActivity,* (November 2005). Retrieved from http//www.oasis-open.org/committees/download.php/15808

FWGrid. (n.d.). Retrieved May 11, 2009, from http://www.fwgrid.ucsd.edu/

GACL. (2008). *Grid Access Control Language.* Retrieved December 5, 2008, from http://www.gridpp.ac.uk/website/gacl.html

Galatopoulos, D., Kalofonos, D. N., & Manolakos, E. (2008). A P2P service oriented architecture enabling group collaboration through service composition. In *Proceedings of the 5th ACM International Conference on Pervasive Services (ICPS'08)* (pp. 111-120).

Gambetta, D. (1998). *Trust: Making and Braking of Cooperative Relations.* Oxford, UK: Basil Blackwell.

Ganesan, P., & Seshadri, M. (2005). On cooperative content distribution and the price of barter. In *25th IEEE International Conference on Distributed Computing Systems* (pp. 81–90).

Ganesan, P., Yang, B., & Garcia-Molina, H. (2004). One Torus to Rule Them All: Multidimensional Queries in P2P Systems. In *Seventh International Workshop on the Web and Databases* (pp. 19-24).

Ganesh, A., Kermarrec, A., & Massoulie, L. (2001). SCAMP: Peer-to-peer lightweight membership service for large-scale group communication. In *Proceedings*

of the 3rd International Workshop on Networked Group Communication.

Gannon, D. (2007). A service architecture for eScience Grid gateways. In *Grid Computing, High-Performance and Distributed Applications (GADA'07).*

Ganz, A., & Chlamtac, I. (1989). Path allocation access control in fiber optic communication systems. *IEEE Transactions on Computers, 38*(10), 1372–1382. doi:10.1109/12.35832

Gara, A., Blumrich, M. A., Chen, D., Chiu, G. L.-T., Coteus, P., Giampapa, M. E., et al. (n.d.). Overview of the Blue Gene/L system architecture. *IBM Journal of Research and Development.* Retrieved on November 9, 2008 from http://www.research.ibm.com/journal/rd49-23.html.

García-Camino, A. (2007). Ignoring, forcing and expecting concurrent events in electronic institutions. In J. Sichman & S. Ossowski (Ed.), *Coordination, organizations, institutions, and norms in agent systems III* (pp. 15-26). Berlin: Springer.

Garlan, D., Siewiorek, D. P., Smailagic, A., & Steenkiste, P. (2002). Project Aura: Toward distraction-free pervasive computing. *IEEE Pervasive Computing / IEEE Computer Society [and] IEEE Communications Society, 1*(3), 22–31. doi:10.1109/MPRV.2002.1012334

GARUDA. (n.d.). Retrieved September 19, 2008, from http://www.garudaindia.in/

Ge, R., Feng, X. Z., & Cameron, K. W. (2005, November). Performance-constrained Distributed DVS Scheduling for Scientific Applications on Power-aware Clusters. In *Proceedings of the ACM/IEEE SC 2005 Conference (Supercomputing 05)* (pp. 34).

g-Eclipse. (2008). g-Eclipse project. Retrieved December 5, 2008, from http://www.geclipse.org/

Gehlert, A., Hielscher, J., Danylevych, O., & Karastoyanova, D. (2008). Online testing, requirements engineering and service faults as drivers for adapting service compositions. In *Proceedings of MONA+ at ServiceWave2008.*

Geldof, M. (2004). *The semantic grid: Will semantic web and grid go hand in hand.* European commission DG Information Society Unit- Grid Technologies. Retrieved May 11, 2009, from http://www.semanticgrid.org/documentsSemantic%20Grid%20report%20public.pdf

Gelenter, D. (1985). Generative Communication in Linda. *ACM Transaction of Prog. Lang. Syst., 1*(7), 80–112. doi:10.1145/2363.2433

Gene Ontology. (n.d.). Retrieved from http://www.geneontology.org/

Genesereth, M. R., & Ketchpel, S. P. (1994). Software agents. *Communications of the ACM, 37*(7), 48–53. doi:10.1145/176789.176794

GENSS Consortium. (2005). *Grid-enabled numerical and symbolic services.* Retrieved November 2008 from http://genss.cs.bath.ac.uk/

Gentry, C. (2003). Certificate-based encryption and the certificate revocation problem. In E. Biham (Ed.), *Advances in Cryptology - Proceedings of EUROCRYPT 2003,* (LNCS Vol. 2656, pp. 272-293). Berlin: Springer-Verlag.

Gentry, C., & Silverberg, A. (2002). Hierarchical ID-based cryptography. In Y. Zheng (Ed.), *Advances in Cryptology - Proceedings of ASIACRYPT 2002,* (LNCS Vol. 2501, pp. 548-566). Berlin: Springer-Verlag.

Gerke, J., Hausheer, D., Mischke, J., & Stiller, B. (2003). An Architecture for a Service Oriented P2P System. *Praxis der Informationsverarbeitung und Kommunikation, 2*(03), 90–95. doi:10.1515/PIKO.2003.90

Germano, G., & Engel, M. (2006). City@home: Monte Carlo derivative pricing distributed on networked computers. In *Grid Technology for Financial Modelling and Simulation, 2006.*

GGF. (2002). Retrieved from http://www.gridforum.org

Ghamri-Doudane, S., & Agoulmine, N. (2007). Enhanced DHT-based P2P architecture for effective resource discovery and management. *Journal of Network and Systems Management, 15*(3), 335–354. doi:10.1007/s10922-007-9067-8

Ghijsen, M., Jansweijer, W., & Wielinga, R. (2007). Towards a framework for agent coordination and reorganization, AgentCore. In J. Sichman & S. Ossowski (Ed.), *Coordination, organizations, institutions, and norms in agent systems III* (pp. 13-24). Berlin: Springer.

Ghodsi, A., Alima, L. O., & Haridi, S. (2005). Symmetric replication for structured peer-to-peer systems. In *Proc. DBISp2p'05, 3rd Int'l VLDB Workshop on Databases, Information Systems and Peer-to-Peer Computing* (LNCS 4125, pp. 74-85). Berlin: Springer.

Gibson, W. (2000). FLASH vs (Simulated) FLASH: Closing the simulation loop. In *ACM Transactions on Modelling and Computer Simulation* (pp. 49-58). New York: ACM.

GigaSpaces Project. (n.d.). Retrieved June 27, 2006, from http://www.psdesign.co.il/gigaspaces/

Gigle Semiconductor. (2009). Retrieved from http://www.gigle.biz/

Gillam, L., & Ahmad, K. *(2005).* Financial data tombs and nurseries: A grid-based text and ontological analysis. In *Proc. of 1st Intl. Workshop on Grid Technology for Financial Modeling and Simulation (Grid in Finance 2006).*

Gillam, L., Ahmad, K., & Dear, G. (2005). Grid-enabling Social Scientists: some infrastructure issues. In *Proc. of 1st Intl. e-Social Science Conference*, Manchester, UK. Globus. (n.d.). Retrieved from http://www.globus.org/

Gillett, F. E. (2004). *Grid Gets Big, But The Term Is Confusing.* Forrester.

Ginits, H. (2000). *Game theory evolving.* NJ: Princeton University Press.

Gkantsidis, C., & Rodriguez, P. (2005). Network coding for large scale content distribution. In *Proceedings of IEEE infocom.*

Gkantsidis, C., & Rodriguez, P. R. (2005). Network Coding for Large Scale Content Distribution. In *24th Annual Joint Conference of the IEEE Computer and Communications Societies (INFOCOM),* (Vol. 4, pp. 2235–2245).

gLite, (2008). *gLite User Guide*. Retrieved December 5, 2008, from http://glite.web.cern.ch/glite/

Globus Alliance. (2005). *Globus Toolkit 4 Java WS Core*. Retrieved from http://www.globus.org/toolkit/docs/4.0/common/javawscore/

Globus Alliance. (n.d.). Retrieved May 1, 2009, from http://www.globus.org/

Globus Toolkit. (n.d.). Retrieved September 15, 2008, from http://www.globus.org/toolkit/

Globus, M. D. S. (2008). *Globus Toolkit MDS: Monitoring & Discovering System*. Retrieved from http://www.globus.org/toolkit/mds

Gnutella Protocol Specification. (n.d.). Retrieved from http://wiki.limewire.org/index.php?title=GDF

Gnutella. (2002). *Gnutella 0.6 specification*. Retrieved June from http://groups.yahoo.com/group/the_gdf/files/Development/GnutellaProtocol-v0.6-200206draft.txt

Gnutella. (2003). *Protocol V.0.6 RFC*. Retrieved from http://rfc-gnutella.sourceforge.net

Godfrey, B. (2008). *Repository of Availability Traces*. Retrieved May 12, 2008 from http://www.eecs.berkeley.edu/~pbg/availability/

GoGrid. (n.d.). *GoGrid cloud hosting services*. Retrieved May 11, 2009, from http://www.gogrid.com/

Golbeck, J., Parisa, B., & Hendler, J. (2003). Trust networks on the Semantic Web. *In Proceedings of Cooperative Intelligent Agents* (pp. 238-249), Helsinki, Finland. Berlin: Springer.

Gomez-Perez, A., Fernandez-Lopez, M., & Corcho, O. (2004). *Ontological Engineering with examples from the areas of Knowledge Management, e-commece and the Semantic Web*. London: Springer-Verlag.

Gong, L. (2001). JXTA: A network programming environment. *IEEE Internet Computing*, 5(3), 88–95. doi:10.1109/4236.935182

González-Castaño, F. J., Gil-Castiñerira, F. J., Rodelgo-Lacruz, M., & Asorey-Cacheda, R. (2005). Off-the-shelf transparent HomePlug range extension. In *Proceedings of the 10th IEEE Symposium on Computers and Communications 2005*, (pp. 179-184).

Google APIs & Tools. (n.d.). Retrieved October 4, 2008, from http://code.google.com/more/#products-products-android

Google. (2008). *Android: an open handset alliance project*. Retrieved November 12, 2008 from http://code.google.com/android/documentation.html.

Google. (n.d.). *Google app engine*. Retrieved May 11, 2009, from http://code.google.com/appengine/

Google. (n.d.). Retrieved from http://www.google.com

Gopalakrishnan, V., Silaghi, B., Bhattacharjee, B., & Keleher, P. (2004). Adaptive replication in peer-to-peer systems. In *Proc. ICDCS 2004, 24th Int'l Conference on Distributed Computing Systems*, Tokyo, Japan (pp. 360-369).

Gounaris, A., Paton, N. W., Sakellariou, R., & Fernandes, A. A. A. (2004). Adaptive query processing and the Grid: Opportunities and challenges. In *Proceedings the 15th International Workshop on Database and Expert Systems Applications*.

Gounaris, A., Paton, N. W., Sakellariou, R., Fernandes, A. A. A., Smith, J., & Watson, P. (2006). Modular adaptive query processing for service-based Grids. In *Proceedings IEEE International Conf. on Autonomic Computing* (pp. 295-296).

Gounaris, A., Paton, N. W., Sakellariou, R., Fernandes, A. A. A., Smith, J., & Watson, P. (2006). Practical adaptation to changing resources in Grid query processing. In *Proceedings 22nd International Conference on Data Engineering*, (pp. 165).

GPFS. (2008). *General Parallel File System*. Retrieved December 5, 2008, from http://www-03.ibm.com/systems/clusters/software/gpfs/index.html

GRAAP-WG. (2008). *OGF Grid Resource Allocation Agreement Protocol Working Group (GRAAP-WG)*. Retrieved December 5, 2008, from http://forge.ogf.org/sf/projects/graap-wg

Grabmeier, J., Kaltofen, E., & Weispfenning, V. (2003). *Computer Algebra Handbook*. Berlin: Springer.

Grace, P., Coulson, G., Blair, G., Mathy, L., Yeung, W. K., Cai, W., et al. (2004, October). GRIDKIT: Pluggable overlay networks for grid computing. In *proceedings of the International Symposium on Distributed Objects and Applications (DOA'04)*, Larnaca, Cyprus (LNCS 3291, pp. 1463-1481). Berlin: Springer.

Grace, P., Hughes, D., Porter, B., Coulson, G., Blair, G., & Taiani, F. (2008). Experiences with Open Overlays: A Middleware Approach to Network Heterogeneity. In *Proceedings of the 3rd ACM International EuroSys Conference* (123-136). New York: ACM Press.

Graham, S., Karmarkar, A., Mischkinsky, J., Robinson, I., & Sedukhin, I. (2006). *Web Services Resource 1.2*. Retrieved October 7, 2008, from http://docs.oasis-open.org/wsrf/wsrf-ws_resource-1.2-spec-os.pdf

Grandison, T. (2007). Conceptions of trust: Definition, constructs, and models. In R. Song, L. Korba, & a. G. Yee, (Eds.), *Trust in e-services: Technologies, practices and challenges* (pp. 1-28). Hershey, PA: IGI Global.

Grandison, T. (2007). Trust management tools. In R. Song, L. Korba, & G. Yee, *Trust in e-services: Technologies, practices and challenges,* (pp. 198-216). Hershey, PA: IGI Global.

Grandison, T., & Sloman, M. (2000). A Survey of Trust in Internet Applications. *IEEE Communications Survey and Tutorials, 4*(4), 2–16. doi:10.1109/COMST.2000.5340804

Granville, L. Z., Rosa, D. M., Panisson, A., Melchiors, C., Almeida, M. J., & Tarouco, L. (2005). Managing Computer Networks Using Peer-to-Peer Technologies. *IEEE Communications Magazine, 43*(10), 62–68. doi:10.1109/MCOM.2005.1522126

Gray, J. (2003). *Distributed computing economics.* Microsoft Research Technical Report: MSRTR-2003-24 (also presented in Microsoft VC Summit 2004, Silicon Valey, April 2004).

Gray, J., & Lamport, L. (2006). Consensus on transaction commit. *ACM Transactions on Database Systems, 31*(1), 133–160. doi:10.1145/1132863.1132867

Gray, J., & Reuter, A. (1993). *Transaction Processing: Concepts and Techniques*. San Francisco: Morgan Kaufmann.

Green 500 list. (2009). Retrieved from http://www.green500.org

GreenCache. (n.d.). Retrieved from http://www.gforceinc.com.cn/greencache.asp?gclid=CMX7oeTM-5gCFRYdewod 8G2amw

GreenGrid. (2008). *The Green Grid – get connected to efficient IT.* Retrieved December 5, 2008, from http://www.thegreengrid.org

Grefen, P., & Angelov, S. (2002). On τ, μ, π and ε-contracting. In C. Bussler, R. Hull, S. McIlraith, M. E. Orlowska, B. Pernici, & J. Yang (Ed.), *Proceedings of the CAiSE Workshop on Web Services, e-Business, and the Semantic Web,* (pp. 68-77). Berlin: Springer.

Grid Datafarm. (n.d.). Retrieved September 16, 2008, from http://datafarm.apgrid.org/

Grid4All. (2008). *Grid4All project*. Retrieved December 5, 2008, from http://www.grid4all.eu/

Grid5000. (2008). *Grid5000 project*. Retrieved December 5, 2008, from https://www.grid5000.fr/

GridBench. (2008). *GridBench A Tool For Benchmarking Grids*. Retrieved December 5, 2008, from http://grid.ucy.ac.cy/gridbench/

Gridbus Project. (n.d.). Retrieved September 18, 2008, from http://www.gridbus.org/

GridBus. (2008). *The GridBus project website*. Retrieved December 5, 2008, from http://www.gridbus.org/

GridCOMP. (2008). *Grid Programming with Components*. Retrieved December 5, 2008, from http://gridcomp.ercim.org/

GridEcon. (2008). *GridEcon project*. Retrieved December 5, 2008, from http://www.gridecon.eu

GridFTP. (2008). *GridFTP project*. Retrieved December 5, 2008, from http://www.globus.org/grid_software/data/gridftp.php

Gridipedia. (2008). *Grid Computing Case Studies*. Retrieved December 5, 2008, from http://www.gridipedia.eu/grid-computing-case-studies.html

GridRPC. (2008). *Grid Remote Procedure Call WG (GRIDRPC-WG)*. Retrieved December 5, 2008, from https://forge.gridforum.org/projects/gridrpc-wg/

Grid-Server. (2008). *DataSynapse GridServer*. Retrieved December 5, 2008, from http://www.datasynapse.com/gridserver

GridSite. (2008). *Grid Security for the Web - Web platforms for Grids*. Retrieved December 5, 2008, from http://www.gridsite.org/

GridTrust. (2008). *GridTrust project*. Retrieved December 5, 2008, from http://www.gridtrust.eu/gridtrust/

Groove Protocol Support. (2008). Retrieved February 15, 2009, from http://technet.microsoft.com/en-us/library/cc261835.aspx

Gruber, R., Keller, V., Kuonen, P., Sawley, M.-C., Schaeli, B., Tolou, A., et al. (2006). Towards an intelligent grid scheduling system. In *Proceedings of PPAM 2005*, (LNCA Vol. 3911, pp. 751–757).

GSI. (2008). *Grid Security Infrastructure*. Retrieved December 5, 2008, from http://www.globus.org/security/overview.html

GTK. (2008). *Globus Toolkit*. Retrieved December 5, 2008, from http://www.globus.org/toolkit/

Gu, X., Nahrstedt, K., & Bin, Yu. (2004). SpiderNet: an integrated peer-to-peer service composition framework. In *Proceedings of the 13th IEEE International Symposium on High performance . Distributed Computing, 2004*, 110–119. doi:10.1109/HPDC.2004.1323507

Guardini, I., Fasano, P., & Girardi, G. (2000). IPv6 Operational Experience within the 6bone. In *Proceedings of the Internet Society Conference*, 2000.

Gudgin, M., Hadley, M., Mendelsohn, N., Moreau, J., Nielsen, H. K., Karmarkar, A., & Lafon, Y. (2007). *SOAP Version 1.2 Part 1: Messaging framework* (2nd Ed.). Retrieved October 11, 2008, from http://www.w3.org/TR/2007/REC-soap12-part1-20070427/

Gulías, V. M., Barreiro, M., & Freire, J. L. (2005). VoDKA: Developing a video-on-demand server using distributed functional programming. *Journal of Functional Programming*, *15*(3), 403–430. doi:10.1017/S0956796805005502

Gunaratne, C., Christensen, K., & Nordman, B. (2005). Managing energy consumption costs in desktop PCs and LAN switches with proxying, split TCP connections, and scaling of link speed. *International Journal of Network Management*, *15*(5), 297–310. doi:10.1002/nem.565

Guo, L., Chen, S., Xiao, Z., Tan, E., Ding, X., & Zhang, X. (2005). Measurements, Analysis and Modeling of BitTorrent-like Systems. In *5th ACM SIGCOMM Conference on Internet Measurement* (pp. 4-4).

Guo, Y., Suh, K., Kurose, J., & Towsley, D. (2003). P2Cast: peer-to-peer patching scheme for VoD service. In *Proceedings of the 12th International Conference on World Wide Web*, (pp. 301-309).

Gupta, A. (2004). *Wireless Sensor Networks Research*. Department of Computer Science, Western Michigan University, USA. Retrieved November 20, 2008, from http://www.cs.wmich.edu/wsn/

Gupta, A., Agrawal, D., & Abbadi, A. E. (2005). Distributed resource discovery in large scale computing systems. In *Proceedings of the 2005 Symposium on Applications and the Internet* (pp. 320-326). Washington, DC: IEEE Computer Society Press.

Gupta, M., & Ammar, M. (2003). Service Differentiation in Peer-to-Peer Networks Utilizing Reputations. In *5th ACM International Workshop on Networked Group Communications* (pp. 70–82).

Gupta, R., Sekhri, V., & Somani, A. K. (2006). CompuP2P: An architecture for Internet computing using peer-to-peer networks. *IEEE Transactions on Parallel and Distributed Systems, 17*(11), 1306–1320. doi:10.1109/TPDS.2006.149

Gupta, S. K. S., Lee, W. C., Purakayastha, A., & Srimani, P. K. (2001). An overview of pervasive computing. *IEEE Personal Communications, 8*(4), 8–9. doi:10.1109/MPC.2001.943997

Gurbani, V., & Marocco, E. (2008). *Application-Layer Traffic Optimization (ALTO) Problem Statement.* IETF Internet-Draft. Retrieved April 14, 2009, from http://tools.ietf.org/html/draft-marocco-alto-problem-statement-02

Gurumurthi, S., Sivasubramaniam, A., Kandemir, M., & Fanke, H. (2003, June). DRPM: Dynamic Speed Control for Power Management in Server Class Disks. In *Proc. Int'l Symp. of Computer Framework* (pp. 169-179).

Gutierrez, D., Torres, L. M., Blasco, F., Carreras, J., & Riveiro, J. C. (2005). In-home plc ready for triple play. In *Proceedings of 2005 International Symposium on Power Line Communications and its Applications,* (pp. 366-370).

Gutmann, P. (2003). Plug-and-play PKI: A PKI your mother can use. In *Proceedings of 12th USENIX Security Symposium,* (pp. 45-58).

Gutscher, A., Heessen, J., & Siemoneit, O. (2008). Possibilities and limitations of modelling trust and reputation. In *Proceedings of the Fifth International Workshop on Philosophy and Informatics (WSPI-2008), Vol. 332, CEUR Workshop Proceedings.*

GVK. (2008). *Grid Visualisation Kernel.* Retrieved December 5, 2008, from http://www.gup.uni-linz.ac.at/gvk/

Haas, H., & Brown, A. (2004). *Web services glossary.* Retrieved October 4, 2008, from http://www.w3.org/TR/ws-gloss/

Haeberlen, A., Mislove, A., & Druschel, P. (2005). Glacier: Highly durable, decentralized storage despite massive correlated failures. In *Proceedings of the 2nd symposium on networked systems design and implementation (nsdi).*

Haenselmann, T. (2006). Sensornetworks. *GFDL Wireless Sensor Network textbook.* Retrieved November 20, 2008, from http://www.informatik.uni-mannheim.de/~haensel/sn_book/

Haghjoo, M. S., & Papazoglou, M. P. (1992). TrActorS: a transactional actor system for distributed query-processing. In *Distributed Computing Systems 1992, Proceedings of the 12th International Conference on,* (pp. 682-689).

Hagstrom, W. O. (1965). *The scientific community.* New York: Basic Books.

Haji, M. H., Gourlay, I., Djemame, K., & Dew, P. M. (2005). A SNAP-based community resource broker using a three-phase commit protocol: A performance study. *The Computer Journal, 48*(3), 333–346. doi:10.1093/comjnl/bxh088

Hammond, K., Al Zain, A., Cooperman, G., Petcu, D., & Trinder, P. (2007). SymGrid: a framework for symbolic computation on the Grid. In A.M. Kermarrec, L. Bouge, & T. Priol (Eds.), *Parallel Processing,* (LNCS 4641, pp.447–456). Berlin: Springer.

Hampshire, A. (2004). Extending the open Grid services architecture to intermittently available wireless networks. *UK eScience All Hands.*

Han, J., & Park, D. (2003). A lightweight personal grid using a supernode network. In *Proceedings of the Third International Conference on Peer-to-Peer Computing (P2P 2003)* (pp. 168-175).

Han, L. (2009). The self-adaptation to dynamic failures for efficient virtual organization formations in Grid computing context. *Chaos, Solitons and Fractals, 14*(3), 1085. Retrieved June 30, 2008, from linkinghub.elsevier.com/retrieve/pii/S0960077908002166

Han, L., & Berry, D. (2008). Semantic-supported and agent-based decentralised Grid resource discovery. *Future Generation Computer Systems, 24*(8), 806–812. doi:10.1016/j.future.2008.04.005

Handley, M. & Jacobson, V. (1998, April). *SDP: session description protocol, RFC 2327.* Internet Engineering Task Force.

Handley, M., Jacobson, V., & Perkins, C. (2006, July). *SDP: Session Description Protocol*. RFC 4566 (Proposed Standard).

Hanson, J. (2005). Event-driven services in SOA. *Javaworld*.

Harihar, K., & Kurkovsky, S. (2005). Using Jini to enable pervasive computing environments. In *Proceedings of the 43rd annual Southeast regional conference, SESSION: Architecture and distributed systems* (pp. 188-193).

Harren, M., Hellerstein, J., Huebsch, R., Loo, B., Shenker, S., & Stoica, I. (2002) Complex Queries in DHT-Based Peer-To-Peer Networks. In *Proceedings of the first International Workshop on P2P Systems (IPTPS'02)*.

Harrison, A., & Taylor, I. J. (2005). *Dynamic Web service deployment using WSPeer*. Retrieved July 7, 2008, from http://www.mardigrasconference.org/conf_2005/2005/Presentations/Harrison.pdf

Hartmann, J., Palma, R., & Sure, Y. (2005). *OMV – Ontology Metadata Vocabulary*

Hasselmeyer, P. (2005). On service discovery process types. In *Service-Oriented Computing - ICSOC 2005* (LNCS 3826, pp. 144-157). Berlin: Springer.

Hausheer, D. (2006). *PeerMart: Secure decentralized pricing and accounting for peer-to-peer systems*. Dissertation No. 16200, ETH Zurich.

Hauswirth, M., & Schmidt, R. (2005). An overlay network for resource discovery in grids. In *Proceedings of the 16th International Workshop on Data Base and Expert Systems Applications*, Copenhagen, Denmark.

Haverinen, H., Siren, J., & Eronen, P. (2007). Energy consumption of always-on applications in wcdma networks. In J. Siren (Ed.), *Proceedings of the 65th IEEE VTC2007-Spring Vehicular Technology Conference*, (pp. 964-968). Dublin, Ireland.

Hayes, B. (2008). Cloud Computing. *Communications of the ACM, 51*(7), 9–11. doi:10.1145/1364782.1364786

Heckmann, O., & Bock, A. (2002). *The eDonkey 2000 protocol*. Retrieved September 6, 2008, from http://www.kom.e-technik.tu-darmstadt.de/publications/abstracts/HB02-1.html

Heflin, J. (2004). *OWL Web Ontology Language*. Retrieved April 2006 from http://www.w3.org/TR/webont-req/

Hei, X., Liu, Y., & Ross, K. W. (2008). IPTV over P2P streaming networks: the mesh-pull approach. *Communications Magazine, 46*(2), 86–92. doi:10.1109/MCOM.2008.4473088

Heine, F., Hovestadt, M., & Kao, O. (2004). Towards ontology-driven P2P Grid resource discovery. In *5th IEEE/ACM International Workshop on Grid Computing* (pp.76-83). Washington, DC: IEEE Computer Society.

Helal, S. (2005). Programming pervasive spaces. *IEEE Pervasive Computing / IEEE Computer Society [and] IEEE Communications Society, 4*(1), 84–87. doi:10.1109/MPRV.2005.22

Helal, S., Mann, W., El-Zabadani, H., King, J., Kaddoura, Y., & Jansen, E. (2005). Gator Tech Smart House: A programmable pervasive space. *IEEE Computer, 38*(3), 50–60.

Helfin, J., & Hendler, J. A. (2000). Dynamic Ontologies on the Web. In *Proceedings of the National Conference on Artificial Intelligence* (AAAI) (pp. 443-449).

Hellerstein, J. L. (2000). Adaptive query processing: technology in evolution. *IEEE Database Engineering Bulletin, 23*(2), 7–18.

Hellerstein, J., Diao, Y., Parekh, S., & Tilbury, D. (2004). *Feedback control of computing systems*. Hoboken, NJ: Wiley-IEEE Press.

Hender, J., & McGuiness, D. L. (2001). DARPA Agent Markup Language. *IEEE Intelligent Systems, 15*(6), 72–73.

Herault, T., Lemarinier, P., Peres, O., Pilard, L., & Beauquier, J. (2007). A Model for Large Scale Self-Stabilization. In Proceedings of *the twenty first International Parallel and Distributed Processing Symposium (IPDPS 2007)*.

Hewitt, C. (2008). ORGs for scalable, robust, privacy-friendly client cloud computing. *IEEE Internet Computing, 12*(5), 96–99. doi:10.1109/MIC.2008.107

Hey, T., & Trefethen, A. E. (2002). The uk e-science core programme and the grid. *Future Generation Computer Systems, 18*(8), 1017–1031. doi:10.1016/S0167-739X(02)00082-1

Heylighen, F. (1997). Self-organization. In *Principia Cybernetica Web'*. Brussels: Principia Cybernetica. Retrieved April 14, 2009, from http://pespmc1.vub.ac.be/SELFORG.html

Hill, J., Szewczyk, R., Woo, A., Hollar, S., Culler, D., & Pister, K. (2000). System Architecture Directions for Networked Sensors. [New York: ACM.]. *ACM SIGPLAN Notice, 35*(11), 93–10. doi:10.1145/356989.356998

Hofmann, U., Pfeiffenberger, T., & Hechenleitner, B. (2000, February). One-way-delay measurements with CM toolset. In *Proceedings of the Performance, Computing and Communications Conference (IPCCC)* (pp. 41–47).

HomePlug Certified Products. (2009). Retrieved from http://www.homeplug.org/kshowcase/view

Hong, T. (2001). Performance. In *Peer-to-Peer: Harnessing the Benefits of a Disruptive Technology,* (pp. 203-241). Sebastopol, CA: O'Reilly Media.

Horwitz, J., & Lynn, B. (2002). Towards hierarchical identity-based encryption. In L.R. Knudsen, (Ed.), *Advances in Cryptology - Proceedings of EUROCRYPT 2002,* (LNCS Vol. 2332, pp. 466-481). Berlin: Springer-Verlag.

Hoßfeld, T., Leibnitz, K., Pries, R., Tutschku, K., Tran-Gia, P., & Pawlikowski, K. (2004). *Information diffusion in eDonkey filesharing networks* (Technical Report No. 341). Germany: University of Würzburg, Institute of Computer Science.

Hotta, Y., Sato, M., Kimura, H., Matsuoka, S., Boku, T., & Takahashi, D. (2006). Profile-based optimization of power performance by using dynamic voltage scaling on a PC cluster. In *Proc. 20th IEEE International Parallel and Distributed Processing Symposium (IPDPS'06)*.

Housley, R., Polk, W., Ford, W. & Solo, D. (2002). Internet X.509 public key infrastructure certificate and certificate revocation list (CRL) profile. *The Internet Engineering Task Force (IETF),* RFC 3280.

HP-Adaptive. (2008). *HP Adaptive Enterprise.* Retrieved December 5, 2008, from http://h41131.www4.hp.com/ph/en/stories/hp-adaptive-enterprise.html

HPC4U. (2008). *HPC4U reliable clusters for Grid.* Retrieved December 5, 2008, from http://www.hpc4u.org/

Hsu, C.-H., & Feng, W.-C. (2005). A power-aware runtime system for high-performance computing. *Proc. ACM/IEEE Supercomputing'05 (SC'05)*.

Hsu, C.-H., & Feng, W.-C. (2005). A feasibility analysis of power awareness in commodity-based high-performance clusters. In *Proc. 2005 IEEE International Conference on Cluster Computing*.

Hua, K., Cai, Y., & Sheu, S. (1998). A multicast technique for true video-on-demand services. In *Proceedings of the 12th ACM International Conference on Multimedia* (pp. 191-200).

Huang, H., & Walker, D. (2003). Extensions to Web Service Techniques for Integrating Jini into a Service-Oriented Architecture for the Grid. In *Proceedings of the International Conference on Computational Science 2003 (ICCS '03),* Melbourne, Australia, (LNCS). Berlin: Springer-Verlag.

Huang, L. (2005). VIRGO: Virtual hierarchical overlay network for scalable Grid computing. In P.M.A. Sloot, et al. (Eds.), *European Grid Conference (EGC2005), Advances in Grid Computing,* (LNCS Vol. 3470, pp. 911-921). Berlin: Springer-Verlag.

Huang, L. (2007). A P2P service discovery strategy based on content catalogues. *Data Science Journal, 6,* S492–S499. doi:10.2481/dsj.6.S492

Huang, L. (2007). Framework for mobile Grid computing by hybridizing structural and un-structural P2P technologies. *International Transactions on Systems Science and Applications, 2*(4), 427–432.

Huang, L. (2008). Resource discovery based on VIRGO P2P distributed DNS framework In M. Bubak, et al, (Eds.), *ICCS 2008, Computational Science – ICCS 2008,* (LNCS Vol. 5103, pp. 501-509). Berlin: Springer-Verlag.

Huang, L. (2008). VIRGO P2P based distributed DNS framework for IP V6 Network. In . *Proceedings of, NCM2008,* 698–702.

Huang, L., & Liu, Y. (2008). Domain classification by granular computing used in a P2P approach for Web service discovery. In *Proceedings of Cyberwords2008.*

Huang, L., Wu, Z., & Pan, Y. (2003). Virtual and dynamic hierarchical architecture for e-Science Grid. *International Journal of High Performance Computing Applications, 17*(3), 329–347. doi:10.1177/1094342003173001

Huang, X., Chen, L., Huang, L., & Li, M. (2005). An identity-based grid security infrastructure model. In R.H. Deng, F. Bao, H. Pang & J. Zhou (Eds.), *Proceedings of the 1ˢᵗ International Conference on Information Security Practice and Experience (ISPEC 2005),* (LNCS Vol. 3439, pp. 314-325). Berlin: Springer-Verlag.

Huang, Y., Mohapatra, S., & Venkatasubramanian, N. (2005). An energy-efficient middleware for supporting multimedia services in mobile Grid environments. In *Proceedings of the International Conference on Information Technology: Coding and Computing.* Las Vegas, NV.

Huedo, E., Montero, R. S., & Llrorent, I. M. (2002). *An experimental framework for executing applications in dynamic Grid environments.* Tech. Rep. No. 2002-43, NASA Langley Research Center.

Hughes, D., Coulson, G., & Walkerdine, J. (2005). Freeriding on Gnutella revisited: The bell tolls? *IEEE Distributed Systems Online,* (6), 1-1.

Hughes, S., & Thorne, D. J. (1998). Broadband in-home networks. *BT Technology Journal, 16*(4), 71–19. doi:10.1023/A:1009639628587

Huhns, M. H., & Singh, M. P. (2005). Service-oriented computing: Key concepts and principles. *IEEE Internet Computing, 9*(1), 75–81. doi:10.1109/MIC.2005.21

Huhns, M.N., Singh, M.P., Burstein, M., Decker, K., Durfee, K.E., Finin, T.et al. (2005) Research Directions for Service-oriented Multiagent Systems. *Internet Computing, IEEE, 9*(6), 65 – 70.

Husker, A., Stubailo, I., Kohler, M., & Davis, P. (2004). *Seismic Network Development Preparations.* Center for Embedded Network Sensing, UCLA, Los Angeles, CA. Retrieved November 20, 2008 from http://www.cens.ucla.edu/Education/RR_Posters/Research%20Review/027_Husker.pdf

Hwagyoo, P., Woojong, S., & Heeseok, L. (2004). A role-driven component-oriented methodology for developing collaborative commerce systems. *Information and Software Technology,* (46): 819–837.

Hwang, J., & Aravamudham, P. (2004). Middleware services for P2P computing in wireless grid networks. *IEEE Internet Computing, 8*(4), 40–46. doi:10.1109/MIC.2004.19

Iamnitchi, A., & Foster, I. (2001). On fully decentralized resource discovery in Grid environments. In *Proceedings of International Workshop on Grid Computing.*

Iamnitchi, A., & Foster, I. (2003). A peer-to-peer approach to resource location in Grid environments. In J. Wrglarz, J. Habrzyski, J. Schopf, & M. Stroinski (Eds.), *Grid resource management: state of the art and future trends* (pp. 413-430). Norwell, MA: Kluwer Academic Publishers.

Iamnitchi, A., & Foster, I. (2003). On Death, Taxes, and the Convergence of Peer-to-Peer and Grid Computing. In *2nd International Workshop on Peer-to-Peer Systems (IPTPS'03)* (pp.118-128).

Iamnitchi, A., Foster, I., & Nurmi, D. C. (2002). A peer-to-peer approach to resource location in Grid environments. In *Proceedings of the 11th IEEE International Symposium on High Performance Distributed Computing,* (pp. 419-426). Washington, DC: IEEE Computer Society.

Iansiti, M., & Levien, R. (2004). *The Keystone Advantage: What the New Dynamics of Business Ecosystems Mean for Strategy, Innovation, and Sustainability* (pp. 304). Cambridge, MA: Harvard Business School Press.

Iberdrola. (2009). Retrieved from http://www.iberdrola. es/

IBM. (2004). *The grid report.* Retrieved May 11, 2009, from http://www-03.ibm.com/grid/pdf/Clabby_Grid_Report_2004_Edition.pdf

IBM. (n.d). Retrieved October 17th, 2008, from http:// www.ibm.com/developerworks/webservices/standards/

IBM-Autonomic. (2008). *IBM autonomic computing.* Retrieved December 5, 2008, from http://www-01.ibm. com/software/tivoli/autonomic/

IBM-Grid. (2008). *IBM Grid Computing.* Retrieved December 5, 2008, from http://www-03.ibm.com/grid/

IBM-Virtualization. (2008). *IBM Virtualization Manager website.* Retrieved December 5, 2008, from http:// www-03.ibm.com/systems/management/director/about/ director52/extensions/vm.html

IBM-WeXs. (2008). IBM WebSphere eXtreme Scale. Retrieved December 5, 2008, from http://www-01.ibm. com/software/webservers/appserv/extremescale/

Ibrohimovna, M., & Heemstra de Groot, S. (2008, July). Proxy-based Fednets for sharing personal services in distributed environments. In [Athens, Greece.]. *Proceedings of, ICWMC2008,* 150–157.

Ibrohimovna, M., & Heemstra de Groot, S. (2008, October). Sharing resources in group-oriented networks: Fednet and related paradigms. In [Valencia, Spain.]. *Proceedings of UBICOMM, 08,* 430–437.

IDC. (2007). *PC market rebounds with strong demand for portables, fueling hopes for holiday sales, according to IDC.* IDC press release December 11, 2007. Retrieved March 15, 2008, from http://www.idc.com/getdoc. jsp?containerId=prUS20995107

Ilyas, M., & Mahgoub, I. (2004). *Handbook of sensor networks: Compact wireless and wired sensing systems.* Boca Raton, FL: CRC Press.

Innovaticus. (n.d.). Retrieved February 13, 2009, from http://www.wglab.net/research

Insight. (2006). Grid Computing: a Vertical Market Perspective 2006-2011. *The Insight Research Corporation.*

Intel. (2004). Enhanced Intel SpeedStep Technology for the Intel Pentium M Processor. *Intel white paper.* Retrieved on February 22, 2008 from ftp://download. intel.com/design/network/papers/30117401.pdf

InteliGrid. (n.d.). Retrieved February 13, 2009, from http://www.inteligrid.com/

Intel-Proactive. (2008). *Intel Proactive Computing.* Retrieved from http://www.intel.com/cd/corporate/ techtrends/emea/eng/209579.htm

Interdisciplinary Wireless Grid Team. (n.d.). Retrieved May 12, 2009, from http://wglab.net/

IOF. *(2007).* External network-network interface (E-NNI) OSPF-based routing-1.0 (intra-carrier) implementation agreement OIF-ENNI-OSPF-01.0 Optical Internetworking Forum (IOF).

Iordache, G.V., Boboila, M.S., Pop, F., Stratan, C., & Cristea, V. (2007). A decentralized strategy for genetic scheduling in heterogeneous environments. *International Journal Multi-agent and Grid Systems, 3*(4).

Ipoque. (2007). *Internet study 2007* (Online Report). Retrieved October 2008 from http://www.ipoque.com/ media/internet_studies/internet_study_2007

iRODS. (2008). *Integrated Rule-Oriented Data System.* Retrieved December 5, 2008, from https://www.irods. org

ISAM. (n.d.). Retrieved June 28, 2006, from http://www. inf.ufrgs.br/~isam/English/

Isenberg, D. (1998). The dawn of the "stupid network". *ACM NetWorker, 2*(1), 24–31. doi:10.1145/280437.280445

ITRS. (2007). *International Technology Roadmap for Semiconductors, 2007 Ed.* Executive Summary. Retrieved from http://public.itrs.net/

ITU-T Recommendation Y.2001. (2004, December). General overview of NGN, December 2004.

ITU-T Recommendation Y.2011. (2004, October). General principles and general reference model for Next Generation Networks.

ITU-T, Recommendation Y.2012. (2006, September). Functional requirements and architecture of the NGN release 1.

ITU-T. (2003). *Architecture for the automatically switched optical network (ASON).* G.8080/Y.1304., International Telecommunications Union (ITU)

Ives, Z., Halevy, A., & Weld, D. (2004). Adapting to source properties in processing data integration queries. In *Proceedings ACM SIGMOD 2004,* (pp. 395-406).

Iyer, S., Rowstron, A., & Druschel, P. (2002). Squirrel: A decentralized peer-to-peer web cache. In *Proceedings of the 21st symposium on principles of distributed computing (podc),* Monterey, CA.

Jackendoff, R. (2007). Compounding in the Parallel Architecture and Conceptual Semantics. In R. Lieber & P. Štekauer (Eds.), *The Oxford handbook of compounding. Oxford handbooks in linguistics.* Oxford, UK: Oxford University Press

JADE. (2005). Retrieved from http://jade.tilab.com/

Jain, M., & Dovrolis, C. (2002). Pathload: A measurement tool for end-to-end available bandwidth. In *Proceedings of Passive and Active Measurements (PAM) Workshop.*

Jain, R., Chiu, D. M., & Hawe, W. (1984). *A Quantitative Measure of Fairness and Discrimination for Resource Allocation in Shared Systems.* DEC Research Report TR-301.

Jakob, M., Pechoucek, M., Chábera, J., Miles, S., & Luck, M. Oren, et al. (2008). Case studies for contract-based systems. In M. Berger, B. Burg, & S. Nishiyama (Eds.), *Proceedings of the 7th International Conference on Autonomous Agents and Multiagent Systems (AAMAS 2008)- Industrial and Applications Track,* (pp. 55-62). INESC.

Jan-David Mol, J., Pouwelse, J. A., Epema, D. H. J., & Sips, H. J. (2008). Free-riding, fairness, and firewalls in p2p file-sharing. In K.Wehrle, W. Kellerer, S. K. Singhal, & R. Steinmetz, (Eds.), *Peer-to-Peer Computing,* (pp. 301–310). Washington, DC: IEEE Computer Society. Retrieved from http://dblp.uni-trier.de/db/conf/p2p/p2p2008.html#MolPES08

Janjic, V., Hammond, K., & Yang, Y. (2008), Using application information to drive adaptive grid middleware scheduling decisions. In Procs. 2nd workshop on Middleware-application interaction. *ACM International Conference Proceeding Series,* (Vol. 306, pp.7-12). New York: ACM Press.

Jannotti, J., Gifford, D. K., Johnson, K. L., Kaashoek, M. F., & O'Toole, J. W. (2000). Overcast: Reliable Multicasting with an Overlay Network. In *Proc. of the Fourth Symposium on Operating System Design and Implementation (OSDI),* October (pp. 197–212).

Jardine, J., Snell, Q., & Clement, M. J. (2001). Livelock avoidance for meta-schedulers. In A. D. Williams (Ed.), *International Symposium on High Performance Distributed Computing* (pp. 141-146). Los Alamitos, CA: IEEE Computer Society.

Jarke, M., & Koch, J. (1984). Query optimization in database systems. *ACM Computing Surveys, 16*(2), 111–152. doi:10.1145/356924.356928

Jefferies, N. (2007). *Global Vision for a Wireless World, Wireless World Research Forum, 18th WWRF meeting,* Helsinki, Finland.

Jeffery, K. G. (2007). Next generation GRIDs for environmental science. *Environmental Modelling & Software, 22*(3), 281–287. doi:10.1016/j.envsoft.2005.07.028

Jelasity, M., Kowalczyk, W., & van Steen, M. (2003). *Newscast computing.* Amsterdam: Vrije Universiteit Amsterdam, Department of Computer Science.

Jennings, N. R., & Wooldridge, M. J. (1998). *Agent technology: Foundations, Applications and Markets.* Berlin: Springer-Verlag.

Jennings, N. R., Norman, T. J., Faratin, P., & Odgers, B. (2000). Autonomous agents for business process management. *International Journal of Applied Intelligence, 14*(2), 145–189.

Jesi, G., Montresor, A., & Babaoglu, O. (2007). Proximity-Aware Superpeer Overlay Topologies. *Network and Service Management . IEEE Transactions on, 4*(2), 74–83. doi:.doi:10.1109/TNSM.2007.070904

Jia, Z., Pei, B., Li, M., & You, J. (2005). A comparison of spread methods in unstructured P2P networks. In *Proc. of ICCSA 2005, Int'l Conference on Computational Science and its Applications* Singapore (pp. 10-18).

JIGSA. (2005). Retrieved from http://www.gridworkflow. org/snips/gridworkflow/space/JIGSA

JINI. (1994). Retrieved from http://www.sun.com/ software/jini/

Jini. (2008). *Jini network technology.* Retrieved November 2, 2008, from http://www.sun.com/software/ jini/specs/

Jones, A. J. I., & Sergot, M. J. (1993). On the Characterisation of Law and Computer Systems: The Normative Systems Perspective. In J.-J.Ch. Meyer & R. J. Wieringa (Ed.), *Deontic logic in computer science: Normative system specification,* (pp. 275–307). New York: John Wiley & Sons.

Jones, W. M., III. W. B. L., & Shrivastava, N. (2006). The impact of information availability and workload characteristics on the performance of job co-allocation in multi-clusters. In *International Conference on Parallel and Distributed Systems* (pp. 123-134). Los Alamitos, CA: IEEE Computer Society.

Jorion, P. (2002). *Value at risk: The new benchmark for managing financial risk* (2nd Ed.). New York: McGraw-Hill.

Josang, A., & Presti, S. L. (2004). Analysing the relationship between risk and trust. In *Trust Management: Second International Conference, iTrust 2004, Proceedings,* (Volume LNCS Vol. 2995/2004, pp. 135–145). Oxford, UK: Springer.

Josang, A., Ismail, R., & Boyd, C. (2005). A Survey of Trust and Reputation Systems for Online Service Provision. *Decision Support Systems, 42*(2), 618–644.

Josang, A., Keser, C., & Dimitrakos, T. (2005). Can we manage trust? In *Trust Management (iTrust*

2005), (LNCS Vol. 3477). Berlin: Springer. Retrieved from http://www.eu-trustcom.com/ViewDocument. php?tipo=Disem&id=248

Joseph, J., & Fellenstein, C. (2003). *Grid computing.* Upper Saddle River, NJ: Prentice Hall PTR.

Joseph, S. (2002). *NeuroGrid: Semantically Routing Queries in Peer-to-Peer Networks.* Paper presented at the International Workshop on Peer-to-Peer Computing, Pisa, Italy.

Joseph, S. (2002). Neurogrid: Semantically routing queries in peer-to-peer networks. In *Proc. Intl. Workshop on Peer-to-Peer Computing* (pp. 202-214).

Joseph, S. (2003). *P2P MetaData Search Layers.* Paper presented at the International Workshop on Agents and Peer-to-Peer Computing, Melbourne, Australia.

Josephson, M. (1962). *The Robber Barons: the Great American Capitalists: 1861-1901.* New York: A Harvest Book.

Jouve, W., Lancia, J., Palix, N., Consel, C., & Lawall, J. (2008). High-level programming support for robust pervasive computing applications. In *Proceedings of the 2008 Sixth Annual IEEE International Conference on Pervasive Computing and Communications* (pp. 252-255).

Joux, A. (2000). A one round protocol for tripartite Diffie-Hellman. In W. Bosma (Ed.), *Proceedings of 4ᵗʰ Algorithmic Number Theory Symposium (ANTS-IV),* (LNCS Vol. 1838, pp. 385-394). Berlin: Springer-Verlag.

Juang, P., Oki, H., Wong, Y., Martonosi, M., Peh, L. S., & Rubenstein, D. (2002). Energy-Efficient Computing for Wildlife Tracking: Design Tradeoffs and Early Experiences with ZebraNet. *The Proceeding of ASPLOS-X,* (pp. 96-107). New York: ACM.

Jue, J. P., & Vokkarane, V. M. (2005). *Optical burst switched networks* (1st ed.). New York: Springer-Verlag.

Jun, S., & Ahamad, M. (2005). Incentives in BitTorrent Induce Free Riding. In *ACM SIGCOMM Workshop on Economics of Peer-to-Peer Systems* (pp. 116–121).

Jung, J., Sit, E., Balakrishnan, H., & Morris, R. (2001). DNS performance and effectiveness of caching. In *Proceedings of SIGCOMM Internet Measurement Workshop*, San Francisco.

JXTA Project. (2008). Retrieved November 15, 2008, from https://jxta.dev.java.net

Kaashoek, M., & Karger, D. (2003). Koorde: A simple degree optimal distributed hash-table. In *Proceedings of IPTPS 2003*.

Kahn, J. M., Katz, R. H., & Pister, K. S. J. (1999). Next century challenge: mobile networking for "Smart Dust." In *Proceedings of the 5th annual ACM/IEEE international conference on Mobile computing and networking*, (pp. 271-278). New York: ACM.

Kalasapur, S., Kumar, M., & Shirazi, B. A. (2007). dynamic service composition in pervasive computing. *IEEE Transactions on Parallel and Distributed Systems*, *18*(7), 907–918. doi:10.1109/TPDS.2007.1039

Kalogeraki, V., Gunopulos, D., & Zeinalipour-Yazti, D. (2002). A Local Search Mechanism for Peer-to-Peer Networks. In *Proceedings of the 11th International Conference on Information and Knowledge Management* (pp. 300-307).

Kalos, M. H., & Paula, A. (1986). *Whitlock, Monte Carlo Methods, Vol. 1: Basics*. Hoboken, NJ: John Wiley & Sons.

Kamienski, C., Fidalgo, J., Dantas, R., Sadok, D., & Ohlman, B. (2007). XACML-Based Composition Policies for Ambient Networks. In *7th IEEE International Workshop on Policies for Distributed Systems and Networks* (pp. 77-86).

Kamienski, C., Sadok, D., Fidalgo, J., Lima, J., & Ohlman, B. (2006). On the Use of Peer-to-Peer Architectures for the Management of Highly Dynamic Environments. In *3rd Intl. Workshop on Mobile Peer-to-Peer Systems* (pp. 135-140).

Kamra, A., Misra, V., & Nahum, E. M. (2004). Yaksha: A self-tuning controller for managing the performance of 3-tiered Web sites. In *Proceedings 12th IEEE International Workshop on Quality of Service*, June.

Kamvar, S. D., Schlosser, M. T., & Garcia-Molina, H. (2003). The eigentrust algorithm for reputation management in p2p networks. In *Proceedings of the Twelfth International World Wide Web Conference*.

Kamvar, S., Schlosser, M., & Molina, H. G. (2003). The eigentrust algorithm for reputation management in p2p networks. In *Proceedings of World Wide Web Conference 2003*, Budapest, Hungary. New York: ACM, Budapest, Hungary.

Kant, K., Iyer, R., & Tewari, V. (2002). A framework for classifying peer-to-peer technologies. In *Proc. of the 2nd IEEE/ACM Int'l Symp. on Cluster Computing and the Grid* (CCGRID02).

Kappiah, N., Lowenthal, D. K., & Freeh, V. W. (2005). Just In Time Dynamic Voltage Scaling: Exploiting Inter-Node Slack to Save Energy in MPI Programs. In *Proceedings of the 2005 ACM/IEEE SC|05 Conference (SC'05)*.

Kappiah, N., Lowenthal, D. K., & Freeh, V. W. (2006). Just in time dynamic voltage scaling: Exploiting Inter-Node Slack to Save Energy in MPI Programs. In *Proceedings of the 2005 ACM/IEEE SC|05 Conference (SC'05)*.

Karastoyanova, D. (2006). *Enhancing flexibility and reusability of Web service flows through parameterization*. PhD Thesis, TU-Darmstadt, Shaker Verlag.

Karastoyanova, D., & Leymann, F. (2009) BPEL'n'Aspects: Adapting service orchestration logic. In *Proceedings of ICWS 2009*.

Karastoyanova, D., et al. (2006). Parameterized BPEL processes: concepts and implementation. In *Proc. of BPM 2006*.

Karastoyanova, D., Houspanossian, A., Cilia, M., Leymann, F., & Buchmann, A. (2005). Extending BPEL for Run Time Adaptability. In *Proceedings of EDOC 2005*.

Karastoyanova, D., Van Lessen, T., Nitzsche, J., Wetzstein, B., Wutke, D., & Leymann, F. (2007). Semantic service bus: Architecture and implementation of a next generation middleware. In *Proceedings of the 2nd International Workshop on Services Engineering (SEIW) 2007, in conjunction with ICDE 2007*.

Karbhari, P., Ammar, M., & Dhamdhere, A. Raj, H., Riley, G., & Zegura, E. (2004). Bootstrapping in Gnutella: A Measurement Study. In *Proceedings of the 2004 Passive and Active Measurement Workshop*.

Karl, H., & Willing, A. (2005). *Protocols and Architectures for Wireless Sensor Networks*. New York: Wiley & Son.

Karonis, N. T., Toonen, B. R., & Foster, I. T. (2003). MPICH-G2: A Grid-enabled implementation of the Message Passing Interface. *Journal of Parallel and Distributed Computing, 63*(5), 551–563. doi:10.1016/S0743-7315(03)00002-9

Karonis, N., Toonen, B., & Foster, I. (2003). MPICH-G2: A Grid-enabled implementation of the message passing interface. *Journal of Parallel and Distributed Computing, 63*(5), 551–563. doi:10.1016/S0743-7315(03)00002-9

Kashani, F. B., Chen, C. C., & Shahabi, C. (2004). WSPDS: Web Services Peer-to-Peer Discovery Service. In *Proceedings of the 2004 International Conference on Internet Computing* (pp. 733-743).

Kashyap, V., & V, B. (2004). Trust but verify: Emergence, trust, and quality in Intelligent Systems. [Washington, DC: IEEE Xplore.]. *IEEE Intelligent Systems*, 85–88.

Kastner, W. (2000). Jini connectivity for fieldbus systems. In *Proceedings of the 2000 IEEE International Symposium on Intelligent Control* (Vol. 1, pp. 229-234).

Kaszuba, T., Rzadca, K., & Wierzbicki, A. (2008). Discovering the most trusted agents without central control. In *proceedings of the Embedded and Ubiquitous Computing (EUC08)*, (Vol. 2, pp. 616-621). Washington, DC: IEEE Computer Society.

Katz, K. Y. D., & Kompella, D. (2003). *Traffic engineering (TE) extensions to OSPF version 2*. RFC 3630, Internet Engineering Task Force (IETF).

Kautz, H., Selman, B., & Shah, M. (1997). Combining Social Networks and Collaborative Filtering. *Communications of the ACM, 40*(3), 63–65. doi:10.1145/245108.245123

Kaye, D. (2003). *Loosely coupled: The missing pieces of Web services*. RDS Press.

Kazaa Home Page. (2001). Retrieved from http://www.kazaa.com

Keidl, M., & Kemper, A. (2004). Towards context-aware adaptable Web services. In *Proceedings of the 13th International World Wide Web Conference* (pp. 55-65).

Keith Edwards, W. (2006). Discovery systems in ubiquitous computing. *IEEE Pervasive Computing / IEEE Computer Society [and] IEEE Communications Society, 5*(2), 70–77. doi:10.1109/MPRV.2006.28

Keller, A., & Badonnel, R. (2004). Automating the provisioning of application services with the BPEL4WS workflow language. In *Proceedings of the 15th IFIP/IEEE International Workshop on Distributed Systems: Operations & Management (DSOM 2004)* (LNCS 3278). Berlin, Germany: Springer Verlag.

Keller, A., & Reinefeld, E. (1998). CCS Resource Management in Networked HPC Systems. In *Proceedings of Heterogeneous Computing Workshop HCW'98 at IPPS*.

Keller, A., Hellerstein, J., Wolf, J., Wu, K., & Krishnan, V. (2004). The CHAMPS system: Change management with planning and scheduling. In *Proceedings of the IEEE/IFIP Network Operations and Management Symposium*. Amsterdam: Kluwer Academic Publishers.

Kenyon, C., & Cheliotis, G. (2002). Architecture requirements for commercializing grid resources. In *11th IEEE International Symposium on High Performance Distributed Computing (HPDC'02)*.

Kenyon, C., & Cheliotis, G. (2003). *Grid resource commercialization: Economic engineering and delivery scenarios*. In J. Nabrzyski, J. Schopf & J. Weglarz (Eds.), *Grid resource management: state of the art and research issues*. Amsterdam: Kluwer.

Kenyon, C., & Cheliotis, G. (2004). Grid resource commercialization: economic engineering and delivery scenarios. In J. Nabrzyski, J. M. Schopf, & J. Weglarz, (Ed.), *Grid resource management: state of the art and future trends*, (pp. 465–478). Norwell, MA: Kluwer Academic Publishers.

Kephart, J. O., & Chess, D. M. (2003). The vision of autonomic computing. *Computer, 36*(1), 41–50. doi:10.1109/MC.2003.1160055

Kephart, J. O., & Chess, D. M. (2003). The vision of autonomic computing. *IEEE Computer Society, 36*(1), 41–52.

Kerberos. (2008). *Kerberos: The Network Authentication Protocol*. Retrieved December 5, 2008, from http://web.mit.edu/Kerberos/

Kermarrec, M., Massouli, L., & Ganesh, A. J. (2003). Probabilistic Reliable Dissemination in Large-Scale Systems. *IEEE Transactions on Parallel and Distributed Systems, 14*(3), 248–258. doi:10.1109/TPDS.2003.1189583

Kerstin, V., Karim, D., Iain, G., & James, P. (2007). *AssessGrid, economic issues underlying risk awareness in Grids,* LNCS. Berlin / Heidelberg: Springer.

Keutzer, K., Shah, N., & Plishker, W. (2003, February). NP-Click: A Programming Model for the Intel IXP1200. In *2nd Workshop on Network Processors (NP-2) at the 9th International Symposium on High Performance Computer Architecture (HPCA-9)*, Anaheim, CA.

Khalaf, R., Karastoyanova, D., & Leymann, F. (2007). Pluggable framework for enabling the execution of extended BPEL behavior. In *Proceedings of the 3rd ICSOC International Workshop on Engineering Service-Oriented Application: Analysis, Design and Composition (WESOA 2007).* New York: Springer.

Khlifi, H., Gregoire, J.-C., & Phillips, J. (2006). VoIP and NAT/firewalls: Issues, traversal techniques, and a real-world solution. *IEEE Communications Magazine, 44*(7), 93–99. doi:10.1109/MCOM.2006.1668388

Kim, S. J., & Browne, J. C. (1988, August). A General Approach to Mapping of Parallel computations upon Multiprocessor Architectures. In *International conference on Parallel Processing*, University Park, Pennsylvania (Vol. 3, pp. 1-8).

Kim, S., Pakzad, S., Culler, D., Demmel, J., Fenves, G., Glaser, S., & Turon, M. (2006). Wireless Sensor Networks for Structural Health Monitoring. In *Conference On Embedded Networked Sensor Systems,* (pp 427-428). ACM: New York.

Kim, W., Reiner, D. S., & Batory, D. S. (Eds.). (1985). *Query processing in database systems*. Berlin: Springer Verlag.

Kimbler, K., & Taylor, M. (2008). *SDP 2.0 – Service Delivery Platforms in the Web2.0 Era*. Egham, UK: The Moriana Group. Retrieved April 14, 2009, from http://www.morianagroup.com

Klinberg, T., & Manfredi, R. (2002, June). Gnutella 0.6. *Gnutella Development Forum*. Retrieved from http://groups.yahoo.com/group/the_gdf

Knecht, L. (1998). *PubMed: Truncation, Automatic Explosion, Mapping, and MeSH Headings* (NLM Technical Bulletin). Retrieved from http://www.nlm.nih.gov/pubs/techbull/mj98/mj98_truncation.html

Koehler, J., & Alonso, G. (2007, July). Service Oriented Computing. *Ercim News, 70*, 15–16.

Kohler, E., Morris, R., Chen, B., Jannotti, J., & Kaashoek, M. F. (2000). The click modular router. *ACM Transactions on Computer Systems, 18*(3), 263–297. doi:10.1145/354871.354874

Komorita, S. S., & Parks, C. D. (1994). *Social Dilemmas*. Madison, WI: Brown and Benchmark.

Komorita, S. S., & Parks, C. D. (1995). Interpersonal relations: Mixed-motive interaction. *Annual Review of Psychology, 46*, 183–207. doi:10.1146/annurev.ps.46.020195.001151

Kon, F. (2000). *Automatic Configuration of Component-Based Distributed Systems*. PhD Thesis, University of Illinois at Urbana-Champaign, Urbana, IL.

Konovalov, A., & Linton, S. (2007). *Symbolic Computation Software Composability Protocol Specification*. CIRCA preprint 2007/5, University of St Andrews. Retrieved November 2008 from http://www-circa.mcs.st-and.ac.uk/preprints.html

Körber, H. J. (2006). *Low Power Wireless Sensor Networks*. Lecture Elektrische Messtechnik, Helmut Schmidt Universität, Universität der Bundeswehr Hamburg.

Retrieved November 20, 2008, from www.hsu-hh.de/download-1.4.1.php?brick_id=YYgNZmeQf1vZvACt

Korkmaz, T., & Krunz, M. (2002). Hybrid flooding and tree-based broadcasting for reliable and efficient link-state dissemination. In *IEEE Global Telecommunications Conference* (pp. 2400-2404).

Kosar, T. (2006). A New Paradigm in Data Intensive Computing: Stork and the Data-Aware Schedulers. In *Challenges of Large Applications in Distributed Environments (CLADE)* (pp. 5-12).

Kostreva, M. M., Ogryczak, W., & Wierzbicki, A. (2004). Equitable aggregations and multiple criteria analysis. *European Journal of Operational Research, 158*(2), 362–377. Retrieved from http://dblp.uni-trier.de/db/journals/eor/eor158.html#KostrevaOW04

Kothari, A., Agrawal, D., Gupta, A., & Suri, S. (2003). Range Addressable Network: A P2P Cache Architecture for Data Ranges. In *Proceedings of the 3rd international Conference on Peer-To-Peer Computing* (pp. 14). Washington, DC: IEEE Computer Society.

Kotowski, N., Lima, A. A. B., Pacitti, E., Valduriez, P., & Mattoso, M. (2008). Parallel query processing for OLAP in Grids. *Concurrency and Computation: Practice and Experience.*

Kotsis, G. (1992). Interconnection Topologies and Routing for Parallel Processing Systems. *ACPC TR 92-19,* 1992.

Koutrouli, E., & Tsalgatidou, A. (2008, August). P2P Reputation Systems Credibility Analysis: Tradeoffs and Design Decisions. In *Proceedings of 12th Pan-Hellenic Conference on Informatics (PCI 2008)*, Samos, Greece (pp. 88-92). Washington, DC: IEEE Computer Society.

Kramer, J., & Magee, J. (1990). The evolving philosophers problem: Dynamic change management. *IEEE Transactions on Software Engineering, 16*(11). doi:10.1109/32.60317

Kraut, R., Fish, R. S., Root, R. W., & Chalfonte, B. L. (1990). Informal communication in organisations: Form, functions, and technology. In R. Baecker (Ed.), *Readings in groupware and computer supported cooperative work: Assisting human to human collaboration.* San Francisco, CA: Morgan Kaufmann Publishers Inc.

Kraut, R., Galegher, J., & Egido, C. (1986). *Relationships and tasks in scientific collaborations.* Paper presented at the The 1986 ACM conference on Computer-supported cooperative work, Austin, Texas.

Krauter, K., Buyya, R., & Maheswaran, M. (2002). A taxonomy and survey of grid resource management systems for distributed computing. *Software, Practice & Experience, 32*(2), 135–164. doi:10.1002/spe.432

Krishnan, S., Wagstrom, P., & Laszewski, G. (2002). *GSFL: A Workflow Framework for Grid Services. Preprint ANL/MCS-P980-0802.* Argonne, IL: Argonne National Laboratory.

Kuba, M., & Krajicek, O. (2006) *Literature search on SOA, Web Services, OGSA and WSRF.* Institute of Computer Science, Masaryk University. Botanická, Brno.

Kubiatowicz, J., Bindel, D., Chen, Y., Czerwinski, S., Eaton, P., Geels, D., et al. (2000). Oceanstore: An architecture for global-scale persistent storage. In *Proceedings of the ninth international conference on architectural support for programming languages and operating systems.*

Kuhn, S. (2008). Prisoner's Dilemma. In E. N. Zalta (Ed.), *The Stanford encyclopedia of philosophy (Winter 2008 Ed.).* Retrieved from http://plato.stanford.edu/archives/win2008/entries/prisoner-dilemma/

Kumar, M., Shirazi, B. A., Das, S. K., Sung, B. Y., Levine, D., & Singhal, M. (2003). PICO: A middleware framework for pervasive computing. *IEEE Pervasive Computing / IEEE Computer Society [and] IEEE Communications Society, 2*, 72–79. doi:10.1109/MPRV.2003.1228529

Kuntschke, R., Scholl, T., Huber, S., Kemper, A., Reiser, A., Adorf, H., et al. (2006). Grid-based data stream processing in e-science. In *Proceedings 2nd IEEE International Conf. on e-Science and Grid Computing.* Amsterdam, The Netherlands.

Kuntschke, R., Stegmaier, B., Kemper, A., & Reiser, A. (2005). StreamGlobe: Processing and Sharing Data Streams in Grid-Based P2P Infrastructures. In *Proceed-*

ings International Conf. on Very Large Data Bases, Rondheim, Norway (pp. 1259-1262).

Kuo, D., & Mckeown, M. (2005). Advance reservation and co-allocation protocol for grid computing. In H. Stockinger, R. Buyya, & R. Perrott (Eds.), *International Conference on e-Science and Grid Technologies* (pp. 164-171). Los Alamitos, CA: IEEE Computer Society.

Kuperberg, G. (2007). Neural mechanisms of language comprehension: Challenges to syntax. *Brain Research*, *1146*, 23–49. doi:10.1016/j.brainres.2006.12.063

Kurdi, H., Li, M., & Al-Raweshidy, H. (2008). A classification of emerging and traditional Grid systems. *IEEE Distributed Systems Online*, *9*(3), 1–1. doi:10.1109/MDSO.2008.8

Kurdi, H., Li, M., & Al-Raweshidy, H. S. (2008). A generic framework for resource scheduling in personal mobile grids based on honeybee colony. In *Proceedings of The IEEE Second International Conference on Next Generation Mobile Applications, Services, and Technologies (ngmast'2008)* (pp. 297-302).

Kurkovsky, S., & Bhagyavati, M. S. (2003). Modeling a computational Grid of mobile devices as a multi-agent system. In *Proceedings of the 2003 International Conference on Artificial Intelligence (IC-AI-03)*. Las Vegas, NV.

Kurkovsky, S., Bhagyavati, & Ray, A. (2004). Modeling a grid-based problem-solving environment for mobile devices. *Journal of Digital Information Management*, *2*(2), 109–114.

Kurkovsky, S., Bhagyavati, M. S., & Ray, A. (2004). A collaborative problem-solving framework for mobile devices. In *ACM-SE 42: Proceedings of the 42nd Annual Southeast Regional Conference*, 5-10. New York: ACM.

KVM. (2008). *Kernel-based Virtual Machine*. Retrieved December 5, 2008, from http://kvm.qumranet.com/kvmwiki

K-Wf Grid. (n.d.). Retrieved February 13, 2009, from http://www.kwfgrid.eu/

K-Wf-Grid. (2008). *The Knowledge-based Workflow System for Grid Applications*. Retrieved December 5, 2008, from http://www.kwfgrid.eu/

Kwok, Y.-K., Song, S., & Hwang, K. (2005). Selfish grid computing: Game-theoretic modeling and nas performance results. In *Proceedings of CCGrid*.

Lacasta, J., Nogueras-Iso, J., Bejar, R., Muro-Medrano, P. R., & Zarazaga-Soria, F. J. (2006). A Web ontology service to facilitate interoperability within a spatial data infrastructure: Applicability to discovery. *Data & Knowledge Engineering*, *63*(3).

Lahiri, K., Raghunathan, A., Dey, S., & Panigrahi, D. (2002). Battery-driven system design: a new frontier in low power design. In A. Raghunathan (Ed.), *Proceedings of the 7th Asia and South Pacific and the 15th International Conference on VLSI Design. Design Automation Conference Proceedings ASP-DAC*, (pp. 261-267). Bangalore, India.

Lai, K., Huberman, B. A., & Fine, L. (2004). *Tycoon: A distributed market-based resource allocation system* (Technical Report CS.DC/0404013). USA: HP Labs.

Lakshminarayanan, K., Rao, A., Stoica, I., & Shenker, S. (2006). End-host controlled multicast routing. *Computer Networks*, *50*(6). doi:10.1016/j.comnet.2005.07.019

Lal, N. (2007). *Enforcing collaboration in a collaborative content distribution network*. Master's thesis, Vrije Universiteit, Amsterdam, The Netherlands.

Lamport, L., & Chandy, M. (1985). Distributed snapshots: Determining global states of a distributed system. *ACM Transactions on Computer Systems*, *3*(1), 63–75. doi:10.1145/214451.214456

Lan, J., Liu, X., Shenoy, P., & Ramamritham, K. (2003). Consistency Maintenance in Peer-to-peer File Sharing Networks. In *Proc. of WIAPP '03, 3rd IEEE Workshop On Internet Applications*, San Jose, CA, USA (pp. 76-85).

Lasek, K., & Rajaravivarma, T. (2007). Design aspects of a hybrid community LAN environment. In . *Proceedings of IEEE SoutheastCon, 2007*, 669–673.

Latip, R., Ibrahim, H., Othman, M., Sulaiman, M. N., & Abdullah, A. (2008). Quorum Based Data Replication in Grid Environment. In *Lecture Notes in Computer Science* (pp. 379-386). Berlin: Springer.

Laure, E., Fisher, S. M., Frohner, A., Grandi, C., Kunszt, P., & Krenek, A. (2006). Programming the Grid with gLite. *Computational Methods in Science and Technology, 12*(1), 33–45.

Laure, E., Hemmer, F., Prelz, F., Beco, S., Fisher, S., Livny, M., et al. Kunszt, Peter Z., Di Meglio, A., Aimar, A., Edlund, A., Groep, D., Pacini, F., Sgaravatto, M., & Mulmo, O. (2004). Middleware for the next generation Grid infrastructure. In A. Aimar, J. Harvey, & N. Knoors (Eds.), *Computing in high energy physics and nuclear physics 2004* (pp.826-829). Geneva, Switzerland: CERN.

Laure, E., Stockinger, H., & Stockinger, K. (2005). Performance engineering in data Grids. *Concurrency and Computation: Practice and Experience, 17*(2- 4), 171-191.

LCG. (2008). *Worldwide LHC Computing Grid.* Retrieved December 5, 2008, from http://lcg.web.cern.ch/LCG/

LCG. (n.d.). Retrieved October 10, 2008, from http://lcg.web.cern.ch/LCG/.

Ledlie, J., & Seltzer, M. (2005). Distributed, Secure Load Balancing with Skew, Heterogeneity and Churn. In *INFOCOM 2005* (pp.419-1430).

Lee, C., Nordstedt, D., & Helal, S. (2003). Enabling smart spaces with OSGi. *IEEE Pervasive Computing / IEEE Computer Society [and] IEEE Communications Society, 2*(3), 89–94. doi:10.1109/MPRV.2003.1228530

Lee, S., Sherwood, R., & Bhattacharjee, B. (2003). Cooperative peer groups in nice. In *Proc. INFOCOM 2003. Twenty-Second Annual Joint Conference of the IEEE Computer and Communications Societies*, (Vol. 2, pp. 1272–1282). Washington, DC: IEEE.

Lee, S., Sherwood, R., & Bhattacharjee, B. (2003). Cooperative peer groups in NICE. *INFOCOM 2003, Twenty-second Annual Joint Conference of the IEEE*

Computer and Communications Societies, (Vol. 2, IEEE, pp. 1272-1282). Washington, DC: IEEE.

Legout, A., Liogkas, N., Kohler, E., & Zhang, L. (2007). Clustering and sharing incentives in bittorrent systems. *SIGMETRICS Perform. Eval. Rev., 35*(1), 301–312. doi: http://doi.acm.org/10.1145/1269899.1254919.

Legout, A., Urvoy-Keller, G., & Michiardi, P. (2006). Rarest first and choke algorithms are enough. In *6th ACM SIGCOMM Conference on Internet Measurement* (pp. 203–216).

Legrand, I. C. (2005). *End user agents: extending the intelligence to the edge in distributed service systems.* Fall 2005 Internet2 Member Meeting, Philadelphia, 2005.

Legrand, I. C., Dobre, C., Voicu, R., Stratan, C., Cirstoiu, C., & Musat, L. (2005). A simulation study for T0/T1 data replication and production activities. In *The 15th International Conference on Control Systems and Computer Science.*

Lehman, T. J., & Kaufman, J. H. (2003, December). OptimalGrid: Middleware for automatic deployment of distributed FEM problems on an internet-based computing grid. In *Proceedings of the IEEE International Conference on Cluster Computing* (pp. 164-171).

Leibowitz, N., Bergman, A., Ben-Shaul, R., & Shavit, A. (2002). Are file swapping networks cacheable? characterizing P2P traffic. In *Proceedings of 7th International Workshop on Web Content Caching and Distribution (WCW '03),* Boulder, CO.

Leighton, F. T. (1992). I*ntroduction to parallel algorithms and architectures: Arrays, trees, and hypercubes.* San Francisco: Morgan Kaufman.

Leong, B., Liskov, B., & Demaine, E. D. (2006). EpiChord: Parallelizing the chord lookup algorithm with reactive routing state management. *Computer Communications, 29*(9), 1243–1259. doi:10.1016/j.comcom.2005.10.002

Leontiadis, E., Dimakopoulos, V. V., & Pitoura, E. (2006). Creating and maintaining replicas in unstructured peer-to-peer systems. In *Proc. of EURO-PAR 2006, 12th Int'l Euro-Par Conference on Parallel Processing* (LNCS 4128, pp. 1015-102). Dresden, Germany: Springer.

Levine, B. N., Shields, C., & Margolin, N. (2006). *A survey of solutions to the Sybil attack* (Technical Report No. 2006-052). USA: University of Massachusetts.

Levis, P., Lee, N., Welsh, M., & Culler, D. (2003). TOS-SIM: Accurate and Scalable Simulation of Entire TinyOS Applications. In *Conference on Embedded Networked Sensor Systems* (pp. 126-137). New York: ACM.

Levis, P., Madden, S., Gay, D., Polastre, J., Szewczyk, R., Woo, A., et al. (2004). The Emergence of Networking Abstractions and Techniques in TinyOS. In *Proceedings of the 1st conference on Symposium on Networked Systems Design and Implementation*, (pp. 1-1). Berkeley, CA: USENIX Association.

Leymann, F. (2005). The (Service) Bus: Services penetrate everyday life. In *Proceedings of ICSOC'2005, Amsterdam, LNCS 3826 Springer-Verlag.*

Leymann, F. (2006). Choreography for the Grid: towards fitting BPEL to the resource framework: research articles. *Journal of Concurrency and Computation: Practice & Experience, 18,* 1201–1217. doi:10.1002/cpe.996

Leymann, F., & Roller, D. (1999). *Production workflow: Concepts and techniques.* Upper Saddle River, NJ: Prentice Hall PTR.

Li, B., Li, W., & Xu, Z. (2003). Personal grid running at the edge of Internet. In *Proceedings of the Second International Workshop on Grid and Cooperative Computing (GCC2003)*, Shanghai, China (pp. 762-769).

Li, J. (2004). *Peerstreaming: A practical receiver-driven peer-to-peer media streaming system.* Microsoft Research, Tech. Rep. MSR-TR-2004-101.

Li, J., & Vuong, S. (2005). A scalable semantic routing architecture for grid resource discovery. In *Proceedings of the 11th International Conference on Parallel and Distributed Systems* (Vol.1, pp. 29-35).

Li, J., & Vuong, S. (2006). Grid resource discovery based on semantic P2P communities. In *Proceedings of the 2006 ACM Symposium on Applied Computing* (pp. 754-758). New York, USA: ACM Press.

Li, J., & Yahyapour, R. (2006). Negotiation model supporting co-allocation for grid scheduling. In D. Gannon, R. M. Badia, & R. Buyya (Eds.), *International Conference on Grid Computing* (pp. 254-261). Los Alamitos, CA: IEEE Computer Society.

Li, J., Sollins, K., & Lim, D. (2005). Implementing aggregation and broadcast over distributed hash tables. *ACM SIGCOMM Computer Communication Review, 35*(1), 81–92. doi:10.1145/1052812.1052813

Li, J., Stribling, J., Morris, R., & Kaashoek, M. F. (2005). *Bandwidth-Efficient Management of DHT Routing Tables.* Paper presented at the 2nd Symposium on Networked Systems Design and Implementation, Boston, MA.

Li, M., & Baker, M. (2005). *The grid: Core technologies.* New York: Wiley.

Li, M., Lee, W. C., & Sivasubramaniam, A. (2004). Semantic small world: an overlay network for peer-to-peer search. In *IEEE International Conference on Network Protocols* (pp. 228–238).

Li, M., Yu, B., Omer, R. F., & Wang, Z. (2008). Grid service discovery with rough sets. *IEEE Transactions on Knowledge and Data Engineering, 20*(6), 851–862. doi:10.1109/TKDE.2007.190744

Li, W. (2001). Overview of fine granularity scalability in mpeg-4 video standard. *IEEE Transactions on Circuits and Systems for Video Technology, 11,* 301–317. doi:10.1109/76.911157

Li, W., Xu, Z., Li, B., & Gong, Y. (2002). The VEGA personal grid: A lightweight grid architecture. In *Proceedings of International Conference on Parallel and Distributed Computing Systems (IASTED2002)* (pp. 6-11).

Li, Z., & Mohapatra, P. (2004a, March). Impact of Topology On Overlay Routing Service. In *INFOCOM* (pp. 418).

Li, Z., & Mohapatra, P. (2004). QRON: QoS-aware routing in overlay networks. *IEEE Journal on Selected Areas in Communications, 22,* 29–40. doi:10.1109/JSAC.2003.818782

Li, Z., & Parashar, M. (2006). *An Infrastructure for Dynamic Composition of Grid Services.* Retrieved from www.caip.rutgers.edu/TASSL/Papers/rudder-grid-06.pdf

Lian, Q., Zhang, Z., Yang, B., Zhao, Y., Dai, Y., & Li, X. (2006). *an empirical study of collusion behavior in the maze P2P file-sharing system* (Technical Report MSR-TR-2006-14). Redmond, WA, USA: Microsoft Research.

Liang, J., Kumar, R., Xi, Y., & Ross, K. (2005). Pollution in P2P file sharing systems. In *24th Annual Joint Conference of the IEEE Computer and Communications Societies (INFOCOM)* (Vol. 2, pp. 1174–1185).

Liang, Z. & Shi, W. (2005). *Pet: A personalized trust model with reputation and risk evaluation for p2p resource sharing.*

Liebeherr, J., Nahas, M., & Si, W. (2002, October). Application Layer Multicasting with Delaunay Triangulation Overlays. *IEEE Journal on Selected Areas in Communications, 20*(8). doi:10.1109/JSAC.2002.803067

Lieberman, H. (1997). Autonomous Interface Agents. In *proceedings of CHI conference on Human Factors in Computer Systems* (pp. 67-74).

Lim, H. W. (2006). *On the Application of Identity-Based Cryptography in Grid Security.* Ph.D thesis, University of London, UK.

Lim, H. W., & Paterson, K. G. (2005). Identity-based cryptography for grid security. In H. Stockinger, R. Buyya & R. Perrott (Eds.), *Proceedings of the 1st IEEE International Conference on e-Science and Grid Computing (e-Science 2005),* (pp. 395-404). Washington, DC: IEEE Computer Society Press.

Lim, H. W., & Robshaw, M. J. B. (2004). On identity-based cryptography and grid computing. In M. Bubak, G.D.v. Albada, P.M.A. Sloot & J.J. Dongarra (Eds), *Proceedings of the 4th International Conference on Computational Science (ICCS 2004),* (LNCS Vol. 3036, pp. 474-477). Berlin: Springer-Verlag.

Lim, H. W., & Robshaw, M. J. B. (2005). A dynamic key infrastructure for grid. In P.M.A. Sloot, A.G. Hoekstra,

T. Priol, A. Reinefeld & M. Bubak (Eds.), *Proceedings of the European Grid Conference (EGC 2005),* (LNCS Vol. 3470, pp. 255-264). Berlin: Springer-Verlag.

Lim, M. Y., Freeh, V. W., & Lowenthal, D. K. (2006). Adaptive, transparent frequency and voltage scaling of communication phases in MPI programs. In *Proc. ACM/IEEE Supercomputing'06 (SC'06).*

Lima, L. S., & Gomes, A. nio, T.A., Ziviani, A., Endler, M., Soares, L. F. G., et al. (2005). Peer-to-peer resource discovery in mobile grids. in *Proceedings of the 3rd International Workshop on Middleware for Grid Computing (MGC'05),* Grenoble, France (pp. 1-6).

Limelight. (n.d.). Retrieved from http://www.limelightnetworks.com

Linsmeier, T. J., & Pearson, N. D. (1996). *Risk measurement: An introduction to value at risk.* University of Illinois.

Linux. The everything as a service (XaaS) model. (2008, December 8). *Linux Magazine.* Retrieved May 11, 2009, from http://www.linux-mag.com/id/7197

Liogkas, N., Nelson, R., Kohler, E. & Zhang, L. (2006). *Exploiting bittorrent for fun (but not profit).*

Litzkow, M., & Livny, M. (1990). Experience with the Condor distributed batch system. In *Proceedings of IEEE Workshop on Experimental Distributed Systems* (pp. 97-101).

Liu, J., Jin, X., & Wang, Y. (2005). Agent-based load balancing on homogeneous minigrids: Macroscopic modeling and characterization. *IEEE Trans. on Parallel and Distributed Systems, 16*(7), 586–598. doi: http://doi.ieeecomputersociety.org/10.1109/TPDS.2005.76

Liu, L., Antonopoulos, N., & Mackin, S. (2007). Fault-tolerant Peer-to-Peer Search on Small-World Networks. *Future Generation Computer Systems, 23*(8), 921–931. doi:10.1016/j.future.2007.03.002

Liu, L., Antonopoulos, N., & Mackin, S. (2007). *Social Peer-to-Peer for Resource Discovery.* Paper presented at the 15th Euromicro International Conference on Parallel, Distributed and Network-based Processing, Naples, Italy.

Liu, L., Antonopoulos, N., Mackin, S., Xu, J., & Russell, D. (2009). Efficient Resource Discovery in Self-organized Unstructured Peer-to-Peer Networks. *Concurrency and Computation, 21*(2), 159–183. doi:10.1002/cpe.1329

Liu, L., Russell, D., Looker, N., Webster, D., Xu, J., Davies, J., et al. (2008). *Evolutionary Service-based Architecture for Network Enabled Capability.* Paper presented at the International Workshop on Verification and Evaluation of Computer and Communication Systems, Leeds, United Kingdom.

Liu, L., Russell, D., Webster, D., Luo, Z., Venters, C., Xu, J., et al. (2009). *Delivering Sustainable Capability on Evolutionary Service-oriented Architecture.* Paper presented at the IEEE International Symposium on Object/component/service-oriented Real-time distributed Computing (ISORC 2009), Tokyo, Japan.

Liu, L., Russell, D., Xu, J., Davies, J., & Irvin, K. (2008). *Agile Properties of Service Oriented Architectures for Network Enabled Capability.* Paper presented at the Realising Network Enabled Capability (RNEC'08), Leeds, United Kingdom.

Liu, L., Zhang, S., Dong Ryu, K., & Dasgupta, P. (2004). R-chain: A selfmaintained reputation management system in p2p networks. In D. A. Bader & A. A. Khokhar, (Eds.), *ISCA PDCS*, (pp. 131–136). Retrieved from http://dblp.uni-trier.de/db/conf/ISCApdcs/ISCApdcs2004.html#LiuZRD04

Liu, S., & Karimi, H. A. (2008). Grid query optimizer to improve query processing in grids. *Future Generation Computer Systems, 24*(5), 342–353. doi:10.1016/j.future.2007.06.003

Liu, X., Zhu, X., Padala, P., Wang, Z., & Singhal, S. (2007). Optimal multivariate control for differentiated services on a shared hosting platform. In *Proceedings 46th IEEE Conference on Decision and Control*, New Orleans, LA.

Liu, Y., & Gorton, I. (2004). *An empirical evaluation of architectural alternatives for j2ee and web services.* Paper presented at the The 11th Asia-Pacific Software Engineering Conference, Busan, Korea.

Liu, Y., Guo, Y., & Liang, C. (2008). A survey on peer-to-peer video streaming systems. *Peer-to-Peer Networking and Applications, 1*(1), 18–28. doi:10.1007/s12083-007-0006-y

Liu, Y., Xiao, L., Liu, X., Ni, L. M., & Zhang, X. (2005). Location Awareness in Unstructured Peer-to-Peer Systems. *IEEE Transactions on Parallel and Distributed Systems, 16*(2), 163–174. doi:10.1109/TPDS.2005.21

Liu, Y., Yang, C., Xu, K., & Chen, H. (2008). A fair utility function for incentive mechanism against free-riding in peer-to-peer networks. In *Next Generation Teletraffic and Wired/Wireless Advanced Networking* (pp. 222–233).

Lo, V. M., Zappala, D., Zhou, D., Liu, Y., & Zhao, S. (2004). Cluster computing on the fly: P2P scheduling of idle cycles in the Internet. In *3rd International Workshop on Peer-to-Peer Systems* (pp. 227–236).

Locher, T., Moor, P., Schmid, S., & Wattenhofer, R. (2006). Free riding in bittorrent is cheap. In *Proc. of HotNets-V.*

Loeser, C., Mueller, W., Berger, F., & Eikerling, H.-J. (2003). Peer-to-peer networks for virtual home environments. *Proceedings 36th Hawaii International Conference on System Sciences, 9*, 282.3.

Loguinov, D., Kumar, A., Rai, V., & Ganesh, S. (2003). Graph-Theoretic Analysis of a Structured Peer-to-Peer System: Routing Distances and Fault Resilience. In *Proc. ACM SIGCOMM 2003*, (pp. 395-406).

Lohr, S. (2001, August 2). Technology, I.B.M. making a commitment to next phase of the Internet. *The New York Times.*

Lomuscio, A., & Sergot, M. (2003). Deontic interpreted systems. *Studia Logica, 75*(1), 63–92. doi:10.1023/A:1026176900459

Loo, B. T., Hellerstein, J. M., Huebsch, R., Shenker, S., & Stoica, I. (2004). Enhancing P2P File-Sharing with an Internet Scale Query Processor. In *Proceedings of the 30th International Conference on Very Large Data Bases* (Vol. 30, pp. 432 – 443)

Lopes Cardoso, H., & Oliveira, E. (2000). Using and evaluating adaptive agents for electronic commerce negotiation. In M. C. Monard & J. Simão Sichman (Ed.), *Proceedings of the International Joint Conference, 7th Ibero-American Conference on AI: Advances in Artificial Intelligence* (pp. 96-105). Berlin: Springer.

Lopes Cardoso, H., & Oliveira, E. (2007). A contract model for electronic institutions. In J. Sichman & S. Ossowski (Ed.), *Coordination, organizations, institutions, and norms in agent systems III,* (pp. 73–84). Berlin: Springer.

Lopez y Lopez, F., Luck, M., & d'Inverno, M. (2005). A normative framework for agent-based systems. *Computational & Mathematical Organization Theory, 12*(2–3), 227–250. doi:10.1007/s10588-006-9545-7

Lorch, J. R., & Smith, A. J. (2001). Improving dynamic voltage scaling algorithms with PACE. *SIGMETRICS/ Performance,* 50-61.

Lorch, J., & Smith, A. (1998, June). Software Strategies for Portable Computer Energy Management. *Institute of Electrical and Electronics Engineers Personal Communication, 5,* 60-73.

Lorch, M., & Kafura, D. (2004). The prima grid authorization system. *Journal of Grid Computing, 2*(3), 279–298. doi:10.1007/s10723-004-5408-y

Loureiro, E., Bublitz, F., Barbosa, N., Perkusich, A., Almeida, H., & Ferreira, G. (2006). A flexible middleware for service provision over heterogeneous pervasive networks. In *Proceedings of the 2006 International Symposium on a World of Wireless, Mobile and Multimedia Networks (WoWMoM'06)* (pp. 609-614).

Lovász, L. (1996). Random walks on graphs: A survey. *Combinatorics, Paul Erdös is Eighty, 2,* 353-398.

Lowekamp, B. B. (2003). Combining active and passive network measurements to build scalable monitoring systems on the Grid. *SIGMETRICS Performance Evaluation Review, 30*(4), 19–26. doi:10.1145/773056.773061

Lua, E. K., Crowcroft, J., Pias, M., Sharma, R., & Lim, S. (2005). A survey and comparison of peer-to-peer overlay network schemes. *IEEE Communications Survey and Tutorial, 7*(2), 72–93. doi:10.1109/COMST.2005.1610546

Lubin, E., Lawrence, E., & Navarro, K. F. (2005). Wireless Remote Healthcare Monitoring with Motes. In *Proceedings of the International Conference on Mobile Business* (pp. 235-241). Washington, DC: IEEE Computer Society.

Luby, M. (2002). LT Codes. In *Proceedings of the 43rd Symposium of Foundations of Computer Science* (p. 271).

Ludwig, H., Keller, A., Dan, A., King, R. P., & Franck, R. (2003). *Web service level agreement (WSLA), language specification.* Tech. Rep. Armonk, NY: IBM Corporation.

Luhmann, N. (1983). *Trust and Power.* Hoboken, NJ: John Wiley & Sons Inc.

Lv, Q., Cao, P., Cohen, E., Li, K., & Shenker, S. (2002). Search and replication in unstructured peer-to-peer networks. *ACM SIGMETRICS Performance Evaluation Review, 30*(1), 258–259. doi:10.1145/511399.511369

Lv, Q., Ratnasamy, S., & Shenker, S. (2002). Can heterogeneity make Gnutella scalable? In *The 1st International Workshop on Peer-to-Peer Systems: Vol. 2429. Revised Papers from the First International Workshop on Peer-to-Peer Systems (IPTPS)* (pp. 94-103). London: Springer-Verlag

Ma, R.T.B., Lee, S.C.M., Lui, J.C.S., & Yau, D.K.Y. (2006). Incentive and service differentiation in P2P networks: A game theoretic approach. *IEEE/ACM Transactions on Networking, 14*(5), 978-991.

Ma, W., Wang, G., & Liu, J. (2007). Scalable semantic search with hybrid concept index over structure peer-to-peer network. In *Proceedings of the 6th International Conference on Grid and Cooperative Computing* (pp. 42-48).

Macariu, G., Cârstea, A., Frîncu, M., & Petcu, D. (2008). Towards a Grid oriented architecture for symbolic computing. In *Procs. ISPDC'08.* Washington, DC: IEEE Computer Society.

MacKenzie, C. M., Laskey, K., McCabe, F., Brown, P. F., Metz, R., & Hamilton, B. A. (2006). *Reference Model for Service Oriented Architecure, 1.0*. Retrieved September 20, 2008, from http://www.oasis-open.org/committees/download.php/19679/soa-rm-cs.pdf

MacKenzie, M., Laskey, K., McCabe, F., Brown, P., & Metz, R. (2006, August 1). *Reference Model for Service Oriented Architecture 1.0*. Retrieved from http://www.oasis-open.org/committees/download.php/19679/soa-rm-cs.pdf

MacKenzie, M., Laskey, K., McCable, F., Brown, P. F., & Metz, R. (2006). *OASIS – Reference Model for Service Oriented Architecture 1.0*. Retrieved from http://www.oasis-open.org/

Maclaren, J., Keown, M. M., & Pickles, S. (2006). Co-allocation, fault tolerance and grid computing. In S. J. Cox (Ed.), *UK e-Science All Hands Meeting* (pp. 155-162). New York: NeSC Press.

Macleod, G., Donachy, P., Harmer, T. J., Perrot, R. H., Conlon, B., Press, J., & Lungu, F. (2005). *Implied volatility Grid: Grid based integration to provide on demand financial risk analysis*. Belfast e-Science Centre, Queen's University of Belfast. NGS ganglia monitoring. (n.d.). Retrieved from http://ganglia.ngs.rl.ac.uk/

MADAM. (n.d.). Retrieved April 30, 2009, from http://www.ist-madam.org/

Maes, P. (1987). Concepts and Experiments in Computational Reflection. In *Proceedings of OOPSLA'87, of ACM SIGPLAN Notices* (Vol. 22, pp. 147-155). New York: ACM Press.

Maesschalck, S. D., Pickavet, M., Colle, D., & Demeester, P. (2003). Multi-layer traffic grooming in networks with an IP/MPLS layer on top of a meshed optical layer. In *IEEE Global Telecommunications Conference* (pp. 2750-2754).

Magnet, I. S. T. *6FP MAGNET*. (2006-2008). Retrieved from http://www.ist-magnet.org, http://magnet.aau.dk/

Magrath, S., Chiang, F., Markovits, S., Braun, R., & Cuervo, F. (2005), Autonomics in telecommunications service activation. In *Autonomous Decentralized Systems 2005,* (pp. 731- 737). New York: IEEE Computer Society.

Maheswaran, M., Ali, S., Siegel, H. J., Hensgen, D., & Freud, R. F. (1999). Dynamic mapping of a class of independent tasks onto heterogeneous computing systems. *Journal of Parallel and Distributed Computing,* (November): 1999.

Maleshefski, T. (2007). *Collanos collaboration software simplifies teamwork*. Retrieved February 15, 2009, from http://www.eweek.com/c/a/Messaging-and-Collaboration/Collanos-Collaboration-Software-Simplifies-Teamwork/

Malkhi, D., Naor, M., & Ratajczak, D. (2002). Viceroy: a scalable and dynamic emulation of the butterfly. In *Proceedings of the twenty-first annual symposium on Principles of distributed computing* (pp. 183-192). Monterey, CA: ACM. doi: 10.1145/571825.571857

Mamei, M., & Zambonelli, F. (2004). Programming pervasive and mobile computing applications with the TOTA middleware. In *Proceedings of the Second IEEE Annual Conference on Pervasive Computing and Communications (PERCOM '04)* (pp. 263-273).

Mannie, E. (Ed.). (2004). *Generalized multi-protocol label switching (GMPLS) architecture*. RFC 3945, Internet Engineering Task Force (IETF).

Manolakos, E. S., Galatopoullos, D., & Funk, A. (2004). Distributed Matlab-based signal and image processing using JavaPorts. In *International Conference on Acoustics, Speech and Signal Processing (ICASSP 2004),* (pp. 217-220).

Manolakos, E. S., Galatopoullos, D., & Funk, A. (2004). Integrating Java and Matlab components into the same parallel and distributed application Using JavaPorts. In *18th International Parallel and Distributed Processing Symposium (IPDPS 2004)* (pp. 14b.1-14b.10).

Manzalini, A. (2008). Tomorrow's open Internet for Telco and Web federations. In *Conference on Complex, Intelligent and Software Intensive Systems* (pp. 567-572). New York: IEEE Computer Society.

Mao, W. (2004). *An Identity-based Non-interactive Authentication Framework for Computational Grids.* HP Lab, Technical Report HPL-2004-96.

MapleConnect. (2006). *MapleNet.* Retrieved November 2008 from http://www.maplesoft.com/products/maplenet

MapleSoft. (2008). *Grid Computing Toolbox.* Retrieved November 2008 from http://www.maplesoft.com/products/toolboxes/Grid-Computing/

March, V., Teo, Y. M., & Wang, X. (2007). DGRID: A DHT-based resource indexing and discovery scheme for computational Grids. In L. Brankovic, P. Coddington, J. F. Roddick, C. Steketee, J. R. Warren, & A. Wendelborn (Eds.), *Proceedings of the Fifth Australasian Symposium on ACSW Frontiers - Volume 68* (pp. 41-48). New York: ACM.

March, V., Teo, Y. M., & Wang, X. (2007). DGRID: A DHT-based resource indexing and discovery scheme for computational grids. In *Proceedings of the Fifth Australasian Symposium on ACSW Frontiers* (pp.41-48). Darlinghurst, Australia: Australian Computer Society, Inc.

Marchal, L., Yang, Y., Casanova, H., & Robert, Y. (2005). A realistic network/application model for scheduling divisible loads on large-scale platforms. In *Proceedings of IPDPS, 01*(48b). doi: http://doi.ieeecomputersociety.org/10.1109/IPDPS.2005.63

Marinescu, D. C., Marinescu, G. M., Ji, Y., Boloni, L., & Siegel, H. J. (2003). Ad hoc grids: Communication and computing in a power constrained environment. In *Proceedings of the IEEE International Performance, Computing, and Communications Conference* (pp. 113-122).

Marples, D., & Kriens, P. (2001). The open services gateway initiative: An introductory overview. *IEEE Communications Magazine, 39*(12), 110–114. doi:10.1109/35.968820

Marsh, S. P. (1994). *Formalising trust as a computational concept.* PhD thesis, University of Stirling, UK.

Martin, T. L. (2001). *Balancing Batteries, Power, and Performance: System Issues in CPU Speed-Setting for Mobile Computing.* PhD thesis, Carnegie Mellon University, Pittsburgh, Pennsylvania.

Martini, B., Campi, A., Baroncelli, F., Martini, V., Torkman, K., Zangheri, F., et al. (2009). *SIP-based Service Platform for On-demand Optical Network Services.* In *OFC 2009. Open Grid Forum.* (n.d.). Retrieved from http://www.ogf.org/

Marzolla, M., Mordacchini, M., & Orlando, S. (2005). Resource discovery in a dynamic grid environment. In *Proceedings. Sixteenth International Workshop on Database and Expert Systems Applications (DEXA'05)* (pp. 356-360).

Marzolla, M., Mordacchini, M., & Orlando, S. (2007). Peer-to-peer systems for discovering resources in a dynamic Grid. *Parallel Computing, 33*(4-5), 339–358. doi:10.1016/j.parco.2007.02.006

Massa, P., & Avesani, P. (2005). Controversial users demand local trust metrics: an experimental study on epinions.com community. In *Proceedings of the 25th American Association for Artificial Intelligence Conference* (pp. 121-126).

Mastroianni, C., Talia, D., & Verta, O. (2005). A super-peer model for resource discovery services in large-scale Grids. *Future Generation Computer Systems, 21*(8), 1235–1248. doi:10.1016/j.future.2005.06.001

Mastroianni, C., Talia, D., & Verta, O. (2005). A super-peer model for resource discovery services in large-scale grids. *Future Generation Computer Systems, 21*(8), 1235–1248. doi:10.1016/j.future.2005.06.001

Matei, R., Iamnitchi, A., & Foster, P. (2002). Mapping the Gnutella network. *Internet Computing, IEEE, 6*(1), 50–57. doi:. doi:10.1109/4236.978369

Mathy, L., Canonico, R., & Hutchison, D. (2001) An Overlay Tree Building Control Protocol. In *Proceedings of Networked Group Communication,* (LNCS Vol. 2233, pp. 76-87). Berlin: Springer.

Matsuoka, S., Shinjo, S., Aoyagi, M., Sekiguchi, S., Usami, H., & Miura, K. (2005). Japanese computational

Grid research project: NAREGI. *Proceedings of the IEEE, 93*(3), 522–533. doi:10.1109/JPROC.2004.842748

Maximilien, E. M., & Singh, M. P. (2004). A framework and ontology for dynamic Web services selection. *IEEE Internet Computing, 8*, 84–93. doi:10.1109/MIC.2004.27

Mayer, C., & Davis, H. (1995). An integrative model of organizational trust. *Academy of Management Review, 20*, 709–734. doi:10.2307/258792

Maymounkov, P. (2002). *Online codes.* New York University, Tech. Rep. TR2002-833.

Maymounkov, P., & Mazières, D. (2002). Kademlia: A peer-to-peer information system based on the XOR metric. []. Heidelberg, Germany: Springer Berlin.]. *Lecture Notes in Computer Science, 2409*, 53–65. doi:10.1007/3-540-45748-8_5

McCann, J., Deering, S., & Mogul, J. (1996, August). *Path MTU Discovery for IP version 6.* RFC 1981 (Draft Standard).

McCanne, S., & Floyd, S. (2008). *The network simulator - NS2.* Retrieved October 15, 2008, from http://www.isi.edu/nsnam/ns/

McKeowen, N., Parulkar, G., & Peterson, L. (2008). OpenFlow: enabling innovation in campus networks. *ACM SIGCOMM Computer Communication Review, 38*(2), 69–74. doi:10.1145/1355734.1355746

McKnight, D. H., & Chervany, N. L. (1996). *The Meaning of Trust.* Technical Report MISRC Working Paper Series 96-04, University of Minnesota. Management Information Systems Research Center.

McKnight, L. W., Howison, J., & Bradner, S. (2004). Guest editors' introduction: Wireless Grids – Distributed resource sharing by mobile, nomadic, and fixed devices. *IEEE Internet Computing, 8*, 24–31. doi:10.1109/MIC.2004.14

Medina, A., Lakhina, A., Matta, I., & Byers, J. W. (2001). BRITE: An approach to universal topology generation. In *Proceedings of the 9th International Workshop on Modeling, Analysis, and Simulation of Computer and Telecommunication Systems* (pp. 346 - 356).

Mellanox Technologies Inc. (2004). Mellanox Performance, Price, Power, Volumn Metric (PPPV). Retrieved on November 9, 2008 from http://www.mellanox.co/products/shared/PPPV.pdf.

Menasce, D. A., & Almeida, V. A. F. (2001). *Capacity Planning for Web Services.* Upper Saddle River, NJ: Prentice Hall.

Meneguzzi, F., Modgil, S., Oren, N., Miles, S., Luck, M., Faci, N., et al. (2009). Monitoring and explanation of contract execution: A case study in the aerospace domain. In *Proceedings of the 8th International Conference on Autonomous Agents and Multiagent Systems (AAMAS 2009) – Industrial and Applications Track.*

Mengotti, T. (2004, March). *GPU, A Framework for Distributed Computing over Gnutella.* Unpublished master's thesis in Computer Science, ETH Zurich, Switzerland.

Merriden, T. (2001). *Irresistible forces: The business legacy of Napster and the growth of the underground Internet.* Capstone Publishing.

Metadata registries. (2004). ISO/IEC 11179, Information Technology -- Metadata registries (MDR). Retrieved October 7, 2008, from http://standards.iso.org/ittf/PubliclyAvailableStandards/c035343_ISO_IEC_11179-1_2004%28E%29.zip

Meulpolder, M., Pouwelse, J.A., Epema, D. H. J., & Sips, H. J. (2008). *Bartercast: Fully distributed sharing-ratio enforcement in bittorrent.*

Michlmayr, E., Graf, S., Siberski, W., & Nejdl, W. (2005). Query Routing with Ants. In *Proceedings of the Workshop on Ontologies in Peer-to-Peer Communities.*

Microsoft Developer Network. (2005, May 1). *Microsoft's Vision for an Identity Metasystem.* Retrieved from http://msdn.microsoft.com/en-us/library/ms996422.aspx

Microsoft Virtual, P. C. (2008). Microsoft VirtualPC website. Retrieved December 5, 2008, from http://www.microsoft.com/windows/products/winfamily/virtualpc/default.mspx

Microsoft-DSI. (2008). *Microsoft Dynamic Systems Initiative.* Retrieved December 5, 2008, from http://www.microsoft.com/business/dsi/default.mspx

Microsystems, S. (1988). *RPC: Remote procedure call protocol specification version 2.* Retrieved September 20, 2008, from http://tools.ietf.org/html/rfc1057

Microsystems, S. S3L. (n.d.). Retrieved from http://dlc.sun.com/pdf/816-0653-10/816-0653-10.pdf

Mietzner, R., & Leymann, F. (2008). Towards provisioning the cloud: On the usage of multi-granularity flows and services to realize a unified provisioning infrastructure for SaaS applications. In *Proceedings of the International Congress on Services, SERVICES 2008.*

Mietzner, R., Karastoyanova, D., & Leymann, F. (2009). Business Grid: Combining Web services and the Grid. *In Special Issue of ToPNoC on Concurrency in Process-Aware Information Systems.* Berlin, Germany: Springer.

Migrating-Desktop. (2008). *Migrating Desktop New Generation Environment for Grid Interactive Application.* Retrieved December 5, 2008, from http://desktop.psnc.pl/

Miles, S., Papay, J., Payne, T., Decker, K., & Moreau, L. (2004). Towards a protocol for the attachment of semantic descriptions to grid services. In *Grid Computing. Second European AcrossGrids Conference, AxGrids 2004. Revised Papers* (pp. 230-239).

Milgram, S. (1967). The small world problem. *Psychology Today, 1*(1), 61–67.

Miller, G. (1990). WordNet: An on-line lexical database. *International Journal of Lexicography, 3*(4), 235–312. doi:10.1093/ijl/3.4.235

Miller, M. (2001). *Discovering P2P.* Alameda, CA: Sybex Inc.

Milojicic, D. S. (2003). *P2P Computing.* Technical Report No. HPL-2002-57. Palo Alto, CA: HP Laboratories Palo Alto.

Minar, N., & Hedlund, M. (2001). A network of peers: Peer-to-peer models through the history of the internet. In A. Oram (Ed.), *Peer-to-peer: Harnessing the benefits of a disruptive technology* (pp. 3-20). Sebastopol, CA: O'Reilly.

Minerva, R., & Moiso, C. (2004). The Death of Network Intelligence? In *15th IEE International Symposium on Services and Local Access* (pp. 157-168). London: IEE.

Miranda, H., & Rodrigues, L. (2003). Friend and foes: Preventing selfishness in open mobile ad hoc networks. In *Proc. of 1st International Workshop on Mobile Distributed Computing* (pp. 440- 445), Providence, RI. Washington, DC: IEEE Computer Society Press.

Misra, J. (1986). Distributed discrete-event simulation. *ACM Computing Surveys, 18*(1), 39–65. doi:10.1145/6462.6485

MIT Project Oxygen. (2004). *Project overview.* Retrieved November 1, 2008, from http://oxygen.csail.mit.edu/Overview.html.

Mitchell, J., & Lapata, M. (2008). Vector-based models of semantic composition. In *Proceedings of ACL-08: HLT* (pp. 236-244). Association for Computational Linguistics.

Mitola, J. (1999). Cognitive Radio for Flexible mobile Multimedia Communications. In *Mobile Multimedia Communications, 1999. (MoMuC '99). IEEE International Workshop on Multimedia Communications* (pp. 3-10).

Miyoshi, A., Lefurgy, C., Hensbergen, E. C., Rajamony, R., & Rajkumar, R. (2002). Critical power slope: understanding the runtime effects of frequency scaling. *Proceedings of the 16th international conference on Supercomputing,* pages 35– 44.

Mockapetris, P. (1987). *Domain names - Implementation and specification.* Specification, RFC1035. Retrieved from http://www.ietf.org/rfc/rfc1035.txt

Modgil, S., Faci, N., Meneguzzi, F., Oren, N., Miles, S., & Luck, M. (2009). A framework for monitoring agent-based normative systems. In *Proceedings of the 8th International Conference on Autonomous Agents and Multiagent Systems (AAMAS 2009).*

Moffat, J. (2003). *Complexity Theory and Network Centric Warfare.* Command and Control Research Program (CCRP) Publications Series.

Mogul, J.C., & Deering, S.E. (1990, November). *Path MTU discovery*. RFC 1191 (Draft Standard).

Mohamed, H. H., & Epema, D. H. J. (2004). An evaluation of the close-to-files processor and data co-allocation policy in multiclusters. In *International Conference on Cluster Computing* (pp. 287-298). Los Alamitos, CA: IEEE Computer Society.

Mohamed, H. H., & Epema, D. H. J. (2005). Experiences with the koala co-allocating scheduler in multiclusters. In *International Symposium on Cluster Computing and the Grid* (pp. 784-791). Los Alamitos, CA: IEEE Computer Society.

Mohamed, H. H., & Epema, D. H. J. (2008). KOALA: a co-allocating grid scheduler. *Concurrency and Computation, 20*(16), 1851–1876. doi:10.1002/cpe.1268

Mokhtar, S. B., Georgantas, N., & Issarny, V. (2006). COCOA: Conversation-based service composition for pervasive computing environments. In *Pervasive Services, ACS/IEEE International Conference* (pp. 29-38).

Mokhtar, S. B., Preuveneers, D., Georgantas, N., Issarny, V., & Berbers, Y. (2008). EASY: Efficient semAntic Service discoverY in pervasive computing environments with QoS and context support. *Journal of Systems and Software, 81*(5), 785–808.

Mondéjar, R., García, P., Pairot, C., & Skarmeta, A. F. G. (2006). Enabling Wide-Area Service Oriented Architecture through the p2pWeb. In *Proceedings of the 15th IEEE International Workshops on Enabling Technologies: Infrastructure for Collaborative Enterprises (WETICE'06)*. Washington, DC: IEEE Computer Society.

Mont, O. K. (2002). Clarifying the concept of product-service system. *Journal of Cleaner Production, 10*(3), 237–245. doi:10.1016/S0959-6526(01)00039-7

Montanelli, S., & Castano, S. (2008). Semantically routing queries in peer-based systems: The h-link approach. *The Knowledge Engineering Review, 23*(1), 51–72. doi:10.1017/S0269888907001257

Montero, R. S., Huedo, E., & Llorente, I. M. (2003). Grid resource selection for opportunistic job migration. In *Proceedings of the 9th International EuroPar Conference* (pp. 366-373). Berlin: Springer.

Montresor, A. (2004, August). A Robust Protocol for Building Superpeer Overlay Topologies. In *Proceedings of the 4th IEEE International Conference on Peer-to-Peer computing (P2P'04)*, Zurich, Switzerland (pp. 202-210).

Moore, B. (2002, August). Taking the data centre power and cooling challenge. *Energy User News*.

Moore, J. F. (1993). Predators and Prey: A New Ecology of Competition. *Harvard Business Review, 71*, 75–83.

MORE. (n.d.). Retrieved February 13, 2009, from http://www.ist-more.org/

Moreira, G. M., Silvestrin, G., Sanchez, R. N., & Gaspary, L. P. (2007). On the Performance of Web Services Management Standards for Network Management - An Evaluation of MUWS and WS-Management. In *IFIP/IEEE International Symposium on Integrated Network Management* (pp. 459-468).

Morrison, D. (1968). PATRICIA - Practical Algorithm To Retrieve Information Coded in Alphanumeric. *Journal of the ACM, 15*(4), 514–534. doi:10.1145/321479.321481

Morselli, R., Bhattacharjee, B., Marsh, M. A., & Srinivasan, A. (2005). Efficient lookup on unstructured topologies. In *Proc. PODC 2005, 24th Symposium on Principles of Distributed Computing*, Las Vegas, NV, USA.

Moschoyiannis, S., & Razavi, A. R. Yongyan Zheng, & Krause, P. (2008). Long-running Transactions: Semantics, schemas, implementation. In *Digital Ecosystems and Technologies, 2008. DEST 2008. 2nd IEEE International Conference on* (pp. 20-27). doi: 10.1109/DEST.2008.4635168.

Moschoyiannis, S., Razavi, A. R., & Krause, P. (2008). Transaction Scripts: Making Implicit Scenarios Explicit. In *ETAPS 2008 - FESCA'08, ENTCS*. New York: Elsevier.

Moser, L. E., Melliar-Smith, P. M., Narasimhan, P., Tewksbury, L., & Kalogeraki, V. (1999). The eternal system: an architecture for enterprise applications. In *International Enterprise Distributed Object Computing Conference (EDOC)* (pp. 214-222). Washington, DC: IEEE Computer Society Press.

Moy, J. (1998). *Ospf version 2*. RFC 2328, Internet Engineering Task Force (IETF).

Mu'alem, A. W., & Feitelson, D. G. (2001). Utilization, predictability, workloads, and user runtime estimates in scheduling the IBM SP2 with backfilling. *IEEE Transactions on Parallel and Distributed Systems, 12*(6), 529–543. doi:10.1109/71.932708

Mui, L. (2002). *Computational Models of Trust and Reputation: Agents, Evolutionary Games, and Social Networks*. PhD thesis, Massachusets Institute of Technology, Cambridge, MA.

Muller, A., Carle, G., & Klenk, A. (2008). Behavior and classification of NAT devices and implications for NAT traversal. *IEEE Network, 22*(5), 14–19. doi:10.1109/MNET.2008.4626227

Muller, I., Kowalczyk, R., & Braun, P. (2006). Towards Agent-based Coalition Formation for Service Composition. In *Proceedings of the IEEE/WIC/ACM International Conference on Intelligent Agent Technology*. Retrieved from ieeexplore.ieee.org/iel5/4052878/4052879/04052901.pdf

Muntaner-Perich, E., de la Rosa, J. L., & Esteva, R. (2007). Towards a formalisation of dynamic electronic institutions. In J. Sichman & S. Ossowski (Ed.), *Coordination, organizations, institutions, and norms in agent systems III*, (pp. 61–72). Berlin: Springer.

Murphy, A. L., Picco, G. P., & Roman, G.-C. (2001). Lime: A middleware for physical and logical mobility. In *Proceedings of the 21ˢᵗ International Conference on Distributed Computing System* (pp. 524-533).

Murphy, G. (1988). Comprehending complex concepts. *Cognitive Science, 12*(4), 529–562.

Myers, M., Ankney, R., Malpani, A., Galperin, S. & Adams, C. (1999). Internet X.509 public key infrastructure online certificate status protocol (OCSP). *The Internet Engineering Task Force (IETF)*, RFC 2560.

myGrid. (n.d.). Retrieved May 1, 2009, from http://www.mygrid.org.uk/

MyProxy. (2008). *MyProxy Credential Management Service*. Retrieved December 5, 2008, from http://grid.ncsa.uiuc.edu/myproxy/

Myspace. (n.d.). Retrieved from http://www.myspace.com

Nachira, F. (2002). *Towards a Network Of Digital Business Ecosystems Fostering the Local Development*.

Nachira, F., Dini, P., Nicolai, A., Louarn, M., & Leon, L. (2007). *Digital Business Ecosystems*. Brussels: European Commission. *OPAALS Website - Opaals Home Page*. (n.d.). Retrieved December 22, 2008, from http://www.opaals.org/

Nakao, A., Peterson, L., Bavier, A.. (2006). Scalable routing overlay networks. *ACM SIGOPS Operating Systems Review*, January .

Naor, M., & Wieder, U. (2003). Novel Architectures for P2P Applications: the continuous discrete approach. *Proceedings of SPAA, 2003*, 50–59.

Napster protocol specification. (2001, March 12). *OpenNap*. Retrieved February 15, 2009, from http://opennap.sourceforge.net/napster.txt

Napster. (n.d.). Wikipedia. Retrieved September 17, 2008, from http://en.wikipedia.org/wiki/Napster

NAREGI. (2008). *NAREGI project*. Retrieved December 5, 2008, from http://www.naregi.org/index_e.html

NAS Parallel Benchmarks. (2007). Retrieved from http://www.nas.nasa.gov/Resources/Software/npb.html

National Research Council. (1993). *National collaboratories: Applying information technology to scientific research*. Washington, DC: National Academy Press.

Natrajan, A., Humphrey, M. A., & Grimshaw, A. S. (2001). Capacity and capability computing using legion. []. Heidelberg, Germany: Springer Berlin.]. *Lecture Notes in Computer Science, 2073*, 273–283. doi:10.1007/3-540-45545-0_36

Nejabati, R. (Ed.). (2008). *Grid optical burst switched networks (GOBS)*. GFD.128.

Neo, H. K., Lin, Q. P., & Liew, K. M. (2005). A grid-based mobile agent collaborative virtual environment. In *Proceedings of the 2005 International Conference on Cyberworlds.* Singapore.

NESSI. (2008). *Networked European Software and Services Initiative.* Retrieved December 5, 2008, from http://www.nessi-europe.com/Nessi/

Nessi-Grid. (2006). Networked European Software and Services Initiative – Grid. *Grid vision and strategic research agenda.* Retrieved from www.nessi-europe.com/

NET. (n.d.). Retrieved September 6, 2008, from http://www.microsoft.com/NET/

NetEqualizer NE serials. (n.d.). Retrieved from http://www.netequalizer.com/nda.htm

Netfilter. (2008). *Netfilter, firewalling, NAT and packet mangling for Linux.* Retrieved from http://www.netfilter.org/

NETGEAR. (2009). Retrieved from http://www.netgear.com/

Netto, M. A. S., & Buyya, R. (2008). Rescheduling co-allocation requests based on flexible advance reservations and processor remapping. In *International Conference on Grid Computing* (p. 144-151). Los Alamitos, CA: IEEE Computer Society.

Netto, M. A. S., & Buyya, R. (2009). Offer-based scheduling of deadline-constrained bag-of-tasks applications for utility computing systems. In *International Heterogeneity in Computing Workshop, in conjunction with the 23rd IEEE International Parallel and Distributed Processing Symposium.* Los Alamitos, CA: IEEE Computer Society.

Network virtualization middleware for large scale distributed applications. (2002). IBM Research. Unpublished.

Network Visibility and Service Management Utilizing Deep Packet Inspection (DPI) Technology [Allot white paper]. (n.d.). Retrieved from http://www.allot.com/index.php?option=com_content &task=view &id=45&Itemid=44

Networked Media of the Future. (2007). White paper available at: http://cordis.europa.eu/fp7/ict/netmedia/publications_en.html

Newcomb, T. M. (1975). *Social Psychology: the Study of Human Interaction* (2nd ed.). London: Routledge and Kegan Paul.

Newcomer, E., & Lomow, G. (2004). Understanding SOA with Web Services (Independent Technology Guides). Reading, MA: Addison-Wesley Professional.

Ng, E., & Zhang, H.. (2002). Predicting Internet Network Distance with Coordinates-based Approaches. *INFOCOM 2002.*

NGG group (Next Generation Grids expert group). (2003). *Next generation grids: European grid research 2005 - 2010 (No. 1).* Retrieved May 1, 2009 from ftp://ftp.cordis.europa.eu/pub/ist/docs/ngg_eg_final.pdf

NGG group (Next Generation Grids expert group). (2004). *Next generation grids 2: Requirements and options for European grids research 2005-2010 and beyond (No. 2).* Retrieved May 1, 2009 from ftp://ftp.cordis.europa.eu/pub/ist/docs/grids/ngg2_eg_final.pdf

NGG group (Next Generation Grids expert group). (2006). *Future for European grids: GRIDs and service oriented knowledge utilities vision and research directions 2010 and beyond (No. 3).* Retrieved May 1, 2009 from ftp://ftp.cordis.europa.eu/pub/ist/docs/grids/ngg3_eg_final.pdf

NGG Report. (2006). Future for European Grids: GRIDs and Service Oriented Knowledge Utilities. *Vision and Research Directions 2010 and Beyond.* Retrieved from semanticgrid.org/NGG3

NGS. (n.d.). Retrieved from http://www.grid-support.ac.uk/

Nichols, J., Demirkan, H., & Goul, M. (2006). Autonomic workflow execution in the grid. *IEEE Transactions on Systems, Man and Cybernetics. Part C, Applications and Reviews, 36*(3), 353–364. doi:10.1109/TSMCC.2006.871574

Niebert, N., Schieder, A., Abramowicz, H., Malmgren, G., Sachs, J., & Horn, U. (2004). Ambient Networks: An Architecture for Communication Networks Beyond

3G. *IEEE Wireless Communications, 11*(2), 14–22. doi:10.1109/MWC.2004.1295733

Niemegeers, I., & Heemstra de Groot, S. (2003). Research issues in ad-hoc distributed personal networking. *Wireless Personal Communications, 26*(2-3), 149–167. doi:10.1023/A:1025522402484

Niemegeers, I., & Heemstra de Groot, S. (2005). FED-NETS: Context-Aware Ad-Hoc Network Federations. *Wireless Personal Communications, 33*(3-4), 305–318. doi:10.1007/s11277-005-0574-1

Nitzsche, J., van Lessen, T., Karastoyanova, D., & Leymann, F. (2008). BPEL^light. In *5th International Conference on Business Process Management (BPM 2007).*

NMI. (2008). *NSF Middlware Initiative.* Retrieved December 5, 2008, from http://www.nsf.gov/news/special_reports/cyber/middleware.jsp

Nordu. (2008). *NorduGrid project.* Retrieved December 5, 2008, from http://www.nordugrid.org/

NORDUGRID. (n.d.). Retrieved October 11, 2008, from http://www.nordugrid.org/

Nwana, H. S., Rosenschein, J., Sandholm, T., Sierra, C., Maes, P., & Guttman, R. (1998). Agent-mediated electronic commerce: Issues, challenges, and some viewpoints. In *Proceedings of 2nd ACM International Conference on Autonomous Agents* (pp. 189-196).

Nwana, S., Lee, L., & Jennings, N. R. (1996). Coordination in Software Agent Systems. *BT Technology Journal, 14*(4).

O'Hara, K., Alani, H., Kalfoglou, Y., & Shadbolt, N. (2004). Trust strategies for the Semantic Web. In *Workshop on Trust, Security, and Reputation on the Semantic Web, 3rd International Semantic Web Conference (ISWC).*

O'Mahony, M. J., Simeonidou, D., Hunter, D., & Tzanakaki, A. (2001). The application of optical packet switching in future communication networks, *IEEE Communication Magazine. Communications Magazine, 39*(3), 128–135. doi:10.1109/35.910600

O'Reilly, T. (2001). Remaking the peer-to-peer meme. In A.Oram (Ed.), *Peer-to-peer: Harnessing the benefits of a disruptive technology* (pp. 38-58). Sebastopol, CA: O'Reilly.

O'Reilly, T. (2005). *What is Web 2.0: Design Patterns and Business Models for the Next Generation of Software.*

O'Sullivan, J., Edmond, D., & ter Hofstede, A. H. M. (2003). *Service Description: A survey of the general nature of services* (Technical Report No. FIT-TR-2003-02). Queensland University of Technology.

OASIS BPEL Technical Committee. (2008). Retrieved from http://www.oasis-open.org/committees/tc_home.php?wg_abbrev=wsbpel

OASIS Consortium. (2008). Retrieved November 15, 2008, from http://www.oasis-open.org

OASIS Web services Resource Framework (WSRF) TC. (2008). Retrieved from http://www.oasis-open.org/committees/documents.php?wg_abbrev=wsrf

OASIS WS-BPEL Extension for People. *(BPEL4People) Technical Committee.* (2008). Retrieved from http://www.oasis-open.org/committees/bpel4people/charter.php

OASIS. (2004). *Web Services Distributed Management: Management Using Web Service (MUWS 1.0) Part 1.* Retrieved November 15, 2008, from http://docs.oasis-open.org/ wsdm/2004/12/wsdm-muws-part1-1.0.pdf

OASIS. (2004, March). *Web Services Security.* Retrieved from http://www-128.ibm.com/developerworks/library/specification/ws-secure/

OASIS. (2005). *eXtensible Access Control Markup Language (XACML) Version 2.0.* Retrieved November 15, 2008, from http://docs.oasis-open.org/xacml/2.0/access_control-xacml-2.0-core-spec-os.pdf

OASIS. (2006). *Reference Model for Service Oriented Architecture 1.0.* Retrieved November 15, 2008, from http://www.oasis-open.org/committees/download.php/19679/ soa-rm-cs.pdf

OASIS. (2007). *Web services business process execution language version 2.0.* Retrieved November 15, 2008, from http://docs.oasis-open.org/wsbpel/2.0/OS/wsbpel-v2.0-OS.html

OASIS. (2008). *OASIS: Advancing open standards for the global information society.* Retrieved November 2, 2008, from http://www.oasis-open.org/home/index.php

OASIS. (2008). *Web service distributed management technical committee.* Retrieved November 15, 2008, from http://www.oasis-open.org/committees/wsdm/

OASIS. (2008, August 01). *SAML specifications.* Retrieved from http://saml.xml.org/saml-specifications

OAuth Workgroup. O. C. (2007, December 4th). *OAuth Core 1.0.* Retrieved December 4th, 2007, from http://oauth.net/core/1.0/

Obreiter, P., & Nimis, J. (2003). *A Taxonomy of Incentive Patterns: The Design Space of Incentives for Cooperation* (Technical Report). Germany: Universität Karlsruhe, Faculty of Informatics.

OGF. (n.d.). Retrieved September 18, 2008, from http://www.ggf.org/.

OGF-RM-WG. (2008). *OGF Reference Model Working Group.* Retrieved December 5, 2008, from http://www.ogf.org/gf/group_info/view.php?group=rm-wg

Ogryczak, W., Kostreva, M. M., & Wierzbicki, A. (2004). Equitable aggregations and multiple criteria analysis. *European Journal of Operational Research, 158,* 362–377. doi:10.1016/j.ejor.2003.06.003

OGSA. (2008). *Open Grid Services Architecture.* Retrieved December 5, 2008, from http://www.globus.org/ogsa/

OGSA-DAI. (2008). *OGSA-DAI project.* Retrieved December 5, 2008, from http://www.ogsadai.org/index.php

Ohara, Y., Bhatia, M., Osamu, N., & Murai, J. (2003). Route flapping effects on OSPF. In *IEEE International Symposium on Applications and the Internet* (pp. 232-237).

Ohta, K., Yoshikawa, T., Nakagawa, T., & Inamura, H. (2005). Design and implementation of mobile Grid middleware for handsets. In *Proceedings of the 11th International Conference on Parallel and Distributed Systems (ICPADS'05)* (pp. 679- 683). Washington, DC: IEEE Computer Society.

Okazaki, T., Kamada, H., Kinoshita, K., Tode, H., & Murakami, K. (2006) Efficient flooding control suitable for multiple requests. In *IEEE International Symposium on Applications and the Internet* (pp. 71-76).

OMII. (2008). *OMII-Europe.* Retrieved December 5, 2008, from http://www.omii-europe.org/

OntoGrid. (n.d.). Retrieved February 13, 2009, from http://www.ontogrid.net/ontogrid/index.jsp

Open Grid Forum. (n.d.). Retrieved February 13, 2009, from http://www.ogf.org/

OpenMath Society. (2004). *OpenMath 2.0.* Retrieved November 2008 from http://www. openmath.org/

OpenNEbula. (2008). OpenNEbula project. Retrieved December 5, 2008, from http://www.opennebula.org/

OpenQRM. (2008). Retrieved from http://www.open-qrm.org/

OPERA. (2009). http://www.ist-opera.org/

Oppenheimer, D., Albrecht, J., Patterson, D., & Vahdat, A. (2004). *Scalable wide-area resource discovery* (Tech. Rep. UCB//CSD-04-1334). Berkeley & San Diego, California: University of California Berkeley, EECS Computer Science Division & University of California San Diego, Department of Computer Science and Engineering.

Oppenheimer, D., Albrecht, J., Patterson, D., & Vahdat, A. (2004). Distributed resource discovery on planetlab with SWORD. In *Proceedings of the First Workshop on Real, Large Distributed Systems (WORLDS 2004).* Retrieved October 10, 2008, from http://sword.cs.williams.edu/pubs/worlds04.pdf

Oppenheimer, D., Albrecht, J., Patterson, D., & Vahdat, A. (2005). Design and implementation tradeoffs for wide-area resource discovery. In *Proceedings of the 14th IEEE International Symposium on High Performance*

Distributed Computing, 2005, HPDC-14, (pp. 113-124). doi: 10.1109/HPDC.2005.1520946

Oracle-11G. (2008). *Oracle database 11G.* Retrieved December 5, 2008, from http://www.oracle.com/database/index.html

Oracle-Coherence. (2008). *Oracle Coherence.* Retrieved December 5, 2008, from http://www.oracle.com/technology/products/coherence/index.html

Oracle-Grid. (2008). *Oracle Grid Computing.* Retrieved December 5, 2008, from http://www.oracle.com/technologies/grid/index.html

Oreizy, P., Medvidovic, N., & Taylor, R. N. (1998). Architecture-based runtime software evolution. In *Proceedings of the 20th international Conference on Software Engineering.*

Osborne, M. J. (2004). *An Introduction to Game Theory.* New York: Oxford University Press.

OSG. (2008). *Open Science Grid project.* Retrieved December 5, 2008, from http://www.opensciencegrid.org

OSGi Alliance. (2003). *OSGi service platform (Release 3).* Amsterdam: IOS Press.

OSOA. (2008). *Open SOA Collaboration.* Retrieved December 5, 2008, from http://www.osoa.org/display/Main/Home

OS-Virtualization. (2008). *Operating System Virtualization.* Retrieved December 5, 2008, from http://en.wikipedia.org/wiki/Operating_system-level_virtualization

Ou, X., Squicciarini, A., Goasguen, S., & Bertino, E. (2006). Authorization Strategies for Virtualized Environments in Grid Computing Systems. In *IEEE Workshop on Web Services Security (WSSS 2006),* Berkeley, CA, U.S.A.

Oualha, N., & Roudier, Y. (2006). *Cooperation Incentive Schemes* (Research Report RR-06-176). France: Institut Eurécom.

Oumanski, G., & Bertok, P. (2005). Wide area service discovery and adaptation for mobile clients in networks with ad-hoc behavior. In *Third International Conference on Information Technology and Applications* (Vol. 2, pp. 334-337).

OurGrid. (n.d.). Retrieved May 1, 2009, from http://www.ourgrid.org/

OverCache. (n.d.). Retrieved from http://www.oversi.com/products/overcache-msp/overcache-p2p.html

OVF. (2008). *Open Virtualization Format Specification V1.0.0.* Retrieved December 5, 2008, from http://www.dmtf.org/standards/published_documents/DSP0243_1.0.0.pdf

OWL-S. (2003). *OWL-S Specifications.* Retrieved December 27, from http://www.daml.org/services/owl-s/1.0/

OWL-S. (2004). *OWL-based Web service ontology.* Retrieved February 20, 2007 from http://www.daml.org/services/owl-s/

P2P-F research group. (n.d.). Retrieved from http://www.p2p-f.edu.cn

PacWoman. (2003). Retrieved from http://www.imec.be/pacwoman

Page, A. J., & Naughton, T. J. (2005). Dynamic task scheduling using genetic algorithms for heterogeneous distributed computing. In *Proceedings of the 19th International Parallel and Distributed Processing Symposium,* Denver, Colorado, USA, 2005.

Page, I., Jacob, T., & Chen, E. (1993, February). Fast Algorithms for Distributed Resource Allocation. *IEEE Transactions on Parallel and Distributed Systems, 4*(2), 188–197. doi:10.1109/71.207594

Page, L., Brin, S., Motwani, R., & Winograd, T. (1998). *The PageRank Citation Ranking: Bringing Order to the Web* (Technical Report). USA: Stanford Digital Libraries.

Pairot, C., García, P., Gómez, A. F., & Skarmeta, S. (2004). Dermi: A New Distributed Hash Table-based Middleware Framework. *IEEE Internet Computing, 8,* 74–84.

Pande, V. S., Bacallado, S., Beberg, A., Bowman, G., Brandman, R., Branson, K., et al. (2009). *Folding@*

home. Retrieved February 15, 2009, from http://folding.stanford.edu/

Pando. (n.d.). Retrieved from http:// www.pando.com

Panisson, A., da Rosa, D. M., Melchiors, C., Granville, L. Z., Almeida, M. J. B., & Tarouco, L. M. R. (2006). Designing the Architecture of P2P-Based Network Management Systems. In *11ᵗʰ IEEE Symposium on Computers and Communications* (pp. 69-75).

Pant, A., & Jafri, H. (2004). Communicating efficiently on cluster based grids with MPICH-VMI. In *International Conference on Cluster Computing* (pp. 23-33). Los Alamitos, CA: IEEE Computer Society.

Paolucci, M., & Sycara, K. (2003). Autonomous Semantic Web services. *Internet Computing, 7*, 34–41. doi:10.1109/MIC.2003.1232516

Paolucci, M., Kawamura, T., Payne, T., & Sycara, K. (2002). Semantic matching of Web service capabilities. In *Proc. First Int'l Semantic Web Conf. (ISWC '02)*, (pp. 333-347).

Papazoglou, M. P. (2003). Service-Oriented Computing: Concepts, Characteristics and Directions. In *Proceedings of the Fourth International Conference on Web Information Systems Engineering* (Vol. 3). Washington, DC: IEEE Computer Society Press., December.

Papazoglou, M. P. (2005). Extending the Service-Oriented Architecture. *Business Integration Journal, 7*(1), 18–21.

Papazoglou, M. P., & Georgakopoulos, D. (2003). Service-Oriented Computing. *Communications of the ACM, 46*(10), 25–28. doi:10.1145/944217.944233

Papazoglou, M. P., Traverso, P., Dustdar, S., & Leymann, F. (2007). Service-oriented computing: State of the art and research challenges. *IEEE Computer, 40*(11), 38–45.

Papazoglou, M., & Dubray, J.-J. (2004). *A Survey of Web Service Technologies* (Technical Report DIT-04-058). University of Trento.

Parallels. (2008). *Parallels optimized computing*. Retrieved December 5, 2008, from http://www.parallels.com/

Parameswaran, M., Susarla, A., & Whinston, A. B. (2001). P2p networking: An information sharing alternative. *Computer, 34*(7), 31–38. doi:10.1109/2.933501

Park, H., Lee, I., Hwang, T., & Kim, N. (2008). Architecture of Home Gateway for Device Collaboration in Extended Home Space. *IEEE Transactions on Consumer Electronics, 54*(4), 1692–1697. doi:10.1109/TCE.2008.4711222

Park, J. (2004). A deadlock and livelock free protocol for decentralized internet resource coallocation. *IEEE Transactions on Systems, Man, and Cybernetics . Part A, 34*(1), 123–131.

Park, S.-M., Ko, Y.-B., & Kim, J.-H. (2003). Disconnected Operation Service in Mobile Grid Computing. In M. E. Orlowska, S. Weerawarana, M. P. Papazoglou, & J. Yang (Eds.) *Service-oriented computing - ICSOC 2003* (pp. 499-513). Berlin/Heidelberg, Germany: Springer.

Particle Physics Data Grid. (n.d.). Retrieved September 18, 2008, from http://www.ppdg.net/

Paschke, A., & Scappiner-Gerull, E. (2006). A categorization scheme for SLA metrics. In *Multi-Conference Information Systems (MKWI06)*, Passau, Germany.

Paterson, K. G. (2005). Cryptography from pairings. In I.F. Blake, G. Seroussi & N.P. Smart (Eds.), *Advances in Elliptic Curve Cryptography. LMS 317*, (pp. 215-251). Cambridge, UK: Cambridge University Press.

Paterson, K. G., & Price, G. (2003). A comparison between traditional public key infrastructures and identity-based cryptography. *Information Security Technical Report, 8*(3), 57–72. doi:10.1016/S1363-4127(03)00308-X

Patriquin, A. (2009). *March Search Market Share: Record query growth and the Yahoo/Microsoft search deal by the numbers*. Retrieved May 7, 2009, from http://blog.compete.com/2009/04/13/search-market-share-march-google-yahoo-msn-live-ask-aol-2/

Pavlou, G., Flegkas, P., Gouveris, S., & Liotta, A. (2004). On management technologies and the potential of Web services. *IEEE Communications Magazine, 42*(7), 58–66. doi:10.1109/MCOM.2004.1316533

Paxson, V., & Floyd, S. (1997). Why we don't know how to simulate the Internet. In *The 29th Conference on Winter Simulation* (pp. 1037-1044). Washington, DC: IEEE Computer Society.

Payton, I. J., Fenner, M., & Lee, W. G. (2002). *Keystone Species: The Concept and Its Relevance for Conservation Management in New Zealand*. Dept. of Conservation.

Pearlman, L., Welch, V., Foster, I., Kesselman, C., & Tuecke, C. (2002). A community authorization service for group collaboration. In *Proceedings of the IEEE 3rd International Workshop on Policies for Distributed Systems and Networks*.

PeerApp UltraBand. (n.d.). Retrieved from http://www.peerapp.com/docs/Carrier-Grade_Peer-to-Peer_Caching.pdf

Peltz, C. (2003). Web services orchestration and choreography. *IEEE Computer, 36*(10), 46–52.

Pendarakis, D., Shi, S., Verma, D., & Waldvogel, M. (2001). ALMI: An Application Level Multicast Infrastructure. In *3rd USNIX Symposium on Internet Technologies and Systems (USITS '01)*, San Francisco, CA, USA (pp. 49–60).

Perez-Sorrosal, F., Patiño-Martinez, M., Jimenez-Peris, R., & Kemme, B. (2007). Consistent and Scalable Cache Replication for Multi-Tier J2EE Applications. In *ACM/IFIP/USENIX 8th Int. Middleware Conference* (pp. 328-347). Berlin: Springer-Verlag.

Perez-Sorrosal, F., Vuckovic, J., Patiño-Martínez, M., & Jiménez-Peris, R. (2006). Highly available long running transactions and activities for J2EE applications. In *IEEE International Conference on Distributed Computing Systems (ICDCS)*. Washington, DC: IEEE Computer Society.

Periorellis, P., Wu, J., & Watson, P. (2006). Security Mechanisms for Data Intensive Systems. In *IEEE Workshop on Web Services Security* (WSSS 2006), Berkeley, CA, U.S.A.

Petcu, D., Cârstea, A., Macariu, G., & Frîncu, M. (2008). Service-oriented symbolic computing with SymGrid. *SCPE, 9*(2), 111–125.

Petcu, D., Tepeneu, D., Paprzycki, M., & Ida, T. (2006). Symbolic computations on Grids. In B. Di Martino, J. Dongarra, A. Hoisie, L. T. Yang, H. Zima, (eds.), *Engineering the Grid,* (pp. 91–107). Valencia, CA: American Scientific Publishers.

Peters, S. (2006). *Hyperglue: An instrastructure for human-centered computing in distributed intelligent environments*. Unpublished doctoral dissertation, Massachusetts Institute of Technology.

Peterson, L., & Culler, D. (2008). PlanetLab testbed. *PlanetLab Consortium*. Retrieved November 16, 2008, from http://www.planet-lab.org

Peterson, L., Anderson, T., Culler, D., & Roscoe, T. (2002). A Blueprint for Introducing Disruptive Technology into the Internet. In *Proceedings of the HotNets-I*, October.

Peyton Young, H. (1994). *Equity: In theory and practice*. NJ: Princeton University Press.

Pham, T. V., Lau, L. M. S., & Dew, P. M. (2007). An ontology-based adaptive approach to p2p resource discovery in distributed scientific communities. *International Transactions on Systems Science and Applications, 2,* 391–404.

Phan, T., Huang, L., & Dulan, C. (2002). Challenge: integrating mobile wireless devices into the computational Grid. In I. F. Akyildiz, J. Y.-B. Lin, R. Jain, V. Bharghavan, & A. T. Campbell (Eds), *MobiCom '02: Proceedings of the 8th Annual International Conference on Mobile Computing and Networking* (pp. 271-278). New York: ACM.

Piango, M. M. J. M. (2006). *The neural basis of semantic compositionality*. paper presented at session hosted by the Yale Interdepartmental Neuroscience Program, Yale University.

Piatek, M., Isdal, T., Anderson, T., Krishnamurthy, A., & Venkataramani, A. (2007). Do incentives build robustness in bittorrent? In *NSDI, USENIX*. Retrieved from http://dblp.uni-trier.de/db/conf/nsdi/nsdi2007.html#PiatekIAKV07.

Pierce, M. E., Youn, C., & Fox, G. (2002). The gateway computational web portal. In *Concurrency and computa-*

tion: Practice and experience. New York: John Wiley & Sons, Ltd.

Pierre, G., & Steen, M. V. (2006). Globule: a collaborative content delivery network. *IEEE Communications Magazine, 44*(8), 127–133. doi:10.1109/MCOM.2006.1678120

Pinango, M. (2006). Understanding the architecture of language: the possible role of neurology. *Trends in Cognitive Sciences, 10*(2), 49–51. doi:10.1016/j.tics.2005.12.003

Pinheiro, E., & Bianchini, R. (2004, June). Energy Conservation Techniques for Disk Array-Based Servers. *Proc. of the 18th International Conference on Supercomputing.*

Piro, R. M., Guarise, A., & Werbrouck, A. (2003). An Economy-based Accounting Infrastructure for the DataGrid. In *the 4th International Workshop on Grid Computing* (pp. 202). Washington, DC: IEEE Computer Society.

Pirro, G., Ruffolo, M., & Talia, D. (2008). Advanced semantic search and retrieval in a collaborative peer-to-peer system. In *Proceedings of the 3rd international workshop on Use of P2P, Grid and Agents for the Development of Content Networks* (pp. 65-72).

Pitoura, T., Ntarmos, N., & Triantafillou, P. (2006). Replication, load balancing and efficient range query processing in DHTs. In *Proc. EDBT 2006,* Munich, Germany (pp. 131-148).

Planetlab. (n.d.). Retrieved from http://www.planet-lab.org

Platform-VM. (2008). *Platform VM Orchestrator.* Retrieved December 5, 2008, from http://www.platform.com/Products/platform-vm-orchestrator

Plaxton, C. G., Rajaraman, R., & Richa, A. (1997). Accessing nearby copies of replicated objects in a distributed environment. In *ACM Symposium on Parallel Algorithms and Architectures* (pp. 311–320).

PNP2008, The Dutch Freeband Communications Project PNP2008. (2004-2008). Retrieved from http://www.freeband.nl

Poikselka, M., et al. (2006). *The IMS: IP Multimedia Concepts and Services* (2nd Ed.). Hoboken, NJ: Wiley.

Polastre, J. (2003). *Design and Implementation of Wireless Sensor Networks for Habitat Monitoring.* Unpublished master thesis, University of California at Berkeley, Department of Electrical Engineering and Computer Sciences.

Polastre, J., Szewczyk, R., Mainwaring, A., Culler, D., & Anderson, J. (2006). Analysis of wireless sensor networks for habitat monitoring. *Wireless Sensor Network,* (pp. 399-423). New York: Springer Science+Buisness Media, LCC.

Ponnekanti, S. R., Johanson, B., Kiciman, E., & Fox, A. (2003). Portability, extensibility and robustness in iROS. In *Proceedings of the 1st IEEE International Conference on Pervasive Computing and Communications (PERCOM ' 03)* (pp. 11-19).

Pop, F. (2008). Communication model for decentralized meta-scheduling in Grid environments. In *Proceedings of The Second International Conference on Complex, Intelligent and Software Intensive System, Second International Workshop on P2P, Parallel, Grid and Internet computing - 3PGIC-2008 (CISIS'08),* March 4-7, 2008, Barcelona, Spain (pp. 315-320).

Pop, F., Tudor, D., Cristea, V., & Cretu, V. (2007). Fault tolerant scheduling framework for MedioGRID system. In *Proceedings of The IEEE Region 8 EUROCON 2007 Conference on Computer as a tool,* September 9-12, 2007, Warsaw, Poland.

Popescu, B. C., Crispo, B., & Tanenbaum, A. S. (2003). Secure data replication over untrusted hosts. In *Proceedings of the 9th Workshop on Hot Topics in Operating Systems.*

Popescu, G. (n.d.). *Graph embedding algorithm for delay optimized distributed indexing networks.* Unpublished paper.

Popescu, G., & Liu, Z. (2002). On Scheduling 3D model transmission in Networked Virtual Environments. In . *Proceedings of IEEE DSRT, 2002,* 127–134.

Popescu, G., & Liu, Z. (2004). Stateless application-level multicast for dynamic group communication. In . *Proceedings of DS-RT, 2004, 20*–28.

Popescu, G., & Liu, Z. (2006). Network overlays for efficient control of large scale dynamic groups. *Proceedings of DS-RT 2006.*

Porto, F., Da Silva, V. F. V., Dutra, M. L., & Schulze, B. (2005). An adaptive distributed query processing Grid service. In *Proceedings the Workshop on Data Management in Grids, VLDB 2005.* (LNCS 3836, pp. 45-57).

Pouwelse, J. A., Garbacki, P., Wang, J., Bakker, A., Yang, J., Iosup, A., et al. (2006). Tribler: A social-based peer-to-peer system. In *The 5th International Workshop on Peer-to-Peer Systems (IPTPS06)*, (pp. 1–6).

Power, M. E., Tilman, D., Estes, J. A., Menge, B. A., Bond, W. J., & Mills, L. S. (1996). Challenges in the quest for keystones. *Bioscience, 46*(8), 609–620. doi:10.2307/1312990

PPLive. (2004). http://www.pplive.com/

Pras, A., Drevers, T., v. d. Meent, R., & Quartel, D. (2004). Comparing the performance of SNMP and Web services-based management. *IEEE Transactions on Network and Service Management, 1*(2).

Pras, A., Schönwälder, J., Burgess, M., Festor, O., Pérez, G. M., Stadler, R., & Stiller, B. (2007). Key Research Challenges in Network Management. *IEEE Communications Magazine, 45*(10), 104–110. doi:10.1109/MCOM.2007.4342832

Presser, A., Canon, L., Canon, D., Conexant, W., Epson, S., & Albright, S. (2008). *UPnP device architecture 1.1.* Retrieved November 22, 2008, from http://www.upnp.org/resources/documents.asp

Price, G. (2005). PKI challenges: An industry analysis. In J. Zhou, M-C. Kang, F. Bao & H-H. Pang (Eds.), *Proceedings of the 4ᵗʰ International Workshop for Applied PKI (IWAP 2005), Vol. 128,* (pp. 3-16). Amsterdam: IOS Press.

Price, G., & Mitchell, C. J. (2005). Interoperation between a conventional PKI and an ID-based infrastructure. In D. Chadwick & G. Zhao (Eds.), *Proceedings of the 2ⁿᵈ European Public Key Infrastructure Workshop (EuroPKI 2005),* (LNCS Vol. 3545, pp. 73-85). Berlin: Springer-Verlag.

ProActive. (2008). *ProActive Parallel suite.* Retrieved December 5, 2008, from http://proactive.inria.fr/

Procera PacketLogic. (n.d.). Retrieved from http://www.proceranetworks.com/products/products-overview.html

Prodan, R., & Fahringer, T. (2005). Dynamic scheduling of scientific workflow application on the Grid: A case study. In *SAC'05: Proceedings of the 2005 ACM Symposium on Applied Computing* (pp. 687-694). New York: ACM Press.

Prudhomme, T., Kesselman, C., Finholt, T., Foster, I., Parsons, D., Abrams, D., et al. (2001). *NEESgrid: A distributed virtual laboratory for advanced earthquake experimentation and simulation: scoping study* (Report No. NEES-2001-02). Retrieved September 19, 2008, from http://www.neesgrid.org/html/TR 2001/NEESgrid TR.2001- 04.pdf

Pubmed. (n.d.). Retrieved from http://www.ncbi.nlm.nih.gov/pubmed/

Puppin, D. Moncelli, S. Baraglia, R. Tonelotto, N., & Silvestri, F. (2005). A Grid information service based on peer to peer. In *Proceedings of 11th Euro-Par Conference (Euro-Per 2005), Lecture Notes in Computer Science* (Vol. 3648, pp. 454-464). Heidelberg, Germany: Springer-Berlin.

Puppin, D., Moncelli, S., Baraglia, R., Tonellotto, N., & Silvestri, F. (2005). A Grid information service based on peer-to-peer. In *Euro-Par 2005 Parallel Processing* (LNCS 3648, pp. 454-464). Berlin, Germany: Springer.

Puri, R., & Ramchandran, K. (1999). Multiple description source coding through forward error correction codes. In *33rd Asilomar Conf. Signals, Systems and Computers.*

Pyun, Y., & Reeves, D. (2004, August). Constructing a Balanced, log(N)-Diameter Super-peer Topology. In

Proceedings of the 4th IEEE International Conference on Peer-to-Peer computing (P2P '04), Zurich, Switzerland (pp. 210-218).

QEMU. (2008). *QEMU Open Source Processor Emulator*. Retrieved December 5, 2008, from http://bellard.org/qemu/

Qi, J., Wei, L., & Bai, Y. (2008). Composition of Concept Lattices. In *7ʰ International conference on machine learning and cybernatics*, Kunming.

Qin, X., & Jiang, H. (2005, August). A Dynamic and Reliability-driven Scheduling Algorithm for Parallel Real-time Jobs on Heterogeneous Clusters. *Journal of Parallel and Distributed Computing, 65*(8), 885–900. doi:10.1016/j.jpdc.2005.02.003

Qin, X., & Jiang, H. (2006, June). A Novel Fault-tolerant Scheduling Algorithm for Precedence Constrained Tasks in Real-Time Heterogeneous Systems. *Parallel Computing, 32*(5-6), 331–356. doi:10.1016/j.parco.2006.06.006

QoS for PNs at home, The Dutch Freeband Communications Project QoS for PNs at home. (2004-2008). Retrieved from http://qos4pn.irctr.tudelft.nl

Qu, X., Zhong, J., & Yang, X. (2006). Towards reliable and trustworthy cooperation in Grid: A pre-evaluating set based trust model. In M. Gavrilova et al. (Eds.), *Lecture Notes in Computer Science* (Vol. 3984, pp. 224–235).

Quasthoff, M. (2008). Enlightenment 2.0: Facilitating user control in distributed collaborative applications. In *Proc. of the 2008 WI-IAT Doctoral Workshop*, Sydney. Washington, DC: IEEE.

Quasthoff, M., Sack, H., & Meinel, C. (2007). Why HTTPS is not enough – A signature-based architecture for trusted content on the social Web. In *Proc. of the 2007 International Conference on Web Intelligence*, (pp. 820-824), Silicon Valley. Washington, DC: IEEE.

Quetier, B., & Capello, F. (2005). *A survey of Grid research tools: Simulators, emulators and real life platforms*. IMACS Survey.

Quix, C., Schoop, M., & Jeusfeld, M. (2002). Business Data Management for Business-To-Business Electronic Commerce. *SIGMOD Record, 31*(1). doi:10.1145/507338.507348

Quocirca. (2006). *Grid Computing Update*. Quocirca Insight Report.

Rabaey, J., & Pedram, M. (Eds.). (1998). *Lower Power Design Methodologies.* Norwell, Massachusetts: Kluwer Academic Publisher.

Raghavan, S., & Garcia-Molina, H. (2001). Crawling the Hidden Web. In *27th VLDB Conference*, Roma, Italy.

Raghavendra, C. S., Sivalingam, K. M., & Znati, T. (2004). *Wireless Sensor Networks*. New York: Springer Science+Buisness Media, LCC.

Ragusa, C., Longo, F., & Puliafito, A. (2008). On the Assessment of the S-Sicilia Infrastructure: a Grid-based Business System. In *International Workshop on Grid Economics & Business Models (GECON)*. (LNCS 5206, pp. 113–124). Berlin: Springer-Verlag.

Rahman, A., & Hailes, S. (2000). Supporting trust in virtual communities. In *Proceedings of the 33rd Annual Hawaii International Conference on System Sciences*, (Vol.6, pp.6007), Hawaii.

Rajagopalan, J. A. D., & Luciani, B. (2004). *IP over optical networks: a framework*. RFC 3717, Internet Engineering Task Force (IETF).

Rajapske, R., & Denham, M. (2006). Text retrieval with more realistic concept matching and reinforcement learning. *Information Processing & Management, 42*, 1260–1275. doi:10.1016/j.ipm.2005.12.005

Ramabhadran, S., Ratnasamy, S., Hellerstein, J., & Shenker, S. (2004). Prefix Hash Tree: An Indexing Data Structure over Distributed Hash Tables. In *Proceedings of the 23rd ACM Symposium on Principles of Distributed Computing.*

Raman, R., Livny, M., & Solomon, M. (1998). Matchmaking: Distributed resource management for high throughput computing. In *HPDC: Proceedings of the 7ʰ IEEE International Symposium on High Performance Distributed Computing* (pp. 140-147). Washington, DC: IEEE Computer Society Press.

Ramasubramanian, V., & Sirer, E. G. (2004). Beehive: O(1) lookup performance for power-law query distributions in peer-to-peer overlays. In *Proc. NSDI'04, 1st Symposium on Networked Systems Design and Implementation*, San Francisco, CA.

Ramaswami, R., & Sivarajan, K. (2001). *Optical networks: A practical perspective* (2nd Ed.). San Francisco: Morgan Kaufman Publishers.

RAMSSD. (2008). *RAM based SSDs*. Retrieved December 5, 2008, from http://www.storagesearch.com/ssd-ram.html

Ranaweera, S., & Agrawal, D. P. (2000, May). A Task Duplication Based Scheduling Algorithm for Heterogeneous Systems. *Parallel and Distributed Processing Symposium*, 445-450.

Ranganathan, A., Chetan, S., Al-Muhtadi, J., Campbell, R. H., & Mickunas, M. D. (2005). Olympus: A high-level programming model for pervasive computing environments. In *Third IEEE International Conference on Pervasive Computing and Communications, PerCom 2005* (pp. 7-16).

Ranjan, R. Lipo, Chan, Harwood, A., Karunasekera, S., & Buyya, R. (2007). Decentralised resource discovery service for large scale federated Grids. In *IEEE International Conference on e-Science and Grid Computing* (pp.379-387). Washington, DC: IEEE Computer Society.

Ranjan, R., Harwood, A., & Buyya, R. (2008). Peer-to-peer-based resource discovery in global Grids: A tutorial. *IEEE Communications Surveys & Tutorials, 10*(2), 6–33. doi:10.1109/COMST.2008.4564477

Rao, W., Chen, L., Fu, A., & Bu, Y. Y. (2007). Optimal Proactive Caching in Peer-to-peer Network: Analysis and Application. In *Proc. CIKM 2007, 15th ACM Int'l Conference on Information and Knowledge Management*, Lisbon, Portugal (pp. 663-672).

Ratnasamy, S., Francis, P., Handley, K., Karp, R., & Shenker, S. (2001). A scalable contentaddressable network. In *Proceedings of the 2001 conference on Applications, technologies, architectures, and protocols for computer communications*, (pp.161 – 172). New York: ACM.

Ratnasamy, S., Handley, M., Karp, R., & Shenker, S. (2002). Topologically-aware overlay construction and server selection. In *Proceedings of IEEE INFOCOM 2002, Twenty-First Annual Joint Conference of the IEEE Computer and Communications Societies,* (Vol. 3, pp. 1190-1199). doi: 10.1109/INFCOM.2002.1019369

Ratnasamy, S., Shenker, S., & McCanne, S. (2005). Towards an evolvable Internet Architecture. In *Proc ACM SIGCOMM* (pp. 313-324).

Raverdy, P.-G., Issarny, V., Chibout, R., & de La Chapelle, A. (2006). A multi-protocol approach to service discovery and access in pervasive environments. In *The 3rd Annual International Conference on Mobile and Ubiquitous Systems: Networking and Services* (pp. 1-9).

Razavi, A. R., & Moschoyiannis, S. (2008). *FESCA WORKSHOP 2009 xml Sources*. Retrieved December 22, 2008, from http://www.computing.surrey.ac.uk/personal/st/S.Moschoyiannis/trnscripts/

Razavi, A. R., Moschoyiannis, S. K., & Krause, P. J. (2007). A Coordination Model for Distributed Transactions in Digital Business EcoSystems. *Digital Ecosystems and Technologies (DEST 2007).* Los Alamitos, CA: IEEE Computer Society Press.

Razavi, A. R., Moschoyiannis, S. K., & Krause, P. J. (2008). A scale-free business network for digital ecosystems. In *Digital Ecosystems and Technologies, 2008. DEST 2008. 2nd IEEE International Conference on,* (pp. 241-246).

Razavi, A. R., Moschoyiannis, S., & Krause, P. (2007). *Preliminary Architecture for Autopoietic P2P Network focusing on Hierarchical Super-Peers, Birth and Growth Models.* OPAALS Project (OPAALS project Deliverable D3.1). Retrieved from http://files.opaals.org/OPAALS/Year_1_Deliverables/WP03/OPAALS_D3.1-final_submitted.pdf

Razavi, A. R., Moschoyiannis, S., & Krause, P. (2007). *Report on formal analysis of autopoietic P2P network, together with predictions of performance.* OPAALS project (Deliverable D3.2). Retrieved from http://files.opaals.org/OPAALS/Year_1_Deliverables/WP03/OPAALS_D3.2_final.pdf

Razavi, A., Krause, P., & Moschoyiannis, S. (2006). Deliverable D24.5: DBE Distributed Transaction Model. *Project Acronym: DBE, European Community, Framework, Contract No: 507953.*

Razavi, A., Moschoyiannis, S., & Krause, P. (2007). Concurrency Control and Recovery Management in Open e-Business Transactions. In *Proc. WoTUG Communicating Process Architectures (CPA 2007),* (pp. 267–285).

RBAC. (2008). *Role-Based Access Control.* Retrieved December 5, 2008, from http://csrc.nist.gov/groups/SNS/rbac/documents/design_implementation/Intro_role_based_access.htm

RDF/XML Syntax Specification. (2004, February 10). W3C Recommendation.

RDFS. (2004). *RDF vocabulary description language 1.0: RDF schema, W3C.* Retrieved October 24, 2006, from http://www.w3.org/TR/rdf-schema/

Recordon, D., & Reed, D. (2006). OpenID 2.0: A platform for user-centric identity management. *Proc. of the 2nd ACM Workshop on Digital Identity Management* (pp. 11-16). Alexandria: ACM.

Rellermeyer, J. S. (2006). *flowSGi: A framework for dynamic fluid applications.* Master's Thesis, ETH Zurich, Switzerland.

Renesse, R., & Bozdog, A. (2005). Willow: DHT, aggregation, and publish/subscribe in one protocol. In *Peer-to-Peer Systems III* (LNCS 3279, pp. 173-183). Berlin, Germany: Springer.

Repastorganization for architecture and development. (2003). Argonne National Laboratory. Retrieved from http://repast.sourceforge.net/docs/docs_main.html

Resendo, L. C., Ribeiro, M. R. N., & Pires, J. J. O. (2008). Optimal multilayer grooming-oriented design for inter-ring traffic protection in DNI multiring WDM networks. *OSA Journal of Optical Networking, 7*(6), 533–549. doi:10.1364/JON.7.000533

RESERVOIR. (2008). *Resources and Services Virtualization without Barriers.* Retrieved December 5, 2008, from http://www.reservoir-fp7.eu/

RFT. (2008). *Reliable Transfer Service.* Retrieved December 5, 2008, from http://www.globus.org/toolkit/docs/3.2/rft/

R-GMA. *Relational Grid Monitoring Architecture.* (2008). Retrieved September 20, 2008, from http://www.r-gma.org/index.html

Rhea, S., Eaton, P., Geels, D., Weatherspoon, H., Zhao, B., & Kubiatowicz, J. (2003). Pond: The oceanstore prototype. In *Proceedings of usenix file and storage technologies (fast).*

Rhea, S., Geels, D., Roscoe, T., & Kubiatowicz, J. (2003). *Handling churn in a DHT* (Report No. UCB//CSD-03-1299). Berkeley: University of California.

Richardson, L., & Ruby, S. (2007). *RESTful Web Services.* Sebastopol, CA: O'Reilly Media, Inc.

Riedel, M., Schuller, B., Mallmann, D., Menday, R., Streit, A., Tweddell, B., et al. Lippert, Th. Snelling, D., van den Berghe, S., Li, V., Drescher, M., Geiger, A., Ohme, G., Benedyczak, K., Bala, P., Ratering, R., & Lukichev, A. (2007). Web services interfaces and open standards integration into the European Unicore 6 Grid middleware. In *Proceedings of 2007 Middleware for Web Services (MWS 2007) Workshop at 11th International IEEE EDOC Conference "The Enterprise Computing Conference"* (pp.57-60). New Jersey: IEEE Computer Society.

Riley, G. F., & Ammar, M. H. (2002). Simulating large networks – How big is big enough? In *The First International Conference on Grand Challenges for Modelling and Simulation.*

Ripeanu, M., Foster, I., & Iamnitchi, A. (2002). Mapping the Gnutella Network: Properties of Large-scale Peer-to-peer Systems and Implications for System Design. *Internet Computing, 6,* 50–57.

Ritter, J. (2001). *Why Gnutella Can't Scale. No, Really.* Retrieved July 17, 2008, from http://www.darkridge.com/~jpr5/doc/gnutella.html

Ritter, J. (2001, February). *Why Gnutella Can't Scale. No Really.* Retrieved from http://www.darkridge.com/~jpr5/doc/gnutella.html

Roach, A. B. (2002, June). *Session Initiation Protocol (SIP)-Specific Event Notification*. RFC 3265 (Proposed Standard).

Roadmap, U. (n.d.). Retrieved September 25, 2008, from http://www.unicore.eu/unicore/roadmap.php

Roblitz, T., & Reinefeld, A. (2005). Co-reservation with the concept of virtual resources. In *International Symposium on Cluster Computing and the Grid* (pp. 398-406). Los Alamitos, CA: IEEE Computer Society.

Roczniak, A., El Saddik, A., & Kouhi, R. (2008). Design of application-specific incentives in P2P networks. In *12th IEEE/ACM International Symposium on Distributed Simulation and Real-Time Applications* (pp. 194-203).

Rodrigues, R., & Liskow, B. (2005). High Availability in DHTs: Erasure Coding vs. Replication. In *Proc. IPTPS 2005,* Ithaca, NY, USA (pp. 226-239).

Rodriguez, P., Tan, S., & Gkantsidis, C. (2006). On the Feasibility of Commercial, Legal P2P Content Distribution. In *ACM SIGCOMM Computer* [New York: ACM.]. *Communication Review, 36,* 75–78.

Roman, M., Hess, C. K., Cerqueira, R., Ranganathan, A., Campbell, R. H., & Nahrsted, K. (2002). Gaia: Middleware infrastructure to enable active spaces. *IEEE Pervasive Computing / IEEE Computer Society [and] IEEE Communications Society, 1*(4), 74–83. doi:10.1109/MPRV.2002.1158281

Römer, K., & Friedemann, M. (2004). The Design Space of Wireless Sensor Networks. *IEEE Communications Society, 11*(6), 54–61.

Roozemond, D. (2008). *OpenMath Content Dictionary: scscp2.* Retrieved November 2008 from http://www.win.tue.nl/SCIEnce/cds/scscp2.html

Rose, B. (2001). Home networks: a standards perspective. *IEEE Communications Magazine, 39*(12), 78–85. doi:10.1109/35.968816

Rosenberg, J., & Schulzrinne, H. (2002). *An offer/answer model with session description protocol (SDP).* RFC 3264, Internet Engineering Task Force, June 2002.

Rosenberg, J., et al. (2002, June). *SIP: Session Initiation Protocol.* IETF RFC 3261.

Rothschild, M. (1995). *Bionomics: Economy As Eco-system* (Reissue., pp. 448). New York: Henry Holt & Company.

Roussopoulos, M., & Baker, M. (2003). CUP: Controlled update propagation in peer-to-peer networks. In *Proc. of the Annual USENIX Technical Conference,* San Antonio, Texas, USA (pp. 167-180).

Rowstron, A. I. T., & Druschel, P. (2001). Pastry: Scalable, Decentralized Object Location, and Routing for Large-Scale Peer-to-Peer Systems. In *Proceedings of the IFIP/ACM International Conference on Distributed Systems Platforms Heidelberg* (pp. 329-350). Berlin: Springer-Verlag.

Rowstron, A., & Druschel, P. (2001). Storage management and caching in PAST, a large-scale, persistent peer-to-peer storage utility. In *Proc. of ACM SOSP '01,* Banff, Canada (pp. 188-201).

Ruohomaa, S., & Kutvonen, L. (2005). Trust management survey. In *iTrust 2005,* (LNCS, pp.77-92)., Berlin: Springer.

Russell, D. J., Dew, P. M., & Djemame, K. (2007). A secure service-based collaborative workflow system. *International Journal of Business Process Integration and Management, 2*(3), 230–244. doi:10.1504/IJBPIM.2007.015497

Russell, D., & Xu, J. (2007). *Service oriented architectures in the provision of military capability.* Paper presented at the UK e-Science All Hands Meeting 2007, Nottingham, UK.

RUS-WG. (2008). *OGSA Resource Usage Service WG.* Retrieved December 5, 2008, from http://forge.gridforum.org/sf/projects/rus-wg

Ruta, M., Di Noia, T., Di Sciascio, E., & Donini, F. M. (2006). Semantic enabled resource discovery, and substitution in pervasive environments. In *Electrotechnical Conference, 2006. MELECON 2006. IEEE Mediterranean* (pp. 754-760).

Rzadca, K., Trystram, D., & Wierzbicki, A. (2007). Fair game-theoretic resource management in dedicated grids. In *CCGRID*, (pp. 343–350). Washington, DC: IEEE Computer Society. Retrieved from http://dblp.uni-trier.de/db/conf/ccgrid/ccgrid2007.html#RzadcaTW07

Rzhetsky, A., & Gomez, S. M. (2001). *Birth of scale-free molecular networks and the number of distinct DNA and protein domains per genome* (Vol. 17, pp. 988-996). Cambridge, UK: Oxford Univ. Press.

Sacha, J., Biskupski, B., Dahlem, D., Cunningham, R., Dowling, J., & Meier, R. (2007). A Service-Oriented Peer-to-Peer Architecture for a Digital Ecosystem. In *Proceedings of the IEEE International Conference on Digital Ecosystems and Technologies (DEST'07)*, Cairns, Australia.

Sacramento, V., Endler, M., Rubinsztejn, H. K., Lima, L. S., Goncalves, K., Nascimento, F. N., & Bueno, G. A. (2004). Moca: A middleware for developing collaborative applications for mobile users. *IEEE Distributed Systems Online*, *5*(10), 2. doi:10.1109/MDSO.2004.26

Sadok, D., Kamienski, C., Kelner, J., & Ohlman, B. (2006). Trends in network and device composition. *IEEE Communications Magazine*, *44*(10), 112–118. doi:10.1109/MCOM.2006.1710422

SAGA. (2008). *Simple API for Grid Applications*. Retrieved December 5, 2008, from http://saga.cct.lsu.edu/

Sagan, H. (1994). *Space-Filling Curves*. Berlin, Germany: Springer-Verlag.

Saha, D., & Mukherjee, A. (2003). Pervasive computing: A paradigm for the 21st century. *IEEE Computer*, *36*(3), 25–31.

Sahin, O. D., Gupta, A., Agrawal, D., & Abbadi, A. E. (2004). A Peer-to-peer framework for caching range queries. In *ICDE'04: Proceedings of the 20th International Conference on Data Engineering* (pp. 165-176). Washington, DC: IEEE Computer Society Press.

Sahin, O. D., Gupta, A., Agrawal, D., & El Abbadi, A. (2004). A Peer-to-peer Framework for Caching Range Queries. In *Proc. ICDE 2004, 20th Int'l Conference on Data Engineering*, Boston, USA (pp. 165 -176).

Sailhan, F., & Issarny, V. (2005). Scalable service discovery for MANET. In *Proceedings of the 3rd IEEE International Conference on Pervasive Computing and Communications*, Kauai Island, Hawaii, USA.

Sajjad, A., Jameel, H., Kalim, U., Han, S., Lee, Y., & Lee, S. (2005). AutoMAGI - an autonomic middleware for enabling mobile access to grid infrastructure. In *Proceedings of the Joint International Conference on Autonomic and Autonomous Systems and International Conference on Networking and Services (ICAS-ICNS 2005)* (pp. 73-79).

Sajjad, A., Kalim, U., Lee, Y.-K., & Lee, S. (2005). A component based architecture for an autonomic middleware enabling mobile access to Grid infrastructure. In T. Enokido, L. Yan, B. Xiao, D. Kim, Y. Dai, & L. T. Yang (Eds.), *Proceedings of the Embedded and Ubiquitous Computing Workshops (EUC 2005)* (pp. 1225-1234). Berlin: Springer.

Sakai, R., Ohgishi, K., & Kasahara, M. (2000). Cryptosystems based on pairing. In *Proceedings of the 2000 Symposium on Cryptography and Information Security (SCIS 2000)*.

Saleh, O., & Hefeeda, M. (2006, May). *Modeling and caching of peer-to-peer traffic* (Technical Report TR 2006-11). Simon Fraser University.

salesforce.com. (n.d.). *Salesforce*. Retrieved May 11, 2009, from http://www.salesforce.com/uk/

Salter, J. (2006). *An Efficient Reactive Model for Resource Discovery in DHT-Based Peer-to-peer Networks*. University of Surrey, Guildford, Surrey.

Salter, J., & Antonopoulos, N. (2005). *ROME: Optimising DHT-based Peer-to-Peer Networks*. Paper presented at the 5th International Network Conference, Samos, Greece.

Salter, J., & Antonopoulos, N. (2007). An Optimised 2-Tier P2P Architecture for Contextualised Keyword Searches. *Future Generation Computer Systems*, *23*(8), 241–251. doi:10.1016/j.future.2006.07.014

Salton, G., & Buckley, C. (1988). Term-weighting approaches in automatic text retrieval. *Information Processing & Management*, 24(5), 513–523. doi:10.1016/0306-4573(88)90021-0

SAML. (2008). *Security Assertion Markup Language*. Retrieved December 5, 2008, from http://www.oasis-open.org/committees/tc_home.php?wg_abbrev=security

Sandhu, R. S., Bellare, M., & Ganesan, R. (2002). Password-enabled PKI: Virtual smartcards versus virtual soft tokens. In *Proceedings of the 1ˢᵗ Annual PKI R&D Workshop*, (pp. 89-96). NIST.

Sangpachatanaruk, C., & Znati, T. (2004). Semantic driven hashing (SDH), An ontology-based search scheme for the semantic aware network (SA Net). In *Proceedings of Fourth International Conference on Peer-to-Peer Computing (P2P'04)* (pp. 270-271). Washington, DC: IEEE Computer Society.

Saraydar, C., Mandayam, N. B., & Goodman, D. J. (2002). Efficient Power Control via Pricing in Wireless Data Networks. *IEEE Transactions on Communications*, 50(2), 291–303. doi:10.1109/26.983324

Saroiu, S. (2004). *Measurement and analysis of internet content delivery systems*. Doctoral Dissertation, University of Washington.

Saroiu, S., Gummadi, K. P., & Gribble, S. D. (2002). *A measurement study of peer-to-peer file sharing systems*, (Tech. Rep. No. UW-CSE-01-06-02). Seattle, WA: University of Washington, Department of Computer Science & Engineering.

Saroiu, S., Gummadi, P. K., & Gribble, S. D. (2002). A measurement study of peer-to-peer file sharing systems. In *Proceedings of the 2002 Multimedia Computing and Networking Conference*.

Satyanarayanan, M. (2001). Pervasive computing: Vision and challenges. *IEEE Personal Communications*, 8(4), 10–17. doi:10.1109/98.943998

Savage, S. (1999). Sting: a TCP-based network measurement tool. In *USITS'99: Proceedings of the 2nd conference on USENIX Symposium on Internet Technologies and Systems*, Berkeley, CA, USA, USENIX Association (pp. 7–7).

Savage, S., Anderson, T., Aggarwal, A., Becker, D., Cardwell, N., & Collins, A. (1999, January). Detour: a case for informed Internet routing and transport. *IEEE Micro*, 19, 50–59. doi:10.1109/40.748796

Savola, P. (2006, April). *MTU and Fragmentation Issues with In-the-Network Tunneling*. RFC 4459 (Informational).

SCA. (2008). *OASIS Service Component Architecture*. Retrieved December 5, 2008, from http://www.oasis-opencsa.org/sca

ScaLAPACK. (2009). *ScaLAPACK Home Page*. Retrieved March 2, 2009, from http://www.netlib.org/scalapack/scalapack_home.html

Scandariato, R., Ofek, Y., Falcarin, P., & Baldi, M. (2008). Application-oriented trust in distributed computing. In *Third International Conference on Availability, Reliability and Security (ARES)* (pp. 434-439).

Schlosser, D., Hossfeld, T., & Tutschku, K. (2006). Comparison of robust cooperation strategies for P2P content distribution networks with multiple source download. In *6th IEEE International Conference Peer-to-Peer Computing* (pp. 31–38).

Schmidt, C., & Parashar, M. (2003). Flexible information discovery in decentralized distributed systems. In *HPDC'03: Proceedings of the 12ᵗʰ IEEE international Symposium on High Performance Distributed Computing*. Washington, DC: IEEE Computer Society Press.

Schmidt, C., & Parashar, M. (2008). Squid: Enabling Search in DHT-Based Systems. *Journal of Parallel and Distributed Computing*, 68(7), 962–975. doi:10.1016/j.jpdc.2008.02.003

Schmitt, C. (2006). *Animal Observation using embedded technologies – Rat movement tracking*. Unpublished diploma thesis, Eberhard-Karls University, Wilhelm-Schickard-Institute for Computer Sciences, Germany, Tuebingen.

Schneier, B. (1996). *Applied cryptography: protocols, algorithms, and source code in C*. New York: John Wiley.

Schulzrinne, H., Rao, A., & Lanphier, R. (1998, April). *Real Time Streaming Protocol(RTSP)*. RFC 2326 (Proposed Standard).

Schumacher, J., Jaekel, U., & Zimmermann, F. (2006). *Grid services for derivatives pricing,* Grid Technology for Financial Modelling and Simulation.

Schwan, N., Strauss, T., & Tomsu, M. (2007). P2P VoIP & MMoIP for Public Services – Requirements and Architecture. In *International Conference on Intelligence in Networks 2007.* Sterling, VA: Neustar. Retrieved Feb. 19, 2009, from www.icin.biz

SDO. (2008). *OASIS Service Data Objects.* Retrieved December 5, 2008, from http://www.oasis-opencsa.org/sdo

Seigneur, J.-M., & Jensen, C. D. (2007). User-centric identity, trust and privacy. In R. Song, L. Korba, & G. Yee, *Trust in e-services: technologies, practices and challenges* (pp. 293-322). Hershey, PA: IGI Global.

Selcuk, A. A., Uzun, E., & Pariente, M. R. (2004). A reputation-based trust management system for p2p networks. In *CCGRID '04: Proceedings of the 2004 IEEE International Symposium on Cluster Computing and the Grid,* (pp. 251–258). Washington, DC: IEEE Computer Society.

Semantic Grid Group. (n.d.). Retrieved February 13, 2009, from http://www.ogf.org/gf/group_info/view.php?group=sem-rg

SENSE. (n.d.). Retrieved February 13, 2009, from http://www.sense-ist.org/

Service Oriented Architecture—SOA. (n.d.). Retrieved July 18, 2008, from http://www-01.ibm.com/software/solutions/soa/

Service-oriented architecture. (n.d.). Wikipedia, the free encyclopedia. Retrieved December 21, 2008, from http://en.wikipedia.org/wiki/Service-oriented_architecture

SESAM Project. (2008), *Self Organization and Spontaneity in Liberalized and Harmonized Markets.* Retrieved Feb. 19, 2009, from http://dsn.tm.uni-karlsruhe.de/english/sesam-project.php

SETI@home Credit overview. (n.d.). Retrieved November 10, 2008, from http://boincstats.com/stats/project_graph.php?pr=sah

Setton, E., Yoo, T., Zhu, X., Goldsmith, A., & Girod, B. (2005). Cross-layer Design of Ad Hoc Networks for Real-Time Video Streaming . *IEEE Wireless Communications Magazine, 12*(4), 59–65. doi:10.1109/MWC.2005.1497859

SGE. (2008). *Sun Grid Engine.* Retrieved December 5, 2008, from http://gridengine.sunsource.net/

Shamir, A. (1984). Identity-based cryptosystems and signature schemes. In G.R. Blakley & D. Chaum (Eds.), *Advances in Cryptology - Proceedings of CRYPTO '84,* (LNCS Vol. 196, pp. 47-53). Berlin: Springer-Verlag.

Shanahan, K., & Freedman, M. (2005). Locality Prediction for Oblivious Clients. In *Peer-to-Peer Systems IV,* (pp. 252-263). doi: 10.1007/11558989

Shands, D., Yee, R., Jacobs, J., & Sebes, E. J. (2001). Secure Virtual Enclaves: Supporting Coalition Use of Distributed Application Technologies. [TISSEC]. *ACM Transactions on Information and System Security, 4*(2), 103–133. doi:10.1145/501963.501964

Sharman Networks. (2005). *How Peer-To-Peer (P2P) and Kazaa Software Works.* Retrieved June 29, 2008, from http://www.kazaa.com/us/help/new_p2p.htm

Shavitt, Y., & Tankel, T. (2003). Big-bang simulation for embedding network distances in Euclidean space. In *Proc. of IEEE Infocom.*

Sheong, C. S. (2008). *Ruby on rails web mashup projects: A step-by-step tutorial to building Web mashups.* Birmingham, UK: Packt Publishing Ltd.

Sherchan, W., Loke, S. W., & Krishnaswamy, S. (2006). A fuzzy model for reasoning about reputation in web services. *Proceedings of the 2006 ACM symposium on Applied computing* (pp. 1886 - 1892). Dijon, France: ACM.

Shi, J., Liang, J., & You, J. (2005). Measurements and Understanding of the KaZaA P2P Network. In Zhang, W., Tong, W. Chen, Z., & Glowinski, R. (Ed.), *Current trends in high performance computing and its applications* (pp.425-429). Heidelberg, Berlin, Germany: Springer.

Shields, M. W. (1997). *Semantics of parallelism.* New York: Springer.

Shirky, C. (2001). Listening to Napster. In A. Oram (Ed.), *Peer-to-Peer: Harnessing the Power of Disruptive Technologies* (pp. 21-37). Sebastopol, CA: O'Reilly and Associates.

Shirky, C. (2001). Listening to napster. In A. Oram (Ed.), *Peer-to-peer: Harnessing the benefits of a disruptive technology* (pp. 21-37). Sebastopol, CA: O'Reilly.

Shivanath, B., & Jennifer, W. (2001). Continuous queries over data streams. *SIGMOD Record, 30*(3), 109–120. doi:10.1145/603867.603884

Shivle, S., Siegel, H. J., Maciejewski, A. A., Banka, T., Chindam, K., Dussinger, S., et al. (2006). Mapping subtasks with multiple versions on an ad-hoc Grid, *Institute of Electrical and Electronics Engineers Heterogeneous Computing Workshop.*

Shivle, S., Siegel, H. J., Maclejewski, A. A., Sugavanam, P., Banka, T., & Castain, R. (2006). Static allocation of resources to communicating subtasks in a heterogeneous ad hoc grid environment. *Journal of Parallel and Distributed Computing, 66*(4), 600–611. doi:10.1016/j.jpdc.2005.10.005

Shokrollahi, A. (2006). Raptor Codes. *IEEE Transactions on Information Theory, 52*(6), 2551–2567. doi:10.1109/TIT.2006.874390

SHOP2. (2004). Retrieved from http://www.cs.umd.edu/projects/shop/

Shu, B., Ooi, Y., Tan, K., & Zhou, A. (2005). Supporting Multi-Dimensional Range Queries in Peer-to-Peer Systems. In *Fifth IEEE International Conference on Peer-to-Peer Computing (P2P 2005)* (pp. 173-180).

Shuen, A. (2008). *Web 2.0: A strategy guide.* Sebastopol, CA: O'Reilly Media, Inc.

Sih, G. C., & Lee, E. A. (1993a, June). Declustering: A New Multiprocessor Scheduling Technique. *Institute of*

Electrical and Electronics Engineers Transaction on Parallel and Distributed System, 4(6), 625–637.

Sih, G. C., & Lee, E. A. (1993b, February). A Compile-Time Scheduling Heuristic for Interconnection-Constrained Heterogeneous Processor Architectures. *Institute of Electrical and Electronics Engineers Transaction on Parallel and Distributed System, 4*(2), 175–186.

Silva, A.P.C., Borges, V.C.M., & Dantas, M.A.R. (2008). A framework for mobile Grid environments based on semantic integration of ontologies and workflow-based applications. *INFOCOMP - Journal of Computer Science 7*(1), 60-69.

Silva, J. F., Gaspary, L. P., Barcellos, M. P., & Detsch, A. (2005). A. policy-based access control in peer-to-peer grid systems. In *The 6th IEEE/ACM International Workshop on Grid Computing* (pp. 107-113).

Sim, K. M. (2007). Relaxed-criteria G-negotiation for grid resource co-allocation. *ACM SIGecom Exchanges, 6*(2), 37–46. doi:10.1145/1228621.1228625

Simeonidou, D., Zervas, G., Nejabati, R., Callegati, F., Campi, A., & Cerroni, W. (2007, September 10-14). SIP empowered OBS Network Architecture for Future IT Services and Applications. In *Proceedings of IEEE Broadnets 2007*, Raleigh, NC.

Simoens, P., De Vleeschauwer, B., Van de Meerssche, W., De Turck, F., Dhoedt, B., Demeester, P., et al. (2007). RTP Connection monitoring for enabling autonomous access network QoS management. In *11th European Conference on Networks and Optical Communications.*

Sinaga, J. M. P., Mohamed, H. H., & Epema, D. H. J. (2004). A dynamic co-allocation service in multicluster systems. In D. G. Feitelson, L. Rudolph, & U. Schwiegelshohn (Eds.), *International Workshop Job Scheduling Strategies for Parallel Processing* (Vol. 3277, p. 194-209). New York: Springer.

Singh, A., & Liu, L. (2003). Trustme: Anonymous management of trust relationships in decentralized p2p systems. In N. Shahmehri, R. Lee Graham, & G. Caronni, (Eds.), *Peer-to-Peer Computing*, (pp. 142–149). Washington, DC: IEEE Computer Society. Retrieved from http://dblp.uni-trier.de/db/conf/p2p/p2p2003.html#SinghL03

Singh, M. P. (2004).Agent-based Abstractions for Software Development - Accommodating Complexity in Open Systems. In F. Bergenti, M.P. Gleizes, F. Zambonelli, (Eds.), *Methodologies and Software Engineering for Agent Systems - The Agent-Oriented Software Engineering Handbook*. Amsterdam: Kluwer Academic Publishers.

Singh, M. P., & Huhns, M. (2005). *Service-Oriented Computing: Semantics, Processes, Agents*. Hoboken, NJ: John Wiley & Sons.

Sipkova, V., & Dobrucky, M. (2008). Towards an advanced distributed computing. In *Proceedings of the 4th International Workshop on Grid Computing for Complex problems (GCCP'2008)* (pp. 128-131).

Sistanizadeh, K. (2005). *Shaping the Future Development of the Networking Industry*. Yipes Enterprise Services Inc.

Sit, E., Haeberlen, A., Dabek, F., Chun, B.-G., Weatherspoon, H., Morris, R., et al. (2006). Proactive replication for data durability. In *the 5th international workshop on peer-to-peer systems*.

Sivaharan, T., Blair, G., & Coulson, G. (2005). GREEN: A configurable and re-configurable publish-subscribe middleware for pervasive computing. In R. Meersaman & Z. Tari (Eds.), *On the Move to Meaningful Internet Systems 2005: CoopIS, DOA, and ODBASE* (LNCS 3760, pp. 732-749). Berlin, Germany: Springer-Verlag.

Skillicorn, D. B. (2002). Motivating computational Grids. In *2nd IEEE/ACM International Symposium on Cluster Computing and the Grid(CCGRID'02)* (pp. 401-406).

SLA@SOI. (2008). *SLA@SOI project*. Retrieved December 5, 2008, from http://www.sla-at-soi.eu/

Sloman, M., & Lupu, E. (2002). Security and Management Policy Specification. *IEEE Network, 16*(2), 10–19. doi:10.1109/65.993218

Slomiski, A. (2006). On using BPEL extensibility to implement OGSI and WSRF Grid workflows. *Concurrency and Computation, 18*, 1229–1241. doi:10.1002/cpe.1004

Slot, M. (2005). Incentives for asymmetric peer-to-peer services. In *12th Americas Conference on Information Systems (AMCIS)*.

Smetters, D. K., & Durfee, G. (2003). Domain-based administration of identity-based cryptosystems for secure email and IPSEC. In *Proceedings of 12th USENIX Security Symposium,* (pp. 215-229).

Smirnova, E., So, C. M., & Watt, S. M. (2004). Providing mathematical Web services using Maple in the MONET architecture. In *Procs. MONET Workshop*. Retrieved November 2008 from http://monet.nag.co.uk/cocoon/monet/proceedings/

Smith, H., & Fingar, P. (2003). *Business Process Management: The Third Wave*. Tampa, FL: Meghan-Kiffer Press.

Smith, J., Watson, P., Gounaris, A., Paton, N. W., Fernandes, A. A. A., & Sakellariou, R. (2003). Distributed query processing on the Grid. *International Journal of High Performance Computing Applications, 17*(4), 353–367. doi:10.1177/10943420030174002

Snell, J. (2001). *Introducing the Web Services Flow Language*. Retrieved from November 10th, 2008, http://www.ibm.com/developerworks/library/ws-ref4/

Snell, Q., Clement, M. J., Jackson, D. B., & Gregory, C. (2000). The performance impact of advance reservation meta-scheduling. In D. G. Feitelson & L. Rudolph (Eds.), *International Workshop on Job Scheduling Strategies for Parallel Processing* (Vol. 1911, pp. 137-153). Berlin: Springer.

SOKU. (2006). Future for European Grids: GRIDs an Service Oriented Knowledge Utilities Vision and Research Directions 2010 and Beyond. *Next Generation GRIDs Expert Group Report,* 3.

Soldatos, J., Dimakis, N., Stamatis, K., & Polymenakos, L. (2007). A breadboard architecture for pervasive context-aware services in smart spaces: middleware components and prototype applications. *Personal and Ubiquitous Computing . Springer London, 11*(3), 193–212.

Solomon, A., & Struble, C. A. (2007). JavaMath - an API for Internet Accessible Mathematical Services. Asian Symposium on Computer Mathematics, Matsuyama, Japan, September 2001. In Shirayangi, K., Yokoyama, K. (Ed.), *Proceedings of Asian Symposium on Computer Mathematics*, (pp.151-160). Singapore: World Scientific

Son S.W., Kandemir, M., and Choudhary A. (2005, April). Software-directed disk power management for scientific applications. *Proc. Int'l Symp. Parallel and Distributed Processing.*

Son, S. W., & Kandemir, M. (2006, May). Energy-aware data prefetching for multi-speed disks. *Proc. ACM International Conference on Computing Frontiers*, Ischia, Italy.

Song, S., Hwang, K., Zhou, R., & Kwok, Y.-K. (2005). Trusted p2p transactions with fuzzy reputation aggregation. *IEEE Internet Computing, 9*(6), 24–34. Retrieved from http://dblp.uni-trier.de/db/journals/internet/internet9.html#SongHZK05

Sonmez, O., Mohamed, H., & Epema, D. (2006). Communication-aware job placement policies for the koala grid scheduler. In *International Conference on e-Science and Grid Computing* (p. 79). Los Alamitos, CA: IEEE Computer Science.

Sopcast. (2008). Retrieved from http://www.sopcast.org

SORMA. (2008). *SORMA - Self-Organizing ICT Resource Management*. Retrieved December 5, 2008, from http://sorma-project.org/

Sotomayor, B., & Childers, L. (2006). *Globus Toolkit 4: Programming Java Services*. San Francisco: Morgan Kauffman publishers.

Sozio, M., Neumann, T., & Weikum, G. (2008). Near-Optimal Dynamic Replication in Unstructured Peer-to-Peer Networks. In *Proc. PODS'08, 27th ACM SIGMOD-SIGACT-SIGART Symposium on Principles of Database Systems*, Vancouver, BC, Canada (pp. 281-290).

Spence, D., & Harris, T. (2003). XenoSearch: distributed resource discovery in the XenoServer open platform. In *Proceedings of the Twelfth IEEE International Symposium on High Performance Distributed Computing* (pp. 216-225). Washington, DC: IEEE Computer Society Press.

Spirent. (2004). *User Guide SmartFlow, Version 4.00.*

Springer, R., Lowenthal, D. K., Rountree, B., & Freeh, V. W. (2006). Minimizing execution time in MPI programs on an energyconstrained,power-scalable cluster. In *Proc. 11th ACM SIGPLAN Symposium on Principles and Practice of Parallel Programming (PPoPP'06)* (pp. 230-238).

Srinivasan, L., & Treadwell, J. (2005). *An overview of service-oriented architecture, web services and grid computing*. HP Software Global Business Unit.

Srinivasan, S. H. (2005, January). Pervasive wireless grid architecture. In *Proceedings of the Second Annual Conference on Wireless on-Demand Network Systems and Services* (pp. 83-88).

Srinivasan, S., & Jha, N. K. (1999, March). Safety and Reliability Driven Task Allocation in Distributed Systems. *Institute of Electrical and Electronics Engineers Transaction on Parallel and Distributed Systems, 10*(3), 238–251.

Sripanidkulchai, K., Maggs, B., & Zhang, H. (2003). *Efficient Content Location Using Interest-Based Locality in Peer-to-Peer Systems*. Paper presented at the IEEE Infocom, San Francisco.

Srisuresh, P., Ford, B., & Kegel, D. (2008). *State of Peer-to-Peer (P2P) Communication across Network Address Translators (NATs)* (Internet RFC 5128). Retrieved November 15, 2008, from http://www.ietf.org/rfc/rfc5128.txt

Srivatsa, M., Xiong, L., & Liu, L. (2005). Trustguard: countering vulnerabilities in reputation management for decentralized overlay networks. In *WWW'05: Proceedings of the 14th international conference on World Wide Web*, (pp. 422–431). New York: ACM. doi:http://doi.acm.org/10.1145/1060745.1060808.

St. Arnaud, B., et al. (2004). A Grid Oriented Lightpath Provisioning System. In *Proc. of Globecom 2004*, Dallas, TX.

St. Arnaud, B., et al. (2006, November). Layer 1 Virtual Private Network Management by Users. *IEEE Comm. Mag.*

Standard Performance Evaluation Corporation CFP2000. (2000). Retrieved from http://www.spec.org/cpu/CFP2000/

Stein, W. (2008). *Sage Mathematics Software.* London: The Sage Group. Retrieved November 2008 from http://www.sagemath.org/

Stoica, I., Adkins, D., Zhuang, S., Shenker, S., & Surana, S. (2002). Internet Indirection Infrastructure. In *Proceedings of SIGCOMM 2002.*

Stoica, I., Morris, R., Karger, D., Kaashoek, F., & Balakrishnan, H. (2001, September). Chord: A scalable peer-to-peer lookup service for internet applications. In *proceedings of ACM SIGCOMM 2001*, San Diego, CA, USA (pp. 149-160). New York: ACM Press.

Stoica, I., Morris, R., Liben-Nowell, D., Karger, D. R., Kaashoek, F. M., Dabek, F., & Balakrishnan, H. (2003). Chord: a scalable peer-to-peer lookup protocol for internet applications. *IEEE/ACM Transactions on Networking, 11*(1) 17-32.

Stone, P., & Veloso, M. (2000). *Multiagent systems: A Survey from a Machine Learning Perspective.* Tech. Rep. CMU-CS-97-193. Pittsburgh, PA: Carnegie Mellon University, School of Computer Science.

Stork. (2008). *Stork project.* Retrieved December 5, 2008, from http://www.storkproject.org/

Storz, O., Friday, A., & Davies, N. (2003). Towards 'ubiquitous' ubiquitous computing: An alliance with 'the Grid'. In *First Workshop on System Support for Ubiquitous Computing Workshop (Ubisys 2003) in association with Fifth International Conference on Ubiquitous Computing*, Seattle, WA.

Strassner, J. (2003). *Policy-Based Network Management: Solutions for the Next Generation.* San Francisco: Morgan Kaufmann.

Stratford, N., & Mortier, R. (1999). An Economic Approach to Adaptive Resource Management. In *7th Workshop on Hot Topics in Operating Systems,* (pp. 142-147). New York: IEEE Computer Society.

Stutzbach, D., & Rejaie, R. (2006). Improving Lookup Performance Over a Widely-Deployed DHT. In *Proceedings INFOCOM 2006, 25th IEEE International Conference on Computer Communications,* (pp. 1-12). doi: 10.1109/INFOCOM.2006.329

Stutzbach, D., & Rejaie, R. (2006). Understanding churn in peer-to-peer networks. In *Proceedings of Internet Measurement Conference* (pp. 189 - 202).

Subramoniam, K., Maheswaran, M., & Toulouse, M. (2002). Towards a micro-economic model for resource allocation in Grid computing systems. In *IEEE Canadian Conference on Electrical and Computer Engineering.*

Suh, K., Diot, C., Kurose, J., Massoulié, L., Neumann, C., Towsley, D. F., & Varvello, M. (2007). Push-to-peer video-on-demand system: Design and evaluation. *IEEE Journal on Selected Areas in Communications, 25*(9), 1706–1716. doi:10.1109/JSAC.2007.071209

Sulistio, A., Yeo, C. S., & Buyya, R. (2004). A taxonomy of computer-based simulations and its mapping to parallel and distributed systems simulation tools. *Software, Practice & Experience, 34*(7), 653–673. doi:10.1002/spe.585

Sun Cluster Grid. (2002). *Sun cluster grid architecture.* Retrieved May 11, 2009, from http://www.sun.com/software/grid/SunClusterGridArchitecture.pdf

Sun Microsystems. (n.d.). Retrieved May 11, 2009, from http://uk.sun.com/

Sun, Q., & Garcia-Molina, H. (2004). SLIC: A selfish link-based incentive mechanism for unstructured P2P networks. In *24th International Conference on Distributed Computing Systems* (pp. 506–515).

Sun, T., & Denko, M. K. (2007), A distributed trust management scheme in the pervasive computing environment. In *Canadian Conference on Electrical and Computer Engineering, CCECE 2007* (pp. 1219-1222).

Sun, X., & Wu, M. (2005). GHS: A Performance System of Grid Computing. In *19th IEEE International Parallel and Distributed Processing Symposium*. Washington, DC: IEEE. Retrieved November 12, 2008, from http://doi.ieeecomputersociety.org/10.1109/IPDPS.2005.234

Sundararaj, A. I., Gupta, A., & Dinda, P. A. (2004). Dynamic topology adaptation of virtual networks of virtual machines. In *LCR '04: Proceedings of the 7th Workshop on Workshop on Languages, Compilers, and Runtime Support for Scalable Systems* (pp. 1-8). New York: ACM Press.

Sun-Edeby. (2008). *Sun Edeby project*. Retrieved December 5, 2008, from http://hedeby.sunsource.net/

Surridge, M. (2002). *A Rough Guide to Grid Security*. Technical Report, IT Innovation Centre.

Surridge, M., Taylor, S., De Roure, D., & Zaluska, E. (2005). Experiences with GRIA — Industrial Applications on a Web Services Grid. In *the First International Conference on e-Science and Grid Computing* (pp. 98-105). Washington, DC: IEEE Press.

Suryanarayana, G., & Taylor, R. (2004). *A survey of trust management and resource discovery technologies in peer-to-peer applications*. ISR Technical Report UCI-ISR-04-06.

Susarla, S., & Carter, J. (2005). Flexible Consistency for Wide Area Peer Replication. In *Proc. ICDCS 2005, 25th IEEE Int'l Conference on Distributed Computing Systems*, Ohio, USA (pp. 199-208).

Sutherland, I. (1968). A futures market in computer time. *Communications of the ACM, 11*(6). The Grid Economy Project. (n.d.). Retrieved from http://www.gridbus.org/ecogrid/index.html

Swallow, G., Drake, J., Ishimatsu, H., & Rekhter, Y. (2005). *Generalized multiprotocol label switching (GMPLS) user-network interface (UNI), resource reservation protocol-traffic engineering (RSVP-TE) support for the overlay model*. RFC 4208, Internet Engineering Task Force (IETF).

SWSI. (2004). *Semantic Web services initiative (SWSI)*. Retrieved February 20, 2007 from http://www.swsi.org/

SWWS. (2004). *Semantic Web enabled Web service*. Digital Enterprise Research Institute (DERI).

Szewczyk, R., Mainwaring, A., Polastre, J., & Culler, D. (2004). An analysis of a large scale habitat monitoring application, *Conference on Embedded Networked Sensor Systems*, (pp. 214-226). New York: ACM.

Sztompka, P. (1999). *Trust: A Sociological Theory*. Cambridge, UK: Cambridge University Press.

Sztompka, P. (2007). *Zaufanie. Fundament Spo?eczen'stwa* (Trust. A Foundation of Society). Wydawnictwo Znak.

Szymaniak, M., Pierre, G., Simons-Nikolova, M., & van Steen, M. (2007). Enabling service adaptability with versatile anycast. *Concurrency and Computation, 19*(13), 1837–1863. doi:10.1002/cpe.1213

Szyperski, C. (1998). *Component Software, Beyond Object-Oriented Programming*. New York: ACM Press/Addison-Wesley.

Takefusa, A., Hayashi, M., Nagatsu, N., Nakada, H., Kudoh, T., & Miyamoto, T. (2006). G-lambda: Coordination of a grid scheduler and lambda path service over GMPLS. *Future Generation Computer Systems, 22*(8), 868–875. doi:10.1016/j.future.2006.03.005

Takefusa, A., Nakada, H., Kudoh, T., Tanaka, Y., & Sekiguchi, S. (2007). GridARS: an advance reservation-based grid co-allocation framework for distributed computing and network resources. In E. Frachtenberg & U. Schwiegelshohn (Eds.), *International Workshop on Job Scheduling Strategies for Parallel Processing*. Berlin: Springer.

Takemiya, H., Tanaka, Y., Sekiguchi, S., Ogata, S., Kalia, R. K., Nakano, A., et al. (2006). Sustainable adaptive grid supercomputing: multiscale simulation of semiconductor processing across the pacific. In *Conference on High Performance Networking and Computing* (p. 106). New York: ACM Press.

Talia, D., & Trunfio, P. (2003). Toward a synergy between P2P and grids. *IEEE Internet Computing, 7*(4), 96–95. doi:10.1109/MIC.2003.1215667

Talia, D., & Trunfio, P. (2004). Web services for peer-to-peer resource discovery on the Grid. In *DELOS Work-*

shop: Digital Library Architectures 2004. (pp.73-84). S. Margherita di Pula, Cagliari, Italy.

Talia, D., & Trunfio, P. (2004). A P2P Grid services-based protocol: Design and evaluation. In *Proceedings of the European Conference on Parallel Computing - EuroPar 2004.* [). Heidelberg, Germany: Springer-Berlin.]. *Lecture Notes in Computer Science, 3149,* 1022–1031.

Talia, D., & Trunfio, P. (2005). Peer-to-peer protocols and Grid services for resource discovery on Grids. In L.Grandinetti (Ed.), *Grid computing: The new frontier of high performance computing, advances in parallel computing* (Vol. 14). Eindhoven, The Netherlands: Elsevier Science.

Talia, D., Trunfio, P., Zeng, J., & Högqvist, M. (2008). A peer-to-peer framework for resource discovery in large-scale Grids. In *Achievements in European Research on Grid Systems* (pp. 123-137). Berlin, Germany: Springer.

Talwar, V., Basu, S., & Kumar, R. (2003). Architecture and environment for enabling interactive grids. *Grid Computing, 1*(3), 231–250. doi:10.1023/B:GRID.0000035188.36288.39

Tang, C., Xu, Z., & Dwarkadas, S. (2003). Peer-to-peer information retrieval using self-organizing semantic overlay networks. In *Proceedings of the ACM SIGCOMM 2003 conference on Applications, Technologies, Architectures, And Protocols for Computer Communications* (pp. 175-186).

Tavares, J., Velez, F. J., & Ferro, J. M. (2008). Application of Wireless Sensor Networks to Automobiles. *Measurement Science Review, 8*(3), 65–70. doi:10.2478/v10048-008-0017-8

Taverna. (2004). Retrieved from http://taverna.sourceforge.net/

Taylor, I. J., et al. (2006). *Workflows for e-Science: Scientific Workflows for Grids.* Berlin, Germany: Springer.

Taylor, I., Wang, I., Shields, M., & Majithia, S. (2005). Distributed computing with triana on the Grid. *Concurrency Computing: Practice Experiment, 17*(9), 1197–1214. doi:10.1002/cpe.901

Taylor, S. J. E., Popescu, G. V., Pullen, J. M., & Turner, S. J. (2004). Distributed Simulation and the Grid: Position Statements. In . *Proceedings of DS-RT, 2004,* 144–149.

Tempich, C., Staab, S., & Wranik, A. (2004). Remindin': semantic query routing in peer-to-peer networks based on social metaphors. In *Proceedings of the 13th international Conference on World Wide Web, WWW '04* (pp. 640-649). New York: ACM

TeraGrid. (2008). *TeraGrid website.* Retrieved December 5, 2008, from http://www.teragrid.org/

Tewari, S., & Kleinrock, L. (2005). Analysis of search and replication in unstructured peer-to-peer networks. In *Proc. of SIGMETRICS 2005,* Banff, Canada (pp 404-405).

Tewari, S., & Kleinrock, L. (2006). Proportional replication in peer-to-peer networks. In *Proc. of INFOCOM 2006,* Barcelona, Spain (pp 1-12).

Thackara, J. (2001). The design challenge of pervasive computing. *Interaction, 8*(3), 46–52. doi:10.1145/369825.369832

Thain, D., Tannenbaum, T., & Livny, M. (2003). Condor and the Grid. In F. Berman, A. J.G. Hey, & G. Fox (Eds.), *Grid computing: Making the global infrastructure a reality.* Hoboken, NJ: John Wiley.

Thatte, S. (2001). *XLANG Web Services for Business Process design.* Retrieved from http://www.ebpml.org/xlang.htm

The Gnutella Protocol Specification v0.4, Document Revision 1.2. (n.d.). Retrieved from http://www9.limewire.com/developer/gnutella_protocol_0.4.pdf

The Gnutella Protocol Specification v0.6, draft. (n.d.). Retrieved from http://rfc-gnutella.sourceforge.net/src/rfc-0_6-draft.html

The OpenNap Protocol Specification. (2000). Retrieved from http://opennap.sourceforge.net/

The P4P Working Group. (n.d.). Retrieved from http://www.pandonetworks.com/p4p

Theocharopoulos, E., & Jackson, M. (2008). *A WS-DAI implementation using OGSA-DAI.* DAIS Working Group Session, OGF22.

Tian, Y., Lau, L. M. S., & Dew, P. M. (2003). *A peer-to-peer knowledge sharing approach for networked research community.* Paper presented at the The Fifth International Conference on Enterprise Information Systems.

Tidwell. (2001). *UDDI4J: Matchmaking for Web services.* Retrieved from http://www.ibm.com/developerworks/library/ws-uddi4j.html

Tiny, O. S. *Homepage* (2004). UC, Berkeley, California, USA. Retrieved November 20, 2008, from http://www.tinyos.net

Tofslie, E. (2002). *OrganicGrid design.* Unpublished thesis. Retrieved May 11, 2009, from http://www.tofslie.com/organicgrid.pdf

Top 100 BOINC participants. (n.d.). Retrieved from http://boinc.berkeley.edu/chart list.php

Top500 Supercomputer List. (2008). Retrieved from http://www.top500.org

Topcuoglu, H., Hariri, S., & Min-You Wu. (2002). Performance-effective and low-complexity task scheduling for heterogeneous computing. *Parallel and Distributed Systems, IEEE Transactions on, 13*(3), 260-274. doi: 10.1109/71.993206.

Traversat, B. (2002). Project JXTA 2.0 Super-Peer Virtual Network. *Project JXTA, Sun Microsystems, Inc.* Retrieved July 8, 2008, from http://www.jxta.org/project/www/docs/JXTA2.0protocols1.pdf

Traversat, B., Abdelaziz, M., & Pouyoul, E. (2003). *Project JXTA: A Loosely-Consistent DHT Rendezvous Walker.* Sun Microsystems, Inc. Retrieved November 16, 2008, from http://research.sun.com/spotlight/misc/jxta-dht.pdf

Treadwell, J. (2005). *Open grid services architecture—Glossary of terms.* Global Grid Forum.

Triana Project. (2003). Retrieved from http://www.trianacode.org/

Triantafillou, P., & Pitoura, T. (2003). Towards a Unifying Framework for Complex Query Processing over Structured Peer-to-Peer Data Networks. In *Proceedings of the First International Workshop on DataBases, Information Systems and Peer-to-Peer Computing (DBISP2P).*

Trivers, R. (1985). *Social Evolution.* Menlo Park, CA: Benjamin Cummings.

Truelove, K. (2000). *To the bandwidth barrier and beyond.* Clip 2, Inc.

Trunfio, P., Talia, D., Papadakis, H., Fragopoulou, P., Mordacchini, M., & Pennanen, M. (2007). Peer-to-peer resource discovery in Grids: models and systems. *Future Generation Computer Systems, 23*(7), 864–878. doi:10.1016/j.future.2006.12.003

TrustCoM. (2008). *The TrustCoM project.* Retrieved December 5, 2008, from http://www.eu-trustcom.com/

Tsoumakos, D., & Roussopoulos, N. (2003). A comparison of peer-to-peer search methods. In *Proceedings of the International Workshop on the Web and Databases.*

Tsoumakos, D., & Roussopoulos, N. (2003). Adaptive probabilistic search for peer-to-peer networks. In *Proceedings of the 3rd IEEE International Conference on P2P Computing* (pp. 102- 109).

Tu, W., Sreenan, C. J., & Jia, W. (2007). Worst-Case Delay Control in Multigroup Overlay Networks. *IEEE Transactions on Parallel and Distributed Systems, 18*(10), 1407–1419. doi:10.1109/TPDS.2007.1074

Tuecke, S., Czajkowski, K., Foster, I., Frey, J., Graham, S., Kesselman, C., & Jennings, N. R. (2002). *Grid Service Specification.* Presented at GGF4, February, 2002. Retrieved from http://www.globus.org/research/papers.html

Tuecke, S., et al. (2003). *Open Grid Services Infrastructure (OGSI) Version 1.0.* Global Grid Forum Draft Recommendation. *SimTech: Stuttgart Research Centre for Simulation Technology at the University of Stuttgart.* (n.d.). Retrieved from http://www.simtech.uni-stuttgart.de/

Tuecke, S., Welch, V., Engert, D., Pearlman, L. & Thompson, M.R. (2004). Internet X.509 public key infrastructure proxy certificate profile. *The Internet Engineering Task Force (IETF),* RFC 3820.

Tuisku, M. (2003). Wireless Java-enabled MIDP devices as peers in a grid infrastructure. In G. Goos, J. Hartmanis, & J. van Leeuwen (Eds.), *Grid Computing* (pp. 273-281). Berlin / Heidelberg, Germany: Springer.

Turner, K. (2000). *Communication Representation Employing Systematic Specification.* Retrieved from http://www.cs.stir.ac.uk/~kjt/research/cress.html

Turner, M., Budgen, D., & Brereton, P. (2003). Turning software into a service. *IEEE Computer, 36*(10), 38–44. doi:10.1109/MCOM.2003.1235593

Tycoon. (2008). *Tycoon project.* Retrieved December 5, 2008, from http://tycoon.hpl.hp.com/

Tyler, T. R., & Smith, H. J. (1998). *The handbook of social psychology,* (Vol. 2, chapter Social justice and social movements, pp. 595–629). Boston: McGraw-Hill.

UK Ministry of Defence. (2005). *Defence Industrial Strategy* (Defence White Paper CM6697).

UK Ministry of Defence. (2005). *Joint Services Publication 777, Edition 1* (pp. 1).

UNICORE. (2008). *Uniform Interface to Computing Resources.* Retrieved December 5, 2008, from http://www.unicore.eu/

Univa. (2008). *Univa Grid MP.* Retrieved December 5, 2008, from http://www.univaud.com/hpc/products/grid-mp/

University of California. (2008), *Open-source software for volunteer computing and grid computing.* Retrieved October 2, 2008, from http://boinc.berkeley.edu/

Uppuluri, P., Jabisetti, N., Joshi, U., & Lee, Y. (2005). P2P Grid: Service oriented framework for distributed resource management. In *Proceedings of the 2005 IEEE International Conference on Services Computing* (Vol. 01, pp.347-350). Washington, DC: IEEE Computer Society.

Uppuluri, P., Jabisetti, N., Joshi, U., & Lee, Y. (2005). P2P Grid: Service Oriented Framework for Distributed Resource Management. In *Proceedings of the 2005 IEEE SCC'05,* (Vol.1, pp. 347-350).

Uribarren, A., Parra, J., Uribe, J. P., Makibar, K., Olalde, I., & Herrasti, N. (2006). Service oriented pervasive applications based on interoperable middleware. In *1st International Workshop on Requirments and Solutions for Pervasive Software Infrastructures (RSPSI).*

Uslaner, E. (2002). *The Moral Foundations of Trust.* UK: Cambridge University Press.

Vadhiyar, S. S., & Dongarra, J. J. (2003). A performance oriented migration framework for the Grid. In *3rd IEEE/ACM International Symposium on Cluster Computing and the Grid (CCGRID'03)* (pp. 130-137).

Van den Berghe, S., Surridge, M., Leonard, T. (2005). *Dynamic resource allocation and accounting in VOs.* NextGRID Deliverable P5.4.3.

van der Aalst, W. M. P., & Jablonski, S. (2000). Dealing with workflow change: identification of issues and solutions. *International Journal of Computer Systems Science and Engineering, 15*(5).

van der Aalst, W., & van Hee, K. (2002). *Workflow Management. Model, Methods and Systems.* Cambridge, MA: MIT Press.

Van der Ham, J., Grosso, P., Dijkstra, F., & de Laat, C. T. (2006, November 11 - 17). Semantics for hybrid networks using the network description language. In *Proceedings of the 2006 ACM/IEEE Conference on Supercomputing,* Tampa, FL.

Van Hoof, J. (2006). *How EDA extends SOA and why it is important.* Retrieved December 5, 2008, from http://jack.vanhoof.soa.eda.googlepages.com/-How_EDA_extends_SOA_and_why_it_is_important_-_Jack_van_Hoof_-_v6.0_-_2006.pdf

van Lessen, T., Nitzsche, J., Dimitrov, M., Konstantinov, M., Karastoyanova, D., & Cekov, L. (2007). An Execution Engine for Semantic Business Process. In *2nd International Workshop on Business Oriented*

Aspects concerning Semantics and Methodologies in Service-oriented Computing (SeMSoC), in conjunction with ICSOC 2007.

Van Renesse, R., Birman, K. P., & Vogels, W. (2003). Astrolabe: A robust and scalable technology for distributed system monitoring, management, and data mining. *ACM Transactions on Computer Systems, 21*(2), 164–206. doi:10.1145/762483.762485

van Renesse, R., Minsky, Y., & Hayden, M. (1998). A Gossip-Based Failure Detection Service. In *Proceedings of Middleware '98, the IFIP International Conference on Distributed Systems Platforms and Open Distributed Processing*, (pp. 55-70).

Vanderhulst, G., Luyten, K., & Coninx, K. (2007). Middleware for ubiquitous service-oriented spaces on the Web. In *Proceedings of the 21st International Conference on Advanced Information Networking and Applications Workshop* (pp. 1001-1006).

Vassiliadis, B., Giotopoulos, K., Votis, K., Sioutas, S., Bogonikolos, N., & Likothanassis, S. (2004). Application Service Provision through the Grid: Business Models and Architectures. In . *Proceedings of International Conference on Information Technology: Coding and Computing, 1*, 367–371. doi:10.1109/ITCC.2004.1286481

Vassiliadis, B., Stefani, A., Tsaknakis, J., & Tsakalidis, A. (2006). From Application Service Provision to Service Oriented Computing: A Study of the IT Outsourcing Evolution. *Telematics and Informatics, 23*, 271–293. doi:10.1016/j.tele.2005.09.001

Vazhkudai, S. (2003). Enabling the co-allocation of grid data transfers. In B. Werner (Ed.), *International Workshop on Grid Computing* (pp. 44-51). Los Alamitos, CA: IEEE Computer Society.

VDT. (2008). Virtual Data Toolkit. Retrieved December 5, 2008, from http://vdt.cs.wisc.edu/

Vecchio, D., & Son, S. H. (2005). Flexible update management in peer-to-peer database systems. In *Proc. IDEAS 2005, Int'l Database Engineering and Applications Symposium*, Montreal, Canada.

Venugopal, S., Buyya, R., & Ramamohanarao, K. (2006). A taxonomy of data grids for distributed data sharing, management and processing. *ACM Computing Surveys, 38*(1), 3. doi:10.1145/1132952.1132955

Verizon. (n.d.). Retrieved from http://www.verizon.com/

Verma, D. C. (2002). Simplifying Network Administration using Policy-Based Management. *IEEE Network, 16*(2), 20–26. doi:10.1109/65.993219

Verma, D. C. (2004). *Legitimate Applications of Peer-to-Peer Networks*. Hoboken, NJ: John Wiley & Sons.

Version, U. D. D. I. *2 Specifications*. (n.d.). Retrieved September 22, 2008, from http://www.oasis-open.org/committees/uddi-spec/doc/tcspecs.htm#uddiv2

Vickrey, W. (1961). Counterspeculation, Auctions, and Competitive Sealed Tenders. *The Journal of Finance, 16*(1), 8–37. doi:10.2307/2977633

Victor, P., Cornelis, C., & Cock, M. (2006). Enhanced recommendations through propagation of trust and distrust. *Proceedings of the 2006 IEEE/WIC/ACM international conference on Web Intelligence and Intelligent Agent Technology*, (pp. 263-266), Hong Kong. Washington, DC: IEEE Computer Society.

Vincent, J.-M., & Legrand, A. (2007). *Discrete event simulation*. Presentation for Laboratory ID-IMAG, France.

Vinod, R., Exarchakos, G., & Antonopoulos, N. (2009). Performance-driven Calibration of Gnutella Reconfiguration. *Peer-to-Peer Networking and Applications*.

Vinoski, S. (2002). Where is middleware? *IEEE Internet Computing, 6*(2), 83–85. doi:10.1109/4236.991448

VirtualBox. (2008). *Sun VirtualBox*. Retrieved December 5, 2008, from http://www.virtualbox.org/

Vishnumurthy, V., Chandrakumar, S., & Sirer, E. G. (2003). KARMA: A secure economic framework for peer-to-peer resource sharing. In *1st Workshop on Economics of Peer-to-Peer Systems*.

Vlavianos, A., Iliofotou, M., & Faloutsos, M. (2006). Bitos: Enhancing bittorent for supporting streaming applications. In . *Proceedings of INFOCOM, 2006*, 1–6.

VMAN. (2008). *DMTF Standards for Virtualization Management*. Retrieved December 5, 2008, from http://www.dmtf.org/initiatives/vman_initiative/

VMware. (2008). *VMware website*. Retrieved December 5, 2008, from http://www.vmware.com/

VMware-ESX. (2008). *VMware ESX website*. Retrieved December 5, 2008, from http://www.vmware.com/products/vi/esx/

Vogels, W. (2003). Web services are not distributed objects. *IEEE Internet Computing, 7*(6), 59–66. doi:10.1109/MIC.2003.1250585

Vogt, F. H., Zambrovski, S., Gruschko, B., Furniss, P., & Green, A. (2005). Implementing Web Service Protocols in SOA: WS-Coordination and WS-BusinessActivity. *CECW, 5*, 21–28.

Volper, D. E., Oh, J. C., & Jung, M. (2004). Game theoretical middleware for cpu sharing in untrusted p2p environment. In *Proceedings of PDCS*.

VOMS. (2008). *Virtual Organization Membership Service*. Retrieved December 5, 2008, from http://www.globus.org/grid_software/security/voms.php

Vratonjic, N., Gupta, P., Knezevic, N., Kostic, D., & Rowstron, A. (2007). Enabling dvd-like features in P2P video-on-demand systems. In *P2P-TV'07: Proceedings of the 2007 workshop on peer-to-peer streaming and IP-TV,* (pp. 329-334).

W3C Consortium. (2008). *Web Services Choreography Description Language Version 1.0*. Retrieved November 15, 2008, from http://www.w3.org/TR/ws-cdl-10

W3C. (2001). *W3C Note: Web services Description Language (WSDL) 1.1*. Retrieved from http://www.w3.org/TR/wsdl

W3C. (2002). *Web Service Choreography Interface (WSCI) 1.0*. Retrieved November 10th, 2008 from http://www.w3.org/TR/wsci/

W3C. (2002). Retrieved from http://www.w3.org

W3C. (2004). *OWL-S: Semantic Markup for Web Services*. Retrieved November 2, 2008, from http://www.w3.org/Submission/OWL-S/

W3C. (2008). *World Wide Web Consortium*. Retrieved November 2, 2008, from http://www.w3.org/

W3C. (n.d.). *W3C member submission: Web services policy framework*. Retrieved from http://www.w3.org/Submission/WS-Policy/

W3C. (n.d.). *Web services architecture*. Retrieved November 11, 2008, from http://www.w3.org/TR/ws-arch/

Wacker, A., Schiele, G., Holzapfel, S., & Weis, T. (2008). A NAT traversal mechanism for peer-to-peer networks. In *Eighth International Conference on Peer-to-Peer Computing* (pp. 81-83, 346-351).

Waloszek, G. (2002). Personal Networks. *SAP AG, Product Design Center*.

Wang, D., & Liu, J. (2008). A dynamic skip list-based overlay for on-demand media streaming with VCR interactions. *IEEE Transactions on Parallel and Distributed Systems, 19*(4), 503–514. doi:10.1109/TPDS.2007.70748

Wang, H., Zhu, Y., & Hu, Y. (2005). To Unify Structured and Unstructured P2P Systems. In *Proceedings of the 19th IEEE International Parallel and Distributed Processing Symposium: Vol. 1* (pp. 104.1). Washington, DC: IEEE Computer Society.

Wang, J., & Zhang, J. (2007). Federation Based Solution for Peer-to-Peer Network Management. In *Computational Science – ICCS 2007* (LNCS 4490, pp. 765-772).

Wang, L. (2007). Toward Agent-Based Grid Computing. In H. Lin (Ed.), *Architectural design of multi-agent systems: technologies and techniques,* (pp. 173-188). Hershey, PA: IGI Global publishing.

Wang, Y., & Vassileva, J. (2003). Trust and Reputation Model in Peer-To-Peer Networks. In *proceedings of the Third International Conference on Peer-to-Peer Computing (P2P'03)*, Linkoping, Sweden (pp. 150-157).

Wang, Y., & Vassileva, J. (2003). Trust and reputation model in peer-to-peer networks. In *P2P '03: Proceedings of the 3rd International Conference on Peer-to-Peer Computing,* (pp. 150). Washington, DC: IEEE Computer Society.

Wang, Z., Das, S. K., Kumar, M., & Shen, H. (2007). An efficient update propagation algorithm for p2p systems. *Computer Communications, 30,* 1106–1115. doi:10.1016/j.comcom.2006.11.005

Wang, Z., Kumar, M., Das, S. K., & Shen, H. (2006). File consistency maintenance through virtual servers in P2P systems. In *Proc. ISCC 2006, 11th IEEE Symposium on Computers and Communications,* Sardinia, Italy (pp. 435-441).

Want, R. (2008). Life, the universe, and the future of mobile computing. Keynote talk. In *Proceedings of the Sixth International Conference on Mobile Systems, Applications, and Services (MobiSys'08)* (p. 1). New York: ACM.

Warneke, B., Last, M., Liebowitz, B., & Pister, K. S. J. (2001). Smart Dust: Communication with a Cubic-Millimeter Computer. *Computer, 34*(1), 44–51. doi:10.1109/2.895117

Warren, M., Weigle, E., & Feng, W. (2002, November). High-density computing: a 240-node Beowulf in one cubic meter. In Proc. *ACM/IEEE Supercomputing'02 (SC'02).*

Waterhouse, S., Doolin, M. D., Kan, G., & Faybishenko, Y. (2002). Distributed Search in P2P Networks. *IEEE Internet Computing, 6*(1), 68–72. doi:10.1109/4236.978371

Watts, D. J. (2003). *Six Degrees: The Science Of A Connected Age.* New York: W.W. Norton & Company.

Watts, D. J., & Strogatz, S. H. (1998). Collective dynamics of 'small-world' networks. *Nature, 393,* 440–442. doi:10.1038/30918

Wax, L. (n.d.). *Aerogility.* Retrieved November 6, 2008, from http://www.aerogility.com/

WCN. *Wireless Community Networks.* (2003). Retrieved from http://wcn.cnt.org

Weatherspoon, H., & Kubiatowicz, J. (2002). Erasure Coding vs. Replication: A Quantitative Comparison. In *Proc. of IPTPS 2002,* Cambridge, MA, USA (pp 328-338).

Web services Notification. (2004). Retrieved from http://www-106.ibm.com/developerworks/library/specification/ws-notification/

Weel, J. (2008). *Gossiptron: Efficient sharing on the grid without central coordination.* Master's thesis, Vrije Universiteit, Amsterdam, The Netherlands.

Weerawarana, S., Curbera, F., Leymann, F., Storey, T., & Ferguson, D. F. (2005). *Web services Platform Architecture.* Upper Saddle River, NJ: Prentice Hall.

Weiser, M. (1991). The computer for the twenty-first century. *Scientific American, 265*(3), 94–101.

Weiser, M., & Brown, J. S. (1997). The coming age of calm technology. In P. Denning & R. Metcalfe (Eds.), *Beyond calculation: The next fifty years of computing.* New York: Springer-Verlag, Inc.

Weiss, G. (1999). *Multiagent Systems: A modern approach to distributed artificial intelligence.* Cambridge, MA: The MIT Press.

Weisstein, E. W. (n.d.). *Voronoi diagram.* From Math-World - A Wolfram Web Resource. Retrieved from http://mathworld.wolfram.com/VoronoiDiagram.html

Welch, V., Foster, I., Kesselman, C., Mulmo, O., Pearlman, L., Tuecke, S., et al. (2004). X.509 proxy certificates for dynamic delegation. In *Proceedings of the 3rd Annual PKI R&D Workshop,* (pp. 42-58). NIST.

Welch, V., Siebenlist, F., Foster, I., Bresnahan, J., Czajkowski, K., Gawor, J., et al. (2003). Security for grid services. In *Proceedings of the 12th IEEE International Symposium on High Performance Distributed Computing (HPDC-12 2003),* (pp. 48-61). Washington, DC: IEEE Computer Society Press.

Wesner, S., Jähnert, J. M., & Aranzazu Toro Escudero, M. (2006). *Mobile collaborative business grids - a short overview of the Akogrimo project.* Whitepaper.

Wierzbicki, A. (2007). The case for fairness of trust management. *Special issue of Electronic Notes in Theoretical Computer Science*.

Wierzbicki, A., & Kaszuba, T. (2007). Practical trust management without reputation in peer-to-peer games. *Multiagent and Grid Systems, 3*(4), 411–428. Retrieved from http://dblp.uni-trier.de/db/journals/mags/mags3.html#WierzbickiK07

Wierzbicki, A., & Kucharski, T. (2004). *P2p scrabble. can p2p games commence?* Retrieved from http://dblp.uni-trier.de/db/conf/p2p/p2p2004.html#WierzbickiK04

Wierzbicki, A., & Nielek, R. (2008). Fairness emergence through simple reputation. In S. Furnell, S. K. Katsikas, & A. Lioy, (Eds.), *Trust, Privacy and Security in Digital Business* (LNCS, pp. 77–89). Berlin: Springer. Retrieved from http://www.springerlink.com/content/951706w307060326/?p=2d15028d80a94e76b1170c3dc1e3d776&pi=0

Wierzbicki, A., Leibowitz, N., Ripeanu, M., & Wozniak, R. (2004, April). Cache replacement policies revisited: The case of p2p traffic. In *Proc of GP2P*, Chicago, IL.

Wildstrom, J., Stone, P., Witchel, E., Mooney, R. J., & Dahlin, M. (2005). Towards self-configuring hardware for distributed computer systems. In *the Second International Conference on Autonomic Computing* (pp. 241-249). Washington, DC: IEEE Computer Society.

Williams, V., & Petrovic, M. (2008). JXTA Framework. *JXTA Community Project*. Retrieved November 16, 2008, from https://jxta.dev.java.net/

Wilson, E. O. (1975). *Sociobiology*. Cambridge, MA: Harvard University Press.

Wi-Max. (2008). *WiMAX Network Deployment - Implementation and Trends*. Retrieved from http://www.companiesandmarkets.com

Winer, D. (2003, June 1). *XML-RPC Specification*. Retrieved from http://www.xmlrpc.com/spec

WiredReach. (n.d.). Retrieved October 7, 2008, from http://www.wiredreach.com/

Wireless Grids. (2008). *Introducing Innovaticus*. Retrieved April 5, 2008 from http://www.wgrids.com/products.html

WL-BOSS. (2008). *WareLite Business Operating Support System*. Retrieved December 5, 2008, from http://www.warelite.net/content/products_home.html

Wolfram Research. (2001). *WebMathematica*. Retrieved November 2008 from http://www.wolfram.com/products/webmathematica/

Wolfram Research. (2003). *gridMathematica*. Retrieved November 2008 from http://www.wolfram.com/products/gridmathematica/

Wolski, R., Brevik, J., Plank, J. S., & Bryan, T. (2003). Grid resource allocation and control using computational economies. In F. Berman, G. Fox, & A. Hey, (Eds.), *Grid Computing: Making The Global Infrastructure a Reality*. Chicester, UK: John Wiley & Sons. Retrieved from http://www.cs.utk.edu/~plank/plank/papers/Grid03.html

Wolski, R., Spring, N. T., & Hayes, J. (1999). The network weather service: A distributed resource performance forecasting service for metacomputing. *Future Generation Computer Systems, 15*(5-6), 757–768. doi:10.1016/S0167-739X(99)00025-4

Wong, T., Katz, R., & McCanne, S. (2000). An evaluation of preference clustering in large scale multicast applications. In *Proceedings of Infocom 2000*.

Woodside, C. M., & Monforton, G. G. (1993, February). Fast Allocation of Processes in Distributed and Parallel systems. *Institute of Electrical and Electronics Engineers Transaction on Parallel and Distributed System, 4*(2), 164–174.

Woolridge, M., & Jennings, N. R. (1995). Intelligent Agents: Theory and Practice. *The Knowledge Engineering Review, 10*(2), 115–152. doi:10.1017/S0269888900008122

WS-Agreement. (2007). *Web Services Agreement Specification*. Retrieved December 5, 2008, from http://www.ogf.org/documents/GFD.107.pdf

WS-BPEL. (2008). *OASIS Web Services Business Process Execution Language (WSBPEL) TC.* Retrieved December 5, 2008, from http://www.oasis-open.org/committees/tc_home.php?wg_abbrev=wsbpel

WSDL2Java. (2000). Retrieved from http://ws.apache.org/axis/java/user-guide.htm

WSDL4J. (2005). Retrieved from http://sourceforge.net/projects/wsdl4j

WSLA. (2008). *Web Service Level Agreements.* Retrieved December 5, 2008, from http://www.research.ibm.com/wsla/

WSML. (2004). Web Service Modeling Language (WSML). Retrieved February 20, 2007 from http://www.wsmo.org/wsml/

WSMO. (2004). *A conceptual comparison between WSMO and OWL-S.* Retrieved November 2, 2008, from http://www.wsmo.org/

WSMO. (2004). *WSMO Working Draft.* Retrieved September 20, 2004 from http://www.wsmo.org/2004/d2/v1.0/

WSMO. (2008). *Web service modeling ontology.* Retrieved November 2, 2008, from http://www.wsmo.org/

WSMX. (2004). Web services execution environment (WSMX). Retrieved February 20, 2007 from http://www.wsmx.org

WS-Policy. (2008). *Web Services Policy Framework.* Retrieved December 5, 2008, from http://www.w3.org/Submission/WS-Policy/

WS-PolicyAttachment. (2008). *Web Services Policy Attachment.* Retrieved December 5, 2008, from http://www.w3.org/Submission/WS-PolicyAttachment/

WS-PolicyConstraints. (2008). *XACML-based Web Services Policy Constraint Language.* Sun Research. Retrieved December 5, 2008, from http://research.sun.com/projects/xacml

WSRF. (2008). *OASIS WSRF standard.* Retrieved December 5, 2008, from http://www.oasis-open.org/committees/tc_home.php?wg_abbrev=wsrf

Wu, C.-L., Liao, C.-F., & Fu, L.-C. (2007). Service-oriented smart-home architecture based on osgi and mobile-agent technology. *IEEE Transactions on Systems, Man and Cybernetics. Part C, Applications and Reviews, 37*(2), 193–205. doi:10.1109/TSMCC.2006.886997

Wu, D., Tian, Y., Ng, K.-W., & Datta, A. (2008). Stochastic analysis of the interplay between object maintenance and churn. *Elsevier Computer Communications, 31*(2), 220–239.

Wu, L., He, Y., Wu, D., & Cui, J. (2008). A novel interoperable model of distributed UDDI. In *International Conference on Networking, Architecture and Storage* (pp. 12-14, 153-154).

Wulf, W. A., & McKee, S. A. (1994). *Hitting the Memory Wall: Implications of the Obvious.* Department of Computer Science, University of Virginia.

X.509. (1999). *Internet X.509 Public Key Infrastructure Certificate Management Protocols.* IETF RFC2510.

X.509-Proxy. (2004). *Internet X.509 Public Key Infrastructure (PKI) Proxy Certificate Profile.* IETF RFC3820.

XACML. (2008). *OASIS eXtensible Access Control Markup Language (XACML) TC.* Retrieved December 5, 2008, from http://www.oasis-open.org/committees/tc_home.php?wg_abbrev=xacml

Xen. (2008). Retrieved December 5, 2008, from http://www.xen.org/

Xen-Server. (2008). *Xen Server website.* Retrieved December 5, 2008, from http://citrix.com/English/ps2/products/product.asp?contentID=683148

Xiao, H., Wu, H., Chi, X., Deng, S., & Zhang, H. (2005). An implementation of interactive jobs submission for grid computing portals. In *Proceedings of the Australasian Workshop on Grid Computing and e-Research (Aus-Grid2005),* (pp. 67-68). Newcastle, Australia.

Xiao, L., Liu, Y., & Ni, L. M. (2005). Improving Unstructured Peer-to-Peer Systems by Adaptive Connection Establishment. *IEEE Transactions on Computers, 54,* 176–184. doi:10.1109/TC.2005.33

Xie, H., Krishnamurthy, A., & Yang, R., et al. (2007, March). *P4P: Proactive Provider Participation for P2P* (YALE/DCS/TR1377). Yale Computer Science.

Xie, H., Krishnamurthy, A., Silberschatz, A., & Yang, Y. R. (2008). *P4P: Explicit Communications for Cooperative Control Between P2P and Network Providers.* Retrieved April 14, 2009, from http://www.dcia.info/documents/P4P_Overview.pdf

Xie, H., Yang, Y. R., Krishnamurthy, A., Liu, Y. G., & Silberschatz, A. (2008). P4P: provider portal for applications. In *Proceedings of the ACM SIGCOMM 2008 conference on Data communication,* (pp. 351-362). Seattle, WA: ACM. doi: 10.1145/1402958.1402999

Xiong, L., & Liu, L. (2002). Building trust in decentralized peer-to-peer electronic communities. In *Fifth International Conference on Electronic Commerce Research (ICECR),* Montreal, Canada.

Xiong, L., & Liu, L. (2003). A reputation-based trust model for peer-to-peer ecommerce communities. In *Proceedings of the Fourth ACM Conference on Electronic Commerce,* San Diego.

Xiong, L., & Liu, L. (2004). Peertrust: Supporting reputation-based trust for peer-to-peer electronic communities. *IEEE Transactions on Knowledge and Data Engineering, 16*(7), 843–857. doi:10.1109/TKDE.2004.1318566

Xiu, D., & Liu, Z. (2005). A dynamic trust model for pervasive computing environments. In *Proceedings of the Fourth Annual Security Conference,* Las Vegas, NV.

XTP. (2008). *Extreme Transaction Processing.* Retrieved December 5, 2008, from http://en.wikipedia.org/wiki/Extreme_Transaction_Processing

Xu, D., Nahrstedt, K., & Wichadakul, D. (2001). QoS and contention-aware multi-resource reservation. *Cluster Computing, 4*(2), 95–107. doi:10.1023/A:1011408729750

Xu, L. (2004). A multi-party contract model. *ACM SIGecom Exchanges, 5*(1), 13–23. doi:10.1145/1120694.1120697

Xu, T., Ye, B., Kubo, M., Shinozaki, A., & Lu, S. (2008). A Gnutella inspired ubiquitous service discovery framework for pervasive computing environment. In *8th IEEE International Conference on Computer and Information Technology, CIT 2008* (pp. 712-717).

Xu, W., Xin, Y., & Lu, G. (2007). A trust framework for pervasive computing environments. In *International Conference on Wireless Communications, Networking and Mobile Computing, WiCom 2007* (pp. 2222-2225).

Xu, Z., Xiao, L., & Liu, X. (2007). Personal grid. In *Proceedings of Network and Parallel Computing (NPC2007)* (pp. 536-540).

Yahya, S., Faiza, N., & Najla, M. (2004). An adaptive cost model for distributed query optimization on the Grid. In *Proceedings OTM 2004 Workshops.* (LNCS 3292, pp. 79-87).

Yajnik, S., Srinivasan, S., & Jha, N. K. (1994, October). TBFT: A Task-Based Fault Tolerance Scheme for Distributed Systems. *International Conference Parallel and Distributed Computer Systems.*

Yalagandula, P., & Dahlin, M. (2004). A scalable distributed information management system. *ACM SIGCOMM Computer Communication Review, 34*(4), 379–390. doi:10.1145/1030194.1015509

Yang, B., & Garcia-Molina, H. (2002). *Efficient Search in Peer-to-Peer Networks.* Paper presented at the International Conference on Distributed Computing Systems, Vienna, Austria.

Yang, B., & Garcia-Molina, H. (2002). Improving search in peer-to-peer networks. In *Proceedings of the 22nd International Conference on Distributed Computing Systems* (pp. 5- 14).

Yang, B., & Garcia-Molina, H. (2003). Designing a super-peer network. In *19th International Conference on Data Engineering* (pp.49-60). Washington, DC: IEEE Computer Society.

Yang, B., Condie, T., Kamvar, S., & Garcia-Molina, H. (2005). Non-cooperation in competitive P2P networks. In *25th IEEE International Conference on Distributed Computing Systems* (pp. 91-100).

Yang, C.-T., Yang, I.-H., Wang, S.-Y., Hsu, C.-H., & Li, K.-C. (2007). A recursively-adjusting co-allocation scheme with cyber-transformer in data grids. *Future Generation Computer Systems*.[INSERT FIGURE 001]Retrieved January 21, 2007, from http://dx.doi.org/doi:10.1016/j.future.2006.11.005.

Yang, H.-I., Jansen, E., & Helal, S. (2006). A comparison of two programming models for pervasive computing. In *Proceedings of Ubiquitous Networking and Enablers to Context Aware Services, International Symposium on Applications and the Internet.*

Yang, J., Li, M., Huang, C., & Gao, C. (2005). WGMDS: A WSRF-compliant information service on wireless Grids. In M. Li (Ed.), *Proceedings of the Sixth International Conference on Parallel and Distributed Computing, Applications and Technologies PDCAT* (pp. 103-105).

Yang, J., Papazoglou, M. P., & van den Heuvel, W. J. (2002). Tackling the Challenges of Service Composition in e-Marketplaces. In *Proceedings of the 12th International Workshop on Research Issues on Data Engineering: Engineering E-Commerce/E-Business Systems (RIDE-2EC 2002)*, San Jose, CA.

Yang, S. (2002). *Wireless sensors from UC Berkeley and Intel researchers help conversation biologists monitor exclusive seabird in Maine*. Berkeley, CA: University of California at Berkeley, Media Relations. Retrieved November 20, 2008, from http://www.universityofcalifornia.edu/news/article/4602

Yankee. (2008). *Virtualization as Enterprise Solution of Choice*. Yankee Group.

Yao, F., Demers, A., & Shenker, S. (1995). A Scheduling Model for Reduced CPU Energy. *Institute of Electrical and Electronics Engineers Annual Foundations of Computer Science*, 374-382.

YarKhan. A., Dongarra, J. & Seymour, K. (2007). GridSolve: The evolution of network enabled solver. In A. Prescott (ed), *Procs. WoCo9, Series IFIP Intern. Federation for Information Processing*, (vol. 239, pp.215–224). Berlin: Springer.

Yavatkar, R., Pendarakis, D., & Guerin, R. (2000). *A Framework for Policy Based Admission Control* (Internet RFC 2753). Retrieved November 15, 2008, from http://www.ietf.org/rfc/rfc2753.txt

Ye, Z., & Zhou, X. (2008). Involvement of cognitive control in sentence comprehension: Evidence from erps. *Brain Research*, *1203*, 103–115. doi:10.1016/j.brainres.2008.01.090

Yeo, C. S., & Buyya, R. (2007). Pricing for Utility-driven Resource Management and Allocation in Clusters. [Sage Publications, Inc. Thousand Oaks, CA, USA.]. *International Journal of High Performance Computing Applications*, *21*(4), 405–418. doi:10.1177/1094342007083776

Yeo, C. S., de Assuncao, M. D., Yu, J., Sulistio, A., Venugopal, S., Placek, M., et al. (2007). Utility computing and global grids. In H. Bidgoli (Ed.), *The handbook of computer networks*. New York: John Wiley & Sons.

Yiu, W. P. K., Jin, X., & Chan, S. H. G. (2007). Vmesh: Distributed segment storage for peer-to-peer interactive video streaming. *IEEE Journal on Selected Areas in Communications*, *25*(9), 1717–1731. doi:10.1109/JSAC.2007.071210

Yoon, H. (2007). A convergence of context-awareness and service-orientation in ubiquitous computing. *IJCSNS International Journal of Computer Science and Network Security*, *7*(3), 253–257.

Yoshimoto, K., Kovatch, P. A., & Andrews, P. (2005). Co-scheduling with user-settable reservations. In D. G. Feitelson, E. Frachtenberg, L. Rudolph, & U. Schwiegelshohn (Eds.), *International Workshop on Job Scheduling Strategies for Parallel Processing* (Vol. 3834, pp. 146-156). Berlin: Springer.

Youtube. (n.d.). Retrieved from http:// www.youtube.com

Yu, B., Singh, M. P., & Sycara, K. (2004). Developing trust in large-scale peer-to-peer systems. In *Proceedings of First IEEE Symposium on Multi-Agent Security and Survivability*, (pp. 1–10). Retrieved from http://jmvidal.cse.sc.edu/library/yu04a.pdf

Yu, C. T., & Meng, W. (1997). *Principles of database query processing for advanced applications*. San Francisco: Morgan Kaufmann.

Yu, J., & Buyya, R. (2005). A taxonomy of workflow management systems for Grid computing. *Journal of*

Grid Computing, 3(3-4), 171–200. doi:10.1007/s10723-005-9010-8

Yu, W., Ginis, G., & Cioffi, J. (2002). Distributed Multiuser Power Control for Digital Subscriber Line. *IEEE Journal on Selected Areas in Communications, 20*(5), 1105–1115. doi:10.1109/JSAC.2002.1007390

Yu-Ju, L., Latchman, H. A., Newman, R. E., & Katar, S. (2003). A comparative performance study of wireless and power line networks. *IEEE Communications Magazine, 41*(4), 54–63. doi:10.1109/MCOM.2003.1193975

Zanikolas, S., & Sakellariou, R. (2005). A taxonomy of grid monitoring systems. *Future Generation Computer Systems*. Retrieved from http://linkinghub.elsevier.com/retrieve/pii/S0167739X04001190

Zao, J. K., Yu-Chih, L., Ming-Hsiao, Y., Sheng-Kun, L., Wei-Yu, C., Ching-Wei, C., et al. (2007). Ubiquitous e-helpers: An UPnP-based home automation platform. In *IEEE International Conference on Systems, Man and Cybernetic* (pp. 3682-3689).

Zeinalipour-Yazti, D., Kalogeraki, V., & Gunopulos, D. (2003). Information Retrieval in Peer-to-Peer Networks. In *International Conference on Computer, Information, and Systems Science, and Engineering CISE 2003.*

Zervas, G., Nejabati, R., Campi, A., Qin, Y., Simeonidou, D., Callegati, F., et al. (2007, September). Demonstration of a Fully Functional Optical Burst Switched Network with Application Layer Resource Reservation Capability. In *33nd European Conference on Optical Communication (ECOC 2007)*, Berlin, Germany.

Zervas, G., Qin, Y., Nejabati, R., Simeonidou, D., Callegati, F., Campi, A., & Cerroni, W. (2008). SIP-enabled Optical Burst Switching architectures and protocols for application-aware optical networks. *Computer Networks.*

Zervas, G., Qin, Y., Nejabati, R., Simeonidou, D., Campi, A., Cerroni, W., & Callegati, F. (2008). Demonstration of Application Layer Service Provisioning Integrated on Full-Duplex Optical Burst Switching Network Test-bed. In *OFC 2008*, California, USA.

Zhang, C., Krishnamurthy, A., & Wang, R. (2005). Brushwood: Distributed Trees in Peer-to-Peer Systems. In . *Proceedings of IPTPS, 2005*, 47–57.

Zhang, H., Goel, A., & Govindan, R. (2004). Using the small-world model to improve Freenet performance. *Computer Networks, 46*, 555–574. doi:10.1016/j.comnet.2004.06.003

Zhang, K., Li, Q., & Sui, Q. (2006). A goal-driven approach of service composition for pervasive computing. In *1st International Symposium on Pervasive Computing and Applications* (pp. 593-598).

Zhang, L., Li, J., & Lam, H. (2004). Toward a Business Process Grid for Utility Computing. *IT Professional, 6*, 62–64. doi:10.1109/MITP.2004.25

Zhang, L., Zhang, J., & Cai, H. (2007). *Services Computing*. Berlin: Co-published by Tsinghua University Press and Springer- Verlag.

Zhang, P., Sadler, C. M., Lyon, S. A., & Mortonosi, M. (2004). Hardware Design Experience in ZebraNet, (n.d.). *Conference On Embedded Networked Sensor Systems*, (pp. 227-238).New York: ACM.

Zhang, Q., Yu, T., & Irwin, K. (2004). A classification scheme for trust functions in reputation-based trust management. In *ISWC Workshop on Trust, Security, and Reputation on the Semantic Web, Vol. 127, CEUR Workshop Proceedings.*

Zhang, X., & Qiao, C. (1998). Wavelength assignment for dynamic traffic in multi-fiber WDM networks. In *IEEE International Conference on Computer Communications and Networks* (pp. 479-485).

Zhang, X., Liu, J., Li, B., & Yum, T. S. (2005). Coolstreaming/donet: A data-driven overlay network for peer-to-peer live media streaming. In . *Proceedings of IEEE INFOCOM, 2005*, 2102–2111.

Zhang, Z., Shi, S., & Zhu, J. (2003). SOMO: Self-organized metadata overlay for resource management in P2P DHT. In *Peer-to-Peer Systems II* (LNCS 2735, pp. 170-182). Berlin, Germany: Springer.

Zhao, B. Y., Huang, L., Stribling, J., Rhea, S. C., Joseph, A. D., & Kubiatowicz, J. D. (2004). Tapestry: a resilient global-scale overlay for service deployment. *IEEE Journal on Selected Areas in Communications, 22*(1), 41–53. doi:10.1109/JSAC.2003.818784

Zhao, H., & Li, X. (2008). H-trust: A robust and light-weight group reputation system for peer-to-peer desktop grid. In *Proc. 28th International Conference on Distributed Computing Systems Workshops ICDCS '08*, (pp. 235–240). doi: 10.1109/ICDCS.Workshops.2008.96.

Zhao, S., Stutzbach, D., & Rejaie, R. (2006). Characterizing files in the modern Gnutella network: A measurement study. In *Proceedings of SPIE/ACM Multimedia Computing and Networking.*

Zheng, X. Y., Chang, G. R., Zhen, L., & Jian, W. (2008). A resource-centric P2P network model for Grid resource discovery. *ISECS International Colloquium on Computing, Communication. Control and Management, 1*(1), 210–214.

Zhou, G., & Yu, J. Chen, R, & Zhang, H. (2007). Scalable Web service discovery on P2P overlay network. In *IEEE International Computing on Services Computing 2007*(pp.122-129). Washington, DC: IEEE Computer Society.

Zhou, R., & Hwang, K. (2007). Gossip-based reputation aggregation for unstructured peer-to-peer networks. *ipdps, 0*(95). doi: http://doi.ieeecomputersociety.org/10.1109/IPDPS.2007.370285

Zhou, R., & Hwang, K. (2007). Powertrust: A robust and scalable reputation system for trusted peer-to-peer computing. *IEEE Trans. Parallel Distrib. Syst., 18*(4), 460–473. Retrieved from http://dblp.uni-trier.de/db/journals/tpds/tpds18.html#ZhouH07

Zhu, C., Liu, Z., Zhang, W., Xiao, W., Xul, Z., & Yang, D. (2004). Decentralized Grid resource discovery based on resource information community. *Journal of Grid Computing, 2*(3), 261–277. doi:10.1007/s10723-004-2810-4

Zhu, F., Mutka, M. W., & Ni, L. M. (2005). Service discovery in pervasive computing environments. *IEEE Pervasive Computing / IEEE Computer Society [and] IEEE Communications Society, 4*(4), 81–90. doi:10.1109/MPRV.2005.87

Zhu, Q., David, F. M., Devaaraj, C. F., Li, Z., Zhou, Y., & Cao, P. (2004). Reducing Energy Consumption of Disk Storage Using Power-Aware Cache Management. *Proc. High-Performance Computer Framework.*

Zhu, X., Zhang, D., Li, W., & Huang, K. (2007). Prediction-based fair replication algorithm in structured p2p Systems. In *Proc. ATC 2007, 4th Int'l Conference on Autonomic and Trusted Computing*, Hong Kong, China (pp. 499-508).

Zimmer, J., Franke, A., & Kohlhase, M. (2006). *MATHWEB-SB: A software bus for MathWeb.* Retrieved November 2008 from http://www.mathweb.org/mathweb/

Zimmermann, H. (1980). Innovations in Internetworking, OSI Reference Model – The ISO Model of Architecture for Open Systems Interconnection. [Norwood, MA: Artech House Inc.]. *IEEE Transactions on Communications*, 425–432. doi:10.1109/TCOM.1980.1094702

Zong, Z.-L., Manzanares, A., Stinar, B., & Qin, X. (2006, September). Energy-Efficient Duplication Strategies for Scheduling Precedence Constrained Parallel Tasks on Clusters. *International Conference Cluster Computing.*

Zugenmaier, A., & Walter, T. (2007). Security in pervasive computing calling for new security principles. In *IEEE International Conference on Pervasive Services* (pp. 96-99).

About the Contributors

Nick Antonopoulos is currently the Head of School of Computing and Assistant Dean (Research) of the Faculty of Business, Computing & Law at the University of Derby, UK. Prior to joining Derby he was a Senior Lecturer (US Associate Professor) at the Department of Computing, University of Surrey, UK. He holds a BSc in Physics (1st class) from the University of Athens in1993, an MSc in Information Technology from Aston University in 1994 and a PhD in Computer Science from the University of Surrey in 2000. Before joining the academia he has worked as a networks consultant and was the co-founder and director of a company developing Web-based management information systems. He has over 10 years of academic experience during which he has designed and has been managing advanced Masters programmes in computer science at the University of Surrey. He has published about 70 articles in fully refereed journals and international conferences. He has received a number of best paper awards in conferences and graduated 6 PhD students. He was the organiser and chair of the 1st International Workshop on Computational P2P networks and the 1st International Workshop on Service-Oriented P2P Networks (as part of IEEE Symposium in Cluster Computing and the Grid, CCGrid 2009). He is currently the organiser and chair of the 1st International Conference on Advances in P2P Systems to take place in Malta, October 2009, sponsored by IEEE. He is on the editorial board of the Springer journal of Peer-to-Peer Networking and Applications and on the advisory editorial board of the IGI Global Handbook of Research on Telecommunications Planning and Management for Business. He is a Fellow of the UK Higher Education Academy and a full member of the British Computer Society. His research interests include emerging technologies such as large scale distributed systems and peer-to-peer networks, software agent architectures and security.

George Exarchakos is a Researcher in P2P Computing having completed his PhD in the Department of Computing at the University of Surrey, in 2009. He successfully completed the BSc in Informatics and Telecommunications of the University of Athens in 2004. The same year joined the MSc in Advanced Computing at Imperial College London to complete it in 2005. He collaborated with Network Operation Centre of the University of Athens from 2003 till 2004. His achievements include one best paper award in the International Network Conference 2006 and a best presentation award in the IEEE DEST 2008: International Conference on Digital Ecosystems and Technologies. Since the start of his PhD in 2005 he has contributed to peer-review journals and international conferences with 10 articles. He is involved in the organisation of a number of conferences such as the ComP2P 2008 (First International Workshop on Computational P2P Networks: Theory and Practice), IEEE CCGrid 2009 International Workshop on Service-Oriented P2P Networks and as chair of the program committee of the International Conference on Advances in P2P systems. His teaching experience the last three years includes tutorials, coursework marking and lab support on Software Agents, P2P networks, Artificial Intelligence and

Object Oriented Programming modules. His research interests cover the areas of decentralized resource sharing technologies like peer-to-peer networks, cloud computing, cluster computing, software agent platforms and network dynamics modelling.

Maozhen Li is a Lecturer in the School of Engineering and Design at Brunel University, United Kingdom. He received the PhD from Institute of Software, Chinese Academy of Sciences in 1997. He joined Brunel University as a full-time lecturer in 2002. His research interests are in the areas of grid computing, intelligent systems, P2P computing, semantic web, information retrieval, content based image retrieval. He has over 60 scientific publications in these areas. He authored "The Grid: Core Technologies", a well-recognized textbook on grid computing which was published by Wiley in 2005. He has served as an IPC member for over 30 IEEE conferences. He is on editorial boards of the International Journal of Grid and High Performance Computing, the International Journal of Distributed Systems and Technologies, and the International Journal on Advances in Internet Technology.

Antonio Liotta holds the Chair of Communication Network Protocols at the Eindhoven University of Technology, The Netherlands. He was previously appointed as a Reader at the University of Essex, were he led the Pervasive Services Team, known for its pioneering work on ubiquitous computing, advanced service management, and systems engineering. Antonio is a Fellow of the U.K. Higher Education Academy and serves a number of senior advisory boards including: the Peer Review College of EPSRC (the U.K. Engineering and Physical Sciences Research Council); the scientific advisory panel of the IWT (the Belgian Research Council); the Board of Editors of the Journal of Network and System Management (Springer); and the advisory board of editors of the International Journal of Network Management (Wiley). He is an active member of the networking and network and service management research communities. He has co-organized and co-chaired several international conferences; has served the Technical Programme Committee of over 90 conferences; and has also contributed as keynote and tutorial speaker. Antonio has over 100 publications to his credit, in the areas of telecommunication services, distributed computing, and autonomic networks and systems. Recent articles have contributed to topical themes including: operator-mediated peer-to-peer systems; P2P streaming; quality of experience management; application-aware networks; context-aware adaptive services; and self-configurable networks.

* * *

Carlos Abalde received his B.A. in computer science from A Coruña University (UDC) in 2001, and has been with the university's Computer Science Department for the past eight years as a member of the MADS research group. At the moment, he combines is assistant lecturer position with the development of its PhD Thesis. Prior to joining UDC as a lecturer, Abalde participated in the development of several projects like VoDKA and ARMISTICE. Abalde's research interests include P2P content distribution networks, functional and object-oriented programming, on-demand video streaming, modeling, performance and availability analysis of functional distributed systems, and design and development of applications with functional kernel and client/server architecture. He has published papers in all of these areas.

Matthew O. Adigun recieved his PhD in Computer Science at Obafemi Awolowo University, Nigeria. He is currently the Professor and Head of the Department of Computer Science, University of Zululand,

South Africa, a position he has held since 1989. His research interests are in Software Engineering and Architecting of Mobile and Pervasive Systems. He has presented papers at national and international conferences in his and related areas of research interests. As a principal investigator, he has led research sponsored by the National Research Foundation under the Research Niche Area titled Software Infrastructure for E-Commerce and E-Business with a group of CS, IS and Business Management researchers from inside and outside of the University of Zululand, South Africa.

Rehab Alnemr is a PhD student at Hasso Plattner Institute, Potsdam University in Germany. She is a graduate of faculty of Computers & Information, Information Technology department, Cairo University in Egypt. On 2006, she has her master degree in the field of security for mobile networks. Since 2007, she is a member of the associated Service-oriented Research School in Hasso Plattner Institute. Her research interests lie in the area of security, semantic web, social networks, and trust management. Her PhD topic is focusing on reputation management systems and the use of service oriented architecture and quality processes to enhance them.

Farag Azzedin is an Assistant Professor in the Department of Information and Computer Science at King Fahd University of Petroleum and Minerals (KFUPM), Saudi Arabia. He obtained his PhD from the University Of Manitoba, Manitoba, Canada in Computer Networks and Distributed Systems. Dr. Azzedin's research interests include Operating Systems, P2P and Grid computing systems, trust and reputation in distributed systems particularly in context-aware computing systems. Dr. Azzedin has published technical papers in these and related areas.

Daniel Batista received a B.Sc. degree in Computer Science from Federal University of Bahia, Brazil in 2004 and his M.Sc. degree in Computer Science from State University of Campinas, Brazil in June 2006. He is now a Ph.D. candidate at the Institute of Computing, State University of Campinas and he is affiliated with the Computer Networks Laboratory at the same University. His research interests include traffic engineering and grid networks. His current research addresses mechanisms to deal with fluctuations and uncertainties in grids.

Kiranmai Bellam received her B.S. degree in Information technology from Madras University, India. She received her M.S. degree in Computer Science from New Mexico Institute of Mining and Technology in 2006. Currently, she is a PhD candidate in the Department of Computer Science and Software Engineering at Auburn University. Her research interests are in energy efficiency, security, storage systems, real-time computing, distributed systems, and reliability.

Amitava Biswas is a practicing technologist with expertise in: networking; information systems; software engineering; and software business. He has worked for nine years in software and hardware industry as a technologist, software development manager and business expert in the USA, Canada and India. Currently, he is completing his PhD in Computer Science at Texas A&M University, USA. He obtained BTech (Hons), MS and MBA from Indian Institute of Technology-Kharagpur, Concordia University, Canada and Indian Institute of Management-Ahmedabad. In past, he has published in area of computer and software engineering and has been a certified Information System Professional in Canada.

Gordon Blair currently holds a Chair in Distributed Systems at Lancaster, and is also an Adjunct Professor at the University of Tromsø in Norway, and a Visiting Researcher at the Simula Research Laboratory in Oslo. He has published over 200 papers in his field and is on the PCs of many major international conferences in middleware and distributed systems. He is on the steering committee of the ACM/ IFIP Middleware series of conferences and was General Chair for this event in 1998.

Rajkumar Buyya is an Associate Professor and Reader of Computer Science and Software Engineering; and Director of the Grid Computing and Distributed Systems (GRIDS) Laboratory at the University of Melbourne, Australia. He is also serving as the founding CEO of Manjrasoft Pty Ltd. He received his B.E and M.E in computer science and engineering from Mysore and Bangalore Universities in 1992 and 1995, respectively; and his Ph.D. in computer science and software engineering from Monash University, Melbourne, Australia, in April 2002. Dr. Buyya served as a speaker in the IEEE Computer Society Chapter Tutorials Program (from 1999-2001), Founding Co-Chair of the IEEE Task Force on Cluster Computing (TFCC) from 1999-2004, Interim Co-Chair of the IEEE Technical Committee on Scalable Computing (TCSC) from 2004-Sept 2005, and member of the Executive Committee of the IEEE Technical Committee on Parallel Processing (TCPP) from 2003-2009. He served as the first elected Chair of the IEEE Technical Committee on Scalable Computing (TCSC) during 2005-2007 and played a prominent role in the creation and execution of several innovative community programs that propelled TCSC into one of the most successful TCs within the IEEE Computer Society. In recognition of these dedicated services to computing community over a decade, President of the IEEE Computer Society presented Dr. Buyya a Distinguished Service Award in 2008. Dr. Buyya recently received the "2009 IEEE Medal for Excellence in Scalable Computing" for pioneering the economic paradigm for utility-oriented distributed computing platforms such as Grids and Clouds.

Franco Callegati is currently serving as an associate professor at the University of Bologna, Italy. He received his Master and Ph.D. in electrical engineering in 1989 and 1992 from the same university. He was a research scientist at the Teletraffic Research Centre of the University of Adelaide, Australia; Fondazione U. Bordoni, Italy; and the University of Texas at Dallas. His research interests are in the field of teletraffic modeling and performance evaluation of telecommunication networks. He has been working in the field of all optical networking since 1994 with particular reference to network architectures and performance evaluation for optical burst and packet switching. He participated in several research project on optical networking at the national and international level, such as ACTS KEOPS, IST DAVID, IST Ephoton/One and IST BONE, often coordinating work packages and research activities.

Aldo Campi received the degree in electronic engineering from the University of Bologna, Italy, in 2004 and obtained his PhD in the same university in 2009. He is currently involved in research on scheduling algorithms for optical burst and packet switching, service oriented networking and collaborative networks. In the year of 2007 he spent 10 months in the University of ESSEX (UK) as visitor researcher working on application aware networking. He has participated in research project on optical networking at international level, such as IST E-Photon/One+ and IST BONE working actively in many workpackages and research activities. His research interests include optical networks, scheduling algorithms, SIP protocol, Grid Networking, Service Oriented and NGN architectures. He is TPC member and reviewer of conferences and journals at international level and IEEE member.

Junwei Cao is currently a Research Professor and Assistant Dean of Research Institute of Information Technology, Tsinghua National Laboratory for Information Science and Technology, Tsinghua University, China. He has been working on advanced computing technologies and applications for more than 10 years. Before joining Tsinghua in 2006, Junwei Cao was a Research Scientist of Massachusetts Institute of Technology, USA and NEC Laboratories Europe, Germany. Junwei Cao got his PhD in Computer Science from University of Warwick, UK, in 2001. He got his Master and Bachelor degrees from Tsinghua University in 1998 and 1996, respectively. Junwei Cao has authored over 80 academic papers and edited 3 books. He is a Senior Member of the IEEE Computer Society and a Member of the ACM and CCF.

Georg Carle is full professor in computer science at Technische Universität München, where he holds the chair on Network Architectures and Services. He conducts research on network security, network measurements, voice and video services over IP. Georg Carle received a M.Sc. degree from Brunel University London in 1989, a diploma degree in electrical engineering from the University Stuttgart in 1992 and a doctoral degree from the faculty of computer science of University Karlsruhe in 1996. In 1997, he worked as postdoctoral researcher at Institut Eurécom, Sophia Antipolis, France. From 1997 to 2002 he has been with the Fraunhofer Institute FOKUS (then GMD) in Berlin. From January 2003 to March 2008, he has been full Professor at University of Tübingen, holding the Chair on Computer Networks and Internet. He is chair of the IFIP Working Group 6.2 on Network and Internetwork Architecture, and has been leading projects funded by EU, national research programs and industry.

Eddy Caron is an assistant professor at Ecole Normale Supérieure de Lyon and holds a position with the LIP laboratory (ENS Lyon, France). He is a member of the GRAAL project and technical manager for the DIET software package. He received his Ph.D. in C.S. from the University de Picardie Jules Verne in 2000. His research interests include parallel libraries for scientific computing on parallel distributed memory machines, problem solving environments, and grid computing.

Alexandru Cârstea, born 23/11/1980, holds a BSc. degree in Mathematics and Computer Sciences from "Transilvania" University of Brasov (2003) and a MSc. in Algorithms and Software products from same university (2004). Currently he is a PhD candidate and junior researcher at the Research Institute e-Austria, Timişoara, Romania and also assistant professor at Informatics Department, Mathematics and Computer Science Faculty, "Transilvania" University of Braşov. Starting from 2006 he is part of the international team working for the European project SCIEnce. His main research interests include distributed computing with emphasis on the Grid architectures, software architectures and computer aided simulation. He is authoring 16 papers in the field of Grid computing, software systems symbolic computing and computer simulation.

Weiwei Chen was born in Guangdong, China, in 1986. He is currently in his fourth year as an undergraduate student of Department of Automation at Tsinghua University. He is now doing the graduation design under the supervision of Professor Junwei Cao. His research interests include fine grained resource allocation, virtualization technology and scientific workflow management in grid. Before that, he was a member of Tsinghua Hephaestus Robot Team and conduct research on multi-robot cooperation and decision making at Robotics Lab, Tsinghua University.

Chunsheng Ni is an Assistant Research Professor in the Network Research Center of Tsinghua University, China. She received her Master degree in Computer Science from Beijing University of Aeronautics and Astronautics (BUAA) in 2002. She then joined Network Research Center of Tsinghua University as a Practice Research Professor as a faculty member from 2002-2005. She is the system manager of TEIN2 (Trans-Eurasia Information Network), CERNET2 (China Education and Research Network) and TUNET (Tsinghua University Network). Her research interests are network management system, P2P computing and network measurement.

Luigi Ciminiera is professor of Computer Engineering at the Dipartimento di Automatica e Informatica of Politecnico di Torino, Italy. His research interests include grids and peer-to-peer networks, distributed software systems, and computer arithmetic. He is a coauthor of two international books and more than 100 contributions published in technical journals and conference proceedings. He is a member of the IEEE.

Geoff Coulson is a Professor of Distributed Computing at Lancaster University, UK. His research interests include distributed systems, adaptive sensor networks, embedded systems, middleware technologies, grids, and component-based software development. Geoff has led many successful projects in the distributed systems/ middleware area. He also serves on numerous PCs in his research areas, has been programme co-chair for the ACM/IFIP Middleware Conference series, and has published over 40 journal and 100 conference papers.

Nelson L.S. da Fonseca received his Electrical Engineer (1984) and M.Sc. in Computer Science (1987) degrees from The Pontifical Catholic University at Rio de Janeiro, Brazil, and the M.Sc. (1993) and Ph.D. (1994) degrees in Computer Engineering from The University of Southern California, USA. Since 1995, he has been affiliated with the Institute of Computing of The State University of Campinas, Campinas Brazil where is currently a Full Professor. He is also a Consulting Professor to the Department of Informatics and Telecommunications of the University of Trento, Italy. He is the Editor-in-Chief of the IEEE Communications Surveys and Tutorials. He served as Editor-in-Chief of the IEEE Communications Society Electronic Newsletter and Editor of the Global Communications Newsletter. He is member of the editorial board of: Computer Networks, IEEE Communications Magazine, IEEE Communications Surveys and Tutorials, and Brazilian Journal of Computer Science. He served on the editorial board of the IEEE Transactions on Multimedia and on the board of the Brazilian Journal on Telecommunications. He is the recipient of Elsevier Computer Networks Editor of the Year 2001, USC International Book award and of the Brazilian Computing Society First Thesis and Dissertations award. He is an active member of the IEEE Communications Society. He served as ComSoc Director of On-line Services (20022003) and served as technical chair for several ComSoc symposia and workshops. His main interests are traffic control, and multimedia services.

Ramide Dantas holds a BSc. degree in Computer Science at the Federal University of Paraíba (UFPB) and in Computer Networks in the Federal Center of Technical Education of Paraíba (CEFET-PB), Brazil, both in 2003. He started his graduate studies in 2004 at the Center of Informatics of the Federal University of Pernambuco (CIn/UFPE), Brazil, and presented his master dissertation on a new Quality of Service (QoS) queuing mechanism at the end of 2005. He is a research fellow of GPRT/UFPE since 2004, working on Peer-to-Peer networks, All-Optical IP networks, Policy-Based Management for Ambient Networks, and IPTV over ADSL, in projects funded by the Brazilian National Research Network (RNP) and Ericsson/EAB. Ramide Dantas is currently a PhD student at CIn/UFPE under the supervision of Prof. Djamel Sadok. His research interests include Network Management and Autonomic Computing.

Anwitaman Datta obtained his Phd from EPFL Switzerland before joining NTU Singapore in 2006, where he works as an assistant professor in the school of computer engineering. He is interested in large-scale networked distributed information systems and social collaboration networks, self-organization and algorithmic issues of these systems and networks and their scalability, resilience and performance.

Sonia Heemstra de Groot received a M.Sc. degree in electrical engineering from Mar del Plata National University, Argentina, a second M.Sc. degree from Netherlands University Federation For International Cooperation (NUFFIC), and a Ph.D. degree in Electrical Engineering from the University of Twente, The Netherlands. From 1991 to 1998 she was a lecturer in the Tele-Informatics and Open Systems group of the Faculty of Electrical Engineering at the University of Twente. From 1999 to 2006 she was an associate professor in the area of wireless networking at the Electrical Engineering, Mathematics and Computer Science (EEMSC) of the same university. In 2001 she joined the Wireless Multimedia Research Group at Ericsson EuroLab Netherlands (ELN). Since 2003 she holds the position of chief scientist at the Twente Institute of Wireless and Mobile Communications, of which she is one of the co-founders. In 2006 she was nominated full-professor at Delft University of Technology, where she holds the part-time chair in Personal and Ambient Networking. She has participated in many national and international projects. She has been project manager of a recently completed Dutch project on 4th generation mobile networks. Currently she is involved in various Dutch and European projects on different issues in future wireless and mobile systems, including the EU IST6FP projects MAGNET, MAGNET Beyond, and HIDENETS, and the Dutch projects PNP2008, Awareness, Easy Wireless and QoS in PN@home. Her present research activities include radio access, future wireless and mobile networks, personal and ad-hoc networks, 4G systems and wireless security. She is a member of the IFIP TC-6 Working Group on Personal Wireless Communication. She has been member of the programme and steering committee of various scientific conferences. She has authored or co-authored more than 100 papers published in international journals or presented at international conferences.

Piet Demeester received the Masters degree in Electro-technical engineering and the Ph.D degree from the Ghent University, Gent, Belgium in 1984 and 1988, respectively. In 1992 he started a new research activity on broadband communication networks resulting in the IBCN-group (INTEC Broadband communications network research group). Since 1993 he became professor at the Ghent University where he is responsible for the research and education on communication networks. The research activities cover various communication networks, including network planning, network and service management, telecom software, internetworking, network protocols for QoS support, etc. Piet Demeester is author of more than 1000 publications in the area of network design, optimization and management. He is member of the editorial board of several international journals and has been member of several technical program committees.

Frédéric Desprez is a director of research at INRIA and holds a position at LIP laboratory (ENS Lyon, France). He received is PhD in C.S. from the Institut National Polytechnique de Grenoble in 1994 and his MS in C.S. from the ENS Lyon in 1990. His research interests include scheduling for large scale distributed platforms, SOA architectures, data management, and grid computing. See http://graal.ens-lyon.fr/~desprez/ for further information.

Peter Dew is a Professor of Computer Science in the School of Computing where he leads Web Science group in the Institute of e-Science. He has published over 90 mostly multidisciplinary research papers relating to system architectures and their applications. Topics span numerical computing, visualization for engineering applications, high performance computing, Grid and P2P computing. He was the lead Leeds investigator for the £3m e-Science demonstrator project entitled "Distributed Aircraft Maintenance Environment (DAME)". He has been the lead academic for two successful University Companies where he was a non-executive director. His current research interests are concerned with the application of large scale Web-based systems (based on P2P) to e-Science, e-Business and e-Law problems. He is also contributing to the emergence of Web Science, a new discipline to increase understanding of the Web.

Bart Dhoedt received a degree in Engineering from the Ghent University in 1990. In September 1990, he joined the Department of Information Technology of the Faculty of Applied Sciences, University of Ghent. His research, addressing the use of micro optics to realize parallel free space optical interconnects, resulted in a PhD degree in 1995. After a 2 year post-doc in opto-electronics, he became professor at the Faculty of Applied Sciences, Department of Information Technology. Since then, he is responsible for several courses on algorithms, programming and software development. His research interests are software engineering and mobile & wireless communications. Bart Dhoedt is author or co-author of more than 300 papers published in international journals or in the proceedings of international conferences. His current research addresses software technologies for communicationnetworks, peer-to-peernetworks, mobile networks and active networks.

Vassilios V. Dimakopoulos received the diploma in Computer Engineering and Informatics from the University of Patras, Greece, and the MASc and PhD degrees in Electrical and Computer Engineering from the University of Victoria, Canada. He is currently an assistant professor in the Department of Computer Science, University of Ioannina, Greece. His research interests lie in the area of parallel and distributed systems, computer architecture, systems software, and performance analysis. He is a member of the IEEE, the IEEE Computer Society, and the Technical Chamber of Greece.

Ciprian Dobre received his PhD in Computer Science at the University POLITEHNICA of Bucharest in 2008. He received his MSc in Computer Science in 2004 and the Engineering degree in Computer Science in 2003, at the same University. His main research interests are Grid Computing, Monitoring and Control of Distributed Systems, Modeling and Simulation, Advanced Networking Architectures, Parallel and Distributed Algorithms. He is member of the RoGRID consortium and is involved in a number of national projects (CNCSIS, GridMOSI, MedioGRID, PEGAF) and international projects (MonALISA, MONARC, VINCI, VNSim, EGEE, SEE-GRID, EU-NCIT). His research activities were awarded with the Innovations in Networking Award for Experimental Applications in 2008 by the Corporation for Education Network Initiatives (CENIC).

Ryota Egashira received the BS degree in mechanical engineering and the MS degree in environmental study from University of Tokyo in 2000 and 2002, respectively. He is currently a Ph.D. candidate in the Donald Bren School of Information and Computer Sciences, University of California, Irvine. His research interests include peer-to-peer applications, distributed search, distributed resource allocation, agent based systems, application of economic principles to networks and network applications.

Mohamed Eltoweissy is an associate professor in the Bradley Department of Electrical and Computer Engineering at Virginia Tech. He also holds a courtesy appointment in the Department of Computer Science. His research projects include the Cell Network Architecture for networks as complex systems, dynamic key management in sensor and ad hoc networks, service-oriented architecture and routing protocols for sensor-actuator networks, reputation management in ad hoc networks and service environments, and authentication management in mobile networks. He has published over 120 manuscripts in refereed journals, books and conference proceedings. Eltoweissy serves on the editorial board of IEEE Transactions on Computers (the flagship and oldest Transactions of the IEEE Computer Society) and the editorial board of the Elsevier Journal of Computer Networks and Applications. Eltoweissy has and continues to participate in the leadership and organization of numerous conferences and workshops.

Akihiro Enomoto received the BE and MI (Master of Informatics) from Kyoto University, Japan, in 2000 and 2002, respectively. He is currently a Ph.D. candidate in the Donald Bren School of Information and Computer Sciences, University of California, Irvine. His research interests include molecular communication, peer-to-peer networks, agent-based computing, and applications of biological concepts to networks and network applications.

Noura Faci is Associate Professor at the Université Claude Bernard (Lyon1) in France. She defended her PhD in Computer Science, on December 2007, at the Université Champagne-Ardenne (Reims), France. She has worked on a IST-CONTRACT european Project in the area of electronic contracting. She is a member of the Service-Oriented Computing research team (SOC) in LIRIS Lab, since October 2008. Her research interests are mainly fault tolerance in multi-agent systems, monitoring for e-contracts, and high availability in service-based applications. She has published in conferences and book chapters related to multi-agent systems area.

Marconi Pereira Fardin was born in Vitória-ES, Brazil, on October 23, 1982. He received the Informatics Technician diploma in 2003 from the Federal Center of Technologic Education of Espírito Santo (CEFET-ES). He graduated as Engenheiro Eletricista from Federal University of Espírito Santo (UFES) at Vitória-ES, Brazil, in 2005 and received the Ms.C. degree from University of Campinas (UNICAMP) at Campinas-SP, Brazil, in 2009, The master developed in (Laboratório de Telecomunicações) LABTEL in UFES and Optical Networking Lab (OptiNet) in UNICAMP. His research interests are in Network Topology, Peer-to-Peer Network, Distributed Hashed Tables (DHT), Distributed Index with Hashing Architecture, and Control Plane for Optical Networks.

Marc E. Frîncu, born 26/04/1983, holds a BSc. degree in Computer Science obtained from the West University of Timisoara Romania (2006) and a MSc. in Artificial Intelligence and Distributed Systems from the same university (2008). Since 2008 he is a PhD student studying distributed scheduling algorithms at the West University of Timisoara and a junior researcher at the e-Austria Research Institute in

Timisoara. Since his graduation in 2006 he has been involved in several international research projects including the FP6 European SCIEnce project. His main research interests include distributed and parallel computing with emphasis on distributed systems, workflows and scheduling algorithms. Despite being in an early stage of his career he has already authored several papers in international conferences and journals.

Jochen Furthmüller received a Diplom-Informatiker degree (comparable to M.Sc in computer science) in 2008 from Universität Karlsruhe, Germany. He is currently scientific staff at Telematics Institute, Universität Karlsruhe and part of a Young Investigator Group led by Dr. Oliver Waldhorst. The Young Investigator Group is a junior research group funded by the 'Concept for the Future' of Karlsruhe Institute of Technology within the framework of the German Excellence Initiative. His research interests include Grid infrastructure for mobile devices, collaboration in spontaneous networks, energy efficiency in distributed systems and wireless sensor networks.

Demetris G. Galatopoullos received his B.S and M.S degrees in Computer Engineering from Boston University and is currently a PhD candidate in Computer Engineering at the Electrical and Computer Engineering Department of Northeastern University in Boston. The principal focus of his research is service-oriented architectures and middleware systems that enable the semantic composition of private and public services over peer-to-peer technologies. Prior to pursuing the PhD degree he was a senior software engineer at Transcore, Inc. During his tenure at Transcore, he served as the software project leader for the Maine TransPass Electronic Toll Collection system. His research interests include Pervasive and Mobile Computing, Internet Computing, Service Oriented Computing, Semantic Web, Distributed and Embedded Systems, and Peer-to-peer technologies. He is a member of IEEE and a regular reviewer for journals, book chapters and IEEE/ACM conference proceedings.

Paul Grace is a senior research associate in the Computing Department at Lancaster University, where he previously received a PhD in Computing in 2004. He has also worked as a research scientist at Katholieke Universiteit Leuven in Belgium where he investigated the relationship of aspect-oriented programming and reflection. His research focuses on the development of middleware solutions for next generation distributed applications with particular interest in: reflection, interoperability mobile and grid computing, component programming, and general distributed systems problems.

Víctor M. Gulías is a lecturer at the Computer Science Department in the University of A Coruña. After one year at the Yale University, Gulías focused his research on distributed systems and its application to the development of multimedia servers implemented using the functional paradigm. He has published more than forty national and international publications on that area, has supervised two Ph.D. Thesis, and has directed a number of public and private funded research projects. Gulias is the head of the MADS research group and also co-founder of the spin-off LambdaStream.

Joan Garcia-Haro is a Professor at the Polytechnic University of Cartagena, Spain. He is author or co-author of more than 160 journal papers mainly in the fields of switching, wireless networking and performance evaluation. From April 2002 to December 2004 he served as EIC of the IEEE Global Communications Newsletter, included in the IEEE Communications Magazine. He is Technical Editor of the same magazine from March 2001. He also holds an Honorable Mention for the IEEE Communications Society Best Tutorial paper award (1995).

Mohammed Hawa graduated from the University of Jordan in 1997 with a B.Sc. degree in Electrical Engineering. He received his M.Sc. degree from University College London in 1999 and his Ph.D. degree from the University of Kansas in 2003. Dr. Hawa is the recipient of the Fulbright Scholarship (1999) and the Shell Centenary Scholarship (1998). He is a published author and a member of the IEEE. He is currently an Assistant Professor of Electrical Engineering at the University of Jordan. His main research interests include: networking, Quality-of-Service and P2P networks.

Camden Holt is a Senior Software Engineer at Lost Wax where he works in the Customer Solutions team for the Aerogility product - the multi-agent decision-support system for the aviation sector. Camden previously worked as a software consultant in the Financial Services industry developing large-scale distributed applications and has applied this experience in developing the core infrastructure for Aerogility, implementing a scalable, enterprise-grade multi-agent system. He has a keen interest in the commercial applications of agent technology and since joining Lost Wax has been involved in a number of research programs involving Aerogility, both academic and private-sector.

Lican Huang works on challenges about e-Science, Grid and P2P computing since the beginning of 2000's. He was mentioned in Marquis Who's Who in the World 2006, Marquis Who's Who in the Science and Engineering 2006-2007, and Marquis Who's Who in Asia 2006-2007 due to his achievement of proposing Virtual and Dynamic Hierarchical Architecture for e-Science, Grid and VIRGO protocols. He is now a Director of Network & Distributed Computing at Zhejiang Sci-Tech University (ZSTU), China. Prior to joining ZSTU, he worked as a Senior Research Associate in the School of Computer Science at Cardiff University since 2004. Before working at Cardiff University, he developed many large software systems in several companies, as technical leader or department manager. He obtained his Ph.D. in Computer Science from Zhejiang University in 2003, Master's Degree from Hangzhou University in 1984 and Bachelor's degree from Nanchang University in 1982.

Danny Hughes is a post-doctoral researcher with the DistriNet research group in the Department of Computer Science of the Katholieke Universiteit Leuven, Belgium. Danny received his PhD in Computer Science from Lancaster University (UK) in the area of adaptable peer-to-peer systems. Since then, his post-doctoral work has focused on the field of wireless sensor networks and in particular providing middleware support for adaptation in sensor network environments. He serves on numerous PCs in his research areas and has published over 40 academic papers.

Malohat Ibrohimovna earned her radio-electronics engineering degree from Tashkent State Technical University (TSTU), Uzbekistan. There she was involved in European Union-funded projects "Training Teachers for Master courses in Information and Communication Technologies" (2000) and "Long Distance Training" (2001), which enabled her to come to the Netherlands, the University of Twente (UT) for several three-month stints. The goal of these projects was applying ICT to educational programs in Uzbekistan and to establish a method by which Uzbek Master students at TSTU and Karshi Engineering Economic Institute can follow courses offered at participating European universities: UT, Technical University of Hamburg-Harburg (Germany), and Aalborg University (Denmark). She has translated into Russian and designed three Master course materials taken from the curriculum of the UT and taught at TSTU during 2001-2002. She received her degree of a Professional Doctor in Engineering from the UT, the faculty of Electrical Engineering, Mathematics and Computer Science, the Chair of Design and Analysis of Communication Systems in 2004. Currently, she is a PhD student at the Chair of Wireless and Mobile Communications, Delft University of Technology, The Netherlands. Her research was funded by the Dutch Freeband project Personal Network Pilot 2008. The topics of her interest are personal communications, cooperative group-oriented networking, access control in sharing personal resources and services.

Johnson Iyilade is a PhD student with the Center for Mobile eServices, Department of Computer Science, University of Zululand, South Africa. He previously holds a B.Sc. (Combine Honours.) in Computer Science with Economics, and M.Sc. in Computer Science from Obafemi Awolowo University, Nigeria. His research interest is in Middleware for Distributed Service Oriented Computing (Web services, Grid, Multi-agent systems and P2P). In particular, he has interest in topics such as: Dynamic Composition of Grid/Web services, Semantic Web Services and Web 2.0 technologies, Service-oriented Multi-agent Systems, Workflow and Business Process Modeling, Pervasive Services and Context-aware Computing, Service Management, Peer-to-peer architectures and Service Grids. His PhD thesis investigates Middleware Infrastructure for Distributed Services Provisioning in a Grid Service ecosystem. He has publications in Journals and Peer-reviewed conference proceedings.

Klaas Kabini is an MSc Student with the Center of Excellence for Mobile eServices, Department of Computer Science, University of Zululand, South Africa. He previously holds a B.Sc. including Honours in Computer Science from the same university. His research interest is in Service Oriented Computing, Multi-agent Systems, Grid computing, P2P and Autonomic Computing. In particular, he has interest in topics such as: dynamic composition of web/ grid services, Business Processes Modeling, Scientific workflows, Knowledge Services, P2P technologies, autonomic grid applications and Service Oriented Multi-agent Systems. His MSc dissertation investigates dynamic composition of grid services using a multi-agent system.

Carlos Alberto Kamienski received his Ph.D. in computer science from the Federal University of Pernambuco (Recife PE, Brazil) in 2003. He is currently an associate professor of computer networks at the Federal University of the ABC (UFABC) in Santo André SP, Brazil, where he is also the coordinator of the graduation program in Information Engineering. Also, he is a research fellow of the Telecommunications and Networking Research Group (GPRT) from the Federal University of Pernambuco. His current research interests include service-oriented architecture, service composition, service creation, peer-to-peer systems, policy-based management, network traffic analysis and virtual worlds. He has been involved in several research and development projects funded by Brazilian agencies and also in partnership with telecom companies and Internet service providers.

Konstantinos Karaoglanoglou received his BSc in Applied Informatics from the University of Macedonia of Thessaloniki in 2006. He received his MSc in Networks-Communications-Systems Architecture from the Department of Informatics at the Aristotle University of Thessaloniki in 2008. Currently he is a PhD student in the Department of Informatics at the Aristotle University of Thessaloniki. His research interests include Grid and Cluster Computing, Resource Discovery in the Grid, and Trust Issues in Distributed Systems and P2P Systems.

Dimka Karastoyanova is a junior professor at the Cluster of Excellence "Simulation Technology" (SimTech) and the Institute of Architecture of Application Systems (IAAS) at the University of Stuttgart, Germany. She holds a Ph.D. in Computer Science from the Technische Universitaet Darmstadt, Germany and M.Sc. degree in Computational Engineering from the University of Erlangen-Nuremberg, Germany. Her research focus is on applying workflow technology for business applications and scientific simulations in a service-oriented environment and on the Grid. Additionally she is interested in extending service-based middleware and the workflow technology to enable flexible service compositions. Her current research work is in the area of service-based scientific workflows, which is one of the major objectives of the research done in the scope of the Excellence Centre in "Simulation Technology" at the University of Stuttgart. She is also a member of several European projects involving industry and academia that deal with open issues in service middleware, BPM (Business Process Management), semantics and fundamental research in SOC (Service-Oriented Computing) driven by the BPM, SOC, Grid and Software Engineering communities.

Helen D. Karatza is an Associate Professor in the Department of Informatics, at the Aristotle University of Thessaloniki, Greece. Her research interests include Computer Systems Modeling and Simulation, Performance Evaluation of Parallel and Distributed Systems, Resource Allocation and Scheduling, Cluster Computing, Grid Computing, Resource Discovery in the Grid, Real-time Distributed Systems and P2P Systems. Dr. Karatza has authored or co-authored over 130 technical papers and book chapters including two papers that earned best paper awards at the 39th Annual Simulation Symposium (ANSS 2006) and the 10th International Symposium on Performance Evaluation of Computer and Telecommunication Systems (SPECTS 2007) respectively. She is a Senior member of the IEEE, and of the Society for Modeling and Simulation International (SCS).

Tomasz Kaszuba is a 3rd year PhD student in Polish-Japanese Institute of Information Technology (PJIIT) Warsaw, Poland. He received his Master's Degree in Computer Science from PJIIT in 2006. His research interests include distributed computing, peer-to-peer networks, reputation and trust management systems, Internet auction platforms.

Salman Ahmad Khwaja has earned his Bachelor's degree in Computer Science from the National University of Computers and Emerging Sciences (NUCES), Lahore. Salman has been involved in the Software industry. He is currently pursuing his Masters in Computer Science at King Fahd University of Petroleum and Minerals (KFUPM) in Saudi Arabia. His research interests are Service Oriented Architecture, Trust, and Honesty in Peer to Peer Systems.

Paul Krause is Professor of Software Engineering at Surrey University. He has over twenty years' experience research experience in software engineering, in both industrial and academic research laboratories. Currently his research work focuses on distributed systems for the Digital Ecosystem and Future Internet domains. He has around 30 journal papers, an extensive list of conference papers and is author of a text book on reasoning under uncertainty.

Heba Kurdi is a lecturer in the Computer Science Department at Al-Imam Mohammad bin Saud University, Riyadh, KSA. Currently, she is a PhD student at the School of Engineering and Design in Brunel University, West London, UK. She received her master degree in Applied Computer Science in

2003 from King Saud University in Riyadh. Her research interests are focused on large scale computer systems, Grid Computing, resource management systems, bee colony optimization and its application in resource scheduling in grid systems. She also has special interest in computer applications for autistic children. During the course of her research work, she has published in various IEEE research conferences and scientific journals. As well, she has participated in submitting several European research projects for the 6th and 7th framework program of the IST initiative.

Lydia Lau is a Lecturer in the School of Computing at the University of Leeds, and a member of the Web Science research group within the School. She was awarded a PhD in Information Systems and a BSc in Computational Science and Management Studies at the University of Leeds. She is a member of the British Computing Society and a Chartered IT Professional. Her research interest is to conceptualise good design principles for collaborative systems and to facilitate new ways for people to interact with each other over the 'virtual world'. She is particularly keen to address the design issues from the infrastructural angle (people, information, processes and systems) with a high level of usability and sustainability. Recent work includes the examination of the use of semantics and social computing for capturing evolving practices and knowledge sharing in communities.

Lee Gillam, PhD in Artificial Intelligence (Surrey, 2004); BSc in Mathematics and Computer Science (Surrey, 1995). Fellow of the British Computer Society (FBCS) and Chartered IT Professional (CITP). Currently a Lecturer in the Department of Computing at the University of Surrey. Previous publications and research in the areas of Ontology Learning, Metadata and Grid Computing Systems. Has worked in and been responsible for a number of research projects supported by the EU's IT Research and Development programmes and UK research programmes under EPSRC and ESRC. Recently, PI on the eContent project LIRICS and currently running a Knowledge Transfer Partnership with a London-based Financial Services provider.

Frank Leymann is a full professor in Computer Science and the director of the Institute of Architecture of Application Systems (IAAS) at the University of Stuttgart. His research and teaching activities are in the fields of workflow technology, middleware, service-oriented computing and architecture, application integration and engineering, scientific and manufacturing workflows and others. Apart from that he takes part in European and national projects investigating the application of service-orientation and workflows in multiple application domains including semantic BPM, Scientific Simulations, Context-aware applications, and fundamental research in SOC in collaboration with scientists from the BPM, SOC, Grid and Software Engineering communities. He is a renowned author of books, conference and journal articles in these major research areas. He has played a major role in industry while he was working for IBM where he was one of the architects of MQ Series Product Suite and has led the pioneer research and product development in workflow management. Additionally, he is an active participant in standardization efforts led by both industry and academia that coin the Web Service specification stack.

Bin Li is a Ph.D. student in the Department of Computing at the University of Surrey. He received his B.Sc. in Computer Science and minor B.A. in Chartered Public Accountancy from JiangXi University of Finance and Economics, China. He received his M.Sc. Internet Computing from the University of Surrey, UK, 2008. His interest in Grid Economics started from his Masters dissertation on Grid based financial risk management. A Ph.D. scholarship from the Department enables his further explorations in this area. Currently he is concentrating on Grid Economics involving prediction, quantification of risk and liability analysis in case of failure. He is also interested in constructing automatic SLAs using financial risk techniques, which might help, in the future, in P2P and Cloud Computing systems.

Liangxiu Han is currently a computer scientist at National eScience Centre in University of Edinburgh and has been working on three large-scale projects including ADMIRE (http://admire1.epcc.ed.ac.uk/), FireGrid (http://www.firegrid.org) and NanoCMOS (http://www.nanocmos.ac.uk) since January 2007, funded by EU-FP7, TSB, EPSRC respectively. Between 2004~2006, Dr. Han worked on an EPSRC-funded project "Performance measurement and management for two-level optimization of networks and peer-to-peer application". During 2002~2004, being a Head of network & system division at Shanghai Development Center of Computer Software Technology, Dr. Han had charged multiple projects funded by both government and IT industry in software R & D, and large-scale network system measurements. To date, Dr. Han has worked in both industrial and academic environments and has extensive research and practical experience in performance modelling and evaluation of large-scale distributed computing systems, software engineering, nonlinear science theory (e.g. chaos, fractal/multifractal), complex network theory, as well as pattern recognition & signal processing (using wavelet transform) in IT field.

Hoon Wei Lim obtained a Ph.D degree in Information Security from Royal Holloway, University of London in 2006. His doctoral research focussed on various key management and security architectural issues for grid computing systems. In particular, he studied how identity-based cryptography can be exploited to design lightweight, flexible and scalable grid security architectures. Upon completion of his PhD, Dr. Lim stayed on at Royal Holloway and worked as a post-doctoral research assistant in an e-Science project funded by the UK EPSRC. In the project, he designed alternative security architectures to PKIs for grid applications, as well as examined various access control and policy management techniques for grid environments. Dr. Lim is now a researcher with SAP Labs France, working on EU-funded projects related to security and privacy.

Lu Liu is a Research Fellow in School of Computing at University of Leeds. He received his PhD Degree from University of Surrey (funded by UK DIF DTC) and MSc Degree from Brunel University. His research interests are in areas of peer-to-peer computing, software engineering and service-oriented computing. He is currently working on NECTISE Project which is an EPSRC/BAE Systems funded research project involving ten UK Universities. Dr Liu has over 20 scientific publications as first author in reputable journals, academic books and international conferences. He won the Best Paper Award at the Realising Network Enabled Capability Conference in 2008. He is the guest editor of the special issue on Dependable Peer-to-Peer Systems of Journal on Peer-to-Peer Networking and Applications. He is on the Editorial Review Board of International Journal of Distributed Systems and Technologies. He served as Co-chair, TPC, and Session Chair of many international conferences and workshops.

Michael Luck is Professor of Computer Science at King's College London, where he leads the Agents and Intelligent Systems group. He has been working in the field of autonomous agents and multiagent systems since its early days, and has over 150 publications (including several books both authored and edited) in areas relating to multiagent systems, intelligent agents, norms and institutions, contract-based systems, and other areas. Michael was Director of AgentLink II and Executive Director of AgentLink III, the European Network of Excellence for Agent-Based Computing. He is also an editorial board member of the journal of Autonomous Agents and Multi-Agent Systems, the International Journal of Agent-Oriented Software Engineering, Web Intelligence and Agent Systems, and ACM Transactions on Autonomous and Adaptive Systems. He will be general co-chair for AAMAS 2010.

Georgiana Macariu received her MSc in Computer Science in 2008 at the "Politehnica" University of Timisoara, Computer Science Department where she is currently a PhD student. Also she carries out her research activities at the eAustria Research Institute in Timisoara. Her work deals with bringing together Symbolic Computing with Grid and distributed computing. Currently she focuses on creating a framework for dynamic composition of symbolic computing services tailored for large scale distributed systems. In addition, she studied the effects of replication for a Grid service layer for Grid shared data programming. Her area of interest also covers embedded systems with a particular interest in task scheduling on multi-core mobile communication systems.

Rabi N. Mahapatra is an associate professor in the Department of Computer Science at Texas A&M University. His research interests are in the area of embedded systems, low-power design, SoC & VLSI Design and computer architecture. He has published more than 130 research papers in international journals/conferences. His research has been funded by NSF, DoT, NASA and other major industries. Currently, he is directing the Hardware-Software Codesign Research group at Texas A&M University and Associate Editor of ACM Transactions on Embedded Computing. He is a Ford Fellow and Senior Member of IEEE Computer Society.

Elias S. Manolakos is an Assoc. Professor with the National and Kapodistrian University of Athens, Dept. of Informatics and Telecommunications. His interests are in parallel and distributed computing, signal processing systems design and implementation, machine learning methods and their applications in multidisciplinary research domains, such as computational biology, ecological modeling, etc. Before joining UoA he was with the faculty of the ECE Department Northeastern University, Boston where he held a tenured appointment. Elias has received the PhD degree from University of Southern California, Los Angeles (1989), the MSc degree from University of Michigan, Ann Arbor and the Dipl. Ing. degree from the Nat. Tech. University of Athens, Greece. As Assist. Professor he has received the NSF Research Initiation Award. Prof. Manolakos has co-authored with his students more than 90 refereed publications in journals and Conference Proceedings and co-edited 3 books. He has led or participated in several funded research projects in Europe (FP6, FP7) and in the USA (NSF, DARPA, EPA etc). He serves or has served in the Editorial Board of several IEEE and other journals and has chaired the technical program of IEEE Conferences and Workshops. He is a Senior Member of the IEEE (1995).

Antonio Manzalini received his M.Sc. degree in electronic engineering at Politecnico of Torino. In 1990 he joined Telecom Italia Lab (formerly CSELT) starting with research activities on technologies and architectures for advanced transport (SDH, DWDM) and networking (IP, GMPL). In 1997-2000 he was Rapporteur in ITU-T. In 2000-2002, he was Project Leader the FP5 IST Project LION. In 2002-2004 he was Project Leader of the FP6 IST Integrated Project NOBEL. In 2003 he was appointed as member of the Scientific Committee of CTTC (Centre Tecnològic de Telecomunicacions de Catalunya). In 2006-2008 he was Project Leader of the FP6 Future Emerging Technology Project CASCADAS whose main goal is developing and demonstrating an architectural vision for autonomic ecosystems. In 2008 he has been awarded with the International Certification of Project Manager by PMI. He has been awarded 5 patents on networking and services systems and methods. Currently he is joining the long term research activities of the Future Centre of Telecom Italia.

Adam Manzanares received his B.S. in Computer Science in 2002 from the New Mexico Institute of Mining and Technology, United States. Currently he is a PhD student in the Department of Computer Science and Software Engineering at Auburn University. During the summers of 2002-2007 he has worked as a student intern at the Los Alamos National Laboratory. His research interests include energy efficient computing, modeling and simulation, and high performance computing.

Marco Papa Manzillo is Ph.D. student at the Department of Control and Computer Engineering of Politecnico di Torino. He got his B.D. and M.D. in Computer Engineering from Politecnico di Torino in 2005 and 2007 respectively. His research interests include Quality of Service in Wireless Systems, traffic control and proximity awareness in peer-to-peer file-sharing systems.

Guido Marchetto is a post-doctoral fellow at the Department of Control and Computer Engineering of Politecnico di Torino. He got his Ph.D. in Computer Engineering in April 2008 and his laurea degree in Telecommunications Engineering in April 2004, both from Politecnico di Torino. His research topics are packet scheduling and Quality of Service in packet switched network, peer-to-peer technologies, and Voice over IP protocols. His interests include network protocols and network architectures.

Spiridoula Margariti received a BSc degree in Electronics in 1992 from the Technological Educational Institute of Lamia, Greece. She received her BSc and MSc degrees in Computer Science in 2002 and 2007 respectively, from the University of Ioannina, Greece. Since April 2007, she is a PhD candidate at the same Department. Her research interests include distributed systems, p2p data management and overlay protocols.

Christoph Meinel is the CEO and President of the Hasso Plattner Institute for IT-Systems Engineering (HPI) and full professor for computer science at the University of Potsdam since 2004. He studied Mathematics and Computer Sciences at the Humboldt-University, received his PhD degree on 1981 and his habilitation on complexity theory on 1988. He worked in Humboldt University in Berlin, Saarbrücken University and Paderborn University. In 1992 he was appointed a full professor for computer science at the University of Trier. He is also a professor both at the School of Computer Science of the Technical University of Beijing (China) and at the Luxembourg Institute of Advanced Studies in Information Technology. He contributed in 7 textbooks and monographs, and more than 300 scientific papers. His research interests focus on in Internet Technology and Systems, particularly in the fields Trust and Security Engineering, Web-University and Secure Telemedicine. He is also chief editor of the scientific electronic journal "Electronic Colloquium on Computational Complexity" and of the "IT-Gipfelblog".

Felipe Meneguzzi is a PhD student at King's College London, previously at the University of Southampton, working on extending agent languages for multiagent domains. Before undertaking PhD research at King's College, Felipe worked on R&D at Hewlett-Packard, working in collaboration with HP Labs in the US and the UK, and was involved in research on digital publishing tools and techniques. Felipe has worked on the development of practical agent architectures, including the integration of planning into BDI interpreters and the adaptation of agent behaviour towards norm compliance. His current research interests include autonomous agents, multiagent systems, normative systems, planning, electronic contracting and artificial intelligence in general.

Simon Miles is a lecturer in Computer Science at King's College London, UK. He has worked on a range of projects in the areas of e-science, agent-oriented software engineering, electronic contracting, and distributed systems, at King's and, previously, at the University of Southampton in the Intelligence, Agent, Multimedia group. He has experience of applying novel open systems technologies to a wide variety of real world use cases, and, as part of his work researching mechanisms for determining the provenance of data, he has collaborated with many international partners. He co-led the International Provenance Challenges, bringing together researchers from around twenty disparate teams in two six-month exercises to compare their systems using a single, medical application. He has published widely in the areas of multi-agent systems and e-science.

Roberto Minerva, manager, focal point for Long Term Research within the Future Center & Technical Communication department of Telecom Italia. He held many responsibilities within Telecom Italia Lab: Network Intelligence, Wireless Architecture and Business Services Area Manager. Roberto has a Master Degree in Computer Science. Since 1987 he has been involved in the development of Service Architectures for Telecom (TINA, OSA/Parlay and SIP), in activities related to IMS, and in the definition of services for the Business market (context-awareness, ambient intelligence and automotive). He is author of several articles and paper presented in international conferences and journals.

Sanjay Modgil is a research associate in the Agents and Intelligent Systems Group, King's College London. He received his PhD in computational logic in 1999 at Imperial College London. His previous research interests lie in the areas of belief revision, non-monotonic logics, modal logics, and their applications in computing science. Other previous research work has included development and application of logic programming techniques for computer aided design and decision support systems. His current work involves: research on argumentation theory; in particular extensions to abstract argumentation systems to accommodate argumentation over preferences and values; applications of argumentation to agent reasoning and communication, and; regulation of agent behaviour through encoding of deontic concepts in electronic contracts.

Suneil Mohan is a PhD student in the Department of Computer Science and Engineering at Texas A&M University. He received his B.E in Electronics and Communication Engineering from Anna University, Chennai, India in 2006. His areas of interest include embedded systems, networking and network security.

Corrado Moiso received his M.Sc degree "cum laude" in Computer Science at University of Torino in 1984; in the same year he joined Telecom Italia Lab (formerly CSELT). In 1984-1991, he studied parallel logic and functional languages. In 1990-1991 he investigated the applicability of Constraint Programming to traffic management. In 1990-1994, he investigated object-oriented distributed platforms and their application to TMN. Since 1994, he has been investigating the introduction of IT in network intelligence: he designed and experimented service platforms based on TINA, investigated Telco/Internet convergence, contributed to Parlay standardization for service exposure, and analysed SOA-based SDP platforms. Currently, in the context of the long term research activities of Telecom Italia Future

Centre, he is studying the adoption in Telco infrastructures of decentralised architectures and autonomic technologies. He joined projects founded by EC and Eurescom. He is author of several papers, and he has been awarded 7 patents on services systems and methods.

Sotiris Moschoyiannis is a Research Fellow at the University of Surrey. He received the BSc degree in Mathematics from the University of Patras, Greece, the MSc in Information Systems and PhD in Computer Science from the University of Surrey, UK. His research work is on the application of mathematical methods to the analysis and design of concurrent and distributed systems, with a particular interest in the behavioural modelling of complex interactions that require transactional guarantees and the underlying network structures to support them. He has worked on several EU and UK research projects and has published a number of papers in peer-reviewed conferences and journals.

Juan Pedro Muñoz-Gea received the Telematics Technical Engineering degree (cum laude) and the Telecommunication Engineering degree (cum laude) in 2003 and 2005 respectively, both from the Polytechnic University of Cartagena, Spain. In 2006 he started working as a research assistant at the Department of Information Technologies and Communications of the Polytechnic University of Cartagena. Since 2008, he is an assistant professor of the Department of Information Technologies and Communications at the Polytechnic University of Cartagena. He is a PhD candidate and his research interest is focused on peer-to-peer systems and privacy enhancing technologies.

Marco A. S. Netto is a PhD student in Computer Science at the University of Melbourne, Australia, and member of GRIDS laboratory. Marco has a Bachelor's (2002) and Master's degree (2004) in Computer Science, both from the Pontifical Catholic University of Rio Grande do Sul (PUCRS), Brazil. He has been working with resource management and job scheduling for high performance computing environments since 2000. Marco has also worked with structural Bioinformatics and Desktop Grids. Marco's current research effort is on co-allocation of space-shared resources for parallel applications. His work considers Quality-of-Service in terms of job's completion time guarantees, and rescheduling aspects, mainly due to inaccurate runtime estimates.

Radoslaw Nielek is a PhD student in Polish-Japanese Institute of Information Technology (PJIIT) Warsaw, Poland. He received his Bachelor's Degree in Production Engineering and Management from Szczecin University of Technology in 2004 and Master's Degree in Computer Science from PJIIT in 2007. His research interests include social simulation, trust management and opinion mining.

Mirto Ntetsika was born in Ioannina, Greece in 1984. She was admitted at the Computer Science Department of the University of Ioannina in 2002 and obtained the BSc degree in 2006. Since then she is an MSc student at the same department. She is a member of the Distributed Management of Data (DMOD) Laboratory since 2007. So far, her research was mainly focused on Databases and Peer-to-Peer systems, with particular interest on issues concerning replication and consistency maintenance on Peer-to-Peer systems with non-uniform overlay topologies, such as power-law networks.

Börje Ohlman is a Senior Research Engineer at Ericsson he received his M.Sc. degree in Computer Science and History of Ideas and Sciences from Uppsala University, Sweden. In the 80's he worked as a computer consultant. He started in telecommunications in the late 80's, when he joined Ericsson, with developing signalling for ATM in the ATMOSPHERIC project of the EU 2nd Framework Programme (FP) RACE as well as in traditional standard bodies (ITU-T, ETSI and ATM Forum). In the mid 90's he moved to IP technology, especially QoS, he was active in IETF in the standardization of DiffServ and Policy based networking. During 2004-2007 he was involved in the EU 6th FP Ambient Networks (AN) project focusing on the overall architecture and the policy framework for AN. He currently leads the Networking of Information workpackage of the EU 7th FP 4WARD. He is also working on goal based policy networking.

Nir Oren is a research associate in the Agents and Intelligent Systems Group at King's College London. He received his PhD in argumentation in 2007 at the University of Aberdeen, investigating how dialogue and argumentation may be used in partially observable, probabilistic domains, and how it may be applied to contract monitoring in such domains. He has previously worked as a research associate within the International Technology Alliance, and as a research assistant on the CONOISE-G project. His research interests include the application of argumentation to normative and practical reasoning, agent reasoning over organisations and institutions, and normative conflict resolution.

Javier Paris received his B.A. in computer science from A Coruña University (UDC) in 2002, and became a member of the Models and Applications of Distributed Systems (MADS). Over the past years Paris has participated in several projects involving distributed systems, networking and network filesystems. At the moment he combines writing his PhD thesis with an assistant position in the A Coruña University. His current line of research includes transparent fault tolerance for connection oriented network protocols, to provide invisible fail-over in distributed systems. This research is part of the group effort to transfer research knowledge in the field of distributed systems to the corporate world.

Dana Petcu holds a MSc in computer science and a PhD in numerical analysis. She is Professor and Director of Computer Science Department of West University of Timisoara, as well as Researcher and Director of Institute e-Austria Timisoara. Her current topics of interests are parallel and distributed computing. Previous research experience is related to computational mathematics, natural computing, expert systems, graphics. She authored in her 20 years of activity around 200 articles and 10 textbooks. She is chief editor of the journal SCPE, member of the editorial board of 6 journals, editor of 12 proceedings. She served as program committee member for around 80 conferences and organized 16 workshops and 3 training events. She is currently leading the Romanian team involved in EC projects related to SOC: FP6 SCIEnce, FP7 DEHEMS and SEE-Grid-SCI, COST Action0805, ESA GiSHEO, Structural-Funds InfraGrid. She received a German award for women in science and education.

Franck Petit received a Ph.D. in computer science from the University of Picardie Jules Verne (Amiens, France) in 1998. He is currently with INRIA as a visiting researcher. He was previously a professor in the University of Picardie Jules Verne, with the MIS Laboratory. His research focuses on algorithmic aspects, fault-tolerance, and dynamicity in distributed systems.

Tran Vu Pham is a lecturer and also the Head of Systems and Networking Department of The Faculty of Computer Science and Engineering, Ho Chi Minh City University of Technology in Vietnam. He is interested in researching for computing infrastructures to efficiently support distributed collaborations and resource sharing employing technologies such as Peer-to-Peer, Grid and cloud computing. Before taking the current post, he spent a year at the Interdisciplinary Centre for Scientific Research in Music at the University of Leeds, UK, to work on an EU funded project named CASPAR. He completed his Master of Science degree in Information Systems and his PhD in Computing also at the University of Leeds. His PhD thesis was on a Collaborative e-Science Architecture for supporting distributed scientific communities. His bachelor degree in Computer Science was awarded by the University of Wollongong, Australia.

Guillaume Pierre is an assistant professor in the Computer Systems group at VU University Amsterdam. His research interests focus on large-scale distributed systems. Pierre has an MSc and a PhD in Computer Science from the University of Evry-val d'Essonne, France. He is the treasurer of EuroSys, the European Professional Society on Computer Systems, and an editorial board member for IEEE DSOnline.

Pedro Jose Piñero-Escuer received the Telecommunication Engineering degree in July 2008 from the Polytechnic University of Cartagena, Spain. In December 2008, he received a pre-doctoral fellowship for the Fundacion Seneca Program FPI. His research activity is focused on channel coding and in the multimedia value-added services over low-voltage PLC networks.

Evaggelia Pitoura received her BSc degree from the University of Patras, Greece in 1990 and her MSc and PhD degrees in Computer Science from Purdue University in 1993 and 1995, respectively. Since September 1995, she has been with the Department of Computer Science of the University of Ioannina, Greece. Her publications include more than 100 articles in international journals and conferences and a book on mobile computing. She has also coauthored two tutorials on mobile computing for IEEE ICDE 2000 and 2003. She has received the best paper award of IEEE ICDE 1999 and two "Recognition of Service Awards" from ACM. She is a member of the IEEE and the IEEE Computer Society.

Florin Pop received PhD in Computer Science with "Magna cum laude" distinction in 2008. The PhD thesis subject was Optimization of Decentralized Scheduling in Grid. His entire research contributions on this topic created DIOGENS system (DIstributed near-Optimal GENEtic algorithm for grid application Scheduling). He is Assistant Professor at Computer Science department in University "Politehnica" of Bucharest. His research interests are oriented to: scheduling in Grid environments, distributed system, parallel and distributed computation, communication protocols and numerical methods. He received engineering degree in Computer Science, in 2005, on Decentralized Scheduling Methods for Grid and MS. He is member of RoGrid consortium and he work as a researcher in some Romania national projects and international projects (e.g. EGEE, SEE-GRID, EU-NCIT).

George Popescu received the Ph.D. degree from Rutgers University, New Brunswick in 2001. He is currently a researcher in performance modeling and analysis at the University Politehnica, Bucharest, Romania. He was with IBM Research from Jan. 2001 to Sept 2004, performing distributed systems research and system modeling and optimization. Between 2004 and 2006 he has been a postdoctoral researcher at Yale University, New Haven. He has developed for his PhD thesis one of the first Internet2 virtual reality telemedicine applications. Subsequently, he has contributed to IBM's advanced network middleware architecture design. He holds several patents in distributed system design. He has published one book chapter and over 35 journal and conference proceedings publications. He has participated in the organization of IEEE VR conference. He is a member of ACM and SIAM and has hold IEEE and INFORMS memberships.

Barry Porter is a research associate at the Computing Department of Lancaster University, from which he also received his PhD in the field of overlay network dependability. His current research focuses on Wireless Sensor Networks, and more generally his interests are in exploring fundamental system building approaches such as component-based design, as well as programming languages in general, and techniques to create adaptive systems.

Xiao Qin (S'99-M'04) received the BS and MS degrees in computer science from Huazhong University of Science and Technology in 1992 and 1999, respectively. He received the PhD degree in computer science from the University of Nebraska-Lincoln in 2004. Currently, he is an Assistant Professor in the Department of Computer Science and Software Engineering at Auburn University. Prior to joining Auburn University in 2007, he had been an assistant professor with New Mexico Institute of Mining and Technology (New Mexico Tech) for three years. He received the NSF CAREER Award in 2009. In 2007, he received an NSF CPA Award and an NSF CSR Award. His research interests include parallel and distributed systems, storage systems, fault tolerance, real-time systems, and performance evaluation. His research is supported by the U.S. National Science Foundation, Auburn University, and Intel Corporation. He had served as a subject area editor of IEEE Distributed System Online (2000-2001). He has been on the program committees of various international conferences, including IEEE Cluster, IEEE IPCCC, and ICPP

Matthias Quasthoff is a research assistant and a PhD student at Hasso Plattner Institute at the University of Potsdam. He graduated at the University of Leipzig in 2006 holding a diploma in Computer Science. His research interests lie in the field of trust and user control in Web-based information systems and social software. His PhD project focuses on helping software developers to integrate standardized, semantic data formats and policies in their applications saving them the trouble of acquiring in-depth knowledge of these technologies.

Carmelo Ragusa received the Laurea degree in computer and electronic engineering from the University of Catania, Italy, in 2001 and the Ph.D. Degree in communication systems from the University of Surrey, U.K., in 2005. From 2005 to 2006, he worked as Research Engineer at the IT Innovation Centre, University of Southampton, U.K., on business models for grid computing. He's currently a Researcher at University of Messina within the Centre on Information Technologies Development and Their Applications (CIA) and he is in charge of the testbed development within the RESERVOIR EU FP7 project. His research interest are in the areas of distributed computing, Grid, Cloud computing, service management, SOA and code mobility.

Omer F. Rana is Professor of Performance Engineering at the School of Computer Science, Cardiff University. He has also been the deputy director of the Welsh eScience Centre. He holds a PhD in Computing from Imperial College, London. His research interests include high performance distributed computing, data mining and multi-agent systems.

Hamed Al-Raweshidy is a research professor and the head of the Wireless Networks & Communications Research Group in the School of Engineering and Design at Brunel University. His research interests include network optimization, mesh and ad hoc networks, radio over fiber, PAN and PN, and IP mobility. He received his PhD for work in spread spectrum multiplexing for communication networks. He holds a number of projects with EPSRC and EU. He's a senior member of the IEEE, an IEE fellow, and a member of New York Academy of Sciences. Contact him at the Wireless Networks & Communications Group, School of Eng. and Design, Brunel Univ., Uxbridge, Middlesex UB8 3PH, UK; hamed. al-raweshidy@brunel.ac.uk.

Amir reza Razavi is a Research Fellow and PhD student at the University of Surrey. He received the BSc in Computer Software engineering from SIU (1996-Iran), the first MSc in Computer Software engineering from IUST (Iranian University Of Science and Technology-1999) and the second MSc in Internet Computing from University of Surrey (2003). During his career, he has taught Database and transactional systems in Shiraz Azad University and Sepidan Azad University (1999-2001). His main interest has been long-running transactions in non-conventional environments. Much of his research has been directed towards analysis and design of the distributed transactional system and the network infrastructure support for SMEs. He has contributed in three EU projects; ASPIC, DBE and OPAALS.

Moisés Renato Nunes Ribeiro was born in Vitória/ES, Brazil, in 1969. He received the B.Sc. degree in electrical engineering from the Instituto Nacional de Telecomunicações, the M.Sc. degree in telecommunications from the Universidade Estadual de Campinas, Brazil, and the Ph.D. degree from the University of Essex, U.K., in 1992, 1996, and 2002, respectively.In 1995, he joined the Department of Electrical Engineering, Federal University of Espírito Santo, Brazil. His research interests include fiber-optic communication devices, systems, and networks.

Fulvio Risso is Assistant Professor at the Department of Control and Computer Engineering of Politecnico di Torino. He got his Ph.D. in Computer and System Engineering from Politecnico di Torino in 2000 with a dissertation on Quality of Service on Packet-Switched Networks. He is author of several papers on quality of service, packet processing, network monitoring, and IPv6. Present research activity focuses on efficient packet processing, network analysis, network monitoring, and peer-to-peer overlays.

Xiaojun Ruan received the B.S. degree in Computer Science from Shandong University in 2005. Currently, he is a PhD student in the department of Computer Science and Software Engineering at Auburn University. His research interests are in parallel and distributed systems, storage systems, real-time computing, performance evaluation, and fault-tolerance. His research interests focus on high-performance parallel cluster computing, storage system, and distributed system.

Duncan Russell is a Senior Research Fellow in the Distributed Systems and Services Group at the University of Leeds, UK. He has worked in research and development for mobile communications, distributed secure workflow and distributed control of networked audio processing. His research activities include distributed systems architectures, systems modelling and design, sustainable through-life management and support, interoperability and collaborative working. Dr Russell has a PhD in secure service-based collaborative workflow, a BEng in Electronic Systems Engineering and 9 years industry

R&D experience. Since November 2005, he has been a lead researcher on the NECTISE (Network Enabled Capability Through Innovative Systems Engineering) Project, investigating the use of SOA for dynamic systems integration in the delivery of military capability.

Djamel F. H. Sadok received his PhD in Computer Science from the University of Kent at Canterbury in 1990. From 1990 to 1992 he was a research fellow in the Computer Science Department, University College London. He is currently a professor of computer networks at the Computer Science Department of the Federal University of Pernambuco, Recife PE, Brazil. His research interests include network management, service-oriented architecture, wireless communications and traffic engineering. He currently coordinates the local Telecommunications and Networking Research Group (www.gprt.ufpe.br) which has a number of research projects with partners from both the Industry and Academia in Brazil, the US and Europe.

Josemaría Malgosa-Sanahuja received the Telecommunication Engineering degree in 1994 from the Polytechnic University of Catalonia (UPC), Spain. In November 2000, he received the Ph.D. degree in Telecommunication from the University of Zaragoza (UZ), Spain. He has been an assistant professor at the Department of Electronic and Communications Engineering (University of Zaragoza) since 1995. In September 1999, he joined the Polytechnic University of Cartagena (UPCT), Spain, as associated professor. He has been involved in several National and International research projects related to switching, multicast technologies, traffic engineering and multimedia value-added services design. He is author of several papers in the fields of switching, multicast technologies and distributed systems. He is regional correspondent of the Global Communications included in the IEEE Communications Magazine since 2002.

Corinna Schmitt studied Bioinformatics at the Eberhard-Karls University in Tübingen until 2006. Afterwards she took part in an internship at Verigy Germany in Böblingen where she developed filter algorithms for interpreting test result of the pin architecture. Followed by a position at the Fraunhofer Institute for Interfacial Engineering and Biotechnology (IGB) in Stuttgart where she worked on a DFG project dealing with microarray annalysis and the development of several other analysis tools and algorithms. The research work as a Ph.D. student started at the chair "Network Architectures and Services" by Prof. Dr.-Ing. G. Carle, Technische Universität München in 2008. Research in the field of wireless sensor network (WSN) was inspired by the diploma theses "Animal observation using embedded technologies" written at the chair of Prof. Dr.-Ing. G. Carle during his position in Tübingen. Currently she deals with security questions in wireless sensor networks and with an implementation of a heterogeneous, hierarchical WSN.

Tatsuya Suda is a Professor in the Donald Bren School of Information and Computer Sciences, University of California, Irvine. He has also served as a Program Director of the Networking Research Program, National Science Foundation from October 1996 to January 1999. He was a visiting Associate Professor at the University of California, San Diego, a Hitachi Professor at the Osaka University, and a NTT Research Professor. He is an Area Editor of the International Journal of Computer and Software Engineering. He is a member of the Editorial Board of the Encyclopedia of Electrical and Electronics Engineering, Wiley. He has been engaged in research in the fields of computer communications and networks, high-speed networks, multimedia systems, ubiquitous networks, distributed systems, object oriented communication systems, network applications, performance modeling and evaluation, and application of biological concepts to networks and network applications.

Xiang Sun is an associate professor with National Engineering and Research Center for Information Technology for Agriculture of China. She was born in 1974 and gained her master degree from Beijing Institute of Technology. Her research interest covers agricultural middleware, distributed processing systems and knowledge engineering.

François Taïani has been a Lecturer in Lancaster's Computing Department since 2005 after an intervening spell at AT&T Labs (NJ). He is interested in developing open and principled middleware solutions for complex systems such as grid and large-scale sensor networks. His research interests include fault-tolerance, resilience, aspect-oriented programming, and computational reflection. Francois has been a co-investigator on a number of national and EU projects in his area. He is currently serving as the Tutorials Chair of the 10th 2009 ACM/IFIP/Usenix International Conference on Middleware, and is the Programme Chair of the Eighth 2010 European Dependable Computing Conference.

Cédric Tedeschi received a PhD. in computer science from the Ecole Normale Supérieure de Lyon in 2008. He is currently a post-doctoral researcher at INRIA Sophia Antipolis - Méditerranée. His research focuses on service discovery in distributed computing, peer-to-peer networking, and fault-tolerance for large scale systems.

Livio Torrero is a post-doctoral fellow at the Department of Control and Computer Engineering of Politecnico di Torino. He got his Ph.D. in Computer Engineering in April 2009 and laurea degree in Computer Engineering from Politecnico di Torino in November 2004. His research topics include the Voice over IP protocols, the IPv6 protocol, peer-to-peer technologies and their NAT/firewall related issues.

Filip De Turck received his M.Sc. degree in Electronic Engineering from the Ghent University, Belgium, in June 1997. In May 2002, he obtained the Ph.D. degree in Electronic Engineering from the same university. At the moment, he is a part-time professor and a post-doctoral fellow of the F.W.O.-V., affiliated with the Department of Information Technology of the Ghent University. Filip De Turck is author or co-author of more than 200 papers published in international journals or in the proceedings of international conferences. His main research interests include scalable software architectures for telecommunication network and service management, performance evaluation and design of new telecommunication services. He is in the program committee of several conferences and regular reviewer for conferences and journals in this field.

Maarten van Steen is full professor at VU University Amsterdam. His research concentrates on large-scale distributed systems, with an emphasis on decentralized solutions, notably epidemic-inspired peer-to-peer systems. Application areas for such solutions include Web-based systems and large-scale wireless ad-hoc networks. He holds an MSc in Applied Mathematics from Twente University and a PhD in Computer Science from Leiden University, both from The Netherlands.

Gary Vickers is an executive director of Lost Wax and responsible for all aspects of the Aerogility product - the multi-agent decision-support system for the aviation industry. Gary has over 25 years experience in the software industry and has worked in a variety of roles. He spent several years with Logica in Australia and the UK, and prior to joining Lost Wax, Gary was a successful independent programme manager delivering five major programmes. Gary has worked closely with the software engineering team at Lost Wax to commercialise agent technology. He was instrumental in defining the Aerogility proposition and leading the business development activities launching the product into the global aerospace market.

Bart De Vleeschauwer obtained a masters degree in computer science from the Ghent University, Belgium, in June 2003. Since August 2003 he is affiliated with the Department of Information Technology of the Ghent University. In September 2008, he obtained the Ph.D. degree in computer science. His research interests include autonomic network and QoE management, the usage of overlay networks as a higher layer routing platform, management platforms for Massively Multiplayer online Gaming applications and QoS and congestion monitoring. His work has been published in more than 35 scientific publications in international conferences and journals.

Oliver Waldhorst received a Diplom-Informatiker degree (comparable to M.Sc. in computer science) in 2000 and a Ph.D. in computer science in 2005 from Universität Dortmund, Germany. He is currently a post doctoral researcher at Universität Karlsruhe, Germany, where he is head of a Young Investigator Group, a junior research group funded by the ‚Concept for the Future' of Karlsruhe Institute of Technology within the framework of the German Excellence Initiative. His research interests include peer-to-peer- and overlay-networks in next-generation communication systems, Grid applications in mobile and hybrid environments as well as modeling and analysis of spontaneous, self-organizing systems.

Helio Waldman received a BSEE from Instituto Tecnológico de Aeronáutica (ITA) at São José dos Campos, Brazil, in 1966, and the M.S. and Ph.D. degrees from Stanford University in 1968 and 1972, respectively. In 1973 he joined the State University of Campinas (UNICAMP), where he was Director of the School of Engineering at Campinas from 1982 to 1986 and Research Vice-President from 1986 to 1990. He is currently Research Vice-President of UFABC – Universidade Federal do ABC, a new Brazilian Federal University currently under construction in the State of São Paulo. Dr. Waldman is a Senior Member of IEEE and a Senior Member of SBrT, where he served as President between 1988 and 1990.

James Walkerdine is a post-doctoral fellow with the Department of Computer Science at Lancaster University, Belgium. James received his PhD from Lancaster University (UK) in Cooperative Query Management. Since then, his post-doctoral work has focused upon software engineering, in particular: Peer-to-Peer systems, Service-Oriented Computing and Internet monitoring.

Jilong Wang is associate professor in the network research center of Tsinghua University, China. He is also the director of network operation center of TEIN2, CERNET2 and TUNET. Dr. Wang received his PhD in Computer Science from Tsinghua University in 2000 and then joined Tsinghua University as assistant professor. His research interests are in the areas of network management, network measurement and internet technologies. During last three years, Wang also preside several china state research projects supported by NSF, 863 and 973 programs. Dr. Wang is also the IT consultant expert of 2008 digital Olympics.

Adam Wierzbicki obtained his Ph.D. from Warsaw University of Technology in 2003. He works as an assistant professor at the Polish-Japanese Institute of Information Technology. He is interested in social informatics, especially trust and fairness management in open, distributed systems, as well as other social phenomena or social concepts that can impact performance, security, or other properties of information systems.

Huarui Wu is the director of computer application department with National Engineering and Research Center for Information Technology for Agriculture of China and an associate professor with it. He was born in 1975 and graduated from Beijing industrial University. He is mainly engaged on the research and application of intelligent agricultural information technology.

Di Wu received his B.S. degree from University of Science and Technology of China (USTC), M.S. degree from Chinese Academy of Sciences, and Ph.D. degree in Computer Science & Engineering from the Chinese University of Hong Kong. He is currently with Polytechnic Institute of New York University, where he is a postdoctoral researcher in the Department of Computer and Information Sciences, advised by Prof. Keith Ross. His recent research interests include networking, distributed systems, multimedia communications, network security, etc. He is a member of IEEE, ACM and Sigma Xi.

Liu Xin is currently a second-year PhD candidate in the Center for Advanced Information System (CAIS), School of Computer Engineering, Nanyang Technological University (NTU), Singapore. He pursues his research work under the guidance of assistant professor Anwitaman Datta. His research interests include peer-to-peer networks and distributed systems, trust and reputation management, publish-subscribe systems and social networks. He received his Bachelor of Science from Jilin University, China in 2007.

Jie Xu is Chair of Computing, Lead of a Peak of Excellence at the University of Leeds, UK and Director of the EPSRC-funded WRG e-Science Centre involving the three White Rose Universities of Leeds, York and Sheffield. He has worked in the field of Distributed Computer Systems for over twenty-four years. He is the recipient of the BCS/IEE Brendan Murphy Prize 2001 for the best work in the area of distributed systems and networks. He has led and co-led many key research projects to the value of over £20M. Professor Xu has published more than 250 edited books, book chapters and academic papers. He received a PhD from the University of Newcastle upon Tyne, and then moved to the University of Durham as the head founder of the Durham Distributed Systems Engineering group. He was professor of Distributed Systems at Durham before he joined the University of Leeds.

Hou Yong is currently a PH.D. Candidate in College of Information Science and Engineering Xinjiang Universtiy. He received his Master degree of Science from Xinjiang Universtiy of China, in 2007. His research focuses on the design and development of distributed query processing, performance evalution and task scheduling system for distributed and grid environment.

Wen Zhang is currently a Ph.D candidate with Tsinghua University. His research covers integrated resource scheduling and management of grid data streaming applications which are more and more popular in science and engineering. Now he is also engaged in cloud computing. Recently, he carries out research and implementation of fine-grained resource allocation for grid and cloud computing with help of control theory based on virtualization technology.

Chunjiang Zhao is the director of National Engineering and Research Center for Information Technology for Agriculture of China and a professor with it. He was born in 1964 and graduated from Chinese Agricultural University. His research interest is mainly focused on application of information technology in agriculture and the technical architecture of refined agriculture, such as agricultural expert system and integration of 3S technology and intelligent equipment technology.

Ziliang Zong received his B.S. and M.S. in Computer Science from Shandong University of China in 2002 and 2005 respectively. He received his PhD degree in computer science from Auburn University, United States in 2008. During Oct.2003 - Oct.2004, he studied as research assistant student in the Artificial Intelligence Lab of Toyama University, Japan. Currently, he is an assistant professor in Mathematics and Computer Science Department of South Dakota School of Mines and Technology. His research interests include multicore technologies, parallel programming, high performance computing and distributed storage systems.

Index

Symbols

2.5 grid generation 22

A

Abstract Workflow Language (AWL) 1068
accelerometers 1083
Access control 254
Access Control in Fednets 980
Accessibility 22, 25, 27, 42
accessible Grids 20, 25, 27
adaptability 382, 383, 384, 385, 386, 387, 392
Adaptive 396, 410, 423
Adaptive Control 394
Adaptive Query Processing 382, 383, 393, 394
Ad-hoc Grids 25, 27, 28
Ad-Hoc Network 1090
ad-hoc wireless networks 948
Advance Reservation 480, 488, 494
Adversary 755, 760, 773
agent-based approach 931
Agent scheduler 576
agility 245, 246, 249, 265
AIDSEC 911, 913, 922, 923, 924, 925, 926, 927, 928, 929, 930
Algorithm 564
allocations 526, 527, 528
Amazon 800, 804, 808, 809
Ambient Intelligence (AmI) 22
Ambient Networks (AN) 210, 224
ambient vibration 1083
AN 199, 210, 211, 212, 217, 224, 225
analog to digital converters (ADC) 1083

anonymity 1, 19
AOP paradigm 638, 649
Application Oriented Modules (AO-M) 897
AQP 382, 383, 384, 385, 391
asset-backed securities (ABSs) 691
Assignment 735, 745
association service 180, 196
asymmetric communication 3, 9
asynchronous collaboration 839
asynchronous collaborative environment 841, 844
audio and video streaming 65
audio-visual contents 1032
augmented transition networks (ATNs) 742
authentication 262
automated control planes 338
automation 253, 259, 273
autonomic computing 254, 260, 274, 276, 277
Autonomic Computing 952, 954, 955
Autonomic Grids 25, 33
Average or Characteristic Path Length 121

B

bandwidth reservation 241, 242
BarterCast algorithm 760, 762
barter-trade pattern 434
Batch Grids 31
Berkeley-Mote Family 1076
BGP protocol 546
binding protocols 2
bindings 984, 999
BitTorrent 425, 433, 434, 436, 437, 438, 439, 440, 442, 443, 445, 446, 447, 449

I

ICT services 937, 942, 943, 951
Identification of shortest paths 106
identity-based approach 818, 822, 830
Identity-Based Cryptography
        817, 820, 823, 835, 837
identity-based cryptography (IBC)
        817, 818, 819
identity-based encryption (IBE) 820
identity-based encryption (IBE) scheme 820
identity-based infrastructure for grid applica-
        tions (IKIG) 822
identity-based key distribution technique 827
identity-based key infrastructure for grid
        (IKIG) 818
identity-based PKI 821, 831
identity-based primitives 832
identity-based security infrastructure 827, 833
identity-based signature (IBS) 820
identity-based signature (IBS) scheme 820
identity-based techniques
        818, 827, 828, 830, 831
identity federation 262
Identity Management
        801, 802, 803, 812, 815
idle CPU cycles 325
impedance mismatch 208
Implementation 547, 564
IMS architecture 895, 939, 940
incentive 425, 426, 427, 428, 429, 430,
        431, 432, 433, 434, 435, 436, 437,
        439, 440, 441, 443, 444, 445, 446,
        448, 449
incremental change model 414, 415, 416
information space 361, 362, 373
Information Technology (IT) 913
Information Technology (IT) investment 913
infrastructure 21, 23, 27, 28, 30, 33, 34,
        36, 37, 40, 41, 42
Infrastructure as a Service (IaaS)
        635, 652, 687
instant messengers 125
integration 15, 16, 17
interaction-based service composition 1026
interaction model 899, 902, 906
interaction paradigms 982, 990, 999

interactive Grids 20
Interactivity 22, 25, 31, 42
interception meta-interface 985
Interconnection 540, 541
interface description languages (IDLs) 639
Interfaces 983
Internal Dependency Graph (IDG) 1016
Internet Assigned Numbers Authority (IANA)
        1061
Internet-based solution 1054, 1055
Internet layered architecture (ISO-OSI) 947
interoperability 316, 326, 332, 451, 462
Inter-Process Communication 494
intersymbol interference (ISI) 1039, 1048
IP approach 938
IP-based communications 830
IP layer 842
IP Multimedia Subsystem (IMS) 894, 938
IP Network 938
IT functions 939
IT security disciplines 796

J

Java Agent Development Environment (JADE)
        928
Java Interface for Network Infrastructure (JINI)
        928
job 520, 521, 525, 526, 541
Job Submission Description Language (JSDL)
        896, 906

K

KANT computer algebra systems 1066
Key Agreement 825, 837
Key-Based Routing (KBR) 987
Key Based Routing (KBR) algorithm 10
Key-Based Routing (KBR) overlay 987
killer application 3
Knowledge Grids 25, 33

L

lambda switch capable 338
language-based simulation tool 675
Large Hadron Collider (LHC) 672
large scale distributed systems 566, 567, 572